Less managing. More teaching. Greater learning.

INSTRUCTORS...

Would you like your **students** to show up for class more **prepared**? *(Let's face it, class is much more fun if everyone is engaged and prepared...)*

Want ready-made application-level **interactive assignments,** student progress reporting, and auto-assignment grading? *(Less time grading means more time teaching...)*

Want an **instant view of student or class performance** relative to learning objectives? *(No more wondering if students understand...)*

Need to **collect data and generate reports** required for administration or accreditation? *(Say goodbye to manually tracking student learning outcomes...)*

Want to **record and post your lectures** for students to view online?

With **McGraw-Hill's *Connect*® *Plus Management*,**

INSTRUCTORS GET:

- Interactive Applications – **book-specific interactive assignments** that require students to APPLY what they've learned.

- Simple **assignment management**, allowing you to spend more time teaching.

- **Auto-graded** assignments, quizzes, and tests.

- **Detailed Visual Reporting** where student and section results can be viewed and analyzed.

- Sophisticated **online testing** capability.

- A **filtering and reporting** function that allows you to easily assign and report on materials that are correlated to accreditation standards, learning outcomes, and Bloom's taxonomy.

- An easy-to-use **lecture capture** tool.

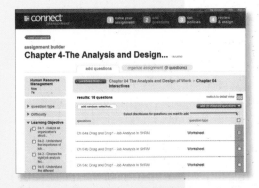

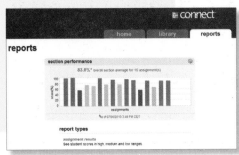

Want an online, **searchable version** of your textbook?

Wish your textbook could be **available online** while you're doing your assignments?

 ### Connect® Plus Management eBook

If you choose to use *Connect® Plus Management*, you have an affordable and searchable online version of your book integrated with your other online tools.

Connect® Plus Management eBook offers features like:

- Topic search
- Direct links from assignments
- Adjustable text size
- Jump to page number
- Print by section

 Want to get more **value** from your textbook purchase?

Think learning management should be a bit more **interesting**?

 ### Check out the STUDENT RESOURCES section under the *Connect®* Library tab.

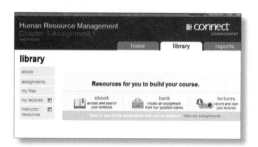

Here you'll find a wealth of resources designed to help you achieve your goals in the course. You'll find things like **quizzes, PowerPoints, and Internet activities** to help you study. Every student has different needs, so explore the STUDENT RESOURCES to find the materials best suited to you.

Human Resource Management

GAINING A COMPETITIVE ADVANTAGE 8e

RAYMOND A. NOE
The Ohio State University

JOHN R. HOLLENBECK
Michigan State University

BARRY GERHART
University of Wisconsin–Madison

PATRICK M. WRIGHT
Cornell University

McGraw-Hill Irwin

The McGraw·Hill Companies

McGraw-Hill
Irwin

HUMAN RESOURCE MANAGEMENT: GAINING A COMPETITIVE ADVANTAGE

Published by McGraw-Hill/Irwin, a business unit of The McGraw-Hill Companies, Inc., 1221 Avenue of the Americas, New York, NY, 10020. Copyright © 2013, 2010, 2008, 2006, 2003, 2000, 1997, 1994 by The McGraw-Hill Companies, Inc. All rights reserved. Printed in the United States of America. No part of this publication may be reproduced or distributed in any form or by any means, or stored in a database or retrieval system, without the prior written consent of The McGraw-Hill Companies, Inc., including, but not limited to, in any network or other electronic storage or transmission, or broadcast for distance learning.

Some ancillaries, including electronic and print components, may not be available to customers outside the United States.

This book is printed on acid-free paper.

3 4 5 6 7 8 9 0 DOW/DOW 1 0 9 8 7 6 5 4 3

ISBN 978-0-07-802925-7
MHID 0-07-802925-2

Vice president and editor-in-chief: *Brent Gordon*
Editorial director: *Paul Ducham*
Executive editor: *John Weimeister*
Executive director of development: *Ann Torbert*
Editorial coordinator: *Heather Darr*
Vice president and director of marketing: *Robin J. Zwettler*
Marketing director: *Amee Mosley*
Marketing manager: *Donielle Xu*
Vice president of editing, design, and production: *Sesha Bolisetty*
Senior project manager: *Diane L. Nowaczyk*
Buyer II: *Debra R. Sylvester*
Lead designer: *Matthew Baldwin*
Senior photo research coordinator: *Keri Johnson*
Photo researcher: *Poyee Oster*
Senior media project manager: *Susan Lombardi*
Senior media project manager: *Bruce Gin*
Media project manager: *Suresh Babu, Hurix Systems Pvt. Ltd.*
Cover design: *Laurie Entringer*
Cover images: *©Getty Images*
Interior design: *Matthew Baldwin*
Typeface: *10.5/12 Goudy*
Compositor: *Laserwords Private Limited*
Printer: *R. R. Donnelley*

Library of Congress Cataloging-in-Publication Data

Human resource management : gaining a competitive advantage / Raymond A. Noe . . . [et al.].—8th ed.
      p. cm.
    Includes index.
    ISBN-13: 978-0-07-802925-7 (alk. paper)
    ISBN-10: 0-07-802925-2 (alk. paper)
    1. Personnel management—United States. I. Noe, Raymond A.

HF5549.2.U5H8 2013
658.3—dc23

                                                                2011043623

www.mhhe.com

In tribute to Karen Liffring Hill
— R. A. N.

To my parents, Harold and Elizabeth, my wife, Patty, and my children, Jennifer, Marie, Timothy, and Jeffrey
— J. R. H.

To my parents, Robert and Shirley, my wife, Heather, and my children, Chris and Annie
— B. G.

To my parents, Patricia and Paul, my wife, Mary, and my sons, Michael and Matthew
— P. M. W.

ABOUT THE AUTHORS

RAYMOND A. NOE is the Robert and Anne Hoyt Designated Professor of Management at The Ohio State University. He was previously a professor in the Department of Management at Michigan State University and the Industrial Relations Center of the Carlson School of Management, University of Minnesota. He received his BS in psychology from The Ohio State University and his MA and PhD in psychology from Michigan State University. Professor Noe conducts research and teaches undergraduate as well as MBA and PhD students in human resource management, managerial skills, quantitative methods, human resource information systems, training, employee development, and organizational behavior. He has published articles in the *Academy of Management Annals, Academy of Management Journal, Academy of Management Review, Journal of Applied Psychology, Journal of Vocational Behavior,* and *Personnel Psychology.* Professor Noe is currently on the editorial boards of several journals including *Personnel Psychology, Journal of Applied Psychology,* and *Journal of Organizational Behavior.* Professor Noe has received awards for his teaching and research excellence, including the Herbert G. Heneman Distinguished Teaching Award in 1991 and the Ernest J. McCormick Award for Distinguished Early Career Contribution from the Society for Industrial and Organizational Psychology in 1993. He is also a fellow of the Society of Industrial and Organizational Psychology.

JOHN R. HOLLENBECK holds the positions of University Distinguished Professor at Michigan State University and Eli Broad Professor of Management at the Eli Broad Graduate School of Business Administration. Dr. Hollenbeck received his PhD in management from New York University in 1984. He served as the acting editor at *Organizational Behavior and Human Decision Processes* in 1995, the associate editor of *Decision Sciences* from 1999 to 2004, and the editor of *Personnel Psychology* from 1996 to 2002. He has published over 80 articles and book chapters on the topics of team decision making and work motivation. According to the Institute for Scientific Information, this body of work has been cited over 2,500 times by other researchers. Dr. Hollenbeck has been awarded over $6 million in external research funding, most of which was granted by the Office of Naval Research and the Air Force Office of Scientific Research. Along with Daniel R. Ilgen, he founded the Michigan State University Team Effectiveness Research Laboratory, and this facility has been dedicated to conducting large sample team research since 1991. Dr. Hollenbeck has been awarded fellowship status in both the Academy of Management and the American Psychological Association, and was recognized with the Career Achievement Award by the HR Division of the Academy of Management (2011) and the Early Career Award by the Society of Industrial and Organizational Psychology (1992). At Michigan State, Dr. Hollenbeck has won several teaching awards including the Michigan State Distinguished Faculty Award, the Michigan State Teacher-Scholar Award, and the Broad MBA Most Outstanding Faculty Member.

BARRY GERHART is Professor of Management and Human Resources and the Bruce R. Ellig Distinguished Chair in Pay and Organizational Effectiveness, School of Business, University of Wisconsin—Madison. He has also served as department chair or area coordinator at Cornell, Vanderbilt, and Wisconsin. His research interests include compensation, human resource strategy, international human resources, and employee retention. Professor Gerhart received his BS in psychology from Bowling Green State University and his PhD in industrial relations from the University of Wisconsin—Madison. His research has been published in a variety of outlets, including the *Academy of Management Annals, Academy of Management Journal, Annual Review of Psychology, Journal of Applied Psychology,* and *Personnel Psychology.* He has co-authored two books in the area of compensation. He serves on the editorial boards of journals such as the *Academy of Management Journal, Industrial and Labor Relations Review, International Journal of Human Resource Management, Journal of Applied Psychology, Management & Organization Review,* and *Personnel Psychology.* Professor Gerhart is a past recipient of the Scholarly Achievement Award and of the International Human Resource Management Scholarly Research Award, both from the Human Resources Division, Academy of Management. He is a Fellow of the American Psychological Association and of the Society for Industrial and Organizational Psychology.

PATRICK M. WRIGHT is the William J. Conaty GE Professor of Strategic Human Resources in the School of Industrial and Labor Relations at Cornell University. He was formerly Associate Professor of Management and Coordinator of the Master of Science in Human Resource Management program in the College of Business Administration and Graduate School of Business at Texas A&M University. He holds a BA in psychology from Wheaton College and an MBA and a PhD in organizational behavior/human resource management from Michigan State University. He teaches, conducts research, and consults in the area of strategic human resource management. His research articles have appeared in journals such as the *Academy of Management Journal, Journal of Applied Psychology, Organizational Behavior and Human Decision Processes, Journal of Management,* and *Human Resource Management Review.* He has served on the editorial boards of *Journal of Applied Psychology, Journal of Management,* and *Academy of Management Review* and currently serves as Senior Associate Editor of *Journal of Management.* He has consulted for a number of organizations, and in 2011 was named by *HR Magazine* as one of the 20 most influential thought leaders in HR.

PREFACE

The U.S. economy—as well as the economies of many other countries across the globe—is struggling to recover from the worldwide recession which officially ended in the summer of 2009. The slow recovery means that both consumers and businesses are carefully considering their spending patterns and investments. Both private- and public-sector employers are delaying calling back laid-off workers or hiring new employees until they see several quarters of increased demand for their products and services. Also, they are continuing to examine how they can improve their "bottom line" while reducing costs. This has resulted in not only considering layoffs, but also purchasing new technology and upgrading equipment, and an increased emphasis on ensuring that management practices and working conditions help employees work harder and smarter.

The gloomy economic conditions have contributed to the demise of familiar companies such as Borders (bookstores) and Blockbuster (video rentals). However, companies in some sectors of the economy are experiencing increased demand for their products and services. For example, Apple, Google, Facebook, Foursquare, McDonald's, Groupon, and Jeni's Ice Creams are expanding, growing, and hiring new employees. Because of increased orders for their products and services, companies in the information technology and fabricated metal manufacturing sectors are struggling to find qualified, talented, and skilled employees despite the many workers available due to the high unemployment rate.

At the same time companies are taking steps to deal with the current economic conditions, they are also paying closer attention to how to engage in business practices that are economically sound but sustainable. That is, business practices that are ethical, protect the environment, and contribute to the communities from which the business draws the financial, physical, and human resources needed to provide its product and services. Consumers are demanding accountability in business practices: making money for shareholders should not involve abandoning ethics, ruining the environment, or taking advantage of employees from developing countries!

Regardless of whether a company's strategic direction involves downsizing, restructuring, growth, or a merger or acquisition, how human resources are managed is crucial for providing "value" to customers, shareholders, employees, and the community in which they are located. Our definition of "value" includes not only profits but also employee growth and satisfaction, additional employment opportunities, stewardship of the environment, and contributions to community programs. If a company fails to effectively use its financial capital, physical capital, and human capital to create "value," it will not survive. The way a company treats its employees (including those who are forced to leave their jobs) will influence the company's public reputation and brand as a responsible business, especially in a poor economy. For example, companies such as Coca-Cola, Caterpillar, and Estée Lauder are sticking with their recruiting, training and development, and employee recognition plans but, at the same time, ensuring that all employees (including top-level managers) make shared sacrifices (such as salary freezes and pay cuts) needed to sustain their businesses.

We believe that all aspects of human resource management—including how companies interact with the environment; acquire, prepare, develop, and compensate employees; and design and evaluate work—can help companies meet their competitive challenges and create value. Meeting challenges is necessary to create value and to gain a competitive advantage.

The Competitive Challenges

The challenges that organizations face today can be grouped into three categories:

- **The sustainability challenge.** Sustainability refers to the ability of a company to survive and succeed in a dynamic competitive environment. Sustainability depends on how well a company meets the needs of those who have an interest in seeing that the company succeeds. Challenges to sustainability include the ability to deal with economic and social changes, engage in responsible and ethical business practices, efficiently use natural resources and protect the environment, provide high-quality products and services, and develop methods and measures (also known as metrics) to determine if the company is meeting stakeholder needs. To compete in today's economy companies use mergers and acquisitions, growth, and downsizing. Companies rely on skilled workers to be productive, creative, and innovative and to provide high-quality customer service; their work is demanding and companies cannot guarantee job security. One issue is how to attract and retain a committed, productive workforce in turbulent economic conditions that offer opportunity for financial success but can also turn sour, making every employee expendable. Forward-looking businesses are capitalizing on the strengths of a diverse multigenerational workforce. The experiences of Enron, *News of the World*, and Lehman Brothers provide vivid examples of how sustainability depends on ethical and responsible business practices, including the management of human resources. Another important issue is how to meet financial objectives through meeting both customer and employee needs. To meet the sustainability challenge companies must engage in human resource management practices that address short-term needs but help ensure the long-term success of the firm. The development and choice of human resource management practices should support business goals and strategy.
- **The global challenge.** Companies must be prepared to compete with companies from around the world either in the United States or abroad. Companies must both defend their domestic markets from foreign competitors and broaden their scope to encompass global markets. Globalization is a continuing challenge as companies look to enter emerging markets in countries such as Brazil and China to provide their products and services.
- **The technology challenge.** Using new technologies such as computer-aided manufacturing, virtual reality, and social networking can give companies an edge. New technologies can result in employees "working smarter" as well as providing higher-quality products and more efficient services to customers. Companies that have realized the greatest gains from new technology have human resource management practices that support the use of technology to create what is known as high-performance work systems. Work, training programs, and reward systems often need to be reconfigured to support employees' use of new technology. The three important aspects of high-performance work systems are (1) human resources and their capabilities, (2) new technology and its opportunities, and (3) efficient work structures and policies that allow employees and technology to interact. Companies are

also using e-HRM (electronic HRM) applications to give employees more owner-ship of the employment relationship through the ability to enroll in and participate in training programs, change benefits, communicate with co-workers and custom-ers online, and work "virtually" with peers in geographically different locations.

We believe that organizations must successfully deal with these challenges to cre-ate and maintain value, and the key to facing these challenges is a motivated, well-trained, and committed workforce.

The Changing Role of the Human Resource Management Function

The human resource management (HRM) profession and practices have undergone substantial change and redefinition. Many articles written in both the academic and practitioner literature have been critical of the traditional HRM function. Unfor-tunately, in many organizations HRM services are not providing value but instead are mired down in managing trivial administrative tasks. Where this is true, HRM departments can be replaced with new technology or outsourced to a vendor who can provide higher-quality services at a lower cost. Although this recommendation is indeed somewhat extreme (and threatening to both HRM practitioners and those who teach human resource management!), it does demonstrate that companies need to ensure that their HRM functions are creating value for the firm.

Technology should be used where appropriate to automate routine activities, and managers should concentrate on HRM activities that can add substantial value to the company. Consider employee benefits: Technology is available to automate the process by which employees enroll in benefits programs and to keep detailed records of benefits usage. This use of technology frees up time for the manager to focus on activities that can create value for the firm (such as how to control health care costs and reduce workers' compensation claims).

Although the importance of some HRM departments is being debated, everyone agrees on the need to successfully manage human resources for a company to maximize its competitiveness. Several themes emerge from our conversations with managers and our review of research on HRM practices. First, in today's organizations, managers themselves are becoming more responsible for HRM practices and most believe that people issues are critical to business success. Second, most managers believe that their HRM departments are not well respected because of a perceived lack of competence, business sense, and contact with operations. A study by Deloitte consulting and *The Economist* Intelligence Unit found that only 23% of business executives believe that HR currently plays a significant role in strategy and operational results. Third, many managers believe that for HRM practices to be effective they need to be related to the strategic direction of the business. This text emphasizes how HRM practices can and should contribute to business goals and help to improve product and service quality and effectiveness.

Our intent is to provide students with the background to be successful HRM profes-sionals, to manage human resources effectively, and to be knowledgeable consumers of HRM products. Managers must be able to identify effective HRM practices to purchase these services from a consultant, to work with the HRM department, or to design and implement them personally. The text emphasizes how a manager can more effectively manage human resources and highlights important issues in current HRM practice.

We think this book represents a valuable approach to teaching human resource management for several reasons:

- The text draws from the diverse research, teaching, and consulting experiences of four authors who have taught human resource management to undergraduates, traditional day MBA students as a required and elective course, and more experienced managers and professional employees in weekend and evening MBA programs. The teamwork approach gives a depth and breadth to the coverage that is not found in other texts.
- Human resource management is viewed as critical to the success of a business. The text emphasizes how the HRM function, as well as the management of human resources, can help companies gain a competitive advantage.
- The book discusses current issues such as social networking, talent management, diversity, and employee engagement, all of which have a major impact on business and HRM practice.
- Strategic human resource management is introduced early in the book and integrated throughout the text.
- Examples of how new technologies are being used to improve the efficiency and effectiveness of HRM practices are provided throughout the text.
- We provide examples of how companies are evaluating HRM practices to determine their value.

Organization

Human Resource Management: Gaining a Competitive Advantage includes an introductory chapter (Chapter 1) and five parts.

Chapter 1 provides a detailed discussion of the global, new economy, stakeholder, and work system challenges that influence companies' abilities to successfully meet the needs of shareholders, customers, employees, and other stakeholders. We discuss how the management of human resources can help companies meet the competitive challenges.

Part 1 includes a discussion of the environmental forces that companies face in attempting to capitalize on their human resources as a means to gain competitive advantage. The environmental forces include the strategic direction of the business, the legal environment, and the type of work performed and physical arrangement of the work.

A key focus of the strategic human resource management chapter is highlighting the role that staffing, performance management, training and development, and compensation play in different types of business strategies. A key focus of the legal chapter is enhancing managers' understanding of laws related to sexual harassment, affirmative action, and accommodations for disabled employees. The various types of discrimination and ways they have been interpreted by the courts are discussed. The chapter on analysis and design of work emphasizes how work systems can improve company competitiveness by alleviating job stress and by improving employees' motivation and satisfaction with their jobs.

Part 2 deals with the acquisition and preparation of human resources, including human resource planning and recruitment, selection, and training. The human resource planning chapter illustrates the process of developing a human resource plan. Also, the strengths and weaknesses of staffing options such as outsourcing, use of contingent workers, and downsizing are discussed. Strategies for recruiting talented employees are emphasized. The selection chapter emphasizes ways to minimize errors in employee selection and placement to improve the company's competitive position. Selection method standards such as validity and reliability are discussed in easily understandable terms without compromising the technical complexity of these issues. The chapter discusses selection methods such as interviews and various types of tests (including personality, honesty, and drug tests) and compares them on measures of validity, reliability, utility, and legality.

We discuss the components of effective training systems and the manager's role in determining employees' readiness for training, creating a positive learning environment, and ensuring that training is used on the job. The advantages and disadvantages of different training methods are described, such as e-learning and mobile training.

Part 3 explores how companies can determine the value of employees and capitalize on their talents through retention and development strategies. The performance management chapter examines the strengths and weaknesses of performance management methods that use ratings, objectives, or behaviors. The employee development chapter introduces the student to how assessment, job experiences, formal courses, and mentoring relationships are used to develop employees. The chapter on retention and separation discusses how managers can maximize employee productivity and satisfaction to avoid absenteeism and turnover. The use of employee surveys to monitor job and organizational characteristics that affect satisfaction and subsequently retention is emphasized.

Part 4 covers rewarding and compensating human resources, including designing pay structures, recognizing individual contributions, and providing benefits. Here we explore how managers should decide the pay rate for different jobs, given the company's compensation strategy and the worth of jobs. The advantages and disadvantages of merit pay, gainsharing, and skill-based pay are discussed. The benefits chapter highlights the different types of employer-provided benefits and discusses how benefit costs can be contained. International comparisons of compensation and benefit practices are provided.

Part 5 covers special topics in human resource management, including labor–management relations, international HRM, and managing the HRM function. The collective bargaining and labor relations chapter focuses on traditional issues in labor–management relations, such as union structure and membership, the organizing process, and contract negotiations; it also discusses new union agendas and less adversarial approaches to labor–management relations. Social and political changes, such as introduction of the euro currency in the European Community, are discussed in the chapter on global human resource management. Selecting, preparing, and rewarding employees for foreign assignments is also discussed. The text concludes with a chapter that emphasizes how HRM practices should be aligned to help the company meet its business objectives. The chapter emphasizes that the HRM function needs to have a customer focus to be effective.

New Feature and Content Changes in This Edition

Chapter I

The chapter opens with an updated story on how Starbucks' HR practices have helped the company weather the recession and prepare for growth. New chapter topics include the shared service model for organizing HR; the strategic value of HR using workforce analytics; and the impact of social networking on HR practices. An updated discussion of the economy, occupational projections, labor force statistics (age, gender, immigration, skills), and their implications for companies and their HR function is provided. New and updated topics include how Google and Southwest Airlines are developing the right mix of HR skills and experience to contribute to the firms' overall business strategies; K&N Management and its 2010 Baldrige Award; lean manufacturing; and Apple's global reputation for auditing its overseas suppliers. End-of-chapter changes include a new Managing People case on skill shortages and an updated Strategy case about online retailer Zappos.

Chapter 2

A new chapter opener discusses HP's new business strategy in the face of increased competition. An updated discussion provides reasons why GM needed to change its business model. The concept of SWOT analysis is described using Google as an example. A new Technology feature focuses on how companies partner with universities to leverage social media. A new Globalization box discusses the talent shortage among millions of college graduates in India. The wisdom of helping rainforest tribes is explored in a new Sustainability feature. Data on layoff events and separations have been updated.

Chapter 3

The chapter-opening case provides updated information on Walmart's discrimination lawsuit and how it is progressing through the courts. A new Globalization box explores how India's lack of privacy laws presents a challenge to BlackBerry users. New and updated discussion is included on how the EEOC has redefined "disability." New examples include a pregnancy discrimination case as well as a disability discrimination suit brought by the EEOC. Updated figures on numbers of discrimination cases in several areas such as disability, sexual harassment, and religion are provided. A new Technology feature provides strategies on how to get doctors to use current technology, and a new Sustainability box focuses on using caution when dealing with whistleblowers.

Chapter 4

The chapter opens with a new vignette on the resurgence of American manufacturing attributable to innovation, flexible team-based structures, and leveraging skills. A new Technology box discusses new computer operations in Silicon Valley that traditionally have been outsourced. A new Globalization feature discusses the "suicide nets" at Foxconn's company-owned worker dormitories in China, highlighting the exploitation of the labor force and the public relations fallout from such abuse. A new Sustainability box highlights "stretched job descriptions" that promote efficiency, on the one hand, but role overload for some and unemployment for others. A new Evidence-Based HR feature describes how pharmaceutical giant Eli Lilly converted a two-stage testing–launching workflow into a more streamlined single-stage process. A revised Strategy case updates Toyota's production problems, and an updated Managing People case highlights IBM's innovation portals for creating new project teams. Additional material has been added on how lean manufacturing techniques have led to reduced layoffs but also reduced hiring, and "just-in-time" inventory management practices and their implications for HR staffing levels. A new safety-focused example describes how UPS used GPS in its delivery trucks to minimize dangerous left-hand turns resulting in more than a million dollars in fuel savings and significantly fewer accidents and driver injuries.

Chapter 5

The new chapter-opening story describes the bidding war for new technical talent among Oracle, Hewlett Packard, Microsoft, and Facebook, and the lengths the companies will go to in recruiting new employees. A new Technology box focuses on how smaller niche-based recruiting sites such as LinkedIn and The Ladders are outcompeting larger recruiting sites such as Monster.com and CareerBuilder. A new Globalization box explains how Dutch and German employers maintain high levels of employment despite the global recession. The Arab Spring uprising is discussed in a new Sustainability feature and how the demonstrations were fueled in part by high unemployment rates among young workers. A new Evidence-Based HR story describes a research study in which applicants who saw company videos as part of their job search rated the companies higher in innovativeness, style, and dominance and lower in terms of cost cutting and thrift. An updated Strategy case shows how the banking industry used federal bailout money to hire more foreign workers as part of H-1B visa programs and the controversy that ensued. In an updated Managing People case, employers discuss how they are trying to keep their older and most experienced workers from retiring. A new section on leading indicators of labor demand suggests that pricing changes are often a good indicator of capacity-related problems. A new example examines the ongoing problems with the development of Boeing's 787 *Dreamliner*—a project that is three years late and billions of dollars over budget— caused by the amount and type of work that was done offshore.

Chapter 6

A new opening vignette describes the selection and composition process involved with SEAL Team 6 and their role in the hunt for Osama bin Laden. A new Technology box describes how computer-adaptive testing is helping to rewrite the process by which test construction is conducted. A new Globalization feature focuses on France's anti-religious rules and how they compare with the notion of freedom of religious practices and evidence of religious discrimination in that country. Rules associated with "retesting" and throwing out test results when they have adverse effects are discussed in a new Sustainability box. A new Evidence-Based HR box discusses how demographic similarity results in biased interviews when interviews are unstructured. An updated Strategy case focuses on security checks and the lack of quality control among many providers of such services. An updated Managing People case highlights computer-generated alternatives to subjective supervisory evaluations when it comes to producing criteria for validation studies. New material has been added on the Walmart sex discrimination lawsuit and how this could be traced to overly autonomous and decentralized decision-making processes. A new discussion has been added on how former "diversity" initiatives have been labeled "inclusive initiatives" and how people react to different frameworks for the same practices. New evidence on discrimination against Muslims among U.S. employers is provided. A new discussion is included in the chapter about how employers are using video-based interviews instead of face-to-face interviews and when this approach works effectively. Recent critiques on the use of personality measures for personnel selection are explored.

Chapter 7

The opening story discusses a chain of car washes in Indiana and Ohio that believes its success comes from its employees and its hiring and training practices. A new discussion of training's role in continuous learning and its competitive advantage includes comments about information learning and knowledge management and an example of Campbell Soup's continuous learning philosophy. A new figure has been added to the chapter that highlights key features of continuous learning. A new table has been included that lists factors that influence a person's motivation to learn. An expanded discussion explains how iPads are being used by Hilton Worldwide for training purposes. A new section has been added on the use of social media for training. New examples of learning management systems are highlighted. A new Strategy case focuses on Farmers Insurance Group and how growth through acquisition helped the company's competitive position. A new Managing People case describes the learning process employed at Wegmans Food Markets.

Chapter 8

A new chapter-opening vignette describes how performance management helped turn around Scripps Health, a private nonprofit community health system in San Diego, California. A new table provides examples of problems with traditional annual performance reviews. A new figure illustrates the performance management process and accompanies an expanded discussion on the topic. A new Globalization feature describes the mix of metrics used by the WD-40 company to support local and company performance. Sprint is featured in a new discussion of strategic performance management. A new discussion of competency models and their use in performance management has been added. A new table features the competency model used by the Luxottica Group, a global leader in fashion, luxury, and sports eyewear. New coverage of SMART goals and balanced scorecards is included. A new discussion describes Just Born's performance management system that is based on a *kaizen* (quality) process. A new Sustainability feature explains that how employees perform is as important as what they accomplish. An expanded text discussion and Technology box describe technology's use in performance management, including a new focus on the use of social networks to provide feedback.

Chapter 9

The chapter begins with a story about Tyson Foods and how the company develops its management staff. A new Globalization box features InterContinental Hotel Group's Leaders' Lounge—a virtual leadership development community. BlueCross BlueShield of North Carolina is featured in a new Evidence-Based HR box about initiating a management development program for all of its formal and emerging leaders. A new table is included that provides examples of mentoring programs. A revised discussion is provided about Myers-Briggs with an example from Hallmark Cards. Updated figures are included about women in management (and their attempt to "melt the glass ceiling"). Succession planning is discussed in a health-system context, along with a new discussion of transparency in the succession planning process with company examples.

Chapter 10

The chapter-opening story is about Steven Slater, the JetBlue flight attendant who quit his job by opening a plane's exit door on an active runway, and the sources of dissatisfaction with his work that led to this act—for which he became a hero. A new Technology box explores how new apps for iPhones and iPads are designed to increase positive moods and job satisfaction. The new Globalization feature discusses the expanded role women are playing in the Indian labor force and the historical reasons why their participation in the workforce was low. A new Sustainability box explains how the Deep Water Horizon disaster, which led to the Gulf oil spill, was triggered by lax standards for worker safety and safe practices. A new Evidence-Based HR box explores when and why some training programs actually create high levels of turnover in organizations, and how to develop training programs with more local value. An updated Strategy case spotlights HR changes at Home Depot. An updated Managing People case discusses the high suicide rates among military recruiters and how this could be traced to HR practices. New material has been added on "bring your gun to work" laws and how they created safety issues for all employees. A new section is included on the role of private investigators as part of the process to establish due process when terminating employment among poor performers. A new section has been added on health-based initiatives that go beyond employees and offer rewards for their spouses and children. A new discussion about whistleblowing has been added and includes the WikiLeaks episode involving Bradley Manning.

Chapter 11

The chapter opens with a story about how rapid wage growth in China is causing some foreign companies to move production out of China. Updated tables are included on earnings by race and gender and on earnings by executives. A new Globalization box describes how Volkswagen is lowering its labor costs by opening its first plant in the United States. A new Sustainability feature describes Google's decision to raise its wage levels for employees to compete better for new talent. A new Technology box explains how sometimes expensive lawyers can be replaced by smart software. Discussion has been added about Chrysler and GM's bankruptcies and how changes to hourly wages will help make their labor costs more competitive going forward. A new Managing People case describes how workers at Harley-Davidson and Sub-Zero were faced with either taking pay cuts or having their jobs moved elsewhere.

Chapter 12

The chapter-opening vignette discusses how companies are gradually restarting their merit increase and bonus programs. A new Globalization box describes how some Asian companies are increasing their reliance on pay-for-performance programs. A new Technology feature explores how BP changed its incentives to highlight safety. A new Sustainability box describes how Goldman Sachs changed its bonus plan to reward performance while avoiding excessive risk-taking by its employees. A section has been added on the newly passed Dodd-Frank Act, including its "Say-on-Pay" requirement.

Chapter 13

The chapter begins with a story about how employers are shifting health care costs to their employees. Updated tables are included on benefit/compensation costs to employers; benefit programs offered by employers; and an international comparison of employee hours worked. A new Evidence-Based HR box deals with analyzing a company's return on investment for employee wellness programs. New discussion has been added about the dangers of investing too much in the stock of the company where you work—the example of Bear Stearns is used. A new Sustainability box describes how some companies are asking higher-paid workers to pay a greater share of health care costs. A new Globalization feature focuses on how Toyota manages the health of its workforce. A new Technology box describes how companies communicate benefits information online. A section has been added that describes how GM, Ford, and Chrysler used a voluntary employee benefits association (VEBA) to remove a substantial part of legacy benefits obligations from their books to improve the companies' financial health. A new Managing People case describes how some companies require employees to follow healthy lifestyles to keep their jobs.

Chapter 14

New chapter opening discusses the two-tier wage system growth and its role at the Big Three Detroit automakers. Updated tables describe the largest labor unions, union membership trends, employer resistance to labor union organizing trends, and work stoppages. A new Technology feature explores the role technology has played in labor union actions in China. A new Globalization box discusses how the legal framework for collective bargaining in China. A new Managing People case describes how Boeing built a plant in South Carolina in hopes of avoiding labor problems but is facing legal challenges in trying to open the facility.

Chapter 15

A new opening vignette discusses GE's shift to a global workforce. New examples are included about the increasingly global nature of business and how many global high performers come from companies headquartered outside the United States. Updated information is included about cross-border mergers and their increasing numbers. New information has been added about the concept of cultural intelligence and the pros and cons of cultural diversity within organizations. A new Technology box discusses how China seeks to solve structural problems before technology boosts unrest among its workers. A new Sustainability feature discusses Coca-Cola in South Africa.

Chapter 16

A new opening case focuses on Google and how the company transformed its HR function. In-depth discussion of Google and its business operations occurs throughout the chapter, including the content of its HR strategy; the company's use of technology and metrics to identify what makes great leaders at Google; and its HR information/social network system which serves as a combination of job posting and a social networking site. A new Technology box discusses "virtual onboarding" at IBM. A new Sustainability feature discusses strategies for managing after layoffs. A new Globalization box compares U.S. and European Chief Human Resource Officers (CHROs) and covers the differences in terms of the challenges of building HR functions based on a 2011 CHRO survey.

Acknowledgments

As this book enters its eighth edition, it is important to acknowledge those who started it all. The first edition of this book would not have been possible if not for the entrepreneurial spirit of two individuals. Bill Schoof, president of Austen Press, gave us the resources and had the confidence that four unproven textbook writers could provide a new perspective for teaching human resource management. John Weimeister, our editor, provided us with valuable marketing information, helped us in making major decisions regarding the book, and made writing this book an enjoyable process. We continue to enjoy John's friendship and hospitality at national meetings. We were fortunate to have the opportunity in the eighth edition to work with John again. We also worked with an all-star development and project management team, including Heather Darr, Diane Nowaczyk, and Michelle Gardner. Their suggestions, patience, gentle prodding, and careful oversight kept the author team focused on providing a high-quality revision while meeting publication deadline. Many thanks to Diane Nowaczyk and Michelle Gardner, project managers, for their careful review of the revised manuscript.

We would also like to thank the professors who gave of their time to review the text and attend focus groups to help craft this eighth edition. Their helpful comments and suggestions have greatly helped to enhance this edition:

Richard Arvey
National University of Singapore

Steve Ash
University of Akron

Carlson Austin
South Carolina State University

Janice Baldwin
The University of Texas at Arlington

Alison Barber
Michigan State University

Kathleen Barnes
University of Wisconsin, Superior

James E. Bartlett, II
University of South Carolina–Columbia

Ron Beaulieu
Central Michigan University

Philip Benson
New Mexico State University

Nancy Bereman
Wichita State University

Chris Berger
Purdue University

Carol Bibly
Triton College

Wendy Boswell
Texas A&M University

Sarah Bowman
Idaho State University

Charles Braun
University of Kentucky

James Browne
University of Southern Colorado

Gerald Calvasina
Southern Utah University

Martin Carrigan
University of Findlay

Georgia Chao
Michigan State University

Fay Cocchiara
Arkansas State University

Walter Coleman
Florida Southern College

Mary Connerley
Virginia Tech University

Donna Cooke
Florida Atlantic University–Davis

Craig Cowles
Bridgewater State College

Michael Crant
University of Notre Dame

Shannon Davis
North Carolina State University

Roger Dean
Washington & Lee University

John Delery
University of Arkansas

Fred Dorn
The University of Mississippi

Jennifer Dose
Messiah College

Tom Dougherty
University of Missouri

Berrin Erdogan
Portland State University

Angela Farrar
University of Nevada–Las Vegas

Dyanne Ferk
University of Illinois–Springfield

Robert Figler
University of Akron

Art Fischer
Pittsburgh State University

Barry Friedman
State University of New York at Oswego

Cynthia Fukami
University of Denver

Daniel J. Gallagher
University of Illinois–Springfield

Donald G. Gardner
University of Colorado at Colorado Springs

Bonnie Fox Garrity
D'Youville College

Sonia Goltz
Michigan Technological University

Bob Graham
Sacred Heart University

Terri Griffith
Washington University

Ken Gross
University of Oklahoma–Norman

John Hannon
University at Buffalo

Bob Hatfield
Indiana University

Alan Heffner
James Monroe Center

Fred Heidrich
Black Hills State University

Rob Heneman
Ohio State University

Gary Hensel
McHenry County College

Kim Hester
Arkansas State University

Nancy Higgins
Montgomery College–Rockville

Wayne Hockwater
Florida State University

Denise Tanguay Hoyer
Eastern Michigan University

Fred Hughes
Faulkner University

Natalie J. Hunter
Portland State University

Sanford Jacoby
University of California, Los Angeles

Frank Jeffries
University of Alaska–Anchorage

Gwen Jones
Fairleigh Dickinson University

Hank Karp
Hampton University

Marianne Koch
University of Oregon

James Kolacek
Palm Beach Atlantic University

Tom Kolenko
Kennesaw State College

Elias Konwufine
Keiser University

Ken Kovach
George Mason University

Vonda Laughlin
Carson-Newman College

Helen LaVan
DePaul University

Renee Lerche
University of Michigan

Nancy Boyd Lillie
University of North Texas

Karen Locke
William & Mary

Larry Mainstone
Valparaiso University

Ann-Marie Majeskey
Mount Olive College

Liz Malatestinic
Indiana University

Patricia Martina
University of Texas–San Antonio

Nicholas Mathys
DePaul University

Lisa McConnell
Oklahoma State University

Liliana Meneses
University of Maryland University College

Jessica Methot
Rutgers University

Stuart Milne
Georgia Institute of Technology

Barbara Minsky
Troy University

Kelly Mollica
University of Memphis

Jim Morgan
California State University–Chico

Gary Murray
Rose State College

Millicent Nelson
Middle Tennessee State University

Lam Nguyen
Palm Beach State College

Cheri Ostroff
Teachers College Columbia

Teresa Palmer
Illinois State University

Robert Paul
Kansas State University

Tracy Porter
Cleveland State University

Gregory Quinet
Southern Polytechnic State University

Sam Rabinowitz
Rutgers University

David Rahn
California State University–Chico

Jude Rathburn
University of Wisconsin–Milwaukee

Katherine Ready
University of Wisconsin

Herbert Ricardo
Indian River State College

Mike Ritchie
University of South Carolina

Gwen Rivkin
Cardinal Stritch University

Mark Roehling
Michigan State University

Mary Ellen Rosetti
Hudson Valley Community College

Miyako Schanely
Jefferson Community College

Robert Schappe
University of Michigan–Dearborn

Joshua Schwarz
Miami University–Ohio

Christina Shalley
Georgia Tech

Richard Simpson
University of Utah

Romila Singh
University of Wisconsin–Milwaukee

Erika Engel Small
Coastal Carolina University

Mark Smith
Mississippi Gulf Coast Community College–Gulfport

Scott Snell
University of Virginia

Howard Stanger
Canisius College

Gary Stroud
Franklin University

Cynthia Sutton
Indiana University–South Bend

Peg Thomas
Pennsylvania State University–Behrend

Steven L. Thomas
Missouri State University

Tom Timmerman
Tennessee Technology University

George Tompson
University of Tampa

Linda Turner
Morrisville State College

Sheng Wang
University of Nevada–Las Vegas

Lynn Wilson
Saint Leo University

We would also like to thank the reviewers and focus group participants who made important suggestions for previous editions of this text. Their comments have helped to develop the book from edition to edition:

Joan Benek-Rivera
University of Pennsylvania–Bloomsburg

Angela Boston
The University of Texas at Arlington

Ronald Brownie
Purdue University–North Central

Jon Bryan
Bridgewater State College

LeAnne Coder
Western Kentucky University

Louis Firenze
Northwood University

Julie Indvik
California State University, Chico

Roy Johnson
Iowa State University

Gwendolyn Jones
University of Akron

Beth Koufteros
Texas A&M University

Chalmer Labig
Oklahoma State University

Patricia Lanier
University of Louisiana at Lafayette

Susan Madsen
Utah Valley University

Sarah Sanders-Smith
Purdue University–North Central

Jack Schoenfelder
Ivy Tech Community College

Pat Setlik
Harper College

Richard Shuey
Thomas More College

Kris Sperstad
Chippewa Valley Technical College

K. J. Tullis
University of Central Oklahoma

Dan Turban
University of Missouri–Columbia

Linda Turner
Morrisville State College

Linda Urbanski
University of Toledo

William Van Lente
Alliant International University

Charles Vance
Loyola Marymount University

Kim Wade
Washington State University

Renee Warning
University of Central Oklahoma

George Whaley
San Jose State University

Daniel Yazak
Montana State University–Billings

Ryan D. Zimmerman
Texas A&M University

Raymond A. Noe
John R. Hollenbeck
Barry Gerhart
Patrick M. Wright

Highlights and Improvements to This Edition

The Eighth Edition of *Human Resource Management: Gaining a Competitive Advantage* was developed to teach students how to face and meet a variety of challenges within their organizations and how to gain a competitive advantage for their companies.

Throughout this text, the pedagogy focuses on HRM practices and strategies companies can employ to be competitive. These boxes, cases, and applications are found in every chapter and provide excellent real business examples to underscore key concepts throughout the text.

Please take a moment to learn about this new edition and its exciting enhancements by paging through this visual guide outlining the text's features.

Twitter Focus creates an excellent opportunity for students to use social media to discuss chapter topics and apply them to chapter cases that can be found on the text website at www.mhhe.com/noe8e.

TWITTER FOCUS: KINAXIS CHOOSES SALES REPS WITH PERSONALITY

Kinaxis is a software company headquartered in Ottawa, Ontario, that sells to clients around the world. Its specialty is software for supply chain management—all the processes and relationships through which companies obtain supplies as needed and get their products to customers on time and at minimal cost. This is a sophisticated type of product, tailored to a company's specific needs. Therefore, Kinaxis depends on salespeople who understand how businesses work, who listen carefully to identify needs, and who provide excellent customer service to maintain long-term business relationships.

Recently, Bob Dolan, vice president for sales at Kinaxis, needed to hire a sales team to serve clients in North America. The company had just one salesperson serving the continent, and Dolan wanted to add four more. He received about 100 résumés and wanted to select from these. He started by reviewing the résumés against job requirements and selected 20 candidates for a first round of interviews. The interview

That meant Dolan still had eight candidates to fill four positions. He asked each one to give him the names of major accounts he or she had signed up in the previous two years. Four candidates were able to come up with three or four large clients. Those were the candidates Dolan hired.

Since then, Dolan says his experience with personality testing has only reinforced his belief that this selection method helps Kinaxis identify the best candidates. For example, one sales rep had scored low on "pace," indicating that the individual might lack the patience needed for the slow cycles required to close a sale of a complex software system. Dolan hoped the issue could be overcome if he provided enough coaching, but in fact, the sales rep sometimes behaved impatiently, annoying prospects. After three years of trying to help him grow into the job, Dolan laid him off.

The company's commitment to careful selection is

The popular boxes **"Competing through Sustainability," "Competing through Globalization,"** and **"Competing through Technology"** have been updated with new references to recent companies and examples. Their practical relevance and timeliness to HR issues are essential for student learning in the classroom.

COMPETING THROUGH SUSTAINABILITY

Volunteerism and Going Green Are Reaping Dividends for Employees, Communities, and the Environment

A growing number of companies have made sustainability an important part of their business strategy. General Electric's health care unit identified maternal and infant mortality as frequent causes of death in India. For example, the infant mortality rate for India, a country with 1.2 billion people is 55 children for every 1,000 births. GE worked with nonprofit organizations and hospitals to understand patient and health care needs. As a result, GE identified opportunities to help as well as gain a potential market for new products. About 700 million people can't afford maternal or birth services. Also, to bring to market a product required overcoming several obstacles including power outages, a lack of money and space in hospitals for large, costly equipment, high levels of dust and pollution, and difficulty of getting replacement parts through government bureaucracy. One of the products GE developed is a baby warmer, called the Lullaby, which provides heat for cradles. The Lullaby is targeted to help people and communities with few financial assets. The Lullaby is easy to use: it uses only buttons with pictures indicating their function. For example, at General Mills, volunteerism is one of the ways that the company lives its corporate values. The CEO and senior leaders serve on nonprofit boards and are involved in the community.

Finance and Information Technology employees from General Mills Canada picked more than 7,000 pounds of apples and pears as part of a team-building exercise. The fruit was donated to food banks in the Niagara region of Canada. General Mills links the expertise of its employees with small and medium-size food processors in Africa. For example, employee volunteers are helping improve the efficiency of a plant in Malawi which produces a high-nutrient peanut butter paste that is distributed to malnourished children across the country. Malawi has 13 million people, most are living in poverty, customer service with Catholic Ch serving meals to people and wor for homeless chi them how to ma diet, leading fitr and helping with as redecorating shelter. Yoplait o ners with the Gr apolis Crisis Nur meals. Kendall J eral Mills' comp chairman, wants to be one of the responsible com companies in th

Pharmaceutical company Novartis supports REPSSI, an African-based philanthropic organization that provides emotional and psychological support for children who lose their parents or guardians to AIDS. The program began in a single district in Tanzania and has expanded to 13 sub-Saharan African countries. The company's trainers provide REPSSI's employees with leadership development training. REPSSI managers need training in communication skills, providing feedback, intercultural skills, and project management. Novartis transformed its corporate training programs into a form useful for REPSSI. The

30

COMPETING THROUGH GLOBALIZATION

Apple Polishes Its Image through Auditing Overseas Suppliers

Apple is known for introducing revolutionary and functional products such as the iphone, Mac Air computers, and the iPad. Although Apple and its products are revered in the United States and around the world, some say that the profits and market share that Apple is earning from these products is due to taking advantage of foreign workers. Apple relies on manufacturing partners in Asia to build its products. Apple Inc. has been criticized by labor groups who have challenged how its manufacturing partners in Asia have treated their employees. Apple has taken these criticisms seriously and is auditing its suppliers and manufacturing facilities to take steps to reduce if not eliminate illegal and poor treatment of workers who are involved in assembling or providing materials for any of its products. Apple is especially focused on

ensuring that its partners don't hire underage workers, provide adequate training, and pay fair wages. For example, Apple's chief operating officer visited a Chinese manufacturing partner to provide advice after several workers committed suicide from jumping from buildings. One of the potential causes of the suicides was the stress the workers experienced as Apple moved to quickly launch the iPad to meet consumer demand for the new product. The chief executive officer and his team interviewed more than 1,000 workers and evaluated the supplier's reactions to the suicides. As a result, Apple recommended that the supplier better train counselors for employees and establish a 24-hour care center. These recommendations were adopted b An audit of anot found underage avoid employing workers Apple is

the supplier to identify fake identification papers. Apple has also required that manufacturers reimburse over 3 million dollars in excessive fees collected from immigrants to recruit and bring them to work in their factories. Apple has also strongly encouraged its manufacturers and suppliers not to purchase minerals such as gold and tin from smelters that get their products from countries known for human rights abuses. Apple has shown that it is serious about its commitment to ensure that its manufacturers and suppliers labor practices are fair, legal, and protect employees from abuse. In those cases in which Apple's recommendations based on its audits were not adopted, the company terminated its relationship with the supplier

New visas are capped at 85,000 per year, 20,000 of ees with U.S. Master's degrees. There is no cap on H the government, universities, and other nonprofit inst H-1B visas are issued for computer-related occupation and Cisco Systems are two of the top 10 companies used by Indian companies such as Infosys Technologie programs are available for lower-skilled temporary or with an annual cap of 66,000 nonagricultural workers

Although companies may be attracted to offshor labor costs, several other issues have emerged that employees in the offshore locations provide a leve as or higher than customers receive from U.S. operat demoralize U.S. employees such that the gains from lower motivation, lower satisfaction, and higher turn adequately trained to motivate and retain offshore

COMPETING THROUGH TECHNOLOGY

Connectedness Enhances HR Practices

Social networks such as Facebook and Twitter help people satisfy their need to be connected to their friends. Recognizing the importance of "connectiveness," companies of all sizes and in various industries are using social networks to enhance many different HR practices including recruiting, training and development, scheduling, and enhancing employees engagement. Recruiters can use social networking to connect and communicate with job candidates, create online communities for job candidates to learn about the company, and monitor news such as store closings or layoffs which can provide a potential group of new employees. Macy's has used Twitter to post job openings and to reach out to recruit merchandise buyers laid off by other retailers who were closing their stores. CareerBuilder.com is using an app that shows its employees which of their Facebook friends would be matches for job openings at the company and encourages them to share that

information. Del Frisco's Steakhouse in Manhattan can quickly create a schedule for its servers on a computer or i-Phone and post it to a website which automatically sends the schedule to all employees' cell phones. Servers can make schedule changes but the system tracks hours to ensure that they do not exceed allowed overtime work hours. Long Realty in Tuscon, Arizona, established Long Connects, an internal social networking site for real estate agents to seek help and discuss issues such as how to deal with a specific bank to secure financing, trends in the current real estate market, and the best way to handle properties sold for less than the amount owed on the mortgage to avoid foreclosure (short sales). Kelly Services is using a tool known as Chatter to help employees more easily share knowledge and best practices. EMC Corporation used its social business network known as EMC/One to ask employees for ideas about how to cut costs. The chief financial officer read the postings and decided to adopt many of the

ideas which helped contribute to EMC's goal to reduce costs by $450 million. IBM's onboarding process known as Succeeding@ IBM is used to help new employees learn about the company and reduce feeling of being overwhelmed. As part of this process new employees are given access to a social networking tool which allows them to collaborate with each other as well as more experienced employees to get personal support, seek career guidance, and find technical expertise.

SOURCES: Based on M. Rafter, "Goin' Mobile," *Workforce Management*, February 2011, pp. 26–27; L. Stevens, "Through the Looking Glass," *Human Resource Executive*, April 2011, pp. 26–29; M. Ciccarelli, "It's Personal," *Human Resource Executive*, September 16, 2010, pp. 1, 14–20; B. Roberts, "Mobile Workforce Management," *HR Magazine*, March 2011, pp. 67–69; G. Kranz, "More to Learn," *Workforce Management*, January 2011, pp. 27–30; S. Ladika, "Socially Evolved," *Workforce Management*, September 2010, pp. 19–22; B. Roberts, "Developing a Social Business Network," *HR Magazine*, October 2010, pp. 54–60; T. Starner, "Big Blue Welcomes You," *Human Resource Executive*, September 16, 2010, pp. 30–33.

customer and determining how they perform their jobs. One of the most popular methods for increasing employee responsibility and control is work teams. *Work teams involve employees with various skills who interact to assemble a product or provide a service.* Work teams may assume many of the activities usually reserved for managers, including selecting new team members, scheduling work, and coordinating activities with customers and other units in the company. To give teams maximum flexibility, cross-training of team members occurs. *Cross-training* refers to training employees in a wide range of skills so they can fill any of the roles needed to be performed on the team.

51

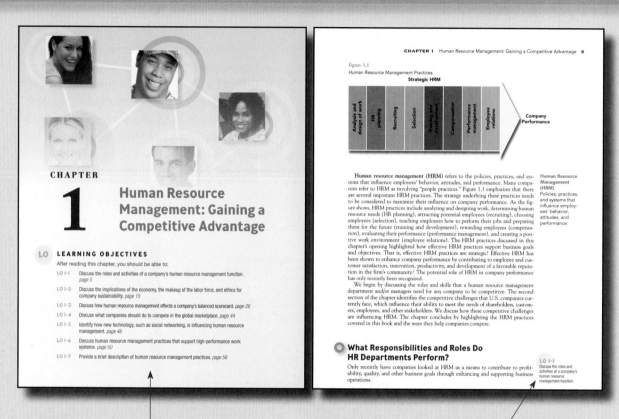

Learning objectives at the beginning of each chapter inform students about the key concepts they should understand after reading through the chapter.

Throughout each chapter, a design element calls out where the learning for each learning objective begins in the text. This element will guide students in their comprehension of the chapter topics and provide a reminder of the learning objectives throughout the chapter.

"Evidence-Based HR" sections within the chapters highlight the growing trend to demonstrate how HR contributes to a company's competitive advantage. Two of the six HR competencies of high-performing HR professionals (credible activist and strategic architect) emphasize the need to influence managers, share information, and develop people strategies that contribute to the business. Evidence-Based HR shows how HR decisions are based on data and not just intuition. The company examples used show how HR practices influence the company's bottom line or key stakeholders including shareholders, employees, customers, or the community.

The **chapter-opening vignettes** are updated with new, relevant examples of real business problems or issues that provide background for the issues discussed in the chapter.

The end-of-chapter segment, **"A Look Back,"** encourages students to recall the chapter's opening vignette and apply it to what they have just learned.

Managing People cases look at incidents and real companies and encourage students to critically evaluate each problem and apply the chapter contents.

ENTER THE WORLD OF BUSINESS

Starbucks: HR Practices Help Focus on the Brew, Weather the Recession, and Prepare for Growth

Starbucks', the Seattle-based coffee store mission is to inspire and nurture the human spirit: one person, one cup, and one neighborhood at a time. The company is well-known for its ethical sourcing of coffee from farmers all over the world, environmental stewardship (by 2015 all cups will be reusable or recyclable), and community involvement through volunteer work in neighborhoods where stores are located. Its stores are designed to be an inviting place for meeting friends and family, reading, working, or as a respite from the hectic pace of daily life. Customers can enjoy fresh-brewed coffee, hot and iced espresso beverages, blended coffee, smoothies, teas, complemented with pastries, sandwiches, salads, oatmeal, yogurt parfaits, and fruit cups. Starbucks had experienced incredible success until 2007 when competition and the recession began to cut into sales and profits. One of the reasons Starbucks struggled during the recession was because customers perceived its beverages as too pricey. The company responded by closing stores, launching a new marketing campaign, and retooling business practices to increase the efficiency in its stores.

Currently, Starbucks has approximately 17,000 stores operating in the United States and in more than 50 countries around the world, including Canada, Bahrain, Sweden, Hong Kong, Singapore, and Brazil. Starbucks has adopted a new growth model that tries to get customers to purchase more coffee regardless of its form, venue, or name on the beans. The new growth model is exemplified by Starbucks new motto: "Great Coffee Everywhere" as well as its new logo that

does not include the company name and the word "coffee." Also, Starbucks is aggressively moving to sell coffee beyond its stores. Consistent with the growth model, since 2010 Starbucks has introduced new products and entered new markets. For example, Starbucks has introduced the Via instant coffee product, placed greater emphasis on selling Seattle Brand Coffee in fast-food chains, supermarkets, and coffee houses (it bought the brand in 2003), and signed deals with Courtesy Products a provider of in-room coffee service to hotels and Green Mountain Coffee Roasters to sell packs of Starbucks for use in single-cup coffee machines. Besides growing the business these actions have helped Starbucks respond to the challenge to its competitive position in the coffee market by the introduction of lower-priced, but tasty coffee by McDonald's, Dunkin' Donuts, and other fast-food chains. Starbucks is also seeking growth of its new products

---

60 CHAPTER 1 Human Resource Management: Gaining a Competitive Advantage

management practice covered in the chapter helps a company gain a competitive advantage by addressing sustainability, global, and technological challenges. Also, each chapter includes an example of a company that demonstrates how HR practices add value (evidence-based HR).

A LOOK BACK

Starbucks is engaged in aggressive business growth focusing on new products and new markets while trying to maintain the customer experience.

Questions

1. What HR practices do you believe are critical for Starbucks to maintain the customer experience and product quality it's known for? Explain.
2. Could Starbucks be successful without its current HR practices? Explain.
3. Do you think that Starbucks' culture and HR practices can also help the bottom line at companies in other industries such as health care, manufacturing, or research and development? Explain why or why not.

Please see the Video that corresponds to this chapter at www.mhhe.com/noe8e.

SUMMARY

This chapter introduced the roles and activities of a company's human resource management function and emphasized that effective management of human resources contribute to a company's business strategy and competitive advantage. HR can be viewed as having product lines: administrative services, strategic services. To successfully m human resources, individuals need personal cred business knowledge, understanding of the business egy, technology knowledge, and the ability to deliv services. Human resource management practices be evidence-based, that is, based on data showin

---

off 124 employees. But Heuti handled the downsizing in a positive way. Laid-off employees with less than two years of service were paid through the end of the year. Everyone received six months of paid health coverage. Zappos also allowed laid-off employees to keep their 40 percent employee discount through Christmas.

To reinforce the importance of the 10 core values Zappos' performance management system asks managers to evaluate how well employees' behaviors demonstrate the core values such as being humble or expressing their personalities. To evaluate task performance managers are asked to regularly provide employees with status reports on such things as how much time they spend on the telephone with customers. The status reports and evaluations of the core values are informational used to identify training needs. Zappos also believes in helping others understand what inspired the company culture. The company created the Zappos.com library which provides a collection of books about creating a passion for customer service, products, and local communities. These books

Questions

1. Zappos seems to be well-positioned to have a competitive advantage over other online retailers. What challenges in Chapter 1 pose the biggest threat to Zappos' ability to maintain and enhance its competitive position? How can human resource management practices help Zappos meet these challenges?
2. Do you think that employees of Zappos have high levels of engagement? Why?
3. Which of Zappos' 10 core values do you believe that human resource practices can influence the most? The least? Why? For each of the core values, identify the HR practices that are related to it. Explain how each of the HR practice(s) you identified is related to the core values.

SOURCES: Based on website for Zappos, www.zappos.com, J. O'Brien, "Zappos Knows How to Kick It," *Fortune*, February 2, 2009, pp. 55–66; M. Moskowitz, R. Levering, and C. Tkaczyk, "100 Best Companies to Work For," *Fortune*, February 7, 2011, pp. 91–101; R. Pyrillis, "The Reviews Are In," *Workforce Management*, May 2011, pp. 20–25.

MANAGING PEOPLE

Skill Shortages Make It Difficult to Fill Positions and Customer Orders

Despite an unemployment rate of around 9%, U.S. manufacturing companies are scrambling to find enough skilled workers. There are several reasons why this is occurring. First, there is increased demand for manufacturing workers. Second, baby boomers (employees 55 or older) making up more than 25% of U.S. manufacturing employees are beginning to retire. Third, the U.S. education system is not developing the math and science skills potential employees need to operate computer-controlled factory equipment like lathes and other metal-shaping equipment. Math and science test scores for U.S. students are significantly lower than those compared to students from countries such as China, Japan, Canada, and Germany. Also, manufacturing jobs suffer from an image problem. Although these jobs often pay from $50,000 to $80,000 per year with benefits and many require advanced math, mechanical drawing, and blueprint reading skills, parents discourage smart children from considering careers in manufacturing, instead emphasizing enrolling in four-year colleges. Also, youth often are unmotivated to train for manufacturing jobs because of miguided stereotypes that they are dirty, unsafe, and boring. Fourth, many manufacturing companies decreased the emphasis they placed on recruiting and finding employees when it was easier to find them in the labor market. For example, Woodward Inc., a parts manufacturer for aircraft and power generation

equipment based in Fort Collins, Colorado, used to operate its own training academy but closed it to lower costs. As a result the company lost its pool of available skilled machinists and technicians. To reestablish a pool of skilled workers Woodward is sponsoring students enrolled in two-year programs in manufacturing skills at local community colleges. The company pays their tuition and other costs and they are paid for working part-time. Woodward's goal is to hire those students for full-time manufacturing jobs after they earn their two-year degree.

Hamill Manufacturing Company, a 127-employee company located near Pittsburgh, Pennsylvania, cuts metal into parts for ships and machinery. The company needs to fill customized orders for small numbers of parts requiring meeting precise specifications. To find workers Hamill works with vocational schools. Employees serve on advisory boards, donate equipment, and even volunteer as guest lecturers. Jeff Kelly, Hamill's chief executive officer, organizes a program in which high school students learn to build fighting robots. These activities have paid off in attracting talented new employees but other larger companies are poaching talented workers away from Hamill Manufacturing. One Hamill employee who won a national competition for metal working skills left for a new job at Curtiss-Wright Corporation, a company that makes pumps and generators and purchases parts

---

XXIII

Exercising Strategy cases at the end of each chapter provide additional cases with discussion questions. These examples pose strategic questions based on real-life practices.

Self-Assessment Exercises at the end of chapters provide a brief exercise for students to complete and evaluate their own skills.

SELF-ASSESSMENT EXERCISE: DO YOU HAVE WHAT IT TAKES TO WORK IN HR?

Instructions: Read each statement and circle yes or no.

Yes No 1. I have leadership and management skills I have developed through prior job experiences, extracurricular activities, community service, or other noncourse activities.

Yes No 2. I have excellent communications, dispute resolution, and interpersonal skills.

Yes No 3. I can demonstrate an understanding of the fundamentals of running a business and making a profit.

Yes No 4. I can use spreadsheets and the World Wide Web, and I am familiar with information systems technology.

Yes No 5. I can work effectively with people of different cultural backgrounds.

Yes No 6. I have expertise in more than one area of human resource management.

Scoring: The greater the number of yes answers, the better prepared you are to work in an HR department. For questions you answered no, you should seek courses and experiences to change your answer to yes—and better prepare yourself for a career in HR!

SOURCE: Based on B. E. Kaufman, "What Companies Want from HR Graduates," HR Magazine, September 1994.

EXERCISING STRATEGY: ZAPPOS FACES COMPETITIVE CHALLENGES

Zappos, based in Las Vegas, is an online retailer with the initial goal of trying to be the best website for buying shoes by offering a wide variety of brands, styles, colors, sizes, and widths. The zappos.com brand has grown to offer shoes, handbags, eyewear, watches, and accessories for online purchase. Zappos' vision is that in the future, online sales will account for 30% of all retail sales in the United States, and Zappos will be the company with the best service and selection. The company's goal is to provide the best service online, not just in shoes but in any product category. Zappos believes that the speed at which a customer receives an online purchase plays a critical role in how that customer thinks about shopping online again in the future, so they are focusing on making sure the items get delivered to our customers as quickly as possible.

In 2009, Zappos was acquired by the Amazon.com, Inc., family of companies which also share a strong passion for customer service. In 2010, Zappos experienced tremendous growth resulting in the need to restructure the company. Zappos was restructured into 10 separate companies under the Zappos family umbrella including Zappos.com, Inc. (the management company) and companies devoted to retail, gift cards, merchandising, and order fulfillment.

Zappos CEO Tony Heish has shaped the company's culture, brand, and business strategy around 10 core values. They are:

Deliver WOW through service.
Embrace and drive change.
Create fun and a little weirdness.
Be adventurous, creative, and open-minded.
Pursue growth and learning.

Build open and honest relationships with communication.
Build a positive team and family spirit.
Do more with less.
Be passionate and determined.
Be humble.

Deliver WOW through Service means that call center employees need to provide excellent customer service. Call center employees encourage callers to order more than one size or color because shipping and return shipping is free. They are also encouraged to use their imaginations to meet customer needs.

Zappos has received many awards for its workplace culture and practices including being recognized as the sixth Best Company to Work for in Fortune magazine's 2011 ranking of the 100 Best Companies to Work For. Zappos' employment practices help perpetuate its company culture. For example, the HR team uses unusual interview questions—such as, How weird are you? and What's your theme song?—to find employees who are creative and have strong individuality. Zappos provides free lunch in the cafeteria (cold cuts) and a full-time life coach (employees have to sit on a red velvet throne to complain), managers are encouraged to spend time with employees outside of the office, and any employee can reward another employee a $50 bonus for good performance. Most employees at Zappos are hourly. All new hires complete four weeks of training, including two weeks working the phones. New recruits are offered $2,000 to leave the company during training to weed out individuals who will not be happy working at the company. Zappos provides free breakfast, lunch, snacks, coffee, tea, and vending machine snacks.

Supplements for Students and Instructors

INSTRUCTOR'S MANUAL

The Instructor's Manual contains a lecture outline and notes, answers to the discussion questions, additional questions and exercises, teaching suggestions, video notes, and answers to the end-of-chapter case questions.

TEST BANK

The test bank has been revised and updated to reflect the content of the 8th edition of the book. Each chapter includes multiple-choice, true/false, and essay questions.

EZ TEST

McGraw-Hill's EZ Test is a flexible and easy-to-use electronic testing program. The program allows instructors to create tests from book-specific items. It accommodates a wide range of question types and instructors may add their own questions. Multiple versions of the test can be created and any test can be exported for use with course management systems such as WebCT, BlackBoard, or PageOut. The program is available for Windows and Macintosh environments.

VIDEOS

Human Resource Management Video DVD volume 3 offers video clips on HRM issues for each chapter of this edition. You'll find a new video produced by the SHRM Foundation, entitled "Once the Deal Is Done: Making Mergers Work." Three new videos specifically address employee benefits: "GM Cuts Benefits and Pay," "Sulphur Springs Teachers," and "Google Employee Perks." Other new videos available for this edition include "E-Learning English" for the chapter on employee development and "Recession Job Growth" for the chapter on HR planning and recruitment.

POWERPOINT

This presentation program features detailed slides for each chapter, which are found on the OLC.

ONLINE LEARNING CENTER (OLC)
www.mhhe.com/noe8e

This text-specific website follows the text chapter by chapter. Instructors and students can access a variety of online teaching and learning tools that are designed to reinforce and build on the text content. Students will have direct access to learning tools such as self-grading quizzes, video clips, and Twitter Focus cases, while instructor materials are password protected.

Technology

McGRAW-HILL *CONNECT MANAGEMENT*

LESS MANAGING. MORE TEACHING. GREATER LEARNING.

McGraw-Hill *Connect Management* is an online assignment and assessment solution that connects students with the tools and resources they'll need to achieve success.

McGraw-Hill *Connect Management* helps prepare students for their future by enabling faster learning, more efficient studying, and higher retention of knowledge.

MCGRAW-HILL *CONNECT MANAGEMENT* FEATURES

Connect Management offers a number of powerful tools and features to make managing assignments easier, so faculty can spend more time teaching. With *Connect Management,* students can engage with their coursework anytime and anywhere, making the learning process more accessible and efficient. *Connect Management* offers you the features described below.

Simple assignment management

With *Connect Management,* creating assignments is easier than ever, so you can spend more time teaching and less time managing. The assignment management function enables you to

- Create and deliver assignments easily with selectable end-of-chapter questions and Test Bank items.
- Streamline lesson planning, student progress reporting, and assignment grading to make classroom management more efficient than ever.
- Go paperless with the eBook and online submission and grading of student assignments.

Smart grading

When it comes to studying, time is precious. *Connect Management* helps students learn more efficiently by providing feedback and practice material when they need it, where they need it. When it comes to teaching, your time also is precious. The grading function enables you to

- Have assignments scored automatically, giving students immediate feedback on their work and side-by-side comparisons with correct answers.
- Access and review each response; manually change grades or leave comments for students to review.
- Reinforce classroom concepts with practice tests and instant quizzes.

Instructor library

The *Connect Management* Instructor Library is your repository for additional resources to improve student engagement in and out of class. You can select and use any asset that enhances your lecture. The *Connect Management* Instructor Library includes

- eBook
- Instructor's Manual
- PowerPoint files
- Videos and instructional notes
- Access to interactive study tools

Student study center

The *Connect Management* Student Study Center is the place for students to access additional resources. The Student Study Center

- Offers students quick access to lectures, practice materials, eBooks, and more.
- Provides instant practice material and study questions easily accessible on the go.
- Gives students access to the Personalized Learning Plan described on the next page.

Student progress tracking

Connect Management keeps instructors informed about how each student, section, and class is performing, allowing for more productive use of lecture and office hours. The progress-tracking function enables you to

- View scored work immediately and track individual or group performance with assignment and grade reports.
- Access an instant view of student or class performance relative to learning objectives.
- Collect data and generate reports required by many accreditation organizations, such as AACSB.

Lecture capture

Increase the attention paid to a lecture discussion by decreasing the attention paid to note-taking. For an additional charge Lecture Capture offers new ways for students to focus on the in-class discussion, knowing they can revisit important topics later. Lecture Capture enables you to

- Record and distribute your lecture with the click of a button.
- Record and index PowerPoint presentations and anything shown on your computer so it is easily searchable, frame by frame.
- Offer access to lectures anytime and anywhere by computer, iPod, or mobile device.
- Increase intent listening and class participation by easing students' concerns about note-taking. Lecture Capture will make it more likely you will see students' faces, not the tops of their heads.

McGraw-Hill *Connect Plus Management*

McGraw-Hill reinvents the textbook learning experience for the modern student with *Connect Plus Management.* A seamless integration of an eBook and *Connect Management, Connect Plus Management* provides all the *Connect Management* features plus the following:

- An integrated eBook, allowing for anytime, anywhere access to the textbook.

- Dynamic links between the problems or questions you assign to your students and the location in the eBook where that problem or question is covered.
- A powerful search function to pinpoint and connect key concepts in a snap.

In short, *Connect Management* offers you and your students powerful tools and features that optimize your time and energies, enabling you to focus on course content, teaching, and student learning. *Connect Management* also offers a wealth of content resources for both instructors and students. This state-of-the-art, thoroughly tested system supports you in preparing students for the world that awaits.

For more information about Connect™, go to www.mcgrawhillconnect.com, or contact your local McGraw-Hill sales representative.

TEGRITY CAMPUS: LECTURES 24/7

 Tegrity Campus is a service that makes class time available 24/7 by automatically capturing every lecture in a searchable format for students to review when they study and complete assignments. With a simple one-click start-and-stop process, you capture all computer screens and corresponding audio. Students can replay any part of any class with easy-to-use browser-based viewing on a PC or Mac.

Educators know that the more students can see, hear, and experience class resources, the better they learn. In fact, studies prove it. With Tegrity Campus, students quickly recall key moments by using Tegrity Campus's unique search feature. This search helps students efficiently find what they need, when they need it, across an entire semester of class recordings. Help turn all your students' study time into learning moments immediately supported by your lecture.

To learn more about Tegrity watch a two-minute Flash demo at http://tegritycampus.mhhe.com.

ASSURANCE OF LEARNING READY

Many educational institutions today are focused on the notion of *assurance of learning,* an important element of some accreditation standards. *Human Resource Management* is designed specifically to support your assurance of learning initiatives with a simple, yet powerful solution.

Each Test Bank question for *Human Resource Management* maps to a specific chapter learning outcome/objective listed in the text. You can use our Test Bank software, EZ Test and EZ Test Online, or in *Connect Management* easily query for learning outcomes/objectives that directly relate to the learning objectives for your course. You can then use the reporting features of EZ Test to aggregate student results in a similar fashion, making the collection and presentation of assurance of learning data simple and easy.

MCGRAW-HILL AND BLACKBOARD

McGraw-Hill Higher Education and Blackboard have teamed up. What does this mean for you?

1. **Your life, simplified.** Now you and your students can access McGraw-Hill's Connect™ and Create™ right from within your Blackboard course—all with one single sign-on. Say goodbye to the days of logging in to multiple applications.
2. **Deep integration of content and tools.** Not only do you get single sign-on with Connect™ and Create™, you also get deep integration of McGraw-Hill content and content engines right in Blackboard. Whether you're choosing a book for your course or building Connect™ assignments, all the tools you need are right where you want them—inside Blackboard.
3. **Seamless gradebooks.** Are you tired of keeping multiple gradebooks and manually synchronizing grades into Blackboard? We

thought so. When a student completes an integrated Connect™ assignment, the grade for that assignment automatically (and instantly) feeds your Blackboard grade center.

4. **A solution for everyone.** Whether your institution is already using Blackboard or you just want to try Blackboard on your own, we have a solution for you. McGraw-Hill and Blackboard can now offer you easy access to industry-leading technology and content, whether your campus hosts it, or we do. Be sure to ask your local McGraw-Hill representative for details.

The **Best** of **Both** Worlds

AACSB STATEMENT

The McGraw-Hill Companies is a proud corporate member of AACSB international. Understanding the importance and value of AACSB accreditation, *Human Resource Management,* 8th edition, recognizes the curricula guidelines detailed in the AACSB standards for business accreditation by connecting selected questions in the Test Bank to the six general-knowledge and skill guidelines in the AACSB standards.

The statements contained in *Human Resource Management,* 8th edition, are provided only as a guide for the users of this textbook. The AACSB leaves content coverage and assessment within the purview of individual schools, the mission of the school, and the faculty. While *Human Resource Management,* 8th edition, and the teaching package make no claim of any specific AACSB qualification or evaluation, we have within *Human Resource Management,* 8th edition, labeled selected questions according to the six general-knowledge and skills areas.

MCGRAW-HILL CUSTOMER CARE CONTACT INFORMATION

At McGraw-Hill, we understand that getting the most from new technology can be challenging. That's why our services don't stop after you purchase our products. You can e-mail our product specialists 24 hours a day to get product-training online. Or you can search our knowledge bank of frequently asked questions on our support website. For customer support, call 800-331-5094, e-mail hmsupport@mcgraw-hill.com, or visit www.mhhe.com/support. One of our technical support analysts will be able to assist you in a timely fashion.

SUPPORT MATERIALS

MCGRAW-HILL'S MANAGEMENT ASSET GALLERY!

McGraw-Hill/Irwin Management is excited to now provide a one-stop shop for our wealth of assets, making it quick and easy for instructors to locate specific materials to enhance their courses.

All of the following can be accessed within the Management Asset Gallery:

MANAGER'S HOT SEAT

This interactive, video-based application puts students in the manager's hot seat, builds critical thinking and decision-making skills, and allows students to apply concepts to real managerial challenges. Students watch as 15 real managers apply their years of experience when confronting unscripted issues such as bullying in the workplace, cyber loafing, globalization, intergenerational work conflicts, workplace violence, and leadership versus management.

Self-Assessment Gallery

Unique among publisher-provided self-assessments, our 23 self-assessments give students background information to ensure that they understand the purpose of the assessment. Students test their values, beliefs, skills, and interests in a wide variety of areas, allowing them to personally apply chapter content to their own lives and careers.

Every self-assessment is supported with PowerPoints® and an instructor manual in the Management Asset Gallery, making it easy for the instructor to create an engaging classroom discussion surrounding the assessments.

Test Your Knowledge

To help reinforce students' understanding of key management concepts, Test Your Knowledge activities give students a review of the conceptual materials followed by application-based questions to work through. Students can choose practice mode, which gives them detailed feedback after each question, or test mode, which provides feedback after the entire test has been completed. Every Test Your Knowledge activity is supported by instructor notes in the Management Asset Gallery to make it easy for the instructor to create engaging classroom discussions surrounding the materials that students have completed.

Management History Timeline

This web application allows instructors to present and students to learn the history of management in an engaging and interactive way. Management history is presented along an intuitive timeline that can be traveled through sequentially or by selected decade. With the click of a mouse, students learn the important dates, see the people who influenced the field, and understand the general management theories that have molded and shaped management as we know it today.

Video Library DVDs

McGraw-Hill/Irwin offers the most comprehensive video support for the Human Resource Management classroom through course library video DVDs. This discipline has library volume DVDs tailored to integrate and visually reinforce chapter concepts. The library volume DVD contains more than 40 clips! The rich video material, organized by topic, comes from sources such as PBS, NBC, BBC, SHRM, and McGraw-Hill. Video cases and video guides are provided for some clips.

DESTINATION CEO VIDEOS

Video clips featuring CEOs on a variety of topics. Accompanying each clip are multiple-choice questions and discussion questions to use in the classroom or assign as a quiz.

Features
CourseSmart eBooks allow students to highlight, take notes, organize notes, and share the notes with other CourseSmart users. Students can also search for terms across all eBooks in their purchased CourseSmart library. CourseSmart eBooks can be printed (five pages at a time).

More info and purchase

Please visit **www.coursesmart.com** for more information and to purchase access to our eBooks. CourseSmart allows students to try one chapter of the eBook, free of charge, before purchase.

Create
Craft your teaching resources to match the way you teach! With McGraw-Hill Create, **www.mcgrawhillcreate .com,** you can easily rearrange chapters, combine material from other content sources, and quickly upload content you have written, like your course syllabus or teaching notes. Find the content you need in Create by searching through thousands of leading McGraw-Hill textbooks. Arrange your book to fit your teaching style. Create even allows you to personalize your book's appearance by selecting the cover and adding your name, school, and course information. Order a Create book and you'll receive a complimentary print review copy in three to five business days or a complimentary electronic review copy (eComp) via e-mail in about one hour. Go to **www .mcgrawhillcreate.com** today and register. Experience how McGraw-Hill Create empowers you to teach *your* students *your* way.

BRIEF CONTENTS

CONTENTS

Human Resource Management

GAINING A COMPETITIVE ADVANTAGE

CHAPTER

1

Human Resource Management: Gaining a Competitive Advantage

LO LEARNING OBJECTIVES

After reading this chapter, you should be able to:

LO 1-1 Discuss the roles and activities of a company's human resource management function. *page 5*

LO 1-2 Discuss the implications of the economy, the makeup of the labor force, and ethics for company sustainability. *page 15*

LO 1-3 Discuss how human resource management affects a company's balanced scorecard. *page 28*

LO 1-4 Discuss what companies should do to compete in the global marketplace. *page 44*

LO 1-5 Identify how new technology, such as social networking, is influencing human resource management. *page 48*

LO 1-6 Discuss human resource management practices that support high-performance work systems. *page 50*

LO 1-7 Provide a brief description of human resource management practices. *page 56*

ENTER THE WORLD OF BUSINESS

Starbucks: HR Practices Help Focus on the Brew, Weather the Recession, and Prepare for Growth

Starbucks', the Seattle-based coffee store mission is to inspire and nurture the human spirit: one person, one cup, and one neighborhood at a time. The company is well-known for its ethical sourcing of coffee from farmers all over the world, environmental stewardship (by 2015 all cups will be reusable or recyclable), and community involvement through volunteer work in neighborhoods where stores are located. Its stores are designed to be an inviting place for meeting friends and family, reading, working, or as a respite from the hectic pace of daily life. Customers can enjoy fresh-brewed coffee, hot and iced espresso beverages, blended coffee, smoothies, teas, complemented with pastries, sandwiches, salads, oatmeal, yogurt parfaits, and fruit cups. Starbucks had experienced incredible success until 2007 when competition and the recession began to cut into sales and profits. One of the reasons Starbucks struggled during the recession was because customers perceived its beverages as too pricey. The company responded by closing stores, launching a new marketing campaign, and retooling business practices to increase the efficiency in its stores.

Currently, Starbucks has approximately 17,000 stores operating in the United States and in more than 50 countries around the world, including Canada, Bahrain, Sweden, Hong Kong, Singapore, and Brazil. Starbucks has adopted a new growth model that tries to get customers to purchase more coffee regardless of its form, venue, or name on the beans. The new growth model is exemplified by Starbucks new motto: "Great Coffee Everywhere" as well as its new logo that does not include the company name and the word "coffee." Also, Starbucks is aggressively moving to sell coffee beyond its stores. Consistent with the growth model, since 2010 Starbucks has introduced new products and entered new markets. For example, Starbucks has introduced the Via instant coffee product, placed greater emphasis on selling Seattle Brand Coffee in fast-food chains, supermarkets, and coffee houses (it bought the brand in 2003), and signed deals with Courtesy Products a provider of in-room coffee service to hotels and Green Mountain Coffee Roasters to sell packs of Starbucks for use in single-cup coffee machines. Besides growing the business these actions have helped Starbucks respond to the challenge to its competitive position in the coffee market by the introduction of lower-priced, but tasty coffee by McDonald's, Dunkin' Donuts, and other fast-food chains. Starbucks is also seeking growth of its new products and stores in global markets in which it already has stores, such as China, as well as new markets such as India.

Starbucks believes its employees, called partners, are the key to the Starbucks experience. Starbucks wants its partners to have coffee knowledge, product expertise, and provide excellent customer service. At the same time it believes in treating its partners with dignity and respect. For example, to ensure that customers were delighted and coffee served high-quality standards, Starbucks went so far as to shut down operations of most of its stores in 2008 for a full-day training event. The training event, known as "Perfect the Art of Espresso," was designed to help baristas deliver high-quality espresso. One activity consisted of pulling an espresso shot and then evaluating the process and the product (Was it the right color? Did it take too long or too short a time?). Staff discussions about how the training would benefit customers were held at each store. Partners were told to greet regular customers by name and not to resteam milk that had been steamed once. Also, Starbucks wants its baristas to slow down and instead focus on making no more than two drinks at a time. This is in response to customer complaints that its beverages are inconsistently prepared from barista to barista and across stores. Starbucks believes the new procedure will lead to fresher, hotter drinks, and reduce the possibility of errors in making drinks and filling customer orders. To maximize the customer experience and increase the freshness of the coffee Starbucks is also asking baristas to grind beans for each batch of coffee as it is needed instead of grinding all of the day's beans first thing in the morning.

Starbucks offers its partners comprehensive health benefits that exceed those provided by many other retailers. Although many partners work part-time they are still eligible for full-time benefits if they work 240 hours a quarter. One estimate is that less than 30 percent of part-time workers in the United States receive health care, paid sick leave, or eligibility for bonuses or stock options. Starbucks Total Pay package includes programs that embrace diversity as a way to conduct business. Starbucks provides all employees and their same-sex or opposite sex partners comprehensive health benefits that include medical, dental, and vision care, as well as tuition reimbursement, stock options and discounted stock purchase plan, vacations, and a 401 (k) retirement plan. Partners are also eligible for free coffee and tea products each week. The high importance placed on partners in Starbucks success is shown by the decision made by Starbucks CEO, Howard Schultz, who was asked by an institutional investor during the worst time for the company during the recent recession to consider cutting its workers health care benefits to save cost. Schultz advised him that he would not do so and that he should consider investing his money elsewhere!

SOURCES: Based on D. Kesmodel, "Starbucks Says Demand Perking Up," *Wall Street Journal,* November, 6, 2009, p. B5; K. Helliker and P. Ziobro, "Starbucks Announces Its First Dividend," *Wall Street Journal,* March 25, 2010, pp. B1, B4; J. Jargon, "Starbucks Signs Deal for Hotel Coffee Machines," *Wall Street Journal,* February 16, 2011, p. B2; J. Jargon, "Starbucks in Pod Pact," *Wall Street Journal,* March 11, 2011, p. B4; Associated Press, "Starbucks Gives Logo New Look," *Columbus Dispatch,* January 9, 2011, p. D6; L. Burkitt, "Starbucks Menu Expands in China," *Wall Street Journal,* March 9, 2011, p. B7; P. Beckett, V. Agarwal, and J. Jargon, "Starbucks Brews Coffee Plan for India," *Wall Street Journal,* January 14, 2011, p. B8; K. Helliker, "Starbucks Targets Regular Joes," *Wall Street Journal,* May 12, 2010, p. B3; "Our Starbucks Mission Statement" from company information from www.starbucks.com; J. Jargon, "At Starbucks, Baristas Told No More than Two Drinks," *Wall Street Journal,* November 13, 2010, pp. B1, B2; "U.S. Total Pay Your Special Blend" from "Working at Starbucks" at www.starbucks.com; M. Weinstein, "Fresh Cup of Training," *Training,* May 2008, p. 10; J. Adamy, "Schultz's Second Act Jolts Starbucks," *Wall Street Journal,* May 19, 2008, pp. A1, A11.

Introduction

Starbucks illustrates the key role that human resource management (HRM) plays in determining the survival, effectiveness, and competitiveness of U.S. businesses. **Competitiveness** refers to a company's ability to maintain and gain market share in its industry. Starbucks' human resource management practices are helping support the company's business strategy and provide services the customer values. The value of a product or service is determined by its quality and how closely the product fits customer needs.

Competitiveness
A company's ability to maintain and gain market share in its industry.

Competitiveness is related to company effectiveness, which is determined by whether the company satisfies the needs of stakeholders (groups affected by business practices). Important stakeholders include stockholders, who want a return on their investment; customers, who want a high-quality product or service; and employees, who desire interesting work and reasonable compensation for their services. The community, which wants the company to contribute to activities and projects and minimize pollution of the environment, is also an important stakeholder. Companies that do not meet stakeholders' needs are unlikely to have a competitive advantage over other firms in their industry.

figure 1.1

Human Resource Management Practices

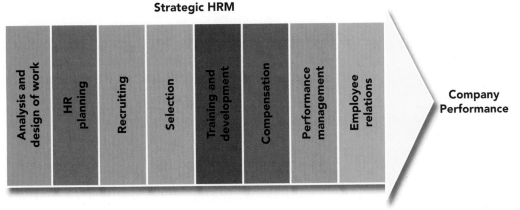

Human resource management (HRM) refers to the policies, practices, and systems that influence employees' behavior, attitudes, and performance. Many companies refer to HRM as involving "people practices." Figure 1.1 emphasizes that there are several important HRM practices. The strategy underlying these practices needs to be considered to maximize their influence on company performance. As the figure shows, HRM practices include analyzing and designing work, determining human resource needs (HR planning), attracting potential employees (recruiting), choosing employees (selection), teaching employees how to perform their jobs and preparing them for the future (training and development), rewarding employees (compensation), evaluating their performance (performance management), and creating a positive work environment (employee relations). The HRM practices discussed in this chapter's opening highlighted how effective HRM practices support business goals and objectives. That is, effective HRM practices are strategic! Effective HRM has been shown to enhance company performance by contributing to employee and customer satisfaction, innovation, productivity, and development of a favorable reputation in the firm's community.[1] The potential role of HRM in company performance has only recently been recognized.

We begin by discussing the roles and skills that a human resource management department and/or managers need for any company to be competitive. The second section of the chapter identifies the competitive challenges that U.S. companies currently face, which influence their ability to meet the needs of shareholders, customers, employees, and other stakeholders. We discuss how these competitive challenges are influencing HRM. The chapter concludes by highlighting the HRM practices covered in this book and the ways they help companies compete.

Human Resource Management (HRM)
Policies, practices, and systems that influence employees' behavior, attitudes, and performance.

What Responsibilities and Roles Do HR Departments Perform?

Only recently have companies looked at HRM as a means to contribute to profitability, quality, and other business goals through enhancing and supporting business operations.

LO 1-1
Discuss the roles and activities of a company's human resource management function.

table 1.1

Responsibilities of
HR Departments

Employment and recruiting	Interviewing, recruiting, testing, temporary labor coordination
Training and development	Orientation, performance management skills training, productivity enhancement
Compensation	Wage and salary administration, job descriptions, executive compensation, incentive pay, job evaluation
Benefits	Insurance, vacation leave administration, retirement plans, profit sharing, stock plans
Employee services	Employee assistance programs, relocation services, outplacement services
Employee and community relations	Attitude surveys, labor relations, publications, labor law compliance, discipline
Personnel records	Information systems, records
Health and safety	Safety inspection, drug testing, health, wellness
Strategic planning	International human resources, forecasting, planning, mergers and acquisitions

SOURCES: Based on Bureau of Labor Statistics, *Occupational Outlook Handbook*, 2010–2011 edition. Washington, DC: Bureau of Labor Statistics, www.bls.gov; and SHRM-BNA Survey No. 66, "Policy and Practice Forum: Human Resource Activities, Budgets, and Staffs, 2000–2001," Bulletin to Management, Bureau of National Affairs Policy and Practice Series, June 28, 2001. Washington, DC: Bureau of National Affairs.

Table 1.1 shows the responsibilities of human resource departments. The average ratio of HR department staff to total number of employees has been 1.0 for every 93 employees served by the department.[2] The median HR department expenditure per employee was $1,409. Labor costs represent approximately 30% of company revenue.

The HR department is solely responsible for outplacement, labor law compliance, record keeping, testing, unemployment compensation, and some aspects of benefits administration. The HR department is most likely to collaborate with other company functions on employment interviewing, performance management and discipline, and efforts to improve quality and productivity. Large companies are more likely than small ones to employ HR specialists, with benefits specialists being the most prevalent. Other common specializations include recruitment, compensation, and training and development.[3]

Many different roles and responsibilities can be performed by the HR department depending on the size of the company, the characteristics of the workforce, the industry, and the value system of company management. The HR department may take full responsibility for human resource activities in some companies, whereas in others it may share the roles and responsibilities with managers of other departments such as finance, operations, or information technology. In some companies the HR department advises top-level management; in others the HR department may make decisions regarding staffing, training, and compensation after top managers have decided relevant business issues.

One way to think about the roles and responsibilities of HR departments is to consider HR as a business within the company with three product lines. Figure 1.2 shows the three product lines of HR. The first product line, administrative services and transactions, is the traditional product that HR has historically provided. The newer HR products—business partner services and the strategic partner role—are the HR functions that are being challenged by top managers to deliver.

figure 1.2

HR as a Business with Three Product Lines

Administrative Services and Transactions: Compensation, hiring, and staffing • Emphasis: Resource efficiency and service quality	**Business Partner Services:** Developing effective HR systems and helping implement business plans, talent management • Emphasis: Knowing the business and exercising influence—problem solving, designing effective systems to ensure needed competencies	**Strategic Partner:** Contributing to business strategy based on considerations of human capital, business capabilities, readiness, and developing HR practices as strategic differentiators • Emphasis: Knowledge of HR and of the business, competition, the market, and business strategies

SOURCE: Adapted from Figure 1, "HR Product Lines," in E. E. Lawler, "From Human Resource Management to Organizational Effectiveness," *Human Resource Management* 44 (2005), pp. 165–69.

HR at SYSCO Corporation, the number one food service marketer and distributor in North America, is successfully delivering business partner services and serving as a strategic partner.[4] The senior vice president and chief administrative officer is responsible for ensuring that HR strategy is aligned with the business strategy. SYSCO tries to differentiate itself from competitors in the marketplace by providing value in its products and customer service to the customer. HR at SYSCO focuses on ensuring that five processes are in place. These processes stress a common understanding of the company's mission, values, and goals, establishment of clear expectations between employees and managers using the performance management process, operating within laws, ensuring that employees are inspired to come to work, and giving every employee the skills and technology needed to contribute to the company. HR, a strategic partner in all of the processes, works together with senior management to develop programs and guidelines to support the processes. It then markets them to line managers, who execute and customize the programs for their specific business. To determine if these processes are working three key dimensions are measured: employee satisfaction, number of employees the company uses per 100,000 cases it sells, and employee retention data for each function in the company. Top executives meet four times each year to review the metrics to see if they are consistent with operating expenses and pretax earnings. For example, since the late 1990s SYSCO has moved the retention rate for its 10,000 marketing associates from 70 to 82%, resulting in more than $70 million saved per year.

Strategic Role of the HRM Function

The amount of time that the HRM function devotes to administrative tasks is decreasing, and its roles as a strategic business partner, change agent, and employee advocate are increasing.[5] HR managers face two important challenges: shifting their focus from current operations to strategies for the future[6] and preparing non-HR managers to develop and implement human resource practices (recall the role of HR in Starbucks' success from the chapter-opening story). To ensure that human resources contributes to the company's competitive advantage many HR departments are organized on

Shared service model
A way to organize the HR function that includes centers of expertise, service centers, and business partners.

the basis of a shared service model. The shared service model can help control costs and improve the business relevance and timeliness of HR practices. A **shared service model** is a way to organize the HR function that includes centers of expertise or excellence, service centers, and business partners.[7] Centers of expertise or excellence include HR specialists in areas such as staffing or training who provide their services companywide. Service centers are a central place for administrative and transactional tasks such as enrolling in training programs or changing benefits that employees and managers can access online. Business partners are HR staff members who work with business-unit managers on strategic issues such as creating new compensation plans or development programs for preparing high-level managers. We will discuss the shared service model is more detail in Chapter 16.

The role of HRM in administration is decreasing as technology is used for many administrative purposes, such as managing employee records and allowing employees to get information about and enroll in training, benefits, and other programs. The availability of the Internet has decreased the HRM role in maintaining records and providing self-service to employees.[8] **Self-service** refers to giving employees online access to information about HR issues such as training, benefits, compensation, and contracts; enrolling online in programs and services; and completing online attitude surveys. For example, General Motors' (GM) goal for its e-HR investment was to create an employee-friendly one-stop shop for employees to enroll in benefits, review their HR data, and get certificates for employee car discounts.[9] The portal, known as "mySocrates," is the place employees go for information about GM. Managers use the system for performance reviews. HR uses it for communications of benefits, training programs, and other programs, which saves time as well as printing and distribution costs. Annual benefits enrollment used to take several days. Now it takes a few minutes.

Self-Service
Giving employees online access to HR information.

Many companies are also contracting with human resource service providers to conduct important but administrative human resource functions such as payroll processing as well as to provide expertise in strategically important practice areas such as recruiting. **Outsourcing** refers to the practice of having another company (a vendor, third party or consultant) provide services. The most commonly outsourced activities include those related to benefits administration (e.g., flexible spending accounts, health plan eligibility status), relocation, and payroll. The major reasons that company executives choose to outsource human resource practices include cost savings, increased ability to recruit and manage talent, improved HR service quality, and protection of the company from potential lawsuits by standardizing processes such as selection and recruitment.[10] ADP, Hewitt, IBM, and Accenture are examples of leading outsource providers.

Outsourcing
The practice of having another company provide services.

Consider the role of outsourcing in several different companies.[11] Olshen's Bottle Supply Company in Portland, Oregon, decided to outsource payroll after an internal audit found mistakes were made in payroll processing. The number of mistakes has decreased since payroll was outsourced. Invision Industries, a small business in Florida with 165 employees who make DVD players for automobiles, avoided the problems associated with administering extended health care benefits for 115 laid-off employees because of the economic stimulus legislation passed by Congress. Its payroll and benefits processor was able to interpret the new legislation and administer the unemployment benefits without errors. Goodyear Tire and Rubber Company reenergized its recruitment and hiring practices through outsourcing recruiting practices. The recruiting outsource provider worked with the company to understand its culture, history, and its employees' recruitment experiences. The recruiting outsourcing service provider was able to help Goodyear streamline the recruiting process through providing hiring managers with online access to create new job requisitions, providing interview feedback, scheduling interviews, generating customized job offer letters, and gaining a real-time perspective on job candidates' progress in the recruitment process. Goodyear recognized several benefits from outsourcing recruitment including improving the timeliness of job offers, diversity and quality of new hires, and reducing turnover.

Traditionally, the HRM department (also known as "Personnel" or "Employee Relations") was primarily an administrative expert and employee advocate. The department took care of employee problems, made sure employees were paid correctly, administered labor contracts, and avoided legal problems. The HRM department ensured that employee-related issues did not interfere with the manufacturing or sales of products or services. Human resource management was primarily reactive; that is, human resource issues were a concern only if they directly affected the business. Although that still remains the case in many companies that have yet to recognize the competitive value of human resource management, other companies believe that HRM is important for business success and therefore have expanded the role of HRM as a change agent and strategic partner.

Other roles such as practice development and strategic business partnering have increased. One of the most comprehensive studies ever conducted regarding HRM concluded that "human resources is being transformed from a specialized, stand-alone function to a broad corporate competency in which human resources and line managers build partnerships to gain competitive advantage and achieve overall business goals."[12] HR managers are increasingly included on high-level committees that are shaping the strategic direction of the company. These managers report directly to the CEO, president, or board of directors and propose solutions to business problems.

Consider the role of HR at McDonald's and VF Corporation.[13] At McDonald's HR is contributing to the company's global expansion. Today, two-thirds of McDonald's workforce is located outside the United States. Most of McDonald's product offerings such as hamburgers are available at locations around the world, but there are some local differences in the menu to accommodate local customs and tastes (for example, you can buy a beer with your hamburger in Munich, Germany!). Similarly McDonald's human resource practices are standardized throughout the company, based on a set of common values and skills sets or competencies. However, while maintaining brand consistency, HR practices are allowed to vary according to cultural norms. For example, a manager in Brazil might decide to invite the parents of a new employee to family orientation night so they can learn more about their son or daughter's job. McDonald's global expansion has changed the role of human resources in the company. To cope with the rapid changes in a global business environment, human resources at McDonald's has to work collaboratively with other business functions. HR plays a key role in the company's Global People Board which includes the heads of global information, technology, and marketing.

The CEO of VF Corporation, a global clothing business including Nautica, Lee, and Wrangler brands, understands that he needs strong finances, winning brands, and talent to drive business growth. HR's role is to develop talent, focusing on the top management group of 1,500 people. The company conducts senior talent assessment reviews two times each year. These reviews include meeting with the company's operating committee, the vice president for human resources, business leaders, and the head of HR for each business unit. Top managers are each individually reviewed to discuss their strengths and weaknesses, how to improve them, and their possibilities for career advancement. This is critical for the company to prepare and have ready the necessary management talent necessary to meet two key growth drivers for the company: global expansion and aggressive acquisitions of other businesses. Also, the vice president for human resources plays a key role in developing the time frame for expansion and preparing managers for international positions. In addition, the vice president for human resources plays an important role in helping understand the available talent in companies targeted for acquisition as well as taking steps to retain talented employees in the acquired company needed to support the brand. The vice president for human resources also is responsible for gathering information about changes in business expectations and growth projects from the vice presidents for human resources at the business unit level and communicating that information to the CEO.

Table 1.2 provides several questions that managers can use to determine if HRM is playing a strategic role in the business. If these questions have not been considered, it is highly unlikely that (1) the company is prepared to deal with competitive challenges or (2) human resources are being used to help a company gain a competitive advantage. The bottom line for evaluating the relationship between human resource management and the business strategy is to consider this question: "What is HR doing to ensure that the right people with the right skills are doing the right things in the jobs that are important for the execution of the business strategy?"[14] We will discuss strategic human resource management in more detail in Chapter 2.

Why have HRM roles changed? Managers see HRM as the most important lever for companies to gain a competitive advantage over both domestic and foreign competitors. We believe this is because HRM practices are directly related to companies' success in meeting competitive challenges. These challenges and their implications for HRM are discussed later in the chapter.

DEMONSTRATING THE STRATEGIC VALUE OF HR: HR ANALYTICS AND EVIDENCE-BASED HR

Evidence-Based HR
Demonstrating that human resource practices have a positive influence on the company's bottom line or key stakeholders (employees, customers, community, shareholders).

For HR to contribute to business goals there is increasing recognition that it is necessary to use data to answer questions such as "Which practices are effective?" "Which practices are cost effective?" and to project the outcomes of changes in practices on employees' attitudes, behavior, and company profits and costs. This helps show that time and money invested in HR programs are worthwhile and HR is as important to the business as finance, marketing, and accounting! **Evidence-based HR** refers to the demonstration that human resources practices have a positive influence on the company's bottom or key stakeholders (employees, customers, community, shareholders).

table 1.2

Questions to Ask: Are Human Resources Playing a Strategic Role in the Business?

1. What is HR doing to provide value-added services to internal clients?
2. What can the HR department add to the bottom line?
3. How are you measuring the effectiveness of HR?
4. How can we reinvest in employees?
5. What HR strategy will we use to get the business from point A to point B?
6. What makes an employee want to stay at our company?
7. How are we going to invest in HR so that we have a better HR department than our competitors?
8. From an HR perspective, what should we be doing to improve our marketplace position?
9. What's the best change we can make to prepare for the future?

SOURCES: Based on A. Halcrow, "Survey Shows HR in Transition," *Workforce*, June 1988, p. 74; P. Wright, *Human Resource Strategy: Adapting to the Age of Globalization* (Alexandria, VA: Society for Human Resource Management Foundation, 2008).

Evidence-based HR requires the use of HR or workforce analytics. **HR or workforce analytics** refers to the practice of using quantitative methods and scientific methods to analyze data from human resource databases, corporate financial statements, employee surveys, and other data sources to make evidence-based human resource decisions and show that HR practices influence the organization's "bottom line" including profits and costs.[15] For example, consider how HR at Superior Energy Services in New Orleans relied on workforce analytics to identify and reduce turnover.[16] The oil industry has an annual turnover rate of approximately 35%. At Superior Energy Services Inc., HR was able to quantify the lost revenue for each job type. This was important because the company's business model operates on billable hours—turnover means lost revenue. HR identified that about half the employees who quit were skilled operators or supervisors. Using a statistical model for predicting the probability of turnover, HR was able to identify that training supervisors on one-to-one coaching skills would have the most significant impact on reducing turnover. Results showed that after training turnover dropped 8%, which translated into less lost revenue. Farmers Group Inc. in Los Angeles used data to better understand the relationship between call center employee personality traits and customer satisfaction.[17] They were able to show that employees with certain personality traits were less likely to have dropped calls and calls that require callbacks, indicators of customer dissatisfaction. As a result, Farmers changed its call center employee selection processes to try to hire more employees with the desirable personality traits. Throughout each chapter of the book we provide examples of companies' use of workforce analytics to make evidence-based HR decisions or to evaluate practices.

HR or Workforce Analytics
The practice of using data from HR databases and other data sources to make evidence-based human resource decisions.

The HRM Profession: Positions, Education, and Competencies

There are many different types of jobs in the HRM profession. Table 1.3 shows various HRM positions and their salaries. A survey conducted by the Society of Human Resource Management to better understand what HR professionals do found that the primary activities of HR professionals are performing the HR generalist role (providing a wide range of HR services), with fewer involved in other activities such as the HR function at the executive level of the company, training and development, HR consulting, and administrative activities.[18] Projections suggest that overall employment in human resource–related positions is expected to grow by 22% between 2008 and 2018, much faster than the occupational average.[19]

POSITION	SALARY
Top HR executive	$189,000
Employee benefits manager	95,700
HR manager	90,000
Compensation analyst	65,000
Professional and technical staff recruiter	64,400
Employee training specialist	59,000
HR generalist	59,300

table 1.3
Median Salaries for HRM Positions

SOURCE: Based on J. Dooney and E. Esen, "The Ups and Downs of HR Salaries," *HR Magazine,* December 2009, pp. 36–41.

Salaries for HR professionals vary according to position, level of experience, training, location, and firm size. As you can see from Table 1.3, some positions involve work in specialized areas of HRM like recruiting, training, or labor and industrial relations. HR generalists usually make between $50,000 and $80,000 depending on their experience and education level. HR generalists perform a wide range of activities including recruiting, selection, training, labor relations, and benefits administration. HR specialists work in one specific functional area such as training or compensation. Although HR generalists tend to be found in smaller companies, many mid- to large-size companies employ HR generalists at the plant or business levels and HR specialists at the corporate, product, or regional levels. Most HR professionals chose HR as a career because they found HR appealing as a career, they wanted to work with people, or they were asked by chance to perform HR tasks and responsibilities.[20]

A college degree is held by the vast majority of HRM professionals, many of whom also have completed postgraduate work. Business typically is the field of study (human resources or industrial relations), although some HRM professionals have degrees in the social sciences (economics or psychology), the humanities, or law. Those who have completed graduate work have master's degrees in HR management, business management, industrial organizational psychology or a similar field. This is important because to be successful in HR, you need to speak the same language as the other business functions. You have to have credibility as a business leader, which means understanding business fundamentals such as how the company makes money and who the competition and customers are. This is necessary to build a business case for HR activities. Professional certification in HRM is less common than membership in professional associations. A well-rounded educational background will likely serve a person well in an HRM position. As one HR professional noted, "One of the biggest misconceptions is that it is all warm and fuzzy communications with the workers. Or that it is creative and involved in making a more congenial atmosphere for people at work. Actually it is both of those some of the time, but most of the time it is a big mountain of paperwork which calls on a myriad of skills besides the 'people' type. It is law, accounting, philosophy, and logic as well as psychology, spirituality, tolerance, and humility."[21]

HR professionals need to have the six competencies shown in Figure 1.3. These are the most recent competencies identified by the Human Resource Competency Study, which has identified HR competencies for more than 15 years. The competencies are shown as a three-tier pyramid with the Credible Activist competency the most important for high performance as an HR professional and effective HR leader. Demonstrating these competencies can help HR professionals show managers that they are capable of helping the HR function create value, contribute to the business strategy, and shape the company culture. They also help the HR department effectively and efficiently provide the three HR products discussed earlier and shown in Figure 1.2. Although great emphasis is placed on the strategic role of HR, effective execution of the operational executor competency—necessary administrative services filling open jobs, paying employees, benefits enrollment, keeping employee records, and completing legally required paperwork (such as W-2 forms and EEO reports)—is still important! As we discuss later in the chapter, technological advances have made available e-HRM and human resource information systems, which make administration of services more efficient and effective and free up time for HR to focus on strategic issues. Successful HR professionals must be able to share information, build relationships, and influence persons both inside and outside the company, including managers, employees, community members, schools, customers, vendors, and suppliers.

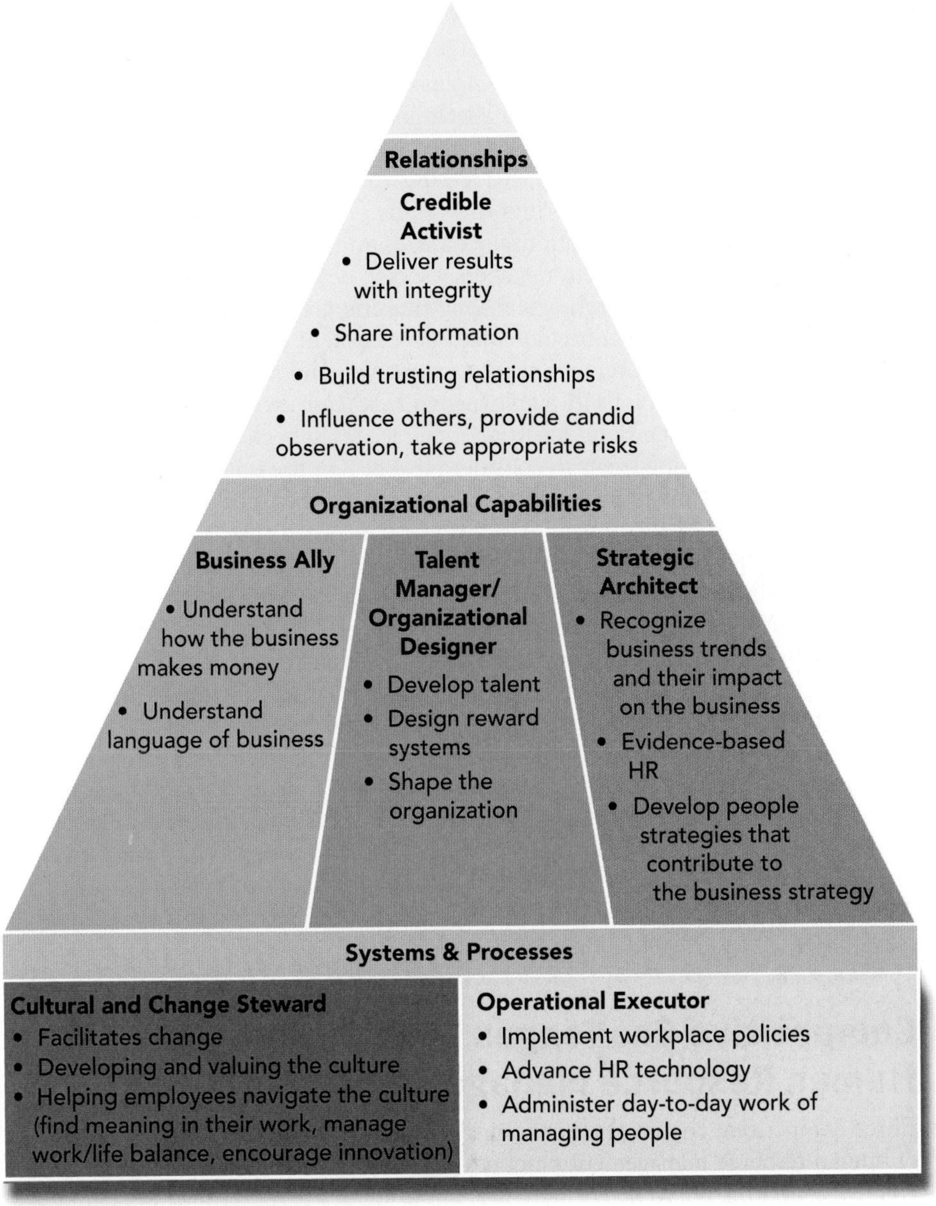

figure 1.3

Six Competencies
for the HR
Profession

Relationships

Credible Activist

- Deliver results with integrity
- Share information
- Build trusting relationships
- Influence others, provide candid observation, take appropriate risks

Organizational Capabilities

Business Ally
- Understand how the business makes money
- Understand language of business

Talent Manager/ Organizational Designer
- Develop talent
- Design reward systems
- Shape the organization

Strategic Architect
- Recognize business trends and their impact on the business
- Evidence-based HR
- Develop people strategies that contribute to the business strategy

Systems & Processes

Cultural and Change Steward
- Facilitates change
- Developing and valuing the culture
- Helping employees navigate the culture (find meaning in their work, manage work/life balance, encourage innovation)

Operational Executor
- Implement workplace policies
- Advance HR technology
- Administer day-to-day work of managing people

SOURCES: Based on R. Grossman, "New Competencies for HR," *HR Magazine* (June 2007): pp. 58–62; D. Ulrich, W. Bruckbank, D. Johnson, K. Sandholtz, and J. Younger, "HR Competencies: Mastery at the Intersection of People and Business" (Alexandria, VA: Society for Human Resource Management +/RBL Group, 2008).

Many top-level managers and HR professionals believe that the best way to develop competencies of the future effective professionals needed in HR is to train employees or put them into experiences that help them understand the business and HR's role in contributing to it. Consider how Google and Southwest Airlines are developing the right mix of HR skills and experience to best contribute to the business.[22] At Google, approximately one-third of the HR team's employees have HR backgrounds and expertise in specialty skill areas such as employment law, compensation, and benefits. Another one-third have little or no human resource experience and were recruited from consulting firms or within Google's engineering or sales functions. The final one-third is a workforce analytics group with employees who have doctorates in finance, statistics, and organizational psychology. Each group has its strengths. For example, HR staff who have limited HR experience are very skilled in problem solving and how the company works outside HR. To capitalize on the unique perspectives and skills that each group brings to working on human resource issues, the vice president of global people operations encourages interactions and knowledge sharing among the entire group of team members. Google develops human resources or key people operations staff through a year-long training program that includes HR specialist training, a business curriculum, and development of skills related to working with clients, communicating with senior executives, and solving business problems. The training is designed for HR employees with at least two years of experience and is taught by People Operations department employees. Google recruits top MBA program graduates, enticing them to consider HR because the opportunity to influence change in the company is greater than is common in other specialty areas and career advancement is faster. Southwest Airlines was concerned that its HR function had become too distant from the company's business units. To develop a stronger team of HR generalists and get them to be valued partners and consultants to operations, managers, and other internal customers, Southwest Airlines retrained and relocated HR specialists into the field. Southwest recognizes that to deal with the fast pace of change in the airline industry HR generalists need to have a continuous improvement philosophy, business savvy, and both interpersonal and strategic skills.

The primary professional organization for HRM is the Society for Human Resource Management (SHRM). SHRM is the world's largest human resource management association with more than 210,000 professional and student members throughout the world. SHRM provides education and information services, conferences and seminars, government and media representation, and online services and publications (such as *HR Magazine*). You can visit SHRM's website to see their services at www.shrm.org.

Competitive Challenges Influencing Human Resource Management

Sustainability
The ability of a company to survive in a dynamic competitive environment. Based on an approach to organizational decision making that considers company's ability to make a profit without sacrificing the resources of its employees, the community, or the environment.

Three competitive challenges that companies now face will increase the importance of human resource management practices: the challenge of sustainability, the global challenge, and the technology challenge. These challenges are shown in Figure 1.4.

THE SUSTAINABILITY CHALLENGE

Traditionally, sustainability has been viewed as one aspect of corporate social responsibility related to the impact of the business on the environment.[23] However, we take a broader view of sustainability. **Sustainability** refers to a company's ability to make a profit without sacrificing the resources of its employees, the community, or the environment.[24] Company success is based on how well the company meets the needs of its stakeholders. **Stakeholders** refers to shareholders, the community, customers, employees, and all of the other parties that have an interest in seeing that the company succeeds. Sustainability includes the ability to deal with economic and social changes, practice environmental responsibility, engage in responsible and ethical business

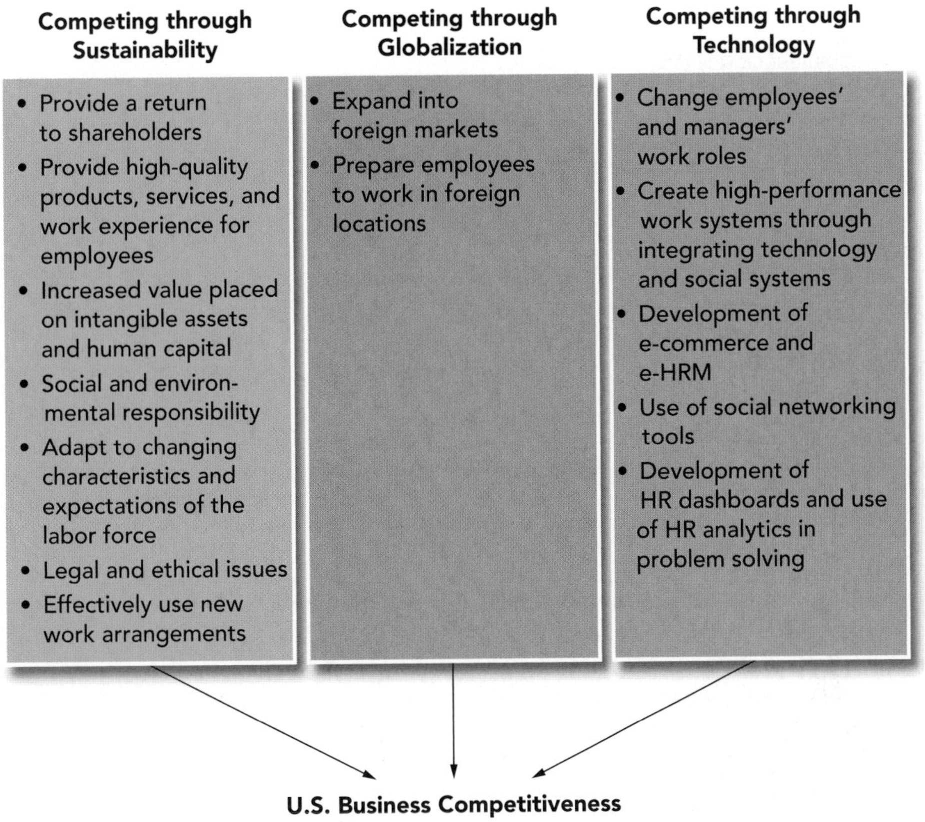

Competing through Sustainability	Competing through Globalization	Competing through Technology
• Provide a return to shareholders • Provide high-quality products, services, and work experience for employees • Increased value placed on intangible assets and human capital • Social and environmental responsibility • Adapt to changing characteristics and expectations of the labor force • Legal and ethical issues • Effectively use new work arrangements	• Expand into foreign markets • Prepare employees to work in foreign locations	• Change employees' and managers' work roles • Create high-performance work systems through integrating technology and social systems • Development of e-commerce and e-HRM • Use of social networking tools • Development of HR dashboards and use of HR analytics in problem solving

U.S. Business Competitiveness

figure 1.4

Competitive Challenges Influencing U.S. Companies

practices, provide high-quality products and services, and put in place methods to determine if the company is meeting stakeholders' needs.

The economy has important implications for human resource management. Some key statistics about the economy and the workforce are shown in Table 1.4. These include the structure of the economy, the development and spread of social networking, and growth in professional and service occupations. Growth in these occupations means that skill demands for jobs have changed, with knowledge becoming more valuable. Not only have skill demands changed, but remaining competitive in a global economy requires demanding work hours and changes in traditional employment patterns. The creation of new jobs, aging employees leaving the workforce, slow population growth, and a lack of employees who have the skills needed to perform the high-demand jobs means that companies need to give more attention to HR practices that influence attracting and retaining employees.

Economic Changes

The recession experienced in the United States was one of the worst ever with the unemployment rate reaching over 10% in October 2009.[25] The U.S. economy continues to struggle due to high unemployment, lack of consumer confidence, and the debt crisis. There are mixed signs that the job market is beginning to recover from the recession which according to economists began in late 2007 and ended in the summer of 2009.[26] One encouraging sign was that in February 2011, the U.S. unemployment rate dropped below 9% for the first time since 2009, suggesting economic recovery.[27] Another positive economic sign is that the number of layoffs has returned close to the

LO 1-2
Discuss the implications of the economy, the makeup of the labor force, and ethics for company sustainability.

Stakeholders
The various interest groups who have relationships with, and consequently, whose interests are tied to the organization (e.g., employees, suppliers, customers, shareholders, community).

table 1.4

Summary of Key Labor Statistics Influencing HRM

- Total employment will increase from 150.9 million in 2008 to 166.2 million by 2018.
- Professional specialty and service occupations will grow the fastest and add the most jobs from 2008 to 2018.
- More job openings are expected from the need to replace workers (34 million), more than twice as many as employment growth (15 million) in the economy.
- The 77 million baby boomers (born between 1946 and 1964) will begin to leave the workforce between 2008 and 2018 as they become eligible for retirement.
- The projected median age of the labor force by 2018 is 42, the highest ever recorded.
- The Hispanic labor force will increase rapidly (2.9% annually) composing 17.6% of the labor force in 2018.

SOURCES: M. Toossi, "Labor Force Projections to 2018; Older Workers Staying More Active," *Monthly Labor Review,* November 2009, pp. 30–51; K. Bartsch, "The Employment Projections for 2008–18," *Monthly Labor Review,* November 2009, pp. 3–10; R. Woods, "Industry Outlook and Employment Projections to 2018," *Monthly Labor Review,* November 2009, pp. 52–84; T. Lacey and B. Wright, "Occupational Employment Projections to 2018," *Monthly Labor Review,* November 2009, pp. 82–123.

levels that existed before the recession. However, the labor force participation rate, which measures those who have jobs or are actively seeking work, was approximately 64% its lowest point since the mid-1980s. Estimates suggest that 4.4 million people have been out of work for over a year. Also, economic recovery has been thwarted by the debt crisis in the United States, Greece and other countries which has created turbulence in the world's financial markets.

There are several implications of this economic period for human resource management. Despite the reduction in number of layoffs, hiring remains slow as many companies are finding ways to increase productivity and efficiency without having to add new employees. Also, companies are waiting for product and service demand to improve and if and when it does they will first call back laid-off employees and restore pay cuts and benefits such as paid holidays before hiring new employees. Sectors such as manufacturing are creating more jobs than they are eliminating for the first time in the last 10 years. Job growth in manufacturing is expected to continue as companies take advantage of government incentives and replace aging equipment.

Although an estimated 14 million people are looking for jobs companies are finding it difficult to fill technical positions such as data, computer, and software engineers, finance and information consultants, and web developers.[28] For example, Gowalla, a Texas-based start-up company that specializes in location-based social networking had to outsource the development of one of its applications because it could not hire enough computer engineers.

Many HR departments are helping companies recover from the recession and preparing them to be well-positioned as business conditions improve. For example, Capital One asks its managers to determine current workloads and staffing needs.[29] HR projects changes in the workforce based on this information. This has allowed Capital One to forecast labor needs with more precision, helping the company avoid hiring new employees only to potentially have to lay them off.

During the recession, Philips Electronics cut its training budget but continued to offer its Inspire program for high-potential employees, emphasizing business strategy and personal leadership topics.[30] Philips believes that investing in leadership development will better position the company to retain top talent and meet demands for managerial talent as business grows and the economy recovers.

Also, companies are under pressure to increase employee productivity to alleviate higher costs such as health care.[31] To control costs and increase the effectiveness of the U.S. health care system, President Obama signed the Patient Protection and Affordable Care Act. However, many provisions of this act are not yet in effect. Companies are uncertain as to the implications of the act for their health care costs, and the basic premises underlying the act are being challenged in court. As a result, companies continue to look for ways to cut costs, including reducing employee and retiree health care benefits and pension contributions, increasing the employee contribution to pay for these benefits, and even hiring and firing employees based on their smoking habits! For example, Scott's Miracle-Gro Company, the lawn care company, banned smoking and encourages employees to complete a health-risk assessment designed to identify employees who are at risk for heart, cancer, and other diseases.[32] Employees at risk are assigned a health coach, who draws up an action plan that may include recommendations such as exercise or change of diet. Employees who refuse the health assessment pay $40 per month more in health care premiums; at-risk employees who refuse to work with a health coach pay an additional $67 per month. We discuss what companies are doing to offset health care and pension costs in Chapter 13, Employee Benefits.

HR programs and the HR function are under pressure to relate to the business strategy and show a return on investment. Customer focus needs to be included in all HRM practices. New technology means that administrative and transactional HR activities will be delivered via technology, creating less need for HR professionals to provide these activities. The aging workforce combined with reduced immigration because of security concerns may lead employers to focus more on retraining employees or encouraging older, skilled workers to delay retirement or work part-time.[33]

U.S. employment is expected to increase from 150. 9 million in 2008 to 166.2 million in 2018 adding 15.3 million jobs. Two service-providing sectors of the U.S. economy, professional and business services and health care and social assistant services are expected to generate more than half the increase in total employment from 2008 to 2018.[34] As a result, most growth is projected for professional and service occupations. Service occupations are expected to increase 13.8 million, rising to 33.6 million jobs by 2018. Professional and related occupations are expected to grow 16.8 percent, resulting in 36.3 million jobs in 2018.[35] Employment in production, farming, fishing, and forestry occupations is expected to decline. For example, employment in production occupations is expected to decline by approximately 349,000 jobs or 3.5%, between 2008 and 2018. Many of these job losses will occur in metal and plastic workers, and textile, apparel, and furnishing occupations. This is occurring for several reasons. First, these occupations are found in businesses producing products with thin profit margins that U.S. companies are abandoning to other nations with lower labor costs. Second, overall employment in manufacturing is also projected to decline between 2008 and 2018.[36] Although the United States is the top manufacturing country in the world it is also the most productive and efficient. This means that fewer workers are needed. Keep in mind that there are likely some exceptions to these projected trends. Companies that require specialized labor to make industrial lathes, computer chips, and health care products requiring specialized skills, plan to expand and locate near towns and cities that have such an available workforce.[37] For example, Greatbatch Inc., which makes medical products, is expanding near Fort Wayne, Indiana, to take advantage of the local workforce's specialized skills.

Table 1.5 shows 10 of the 30 fastest growing occupations between 2008 and 2018. Of the 30 fastest growing occupations, 17 are in professional and related occupations, 7 include health care practitioners and technical occupations (such as physicians'

table 1.5

Examples of the Fastest Growing Occupations

| OCCUPATION | EMPLOYMENT CHANGE 2008–2018 | | MOST SIGNIFICANT EDUCATION OR TRAINING |
	NUMBER (IN THOUSANDS)	PERCENT	
Biomedical engineers	12	72	Bachelor's degree
Network systems and data communication analysts	156	53	Bachelor's degree
Home health care aides	461	50	Short-term on-the-job training
Personal and home health care aides	376	46	Short-term on-the-job training
Financial examiners	11	41	Bachelor's degree
Medical scientists, except epidemiologists	44	40	Doctoral degree
Physicians' assistants	29	39	Master's degree
Skin care specialists	15	38	Postsecondary vocational
Biochemists and biophysicists	9	37	Doctoral degree
Athletic trainers	6	37	Bachelor's degree

SOURCE: Based on T. Lacey and B. Wright, "Occupational Employment Projections to 2018," *Monthly Labor Review,* November 2009, pp. 82–123.

assistants and biomedical engineers), 10 are service occupations (such as fitness trainers, aerobics instructors, and occupational therapists), and 3 are management occupations (business and financial occupations such as financial advisers and examiners). Many of the growing occupations are related to health care. This is because as the U.S. population ages, more inpatient and outpatient medical-related services are necessary. Also, technicians and assistants are providing many types of basic medical care allowing more highly paid physicians, surgeons, and pharmacists to focus on more complex patient needs and treatments. Over two-thirds of the 30 fastest growing occupations require education beyond high school and slightly less than half require at least a Bachelor's degree or higher as their most significant source of education and training. This is not surprising because occupations that involve a postsecondary award or degree will see faster employment growth than occupations requiring on-the-job training. Almost 51 million job openings are expected to occur between 2008 and 2018, half in jobs with high turnover that require on-the-job training such as cashiers and customer service representatives. Farmers and ranchers, sewing machine operators, order clerks, and postal service mail sorters and processors are expected to have the largest declines in the number of jobs between 2008 and 2018.

The future U.S. labor market will be both a knowledge economy and a service economy.[38] There will be many high-education professional and managerial jobs and low-education service jobs. High-tech manufacturing jobs will require specialized skills such as blue print reading, repair, troubleshooting, operations of computerized machines, and

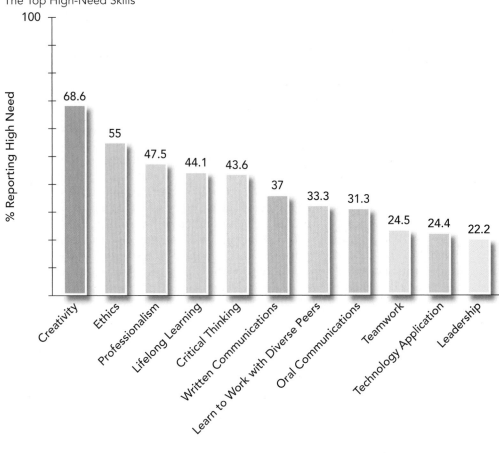

figure 1.5

The Top High-Need Skills

SOURCE: Data from J. Casner-Lotto, E. Rosenblum and M. Wright, "The Ill-Prepared US Workforce," Conference Board.

understanding how to improve quality and productivity on the factory floor. Boundaries between knowledge and service work are blurring, creating "technoservice" occupations that combine service technology and software application. Software application engineers, technical support, engineering, and scientific consulting jobs work directly with customers, and customers influence the product design process.

Figure 1.5 shows the top high-need applied skills for employers. However, new entrants to the workplace lack these and other skills needed for companies to compete in the global economy. Several studies illustrate the skill deficit companies are experiencing.[39] A study by the Business Roundtable found that 62% of employers report they are having difficulty finding qualified job applicants to fill job openings. More than half indicated that at least 16% of their workforce has skills gaps that adversely affect productivity. Similarly a study by a consortium of Society for Human Resource Management, American Society for Training and Development, The Conference Board, and Corporate Voices for Working Families found that regardless of their education level only half the companies surveyed rated new employees as adequately prepared for work. Companies' greatest basic skills needs were in reading, writing, and math.

Also, business leaders such as Bill Gates have expressed their concern at the comparatively low numbers of U.S. students in the science and engineering fields. China graduates about four times the number of engineers as the United States, although they are not all trained at the same level as U.S. engineers.[40] Japan graduates twice as many engineers and South Korea graduates nearly as many engineers as the United States. This has resulted in a shortage of engineering and other technical professionals.

Companies are involved in training current employees as well as establishing partnerships with schools to help improve the skills of the current and future U.S. workforce. For example, at Whirlpool, building a dishwasher requires that the sheet of steel used on the sides of the machine be the correct width.[41] Employees must be able to ensure that the steel meets specifications by calibrating equipment, which requires algebra-level math knowledge. Whirlpool is finding that employees lack the math problem-solving skills needed to perform the job. As a result, Whirlpool has developed training programs to improve workforce skills. About 25 percent of the programs focus on remedial skills. IBM, Hewlett-Packard, and Advanced Micro Devices are making efforts to increase the skills of the workforce by investing in local secondary schools.[42] IBM's Transition to Teaching program allows employees to take leaves of absences to student teach for three months. Eligible employees must meet certain requirements such as 10 years of service with IBM; a bachelor's degree in math or science, or a higher degree in a related field; and some experience teaching, tutoring, or volunteering in schools. IBM hopes that many of its experienced employees with math and engineering backgrounds will take advantage of the program, providing high-quality math and science teachers for public schools.

Increased Value Placed on Intangible Assets and Human Capital. Today more and more companies are interested in using intangible assets and human capital as a way to gain an advantage over competitors. A company's value includes three types of assets that are critical for the company to provide goods and services: financial assets (cash and securities), physical assets (property, plant, equipment), and intangible assets. Table 1.6 provides examples of intangible assets. **Intangible assets** include human capital, customer capital, social capital, and intellectual capital. Intangible assets are equally or even more valuable than financial and physical assets but they are difficult to duplicate or imitate.[43] By one estimate, up to 75 percent of the source of value in a company is in intangible assets.[44]

Intangible Assets
A type of company asset including human capital, customer capital, social capital, and intellectual capital.

Intangible assets have been shown to be responsible for a company's competitive advantage. Human resource management practices such as training, selection, performance management, and compensation have a direct influence on human and social capital through influencing customer service, work-related know-how and competence, and work relationships. Consider the effort that Macy's is undertaking to develop human capital, social capital, and customer capital.[45] Almost half of Macy's department store customer complaints are focused on interactions with sales associates. To cut costs to survive during the recession Macy's closed stores and invested in technology to improve efficiency which diverted attention away from customer service. But now Macy's is making a considerable investment in training its sales associates to provide better customer service and to help the company meet sales growth targets. The new training program requires new sales associates to attend a three-hour training session and includes refresher courses and coaching from managers when they are working on the sales floor. The Magic Selling Program (Magic stands for meet and make a connection, ask questions and listen, give options and advice, inspire to buy, and celebrate the purchase) is designed to help sales associates make more personal connections with shoppers. Positive interactions with sales associates

table 1.6

Examples of
Intangible Assets

Human capital
- Tacit knowledge
- Education
- Work-related know-how
- Work-related competence

Customer capital
- Customer relationships
- Brands
- Customer loyalty
- Distribution channels

Social capital
- Corporate culture
- Management philosophy
- Management practices
- Informal networking systems
- Coaching/mentoring relationships

Intellectual capital
- Patents
- Copyrights
- Trade secrets
- Intellectual property

SOURCES: Based on L. Weatherly, *Human Capital: The Elusive Asset* (Alexandria, VA: 2003 SHRM Research Quarterly); E. Holton and S. Naquin, "New Metrics for Employee Development," *Performance Improvement Quarterly* 17 (2004), pp. 56–80; M. Huselid, B. Becker, and R. Beatty, *The Workforce Scorecard* (Boston: Harvard University Press, 2005).

contribute to the number of items that a customer purchases and can help enhance Macy's service reputation as customers share experiences on social network sites such as Twitter and Facebook.

Intangible assets have been shown to be related to a company's bottom line. A study by the American Society for Training and Development of more than 500 publicly traded U.S-based companies found that companies that invested the most in training and development had a shareholder return 86% higher than companies in the bottom half and 46% higher than the market average.[46]

One way companies try to increase intangible assets is through attracting, developing, and retaining knowledge workers. **Knowledge workers** are employees who contribute to the company not through manual labor, but through what they know about customers or a specialized body of knowledge. Employees cannot simply be ordered to perform tasks; they must share knowledge and collaborate on solutions. Knowledge workers contribute specialized knowledge that their managers may not have, such as information about customers. Managers depend on them to share information. Knowledge workers have many job opportunities. If they choose, they can leave a company and take their knowledge to a competitor. Knowledge workers are in demand because companies need their skills and jobs requiring them are growing (see Table 1.5).

To completely benefit from employees' knowledge requires a management style that focuses on developing and empowering employees. **Empowering** means giving employees responsibility and authority to make decisions regarding all aspects of product development or customer service.[47] Employees are then held accountable for products and services; in return, they share the rewards and losses of the results. For empowerment to be successful, managers must be trained to link employees to

Knowledge Workers
Employees who own the intellectual means of producing a product or service.

Empowering
Giving employees responsibility and authority to make decisions.

resources within and outside the company (people, websites, etc.), help employees interact with their fellow employees and managers throughout the company, and ensure that employees are updated on important issues and cooperate with each other. Employees must also be trained to understand how to use the Web, e-mail, and other tools for communicating, collecting, and sharing information.

Learning Organization
Employees are continually trying to learn new things.

As more companies become knowledge-based, it's important that they promote and capture learning at the employee, team, and company levels. A **learning organization** embraces a culture of lifelong learning, enabling all employees to continually acquire and share knowledge. Improvements in product or service quality do not stop when formal training is completed.[48] Employees need to have the financial, time, and content resources (courses, experiences, development opportunities) available to increase their knowledge. Managers take an active role in identifying training needs and helping to ensure that employees use training in their work. Also, employees should be actively encouraged to identify problems, make decisions, continuously experiment, and improve.

At Cheesecake Factory Inc., which operates about 160 restaurants in the United States, learning is less about formal programs and courses and more about being available on an as-needed basis and driven by employees.[49] The company is focused on driving continuous learning related to guest satisfaction, perfect food, and execution of the many dishes on its menu. To do so, the company is creating interactive learning content that employees access at work. Through the the VideoCafe employees can upload and share short videos on topics such as customer greetings and food preparation. The company plans to develop interactive games including a simulation for building the perfect hamburger. Hands-on employee-driven learning is supported by managers observing employees and providing coaching and feedback to help them develop new skills and reinforce their use in the workplace.

Social collaboration and social networking technology are also contributing to the development of a learning organization.[50] CareSource uses Wikis, websites with content created by users, and discussion boards to encourage employees to engage in critical thinking and learn from each other by sharing ideas about how to apply skills that they have acquired in formal training programs. Coldwell Banker encourages its real estate professionals to develop and share videos of best sales techniques using the company's video portal. Coldwell Banker also uses communities of practice to encourage employees to share best practices and provide insights on how to best approach specific types of job assignments. inVentiv Health Inc. uses tools on Facebook to help sales employees share information and update lessons learned.

Psychological Contract
Expectations of employee contributions and what the company will provide in return.

Adapting to Change and Its Effect on the Employment Relationship. *Change* refers to the adoption of a new idea or behavior by a company. Technological advances, changes in the workforce or government regulations, globalization, and new competitors are among the many factors that require companies to change. Change is inevitable in companies as products, companies, and entire industries experience shorter life cycles.[51] This has played a major role in reshaping the employment relationship.[52] New or emergent business strategies that result from these changes cause companies to merge, acquire new companies, grow, and in some cases downsize and restructure. This has resulted in changes in the employment relationship. The **psychological contract** describes what an employee expects to contribute and what the company will provide to the employee for these contributions.[53] Unlike a sales contract, a psychological contract is not written. Consider how the psychological contract in today's workplace has shaped both the company and its employees' expectations.[54] Companies demand excellent customer service and high productivity levels. Employees are expected to take more responsibility for their own careers, from seeking training to balancing work and family. In exchange for top performance and working longer hours without job security, employees want companies to provide flexible work schedules, comfortable working conditions, more autonomy in accomplishing work, training and development opportunities, and financial incentives based on how the company performs. Employees realize that companies cannot provide employment security, so they want employability—that is, they want their company to provide training and job experiences to help ensure that employees can find other employment opportunities. The human resource management challenge is how to build a committed, productive workforce in economic conditions that offer opportunity for financial success but can also quickly turn sour, making every employee expendable.

Consider how NASA is adapting to change and helping employees cope with the realities of today's psychological contract. NASA's space shuttle program has ended after 29 years.[55] Because of cuts in its budget, there is not enough money to pay for costs related to flying the space shuttle and operating the International Space Station. This will have a major impact on communities in which the space program is located, NASA employees, as well as employees from its contractors for space shuttle operations such as Lockheed-Martin and United Space Alliance. The shuttle's last flight means that NASA and contract engineers will need to either seek other employment or put their skills to work on new space vehicles and new planetary missions such as to Mars. NASA must decide which employees and skills it needs and then use retirement, attrition, or layoffs to reduce head count. To cope with the change, NASA is trying to determine the skills they need for the next program and how they relate to human resource requirements, and identify skill excesses and weaknesses in the current workforce as they relate to the new requirements. NASA estimates that slightly more than half the 13,000 shuttle contractor employees could lose their jobs as the program ends following the last flight in 2011. To help employees and contract workers cope with the change, NASA has improved communications to make sure they know what training will be available for new skills. Websites at Johnson and Kennedy space centers are used to provide information on the transition and help employees find positions that need their skills or help them transition to positions outside of NASA (such as with defense contractors). NASA and its subcontractors are also providing career planning, skills training, and counseling for employees to help them deal with anxiety and grief associated with the ending of the shuttle program.

Concerns with Employee Engagement. **Employee engagement** refers to the degree to which employees are fully involved in their work and the strength of their commitment to their job and the company.[56] Employees who are engaged in their work and committed to the company they work for give companies competitive advantage including higher productivity, better customer service, and lower turnover.[57] What is the state of employee engagement in U.S. companies? One survey of 50,000 employees across different companies showed that about 13 percent of employees are disengaged, poor performers who put in minimal effort on the job and are likely to leave the organization. Some 76% of employees exhibit moderate engagement; that is, they are marginally committed to the company and perform their jobs to the level expected by their manager. Only 11% of employees had high levels of engagement: they exhibited strong commitment to the company and were high performers who helped other employees with their work, volunteered for new responsibilities, and were constantly looking for ways to perform their jobs better.[58]

Perhaps the best way to understand engagement is to consider how companies measure employee engagement. Companies measure employees' engagement levels with attitude or opinion surveys (we discuss these in detail in Chapter 10). Although the types of questions asked on these surveys vary from company to company, research

Employee Engagement
The degree to which employees are fully involved in their work and the strength of their job and company commitment.

table 1.7

Common Themes
of Employee
Engagement

Pride in employer
Satisfaction with employer
Satisfaction with the job
Opportunity to perform challenging work
Recognition and positive feedback from contributions
Personal support from manager
Effort above and beyond the minimum
Understanding the link between one's job and the company's mission
Prospects for future growth with the company
Intention to stay with the company

SOURCE: Based on R. Vance, *Employee Engagement and Commitment* (Alexandria, VA: Society for Human Resource Management, 2006).

suggests the questions generally measure 10 common themes shown in Table 1.7. As you probably realize after reviewing the themes shown in Table 1.7, employees' engagement is influenced by how managers treat employees as well as human resource practices such as recruiting, selection, training and development, performance management, work design, and compensation. For example, companies should recruit and select employees who are able to perform the job, are willing to work toward achieving the company strategy, and will react favorably to the work environment. Performance management systems need to provide employees with opportunities to receive performance feedback and recognition for their accomplishments. Compensation including incentives, benefits, and nonfinancial perks such as on-site day care or travel discounts contribute to employee engagement. Training and development gives employees the opportunity for personal growth within the company. Work that is designed to be meaningful and allows employees to use a variety of their skills relates to several different aspects of engagement including satisfaction, intention to stay, pride, and opportunity to perform challenging work.

EVIDENCE-BASED HR

United Health Care consists of six businesses focusing on individual, community, and state health care plans and services.[59] The company's mission is to help people live healthier lives. United Health Care Group uses engagement surveys to help identify changes in HR practices as well as to ensure that HR practices align with and support the company's business strategy. Recent survey results suggested that managers' performance, communication, and understanding of how each employee's job contributes to the business strategy were areas in need of improvement. Based on the survey results, the executive vice president of human capital has personal and monthly communications with managers about how to engage employees and explain what employees can do in their jobs to positively impact the business strategy. Underscoring the importance of employee engagement, recent increases in employee engagement survey scores have been found to correlate to a decrease in turnover of 9%, a 6% drop in turnover of key employees, a 13% increase in internal promotion rates, and a 10% drop in the number of employees who leave the company in their first year of employment. Also, increases in engagement scores have been accompanied by an increase in customer and provider satisfaction and higher company revenues.

Talent Management. **Talent management** refers to the systematic planned strategic effort by a company to use bundles of human resource management practices including acquiring and assessing employees, learning and development, performance management, and compensation to attract, retain, develop, and motivate highly skilled employees and managers. This means recognizing that all HR practices are inter-related, aligned with business needs, and help the organization manage talent to meet business goals. For example, at Qualcomm, a San Diego company, talent management is organized around core values that emphasize recruiting smart, motivated employees and creating a work environment that allows them to innovate, execute, partner, and lead.[60] When Qualcomm wanted to introduce technology for its performance management process human resources generalists worked together with organizational development and information technology specialists to ensure that what employees were being evaluated on (performance management) and what employees were paid and rewarded for (compensation and rewards) were aligned. HR trained managers to use the performance management system and now focus on identifying employee skills gaps to identify opportunities to improve performance.

Survey results suggest that opportunities for career growth, learning, and development and performing exciting and challenging work are some of the most important factors in determining employees' engagement and commitment to their current employer.[61] As the economy improves, high-achieving employees may be looking to leave companies if they do not feel they have adequate opportunities to develop or move to positions in which they can best utilize their skills. Hilton Worldwide has been changing its talent management strategy to create a culture that allows all employees to capitalize on their talent.[62] At Hilton, top performers are identified through manager and peer nomination programs. Hilton's career pathing program provides employees with online access to information on roles within different departments and training programs for skills development. Hilton is also using surveys, town hall meetings, newsletters, and online videos to help enhance employees' engagement. Hilton believes the key for retaining high-performing employees is that they need to feel they are fairly paid, have opportunities to learn and develop, and have fun in their jobs. CVS Caremark is also taking steps to show top performers they are valued, are an important part of the business, and are aware of development and promotion opportunities. CVS Caremark introduced a companywide leadership development curriculum for senior director to vice president–level employees who were identified as high potential employees by their managers and HR leaders. The program is designed to provide them with a better understanding of the entire business and how they can contribute to business goals. The program includes face-to-face meetings and assignments focused on developing leadership skills. CVS Caremark has found on employee surveys that program participants give higher scores on engagement measures including feeling like an important part of the company, believing that their work makes an important contribution to the company's success, and reporting they are less likely to leave the company.

Use of Alternative Work Arrangements. **Alternative work arrangements** include independent contractors, on-call workers, temporary workers, and contract company workers. The Bureau of Labor Statistics estimates that alternative work arrangements make up 11% of total employment.[63] There are 10.3 million independent contractors, 2.5 million on-call workers, 1.2 million temporary help agency workers, and

Talent Management
A systematic planned strategic effort by a company to attract, retain, develop, and motivate highly skilled employees and managers.

Alternative Work Arrangements
Independent contractors, on-call workers, temporary workers, and contract company workers who are not employed full-time by the company.

approximately 813,000 workers employed by contract firms. Contingent workers, or workers who do not expect their jobs to last or who believe their jobs are temporary, account for approximately 2 to 4% of total employment. Companies that provide temporary employees, such as Manpower, Kelly Services, and Adecco are reporting high demand for their services.[64] One of the reasons for the growth of the use of contingent workers is because companies are adding temporary workers as the economy begins to improve but are delaying adding new permanent employees until economic growth is more stable and certain. Also, companies want to avoid going through the painful layoffs that occurred during the recession.

More workers in alternative employment relationships are choosing these arrangements. Alternative work arrangements can benefit both individuals and employers. More and more individuals don't want to be attached to any one company. They want the flexibility to work when and where they choose. They may want to work fewer hours to effectively balance work and family responsibilities. Also, individuals who have been downsized may choose alternative work arrangements while they are seeking full-time employment. From the company perspective, it is easier to add temporary employees when they are needed and easier to terminate their employment when they are not needed. Part-time workers can be a valuable source of skills that current employees may not have and are needed for a specific project that has a set completion date. Part-time workers can be less expensive than permanent employees because they do not receive employer health benefits or participate in pension plans. Employing part-time workers such as interns allows the company to determine if the worker meets performance requirements and fits in with the company culture, and if so, to offer the employee a permanent position. For example, Verigy, a semiconductor manufacturer in California, employs only a small number of permanent employees and nonessential jobs are outsourced. When demand for its products increases, engineers and other high-tech employees are hired through staffing companies or as independent contractors.[65]

Also, the use of alternative work arrangements has resulted in the development of co-working sites where diverse workers such as designers, artists, freelancers, consultants, and other independent contractors pay a daily or monthly fee for a guaranteed work space.[66] The co-working site is equipped with desks and wireless Internet and some provide access to copy machines, faxes, and conference rooms. Co-working sites help facilitate independent contractors and, employees working at home, traveling, or telecommuting, who have feelings of isolation, and give them the ability to collaborate and interact, provide a more professional working atmosphere than coffee shops, and help decrease traffic and pollution.

Demanding Work, but with More Flexibility. The globalization of the world economy and the development of e-commerce have made the notion of a 40-hour work week obsolete. As a result, companies need to be staffed 24 hours a day, seven days a week. Employees in manufacturing environments and service call centers are being asked to move from 8- to 12-hour days or to work afternoon or midnight shifts. Similarly, professional employees face long hours and and work demands that spill over into their personal lives. Personal digital assistants (PDAs), pagers, and iPhones bombard employees with information and work demands. In the car, on vacation, on planes, and even in the bathroom, employees can be interrupted by work demands. More demanding work results in greater employee stress, less satisfied employees, loss of productivity, and higher turnover—all of which are costly for companies.

One study found that because of work demands 75% of employees report having not enough time for their children, and 61% report not having enough time for their husbands and wives. However, only half of employees in the United States strongly agree that they have the flexibility they need to successfully manage their work and personal or family lives.[67] Many companies are recognizing the benefits that can be gained by both the company and employees through providing flexible work schedules, protecting employees' free time, and more productively using employees' work time.[68] The benefits include the ability to have an advantage in attracting and retaining talented employees, reduced stress resulting in healthier employees, and a rested workforce that can maximize the use of their skills. AmerisureMutual Insurance in Farmington Hills, Michigan, built a work environment and provides flexible programs designed to increase employee retention and engagement.[69] A new computer system makes it easier for employees to work at home by giving them access to work files using their home computers. Employees meet with their managers to discuss the feasibility of working off-site and how their performance will be evaluated. Amerisure also allows employees to take days off each year for volunteer work, and provides five paid days each year for family commitments related to medical care such as ill grandparents and immediate family members. The company's turnover rate has dropped from 18% to 10% and employee engagement survey scores have increased. Fenwick & West LLP, a law firm in San Francisco, California, with 245 employees has created special positions known as "workflow coordinators" and "balanced hour advisors" who regularly review attorney's hours to ensure that employees on reduced assignments are not overworked or overlooked for key assignments. KPMG uses Wellness Scorecards to determine if consultants are working too much overtime or skipping vacations. RSM McGladrey, a consulting firm in Rochester, Minnesota, gives employees multiple flextime options including FlexYear, which provides a schedule similar to a teacher, and FlexCareer, which enables employees to take up to five years' leave for personal reasons and provides resources such as training to keep employees connected with the firm and the industry so they can more easily transition back to work.

Meeting the Needs of Stakeholders, Shareholders, Customers, Employees, and Community

As we mentioned earlier, company effectiveness and competitiveness are determined by whether the company satisfies the needs of stakeholders. Stakeholders include stockholders (who want a return on their investment), customers (who want a high-quality product or service), and employees (who desire interesting work and reasonable compensation for their services). The community, which wants the company to contribute to activities and projects and minimize pollution of the environment, is also an important stakeholder.

Measuring Performance to Stakeholders: The Balanced Scorecard. The **balanced scorecard** gives managers an indication of the performance of a company based on the degree to which stakeholder needs are satisfied; it depicts the company from the perspective of internal and external customers, employees, and shareholders.[70] The balanced scorecard is important because it brings together most of the features that a company needs to focus on to be competitive. These include being customer-focused, improving quality, emphasizing teamwork, reducing new product and service development times, and managing for the long term.

The balanced scorecard differs from traditional measures of company performance by emphasizing that the critical indicators chosen are based on the company's

Balanced Scorecard
A means of performance measurement that gives managers a chance to look at their company from the perspectives of internal and external customers, employees, and shareholders.

LO 1-3
Discuss how human resource management affects a company's balanced scorecard.

business strategy and competitive demands. Companies need to customize their balanced scorecards based on different market situations, products, and competitive environments.

The balanced scorecard should be used to (1) link human resource management activities to the company's business strategy and (2) evaluate the extent to which the HRM function is helping the company meet its strategic objectives. Communicating the scorecard to employees gives them a framework that helps them see the goals and strategies of the company, how these goals and strategies are measured, and how they influence the critical indicators. Measures of HRM practices primarily relate to productivity, people, and process.[71] Productivity measures involve determining output per employee (such as revenue per employee). Measuring people includes assessing employees' behavior, attitudes, or knowledge. Process measures focus on assessing employees' satisfaction with people systems within the company. People systems can include the performance management system, the compensation and benefits system, and the development system. To show that HRM activities contribute to a company's competitive advantage, managers need to consider the questions shown in Table 1.8 and be able to identify critical indicators or metrics related to human resources. As shown in the last column of Table 1.8, critical indicators of HR practices primarily relate to people, productivity, and processes.

For example, at Tellabs, a company that provides communication service products (such as optical networking) around the world, key results tracked on the balanced scorecard include revenue growth, customer satisfaction, time to market for new products, and employee satisfaction.[72] Every employee has a bonus plan; bonuses are tied to performance as measured by the scorecard. The performance appraisal process

table 1.8

The Balanced Scorecard

PERSPECTIVE	QUESTIONS ANSWERED	EXAMPLES OF CRITICAL BUSINESS INDICATORS	EXAMPLES OF CRITICAL HR INDICATORS
Customer	How do customers see us?	Time, quality, performance, service, cost	Employee satisfaction with HR department services Employee perceptions of the company as an employer
Internal	What must we excel at?	Processes that influence customer satisfaction, availability of information on service and/or manufacturing processes	Training costs per employee, turnover rates, time to fill open positions
Innovation and learning	Can we continue to improve and create value?	Improve operating efficiency, launch new products, continuous improvement, empowering of workforce, employee satisfaction	Employee/skills competency levels, engagement survey results, change management capability
Financial	How do we look to shareholders?	Profitability, growth, shareholder value	Compensation and benefits per employee, turnover costs, profits per employee, revenues per employee

SOURCE: Based on B. Becker, M. Huselid, and D. Ulrich, *The HR Scorecard: Linking People, Strategy, and Performance* (Boston: Harvard Business School Press, 2001).

measures employee performance according to departmental objectives that support the scorecard. At quarterly meetings, how employee performance is evaluated according to the scorecard is shared with every employee, and the information is also available on the company intranet website.

Social Responsibility. Increasingly, companies are recognizing that social responsibility can help boost a company's image with customers, gain access to new markets, and help attract and retain talented employees. Companies thus try to meet shareholder and general public demands that they be more socially, ethically, and environmentally responsible. For example, Bill Gates, former chief executive officer and Microsoft Corporation founder, through personal involvement in a charitable foundation dedicated to bringing science and technology to improve lives around the world, has improved Microsoft's corporate reputation. Danone, a company that makes yogurts (Dannon) and mineral waters (Evian), recently invested in a factory in Bangladesh to make a yogurt fortified to help stop malnutrition and priced at seven cents to be affordable.[73] This investment gives Danone access to a large market for its products, demonstrates the company is socially responsible, and at the same time helps alleviate local malnutrition as well as creating jobs. Companies are realizing that helping to protect the planet can also save money.[74] International Paper, a global paper and packaging company, has focused on using less water and energy at its manufacturing operations. International Paper cut fossil fuel purchases by 21% by burning tree limbs and debris from tree processing. PepsiCo is introducing use of all-electric trucks in several places including California and Texas. The trucks will cut PepsiCo's diesel consumption by 500,000 gallons per year, significantly reduce annual maintenance costs, and help preserve the climate by reducing greenhouse gas emissions. Other companies such as Halliburton and BP are viewed less positively due to perceptions that they are responsible for environmental damage.

The "Competing through Sustainability" box highlights the sustainable business practices of several companies.

Customer Service and Quality Emphasis

Companies' customers judge quality and performance. As a result, customer excellence requires attention to product and service features as well as to interactions with customers. Customer-driven excellence includes understanding what the customer wants and anticipating future needs. Customer-driven excellence includes reducing defects and errors, meeting specifications, and reducing complaints. How the company recovers from defects and errors is also important for retaining and attracting customers.

Due to increased availability of knowledge and competition, consumers are very knowledgeable and expect excellent service. This presents a challenge for employees who interact with customers. The way in which clerks, sales staff, front-desk personnel, and service providers interact with customers influences a company's reputation and financial performance. Employees need product knowledge and service skills, and they need to be clear about the types of decisions they can make when dealing with customers.

To compete in today's economy, whether on a local or global level, companies need to provide a quality product or service. If companies do not adhere to quality standards, their ability to sell their product or service to vendors, suppliers, or customers will be restricted. Some countries even have quality standards that companies must meet to conduct business there. **Total quality management (TQM)** is a companywide

Total Quality Management (TQM)
A cooperative form of doing business that relies on the talents and capabilities of both labor and management to continually improve quality and productivity.

Volunteerism and Going Green Are Reaping Dividends for Employees, Communities, and the Environment

A growing number of companies have made sustainability an important part of their business strategy. General Electric's health care unit identified maternal and infant mortality as frequent causes of death in India. For example, the infant mortality rate for India, a country with 1.2 billion people is 55 children for every 1,000 births. GE worked with non-profit organizations and hospitals to understand patient and health care needs. As a result, GE identified opportunities to help as well as gain a potential market for new products. About 700 million people can't afford maternal or birth services. Also, to bring to market a product required overcoming several obstacles including power outages, a lack of money and space in hospitals for large, costly equipment, high levels of dust and pollution, and difficulty of getting replacement parts through government bureaucracy. One of the products GE developed is a baby warmer, called the Lullaby, which provides heat for cradles. The Lullaby is targeted to help people and communities with few financial assets. The Lullaby is easy to use: it uses only buttons with pictures indicating their function. For example, at General Mills, volunteerism is one of the ways that the company lives its corporate values. The CEO and senior leaders serve on non-profit boards and are involved in the community.

Finance and Information Technology employees from General Mills Canada picked more than 7,000 pounds of apples and pears as part of a team-building exercise. The fruit was donated to food banks in the Niagara region of Canada. General Mills links the expertise of its employees with small and medium-size food processors in Africa. For example, employee volunteers are helping improve the efficiency of a plant in Malawi which produces a high-nutrient peanut butter paste that is distributed to malnourished children across the country. Malawi has 13 million people, most are farm families living in poverty. General Mills' customer service center works with Catholic Charities USA, serving meals to homeless people and working at a shelter for homeless children—teaching them how to maintain a healthy diet, leading fitness activities, and helping with projects such as redecorating rooms in the shelter. Yoplait employees, partners with the Greater Minneapolis Crisis Nursery, help cook meals. Kendall J. Powell, General Mills' company CEO and chairman, wants General Mills to be one of the most socially responsible consumer food companies in the world.

Pharmaceutical company Novartis supports REPSSI, an African-based philanthropic organization that provides emotional and psychological support for children who lose their parents or guardians to AIDS. The program began in a single district in Tanzania and has expanded to 13 sub-Saharan African countries. The company's trainers provide REPSSI's employees with leadership development training. REPSSI managers need training in communication skills, providing feedback, intercultural skills, and project management. Novartis transformed its corporate training programs into a form useful for REPSSI. The training content is delivered through instructor-led courses and e-learning. Novartis and training vendor partners, including business schools, send speakers at their own expense to Africa. Instructors are also available for follow-up after each course is completed.

SOURCES: Based on M. Weinstein, "Charity Begins @ Work," *Training*, May 2008, pp. 56–58; M. Laff, "Triple Bottom Line," *T + D*, February 2009, pp. 34–39; M. Bahree, "GE Remodels Business in India," *The Wall Street Journal*, April 26, 2011, p. B8; Welcome to Citizenship@Novartis from www.corporatecitizenship.novartis.com, April 26, 2011; General Mills Corporate Social Responsibility Report 2011, from www.generalmills.com, accessed April 26, 2011.

effort to continuously improve the ways people, machines, and systems accomplish work.[75] Core values of TQM include the following:[76]

- Methods and processes are designed to meet the needs of internal and external customers.
- Every employee in the company receives training in quality.
- Quality is designed into a product or service so that errors are prevented from occurring rather than being detected and corrected.
- The company promotes cooperation with vendors, suppliers, and customers to improve quality and hold down costs.
- Managers measure progress with feedback based on data.

There is no universal definition of quality. The major differences in its various definitions relate to whether customer, product, or manufacturing process is emphasized. For example, quality expert W. Edwards Deming emphasized how well a product or service meets customer needs. Phillip Crosby's approach emphasizes how well the service or manufacturing process meets engineering standards.

The emphasis on quality is seen in the establishment of the **Malcolm Baldrige National Quality Award** and the **ISO 9000:2000** quality standards. The Baldrige award, created by public law, is the highest level of national recognition for quality that a U.S. company can receive. To become eligible for the Baldrige, a company must complete a detailed application that consists of basic information about the firm as well as an in-depth presentation of how it addresses specific criteria related to quality improvement.[77] The categories and point values for the Baldrige Award are found in Table 1.9. The award is not given for specific products or services. Organizations can compete for the Baldrige Award in one of six categories: manufacturing, service, small business, education, health care and non-profit. The Baldrige Award is given annually in each of the categories with a total limit each year of 18 awards. All applicants for the Baldrige Award undergo a rigorous examination process that takes from 300 to 1,000 hours. Applications are reviewed by an independent board of about 400 examiners who come primarily from the private sector. One of the major benefits of applying for the Baldrige Award is the feedback report from the examining team noting the company's strengths and areas for improvement.[78]

The Baldrige Award winners usually excel at human resource practices. For example consider the human resource practices of two recent Baldrige Award winners.[79] K&N Management, a 2010 Award winner in the Small Business category, employs 454 employees in the Austin, Texas, area. They are developers for two fast-causal restaurant concepts: Rudy's Country Store & Bar-B-Q and Mighty Fine Burgers, Fries, and Shakes. Both restaurants have exceeded the industry standard for profits for several years. This can be attributed to the restaurants' focus on delighting the guests which includes giving customers access to store information and events through websites and Facebook and Twitter as well as giving the customers the opportunity to provide feedback tableside using an electronic tablet that administers short surveys. All managers and owners carry a personal digital assistant (PDA) to give them access to customer complaints and performance results. This data has been used to develop new products and services such as a breakfast taco and group meal service with pickup pavilions. To ensure that guests receive consistently high service and delicious food, K&N has taken steps to retain its employees by offering above-market benefits to all employees who work on average 30 hours per week, including a 90% paid comprehensive health care plan and a company-matched retirement plan. Turnover rates are less than 50% (compared to the industry average of 85%)

Malcolm Baldrige National Quality Award
An award established in 1987 to promote quality awareness, to recognize quality achievements of U.S. companies, and to publicize successful quality strategies.

ISO 9000:2000
Quality standards adopted worldwide.

table 1.9

Categories and Point Values for the Malcolm Baldrige National Quality Award Examination

Leadership The way senior executives create and sustain vision, values, and mission; promote legal and ethical behavior; create a sustainable company and communicate with and engage the workforce.	120
Measurement, Analysis, and Knowledge Management The way the company selects, gathers, analyzes, manages, and improves its data, information, and knowledge assets	90
Strategic Planning The way the company sets strategic direction, how it determines action plans, how it changes strategy and action plans if required, and how it measures progress	85
Workforce Focus Company's efforts to develop and utilize the workforce to achieve high performance; how the company engages, manages, and develops the potential of the workforce in alignment with company goals	85
Operations Focus Design, management, and improvement of work systems and work processes to deliver customer value and achieve company success and sustainability	85
Results Company's performance and improvement in key business areas (product, service, and supply quality; productivity; and operational effectiveness and related financial indicators)	450
Customer Focus Company's knowledge of the customer, customer service systems, current and potential customer concerns, customer satisfaction and engagement	85
Total Points	1,000

SOURCE: Based on "2011–2012 Criteria for Performance Excellence" from the website for the National Institute of Standards and Technology, www.nist/gov/baldrige.

and absenteeism is slightly less than 1%. AtlantiCare, a health provider located in New Jersey with about 5,100 employees, won the award in 2009. Part of the reason that nurse turnover is below the local norm and patient volume and satisfaction are high is due to AtlantiCare's human resource practices which result in high levels of employee engagement and an understanding of how each employee's job influences the customer. For example, new hires at AtlantiCare receive a strategy map showing how company goals such as building customer loyalty relate to company values such as safety and team spirit. Employees are asked to frequently review the map and to consider ways they can contribute to performance excellence. AtlantiCare's emphasis on recognizing employee accomplishments also contributes to employee satisfaction which translates into high-quality customer service. Managers both publicly and privately recognize employees' and work groups' accomplishments in newsletters, at annual rewards dinners, and by sending thank-you cards, and awarding gift cards, cash bonuses, and preferred parking spaces. AtlantiCare expects its HR staff to keep abreast of employees' needs in order to continuously improve its services and practices. One way is through requiring most of the HR staff to visit its health care facilities to ensure that employees' HR needs are being met. Also, AtlantiCare strategically uses results of employee surveys to make changes in HR practices. For example, in response to survey results showing positive but lower engagement for employees with 6 to 10 years of tenure, managers are considering offering training that would give employees greater opportunities to change jobs.

ISO (International Organization for Standardization), a network of national standards institutes including 160 countries with a central governing body in Geneva, Switzerland, is the world's largest developer and publisher of international standards.[80] The ISO develops standards related to management, as well as a wide variety of other areas including education, music, ships, and even protecting children! ISO standards are voluntary but countries may decide to adopt ISO standards in their regulations and as a result they may become a requirement to compete in the market. The ISO 9000 is a family of standards related to quality (ISO 9000, 9001, 9004, and 10011). The ISO 9000 quality standards address what the company does to meet regulatory requirements and the customer's quality requirements while striving to improve customer satisfaction and continuous improvement. The standards represent an international consensus on quality management practices. ISO 9000:2000 has been adopted as the quality standard in nearly 100 counties around the world meaning that companies have to follow the standards to conduct business in those countries. The quality management standards of the ISO 9000 are based on eight quality management principles including customer focus, leadership, people involvement, a process approach, a systems approach to management, continuous improvement, using facts to make decisions, and establishing mutually beneficial relationships with suppliers. ISO 9001:2008 is the most comprehensive standard because it provides a set of requirements for a quality management system for all organizations both private and public. The ISO 9001:2008 has been implemented by over 1 million organizations in 176 countries. ISO 9004 provides a guide for companies that want to improve.

Why are standards useful? Customers may want to check that the product they ordered from a supplier meets the purpose for which it is required. One of the most efficient ways to do this is when the specifications of the product have been defined in an International Standard. That way, both supplier and customer are on the same wavelength, even if they are based in different countries, because they are both using the same references. Today, many products require testing for conformance with specifications or compliance with safety or other regulations before they can be put on many markets. Even simpler products may require supporting technical documentation that includes test data. With so much trade taking place across borders, it may just not be practical for these activities to be carried out by suppliers and customers, but rather by specialized third parties. In addition, national legislation may require such testing to be carried out by independent bodies, particularly when the products concerned have health or environmental implications. One example of an ISO standard is on the back cover of this book and nearly every other book. On the back cover is something called an ISBN. ISBN stands for International Standard Book Number. Publishers and booksellers are very familiar with ISBNs, because they are the method through which books are ordered and bought. Try buying a book on the Internet, and you will soon learn the value of the ISBN—there is a unique number for the book you want! And it is based on an ISO standard.

In addition to competing for quality awards and seeking ISO certification, many companies are using the Six Sigma process and lean thinking. The **Six Sigma process** refers to a process of measuring, analyzing, improving, and then controlling processes once they have been brought within the narrow Six Sigma quality tolerances or standards. The objective of Six Sigma is to create a total business focus on serving the customer, that is, to deliver what customers really want when they want it. For example, at General Electric introducing the Six Sigma quality initiative meant

Six Sigma Process
System of measuring, analyzing, improving, and controlling processes once they meet quality standards.

going from approximately 35,000 defects per million operations—which is average for most companies, including GE—to fewer than four defects per million in every element of every process GE businesses perform—from manufacturing a locomotive part to servicing a credit card account to processing a mortgage application to answering a phone.[81]

Training is an important component of quality programs because it teaches employees statistical process control and how to engage in "lean thinking." For example, Six Sigma involves highly trained employees known as Champions, Master Black Belts, Black Belts, and Green Belts who lead and teach teams that are focusing on an ever-growing number of quality projects. The quality projects focus on improving efficiency and reducing errors in products and services. The Six Sigma quality initiative has produced more than $2 billion in benefits for GE. In the past three years, Cardinal Fastener & Specialty Co. Inc.'s sales to wind turbine manufacturers have grown more than 900%.[82] The growth of the Cleveland, Ohio, based company started over 10 years ago when under the leadership of the company's founder and president, Cardinal began using "Lean Thinking," involving all employees in the process of what they referred to as "blowing up the company." The goal was to eliminate waste from the entire operation including manufacturing, administration, and sales. As a result, manufacturing lead times went from six weeks to five days, productivity improvement increased 50%, and half of all sales now come from orders that are manufactured and shipped the same day the order is taken. Because of the company's reputation for fast turnaround of specialty manufactured fasteners they received an order for a wind turbine project in Iowa. The company quickly realized that there was an opportunity to expand into the global marketplace of renewable energy, and in early 2009, the company's accomplishments were recognized by a visit from newly elected President Obama. **Lean thinking** is a way to do more with less effort, time, equipment, and space, but still provide customers with what they need and want. Part of lean thinking includes training workers in new skills or how to apply old skills in new ways so they can quickly take over new responsibilities or use new skills to help fill customer orders. As a result of lean thinking, machines were moved so that operators could make a bolt or fastener complete from start to finish, resulting in a decrease in the time it takes to make a finished product. Quality is near perfect, and inventory has been reduced 54%.

In addition to developing products or providing services that meet customer needs, one of the most important ways to improve customer satisfaction is to improve the quality of employees' work experiences. Research shows that satisfied employees are more likely to provide high-quality customer service. Customers who receive high-quality service are more likely to be repeat customers. As Table 1.10 shows, companies that are recognized as providing elite customer service emphasize state-of-the-art human resource practices including rigorous employee selection, employee loyalty, training, and keeping employees satisfied by offering generous benefits.

Lean Thinking
A process used to determine how to use less effort, time, equipment, and space but still meet customers' requirements.

Internal Labor Force
Labor force of current employees.

External Labor Market
Persons outside the firm who are actively seeking employment.

Changing Demographics and Diversity of the Workforce

Company performance on the balanced scorecard is influenced by the characteristics of its labor force. The labor force of current employees is often referred to as the **internal labor force.** Employers identify and select new employees from the external labor market through recruiting and selection. The **external labor market** includes persons actively seeking employment. As a result, the skills and motivation of a company's internal labor force are influenced by the composition of the available labor

table 1.10

Examples of HR
Practices That
Enhance Customer
Service

Wegmans

Gives away $59 million in scholarships to 19,000 employees. Senior managers sit side-by-side with employees listening in on phones in the company's call center.

Ritz Carlton

Despite having 20 service standards, front-line employees have flexibility to make customers' experiences more personal, unusual, and memorable.

Four Seasons Hotels

No employee gets a job before passing four interviews. Each employee receives a free nights' stay for himself or herself and a guest, along with free dinner at employee orientation. The free stay helps employees, most of whom otherwise could not afford to stay at the hotel, understand what being a customer feels like. They grade the hotel services such as time for room service to arrive and number of times a phone rings when calling the front desk.

Cadillac

Performance of repair technicians is carefully monitored to ensure they are not repeating mistakes in repairs. Dealers who maintain good customer service ratings based on customer surveys receive cash rewards.

Starbucks

Entry-level baristas get 24 hours of training that prepares them to stay calm and courteous in busy times.

Publix Super Markets

Employees receive bonuses based on their unit's performance and share grants as part of their incentive plans.

Cabela

Job candidates must pass a difficult 150-question test that measures their outdoor sports expertise.

SOURCE: Based on J. McGregor, "Customer Service Champs," *BusinessWeek*, March 5, 2007, pp. 52–64.

market (the external labor market). The skills and motivation of a company's internal labor force determine the need for training and development practices and the effectiveness of the company's compensation and reward systems.

Three important changes in the demographics and diversity of the workforce are projected. First, the average age of the workforce will increase. Second, the workforce will become more diverse in terms of gender and racial composition, and third, immigration will continue to affect the size and diversity of the workforce.

Aging of the Workforce. The labor force will continue to age, and the size of the 16–24 youth labor force will decrease to its lowest level in 30 years. Figure 1.6 compares the projected distribution of the age of the workforce in 2008 and 2018. The 55 and older age group is expected to grow by approximately 12M to 40M in 2018, representing a 43% increase between 2008 and 2018. This 12 million is nearly all the 12.6 million workers who are projected to be added to the workforce by 2018![83] The labor force participation of those 55 years and older is expected to grow because older individuals are leading healthier and longer lives than in the past, providing the opportunity to work more years; the high cost of health insurance and decrease in health benefits causes many employees to keep working to keep their employer-based insurance or to return to work after retirement to obtain health insurance through their employer; and the trend toward pension plans based on individuals' contributions to them rather than years of service provides an incentive for older employees

figure 1.6

Comparison of the Age Distribution of the 2008 and 2018 Labor Force

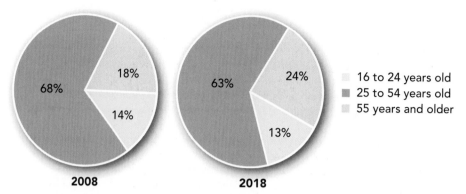

SOURCE: Based on M. Toossi, "Labor Force Projections to 2018: Older Workers Staying More Active," *Monthly Labor Review*, November 2009, pp. 30–51.

to continue working. The aging labor force means companies are likely to employ a growing share of older workers—many in their second or third career. Older people want to work and many say they plan a working retirement. Despite myths to the contrary, worker performance and learning are not adversely affected by aging.[84] Older employees are willing and able to learn new technology. An emerging trend is for qualified older workers to ask to work part-time or for only a few months at a time as a means to transition to retirement. Employees and companies are redefining the meaning of retirement to include second careers as well as part-time and temporary work assignments. An aging workforce means that employers will increasingly face HRM issues such as career plateauing, retirement planning, and retraining older workers to avoid skill obsolescence. Companies will struggle with how to control the rising costs of benefits and health care. Companies face competing challenges with older workers. Companies will have to ensure that older workers are not discriminated against in hiring, training, and workforce reduction decisions. At the same time companies will want to encourage retirement and make it financially and psychologically acceptable.

Consider the programs that several companies are offering to capitalize on older employees' skills and accommodate their needs.[85] SC Johnson offers retirees temporary work assignments, consulting and contract work, telecommuting, and part-time work. Centegra Health System's phased retirement program offers flexible scheduling including part-time work, compressed work weeks, job sharing, summers off, and long-distance contract work. LL Bean allows employees to trade, take on or give away work shifts, and volunteer to stay late or leave early.

As many older workers leave the workforce permanently or decide to work part-time, another challenge companies face is how to capture their unique knowledge and expertise so it can be used and shared with remaining employees. Recognizing that many talented employees would soon be retiring and their knowledge would be lost or forgotten, LyondellBasell, a polymer manufacturer located in Clinton, Iowa, asked key employees to record what they had learned during their tenure, especially knowledge that they knew was not already documented. Employees were interviewed to better understand difficult tasks that lacked well-documented procedures. For example, an interview with a chemical specialist revealed that when a chemical reaches a specific fluidity and color it is ready to use. That part of the interview was taped so that future employees would have a reference to the correct color of the solution.[86] Special People in Northeast, Inc. (SPIN), a nonprofit that provides services for persons with disabilities, uses "electronic how-to" manuals and flowcharts provided by key employees

figure 1.7

The U.S. Workforce, 2018

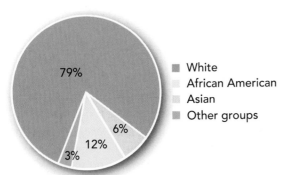

- White
- African American
- Asian
- Other groups

79%

6%

12%

3%

SOURCE: Based on M. Toossi, "Labor Force Projections to 2018: Older Workers Staying More Active," *Monthly Labor Review,* November 2009, pp. 33–51.

to ensure that current practices and procedures are available to employees with less experience who are succeeding expert employees who are leaving the organization.[87]

Increased Diversity of Workforce. As Figure 1.7 shows, by 2018 the workforce is expected to be 79% white, 12% African American, 6% Asian, and 3% other groups, which includes individuals of multiple racial origin, American Indian, Alaskan Native or Native Hawaiian, and other Pacific Islanders.[88] The diversity of the workforce is expected to increase from 2008 to 2018. As a result of different fertility rates and differences in immigration patterns, race and ethnic groups will show different trends in labor force growth. Between 2008 and 2018 the projected annual growth rates for Hispanics (2.9%) and Asians (2.6%) are higher than for African Americans and other groups. As a result, the 2018 labor force is expected to become more diverse.[89]

Influence of Immigration. Many U.S. industries, including meatpacking, construction, farming, and service, rely on immigrants from Mexico and other countries to perform short-term or labor-intensive jobs. Although determining exactly the number of illegal workers in the United States is difficult, estimates are that of the hotel industry's 1.5 million employees, 150,000 are illegal immigrants, in the roofing industry one in three workers are thought to be illegal immigrants, and one-third of restaurant workers are Hispanic. While the U.S. government is debating how to deal with illegal immigration, many companies would face a labor crisis if they were forced to terminate employment of illegal immigrants, many of whom have lived and worked in the United States for years but lack the work authorizations and visas needed to work legally in this country. For example, an oyster-processing operation in Maryland brings in workers from Mexico to perform the dirty and smelly work needed to shuck oysters from October to February. The family-owned business has tried to hire U.S. workers but so far has had little success although the typical worker makes $12 per hour.[90] Many business owners believe the annual cap on visas is too low because they cannot find enough employees to fill their jobs.

There is considerable debate about how and if immigrants fit into the U.S. workforce. Many employers argue that most of the immigrants are hard-working and loyal and deserve to be granted legal status and citizenship. Others argue that illegal immigrants should be jailed or immediately extradited to their home country. While the national debate over this issue continues it is important to note that many midsized to small companies in the hotel, building cleaning, roofing, poultry, and construction industries could face a severe labor shortage crippling their businesses if immigration reform requires illegal immigrants to quit their jobs or return to their home countries before applying for work permits.[91] U.S. immigration and customs officials are increasing efforts to stop illegal immigration. Three top executives of a national cleaning service were arrested for allegedly employing illegal immigrants as well as nearly 200 employees believed to be illegal immigrants.[92]

Besides women and minorities another source of diversity in the workforce is disabled workers. Disabled workers can also be a source of competitive advantage. Wiscraft Inc., a Milwaukee company, contracts with companies such as Briggs & Stratton Corporation and Harley-Davidson to do assembly, packaging, and machining work.[93] At least 75 percent of Wiscraft's employees are legally blind. But the company is not a charity. It competes with other companies for contracts. It receives no subsidies from local, state, or federal governments. Employees have to rely on public transportation or friends or relatives to get to work. Kathy Walters said she could have worked at another company but chose Wiscraft because of its supportive culture. Walters, who is legally blind, believes she would have had trouble finding a job that offered health benefits and paid as well as her job at Wiscraft. The company has received ISO 9001:2000 certification, evidence that it provides high-quality work and can compete internationally.

The heterogeneous composition of the workforce challenges companies to create HRM practices that ensure that the talents, skills, and values of all employees are fully utilized to help deliver high-quality products and services.

Because the workforce is predicted to become more diverse in terms of age, ethnicity, and racial background, it is unlikely that one set of values will characterize all employees. For example, the "Silent Generation," born between 1925 and 1945, tend to be uncomfortable challenging the status quo and authority. They value income and employment security. "Baby Boomers," born between 1946 and 1964, value unexpected rewards for work accomplishments, opportunities to learn new things, praise, recognition, and time with the manager. "Generation X," born between 1965 and 1980, experienced the collapse of major institutions such as marriage, family, companies, and the economy. As a result, they tend to be pragmatic, cynical, and have well-developed self-management skills. "Millennials," born between 1981 and 1995, love the latest technology, are ambitious and goal-oriented, and seek meaningful work. They want to be noticed, respected, and involved. Millennials work to live while boomers live to work. Personality differences between the generations can potentially cause problems.[94] For example, Millennials can be underwhelmed by Generation X's aloof management style. Millennials are used to being mentored but Generations Xers tend to value self-reliance. Millennials think baby boomers are too rigid, rule-oriented, too slow to adapt to new social media tools, and value tenure over knowledge and performance.

Companies are being proactive to help employees and managers understand generational differences. A survey conducted at Ernst & Young LLC found that Generation Y employees (born after 1980) want and ask for more frequent and candid feedback than baby boomers (born between 1946 and 1964).[95] As a result, Ernst & Young developed an online "Feedback Zone" where employees can provide or ask for feedback at any time. Also, the company assigns every employee a mentor and offers training for managers on how to give effective feedback. To make sure employees understand generational differences and how to connect and communicate with employees from different generations, Aflac, the insurance provider, offers a training program called "Connecting Generations."[96] Aflac believes that employees in all age groups will be more effective if they understand how members of each generation approach their jobs. The program reviews the characteristics of each generation represented in the workplace. It also describes the effects of family and world events on each generation, analyzes their work styles and employment characteristics, and helps show connections to bridge generation gaps.

Keep in mind that apparent differences in personality differences and values between generations may be due to differences in age and experience. As a result, it is unwise to stereotype employees of a certain generation, i.e., expect them to have similar values. Most employees value several aspects of work regardless of their background. Employees view work as a means to self-fulfillment—that is, a means to more fully use their skills and abilities, meet their interests, and allow them to live a desirable lifestyle.[97] Because many employees place more value on the quality of nonwork activities and family life than on pay and production, employees will demand more flexible work policies that allow them to choose work hours and locations where work is performed.

The implications of the changing labor market for managing human resources are far-reaching. Because labor market growth will be primarily in female and minority populations, U.S. companies will have to ensure that employees and human resource management systems are free of bias to capitalize on the perspectives and values that women and minorities can contribute to improving product quality, customer service, product development, and market share. Managing cultural diversity involves many different activities, including creating an organizational culture that values diversity, ensuring that HRM systems are bias-free, facilitating higher career involvement of women, promoting knowledge and acceptance of cultural differences, ensuring involvement in education both within and outside the company, and dealing with employees' resistance to diversity.[98] Table 1.11 presents ways that managing cultural diversity can provide a competitive advantage. As Table 1.11 illustrates, the implications of successfully managing a diverse workforce go beyond legal concerns. How diversity issues are managed has implications for creativity, problem solving, retaining good employees, and developing markets for the firm's products and services. To successfully manage a diverse workforce, managers must develop a new set of skills, including:

1. Communicating effectively with employees from a wide variety of cultural backgrounds.
2. Coaching and developing employees of different ages, educational backgrounds, ethnicity, physical ability, and race.
3. Providing performance feedback that is based on objective outcomes rather than values and stereotypes that work against women, minorities, and handicapped persons by prejudging these persons' abilities and talents.
4. Creating a work environment that makes it comfortable for employees of all backgrounds to be creative and innovative.
5. Recognizing and responding to generational issues.[99]

Diversity is important for tapping all employees' creative, cultural, and communication skills and using those skills to provide competitive advantage as shown in Table 1.11. For example, the Latino Employee Network at Frito-Lay played a key role during the development of Doritos Guacamole Flavored Tortilla Chips.[100] The chips generated more than $500 million in sales during their first year, making this one of the most successful product launches in the company's history. Network members provided feedback on the taste and packaging to ensure that the product would be seen as authentic in the Latino community. Florida Power and Light Company recognized that workers with expertise in nuclear energy were aging and soon would be

table 1.11

How Managing
Cultural Diversity
Can Provide
Competitive
Advantage

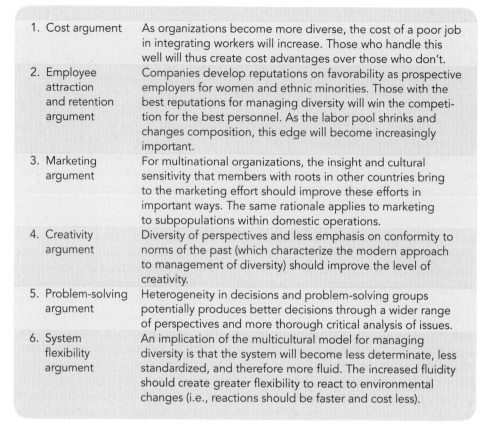

1.	Cost argument	As organizations become more diverse, the cost of a poor job in integrating workers will increase. Those who handle this well will thus create cost advantages over those who don't.
2.	Employee attraction and retention argument	Companies develop reputations on favorability as prospective employers for women and ethnic minorities. Those with the best reputations for managing diversity will win the competition for the best personnel. As the labor pool shrinks and changes composition, this edge will become increasingly important.
3.	Marketing argument	For multinational organizations, the insight and cultural sensitivity that members with roots in other countries bring to the marketing effort should improve these efforts in important ways. The same rationale applies to marketing to subpopulations within domestic operations.
4.	Creativity argument	Diversity of perspectives and less emphasis on conformity to norms of the past (which characterize the modern approach to management of diversity) should improve the level of creativity.
5.	Problem-solving argument	Heterogeneity in decisions and problem-solving groups potentially produces better decisions through a wider range of perspectives and more thorough critical analysis of issues.
6.	System flexibility argument	An implication of the multicultural model for managing diversity is that the system will become less determinate, less standardized, and therefore more fluid. The increased fluidity should create greater flexibility to react to environmental changes (i.e., reactions should be faster and cost less).

SOURCES: *Academy of Management Executive*, by T. H. Cox and S. Blake, 1991; N. Lockwood, *Workplace Diversity: Leveraging the Power of Difference for Competitive Advantage* (Alexandria, VA: Society for Human Resource Management, 2005).

eligible for retirement.[101] To identify and develop talent for its nuclear plant in South Florida, which is located in a predominantly Hispanic community, Florida Light and Power teamed up with Miami Dade College. Students complete a two-year Associate's degree in electric power technology, gaining experience at Florida Power and Light through summer work experience. They return to Miami Dade to work on a specific area of expertise in the nuclear industry. The program is a win–win for the company and the community. The partnership saves the power company recruiting costs and reduces the need for on-the-job training. Also, it provides a college degree and jobs for talented members of the local Hispanic community.

To reach high-performing, high-potential multicultural women and women of color, Johnson & Johnson created a program called "Crossing the Finish Line." The program includes a two and one-half day project assignment in which participants have open conversations with their managers and executives including the CEO and the vice chair of the company. The program helps Johnson & Johnson identify women who should be given new development opportunities as well as help them understand that they must be visible, establish networks, and take the initiative for development assignments. Through the program managers are educated about cultural differences and creates an awareness of how an employee's culture might affect his or her career.[102]

The bottom line is that to gain a competitive advantage, companies must harness the power of the diverse workforce. These practices are needed not only to meet employee needs but to reduce turnover costs and ensure that customers receive the best service possible. The implication of diversity for HRM practices will be highlighted throughout this book. For example, from a staffing perspective, it is important to ensure that tests used to select employees are not biased against minority groups. From a work design perspective, employees need flexible schedules that allow them to meet nonwork needs. From a training perspective, it is clear that all employees need to be made aware of the potential damaging effects of stereotypes. From a compensation perspective, new benefits such as elder care and day care need to be included in reward systems to accommodate the needs of a diverse workforce.

Legal Issues

Five main areas of the legal environment have influenced human resource management over the past 25 years.[103] These areas are equal employment opportunity legislation, employee safety and health, employee pay and benefits, employee privacy, and job security. Attention is likely to continue to be paid to age, race, and religious discrimination, and discrimination against physically challenged employees.

There is also likely to be continued discussion about legislation to prohibit discrimination by employers and health insurers against employees based on their genetic makeup. Advances in medicine and genetics allow scientists to predict from DNA samples a person's likelihood of contracting certain diseases. To reduce health care costs, companies may want to use this information to screen out job candidates or reassign current employees who have a genetic predisposition to a disease that is triggered by exposure to certain working conditions. The Genetic Information Nondiscrimination Act of 2008 is the first federal law prohibiting health insurers from denying coverage or charging higher premiums based on genetic information. It also prohibits companies from using genetic information to make hiring, firing, and other job placement decisions.

The number of court battles over company policies to reduce health care and other benefits costs is likely to increase. Many companies (such as IBM, Microsoft, and Harrah's Entertainment) are calculating the health care premiums that employees pay on the basis of their health and habits and participation in wellness programs (e.g., counseling, weight loss, smoking cessation, physical fitness). The passage of federal health care legislation means that companies need to ensure that HR professionals are working with legal counsel and benefits experts to understand the details and implications of the new law, conducting cost analyses to determine the financial impact of the new law on the business, and helping determine if health care will be provided and what form it will take. A key issue is whether companies will decide to drop health care coverage.

Although women and minorities are advancing into top management ranks, "glass ceilings" are still keeping women and minorities from getting the experiences necessary to move to top management positions.[104] A survey showed that women held only 10% of all of the corporate officer positions in the *Fortune* top 50 companies.[105] We are likely to see more challenges to sex and race discrimination focusing on lack of access to training and development opportunities that are needed to be considered for top management positions.

Scrutiny of companies who employ unlawful immigrants or abuse laborers will continue to increase. One reason is because President Obama shifted the emphasis from arresting illegal workers to preventing companies from hiring them. Companies can face criminal charges if immigration and customs officials can show that they knowingly employed undocumented and illegal immigrants. In 2010, Immigration and Customs Enforcement (ICE) filed charges against a record number of owners, managers, and senior company officials. From 2009 to 2010 the number of work site cases initiated by ICE doubled. For example, the owners of 15 Chuy's Mesquite Broiler restaurants in California and Arizona were arrested and suspected illegal immigrants were detained. Also, the federal government is investigating whether Chipotle Mexican Grill hired illegal immigrants at its U.S. restaurants.[106]

An area of litigation that will continue to have a major influence on HRM practices involves job security. As companies are forced to close plants and lay off employees because of restructuring, technology changes, or financial crisis, cases dealing with the illegal discharge of employees have increased. The issue of what constitutes employment at will—that is, employment that can be terminated at any time without notice—will be debated. As the age of the workforce increases, the number of cases dealing with age discrimination in layoffs, promotions, and benefits will likely rise. Employers' work rules, recruitment practices, and performance evaluation systems will need to be revised to ensure that these systems do not falsely communicate employment agreements the company does not intend to honor (such as lifetime employment) or discriminate on the basis of age.

It is likely that state and federal laws may be introduced that are related to the use of background and credit checks for job applicants, hours worked and wages related to overtime pay, and regulations that clarify or define what classifies a worker as an independent contractor.[107] Because of the emphasis on reducing the federal deficit, there may be changes in how health care and retirement benefits are taxed and the eligibility age for employees to receive Social Security may be extended. In countries experiencing skill shortages, such as the United States, there may be increases in the number of skilled foreign workers who are eligible for visas, for example, the H-1-B visa for occupations that require highly specialized knowledge and advanced degrees. Also, restrictions that discourage foreign citizens who come to the United States to study for advanced degrees from staying and applying for U.S. citizenship may be eased.

The publication of classified documents by WikiLeaks and Wall Street insider trading probes have resulted in companies more carefully scrutinizing data-security practices and increased concerns about protecting intellectual property. This will likely influence human resource practices related to performance management such as the use of electronic monitoring and surveillance of knowledge workers. We may see more litigation related to employee privacy rights and intellectual property rights as a result of companies terminating employees or taking disciplinary action against them for data-security breaches or sharing or stealing intellectual property for personal gain.

Ethical Issues

Many decisions related to managing human resources are characterized by uncertainty. Ethics can be considered the fundamental principles by which employees and companies interact.[108] These principles should be considered in making business decisions and interacting with clients and customers. Ethical, successful companies can be characterized by four principles.[109] First, in their relationships with customers, vendors, and clients, these companies emphasize mutual benefits. Second, employees assume responsibility for the actions of the company. Third, such companies have a sense of purpose or vision the employees value and use in their day-to-day work. Finally, they emphasize fairness; that is, another person's interests count as much as their own. Recent surveys suggest that business ethics improved during the most recent recession. Forty-nine percent of employees report having witnessed unethical behavior on the job, 63% of employees say they reported unethical behavior they observed, and only 10% of employees report perceived retaliation as a result of reporting an ethics violation.[110] The decrease in unethical behavior may be because during a recession management emphasizes high standards and enforcement and all employees are less likely to commit ethical violations because of concerns they would negatively affect the company's image to its customers and therefore its survival. It is important to note that ethics refers to behavior that is not clearly right or wrong. Compliance means that the company is not violating legal regulations. But a company can be compliant and still have employees engaging in unethical practices.

The **Sarbanes-Oxley Act of 2002** sets strict rules for corporate behavior and sets heavy fines and prison terms for noncompliance: organizations are spending millions of dollars each year to comply with regulations under the Sarbanes-Oxley Act, which imposes criminal penalties for corporate governing and accounting lapses, including retaliation against whistle-blowers reporting violations of Security and Exchange Commission rules.[111] Due to Sarbanes-Oxley and new Security and Exchange Commission regulations that impose stricter standards for disclosing executive pay, corporate boards are paying more attention to executive pay as well as issues like leadership development and succession planning.[112] This has resulted in an increase in the number of HR executives and individuals with HR expertise who are being asked to serve on corporate boards to provide data and analysis. For example, a CEO or chief financial officer (CFO) who falsely represents company finances may be fined up to $1 million and/or imprisoned for up to 10 years. The penalty for willful violations is up to $5 million and/or 20 years imprisonment. The law requires CEOs and CFOs to certify corporate financial reports, prohibits personal loans to officers and directors, and prohibits insider trading during pension fund blackout periods.[113] A "blackout" is any period of more than three consecutive business days during which the company temporarily stops 50% or more of company plan participants or beneficiaries from acquiring, selling, or transferring an interest in any of the company's equity securities in the pension plan. The law also requires retention of all documents relevant to a government investigation.

The law also has a number of provisions that directly affect the employer–employee relationship.[114] For example, the act prohibits retaliation against whistle-blowers (individuals who have turned in the company or one of its officers for an illegal act) and government informants. The act also requires that publically traded companies disclose whether they have a code of ethics.[115] Other federal guidelines such as the Federal Acquisition Regulation also require or provide incentives to encourage all businesses to adopt codes of conduct, train employees on these codes, and create effective ways to audit and report ethical and unethical behavior. This means that companies, with HR taking the lead, should develop codes of conduct that clearly define ethics and professional responsibility. HR professionals along with other top-level managers usually play a key role in helping conduct ethics audits, develop ethical codes of conduct, and respond to ethical violations. Guidelines for disciplinary actions for employees guilty of unethical behavior and conduct need to be developed. Managers and employees will need to be trained on ethics policies to ensure that business processes and procedures are correctly followed. HR professionals will need to document the fact that employees have received these policies and have attended training to ensure their compliance with the act. Because of the potential liability for

Sarbanes-Oxley Act of 2002
A congressional act passed in response to illegal and unethical behavior by managers and executives. The act sets stricter rules for business especially accounting practices including requiring more open and consistent disclosure of financial data, CEOs' assurance that the data is completely accurate, and provisions that affect the employee–employer relationship (e.g., development of a code of conduct for senior financial officers).

retaliation in the context of discrimination and harassment, policies should include assurances that an employee will not be retaliated against for making a complaint or for serving as a witness. Executive compensation programs will need to be monitored to ensure that the program is in compliance with the no personal loans and no sales of pension funds during blackout period provisions.

Consider the policies and practices that companies are using to help ensure an ethical workplace.[116] Nabholz Construction, an Arkansas-based company established an ethics committee with representatives from legal, human resources, finance, and operations. The committee is responsible for monitoring and investigating the company's ethics hotline and e-mails. The committee conducts annual ethics audits as part of an internal audit process. Nabholz will also use a small team of managers, including an HR manager, to conduct spot audits in response to a specific incident. Cisco Systems has taken steps to make its ethics and compliance programs more engaging and interesting for employees. Cisco worked with a consulting firm to create a four-episode training module based on the *American Idol* popular television show. The episodes involve decisions related to sharing proprietary information from former employers, how to pick new vendors, entertaining potential customers, and accepting gifts from vendors. Employees watch each of the "contestants" talk about a different ethical situation and listen while the three judges each provide their opinion. Employees are then asked to vote on which of the three judges gave the best response to each situation and they can instantly see how their response matched up to the responses of other Cisco employees who have participated in the ethics training. At the end of each episode Cisco's ethics office provides the correct response to the situation based on the company's ethics and compliance standards. The new training program helped increase the visibility of Cisco's ethics office and raised employees' awareness that the right answer to each ethical dilemma they may encounter is not always obvious.

Nationwide, an insurance provider located in Columbus, Ohio, developed and adopted a detailed Code of Conduct.[117] The Code of Conduct applies to all employees, it protects employees who report code violations from retaliation, and it guides employees' decision making when the correct action is unclear. The Code of Conduct covers discrimination, conflicts of interest, financial reporting, business records, honesty in business communications, handling company assets, and political activities including gifts to public officials. Nationwide has established an Office of Ethics and code violations can be reported to them using e-mail, fax, or telephone.

Human resource managers must satisfy three basic standards for their practices to be considered ethical.[118] First, HRM practices must result in the greatest good for the largest number of people. Second, employment practices must respect basic human rights of privacy, due process, consent, and free speech. Third, managers must treat employees and customers equitably and fairly. Throughout the book we highlight ethical dilemmas in human resource management practices.

THE GLOBAL CHALLENGE

LO I-4
Discuss what companies should do to compete in the global marketplace.

Companies are finding that to survive they must compete in international markets as well as fend off foreign corporations' attempts to gain ground in the United States. To meet these challenges, U.S. businesses must develop global markets, use their practices to improve global competitiveness, and better prepare employees for global assignments.

Every business must be prepared to deal with the global economy. Global business expansion has been made easier by technology. The Internet allows data and information to be instantly accessible and sent around the world. The Internet, e-mail, social networking, and video conferencing enable business deals to be completed between companies thousands of miles apart.

Globalization is not limited to any particular sector of the economy, product market, or company size.[119] Companies without international operations may buy or use goods that have been produced overseas, hire employees with diverse backgrounds, or compete with foreign-owned companies operating within the United States.

Businesses around the world are attempting to increase their competitiveness and value by increasing their global presence, often through mergers and acquisitions. The "Competing through Globalization" box shows how Apple ensured that its global suppliers engaged in human rights and environmental protection.

Entering International Markets

Many companies are entering international markets by exporting their products overseas, building manufacturing facilities or service centers in other countries, entering into alliances with foreign companies, and engaging in e-commerce. One estimate is that developing economies and emerging markets such as those found in the BRIC nations (Brazil, Russia, India, and China) will be responsible for 68% of the growth of the world's economy.[120] The importance of globalization is seen in recent hiring patterns of large U.S. multinational corporations that have increased their overseas workforce, particularly in Asia.[121] For example, Oracle, the business hardware and software developer, added twice as many workers overseas over the past five years than in the United States. Sixty-three percent of its employees are outside the United States. Markets in Brazil, China, and India have resulted in 60% of General Electric's business outside the United States with 54% of employees overseas. Clothing retailer Gap Inc. plans to open 11 stores this year in Hong Kong and China.[122] This will add to the new four stores and e-business website opened in China in November 2010. This expands the Gap's Asian presence which already includes Gap and Banana Republic stores in Japan. Gap believes it needs to expand its international presence because the U.S. market is maturing and has many competitors. Yum! Brands, parent company of KFC and Pizza Hut has over 3,700 stores in China contributing to over 40% of its operating income in 2010.[123]

Global companies are struggling both to find and retain talented employees, especially in emerging markets. Companies are moving into China, India, eastern Europe, the Middle East, Southeast Asia, and Latin America, but the demand for talented employees exceeds supply. Also, companies often place successful U.S. managers in charge of overseas operations, but these managers lack the cultural understanding necessary to attract, motivate, and retain talented employees. To cope with these problems, companies are taking actions to better prepare their managers and their families for overseas assignments and to ensure that training and development opportunities are available for global employees. Cross-cultural training prepares employees and their families to understand the culture and norms of the country they are being relocated to and to return to their home country after the assignment. Cross-cultural training is discussed in Chapter 10.

McDonald's has built a new Hamburger University near Shanghai to train future managers in store operations, leadership, and staff management skills which are needed for the company's planned expansion in China. McDonald's opened 165 stores in China in 2010 and plans to open 1,000 more by the end of 2013.[124]

IBM obtains more than two-thirds of its revenue from outside the United States and is seeking to build team leadership in order to compete in emerging markets around the world. IBM's Corporate Service Program donates the time and service of about 600 employees for projects in countries such as Turkey, Romania, Ghana, Vietnam, the Phillipines, and Tanzania.[125] The goal of the program is to develop a leadership team that learns about the needs and culture of these countries, at the same time providing valuable community service. For example, eight IBM employees from five countries traveled to Timisoara, Romania. Each employee was assigned to help a different company or nonprofit organization. One software-development manager helped Green-Forest, a manufacturer of office, hotel, school, and industrial furniture, reach its goal of cutting costs and becoming more efficient by recommending computer equipment and systems needed to increase production and exports to western Europe. Another employee worked with a nonprofit organization that offers services to disabled adults. Besides benefiting the companies, the employees have also found that the experience has helped them understand cultural differences, improve their communication and teamwork skills, and gain insights on global marketing and strategy.

Offshoring

Offshoring
Exporting jobs from developed to less developed countries.

Offshoring refers to the exporting of jobs from developed countries, such as the United States, to countries where labor and other costs are lower. India, Canada, China, Russia, Ireland, Mexico, Brazil, and the Philippines are some of the destination countries for offshored jobs. Why are jobs offshored?[126] The main reason is labor costs. Workers in other countries earn a fraction of the wages of American workers performing the same job. For example, Indian computer programmers receive about $10 an hour compared to $60 per hour earned by U.S. programmers. Other reasons include the availability of a highly skilled and motivated workforce. Both India and China have high numbers of engineering and science graduates. China graduates about four times as many engineers as the United States, although they are not all trained at the same level as U.S. engineers.[127] Japan graduates twice as many engineers and South Korea graduates nearly as many engineers as the United States. Each year, India graduates 2 million English-speaking students with strong technical and quantitative skills.[128] Finally, cheap global telecommunications costs allow companies with engineers 6,000 miles away to complete design work and interact with other engineers as if they were located in the office down the hall.

Initially, offshoring involved low-skilled manufacturing jobs with repeatable tasks and specific guidelines for how the work was to be completed. Offshoring now includes high-skilled manufacturing jobs and is also prevalent in the service and information technology sectors, for example, telephone call center, accounting bookkeeping and payroll, legal research, software engineers, architecture, and design. Gen3Partners, a Boston-based product innovation company, has a research and development lab in St. Petersburg, Russia, with 90 scientists and engineers, all with advanced degrees.[129] Russia has a tradition of scientific excellence, and comparable talent costs less than in the United States. For small companies such as Cobalt Group, a Seattle, Washington, automotive online services company, labor costs for its 50 research and development engineers who work in a technology center in India are about one-third of the U.S. costs.

Immigration rules have made it difficult for immigrants to seek employment. Also, visa limits have restricted the number of highly skilled professionals and technical employees who can work in the United States. The H-1B Visa Program is for persons in highly skilled and technical occupations requiring completion of higher education.

COMPETING THROUGH GLOBALIZATION

Apple Polishes Its Image through Auditing Overseas Suppliers

Apple is known for introducing revolutionary and functional products such as the iphone, Mac Air computers, and the iPad. Although Apple and its products are revered in the United States and around the world, some say that the profits and market share that Apple is earning from these products is due to taking advantage of foreign workers. Apple relies on manufacturing partners in Asia to build its products. Apple Inc. has been criticized by labor groups who have challenged how its manufacturing partners in Asia have treated their employees. Apple has taken these criticisms seriously and is auditing its suppliers and manufacturing facilities to take steps to reduce if not eliminate illegal and poor treatment of workers who are involved in assembling or providing materials for any of its products. Apple is especially focused on

ensuring that its partners don't hire underage workers, provide adequate training, and pay fair wages. For example, Apple's chief operating officer visited a Chinese manufacturing partner to provide advice after several workers committed suicide from jumping from buildings. One of the potential causes of the suicides was the stress the workers experienced as Apple moved to quickly launch the iPad to meet consumer demand for the new product. The chief executive officer and his team interviewed more than 1,000 workers and evaluated the supplier's reactions to the suicides. As a result, Apple recommended that the supplier better train counselors for employees and establish a 24-hour care center. These recommendations were adopted by the supplier. An audit of another supplier found underage workers. To avoid employing underage workers Apple is working with

the supplier to identify fake identification papers. Apple has also required that manufacturers reimburse over 3 million dollars in excessive fees collected from immigrants to recruit and bring them to work in their factories. Apple has also strongly encouraged its manufacturers and suppliers not to purchase minerals such as gold and tin from smelters that get their products from countries known for human rights abuses. Apple has shown that it is serious about its commitment to ensure that its manufacturers and suppliers labor practices are fair, legal, and protect employees from abuse. In those cases in which Apple's recommendations based on its audits were not adopted, the company terminated its relationship with the supplier.

SOURCE: Based on I. Sherr, "Apple Says China Partner Made Changes for Workers," *The Wall Street Journal*, February 15, 2011, p. B5.

New visas are capped at 85,000 per year, 20,000 of which are reserved for employees with U.S. Master's degrees. There is no cap on H-1Bs for employees working for the government, universities, and other nonprofit institutions. The largest number of H-1B visas are issued for computer-related occupations (43%). U.S.-based Microsoft and Cisco Systems are two of the top 10 companies using H-1B visas but most are used by Indian companies such as Infosys Technologies and Wipro Ltd.[130] Other visa programs are available for lower-skilled temporary or seasonal workers (H-2A, H-2B) with an annual cap of 66,000 nonagricultural workers.

Although companies may be attracted to offshoring because of potential lower labor costs, several other issues have emerged that are also important. First, can employees in the offshored locations provide a level of customer service the same as or higher than customers receive from U.S. operations? Second, would offshoring demoralize U.S. employees such that the gains from offshoring would be negated by lower motivation, lower satisfaction, and higher turnover? Third, are local managers adequately trained to motivate and retain offshore employees? Fourth, what is the potential effect, if any, of political unrest in the countries in which operations are offshored? Fifth, what effect would offshoring have on the public image of the company? Would customers or potential customers avoid purchasing products or services because they believe offshoring costs U.S. employees their jobs? Would offshoring have an adverse effect on recruiting new employees?

Because of the disadvantages of offshoring discussed above and the total costs of working with different languages, cultures, and time zones, many companies are **onshoring,** or moving jobs to rural America.[131] Onshoring may be most attractive to companies that have brands tied to the United States because they fear the political fallout related to offshoring. Dell opened a call center in Twin Falls, Idaho, after closing one in India because of customer complaints. US Bank considered opening a call center in India but decided against it because of the bad publicity that would have resulted. US Bank chose instead to put the call center in Coeur d'Alene, Idaho, where the 500 new jobs would reduce the area's unemployment rate and make a difference in the quality of life in the community.[132] Whirlpool decided to replace and build a new cooking appliances plant in Cleveland, Tennessee, rather than move production to Mexico where it has several factories.[133] The new plant, which will grow the size of its local workforce, will be Whirlpool's first U.S. factory since the mid-1990s. Although labor costs would be lower in Mexico, Whirlpool decided to build the new plant because it already has a trained workforce, it wouldn't have to pay layoff costs, it received tax breaks and incentives from state and local government, and shipping costs would be lower because most of the products are sold in the United States.

Onshoring
Exporting jobs to rural parts of the United States.

THE TECHNOLOGY CHALLENGE

Technology has reshaped the way we play, communicate, plan our lives, and where we work. Many companies' business models include e-commerce which allows consumers to purchase products and services online. The Internet is a global collection of computer networks that allows users to exchange data and information. Americans' use of the Internet has doubled over the last five years with 48% reporting using the Internet more than one hour per day. Sixty percent visit Google during the week and 43% have a Facebook page.[134] Using Facebook, Twitter, LinkedIn, and other social networking tools available on the Internet accessed through iPhones, Blackberries, or personal computers, companies can connect with job candidates and employers can connect with friends, family, and co-workers.

How and Where People Work

LO 1-5
Identify how new technology, such as social networking, is influencing human resource management.

Social Networking
Websites and blogs that facilitate interactions between people.

Advances in sophisticated technology along with reduced costs for the technology are changing many aspects of human resource management. Technological advances in electronics and communications software have made possible mobile technology such as personal digital assistants (PDAs), iPads, and iPods and enhanced the Internet through developing enhanced capability for social networking. **Social networking** refers to websites such as Facebook, Twitter, and LinkedIn, Wikis, and blogs that facilitate interactions between people usually around shared interests. Table 1.12 shows some of the potential issues that can be addressed by using social networking.[135] In general, social networking facilitates communications, decentralized decision making, and collaboration. Social networking can be useful for connecting to customers and valuable for busy employees to share knowledge and ideas with their peers and managers with whom they may not have much time to interact face-to-face on a daily

ISSUES	USE
Loss of expert knowledge due to retirement	Knowledge sharing, capturing, and storing
Employee engagement	Collect employees' opinions
Identify and promote employee expertise	Create online expert communities
Promote innovation and creativity	Encourage participation in online discussions
Reinforce learning	Share best practices, applications, learning, points, links to articles and webinars
Employees need coaching and mentoring	Interact with mentors and coaching peers
Need to identify and connect with promising job candidates	Distribute job postings, respond to candidates' questions

table 1.12

Potential Uses of Social Networking

SOURCES: Based on P. Brotherson, "Social Networks Enhance Employee Learning," *T + D*, April 2011, pp. 18–19; T. Bingham and M. Connor, *The New Social Learning* (Alexandria, VA: American Society for Training & Development, 2010); M. Derven, "Social Networking: A Frame for Development," *T + D*, July 2009, pp. 58–63; M. Weinstein, "Are You Linked In?" *Training*, September/October, 2010, pp. 30–33.

basis. Employees, especially young workers from the Millennial or Gen-Y generations have learned to use social networking tools such as Facebook throughout their lives and see them as valuable tools for both their work and nonwork lives. The "Competing through Technology" box shows how companies are using social networking for HR practices including recruiting, training and development, scheduling, and measuring employee attitudes.

Despite its potential advantages, many companies are uncertain as to whether they should embrace social networking.[136] They fear that social networking will result in employees wasting time or offending or harassing their co-workers. Other companies believe that the benefits of using social networking for HR practices and allowing employees to access social networks at work outweigh the risks. They trust employees to use social networking productively and are proactive in developing policies about personal use and training employees about privacy settings and social network etiquette. They realize that employees will likely check their Twitter, Facebook, or LinkedIn accounts but ignore it unless productivity is decreasing. In some ways, social networking has become the electronic substitute for daydreaming at one's desk or walking to the break room to socialize with co-workers!

Robotics, computer-assisted design, radio frequency identification, and nanotechnology are transforming work.[137] Technology has also made it easier to monitor environmental conditions and operate equipment. For example, consider working a grader construction vehicle (which is used to smooth and level dirt on roadways and other construction projects). Older vehicle models required operating as many as 15 levers in addition to a steering wheel and several foot pedals. As a result, working the grader usually left operators with sore backs and shoulders at the end of the day. Caterpillar's latest version of the grader includes redesigned controls that use only two joysticks and eliminate the physical demands of pushing pedals and turning a steering wheel. Besides reducing the physical demands, the redesign of the grader without a steering wheel resulted in operators having better visibility of the steel blade and switches for lights, windshield wipers, and the parking brake and these could be grouped together in one place in the cab. A Japanese commercial farm, Shinpuku Seika, relies on computer readings from monitors placed out in the fields which report temperature, soil, and moisture levels to the farmers.[138] Computer analysis of these data alerts farmers when to start planting or identifies specific crops that may grow best in each field. Farmers can use cameras in the fields to examine crops. Farm workers can also use their mobile phones to take pictures of potential diseased or infected crops which are uploaded to the computer for diagnosis by crop experts. The workers' phones also include a global positioning system, allowing the company to determine if workers are taking the most efficient routes between fields or slacking off on the job.

Human Resource Information System (HRIS)
A system used to acquire, store, manipulate, analyze, retrieve, and distribute HR information.

Companies continue to use human resource information systems to store large quantities of employee data including personal information, training records, skills, compensation rates, absence records, and benefits usages and costs. A **human resource information system (HRIS)** is a computer system used to acquire, store, retrieve, and distribute information related to a company's human resources.[139] An HRIS can support strategic decision making, help the company avoid lawsuits, provide data for evaluating policies and programs, and support day-to-day HR decisions. Florida Power & Light Company, based in Juno Beach, Florida, uses HRIS applications to provide information to employees and to support decision making by managers. More than 10,000 employees in 20 states can use the information system to learn about their benefits. Managers use the system to track employees' vacation and sick days and to make changes in staffing and pay. Using the HRIS, managers can request the HRIS system to automatically prepare a personnel report; they no longer have to contact the HR department to request one.[140]

High-Performance Work Systems

High-Performance Work Systems
Work systems that maximize the fit between the company's social system and technical system.

New technology causes changes in skill requirements and work roles and often results in redesigning work structures (e.g., using work teams).[141] **High-performance work systems** maximize the fit between the company's social system (employees) and its technical system.[142] For example, computer-integrated manufacturing uses robots and computers to automate the manufacturing process. The computer allows the production of different products simply by reprogramming the computer. As a result, laborer, material handler, operator/assembler, and maintenance jobs may be merged into one position. Computer-integrated manufacturing requires employees to monitor equipment and troubleshoot problems with sophisticated equipment, share information with other employees, and understand the relationships between all components of the manufacturing process.[143] Consider the changes Canon Inc., known for office imaging, computer peripherals, and cameras, has made to speed up the development and production process.[144] Canon is using a procedure called concurrent engineering, where production engineers work together with designers. This allows them to more easily exchange ideas to improve a product or make it easier to manufacture. Canon also now has production employees work in "cells," where they perform multiple tasks and can more easily improve the production process. Previously, employees worked in an assembly line controlled by a conveyor belt. The new cell system requires lower parts inventory and less space, cutting factory operating and real estate costs. Also, employees are more satisfied working in cells because they feel more responsibility for their work.

LO 1-6
Discuss human resource management practices that support high-performance work systems.

Working in Teams. Through technology, the information needed to improve customer service and product quality becomes more accessible to employees. This means that employees are expected to take more responsibility for satisfying the

COMPETING THROUGH TECHNOLOGY

Connectiveness Enhances HR Practices

Social networks such as Facebook and Twitter help people satisfy their need to be connected to their friends. Recognizing the importance of "connectiveness," companies of all sizes and in various industries are using social networks to enhance many different HR practices including recruiting, training and development, scheduling, and enhancing employees engagement. Recruiters can use social networking to connect and communicate with job candidates, create online communities for job candidates to learn about the company, and monitor news such as store closings or layoffs which can provide a potential group of new employees. Macy's has used Twitter to post job openings and to reach out to recruit merchandise buyers laid off by other retailers who were closing their stores. CareerBuilder.com is using an app that shows its employees which of their Facebook friends would be matches for job openings at the company and encourages them to share that

information. Del Frisco's Steakhouse in Manhattan can quickly create a schedule for its servers on a computer or i-Phone and post it to a website which automatically sends the schedule to all employees' cell phones. Servers can make schedule changes but the system tracks hours to ensure that they do not exceed allowed overtime work hours. Long Realty in Tuscon, Arizona, established Long Connects, an internal social networking site for real estate agents to seek help and discuss issues such as how to deal with a specific bank to secure financing, trends in the current real estate market, and the best way to handle properties sold for less than the amount owed on the mortgage to avoid foreclosure (short sales). Kelly Services is using a tool known as Chatter to help employees more easily share knowledge and best practices. EMC Corporation used its social business network known as EMC/One to ask employees for ideas about how to cut costs. The chief financial officer read the postings and decided to adopt many of the

ideas which helped contribute to EMC's goal to reduce costs by $450 million. IBM's onboarding process known as Succeeding@ IBM is used to help new employees learn about the company and reduce feeling of being overwhelmed. As part of this process new employees are given access to a social networking tool which allows them to collaborate with each other as well as more experienced employees to get personal support, seek career guidance, and find technical expertise.

SOURCES: Based on M. Rafter, "Goin' Mobile," *Workforce Management,* February 2011, pp. 26–27; L. Stevens, "Through the Looking Glass," *Human Resource Executive,* April 2011, pp. 26–29; M. Ciccarelli, "It's Personal," *Human Resource Executive,* September 16, 2010, pp. 1, 14–20; B. Roberts, "Mobile Workforce Management," *HR Magazine,* March 2011, pp. 67–69; G. Kranz, "More to Learn," *Workforce Management,* January 2011, pp. 27–30; S. Ladika, "Socially Evolved," *Workforce Management,* September 2010, pp. 19–22; B. Roberts, "Developing a Social Business Network," *HR Magazine,* October 2010, pp. 54–60; T. Starner, "Big Blue Welcomes You," *Human Resource Executive,* September 16, 2010, pp. 30–33.

customer and determining how they perform their jobs. One of the most popular methods for increasing employee responsibility and control is work teams. *Work teams* involve employees with various skills who interact to assemble a product or provide a service. Work teams may assume many of the activities usually reserved for managers, including selecting new team members, scheduling work, and coordinating activities with customers and other units in the company. To give teams maximum flexibility, cross-training of team members occurs. *Cross-training* refers to training employees in a wide range of skills so they can fill any of the roles needed to be performed on the team.

Use of new technology and work designs such as work teams needs to be supported by specific human resource management practices. These practices include the following actions:

- Employees choose or select new employees or team members.
- Employees receive formal performance feedback and are involved in the performance improvement process.
- Ongoing training is emphasized and rewarded.
- Rewards and compensation are linked to company performance.
- Equipment and work processes encourage maximum flexibility and interaction between employees.
- Employees participate in planning changes in equipment, layout, and work methods.
- Employees understand how their jobs contribute to the finished product or service.

Changes in Skill Requirements. High-performance work systems have implications for employee selection and training. Employees need job-specific knowledge and basic skills to work with the equipment created with the new technology. Because technology is often used as a means to achieve product diversification and customization, employees must have the ability to listen and communicate with customers. Interpersonal skills, such as negotiation and conflict management, and problem-solving skills are more important than physical strength, coordination, and fine-motor skills—previous job requirements for many manufacturing and service jobs. Although technological advances have made it possible for employees to improve products and services, managers must empower employees to make changes.

Working in Partnerships. Besides changing the way that products are built or services are provided within companies, technology has allowed companies to form partnerships with one or more other companies. **Virtual teams** refer to teams that are separated by time, geographic distance, culture, and/or organizational boundaries and that rely almost exclusively on technology (e-mail, Internet, videoconferencing) to interact and complete their projects. Virtual teams can be formed within one company whose facilities are scattered throughout the country or the world. A company may also use virtual teams in partnerships with suppliers or competitors to pull together the necessary talent to complete a project or speed the delivery of a product to the marketplace. PricewaterhouseCoopers's learning and education department has 190 employees who are located in 70 offices in different cities.[145] These employees work together on virtual teams that range in size from 5 to 50 people. Shared databases are used for background information and developing work; each office has videoconferencing and software is used to track calendars and connect employees via their personal computers to their virtual teams.

Software developers are positioning employees around the world with clusters of three or four facilities, six to eight hours apart, to keep projects moving 24 hours a day.[146] The intent is to increase productivity and reduce project completion time by allowing employees to focus continuously on projects through using highly talented engineers who can work in their own time zone and location without having to move to a different country or work inconvenient hours. Also, globally distributed projects can draw on employees from many different cultures, backgrounds, and perspectives helping to produce services and products that can better meet the needs of global customers. The challenges are how to organize work so that teams in different locations and different work shifts can share tasks with minimum interaction.

Virtual Teams
Teams that are separated by time, geographic distance, culture and/ or organizational boundaries and rely exclusively on technology for interaction between team members.

Employees must be trained in principles of employee selection, quality, and customer service. They need to understand financial data so they can see the link between their performance and company performance.

Changes in Company Structure and Reporting Relationships. The traditional design of U.S. companies emphasizes efficiency, decision making by managers, and dissemination of information from the top of the company to lower levels. However, this structure will not be effective in the current work environment, in which personal computers give employees immediate access to information needed to complete customer orders or modify product lines. In the adaptive organizational structure, employees are in a constant state of learning and performance improvement. Employees are free to move wherever they are needed in the company. The adaptive organization is characterized by a core set of values or a vital vision that drives all organizational efforts.[147] Previously established boundaries between managers and employees, employees and customers, employees and vendors, and the various functions within the company are abandoned. Employees, managers, vendors, customers, and suppliers work together to improve service and product quality and to create new products and services. Line employees are trained in multiple jobs, communicate directly with suppliers and customers, and interact frequently with engineers, quality experts, and employees from other functions.

One of the jobs at General Electric's Greenville Airfoils Facility in Piedmont, South Carolina, involves using a computer-controlled machine to burn small cooling holes in 3-inch long turbine blades for jet engines.[148] Most of the holes in each blade are thinner than a human hair! Employees are responsible for choosing who gets hired. They interview job candidates and observe them in "games" that involve working in a team to build a helicopter from blocks. Employee teams can adjust the line operation to remove bottlenecks and maximize productivity. For example, a team identified a way to increase the speed of washing turbine blades. The plant leader allowed the team to buy equipment to wash the blades based on their recommendations.

Increased Use and Availability of e-HRM and HRM Dashboards. Electronic human resource management (e-HRM) refers to the processing and transmission of digitized information used in HRM, including text, sound, and visual images from one computer or electronic device to another. e-HRM includes the use of software, social networks, and mobile technologies such as iPhones, iPods, and handheld and notebook computers. For example, Capital One, a financial service company, uses an audio learning program that allows employees to learn through their iPods at their own convenience.[149] The company has also developed a mobile audio learning channel. The channel supplements competency-based and leadership and management programs and other existing company training courses. It is also used to ensure that employees receive information when they need it. The Federal Aviation Administration (FAA) has 50,000 employees spread throughout the country.[150] Proposals that required input from these employees took years to complete. New software allows the FAA to create virtual shared workspaces for employees. FAA employees and industry experts can now interact in virtual "rooms" to debate ideas and work on shared documents. The virtual rooms have saved the FAA more than $3 million in travel costs and $2 million in employee time, and they have reduced the time needed for most proposals to become rules to one year. United Parcel Service (UPS) implemented a software system that each evening maps out the next day's schedule for its drivers.[151] The software designs each route to minimize the number of left turns, reducing the

Electronic Human Resource Management (e-HRM)
The processing and transmission of digitized information used in HRM.

time and gas that drivers waste at traffic lights. Customers get their packages on time and drivers can make it home in the evening for dinner.

The use of company intranets, a network that uses Internet tools but limits access to authorized users in the company, and web portals designed to serve as gateways to the Internet that highlight links to relevant information are becoming common practice. As we mentioned earlier in the chapter (in the discussion of how HR's role in administration is decreasing), company intranets and web portals allow employees and managers online access to information about HR issues, offer self-enrollment programs, and provide feedback through surveys (self-service). Employees can look up workplace policies and information about training programs and enroll online, choose benefits and change salary deductions, and review employment contracts. Self-service at Mapics, a software developer based in Atlanta, allows managers and employees to keep track of vacation time.[152] This helps with scheduling and enables managers to encourage employees to use their remaining vacation time. Mapics changed its vacation policy to require that employees take their vacation time or lose it at the end of the year. Before self-service, Mapics lacked reliable information on company vacation time, resulting in a liability of a million dollars worth of accrued, unused vacation time. Self-service improved management and employee satisfaction with HR services at the same time it cut costs.

More sophisticated systems extend management applications to decision making in areas such as compensation and performance management. Managers can schedule job interviews or performance appraisals, guided by the system to provide the necessary information and follow every step called for by the procedure.[153] One of the most important uses of Internet technology is the development of HR dashboards. An **HR dashboard** is a series of indicators or metrics that managers and employees have access to on the company intranet or human resource information system. The HR dashboard provides access to important HR metrics for conducting workforce analytics. HR dashboards are important for determining the value of HR practices and how they contribute to business goals. As a result, the use of dashboards is critical for evidence-based HR discussed earlier in the chapter. For example, Cisco Systems views building talent as a priority so it has added to its dashboard of people measures a metric to track how many people move and the reasons why.[154] This allows Cisco to identify divisions that are developing new talent.

Competitiveness in High-Performance Work Systems. Unfortunately, many managers have tended to consider technological and structural innovations independent of each other. That is, because of immediate demands for productivity, service, and short-term profitability, many managers implement a new technology (such as a networked computer system) or a new work design (like service teams organized by product) without considering how a new technology might influence the efficiency or effectiveness of the way work is organized.[155] Without integrating technology and structure, a company cannot maximize production and service.

Human resource management practices that support high-performance work systems are shown in Table 1.13. The HRM practices involved include employee selection, performance management, training, work design, and compensation. These practices are designed to give employees skills, incentives, knowledge, and autonomy. Research studies suggest that high-performance work practices are usually associated with increases in productivity and long-term financial performance.[156] Research also suggests that it is more effective to improve HRM practices as a whole, rather than focus on one or two isolated practices (such as the pay system or selection system).[157] There may be a best HRM system, but whatever the company does, the practices

HR Dashboard
HR metrics such as productivity and absenteeism that are accessible by employees and managers through the company intranet or human resource information system.

table 1.13

How HRM Practices
Support High-
Performance Work
Systems

Staffing	• Employees participate in selecting new employees, e.g., peer interviews.
Work Design	• Employees understand how their jobs contribute to the finished product or service.
	• Employees participate in planning changes in equipment, layout, and work methods.
	• Work may be organized in teams.
	• Job rotation used to develop skills.
	• Equipment and work processes are structured and technology is used to encourage flexibility and interaction between employees.
	• Work design allows employees to use a variety of skills.
	• Decentralized decision making, reduced status distinctions, information sharing.
	• Increased safety.
Training	• Ongoing training emphasized and rewarded.
	• Training in finance and quality control methods.
Compensation	• Team-based performance pay.
	• Part of compensation may be based on company or division financial performance.
Performance Management	• Employees receive performance feedback and are actively involved in the performance improvement process.

SOURCES: Based on K. Birdi, C. Clegy, M. Patterson, A. Robinson, C. Stride, T. Wall, and S. Wood, "The Impact of Human Resource and Operational Management Practices on Company Productivity: A Longitudinal Study," *Personnel Psychology* 61(2008), pp. 467–501; A. Zacharatos, J. Barling, and R. Iverson, "High Performance Work Systems and Occupational Safety," *Journal of Applied Psychology* 90 (2005), pp. 77–93; S. Way, "High Performance Work Systems and Intermediate Indicators of Performance within the U.S. Small Business Sector," *Journal of Management* 28 (2002), pp. 765–85; M. A. Huselid, "The Impact of Human Resource Management Practices on Turnover, Productivity, and Corporate Financial Performance," *Academy of Management Journal* 38 (1995), pp. 635–72.

must be aligned with each other and be consistent with the system if they are to positively affect company performance.[158] We will discuss this alignment in more detail in Chapters 2 and 16.

Consider how human resource management practices support the high-performance work system at the Global Engineering Manufacturing Alliance (GEMA) plant in Dundee, Michigan.[159] GEMA is a wholly owned subsidiary of Chrysler LLC/Fiat. The plant is more automated and employs fewer workers than most engine plants, 275 compared with 600 to 2,000 employees at other engine plants. The goal of the plant is to be the most productive engine plant in the world. The UAW endorsed the high-performance workplace because it recognized that the company needs to be competitive to avoid losing jobs. Chryler Group LLC will invest $179 million to launch production of a fuel-efficient engine for the North American market that will be built at GEMA. The implications of this work system for labor relations is discussed in Chapter 14.

The plant's hourly employees rotate jobs and shifts, increasing the company's flexibility. The plant's culture emphasizes problem solving and that anyone can do anything, anytime, anywhere. Everyone has the same title: team member or team leader. By rotating jobs the plant wants to keep workers motivated in their work and avoid injuries. Team leaders and engineers don't stay in their offices; they are expected to work on the shop floor as part of six-person teams. Contractors are also seen as part of the team, working alongside assembly workers and engineers and wearing the same uniforms. Most auto plants have a day and night shift with senior workers usually choosing to work the day shift. At GEMA, employees rotate shifts in crews of three, working 10 hours per day, four days per week, alternating between days and nights. Every third week of their rotation they get five days off in addition to any vacation time. Counseling is available to help employees adjust to the rotating work schedule. The work schedule allows the plant to be in operation 21 hours per day, 6 days per week, 294 days a year. But employees work only 196 days a year. The alternating shifts also help employees to know and work with each other and salaried employees, who work only during daytime.

To hire employees who could work in a team environment emphasizing problem solving and flexibility, GEMA recruited using local newspapers within 70 miles of Dundee. GEMA worked with local civil rights organizations to find diverse candidates. Nonexempt employees whose wages start at $21 and increase to $30 within five years must have a two-year technical degree, a skilled journeyman's card, or five years' experience in advanced machining.

Job candidates have to make it through a difficult screening process that takes 12 hours. The process requires candidates to take tests, participate in team activities in which they confront challenges facing the plant (e.g., process in the plant is inefficient), and interviews with operations managers and team leaders. When the plant is ahead of its production schedule employees receive training in class and on the shop floor in topics such as how to assemble an engine to math skills.

GEMA gives employees access to technology that helps them monitor productivity. Large electronic screens hanging from the plant ceiling provide alerts of any machinery parts that are ending their life span and need to be replaced before they malfunction. A performance management system available on personal computers, as well as a display board, alerts employees to delays or breakdowns in productivity. This is different from most engine plants where only managers have access to this information. The technology empowers all employees to fix problems, not just managers or engineers. GEMA provides rewards and bonuses for employees who develop innovative problem solutions.

Meeting Competitive Challenges through HRM Practices

LO 1-7
Provide a brief description of human resource management practices.

We have discussed the global, stakeholder, new economy, and high-performance work system challenges U.S. companies are facing. We have emphasized that management of human resources plays a critical role in determining companies' success in meeting these challenges. HRM practices have not traditionally been seen as providing economic value to the company. Economic value is usually associated with equipment, technology, and facilities. However, HRM practices have been shown to be valuable. Compensation, staffing, training and development, performance management, and other HRM practices are investments that directly affect employees' motivation and ability to provide products and services that are valued by customers. Research has shown that companies that attempt to increase their competitiveness by investing in new technology and becoming involved in the quality movement also invest in state-of-the-art staffing, training, and compensation practices.[160] Figure 1.8 shows examples of human resource management practices that help companies deal with the

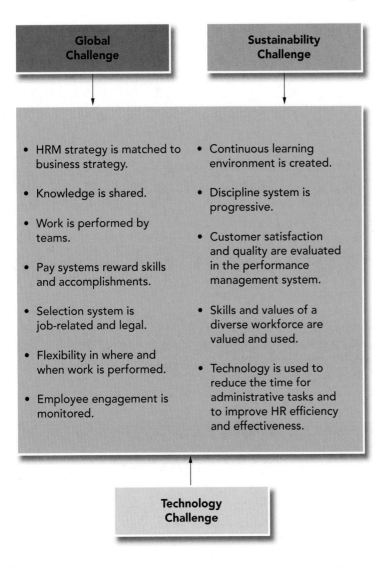

figure 1.8

Examples of How HRM Practices Can Help Companies Meet Competitive Challenges

Global Challenge

Sustainability Challenge

- HRM strategy is matched to business strategy.
- Knowledge is shared.
- Work is performed by teams.
- Pay systems reward skills and accomplishments.
- Selection system is job-related and legal.
- Flexibility in where and when work is performed.
- Employee engagement is monitored.

- Continuous learning environment is created.
- Discipline system is progressive.
- Customer satisfaction and quality are evaluated in the performance management system.
- Skills and values of a diverse workforce are valued and used.
- Technology is used to reduce the time for administrative tasks and to improve HR efficiency and effectiveness.

Technology Challenge

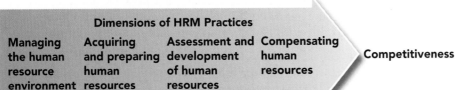

figure 1.9

Major Dimensions of HRM Practices Contributing to Company Competitiveness

Dimensions of HRM Practices

Managing the human resource environment	Acquiring and preparing human resources	Assessment and development of human resources	Compensating human resources

Competitiveness

three challenges. For example, to meet the sustainability challenge, companies need to identify through their selection processes whether prospective employees value customer relations and have the levels of interpersonal skills necessary to work with fellow employees in teams. To meet all three challenges, companies need to capitalize on the diversity of values, abilities, and perspectives that employees bring to the workplace.

HRM practices that help companies deal with the competitive challenges can be grouped into the four dimensions shown in Figure 1.9. These dimensions include the human resource environment, acquiring and preparing human resources, assessment and development of human resources, and compensating human resources. In addition, some companies have special issues related to labor–management relations, international human resource management, and managing the human resource function.

Managing the Human Resource Environment

Managing internal and external environmental factors allows employees to make the greatest possible contribution to company productivity and competitiveness. Creating a positive environment for human resources involves

- Linking HRM practices to the company's business objectives—that is, strategic human resource management.
- Ensuring that HRM practices comply with federal, state, and local laws.
- Designing work that motivates and satisfies the employee as well as maximizes customer service, quality, and productivity.

Acquiring and Preparing Human Resources

Customer needs for new products or services influence the number and type of employees businesses need to be successful. Terminations, promotions, and retirements also influence human resource requirements. Managers need to predict the number and type of employees who are needed to meet customer demands for products and services. Managers must also identify current or potential employees who can successfully deliver products and services. This area of human resource management deals with

- Identifying human resource requirements—that is, human resource planning, recruiting employees, and selecting employees.
- Training employees to have the skills needed to perform their jobs.

Assessment and Development of Human Resources

Managers need to ensure that employees have the necessary skills to perform current and future jobs. As we discussed earlier, because of new technology and the quality movement, many companies are redesigning work so that it is performed by teams. As a result, managers and employees may need to develop new skills to succeed in a team environment. Companies need to create a work environment that supports employees' work and nonwork activities. This area of human resource management addresses

- Measuring employees' performance.
- Preparing employees for future work roles and identifying employees' work interests, goals, values, and other career issues.
- Creating an employment relationship and work environment that benefits both the company and the employee.

Compensating Human Resources

Besides interesting work, pay and benefits are the most important incentives that companies can offer employees in exchange for contributing to productivity, quality, and customer service. Also, pay and benefits are used to reward employees' membership in the company and attract new employees. The positive influence of new work designs, new technology, and the quality movement on productivity can be damaged if employees are not satisfied with the level of pay and benefits or believe pay and benefits are unfairly distributed. This area of human resource management includes

- Creating pay systems.
- Rewarding employee contributions.
- Providing employees with benefits.

Special Issues

In some companies, employees are represented by a labor union. Managing human resources in a union environment requires knowledge of specific laws, contract administration, and the collective bargaining process.

Many companies are globally expanding their business through joint ventures, mergers, acquisitions, and establishing new operations. Successful global expansion depends on the extent to which HRM practices are aligned with cultural factors as well as management of employees sent to work in another country. Human resource management practices must contribute to organizational effectiveness.

Human resource management practices of both managers and the human resource function must be aligned and contribute to the company's strategic goals. The final chapter of the book explains how to effectively integrate human resource management practices.

Organization of This Book

The topics in this book are organized according to the four areas of human resource management and special issues. Table 1.14 lists the chapters covered in the book.

The content of each chapter is based on academic research and examples of effective company practices. Each chapter includes examples of how the human resource

table 1.14

Topics Covered in This Book

1   Human Resource Management: Gaining a Competitive Advantage
I The Human Resource Environment
2   Strategic Human Resource Management
3   The Legal Environment: Equal Employment Opportunity and Safety
4   The Analysis and Design of Work
II Acquisition and Preparation of Human Resources
5   Human Resource Planning and Recruitment
6   Selection and Placement
7   Training
III Assessment and Development of HRM
8   Performance Management
9   Employee Development
10   Employee Separation and Retention
IV Compensation of Human Resources
11   Pay Structure Decisions
12   Recognizing Employee Contributions with Pay
13   Employee Benefits
V Special Topics in Human Resource Management
14   Collective Bargaining and Labor Relations
15   Managing Human Resources Globally
16   Strategically Managing the HRM Function

management practice covered in the chapter helps a company gain a competitive advantage by addressing sustainability, global, and technological challenges. Also, each chapter includes an example of a company that demonstrates how HR practices add value (evidence-based HR).

A Look Back

Starbucks is engaged in aggressive business growth focusing on new products and new markets while trying to maintain the customer experience.

Questions

1. What HR practices do you believe are critical for Starbucks to maintain the customer experience and product quality it's known for?
2. Could Starbucks be successful without its current HR practices? Explain.
3. Do you think that Starbucks' culture and HR practices can also help the bottom line at companies in other industries such as health care, manufacturing, or research and development? Explain why or why not.

 Please see the Video that corresponds to this chapter at www.mhhe.com/noe8e.

Summary

This chapter introduced the roles and activities of a company's human resource management function and emphasized that effective management of human resources can contribute to a company's business strategy and competitive advantage. HR can be viewed as having three product lines: administrative services, business partner services, and strategic services. To successfully manage human resources, individuals need personal credibility, business knowledge, understanding of the business strategy, technology knowledge, and the ability to deliver HR services. Human resource management practices should be evidence-based, that is, based on data showing the relationship between the practice and business outcomes related to key company stakeholders (customers, shareholders, employees, community). In addition to contributing to a company's business strategy, human resource practices are important for helping companies deal with sustainability, globalization, and technology challenges. The sustainability challenges are related to the economy, the characteristics and expectations of the labor force, how and where work is done, the value placed on intangible assets and human capital, and meeting stakeholder

needs (ethical practices, high-quality products and services, return to shareholders, and social responsibility). Global challenges include entering international markets, immigration, and offshoring. Technology challenges include using new technologies to support flexible and virtual work arrangements, high-performance work systems, and implementing social networking and human resource information systems.

The chapter concludes by showing how the book is organized. The book includes four topical areas: the human resource environment (strategic HRM, legal, analysis and design of work), acquisition and preparation of human resources (HR planning and recruitment, selection, training), assessment and development of human resources (performance management, development, training), compensation of human resources (pay structures, recognizing employee contributions with pay, benefits), and special topics (collective bargaining and labor relations, managing human resources globally, and strategically managing the HR function). All of the topical areas are important for companies to deal with the competitive challenges and contribute to business strategy.

● KEY TERMS

Competitiveness, 4
Human resource management (HRM), 5
Shared service model, 8
Self-service, 8
Outsourcing, 8
Evidence-based HR, 10
HR or workforce analytics, 11
Sustainability, 14
Stakeholders, 14
Intangible assets, 20
Knowledge workers, 21
Empowering, 21

Learning organization, 22
Psychological contract, 22
Employee engagement, 23
Talent management, 25
Alternative work arrangements, 25
Balanced scorecard, 27
Total quality management (TQM), 29
Malcolm Baldrige National Quality Award, 31
ISO 9000:2000, 31
Six Sigma process, 33
Lean thinking, 34

Internal labor force, 34
External labor market, 34
Sarbanes-Oxley Act of 2002, 43
Offshoring, 46
Onshoring, 48
Social networking, 48
Human resource information system (HRIS), 50
High-performance work systems, 50
Virtual teams, 52
Electronic human resource management (e-HRM), 53
HR dashboard, 54

● DISCUSSION QUESTIONS

1. Traditionally, human resource management practices were developed and administered by the company's human resource department. Line managers are now playing a major role in developing and implementing HRM practices. Why do you think non-HR managers are becoming more involved in developing and implementing HRM practices?

2. Staffing, training, compensation, and performance management are important HRM functions. How can each of these functions help companies succeed in meeting the global challenge, the challenge of using new technology, and the sustainability challenge?

3. What are intangible assets? How are they influenced by human resource management practices?

4. What is "evidence-based HR"? Why might an HR department resist becoming evidence-based?

5. What types of workforce analytics would you collect and analyze to understand why an employer was experiencing a high turnover rate?

6. Which HR practices can benefit by the use of social collaboration tools like Twitter and Facebook? Identify the HR practices and explain the benefits gained.

7. Do you agree with the statement "Employee engagement is something companies should be concerned about only if they are making money"? Explain.

8. This book covers four human resource management practice areas: managing the human resource environment, acquiring and preparing human resources, assessment and development of human resources, and compensating human resources. Which area do you believe contributes most to helping a company gain a competitive advantage? Which area do you believe contributes the least? Why?

9. What is the balanced scorecard? Identify the four perspectives included in the balanced scorecard. How can HRM practices influence the four perspectives?

10. Is HRM becoming more strategic? Explain your answer.

11. What is sustainability? How can HR practices help a company become more socially and environmentally conscious?

12. Explain the implications of each of the following labor force trends for HRM: (1) aging workforce, (2) diverse workforce, (3) skill deficiencies.

13. What role do HRM practices play in a business decision to expand internationally?

14. What might a quality goal and high-performance work systems have in common in terms of HRM practices?

15. What disadvantages might result from outsourcing HRM practices? From employee self-service? From increased line manager involvement in designing and using HR practices?

16. What factors should a company consider before offshoring? What are the advantages and disadvantages of offshoring?

● SELF-ASSESSMENT EXERCISE: DO YOU HAVE WHAT IT TAKES TO WORK IN HR?

Instructions: Read each statement and circle *yes* or *no*.

Yes   No   1. I have leadership and management skills I have developed through prior job experiences, extracurricular activities, community service, or other noncourse activities.

Yes   No   2. I have excellent communications, dispute resolution, and interpersonal skills.

Yes   No   3. I can demonstrate an understanding of the fundamentals of running a business and making a profit.

Yes   No   4. I can use spreadsheets and the World Wide Web, and I am familiar with information systems technology.

Yes   No   5. I can work effectively with people of different cultural backgrounds.

Yes   No   6. I have expertise in more than one area of human resource management.

Scoring: The greater the number of yes answers, the better prepared you are to work in an HR department. For questions you answered *no*, you should seek courses and experiences to change your answer to *yes*—and better prepare yourself for a career in HR!

SOURCE: Based on B. E. Kaufman, "What Companies Want from HR Graduates," *HR Magazine*, September 1994.

● EXERCISING STRATEGY: ZAPPOS FACES COMPETITIVE CHALLENGES

Zappos, based in Las Vegas, is an online retailer with the initial goal of trying to be the best website for buying shoes by offering a wide variety of brands, styles, colors, sizes, and widths. The zappos.com brand has grown to offer shoes, handbags, eyewear, watches, and accessories for online purchase. Zappos' vision is that in the future, online sales will account for 30% of all retail sales in the United States, and Zappos will be the company with the best service and selection. The company's goal is to provide the best service online, not just in shoes but in any product category. Zappos believes that the speed at which a customer receives an online purchase plays a critical role in how that customer thinks about shopping online again in the future, so they are focusing on making sure the items get delivered to our customers as quickly as possible.

In 2009, Zappos was acquired by the Amazon.com, Inc., family of companies which also share a strong passion for customer service. In 2010, Zappos experienced tremendous growth resulting in the need to restructure the company. Zappos was restructured into 10 separate companies under the Zappos family umbrella including Zappos.com, Inc. (the management company) and companies devoted to retail, gift cards, merchandising, and order fulfillment.

Zappos CEO Tony Heish has shaped the company's culture, brand, and business strategy around 10 core values. They are:

Deliver WOW through service.
Embrace and drive change.
Create fun and a little weirdness.
Be adventurous, creative, and open-minded.
Pursue growth and learning.

Build open and honest relationships with communication.
Build a positive team and family spirit.
Do more with less.
Be passionate and determined.
Be humble.

Deliver WOW through Service means that call center employees need to provide excellent customer service. Call center employees encourage callers to order more than one size or color because shipping and return shipping is free. They are also encouraged to use their imaginations to meet customer needs.

Zappos has received many awards for its workplace culture and practices including being recognized as the sixth Best Company to Work for in *Fortune* magazine's 2011 ranking of the 100 Best Companies to Work For. Zappos' employment practices help perpetuate its company culture. For example, the HR team uses unusual interview questions—such as, How weird are you? and What's your theme song?—to find employees who are creative and have strong individuality. Zappos provides free lunch in the cafeteria (cold cuts) and a full-time life coach (employees have to sit on a red velvet throne to complain), managers are encouraged to spend time with employees outside of the office, and any employee can reward another employee a $50 bonus for good performance. Most employees at Zappos are hourly. All new hires complete four weeks of training, including two weeks working the phones. New recruits are offered $2,000 to leave the company during training to weed out individuals who will not be happy working at the company. Zappos provides free breakfast, lunch, snacks, coffee, tea, and vending machine snacks.

Similar to other companies trying to survive the 2009 recession, Zappos was forced to cut costs, including laying off 124 employees. But Heish handled the downsizing in a positive way. Laid-off employees with less than two years of service were paid through the end of the year. Everyone received six months of paid health coverage. Zappos also allowed laid-off employees to keep their 40 percent employee discount through Christmas.

To reinforce the importance of the 10 core values Zappos' performance management system asks managers to evaluate how well employees' behaviors demonstrate the core values such as being humble or expressing their personalities. To evaluate task performance managers are asked to regularly provide employees with status reports on such things as how much time they spend on the telephone with customers. The status reports and evaluations of the core values are informational or used to identify training needs. Zappos also believes in helping others understand what inspired the company culture. The company created the Zappos.com library which provides a collection of books about creating a passion for customer service, products, and local communities. These books can be found in the front lobby of Zappos offices and are widely read and discussed by company employees.

Questions

1. Zappos seems to be well-positioned to have a competitive advantage over other online retailers. What challenges discussed in Chapter 1 pose the biggest threat to Zappos' ability to maintain and enhance its competitive position? How can human resource management practices help Zappos meet these challenges?
2. Do you think that employees of Zappos have high levels of engagement? Why?
3. Which of Zappos' 10 core values do you believe that human resource practices can influence the most? The least? Why? For each of the core values, identify the HR practices that are related to it. Explain how each of the HR practice(s) you identified is related to the core values.

SOURCES: Based on website for Zappos, www.zappos.com; J. O'Brien, "Zappos Knows How to Kick It," *Fortune*, February 2, 2009, pp. 55–66; M. Moskowitz, R. Levering, and C. Tkaczyk, "100 Best Companies to Work For," *Fortune*, February 7, 2011, pp. 91–101; R. Pyrillis, "The Reviews Are In," *Workforce Management*," May 2011, pp. 20–25.

● MANAGING PEOPLE

Skill Shortages Make It Difficult to Fill Positions and Customer Orders

Despite an unemployment rate of around 9%, U.S. manufacturing companies are scrambling to find enough skilled workers. There are several reasons why this is occurring. First, there is increased demand for manufacturing workers. Second, baby boomers (employees 55 or older) making up more than 25% of U.S. manufacturing employees are beginning to retire. Third, the U.S. education system is not developing the math and science skills potential employees need to operate computer-controlled factory equipment like lathes and other metal-shaping equipment. Math and science test scores for U.S. students are significantly lower than those compared to students from countries such as China, Japan, Canada, and Germany. Also, manufacturing jobs suffer from an image problem. Although these jobs often pay from $50,000 to $80,000 per year with benefits and many require advanced math, mechanical drawing, and blueprint reading skills, parents discourage smart children from considering careers in manufacturing, instead emphasizing enrolling in four-year colleges. Also, youth often are unmotivated to train for manufacturing jobs because of misguided stereotypes that they are dirty, unsafe, and boring. Fourth, many manufacturing companies decreased the emphasis they placed on recruiting and finding employees when it was easier to find them in the labor market. For example, Woodward Inc., a parts manufacturer for aircraft and power generation equipment based in Fort Collins, Colorado, used to operate its own training academy but closed it to lower costs. As a result the company lost its pool of available skilled machinists and technicians. To reestablish a pool of skilled workers Woodward is sponsoring students enrolled in two-year programs in manufacturing skills at local community colleges. The company pays their tuition and other costs and they are paid for working part-time. Woodward's goal is to hire those students for full-time manufacturing jobs after they earn their two-year degree.

Hamill Manufacturing Company, a 127-employee company located near Pittsburgh, Pennsylvania, cuts metal into parts for ships and machinery. The company needs to fill customized orders for small numbers of parts requiring meeting precise specifications. To find workers Hamill works with vocational schools. Employees serve on advisory boards, donate equipment, and even volunteer as guest lecturers. Jeff Kelly, Hamill's chief executive officer, organizes a program in which high school students learn to build fighting robots. These activities have paid off in attracting talented new employees but other larger companies are poaching talented workers away from Hamill Manufacturing. One Hamill employee who won a national competition for metal working skills left for a new job at Curtiss-Wright Corporation, a company that makes pumps and generators and purchases parts from Hamill. Curtiss-Wright pays him 40% more than he earned at Hamill and because it is a larger company it has more career opportunities. To try and discourage skilled employees from leaving Hamill, Jeff Kelly increased wages 18 to 25%. Despite the pay increases, over the past two years Hamill has lost 10 employees to Curtiss-Wright.

Besides poaching and involvement with community colleges other manufacturing companies are relying on creative sources for skilled workers. Swift-Cor Aerospace is hiring former prisoners for its airplane parts plants near Los Angeles. San Quentin prison in California is using its machine shop to train prisoners skills in operating computer-controlled lathes and mills. Some prisoners also take classes in calculus and trigonometry to help them work with machinery. Advanced Technology Services of Peoria, Illinois, hires employees with military backgrounds because they have acquired the skills needed to

fix equipment through repairing tanks and airplanes and have a strong work ethic.

Questions

1. If you worked in a manufacturing company what evidence would you look for to determine if involvement in community colleges and recruiting employees with ex-military backgrounds and inmates was an effective human resource practice?
2. Besides the ideas discussed in the case what other ideas should a manufacturing company consider to identify, prepare, and attract skilled manufacturing employees?
3. What HR practices might help a small manufacturing company retain skilled manufacturing employees who are being recruited by other companies?

SOURCE: Based on J. Hagerty, "Help Wanted on Factory Floor," *The Wall Street Journal*, May 9, 2011, pp. A1, A12.

● TWITTER FOCUS: MANAGING HR AT A SERVICES FIRM

Using Twitter, continue the conversation about how HR helps companies gain competitive advantage by reading the case about managing HR at a services firm at www.mhhe.com/noe8e.

Helping others and making her company a positive place to work has helped Susan Dubin create a successful career in human resource management. When a local insurance agent decided to open her own services firm, Dubin signed on as the firm's HR manager because she was

so impressed with the business owner's commitment to client services and to her own employees. Dubin understands that employees who are happy at work are more productive and play a major role in growing any successful business.

Engage with your classmates and instructor via Twitter to chat about Dubin's success using the case questions posted on the Noe website. Don't have a Twitter account yet? See the instructions for getting started on the Online Learning Center.

● NOTES

1. A. S. Tsui and L. R. Gomez-Mejia, "Evaluating Human Resource Effectiveness," in *Human Resource Management: Evolving Rules and Responsibilities*, ed. L. Dyer (Washington, DC: BNA Books, 1988), pp. 1187–227; M. A. Hitt, B. W. Keats, and S. M. DeMarie, "Navigating in the New Competitive Landscape: Building Strategic Flexibility and Competitive Advantage in the 21st Century," *Academy of Management Executive* 12, no. 4 (1998), pp. 22–42; J. T. Delaney and M. A. Huselid, "The Impact of Human Resource Management Practices on Perceptions of Organizational Performance," *Academy of Management Journal* 39 (1996), pp. 949–69.
2. F. Hansen, "2006 Data Bank Annual," *Workforce Management*, December 11, 2006, p. 48.
3. SHRM-BNA Survey No. 66, "Policy and Practice Forum: Human Resources Activities, Budgets, and Staffs: 2000–2001," Bulletin to Management, Bureau of National Affairs Policy and Practice Series, June 28, 2001 (Washington, DC: Bureau of National Affairs).
4. W. Cascio, "From Business Partner to Driving Business Success: The Next Step in the Evolution of HR Management," *Human Resource Management* 44 (2005), pp. 159–63.
5. A. Halcrow, "Survey Shows HRM in Transition," *Workforce*, June 1998, pp. 73–80: J. Laabs, "Why HR Can't Win Today," *Workforce*, May 1998, pp. 62–74; C. Cole, "Kodak Snapshots," *Workforce*, June 2000, pp. 65–72; W. Ruona and S. Gibson, "The Making of Twenty-First Century HR: An Analysis of the Convergence of HRM, HRD, and OD," *Human Resource Management* 43 (2004), pp. 49–66.
6. Towers Perrin, *Priorities for Competitive Advantage: An IBM Study Conducted by Towers Perrin*, 1992.
7. R. Grossman, "Saving Shared Services," *HR Magazine*, September 2010, pp. 26–31.
8. S. Greengard, "Building a Self-Service Culture That Works," *Workforce*, July 1998, pp. 60–64.
9. G. Yohe, "Building Your Case," *Human Resource Executive*, March 2, 2003, pp. 22–26.
10. K. Kramer, "Industrial-Organizational (I-O) Psychology's Contribution to Strategic Human Resources Outsourcing (HRO): How Can We Shape the Future of HR?" *The Industrial-Organizational Psychologist*, January 2011, pp. 13–20.
11. B. Roberts, "Outsourcing in Turbulent Times," *HR Magazine*, November 2009, pp. 42–47; The Right Thing, "The Goodyear

Tire and Rubber Company Discovers Key to Successful Outsourcing Partnerships," *Workforce Management*, March 2011, p. S2.

12. Towers Perrin, *Priorities for Competitive Advantage*.

13. F. Hansen, "Chief Concern: Leaders," *Workforce Management*, July 20, 2009, pp. 17–20; J. Wiscombe, "McDonald's Corp.," *Workforce Management*, November 2010, pp. 38–40.

14. P. Wright, *Human Resource Strategy: Adapting to the Age of Globalization* (Alexandria, VA: Society for Human Resource Management Foundation, 2008).

15. E. Frauenheim, "Numbers Game," *Workforce Management*, March 2011, pp. 20–21; P. Gallagher, "Rethinking HR," *Human Resource Executive*, September 2, 2009, pp. 1, 18–23.

16. B. Roberts, "Analyze This!" *HR Magazine*, October 2009, pp. 35–41.

17. B. Roberts, "How to Put Analytics 'On Your Side,'" *HR Magazine*, October 2009, pp. 43–46.

18. L. Claus and J. Collison, *The Maturing Profession of Human Resources: Worldwide and Regional View* (Alexandria, VA: Society for Human Resource Management, 2005).

19. Bureau of Labor Statistics, *Occupational Outlook Handbook*, 2010–2011 edition (Washington, DC: Bureau of Labor Statistics), www.bls.gov.

20. Ibid; E. Krell, "Become a Master of Expertise and Credibility," *HR Magazine*, May 2010, pp. 53–63.

21. J. Wiscombe, "Your Wonderful, Terrible HR Life," *Workforce*, June 2001, pp. 32–38.

22. D. Zielinski, "Building a Better HR Team," *HR Magazine*, August 2010, pp. 65–68.

23. A. Jones, "Evolutionary Science, Work/Life Integration, and Corporate Responsibility," *Organizational Dynamics* 32 (2002), pp. 17–31.

24. A. Fox, "Get in the Business of Being Green," *HR Magazine*, June 2008, p. 45.

25. I. Wyatt and K. Byun, "The U.S. Economy to 2018: From Recession to Recovery," *Monthly Labor Review*, November 2009, pp. 11–29.

26. J. Hagerty, "U.S. Factories Buck Decline," *Wall Street Journal*, January 19, 2011, pp. A1–A2; J. Lahart, "Layoffs Ease, but Hiring Is Still Slow," *Wall Street Journal*, February 9, 2011, pp. A2; I. Katz and Bob Willis, "A CEO's Dilemma: When Is It Safe to Hire Again?" *Bloomberg Businessweek*, January 17–January 23, 2011, pp. 22–24; M. Hulbert, "It's Dippy to Fret about a Double-Dip Recession," *Barron's Online*, http://online.barrons.com, accessed May 1, 2011.

27. S. Reddy and S. Murray, "Jobless Rate Falls Further," *Wall Street Journal*, March 5–6, 2011, pp. A1, A2.

28. J. Light, "Labor Shortage Persists in Some Fields," *Wall Street Journal*, February 7, 2011, p. B6.

29. S. Wells, "Managing a Downturn," *HR Magazine*, May 2008, pp. 48–52.

30. D. Mattioli, "Despite Cutbacks, Firms Invest in Developing Leaders," *The Wall Street Journal*, February 9, 2009, p. B4.

31. Society for Human Resource Management, "HR Insight into the Economy," *Workplace Visions* 4 (2008), p. 4; Society for Human Resource Management, "Workplace Trends: An Overview of the Findings of the Latest SHRM Workplace Forecast," *Workplace Visions* 3 (2008), pp. 1–6.

32. M. Conlin, "Get Healthy or Else," *BusinessWeek*, February 26, 2007, pp. 58–69.

33. SHRM Workplace Forecast (Alexandria, VA: Society for Human Resource Management, 2008).

34. R. Woods, "Industry Output and Employment Projections to 2018," *Monthly Labor Review*, November 2009, pp. 52–81.

35. T. Lacey and B. Wright, "Occupational Employment Projections to 2018," *Monthly Labor Review*, November 2009, pp. 82–123.

36. R. Woods, "Industry Output and Employment Projections to 2018," *Monthly Labor Review*, November 2009, pp. 52–81.

37. P. Wiseman, "U.S. a Lean, Mean Factory Machine," *Columbus Dispatch*, January 31, 2011, p. A3.

38. M. Hilton, "Skills for Work in the 21st Century: What Does the Research Tell Us?" *Academy of Management Executive*, November 2008, pp. 63–78; "Manufacturing: Engine of US Innovation," *National Association of Manufacturing* (October 4, 2006), available at www.nam.org (accessed January 21, 2009).

39. M. Schoeff Jr., "Companies Report Difficulty Finding Qualified Employees," *Workforce Management*, October 19, 2009, p. 14; J. Casner-Lotto, E. Rosenblum, and M. Wright, The Ill-Prepared U.S. Workforce (New York: The Conference Board).

40. National Science Board, *Science and Engineering Indicators*, vol. 1 (Arlington, VA: National Science Foundation, 2006).

41. M. Schoeff, "Amid Calls to Bolster U.S. Innovation, Experts Lament Paucity of Basic Math Skills," *Workforce Management*, March 2006, pp. 46–49.

42. J. Barbian, "Get 'em While They're Young," *Training*, January 2004, pp. 44–46; E. Frauenheim, "IBM Urged to Take Tech Skills to Classrooms," *Workforce Management*, October 24, 2005, pp. 8–9; K. Maher, "Skills Shortage Gives Training Programs New Life," *The Wall Street Journal*, June 3, 2005, p. A2; "IBMers Pursue Second Careers in Math and Science Education," from www.ibm.com/ibm/responsibility/teaching.shtml, accessed May 10, 2011.

43. J. Barney, *Gaining and Sustaining a Competitive Advantage* (Upper Saddle River, NJ: Prentice Hall, 2002).

44. L. Weatherly, *Human Capital: The Elusive Asset* (Alexandria, VA: 2003 SHRM Research Quarterly).

45. R. Dodes, "At Macy's, a Makeover on Service," *Wall Street Journal*, April 11, 2011, p. B10.

46. L. Bassi, J. Ludwig, D. McMurrer, and M. Van Buren, *Profiting from Learning: Do Firms' Investments in Education and Training Pay Off?* (Alexandria, VA: American Society for Training and Development, September 2000).

47. T. J. Atchison, "The Employment Relationship: Untied or Re-Tied," *Academy of Management Executive* 5 (1991), pp. 52–62.

48. D. Senge, "The Learning Organization Made Plain and Simple," *Training and Development Journal*, October 1991, pp. 37–44.

49. G. Kranz, "More to Learn," *Workforce Management*, January 2011, pp. 27–30.

50. M. Weinstein, "Are You Linked In?" *Training*, September/October 2010, pp. 30–33.

51. SHRM Workplace Forecast.

52. J. O'Toole and E. Lawler III, *The New American Workplace* (New York: Palgrave McMillan, 2006).

53. D. M. Rousseau, "Psychological and Implied Contracts in Organizations," *Employee Rights and Responsibilities Journal* 2 (1989), pp. 121–29.

54. D. Rousseau, "Changing the Deal While Keeping the People," *Academy of Management Executive* 11 (1996), pp. 50–61; M. A. Cavanaugh and R. Noe, "Antecedents and Consequences of the New Psychological Contract," *Journal of Organizational Behavior* 20 (1999), pp. 323–40.

55. B. Testa, "New Orbit," *Workforce Management*, August 17, 2009, pp. 16–20.

56. R. Vance, *Employee Engagement and Commitment* (Alexandria, VA: Society for Human Resource Management, 2006).

57. For examples see M. Huselid, "The Impact of Human Resource Management Practices on Turnover, Productivity,

and Corporate Financial Performance," *Academy of Management Journal* 38 (1995), pp. 635–72; S. Payne and S. Webber, "Effects of Service Provider Attitudes and Employment Status on Citizenship Behaviors and Customers' Attitudes and Loyalty Behavior," *Journal of Applied Psychology* 91 (2006), pp. 365–68; J. Hartner, F. Schmidt, and T. Hayes, "Business-Unit Level Relationship between Employee Satisfaction, Employee Engagement, and Business Outcomes: A Meta-Analysis," *Journal of Applied Psychology* 87 (2002), pp. 268–79; I. Fulmer, B. Gerhart, and K. Scott, "Are the 100 Best Better? An Empirical Investigation of the Relationship between Being a 'Great Place to Work' and Firm Performance," *Personnel Psychology* 56 (2003), pp. 965–93; "Working Today: Understanding What Drives Employee Engagement," *Towers Perrin Talent Report* (2003).

58. Corporate Leadership Council, *Driving Performance and Retention through Employee Engagement* (Washington, DC: Corporate Executive Board, 2004).

59. A. Fox, "Raising Engagement," *HR Magazine*, May 2010, pp. 34–40; www.unitedhealthgroup.com, website for United Health Group.

60. M. Ciccarelli, "Keeping the Keepers," *Human Resource Executive*, January/February 2011, pp. 1, 20–23.

61. P. Cappelli, "Talent Management for the Twenty-First Century," *Harvard Business Review*, March 2008, pp. 74–81.

62. M. Ciccarelli, "Keeping the Keepers."

63. Bureau of Labor Statistics, "Contingent and Alternative Employment Arrangements, February 2005," from www.bls.gov (accessed January 21, 2009).

64. I. Speizer, "Contingency Plan," *Workforce Management*, October 2010, pp. 28–34; K. Evans, "Permanent Boost for a 'Temp' Company?" *Wall Street Journal*, February 2, 2011, p. C1.

65. R. Zeidner, "Heady Debate," *HR Magazine*, February 2010, pp. 28–33.

66. A. Fox, "At Work in 2020," *HR Magazine*, January 2010, pp. 18–23.

67. C. Patton, "On the Frontier of Flexibility," *Human Resource Executive*, May 2, 2009, pp. 48–51.

68. A. Fox, "Achieving Integration," *HR Magazine*, April 2011, pp. 42–47.

69. Families and Work Institute, *2009 Guide to Bold Ideas for Making Work Work* (New York: Families and Work Institute, 2009); S. Shellenberger, "Time-Zoned: Working Round the Clock Workforce," *Wall Street Journal*, February 15, 2007, p. D1.

70. R. S. Kaplan and D. P. Norton, "The Balanced Scorecard—Measures That Drive Performance," *Harvard Business Review*, January–February 1992, pp. 71–79; R. S. Kaplan and D. P. Norton, "Putting the Balanced Scorecard to Work," *Harvard Business Review*, September–October 1993, pp. 134–47.

71. S. Bates, "The Metrics Maze," *HR Magazine*, December 2003, pp. 50–55; D. Ulrich, "Measuring Human Resources: An Overview of Practice and a Prescription for Results," *Human Resource Management* 36 (1997), pp. 303–20.

72. E. Raimy, "A Plan for All Seasons," *Human Resource Executive*, April 2001, pp. 34–38.

73. S. Prasso, "Saving the World One Cup of Yogurt at a Time," *Fortune*, February 19, 2007, pp. 96–102.

74. D. Stanford, "Sustainability Meets the Profit Motive," *Bloomberg Businessweek*, April 4–April 10, 2011, pp. 25–26.

75. J. R. Jablonski, *Implementing Total Quality Management: An Overview* (San Diego: Pfeiffer, 1991).

76. R. Hodgetts, F. Luthans, and S. Lee, "New Paradigm Organizations: From Total Quality to Learning World-Class," *Organizational Dynamics*, Winter 1994, pp. 5–19.

77. National Institute of Standards and Technology (NIST), Baldrige Performance Excellence Program, "Baldrige Frequently Asked Questions," from www.nist.gov/baldrige, accessed April 8, 2011.

78. A. Pomeroy, "Winners and Learners," *HR Magazine*, April 2006, pp. 62–67.

79. K&N Management, "Malcolm Baldrige National Quality Award 2010 Award Recipient, Small Business Category," accessed April 8, 2011, from www.nist.gov/baldrige/award_recipients/ website for The National Institute of Standards and Technology (NIST); R. Zeidner, "Questing for Quality," *HR Magazine*, July 2010, pp. 25–28.

80. "ISO in One Page," "Quality Management Principles," "ISO 9000 Essentials," and "Management and Leadership Standards" from www.iso.org, the website from the International Organization for Standardization, accessed April 9, 2011.

81. General Electric 1999 Annual Report, www.ge.com/annual99.

82. "Capitalizing on Opportunities," *Smart Business*, February 16, 2011, accessed on April 9, 2011, from www.sbnonline.com, website of SmartBusiness; D. Arnold, "Cardinal Fastener Soars with Lean Thinking," from www.cardinalfastener.com, accessed January 19, 2008.

83. M. Toosi, "Labor Force Projections to 2018: Older Workers Staying More Active," *Monthly Labor Review*, November 2009, pp. 30–51.

84. N. Lockwood, *The Aging Workforce* (Alexandria, VA: Society for Human Resource Management, 2003).

85. AARP website, www.aarp.org, "2009 AARP Best Employers for Workers over 50," accessed May 6, 2011.

86. J. Thilmany, "Passing on Knowledge," *HR Magazine*, June 2008, pp. 100–104.

87. M. Weinstein, "Netting Know-How," *Training*, September/October 2010, pp. 26–29.

88. M. Toosi, "Labor Force Projections to 2018: Older Workers Staying More Active," *Monthly Labor Review*, November 2009, pp. 30–51.

89. Ibid.

90. R. Zeidner, "Does the United States Need Foreign Workers?" *HR Magazine*, June 2009, pp. 42–47.

91. M. Jordan, J. Kronholz, and B. Newman, "Off the Job, onto the Streets," *The Wall Street Journal*, April 11, 2006, pp. B1, B4; I. Speizer, "Roots of the Immigration Debate," *Workforce Management*, August 14, 2006, pp. 1, 18–26.

92. R. Block, "Homeland Security Strategy Hits Executives, Illegal Workers," *The Wall Street Journal*, February 23, 2007, p. A5.

93. M. Johnson, "Blind Workers Find Fulfillment at Wiscraft Inc.," *Columbus Dispatch*, February 18, 2006, p. F2.

94. A. Fox, "Mixing It Up," *HR Magazine*, May 2011, pp. 22–27.

95. B. Hite, "Employers Rethink How They Give Feedback," *The Wall Street Journal*, October 13, 2008, p. B5; E. White, "Age Is as Age Does: Making the Generation Gap Work for You," *The Wall Street Journal*, June 30, 2008, p. B3; P. Harris, "The Work War," *TD*, May 2005, pp. 45–48; C. Hirshman, "Here They Come," *HR Executive*, July 2006, pp. 1, 22–26.

96. M. Rowh, "Older and Wiser," *Human Resource Executive*, August 2008, pp. 35–37.

97. B. Wooldridge and J. Wester, "The Turbulent Environment of Public Personnel Administration: Responding to the Challenge of the Changing Workplace of the Twenty-First Century," *Public Personnel Management* 20 (1991), pp. 207–24; J. Laabs, "The New Loyalty: Grasp It. Earn It. Keep It," *Workforce*, November 1998, pp. 34–39.

98. T. H. Cox and S. Blake, "Managing Cultural Diversity: Implications for Organizational Competitiveness," *The Executive* 5 (1991), pp. 45–56.

99. M. Loden and J. B. Rosener, *Workforce America!* (Homewood, IL: Business One Irwin, 1991); N. Lockwood, *Workplace Diversity: Leveraging the Power of Difference for Competitive Advantage* (Alexandria, VA: Society for Human Resource Management, 2005).

100. R. Rodriguez, "Diversity Finds Its Place," *HR Magazine,* August 2006, pp. 56–61.

101. C. Huff, "Powering Up a Hispanic Workforce," *Workforce Management,* May, 18, 2009, pp. 25–29.

102. J. Salopek, "Retaining Women," *T + D,* September 2008, pp. 24–27.

103. J. Ledvinka and V. G. Scarpello, *Federal Regulation of Personnel and Human Resource Management,* 2nd ed. (Boston: PWS-Kent, 1991).

104. N. Lockwood, *The Glass Ceiling: Domestic and International Perspectives* (Alexandria, VA: Society for Human Resource Management, 2004).

105. *Women in U.S. Corporate Leadership: 2003* (New York: Catalyst, 2003).

106. M. Jordan and J. Jargon, "Cases Target Illegal Labor," *Wall Street Journal,* April 21, 2010, p. A3; B. Leonard, "When HR Goes Bad," *HR Magazine,* January 2011, pp. 30–32.

107. Society for Human Resource Management, *SHRM Workplace Forecast: The Top Trends According to Workplace Professionals* (Alexandria, VA: SHRM, 2009).

108. M. Pastin, *The Hard Problems of Management: Gaining the Ethics Edge* (San Francisco: Jossey-Bass, 1986); T. Thomas, J. Schermerhorn, Jr., and J. Dienhart, "Strategic Leadership of Ethical Behavior in Business," *Academy of Management Executive* 18 (2004), pp. 56–66.

109. Ibid.

110. E. Krell, "How to Conduct an Ethics Audit," *HR Magazine,* April 2010, pp. 48–50; B. Leonard, "When HR Goes Bad"; S. Bates, "Survey: Business Ethics Improved during Recession," *HR Magazine,* January 2010, p. 13.

111. K. Gurchiek, "Sarbanes-Oxley Compliance Costs Rising," *HR Magazine,* January 2005, pp. 29, 33.

112. R. Grossman, "HR and the Board," *HR Magazine,* January 2007, pp. 52–58.

113. J. Segal, "The 'Joy' of Uncooking," *HR Magazine* 47 (11) (2002).

114. D. Buss, "Corporate Compasses," *HR Magazine* 49 (6) (2004), pp. 126–32.

115. E. Krell, "How to Conduct an Ethics Audit," *HR Magazine,* April 2010, pp. 48–50.

116. M. O'Brien, "'Idol'-izing Ethics," *Human Resource Executive,* May 16, 2009, pp. 32–34.

117. www.nationwide.com Code of Conduct.

118. G. F. Cavanaugh, D. Moberg, and M. Velasquez, "The Ethics of Organizational Politics," *Academy of Management Review* 6 (1981), pp. 363–74.

119. "Manufacturing: Engine of US Innovation," *National Association of Manufacturing* (October 4, 2006), available at www.nam.org (accessed January 21, 2009).

120. S. Kennedy, "U.S. Won't Dominate New World Economy," *The Columbus Dispatch,* January 16, 2011, p. G2.

121. D. Wessel, "Big U.S. Firms Shift Hiring Abroad," *Wall Street Journal,* April 19, 2011, pp. B1, B2.

122. M. Sanchanta, "Gap Expands Japan Push," *Wall Street Journal,* March 2, 2011, p. B8.

123. M. Wei, "East Meets West at Hamburger University," *Bloomberg Businessweek,* January 31–February 6, 2011 pp. 22–23.

124. Ibid.

125. C. Hymowitz, "IBM Combines Volunteer Service, Teamwork to Cultivate Emerging Markets," *The Wall Street Journal,* August 4, 2008, p. B6.

126. J. Schramm, "Offshoring," *Workplace Visions 2* (Alexandria, VA: Society for Human Resource Management, 2004); P. Babcock, "America's Newest Export: White Collar Jobs," *HR Magazine* 49 (4) 2004, pp. 50–57.

127. "Manufacturing: Engine of U.S. Innovation", National Association of Manufacturing, October 4, 2006. Available at website www.nam.org, January 21, 2009.

128. F. Hansen, "U.S. Firms Going Wherever the Knowledge Workers Are," *Workforce Management,* October 2005, pp. 43–44.

129. Ibid.

130. R. Zeidner, "Does the United States Need Foreign Workers?" *HR Magazine,* June 2009, pp. 42–47; U.S. Department of Homeland Security, *Yearbook of Immigration Statistics: 2009* (Washington, DC: U.S. Department of Homeland Security, Office of Immigration Statistics, 2010).

131. J. Marquez, "Going Rural: A U.S. Alternative to Offshoring," *Workforce Management,* September 2005, pp. 16–17.

132. R. Chittum, "Call Centers Phone Home," *The Wall Street Journal,* June 9, 2004, pp. B1, B8.

133. J. Hagerty, "U.S. Factories Buck Decline," *Wall Street Journal,* January 19, 2011, pp. A1–A2.

134. L. Morales, "Nearly Half of Americans Are Frequent Internet Users," January 2, 2009, www.gallup.com; L. Morales, "Google and Facebook Users, Skew Young, Affluent and Educated," February 17, 2011, www.gallup.com.

135. M. Derven, "Social Networking: A Frame for Development," *T + D,* July 2009, pp. 58–63; J. Arnold, "Twittering and Facebooking While They Work," *HR Magazine,* December 2009, pp. 53–55.

136. C. Goodman, "Employers Wrestle with Social-Media Policies," *The Columbus Dispatch,* January 30, 2011, p. D3.

137. I. Brat, "A Joy(stick) to Behold," *The Wall Street Journal,* June 23, 2008, p. R5.

138. D. Wakabayashi, "Japanese Farms Look to the 'Cloud,'" *Wall Street Journal,* January 18, 2011, p. B5.

139. M. J. Kavanaugh, H. G. Guetal, and S. I. Tannenbaum, *Human Resource Information Systems: Development and Application* (Boston: PWS-Kent, 1990).

140. Bill Roberts, "Empowerment or Imposition?" *HR Magazine,* June 2004, downloaded from Infotrac at http://web7.infotrac.galegroup.com.

141. P. Choate and P. Linger, *The High-Flex Society* (New York: Knopf, 1986); P. B. Doeringer, *Turbulence in the American Workplace* (New York: Oxford University Press, 1991).

142. J. A. Neal and C. L. Tromley, "From Incremental Change to Retrofit: Creating High-Performance Work Systems," *Academy of Management Executive* 9 (1995), pp. 42–54.

143. K. A. Miller, *Retraining the American Workforce* (Reading, MA: Addison-Wesley, 1989).

144. S. Moffett, "Separation Anxiety," *The Wall Street Journal,* September 27, 2004, p. R11.

145. J. Gordon, "Do Your Virtual Teams Deliver Only Virtual Performance?" *Training,* June 2005, pp. 20–25.

146. A. Gupta, "Expanding the 24-Hour Workplace," *The Wall Street Journal,* September 15–16, 2007, pp. R9, R11.

147. T. Peters, "Restoring American Competitiveness: Looking for New Models of Organizations," *The Executive* 2 (1988), pp. 103–10.

148. P. Coy, "A Renaissance in U.S. Manufacturing," *Bloomberg Businessweek,* May 9–15, 2011, pp. 11–13.

149. "Outstanding Training Initiatives: Capital One: Audio Learning in Stereo," *Training*, March 2006, p. 64.

150. J. Marquez, "Firms Tap Virtual Work Spaces to Ease Collaboration, Debate among Scattered Employees," *Workforce Management*, May 22, 2006, pp. 38–39.

151. D. Foust, "How Technology Delivers for UPS," *BusinessWeek*, March 5, 2007, p. 60.

152. Roberts, "Empowerment or Imposition."

153. L. Weatherly, "HR Technology: Leveraging the Shift to Self-Service," *HR Magazine*, March 2005.

154. N. Lockwood, *Maximizing Human Capital: Demonstrating HR Value with Key Performance Indicators* (Alexandria, VA: SHRM Research Quarterly, 2006).

155. R. N. Ashkenas, "Beyond the Fads: How Leaders Drive Change with Results," *Human Resource Planning* 17 (1994), pp. 25–44.

156. M. A. Huselid, "The Impact of Human Resource Management Practices on Turnover, Productivity, and Corporate Financial Performance," *Academy of Management Journal* 38 (1995), pp. 635–72; U.S. Dept. of Labor, *High-Performance Work Practices and Firm Performance* (Washington, DC: U.S. Government Printing Office, 1993); J. Combs, Y. Liu, A. Hall, and D. Ketchen, "How Much Do High-Performance Work Practices Matter? A Meta-analysis of Their Effects on Organizational Performance," *Personnel Psychology* 59 (2006), pp. 501–28.

157. B. Becker and M. A. Huselid, "High-Performance Work Systems and Firm Performance: A Synthesis of Research and Managerial Implications," in *Research in Personnel and Human Resource Management* 16, ed. G. R. Ferris (Stamford, CT: JAI Press, 1998), pp. 53–101; A. Zacharatos, J. Barling, and R. Iverson, "High Performance Work Systems and Occupational Safety," *Journal of Applied Psychology* 90 (2005), pp. 77–93.

158. B. Becker and B. Gerhart, "The Impact of Human Resource Management on Organizational Performance: Progress and Prospects," *Academy of Management Journal* 39 (1996), pp. 779–801.

159. J. Marquez, "Engine of Change," *Workforce Management*, July 17, 2006, pp. 20–30; from Global Engineering Manufacturing Alliance website at www.gemaengine.com.

160. S. A. Snell and J. W. Dean, "Integrated Manufacturing and Human Resource Management: A Human Capital Perspective," *Academy of Management Journal* 35 (1992), pp. 467–504; M. A. Youndt, S. Snell, J. W. Dean Jr., and D. P. Lepak, "Human Resource Management, Manufacturing Strategy, and Firm Performance," *Academy of Management Journal* 39 (1996), pp. 836–66.

PART 1

The Human Resource Environment

CHAPTER

2

Strategic Human Resource Management

LO LEARNING OBJECTIVES

After reading this chapter, you should be able to:

LO 2-1   Describe the differences between strategy formulation and strategy implementation. *page 74*

LO 2-2   List the components of the strategic management process. *page 75*

LO 2-3   Discuss the role of the HRM function in strategy formulation. *page 77*

LO 2-4   Describe the linkages between HRM and strategy formulation. *page 78*

LO 2-5   Discuss the more popular typologies of generic strategies and the various HRM practices associated with each. *page 83*

LO 2-6   Describe the different HRM issues and practices associated with various directional strategies. *page 92*

ENTER THE WORLD OF BUSINESS

HP's New Strategy

In the face of increasing competition, the largest producer of PCs and laptops, Hewlett Packard, recently decided to get out of the PC business altogether. After outdueling Dell to become the world's largest manufacturer of computers (HP shipped over 64 million PCs in 2010), the company has announced its intention to spin or sell its personal-systems group, a division that brought in $40.74 billion in sales in 2010. CEO Leo Apotheker concluded that, "to be successful in the consumer device business we would have had to invest a lot of capital and I believe we can invest it in better places."

These investments seem to be taking HP further into markets that target businesses as customers. The thinking is that such businesses provide higher potential profit margins. For instance, in 2008 the company acquired the tech services company Electronic Data Systems for $13.9 billion in an effort to compete against IBM's tech-services division. In 2010 it also acquired 3Com in an effort to compete with Cisco Systems' network-equipment business. HP recently announced a $10.25 billion purchase of British enterprise software company Autonomy, which will compete against Mr. Apotheker's former employer, SAP.

Industry analysts agree that the conditions of the PC market make it a business which is hard to run. Margins for PCs run in the 2–6% range, much lower than HP thinks it can generate by focusing on software and services.

Interestingly, this is not the first time that the markets have questioned the wisdom of HP's strategy. Ten years ago HP made headlines for making a controversial $25 billion acquisition. What was the acquisition? Ironically in light of today's strategy, HP bought PC maker Compaq in an effort to strengthen its position in the PC market.

SOURCE: From Y. Kane and N. Wingfield, "Pioneering Firm Bows to Post-PC World," *Wall Street Journal*, August 19, 2011. Reproduced with permission of Dow Jones & Company, Inc. via Copyright Clearance Center.

Introduction

As the HP example just illustrated, business organizations exist in an environment of competition. They can use a number of resources to compete with other companies. These resources are physical (such as plant, equipment, technology, and geographic location), organizational (the structure, planning, controlling, and coordinating systems, and group relations), and human (the experience, skill, and intelligence of employees). It is these resources under the control of the company that provide competitive advantage.[1]

The goal of strategic management in an organization is to deploy and allocate resources in a way that gives it a competitive advantage. As you can see, two of the three classes of resources (organizational and human) are directly tied to the human resource management function. As Chapter 1 pointed out, the role of human resource management is to ensure that a company's human resources provide a competitive advantage. Chapter 1 also pointed out some of the major competitive challenges that companies face today. These challenges require companies to take a proactive, strategic approach in the marketplace.

To be maximally effective, the HRM function must be integrally involved in the company's strategic management process.[2] This means that human resource managers should (1) have input into the strategic plan, both in terms of people-related issues and in terms of the ability of the human resource pool to implement particular strategic alternatives; (2) have specific knowledge of the organization's strategic goals; (3) know what types of employee skills, behaviors, and attitudes are needed to support the strategic plan; and (4) develop programs to ensure that employees have those skills, behaviors, and attitudes.

We begin this chapter by discussing the concepts of business models and strategy and by depicting the strategic management process. Then, we discuss the levels of integration between the HRM function and the strategic management process in strategy formulation. Next, we review some of the more common strategic models and, within the context of these models, discuss the various types of employee skills, behaviors, and attitudes, and the ways HRM practices aid in implementing the strategic plan. Finally, we discuss the role of HR in creating competitive advantage.

 ## What Is a Business Model?

A business model is a story of how the firm will create value for customers and, more important, how it will do so profitably. We often hear or read of companies that have "transformed their business model" in one way or another, but what that means is not always clear. To understand this, we need to grasp a few basic accounting concepts.

First, fixed costs are generally considered the costs that are incurred regardless of the number of units produced. For instance, if you are producing widgets in a factory, you have the rent you pay for the factory, depreciation of the machines, the utilities, the property taxes, and so on. In addition, you generally have a set number of employees who work a set number of hours with a specified level of benefits, and while you might be able to vary these over time, on a regular basis you pay the same total labor costs whether your factory runs at 70% capacity or 95% capacity.

Second, you have a number of variable costs, which are those costs that vary directly with the units produced. For instance, all of the materials that go into the widget might cost a total of $10, which means that you have to charge at least $10 per widget, or you cannot even cover the variable costs of production.

Third is the concept of "contribution margins," or margins. Margins are the difference between what you charge for your product and the variable costs of that product. They are called contribution margins because they are what contributes to your ability to cover your fixed costs. So, for instance, if you charged $15 for each widget, your contribution margin would be $5 ($15 price – $10 variable cost).

Fourth, the gross margin is the total amount of margin you made and is calculated as the number of units sold times the contribution margin. If you sold 1,000,000 units, your gross margin would then be $5,000,000. Did you make a profit? That depends. Profit refers to what is left after you have paid your variable costs and your fixed costs. If your gross margin was $5,000,000, and your fixed costs were $6,000,000, then you lost $1,000,000.

GM'S ATTEMPT TO SURVIVE

Let's look at how a business model plays out with the recent challenges faced by General Motors (GM). Critics of GM talk about the fact that GM has higher labor costs than their foreign competitors. This is true, but misleading. GM's average hourly wage for their existing workforce is reasonably competitive. However, the two aspects that make GM uncompetitive are their benefit costs (in particular, health care) and most important, the cost of their legacy workforce.

A legacy workforce describes the former workers (i.e., those no longer working for the company) to whom the firm still owes financial obligations. GM and the United Auto Workers (UAW) union have negotiated contracts over the years that provide substantial retirement benefits for former GM workers. In particular, retired GM workers have defined benefit plans that guarantee a certain percentage of their final (preretirement) salary as a pension payment as long as they live as well as having the company pay for their health insurance. In addition, the contract specifies that workers are entitled to retire at full pension after 30 years of service.

This might have seemed sustainable when the projections were that GM would continue growing its sales and margins. However, since the 1970s, foreign competitors have been eating away at GM's market share to the extent that GM's former 50% of the market has shrunk to closer to 20%. In addition, with the current economic crisis, the market itself has been shrinking, leaving GM with a decreasing percentage of a decreasing market. For instance, in December of 2005, GM sold 26% of the cars in the global market of almost 1.5 million, but by January of 2009, the market had shrunk to 656,000, and GM was down to 20% of those sales. Thus, in addition to the legacy workforce, they had a significant number of plants with thousands of employees that were completely unnecessary, given the volume of cars GM can produce and sell.[3,4]

If you look at Figure 2.1, you'll see that the solid lines represent the old GM business model, which was based on projections that GM would be able to sell 4 million units at a reasonably high margin, and thus completely cover its fixed costs to make a strong profit. However, the reality was that its products didn't sell at the higher prices, so to try to sell 4 million vehicles, GM offered discounts, which cut into its margins. When GM ended up selling only 3.5 million vehicles, and those were sold at a lower margin, the company could not cover its fixed costs, resulting in a $9 billion loss in 2008 (this is illustrated by the dotted blue line in the figure). So, when GM refers to the "redesigned business model," what it is referring to is a significant reduction in fixed costs (through closing plants and cutting workers) to get the fixed-cost base low enough (the dotted red line) to be able to still be profitable selling fewer cars at lower margins (again, the dotted blue line).

One can easily see how, given the large component that labor costs are to most companies, reference to business models almost inevitably leads to discussions of

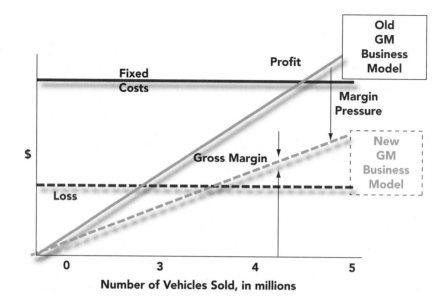

figure 2.1

An Illustration of a
Business Model for
GM

Number of Vehicles Sold, in millions

labor costs. These can be the high cost associated with current unionized employees
in developed countries within North America or Europe or, in some cases, the high
costs associated with a legacy workforce. For instance, the Big Three automakers have
huge numbers of retired or laid-off workers for whom they still have the liability of
paying pensions and health care benefits. This is a significant component of their
fixed-cost base, which makes it difficult for them to compete with other automakers
that either have fewer retirees to cover or have no comparable costs because their
home governments provide pensions and health care.

What Is Strategic Management?

LO 2-1
Describe the differences
between strategy
formulation and strategy
implementation.

Many authors have noted that in today's competitive market, organizations must
engage in strategic planning to survive and prosper. Strategy comes from the Greek
word *strategos*, which has its roots in military language. It refers to a general's grand
design behind a war or battle. In fact, *Webster's New American Dictionary* defines strategy as the "skillful employment and coordination of tactics" and as "artful planning
and management."

Strategic management is a process, an approach to addressing the competitive
challenges an organization faces. It can be thought of as managing the "pattern or
plan that integrates an organization's major goals, policies, and action sequences into
a cohesive whole."[5] These strategies can be either the generic approach to competing
or the specific adjustments and actions taken to deal with a particular situation.

First, business organizations engage in generic strategies that often fit into some
strategic type. One example is "cost, differentiation, or focus."[6] Another is "defender,
analyzer, prospector, or reactor."[7] Different organizations within the same industry
often have different generic strategies. These generic strategy types describe the consistent way the company attempts to position itself relative to competitors.

However, a generic strategy is only a small part of strategic management. The second aspect of strategic management is the process of developing strategies for achieving
the company's goals in light of its current environment. Thus, business organizations
engage in generic strategies, but they also make choices about such things as how to

scare off competitors, how to keep competitors weaker, how to react to and influence pending legislation, how to deal with various stakeholders and special interest groups, how to lower production costs, how to raise revenues, what technology to implement, and how many and what types of people to employ. Each of these decisions may present competitive challenges that have to be considered.

Strategic management is more than a collection of strategic types. It is a process for analyzing a company's competitive situation, developing the company's strategic goals, and devising a plan of action and allocation of resources (human, organizational, and physical) that will increase the likelihood of achieving those goals. This kind of strategic approach should be emphasized in human resource management. HR managers should be trained to identify the competitive issues the company faces with regard to human resources and think strategically about how to respond.

Strategic human resource management (SHRM) can be thought of as "the pattern of planned human resource deployments and activities intended to enable an organization to achieve its goals."[8] For example, many firms have developed integrated manufacturing systems such as advanced manufacturing technology, just-in-time inventory control, and total quality management in an effort to increase their competitive position. However, these systems must be run by people. SHRM in these cases entails assessing the employee skills required to run these systems and engaging in HRM practices, such as selection and training, that develop these skills in employees.[9] To take a strategic approach to HRM, we must first understand the role of HRM in the strategic management process.

Strategic Human Resource Management (SHRM)
A pattern of planned human resource deployments and activities intended to enable an organization to achieve its goals.

COMPONENTS OF THE STRATEGIC MANAGEMENT PROCESS

The strategic management process has two distinct yet interdependent phases: strategy formulation and strategy implementation. During **strategy formulation** the strategic planning groups decide on a strategic direction by defining the company's mission and goals, its external opportunities and threats, and its internal strengths and weaknesses. They then generate various strategic alternatives and compare those alternatives' ability to achieve the company's mission and goals. During **strategy implementation,** the organization follows through on the chosen strategy. This consists of structuring the organization, allocating resources, ensuring that the firm has skilled employees in place, and developing reward systems that align employee behavior with the organization's strategic goals. Both of these strategic management phases must be performed effectively. It is important to note that this process does not happen sequentially. As we will discuss later with regard to emergent strategies, this process entails a constant cycling of information and decision making. Figure 2.2 presents the strategic management process.

In recent years organizations have recognized that the success of the strategic management process depends largely on the extent to which the HRM function is involved.[10]

LO 2-2
List the components of the strategic management process.

Strategy Formulation
The process of deciding on a strategic direction by defining a company's mission and goals, its external opportunities and threats, and its internal strengths and weaknesses.

Strategy Implementation
The process of devising structures and allocating resources to enact the strategy a company has chosen.

LINKAGE BETWEEN HRM AND THE STRATEGIC MANAGEMENT PROCESS

The strategic choice really consists of answering questions about competition—that is, how the firm will compete to achieve its missions and goals. These decisions consist of addressing the issues of where to compete, how to compete, and with what to compete, which are described in Figure 2.3.

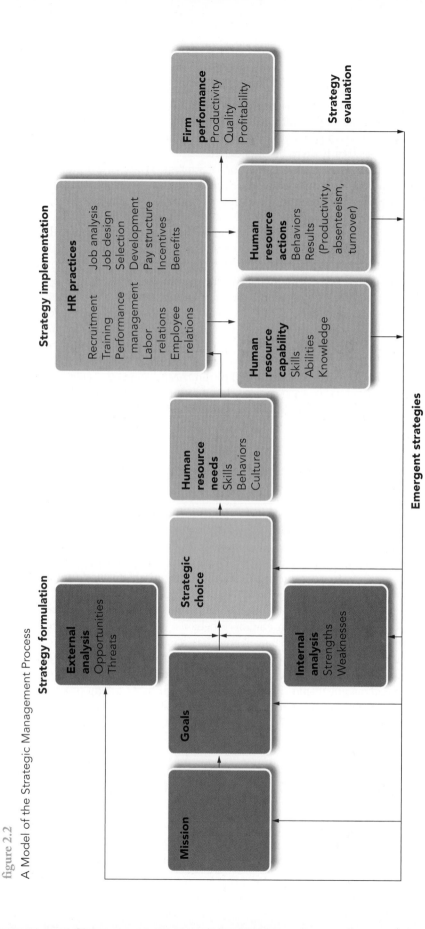

figure 2.2

A Model of the Strategic Management Process

1. Where to compete?
   In what market or markets (industries, products, etc.) will we compete?
2. How to compete?
   On what criterion or differentiating characteristic(s) will we compete? Cost?
   Quality? Reliability? Delivery?
3. With what will we compete?
   What resources will allow us to beat our competition?
   How will we acquire, develop, and deploy those resources to compete?

figure 2.3

Strategy—Decisions about Competition

Although these decisions are all important, strategic decision makers often pay less attention to the "with what will we compete" issue, resulting in poor strategic decisions. For example, PepsiCo in the 1980s acquired the fast-food chains of Kentucky Fried Chicken, Taco Bell, and Pizza Hut ("where to compete" decisions) in an effort to increase its customer base. However, it failed to adequately recognize the differences between its existing workforce (mostly professionals) and that of the fast-food industry (lower skilled people and high schoolers) as well as its ability to manage such a workforce. This was one reason that PepsiCo, in 1998, spun off the fast-food chains. In essence, it had made a decision about where to compete without fully understanding what resources would be needed to compete in that market.

Boeing illustrates how failing to address the "with what" issue resulted in problems in its "how to compete" decisions. When the aerospace firm's consumer products division entered into a price war with Airbus Industrie, it was forced to move away from its traditional customer service strategy toward emphasizing cost reduction.[11] The strategy was a success on the sales end as Boeing received large numbers of orders for aircraft from firms such as Delta, Continental, Southwest, and Singapore Airlines. However, it had recently gone through a large workforce reduction (thus, it didn't have enough people to fill the orders) and did not have the production technology to enable the necessary increase in productivity. The result of this failure to address "with what will we compete" in making a decision about how to compete resulted in the firm's inability to meet delivery deadlines and the ensuing penalties it had to pay to its customers. The end result is that after all the travails, for the first time in the history of the industry, Airbus sold more planes than Boeing in 2003. Luckily, Boeing was able to overcome this stumble, in large part because of a number of stumbles on the part of its chief rival, Airbus. Boeing's 787 Dreamliner has generated a number of orders, while Airbus's behemoth A380 has been beset by a number of production delays, enabling Boeing to regain its market lead. The "Competing through Globalization" box illustrates how firms face a "with what to compete" question in India in terms of talent.

ROLE OF HRM IN STRATEGY FORMULATION

As the preceding examples illustrate, often the "with what will we compete" questions present ideal avenues for HRM to influence the strategic management process. This might be through either limiting strategic options or forcing thoughtfulness among the executive team regarding how and at what cost the firm might gain or develop the human resources (people) necessary for such a strategy to be successful. For example, HRM executives at PepsiCo could have noted that the firm had no expertise in managing the workforce of fast-food restaurants. The limiting role would have been for these executives to argue against the acquisition because of this lack of resources. On

LO 2-3
Discuss the role of the HRM function in strategy formulation.

the other hand, they might have influenced the decision by educating top executives as to the costs (of hiring, training, and so on) associated with gaining people who had the right skills to manage such a workforce.

A firm's strategic management decision-making process usually takes place at its top levels, with a strategic planning group consisting of the chief executive officer, the chief financial officer, the president, and various vice presidents. However, each component of the process involves people-related business issues. Therefore, the HRM function needs to be involved in each of those components. One recent study of 115 strategic business units within *Fortune* 500 corporations found that between 49 and 69% of the companies had some link between HRM and the strategic planning process.[12] However, the level of linkage varied, and it is important to understand these different levels.

Four levels of integration seem to exist between the HRM function and the strategic management function: administrative linkage, one-way linkage, two-way linkage, and integrative linkage.[13] These levels of linkage will be discussed in relation to the different components of strategic management. The linkages are illustrated in Figure 2.4.

Administrative Linkage

LO 2-4
Describe the linkages between HRM and strategy formulation.

In administrative linkage (the lowest level of integration), the HRM function's attention is focused on day-to-day activities. The HRM executive has no time or opportunity to take a strategic outlook toward HRM issues. The company's strategic business planning function exists without any input from the HRM department. Thus, in this level of integration, the HRM department is completely divorced from any component of the strategic management process in both strategy formulation and strategy implementation. The department simply engages in administrative work unrelated to the company's core business needs.

One-Way Linkage

In one-way linkage, the firm's strategic business planning function develops the strategic plan and then informs the HRM function of the plan. Many believe this level of integration constitutes strategic HRM—that is, the role of the HRM function is to design systems and/or programs that implement the strategic plan. Although one-way

figure 2.4

Linkages of Strategic Planning and HRM

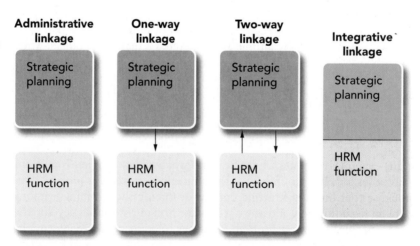

SOURCE: Adapted from K. Golden and V. Ramanujam, "Between a Dream and a Nightmare: On the Integration of the Human Resource Function and the Strategic Business Planning Process," *Human Resource Management* 24 (1985), pp. 429–51.

linkage does recognize the importance of human resources in implementing the strategic plan, it precludes the company from considering human resource issues while formulating the strategic plan. This level of integration often leads to strategic plans that the company cannot successfully implement.

Two-Way Linkage

Two-way linkage allows for consideration of human resource issues during the strategy formulation process. This integration occurs in three sequential steps. First, the strategic planning team informs the HRM function of the various strategies the company is considering. Then HRM executives analyze the human resource implications of the various strategies, presenting the results of this analysis to the strategic planning team. Finally, after the strategic decision has been made, the strategic plan is passed on to the HRM executive, who develops programs to implement it. The strategic planning function and the HRM function are interdependent in two-way linkage.

Integrative Linkage

Integrative linkage is dynamic and multifaceted, based on continuing rather than sequential interaction. In most cases the HRM executive is an integral member of the senior management team. Rather than an iterative process of information exchange, companies with integrative linkage have their HRM functions built right into the strategy formulation and implementation processes. It is this role that we will discuss throughout the rest of this chapter.

Thus, in strategic HRM, the HRM function is involved in both strategy formulation and strategy implementation. The HRM executive gives strategic planners information about the company's human resource capabilities, and these capabilities are usually a direct function of the HRM practices.[14] This information about human resource capabilities helps top managers choose the best strategy because they can consider how well each strategic alternative would be implemented. Once the strategic choice has been determined, the role of HRM changes to the development and alignment of HRM practices that will give the company employees having the necessary skills to implement the strategy.[15] In addition, HRM practices must be designed to elicit actions from employees in the company.[16] In the next two sections of this chapter we show how HRM can provide a competitive advantage in the strategic management process.

Strategy Formulation

Five major components of the strategic management process are relevant to strategy formulation.[17] These components are depicted in Figure 2.5. The first component is the organization's mission. The mission is a statement of the organization's reason for being; it usually specifies the customers served, the needs satisfied and/or the values received by the customers, and the technology used. The mission statement is often accompanied by a statement of a company's vision and/or values. For example, Table 2.1 illustrates the mission and values of Merck & Co., Inc.

An organization's **goals** are what it hopes to achieve in the medium- to long-term future; they reflect how the mission will be operationalized. The overarching goal of most profit-making companies in the United States is to maximize stockholder wealth. But companies have to set other long-term goals in order to maximize stockholder wealth.

Goals
What an organization hopes to achieve in the medium- to long-term future.

figure 2.5

Strategy Formulation

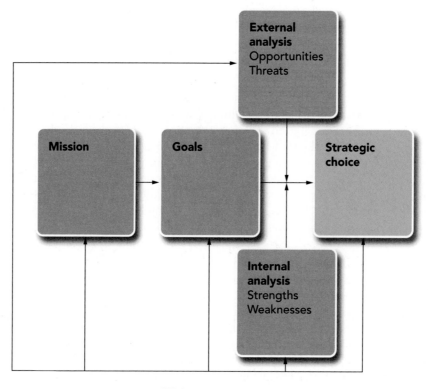

HR input

SOURCE: Adapted from K. Golden and V. Ramanujam, "Between a Dream and a Nightmare," *Human Resource Management* 24 (1985), pp. 429–51.

External Analysis
Examining the organization's operating environment to identify strategic opportunities and threats.

Internal Analysis
The process of examining an organization's strengths and weaknesses.

Strategic Choice
The organization's strategy; the ways an organization will attempt to fulfill its mission and achieve its long-term goals.

External analysis consists of examining the organization's operating environment to identify the strategic opportunities and threats. Examples of opportunities are customer markets that are not being served, technological advances that can aid the company, and labor pools that have not been tapped. Threats include potential labor shortages, new competitors entering the market, pending legislation that might adversely affect the company, and competitors' technological innovations.

Internal analysis attempts to identify the organization's strengths and weaknesses. It focuses on the quantity and quality of resources available to the organization—financial, capital, technological, and human resources. Organizations have to honestly and accurately assess each resource to decide whether it is a strength or a weakness.

External analysis and internal analysis combined constitute what has come to be called the SWOT (strengths, weaknesses, opportunities, threats) analysis. Table 2.2 shows an example of a SWOT analysis for Google. After going through the SWOT analysis, the strategic planning team has all the information it needs to generate a number of strategic alternatives. The strategic managers compare these alternatives' ability to attain the organization's strategic goals; then they make their **strategic choice.** The strategic choice is the organization's strategy; it describes the ways the organization will attempt to fulfill its mission and achieve its long-term goals.

Many of the opportunities and threats in the external environment are people-related. With fewer and fewer highly qualified individuals entering the labor market,

MISSION STATEMENT

Merck & Co., Inc. is a leading research-driven pharmaceutical products and services company. Merck discovers, develops, manufactures and markets a broad range of innovative products to improve human and animal health. The Merck-Medco Managed Care Division manages pharmacy benefits for more than 40 million Americans, encouraging the appropriate use of medicines and providing disease management programs.

Our Mission

The mission of Merck is to provide society with superior products and services—innovations and solutions that improve the quality of life and satisfy customer needs—to provide employees with meaningful work and advancement opportunities and investors with a superior rate of return.

Our Values

1. **Our business is preserving and improving human life.** All of our actions must be measured by our success in achieving this goal. We value above all our ability to serve everyone who can benefit from the appropriate use of our products and services, thereby providing lasting consumer satisfaction.

2. **We are committed to the highest standards of ethics and integrity.** We are responsible to our customers, to Merck employees and their families, to the environments we inhabit, and to the societies we serve worldwide. In discharging our responsibilities, we do not take professional or ethical shortcuts. Our interactions with all segments of society must reflect the high standards we profess.

3. **We are dedicated to the highest level of scientific excellence and commit our research to improving human and animal health and the quality of life.** We strive to identify the most critical needs of consumers and customers; we devote our resources to meeting those needs.

4. **We expect profits, but only from work that satisfies customer needs and benefits humanity.** Our ability to meet our responsibilities depends on maintaining a financial position that invites investment in leading-edge research and that makes possible effective delivery of research results.

5. **We recognize that the ability to excel—to most competitively meet society's and customers' needs—depends on the integrity, knowledge, imagination, skill, diversity, and teamwork of employees, and we value these qualities most highly.** To this end, we strive to create an environment of mutual respect, encouragement, and teamwork—a working environment that rewards commitment and performance and is responsive to the needs of employees and their families.

SOURCE: Courtesy of Merck.

STRENGTHS	WEAKNESSES
Expanding Liquidity	Issues with Chinese Government
Operational Efficiency	Dependence on Advertising Segment
Broad Range of Services Portfolio	Losses at YouTube

OPPORTUNITIES	THREATS
Growing Demand for Online Video	Weak Economic Outlook
Growth in Internet Advertising Market	Invalid Clicks
Inorganic Growth	Microsoft–Yahoo! Deal

SOURCE: GlobalData.

COMPETING THROUGH GLOBALIZATION

A Talent Shortage among Millions of Graduates

We often hear about how many firms have moved call center and technology operations to India because of the large supply of college graduate talent. For example, universities in India have seats for 1.5 million engineering students, up from 390,000 in 2000. However, according to assessment tests administered by the National Association of Software and Services Companies, 75% of technical graduates and 85% of general graduates are unemployable in the information technology and call center industries.

The problem is multifaceted. First, because faculty are paid so low, they do not put much effort into teaching. For instance, Pradeep Singh, a 23-year-old engineering graduate, quickly learned that they need not go to classes. "The faculty take it very casually, and the students take it very casually, like they've all agreed not to be bothered too much," he says.

In addition, cheating, often encouraged by the graders, is widespread. For instance, Deepack Sharma says he failed several exams until he found the secret: putting his cell phone number on his exam. After doing this he says he got a call from the examiner who offered to pass him and his friends if they paid 10,000 rupees each (about $250). After getting the money together and paying the examiner, they all passed the test. He says, "I feel almost certain that if I didn't pay the money, I would have failed the exam again."

Large Indian companies such as Wipro and Tata have attempted to bridge the wide gap between job requirements and skills of graduates through developing significant internal training programs. For instance, Tata puts recent graduates though a 72-day training process and Wipro has developed a 90-day program.

As human capital (or talent) continues to become one of the critical assets that companies must manage to be competitive, firms doing business in India may have to think twice before they let the idea of millions of college graduates entice them to make investments.

SOURCE: From G. Anand, "India Graduates Millions, but Too Few Are Fit to Hire," *Wall Street Journal Online*, April 6, 2011. Reproduced with permission of Dow Jones & Company, Inc. via Copyright Clearance Center.

---

organizations compete not just for customers but for employees. It is HRM's role to keep close tabs on the external environment for human resource–related opportunities and threats, especially those directly related to the HRM function: potential labor shortages, competitor wage rates, government regulations affecting employment, and so on. For example, as discussed in Chapter 1, U.S. companies are finding that more and more high school graduates lack the basic skills needed to work, which is one source of the "human capital shortage."[18] However, not recognizing this environmental threat, many companies have encouraged the exit of older, more skilled workers while hiring less skilled younger workers who require basic skills training.[19] In fact, the "Competing through Globalization" box illustrates how a skill shortage exists in India, in spite of the huge number of college graduates.

An analysis of a company's internal strengths and weaknesses also requires input from the HRM function. Today companies are increasingly realizing that their human resources are one of their most important assets. In fact, one estimate is that over one-third of the total growth in U.S. gross national product (GNP) between 1943 and 1990 was the result of increases in human capital. A company's failure to consider the strengths and weaknesses of its workforce may result in its choosing strategies it is not capable of pursuing.[20] However, some research has demonstrated that few companies have achieved this level of linkage.[21] For example, one company chose a strategy of cost reduction through technological improvements. It built a plant designed around a computer-integrated manufacturing system with statistical process controls. Although this choice may seem like a good one, the company soon learned otherwise. It discovered that its employees could not operate the new equipment because 25% of the workforce was functionally illiterate.[22]

Thus, with an integrative linkage, strategic planners consider all the people-related business issues before making a strategic choice. These issues are identified with regard to the mission, goals, opportunities, threats, strengths, and weaknesses, leading the strategic planning team to make a more intelligent strategic choice. Although this process does not guarantee success, companies that address these issues are more likely to make choices that will ultimately succeed.

Recent research has supported the need to have HRM executives integrally involved in strategy formulation. One study of U.S. petrochemical refineries found that the level of HRM involvement was positively related to the refinery manager's evaluation of the effectiveness of the HRM function.[23] A second study of manufacturing firms found that HRM involvement was highest when top managers viewed employees as a strategic asset and associated them with reduced turnover.[24] However, both studies found that HRM involvement was unrelated to operating unit financial performance.

Research has indicated that few companies have fully integrated HRM into the strategy formulation process.[25] As we've mentioned before, companies are beginning to recognize that in an intensely competitive environment, managing human resources strategically can provide a competitive advantage. Thus, companies at the administrative linkage level will either become more integrated or face extinction. In addition, companies will move toward becoming integratively linked in an effort to manage human resources strategically.

It is of utmost importance that all people-related business issues be considered during strategy formulation. These issues are identified in the HRM function. Mechanisms or structures for integrating the HRM function into strategy formulation may help the strategic planning team make the most effective strategic choice. Once that strategic choice is determined, HRM must take an active role in implementing it. This role will be discussed in the next section.

Strategy Implementation

After an organization has chosen its strategy, it has to execute that strategy—make it come to life in its day-to-day workings. The strategy a company pursues dictates certain HR needs. For a company to have a good strategy foundation, certain tasks must be accomplished in pursuit of the company's goals, individuals must possess certain skills to perform those tasks, and these individuals must be motivated to perform their skills effectively.

The basic premise behind strategy implementation is that "an organization has a variety of structural forms and organizational processes to choose from when implementing a given strategy," and these choices make an economic difference.[26] Five important variables determine success in strategy implementation: organizational structure; task design; the selection, training, and development of people; reward systems; and types of information and information systems.

LO 2-5
Discuss the more popular typologies of generic strategies and the various HRM practices associated with each.

figure 2.6

Variables to
Be Considered
in Strategy
Implementation

As we see in Figure 2.6, HRM has primary responsibility for three of these five implementation variables: task, people, and reward systems. In addition, HRM can directly affect the two remaining variables: structure and information and decision processes. First, for the strategy to be successfully implemented, the tasks must be designed and grouped into jobs in a way that is efficient and effective.[27] In Chapter 4 we will examine how this can be done through the processes of job analysis and job design. Second, the HRM function must ensure that the organization is staffed with people who have the necessary knowledge, skill, and ability to perform their part in implementing the strategy. This goal is achieved primarily through recruitment, selection and placement, training, development, and career management—topics covered in Chapters 5, 6, 7, and 9. In addition, the HRM function must develop performance management and reward systems that lead employees to work for and support the strategic plan. The specific types of performance management systems are covered in Chapter 8, and the many issues involved in developing reward systems are discussed in Chapters 11 through 13. In other words, the role of the HRM function becomes one of (1) ensuring that the company has the proper number of employees with the levels and types of skills required by the strategic plan[28] and (2) developing "control" systems that ensure that those employees are acting in ways that promote the achievement of the goals specified in the strategic plan.[29]

In essence, this is what has been referred to as the "vertical alignment" of HR with strategy. Vertical alignment means that the HR practices and processes are aimed at addressing the strategic needs of the business. But the link between strategy and HR practices is primarily through people. For instance, as IBM moved from being a manufacturer of personal computers to being a fully integrated service provider, the types of people it needed changed significantly. Instead of employing thousands of workers in manufacturing or assembly plants, IBM increasingly needed software engineers to help write new "middleware" programs, and an army of consultants who could help their corporate customers to implement these systems. In addition, as IBM increasingly differentiated itself as being the "integrated solutions" provider (meaning it could sell

Helping the Rainforest Tribes?

As many firms seek to promote the welfare of their suppliers, some firms have gone far back into the supply chain. Many firms develop partnerships with rainforest villages as a way to seek to profit while helping the planet. For instance, Aveda, the cosmetics company which is a unit of Estee Lauder, has established a partnership with the Yawanawa' Indian tribe in the rainforest of western Brazil. Aveda uses pictures of the Indian tribe members to promote its popular Uruku line of lipsticks, eye shadows, and facial bronzers that are supposed to use urukum, a fruit the tribe uses to make body paint. The "green/sustainability" emphasis allows them to charge a premium price to consumers.

However, the tribe has not delivered any urukum to Aveda between 2008 and 2010 since it is more commonly referred to as "annatto" which is grown commercially all over the globe. This does not mean that Aveda has not helped the village; it has improved access to health care, education, and government services. They provided $50,000 for the tribe to buy seedlings to grow urukum on a larger scale. The provided additional funds for the tribe to buy food, clothing, and other supplies. They helped build a new village, a school, and a health clinic.

However, the tribe soon lost interest in the required weeding and caring for the plants to the point that the plants were in a "state of crisis" according to the director of the zoo-botanical park of the Federal University of Acre Flavio Rodriques. In addition, an internal tribal squabble created division regarding whether or not the tribe should even continue the partnership.

While one can certainly admire the motivation of Aveda to do well by doing good, given that the market crop for urukum is about $500 annually, it by no means provides enough to make the village self-sufficient. This led Mr. Rodrigues to write in a 2001 report that "The project probably does not have economic viability. The impression that remained with the technical team is that the multinational has more interest in the marketing aspect of working with an indigenous community in the Amazon than it does in the production of annatto."

SOURCE: From John Lyons, "Skin-Deep Gains for Amazon Tribe, *Wall Street Journal Online*, May 5, 2011. Reproduced with permission of Dow Jones & Company, Inc. via Copyright Clearance Center.

the hardware, software, consulting, and service for a company's entire information technology needs), employees needed a new mindset which emphasized cooperating across different business divisions rather than running independently. Thus, the change in strategy required different kinds of skills, different kinds of employees, and different kinds of behaviors. The "Competing through Sustainability" box illustrates how the cosmetics company Aveda sought to support an Amazonian tribe through sourcing cosmetic raw materials from them.

How does the HRM function implement strategy? As Figure 2.7 shows, it is through administering HRM practices: job analysis/design, recruitment, selection systems, training and development programs, performance management systems, reward systems, and labor relations programs. The details of each of these HRM practices are the focus of the rest of this book. However, at this point it is important to present a general overview of the HRM practices and their role in strategy implementation. We then discuss the various strategies companies pursue and the types of HRM systems congruent with those strategies. First we focus on how the strategic types are implemented; then we discuss the HRM practices associated with various directional strategies.

figure 2.7

Strategy Implementation

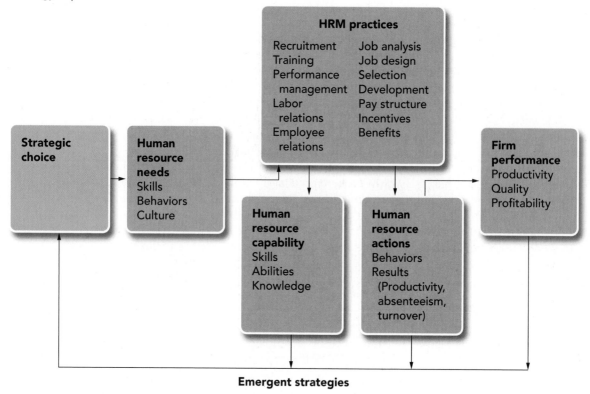

HRM PRACTICES

The HRM function can be thought of as having six menus of HRM practices, from which companies can choose the ones most appropriate for implementing their strategy. Each of these menus refers to a particular functional area of HRM: job analysis/ design, recruitment/selection, training and development, performance management, pay structure/incentives/benefits, and labor–employee relations.[30] These menus are presented in Table 2.3.

Job Analysis and Design

Job Analysis
The process of getting detailed information about jobs.

Companies produce a given product or service (or set of products or services), and the manufacture of these products requires that a number of tasks be performed. These tasks are grouped together to form jobs. **Job analysis** is the process of getting detailed information about jobs. **Job design** addresses what tasks should be grouped into a particular job. The way that jobs are designed should have an important tie to the strategy of an organization because the strategy requires either new and different tasks or different ways of performing the same tasks. In addition, because many strategies entail the introduction of new technologies, this affects the way that work is performed.[31]

Job Design
The process of defining the way work will be performed and the tasks that will be required in a given job.

In general, jobs can vary from having a narrow range of tasks (most of which are simplified and require a limited range of skills) to having a broad array of complex tasks requiring multiple skills. In the past, the narrow design of jobs has been used to increase efficiency, while the broad design of jobs has been associated with efforts to

table 2.3

Menu of HRM
Practice Options

Job Analysis and Design

Few tasks	↔	Many tasks
Simple tasks	↔	Complex tasks
Few skills required	↔	Many skills required
Specific job descriptions	↔	General job descriptions

Recruitment and Selection

External sources	↔	Internal sources
Limited socialization	↔	Extensive socialization
Assessment of specific skills	↔	Assessment of general skills
Narrow career paths	↔	Broad career paths

Training and Development

Focus on current job skills	↔	Focus on future job skills
Individual orientation	↔	Group orientation
Train few employees	↔	Train all employees
Spontaneous, unplanned	↔	Planned, systematic

Performance Management

Behavioral criteria	↔	Results criteria
Developmental orientation	↔	Administrative orientation
Short-term criteria	↔	Long-term criteria
Individual orientation	↔	Group orientation

Pay Structure, Incentives, and Benefits

Pay weighted toward salary and benefits	↔	Pay weighted toward incentives
Short-term incentives	↔	Long-term incentives
Emphasis on internal equity	↔	Emphasis on external equity
Individual incentives	↔	Group incentives

Labor and Employee Relations

Collective bargaining	↔	Individual bargaining
Top-down decision making	↔	Participation in decision making
Formal due process	↔	No due process
View employees as expense	↔	View employees as assets

SOURCES: Adapted from R. S. Schuler and S. F. Jackson, "Linking Competitive Strategies with Human Resource Management Practices," *Academy of Management Executive* 1 (1987), pp. 207–19; and C. Fisher, L. Schoenfeldt, and B. Shaw, *Human Resource Management*, 2nd ed. (Boston: Houghton Mifflin, 1992).

increase innovation. However, with the advent of total quality management methods and a variety of employee involvement programs such as quality circles, many jobs are moving toward the broader end of the spectrum.[32]

Employee Recruitment and Selection

Recruitment is the process through which the organization seeks applicants for potential employment. **Selection** refers to the process by which it attempts to identify applicants with the necessary knowledge, skills, abilities, and other characteristics that will help the company achieve its goals. Companies engaging in different strategies need different types and numbers of employees. Thus, the strategy a company is pursuing will have a direct impact on the types of employees that it seeks to recruit and select.[33]

Recruitment
The process of seeking applicants for potential employment.

Selection
The process by which an organization attempts to identify applicants with the necessary knowledge, skills, abilities, and other characteristics that will help it achieve its goals.

Employee Training and Development

A number of skills are instilled in employees through training and development. **Training** refers to a planned effort to facilitate the learning of job-related knowledge, skills, and behavior by employees. **Development** involves acquiring knowledge, skills, and behavior that improve employees' ability to meet the challenges of a variety of existing jobs or jobs that do not yet exist. Changes in strategies often require changes in the types, levels, and mixes of skills. Thus, the acquisition of strategy-related skills is an essential element of the implementation of strategy. For example, many companies have recently emphasized quality in their products, engaging in total quality management programs. These programs require extensive training of all employees in the TQM philosophy, methods, and often other skills that ensure quality.[34]

Through recruitment, selection, training, and development, companies can obtain a pool of human resources capable of implementing a given strategy.[35] In fact, as the "Competing through Technology" box illustrates, companies are partnering with universities to develop students while obtaining important information.

Performance Management

Performance management is used to ensure that employees' activities and outcomes are congruent with the organization's objectives. It entails specifying those activities and outcomes that will result in the firm's successfully implementing the strategy. For example, companies that are "steady state" (not diversified) tend to have evaluation systems that call for subjective performance assessments of managers. This stems from the fact that those above the first-level managers in the hierarchy have extensive knowledge about how the work should be performed. On the other hand, diversified companies are more likely to use quantitative measures of performance to evaluate managers because top managers have less knowledge about how work should be performed by those below them in the hierarchy.[36]

Similarly, executives who have extensive knowledge of the behaviors that lead to effective performance use performance management systems that focus on the behaviors of their subordinate managers. However, when executives are unclear about the specific behaviors that lead to effective performance, they tend to focus on evaluating the objective performance results of their subordinate managers.[37]

An example of how performance management can be aligned with strategy is provided in Figure 2.8. This comes from a firm in the health care industry whose strategy

Training
A planned effort to facilitate the learning of job-related knowledge, skills, and behavior by employees.

Development
The acquisition of knowledge, skills, and behaviors that improve an employee's ability to meet changes in job requirements and in client and customer demands.

Performance Management
The means through which managers ensure that employees' activities and outputs are congruent with the organization's goals.

figure 2.8

Percentage of Objectives Identified in Individual Performance Plans That Are Tied to Each Strategic Imperative

Strategic Imperative	Business A	Business B	International	Investment	Finance	Legal	IT	HR&S	Enterprise
Achieve superior medical performance	10.5%	12.5%	2.7%	7.6%	3.1%	2.7%	11.4%	2.1%	10.0%
Effectively serve our customers	24.7%	27.2%	36.7%	12.2%	10.3%	27.2%	18.9%	19.5%	23.7%
Create great products and services	5.6%	6.1%	10.1%	9.8%	5.0%	10.1%	15.3%	8.9%	6.9%
Create a winning environment	27.7%	29.7%	30.1%	29.9%	30.3%	33.7%	22.4%	39.4%	27.7%
Establish a cost advantage	31.5%	24.5%	20.5%	40.5%	51.3%	26.3%	32%	30.0%	31.7%
Total	100%	100%	100%	100%	100%	100%	100%	100%	100%

Tweet Your Way to a Degree

The new social media technologies such as Twitter and Facebook have transformed communications among the current generation of college students. However, because firms are still led by those from earlier generations who grew up with landline phones who do not fully comprehend the ways in which these technologies can be used, some firms have found that partnering with universities can help to provide students with the experience they will need to land a job while giving the firms access to the social media expertise they lack.

For instance, Sprint has partnered with an online marketing course at Emerson College called Emerson Social Media, or #ESM as students refer to it on Twitter. Emerson provided the class with 10 smartphones and unlimited wireless access in exchange for them blogging, tweeting, producing YouTube videos, and posting Facebook updates about Sprint's 4G network launch in Boston.

At Arizona State University's Walter Cronkite School of Journalism student teams sought to revamp FoxSportsArizona.com, the website for Fox Sports Net's affiliate. One team suggested to Fox Sports Net executives that viewers be able to build their own pages, posting videos and photos of themselves and friends celebrating their favorite local teams and athletes. The networks like the idea so much they are currently implementing the strategy. Kyle Daly, one of the team members whose ideas Fox liked, feels like this will give him an advantage in a tight job market. "I've already updated my resume," he says.

SOURCE: From K. Rosman, "Here, Tweeting Is a Class Requirement," *Wall Street Journal Online*, March 9, 2011. Reproduced with permission of Dow Jones & Company, Inc. via Copyright Clearance Center.

consisted of five "strategic imperatives," or things that the company was trying to accomplish. In this company all individuals set performance objectives each year, and each of their objectives have to be tied to at least one of the strategic imperatives. The senior VP of HR used the firm's technology system to examine the extent to which each business unit or function was focused on each of the imperatives. The figure illustrates the percentage of objectives that were tied to each imperative across the different units. It allows the company to determine if the mix of objectives is right enterprisewide as well as within each business unit or function.

Pay Structure, Incentives, and Benefits

The pay system has an important role in implementing strategies. First, a high level of pay and/or benefits relative to that of competitors can ensure that the company attracts and retains high-quality employees, but this might have a negative impact on the company's overall labor costs.[38] Second, by tying pay to performance, the company can elicit specific activities and levels of performance from employees.

In a study of how compensation practices are tied to strategies, researchers examined 33 high-tech and 72 traditional companies. They classified them by whether they were in a growth stage (greater than 20% inflation-adjusted increases in annual sales) or a maturity stage. They found that high-tech companies in the growth stage used compensation systems that were highly geared toward incentive pay, with a lower percentage of total pay devoted to salary and benefits. On the other hand, compensation systems among mature companies (both high-tech and traditional) devoted a lower percentage of total pay to incentives and a high percentage to benefits.[39]

Labor and Employee Relations

Whether companies are unionized or not, the general approach to relations with employees can strongly affect their potential for gaining competitive advantage. In the late 1970s Chrysler Corporation was faced with bankruptcy. Lee Iacocca, the new president of Chrysler, asked the union for wage and work-rule concessions in an effort to turn the company around. The union agreed to the concessions, in return receiving profit sharing and a representative on the board. Within only a few years, the relationship with and support from the union allowed Chrysler to pull itself out of bankruptcy and into record profitability.[40]

Companies can choose to treat employees as an asset that requires investment of resources or as an expense to be minimized.[41] They have to make choices about how much employees can and should participate in decision making, what rights employees have, and what the company's responsibility is to them. The approach a company takes in making these decisions can result in it either successfully achieving its short- and long-term goals or ceasing to exist.

Recent research has begun to examine how companies develop sets of HRM practices that maximize performance and productivity. For example, one study of automobile assembly plants around the world found that plants that exhibited both high productivity and high quality used "HRM best practices," such as heavy emphasis on recruitment and hiring, compensation tied to performance, low levels of status differentiation, high levels of training for both new and experienced employees, and employee participation through structures such as work teams and problem-solving groups.[42] Another study found that HRM systems composed of selection testing, training, contingent pay, performance appraisal, attitude surveys, employee participation, and information sharing resulted in higher levels of productivity and corporate financial performance, as well as lower employee turnover.[43] Finally, a recent study found that companies identified as some of the "best places to work" had higher financial performances than a set of matched companies that did not make the list.[44] Similar results have also been observed in a number of other studies.[45]

In addition to the relationship between HR practices and performance in general, in today's fast-changing environment, businesses have to change quickly, requiring changes in employees' skills and behaviors. In one study the researchers found that the flexibility of HR practices, employee skills, and employee behaviors were all positively related to firm financial performance, but only the skill flexibility was related to cost efficiency.[46] While these relationships are promising, the causal direction has not yet been proven. For instance, while effective HR practices should help firms perform better, it is also true that highly profitable firms can invest more in HR practices.[47] The research seems to indicate that while the relationship between practices and performance is consistently positive, we should not go too far out on a limb arguing that increasing the use of HRM practices will automatically result in increased profitability.[48]

STRATEGIC TYPES

As we previously discussed, companies can be classified by the generic strategies they pursue. It is important to note that these generic "strategies" are not what we mean by a strategic plan. They are merely similarities in the ways companies seek to compete in their industries. Various typologies have been offered, but we focus on the two generic strategies proposed by Porter: cost and differentiation.[49]

According to Michael Porter of Harvard, competitive advantage stems from a company's being able to create value in its production process. Value can be created in one of two ways. First, value can be created by reducing costs. Second, value can be created by differentiating a product or service in such a way that it allows the company to charge a premium price relative to its competitors. This leads to two basic strategies. According to Porter, the "overall cost leadership" strategy focuses on becoming the lowest cost producer in an industry. This strategy is achieved by constructing efficient large-scale facilities, by reducing costs through capitalizing on the experience curve, and by controlling overhead costs and costs in such areas as research and development, service, sales force, and advertising. This strategy provides above-average returns within an industry, and it tends to bar other firms' entry into the industry because the firm can lower its prices below competitors' costs.

The "differentiation" strategy, according to Porter, attempts to create the impression that the company's product or service is different from that of others in the industry. The perceived differentiation can come from creating a brand image, from technology, from offering unique features, or from unique customer service. If a company succeeds in differentiating its product, it will achieve above-average returns, and the differentiation may protect it from price sensitivity. For instance, Dell Computer Company built its reputation on providing the lowest cost computers through leveraging its supply chain and direct selling model. However, recently they have seen share eroding as the consumer market grows and HP has offered more differentiated, stylish-looking computers sold through retail outlets where customers can touch and feel them. In addition, Apple has differentiated itself through its own operating system that integrates well with peripheral devices such as the iPod and iPhone. In both cases, these companies can charge a premium (albeit higher for Apple) over Dell's pricing.[50]

HRM NEEDS IN STRATEGIC TYPES

While all of the strategic types require competent people in a generic sense, each of the strategies also requires different types of employees with different types of behaviors and attitudes. As we noted earlier, different strategies require employees with specific skills and also require these employees to exhibit different "role behaviors."[51] **Role behaviors** are the behaviors required of an individual in his or her role as a jobholder in a social work environment. These role behaviors vary on a number of dimensions. Additionally, different role behaviors are required by the different strategies. For example, companies engaged in a cost strategy require employees to have a high concern for quantity and a short-term focus, to be comfortable with stability, and to be risk averse. These employees are expected to exhibit role behaviors that are relatively repetitive and performed independently or autonomously.

Thus, companies engaged in cost strategies, because of the focus on efficient production, tend to specifically define the skills they require and invest in training employees in these skill areas. They also rely on behavioral performance management systems with a large performance-based compensation component. These companies promote internally and develop internally consistent pay systems with high pay differentials between superiors and subordinates. They seek efficiency through worker participation, soliciting employees' ideas on how to achieve more efficient production.

On the other hand, employees in companies with a differentiation strategy need to be highly creative and cooperative; to have only a moderate concern for quantity, a long-term focus, and a tolerance for ambiguity; and to be risk takers. Employees

Role Behaviors
Behaviors that are required of an individual in his or her role as a jobholder in a social work environment.

in these companies are expected to exhibit role behaviors that include cooperating with others, developing new ideas, and taking a balanced approach to process and results.

Thus differentiation companies will seek to generate more creativity through broadly defined jobs with general job descriptions. They may recruit more from outside, engage in limited socialization of newcomers, and provide broader career paths. Training and development activities focus on cooperation. The compensation system is geared toward external equity, as it is heavily driven by recruiting needs. These companies develop results-based performance management system and divisional–corporate performance evaluations to encourage risk taking on the part of managers.[52]

EVIDENCE-BASED HR

A study of HRM among steel minimills in the United States found that mills pursuing different strategies used different systems of HRM. Mills seeking cost leadership tended to use control-oriented HRM systems that were characterized by high centralization, low participation, low training, low wages, low benefits, and highly contingent pay, whereas differentiator mills used "commitment" HRM systems, characterized as the opposite on each of those dimensions. A later study from the same sample revealed that the mills with the commitment systems had higher productivity, lower scrap rates, and lower employee turnover than those with the control systems.

SOURCE: J. Arthur, "The Link between Business Strategy and Industrial Relations Systems in American Steel Mini-Mills," *Industrial and Labor Relations Review* 45 (1992), PP. 488–506.

DIRECTIONAL STRATEGIES

LO 2-6
Describe the different HRM issues and practices associated with various directional strategies.

As discussed earlier in this chapter, strategic typologies are useful for classifying the ways different organizations seek to compete within an industry. However, it is also necessary to understand how increasing size (growth) or decreasing it (downsizing) affects the HRM function. For example, the top management team might decide that they need to invest more in product development or to diversify as a means for growth. With these types of strategies, it is more useful for the HRM function to aid in evaluating the feasibility of the various alternatives and to develop programs that support the strategic choice.

Companies have used four possible categories of directional strategies to meet objectives.[53] Strategies emphasizing market share or operating costs are considered "concentration" strategies. With this type of strategy, a company attempts to focus on what it does best within its established markets and can be thought of as "sticking to its knitting." Strategies focusing on market development, product development, innovation, or joint ventures make up the "internal growth" strategy. Companies with an internal growth strategy channel their resources toward building on existing strengths. Those attempting to integrate vertically or horizontally or to diversify are exhibiting an **"external growth" strategy,** usually through mergers or acquisitions. This strategy attempts to expand a company's resources or to strengthen its market position through acquiring or creating new businesses. Finally, a "divestment," or downsizing, strategy is one made up of retrenchment, divestitures, or liquidation. These strategies are observed among companies facing serious economic difficulties and seeking to pare down their operations. The human resource implications of each of these strategies are quite different.

External Growth Strategy
An emphasis on acquiring vendors and suppliers or buying businesses that allow a company to expand into new markets.

Concentration Strategies

Concentration strategies require that the company maintain the current skills that exist in the organization. This requires that training programs provide a means of keeping those skills sharp among people in the organization and that compensation programs focus on retaining people who have those skills. Appraisals in this strategy tend to be more behavioral because the environment is more certain, and the behaviors necessary for effective performance tend to be established through extensive experience.

Internal Growth Strategies

Internal growth strategies present unique staffing problems. Growth requires that a company constantly hire, transfer, and promote individuals, and expansion into different markets may change the necessary skills that prospective employees must have. In addition, appraisals often consist of a combination of behaviors and results. The behavioral appraisal emphasis stems from the knowledge of effective behaviors in a particular product market, and the results appraisals focus on achieving growth goals. Compensation packages are heavily weighted toward incentives for achieving growth goals. Training needs differ depending on the way the company attempts to grow internally. For example, if the organization seeks to expand its markets, training will focus on knowledge of each market, particularly when the company is expanding into international markets. On the other hand, when the company is seeking innovation or product development, training will be of a more technical nature, as well as focusing on interpersonal skills such as team building. Joint ventures require extensive training in conflict resolution techniques because of the problems associated with combining people from two distinct organizational cultures.

Mergers and Acquisitions

Increasingly we see both consolidation within industries and mergers across industries. For example, British Petroleum's acquisition of Amoco Oil represented a consolidation, or reduction in the number of firms within the industry. On the other hand, Citicorp's merger with Traveller's Group to form Citigroup represented firms from different industries (pure financial services and insurance) combining to change the dynamics within both. Whatever the type, one thing is for sure—mergers and acquisitions are on the increase, and HRM needs to be involved.[54] In addition, these mergers more frequently consist of global megamergers, in spite of some warnings that these might not be effective.

According to a report by the Conference Board, "people issues" may be one of the major reasons that mergers do not always live up to expectations. Some companies now heavily weigh firm cultures before embarking on a merger or acquisition. For example, prior to acquiring ValueRx, executives at Express Scripts Inc. interviewed senior executives and middle managers at the potential target firm in order to get a sense of its culture.[55] In spite of this, fewer than one-third of the HRM executives surveyed said that they had a major influence in how mergers are planned, yet 80 percent of them said that people issues have a significant impact after the deals are finalized.[56]

In addition to the desirability of HRM playing a role in evaluating a merger opportunity, HRM certainly has a role in the actual implementation of a merger or acquisition. Training in conflict resolution is also necessary when companies engage in an external growth strategy. All the options for external growth consist of acquiring or developing new businesses, and these businesses often have distinct cultures. Thus many HRM

Concentration Strategy
A strategy focusing on increasing market share, reducing costs, or creating and maintaining a market niche for products and services.

Internal Growth Strategy
A focus on new market and product development, innovation, and joint ventures.

programs face problems in integrating and standardizing practices across the company's businesses. The relative value of standardizing practices across businesses must be weighed against the unique environmental requirements of each business and the extent of desired integration of the two firms. For example, with regard to pay practices, a company may desire a consistent internal wage structure to maintain employee perceptions of equity in the larger organization. In a recent new business developed by IBM, the employees pressured the company to maintain the same wage structure as IBM's main operation. However, some businesses may function in environments where pay practices are driven heavily by market forces. Requiring these businesses to adhere to pay practices in other environments may result in an ineffective wage structure.

Downsizing

Downsizing
The planned elimination of large numbers of personnel, designed to enhance organizational effectiveness.

Of increasing importance to organizations in today's competitive environment is HRM's role in **downsizing** or "rightsizing." The number of organizations undergoing downsizing increased significantly from the third to the fourth quarter of 2008, and while this trend has slowed, layoffs are still significant (see Figure 2.9).[57]

One would have great difficulty ignoring the massive "war for talent" that went on during the late 1990s, particularly with the notable dot-com craze. Firms during this time sought to become "employers of choice," to establish "employment brands," and to develop "employee value propositions" as ways to ensure that they would be able to attract and retain talented employees.

figure 2.9

Layoff Events and Separations 2004–2011

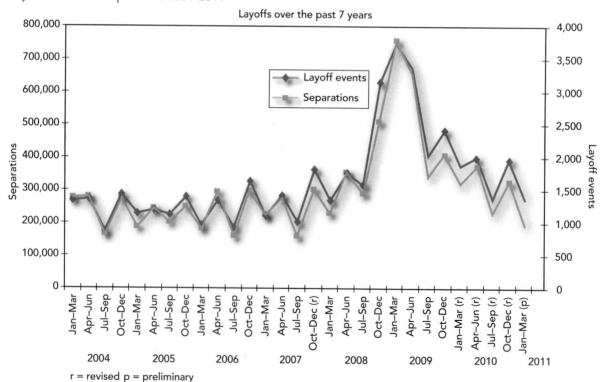

r = revised p = preliminary

SOURCE: http://www.bls.gov/news.release/mslo.nr0.htm.

The current economic crisis means that one important question facing firms is, How can we develop a reputation as an employer of choice, and engage employees to the goals of the firm, while laying off a significant portion of our workforce? How firms answer this question will determine how they can compete by meeting the stakeholder needs of their employees.

In spite of the increasing frequency of downsizing, research reveals that it is far from universally successful for achieving the goals of increased productivity and increased profitability. For example, Table 2.4 illustrates the results of a survey conducted by the American Management Association indicating that only about one-third of the companies that went through downsizings actually achieved their goal of increased productivity. Another survey by the AMA found that over two-thirds of the companies that downsize repeat the effort a year later.[58] Also, research by the consulting firm Mitchell & Company found that companies that downsized during the 1980s lagged the industry average stock price in 1991.[59] Thus it is important to understand the best ways of managing downsizings, particularly from the standpoint of HRM.

Downsizing presents a number of challenges and opportunities for HRM.[60] In terms of challenges, the HRM function must "surgically" reduce the workforce by cutting only the workers who are less valuable in their performance. Achieving this is difficult because the best workers are most able (and often willing) to find alternative employment and may leave voluntarily prior to any layoff. For example, in 1992 General Motors and the United Auto Workers agreed to an early retirement program for individuals between the ages of 51 and 65 who had been employed for 10 or more years. The program provided those who agreed to retire their full pension benefits, even if they obtained employment elsewhere, and as much as $13,000 toward the purchase of a GM car.[61] As mentioned earlier in the chapter, this is part of GM's labor cost problem.

Early retirement programs, although humane, essentially reduce the workforce with a "grenade" approach. This type of reduction does not distinguish between

DESIRED OUTCOME	PERCENTAGE THAT ACHIEVED DESIRED RESULT
Reduced expenses	46%
Increased profits	32
Improved cash flow	24
Increased productivity	22
Increased return on investment	21
Increased competitive advantage	19
Reduced bureaucracy	17
Improved decision making	14
Increased customer satisfaction	14
Increased sales	13
Increased market share	12
Improved product quality	9
Technological advances	9
Increased innovation	7
Avoidance of a takeover	6

table 2.4

Effects of Downsizing on Desired Outcomes

SOURCE: From *Wall Street Journal*, June 6, 1991. Reproduced with permission of Dow Jones & Company, Inc. via Copyright Clearance Center.

good and poor performers but rather eliminates an entire group of employees. In fact, recent research indicates that when companies downsize by offering early retirement programs, they usually end up rehiring to replace essential talent within a year. Often the company does not achieve its cost-cutting goals because it spends 50 to 150% of the departing employee's salary in hiring and retraining new workers.[62]

Another HRM challenge is to boost the morale of employees who remain after the reduction; this is discussed in greater detail in Chapter 5. Survivors may feel guilt over keeping their jobs when their friends have been laid off, or they may envy their friends who have retired with attractive severance and pension benefits. Their reduced satisfaction with and commitment to the organization may interfere with work performance. Thus the HRM function must maintain open communication with remaining employees to build their trust and commitment rather than with-holding information.[63] All employees should be informed of the purpose of the downsizing, the costs to be cut, the duration of the downsizing, and the strategies to be pursued. In addition, companies going through downsizing often develop compensation programs that tie the individual's compensation to the company's success. Employee ownership programs often result from downsizing, and gainsharing plans such as the Scanlon plan (discussed in Chapter 12) originated in companies facing economic difficulties.

In spite of these challenges, downsizing provides opportunities for HRM. First, it often allows the company to "get rid of dead wood" and make way for fresh ideas. In addition, downsizing is often a unique opportunity to change an organization's culture. In firms characterized by antagonistic labor–management relations, down-sizing can force the parties to cooperate and to develop new, positive relation-ships.[64] Finally, downsizing can demonstrate to top-management decision makers the value of the company's human resources to its ultimate success. The role of HRM is to effectively manage the process in a way that makes this value undeni-able. We discuss the implications of downsizing as a labor force management strat-egy in Chapter 5.

STRATEGY EVALUATION AND CONTROL

A final component to the strategic management process is that of strategy evalua-tion and control. Thus far we have focused on the planning and implementation of strategy. However, it is extremely important for the firm to constantly monitor the effectiveness of both the strategy and the implementation process. This monitoring makes it possible for the company to identify problem areas and either revise existing structures and strategies or devise new ones. In this process we see emergent strategies appear as well as the critical nature of human resources in competitive advantage.

The Role of Human Resources in Providing Strategic Competitive Advantage

Thus far we have presented the strategic management process as including a step-by-step procedure by which HRM issues are raised prior to deciding on a strategy and then HRM practices are developed to implement that strategy. However, we must note that human resources can provide a strategic competitive advantage in two addi-tional ways: through emergent strategies and through enhancing competitiveness.

EMERGENT STRATEGIES

Having discussed the process of strategic management, we also must distinguish between intended strategies and emergent strategies. Most people think of strategies as being proactive, rational decisions aimed toward some predetermined goal. The view of strategy we have presented thus far in the chapter focuses on intended strategies. Intended strategies are the result of the rational decision-making process used by top managers as they develop a strategic plan. This is consistent with the definition of strategy as "the pattern or plan that integrates an organization's major goals, policies, and action sequences into a cohesive whole."[65] The idea of emergent strategies is evidenced by the feedback loop in Figure 2.2.

Most strategies that companies espouse are intended strategies. For example, when Howard Schultz founded Starbucks, he had the idea of creating a third place (between work and home) where people could enjoy traditional Italian-style coffee. He knew that the smell of the coffee and the deeper, darker, stronger taste would attract a new set of customers to enjoy coffee the way he thought it should be enjoyed. This worked, but as Starbucks grew, customers began asking if they could have non-fat milk in their lattes, or if they could get flavor shots in their coffees. Schultz swore that such things would essentially pollute the coffee and refused to offer them. Finally, after repeated requests from his store managers who kept hearing customers demanding such things, Schultz finally relented.[66]

Emergent strategies, on the other hand, consist of the strategies that evolve from the grassroots of the organization and can be thought of as what organizations actually do, as opposed to what they intend to do. Strategy can also be thought of as "a pattern in a stream of decisions or actions."[67] For example, when Honda Motor Company first entered the U.S. market with its 250-cc and 350-cc motorcycles in 1959, it believed that no market existed for its smaller 50-cc bike. However, the sales on the larger motorcycles were sluggish, and Japanese executives running errands around Los Angeles on Honda 50's attracted a lot of attention, including that of a buyer with Sears, Roebuck. Honda found a previously undiscovered market as well as a new distribution outlet (general retailers) that it had not planned on. This emergent strategy gave Honda a 50% market share by 1964.[68]

The distinction between intended and emergent strategies has important implications for human resource management.[69] The new focus on strategic HRM has tended to focus primarily on intended strategies. Thus HRM's role has been seen as identifying for top management the people-related business issues relevant to strategy formulation and then developing HRM systems that aid in the implementation of the strategic plan.

However, most emergent strategies are identified by those lower in the organizational hierarchy. It is often the rank-and-file employees who provide ideas for new markets, new products, and new strategies. HRM plays an important role in facilitating communication throughout the organization, and it is this communication that allows for effective emergent strategies to make their way up to top management. For example, Starbucks' Frappucino was a drink invented by one of the store employees in California; Starbucks leaders (including Schultz) thought it was a terrible idea. They fought it in a number of meetings, but the employee kept getting more and more information supporting her case for how much customers seemed to like it. The leaders finally gave the go-ahead to begin producing it, and it has become a $1 billion a year product, and one that has contributed to the Starbucks brand.[70]

ENHANCING FIRM COMPETITIVENESS

A related way in which human resources can be a source of competitive advantage is through developing a human capital pool that gives the company the unique ability to adapt to an ever-changing environment. Recently managers have become interested in the idea of a "learning organization," in which people continually expand their capacity to achieve the results they desire.[71] This requires the company to be in a constant state of learning through monitoring the environment, assimilating information, making decisions, and flexibly restructuring to compete in that environment. Companies that develop such learning capability have a competitive advantage. Although certain organizational information-processing systems can be an aid, ultimately the people (human capital) who make up the company provide the raw materials in a learning organization.[72]

Thus, the role of human resources in competitive advantage should continue to increase because of the fast-paced change characterizing today's business environment. It is becoming increasingly clear that even as U.S. automakers have improved the quality of their cars to compete with the Japanese, these competitors have developed such flexible and adaptable manufacturing systems that they can respond to customer needs more quickly.[73] This flexibility of the manufacturing process allows the emergent strategy to come directly from the marketplace by determining and responding to the exact mix of customer desires. It requires, however, that the company have people in place who have the skills to similarly adapt quickly.[74] As Howard Schultz, the founder and chairman of Starbucks, says, "If people relate to the company they work for, if they form an emotional tie to it and buy into its dreams, they will pour their heart into making it better. When employees have self-esteem and self-respect they can contribute so much more; to their company, to their family, to the world."[75] This statement exemplifies the increasing importance of human resources in developing and maintaining competitive advantage.[76]

A LOOK BACK

HP'S WAY FORWARD

As you have seen, any business strategy has a number of implications for the workforce, and the HR function plays a critical role in implementing the strategy through providing systems and solutions to these people issues. As the opening case illustrated, HP's strategy is being driven by a number of dynamics in the industry. As margins for PCs decrease, HP has to find higher margin businesses to enter. However, entry often requires the acquisition of an existing company that already has the human capital and organizational capabilities to compete in that market. Thus, HP's acquisitions over the past few years make sense strategically, but will create a host of problems. Merging cultures, policies, compensation systems, information systems, business processes, etc. is not easy with two companies, but HP will be doing it with three. In addition, one can expect HP to have to eliminate some redundant jobs resulting in layoffs. With all the changes required and the uncertainty arising about the future, one can expect that employee morale issues will soon surface. So, while the formulation of this strategy makes sense on paper, the effectiveness of the strategy will depend largely on how well it is implemented. In other words, many argued that HP's decision to acquire

Compaq was not the right one. Now, how the people react may largely determine whether or not this decision about the PC market is the right one.

Questions

1. What do you think of HP's decision to get rid of its PC business?
2. What do you think are the major human resource issues facing HP?
3. What are the major human resource implications of HP's new strategy?

SOURCE: Y. Kane and N. Wingfield, "Pioneering Firm Bows to "Post-PC World," *The Wall Street Journal*, www.online.wsj.com, accessed August 19, 2011.

 Please see the Video that corresponds to this chapter at www.mhhe.com/noe8e.

SUMMARY

A strategic approach to human resource management seeks to proactively provide a competitive advantage through the company's most important asset: its human resources. While human resources are the most important asset, they are also usually the single largest controllable cost within the firm's business model. The HRM function needs to be integrally involved in the formulation of strategy to identify the people-related business issues the company faces. Once the strategy has been determined, HRM has a profound impact on the implementation of the plan by developing and aligning HRM practices that ensure that the company has motivated employees with the necessary skills. Finally, the emerging strategic role of the HRM function requires that HR professionals in the future develop business, professional–technical, change management, and integration competencies. As you will see more clearly in later chapters, this strategic approach requires more than simply developing a valid selection procedure or state-of-the-art performance management systems. Only through these competencies can the HR professional take a strategic approach to human resource management.

KEY TERMS

Strategic human resource management (SHRM), 75
Strategy formulation, 75
Strategy implementation, 75
Goals, 79
External analysis, 80
Internal analysis, 80

Strategic choice, 80
Job analysis, 86
Job design, 86
Recruitment, 87
Selection, 87
Training, 88
Development, 88

Performance management, 88
Role behaviors, 91
External growth strategy, 92
Concentration strategy, 93
Internal growth strategy, 93
Downsizing, 94

DISCUSSION QUESTIONS

1. Pick one of your university's major sports teams (like football or basketball). How would you characterize that team's generic strategy? How does the composition of the team members (in terms of size, speed, ability, and so on) relate to that strategy? What are the strengths and weaknesses of the team? How do they dictate the team's generic strategy and its approach to a particular game?

2. Do you think that it is easier to tie human resources to the strategic management process in large or in small organizations? Why?

3. Consider one of the organizations you have been affiliated with. What are some examples of human resource practices that were consistent with that organization's strategy? What are examples of practices that were inconsistent with its strategy?

4. How can strategic management within the HRM department ensure that HRM plays an effective role in the company's strategic management process?

5. What types of specific skills (such as knowledge of financial accounting methods) do you think HR professionals will need to have the business, professional-technical, change management, and integrative competencies necessary in the future? Where can you develop each of these skills?

6. What are some of the key environmental variables that you see changing in the business world today? What impact will those changes have on the HRM function in organizations?

SELF-ASSESSMENT EXERCISE

Think of a company you have worked for, or find an annual report for a company you are interested in working for. (Many companies post their annual reports online at their website.) Then answer the following questions.

Questions

1. How has the company been affected by the trends discussed in this chapter?

2. Does the company use the HR practices recommended in this chapter?

3. What else should the company do to deal with the challenges posed by the trends discussed in this chapter?

EXERCISING STRATEGY: STRATEGY AND HRM AT DELTA AIRLINES

In 1994 top executives at Delta Air Lines faced a crucial strategic decision. Delta, which had established an unrivaled reputation within the industry for having highly committed employees who delivered the highest quality customer service, had lost more than $10 per share for two straight years. A large portion of its financial trouble was due to the $491 million acquisition of Pan Am in 1991, which was followed by the Gulf War (driving up fuel costs) and the early 1990s recession (causing people to fly less). Its cost per available seat mile (the cost to fly one passenger one mile) was 9.26 cents, among the highest in the industry. In addition, it was threatened by new discount competitors with significantly lower costs—in particular, Valujet, which flew out of Delta's Atlanta hub. How could Delta survive and thrive in such an environment? Determining the strategy for doing so was the top executives' challenge.

Chairman and chief executive officer Ron Allen embarked upon the "Leadership 7.5" strategy, whose goal was to reduce the cost per available seat mile to 7.5 cents, comparable with Southwest Airlines. Implementing this strategy required a significant downsizing over the following three years, trimming 11,458 people from its 69,555-employee workforce (the latter number representing an 8% reduction from two years earlier). Many experienced customer service representatives were laid off and replaced with lower paid, inexperienced, part-time workers. Cleaning service of planes as well as baggage handling were outsourced, resulting in layoffs of long-term Delta employees. The numbers of maintenance workers and flight attendants were reduced substantially.

The results of the strategy were mixed as financial performance improved but operational performance plummeted. Since it began its cost cutting, its stock price more than doubled in just over two years and its debt was upgraded. On the other hand, customer complaints about dirty airplanes rose from 219 in 1993 to 358 in 1994 and 634 in 1995. On-time performance was so bad that passengers joked that Delta stands for "Doesn't Ever Leave The Airport." Delta slipped from fourth to seventh among the top 10 carriers in baggage handling. Employee morale hit an all-time low, and unions were beginning to make headway toward organizing some of Delta's employee groups. In 1996 CEO Allen was quoted as saying, "This has tested our people. There have been some morale problems. But so be it. You go back to the question of survival, and it makes the decision very easy."

Shortly after, employees began donning cynical "so be it" buttons. Delta's board saw union organizers stirring blue-collar discontent, employee morale destroyed, the customer service reputation in near shambles, and senior managers exiting the company in droves. Less than one year later, Allen was fired despite Delta's financial turnaround. His firing was "not because the company was going broke, but because its spirit was broken."

Delta's Leadership 7.5 strategy destroyed the firm's core competence of a highly experienced, highly skilled, and highly committed workforce that delivered the highest quality customer service in the industry. HRM might have affected the strategy by pointing out the negative impact that this strategy would have on the firm. Given the strategy and competitive environment, Delta might have sought to implement the cost cutting differently to reduce the cost structure but preserve its source of differentiation.

The present state of Delta provides further support to these conclusions. With the family atmosphere dissolved and the bond between management and rank-and-file employees broken, employees have begun to seek other ways to gain voice and security. By fall 2001 Delta had two union organizing drives under way with both the flight attendants and the mechanics. In addition, labor costs have been driven up as a result of the union activity. The pilots signed a lucrative five-year contract that will place them at the highest pay in the industry. In an effort to head off the organizing drive, the mechanics were recently given raises to similarly put them at the industry top. Now the flight attendants are seeking industry-leading pay regardless of, but certainly encouraged by, the union drive.[77]

The Delta Air Lines story provides a perfect example of the perils that can await firms that fail to adequately address human resource issues in the formulation and implementation of strategy.

Questions

1. How does the experience of Delta Air Lines illustrate the interdependence between strategic decisions of "how to compete" and "with what to compete"? Consider this with regard to both strategy formulation and strategy implementation.

2. If you were in charge of HRM for Delta Air Lines now, what would be your major priorities?

SOURCES: M. Brannigan and E. De Lisser, "Cost Cutting at Delta Raises the Stock Price but Lowers the Service," *The Wall Street Journal*, June 20, 1996, pp. A1, A8; M. Brannigan and J. White, "So Be It: Why Delta Air Lines Decided It Was Time for CEO to Take Off," *The Wall Street Journal*, May 30, 1997, p. A1.

● MANAGING PEOPLE

Is Dell Too Big for Michael Dell?

He's back in charge—and he may have the toughest job in the computer business. Welcome back, Michael. Don't get too comfortable.

By returning to the top job at Dell Inc., replacing departing chief executive Kevin Rollins, founder Michael S. Dell takes on perhaps the toughest job in the computer industry. Since mid-2005 the PC maker has battled problems with customer service, quality, and the effectiveness of its direct-sales model. Lately, rivals Hewlett-Packard Co. and Apple Inc. have been gaining in sales and market share. On January 31, the day Rollins's departure was announced, the Round Rock (Texas) company disclosed that its fourth-quarter earnings and sales would fall short of analyst estimates. It's also under scrutiny by the Securities & Exchange Commission and a U.S. attorney for accounting irregularities.

As recently as last November, Dell insisted to *BusinessWeek* that Rollins's job was safe. Now, in an interview, he insists the decision to push Rollins out started with him. "I recommended to our board that I become the CEO," Dell says. For years, Dell and Rollins were held up as a prime example of the company's "two-in-a-box" management structure, in which two leaders worked together in lockstep. When Rollins was president, Michael Dell was CEO; when Rollins was promoted to CEO in 2004, Michael remained chairman. But financial performance has been deteriorating for a while now, and Michael Dell apparently ran out of patience in light of the latest disappointment. "People are looking forward to a change," said an analyst at one of Dell's largest institutional shareholders. Indeed, the company's share price jumped 3.6% in the couple of hours after the shift was announced.

But does Michael Dell have what it takes to turn the company around? It's been years since he shouldered day-to-day operational responsibility on his own. Since the early 1990s, Dell has always had a strong No. 2; back then, the company had less than $3 billion in yearly sales. Today it is a $60 billion company. But Dell says he has a clear plan. He believes the company's supply chain and manufacturing can be improved. "I think you're going to see a more streamlined organization, with a much clearer strategy."

But none of the paths to improve performance will be easy. Dell doesn't have the innovation DNA of an Apple or even an HP, should it want to overhaul its utilitarian products and services. Any effort to crank up R&D would crimp margins. Trying to win over more consumers, the fastest-growing part of the market, may well require a move away from its direct-sales model into retail. That could prove costly as well. Dell himself says he doesn't anticipate leaving the direct-sales model behind: "It's a significant strength of the company." Nor does a big acquisition seem to be an option, given that Dell has never done one in the past.

Slots to fill But standing in place also looks hazardous, since Dell may now be slipping in its core corporate business, too. According to a January 30 study done by Goldman, Sachs & Co., Dell is losing share in business spending for PCs. (Hewlett-Packard is also losing share of spending, while Lenovo and Apple are gaining.) "Dell's troubles seem to be bleeding into its corporate business, which, up until now, had been a stronghold," the report said. Dell has also lost the top spot in the worldwide PC market-share rankings. In the fourth quarter, Hewlett-Packard's worldwide market share grew to 18.1%, while Dell's share dropped to 14.7%, according to market researcher IDC.

Dell also has several slots to fill in the executive suite; Rollins is only the latest departure among key managers. But for the first time in years, the tough choices will be solely in the lap of the man who started the company in his University of Texas dorm room back in 1984. "I'm not hiring a COO or a CEO," Dell says, "I'm going to be the CEO for the next several years." He adds: "We're going to fix this business."

Questions

1. How does the case describe Dell's transformed strategy over the years in terms of where to compete, how to compete, and with what to compete?
2. What are the major people issues that exist as Michael Dell retakes the reins at Dell?
3. How would HR help in addressing the issues that Dell faces?

SOURCE: From L. Lee and P. Burrows, "Is Dell Too Big for Michael Dell?" *BusinessWeek*, April 4, 2007. Used with permission of Bloomberg L. P. Copyright © 2007. All rights reserved.

TWITTER FOCUS: RADIO FLYER ROLLS FORWARD

Using Twitter, continue the conversation about strategic HR management by reading the Radio Flyer case at www .mhhe.com/noe8e.

Famous for its little red wagons, Radio Flyer had a difficult time in the mid-2000s. The company spent hundreds of thousands of dollars on a product idea that failed miserably, and it made a tough decision to shift manufacturing jobs to China as a way of keeping costs down. During this difficult time, senior management never lost

track of what made the company successful: its employees. Radio Flyer focused its corporate energies on building morale among its global employees, and the company has never looked back.

Engage with your classmates and instructor via Twitter to chat about Radio Flyer using the case questions posted on the Noe website. Don't have a Twitter account yet? See the instructions for getting started on the Online Learning Center.

NOTES

1. J. Barney, "Firm Resources and Sustained Competitive Advantage," *Journal of Management* 17 (1991), pp. 99–120.
2. L. Dyer, "Strategic Human Resource Management and Planning," in *Research in Personnel and Human Resources Management*, ed. K. Rowland and G. Ferris (Greenwich, CT: JAI Press, 1985), pp. 1–30.
3. P. Ingrassia, "GM's Plan: Subsidize Our 48-Year-Old Retirees," *Wall Street Journal*, February 19, 2009, http://online.wsj.com/article/SB123500874299418721.html.
4. S. Terlep, and N. King, "Bondholders say GM's Plan Fails to Tackle Issues," *The Wall Street Journal*, February 19, 2009, http://online.wsj.com/article/SB123500467245718075.html?mod=testMod.
5. J. Quinn, *Strategies for Change: Logical Incrementalism* (Homewood, IL: Richard D. Irwin, 1980).
6. M. Porter, *Competitive Strategy: Techniques for Analyzing Industries and Competitors* (New York: Free Press, 1980).
7. R. Miles and C. Snow, *Organizational Strategy, Structure, and Process* (New York: McGraw-Hill, 1978).
8. P. Wright and G. McMahan, "Theoretical Perspectives for Strategic Human Resource Management," *Journal of Management* 18 (1992), pp. 295–320.
9. D. Guest, "Human Resource Management, Corporate Performance and Employee Well-Being: Building the Worker into HRM," *Journal of Industrial Relations* 44 (2002), pp. 335–58; B. Becker, M. Huselid, P. Pinckus, and M. Spratt, "HR as a Source of Shareholder Value: Research and Recommendations," *Human Resource Management* 36 (1997), pp. 39–47.
10. P. Boxall and J. Purcell, *Strategy and Human Resource Management* (Basingstoke, Hants, U.K.: Palgrave MacMillan, 2003).
11. F. Biddle and J. Helyar, "Behind Boeing's Woes: Chunky Assembly Line, Price War with Airbus," *The Wall Street Journal*, April 24, 1998, pp. A1, A16.
12. K. Martell and S. Carroll, "How Strategic Is HRM?" *Human Resource Management* 34 (1995), pp. 253–67.
13. K. Golden and V. Ramanujam, "Between a Dream and a Nightmare: On the Integration of the Human Resource Function and the Strategic Business Planning Process," *Human Resource Management* 24 (1985), pp. 429–51.
14. P. Wright, B. Dunford, and S. Snell, "Contributions of the Resource-Based View of the Firm to the Field of Strategic HRM: Convergence of Two Fields," *Journal of Management* 27 (2001), pp. 701–21.
15. J. Purcell, N. Kinnie, S. Hutchinson, B. Rayton, and J. Swart, *Understanding the People and Performance Link: Unlocking the Black Box* (London: CIPD, 2003).
16. P. M. Wright, T. Gardner, and L. Moynihan, "The Impact of Human Resource Practices on Business Unit Operating and Financial Performance," *Human Resource Management Journal* 13, no. 3 (2003), pp. 21–36.
17. C. Hill and G. Jones, *Strategic Management Theory: An Integrated Approach* (Boston: Houghton Mifflin, 1989).
18. W. Johnston and A. Packer, *Workforce 2000: Work and Workers for the Twenty-First Century* (Indianapolis, IN: Hudson Institute, 1987).

19. "Labor Letter," *The Wall Street Journal*, December 15, 1992, p. A1.

20. P. Wright, G. McMahan, and A. McWilliams, "Human Resources and Sustained Competitive Advantage: A Resource-Based Perspective," *International Journal of Human Resource Management* 5 (1994), pp. 301–26.

21. P. Buller, "Successful Partnerships: HR and Strategic Planning at Eight Top Firms," *Organizational Dynamics* 17 (1988), pp. 27–42.

22. M. Hitt, R. Hoskisson, and J. Harrison, "Strategic Competitiveness in the 1990s: Challenges and Opportunities for U.S. Executives," *The Executive* 5 (May 1991), pp. 7–22.

23. P. Wright, G. McMahan, B. McCormick, and S. Sherman, "Strategy, Core Competence, and HR Involvement as Determinants of HR Effectiveness and Refinery Performance." Paper presented at the 1996 International Federation of Scholarly Associations in Management, Paris, France.

24. N. Bennett, D. Ketchen, and E. Schultz, "Antecedents and Consequences of Human Resource Integration with Strategic Decision Making." Paper presented at the 1995 Academy of Management Meeting, Vancouver, BC, Canada.

25. Golden and Ramanujam, "Between a Dream and a Nightmare."

26. J. Galbraith and R. Kazanjian, *Strategy Implementation: Structure, Systems, and Process* (St. Paul, MN: West, 1986).

27. B. Schneider and A. Konz, "Strategic Job Analysis," *Human Resource Management* 27 (1989), pp. 51–64.

28. P. Wright and S. Snell, "Toward an Integrative View of Strategic Human Resource Management," *Human Resource Management Review* 1 (1991), pp. 203–25.

29. S. Snell, "Control Theory in Strategic Human Resource Management: The Mediating Effect of Administrative Information," *Academy of Management Journal* 35 (1992), pp. 292–327.

30. R. Schuler, "Personnel and Human Resource Management Choices and Organizational Strategy," in *Readings in Personnel and Human Resource Management*, 3rd ed., ed. R. Schuler, S. Youngblood, and V. Huber (St. Paul, MN: West, 1988).

31. J. Dean and S. Snell, "Integrated Manufacturing and Job Design: Moderating Effects of Organizational Inertia," *Academy of Management Journal* 34 (1991), pp. 776–804.

32. E. Lawler, *The Ultimate Advantage: Creating the High Involvement Organization* (San Francisco: Jossey-Bass, 1992).

33. J. Olian and S. Rynes, "Organizational Staffing: Integrating Practice with Strategy," *Industrial Relations* 23 (1984), pp. 170–83.

34. G. Smith, "Quality: Small and Midsize Companies Seize the Challenge—Not a Moment Too Soon," *BusinessWeek*, November 30, 1992, pp. 66–75.

35. J. Kerr and E. Jackofsky, "Aligning Managers with Strategies: Management Development versus Selection," *Strategic Management Journal* 10 (1989), pp. 157–70.

36. J. Kerr, "Strategic Control through Performance Appraisal and Rewards," *Human Resource Planning* 11 (1988), pp. 215–23.

37. Snell, "Control Theory in Strategic Human Resource Management."

38. B. Gerhart and G. Milkovich, "Employee Compensation: Research and Practice," in *Handbook of Industrial and Organizational Psychology*, 2nd ed., ed. M. Dunnette and L. Hough (Palo Alto, CA: Consulting Psychologists Press, 1992), pp. 481–569.

39. D. Balkin and L. Gomez-Mejia, "Toward a Contingency Theory of Compensation Strategy," *Strategic Management Journal* 8 (1987), pp. 169–82.

40. A. Taylor, "U.S. Cars Come Back," *Fortune*, November 16, 1992, pp. 52, 85.

41. S. Cronshaw and R. Alexander, "One Answer to the Demand for Accountability: Selection Utility as an Investment Decision," *Organizational Behavior and Human Decision Processes* 35 (1986), pp. 102–18.

42. P. MacDuffie, "Human Resource Bundles and Manufacturing Performance: Organizational Logic and Flexible Production Systems in the World Auto Industry," *Industrial and Labor Relations Review* 48 (1995), pp. 197–221; P. McGraw, "A Hard Drive to the Top," *U.S. News & World Report* 118 (1995), pp. 43–44.

43. M. Huselid, "The Impact of Human Resource Management Practices on Turnover, Productivity, and Corporate Financial Performance," *Academy of Management Journal* 38 (1995), pp. 635–72.

44. B. Fulmer, B. Gerhart, and K. Scott, "Are the 100 Best Better? An Empirical Investigation of the Relationship between Being a 'Great Place to Work' and Firm Performance," *Personnel Psychology* 56 (2003), pp. 965–93.

45. J. E. Delery and D. H. Doty, "Modes of Theorizing in Strategic Human Resource Management: Tests of Universalistic, Contingency and Configurational Performance Predictions," *Academy of Management Journal* 39 (1996), pp. 802–83; D. Guest, J. Michie, N. Conway, and M. Sheehan, "Human Resource Management and Corporate Performance in the UK," *British Journal of Industrial Relations* 41 (2003), pp. 291–314; J. Guthrie, "High Involvement Work Practices, Turnover, and Productivity: Evidence from New Zealand," *Academy of Management Journal* 44 (2001), pp. 180–192; J. Harter, F. Schmidt, and T. Hayes, "Business-Unit-Level Relationship between Employee Satisfaction, Employee Engagement, and Business Outcomes: A Meta-analysis," *Journal of Applied Psychology* 87 (2002), pp. 268–79; Watson Wyatt, Worldwide, "Human Capital Index®: Human Capital as a Lead Indicator of Shareholder Value" (2002).

46. M. Bhattacharya, D. Gibson, and H. Doty, "The Effects of Flexibility in Employee Skills, Employee Behaviors, and Human Resource Practices on Firm Performance," *Journal of Management* 31 (2005), pp. 622–40.

47. D. Guest, J. Michie, N. Conway, and M. Sheehan, "Human Resource Management and Corporate Performance in the UK," *British Journal of Industrial Relations* 41 (2003), pp. 291–314; P. Wright, T. Gardner, L. Moynihan, and M. Allen, "The HR–Performance Relationship: Examining Causal Direction," *Personnel Psychology* 58 (2005), pp. 409–76.

48. P. Wright, *No Strategy: Adaptive to the Age of Globalization* (Arlington, VA: SHRM Foundation, 2008).

49. M. Porter, *Competitive Advantage* (New York: Free Press, 1985).

50. C. Lawton, "How HP Reclaimed Its PC Lead over Dell," June 2007; "Can Dell's Turnaround Strategy Keep HP at Bay?" September 2007, *Knowledge@Wharton*, http://knowledge.wharton .upenn.edu/article.cfm?articleid=1799.

51. R. Schuler and S. Jackson, "Linking Competitive Strategies with Human Resource Management Practices," *Academy of Management Executive* 1 (1987), pp. 207–19.

52. R. Miles and C. Snow, "Designing Strategic Human Resource Management Systems," *Organizational Dynamics* 13, no. 1 (1984), pp. 36–52.

53. A. Thompson and A. Strickland, *Strategy Formulation and Implementation: Tasks of the General Manager*, 3rd ed. (Plano, TX: BPI, 1986).

54. J. Schmidt, *Making Mergers Work: The Strategic Importance of People* (Arlington, VA: SHRM Foundation, 2003).

55. G. Fairclough, "Business Bulletin," *The Wall Street Journal*, March 5, 1998, p. A1.

56. P. Sebastian, "Business Bulletin," *The Wall Street Journal*, October 2, 1997, p. A1.

57. www.bls.gov/news.release/mslo.nro.gov.

58. S. Pearlstein, "Corporate Cutback Yet to Pay Off," *Washington Post*, January 4, 1994, p. B6.

59. K. Cameron, "Guest Editor's Note: Investigating Organizational Downsizing—Fundamental Issues," *Human Resource Management* 33 (1994), pp. 183–88.

60. W. Cascio, *Responsible Restructuring: Creative and Profitable Alternatives to Layoffs* (San Francisco: Berrett-Koehler, 2002).

61. N. Templin, "UAW to Unveil Pact on Slashing GM's Payroll," *The Wall Street Journal*, December 15, 1992, p. A3.

62. J. Lopez, "Managing: Early-Retirement Offers Lead to Renewed Hiring," *The Wall Street Journal*, January 26, 1993, p. B1.

63. A. Church, "Organizational Downsizing: What Is the Role of the Practitioner?" *Industrial–Organizational Psychologist* 33, no. 1 (1995), pp. 63–74.

64. N. Templin, "A Decisive Response to Crisis Brought Ford Enhanced Productivity," *The Wall Street Journal*, December 15, 1992, p. A1.

65. Quinn, *Strategies for Change*.

66. H. Schultz and D. Yang, *Pour Your Heart Into It* (New York: Hyperion, 1987).

67. R. Pascale, "Perspectives on Strategy: The Real Story behind Honda's Success," *California Management Review* 26 (1984), pp. 47–72.

68. Templin, "A Decisive Response to Crisis."

69. P. Wright and S. Snell, "Toward a Unifying Framework for Exploring Fit and Flexibility in Strategic Human Resource Management," *Academy of Management Review* 23, no. 4 (1998), pp. 756–72.

70. H. Behar, *It's Not about the Coffee: Lessons for Putting People First from a Life at Starbucks* (New York, NY: Penguin Group, 2007).

71. T. Stewart, "Brace for Japan's Hot New Strategy," *Fortune*, September 21, 1992, pp. 62–76.

72. B. Dunford, P. Wright, and S. Snell, "Contributions of the Resource-Based View of the Firm to the Field of Strategic HRM: Convergence of Two Fields," *Journal of Management* 27 (2001), pp. 701–21.

73. C. Snow and S. Snell, *Staffing as Strategy*, vol. 4 of *Personnel Selection* (San Francisco: Jossey-Bass, 1992).

74. T. Batten, "Education Key to Prosperity—Report," *Houston Chronicle*, September 7, 1992, p. 1B.

75. Schultz and Yang, *Pour Your Heart Into It*.

76. G. McMahan, University of Texas at Arlington, personal communications.

77. M. Brannigan, "Delta Lifts Mechanics' Pay to Top of Industry Amid Push by Union," *The Wall Street Journal Interactive*, August 16, 2001; M. Adams, "Delta May See Second Big Union," *USA Today*, August 27, 2001, p. 1B.

CHAPTER

3

The Legal Environment: Equal Employment Opportunity and Safety

LO LEARNING OBJECTIVES

After reading this chapter, you should be able to:

LO 3-1 Identify the three branches of government and the role each plays in influencing the legal environment of human resource management. *page 108*

LO 3-2 List the major federal laws that require equal employment opportunity and the protections provided by each of these laws. *page 110*

LO 3-3 Discuss the roles, responsibilities, and requirements of the federal agencies responsible for enforcing equal employment opportunity laws. *page 118*

LO 3-4 Identify the three theories of discrimination under Title VII of the Civil Rights Act and apply these theories to different discrimination situations. *page 121*

LO 3-5 Discuss the legal issues involved with preferential treatment programs. *page 132*

LO 3-6 Identify behavior that constitutes sexual harassment, and list things that an organization can do to eliminate or minimize it. *page 133*

LO 3-7 Identify the major provisions of the Occupational Safety and Health Act (1970) and the rights of employees that are guaranteed by this act. *page 139*

ENTER THE WORLD OF BUSINESS

Wal-Mart's Legal Problems

One of the largest discrimination lawsuits in the history of U.S. employment law is currently working its way through the court system.

Wal-Mart has become one of the largest, most admired, and ironically, most detested companies in the world. Its "Always Low Prices, Always" motto and business model have enabled it to become the world's largest private employer with retail outlets all over the world. This success has led to its frequent inclusion on *Fortune*'s Most Admired Companies list. However, its positive reputation has taken serious blows over the past few years, at least in part because of its practices for managing people.

Union leaders criticize Wal-Mart for its low pay and modest health insurance. Wal-Mart defends itself by noting that it pays competitively with similar organizations. However, what undeniably has hurt Wal-Mart's image is the large number of discrimination suits that it has faced over the past 10 years. For instance, it recently settled a class-action race discrimination suit regarding its hiring of drivers, agreeing to a $17.5 million settlement while denying that it had engaged in any pattern or practice of discrimination. The most important one is a class-action suit brought on behalf of 2 million former female Wal-Mart employees. The suit, known as *Dukes v. Wal-Mart,* alleges that Wal-Mart discouraged the promotion of women store employees to managerial positions and that it paid them less than men across all jobs. The plaintiff's lawyers argued that women made up 63.4% of Wal-Mart's nonmanagerial workers, but only 33.6% of the store's salaried managers. They also suggest that the 33.6% is far below the 56.5% of female managers at Wal-Mart's top 20 competitors.

An earlier analysis of liability in the lawsuit by the Goldman Sachs Group Inc., based on a potential plaintiff group of 1.6 million workers, estimated potential damages at $1.5 billion to $3.5 billion if Wal-Mart loses. Punitive damages potentially push the figure to a range of $13.5 billion to $31.5 billion, the analysis said. In March 2011, the Supreme Court heard arguments regarding whether or not the plaintiffs can file as a class-action suit representing all women who had worked at Wal-Mart. Wal-Mart contends that the alleged victims, who worked in 170 job classifications across 3,400 stores do not have enough in common to qualify as a single class action. Did Wal-Mart really discriminate against 2 million of its former employees, and if so, how would you know?

SOURCES: Bloomberg News, "Wal-Mart to Settle Bias Lawsuit," *Los Angeles Times*, February 21, 2009, p. C3; R. Parloff and S. Kaufman, "The War Over Unconscious Bias," *Fortune*, October 15, 2007, p. 90.

Introduction

In the opening chapter, we discussed the environment of the HRM function, and we noted that several environmental factors affect an organization's HRM function. One is the legal environment, particularly the laws affecting the management of people. As the troubles at Wal-Mart indicate, legal issues can cause serious problems for a company's success and survival. In this chapter, we first present an overview of the U.S. legal system, noting the different legislative bodies, regulatory agencies, and judicial bodies that determine the legality of certain HRM practices. We then discuss the major laws and executive orders that govern these practices.

One point to make clear at the outset is that managers often want a list of "dos and don'ts" that will keep them out of legal trouble. They rely on rules such as "Don't ever ask a female applicant if she is married" without understanding the "why" behind these rules. Clearly, certain practices are illegal or inadvisable, and this chapter will provide some valuable tips for avoiding discrimination lawsuits. However, such lists are not compatible with a strategic approach to HRM and are certainly not the route to developing a competitive advantage. They are simply mechanical reactions to the situations. Our goal is to provide an understanding of how the legislative, regulatory, and judicial systems work to define equal employment opportunity law. Armed with this understanding, a manager is better prepared to manage people within the limits imposed by the legal system. Doing so effectively is a source of competitive advantage. Doing so ineffectively results in competitive disadvantage. Rather than viewing the legal system as a constraint, firms that embrace the concept of diversity can often find that they are able to leverage the differences among people as a tremendous competitive tool.

The Legal System in the United States

LO 3-1
Identify the three branches of government and the role each plays in influencing the legal environment of human resource management.

The foundation for the U.S. legal system is set forth in the U.S. Constitution, which affects HRM in two ways. First, it delineates a citizen's constitutional rights, on which the government cannot impinge.[1] Most individuals are aware of the Bill of Rights, the first 10 amendments to the Constitution; but other amendments, such as the Fourteenth Amendment, also influence HRM practices. The Fourteenth Amendment, called the equal protection clause, states that all individuals are entitled to equal protection under the law.

Second, the Constitution established three major governing bodies: the legislative, executive, and judicial branches. The Constitution explicitly defines the roles and responsibilities of each of these branches. Each branch has its own areas of authority, but these areas have often overlapped, and the borders between the branches are often blurred.

LEGISLATIVE BRANCH

The legislative branch of the federal government consists of the House of Representatives and the Senate. These bodies develop laws that govern many HRM activities. Most of the laws stem from a perceived societal need. For example, during the civil rights movement of the early 1960s, the legislative branch moved to ensure that various minority groups received equal opportunities in many areas of life. One of these areas was employment, and thus Congress enacted Title VII of the Civil Rights Act.

Similar perceived societal needs have brought about labor laws such as the Occupational Safety and Health Act, the Employee Retirement Income Security Act, the Age Discrimination in Employment Act, and, more recently, the Americans with Disabilities Act of 1990 and the Civil Rights Act of 1991.

EXECUTIVE BRANCH

The executive branch consists of the president of the United States and the many regulatory agencies the president oversees. Although the legislative branch passes the laws, the executive branch affects these laws in many ways. First, the president can propose bills to Congress that, if passed, would become laws. Second, the president has the power to veto any law passed by Congress, thus ensuring that few laws are passed without presidential approval—which allows the president to influence how laws are written.

Third, the regulatory agencies, under the authority of the president, have responsibility for enforcing the laws. Thus, a president can influence what types of violations are pursued. For example, many laws affecting employment discrimination are enforced by the Equal Employment Opportunity Commission under the Department of Justice. During President Jimmy Carter's administration, the Department of Justice brought a lawsuit against Birmingham, Alabama's, fire department for not having enough black firefighters. This suit resulted in a consent decree that required blacks to receive preferential treatment in hiring and promotion decisions. Two years later, during Ronald Reagan's administration, the Department of Justice sided with white firefighters in a lawsuit against the city of Birmingham, alleging that the preferential treatment required by the consent decree discriminated against white firefighters.[2]

Fourth, the president can issue executive orders, which sometimes regulate the activities of organizations that have contracts with the federal government. For example, Executive Order 11246, signed by President Lyndon Johnson, required all federal contractors and subcontractors to engage in affirmative action programs designed to hire and promote women and minorities within their organizations. Fifth, the president can influence the Supreme Court to interpret laws in certain ways. When particularly sensitive cases come before the Court, the attorney general, representing the executive branch, argues for certain preferred outcomes. For example, one court case involved a white female schoolteacher who was laid off from her job in favor of retaining a black schoolteacher with equal seniority and performance with the reason given as "diversity." The white woman filed a lawsuit in federal court and the (first) Bush administration filed a brief on her behalf, arguing that diversity was not a legitimate reason to use race in decision making. She won in federal court, and the school district appealed. The Clinton administration, having been elected in the meantime, filed a brief on behalf of the school district, arguing that diversity was a legitimate defense.

Finally, the president appoints all the judges in the federal judicial system, subject to approval from the legislative branch. This affects the interpretation of many laws.

JUDICIAL BRANCH

The judicial branch consists of the federal court system, which is made up of three levels. The first level consists of the U.S. District Courts and quasi-judicial administrative agencies. The district courts hear cases involving alleged violations of federal laws. The quasi-judicial agencies, such as the National Labor Relations Board (or NLRB, which is actually an arm of the executive branch, but serves a judicial function), hear cases regarding their particular jurisdictions (in the NLRB's case, disputes between unions and management). If neither party to a suit is satisfied with the decision of the court at this level, the parties can appeal the decision to the U.S. Courts of Appeals. These courts were originally set up to ease the Supreme Court's caseload, so appeals generally go from the federal trial level to one of the 13 appellate courts before they can be heard by the highest level, the Supreme Court. The Supreme Court must grant certiorari before hearing an appealed case. However, this is not usually granted unless two appellate courts have come to differing decisions on the same point of law or if the case deals with an important interpretation of constitutional law.

The Supreme Court serves as the court of final appeal. Decisions made by the Supreme Court are binding; they can be overturned only through legislation. For example, Congress, dissatisfied with the Supreme Court's decisions in certain cases such as *Wards Cove Packing v. Atonio*, overturned those decisions through the Civil Rights Act of 1991.[3]

Having described the legal system that affects the management of HR, we now explore some laws that regulate HRM activities, particularly equal employment opportunity laws. We first discuss the major laws that mandate equal employment opportunity in the United States. Then we examine the agencies involved in enforcing these laws. This leads us into an examination of the four theories of discrimination, with a discussion of some relevant court cases. Finally, we explore some equal employment opportunity issues facing today's managers.

The right to privacy is a well-accepted right within the judicial system in the United States, but as the "Competing through Globalization" box illustrates, this is not necessarily true in India and is causing difficulties for companies.

Equal Employment Opportunity

LO 3-2
List the major federal laws that require equal employment opportunity and the protections provided by each of these laws.

Equal employment opportunity (EEO) refers to the government's attempt to ensure that all individuals have an equal chance for employment, regardless of race, color, religion, sex, age, disability, or national origin. To accomplish this, the federal government has used constitutional amendments, legislation, and executive orders, as well as the court decisions that interpret these laws. (However, equal employment laws are not the same in all countries.) The major EEO laws we discuss are summarized in Table 3.1.

Equal Employment Opportunity (EEO)
The government's attempt to ensure that all individuals have an equal opportunity for employment, regardless of race, color, religion, sex, age, disability, or national origin.

CONSTITUTIONAL AMENDMENTS

Thirteenth Amendment

The Thirteenth Amendment of the Constitution abolished slavery in the United States. Though one might be hard-pressed to cite an example of race-based slavery in the United States today, the Thirteenth Amendment has been applied in cases where the discrimination involved the "badges" (symbols) and "incidents" of slavery.

Fourteenth Amendment

The Fourteenth Amendment forbids the states from taking life, liberty, or property without due process of law and prevents the states from denying equal protection of the laws. Passed immediately after the Civil War, this amendment originally applied

India's Lack of Privacy Laws Presents a Challenge to BlackBerrys

As mentioned in the text, a country's regulatory environment can influence how attractive that country is for multinational companies to do business there. As a case in point, Research in Motion (RIM), the maker of the BlackBerry, faces a dilemma for sales in India. Indian security agencies demand increased power to monitor e-mail and other data traffic. India's Home Ministry, that oversees domestic security, seeks the ability to intercept any communication on any Indian network in real-time. This would include BlackBerry's highly secure corporate e-mail service, which raises a number of privacy concerns for Black-Berry and its customers.

Robert Crow, VP of industry and government relations for RIM, says that such a broad requirement suggests the government believes virtually no communications are off-limits. "You connect those dots and you're saying 'Holy Smokes.' This claim is made in an environment where we don't really have any privacy- or data-protection laws—and where we have a pretty poor administrative record of keeping similar things like wiretaps secure."

The Indian government has stated that it seeks to ensure that terrorists and other criminals cannot use new technologies to elude government surveillance. However, in the absence of well-defined regulations on data protection and privacy, such efforts make multinational companies anxious about doing business in India. As Mr. Crow states, "It will be one of those factors that people talk about in the Indian business environment—not one that will be seen in India's favor in international comparison."

SOURCE: From A. Sharma, "RIM Hits India's Demands to Monitor Email," *Wall Street Journal,* March 14, 2011, p. B3. Reproduced with permission of Dow Jones & Company, Inc. via Copyright Clearance Center.

only to discrimination against blacks. It was soon broadened to protect other groups such as aliens and Asian-Americans, and more recently it has been applied to the protection of whites in allegations of reverse discrimination. In *Bakke v. California Board of Regents*, Alan Bakke alleged that he had been discriminated against in the selection of entrants to the University of California at Davis medical school.[4] The university had set aside 16 of the available 100 places for "disadvantaged" applicants who were members of racial minority groups. Under this quota system, Bakke was able to compete for only 84 positions, whereas a minority applicant was able to compete for all 100. The court ruled in favor of Bakke, noting that this quota system had violated white individuals' right to equal protection under the law.

One important point regarding the Fourteenth Amendment is that it is applicable only to "state actions." This means that only the decisions or actions of the government or of private groups whose activities are deemed state actions can be construed as violations of the Fourteenth Amendment. Thus, one could file a claim under the Fourteenth Amendment if one were fired from a state university (a government organization) but not if one were fired by a private employer.

CONGRESSIONAL LEGISLATION

The Reconstruction Civil Rights Acts (1866 and 1871)

The Thirteenth Amendment eradicated slavery in the United States, and the Reconstruction Civil Rights Acts were attempts to further this goal. The Civil Rights Act passed in 1866 was later broken into two statutes. Section 1982 granted all persons the same property rights as white citizens. Section 1981 granted other rights, including the right to enter into and enforce contracts. Courts have interpreted Section

table 3.1

Summary of Major EEO Laws and Regulations

ACT	REQUIREMENTS	COVERS	ENFORCEMENT AGENCY
Thirteenth Amendment	Abolished slavery	All individuals	Court system
Fourteenth Amendment	Provides equal protection for all citizens and requires due process in state action	State actions (e.g., decisions of government organizations)	Court system
Civil Rights Acts (CRAs) of 1866 and 1871 (as amended)	Grants all citizens the right to make, perform, modify, and terminate contracts and enjoy all benefits, terms, and conditions of the contractual relationship	All individuals	Court system
Equal Pay Act of 1963	Requires that men and women performing equal jobs receive equal pay	Employers engaged in interstate commerce	EEOC
Title VII of CRA	Forbids discrimination based on race, color, religion, sex, or national origin	Employers with 15 or more employees working 20 or more weeks per year; labor unions; and employment agencies	EEOC
Age Discrimination in Employment Act of 1967	Prohibits discrimination in employment against individuals 40 years of age and older	Employers with 15 or more employees working 20 or more weeks per year; labor unions; employment agencies; federal government	EEOC
Rehabilitation Act of 1973	Requires affirmative action in the employment of individuals with disabilities	Government agencies; federal contractors and subcontractors with contracts greater than $2,500	OFCCP
Americans with Disabilities Act of 1990	Prohibits discrimination against individuals with disabilities	Employers with more than 15 employees	EEOC
Pregnancy Discrimination Act	Prohibits discrimination on the basis of pregnancy, childbirth, or related medical conditions	Employers with more than 15 employees	EEOC
Executive Order 11246	Requires affirmative action in hiring women and minorities	Federal contractors and subcontractors with contracts greater than $10,000	OFCCP
Civil Rights Act of 1991	Prohibits discrimination (same as Title VII)	Same as Title VII, plus applies Section 1981 to employment discrimination cases	EEOC

1981 as granting individuals the right to make and enforce employment contracts. The Civil Rights Act of 1871 granted all citizens the right to sue in federal court if they felt they had been deprived of some civil right. Although these laws might seem outdated, they are still used because they allow the plaintiff to recover both compensatory and punitive damages.

In fact, these laws came to the forefront in a Supreme Court case: *Patterson v. McClean Credit Union.*[5] The plaintiff had filed a discrimination complaint under Section 1981 for racial harassment. After being hired by McClean Credit Union, Patterson failed to receive any promotions or pay raises while she was employed there. She was also told that "blacks work slower than whites." Thus, she had grounds to prove discrimination and filed suit under Section 1981, arguing that she had been discriminated against in the making and enforcement of an employment contract. The Supreme Court ruled that this situation did not fall under Section 1981 because it did not involve the making and enforcement of contracts. However, the Civil Rights Act of 1991 amended this act to include the making, performance, modification, and termination of contracts, as well as all benefits, privileges, terms, and conditions of the contractual relationship.

The Equal Pay Act of 1963

The Equal Pay Act, an amendment to the Fair Labor Standards Act, requires that men and women in the same organization who are doing equal work must be paid equally. The act defines equal in terms of skill, effort, responsibility, and working conditions. However, the act allows for reasons why men and women performing the same job might be paid differently. If the pay differences are the result of differences in seniority, merit, quantity or quality of production, or any factor other than sex (such as shift differentials or training programs), then differences are legally allowable.

Title VII of the Civil Rights Act of 1964

This is the major legislation regulating equal employment opportunity in the United States. It was a direct result of the civil rights movement of the early 1960s, led by such individuals as Dr. Martin Luther King Jr. It was Dr. King's philosophy that people should "not be judged by the color of their skin but by the content of their character." To ensure that employment opportunities would be based on character or ability rather than on race, Congress wrote and passed Title VII, which President Lyndon Johnson signed into law.

Title VII states that it is illegal for an employer to "(1) fail or refuse to hire or discharge any individual, or otherwise discriminate against any individual with respect to his compensation, terms, conditions, or privileges of employment because of such individual's race, color, religion, sex, or national origin, or (2) to limit, segregate, or classify his employees or applicants for employment in any way that would deprive or tend to deprive any individual of employment opportunities or otherwise adversely affect his status as an employee because of such individual's race, color, religion, sex, or national origin." The act applies to organizations with 15 or more employees working 20 or more weeks a year that are involved in interstate commerce, as well as state and local governments, employment agencies, and labor organizations.

Age Discrimination in Employment Act (ADEA)

Passed in 1967 and amended in 1986, this act prohibits discrimination against employees over the age of 40. The act almost exactly mirrors Title VII in terms of its substantive provisions and the procedures to be followed in pursuing a case.[6] As with Title VII, the EEOC is responsible for enforcing this act.

The ADEA was designed to protect older employees when a firm reduces its workforce through layoffs. By targeting older employees, who tend to have higher pay, a firm can substantially cut labor costs. Recently, firms have often offered early retirement incentives, a possible violation of the act because of the focus on older employees. Early retirement incentives require employees to sign an agreement waiving their rights to sue under the ADEA. Courts have tended to uphold the use of early retirement incentives and waivers as long as the individuals were not coerced into signing the agreements, the agreements were presented in a way that the employees could understand, and the employees were given enough time to make a decision.[7]

However, age discrimination complaints make up a large percentage of the complaints filed with the Equal Employment Opportunity Commission, and the number of complaints continues to grow whenever the economy is slow. For example, as we see in Figure 3.1, the cases increased during the early 1990s when many firms were downsizing, but the number of cases decreased as the economy expanded. The number of charges increased again as the economy began slowing again in 2000 and again with the recent recession in 2008. This often stems from firms seeking to lay off older (and thus higher paid) employees when they are downsizing. These cases can be costly; most cases are settled out of court, but such settlements run from $50,000 to $400,000 per employee.[8] In one recent case, Schering-Plough fired 35-year employee Fred Maiorino after he twice failed to accept an early retirement offer made to all sales representatives. After hearing testimony that Maiorino's boss had plastered his file with negative paperwork aimed at firing him, rather than trying to help him improve his performance, the jurors unanimously decided he had been discriminated against because of his age. They awarded him $435,000 in compensatory damages and $8 million in punitive damages.[9]

figure 3.1

Age Discrimination Complaints, 1991–2010

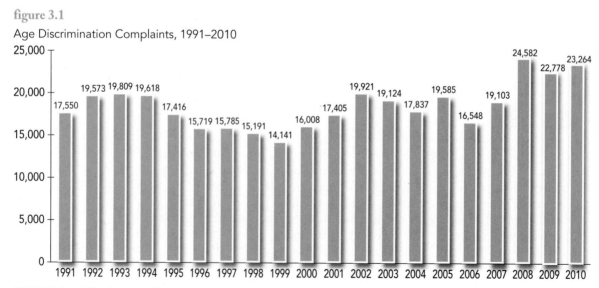

SOURCE: Equal Employment Opportunity Commission, at http://eeoc.gov/stats/adea.html.

The Vocational Rehabilitation Act of 1973

This act covers executive agencies and contractors and subcontractors that receive more than $2,500 annually from the federal government. It requires them to engage in affirmative action for individuals with disabilities. Congress designed this act to encourage employers to actively recruit qualified individuals with disabilities and to make reasonable accommodations to allow them to become active members of the labor market. The Employment Standards Administration of the Department of Labor enforces this act.

Vietnam Era Veteran's Readjustment Act of 1974

Similar to the Rehabilitation Act, this act requires federal contractors and subcontractors to take affirmative action toward employing Vietnam veterans (those serving between August 5, 1964, and May 7, 1975). The Office of Federal Contract Compliance Programs (OFCCP), discussed later in this chapter, has authority to enforce this act.

Pregnancy Discrimination Act

The Pregnancy Discrimination Act is an amendment to Title VII of the Civil Rights Act. It makes illegal discrimination on the basis of pregnancy, childbirth, or related medical conditions as a form of unlawful sex discrimination. An employer cannot refuse to hire a pregnant woman because of her pregnancy, a pregnancy-related condition, or the prejudices of co-workers, clients, or customers. For instance, in a recent court case, the retail store Motherhood Maternity, a Philadelphia-based maternity clothes retailer, settled a pregnancy discrimination and retaliation lawsuit brought by the Equal Employment Opportunity Commission (EEOC). The EEOC had charged that the company refused to hire qualified female applicants because they were pregnant. As a result of the settlement, Motherhood Maternity agreed to a three-year consent decree requiring them to pay plaintiffs $375,000, adopt and distribute an antidiscrimination policy specifically prohibiting discrimination on the basis of pregnancy, train its Florida employees on the new policy, post a notice of resolution of the lawsuit, and provide twice a year reports to the EEOC on any pregnancy discrimination complaints.[10]

In addition, regarding pregnancy and maternity leave, employers may not single out pregnancy-related conditions for special procedures to determine an employee's ability to work, and if an employee is temporarily unable to perform during her pregnancy, the employer must treat her the same as any temporarily disabled employees. The act also requires that any health insurance must cover expenses for pregnancy-related conditions on the same basis as costs for other medical conditions. Finally, pregnancy-related benefits cannot be limited to married employees, and if an employer provides any benefits to workers on leave, they must also provide the same benefits for those on leave for pregnancy-related conditions.

Recently the EEOC filed suit against HCS Medical Staffing, Inc., for allegedly discriminating against a pregnant employee and then firing her while she was on maternity leave. According to the EEOC's suit, owner Charles Sisson engaged in escalating negative comments about the upcoming maternity leave of HCS bookkeeper Roxy Leger. He allegedly insisted that Leger's pregnancy was a joke, described her maternity leave as "vacation," and insisted that maternity leave should be no longer than two days. Sisson then allegedly terminated Leger, who had no prior negative comments on her work performance, seven days after she gave birth by caesarean section.[11]

Civil Rights Act of 1991

The Civil Rights Act of 1991 (CRA 1991) amends Title VII of the Civil Rights Act of 1964, Section 1981 of the Civil Rights Act of 1866, the Americans with Disabilities Act, and the Age Discrimination in Employment Act of 1967. One major change in EEO law under CRA 1991 has been the addition of compensatory and punitive damages in cases of discrimination under Title VII and the Americans with Disabilities Act. Before CRA 1991, Title VII limited damage claims to equitable relief such as back pay, lost benefits, front pay in some cases, and attorneys' fees and costs. CRA 1991 allows compensatory and punitive damages when intentional or reckless discrimination is proven. Compensatory damages include such things as future pecuniary loss, emotional pain, suffering, and loss of enjoyment of life. Punitive damages are meant to discourage employers from discriminating by providing for payments to the plaintiff beyond the actual damages suffered.

Recognizing that one or a few discrimination cases could put an organization out of business, thus adversely affecting many innocent employees, Congress has put limits on the amount of punitive damages. Table 3.2 depicts these limits. As can be seen, damages range from $50,000 to $300,000 per violation, depending on the size of the organization. Punitive damages are available only if the employer intentionally discriminated against the plaintiff(s) or if the employer discriminated with malice or reckless indifference to the employee's federally protected rights. These damages are excluded for an employment practice held to be unlawful because of its disparate impact.[12]

The addition of damages to CRA 1991 has had two immediate effects. First, by increasing the potential payoff for a successful discrimination suit, it has increased the number of suits filed against businesses. Second, organizations are now more likely to grant all employees an equal opportunity for employment, regardless of their race, sex, religion, or national origin. Many organizations have felt the need to make the composition of their workforce mirror the general population to avoid costly lawsuits. This act adds a financial incentive for doing so.

Americans with Disabilities Act (ADA) of 1990

Americans with Disabilities Act (ADA) of 1990
A 1990 act prohibiting individuals with disabilities from being discriminated against in the workplace.

One of the most far-reaching acts concerning the management of human resources is the **Americans with Disabilities Act.** This act protects individuals with disabilities from being discriminated against in the workplace. It prohibits discrimination based on disability in all employment practices such as job application procedures, hiring, firing, promotions, compensation, and training—in addition to other employment activities such as advertising, recruitment, tenure, layoff, leave, and fringe benefits. Because this act is so new, we will cover its various stipulations individually.

The ADA defines a disability as a physical or mental impairment that substantially limits one or more major life activities, a record of having such an impairment, or being regarded as having such an impairment. The first part of the definition refers

table 3.2

Maximum Punitive Damages Allowed under the Civil Rights Act of 1991

EMPLOYER SIZE	DAMAGE LIMIT
14 to 100 employees	$ 50,000
101 to 200 employees	100,000
201 to 500 employees	200,000
More than 500 employees	300,000

to individuals who have serious disabilities—such as epilepsy, blindness, deafness, or paralysis—that affect their ability to perform major life activities such as walking, seeing, performing manual tasks, learning, caring for oneself, and working. The second part refers to individuals who have a history of disability, such as someone who has had cancer but is currently in remission, someone with a history of mental illness, and someone with a history of heart disease. The third part of the definition, "being regarded as having a disability," refers, for example, to an individual who is severely disfigured and is denied employment because an employer fears negative reactions from others.[13]

Thus the ADA covers specific physiological disabilities such as cosmetic disfigurement and anatomical loss affecting the neurological, musculoskeletal, sensory, respiratory, cardiovascular, reproductive, digestive, genitourinary, hemic, or lymphatic systems. In addition, it covers mental and psychological disorders such as mental retardation, organic brain syndrome, emotional or mental illness, and learning disabilities. However, conditions such as obesity, substance abuse, eye and hair color, and lefthandedness are not covered.[14]

In addition, the Americans with Disabilities Act Amendments Act (ADAAA), effective January 1, 2009, broadened the scope of who is considered to be an individual with a disability. It states that the definition of disability should be broadly construed and that the "question of whether an individual's impairment is a disability under the ADA should not demand extensive analysis." The Supreme Court had interpreted the term "substantially limited" in a major life activity to require the individual to be "significantly restricted," but the ADAAA states that this is too high a standard and directs the EEOC to revise its regulations to set a lower standard. Also, regarding the term "regarded as disabled," previously employers could avoid liability by showing that the impairment did not substantially limit a major life activity. However, the ADAAA states that an employee can prove he or she was subjected to an illegal act "because of an actual or perceived physical or mental impairment whether or not the impairment limits or is perceived to limit a major life activity." In fact, in response to the ADAAA, the EEOC has clarified and somewhat redefined "disability." According to their most recent guidelines, a disability is defined along three so-called "prongs": a physical or mental impairment that "substantially limits one or more major life activity," a record or past history of such an impairment; and/or being "regarded as" having a disability by an employer whether you have one or not, usually in terms of hiring, firing, or demotion. In essence, a person is considered disabled not only if he or she cannot DO something, but just because he or she has a medical condition whether or not it impairs functioning.[15]

EXECUTIVE ORDERS

Executive orders are directives issued and amended unilaterally by the president. These orders do not require congressional approval, yet they have the force of law. Two executive orders directly affect HRM.

Executive Order 11246

President Johnson issued this executive order, which prohibits discrimination based on race, color, religion, sex, and national origin. Unlike Title VII, this order applies only to federal contractors and subcontractors. Employers receiving more than $10,000 from the federal government must take affirmative action to ensure against discrimination, and those with contracts greater than $50,000 must develop a written affirmative action plan for each of their establishments within 120 days of the beginning of the contract. The Office of Federal Contract Compliance Programs enforces this executive order.

Executive Order 11478

President Richard M. Nixon issued this order, which requires the federal government to base all its employment policies on merit and fitness, and specifies that race, color, sex, religion, and national origin should not be considered. (The U.S. Office of Personnel Management is in charge of this.) The order also extends to all contractors and subcontractors doing $10,000 worth of business with the federal government. (The relevant government agencies have the responsibility to ensure that the contractors and subcontractors comply with the order.)

Enforcement of Equal Employment Opportunity

LO 3-3
Discuss the roles, responsibilities, and requirements of the federal agencies responsible for enforcing equal employment opportunity laws.

As discussed previously, the executive branch of the federal government bears most of the responsibility for enforcing all EEO laws passed by the legislative branch. In addition, the executive branch must enforce the executive orders issued by the president. The two agencies responsible for the enforcement of these laws and executive orders are the Equal Employment Opportunity Commission and the Office of Federal Contract Compliance Programs, respectively.

Equal Employment Opportunity Commission (EEOC)
The government commission to ensure that all individuals have an equal opportunity for employment, regardless of race, color, religion, sex, age, disability, or national origin.

EQUAL EMPLOYMENT OPPORTUNITY COMMISSION (EEOC)

An independent federal agency, the EEOC is responsible for enforcing most of the EEO laws, such as Title VII, the Equal Pay Act, and the Americans with Disabilities Act. The EEOC has three major responsibilities: investigating and resolving discrimination complaints, gathering information, and issuing guidelines.

Investigation and Resolution

Individuals who feel they have been discriminated against must file a complaint with the EEOC or a similar state agency within 180 days of the incident. Failure to file a complaint within the 180 days results in the case's being dismissed immediately, with certain exceptions, such as the enactment of a seniority system that has an intentionally discriminatory purpose. For instance, the recent Lilly Ledbetter Fair Pay Act signed by President Obama was crafted in direct response to the 180-day window. Ledbetter had been an area manager at the Goodyear Tire and Rubber plant in Alabama from 1979 to 1998, during which time she received lower raises than the males. The differences were such that by the end of her career she was making $6,700 less per year than her male counterparts, and because pension payments were related to the salary at the time of retirement, she received smaller pension payments. When she filed the lawsuit, the Supreme Court ruled that the illegal acts were the pay raise decisions themselves (which fell far outside the 180-day window); Ledbetter wanted to argue that every time she received a pension check lower than her peers it served as an act of discrimination. Thus,

Congress passed the act specifying that an "illegal act" occurs when (1) a discriminatory compensation decision is adopted; (2) an employee becomes subject to the decision; or (3) an employee is affected by it application, including each time compensation is paid.

Once the complaint is filed, the EEOC takes responsibility for investigating the claim of discrimination. The complainant must give the EEOC 60 days to investigate the complaint. If the EEOC either does not believe the complaint to be valid or fails to complete the investigation, the complainant may sue in federal court. If the EEOC determines that discrimination has taken place, its representatives will attempt to provide a reconciliation between the two parties without burdening the court system with a lawsuit. Sometimes the EEOC enters into a consent decree with the discriminating organization. This decree is an agreement between the agency and the organization that the organization will cease certain discriminatory practices and possibly institute additional affirmative action practices to rectify its history of discrimination.

If the EEOC cannot come to an agreement with the organization, it has two options. First, it can issue a "right to sue" letter to the alleged victim, which certifies that the agency has investigated and found validity in the victim's allegations. Second, although less likely, the agency may aid the alleged victim in bringing suit in federal court.

Information Gathering

The EEOC also plays a role in monitoring the hiring practices of organizations. Each year organizations with 100 or more employees must file a report (EEO-1) with the EEOC that provides the number of women and minorities employed in nine different job categories. The EEOC computer analyzes these reports to identify patterns of discrimination that can then be attacked through class-action suits.

Issuance of Guidelines

A third responsibility of the EEOC is to issue guidelines that help employers determine when their decisions are violations of the laws enforced by the EEOC. These guidelines are not laws themselves, but the courts give great deference to them when hearing employment discrimination cases.

For example, the *Uniform Guidelines on Employee Selection Procedures* is a set of guidelines issued by the EEOC, the Department of Labor, the Department of Justice, and the U.S. Civil Service Commission.[16] This document provides guidance on the ways an organization should develop and administer selection systems so as not to violate Title VII. The courts often refer to the *Uniform Guidelines* to determine whether a company has engaged in discriminatory conduct or to determine the validity of the procedures it used to validate a selection system. Another example: Since the passage of the ADA, employers have been somewhat confused about the act's implications for their hiring procedures. Therefore, the EEOC issued guidelines in the *Federal Register* that provided more detailed information regarding what the agency will consider legal and illegal employment practices concerning disabled individuals. Although companies are well advised to follow these guidelines, it is possible that courts will interpret the ADA differently from the EEOC. Thus, through the issuance of guidelines the EEOC gives employers directions for making employment decisions that do not conflict with existing laws.

OFFICE OF FEDERAL CONTRACT COMPLIANCE PROGRAMS (OFCCP)

The OFCCP is the agency responsible for enforcing the executive orders that cover companies doing business with the federal government. Businesses with contracts for more than $50,000 cannot discriminate in employment based on race, color, religion, national origin, or sex, and they must have a written affirmative action plan on file.

Utilization Analysis
A comparison of the race, sex, and ethnic composition of an employer's workforce with that of the available labor supply.

These plans have three basic components.[17] First, the **utilization analysis** compares the race, sex, and ethnic composition of the employer's workforce with that of the available labor supply. For each job group, the employer must identify the percentage of its workforce with that characteristic (e.g., female) and identify the percentage of workers in the relevant labor market with that characteristic. If the percentage in the employer's workforce is much less than the percentage in the comparison group, then that minority group is considered to be "underutilized."

Goals and Timetables
The part of a written affirmative action plan that specifies the percentage of women and minorities that an employer seeks to have in each job group and the date by which that percentage is to be attained.

Second, the employer must develop specific **goals and timetables** for achieving balance in the workforce concerning these characteristics (particularly where underutilization exists). Goals and timetables specify the percentage of women and minorities that the employer seeks to have in each job group and the date by which that percentage is to be attained. These are not to be viewed as quotas, which entail setting aside a specific number of positions to be filled only by members of the protected class. Goals and timetables are much more flexible, requiring only that the employer have specific goals and take steps to achieve those goals. In fact, one study that examined companies with the goal of increasing black employment found that only 10% of them actually achieved their goals. Although this may sound discouragingly low, it is important to note that these companies increased their black employment more than companies that set no such goals.[18]

Action Steps
The written affirmative plan that specifies what an employer plans to do to reduce underutilization of protected groups.

Third, employers with federal contracts must develop a list of **action steps** they will take toward attaining their goals to reduce underutilization. The company's CEO must make it clear to the entire organization that the company is committed to reducing underutilization, and all management levels must be involved in the planning process. For example, organizations can communicate job openings to women and minorities through publishing the company's affirmative action policy, recruiting at predominantly female or minority schools, participating in programs designed to increase employment opportunities for underemployed groups, and removing unnecessary barriers to employment. Organizations must also take affirmative steps toward hiring Vietnam veterans and individuals with disabilities.

The OFCCP annually audits government contractors to ensure that they actively pursue the goals in their plans. These audits consist of (1) examining the company's affirmative action plan and (2) conducting on-site visits to examine how individual employees perceive the company's affirmative action policies. If the OFCCP finds that the contractors or subcontractors are not complying with the executive order, then its representatives may notify the EEOC (if there is evidence that Title VII has been violated), advise the Department of Justice to institute criminal proceedings, request that the Secretary of Labor cancel or suspend any current contracts, and forbid the firm from bidding on future contracts. This last penalty, called debarment, is the OFCCP's most potent weapon.

Having discussed the major laws defining equal employment opportunity and the agencies that enforce these laws, we now address the various types of discrimination and the ways these forms of discrimination have been interpreted by the courts in a number of cases.

Types of Discrimination

How would you know if you had been discriminated against? Assume that you have applied for a job and were not hired. How do you know if the organization decided not to hire you because you are unqualified, because you are less qualified than the individual ultimately hired, or simply because the person in charge of the hiring decision "didn't like your type"? Discrimination is a multifaceted issue. It is often not easy to determine the extent to which unfair discrimination affects an employer's decisions.

Legal scholars have identified three theories of discrimination: disparate treatment, disparate impact, and reasonable accommodation. In addition, there is protection for those participating in discrimination cases or opposing discriminatory actions. In the act, these theories are stated in very general terms. However, the court system has defined and delineated these theories through the cases brought before it. A comparison of the theories of discrimination is given in Table 3.3.

LO 3-4
Identify the three theories of discrimination under Title VII of the Civil Rights Act and apply these theories to different discrimination situations.

DISPARATE TREATMENT

Disparate treatment exists when individuals in similar situations are treated differently and the different treatment is based on the individual's race, color, religion, sex, national origin, age, or disability status. If two people with the same qualifications

Disparate Treatment
A theory of discrimination based on different treatments given to individuals because of their race, color, religion, sex, national origin, age, or disability status.

table 3.3

Comparison of Discrimination Theories

TYPES OF DISCRIMINATION	DISPARATE TREATMENT	DISPARATE IMPACT	REASONABLE ACCOMMODATION
Show intent?	Yes	No	Yes
Prima facie case	Individual is member of a protected group, was qualified for the job, and was turned down for the job, and the job remained open	Statistical disparity in the effects of a facially neutral employment practice	Individual has a belief or disability, provided the employer with notice (request to accommodate), and was adversely affected by a failure to be accommodated
Employer's defense	Produce a legitimate, nondiscriminatory reason for the employment decision or show bona fide occupational qualification (BFOQ)	Prove that the employment practice bears a manifest relationship with job performance	Job-relatedness and business necessity, undue hardship, or direct threat to health or safety
Plaintiff's rebuttal	Reason offered was merely a "pretext" for discrimination	Alternative procedures exist that meet the employer's goal without having disparate impact	
Monetary damages	Compensatory and punitive damages	Equitable relief (e.g., back pay)	Compensatory and punitive damages (if discrimination was intentional or employer failed to show good faith efforts to accommodate)

apply for a job and the employer decides whom to hire based on one individual's race, the individual not hired is a victim of disparate treatment. In the disparate treatment case the plaintiff must prove that there was a discriminatory motive—that is, that the employer intended to discriminate.

Whenever individuals are treated differently because of their race, sex, or the like, there is disparate treatment. For example, if a company fails to hire women with school-age children (claiming the women will be frequently absent) but hires men with school-age children, the applicants are being treated differently based on sex. Another example would be an employer who checks the references and investigates the conviction records of minority applicants but does not do so for white applicants. Why are managers advised not to ask about marital status? Because in most cases, a manager will either ask only the female applicants or, if the manager asks both males and females, he or she will make different assumptions about females (such as "She will have to move if her husband gets a job elsewhere") and males (such as "He's very stable"). In all these examples, notice that (1) people are being treated differently and (2) there is an actual intent to treat them differently.[19]

For instance, The Timken Company recently agreed to a $120,000 settlement over a sex and disability discrimination suit. In 2007, Carmen Halloran applied for a full-time position at The Timken Company, after having worked at the facility as a part-time process associate for four years. The EEOC alleged that the company refused to hire Halloran because managers believed that Halloran, who is the mother of a disabled child, would be unable to work full-time and care for her disabled child. They also alleged that this decision was based on an unfounded gender stereotype that the mother of a disabled child would necessarily be the primary caregiver because they did hire men with disabled children. "The EEOC is committed to fighting discrimination in the workplace," said Lynette A. Barnes, regional attorney for the EEOC's Charlotte District Office. "Employers must be careful not to apply stereotypes against women based on perceptions that they must always be the primary caregivers and therefore are unreliable employees."[20]

To understand how disparate treatment is applied in the law, let's look at how an actual court case, filed under disparate treatment, would proceed.

The Plaintiff's Burden

As in any legal case, the plaintiff has the burden of proving that the defendant has committed an illegal act. This is the idea of a "prima facie" case. In a disparate treatment case, the plaintiff meets the prima facie burden by showing four things:

1. The plaintiff belongs to a protected group.
2. The plaintiff applied for and was qualified for the job.
3. Despite possessing the qualifications, the plaintiff was rejected.
4. After the plaintiff was rejected, the position remained open and the employer continued to seek applicants with similar qualifications, or the position was filled by someone with similar qualifications.

Although these four elements may seem easy to prove, it is important to note that what the court is trying to do is rule out the most obvious reasons for rejecting the plaintiff's claim (for example, the plaintiff did not apply or was not qualified, or the position was already filled or had been eliminated). If these alternative explanations are ruled out, the court assumes that the hiring decision was based on a discriminatory motive.

The Defendant's Rebuttal

Once the plaintiff has made the prima facie case for discrimination, the burden shifts to the defendant. The burden is different depending on whether the prima facie case presents only circumstantial evidence (there is no direct evidence of discrimination such as a formal policy to discriminate, but rather discriminatory intent must be inferred) or direct evidence (a formal policy of discrimination for some perceived legitimate reason). In cases of circumstantial evidence, the defendant simply must produce a legitimate, nondiscriminatory reason, such as that, although the plaintiff was qualified, the individual hired was more qualified.

However, in cases where direct evidence exists, such as a formal policy of hiring only women for waitress jobs because the business is aimed at catering to male customers, then the defendant is more likely to offer a different defense. This defense argues that for this job, a factor such as sex or religion was a **bona fide occupational qualification (BFOQ).** For example, if one were hiring an individual to hand out towels in a women's locker room, being a woman might be a BFOQ. However, there are very few cases in which sex qualifies as a BFOQ, and in these cases it must be a necessary, rather than simply a preferred characteristic of the job.

Bona Fide Occupational Qualification (BFOQ)
A job qualification based on sex, religion, and so on, that an employer asserts is a necessary qualification for the job.

UAW v. Johnson Controls, Inc., illustrates the difficulty in using a BFOQ as a defense.[21] Johnson Controls, a manufacturer of car batteries, had instituted a "fetal protection" policy that excluded women of childbearing age from a number of jobs in which they would be exposed to lead, which can cause birth defects in children. The company argued that sex was a BFOQ essential to maintaining a safe workplace. The Supreme Court did not uphold the company's policy, arguing that BFOQs are limited to policies that are directly related to a worker's ability to do the job.

Interestingly, some factors are by no means off-limits when it comes to discrimination. For instance, a recent survey by *Newsweek* of 202 hiring managers revealed that almost 60% said that qualified, yet unattractive, applicants face a harder time getting hired. In addition, two-thirds believe that managers hesitate before hiring qualified, but overweight, candidates.[22]

The Plaintiff's Rebuttal

If the defendant provides a legitimate, nondiscriminatory reason for its employment decision, the burden shifts back to the plaintiff. The plaintiff must now show that the reason offered by the defendant was not in fact the reason for its decision but merely a "pretext" or excuse for its actual discriminatory decision. This could entail providing evidence that white applicants with very similar qualifications to the plaintiff have often been hired while black applicants with very similar qualifications were all rejected. To illustrate disparate treatment, let's look at the first major case dealing with disparate treatment, *McDonnell Douglas Corp. v. Green.*

McDonnell Douglas Corp. v. Green. This Supreme Court case was the first to delineate the four criteria for a prima facie case of discrimination. From 1956 to 1964, Green had been an employee at McDonnell Douglas, a manufacturing plant in St. Louis, Missouri, that employed about 30,000 people. In 1964 he was laid off during a general workforce reduction. While unemployed, he participated in some activities that the company undoubtedly frowned upon: a "lock-in," where he and others placed a chain and padlock on the front door of a building to prevent the employees from leaving; and a "stall-in," where a group of employees stalled their cars at the gates of the plant so that no one could enter or leave the parking lot. About three weeks after the lock-in, McDonnell Douglas advertised for qualified mechanics, Green's trade, and he reapplied. When the company rejected his application, he sued, arguing that the company didn't hire him because of his race and because of his persistent involvement in the civil rights movement.

In making his prima facie case, Green had no problem showing that he was a member of a protected group, that he had applied for and was qualified for the job (having already worked in the job), that he was rejected, and that the company continued to advertise the position. The company's defense was that the plaintiff was not hired because he participated in the lock-in and the stall-in. In other words, the company was merely refusing to hire a troublemaker.

The plaintiff responded that the company's stated reason for not hiring him was a pretext for discrimination. He pointed out that white employees who had participated in the same activities (the lock-in and stall-in) were rehired, whereas he was not. The court found in favor of the plaintiff.

This case illustrates how similarly situated individuals (white and black) can be treated differently (whites were hired back whereas blacks were not) with the differences in treatment based on race. As we discuss later, most plaintiffs bring cases of sexual harassment under this theory of discrimination, sexual harassment being a situation where individuals are treated differently because of their sex.

Mixed-Motive Cases

In a mixed-motive case, the defendant acknowledges that some discriminatory motive existed but argues that the same hiring decision would have been reached even without the discriminatory motive. In *Hopkins v. Price Waterhouse*, Ann Hopkins was an accountant who had applied for partnership in her firm. Although she had brought in a large amount of business and had received high praise from her clients, she was turned down for a partnership on two separate occasions. In her performance reviews, she had been told to adopt more feminine dress and speech and received many other comments that suggested gender-based stereotypes. In court, the company admitted that a sex-based stereotype existed but argued that it would have come to the same decision (not promoted Hopkins) even if the stereotype had not existed.

One of the main questions that came out of this case was, Who has the burden of proof? Does the plaintiff have to prove that a different decision would have been made (that Hopkins would have been promoted) in the absence of the discriminatory motive? Or does the defendant have to prove that the same decision would have been made?

According to CRA 1991, if the plaintiff demonstrates that race, sex, color, religion, or national origin was a motivating factor for any employment practice, the prima facie burden has been met, and the burden of proof is on the employer to demonstrate that the same decision would have been made even if the discriminatory motive had not been present. If the employer can do this, the plaintiff cannot collect compensatory or punitive damages. However, the court may order the employer to quit using the discriminatory motive in its future employment decisions.

Disparate Impact
A theory of discrimination based on facially neutral employment practices that disproportionately exclude a protected group from employment opportunities.

DISPARATE IMPACT

The second type of discrimination is called **disparate impact.** It occurs when a facially neutral employment practice disproportionately excludes a protected group from employment opportunities. A facially neutral employment practice is one that lacks obvious discriminatory content yet affects one group to a greater extent than other groups, such as an employment test. Although the Supreme Court inferred disparate impact from Title VII in the *Griggs v. Duke Power* case, it has since been codified into the Civil Rights Act of 1991.

There is an important distinction between disparate impact and disparate treatment discrimination. For there to be discrimination under disparate treatment, there has to be intentional discrimination. Under disparate impact, intent is irrelevant. The important criterion is that the consequences of the employment practice are discriminatory.

For example, if, for some practical reason, you hired individuals based on their height, you may not have intended to discriminate against anyone, and yet using height would have a disproportionate impact on certain protected groups. Women tend to be shorter than men, so fewer women will be hired. Certain ethnic groups, such as those of Asian ancestry, also tend to be shorter than those of European ancestry. Thus, your facially neutral employment practice will have a disparate impact on certain protected groups.

This is not to imply that simply because a selection practice has disparate impact, it is necessarily illegal. Some characteristics (such as height) are not equally distributed across race and gender groups; however, the important question is whether the characteristic is related to successful performance on the job. To help you understand how disparate impact works, let's look at a court proceeding involving a disparate impact claim.

The Plaintiff's Burden

In a disparate impact case, the plaintiff must make the prima facie case by showing that the employment practice in question disproportionately affects a protected group relative to the majority group. To illustrate this theory, let's assume that you are a manager who has 60 positions to fill. Your applicant pool has 80 white and 40 black applicants. You use a test that selects 48 of the white and 12 of the black applicants. Is this a disparate impact? Two alternative quantitative analyses are often used to determine whether a test has adverse impact.

The **four-fifths rule** states that a test has disparate impact if the hiring rate for the minority group is less than four-fifths (or 80%) of the hiring rate for the majority group. Applying this analysis to the preceding example, we would first calculate the hiring rates for each group:

$$\text{Whites} = 48/80 = 60\%$$
$$\text{Blacks} = 12/40 = 30\%$$

Then we would compare the hiring rate of the minority group (30%) with that of the majority group (60%). Using the four-fifths rule, we would determine that the test has adverse impact if the hiring rate of the minority group is less than 80% of the hiring rate of the majority group. Because it is less (i.e., 30%/60% = 50%, which is less than 80%), we would conclude that the test has adverse impact. The four-fifths rule is used as a rule of thumb by the EEOC in determining adverse impact.

The **standard deviation rule** uses actual probability distributions to determine adverse impact. This analysis uses the difference between the expected representation (or hiring rates) for minority groups and the actual representation (or hiring rate) to determine whether the difference between these two values is greater than would occur by chance. Thus, in our example, 33% (40 of 120) of the applicants were

Four-Fifths Rule
A rule that states that an employment test has disparate impact if the hiring rate for a minority group is less than four-fifths, or 80 percent, of the hiring rate for the majority group.

Standard Deviation Rule
A rule used to analyze employment tests to determine disparate impact; it uses the difference between the expected representation for minority groups and the actual representation to determine whether the difference between the two is greater than would occur by chance.

blacks, so one would expect 33% (20 of 60) of those hired to be black. However, only 12 black applicants were hired. To determine if the difference between the expected representation and the actual representation is greater than we would expect by chance, we calculate the standard deviation (which, you might remember from your statistics class, is the standard deviation in a binomial distribution):

$$\sqrt{\text{Number hired} \times \frac{\text{Number of minority applicants}}{\text{Number of total applicants}} \times \frac{\text{Number of nonminority applicants}}{\text{Number of total applicants}}}$$

or in this case:

$$\sqrt{60 \times \frac{40}{120} \times \frac{80}{120}} = 3.6$$

If the difference between the actual representation and the expected representation ($20 - 12 = 8$ in this case) of blacks is greater than 2 standard deviations ($2 \times 3.6 = 7.2$ in this case), we would conclude that the test had adverse impact against blacks, because we would expect this result less than 1 time in 20 if the test were equally difficult for both whites and blacks.

The *Wards Cove Packing Co. v. Atonio* case involved an interesting use of statistics. The plaintiffs showed that the jobs in the cannery (lower paying jobs) were filled primarily with minority applicants (in this case, American Eskimos). However, only a small percentage of the noncannery jobs (those with higher pay) were filled by nonminorities. The plaintiffs argued that this statistical disparity in the racial makeup of the cannery and noncannery jobs was proof of discrimination. The federal district, appellate, and Supreme Courts all found for the defendant, stating that this disparity was not proof of discrimination.

Once the plaintiff has demonstrated adverse impact, he or she has met the burden of a prima facie case of discrimination.[23]

Defendant's Rebuttal

According to CRA 1991, once the plaintiff has made a prima facie case, the burden of proof shifts to the defendant, who must show that the employment practice is a "business necessity." This is accomplished by showing that the practice bears a relationship with some legitimate employer goal. With respect to job selection, this relationship is demonstrated by showing the job relatedness of the test, usually by reporting a validity study of some type, to be discussed in Chapter 6. For now, suffice it to say that the employer shows that the test scores are significantly correlated with measures of job performance.

Measures of job performance used in validation studies can include such things as objective measures of output, supervisor ratings of job performance, and success in training.[24] Normally, performance appraisal ratings are used, but these ratings must be valid for the court to accept the validation results. For example, in *Albermarle Paper v. Moody*, the employer demonstrated that the selection battery predicted performance (measured with supervisors' overall rankings of employees) in only some of the 13 occupational groups in which it was used. In this case, the court was especially critical of the supervisory ratings used as the measure of job performance. The court stated, "There is no way of knowing precisely what criteria of job performance the supervisors were considering."[25]

Plaintiff's Rebuttal

If the employer shows that the employment practice is the result of some business necessity, the plaintiff's last resort is to argue that other employment practices could sufficiently meet the employer's goal without adverse impact. Thus, if a plaintiff can demonstrate that selection tests other than the one used by the employer exist, do not have adverse impact, and correlate with job performance as highly as the employer's test, then the defendant can be found guilty of discrimination. Many cases deal with standardized tests of cognitive ability, so it is important to examine alternatives to these tests that have less adverse impact while still meeting the employer's goal. At least two separate studies reviewing alternative selection devices such as interviews, biographical data, assessment centers, and work sample tests have concluded that none of them met both criteria.[26] It seems that when the employment practice in question is a standardized test of cognitive ability, plaintiffs will have a difficult time rebutting the defendant's rebuttal.

Griggs v. Duke Power. To illustrate how this process works, let's look at the *Griggs v. Duke Power* case.[27] Following the passage of Title VII, Duke Power instituted a new system for making selection and promotion decisions. The system required either a high school diploma or a passing score on two professionally developed tests (the Wonderlic Personnel Test and the Bennett Mechanical Comprehension Test). A passing score was set so that it would be equal to the national median for high school graduates who had taken the tests.

The plaintiffs met their prima facie burden showing that both the high school diploma requirement and the test battery had adverse impacts on blacks. According to the 1960 census, 34% of white males had high school diplomas, compared with only 12% of black males. Similarly, 58% of white males passed the test battery, whereas only 6% of blacks passed.

Duke Power was unable to defend its use of these employment practices. A company vice president testified that the company had not studied the relationship between these employment practices and the employees' ability to perform the job. In addition, employees already on the job who did not have high school diplomas and had never taken the tests were performing satisfactorily. Thus, Duke Power lost the case.

It is interesting to note that the court recognized that the company had not intended to discriminate, mentioning that the company was making special efforts to help undereducated employees through financing two-thirds of the cost of tuition for high school training. This illustrates the importance of the consequences, as opposed to the motivation, in determining discrimination under the disparate impact theory.

PATTERN AND PRACTICE

In showing class action pattern and practice lawsuits, the plaintiffs attempt to show three things. First, they show some statistical disparities between the composition of some group within the company compared to some other relevant group. For instance, the opening case described how the plaintiff's lawyers pointed to two comparative statistics as evidence of discrimination. First, they compared the female representation in the non-managerial (63.4%) vs the managerial (33.6%) employee groups. They also compared the female representation in the managerial group (again, 33.6%) with that in their top 20 competitors (56.5%). They also calculated that hourly female workers were paid, on average, $1,100 less than men and salaried women received $14,500 less. However, Wal-Mart disputes the list of comparison companies, arguing that if a broader group is used, reflecting Wal-Mart's wide geographic footprint and variety of products offered, it does not differ from that group. It also claims that if it had claimed its highest-level hourly-wage supervisors as "managers" on its EEO-1 forms, as many of the comparison companies do, the entire disparity disappears. They also note that of the applicants for managerial positions, only 15% are female, and that of those promoted, 18% are female. Finally, regarding pay, Wal-Mart's experts suggested that the plaintiff's pay comparisons did not account for crucial factors such as the number of hours worked or whether the work was night-shift work, which pays more. Their analyses suggested that when pay was compared at the department level, where pay decisions are determined, 92.8% of all stores showed no statistically significant pay disparities, and that of the remainder, 5.2% showed disparities favoring men while 2.0% showed disparities favoring women.

Second, the plaintiff tries to show that there are individual acts of intentional discrimination that suggest that the statistical disparity is a function of the larger culture. In the Dukes case, the plaintiffs argued that at Monday morning meetings of high-level Sam's Club executives, female store employees were referred to as "Janie Q's," and that this continued even after a woman executive complained that she found the term demeaning.

Finally, the plaintiff usually tries to make the case that the promotion and/or pay procedures leave too much discretion to managers, providing the avenue through which their unconscious biases can play a part. In the Dukes case the plaintiffs brought in expert witnesses to argue that the performance management processes were extremely subjective, and that male managers have subconscious tendencies to favor male over female employees.

REASONABLE ACCOMMODATION

Reasonable Accommodation
Making facilities readily accessible to and usable by individuals with disabilities.

Reasonable accommodation presents a relatively new theory of discrimination. It began with regard to religious discrimination, but has recently been both expanded and popularized with the passage of the ADA. Reasonable accommodation differs from these two theories in that rather than simply requiring an employer to refrain from some action, reasonable accommodation places a special obligation on an employer to affirmatively do something to accommodate an individual's disability or religion. This theory is violated when an employer fails to make reasonable accommodation, where that is required, to a qualified person with a disability or to a person's religious observation and/or practices.

Religion and Accommodation

Often individuals with strong religious beliefs find that some observations and practices of their religion come into direct conflict with their work duties. For example, some religions forbid individuals from working on the sabbath day when the employer schedules them for work. Others might have beliefs that preclude them from shaving, which might conflict with a company's dress code. Although Title VII forbids discrimination on the basis of religion just like race or sex, religion also receives special treatment requiring employers to exercise an affirmative duty to accommodate individuals' religious beliefs and practices. As Figure 3.2 shows, the number of religious discrimination charges has consistently increased over the past few years.

In cases of religious discrimination, an employee's burden is to demonstrate that he or she has a legitimate religious belief and provided the employer with notice of the need to accommodate the religious practice, and that adverse consequences occurred due to the employer's failure to accommodate. In such cases, the employer's major defense is to assert that to accommodate the employee would require an undue hardship.

Examples of reasonably accommodating a person's religious obligations might include redesigning work schedules (most often accommodating those who cannot work on their sabbath), providing alternative testing dates for applicants, not requiring union membership and/or allowing payment of "charitable contributions" in lieu of union dues, or altering certain dress or grooming requirements. Note that although an employer is required to make a reasonable accommodation, it need not be the one that is offered by the employee.[28]

In one case, Wal-Mart agreed to settle with a former employee who alleged that he was forced to quit in 1993 after refusing to work on Sunday. Wal-Mart agreed to pay the former employee unspecified damages, to instruct managers on employees' rights to have their religious beliefs accommodated, and to prepare a computer-based manual describing employees' rights and religious harassment.[29]

figure 3.2

Religious Discrimination Complaints, 1991–2010

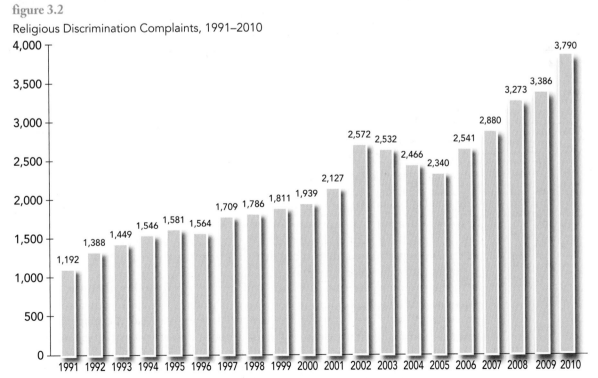

SOURCE: www.eeoc.gov/stats/religion.html.

Following the attack of 9/11, a number of cases sprang up with regard to discrimination against Muslims, partly accounting for the significant increase in religious discrimination complaints in 2002. In one case, the EEOC and Electrolux Group settled a religious accommodation case brought by Muslim workers from Somalia. The Islamic faith requires Muslims to offer five prayers a day, with two of these prayers offered within restricted time periods (early morning and sunset). Muslim employees alleged that they were disciplined for using an unscheduled break traditionally offered to line employees on an as-needed basis to observe their sunset prayer. Electrolux worked with the EEOC to respect the needs of its Muslim workers without creating a business hardship by affording them with an opportunity to observe their sunset prayer.[30]

Religion and accommodation also bring up the question as to what to do when different rights collide. For instance, John Nemecek had been a respected business professor at Spring Arbor University for 15 years. Spring Arbor is an evangelical college in Michigan which began to take issue with some of his behavior. After he began wearing earrings and makeup and asking friends to call him "Julie" he found himself demoted and fired because his womanly appearance violated "Christian behavior." In 2004 a doctor diagnosed Prof. Nemecek with a "gender-identity disorder," in which one's sexual identity differs from one's body. Soon after, the school began taking away some of his responsibilities, and then issued him a contract revoking his dean's post, reassigning him to a non-tenure-track role in which he would work from home, teaching online. It also required him to not wear any makeup or female clothing or to display any outward signs of femininity when visiting campus. Gayle Beebe, the university's president, said "We felt through a job reassignment we could give him the space to work on this issue." Prof. Nemecek signed the contract but then violated it by showing up on campus with earrings and makeup on four separate occasions. The professor filed his complaint with the EEOC and the university then declined to renew his contract. Prof. Nemecek, whose Baptist church also asked him to leave the congregation, says of the university, "Essentially, they're saying they can define who is a Christian. I don't agree that our biology determines our gender."[31]

Disability and Accommodation

As previously discussed, the ADA made discrimination against individuals with disabilities illegal. However, the act itself states that the employer is obligated not just to refrain from discriminating, but to take affirmative steps to accommodate individuals who are protected under the act.

Under disability claims, the plaintiff must show that she or he is a qualified applicant with a disability and that adverse action was taken by a covered entity. The employer's defense then depends on whether the decision was made without regard to the disability or in light of the disability. For example, if the employer argues that the plaintiff is not qualified, then it has met the burden, and the question of reasonable accommodation becomes irrelevant.

If, however, the decision was made "in light of" the disability, then the question becomes one of whether the person could perform adequately with a reasonable accommodation. This leads to three potential defenses. First, the employer could allege job-relatedness or business necessity through demonstrating, for example, that it is using a test that assesses ability to perform essential job functions. However, then the question arises of whether the applicant could perform the essential job functions with a reasonable accommodation. Second, the employer could claim an undue hardship to accommodate the individual. In essence, this argues that the accommodation necessary is an action requiring significant difficulty or expense. Finally, the employer could argue that the individual with the disability might pose a direct threat to his own or others' health or safety in the workplace. This requires examining the duration of the risk, the nature and severity of potential harm, the probability of the harm occurring, and the imminence of the potential harm. For instance, Wal-Mart was sued by one of its employees who was a fitting room attendant with cerebral palsy and confined to a wheelchair. The employee requested to use a grabber and a shopping cart to help her pick up and hold clothes. However, she was prevented from using both by the manager, who then implemented progressive discipline ending in the attendant's termination.[32]

What are some examples of reasonable accommodation with regard to disabilities? First is providing readily accessible facilities such as ramps and/or elevators for disabled individuals to enter the workplace. Second, job restructuring might include eliminating marginal tasks, shifting these tasks to other employees, redesigning job procedures, or altering work schedules. Third, an employer might reassign a disabled employee to a job with essential job functions he or she could perform. Fourth, an employer might accommodate applicants for employment who must take tests through providing alternative testing formats, providing readers, or providing additional time for taking the test. Fifth, readers, interpreters, or technology to offer reading assistance might be given to a disabled employee. Sixth, an employer could allow employees to provide their own accommodation such as bringing a guide dog to work.[33] Note that most accommodations are inexpensive. A study by Sears Roebuck & Co. found that 69% of all accommodations cost nothing, 29% cost less than $1,000, and only 3% cost more than $1,000.[34]

EVIDENCE-BASED HR

As information technology becomes more and more ubiquitous in the workplace, some have begun to explore the implications for people with disabilities. Researchers at the Employment and Disability Institute at Cornell University recently reviewed the accessibility of 10 job boards and 31 corporate e-recruiting websites using Bobby 3.2, a software program designed to check for errors that cause accessibility concerns. They found that none of the job boards and only a small minority of the e-recruiting sites met the Bobby standards.

In phase 2 of the study, they surveyed 813 HR professionals who were members of the Society for Human Resource Management (SHRM). Between 16 and 46% of the HR professionals were familiar with six of the most common assistive technologies to adapt computers for disabled individuals (screen magnifiers, speech recognitions software, video captioning, Braille readers/displays, screen readers, guidelines for web design). In addition, only 1 in 10 said they knew that their firm had evaluated the websites for accessibility to people with disabilities.

This study indicates that while firms may not have any intention of discriminating against people with disabilities, the rapid expansion of information technology combined with an inattention to and/or lack of education regarding accessibility issues may accidentally lead them to do so.

SOURCE: S. Bruyere, S. Erickson, and S. VanLooy, "Information Technology and the Workplace: Implications for Persons with Disabilities," *Disability Studies Quarterly* 25, no. 2 (Spring 2005), at www.dsq-sds.org.

LO 3-5
Discuss the legal issues
involved with preferential
treatment programs.

Retaliation for Participation and Opposition

Suppose you overhear a supervisor in your workplace telling someone that he refuses to hire women because he knows they are just not cut out for the job. Believing this to be illegal discrimination, you face a dilemma. Should you come forward and report this statement? Or if someone else files a lawsuit for gender discrimination, should you testify on behalf of the plaintiff? What happens if your employer threatens to fire you if you do anything?

Title VII of the Civil Rights Act of 1964 protects you. It states that employers cannot retaliate against employees for either "opposing" a perceived illegal employment practice or "participating in a proceeding" related to an alleged illegal employment practice. Opposition refers to expressing to someone through proper channels that you believe that an illegal employment act has taken place or is taking place. Participation refers to actually testifying in an investigation, hearing, or court proceeding regarding an illegal employment act. Clearly, the purpose of this provision is to protect employees from employers' threats and other forms of intimidation aimed at discouraging the employees from bringing to light acts they believe to be illegal.

Recently the EEOC filed suit against Dillard's, a major department store chain, for firing a business manager as retaliation for filing a discrimination charge. In 2008, Shontel Mayfield filed a charge with the EEOC in which she alleged that Dillard's management had discriminated against her because of her race. She had begun working for Dillard's in July 2001, and earned a promotion to business manager of the Estee Lauder counter in 2006. However, in September 2008, Mayfield complied with a Jefferson County, Texas, mandatory evacuation order and evacuated the area in advance of Hurricane Ike. She returned to Jefferson County consistent with the directives of the county's "disaster declarations." After Mayfield returned to work she was told that she was being fired for the stated reason of "excessive absenteeism." On her termination paperwork, she was accused of having "failed to maintain verbal communication concerning her absences with either the store manager or the operations manager." Yet telephone records showed that Mayfield placed numerous calls to Dillard's "disaster recovery" number, as well as to the cellular telephones of the store manager and the operations manager during the evacuation period.[35]

These cases can be extremely costly for companies because they are alleging acts of intentional discrimination, and therefore plaintiffs are entitled to punitive damages. For example, a 41-year-old former Allstate employee who claimed that a company official told her that the company wanted a "younger and cuter" image was awarded $2.8 million in damages by an Oregon jury. The jury concluded that the employee was forced out of the company for opposing age discrimination against other employees.[36]

In one case, Target Corporation agreed to pay $775,000 to a group of black workers who charged that at one store, the company condoned a racially hostile work environment exemplified by inappropriate comments and verbal berating based on race. When one of the black employees objected to this treatment, he was allegedly retaliated against, forcing him to resign.[37]

This does not mean that employees have an unlimited right to talk about how racist or sexist their employers are. The courts tend to frown on employees whose activities result in a poor public image for the company unless those employees had attempted to use the organization's internal channels—approaching one's manager, raising the issue with the HRM department, and so on—before going public.

It is important to note that deciding when an employee has done something wrong is often difficult to both know and prove. The "Competing through Sustainability"

Caution with Whistleblowers

Recent corporate scandals have heightened firms' sensitivity to potential ethical breaches among senior executives. Through developing and communicating whistleblower policies, firms often hope to surface potential ethical lapses to quickly exit those involved. However, Renault recently learned that not every allegation is true, and that often it is better to presume innocence until guilt has been proven.

In August of 2010 an anonymous letter was sent to a number of senior managers alleging that three leaders of Renault's electric-vehicle program had negotiated a bribe. An internal investigation revealed that the three men held accounts in Switzerland and Liechtenstein, and it was believed that these accounts were used to funnel bribes to them. The three executives were fired in January 2011 with CEO Carlos Ghosn suggesting that the company had evidence that these individuals were passing along confidential business information to competitors.

However, state prosecutor Jean-Claude Marin found that the three executives did not have accounts in these countries and suggested that some organized effort had been made to defraud Renault. He stated, "At this stage we do not know whether this is just fraud or a deliberate attempt to destabilize Renault. If there was any suspicious espionage, it was not done through the networks identified by Renault."

CEO Ghosn apologized to the three fired executives in a televised press conference, and offered to meet with them to invite them to rejoin the company. He also noted that Renault would offer them compensation "taking into account the serious hurt that they and their families have suffered."

SOURCE: From S. Moffett and D. Pearson, "Renault Apologizes in Spy Case," *Wall Street Journal*, March 15, 2011, B1, B2. Reproduced with permission of Dow Jones & Company, Inc. via Copyright Clearance Center.

box illustrates an ethical problem French automaker Renault faced when it suspected some employees were engaged in corporate espionage and tried to discipline them.

Current Issues Regarding Diversity and Equal Employment Opportunity

Because of recent changes in the labor market, most organizations' demographic compositions are becoming increasingly diverse. A study by the Hudson Institute projected that 85% of the new entrants into the U.S. labor force over the next decade will be females and minorities.[38] Integrating these groups into organizations made up predominantly of able-bodied white males will bring attention to important issues like sexual harassment, affirmative action, and the "reasonable accommodation" of employees with disabilities.

LO 3-6
Identify behavior that constitutes sexual harassment, and list things that an organization can do to eliminate or minimize it.

SEXUAL HARASSMENT

Clarence Thomas's Supreme Court confirmation hearings in 1991 brought the issue of sexual harassment into increased prominence. Anita Hill, one of Thomas's former employees, alleged that he had sexually harassed her while she was working under his supervision at the Department of Education and the Equal Employment Opportunity Commission. Although the allegations were never substantiated, the hearing made many people more aware of how often employees are sexually harassed in the workplace and, combined with other events, resulted in a tremendous increase in the number of sexual harassment complaints being filed with the EEOC, as we see in Figure 3.3. In addition, after President Clinton took office and faced a sexual harassment lawsuit by Paula Corbin Jones for his alleged proposition to her in a Little Rock hotel room, the number of sexual harassment complaints took another jump from 1993 to 1994—again, potentially due to the tremendous amount of publicity regarding sexual harassment. However, the number of cases filed has actually decreased substantially since 2000.

Sexual harassment refers to unwelcome sexual advances (see Table 3.4). It can take place in two basic ways. "Quid pro quo" harassment occurs when some kind of benefit (or punishment) is made contingent on the employee's submitting (or not submitting) to sexual advances. For example, a male manager tells his female secretary that if she has sex with him, he will help her get promoted, or he threatens to fire her if she fails to do so; these are clearly cases of quid pro quo sexual harassment.

The *Bundy v. Jackson* case illustrates quid pro quo sexual harassment.[39] Sandra Bundy was a personnel clerk with the District of Columbia Department of Corrections. She received repeated sexual propositions from Delbert Jackson, who was at the time a fellow employee (although he later became the director of the agency). She later began to receive propositions from two of her supervisors: Arthur Burton and James Gainey. When she raised the issue to their supervisor, Lawrence Swain, he dismissed her complaints, telling her that "any man in his right mind would want to rape you," and asked her to begin a sexual relationship with him. When Bundy became eligible for a promotion, she was passed over because of her "inadequate work performance," although she had never been told that her work performance was unsatisfactory. The U.S. Court of Appeals found that Bundy had been discriminated against because of her sex, thereby extending the idea of discrimination to sexual harassment.

A more subtle, and possibly more pervasive, form of sexual harassment is "hostile working environment." This occurs when someone's behavior in the workplace creates an environment that makes it difficult for someone of a particular sex to work. Many plaintiffs in sexual harassment lawsuits have alleged that men ran their fingers

figure 3.3

Sexual Harassment Charges, 1991–2010

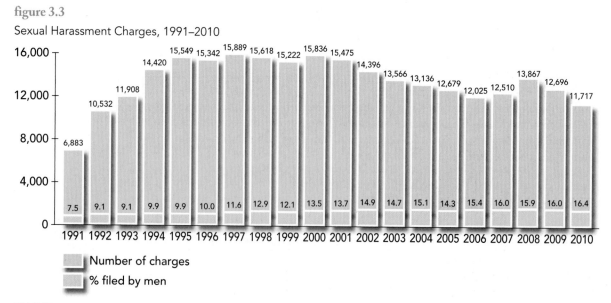

SOURCE: www.eeoc.gov/stats/harass.html.

table 3.4

EEOC Definition of
Sexual Harassment

Unwelcome sexual advances, requests for sexual favors, and other verbal or physical contact of a sexual nature constitute sexual harassment when

1. Submission to such conduct is made either explicitly or implicitly a term or condition of an individual's employment,
2. Submission to or rejection of such conduct by an individual is used as the basis for employment decisions affecting such individual, or
3. Such conduct has the purpose or effect of unreasonably interfering with an individual's work performance or creating an intimidating, hostile, or offensive working environment.

SOURCE: EEOC guideline based on the Civil Rights Act of 1964, Title VII.

through the plaintiffs' hair, made suggestive remarks, and physically assaulted them by touching their intimate body parts. Other examples include having pictures of naked women posted in the workplace, using offensive sexually explicit language, or using sex-related jokes or innuendoes in conversations.[40]

Note that these types of behaviors are actionable under Title VII because they treat individuals differently based on their sex. In addition, although most harassment cases involve male-on-female harassment, any individual can be harassed. For example, male employees at Jenny Craig alleged that they were sexually harassed, and a federal jury found that a male employee had been sexually harassed by his male boss.[41]

In addition, Ron Clark Ford of Amarillo, Texas, recently agreed to pay $140,000 to six male plaintiffs who alleged that they and others were subjected to a sexually hostile work environment and different treatment because of their gender by male managers. Evidence gathered showed that the men were subjected to lewd, inappropriate comments of a sexual nature, and had their genitals and buttocks grabbed against their will by their male managers. The defendants argued that the conduct was "harmless horseplay."[42]

Finally, Babies 'R' Us agreed to pay $205,000 to resolve a same-sex suit. The lawsuit alleged that Andres Vasquez was subjected to a sexually hostile working environment and was the target of unwelcome and derogatory comments as well as behavior that mocked him because he did not conform to societal stereotypes of how a male should appear or behave.

Sexual harassment charge filings with the EEOC by men have increased to 16.4% of all filings in 2010, from 10% of filings in 1994. While the commission does not track same-sex, male-on-male charges, anecdotal evidence shows that most harassment allegations by men are against other men.[43]

There are three critical issues in these cases. First, the plaintiff cannot have "invited or incited" the advances. Often the plaintiff's sexual history, whether she or he wears provocative clothing, and whether she or he engages in sexually explicit conversations are used to prove or disprove that the advance was unwelcome. However, in the absence of substantial evidence that the plaintiff invited the behavior, courts usually lean toward assuming that sexual advances do not belong in the workplace and thus are unwelcome. In *Meritor Savings Bank v. Vinson*, Michelle Vinson claimed that during the four years she worked at a bank she was continually harassed by the bank's vice president, who repeatedly asked her to have sex with him (she eventually agreed) and sexually assaulted her.[44] The Supreme Court ruled that the victim's voluntary participation in sexual relations was not the major issue, saying that the focus of the case was on whether the vice president's advances were unwelcome.

A second critical issue is that the harassment must have been severe enough to alter the terms, conditions, and privileges of employment. Although it has not yet been consistently applied, many courts have used the "reasonable woman" standard in determining the severity or pervasiveness of the harassment. This consists of assessing whether a reasonable woman, faced with the same situation, would have reacted similarly. The reasonable woman standard recognizes that behavior that might be considered appropriate by a man (like off-color jokes) might not be considered appropriate by a woman.

The third issue is that the courts must determine whether the organization is liable for the actions of its employees. In doing so, the court usually examines two things. First, did the employer know about, or should he or she have known about, the harassment? Second, did the employer act to stop the behavior? If the employer knew about it and the behavior did not stop, the court usually decides that the employer did not act appropriately to stop it.

To ensure a workplace free from sexual harassment, organizations can follow some important steps. First, the organization can develop a policy statement that makes it very clear that sexual harassment will not be tolerated in the workplace. Second, all employees, new and old, can be trained to identify inappropriate workplace behavior. Third, the organization can develop a mechanism for reporting sexual harassment that encourages people to speak out. Fourth, management can prepare to take prompt disciplinary action against those who commit sexual harassment as well as appropriate action to protect the victims of sexual harassment.[45]

AFFIRMATIVE ACTION AND REVERSE DISCRIMINATION

Few would disagree that having a diverse workforce in terms of race and gender is a desirable goal, if all individuals have the necessary qualifications. In fact, many organizations today are concerned with developing and managing diversity. To eliminate discrimination in the workplace, many organizations have affirmative action programs to increase minority representation. Affirmative action was originally conceived as a way of taking extra effort to attract and retain minority employees. This was normally done by extensively recruiting minorities on college campuses, advertising in minority-oriented publications, and providing educational and training opportunities to minorities.[46] However, over the years, many organizations have resorted to quotalike hiring to ensure that their workforce composition mirrors that of the labor market. Sometimes these organizations act voluntarily; in other cases, the quotas are imposed by the courts or by the EEOC. Whatever the impetus for these hiring practices, many white and/or male individuals have fought against them, alleging what is called reverse discrimination.

An example of an imposed quota program is found at the fire department in Birmingham, Alabama. Having admitted a history of discriminating against blacks, the department entered into a consent decree with the EEOC to hold 50% of positions at all levels in the fire department open for minorities even though minorities made up only 28% of the relevant labor market. The result was that some white applicants were denied employment or promotion in favor of black applicants who scored lower on a selection battery. The federal court found that the city's use of the inflexible hiring formula violated federal civil rights law and the constitutional guarantee of equal protection. The appellate court agreed, and the Supreme Court refused to hear the case, thus making the decision final.

Ricci v. DeStefano represents another recent case that has been appealed to the Supreme Court regarding the potential for reverse discrimination based on a situation in New Haven, Connecticut. In this case a professional consulting firm developed a firefighter test specifically eliminating questions that had adverse impact against minority members (based on pilot study testing). However, when the test was given, no blacks made the promotion list, so the city simply ignored the test and promoted no one. White and Hispanic firefighters who would have been on the promotion list sued, stating that the failure to use the test results discriminated against them because of their race. The district and appellate courts ruled that because no blacks were promoted either (because there were no promotions), there had been no discrimination.

The entire issue of affirmative action should evoke considerable attention and debate over the next few years. Although most individuals support the idea of diversity, few argue for the kinds of quotas that have to some extent resulted from the present legal climate. In fact, one recent survey revealed that only 16% of the respondents favored affirmative action with quotas, 46% favored it without quotas, and 28% opposed all affirmative action programs. One study found that people favor affirmative action when it is operationalized as recruitment, training, and attention to applicant qualifications but oppose it when it consists of discrimination, quotas, and preferential treatment.[47]

OUTCOMES OF THE AMERICANS WITH DISABILITIES ACT

The ADA was passed with the laudable goals of providing employment opportunities for the truly disabled who, in the absence of legislation, were unable to find employment. Certainly, some individuals with disabilities have found employment as a result of its passage. However, as often occurs with legislation, the impact is not necessarily what was intended. First, there has been increased litigation. The EEOC reports that more than 200,000 complaints have been filed since passage of the act. Approximately 50% of the complaints filed have been found to be without reasonable cause. For example, in one case a company fired an employee for stealing from other employees and bringing a loaded gun to work. The fired employee sued for reinstatement under the ADA, claiming that he was the victim of a mental illness and thus should be considered disabled.[48]

A second problem is that the kinds of cases being filed are not what Congress intended to protect. Although the act was passed because of the belief that discrimination against individuals with disabilities occurred in the failure to hire them, 52.2% of the claims deal with firings, 28.9% with failure to make reasonable accommodation, and 12.5% with harassment. Only 9.4% of the complaints allege a failure to hire or rehire.[49] In addition, although the act was passed to protect people with major disabilities such as blindness, deafness, lost limbs, or paralysis, these disabilities combined account for a small minority of the disabilities claimed. As we see in Table 3.5, the biggest disability category is "other," meaning that the plaintiff claims a disability that is not one of the 35 types of impairment listed in the EEOC charge data system. The second largest category is "being regarded as disabled" accounting for 12.8% of all charges, followed by "back impairment" claims at 9.7%. As an example, recently a fired employee sued IBM asking for $5 million in damages for violation of the Americans with Disabilities Act. The employee had been fired for spending hours at work visiting adult chat rooms on his computer. He alleged that his addiction to sex and the Internet stemmed from trauma experienced by seeing a friend killed in 1969 during an Army patrol in Vietnam.[50]

Finally, the act does not appear to have had its anticipated impact on the employment of Americans with disabilities. According to the National Organization on Disability, 22 million of the 54 million disabled Americans are unemployed.[51]

table 3.5

Sample of Complaints Filed under the ADA

	1997	1998	1999	2000	2001	2002	2003	2004	2005	2006	2007	2008	2009	2010
Number of complaints	18,108	17,806	17,007	15,864	16,470	15,964	15,377	15,576	14,893	15,575	17,734	19,453	21,451	25,165
% dealing with*														
Asthma	1.5%	1.9%	1.8%	2.0%	1.6%	1.6%	1.6%	1.5%	1.6%	1.7%	1.0%	1.7	1.6	1.7
Back impairment	14.9	12.9	12.2	10.2	9.3	9.5	8.6	8.0	8.4	8.1	8.3	9.3	9.9	9.7
Cancer	2.5	2.6	2.3	2.7	2.8	2.9	2.9	2.8	2.7	3.2	3.3	3.6	3.7	3.9
Diabetes	3.7	3.7	4.0	4.1	4.3	4.7	4.8	4.7	4.5	4.8	5.1	5.6	5.5	5.4
Hearing	2.8	2.9	2.9	3.1	2.9	3.2	3.1	3.4	3.2	3.3	3.0	3.3	3.3	3.1
Vision	2.4	2.4	2.5	2.3	2.3	2.6	2.6	2.5	2.3	2.3	2.5	2.6	2.2	2.3
Heart	3.7	3.8	3.8	3.3	3.6	4.0	3.7	3.5	3.3	3.4	3.7	3.8	3.8	4.2
Regarded as disabled	11.4	11.1	11.6	13.7	12.8	13.7	16.8	18.2	17.4	17.2	17.7	16.7	14.1	12.8
Drug addiction	0.8	0.7	0.5	0.6	0.5	0.6	0.6	0.5	0.3	0.5	0.5	0.7	0.6	0.5
Anxiety	2.5	3.0	3.0	3.4	3.4	4.1	3.5	2.4	2.2	2.2	2.8	4.5	5.3	5.3
Depression	7.6	9.9	7.5	7.8	7.5	7.6	7.7	6.9	8.7	6.3	6.8	7.3	7.1	7.1
Other	20.0	20.2	21.4	22.2	22.3	23.7	18.1	12.3	14.7	15.7	16.4	20.2	24.4	26.3

*Not all complaints are listed.

SOURCE: EEOC, http://www.eeoc.gov/stats/ada-receipts.html.

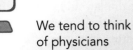

Getting Doctors to Use Technology

We tend to think of physicians as being among the best-educated occupations and, in terms of years of education, such a conclusion is justified. However, in response to the fast-rising health care costs, the medical community has turned to increasingly leveraging technology as a cost-saving device, and the biggest impediment to successful implementation may be doctors.

Hospitals spent millions of dollars implementing electronic medical records. Such record keeping allows doctors to enter orders for medication on the computer and to take patients' medical histories on the computer. However, doing so requires doctors to change their work habits, and it is not clear they are on board. For instance, rather than waiting until the end of a child's examination to check on vaccinations, they now have to do that at the beginning to order the shots on their computer so a nurse will have them ready at the end. Sarah Corley, the chief medical officer at NextGen Healthcare, suggests that many hospitals "have underestimated how hard it can be to get full participation by staff." This lack of participation comes, in part, because many doctors are skeptical about the extent to which electronic records can improve productivity and patient care.

However, even if a health care organization succeeds in getting buy-in, there will still be the need to train those using the technologies in how to do so. This creates another challenge as doctors are not usually fans of large classroom training. George Reynolds, chief information officer at Children's Hospital and Medical Center in Omaha, Nebraska, states, "No one likes to feel that they're not masters of the material, and they're frankly uncomfortable about being perceived as less than masterful."

This has led many hospitals to focus on more smaller-group training settings. So, Children's Hospital provides 8 to 10 hours of training in groups as small as two-to-four physicians at a time. Other hospitals are finding that physicians would rather be trained by other physicians, and at times that work in their schedules. Thus one doctor requested and received training at 3 AM.

Electronic medical records have been proposed as one critical aspect of the transformation of the health care delivery system. Hopefully it won't be the doctors that stand in the way.

SOURCE: K. Hobson, "Getting Docs to Use PCs," *The Wall Street Journal*, March 15, 2011, http://online.wsj.com.

For these reasons, Congress has explored the possibility of amending the act to more narrowly define the term disability.[52] The debate continues regarding the effectiveness of the ADA.

The "Competing through Technology" box describes the difficulties that hospitals are having to get doctors to use technology systems that are purported to reduce health care costs.

Employee Safety

In March 2005, officials at the BP refinery in Texas City, Texas, were aware of the fact that some repairs needed to be done on some of the equipment in an octane-boosting processing unit. On March 23, knowing that some of the key alarms were not working, managers authorized a start-up of the unit. The start-up resulted in the deadliest petrochemical accident in 15 years, killing 15 people and injuring an additional 170.[53]

LO 3-7
Identify the major provisions of the Occupational Safety and Health Act (1970) and the rights of employees that are guaranteed by this act.

Like equal employment opportunity, employee safety is regulated by both the federal and state governments. However, to fully maximize the safety and health of workers, employers need to go well beyond the letter of the law and embrace its spirit. With this in mind, we first spell out the specific protections guaranteed by federal legislation and then discuss various kinds of safety awareness programs that attempt to reinforce these standards.

THE OCCUPATIONAL SAFETY AND HEALTH ACT (OSHA)

Occupational Safety and Health Act (OSHA)
The law that authorizes the federal government to establish and enforce occupational safety and health standards for all places of employment engaging in interstate commerce.

Although concern for worker safety would seem to be a universal societal goal, the **Occupational Safety and Health Act (OSHA)**—the most comprehensive legislation regarding worker safety—did not emerge in this country until the early 1970s. At that time, there were roughly 15,000 work-related fatalities every year.

OSHA authorized the federal government to establish and enforce occupational safety and health standards for all places of employment engaging in interstate commerce. The responsibility for inspecting employers, applying the standards, and levying fines was assigned to the Department of Labor. The Department of Health was assigned responsibility for conducting research to determine the criteria for specific operations or occupations and for training employers to comply with the act. Much of this research is conducted by the National Institute for Occupational Safety and Health (NIOSH).

Employee Rights under OSHA

General Duty Clause
The provision of the Occupational Safety and Health Act that states that an employer has an overall obligation to furnish employees with a place of employment free from recognized hazards.

The main provision of OSHA states that each employer has a general duty to furnish each employee a place of employment free from recognized hazards that cause or are likely to cause death or serious physical harm. This is referred to as the **general duty clause.** Some specific rights granted to workers under this act are listed in Table 3.6. The Department of Labor recognizes many specific types of hazards, and employers are required to comply with all the occupational safety and health standards published by NIOSH.

A recent example is the development of OSHA standards for occupational exposure to blood-borne pathogens such as the AIDS virus. These standards identify 24 affected industrial sectors, encompassing 500,000 establishments and 5.6 million workers. Among other features, these standards require employers to develop an exposure control plan (ECP). An ECP must include a list of jobs whose incumbents might be exposed to blood, methods for implementing precautions in these jobs, postexposure follow-up plans, and procedures for evaluating incidents in which workers are accidentally infected.

table 3.6

Rights Granted to Workers under the Occupational Safety and Health Act

Employees have the right to
1. Request an inspection.
2. Have a representative present at an inspection.
3. Have dangerous substances identified.
4. Be promptly informed about exposure to hazards and be given access to accurate records regarding exposures.
5. Have employer violations posted at the work site.

Although NIOSH publishes numerous standards, regulators clearly cannot anticipate all possible hazards that could occur in the workplace. Thus, the general duty clause requires employers to be constantly alert for potential sources of harm in the workplace (as defined by the standards of a reasonably prudent person) and to correct them. For example, managers at Amoco's Joliet, Illinois, plant realized that over the years some employees had created undocumented shortcuts and built them into their process for handling flammable materials. These changes appeared to be labor saving but created a problem: workers did not have uniform procedures for dealing with flammable products. This became an urgent issue because many of the experienced workers were reaching retirement age, and the plant was in danger of losing critical technical expertise. To solve this problem, the plant adopted a training program that met all the standards required by OSHA. That is, it conducted a needs analysis highlighting each task new employees had to learn and then documented these processes in written guidelines. New employees were given hands-on training with the new procedures and were then certified in writing by their supervisor. A computer tracking system was installed to monitor who was handling flammable materials, and this system immediately identified anyone who was not certified. The plant met requirements for both ISO 9000 standards and OSHA regulations and continues to use the same model for safety training in other areas of the plant.[54]

● OSHA is responsible for inspecting businesses, applying safety and health standards, and levying fines for violations. OSHA regulations prohibit notifying employers of inspections in advance.

OSHA Inspections

OSHA inspections are conducted by specially trained agents of the Department of Labor called compliance officers. These inspections usually follow a tight "script." Typically, the compliance officer shows up unannounced. For obvious reasons, OSHA's regulations prohibit advance notice of inspections. The officer, after presenting credentials, tells the employer the reasons for the inspection and describes, in a general way, the procedures necessary to conduct the investigation.

An OSHA inspection has four major components. First, the compliance officer reviews the employer's records of deaths, injuries, and illnesses. OSHA requires this kind of record keeping from all firms with 11 or more full- or part-time employees. Second, the officer, typically accompanied by a representative of the employer (and perhaps by a representative of the employees), conducts a "walkaround" tour of the employer's premises. On this tour, the officer notes any conditions that may violate specific published standards or the less specific general duty clause. The third component of the inspection, employee interviews, may take place during the tour. At this time, any person who is aware of a violation can bring it to the attention of the officer. Finally, in a closing conference the compliance officer discusses the findings with the employer, noting any violations. The employer is given a reasonable time frame in which to correct these violations. If any violation represents imminent danger (that is, could cause serious injury or death before being eliminated through the normal enforcement procedures), the officer may, through the Department of Labor, seek a restraining order from a U.S. district court. Such an order compels the employer to correct the problem immediately.

Citations and Penalties

If a compliance officer believes that a violation has occurred, he or she issues a citation to the employer that specifies the exact practice or situation that violates the act. The employer is required to post this citation in a prominent place near the location of the violation—even if the employer intends to contest it. Nonserious violations may be assessed up to $1,000 for each incident, but this may be adjusted downward if the employer has no prior history of violations or if the employer has made a good-faith effort to comply with the act. Serious violations of the act or willful, repeated violations may be fined up to $10,000 per incident. Fines for safety violations are never levied against the employees themselves. The assumption is that safety is primarily the responsibility of the employer, who needs to work with employees to ensure that they use safe working procedures.

In addition to these civil penalties, criminal penalties may also be assessed for willful violations that kill an employee. Fines can go as high as $20,000, and the employer or agents of the employer can be imprisoned. Criminal charges can also be brought against anyone who falsifies records that are subject to OSHA inspection or anyone who gives advance notice of an OSHA inspection without permission from the Department of Labor.

The Effect of OSHA

OSHA has been unquestionably successful in raising the level of awareness of occupational safety. Table 3.7 presents recent data on occupational injuries and illnesses. Yet legislation alone cannot solve all the problems of work site safety.[55] Many industrial accidents are a product of unsafe behaviors, not unsafe working conditions. Because the act does not directly regulate employee behavior, little behavior change can be expected unless employees are convinced of the standards' importance.[56] This has been recognized by labor leaders. For example, Lynn Williams, president of the United Steelworkers of America, noted, "We can't count on government. We can't count on employers. We must rely on ourselves to bring about the safety and health of our workers."[57]

table 3.7

Some of the Most Recent Statistics Provided by the Bureau of Labor Statistics Regarding Workplace Illnesses and Injuries

NONFATAL INJURIES AND ILLNESSES, PRIVATE INDUSTRY	FATAL WORK-RELATED INJURIES
Total recordable cases: 3,900,000 in 2009	Total fatalities (all sectors): 4,551(p) in 2009
Cases involving days away from work: 1,238,490 in 2009	Total fatalities (private industry): 4,956(p) in 2009
Cases involving sprains, strains, tears: 493,170 in 2009	Highway incidents (private industry): 985(p) in 2009
Cases involving injuries to the back: 242,380 in 2009	Falls (private industry): 645(p) in 2009
Cases involving falls: 265,680 in 2009	Homicides (private industry): 542(p) in 2009

p=preliminary
SOURCE: www.bls.gov.

Because conforming to the statute alone does not necessarily guarantee safety, many employers go beyond the letter of the law. In the next section we examine various kinds of employer-initiated safety awareness programs that comply with OSHA requirements and, in some cases, exceed them.

SAFETY AWARENESS PROGRAMS

Safety awareness programs go beyond compliance with OSHA and attempt to instill symbolic and substantive changes in the organization's emphasis on safety. These programs typically focus either on specific jobs and job elements or on specific types of injuries or disabilities. A safety awareness program has three primary components: identifying and communicating hazards, reinforcing safe practices, and promoting safety internationally.

Identifying and Communicating Job Hazards

Employees, supervisors, and other knowledgeable sources need to sit down and discuss potential problems related to safety. The **job hazard analysis technique** is one means of accomplishing this.[58] With this technique, each job is broken down into basic elements, and each of these is rated for its potential for harm or injury. If there is consensus that some job element has high hazard potential, this element is isolated and potential technological or behavioral changes are considered.

Another means of isolating unsafe job elements is to study past accidents. The **technic of operations review (TOR)** is an analysis methodology that helps managers determine which specific element of a job led to a past accident.[59] The first step in a TOR analysis is to establish the facts surrounding the incident. To accomplish this, all members of the work group involved in the accident give their initial impressions of what happened. The group must then, through group discussion, reach a consensus on the single, systematic failure that most contributed to the incident as well as two or three major secondary factors that contributed to it.

An analysis of jobs at Burger King, for example, revealed that certain jobs required employees to walk across wet or slippery surfaces, which led to many falls. Specific corrective action was taken based on analysis of where people were falling and what conditions led to these falls. Now Burger King provides mats at critical locations and has generally upgraded its floor maintenance. The company also makes slip-resistant shoes available to employees in certain job categories.[60]

Communication of an employee's risk should take advantage of several media. Direct verbal supervisory contact is important for its saliency and immediacy. Written memos are important because they help establish a "paper trail" that can later document a history of concern regarding the job hazard. Posters, especially those placed near the hazard, serve as a constant reminder, reinforcing other messages.

In communicating risk, it is important to recognize two distinct audiences. Sometimes relatively young or inexperienced workers need special attention. Research by the National Safety Council indicates that 40% of all accidents happen to individuals in the 20-to-29 age group and that 48% of all accidents happen to workers during their first year on the job.[61] The employer's primary concern with respect to this group is to inform them. However, the employer must not overlook experienced workers. Here the key concern is to remind them. Research indicates that long-term exposure to and familiarity with a specific threat lead to complacency.[62] Experienced employees need retraining to jar them from complacency about the real dangers associated with their work. This is especially the case if the hazard in question poses a greater threat to older employees. For example, falling off a ladder is a greater threat to older

---

Safety Awareness Programs
Employer programs that attempt to instill symbolic and substantive changes in the organization's emphasis on safety.

Job Hazard Analysis Technique
A breakdown of each job into basic elements, each of which is rated for its potential for harm or injury.

Technic of Operations Review (TOR)
Method of determining safety problems via an analysis of past accidents.

workers than to younger ones. More than 20% of such falls lead to a fatality for workers in the 55-to-65 age group, compared with just 10% for all other workers.[63]

Reinforcing Safe Practices

One common technique for reinforcing safe practices is implementing a safety incentive program to reward workers for their support and commitment to safety goals. Initially, programs are set up to focus on improving short-term monthly or quarterly goals or to encourage safety suggestions. These short-term goals are later expanded to include more wide-ranging, long-term goals. Prizes are typically distributed in highly public forums (like annual meetings or events). These prizes usually consist of merchandise rather than cash because merchandise represents a lasting symbol of achievement. A good deal of evidence suggests that such programs are effective in reducing injuries and their cost.[64]

Whereas the safety awareness programs just described focus primarily on the job, other programs focus on specific injuries or disabilities. Lower back disability (LBD), for example, is a major problem that afflicts many employees. LBD accounts for approximately 25% of all workdays lost, costing firms nearly $30 billion a year.[65] Human resource managers can take many steps to prevent LBD and rehabilitate those who are already afflicted. Eye injuries are another target of safety awareness programs. The National Society to Prevent Blindness estimates that 1,000 eye injuries occur every day in occupational settings.[66] A 10-step program to reduce eye injuries is outlined in Table 3.8. Similar guidelines can be found for everything from chemical burns to electrocution to injuries caused by boiler explosions.[67]

Promoting Safety Internationally

Given the increasing focus on international management, organizations also need to consider how to best ensure the safety of people regardless of the nation in which they operate. Cultural differences may make this more difficult than it seems. For example, a recent study examined the impact of one standardized corporationwide safety policy on employees in three different countries: the United States, France, and Argentina. The results of this study indicated that the same policy was interpreted differently because of cultural differences. The individualistic, control-oriented culture of the United States stressed the role of top management in ensuring safety in a top-down

table 3.8

A 10-Step Program
for Reducing
Eye-Related Injuries

1. Conduct an eye hazard job analysis.
2. Test all employees' vision to establish a baseline.
3. Select protective eyewear designed for specific operations.
4. Establish a 100% behavioral compliance program for eyewear.
5. Ensure that eyewear is properly fitted.
6. Train employees in emergency procedures.
7. Conduct ongoing education programs regarding eye care.
8. Continually review accident prevention strategies.
9. Provide management support.
10. Establish written policies detailing sanctions and rewards for specific results.

SOURCE: From T. W. Turrif, "NSPB Suggests 10-Step Program to Prevent Eye Injury," *Occupational Health and Safety 60* (1991), pp. 62–66. Copyright © Media Inc. Reprinted with permission.

The Gap's Focus on Its Global Supply Chain

How do you manage a global supply chain consisting of thousands of independent vendors scattered across the globe in a way that ensures they provide safe workplaces that respect human rights?

In 2003 The Gap Inc. was the first retailer to release a social responsibility report, offering a comprehensive overview of its approach to social responsibility with a particular focus on the workplace practices of vendors in its global supply chain. The report was broadly lauded for its openness and honesty about both the successes and failures in this arena. In fact, this report won *Business Ethics* magazine's Social Reporting Award for "unprecedented honesty in reporting on factory conditions."

The Gap's 2004 Social Responsibility Report continued that discussion and provided new information on the company's progress, challenges, and new initiatives. Eva Sage-Gavin is the executive vice president of Human Resources and Corporate Communications at Gap, and here's how she describes its CSR efforts.

"There are really four key areas, and we think of corporate social responsibility across Gap, Inc., in these four strategic ways. The first one is this whole idea of sustainable solutions in our supply chain. This consists of working on a four-part strategy to improve working conditions,

monitor factories, integrate labor standards into our business practices, and the whole idea of collaborating with outside partners to drive industry-wide change. So that's the first big centerpiece of how we think about CSR. The second is with our employees and making Gap, Inc., a place where people can really flourish and build their careers in a positive work environment. The third is community involvement, including everything from our foundation to our volunteerism. And the fourth key area in corporate social responsibility for us is environment, health, and safety. This is everything from the average store energy consumption to the safety of our stores for customers and employees to a high-level environmental impact assessment for all of our business operations.

"We think that this is critical to our long-term growth and the sustainability of our business. We see there are three elements to the benefits. First is the idea of our employee attraction and retention. Our employees tell us they want to work for a company that's socially responsible and they tell us through a variety of channels that they love working for a company that they believe is doing what's right. The second piece for us is a better supply chain. We know that better factory working conditions lead to better factories, and better factories make better products. The sourcing team can also

select and make better buying decisions. We also introduced an integrated scorecard into the retail industry that gives factories feedback and scores on criteria such as quality, innovation, speed to market, and cost, and it considers the manufacturers' compliance history. Finally, our focus on sustainability creates win-win scenarios for everyone involved in our environmental impact. When we reduce our energy usage we also reduce cost. Obviously that's a win-win all the way around.

"I can say confidently that it's a critical part of our long-term growth and sustainability of our business. We know that our success depends on our employees and it depends on creating value for our shareholders, but ultimately it's about the customer experience and their desire to purchase great products. We know that we won't do that without employees who are engaged, satisfied, proud to work here—employees that want to exceed our customers' expectations. It's a very competitive global environment. We also know that improved factory working conditions lead to better factories, and that leads to a better supply chain."

SOURCE: Reprinted with permission from E. Sage-Gavin and P. Wright, "Corporate Social Responsibility at Gap," Inc., An Interview with Eva Sage-Gavin," *Human Resource Planning*, Vol. 30, No. 1, 2007, pp. 45–48. Published by HR People & Strategy. All rights reserved, www.hrps.org.

fashion. However, this policy failed to work in Argentina, where the collectivist culture made employees feel that safety was everyone's joint concern; therefore, programs needed to be defined from the bottom up.[68]

At the beginning of this section we discussed a horrific accident at BP's Texas City refinery. After examining the causes of the explosion, the U.S. Chemical Safety and Hazard Investigation Board asked BP to set up an independent panel that would focus on overseeing radical changes in BP's safety procedures. This panel was tasked with investigating the safety culture at BP along with the procedures for inspecting equipment and reporting near-miss accidents. The panel's charter is not just to oversee the Texas City refinery, but also to look at the safety practices in refineries that BP has acquired over the years.[69]

The "Competing through Globalization" box illustrates how The Gap has strategically managed a measurement and reporting system with regard to its suppliers to ensure that it is being socially responsible. This reporting system reveals The Gap's concern with human rights and safety in the workplace, usually the workplaces of their suppliers, scattered all across the globe.

A LOOK BACK

WAL-MART'S DISCRIMINATION?

At the opening and throughout this chapter, we have referred to the *Dukes v. Wal-Mart* case because it will be a watershed case for deciding the future of class-action discrimination suits. After reading about how pattern and practice discrimination suits proceed, do you think Wal-Mart has discriminated against 2 million female former employees?

Regardless of the merits of this particular suit, Wal-Mart has heard the message that it has problems—and has responded accordingly. For instance, in 2006 the company began hiring 300 human resource managers to work in the field, in addition to the 100 executives in its Bentonville, Arkansas, headquarters. Now their HR field structure contains five divisional heads, 27 regional HR directors, and 342 field HR managers. By placing more HR professionals side-by-side with store managers, they hope to provide more discipline to workforce decisions to ensure better compliance with the legal requirements.

However, this case continues to unfold. As the Supreme Court justices questioned the plaintiffs and defendants over the class-action question, they seemingly split along political lines. Conservative Justice Samuel Alito asked the plaintiffs, who base their claim on a simply statistical disparity, if that meant that "every single company" in the country could potentially be in violation of the Civil Rights Act. Liberal Justice Elena Kagan, on the other hand, suggested that to qualify as a class action the plaintiffs only need to show "that there is a practice, a policy of subjectivity that on the whole results in discrimination against women, not that each one of those women in the class were themselves discriminated against."

Questions

1. Based on what you read, do you think that Wal-Mart will win or lose the class-action discrimination case brought against it?

2. Assume that you have taken over the HR function at Wal-Mart and want to make sure that your pay system is fair, so you commission a salary study that

reveals pay differences between men and women. If you publicize the data and try to fix the problem, you open the company up to liability for past discrimination. What will you do?

3. What do you think? Is a statistical disparity proof of discrimination, and if one exists, does that open every member of the protected group up to a remedy, even if they had not individually been discriminated against?

SOURCES: J. Marquez, "Wal-Mart Puts on a New Face," *Workforce Management*, August 14, 2006, p. 29; R. Parloff and S. Kaufman, "The War Over Unconscious Bias," *Fortune*, October 15, 2007, p. 90.

 Please see the Video that corresponds to this chapter at www.mhhe.com/noe8e.

Summary

Viewing employees as a source of competitive advantage results in dealing with them in ways that are ethical and legal as well as providing a safe workplace. An organization's legal environment—especially the laws regarding equal employment opportunity and safety—has a particularly strong effect on its HRM function. HRM is concerned with the management of people, and government is concerned with protecting individuals. One of HRM's major challenges, therefore, is to perform its function within the legal constraints imposed by the government. Given the multimillion-dollar settlements resulting from violations of EEO laws (and the moral requirement to treat people fairly regardless of their sex or race) as well as the penalties for violating OSHA, HR and line managers need a good understanding of the legal requirements and prohibitions in order to manage their businesses in ways that are sound, both financially and ethically. Organizations that do so effectively will definitely have a competitive advantage.

Key Terms

Equal employment opportunity (EEO), 110
Americans with Disabilities Act (ADA) of 1990, 116
Equal Employment Opportunity Commission (EEOC), 118
Utilization analysis, 120
Goals and timetables, 120

Action steps, 120
Disparate treatment, 121
Bona fide occupational qualification (BFOQ), 123
Disparate impact, 124
Four-fifths rule, 125
Standard deviation rule, 125
Reasonable accommodation, 128

Occupational Safety and Health Act (OSHA), 140
General duty clause, 140
Safety awareness programs, 143
Job hazard analysis technique, 143
Technic of operations review (TOR), 143

Discussion Questions

1. Disparate impact theory was originally created by the court in the *Griggs* case before finally being codified by Congress 20 years later in the Civil Rights Act of 1991. Given the system of law in the United States, from what branch of government should theories of discrimination develop?

2. Disparate impact analysis (the four-fifths rule, standard deviation analysis) is used in employment discrimination cases. The National Assessment of Education Progress conducted by the U.S. Department of Education found that among 21- to 25-year-olds (a) 60% of whites, 40% of Hispanics, and 25% of blacks could locate information in a news article or almanac; (b) 25% of whites, 7% of Hispanics, and 3% of blacks could decipher a bus schedule; and (c) 44% of whites, 20% of Hispanics, and 8% of blacks could correctly determine the change they were due from the purchase of a two-item restaurant

meal. Do these tasks (locating information in a news article, deciphering a bus schedule, and determining correct change) have adverse impact? What are the implications?

3. Many companies have dress codes that require men to wear suits and women to wear dresses. Is this discriminatory according to disparate treatment theory? Why?

4. Cognitive ability tests seem to be the most valid selection devices available for hiring employees, yet they also have adverse impact against blacks and Hispanics. Given the validity and adverse impact, and considering that race norming is illegal under CRA 1991, what would you say in response to a recommendation that such tests be used for hiring?

5. How might the ADA's reasonable accommodation requirement affect workers such as law enforcement officers and firefighters?

6. The reasonable woman standard recognizes that women have different ideas than men of what constitutes appropriate behavior. What are the implications of this distinction? Do you think it is a good or bad idea to make this distinction?

7. Employers' major complaint about the ADA is that the costs of making reasonable accommodations will reduce their ability to compete with businesses (especially foreign ones) that do not face these requirements. Is this a legitimate concern? How should employers and society weigh the costs and benefits of the ADA?

8. Many have suggested that OSHA penalties are too weak and misdirected (aimed at employers rather than employees) to have any significant impact on employee safety. Do you think that OSHA-related sanctions need to be strengthened, or are existing penalties sufficient? Defend your answer.

SELF-ASSESSMENT EXERCISE

Take the following self-assessment quiz. For each statement, circle T if the statement is true or F if the statement is false.

What do you know about sexual harassment?

1. A man cannot be the victim of sexual harassment.   T   F

2. The harasser can only be the victim's manager or a manager in another work area.   T   F

3. Sexual harassment charges can be filed only by the person who directly experiences the harassment.   T   F

4. The best way to discourage sexual harassment is to have a policy that discourages employees from dating each other.   T   F

5. Sexual harassment is not a form of sex discrimination.   T   F

6. After receiving a sexual harassment complaint, the employer should let the situation cool off before investigating the complaint.   T   F

7. Sexual harassment is illegal only if it results in the victim being laid off or receiving lower pay.   T   F

EXERCISING STRATEGY: HOME DEPOT'S BUMPY ROAD TO EQUALITY

Home Depot is the largest home products firm selling home repair products and equipment for the "do-it-yourselfer." Founded 20 years ago, it now boasts 100,000 employees and more than 900 warehouse stores nationwide. The company's strategy for growth has focused mostly on one task: build more stores. In fact, an unwritten goal of Home Depot executives was to position a store within 30 minutes of every customer in the United States. They've almost made it. In addition, Home Depot has tried hard to implement a strategy of providing superior service to its customers. The company has prided itself on hiring people who are knowledgeable about home repair and who can teach customers how to do home repairs on their own. This strategy, along with blanketing the country with stores, has led to the firm's substantial advantage over competitors, including the now-defunct Home Quarters (HQ) and still-standing Lowe's.

But Home Depot has run into some legal problems. During the company's growth, a statistical anomaly has emerged. About 70% of the merchandise employees (those directly involved in selling lumber, electrical supplies, hardware, and so forth) are men, whereas about 70% of operations employees (cashiers, accountants, back office staff, and so forth) are women. Because of this difference, several years ago a lawsuit was filed on behalf of 17,000 current and former employees as well as up to 200,000 rejected applicants. Home Depot explained the disparity by noting that most female job applicants have experience as cashiers, so they are placed in cashier positions; most male applicants express an interest in or aptitude for home repair work such as carpentry or plumbing. However, attorneys argued that Home Depot was reinforcing gender stereotyping by hiring in this manner.

More recently, five former Home Depot employees sued the company, charging that it had discriminated against African American workers at two stores in southeast Florida. The five alleged that they were paid less than white workers, passed over for promotion, and given critical performance reviews based on race. "The company takes exception to the charges and believes they are without merit," said Home Depot spokesman Jerry Shields. The company has faced other racial discrimination suits as well, including one filed by the Michigan Department of Civil Rights.

To avoid such lawsuits in the future, Home Depot could resort to hiring and promoting by quota, ensuring an equal distribution of employees across all job categories—something that the company has wanted to avoid because it believes such action would undermine its competitive advantage. However, the company has taken steps to broaden and strengthen its own nondiscrimination policy by adding sexual orientation to the written policy. In addition, company president and CEO Bob Nardelli announced in the fall of 2001 that Home Depot would take special steps to protect benefits for its more than 500 employees who serve in the Army reserves and had been activated. "We will make up any difference between their Home Depot pay and their military pay if it's lower," said Nardelli. "When they come home [from duty], their jobs and their orange aprons are waiting for them."

In settling the gender discrimination suit the company agreed to pay $65 million to women who had been steered to cashiers' jobs and had been denied promotions. In addition, the company promised that every applicant would get a "fair shot." Home Depot's solution to this has been to leverage technology to make better hiring decisions that ensure the company is able to maximize diversity.

Home Depot instituted its Job Preference Program, an automated hiring and promotion system, across its 900 stores at a cost of $10 million. It has set up kiosks where potential applicants can log on to a computer, complete an application, and undergo a set of prescreening tests. This process weeds out unqualified applicants. Then the system prints out test scores along with structured interview questions and examples of good and bad answers for the managers interviewing those who make it through the prescreening. In addition, the Home Depot system is used for promotions. Employees are asked to constantly update their skills and career aspirations so they can be considered for promotions at nearby stores.

The system has been an unarguable success. Managers love it because they are able to get high-quality applicants without having to sift through mounds of résumés. In addition, the system seems to have accomplished its main purpose. The number of female managers has increased 30% and the number of minority managers by 28% since the introduction of the system. In fact, David Borgen, the co-counsel for the plaintiffs in the original lawsuit, states, "No one can say it can't be done anymore, because Home Depot is doing it bigger and better than anyone I know."

Questions

1. If Home Depot was correct in that it was not discriminating, but simply filling positions consistent with those who applied for them (and very few women were applying for customer service positions), given your reading of this chapter, was the firm guilty of discrimination? If so, under what theory?
2. How does this case illustrate the application of new technology to solving issues that have never been tied to technology? Can you think of other ways technology might be used to address diversity/EEO/affirmative action issues?

SOURCES: "Home Depot Says Thanks to America's Military; Extends Associates/Reservists' Benefits, Announces Military Discount," company press release, October 9, 2001; S. Jaffe, "New Tricks in Home Depot's Toolbox?" *BusinessWeek* Online, June 5, 2001, at www.businessweek.com; "HRC Lauds Home Depot for Adding Sexual Orientation to Its Non-discrimination Policy," Human Rights Campaign, May 14, 2001, at www.hrc.org; "Former Home Depot Employees File Racial Discrimination Lawsuit," Diversity at Work, June 2000, at www.diversityatwork.com; "Michigan Officials File Discrimination Suit against Home Depot," Diversity at Work, February 2000, at www.diversityatwork.com; M. Boot, "For Plaintiffs' Lawyers, There's No Place Like Home Depot," *The Wall Street Journal*, interactive edition, February 12, 1997.

● Managing People

Brown v. Board of Education: A Bittersweet Birthday

Decades of progress on integration have been followed by disturbing slippage

May 17 marks the 50th anniversary of *Brown v. Board of Education*, the landmark Supreme Court ruling that declared racially segregated "separate but equal" schools unconstitutional. The case is widely regarded as one of the court's most important decisions of the 20th century, but the birthday celebration will be something of a bittersweet occasion. There's no question that African Americans have made major strides since—economically, socially, and educationally. But starting in the late 1980s, political backlash brought racial progress to a halt. Since then, schools have slowly been resegregating, and the achievement gap between white and minority schoolchildren has been widening again. Can the United States ever achieve the great promise of integration? Some key questions follow.

What did the court strike down in 1954? Throughout the South and in border states such as Delaware, black and white children were officially assigned to separate schools. In Topeka, Kansas, the lead city in the famous case, there were 18 elementary schools for whites and just 4 for blacks, forcing many African American children to travel a long way to school. The idea that black schools were "equal" to those for whites was a cruel fiction, condemning most black kids to a grossly inferior education.

Surely we've come a long way since then? Yes, though change took a long time. Over 99% of Southern black children were still in segregated schools in 1963. The 1960s civil rights movement eventually brought aggressive federal policies such as busing and court orders that forced extensive integration, especially in the South. So by 1988, 44% of Southern black children were attending schools where a majority of students were white, up from 2% in 1964. "We cut school desegregation almost in half between 1968 and 1990," says John Logan, director of the Lewis Mumford Center for Comparative Urban and Regional Research at State University of New York at Albany.

What's the picture today? There have been some real gains. The share of blacks graduating from high school has nearly quadrupled since *Brown,* to 88% today, while the share of those ages 25 to 29 with a college degree has increased more than sixfold, to 18%.

Another important trend is in housing, which in turn helps determine the characteristics of school districts. Residential integration is improving, albeit at a glacial pace. There's still high housing segregation in major metropolitan areas, but it has fallen four percentage points, to 65%, on an index developed by the Mumford Center. Some of the gains are happening in fast-growing new suburbs where race lines aren't so fixed. A few big cities have improved, too. In Dallas, for example, black–white residential segregation fell from 78% in 1980 to 59% in 2000.

Why haven't schools continued to desegregate, too? The increased racial mixing in housing hasn't been nearly large enough to offset the sheer increase in the ranks of minority schoolchildren. While the number of white elementary school kids remained flat, at 15.3 million, between 1990 and 2000, the number of black children climbed by 800,000, to 4.6 million, while Hispanic kids jumped by 1.7 million, to 4.3 million. The result: Minorities now comprise 40% of public school kids, vs. 32% in 1990. And as the nonwhite population has expanded, so have minority neighborhoods—and schools.

So minorities have lost ground? Yes, in some respects. By age 17, black students are still more than three years behind their white counterparts in reading and math. And whites are twice as likely to graduate from college. Taken as a whole, U.S. schools have been resegregating for

15 years or so, according to studies by the Harvard University Civil Rights Project. "We're celebrating [Brown] at a time when schools in all regions are becoming increasingly segregated," says project co-director Gary Orfield.

What role has the political backlash against integration played? The courts and politicians have been pulling back from integration goals for quite a while. In 1974, the Supreme Court ruled that heavily black Detroit didn't have to integrate its schools with the surrounding white suburbs. Then, in the 1980s, the growing backlash against busing and race-based school assignment led politicians and the courts to all but give up on those remedies, too.

So what are the goals now? The approach has shifted dramatically. Instead of trying to force integration, the United States has moved toward equalizing education. In a growing number of states, the courts have been siding with lawsuits that seek equal or "adequate" funding for minority and low-income schools.

The No Child Left Behind Act goes even further. It says that all children will receive a "highly qualified" teacher by 2006 and will achieve proficiency in math and reading by 2014. It specifically requires schools to meet these goals for racial subgroups. Paradoxically, it sounds like separate but equal again. Both the equal-funding suits and No Child Left Behind aim to improve all schools, whatever their racial composition. Integration is no longer the explicit goal.

Can schools equalize without integrating? It's possible in some cases, but probably not for the United States as a whole. The Education Trust, a nonprofit group in Washington, D.C., has identified a number of nearly all-black, low-income schools that have achieved exceptional test results. But such success requires outstanding leadership, good teachers, and a fervent commitment to high standards.

These qualities are far more difficult to achieve in large urban schools with many poor kids—the kind most black and Hispanic students attend. The average minority student goes to a school in which two-thirds of the students are low-income. By contrast, whites attend schools that are just 30% low-income.

So are black–white achievement gaps as much about poverty as race? Yes, which is why closing them is difficult with or without racial integration. Studies show that middle-class students tend to have higher expectations, more engaged parents, and better teachers. Poor children, by contrast, often come to school with far more personal problems. Yet poor schools are more likely to get inferior teachers, such as those who didn't major in the subject they teach. Many poor schools also lose as many as 20% of their teachers each year, while most middle-class suburban schools have more stable teaching staffs. "Research suggests that when low-income students attend middle-class schools, they do substantially better," says Richard Kahlenberg, senior fellow at the Century Foundation, a public policy think tank in New York City.

Is it possible to achieve more economic integration? There are a few shining examples, but they take enormous political commitment. One example that education-system reformers love to highlight is Wake County, N.C., whose 110,000-student school district includes Raleigh. In 2000, it adopted a plan to ensure that low-income students make up no more than 40% of any student body. It also capped those achieving under grade level at 25%. Moreover, it used magnet schools offering specialized programs, such as one for gifted children, to help attract middle-income children to low-income areas.

Already, 91% of the county's third- to eighth-graders work at grade level in math and reading, up from 84% in 1999. More impressive, 75% of low-income kids are reading at grade level, up from just 56% in 1999, as are 78% of black children, up from 61%. "The academic payoff has been pretty incredible," says Walter C. Sherlin, a 28-year Wake County schools veteran and interim director of the nonprofit Wake Education Partnership.

Could this serve as a national model? For that to happen in many cities, school districts would have to merge with the surrounding suburbs. Wake County did this, but that was back in the 1970s and part of a long-term plan to bring about racial integration. In the metro Boston area, by contrast, students are balkanized into dozens of tiny districts, many of which are economically homogeneous. The result: Some 70% of white students attend schools that are over 90% white and overwhelmingly middle-class. Meanwhile, 97% of the schools that are over 90% minority are also high-poverty. Similar patterns exist in most major cities, but most affluent white suburbs aren't likely to swallow a move like Wake County's.

How important is funding equality within states? It's critical, especially if segregation by income and race persists. Massachusetts, for instance, has nearly tripled state aid to schools since 1993, with over 90% of the money going to the poorest towns. That has helped make Massachusetts a national leader in raising academic achievement.

Nationally, though, there are still huge inequities in school spending, with the poorest districts receiving less money than the richest—even though low-income children are more expensive to educate. Fixing these imbalances would be costly. Even in Massachusetts, a lower court judge ruled on April 26 that the system still shortchanges students in the poorest towns. Nationally, it would cost more than $50 billion a year in extra funding to correct inequities enough to meet the goals of No Child, figures Anthony P. Carnevale, a vice president at Educational Testing Service.

If, somehow, the United States could achieve more economic integration, would racial integration still be necessary? Proficiency on tests isn't the only aim. As the Supreme Court said last year in a landmark decision on affirmative action in higher education: "Effective participation by members of all racial and ethnic groups in the civic life of our nation is essential if the dream of one nation, indivisible, is to be realized." It's hard to see how students attending largely segregated schools, no matter how proficient, could be adequately prepared for life in an increasingly diverse country. In this sense, integrating America's educational system remains an essential, though still elusive, goal.

Questions

1. While segregation of public schools has been outlawed, the article notes that schools are not necessarily "desegregating" (i.e., there are still predominantly minority and predominantly nonminority schools). If students are to work in increasingly diverse workforces, is the current system failing them? Why or why not?

2. The black–white gap continues to exist with regard to reading, math, and graduation rates. What are the implications of this on organizations' selection systems (i.e., disparate impact)?

3. Given the lack of a "diverse" educational experience for a large percentage of black children, and the gap between them and their white counterparts, what must organizations do to leverage diversity as a source of competitive advantage?

SOURCE: From W. Symonds, "A Bittersweet Birthday," *BusinessWeek*, May 17, 2004, pp. 62–66. Used with permission of Bloomberg L. P. Copyright © 2004. All rights reserved.

TWITTER FOCUS: COMPANY FAILS FAIR-EMPLOYMENT TEST

Using Twitter, continue the conversation about companies complying with federal, state, and local laws by reading the fair-employment case at www.mhhe.com/noe8e.

A medical-testing company fired a female sales rep when she called in sick because of her daughter's contagious illness. The employee also discovered that female colleagues who did not have children were routinely paid more than female workers who had children. She sought help from the Chicago Human Relations Commission, which could find no performance-related problems that would justify her dismissal. The terminated employee was awarded a substantial settlement.

Engage with your classmates and instructor via Twitter to chat about the employee's experience using the case questions posted on the Noe website. Don't have a Twitter account yet? See the instructions for getting started on the Online Learning Center.

● NOTES

1. J. Ledvinka, *Federal Regulation of Personnel and Human Resource Management* (Boston: Kent, 1982).
2. *Martin v. Wilks*, 49 FEP Cases 1641 (1989).
3. *Wards Cove Packing Co. v. Atonio*, FEPC 1519 (1989).
4. *Bakke v. Regents of the University of California*, 17 FEPC 1000 (1978).
5. *Patterson v. McLean Credit Union*, 49 FEPC 1814 (1987).
6. J. Friedman and G. Strickler, *The Law of Employment Discrimination: Cases and Materials*, 2nd ed. (Mineola, NY: Foundation Press, 1987).
7. "Labor Letter," *The Wall Street Journal*, August 25, 1987, p. 1.
8. J. Woo, "Ex-Workers Hit Back with Age-Bias Suits," *The Wall Street Journal*, December 8, 1992, p. B1.
9. W. Carley, "Salesman's Treatment Raises Bias Questions at Schering-Plough," *The Wall Street Journal*, May 31, 1995, p. A1.
10. http://www.eeoc.gov/press/1-8-07.html.
11. http://www.eeoc.gov/eeoc/newsroom/release/4-27-11b.cfm.
12. Special feature issue: "The New Civil Rights Act of 1991 and What It Means to Employers," *Employment Law Update* 6 (December 1991), pp. 1–12.
13. "ADA: The Final Regulations (Title I): A Lawyer's Dream/An Employer's Nightmare," *Employment Law Update* 16, no. 9 (1991), p. 1.
14. "ADA Supervisor Training Program: A Must for Any Supervisor Conducting a Legal Job Interview," *Employment Law Update* 7, no. 6 (1992), pp. 1–6.
15. http://www.hreonline.com/HRE/story.jsp?storyId=533335303.
16. Equal Employment Opportunity Commission, "Uniform Guidelines on Employee Selection Procedures," *Federal Register* 43 (1978), pp. 38290–315.
17. Ledvinka, *Federal Regulation*.
18. R. Pear, "The Cabinet Searches for Consensus on Affirmative Action," *The New York Times*, October 27, 1985, p. E5.
19. *McDonnell Douglas v. Green*, 411 U.S. 972 (1973).
20. http://www.eeoc.gov/eeoc/newsroom/release/4-29-11.cfm.
21. *UAW v. Johnson Controls, Inc.* (1991).
22. M. O'Brien, "Ugly People Need Not Apply?" *HR Executive*, September 16, 2010, p. 12.
23. Special feature issue: "The New Civil Rights Act of 1991," pp. 1–6.
24. *Washington v. Davis*, 12 FEP 1415 (1976).
25. *Albermarle Paper Company v. Moody*, 10 FEP 1181 (1975).
26. R. Reilly and G. Chao, "Validity and Fairness of Some Alternative Employee Selection Procedures," *Personnel Psychology* 35 (1982), pp. 1–63; J. Hunter and R. Hunter, "Validity and Utility of Alternative Predictors of Job Performance," *Psychological Bulletin* 96 (1984), pp. 72–98.
27. *Griggs v. Duke Power Company*, 401 U.S. 424 (1971).
28. B. Lindeman and P. Grossman, *Employment Discrimination Law* (Washington, DC: BNA Books, 1996).
29. M. Jacobs, "Workers' Religious Beliefs May Get New Attention," *The Wall Street Journal*, August 22, 1995, pp. B1, B8.
30. EEOC, "EEOC and Electrolux Reach Voluntary Resolution in Class Religious Accommodation Case," at www.eeoc.gov/press/9-24-03.
31. S. Sataline, "Who's Wrong When Rights Collide?" *The Wall Street Journal*, March 6, 2007, p. B1.
32. "Manager's Failure to Accommodate Creates Liability for Store," *Disability Compliance Bulletin*, January 15, 2009.
33. Lindeman and Grossman, *Employment Discrimination Law*.
34. J. Reno and D. Thornburgh, "ADA—Not a Disabling Mandate," *The Wall Street Journal*, July 26, 1995, p. A12.
35. http://www.eeoc.gov/eeoc/newsroom/release/4-28-11.cfm.
36. Woo, "Ex-Workers Hit Back."
37. EEOC, "Target Corp. to Pay $775,000 for Racial Harassment: EEC Settles Suit for Class of African American Employees; Remedial Relief Included," at www.eeoc.gov/press/1-26-07.html.
38. W. Johnston and A. Packer, *Workforce 2000* (Indianapolis, IN: Hudson Institute, 1987).
39. *Bundy v. Jackson*, 641 F.2d 934, 24 FEP 1155 (D.C. Cir., 1981).
40. L. A. Graf and M. Hemmasi, "Risqué Humor: How It Really Affects the Workplace," *HR Magazine*, November 1995, pp. 64–69.
41. B. Carton, "At Jenny Craig, Men Are Ones Who Claim Sex Discrimination," *The Wall Street Journal*, November 29, 1995, p. A1; "Male-on-Male Harassment Suit Won," *Houston Chronicle*, August 12, 1995, p. 21A.
42. EEOC, "Texas Car Dealership to Pay $140,000 to Settle Same-Sex Harassment Suit by EEOC," at www.eeoc.gov/press/10-28-02.
43. EEOC, "Babies 'R' Us to Pay $205,000, Implement Training Due to Same-Sex Harassment of Male Employee," at www.eeoc.gov/press/1-15-03.
44. *Meritor Savings Bank v. Vinson* (1986).
45. R. Paetzold and A. O'Leary-Kelly, "The Implications of U.S. Supreme Court and Circuit Court Decisions for Hostile Environment Sexual Harassment Cases," in *Sexual Harassment: Perspectives, Frontiers, and Strategies*, ed. M. Stockdale (Beverly Hills, CA: Sage); R. B. McAfee and D. L. Deadrick, "Teach Employees to Just Say 'No'!" *HR Magazine*, February 1996, pp. 586–89.
46. C. Murray, "The Legacy of the 60's," *Commentary*, July 1992, pp. 23–30.
47. D. Kravitz and J. Platania, "Attitudes and Beliefs about Affirmative Action: Effects of Target and of Respondent Sex and Ethnicity," *Journal of Applied Psychology* 78 (1993), pp. 928–38.
48. J. Mathews, "Rash of Unintended Lawsuits Follows Passage of Disabilities Act," *Houston Chronicle*, May 16, 1995, p. 15A.
49. C. Bell, "What the First ADA Cases Tell Us," *SHRM Legal Report* (Winter 1995), pp. 4–7.
50. J. Fitzgerald, "Chatty IBMer Booted," *New York Post*, February 18, 2007.
51. National Organization on Disability 2006 Annual Report at www.nod.org.
52. K. Mills, "Disabilities Act: A Help, or a Needless Hassle," *B/CS Eagle*, August 23, 1995, p. A7.

53. C. Cummins and T. Herrick, "Investigators Fault BP for More Lapses in Refinery Safety," *The Wall Street Journal*, August 18, 2005, p. A3.

54. V. F. Estrada, "Are Your Factory Workers Know-It-All?" *Personnel Journal*, September 1995, pp. 128–34.

55. R. L. Simison, "Safety Last," *The Wall Street Journal*, March 18, 1986, p. 1.

56. J. Roughton, "Managing a Safety Program through Job Hazard Analysis," *Professional Safety* 37 (1992), pp. 28–31.

57. M. A. Verespec, "OSHA Reform Fails Again," *Industry Week*, November 2, 1992, p. 36.

58. R. G. Hallock and D. A. Weaver, "Controlling Losses and Enhancing Management Systems with TOR Analysis," *Professional Safety* 35 (1990), pp. 24–26.

59. H. Herbstman, "Controlling Losses the Burger King Way," *Risk Management* 37 (1990), pp. 22–30.

60. L. Bryan, "An Ounce of Prevention for Workplace Accidents," *Training and Development Journal* 44 (1990), pp. 101–2.

61. J. F. Mangan, "Hazard Communications: Safety in Knowledge," *Best's Review* 92 (1991), pp. 84–88.

62. T. Markus, "How to Set Up a Safety Awareness Program," *Supervision* 51 (1990), pp. 14–16.

63. J. Agnew and A. J. Saruda, "Age and Fatal Work-Related Falls," *Human Factors* 35 (1994), pp. 731–36.

64. R. King, "Active Safety Programs, Education Can Help Prevent Back Injuries," *Occupational Health and Safety* 60 (1991), pp. 49–52.

65. J. R. Hollenbeck, D. R. Ilgen, and S. M. Crampton, "Lower Back Disability in Occupational Settings: A Review of the Literature from a Human Resource Management View," *Personnel Psychology* 45 (1992), pp. 247–78.

66. T. W. Turriff, "NSPB Suggests 10-Step Program to Prevent Eye Injury," *Occupational Health and Safety* 60 (1991), pp. 62–66.

67. D. Hanson, "Chemical Plant Safety: OSHA Rule Addresses Industry Concerns," *Chemical and Engineering News* 70 (1992), pp. 4–5; K. Broscheit and K. Sawyer, "Safety Exhibit Teaches Customers and Employees about Electricity," *Transmission and Distribution* 43 (1992), pp. 174–79; R. Schuch, "Good Training Is Key to Avoiding Boiler Explosions," *National Underwriter* 95 (1992), pp. 21–22.

68. M. Janssens, J. M. Brett, and F. J. Smith, "Confirmatory Cross-Cultural Research: Testing the Viability of a Corporation-wide Safety Policy," *Academy of Management Journal* 38 (1995), pp. 364–82.

69. Cummins and Herrick, "Investigators Fault BP."

CHAPTER

4

The Analysis and Design of Work

LO **LEARNING OBJECTIVES**

After reading this chapter, you should be able to:

LO 4-1 Analyze an organization's structure and work-flow process, identifying the output, activities, and inputs in the production of a product or service. *page 157*

LO 4-2 Understand the importance of job analysis in strategic human resource management. *page 170*

LO 4-3 Choose the right job analysis technique for a variety of human resource activities. *page 173*

LO 4-4 Identify the tasks performed and the skills required in a given job. *page 175*

LO 4-5 Understand the different approaches to job design. *page 177*

LO 4-6 Comprehend the trade-offs among the various approaches to designing jobs. *page 183*

ENTER THE WORLD OF BUSINESS

Working Smarter: U.S. Manufacturers Stage a Comeback

Dave Laws loves his U.S. manufacturing job. He works at the Greenville Airfoils Facility in Piedmont, South Carolina, helping produce turbine blades for jet engines that General Electric (GE) sells all over the world. Laws is well paid, making over $30 an hour, and he has an excellent benefits package. Still, the best feature of his work is that his opinions on how to increase the efficiency and quality at the plant are constantly solicited. "At other jobs I've had, it was just a paycheck. Here you have a say-so. Out of all the places I have worked, this is by far the best one."

This ability to tap into worker expertise to make on-the-job improvements has been one of the major factors contributing to the resurgence in U.S. manufacturing. In an age when global corporations like GE can move jobs to any country promising the lowest wages, the only way American factory workers can save their jobs is to compete in ways other than price. For example, at the Piedmont plant, line workers like Dave Laws work together as part of cross-trained, cross-functional teams who are empowered to design their own work processes. In fact, the workers of these teams have come up with so many different ideas for enhancing productivity, that management often lets two different teams doing essentially the same work do it in totally different ways.

Often these gains have to be achieved without large new cash outlays for new machinery. For example, at K & S Tool and Manufacturing in High Point, North Carolina, the company brought together a team of workers who generated over 20 new ideas for small fixes to problems associated with manufacturing forklifts, that, when taken together, boosted productivity enough to stay price competitive internationally even though paying higher wages. This was despite the fact that, in the words of chief executive William Jasper, "every piece of equipment we have here is pre-2000, and so we have to find out how to be more effective with what we have."

In fact, even industries like apparel and clothing—where U.S. manufacturing was written off for dead—are experiencing a renaissance. For example, Boathouse Sports, a manufacturer of jerseys, uniforms, and jackets in Philadelphia, Pennsylvania, relies on flexible manufacturing teams and finds its own unique competitive advantage in adaptively responding to small orders, and then delivering results with the kind of speed that simply cannot be matched by offshore producers. Indeed, even though Boathouse prices are 10 to 15% higher, they can deliver on most small orders in four weeks, compared to Chinese manufacturers who would take over eight weeks. Indeed, the high cost of shipping expenses due to the recent spike in oil prices is even cutting into the price differential. Thus, although some have suggested that global competition is eliminating high wage manufacturing jobs where workers have a strong voice in how the work gets accomplished, in many corners of the economy, high priced and empowered workers are more than earning their own way.

Sources: P. Coy, "A Renaissance in U.S. Manufacturing," *Bloomberg Businessweek*, May 9, 2011, pp. 11–12; J. Lahart, "Moment of Truth for Productivity Boom," *The Wall Street Journal*, May 5, 2010, p. B1; N. Leiber, "Suddenly, Made in the USA Looks Like a Strategy," *Bloomberg Businessweek*, March 28, 2011, pp. 57–58.

Introduction

In Chapter 2 we discussed the processes of strategy formulation and strategy implementation. Strategy formulation is the process by which a company decides how it will compete in the marketplace; this is often the energizing and guiding force for everything it does. Strategy implementation is the way the strategic plan gets carried out in activities of organizational members. We noted five important components in the strategy implementation process, three of which are directly related to the human resource management function and one of which we will discuss in this chapter: the task or job.

Many central aspects of strategy formulation address how the work gets done, in terms of individual job design as well as the design of organizational structures that link individual jobs to each other and the organization as a whole. The way a firm competes can have a profound impact on the ways jobs are designed and how they are linked via organizational structure. In turn, the fit between the company's structure and environment can have a major impact on the firm's competitive success.

For example, if a company decides to compete on cost, and hence hire low-cost offshore labor, the jobs have to be designed so that they can be performed by minimally skilled people who will require little training. The organization in this case needs to have a centralized structure so that low-level workers are not forced into making too many decisions and the workers should work independently to prevent errors from cascading through the system. In contrast, if the organization is going to compete by differentiating its product, and hence hiring high-wage labor, it has to design the jobs in a different way. As we saw in our opening vignette, organizations that employ high-wage U.S. labor have to leverage the higher skills of their workforce by broadening job descriptions and creating flexible role responsibilities. The organizational structure has to be decentralized so that these high-skill workers, often working together closely in interdependent teams, can make their own individual and team decisions.[1]

Throughout this chapter, we provide examples of the kinds of decisions that need to be made with regard to how organizations should be structured and to the jobs that exist within these organizations, so you can learn how these choices affect a number of outcomes. This includes not just quantity and quality of production, but also outcomes like coordination; innovation; and worker attraction, motivation, and retention. In many cases, there are trade-offs associated with the choices, and the more you know about these trade-offs, the better decisions you can make in terms of making your team or organization more competitive.

Thus, it should be clear from the outset of this chapter that there is no "one best way" to design jobs and structure organizations. The organization needs to create a fit between its environment, competitive strategy, and philosophy on the one hand, with its jobs and organizational design on the other. Failing to design effective organizations and jobs has important implications for competitiveness. Many years ago, some believed that the difference between U.S. auto producers and their foreign competitors could be traced to American workers; however, when companies like Toyota and Honda came into the United States and demonstrated clearly that they could run profitable car companies with American workers, the focus shifted to processes and organization. It is now clear that the success of many of these non-U.S. firms was attributable to how they structured the work and designed their organizations. For example, Toyota's new plant in San Antonio, Texas, differs in many ways from the General Motors plant in Arlington, Texas, but the nature of the workforce is not one of them.[2]

This chapter discusses the analysis and design of work and, in doing so, lays out some considerations that go into making informed decisions about how to create and link jobs. The chapter is divided into three sections, the first of which deals with "big-picture" issues related to work-flow analysis and organizational structure. The remaining two sections deal with more specific, lower-level issues related to job analysis and job design.

The fields of job analysis and job design have extensive overlap, yet in the past they have been treated differently.[3] Job analysis has focused on analyzing existing jobs to gather information for other human resource management practices such as selection, training, performance appraisal, and compensation. Job design, on the other hand, has focused on redesigning existing jobs to make them more efficient or more motivating to jobholders. Thus job design has had a more proactive orientation toward changing the job, whereas job analysis has had a passive, information-gathering orientation.

Work-Flow Analysis and Organization Structure

Work-flow design is the process of analyzing the tasks necessary for the production of a product or service, prior to allocating and assigning these tasks to a particular job category or person. Only after we thoroughly understand work-flow design can we make informed decisions regarding how to initially bundle various tasks into discrete jobs that can be executed by a single person.

LO 4-1
Analyze an organization's structure and work-flow process, identifying the output, activities, and inputs in the production of a product or service.

Organization structure refers to the relatively stable and formal network of vertical and horizontal interconnections among jobs that constitute the organization. Only after we understand how one job relates to those above (supervisors), below (subordinates), and at the same level in different functional areas (marketing versus production) can we make informed decisions about how to redesign or improve jobs to benefit the entire organization.

Finally, work-flow design and organization structure have to be understood in the context of how an organization has decided to compete. Both work-flow design and organization structure can be leveraged to gain competitive advantage for the firm, but how one does this depends on the firm's strategy and its competitive environment.

WORK-FLOW ANALYSIS

All organizations need to identify the outputs of work, to specify the quality and quantity standards for those outputs, and to analyze the processes and inputs necessary for producing outputs that meet the quality standards. This conception of the work-flow process is useful because it provides a means for the manager to understand all the tasks required to produce a number of high-quality products as well as the skills necessary to perform those tasks. This work-flow process is depicted in Figure 4.1.

Analyzing Work Outputs

Every work unit—whether a department, team, or individual—seeks to produce some output that others can use. An output is the product of a work unit and, within manufacturing realms like those discussed in our opening story, this is often an identifiable object such as a jet engine blade, a forklift, or a football jersey. However, an output

figure 4.1

Developing a Work–Unit Activity Analysis

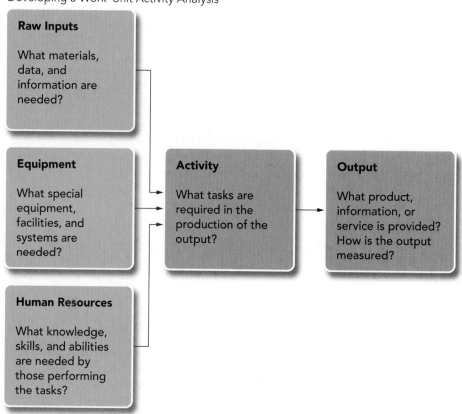

Raw Inputs

What materials, data, and information are needed?

Equipment

What special equipment, facilities, and systems are needed?

Human Resources

What knowledge, skills, and abilities are needed by those performing the tasks?

Activity

What tasks are required in the production of the output?

Output

What product, information, or service is provided? How is the output measured?

can also be a service, such as the services provided by an airline that transports you to some destination, a housecleaning service that maintains your house, or a babysitter who watches over your children.

We often picture an organization only in terms of the product that it produces, and then we focus on that product as the output. Merely identifying an output or set of outputs is not sufficient. Once these outputs have been identified, it is necessary to specify standards for the quantity or quality of these outputs. For example, a productivity improvement technique known as ProMES (productivity measurement and evaluation system) focuses attention on both identifying work-unit outputs and specifying the levels of required performance for different levels of effectiveness.[4] With ProMES, the members of a work unit identify each of the products (outputs) of the work unit for the various customers. They then evaluate the effectiveness of each level of products in the eyes of their customers. A recent large-scale review of more than 80 studies of firms that have applied the ProMES system suggests that the use of this system for improving work flow results in large improvements in productivity that can last for many years.

Analyzing Work Processes

Once the outputs of the work unit have been identified, it is possible to examine the work processes used to generate the output. The work processes are the activities that members of a work unit engage in to produce a given output. Every process consists of operating procedures that specify how things should be done at each stage of the development of the product. These procedures include all the tasks that must be performed in the production of the output. The tasks are usually broken down into those performed by each person in the work unit. Of course, in many situations where the work that needs to be done is highly complex, no single individual is likely to have all the required skills. In these situations, the work may be assigned to a team, and team-based job design is becoming increasingly popular in contemporary organizations. In addition to providing a wider set of skills, team members can back each other up, share work when any member becomes overloaded, and catch each other's errors.

Teams are not a panacea, however, and for teams to be effective, it is essential that the level of task interdependence (how much they have to cooperate) matches the level of outcome interdependence (how much they share the reward for task accomplishment).[5] That is, if work is organized around teams, team bonuses rather than individual pay raises need to play a major role in terms of defining rewards. Teams also have to be given the autonomy to make their own decisions in order to maximize the flexible use of their skill and time and thus promote problem solving.[6] In addition, some members of teams may lean too much on the other team members and fail to develop their own skills or take responsibility for their own tasks, and so even in teams it is critical to establish individual accountability of behavior.[7]

For example, Louis Vuitton, the maker of top-of-the-line bags and purses, used to design work processes centered on individuals. In this old system, each Vuitton worker did a highly specialized task (cutting leather and canvas, stitching seams, attaching the handle, and so on), and then, when each person was finished, he or she would sequentially send the bag to the next person in line. A typical line would be staffed by 20 to 30 people. In 2006, the company switched to a team-based design where teams of six to nine people all work together simultaneously to assemble the bags. Workers are cross-trained in multiple tasks and can flexibly change roles and shift production from one bag to another if any one bag becomes a "hit" and another becomes a "dud." The length of time it took to produce the same bags dropped from eight days to one day, and Vuitton customers, who had often had to be placed on waiting lists for their most popular products, were able to get their hands on the product much more quickly. This speed to market is critical given the emotional nature of this purchase—after all, if one is ready to spend $700 on a tote bag, it is best not to have to delay that decision.[8]

Again, to design work systems that are maximally efficient, a manager needs to understand the processes required in the development of the products for that work unit. The ability to balance the productivity-enhancing benefits of small workforces, while at the same time not pushing people to the limits of their capacities, is a critical need. Most managers, because they are not always central to the workflow, cannot do this by themselves, and thus, they often have to develop trusting relationships with highly experienced front-line workers.[9] Without a clear understanding of the tasks necessary to the production of an output, it is difficult to determine whether the work unit has become overstaffed. Understanding the tasks required allows the manager to specify which tasks are to be carried out by which individuals and eliminate tasks that are not necessary for the desired end.

Organizations often work hard to minimize overstaffing via lean production techniques. Lean production refers to processes developed in Japan, but then adopted worldwide, emphasizing manufacturing goods with a minimum amount of time, materials, money—and most important—people. Lean production tries to leverage technology, along with small numbers of flexible, well-trained, and skilled personnel

● This job may look tedious or possibly even uninteresting. Considering how to engage employees in seeing the benefits of their work outside of the lab is an important way to motivate them through their day.

in order to produce more custom-based products at less cost. This can be contrasted with more traditional "batch work" methods, where large groups of low-skilled employees churn out long runs of identical mass products that are stored in inventories for later sale. In lean production systems, there are fewer employees to begin with, and the skill levels of those employees are so high that the opportunity to cuts costs by laying off employees is simply less viable.

Indeed, a paradox of the most recent recession in 2008–2009 was how small many of the layoffs in the manufacturing sector of the economy were given the huge drop in production levels. For example, 14 months into the recession of 2000, manufacturers cut 9.5% of their employees in response to a *2% cut* in production. In contrast, 14 months into the most recent recession, the same 9.5% of employees were laid off in response to a *12% cut* in production. If the same ratio of job cuts to production cuts from the year 2000 held in the year 2009, this would have resulted in an astounding layoff rate of over 50% of manufacturing employees. Many have attributed the lower "job cut" to a "production cut" ratio experienced in the most recent recession to the use of job redesign initiatives that emphasize lean production over more traditional approaches.

For example, at Parker Hannifan Corporation's plastics manufacturing plant in South Carolina, lean production techniques have cut the number of people required to run the plant to such a small number that permanently pulling one highly trained person off the line saves very little money, and yet makes it impossible to sustain production at all. In addition, the work has been restructured to create smaller production runs that result in reduced inventories, so that when a downturn hits, it is noticed more quickly and can be responded to more gradually. In the past, by the time a recession was detected, inventories had bulged to such a level that more employees had to be laid off more quickly and for longer time periods.[10]

Analyzing Work Inputs

The final stage in work-flow analysis is to identify the inputs used in the development of the work unit's product. As shown in Figure 4.1, these inputs can be broken down into the raw materials, equipment, and human skills needed to perform the tasks. *Raw materials* consist of the materials that will be converted into the work unit's product.

Organizations that try to increase efficiency via lean production techniques often try to minimize the stockpile of inputs via "just-in-time" inventory control procedures. Indeed, in some cases, inventories are being abandoned altogether, and companies at the edge of the lean production process do not even manufacture any products until customers actually place an order for them. For example, surgical device maker Conmed used to forecast demand for their products one to two months ahead, and when those forecasts turned out to be inaccurate they would either lose sales or stockpile inventories. Today, because the length of time it takes to produce their devices has decreased from 6 weeks to 48 hours, they do not even manufacture any products that are not already sold. The impact of this can be seen at Conmed's plant in Utica, New York, where a $93,000 inventory that used to take up 3,300 square feet on the factory floor has been all but eliminated. This allowed the company to take back lost sales from Chinese competitors whom, despite their lower labor costs, face the costs of long lead times, inventory pileups, and quality problems and transportation costs. As David Johnson, Vice President for Global Operations at Conmed notes, "If more U.S. companies deploy these job design methods we can compete with anybody and still provide security to our workforce."[11]

However, there are also downsides to "just-in-time" inventory management practices. Specifically, the efficiency gained from maintaining an inventory measured in days rather than weeks creates a of lack of flexibility. An example of this can be seen in the aftermath of the earthquake that struck northern Japan in 2011. This region of Japan was home to a number of suppliers who had to unexpectedly halt all production overnight on March 22. This disruption rippled through the entire global economy that relied on "just-in-time" practices when organizations as varied as Boeing, General Motors, John Deere, Hewlett-Packard, and Dell had to halt their own production lines after running out of inputs. As one analyst noted, "If supply is disrupted in this situation, there's nowhere to get inputs."[12]

Equipment refers to the technology and machinery necessary to transform the raw materials into the product, but the final input in the work-flow process is the *human skills* and efforts necessary to perform the tasks. Obviously, the human skills consist of the workers available to the company, but increasingly organizations are recruiting the inputs of customers as a critical input for designing processes and products. For example, at Xerox, the organization was developing a two-engine model of a copier, with one engine driving standard black-and-white printing tasks, and the second one driving color tasks. One of the customers noted that what would be better was a two-engine model, where the second engine could drive both tasks in emergency cases when the first engine shut down. All of the customers on the design team loved this idea, which had never really crossed the minds of the engineering team. The result was the new Nuvera 288 Digital Perfecting System, that became one of Xerox's top-selling models. As team leader Steve Hoover noted, "the team had a certain idea of what customers wanted, but actually talking to them really changed that."[13]

To compete successfully, organizations often have to scour the world for the best raw materials, the best equipment, and the people with the best skills, and then try to integrate all of this seamlessly in the work processes that merge all these factors. As we have seen, IBM has been on the forefront of incorporating new technological equipment in the processes, in order to eliminate office space and reduce middle layers of management. This company has also searched high and wide for people with the best sets of skills as well. For example, symbolically, IBM's 2006 Annual Investors Meeting was held in Bangalore, India.

India is central to IBM's future because it is a source of high-skilled, low-cost talent, especially in the area of software development. Indeed, the size of IBM's staff in India surged from 9,000 to 43,000 between 2003 and 2006. However, this is just one part of the puzzle. Some of IBM operations require high-skill employees who have to work on-site with hardware issues in close proximity to U.S. customers, and hence IBM also opened a new center in Boulder, Colorado. IBM also needs the very narrow skills of people with doctorates in the hard sciences, and thus it opened a research lab in Yorktown Heights, New York. Some low-skill jobs that IBM needs are done by workers from China, Brazil, or eastern Europe, depending on where the call originates and the language spoken by the customer. The key to this strategy is not just going where one can get cheap labor, but, instead, going where one can get just the exact kind of labor needed at the best price. As noted by Robert Moffat, IBM's senior vice president, "Some people think the world is centered in India and that's it. Globalization is more than that. Our customers need the right skills, in the right place at the right time."[14]

ORGANIZATION STRUCTURE

Whereas work-flow design provides a longitudinal overview of the dynamic relationships by which inputs are converted into outputs, organization structure provides a cross-sectional overview of the static relationships between individuals and units that create the outputs. Organization structure is typically displayed via organizational charts that convey both vertical reporting relationships and horizontal functional responsibilities.

Dimensions of Structure

Centralization
Degree to which decision-making authority resides at the top of the organizational chart.

Departmentalization
Degree to which work units are grouped based on functional similarity or similarity of work flow.

Two of the most critical dimensions of organization structure are centralization and departmentalization. **Centralization** refers to the degree to which decision-making authority resides at the top of the organizational chart as opposed to being distributed throughout lower levels (in which case authority is *decentralized*). **Departmentalization** refers to the degree to which work units are grouped based on functional similarity or similarity of work flow.

For example, a school of business could be organized around functional similarity so that there would be a marketing department, a finance department, and an accounting department, and faculty within these specialized departments would each teach their area of expertise to all kinds of students. Alternatively, one could organize the same school around work-flow similarity, so that there would be an undergraduate unit, a graduate unit, and an executive development unit. Each of these units would have its own marketing, finance, and accounting professors who taught only their own respective students and not those of the other units.

Structural Configurations

Although there are an infinite number of ways to combine centralization and departmentalization, two common configurations of organization structure tend to emerge in organizations. The first type, referred to as a *functional structure*, is shown in Figure 4.2. A functional structure, as the name implies, employs a functional departmentalization scheme with relatively high levels of centralization. High levels of centralization tend to go naturally with functional departmentalization because individual units in the structures are so specialized that members of the unit may have a weak conceptualization of the overall organization mission. Thus, they tend to identify with their department and cannot always be relied on to make decisions that are in the best interests of the organization as a whole.

Alternatively, a second common configuration is a *divisional structure*, three examples of which are shown in Figures 4.3, 4.4, and 4.5. Divisional structures combine a divisional departmentalization scheme with relatively low levels of centralization. Units in these structures act almost like separate, self-sufficient, semi-autonomous organizations. The organization shown in Figure 4.3 is divisionally organized around different products; the organization shown in Figure 4.4 is divisionally organized

figure 4.2

The Functional Structure

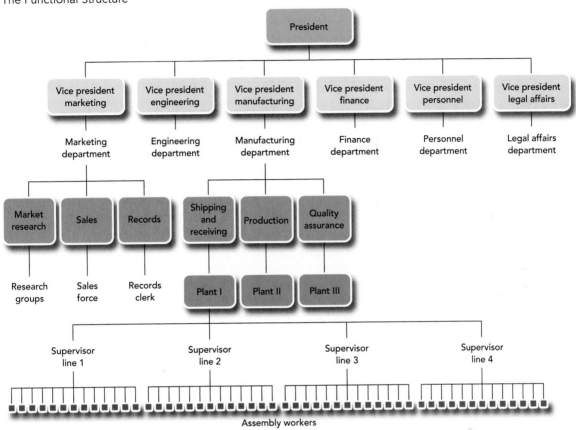

SOURCE: Adapted from J. A. Wagner and J. R. Hollenbeck, *Organizational Behavior: Securing Competitive Advantage*, 3rd ed. (New York: Prentice Hall, 1998).

around geographic regions; and the organization shown in Figure 4.5 is divisionally organized around different clients.

Because of their work-flow focus, their semi-autonomous nature, and their proximity to a homogeneous consumer base, divisional structures tend to be more flexible and innovative. They can detect and exploit opportunities in their respective consumer base faster than the more centralized functionally structured organizations. The perceived autonomy that goes along with this kind of structure also means that most employees prefer it and feel they are more fairly treated than when they are subject to centralized decision-making structures.[15] A good example of the interplay of alternative structures can be seen in recent developments in the computer industry. Historically, the computer industry started with large and divisionally structured companies like IBM, that over time splintered off into increasingly smaller and functionally specialized organizations. Technology companies focused in narrowly on hardware *or* software *or* data storage *or* IT consulting services, but no one company was interested in providing all of these services. The thought was that specialization would boost efficiency and technical innovation. Indeed, as one analyst noted, "today, a typical corporate computer system might be assembled by Accenture PLC with data storage

figure 4.3

Divisional Structure: Product Structure

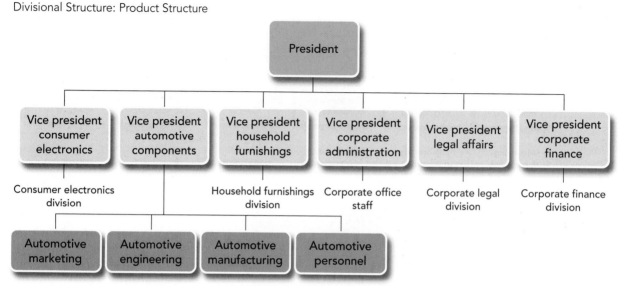

SOURCE: Adapted from J. A. Wagner and J. R. Hollenbeck, *Organizational Behavior: Securing Competitive Advantage,* 3rd ed. (New York: Prentice Hall, 1998).

figure 4.4

Divisional Structure: Geographic Structure

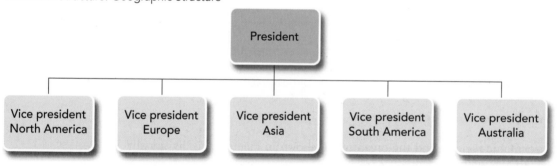

SOURCE: Adapted from J. A. Wagner and J. R. Hollenbeck, *Organizational Behavior: Securing Competitive Advantage,* 3rd ed. (New York: Prentice Hall, 1998).

systems from EMC Corporation and computers from Hewlett-Packard that use chips from Intel Corporation to run Oracle software."

However, Oracle recently announced that they were going to reverse that trend with their announcement to purchase Sun Microsystems Inc., making them both a software producer and a hardware manufacturer. Oracle now plans on selling complete systems made of chips, computers, storage devices, and software—highlighting a competitive strategy that is based on the idea that corporate customers are tired of assembling and integrating different technological components from multiple suppliers. In similar moves, Hewlett-Packard announced just a few months after this that they were going to purchase Electronic Data Systems, thus entering the data storage industry and Apple announced it was making a move to enter the semiconductor chip business by buying chip maker P.A. Semi.

figure 4.5

Divisional Structure: Client Structure

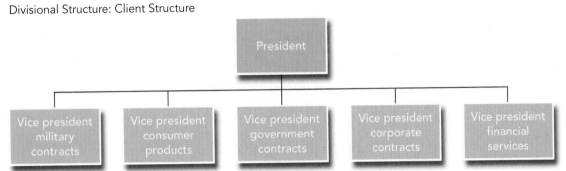

SOURCE: Adapted from J. A. Wagner and J. R. Hollenbeck, *Organizational Behavior: Securing Competitive Advantage*, 3rd ed. (New York: Prentice Hall, 1998).

The temptation toward this type of "vertical integration" can be strong because one of the virtues of divisional structures is that they allow one to control all aspects of an entire business, making one's former supplier part of the team, as opposed to an unpredictable element of the business environment. Vertical integration also tends to generate large-scale operations that would not naturally evolve organically from smaller organizations, and with size comes some degree of power. Indeed, Oracle's CEO, Larry Ellison directly invoked the old 1960s IBM model by stating, "we want to be T. J. Watson's IBM, which was the greatest company in the history of enterprise in America because its hardware and software ran most companies."[16] Time will tell whether this strategy is effective, or like the old IBM, whether Oracle will learn that there are real limits associated with divisional structures as well.

Divisional structures are not very efficient because of the redundancy associated with each group carrying its own functional specialists. Also, divisional structures can "self-cannibalize" if the gains achieved in one unit come at the expense of another unit. For example, Kinko's stores are structured divisionally with highly decentralized control. Each manager can set his or her own price and has autonomy to make his or her own decisions. But the drawback to this is lack of coordination in the sense that "every Kinko's store considers every other Kinko's store a competitor; they vie against each other for work, they bid against each other competing on price."[17] The exact same problem has been cited at Whole Foods Markets, which operates 189 stores throughout the United States. Whole Foods' stores emphasize organic produce, and individual store managers are encouraged to be entrepreneurial, with little guidance from central headquarters. Same-store sales growth at Whole Foods was averaging 15% in 2004 but was down to 6% in 2006, largely because of competition between one Whole Foods store and another.[18]

Lack of coordination caused by decentralized and divisional structures can be especially problematic with new and emerging organizations that do not have a great deal of history or firmly established culture. Higher levels of centralization and more functional design of work make it easier in this context to keep everyone on the same page while the business builds experience.[19] Decentralized and divisional structures can also create problems if the stand-alone divisions start making decisions that are overly risky or out of line with the organization's larger goals. For example, many analysts felt that many of the problems associated with the near bankruptcy of

Citibank in 2009 were caused by excessive risk taking in several autonomous divisions that were not being closely monitored by any centralized authority. This was especially the case with the division that managed collateralized debt obligations (CDOs). Many conservative banking analysts warned that CDOs and other similar derivatives spread risk and uncertainty throughout the economy more widely and did little to reduce risk through diversification. This belief was validated in the 2008 recession, when the housing market crashed and thousands of people defaulted on their mortgages.[20]

Alternatively, functional structures are very efficient, with little redundancy across units, and provide little opportunity for self-cannibalization or for rogue units running wild. Also, although the higher level of oversight in centralized structures tends to reduce the number of errors made by lower level workers, when errors do occur in overly centralized systems, they tend to cascade through the system as a whole more quickly and can, therefore, be more debilitating. For example, when there was a blackout throughout a large part of the East and Midwest in the summer of 2003, many felt that the overly centralized nature of the nation's power grid was a major source of this crisis.[21] Moreover, these structures tend to be inflexible and insensitive to subtle differences across products, regions, or clients.

Functional structures are most appropriate in stable, predictable environments, where demand for resources can be well anticipated and coordination requirements between jobs can be refined and standardized over consistent repetitions of activity. This type of structure also helps support organizations that compete on cost, because efficiency is central to making this strategy work. Divisional structures are most appropriate in unstable, unpredictable environments, where it is difficult to anticipate demands for resources, and coordination requirements between jobs are not consistent over time. This type of structure also helps support organizations that compete on differentiation or innovation, because flexible responsiveness is central to making this strategy work. Of course, designing an organizational structure is not an either–or phenomenon, and some research suggests that "middle-of-the-road" options that combine functional and divisional elements are often best. For example, the use of team-based structures composed of "semi-isolated workgroups" often allows organizations to simultaneously achieve the virtues of both worlds. These "loosely coupled" teams have enough autonomy to perform broad missions but, at the same time, enough specialization to support innovation and efficiency.[22] The problem with these team-based structures, however, is that they become so loosely coupled that they fail to integrate their work with other teams.[23] Indeed, it is often the case that teams that are very high in team cohesion often have difficulty managing the between-team coordination that is also critical in team-based structures.[24] Finally, any thoughts of changing one's structure has to be made with the realization that moves that give workers or teams greater autonomy are probably easier to execute relative to changes than centralized moves that reduce discretion at the individual or team level.[25] Still, as the "Competing through Technology" box illustrates, the use of team-based structures that keep different subteams close and cohesive can be a powerful means of promoting speed and innovation.

Structure and the Nature of Jobs

Finally, moving from big-picture issues to lower-level specifics, the type of organization structure also has implications for the design of jobs. Jobs in functional structures need to be narrow and highly specialized. Workers in these structures (even

COMPETING THROUGH TECHNOLOGY

Serving Up Speed, Flexibility, and Innovation

When it comes to computer servers, the heavy-weight division includes the likes of Hewlett-Packard, IBM, and Dell. The servers sold by these giants are mass marketed as standardized products built to meet the predictable needs of a large customer base. Most of these customers use these servers for large volume data storage and retrieval, and the Intel chips that serve at the core of these machines are very powerful. HP, IBM, and Dell tend to compete on price within this market, and in order to keep prices competitive, all of their manufacturing takes place in low wage countries in Asia.

Many new web-based companies, however, have demands that differ from a traditional mass storage and retrieval system. Web companies need to quickly fulfill requests for small amounts of data, such as an image on Google or Facebook, and they do not face the same demands for computing power that might characterize a large bank or credit card company. Santa Clara–based SeaMicro was one of the first companies to recognize this distinction, and they quickly moved into

this market with new servers that were built not in China, but rather built a half mile down the road in Santa Clara.

Indeed, although the name, "Silicon Valley" is synonymous with computers, in fact, when it comes to hardware, very little manufacturing has taken place within the valley since the 1980s. The strategic decision by SeaMicro to build its servers in California, as opposed to Asia, was based on the way they designed the work and the need to stay at the cutting edge of innovation in order to quickly respond to changes in technological developments. For example, the key to SeaMicro's success is that they start with smaller energy efficient chips such as those that might power a smartphone, and then surround these with custom made hardware and software that allows a large number of these smaller engines to act like a much more powerful engine, while only using 25% as much energy as a standard server.

This kind of successful innovation requires that the cross-functional teams of hardware, software, and manufacturing engineers at SeaMicro

constantly experiment with the latest components, and this type of experimentation requires rich, face-to-face communication in real time that only can be supported by having design and manufacturing side-by-side. Eliminating the need to ship materials speeds the transition from design to production, and although the cost of high skilled California labor might seem prohibitive, SeaMicro can offset this via a strong revenue stream. The energy cost savings for its customers are such that the systems essentially pay for themselves in just over a year, allowing for a healthy gross margin of over 60% for each unit, which makes this small company highly competitive in their battle with much larger competitors. As John Turk, Vice President of Operations notes, "It's not about us getting big, but rather it's how we stay flexible. That is what the big guys don't have."

SOURCES: L. Wood, "SeaMicro Breaks New Ground with Atom Server," *InformationWeek*, March 1, 2011, p. 23; C. Debaise, "The Top 10 Clean-tech Companies," *The Wall Street Journal*, March 4, 2011, p. B1; A. Vance, "Stars and Stripes and Servers Forever," *Bloomberg Businessweek*, February 28, 2011, pp. 33–35.

middle managers) tend to have little decision-making authority or responsibility for managing coordination between themselves and others. For example, at Nucor Steel, production at its 30 minimill plants has doubled almost every two years and profit margins have pushed beyond 10% largely because of its flat, divisional structure. At Nucor, individual plant managers have wide autonomy in how to design work at their own mills. Nucor plants sometimes compete against each other, but the CEO makes sure that the competition is healthy and that best practices are distributed throughout the organization as fast as possible, preventing any long-term sustainable advantage to any one plant. Moreover, the profit-sharing plan that makes up the largest part of people's pay operates at the organizational level, which also promotes collaboration among managers who want to make sure that every plant is successful. Thus, after taking over a new mill for the first time, one new plant manager got a call or visit from every other manager, offering advice and assistance. As the new manager noted, "It wasn't idle politeness. I took them up on it. My performance impacted their paycheck."[26]

Nucor employs just four levels of management and operates a headquarters of just 66 people, compared to one of its competitors, U.S. Steel, which has over 20 levels and 1,200 people at its headquarters. This gives Nucor a long-term sustainable competitive advantage, which it has held for close to 15 years. Sales at Nucor grew from $4.5 billion in 2000 to over $13 billion in 2006. During the same period, U.S. Steel's volume decreased by 6%. This has translated into success for both investors (roughly 400% return on investment in the last five years) and workers, whose wages average $100,000 a year, compared to $70,000 a year at U.S. Steel. As one industry analyst notes, "In terms of a business model, Nucor has won this part of the world," and much of that victory can be explained by their superior structure and process for managing work.[27]

The choice of structure also has implications for people who would assume the jobs created in functional versus divisional structures. For example, managers of divisional structures often need to be more experienced or high in cognitive ability relative to managers of functional structures.[28] The relatively smaller scope and routine nature of jobs created in centralized and functional structures make them less sensitive to individual differences between workers. The nature of the structure also has implications for relationships, in the sense that in centralized and functional structures people tend to think of fairness in terms of rules and procedures, whereas in decentralized and divisional structures, they tend to think of fairness in terms of outcomes and how they are treated interpersonally.[29] For example, Netflix, the online video rental service, is widely recognized as an employer that tends to give a wide degree of autonomy to managers. CEO Reed Hastings tends to pay managers very well and gives them unlimited vacation time. They are also free to structure their own compensation package (cash versus stock) as well as the way they do their own work. In return, Hastings expects extremely high performance and accountability. Indeed, as marketing manager Heather McIlhany notes, "Netflix has a tough but fulfilling culture that will only work with fully formed adults who are not looking for a place to hide or pass the buck." This combination of freedom and responsibility among its workers has helped Netflix fight off many competitors, including Walmart, who briefly ventured into the online video rental business. Many thought that Walmart would put an end to Netflix, but after several years of failing to make inroads into this market, Walmart pulled out in 2007 and referred all of its former customers to Netflix.[30]

Flatter structures also have implications for organizational culture in terms of ethics and accountability. For example, in a highly public scandal, Putnam Investments was fined $110 million for engaging in "market timing," that is, jumping quickly in and out of funds in order to take advantage of momentary market inefficiencies. This is considered an unethical practice within the industry because it increases fund expenses which, in turn, harms long-term investors. Many long-term investors left the organization, some of whom had more than $800 million being managed by Putnam.

According to Putnam insiders, the organization's tall and narrow organizational structure created a situation in which too many people were managing other people and telling them what they had to do to get promoted. Because the only way to earn more money at Putnam was to climb the corporate ladder, too much pressure was put on managers and employees alike to boost short-term results in order to attract the attention of those high above. The culture was one where people tended to ask "What is the fine for this?" instead of "What does this do to help my clients?" When new CEO Ed Haldeman was brought in to repair the damage, one of his first steps was to remove hundreds of salespeople, and then flatten the structure. The goal was to attract a different kind of employee, who would be less interested in short-term gains and hierarchical promotions handed out by others and more interested in establishing personal long-term relationships with customers and more collaborative relationships with colleagues. In Haldeman's words, "To retain and attract the best people, it's necessary to provide them with autonomy and independence to make their own decisions."[31]

In our next section, we cover specific approaches for analyzing and designing jobs. Although all of these approaches are viable, each focuses on a single, isolated job. These approaches do not necessarily consider how that single job fits into the overall work flow or structure of the organization. Whereas the Putnam Investments example shows how a firm moved from a functional structure to a divisional structure, the Evidence-Based HR example shows how Eli Lilly changed their structure in just the opposite direction, and this reinforces our general principle that there is no "one best way" when it comes to organizational structure. Without this big-picture appreciation, we might redesign a job in a way that might be good for that one job but out of line with the work flow, structure, or strategy of the organization. In an effectively structured organization, people not only know how their job fits into the bigger picture, they know how everyone else fits as well.

EVIDENCE-BASED HR

An example of how restructuring the work can help increase speed of operations is provided by pharmaceutical giant Eli Lilly. Because patents for well-established drugs run out after a set time period, a company like Eli Lilly can only survive by inventing new products before the time bomb represented by their older drugs goes off. Faced with the prospect of losing the patent on its $5 billion a year schizophrenia pill, Zyprexa, this company restructured operations in a functional direction in order to create new products more quickly and efficiently. For example, every person who was responsible for converting molecules into medicine were taken out of their home departments and placed under one roof in the new Development Center for Excellence.

This group of intensely focused specialists, who were all working together for the first time, came up with an innovative new method for launching and testing drugs. This group took a formerly sequential two-stage process for determining general effectiveness and then the optimal dosage, and converted it into a single-stage process where multiple dose levels were tested all at once and compared to each other. This process shaved 14 months off the process of developing a new drug for diabetes, and was then generalized to other therapeutic causes.

SOURCES: A. Weintraub and M. Tirrell, "Eli Lilly's Drug Assembly Line," *Bloomberg Businessweek,* February 25, 2010, pp. 34–35.

Job Analysis

Job Analysis
The process of getting detailed information about jobs.

Job analysis refers to the process of getting detailed information about jobs. It is important for organizations to understand and match job requirements and people to achieve high-quality performance. This is particularly true in today's competitive marketplace.

THE IMPORTANCE OF JOB ANALYSIS

LO 4-2
Understand the importance of job analysis in strategic human resource management.

Job analysis is the building block of everything that human resource managers do. Almost every human resource management program requires some type of information that is gleaned from job analysis: selection, performance appraisal, training and development, job evaluation, career planning, work redesign, and human resource planning.

Work Redesign. As previously discussed, job analysis and job design are interrelated. Often a firm will seek to redesign work to make it more efficient or effective. To redesign the work, detailed information about the existing job(s) must be available. In addition, redesigning a job will, in fact, be similar to analyzing a job that does not yet exist.

Human Resource Planning. In human resource planning, managers analyze an organization's human resource needs in a dynamic environment and develop activities that enable a firm to adapt to change. This planning process requires accurate information about the levels of skill required in various jobs to ensure that enough individuals are available in the organization to meet the human resource needs of the strategic plan.

Selection. Human resource selection identifies the most qualified applicants for employment. To identify which applicants are most qualified, it is first necessary to determine the tasks that will be performed by the individual hired and the knowledge, skills, and abilities the individual must have to perform the job effectively. This information is gained through job analysis.

Training. Almost every employee hired by an organization will require training. Some training programs may be more extensive than others, but all require the trainer to have identified the tasks performed in the job to ensure that the training will prepare individuals to perform their jobs effectively.

Performance Appraisal. Performance appraisal deals with getting information about how well each employee is performing in order to reward those who are effective, improve the performance of those who are ineffective, or provide a written justification for why the poor performer should be disciplined. Through job analysis, the organization can identify the behaviors and results that distinguish effective performance from ineffective performance.

Career Planning. Career planning entails matching an individual's skills and aspirations with opportunities that are or may become available in the organization. This matching process requires that those in charge of career planning know the skill requirements of the various jobs. This allows them to guide individuals into jobs in which they will succeed and be satisfied.

Job Evaluation. The process of job evaluation involves assessing the relative dollar value of each job to the organization to set up internally equitable pay structures. If pay structures are not equitable, employees will be dissatisfied and quit, or they will not see the benefits of striving for promotions. To put dollar values on jobs, it is necessary to get information about different jobs to determine which jobs deserve higher pay than others.

THE IMPORTANCE OF JOB ANALYSIS TO LINE MANAGERS

Job analysis is clearly important to the HR department's various activities, but why it is important to line managers may not be as clear. There are many reasons. First, managers must have detailed information about all the jobs in their work group to understand the work-flow process. Second, managers need to understand the job requirements to make intelligent hiring decisions. Very seldom do employees get hired by the human resource department without a manager's input. Third, a manager is responsible for ensuring that each individual is performing satisfactorily (or better). This requires the manager to evaluate how well each person is performing and to provide feedback to those whose performance needs improvement. Finally, it is also the manager's responsibility to ensure that the work is being done safely, knowing where potential hazards might manifest themselves and creating a climate where people feel free to interrupt the production process if dangerous conditions exist.[32]

JOB ANALYSIS INFORMATION
Nature of Information

Two types of information are most useful in job analysis: job descriptions and job specifications. A **job description** is a list of the tasks, duties, and responsibilities (TDRs) that a job entails. TDRs are observable actions. For example, a clerical job requires the jobholder to type. If you were to observe someone in that position for a day, you would certainly see some typing. When a manager attempts to evaluate job performance, it is most important to have detailed information about the work performed in the job (that is, the TDRs). This makes it possible to determine how well an individual is meeting each job requirement. Table 4.1 shows a sample job description. On the one hand, job descriptions need to be written broadly because overly restrictive descriptions make it easy for someone to claim that some important task, perhaps unforeseen, "is not my job." On the other hand, lack of specificity can also result in disagreement and conflict between people about the essential elements of what the job entails.[33] Thus, it is critical to strike an effective balance between breadth and specificity when constructing job descriptions.

> **Job Description**
> A list of the tasks, duties, and responsibilities (TDRs) that a job entails.

A **job specification** is a list of the knowledge, skills, abilities, and other characteristics (KSAOs) that an individual must have to perform the job. *Knowledge* refers to factual or procedural information that is necessary for successfully performing a task. A *skill* is an individual's level of proficiency at performing a particular task. *Ability* refers to a more general enduring capability that an individual possesses. Finally, *other characteristics* might be personality traits such as one's achievement motivation or persistence. Thus KSAOs are characteristics about people that are not directly observable; they are observable only when individuals are carrying out the TDRs of the job. If someone applied for the clerical job discussed, you could not simply look at the individual to determine whether he or she possessed typing skills. However, if you were to observe that individual typing something, you could assess the level of typing skill. When a manager is attempting to fill a position, it is important to have accurate information about the characteristics a successful jobholder must have. This requires focusing on the KSAOs of each applicant.

> **Job Specification**
> A list of the knowledge, skills, abilities, and other characteristics (KSAOs) that an individual must have to perform a job.

table 4.1

A Sample Job
Description

> **Job Title:** Maintenance Mechanic
> **General Description of Job:** General maintenance and repair of all equipment used in the operations of a particular district. Includes the servicing of company vehicles, shop equipment, and machinery used on job sites.
> 1. *Essential Duty (40%): Maintenance of Equipment*
>   Tasks: Keep a log of all maintenance performed on equipment. Replace parts and fluids according to maintenance schedule. Regularly check gauges and loads for deviances that may indicate problems with equipment. Perform nonroutine maintenance as required. May involve limited supervision and training of operators performing maintenance.
> 2. *Essential Duty (40%): Repair of Equipment*
>   Tasks: Requires inspection of equipment and a recommendation that a piece be scrapped or repaired. If equipment is to be repaired, mechanic will take whatever steps are necessary to return the piece to working order. This may include a partial or total rebuilding of the piece using various hand tools and equipment. Will primarily involve the overhaul and troubleshooting of diesel engines and hydraulic equipment.
> 3. *Essential Duty (10%): Testing and Approval*
>   Tasks: Ensure that all required maintenance and repair has been performed and that it was performed according to manufacturer specifications. Approve or reject equipment as being ready for use on a job.
> 4. *Essential Duty (10%): Maintain Stock*
>   Tasks: Maintain inventory of parts needed for the maintenance and repair of equipment. Responsible for ordering satisfactory parts and supplies at the lowest possible cost.
> *Nonessential Functions*
> Other duties as assigned.

Sources of Job Analysis Information

In performing the job analysis, one question that often arises is, Who should be responsible for providing the job analysis information? Whatever job analysis method you choose, the process of job analysis entails obtaining information from people familiar with the job. We refer to these people as *subject-matter experts* because they possess deep knowledge of the job.

In general, it will be useful to go to the job incumbent to get the most accurate information about what is actually done on the job. This is especially the case when it is difficult to monitor the person who does the job. The ratings of multiple job incumbents that are doing the same job do not always agree, however, especially if the job is complex and does not involve standardized equipment or tight scripts for customer contact.[34] Thus, you will also want to ask others familiar with the job, such as supervisors, to look over the information generated by the job incumbent. This serves as a check to determine whether what is being done is congruent with what is supposed to be done in the job. One conclusion that can be drawn from this research is that incumbents may provide the most accurate estimates of the actual time spent performing job tasks. However, supervisors may be a more accurate source of information about the importance of job duties. Incumbents also seem more accurate in terms of assessing safety-related risk factors associated with various aspects of work, and in general the further one moves up the organizational hierarchy, the less accurate the risk assessments.[35] Although job incumbents and supervisors are the most obvious and frequently used sources of job analysis information, other sources, such as customers, can be helpful, particularly for service jobs. Finally, when it comes to analyzing skill levels, external job analysts who have more experience rating a wide range of jobs may be the best source.[36]

JOB ANALYSIS METHODS

There are various methods for analyzing jobs and no "one best way." In this section, we discuss two methods for analyzing jobs: the position analysis questionnaire and the Occupational Information Network (O*NET). Although most managers may not have time to use each of these techniques in the exact manner suggested, the two provide some anchors for thinking about broad approaches, task-focused approaches, and person-oriented approaches to conducting job analysis.

LO 4-3
Choose the right job analysis technique for a variety of human resource activities.

Position Analysis Questionnaire (PAQ)

We lead this section off with the PAQ because this is one of the broadest and most well-researched instruments for analyzing jobs. Moreover, its emphasis on inputs, processes, relationships, and outputs is consistent with the work-flow analysis approach that we used in leading off this chapter (Figure 4.1).

The PAQ is a standardized job analysis questionnaire containing 194 items.[37] These items represent work behaviors, work conditions, and job characteristics that can be generalized across a wide variety of jobs. They are organized into six sections:

1. *Information input*—Where and how a worker gets information needed to perform the job.
2. *Mental processes*—The reasoning, decision making, planning, and information processing activities that are involved in performing the job.
3. *Work output*—The physical activities, tools, and devices used by the worker to perform the job.
4. *Relationships with other persons*—The relationships with other people required in performing the job.
5. *Job context*—The physical and social contexts where the work is performed.
6. *Other characteristics*—The activities, conditions, and characteristics other than those previously described that are relevant to the job.

The job analyst is asked to determine whether each item applies to the job being analyzed. The analyst then rates the item on six scales: extent of use, amount of time, importance to the job, possibility of occurrence, applicability, and special code (special rating scales used with a particular item). These ratings are submitted to the PAQ headquarters, where a computer program generates a report regarding the job's scores on the job dimensions.

Research has indicated that the PAQ measures 12 overall dimensions of jobs (listed in Table 4.2) and that a given job's scores on these dimensions can be very useful. The significant database has linked scores on certain dimensions to scores on subtests of the General Aptitude Test Battery (GATB). Thus, knowing the dimension scores provides some guidance regarding the types of abilities that are necessary to perform the job. Obviously, this technique provides information about the work performed in a format that allows for comparisons across jobs, whether those jobs are similar or dissimilar. Another advantage of the PAQ is that it covers the work context as well as inputs, outputs, and processes.

table 4.2

Overall Dimensions
of the Position
Analysis
Questionnaire

Decision/communication/general responsibilities
Clerical/related activities
Technical/related activities
Service/related activities
Regular day schedule versus other work schedules
Routine/repetitive work activities
Environmental awareness
General physical activities
Supervising/coordinating other personnel
Public/customer/related contact activities
Unpleasant/hazardous/demanding environment
Nontypical work schedules

In spite of its widespread use, the PAQ is not without problems. One problem is that to fill out the test, an employee needs the reading level of a college graduate; this disqualifies some job incumbents from the PAQ. In fact, it is recommended that only job analysts trained in how to use the PAQ should complete the questionnaire, rather than job incumbents or supervisors. Indeed, the ratings of job incumbents tend to be lower in reliability relative to ratings from supervisors or trained job analysts.[38] A second problem associated with the PAQ is that its general, standardized format leads to rather abstract characterizations of jobs. Thus it does not lend itself well to describing the specific, concrete task activities that comprise the actual job, and it is not ideal for developing job descriptions or redesigning jobs. Methods that do focus on this aspect of the work are needed if this is the goal.

The Occupational Information Network (O*NET)

The *Dictionary of Occupational Titles* (DOT) was born during the 1930s and served as a vehicle for helping the new public employment system link the demand for skills and the supply of skills in the U.S. workforce. Although this system served the country well for more than 60 years, it became clear to officials at the U.S. Department of Labor that jobs in the new economy were so qualitatively different from jobs in the old economy, that the DOT no longer served its purpose. Technological changes in the nature of work, global competition, and a shift from stable, fixed manufacturing jobs to a more flexible, dynamic, service-based economy were quickly making the system obsolete.[39]

For all these reasons, the Department of Labor abandoned the DOT in 1998 and developed an entirely new system for classifying jobs referred to as the Occupational Information Network, or O*NET. Instead of relying on fixed job titles and narrow task descriptions, the O*NET uses a common language that generalizes across jobs to describe the abilities, work styles, work activities, and work context required for various occupations that are more broadly defined (e.g., instead of the 12,000 jobs in the DOT, the O*NET describes only 1,000 occupations).[40] Although it was developed to analyze jobs in the U.S. economy, research suggests that the ratings tend to be transportable across countries. That is, if one holds the job title constant (e.g., first-line supervisor, office clerk, computer programmer), the ratings of the job tend to be the same even if the job is located in a different country.[41]

The O*NET is being used by many employers and employment agencies. For example, after closing its Seattle-based headquarters, Boeing used the O*NET system to help find new jobs for the workers who were laid off because of the impending move.[42] The State of Texas has used the O*NET to identify emerging occupations within the state whose requisite knowledge, skills, and abilities are underrepresented in the current occupational system. This information will be used to help train Texas residents to be prepared for the jobs of the future.

Although these examples show its value for employers, the O*NET was also designed to help job seekers. For example, the O*NET seems particularly well suited to describing the literacy requirements associated with alternative jobs. Thus, individuals who want to improve their ability to find employment can obtain relatively accurate information about what jobs they are qualified for given their current literacy level from the O*NET. They can also see how much their literacy skills would have to improve if they wanted to apply for higher-level jobs characterized by higher levels of complexity.[43] To see if you think this new system meets the goal of promoting "the effective education, training, counseling, and employment needs of the American workforce," visit its website yourself at http://online.onetcenter.org/ and see if the skills it lists for your current job or your "dream job" match what you know from your own experiences and expectations.

DYNAMIC ELEMENTS OF JOB ANALYSIS

Although we tend to view jobs as static and stable, in fact, jobs tend to change and evolve over time. Those who occupy or manage the jobs often make minor, cumulative adjustments to the job that try to match either changing conditions in the environment or personal preferences for how to conduct the work.[44] Indeed, although there are numerous sources for error in the job analysis process,[45] most inaccuracy is likely to result from job descriptions simply being outdated. For this reason, in addition to statically defining the job, the job analysis process must also detect changes in the nature of jobs.

LO 4-4
Identify the tasks performed and the skills required in a given job.

For example, in today's world of rapidly changing products and markets, some people have begun to question whether the concept of "the job" is simply a social artifact that has outlived its usefulness. Indeed, many researchers and practitioners are pointing to a trend referred to as "dejobbing" in organizations. This trend consists of viewing organizations as a field of work needing to be done rather than a set of discrete jobs held by specific individuals. For example, at Amazon.com, HR director Scott Pitasky notes, "Here, a person might be in the same 'job,' but three months later be doing completely different work."[46] This means Amazon.com puts more emphasis on broad worker specifications ("entrepreneurial and customer-focused") than on detailed job descriptions ("C++ programming") that may not be descriptive one year down the road.

Also, jobs tend to change with changes in the economy in the sense that economic downturns tend to be associated with organizational downsizing efforts. Research suggests that successful downsizing efforts almost always entail some changes in the nature, and not just the number, of jobs.[47] Indeed, as the "Competing through Sustainability" box shows, this seems to be the exact situation confronting many employers and employees coming out of the most recent recession, where job descriptions are being stretched to the breaking point. Failure to take into consideration the nature of the new jobs created after downsizing events is critical because, without support from HR, survivors of downsizing events tend to be less committed to the organization and have higher rates of subsequent turnover when the economy returns to normal.[48]

Stretching the Job Description

The economic data that was being reported in 2010 made it quite clear that the U.S. economy was coming out of the recession. Profits, as well as productivity, were at near record levels, and yet there was still very little evidence as late as the spring of 2011 that employers were showing any sign of hiring new workers. Although hiring always lags a recovery somewhat, the lag this time was more extended than ever, and some were concerned whether there would ever be an uptick in new jobs. This was reinforced in messages from employers like Wendy Goldstein, CEO of Costume Specialists, a small jewelry manufacturer who noted that "The jobs I cut aren't going to come back just because business is better."

Employers were reluctant to engage in new hiring for a whole host of reasons. For one, many employers were suspicious of the recovery, and concerned that increases in demand for products was going to be short lived. Rather than reflecting true growth in market demand, many employers feared that they were seeing just a one time restocking of their customers' depleted inventories. Second, there was uncertainty regarding how the nation's debates about health care were going to play out for employers. Thus, it is difficult to calculate the cost of labor due too the high and growing cost of insurance coverage that would have to be offered to any new hire under some of the proposed federal plans. Finally, and most critically, however, some employers during the recession just learned how to get more work out of fewer employees and liked it that way. In fact, one 2011 survey indicated that over 50% of workers reported that they had taken on new duties over the last year with no hike in pay.

Indeed, the most recent economic recovery was witness to a great deal of "work redistribution" and as one analyst noted, "job descriptions are written in sand, and the wind is blowing." In some cases, work was redistributed horizontally, as people who survived the layoffs simply took on the jobs of those that used to work alongside them. For example, at D'Addario & Co., a manufacturer of guitar strings, inspector jobs were eliminated, and line workers were taught how to inspect their own work. In other cases, work was redistributed vertically, as executives and managers had to pick up the work of junior staff or line workers that were let go. For example, marketing director Carol Firth found herself not only doing more copy production and copy-editing, she even wound up being responsible for the work of laid off security guards and was responsible for punching in the codes to open the parking lot gates every morning.

The gains in efficiency achieved by stretching job descriptions like this however is offset by certain costs. For example, with respect to vertical redistribution, executives like Firth worry that "it was hard to find time to meet with customers." Horizontal planning often places people in roles that they were not hired to fill and may not fit with their skills set. One can assign an effective but shy computer programmer to do sales work, but one may wind up with a lousy salesperson and ineffective programmer. Moreover, there are mental costs associated with switching back and forth from qualitatively different tasks that tire workers out and can result in errors, accidents, and misplaced priorities. Ultimately, there is a price to be paid for this kind of job stretching, and at some point a stretch can become a snap.

SOURCES: A. Kadet, "'Superjobs': Why You Work More, Enjoy It Less," *The Wall Street Journal*, May 8, 2011, pp. B1 and B7; T. Aeppel and C. Dougherty, "Employers Hold Off on Hiring," *The Wall Street Journal*, October 20, 2009, p. A3; S. E. Needleman, "Entrepreneurs Prefer to Keep Staffs Lean," *The Wall Street Journal*, March 2, 2010, p. B5.

Job Design

So far we have approached the issue of managing work in a passive way, focusing only on understanding what gets done, how it gets done, and the skills required to get it done. Although this is necessary, it is a very static view of jobs, in that jobs must already exist and that they are already assumed to be structured in the one best way. However, a manager may often be faced with a situation in which the work unit does not yet exist, requiring jobs within the work unit to be designed from scratch. Sometimes work loads within an existing work unit are increased, or work group size is decreased while the same work load is required. Finally, sometimes the work is not being performed in the most efficient manner. In these cases, a manager may decide to change the way that work is done in order for the work unit to perform more effectively and efficiently. This requires redesigning the existing jobs.

Job design is the process of defining how work will be performed and the tasks that will be required in a given job. **Job redesign** refers to changing the tasks or the way work is performed in an existing job. To effectively design jobs, one must thoroughly understand the job as it exists (through job analysis) and its place in the larger work unit's work-flow process (work-flow analysis). Having a detailed knowledge of the tasks performed in the work unit and in the job, a manager then has many alternative ways to design a job. This can be done most effectively through understanding the trade-offs between certain design approaches.

Research has identified four basic approaches that have been used among the various disciplines (such as psychology, management, engineering, and ergonomics) that have dealt with job design issues.[49] All jobs can be characterized in terms of how they fare according to each approach; thus a manager needs to understand the trade-offs of emphasizing one approach over another. In the following sections we discuss each of these approaches and examine the implications of each for the design of jobs. Table 4.3 displays how jobs are characterized along each of these dimensions, and

LO 4-5
Understand the different approaches to job design.

Job Design
The process of defining the way work will be performed and the tasks that will be required in a given job.

Job Redesign
The process of changing the tasks or the way work is performed in an existing job.

The mechanistic approach
    Specialization
    Skill variety
    Work methods autonomy
The motivational approach
    Decision-making autonomy
    Task significance
    Interdependence
The biological approach
    Physical demands
    Ergonomics
    Work conditions
The perceptual approach
    Job complexity
    Information processing
    Equipment use

table 4.3
Major Elements of Various Approaches to Job Design

SOURCE: From Michael A. Campion and Paul W. Thayer, "Job Design: Approaches, Outcomes, and Trade-Offs," *Organizational Dynamics*, Winter 1987, Vol. 15, No. 3. Copyright © 1987, with permission from Elsevier.

the Work Design Questionnaire (WDQ), a specific instrument that reliably measures these and other job design characteristics, is available for use by companies wishing to comprehensively assess their jobs on these dimensions.[50]

MECHANISTIC APPROACH

The mechanistic approach has roots in classical industrial engineering. The focus of the mechanistic approach is identifying the simplest way to structure work that maximizes efficiency. This most often entails reducing the complexity of the work to provide more human resource efficiency—that is, making the work so simple that anyone can be trained quickly and easily to perform it. This approach focuses on designing jobs around the concepts of task specialization, skill simplification, and repetition.

For example at Chili's Restaurants, cooks used to cut up vegetables, meats, and other ingredients as part of preparing a meal. In order to increase efficiency, however, the organization decided to break this job into two smaller parts: one job, called "prep cooks" who come in the morning and do all the cutting up, and the second job, "line cooks" who take these prepared ingredients and use them to assemble the final meal.[51]

Scientific management was one of the earliest and best-known statements of the mechanistic approach.[52] According to this approach, productivity could be maximized by taking a scientific approach to the process of designing jobs. Scientific management first sought to identify the "one best way" to perform the job. This entailed performing time-and-motion studies to identify the most efficient movements for workers to make. Once the best way to perform the work is identified, workers should be selected based on their ability to do the job, they should be trained in the standard "one best way" to perform the job, and they should be offered monetary incentives to motivate them to work at their highest capacity.

The scientific management approach was built upon in later years, resulting in a mechanistic approach that calls for jobs to be designed so that they are very simple and lack any significant meaningfulness. By designing jobs in this way, the organization reduces its need for high-ability individuals and thus becomes less dependent on individual workers. Individuals are easily replaceable—that is, a new employee can be trained to perform the job quickly and inexpensively.

Many jobs structured this way are performed in developing countries where low-skilled and inexpensive labor is abundant. As one might expect, this includes a host of "low-tech" manufacturing and assembly jobs, but increasingly this also involves "digital factory jobs." For example, *ProQuest Historical Newspaper* provides a service where subscribers can access the contents of any article ever published by one of nine major U.S. newspapers simply by entering an author name, keyword, or image. You might wonder how all of this historical, nondigital information and text is entered into this digital database, and the answer would be found in Madras, Spain. Here workers take this material and enter the headline, author, major key words, and first paragraph of the work by hand into the database, and then run a program to attach a visual file to the rest of the article. This menial work is conducted by 850 workers, who comprise three 8-hour shifts that work 24 hours a day, 7 days a week.[53] It would be difficult, if not impossible to find workers in the United States willing to put up with work this boring. In fact, as the "Competing through Globalization" box documents, few workers, even those in countries that specialize in low-cost labor, respond well to work that is overly routine and devoid of meaning.

In some cases, jobs designed via mechanistic practices result in work that is so simple that a child could do it, and this is exactly what can happen in some undeveloped

COMPETING THROUGH GLOBALIZATION

The Price Paid for Low Prices

Foxconn's Longhua factory campus in Shenzhen, China, is as much a city as it is a place of work. The 400,000 employees who work here spend 12 hour shifts in the company-owned plant manufacturing iPads, Playstations, and other high tech toys and electronic devices. After work, they retreat to their company-owned dormitories. From the outside, one of these dormitories looks like any other normal apartment building, except for the nets. Protruding horizontally from each of the buildings on both sides of the road are 15 foot poles that support yellow nets. In fact, there is 3.0 million square meters of such netting within the campus, all with one single purpose—catching potential suicide victims from jumping to their deaths.

The Foxconn suicide nets were put in place after 11 workers at the facility took their own lives in the summer of 2010, many of whom complained of having to work forced overtime, doing mindlessly repetitive work, under military-style rigor and discipline. This stress was exacerbated by the fact that most of the workers were poor,

uneducated teenagers and young adults from rural areas who had never been away from their homes prior to working at Foxconn. The tough culture in place at Foxconn is no accident and, their ruthlessly efficient operations helped the company become the world's largest electronics contract manufacturer by revenue and its CEO, Terry Guo, the richest man in Taiwan. The Longhua plant alone produces 137,000 iPhones a day. The secret to Foxconn's success, according to one industry analyst is simple; "It's the prices. Their prices are lower for high quality work."

The suicide nets of Shenzhen make it clear why the marvelous technology represented by an Apple iPod or iPhone or iPad can be obtained for such a small purchase price, in the sense that the real price was being paid by the workers who build the device. For example, Li Caihe, a 19 year old from Gansu province works 12 hour shifts where she attaches the same nine parts to the same motherboard of a smartphone each and every day, and then retreats to her dorm room that she shares with seven other girls

at night. Li notes that "youth, especially those born after 1990 are less able to endure suffering relative to our parents." Li also notes that when she gets to speak to her parents, often just once a week, "I try to sound happy. I don't speak about my stress."

The negative publicity from the Foxconn suicides proved to be a public relations nightmare for Apple and other U.S. companies. Steve Jobs, the former CEO of Apple, stressed that the news of the deaths was "very troubling" and that "we are all over this" in terms of rectifying the situation. This negative attention led to a 30% increase in wages and other worker-friendly initiatives at the plant, including counseling and a 24 hour suicide hotline. Of course, these amenities don't come for free—they all resulted in a 1% increase in the price of the finished product—roughly $4 per iPad.

SOURCES: J. Ye, "Suicides Spark Inquires," *The Wall Street Journal,* May 27, 2010, pp. B1 & B7; S. Wong, "Life and Death at the iPad Factory," *Bloomberg Businessweek,* June 7, 2010, pp. 35–36; F. Balfour, "Chairman Gou," *Bloomberg Businessweek,* September 13, 2010, pp. 57–69.

countries. This can lead to a backlash against companies that benefit from this unethical practice, and increasingly, organizations are taking the lead in preventing these kinds of practices. For example, when it learned that Uzbekistan cotton growers were using child labor to pick their crops, Walmart used its power to force them to abandon this practice. Working with other large U.S. retailers, Walmart took the lead to create the first system for tracking where cotton came from and organized a boycott against Uzbekistan, which quickly acquiesced to the corporate giant's pressure, freeing the children to return to school.[54] At the time, almost everyone else perceived that Walmart was a corporate villain and bully, assaulting workers, the environment, and consumers. Over the course of his tenure as the Walmart CEO, H. Lee Scott dramatically reversed this perception, and now Walmart is routinely listed as one of the most sustainable and corporately responsible organizations in the United States.[55]

MOTIVATIONAL APPROACH

The motivational approach to job design has roots in organizational psychology and management literature and, in many ways, emerged as a reaction to mechanistic approaches to job design. It focuses on the job characteristics that affect psychological meaning and motivational potential, and it views attitudinal variables (such as satisfaction, intrinsic motivation, job involvement, and behavioral variables such as attendance and performance) as the most important outcomes of job design. The prescriptions of the motivational approach focus on increasing the meaningfulness of jobs through such interventions as job enlargement, job enrichment, and the construction of jobs around sociotechnical systems.[56]

A model of how job design affects employee reactions is the "Job Characteristics Model."[57] According to this model, jobs can be described in terms of five characteristics. *Skill variety* is the extent to which the job requires a variety of skills to carry out the tasks. *Task identity* is the degree to which a job requires completing a "whole" piece of work from beginning to end. *Autonomy* is the degree to which the job allows an individual to make decisions about the way the work will be carried out. *Feedback* is the extent to which a person receives clear information about performance effectiveness from the work itself. *Task significance* is the extent to which the job has an important impact on the lives of other people. Although all five characteristics are important, the belief that the task is significant because performing it well leads to outcomes one values may be the most critical motivational aspect of work.[58] This can often be enhanced by making it clear to the worker how his or her job affects other people, whether they be customers, co-workers or society in general.[59]

These five job characteristics determine the motivating potential of a job by affecting the three critical psychological states of "experienced meaningfulness," "responsibility," and "knowledge of results." According to the model, when the core job characteristics (and thus the critical psychological states) are high, individuals will have a high level of internal work motivation. This is expected to result in higher quantity and quality of work as well as higher levels of job satisfaction.[60] Of the three critical psychological states, research suggests that "experienced meaningfulness may be the most important when it comes to managing work-related stress."[61]

Job design interventions emphasizing the motivational approach tend to focus on increasing the meaningfulness of jobs. Much of the work on job enlargement (broadening the types of tasks performed), job enrichment (empowering workers by adding more decision-making authority to jobs), and self-managing work teams has its roots in the motivational approach to job design. In enriched jobs, leadership is not the sole prerogative of one person, but rather is distributed throughout the team, and research shows that this can enhance group performance—especially in service jobs where there is a great deal of direct interpersonal interaction between team members and clients.[62] Not all workers respond positively to enriched jobs like these because it requires some degree of flexibility and responsiveness to other people, but with the right workers, interventions such as these have been found to have dramatic effects on employee motivation.[63]

In some cases, even work that may not be that interesting can be made significant by clarifying the link between what workers do and the outcomes of their work, perhaps far down the chain. For example, in medicine, a stent is an expandable wire form or perforated tube that is inserted into an artery to help promote blood flow after a heart operation. The actual work that goes into stent production is an assembly line process where each worker does a very small and, some might argue, boring task. To help increase the meaningfulness of this work, however, the company sponsors a party each year where line workers get to meet people whose lives were saved by the stents that were produced on that line. This is often a moving emotional experience for both parties and helps the employees see the impact of their work in a context where this would not naturally happen.[64] Thus, although at some point it might be necessary to pay workers in order to motivate them, it is even more important to show job incumbents why their jobs are important. Indeed, one of the secrets behind effective transformational leaders is their ability to help workers see the larger meaning in what they are doing on a day-to-day basis.[65]

BIOLOGICAL APPROACH

The biological approach to job design comes primarily from the sciences of biomechanics (i.e., the study of body movements), work physiology, and occupational medicine, and it is usually referred to as *ergonomics*. **Ergonomics** is concerned with examining the interface between individuals' physiological characteristics and the physical work environment. The goal of this approach is to minimize physical strain on the worker by structuring the physical work environment around the way the human body works. It therefore focuses on outcomes such as physical fatigue, aches and pains, and health complaints. Research in this tradition looks a bit more on the context in which it takes place rather than the work itself, and hence issues like lighting, space, and hours worked become more salient from this perspective.[66]

Ergonomics
The interface between individuals' physiological characteristics and the physical work environment.

The biological approach has been applied in redesigning equipment used in jobs that are physically demanding. Such redesign is often aimed at reducing the physical demands of certain jobs so that anyone can perform them. In addition, many biological interventions focus on redesigning machines and technology, such as adjusting the height of the computer keyboard to minimize occupational illnesses (like carpal tunnel syndrome). The design of chairs and desks to fit posture requirements is very important in many office jobs and is another example of the biological approach to job design. In addition to the direct effects of these kinds of interventions on worker well-being, these types of programs also have a positive psychological effect on workers by emphasizing an organizational climate that values safety and health.[67]

Often redesigning work to make it more worker-friendly also leads to increased efficiencies. For example, at International Truck and Engine Corporation, one of the most difficult aspects of truck production was pinning the axles to the truck frame. Traditionally, the frame was lowered onto the axle and a crew of six people, armed with oversized hammers and crowbars, forced the frame onto the axle. Because the workers could not see the bolts they had to tighten under the frame, the bolts were often not fastened properly, and many workers injured themselves in the process. After a brainstorming session, the workers and engineers figured that it would be better to flip the frame upside down and attach the axles from above instead of below. The result was a job that could be done twice as fast by half as many workers, who were much less likely to make mistakes or get injured.[68]

PERCEPTUAL–MOTOR APPROACH

The perceptual–motor approach to job design has roots in human-factors literature. Whereas the biological approach focuses on physical capabilities and limitations, the perceptual–motor approach focuses on human mental capabilities and limitations. The goal is to design jobs in a way that ensures they do not exceed people's mental capabilities and limitations. This approach generally tries to improve reliability, safety, and user reactions by designing jobs to reduce their information-processing requirements. In designing jobs, one looks at the least capable worker and then constructs job requirements that an individual of that ability level could meet. Similar to the mechanistic approach, this approach generally decreases the job's cognitive demands.

For example, although it may seem inconsequential, the practice of turning a truck left against traffic can be a dangerous act. The odds of an accident occurring on any single left turn against traffic is very small, of course, but for a company like UPS, that employs thousands or drivers covering millions of miles, these odds add up over time. Thus, UPS attached GPS devices to their trucks that were programmed, within some limits, to plan routes that minimized those types of turns. In addition to reducing accidents and injuries due to driver errors, the program also wound up saving $1.4 million in fuel costs.[69]

Recent changes in technological capacities hold the promise of helping to reduce job demands and errors, but in some cases, these developments have actually made the problem worse. The term "absence presence" has been coined to refer to the reduced attentive state that one might experience when simultaneously interacting with multiple media. For example, someone might be talking on a cell phone while driving a car, or surfing the net while attending a business meeting, or checking e-mail while preparing a presentation. In all these cases, the new technology serves as a source of distraction from the primary task, reducing performance and increasing the opportunities for errors.[70] Indeed, research shows that on complex tasks, even very short interruptions can break one's train of thought and derail performance. Thus, e-mail servers that have a feature that signals the arrival of each incoming message might best be turned off if the job incumbent cannot resist the temptation this creates to interrupt ongoing activity.[71]

In addition to external disruptions, information processing errors are also increased in any context that requires a "handoff" of information from one person to another. Indeed, problems with handoffs have become a major concern in the field of medicine. As Mike Leonard, physician leader for patient safety at Kaiser Colorado Hospital, notes, "In almost all serious avoidable episodes of patient harm, communication failures play a central role." This would include information that fails to get handed off from nurses, doctors, and medical technicians to one another (e.g., the results of the most recent test that was handed to the attending doctor does not get handed to the attending nurse) or information that fails to get handed off from one work shift to another (e.g., a patient who has already received medication from one shift gets it again from the next shift). Problems between shifts are especially likely due to fatigue and burnout, which may be present at the end of a shift for workers in stressful jobs.[72]

Increasingly, hospitals are borrowing the "SBAR" method, originally developed in commercial and military aviation as a means to hand off an airplane moving through different people's airspace, to standardize communication protocols at the handoff point in medical contexts. SBAR stands for situation, background, assessment, and recommendation, which constitute the four components of every successful handoff. That is, in a few seconds, the person handing off the patient needs to get control of the situation by demanding the listener's attention (situation), then relay enough information to establish the context or the problem (background), then give an overall evaluation of the condition (assessment), and finally make a specific suggestion about the next best course of action (recommendation). At one hospital that introduced this procedure, the rate of adverse events (i.e., unexpected medical problems that cause harm) was reduced by more than half, from 90 to 40 for every 1,000 patients treated.[73]

TRADE-OFFS AMONG DIFFERENT APPROACHES TO JOB DESIGN

A great deal of research has aimed at understanding the trade-offs and implications of these different job design strategies.[74] Many authors have called for redesigning jobs according to the motivational approach so that the work becomes more psychologically meaningful. However, one study examined how the various approaches to job design are related to a variety of work outcomes. For example, in this study, job incumbents expressed higher satisfaction with jobs scoring high on the motivational approach. Also, jobs scoring high on the biological approach were ones for which incumbents expressed lower physical requirements. Finally, the motivational and mechanistic approaches were negatively related to each other, suggesting that designing jobs to maximize efficiency very likely results in a lower motivational component to those jobs.

LO 4-6
Comprehend the trade-offs among the various approaches to designing jobs.

Although the motivational and mechanistic approaches to job design do work against one another somewhat, at the same time there is not a tight, one-on-one correspondence between the two. Thus, not all efficiency-producing changes result in dissatisfying work, and not all changes that promote satisfaction create inevitable inefficiencies. By carefully and simultaneously attending to both efficiency and satisfaction aspects of job redesign, managers can sometimes achieve the best of both worlds.[75] For example, at the new Indiana Heart Hospital in Indianapolis, much of the work was digitized in order to create a paperless organization. There are more than 600 computer terminals placed throughout the facility, and the doctors and staff directly enter or access information from these terminals as needed. This has eliminated the need for nurses' stations, chart racks, medical records departments, file storage rooms, and copiers and has cut down paperwork, resulting in an increase in efficiency, but also increased job satisfaction by eliminating bureaucracy, allowing the staff more immediate access to needed information. This has affected the bottom line by reducing the length of time a patient stays in the hospital from an average of five days at other hospitals to three days at Indiana Heart Hospital. This allows the hospital to process more patients per bed relative to the competition, giving them a direct source of competitive advantage.[76]

A LOOK BACK

WORK DESIGN & ORGANIZATIONAL STRUCTURE

This chapter opened with a vignette that illustrated U.S. manufacturing was making a comeback, despite the fact that wages in the United States are higher than many other countries where work might be outsourced. We showed how three different companies tapped into the ideas of their high-wage workforce to help reduce costs, increase innovation, and speed the delivery of service in ways that offset labor–price differentials. Then throughout this chapter we provided numerous methods and examples of how organizations can successfully compete via the more effective design of work flows, organizational structures, and individual jobs.

Questions

1. The analysis of work-flow design traditionally starts at the end of the process, with the final product or service that is to be rendered. One then works back to determine the best process for this, and then determines the appropriate inputs. If an employer is totally committed to a specific type of input, like high-wage labor or existing equipment or easy access to certain raw materials, how could the process of work-flow design play out and how might the results be different?

2. Although there are advantages and disadvantages to different structural configurations, why might it be more difficult to change one's structure in some directions than others? Specifically, how are the HR challenges associated with moving from centralized and functional structures to decentralized and divisional different from the challenge of moving one's structure in the alternative direction?

3. We have seen throughout this chapter that many ways of reducing the cost of getting jobs done, often comes at some price to workers who have to do those jobs. What can be done to promote a more just, fair, humane, and sustainable workforce in all corners of the world? Does the competitive nature of product or labor markets mean that "nice guys always finish last"?

 Please see the Video that corresponds to this chapter at www.mhhe.com/noe8e.

SUMMARY

The analysis and design of work is one of the most important components to developing and maintaining a competitive advantage. Strategy implementation is virtually impossible without thorough attention devoted to work-flow analysis, job analysis, and job design. Managers need to understand the entire work-flow process in their work unit to ensure that the process maximizes efficiency and effectiveness. To understand this process, managers also must have clear, detailed information about the jobs that exist in the work unit, and the way to gain this information is through job analysis. Equipped with an understanding of the work-flow process and the existing job, managers can redesign jobs to ensure that the work unit is able to achieve its goals while individuals within the unit benefit from the various work outcome dimensions such as motivation, satisfaction, safety, health, and achievement. This is one key to competitive advantage.

KEY TERMS

Centralization, 162
Departmentalization, 162
Job analysis, 170

Job description, 171
Job specification, 171
Job design, 177

Job redesign, 177
Ergonomics, 181

● DISCUSSION QUESTIONS

1. Assume you are the manager of a fast-food restaurant. What are the outputs of your work unit? What are the activities required to produce those outputs? What are the inputs?

2. Based on Question 1, consider the cashier's job. What are the outputs, activities, and inputs for that job?

3. Consider the "job" of college student. Perform a job analysis on this job. What are the tasks required in the job? What are the knowledge, skills, and abilities necessary to perform those tasks? What environmental trends or shocks (like computers) might change the job, and how would that change the skill requirements?

4. Discuss how the following trends are changing the skill requirements for managerial jobs in the United States: (a) increasing use of computers, (b) increasing international competition, (c) increasing work–family conflicts.

5. Why is it important for a manager to be able to conduct a job analysis? What are the negative outcomes that would result from not understanding the jobs of those reporting to the manager?

6. What are the trade-offs between the different approaches to job design? Which approach do you think should be weighted most heavily when designing jobs?

7. For the cashier job in Question 2, which approach to job design was most influential in designing that job? In the context of the total work-flow process of the restaurant, how would you redesign the job to more heavily emphasize each of the other approaches?

● SELF-ASSESSMENT EXERCISE

The chapter described how the Department of Labor's Occupational Information Network (O*NET) can help employers. The system was also designed to help job seekers. To see if you think this new system meets the goal of promoting "the effective education, training, counseling, and employment needs of the American workforce," visit O*NET's website at http://online .onetcenter.org/.

Look up the listing for your current job or dream job. List the skills identified for that job. For each skill, evaluate how well your own experiences and abilities enable you to match the job requirements.

● EXERCISING STRATEGY: THE TROUBLE AT TOYOTA: WHEN AMBITION TRUMPS TRADITION

In 2007, Toyota Motor Corporation surpassed General Motors as the world's largest carmaker. This was the accomplishment of a long-term goal that could only be obtained by a strong focus on rapid growth and expansion. However, in the process of focusing on this goal, many insiders at Toyota believed that the organization was straying from some of its core values, especially as this related to the organization's structure and design of jobs. In fact, in 2009, Toyota reported its first annual operating loss since 1938, and due to the economic recession, the company had so much overcapacity that they had to lay off workers for the first time since 1950. As one industry observer, Tokai Gakuin, noted, "Toyota was so focused on becoming the world's largest automaker that it failed to cut production quickly enough in 2008, as the economic crisis struck the U.S., its largest market."

Matters became even worse when the focus on growth and expansion started resulting in problems with safety that landed the company in the sights of the U.S. Congress. Standards at Toyota had slipped so far by this point that by 2010, it had recalled 8 million vehicles due to mechanical failures that were attributable for at least 51 deaths. The most famous of these was the unexpected acceleration issues that caused "runaway cars." Safety inspectors found over 2,000 cases where Camry, Prius, and Lexus owners reported that their cars surged without warning up to speeds of 100 miles per hour. By March of 2010, Toyota was involved in 109 class-action suits and 32 individual cases in U.S. courts.

The steps that the company took to restore profitability provide a lesson in how to compete via organizational design and job design. First, with respect to manufacturing jobs, the fast-paced expansion of Toyota's plants both in Japan and the United States was, in some cases, purchased at the price of reduced quality standards. In response to this, the company streamlined jobs, tightened job descriptions, and enhanced training programs in a way that slowed production, but also increased quality. For example, quality control inspectors were required to put on gloves and massage the door of every Camry in a soft circular motion in search of tiny dents for roughly 15 minutes prior to sending the car further down the production line.

With respect to sales jobs, because of Toyota's ambitious quotas, sales personnel often used high-pressure techniques to get customers to purchase cars more quickly, and then, after the sale was made, often handed over the cars without properly inspecting them. Thus, even when customers loved their cars, they often hated their car-buying experience. Toyota quickly responded to this problem by sending out five-person SWAT teams to sales units that were ranked low in customer satisfaction and reanalyzed all the jobs in those units, all the way from the top manager to the car washer. In each case, the team tried to create a personal link between each customer and each person who was responsible for the car, all of which resulted in slower sales, but happier customers.

Finally, with respect to managerial jobs, Toyota's middle-level managers made the case that in contrast to the organization's traditional, slow, consensus-based decision-making process with a long-term focus, too many recent decisions were made single-handedly by the President Katsuaki Watanabe. For example, middle-level managers noted how Watanabe quickly flip-flopped on where to build factories, first increasing production overseas when the Japanese yen was strong (and hence made production in Japan more expensive), and then quickly reverting production back within the country when the yen lost value. Because currency exchange rates fluctuate a great deal over short time periods, the short-term gain in profitability often resulted in long-term inefficiencies associated with starting up and closing factories. Watanabe was eventually replaced as president by Akio Toyoda, the grandson of the organization's founder, Kiichiro Toyoda, who promised to restore the organization's traditional approach to organizational structure and job design.

Questions

1. How would you characterize the traditional and historical organizational structure at Toyota in terms of centralization and departmentation?
2. How and why did the organizational structure change over time, and in what ways were some of these changes responsible for some of their recent problems?
3. Are there inevitable trade-offs between quantity and quality of production and in what ways can job analysis and job redesign help manage these trade-offs?

SOURCES: A. Ohnsman, J. Green, and K. Inoue, "The Humbling of Toyota," *Bloomberg Businessweek*, March 22, 2010, pp. 33–36; I. Rowley, "Even Toyota Isn't Perfect," *BusinessWeek*, January 11, 2007, pp. 33–36; N. Shirouzu, "Toyota to Change Leader amid Sales Slump," *The Wall Street Journal*, December 28, 2008, pp. A1–A2; N. Shirouzu and J. Murphy, "A Scion Drives Toyota Back to the Basics," *The Wall Street Journal*, February, 24, 2009, pp. B1–B3.

● MANAGING PEOPLE

Portals and Mashups: Creating Opportunities for Global Teams

Due to the increased complexity of work, as well as the increased demand to compete based upon speed, most organizations have changed the job design process from one focused on individual stand-alone jobs, toward jobs that are designed for teams. Increasingly, however, the globalization of product and labor markets has created an additional pressure for quick collaboration within global teams. One response to this demand has been the creation of technology that helps individual employees with a problem or innovative idea to tap into the global network of talent within the organization or even outside its own boundaries.

For example, web portals provide users with a single, security-rich, personalized interface that combines numerous sources of information from within a company's firewall and from the Internet at large. The right portal can help employees and business partners work more efficiently—streamlining business processes and enabling companies to implement new, highly responsive product and service delivery offerings. At IBM, portals take the form of specially designated "chat rooms" where any employee with a new idea or project can recruit team members, line up resources, and tap into market research or engineering skills available anywhere within this large and sprawling multinational firm. An entrepreneurial IBM employee can often create a virtual global team with cross-functional skills to tackle some problem in as little as two hours. For example, in one case, when a client needed to launch a new service that would allow video streaming for cell phones, an IBM project leader was able to organize a 20-person team that included staff from 10 different countries in just two weeks. The entire project was completed within two months.

Portals are often combined with mashups that are platforms that support development of quick applications that can be rapidly assembled and shared by individuals and teams. Typically, mashups are relatively simple, tactical applications built to solve a specific business need and enable more flexibility for business users to work with their own targeted applications and innovate in a protected environment that doesn't interfere with mission-critical applications. Because of its size and global scope, IBM tends to use its portals and mashups to create teams where all the members are IBM employees. On average,

IBM's own internal research suggests that the use of such portals has decreased the length of time it takes to get projects up and running from 6 months to 30 days. In the last three years alone, IBM has employed over 90,000 workers in such global teams, and these groups have been responsible for leading 70 new businesses and creating 10 new products.

This is often not an option for smaller firms that are not international in their scope. Hence, many smaller firms use portals and mashups to link specialists within their own companies to independent contractors or specialists in other companies. There are many different models for such global collaboration but the key dimensions by which most differ deal with how well-structured the problem is and how dominant any one member of the team is in terms of command and control. For example, the "Orchestra Model" of global teams is one where there is a well-structured problem and one dominant member of the team that controls the process. For example, the Boeing 787 Project used a portal owned by Boeing to recruit partners from its own list of suppliers, but also independent contractors to help develop components for Boeing's new airplane. Boeing was clearly in control of this well-scripted and planned project, but was able to reach far outside its own local talent base to create global teams for accomplishing complex tasks.

Alternatively, portals and mashups follow a "Jam Session Model" of global teaming where the problem is unstructured and there are no dominant members. For example, the Tropical Disease Initiative was an innovation portal project where many different academics and scientists concerned about fighting global diseases came together to take on diseases that were not widespread enough to create a strong profit potential for commercial pharmaceutical teams. This democratically led community of scientists tends to focus not on well-structured problems (e.g., curing Malaria), but instead focused on emergent opportunities where some new finding in the scientific literature was studied for its potential to provide assistance in treating any of a large number of diseases off a fixed list of "unprofitable diseases." Regardless of what model one employs, portals and mashups create opportunities to create global teams that can accomplish tasks that are well beyond the scope of any one of its members.

Questions

1. In what way does the existence of portals and mashups change the way one might design jobs today relative to just 10 years ago?

2. In what sense does every technological change that is introduced into the world have potential to change the way work is done?

3. What are some changes occurring in the technological landscape today that might have a major impact on the ways jobs are designed 10 years from now?

SOURCES: J. Addison, "Integrating IBM WebSphere Portal and IBM Mashup Center Software," *Bloomberg Businessweek*, May 17, 2011, p. 20; "P. Engardio, "Managing a Global Workforce," *BusinessWeek*, August 20, 2007, pp. 48–51; J. Marquez, "Connecting a Virtual Workforce," *Workforce Management*, September 22, 2008, pp. 18–28; S. Nambison and M. Sawhney, *The Global Brain* (Philadelphia, PA: Wharton School Publishing, 2008).

TWITTER FOCUS: INCLUSIVITY DEFINES BRAUNABILITY'S PRODUCTS AND ITS JOBS

Using Twitter, continue the conversation about job analysis and design by reading the BraunAbility case at www.mhhe.com/noe8e.

Diagnosed with spinal muscular atrophy, Ralph Braun needed a wheelchair to get around when he was a teenager. He developed a strong mechanical aptitude, which eventually led him to build a battery-powered scooter. Then he figured out how to modify a van with a lift so he could drive the van. When people saw the van, they asked him to build something similar for them. He used his earnings to start a company that became the world's largest maker of wheelchair-accessible vans. Based on his personal experience, Braun has a great appreciation for the potential of disabled workers. Braun's passion and purposefulness are reflected in the job design and work structure at his company, BraunAbility.

Engage with your classmates and instructor via Twitter to chat about Ralph Braun and his company using the case questions posted on the Noe website. Don't have a Twitter account yet? See the instructions for getting started on the Online Learning Center.

NOTES

1. K. M. Eisenhardt, N. R. Furr, and C. B. Bingham, "Microfoundations of Performance: Balancing Efficiency and Flexibility in Dynamic Environments," *Organization Science* 21 (2010), pp. 1263–73.

2. L. Hawkins and N. Shirouzo, "A Tale of Two Auto Plants," *The Wall Street Journal*, May 24, 2006, pp. B1–B2.

3. D. Ilgen and J. Hollenbeck, "The Structure of Work: Job Design and Roles," in *Handbook of Industrial & Organizational*

Psychology, 2nd ed., ed. M. Dunnette and L. Hough (Palo Alto, CA: Consulting Psychologists Press, 1991), pp. 165–208.

4. R. D. Pritchard, M. M. Harrell, D. Diaz Granados, and M. J. Guzman, "The Productivity Measurement and Enhancement System: A Meta-analysis," *Journal of Applied Psychology* 93 (2008), pp. 540–67.

5. G. S. Van der Vegt, B. J. M. Emans, and E. Van de Vliert, "Patterns of Interdependence in Work Teams: A Two-Level Investigation of the Relations with Job and Team Satisfaction," *Personnel Psychology* 54 (2001), pp. 51–70.

6. F. P. Morgeson, M. D. Johnson, M. A. Campion, G. J. Medsker, and T. V. Mumford, "Understanding Reactions to Job Redesign: A Quasi-Experimental Investigation of the Moderating Effects of Organizational Context on Perceptions of Performance and Behavior," *Personnel Psychology* 59 (2006), pp. 333–63.

7. C. M. Barnes, J. R. Hollenbeck, D. T. Wagner, D. S. DeRue, J. D. Nahrgang, and K. M. Schwind, "Harmful Help: The Costs of Backing-up Behaviors in Teams," *Journal of Applied Psychology* 93 (2008), pp. 529–39.

8. C. Passariello, "Louis Vuitton Tries Modern Methods on Factory Line," *The Wall Street Journal,* October 9, 2006, pp. A1, A15.

9. V. Venkataramani and S. Tangirala, "When and Why Do Central Employees Speak Up? An Examination of Mediating and Moderating Variables," *Journal of Applied Psychology* 95 (2010), pp. 582–91.

10. T. Aeppel and J. Lahart, "Lean Factories Find It Hard to Cut Jobs Even in a Slump," *The Wall Street Journal,* March 9, 2009, pp. B2–B3.

11. P. Engardio, "Lean and Mean Gets Extreme," *Bloomberg Businessweek,* March 23, 2009, pp. 60–62.

12. T. Black, "Downsides of Just-in-Time Inventory," *Bloomberg Businessweek,* March 28, 2011, pp. 17–18.

13. N. Byrnes, "Xerox' New Design Team: Customers," *BusinessWeek,* May, 7, 2007, p. 72.

14. S. Hamm, "Big Blue Shift," *BusinessWeek,* June 5, 2006, pp. 108–10.

15. M. Schminke, M. L. Ambrose, and R. S. Cropanzano, "The Effect of Organizational Structure on Perceptions of Procedural Fairness," *Journal of Applied Psychology* 85 (2000), pp. 294–304.

16. B. Worthen, C. Tuna, and J. Scheck, "Companies More Prone to Go Vertical," *The Wall Street Journal* November 30, 2009, pp. A1 and A16.

17. T. Neff and J. Citrin, "You're in Charge: Now What?" *Fortune,* January 24, 2005, pp. 109–20.

18. S. Gray, "Natural Competitor," *The Wall Street Journal,* December 4, 2006, pp. B1, B3.

19. W. D. Sine, H. Mitsuhashi, and D. A. Kirsch, "Revisiting Burns and Stalker: Formal Structure and New Venture Performance in Emerging Economic Sectors," *Academy of Management Journal* 49 (2006), pp. 121–32.

20. J. Marquez, "Banking on a New Culture at Citibank," *Workforce Management,* May 19, 2008, pp. 1–3.

21. B. Nussaum, "Technology, Just Make It Simpler," *BusinessWeek,* September 8, 2003, p. 38.

22. C. Fang, J. Lee, and M. A. Schilling, "Balancing Exploration and Exploitation through Structural Design: The Isolation of Subgroups and Organizational Learning," *Organization Science* 21 (2010), pp. 625–42.

23. J. D. Sherman and R. T. Keller, "Suboptimal Assessment of Interunit Task Interdependence: Modes of Integration and Information Processing for Coordination Performance," *Organization Science* 22 (2011), pp. 245–61.

24. R. Davison, J. R. Hollenbeck, C. M. Barnes, D. Sleesman, and D. R. Ilgen, "Coordinated Action in Multiteam Systems," *Journal of Applied Psychology* 96 (2011), pp. 650–63.

25. J. R. Hollenbeck, A. P. J. Ellis, S. E. Humphrey, A. Garza, and D. R. Ilgen, "Asymmetry in Structural Adaptation: The Differential Impact of Centralizing versus Decentralizing Team Decision-Making Structures," *Organizational Behavior and Human Decision Processes* 20 (2011) pp. 64–74.

26. P. Glader, "It's Not Easy Being Lean," *The Wall Street Journal,* June 19, 2006, pp. B1, B3.

27. N. Byrnes, "The Art of Motivation," *BusinessWeek,* May 1, 2006, pp. 57–62.

28. J. R. Hollenbeck, H. Moon, A. Ellis, B. West, D. R. Ilgen, L. Sheppard, C. O. Porter, and J. A. Wagner, "Structural Contingency Theory and Individual Differences: Examination of External and Internal Person–Team Fit," *Journal of Applied Psychology* 87 (2002), pp. 599–606.

29. M. L. Ambrose and M. Schminke, "Organization Structure as a Moderator of the Relationship between Procedural Justice, Interactional Justice, Perceived Organizational Support, and Supervisory Trust," *Journal of Applied Psychology* 88 (2003), pp. 295–305.

30. M. Conlin, "Netflix: Flex to the Max," *BusinessWeek,* September 24, 2007, pp. 72–74.

31. J. A. Marquez, "Taking a Longer View," *Workforce Management,* May 21, 2006, pp. 18–22.

32. D. A. Hofmann, F. P. Morgeson, and S. J. Gerras, "Climate as a Moderator of the Relationship between Leader–Member Exchange and Content-Specific Citizenship: Safety Climate as an Exemplar," *Journal of Applied Psychology* 88 (2003), pp. 170–78.

33. E. C. Dierdorf and F. P. Morgeson, "Effects of Descriptor Specificity and Observability on Incumbent Work Analysis Ratings," *Personnel Psychology* 62 (2009), pp. 601–28.

34. P. Lievens, J. I. Sanchez, D. Bartram, and A. Brown, "Lack of Consensus among Competency Ratings of the Same Occupation: Noise or Substance," *Journal of Applied Psychology* 95 (2010), pp. 562–71.

35. A. K. Weyman, "Investigating the Influence of Organizational Role on Perceptions of Risk in Deep Coal Mines," *Journal of Applied Psychology* 88 (2003), pp. 404–12.

36. L. E. Baranowski and L. E. Anderson, "Examining Rater Source Variation in Work Behavior to KSA Linkages," *Personnel Psychology* 58 (2005), pp. 1041–54.

37. E. McCormick and R. Jeannerette, "The Position Analysis Questionnaire," in *The Job Analysis Handbook for Business, Industry, and Government,* pp. 880–901.

38. E. C. Dierdorff and M. A. Wilson, "A Meta-analysis of Job Analysis Reliability," *Journal of Applied Psychology* 88 (2003), pp. 635–46.

39. N. G. Peterson, M. D. Mumford, W. C. Borman, P. R. Jeanneret, and E. A. Fleishman, *An Occupational Information System for the 21st Century: The Development of O*NET* (Washington, DC: American Psychological Association, 1999).

40. N. G. Peterson, M. D. Mumford, W. C. Borman, P. R. Jeanneret, E. A. Fleishman, K. Y. Levin, M. A. Campion, M. S. Mayfield, F. P. Morgeson, K. Pearlman, M. K. Gowing, A. R. Lancaster, M. B. Silver, and D. M. Dye, "Understanding Work Using the Occupational Information Network (O*NET): Implications for Practice and Research," *Personnel Psychology* 54 (2001), pp. 451–92.

41. P. J. Taylor, W. D. Li, K. Shi, and W. C. Borman, "The Transportability of Job Information Across Countries," *Personnel Psychology* 61 (2008), pp. 69–111.

42. S. Holmes, "Lots of Green Left in the Emerald City," *Business-Week Online* (March 28, 2000).

43. C. C. Lapolice, G. W. Carter, and J. W. Johnson, "Linking O*NET Descriptors to Occupational Literacy Requirements Using Job Component Validation," *Personnel Psychology* 61 (2008), pp. 405–441.

44. M. K. Lindell, C. S. Clause, C. J. Brandt, and R. S. Landis, "Relationship between Organizational Context and Job Analysis Ratings," *Journal of Applied Psychology* 83 (1998), pp. 769–76.

45. F. P. Morgeson and M. A. Campion, "Social and Cognitive Sources of Potential Inaccuracy in Job Analysis," *Journal of Applied Psychology* 82 (1997), pp. 627–55.

46. S. Caudron, "Jobs Disappear When Work Becomes More Important," *Workforce,* January 2000, pp. 30–32.

47. D. S. DeRue, J. R. Hollenbeck, M. D. Johnson, D. R. Ilgen, and D. K. Jundt, "How Different Team Downsizing Approaches Influence Team-level Adaptation and Performance," *Academy of Management Journal* 51 (2008), pp. 182–96.

48. C. O. Trevor and A. J. Nyberg, "Keeping Your Headcount When All About You Are Losing Theirs: Downsizing, Voluntary Turnover Rates, and the Moderating Role of HR Practices," *Academy of Management Journal* 51 (2008), pp. 259–76.

49. M. Campion and P. Thayer, "Development and Field Evaluation of an Interdisciplinary Measure of Job Design," *Journal of Applied Psychology* 70 (1985), pp. 29–34.

50. F. P. Morgeson and S. E. Humphrey, "The Work Design Questionnaire (WDQ): Developing and Validating a Comprehensive Measure for Assessing Job Design and the Nature of Work," *Journal of Applied Psychology* 91 (2006), pp. 1312–39.

51. J. Jargon, "Chili's Feels Heat to Pare Costs," *The Wall Street Journal,* January 28, 2011, pp. B.8.

52. F. Taylor, *The Principles of Scientific Management* (New York: W. W. Norton, 1967) (originally published in 1911 by Harper & Brothers).

53. B. Helm, "Life on the Web's Factory Floor," *BusinessWeek,* May 22, 2006, pp. 70–71.

54. M. Gunther, "Wal-Mart: A Bully Benefactor," CNNMoney.com, December 5, 2008, p. 1.

55. L. Delevevigne, "Surprising Corporate Do-gooders," CNN .Money.com, January 20, 2009, p. 1.

56. R. Griffin and G. McMahan, "Motivation through Job Design," in *OB: The State of the Science,* ed. J. Greenberg (Hillsdale, NJ: Lawrence Erlbaum Associates, 1993).

57. R. Hackman and G. Oldham, *Work Redesign* (Boston: Addison-Wesley, 1980).

58. A. M. Grant, "The Significance of Task Significance," *Journal of Applied Psychology* 93 (2007), pp. 108–24.

59. A. M. Grant, E. M. Campbell, G. Chen, K. Cottone, D. Lapedia, and K. Lee, "Impact and Art of Motivation Maintenance: The Effects of Contact with Beneficiaries on Persistence Behavior," *Organizational Behavior and Human Decision Processes* 103 (2007), pp. 53–67.

60. M. Schrage, "More Power to Whom?" *Fortune* (July 23, 2001), p. 270.

61. A. A. Grandey, G. M. Fisk, and D. D. Steiner, "Must 'Service with a Smile' Be Stressful?" *Journal of Applied Psychology* 90, (2005), pp. 893–904.

62. J. B. Carson, P. E. Tesluk, and J. A. Marrone, "Shared Leadership in Teams: An Investigation of Antecedent Conditions and Performance," *Academy of Management Journal* 50 (2007), pp. 1217–34.

63. F. W. Bond, P. E. Flaxman, and D. Bunce, "The Influence of Psychological Flexibility on Work Redesign: Mediated Moderation of a Work Reorganization Intervention," *Journal of Applied Psychology* 93 (2008), pp. 645–54.

64. W. E. Byrnes, "Making the Job Meaningful All the Way Down the Line," *BusinessWeek,* May 1, 2006, p. 60.

65. J. A. Colquitt and R. F. Piccalo, "Transformational Leadership and Job Behaviors: The Mediating Role of Core Job Characteristics," *Academy of Management Journal* 49 (2006), pp. 327–40.

66. S. Sonnentag and F. R. H. Zijistra, "Job Characteristics and Off-the-Job Activities as Predictors of Need for Recovery, Well-Being, and Fatigue," *Journal of Applied Psychology* 91 (2006), pp. 330–50.

67. S. Mewman, M. A. Griffen, and C. Mason, "Safety in Work Vehicles: A Multilevel Study Linking Safety Values and Individual Predictors to Work-related Driving Crashes," *Journal of Applied Psychology* 93 (2008), pp. 632–44.

68. S. F. Brown, "International's Better Way to Build Trucks," *Fortune,* February 19, 2001, pp. 210k–210v.

69. C. Torres, "Campbell's Quest for Productivity," *Bloomberg Businessweek,* November, 29, 2010, pp. 17–18.

70. D. K. Berman, "Technology Has Us So Plugged into Data, We Have Turned Off," *The Wall Street Journal,* November 10, 2003, pp. A1–A2.

71. J. Baker, "From Open Doors to Gated Communities," *Business-Week,* September 8, 2003, p. 36.

72. L. E. LaBlanc, J. J. Hox, W. B. Schaufell, T. W. Taris, and M. C. W. Peters, "Take Care! The Evaluation of a Team-Based Burnout Intervention Program for Oncology Health Care Providers," *Journal of Applied Psychology* 92 (2007), pp. 213–27.

73. L. Landro, "Hospitals Combat Errors at the 'Hand-Off,'" *The Wall Street Journal,* June 28, 2006, pp. D1, D2.

74. J. R. Edwards, J. A. Scully, and M. D. Brteck, "The Nature and Outcomes of Work: A Replication and Extension of Interdisciplinary Work-Design Research," *Journal of Applied Psychology* 85 (2000), pp. 860–68.

75. F. P. Morgeson and M. A. Campion, "Minimizing Trade-Offs When Redesigning Work: Evidence from a Longitudinal Quasi-Experiment," *Personnel Psychology* 55 (2002), pp. 589–612.

76. E. Florian, "IT Takes on the ER," *Fortune,* November 24, 2003, pp. 193–200.

PART 2

Acquisition and Preparation of Human Resources

Chapter 5
Human Resource Planning and Recruitment

Chapter 6
Selection and Placement

Chapter 7
Training

CHAPTER

5

Human Resource Planning and Recruitment

LO LEARNING OBJECTIVES

After reading this chapter, you should be able to:

LO 5-1 Discuss how to align a company's strategic direction with its human resource planning. *page 194*

LO 5-2 Determine the labor demand for workers in various job categories. *page 195*

LO 5-3 Discuss the advantages and disadvantages of various ways of eliminating a labor surplus and avoiding a labor shortage. *page 198*

LO 5-4 Describe the various recruitment policies that organizations adopt to make job vacancies more attractive. *page 212*

LO 5-5 List the various sources from which job applicants can be drawn, their relative advantages and disadvantages, and the methods for evaluating them. *page 216*

LO 5-6 Explain the recruiter's role in the recruitment process, the limits the recruiter faces, and the opportunities available. *page 222*

The Competition for Technical Talent

Although many job categories experienced an increase in demand for labor at the end of the last recession, nowhere was the battle for talent more intense than in the technology industry. The fast growth of opportunities in social media, mobile cell applications, and e-commerce has created a huge need for people with skills in the area of hardware and software development. Jobs posting data for technical workers indicates that while the number of new listings in this category dropped 50% from January of 2008 to May of 2009, between May of 2009 and October of 2010, the number of openings increased by 90%. This in turn has ignited a bidding war that illustrates the lengths that companies will go to compete when recruiting new employees.

In some cases, the battle reflects a "Clash of Titans," and takes place between large and well-known players such as Oracle, Hewlett Packard, Microsoft, and Facebook, who often raid each other in an effort to poach the best workers. From a competitive standpoint, poaching is a powerful weapon because one increases one's own advantage while at the same time, weakening one's competitors. For example, Juniper Networks snatched multiple executives from Cisco systems in 2011, drastically changing the balance of power in that sector of the industry. Twitter started courting Google's product development vice-president, Sundar Pichae, but was turned away when a $5 million counter-offer was placed on the table. As search firm executive Jeff Sanders notes, "Employers are really taking a look at the top 10% of performers and asking, 'Are we locked in?'"

In other cases, the fight takes on a more "David versus Goliath" theme as small startups with big ideas but small budgets struggle to lure highly skilled workers from more well established firms with strong social reputations. For example, Casual Collective, a small 14-person gaming company, raided Adobe Systems and stole engineering product manager Danielle Deibler who took a cut in salary to make the move from large to small. This was more than offset, however, by the larger role that she would play with her new employer. "In a large company it's hard to have a lot of impact on the direction of a product or the strategy," Diebler noted, and the stock options she received would make her a millionaire if the small startup ever was successful enough to go public.

In still other cases, the struggle is one of "Apples and Oranges," in the sense that employers who are not themselves in the tech industry, still require that type of talent and thus have to compete against tech-based rivals that are a more obvious fit for people who are being recruited. For example, the growth of high frequency trading firms in the financial industry has created an unprecedented demand for hardware and software specialists, however, the people with the right kind of skills have never even considered working on Wall Street as a potential career. Financial firms have to pay a great deal more to lure the best talent, and even then it is sometimes an uphill struggle. Especially in the wake of the recent financial crisis, many applicants are leery of working in the finance industry. "I've had people at interviews ask me point-blank, what the social value is that we're adding" states a recruiter for Knight Capital Group's electronic-trading firm. "It's very hard to compete with the well-known startups here."

SOURCES: J. Tozzi, "The Struggle to Recruit Tech Talent," *Bloomberg Businessweek*, October, 28, 2010, pp. 70–71.; J. Helyar and D. MacMillan, "In Tech, Poaching Is the Highest Form of Flattery," *Bloomberg Businessweek*, March 7, 2011, pp. 17–18; B. Saporito, "Where the Jobs Are," *Time*, January 17, 2011, pp. 26–34; and K. Peterson, "Battle for Techies: Wall Street versus Silicon Valley," *The Wall Street Journal*, January 18, 2011, p. C8.

Introduction

Human resource managers are the frontline troops in the war for talent. In the case of labor shortages, as those illustrated in the opening vignette about the technology industry, the ability to find and recruit the best talent can make the difference in a firm's ability to compete against its rivals. For some large and well-established companies, their strong reputation and the prestige associated with working with them gives them the edge. For smaller employers, the chance to offer someone a chance to have a large and immediate impact on a nascent and growing venture gives them their edge. For others, their edge is purchased with high pay, lucrative benefits, and salient perks. Each employer needs to find an edge in this competition to secure talent when there is a labor shortage, but beyond this, each employer must also learn how quickly, cheaply, and painlessly to shed workers when confronted with a labor surplus. Firms that win out in this competition grow and prosper, while those that fail to forecast the future and plan accordingly run the risk of going out of business.

The purpose of this chapter is to examine factors that influence the supply and demand for labor, and, in particular, focus on what human resources managers can do in terms of planning and executing human resource policies that give their firms competitive advantage in a dynamic environment.

Two of the major ways that societal trends and events affect employers are through (1) consumer markets, which affect the demand for goods and services, and (2) labor markets, which affect the supply of people to produce goods and services. In some cases, as we saw in the opening story, the market might be characterized by a labor shortage. In other cases, the market may be characterized by a surplus of labor. Reconciling the difference between the supply and demand for labor presents a challenge for organizations, and how they address this will affect their overall competitiveness.

There are three keys to effectively utilizing labor markets to one's competitive advantage. First, companies must have a clear idea of their current configuration of human resources. In particular, they need to know the strengths and weaknesses of their present stock of employees. Second, organizations must know where they are going in the future and be aware of how their present configuration of human resources relates to the configuration that will be needed. Third, where there are discrepancies between the present configuration and the configuration required for the future, organizations need programs that will address these discrepancies.

This chapter looks at tools and technologies that can help an organization develop and implement effective strategies for leveraging labor market "threats" into opportunities to gain competitive advantage. In the first half of the chapter, we lay out the actual steps that go into developing and implementing a human resource plan. Through each section, we focus especially on recent trends and practices (like downsizing, employing temporary workers, and outsourcing) that can have a major impact on the firm's bottom line and overall reputation. In the second half of the chapter, we familiarize you with the process by which individuals find and choose jobs and the role of personnel recruitment in reaching these individuals and shaping their choices.

The Human Resource Planning Process

LO 5-1
Discuss how to align a company's strategic direction with its human resource planning.

An overview of human resource planning is depicted in Figure 5.1. The process consists of forecasting, goal setting and strategic planning, and program implementation and evaluation. We discuss each of these stages in the next sections of this chapter.

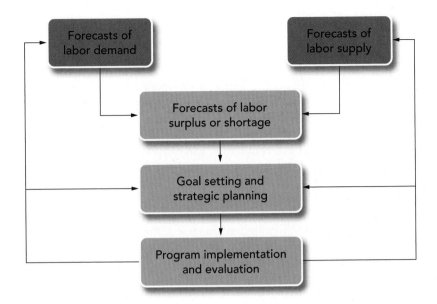

figure 5.1
Overview of the
Human Resource
Planning Process

FORECASTING

The first step in the planning process is **forecasting**, as shown in the top portion of Figure 5.1. In personnel forecasting, the HR manager attempts to ascertain the supply of and demand for various types of human resources. The primary goal is to predict areas within the organization where there will be future labor shortages or surpluses.

Forecasting, on both the supply and demand sides, can use either statistical methods or judgmental methods. Statistical methods are excellent for capturing historic trends in a company's demand for labor, and under the right conditions they give predictions that are much more precise than those that could be achieved through subjective judgments of a human forecaster. On the other hand, many important events that occur in the labor market have no historical precedent; hence, statistical methods that work from historical trends are of little use in such cases. With no historical precedent, one must rely on the pooled subjective judgments of experts, and their "best guesses" might be the only source from which to make inferences about the future. Typically, because of the complementary strengths and weaknesses of the two methods, companies that engage in human resource planning use a balanced approach.

Determining Labor Demand

Typically, demand forecasts are developed around specific job categories or skill areas relevant to the organization's current and future state. Once the job categories or skills are identified, the planner needs to seek information that will help predict whether the need for people with those skills or in that job category will increase or decrease in the future. Organizations differ in the sophistication with which such forecasts are derived.

At the most sophisticated level, an organization might have statistical models that predict labor demand for the next year given relatively objective statistics on leading indicators from the previous year. A **leading indicator** is an objective measure that accurately predicts future labor demand. For example, changes in price are often a

Forecasting
The attempts to determine the supply of and demand for various types of human resources to predict areas within the organization where there will be future labor shortages or surpluses.

LO 5-2
Determine the labor demand for workers in various job categories.

Leading Indicator
An objective measure that accurately predicts future labor demand.

good indicator of capacity-related problems, which in turn, is a good predictor of demand for labor. Thus, when prices for many manufactured goods fell over 5% in early 2007, this was an indicator that retailers had too many products piling up in inventories, and this was predictive of the recession in 2008. In contrast, to the manufacturing sector, however, prices in the service sector of the economy that year actually went up by 3%, suggesting there was less of an overcapacity problem in that sector. Human resource professionals need to recognize how prices for their product predict future demand for labor so they can react quickly to oversupply problems.[1]

Similarly, the demand for nurses in a community can historically be predicted very well by knowing the average age of the community members. Thus, if the average age of American citizens is going up, which it is, then one can expect an increase in the need for nurses. Studies based on these historical trends suggest that by the year 2014, our economy will need 1.2 million more nurses relative to what is available today.[2]

Statistical planning models are useful when there is a long, stable history that can be used to reliably detect relationships among variables. However, these models almost always have to be complemented by subjective judgments of people who have expertise in the area. There are simply too many "once-in-a-lifetime" changes that have to be considered and that cannot be accurately captured in statistical models. For example, based upon statistical history of the relationship between output (as measured with the gross domestic product) and unemployment, the Obama Administration predicted that unemployment rates in 2010 would come in at around 8%. However, to people's surprise, the actual figure was closer to 9.5%, and the failure of this formerly accurate leading indicator to predict actual employment levels was attributed to historically unprecedented events. Christina Romer, Chair of the White House Council of Economic Advisors noted that "the fact that the recession was caused by a financial crisis made it an unusual event, and firms may have reacted more forcefully than was usual out of fear of the unknown. Also firms that couldn't get credit may have had to lay more people off than normally."[3]

Determining Labor Supply

Once a company has projected labor demand, it needs to get an indicator of the firm's labor supply. Determining the internal labor supply calls for a detailed analysis of how many people are currently in various job categories (or who have specific skills) within the company. This analysis is then modified to reflect changes in the near future caused by retirements, promotions, transfers, voluntary turnover, and terminations.

As in the case of labor demand, projections for labor supply can be derived either from historical statistical models or through judgmental techniques. One type of statistical procedure that can be employed for this purpose involves transitional matrices. **Transitional matrices** show the proportion (or number) of employees in different job categories at different times. Typically these matrices show how people move in one year from one state (outside the organization) or job category to another state or job category.

Table 5.1 shows a hypothetical transitional matrix for a hypothetical manufacturer, focusing on seven job categories. Although these matrices look imposing at first, you will see that they are easy to read and use in determining the internal labor supply. A matrix like the one in this table can be read in two ways. First, we can read the rows to answer the question "Where did people in this job category in 2009 go by 2012?" For example, 70% of those in the clerical job category (row 7) in 2009 were

Transitional Matrix
Matrix showing the proportion (or number) of employees in different job categories at different times.

2009	2012							
	(1)	(2)	(3)	(4)	(5)	(6)	(7)	(8)
(1) Sales manager	.95							.05
(2) Sales representative	.05	.60						.35
(3) Sales apprentice		.20	.50					.30
(4) Assistant plant manager				.90	.05			.05
(5) Production manager				.10	.75			.15
(6) Production assembler					.10	.80		.10
(7) Clerical							.70	.30
(8) Not in organization	.00	.20	.50	.00	.10	.20	.30	

still in this job category in 2012, and the remaining 30% had left the organization. For the production assembler job category (row 6), 80% of those in this position in 2009 were still there in 2012. Of the remaining 20%, half (10%) were promoted to the production manager job category, and the other half (10%) left the organization. Finally, 75% of those in the production manager job category in 2009 were still there in 2012, while 10% were promoted to assistant plant manager and 15% left the organization.

Reading these kinds of matrices across rows makes it clear that there is a career progression within this firm from production assembler to production manager to assistant plant manager. Although we have not discussed rows 1 through 3, it might also be noted that there is a similar career progression from sales apprentice to sales representative to sales manager. In this organization, the clerical category is not part of any career progression. That is, this job category does not feed any other job categories listed in Table 5.1.

A transitional matrix can also be read from top to bottom (in the columns) to answer the question "Where did the people in this job category in 2012 come from (Where were they in 2009)?" Again, starting with the clerical job (column 7), 70% of the 2012 clerical positions were filled by people who were also in this position in 2009, and the remaining 30% were external hires (they were not part of the organization in 2009). In the production assembler job category (column 6), 80% of those occupying this job in 2012 occupied the same job in 2009, and the other 20% were external hires. The most diversely staffed job category seems to be that of production manager (column 5): 75% of those in this position in 2012 held the same position in 2009; however, 10% were former production assemblers who were promoted, 5% were former assistant plant managers who were demoted, and 10% were external hires who were not with the company in 2009.

Matrices such as these are extremely useful for charting historical trends in the company's supply of labor. More important, if conditions remain somewhat constant, they can also be used to plan for the future. For example, if we believe that we are going to have a surplus of labor in the production assembler job category in the next three years, we note that by simply initiating a freeze on external hires, the ranks of this position will be depleted by 20% on their own. Similarly, if we believe that we will have a labor shortage in the area of sales representatives, the matrix informs us that we may want to (1) decrease the amount of voluntary turnover in this position, since 35% of those in this category leave every three years, (2) speed the training of those in the sales apprentice job category so that they can be promoted more quickly than in the past, and/or (3) expand external recruitment of individuals for this job category, since the usual 20% of job incumbents drawn from this source may not be sufficient to meet future needs.

As with labor demand, historical precedents for labor supply may not always be reliable indicators of future trends. For example, it is typically the case that when unemployment is high, applications for any open positions increase dramatically compared to what might be experienced when the unemployment rate is low. However, in 2010, many employers who were posting open positions found that there were very few people actually applying for jobs. This was attributed to the fact that unemployment benefits had been extended to unprecedented lengths (99 weeks) and because the collapse of the housing market made it impossible for people to sell their homes, leaving them locked into their current location.[4] In addition, many of the new jobs that were opening up paid less than people's former jobs and thus there was a reluctance to "trade-down" with respect to occupational pay.[5] Finally, even many of the openings in jobs that were highly paid required technical skills or involved hardships that people who were formerly in white collar occupations were unwilling to take on. For example, there was a huge shortage of mine workers in 2010, and even though this is a well-paid occupation, for obvious reasons, most of the jobs in this field were going unfilled.[6]

Determining Labor Surplus or Shortage

LO 5-3
Discuss the advantages and disadvantages of various ways of eliminating a labor surplus and avoiding a labor shortage.

Once forecasts for labor demand and supply are known, the planner can compare the figures to ascertain whether there will be a labor shortage or labor surplus for the respective job categories. When this is determined, the organization can determine what it is going to do about these potential problems. For example, in our opening vignette, the introduction of new forms of electronic trading created an unprecedented level of demand for technical workers in the financial trading industry. This meant that there was likely to be a shortage of workers in that job category for that industry, and hence the firms that forecast this problem the soonest and had the best plans in place for solving that problem had a major competitive advantage relative to firms that learned of this very late in the game.

GOAL SETTING AND STRATEGIC PLANNING

The second step in human resource planning is goal setting and strategic planning, as shown in the middle of Figure 5.1. The purpose of setting specific quantitative goals is to focus attention on the problem and provide a benchmark for determining the relative success of any programs aimed at redressing a pending labor shortage or surplus. The goals should come directly from the analysis of labor supply and demand and should include a specific figure for what should happen with the job category or skill area and a specific timetable for when results should be achieved.

The hypothetical manufacturer described in Table 5.1, for instance, might set a goal to reduce the number of individuals in the production assembler job category by 50% over the next three years. Similarly, the firm might set a goal to increase the number of individuals in the sales representative job category by 25% over the next three years.

Once these goals are established, the firm needs to choose from the many different strategies available for redressing labor shortages and surpluses. Table 5.2 shows some of the options for a human resource planner seeking to reduce a labor surplus. Table 5.3 shows some options available to the same planner intent on avoiding a labor shortage.

OPTION	SPEED	HUMAN SUFFERING
1. Downsizing	Fast	High
2. Pay reductions	Fast	High
3. Demotions	Fast	High
4. Transfers	Fast	Moderate
5. Work sharing	Fast	Moderate
6. Hiring freeze	Slow	Low
7. Natural attrition	Slow	Low
8. Early retirement	Slow	Low
9. Retraining	Slow	Low

table 5.2

Options for Reducing an Expected Labor Surplus

OPTION	SPEED	REVOCABILITY
1. Overtime	Fast	High
2. Temporary employees	Fast	High
3. Outsourcing	Fast	High
4. Retrained transfers	Slow	High
5. Turnover reductions	Slow	Moderate
6. New external hires	Slow	Low
7. Technological innovation	Slow	Low

table 5.3

Options for Avoiding an Expected Labor Shortage

This stage is critical because the many options available to the planner differ widely in their expense, speed, effectiveness, amount of human suffering, and revocability (how easily the change can be undone). For example, if the organization can anticipate a labor surplus far enough in advance, it may be able to freeze hiring and then just let natural attrition adjust the size of the labor force. If successful, an organization may be able to avoid layoffs altogether, so that no one has to lose a job.

Unfortunately for many workers, in the past decade the typical organizational response to a surplus of labor has been downsizing, which is fast but high in human suffering. The human suffering caused by downsizing has both an immediate and a long-term element. In the short term, the lack of pay, benefits, and meaningful work has negative implications for financial, physical, and psychological aspects of individuals, causing bankruptcies, illnesses, and depression. Then, even if one can survive these immediate problems, in the long term, an extended bout of unemployment (e.g., lasting over six months) can stigmatize the individual, thus reducing future opportunities. In particular, in job categories where skills are perishable and need to be constantly updated, many laid-off workers will take any work within their area—even unpaid volunteer work—in order to prevent a gap in their employment history.[7] Indeed, the term "adult intern" has been coined to describe people who are willing to work for free while trying to break into a new career field.[8] The typical organizational response to a labor shortage has been either hiring temporary employees or outsourcing, responses that are fast and high in revocability. Given the pervasiveness of these choices, we will devote special subsections of this chapter to each of these options.

Downsizing

Downsizing
The planned elimination of large numbers of personnel designed to enhance organizational effectiveness.

We define **downsizing** as the planned elimination of large numbers of personnel designed to enhance organizational effectiveness. Although one tends to think of downsizing as something that a company turns to in times of recession like we saw in 2008 and 2009, if fact, many organizations engaged in downsizing in the 2002–2007 time period. During that period, in more than 80% of the cases where downsizing took place, the organizations initiating the cutbacks were making a profit at the time.

Surveys indicate three major reasons that organizations engage in downsizing. First, many organizations are looking to reduce costs, and because labor costs represent a big part of a company's total costs, this is an attractive place to start. For example, when the financial industry collapsed in 2008, firms in that industry were forced to slash payrolls.

Second, in some organizations, closing outdated plants or introducing technological changes to old plants reduced the need for labor. For example, Eastman Machine is a Buffalo, New York–based manufacturer of equipment that is used for cutting fabric. In order to stave off low-priced competition from Chinese rivals, Eastman expanded heavily into the market for highly automated, computer-driven cutting machines that are not currently available in Asia. This eliminated much of the manual work that was formerly performed at the plant, and now, the same amount of product and revenue that was once generated by a 120-person workforce can be produced with a staff of 80, requiring a downsizing of one-third of the workforce.[9] In fact, economywide, the ratio of spending on capital (plants, equipment, and machinery) increased by over 300% between 1990 and 2010, indicating that employers across the board were substituting technology for human labor.[10]

A third reason for downsizing was that, for economic reasons, many firms changed the location of where they did business. Some of this shift was from one region of the United States to another—in particular, many organizations moved from the Northeast, the Midwest, and California to the South and the mountain regions of the West. In some cases, technology is employed to move work that one might think was not that mobile. For example, the McDonald's restaurant chain experimented with drive-up windows in Michigan that were staffed with lower-wage workers located in Fargo, North Dakota. What looked like a standard drive-up squawk box was actually a long-distance connection, where Michigan orders were taken down by a worker in North Dakota who then relayed the order information back to the Michigan staff.[11]

Although downsizing has an immediate effect on costs, much of the evidence suggests that it has negative effects on long-term organizational effectiveness, especially for some types of firms. For example, in firms that are high in research and development intensity, downsizing has been linked to lower long-term organizational profits.[12] Also, the negative effects of downsizing seem to be exacerbated in service industries characterized by high levels of customer contact.[13] In addition, when downsizing efforts are not complemented by changes in the nature of work roles, then performance also tends to suffer.[14] The negative effect of downsizing on performance was especially high among firms that engaged in high-involvement work practices, such as employing teams and pay-for-performance incentives. Thus, the more a firm attempts to compete through its human resources, the more devastating the impact of layoffs is on productivity.[15]

Still, many employers engage in this tactic and hence it is important to understand what goes into an effective versus ineffective downsizing campaign. There seem to be a number of reasons for the failure of most downsizing efforts to live up to expectations in terms of enhancing firm performance. First, although the initial cost savings are a short-term plus, the long-term effects of an improperly managed downsizing effort can be negative. Downsizing not only leads to a loss of talent, but in many cases it disrupts the social networks needed to promote creativity and flexibility.[16] Second, many downsizing campaigns let go of people who turn out to be irreplaceable assets. In fact, one survey indicated that in 80% of the cases, firms wind up replacing some of the very people who were let go. Indeed, the practice of hiring back formerly laid-off workers has become so routine that many organizations are increasingly using software formerly used for tracking job applicants to track their laid-off employees.[17]

A third reason downsizing efforts often fail is that employees who survive the purges often become narrow-minded, self-absorbed, and risk-averse. Motivation levels drop off because any hope of future promotions—or even a future—with the company dies out. Many employees also start looking for alternative employment opportunities.[18] The negative publicity associated with a downsizing campaign can also hurt the company's image in the labor market, making it more difficult to recruit employees later. Especially in an age of blogs and text messaging, the once-private practice of laying off employees is becoming increasingly transparent, and any organizational mistake that gets made in the process is likely to become highly public.[19] The key to avoiding this kind of reputation damage is to ensure that the need for the layoff is well explained and that procedures for implementing the layoff are fair. Although this may seem like common sense, many employers execute layoffs in ways that make matters worse. For example, in September 2006, Radio Shack human resource managers decided to inform 400 people that they were laid off by e-mail.[20] This makes a dehumanizing event even more humiliating, and the negative publicity that attended this decision hurt the company's future recruitment efforts. This also increases the likelihood that disgruntled employees are likely to sue for loss of wages. Angry ex-employees often bring suit based upon the Worker Adjustment and Retraining Notification Act. This act requires that employers give workers 60 days warning regarding layoffs, as well as severance pay. Many employers seem to be unaware of this act, and because of the recession, there was a spike in lawsuits in 2009 based upon this act.[21]

The key to a successful downsizing effort is to avoid indiscriminant across-the-board reductions, and instead perform surgical strategic cuts that not only reduce costs, but also improve the firm's competitive position. For example, Raven Industries, a Sioux Falls manufacturer of a wide variety of plastic products, had to cut its workforce, but went about the process in a manner that would help make the company "China proof." They went from having 10 different divisions to 4, eliminating manufacturing of certain low-margin products that could be produced cheaper in China (e.g., generic plastic covers for pickup trucks) and pouring more resources into more profitable custom-made covers for widely different agricultural machines. In the process, the organization decreased in size almost by half (from 1,500 workers to 750), but revenue was off by less than 20%. Two years after this strategic downsizing effort, the company's share price increased from $4.50 to over $30.[22]

Early Retirement Programs and Buyouts

Another popular means of reducing a labor surplus is to offer an early retirement program. As shown in Figure 5.2, the average age of the U.S. workforce is increasing. But although many baby boomers are approaching traditional retirement age, early indications are that this group has no intention of retiring any time soon.[23] Several

figure 5.2

Aging of the U.S. Population, 2000–2020

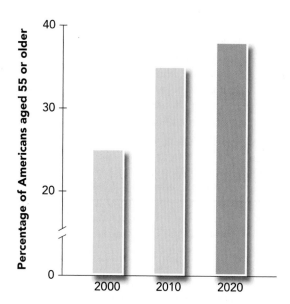

forces fuel the drawing out of older workers' careers. First, the improved health of older people in general, in combination with the decreased physical labor in many jobs, has made working longer a viable option. Second, this option is attractive for many workers because they fear Social Security will be cut, and many have skimpy employer-sponsored pensions that may not be able to cover their expenses. Third, age discrimination legislation and the outlawing of mandatory retirement ages have created constraints on organizations' ability to unilaterally deal with an aging workforce. Fourth, the combined collapse of the financial market and housing markets deeply cut into the wealth of many older workers, making it economically unviable to retire. Finally, many employers are increasingly concerned about losing the wealth of experience that older workers bring to their companies.

Although an older workforce has some clear advantages for employers in terms of experience and stability, it also poses problems. First, older workers are sometimes more costly than younger workers because of their higher seniority, higher medical costs, and higher pension contributions. When the value of the experience offsets these costs, then employers are fine; but if it does not, it becomes difficult to pass these costs to consumers. Second, because older workers typically occupy the best-paid jobs, they sometimes prevent the hiring or block the advancement of younger workers. This is frustrating for the younger workers and leaves the organization in a perilous position whenever the older workers decide to retire.

Indeed, although a weak economy hurts the prospects of all workers, the impact is especially hard on young people who have limited work experience and skills. In fact, simply graduating into a bad economy can have lasting negative effects on workers. For example, one study found that for each percentage point rise in the unemployment rate, those who graduated during a recession earn 7% less in their first year on the job, and 3% less even 15 years later, relative to peers who just happened to graduate in better economic times.[24] Moreover, the impact of youth unemployment can also have powerful effects that can ripple through an entire society, as illustrated in the "Competing through Sustainability" box.

COMPETING THROUGH SUSTAINABILITY

Youth Unemployment and the Arab Spring

What will forever be known as the Arab Spring of 2011 began with a 26-year-old Tunisian named Mohamed Bouzizi, a well-educated, but unemployed young man who took to selling fruits and vegetables from a rickety old cart in order to make a living. When the government officials in the city of Sidi Bouzid ruled his cart illegal, and then confiscated it, Bouzizi, in a fit of depression and desperation, set himself on fire. His story spread quickly throughout Tunisia and the rest of the world via Twitter, YouTube, blogs, and other social media, igniting a firestorm of protests and riots that would bring down not only the government of Tunisia, but also neighboring Egypt as well. Although there were multiple underlying causes behind these large revolts, there is wide consensus that high unemployment rates among young workers was one of the root causes.

Unemployment rates for young workers in the 16-to-24 age range throughout the Middle East were over 25% at the time of the riots. This level of unemployment leaves way too many young, energetic people bored and with much too much time on their hands. Indeed, although the problem is most dramatic in this part of the world, this is a global predicament. Youth unemployment rates in Europe and the United States ranged between 15% and 20% that same spring, and unrest was evident in these locations as well. For example, protesting British students attacked the headquarters of the Conservative Party headquarters in London that spring, and students in Oakland, California, shut down Interstate 880 contesting tuition increases and lack of job opportunities.

Indeed, the fact that many of the protestors are well-educated points to the fact that the typical "solution" to youth unemployment—promoting higher education—is no longer working. For example, Egypt had traditionally coped with high youth unemployment rates by subsidizing college enrollments, and many of the youths protesting in Liberation Square in Cairo had graduate degrees from diploma mills. The problem was that the skills that were being taught in these schools were light in the areas of technology and language abilities that were most sought after by employers in the region, and that the economy was not growing fast enough to absorb the large demographic bulge of young workers regardless of their education.

The size and scope of this problem defies any one solution, but governments and organizations throughout the world are trying to respond in ways that would promote a sustainable means of easing the transition to work for younger workers. On the government side, the use of short-term, subminimum wages for new workers are being considered, to help reduce this specific barrier to employment. On the employer side, a key to success seems to rest on creating a tight link between young workers and employers as soon as possible. In some countries like Germany, the use of apprenticeship programs that link new workers to older and established workers has been found to increase the efficiency of experienced workers (who can off-load simpler tasks), but also cheaply train the next generation of workers. In a similar vein, AT&T has instituted a job shadowing program where teenagers observe employees in action, in order to give insights into the demands of a modern workplace. Finally, programs that promote and sustain young entrepreneurs, as opposed to shutting them down, as was the case in Sidi Bouzid, are critical because this is the source of new ideas and new job opportunities.

SOURCES: S. Reed, "Youth Unemployment Shakes the Arab World," *Bloomberg Businessweek*, January 24, 2011, pp. 13–14; P. Coy, "The Lost Generation," *BusinessWeek*, October, 19, 2009, pp. 33–35; "The Youth Unemployment Bomb," *Bloomberg Businessweek*, February 2, 2011, pp. 27–31.

In the face of such demographic pressures, many employers try to induce voluntary attrition among their older workers through early retirement incentive programs. Although some research suggests that these programs do induce attrition among lower-performing older workers, to a large extent, such programs' success is contingent upon accurate forecasting. For example, at FedEx, the company had to scramble to find workers for the busy holiday season in 2003, when more people opted to take early retirement packages than anticipated. In contrast, at Electronic Data Systems, only one-third of the number of anticipated people opted to accept buyouts in a 2004 program that had to be reapplied in 2005 with a more lucrative set of enticements. Although mistakes in either direction can be costly, an underenrolled program creates an additional set of problems if employees start to think that they should wait it out and hope for an even better package further down the line. This makes the process of calculating one's future labor supply much more complex. As one HR manager notes, "It's a very dicey issue. You have to encourage people to leave and tell them this is the best offer you are going to get."[25]

For this and other reasons, many early retirement programs are simply converted into buyouts for specific workers that have nothing to do with age. For example, in 2006, Ford reduced the size of its unionized workforce by close to 50% using across-the-board buyouts of workers. Depending on the length of service, some employees received as little as $35,000 to leave, whereas those with the longest tenure received as much as $145,000.[26]

In contrast to Ford, one part of the plan at General Motors was to reduce the surplus of labor by buying out the contracts of long tenured workers. In this most recent buyout plan at GM, 22,000 of its 62,000 unionized workers were offered $20,000 plus a $25,000 voucher toward the purchase of a GM car if they were willing to retire. This offer was much less lucrative relative to previous buyouts announced at the company, and for that reason, many outsiders thought that this part of their plan was also unrealistic in terms of generating its hoped for benefits.[27] A similar program at the *Washington Post* offered workers roughly a year and a half in salary, and this offer seemed to be more in line with what it generally takes to get people to leave voluntarily. Interestingly, while the *Post* was cutting the number of employees, the *New York Times* decided to reduce pay levels by roughly 3% and not layoff or buyout any employees. Rather than seeing size as a liability, Executive Editor Bill Keller saw it as a source of unique competitive advantage for the *Times* (in fact, the largest newsroom in the country), describing his current stock of employees as "the engine of our long term success."[28]

Employing Temporary Workers

Whereas downsizing has been a popular method for reducing a labor surplus, hiring temporary workers and outsourcing has been the most widespread means of eliminating a labor shortage. Temporary employment afforded firms the flexibility needed to operate efficiently in the face of swings in the demand for goods and services. In fact, a surge in temporary employment often preceded a jump in permanent hiring, and was often a leading indicator that the economy was expanding. However, that no longer seems to be the case. Hiring of temporary workers rose each month from October of 2009 to August of 2010, but there were no signs that the hiring of permanent workers was expanding. Many analysts pointed to concerns regarding the stability of the economic recovery and uncertainty regarding pending health care legislation (and its impact on the costs associated with full-time workers) as the major reason why employers avoided real hiring. However, others suggested that employers had simply come to enjoy the idea of matching quick changes in consumer demands for products with quick changes in the supply of labor. As one CEO notes, "You need the flexibility in your manpower costs since sales can fluctuate more."[29]

In addition to flexibility, hiring temporary workers offers several other advantages:

- The use of temporary workers frees the firm from many administrative tasks and financial burdens associated with being the "employer of record."
- Small companies that cannot afford their own testing programs often get employees who have been tested by a temporary agency.
- Many temporary agencies train employees before sending them to employers, which reduces training costs and eases the transition for both the temporary worker and the company.
- Because the temporary worker has little experience in the host firm, she brings an objective perspective to the organization's problems and procedures that is sometimes valuable. Also, since the temporary worker may have a great deal of experience in other firms, she can sometimes identify solutions to the host organization's problems that were confronted at a different firm.

Certain disadvantages to employing temporary workers need to be overcome to effectively use this source of labor. For example, in the service sector of the economy, low levels of commitment to the organization and its customers on the part of temporary employees, often spills over and reduces the level of customer loyalty.[30] Instead of replacing long-term employees with temporary employees, many organizations try to buffer their "core employees" from wild swings in demand by supplementing their core staff with a small set of temporary workers. For example, in 2009, Boeing cut 1,500 temporary workers from one of its divisions, but retained all of its permanent workers. HR executive Jim Proulx noted that, "The first imperative was to reduce all of the contract and contingent labor that we possibly could to shield our regular employees."[31]

In addition, there is often tension between a firm's temporary employees and its full-time employees. Surveys indicate that 33% of full-time employees perceive the temporary help as a threat to their own job security. This can lead to low levels of cooperation and, in some cases, outright sabotage if not managed properly.[32]

There are several keys to managing this problem. First, the organization needs to have bottomed out in terms of any downsizing effort before it starts bringing in temporaries. A downsizing effort is almost like a death in the family for employees who survive, and a decent time interval needs to exist before new temporary workers are introduced into this context. Without this time delay, there will be a perceived association between the downsizing effort (which was a threat) and the new temporary employees (who may be perceived by some as outsiders who have been hired to replace old friends). Any upswing in demand for labor after a downsizing effort should probably first be met by an expansion of overtime granted to core full-time employees. If this demand persists over time, one can be more sure that the upswing is not temporary and that there will be no need for future layoffs. The extended stretches of overtime will eventually tax the full-time employees, who will then be more receptive to the prospect of hiring temporary employees to help lessen their load.

Second, if the organization is concerned about the reactions of full-time workers to the temporaries, it may want to go out of its way to hire "nonthreatening" temporaries. For example, although most temporary workers want their temporary assignments to turn into full-time work (75% of those surveyed expressed this hope), not all do. Some prefer the freedom of temporary arrangements. These workers are the ideal temporaries for a firm with fearful full-time workers.[33] In many cases, temporary staffing firms have access to this type of employee, and this explains the massive growth rate for firms in that industry. For example, Manpower Inc., one of the larger temporary employment agencies, has seen an increase in stock price of more than 35% between 2005 and 2007.[34]

Of course, in attempting to convince full-time employees that they are valued and not about to be replaced by temporary workers, the organization must not create the perception that temporary workers are second-class organizational citizens. HR staff can also prevent feelings of a two-tiered society by ensuring that the temporary agency provides benefits to the temporaries that are at least minimally comparable to those enjoyed by the full-time workers with whom they interact. This not only reduces the benefit gap between the full-time and part-time workers but also helps attract the best part-time workers in the first place.

Outsourcing, Offshoring, and Immigration

Outsourcing

An organization's use of an outside organization for a broad set of services.

Whereas a temporary employee can be brought in to manage a single job, in other cases a firm may be interested in getting a much broader set of services performed by an outside organization; this is called **outsourcing**. Outsourcing is a logical choice when a firm simply does not have certain expertise and is not willing to invest time and effort into developing it. For example, ironically, companies increasingly outsource many of their human resource management tasks to outside vendors who specialize in efficiently performing many of the more routine administrative tasks associated with this function. Figure 5.3 shows a forecast for growth rates in the human resource outsourcing (HRO) industry. Cost savings in this area are easily obtained because rather than purchase and maintain their own specialized hardware and software, as well as specialized staff to support such systems, companies can time-share the facilities and expertise of a firm that focuses on this technology.

Thus, a moderate-size company that might otherwise need to have a 15- to 30-person HR staff can get by with just 5 to 7 people devoted to HR because they share services with outside firms like Accenture,[35] thus benefiting from economies of scale. In addition to managing the size of the HR unit, the hope is also that this frees up HR managers to focus on more strategic issues. As Samuel Borgese, VP of HR for Catalina Restaurant Group, notes, "This allows us to keep strategic tasks in-house with tactical support form the outsourcing vendor. It's very difficult for a VP of HR to be a strategic player if he or she is managing the HR infrastructure."[36]

Offshoring

A special case of outsourcing where the jobs that move actually leave one country and go to another.

In other cases, outsourcing is aimed at simply reducing costs by hiring less expensive labor to do the work, and, more often than not, this means moving the work outside the country. **Offshoring** is a special case of outsourcing where the jobs that move actually leave one country and go to another. This kind of job migration has always taken place; however, rapid technological changes have made the current trends in this area historically unprecedented. Offshoring is controversial because close to 800,000 white-collar jobs have moved from the United States to India, eastern Europe, Southeast Asia, and China in the last 10 years. In addition to restricting job growth in the United States this has also affected wages, in the sense that while the average rate of salary growth during an economic recovery is usually around 6–8%, because of offshoring, salary growth in the most recent recovery was actually negative (−1%).

Although initially many jobs that were outsourced were low scope and simple jobs, increasingly, higher skilled work is being done overseas. For example, in 2006, DuPont moved legal services associated with its $100 million asbestos case litigation to a team of lawyers working in the Philippines. Some of this work reflects the sort of

NelsonHall puts the market for multiprocess HRO at $1.475 billion by 2010 for the midmarket, which it defines as companies with 1,000–10,000 employees. NelsonHall defines multiprocess HRO as two or more major HR tasks outsourced to a single vendor, so this market is broader than the market for comprehensive HRO.

figure 5.3

U.S. Multiprocess
HR Outsourcing
Forecast

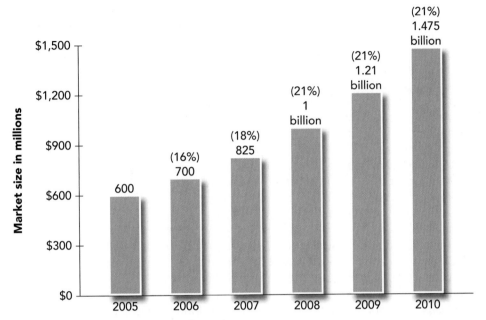

Note: Percentage = compound annual growth rate.
SOURCE: NelsonHall, "Multiple HR Outsourcing in the U.S.: Market Assessment," June 2006.

tedious copying of documents (more than 2 million pages) that is associated with a typical offshoring project, but much of the work requires actual legal judgments (e.g., determining the relevance of the document to the case or its need for confidentiality) that normally would be performed by U.S. lawyers. Paralegal work by U.S. firms can run up to $150 an hour versus $30 in the Philippines, and lawyers' salaries in the Philippines are one-fifth of their counterparts' in the United States.[37]

Indeed, the stereotype that "call center" staffing is the only type of work being offshored is increasingly invalid, as countries like China, India, and those in eastern Europe try to climb the skill ladder of available work. In India alone, whereas 85% of the work offshored there in 2000 reflected call center work, by 2006 this was reduced to 35%. The growth in India is now in higher-paying contracts dealing with business process improvement, processing mortgages, handling insurance claims, overseeing payrolls, and reading X-rays and other medical tests.[38] Many of the simple call center jobs that moved to India are either moving deeper into the rural Indian villages[39] or, ironically, moving back to the United States. Indeed, call center jobs are increasingly being performed by U.S. workers who are now operating out of their own homes instead of massive call centers like those run overseas. One recent survey indicated that 25% of call center employees are based in their own homes, and some have estimated that this will grow by another 25% between 2006 and 2010.[40]

Although this may seem problematic for U.S. employers, in fact, if effectively managed, firms that offshore certain aspects of work gain an undeniable competitive advantage over their rivals. Ignoring this source of advantage is self-defeating, and akin to putting one's head in the sand. For example, Levi-Strauss tried for years to compete against other low-cost jeans manufacturers who offshored their labor. However, after years of one plant shutdown after another, in 2003 the firm finally gave up and closed down all of its U.S. manufacturing plants. The move, which many saw as inevitable, was long overdue and had it been made earlier, the company might have been able to avoid losing over $20 million.

When making the decision to offshore some product or service, organizations should consider several critical factors. Many who failed to look before they leaped onto the offshoring bandwagon have been disappointed by their results. Quality control problems, security violations, and poor customer service experiences have in many cases wiped out all the cost savings attributed to lower wages and more. For example, problems with the development of Boeing's 787 Dreamliner, a project that is three years overdue and billions of dollars over budget, have been attributed to both the amount and type of work that was offshored. With respect to the amount of outsourced work, the 787 had more foreign content (30%) than any plane Boeing ever built (where the average is 5%), and many of the component parts manufactured by far-flung suppliers did not fit together very well. In terms of the nature of the work, Boeing took on final assembly of the plane, but this is the activity that provided the least amount of value added.[41] Jim Albaugh, the company's chief of aviation, admitted that "We gave too much work to people that had never really done this before, and then we didn't provide the oversight that was necessary. In hindsight, we spent a lot more money than we ever would have spent if we tried to keep many of the key technologies closer to Boeing. The pendulum swung too far."[42]

Indeed, these kinds of problems have led to a resurgence of outsourcing activity that keeps the work within the boundaries of the United States. For example, many rural areas of the United States that have been victims of lost manufacturing jobs have retooled themselves in an effort to attract work that is currently being shipped overseas. The value proposition offered by these firms is that "We cost less than cities on the East or West Coast, and we're easier to deal with than India."[43] Ironically, some of the growth in rural outsourcing has come from firms in India opening up U.S. facilities. For example, several of the large Indian outsourcing firms such as Tata, Wipro, and Infosys have opened up shop in rural Ohio using American workers. Privacy laws prevent certain data from being shipped overseas and hence being local allows these firms to do work with the U.S. government and health care providers that they could not do otherwise. Moreover, local workers have a more nuanced understanding of the language and culture that supports working on more complicated on-site business problems versus simply writing batch code.[44]

There are several steps a company should take to ensure the success of outsourcing. First, when choosing an outsourcing vendor, it is usually the bigger and older the better. Small overseas upstarts often promise more than they can deliver and take risks that one is not likely to see in larger, more established contractors.[45] Second, do not offshore any work that is proprietary or requires tight security. One software developer that hired an Indian firm to debug its programs later found that the firm copied the software and sold it under its own brand name.[46] In general, the work that is outsourced needs to be "modular" in the sense that the work is self-contained and does not require the outsourcing firm to provide any information that is best kept secret for competitive reasons.[47] Third, it is generally a good idea to start small and then monitor the work very closely, especially in the beginning. Typically, if problems are going to develop, they manifest themselves quickly to those who are paying close attention.[48]

Finally, rather than treating offsourced work as just a cost-containment strategy, firms are increasingly looking for "transformational offshoring," which promotes growth and opens up avenues of new revenue. That is, the increased sophistication of outsourcing firms means that they are better able to partner with companies on an equal basis in developing innovative and unique ways to do business. This development has prompted one CEO to note that "I think we will end up with companies that deliver products faster, at lower cost, and are better able to compete against anyone in the world."

If one cannot take the work overseas, but still wishes to tap into less-expensive global talent to fill a labor shortage, then one might simply bring foreign workers into the country. Immigration has always been a vital part of the American economy, and many foreign workers are happy to leave their home and pursue their own American dream.[49] However, entrance of foreign workers into the United States to fill jobs is federally regulated, so there are limits to what can be accomplished here. Employers wishing to hire foreign workers need to help them secure work visas and show that there are no qualified Americans who could do the same work.[50]

● Employees at Pella Windows agreed to a four-day workweek to avoid massive layoffs in the midst of a labor surplus.

Although most companies that go this route behave ethically, there have been numerous recent cases where headhunting firms have violated U.S. laws and exploited foreign workers through a host of schemes that include (a) making the worker pay exorbitant fees for their visa, (b) falsifying résumés, employment records, and education records, (c) failing to provide a job after the foreign worker shows up, and (d) taking an illegal cut of the workers' pay when they are working.[51] Scrutiny of the behavior of hiring agencies and employers who recruit foreign workers becomes especially high during recessions, when many Americans are out of work. This has certainly been the case recently, as the number of employer audits conducted by the U.S. Immigration and Customs Enforcement, a division of Department of Homeland Security, doubled between 2009 and 2010.[52]

Altering Pay and Hours

Companies facing a shortage of labor may be reluctant to hire new full-time or part-time employees. Under some conditions, these firms may have the option of trying to garner more hours out of the existing labor force. Despite having to pay workers time-and-a-half for overtime production, employers see this as preferable to hiring and training new employees—especially if they are afraid that current demand for products or services may not extend to the future. Also, for a short time at least, many workers enjoy the added compensation. However, over extended periods, employees experience stress and frustration from being overworked in this manner.

In the face of a labor surplus, organizations can sometimes avoid layoffs if they can get their employees to take pay cuts. For example, Hewlett-Packard cut salaries between 3% and 20% and reduced their contributions to 401(k) plans in the face of the last recession, and many other firms engaged in the same sort of practices.[53] Alternatively, one can avoid layoffs and hold the pay rate constant but reduce the number of hours of all the workers. For example, during the recent recession, Pella Windows shifted from a five-day workweek to a four-day workweek, but kept each and every worker on the payroll. Although most of Pella's employees would prefer to work the full week, most also agreed that this was a more humane way to reduce the surplus of labor relative to laying off 20% of the workforce altogether. Moreover, Pella believed that the recession was going to be short and that government bailout money aimed at improving the nation's infrastructure would eventually translate into increased sales of their windows.

By not laying off workers, the company would be able to ramp up more quickly and take advantage of a forecasted spike in demand shortly down the road.[54] This practice of cutting hours is not very common in the United States, however, as one can see in the "Competing through Globalization" box, this has been a key tactic that other countries, especially the Netherlands, have used to minimize unemployment rates.

While these kinds of swings in labor supply and demand are not historically uncommon in the manufacturing industry, one unique aspect of the recession of 2008–2009 was the degree to which similar methods were aimed at professional workers. A "furlough" is a short-term elimination of paid workdays applied to salaried workers, as opposed to "hourly workers." For example, at Arizona State University and the University of Maryland, professional workers were furloughed for between 9 to 15 days, saving the institutions roughly $25 million.[55] Furloughs are perceived as a good strategy to employ when the employer has an immediate need to conserve money and protect cash flow, but also believes that need will be short term and the employees involved have skills that make them hard to replace in the long term.[56]

Furloughs are controversial because, unlike most hourly workers who go home after the assembly line stops running, the work of most white-collar professionals simply piles up when they leave the office for extended periods of time. Indeed, at Arizona State and Maryland, most of the professional workers came to work anyway, meaning that the furloughs were actually pay cuts, not reductions in hours. Also furloughs are controversial because they hit higher-paid employees harder than lower-paid employees, and if these pay differences were a result of some type of pay-for-performance system, this means that the best employees take the biggest hit. On the other hand, some argue that this aspect of furloughs is actually desirable in the sense that those at the bottom of the pay grade are more likely to need the money to meet basic needs like food and rent relative to those at the top of the pay system.

PROGRAM IMPLEMENTATION AND EVALUATION

The programs developed in the strategic-choice stage of the process are put into practice in the program-implementation stage, shown at the bottom of Figure 5.1. A critical aspect of program implementation is to make sure that some individual is held accountable for achieving the stated goals and has the necessary authority and resources to accomplish this goal. It is also important to have regular progress reports on the implementation to be sure that all programs are in place by specified times and that the early returns from these programs are in line with projections. The final step in the planning process is to evaluate the results.

THE SPECIAL CASE OF AFFIRMATIVE ACTION PLANNING

Workforce Utilization Review
A comparison of the proportion of workers in protected subgroups with the proportion that each subgroup represents in the relevant labor market.

Human resource planning is an important function that should be applied to an organization's entire labor force. It is also important to plan for various subgroups within the labor force. For example, affirmative action plans forecast and monitor the proportion of various protected group members, such as women and minorities, that are in various job categories and career tracks. The proportion of workers in these subgroups can then be compared with the proportion that each subgroup represents in the relevant labor market. This type of comparison is called a **workforce utilization review**. This process can be used to determine whether there is any subgroup whose proportion in the relevant labor market is substantially different from the proportion in the job category.

COMPETING THROUGH GLOBALIZATION

Short-Work Programs Buffer Workers and Firms

Although the global economic recession of 2007–2008 hit all countries hard, some nations were able to weather this storm better than others, at least with respect to layoffs and unemployment. For example, in Holland, even at the peak of the recession, the Dutch unemployment rate was at just 3.7%, well below the double-digit numbers experienced in the United States. Much of the credit for this can be traced to so-called short-work programs established in the Netherlands, where government intervention and subsidies help soften the blows associated with sharp swings in labor demand and supply.

Short-work programs were historically introduced in Holland during the Nazi occupation in the 1940s but they were often reintroduced after the Second World War during times of dire need. In the most recent recession, to qualify for a subsidy, employers had to show that their organization experienced a 30% drop in revenue over a two-month period, thus qualifying as a "sharp swing." Rather than resorting to layoffs, the company simply reduces the hours each person works, and then the government pays workers for a large percentage of the hours that were lost. For example, at DAF Trucks, even though demand for trucks dropped by over 50% in 2009, the company maintained over 80% of its full-time staff.

Although pay is off slightly relative to normal, most employees on a short week take home about 85% of what they would normally make, and as one DAF worker noted, "it sure beats being unemployed." The practice also helps the employer, who gets to retain highly trained workers that might otherwise be lost forever. Especially during short-term shocks, valued employees might be unavailable for rehire once the demand for labor rebounds, and hence a short-term shock results in a long-term, irrevocable loss. Indeed, not only do the companies get to retain valued employees, in many cases these same workers wind up using the time off to upgrade their skills. Finally, although there are some up-front costs for the government when they provide the subsidies (roughly 2 million euros for the Dutch), this is somewhat offset by the reduction in costs associated with unemployment compensation that are also borne by the government.

Short-work programs do have their critics, however. Some of the criticism is strictly financial, in the sense that it results in a deficit spending model for the government. For example, in Holland, the country went from having a government surplus of 1% GDP to a deficit of 5% in a single year. Some of the criticism is more ideological, in the sense that the programs seem to have a communist tinge to them. For example, Rick Van der Ploeg, an economics professor at Oxford University, claims that "this is sharing poverty plain and simple." Finally, some of the criticism hinges on competitive dynamics, in the sense that if the downturn is not just a short-term cyclical drop, but rather a long term structural change in the economy, this practice "locks" people into obsolete jobs. Clearly, the debate about the costs and benefits of such programs will go on in other countires, but in the meantime, the Dutch have a long-term commitment to short-work programs.

SOURCES: A. Cohen, "A Dutch Formula Holds Down Joblessness," *The Wall Street Journal*, December 28, 2009, p. A10; J. Smith, "Making Short-Work of Things," *The Economist*, August 4, 2010, p. 23; P. Jones, "Short-Time Work Plans Saved Jobs," *The Wall Street Journal*, January 4, 2011, p. C3.

If such an analysis indicates that some group—for example, African Americans—makes up 35% of the relevant labor market for a job category but that this same group constitutes only 5% of the actual incumbents in that job category in that organization, then this is evidence of underutilization. Underutilization could come about because of problems in selection or from problems in internal movement, and this could be seen via the transitional matrices discussed earlier in this chapter.

These kinds of affirmative programs are often controversial because they are seen as unfair by many nonminorities.[57] Indeed, even some minorities feel that these kinds of programs unfairly stigmatize the most highly qualified minority applicants because of perceptions that their hiring was based on something other than their skills and abilities.[58] However, when the evidence provided from a workforce utilization review makes it clear that a specific minority group has been historically underrepresented because of past discrimination, and that increasing the level of representation will benefit workforce diversity and competitiveness, then these kinds of programs are easier to justify to all involved.[59] Organizations need to realize, however, that affirmative action plans need to be complemented with communication programs that clearly spell out the needs and benefits that these programs bring to the organization and the larger society.[60]

The Human Resource Recruitment Process

Human Resource Recruitment
The practice or activity carried on by the organization with the primary purpose of identifying and attracting potential employees.

As the first half of this chapter shows, it is difficult to always anticipate exactly how many (if any) new employees will have to be hired in a given year in a given job category. The role of human resource recruitment is to build a supply of potential new hires that the organization can draw on if the need arises. Thus, **human resource recruitment** is defined as any practice or activity carried on by the organization with the primary purpose of identifying and attracting potential employees. It thus creates a buffer between planning and actual selection of new employees, which is the topic of our next chapter.

The goal of the recruiting is not simply to generate large numbers of applicants. If the process generates a sea of unqualified applicants, the organization will incur great expense in personnel selection, but few vacancies will actually be filled. This problem of generating too many applicants is often promulgated by the use of wide-reaching technologies like the Internet to reach people. For example, when Trend Micro was trying to fill a management position, it posted an advertisement on several online job boards, which resulted in a flood of nearly 1,000 resumes.[61]

The goal of personnel recruitment is not to finely discriminate among reasonably qualified applicants either. Recruiting new personnel and selecting new personnel are both complex processes. Organizations explicitly trying to do both at the same time will probably not do either well. For example, research suggests that recruiters provide less information about the company when conducting dual-purpose interviews (interviews focused on both recruiting and selecting applicants).[62] Also, applicants apparently remember less information about the recruiting organization after dual-purpose interviews.[63]

In general as shown in Figure 5.4, all companies have to make decisions in three areas of recruiting: (1) personnel policies, which affect the kinds of jobs the company has to offer; (2) recruitment sources used to solicit applicants, which affect the kinds of people who apply; and (3) the characteristics and behaviors of the recruiter. These, in turn, influence both the nature of the vacancies and the nature of the people applying for jobs in a way that shapes job choice decisions.

LO 5-4
Describe the various recruitment policies that organizations adopt to make job vacancies more attractive.

PERSONNEL POLICIES

Personnel policies is a generic term we use to refer to organizational decisions that affect the nature of the vacancies for which people are recruited. If the research on recruitment makes one thing clear, it is that characteristics of the vacancy are more important than recruiters or recruiting sources when it comes to predicting job choice.

Job Choice

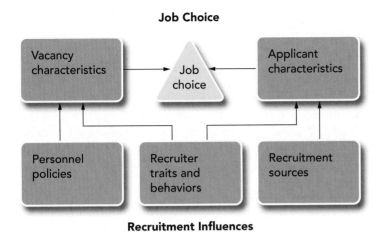

Recruitment Influences

figure 5.4

Overview of
the Individual
Job Choice—
Organizational
Recruitment Process

Internal versus External Recruiting: Job Security

One desirable feature of a vacancy is that it provides ample opportunity for advancement and promotion. One organizational policy that affects this is the degree to which the company "promotes from within"—that is, recruits for upper-level vacancies internally rather than externally. Indeed, a survey of MBA students found that this was their top consideration when evaluating a company.[64] Promote-from-within policies make it clear to applicants that there are opportunities for advancement within the company. These opportunities spring not just from the first vacancy but from the vacancy created when a person in the company fills that vacancy.

A good example of the power of tapping internal sources of recruits is provided by Edwards Lifesciences, a medical device maker that has grown an average of 7% a year for the last 10 years. Edwards Lifesciences' workforce planning model begins with the identification of the 75 most critical jobs in the company and then identifies two or three individuals that would serve as potential excellent replacements or successors for the person currently occupying that job. Identifying these internal candidates early allows the firm to invest in them slowly, but surely, providing them with extra training both in technical areas and general leadership skills. This gives the company a deep "bench" from which to draw talent, and indeed more than 70% of its most critical jobs are staffed from this bench.[65] The potential for extra training and the hope of upward advancement is a highly motivating element of the culture and helps keep attrition and turnover to some of the lowest rates in the industry.

In addition to employing promote from within and internal recruiting sources, perceptions of job security and long-term commitment to the organization are also promoted by "due process policies." **Employment-at-will policies** state that either party in the employment relationship can terminate that relationship at any time, regardless of cause. Companies that do not have employment-at-will provisions typically have extensive due process policies. **Due process policies** formally lay out the steps an employee can take to appeal a termination decision. Organizational recruiting materials that emphasize due process, rights of appeal, and grievance mechanisms send a message that job security is high; employment-at-will policies suggest the opposite. Research indicates that job applicants find companies with due process policies more attractive than companies with employment-at-will policies.[66]

Employment-at-Will Policies
Policies which state that either an employer or an employee can terminate the employment relationship at any time, regardless of cause.

Due Process Policies
Policies by which a company formally lays out the steps an employee can take to appeal a termination decision.

Extrinsic and Intrinsic Rewards

Because pay is an important job characteristic for almost all applicants, companies that take a "lead-the-market" approach to pay—that is, a policy of paying higher-than-current-market wages—have a distinct advantage in recruiting. Thus, as we saw in the vignette that opened this chapter, firms in the financial sector of the economy often had to pay higher wages to lure technical talent away from more well-established companies in the technology sector. Pay can also make up for a job's less desirable features—for example, paying higher wages to employees who have to work midnight shifts. These kinds of specific shift differentials and other forms of more generic compensating differentials will be discussed in more detail in later chapters that focus on compensation strategies. We merely note here that "lead" policies make any given vacancy more attractive to applicants.

There are limits to what can be done in terms of using pay to attract people to certain jobs, however. For example, the U.S. Army, because of the ongoing wars in Iraq and Afghanistan, struggled and failed to meet its recruiting goals for new soldiers, despite offering a $20,000 signing bonus and a $400 a month raise in base pay for infantry positions. As General Michael Rochelle, head of Army recruiting, notes, "We can't get started down a slippery slope where we are depending on money to lure people in. The reality is that while we have to remain at least competitive, we're never going to be able to pay as much as the private sector." To offset this disadvantage in extrinsic financial rewards, the Army has to rely on more intrinsic rewards related to patriotism and personal growth opportunities that people associate with military service. For example, Rochelle suggests that "the idea that being a soldier strengthens you for today and for tomorrow, for whatever you go on to do in life, that clearly resonates with them," and thus this serves as an alternative means of appealing to recruits.[67] The Army's Partnership for Youth Success Program uses this idea to match recruits with private-sector employers who are interested in hiring former soldiers who have received the skills and experiences that the Army provides.

The Army also uses partnerships to help retain current soldiers, and one of these focuses on spouses. Because of the short-term nature of military deployments, spouses in the military have often struggled to find stable employment, and because marital discord is a primary negative influence on reenlistment, helping the spouses of soldiers can in turn promote retention. The Army partners with firms like Home Depot, Sprint, CVS, Sears, and Dell because these employers have many branches in different parts of the country. Thus, if the soldier is forced to redeploy from one base to another, the private company may well have openings that would allow the spouse to simply transfer from one branch to another. Partnerships like this help support soldiers but do not necessarily result in direct competition on pay with respect to private employers.[68]

Home Depot has this same type of recruiting partnership with other organizations such as the American Association of Retired Persons (AARP). The AARP signs up interested members as part of a database and then works with Home Depot to find suitable jobs for its members. Because many AARP members have outside income from pensions or Social Security, competition on wages is not as significant a factor for this segment of the labor force as it is for younger workers who are raising families. Moreover, Home Depot's own research makes it clear that the turnover and absenteeism rates are lower for older workers than for their younger colleagues. As Home Depot's CEO notes, "When you look at the knowledge and career experience, and the passion of the members of the AARP, this is a gold mine of resources to draw upon, and this helps us gain competitive advantage."[69]

Image Advertising

Organizations often advertise specific vacancies (discussed next in the section "Recruitment Sources"). Sometimes, however, organizations advertise just to promote themselves as a good place to work in general. Image advertising is particularly important for companies in highly competitive labor markets that perceive themselves as having a bad image. Indeed, research evidence suggests that the impact of company image on applicant reactions ranks second only to the nature of the work itself.[70]

Even though it does not provide any information about any specific job, image advertising is often effective because job applicants develop ideas about the general reputation of the firm (i.e., its brand image) and then this spills over to influence their expectations about the nature of specific jobs or careers at the organization.[71] Research suggests that the language associated with the organization's brand image is often similar to personality trait descriptions that one might more commonly use to describe another person (such as innovative or competent or sincere).[72] These perceptions then influence the degree to which the person feels attracted to the organization, especially if there appears to be a good fit between the traits of the applicant and the traits that describe the organization.[73] Applicants seem particularly sensitive to issues of diversity and inclusion in these types of advertisements, and hence organizations that advertise their image need to go out of their way to ensure that the actors in their advertisements reflect the broad nature of the labor market constituencies that they are trying to appeal to in terms of race, gender, and culture.[74]

EVIDENCE-BASED HR

There are an infinite number of ways for firms to try to project their image, but increasingly this is being accomplished at the organizations' own websites. In fact, one recent study tried to determine if the media used (pictures versus video) and the nature of the people portrayed in the media (homogenous or diverse) had an impact on applicant reactions to a firm's website. In this study, researchers randomly assigned a large sample of upper-level college students who were seeking jobs to one of four different experimental websites that included (a) text and pictures of current employees who were homogenous, (b) text and pictures of current employees who were racially diverse, (c) videos of current employees who were homogenous, or (d) videos of current employees who were racially diverse. The students were then asked to respond to a number of items that dealt with their perceptions of the company's image.

The results of this study proved that applicants who saw videos rated the company higher in innovativeness, style, and dominance, and lower in terms of cost cutting and thrift. In addition, for applicants that were racial minorities, the websites that presented a diverse set of employees also resulted in higher ratings of innovativeness and style, and lower ratings in terms of cost cutting and thrift. Thus, it seems that there is real value added in terms of image projection by the added expense of producing videos, especially those involving racially diverse employees.

SOURCE: H. J. Walker, H. S. Field, W. F. Giles, J. B. Bernerth, and J. C. Short, "So What Do You Think of the Organization?" *Organizational Behavior and Human Decision Processes* 114 (2011), pp. 165–78.

RECRUITMENT SOURCES

LO 5-5

List the various sources from which job applicants can be drawn, their relative advantages and disadvantages, and the methods for evaluating them.

The sources from which a company recruits potential employees are a critical aspect of its overall recruitment strategy. The type of person who is likely to respond to a job advertised on the Internet may be different from the type of person who responds to an ad in the classified section of a local newspaper. In this section we examine the different sources from which recruits can be drawn, highlighting the advantages and disadvantages of each.

Internal versus External Sources

We discussed internal versus external sources of recruits earlier in this chapter and focused on the positive effects that internal recruiting can have on recruits' perceptions of job security. We will now discuss this issue again, but with a focus on how using internal sources affects the kinds of people who are recruited.

In general, relying on internal sources offers a company several advantages. First, it generates a sample of applicants who are well known to the firm. Second, these applicants are relatively knowledgeable about the company's vacancies, which minimizes the possibility of inflated expectations about the job. Third, it is generally cheaper and faster to fill vacancies internally.

With all these advantages, you might ask why any organization would ever employ external recruiting methods. There are several good reasons why organizations might decide to recruit externally. First, for entry-level positions and perhaps even for some specialized upper-level positions, there may not be any internal recruits from which to draw. Second, bringing in outsiders may expose the organization to new ideas or new ways of doing business. Using only internal recruitment can result in a workforce whose members all think alike and who therefore may be poorly suited to innovation. For example, for most of its 100-year history, retailer JCPenney followed a practice of strictly promoting from within. This led to a very strong culture that in many ways was still closely related to the one first established by JCPenney himself in the late 1800s. The company's image was very conservative, and the behavior and attire of the employees was very formal. This culture made it difficult to attract and retain younger workers, however, and the accounting department estimated that turnover was costing the company $400 million a year. To stem the tide, JCPenney brought in an outsider, Mike Ullman, as the new CEO in 2006, and his first steps in redirecting the company were to loosen up the culture and hire more outsiders into key management positions. This was central to the CEO's new competitive strategy, in the sense that, in Ullman's own words, "In retailing today, you have to realize there is too much property and too much merchandise—what there isn't enough of is talent. If I had a choice to honor the past and lose, or move forward and win, I pick winning."[75]

Finally, recruiting from outside sources is a good way to strengthen one's own company and weaken one's competitors at the same time. This strategy seems to be particularly effective during bad economic times, where "counter cyclical hiring" policies create once-in-a-lifetime opportunities for acquiring talent.[76] For example, during the most recent recession, many firms that were top performers—and hence able to weather the storm better than their lower-performing competitors—viewed this as an excellent opportunity to poach the highest-performing individuals within struggling companies.[77] Thus, for many organizations, times of crisis and turbulence are actually the best time for them to shine by leveraging their current talent and success to bring in more talent and achieve even greater success over the long term.[78]

Direct Applicants and Referrals

Direct applicants are people who apply for a vacancy without prompting from the organization. **Referrals** are people who are prompted to apply by someone within the organization. These two sources of recruits share some characteristics that make them excellent sources from which to draw.

First, many direct applicants are to some extent already "sold" on the organization. Most of them have done some homework and concluded that there is enough fit between themselves and the vacancy to warrant their submitting an application. This process is called *self-selection*. A form of aided self-selection occurs with referrals. Many job seekers look to friends, relatives, and acquaintances to help find employment, and evoking these social networks can greatly aid the job search process for both the job seeker and the organization. Current employees (who are knowledgeable of both the vacancy and the person they are referring) do their homework and conclude that there is a fit between the person and the vacancy; they then sell the person on the job. These kinds of "word-of-mouth" endorsements from credible sources seem to have a particularly strong effect early in the recruitment process when people are still unfocused in their search process.[79] Ironically, as more and more recruiting is accomplished via impersonal sources like the Internet, the ability to draw on personal sources of information on recruits is becoming even more valuable. At companies like Sprint, the percentage of new hires from this source has gone from 8% to 34% in the last three years alone.[80]

In the war for talent, some employers who try to entice one new employee from a competitor will often try to leverage that one person to try to entice even more people away. The term "liftout" has been coined for this practice of trying to recruit a whole team of people. For example, when Mike Mertz was recruited as the new chief executive at Optimus, a computer servicing outfit, within hours of leaving his former employer, he in turn recruited seven other former colleagues to join Optimus. Liftouts are seen as valuable because in recruiting a whole intact group, as Mertz notes, "You get the dynamics of a functioning team without having to create that yourself."[81] Indeed, the team chemistry and coordination that often takes years to build is already in place after a liftout, and this kind of speed provides competitive advantage. Of course, having a whole team lifted out of your organization is devastating, because customers are frequently next to leave, following the talent rather than standing pat, and hence firms have to work hard to make sure that they can retain their critical teams.

Advertisements in Newspapers and Periodicals

Advertisements to recruit personnel are ubiquitous, even though they typically generate less desirable recruits than direct applications or referrals—and do so at greater expense. However, because few employers can fill all their vacancies with direct applications and referrals, some form of advertising is usually needed. Moreover, an employer can take many steps to increase the effectiveness of this recruitment method.

The two most important questions to ask in designing a job advertisement are, What do we need to say? and To whom do we need to say it? With respect to the first question, many organizations fail to adequately communicate the specifics of the vacancy. Ideally, persons reading an ad should get enough information to evaluate the job and its requirements, allowing them to make a well-informed judgment regarding their qualifications. This could mean running long advertisements, which costs more. However, these additional costs should be evaluated against the costs of processing a huge number of applicants who are not reasonably qualified or who would not find the job acceptable once they learn more about it.

Direct Applicants
People who apply for a job vacancy without prompting from the organization.

Referrals
People who are prompted to apply for a job by someone within the organization.

In terms of whom to reach with this message, the organization placing the advertisement has to decide which medium it will use. The classified section of local newspapers is the most common medium. It is a relatively inexpensive means of reaching many people within a specified geographic area who are currently looking for work (or at least interested enough to be reading the classifieds). On the downside, this medium does not allow an organization to target skill levels very well. Typically, classified ads are read by many people who are either over- or underqualified for the position. Moreover, people who are not looking for work rarely read the classifieds, and thus this is not the right medium for luring people away from their current employers. Specially targeted journals and periodicals may be better than general newspapers at reaching a specific part of the overall labor market. In addition, employers are increasingly using television—particularly cable television—as a reasonably priced way of reaching people.

Electronic Recruiting

The growth of the information superhighway has opened up new vistas for organizations trying to recruit talent. There are many ways to employ the Internet, and increasingly organizations are refining their use of this medium. Obviously, one of the easiest ways to get into "e-cruiting" is to simply use the organization's own web page to solicit applications. By using their own web page, organizations can highly tune their recruitment message and focus in on specific people. For example, the interactive nature of this medium allows individuals to fill out surveys that describe what they are looking for and what they have to offer the organizations. These surveys can be "graded" immediately and recruits can be given direct feedback about how well they are matched for the organization. Indeed, customizing e-recruiting sites to maximize their targeted potential for helping people effectively match their own values with the organization's values, and their skills with the demands of the job is probably their best feature.[82] The value of steering recruits to company websites is so high that many employers will pay to have their sites rise to the top of the list in certain search engines when certain terms are entered. For example, PricewaterhouseCoopers (PwC) struck a deal with the career networking site LinkedIn so that if any student from one of the 60 schools it recruits does a search of accounting-related jobs, PwC pops up first and is listed as "the featured job." PwC also gets space on the page to promote the organization that includes videos of current employees extolling the virtues of working at that company.[83]

Of course, smaller and less well-known organizations may not attract any attention to their own websites, and thus for them this is not a good option. A second way for organizations to use the web is to interact with the large, well-known job sites such as Monster.com, HotJobs.com, or CareerBuilder.com. These sites attract a vast array of applicants, who submit standardized résumés that can be electronically searched using key terms. Applicants can also search for companies in a similar fashion. The biggest downside to these large sites, however, is their sheer size and lack of differentiation. In fact, as the "Competing through Technology" box illustrates, this problem has opened the door to new competition that is threatening to make job boards obsolete.

The increased familiarity of web devotees with web logs or "blogs" has created other opportunities for recruiters to reach out and have public or semi-public conversations with recruits. Microsoft's senior recruiter for marketing, Heather Hamilton, manages a blog that describes what it is like to work at a marketing career at Microsoft. Interested candidates can read what she posts, and then ask questions or provide their own information. This allows many other "passive" applicants to see the answers

Monster Slayed?

With $1 billion in sales revenues and 80 million résumés on file, Monster.com is at the top of the job board industry, just ahead of the other major job boards, CareerBuilder and Yahoo!HotJobs. However, rapid changes in technology are threatening the entire business model that underlies the big job boards, and some say all the signs are pointing in other directions when it comes to using the Internet for recruiting. For example, a recent survey in 2011 indicated that 25% of companies were planning on decreasing their usage of job boards, and 80% were planning on increasing their use of alternative methods. In fact, Bill Warren, the founder of the start-up company that eventually turned into Monster has boldly proclaimed that "the days of the big expensive job boards are over."

There are many major threats facing the big job boards. First, social networking sites, such as LinkedIn are now the preferred vehicle for Internet recruiting for many employers searching for professional workers. LinkedIn is much less expensive to use, and has close to 42 million people online. Most importantly, though, unlike the big job boards, almost all of these individuals are "passive"

job seekers, that is, people who already have jobs. Many recruiters prefer passive job seekers due to the belief that most of the truly good workers already have jobs.

Niche boards also pose a threat to the big boards because although they have fewer résumés online, the fit of those résumés for specific jobs is much higher relative to what one finds on Monster or CareerBuilder. For example, TheLadders, which targets only high wage earners (over $100,000 a year), trades quality for quantity when it comes to competing for recruiters' attention. Many recruiters complain that the big job boards generate so many unqualified applicants that the time it takes to sift through the haystack to find that one needle simply is not justified. Niche boards pre-screen applicants and thus generate a higher "signal to noise ratio" for many harried HR executives.

Search engine sites like Google are also entering into the mix when it comes to recruiting. Employers can pay to have their advertisements pop up whenever users type in certain terms to their search engines. For example, when it needed to hire additional truck drivers for the Christmas rush, United Parcel Service launched

a search engine campaign so that anyone who entered the terms "seasonal jobs" or "part-time jobs" were directed to an advertisement for UPS jobs and the UPS website. Mathew Lavery, Director of Workforce Planning reports that UPS received more than 150,000 applications from the program, and is sold on the fact that "Google is outperforming other online media" when it comes to recruiting.

Of course, this Monster is not exactly asleep, and CEO Sal Iannuzzi is fighting back. Monster has cut prices, hired more salespeople, introduced new algorithms that rank order candidates, and streamlined processes so that it takes just four steps (as opposed to 20) to upload a listing. Indeed, as one industry analyst has noted, "If the job boards don't innovate more often and more quickly, they are going to have a very difficult time just holding their business, let alone growing their business."

SOURCES: J. Light, "Recruiters Rethink Online Playbook," *The Wall Street Journal*, January 18, 2011, p. C2.; M. Boyle, "Enough to Make a Monster Tremble," *BusinessWeek*, July 6, 2009, pp. 43–45; S. E. Needleman, "Recruiters Use Search Engines to Lure Job Hunters," *The Wall Street Journal*, March, 9, 2009, p. B4; J. De Avila, "Beyond Job Boards: Targeting the Source," *The Wall Street Journal*, July 2, 2010, p. D1.

to previous questions or what other people who are applying to the organization are like. In one week alone, this blog was viewed by over 25,000 people, and as Hamilton notes, "the big thing for me is reach. . . . As a recruiter, I could be on the phone all day every day and not be able to reach that many people."[84]

The growing use of iPods and iPads has also opened up a new and rich avenue to get information from employer to applicant via podcasts. A podcast is an audio or audio/visual program that can be placed on the web by an employer and then downloaded for subsequent viewing. Podcasts are like e-mails in the sense that they can be used to reach out to a large number of people; however, the rich nature of the media—which employs color, sound, and video—is much more powerful than a simple text-only e-mail. "Podcasts really make the job description comes alive," notes Dan Finnigan, a general manager at HotJobs.com, and the ability to describe the organization's culture is so much more emotionally charged with this media relative to mere words on a page.[85]

Social networking sites such as Facebook and MySpace.com are yet another avenue for employers to reach out to younger workers in their own environments. Neither Facebook nor MySpace allow employers to create pages as members, but it does allow them to purchase pages in order to create what is called a "sponsored group." Ernst & Young's sponsored group page has been joined by more than 5,000 Facebook users, who can access information about Ernst & Young and chat with recruiters from the company in a blog-like manner.[86] Unlike more formal media, the conversations held here are very informal and serve as an easy first step for potential recruits to take in their relationship with the company. New entrants to this market like the site BranchOut take this informal format even further, and allow its members to rate other workers in a "Hot or Not" format. That is, users are shown the pictures of two of their Facebook friends and then asked to choose which one they would rather work with. Scores accumulate over time and founder Rick Marini suggests that "it provides a realistic, crowd sourced assessment of a candidate that recruiters might find hard to come by on their own."[87]

As with any new and developing technology, all of these approaches present some unique challenges. From an employer's perspective, the interactive, dynamic, and unpredictable nature of blogs and social networking sites means that sometimes people who have negative things to say about the organization join in on the conversations, and this can be difficult to control. The biggest liability from the applicant's perspective is the need to protect his or her identity, because this medium has also been a haven for identity thieves, who post false openings in the hope of getting some applicant to provide personal information.[88] In general, an applicant interacting with these types of sites should never provide Social Security numbers or set up bank accounts or submit to security checks until they have visited the employer and met them in person.

Public and Private Employment Agencies

The Social Security Act of 1935 requires that everyone receiving unemployment compensation be registered with a local state employment office. These state employment offices work with the U.S. Employment Service (USES) to try to ensure that unemployed individuals eventually get off state aid and back on employer payrolls. To accomplish this, agencies collect information from the unemployed about their skills and experiences.

Employers can register their job vacancies with their local state employment office, and the agency will attempt to find someone suitable using its computerized inventory of local unemployed individuals. The agency makes referrals to the organization at no charge, and these individuals can be interviewed or tested by the employer for potential vacancies. Because of certain legislative mandates, state unemployment offices often have specialized "desks" for minorities, handicapped individuals, and

Vietnam-era veterans. Thus, this is an excellent source for employers who feel they are currently underutilizing any of these subgroups.

Public employment agencies serve primarily the blue-collar labor market; private employment agencies perform much the same service for the white-collar labor market. Unlike public agencies, however, private employment agencies charge the organization for the referrals. Another difference between private and public employment agencies is that one doesn't have to be unemployed to use a private employment agency.

One special type of private employment agency is the so-called executive search firm (ESF). These agencies are often referred to as *headhunters* because, unlike the other sources we have examined, they operate almost exclusively with people who are currently employed. Dealing with executive search firms is sometimes a sensitive process because executives may not want to advertise their availability for fear of their current employer's reaction. Due to the sensitive nature of this process, the most successful ESFs tend to develop trusting, long-term relationships with high-skilled employees, and serving as the buffer between the employer and the recruit becomes the core of their business model.[89] Along with newspapers and classified advertisements, ESFs may have suffered the most damage in recent years due to the combination of reduced employment levels because of the recent recession on the one hand and increased use of low cost electronic search vehicles on the other. Many have questioned whether the ESFs have a viable business model, given the recent changes in the economy and in technology.[90]

Colleges and Universities

Most colleges and universities have placement services that seek to help their graduates obtain employment. Indeed, on-campus interviewing is the most important source of recruits for entry-level professional and managerial vacancies. Organizations tend to focus especially on colleges that have strong reputations in areas for which they have critical needs (chemical engineering, public accounting, or the like).

Many employers have found that to effectively compete for the best students, they need to do more than just sign prospective graduates up for interview slots. One of the best ways to establish a stronger presence on a campus is with a college internship program. These kinds of programs allow an organization to get early access to potential applicants and to assess their capacities directly. These programs also allow applicants to gain firsthand experience with the employer, so that both parties can make well-informed choices about fit with relatively low costs and commitment.[91]

Another way of increasing one's presence on campus is to participate in university job fairs. In general, a job fair is a place where many employers gather for a short time to meet large numbers of potential job applicants. Although job fairs can be held anywhere (such as at a hotel or convention center), campuses are ideal locations because of the many well-educated, yet unemployed, individuals who live there. Job fairs are a rather inexpensive means of generating an on-campus presence and can even provide one-on-one dialogue with potential recruits—dialogue that could not be achieved through less interactive media like newspaper ads.

Evaluating the Quality of a Source

Because there are few rules about the quality of a given source for a given vacancy, it is generally a good idea for employers to monitor the quality of all their recruitment sources. One means of accomplishing this is to develop and compare yield ratios for each source. Yield ratios express the percentage of applicants who successfully move from one stage of the recruitment and selection process to the next. Comparing yield ratios for different sources helps determine which is best or most efficient for the type of vacancy being investigated. Data on cost per hire are also useful in establishing the efficiency of a given source.[92]

Table 5.4 shows hypothetical yield ratios and cost-per-hire data for five recruitment sources. For the job vacancies generated by this company, the best two sources of recruits are local universities and employee referral programs. Newspaper ads generate the largest number of recruits, but relatively few of these are qualified for the position. Recruiting at nationally renowned universities generates highly qualified applicants, but relatively few of them ultimately accept positions. Finally, executive search firms generate a small list of highly qualified, interested applicants, but this is an expensive source compared with other alternatives.

RECRUITERS

LO 5-6
Explain the recruiter's role in the recruitment process, the limits the recruiter faces, and the opportunities available.

The last part of the model presented in Figure 5.4 that we will discuss is the recruiter. We consider the recruiter this late in the chapter to reinforce our earlier observation that the recruiter often gets involved late in the process. In many cases, by the time a recruiter meets some applicants, they have already made up their minds about what they desire in a job, what the current job has to offer, and their likelihood of receiving a job offer.

Moreover, many applicants approach the recruiter with some degree of skepticism. Knowing that it is the recruiter's job to sell them on a vacancy, some applicants may discount what the recruiter says relative to what they have heard from other sources (like friends, magazine articles, and professors). For these and other reasons, recruiters' characteristics and behaviors seem to have less impact on applicants' job choices than we might expect.

table 5.4

Hypothetical Yield Ratios for Five Recruitment Sources

	RECRUITING SOURCE				
	LOCAL UNIVERSITY	RENOWNED UNIVERSITY	EMPLOYEE REFERRALS	NEWSPAPER AD	EXECUTIVE SEARCH FIRMS
Résumés generated	200	400	50	500	20
Interview offers accepted	175	100	45	400	20
Yield ratio	87%	25%	90%	80%	100%
Applicants judged acceptable	100	95	40	50	19
Yield ratio	57%	95%	89%	12%	95%
Accept employment offers	90	10	35	25	15
Yield ratio	90%	11%	88%	50%	79%
Cumulative yield ratio	90/200 45%	10/400 3%	35/50 70%	25/500 5%	15/20 75%
Cost	$30,000	$50,000	$15,000	$20,000	$90,000
Cost per hire	$333	$5,000	$428	$800	$6,000

Recruiter's Functional Area. Most organizations must choose whether their recruiters are specialists in human resources or experts at particular jobs (supervisors or job incumbents). Some studies indicate that applicants find a job less attractive and the recruiter less credible when he is a personnel specialist.[93] This does not completely discount personnel specialists' role in recruiting, but it does indicate that such specialists need to take extra steps to ensure that applicants perceive them as knowledgeable and credible.

Recruiter's Traits. Two traits stand out when applicants' reactions to recruiters are examined. The first, which could be called "warmth," reflects the degree to which the recruiter seems to care about the applicant and is enthusiastic about her potential to contribute to the company. The second characteristic could be called "informativeness." In general, applicants respond more positively to recruiters who are perceived as warm and informative. These characteristics seem more important than such demographic characteristics as age, sex, or race, which have complex and inconsistent effects on applicant responses.[94]

Recruiter's Realism. Perhaps the most well-researched aspect of recruiting deals with the level of realism that the recruiter incorporates into his message. Because the recruiter's job is to attract candidates, there is some pressure to exaggerate the positive features of the vacancy while downplaying the negative features. Applicants are highly sensitive to negative information. On the other hand, if the recruiter goes too far in a positive direction, the candidate can be misled and lured into taking the job under false pretenses. This can lead to a serious case of unmet expectations and a high turnover rate. In fact, unrealistic descriptions of a job may even lead new job incumbents to believe that the employer is deceitful.[95]

Many studies have looked at the capacity of "realistic job previews" to circumvent this problem and help minimize early job turnover. On the whole, the research indicates that realistic job previews do lower expectations and can help reduce future turnover in the workforce.[96] Certainly, the idea that one can go overboard in selling a vacancy to a recruit has merit. However, the belief that informing people about the negative characteristics of the job will totally "inoculate" them to such characteristics seems unwarranted, based on the research conducted to date.[97] Thus we return to the conclusion that an organization's decisions about personnel policies that directly affect the job's attributes (pay, security, advancement opportunities, and so on) will probably be more important than recruiter traits and behaviors in affecting job choice. Still, helping applicants better understand their own needs and qualifications and then linking this to the true nature of current openings may be best in the long run for all concerned, even if it does not result in an immediate hire.[98]

Enhancing Recruiter Impact. Although research suggests that recruiters do not have much influence on job choice, this does not mean recruiters cannot have an impact. Organizations can take steps to increase the impact that recruiters have on those they recruit. First, recruiters can provide timely feedback. Applicants react very negatively to delays in feedback, often making unwarranted attributions for the delays (such as, the organization is uninterested in my application).[99] Second, recruiting can be done in teams rather than by individuals. As we have seen, applicants tend to view line personnel (job incumbents and supervisors) as more credible than personnel specialists, so these kinds of recruiters should be part of any team. On the other hand, personnel specialists have knowledge that is not shared by line personnel (who may perceive recruiting as a small part of their "real" jobs), so they should be included as well.

A LOOK BACK

SECURING TECHNICAL TALENT

We opened this chapter with a story of how different companies in different industries competed for the same valued resource: technical talent. Each organization was seeking some competitive edge that would result in their securing the most talented individuals, and each company had a different strategy depending upon the company's size, its social reputation, and the nature of the work itself.

Questions

1. Assume for a moment that you were a small new company seeking talent that was in high demand. Based on the material in this chapter, how might you go about competing against larger and more established firms in terms of how, where, when, and who you would use to recruit the best employees?

2. Assume for a moment that you were a large and well-established company, but learned recently that many of the people you were recruiting were choosing to go to smaller and less well-known upstarts. How might you go about competing against these smaller companies in terms of how, where, when, and who you would use to recruit the best employees?

3. Assume you were a large and well-established company that was now facing a labor surplus in some job category. Why might it be in your best interest to use some method other than layoffs to reduce this surplus, and in what sense are your options here a function of how well you did in terms of forecasting labor demand and supply?

 Please see the Video that corresponds to this chapter at www.mhhe.com/noe8e.

SUMMARY

Human resource planning uses labor supply and demand forecasts to anticipate labor shortages and surpluses. It also entails programs that can be utilized to reduce a labor surplus (such as downsizing and early retirement programs) and eliminate a labor shortage (like bringing in temporary workers or expanding overtime). When done well, human resource planning can enhance the success of the organization while minimizing the human suffering resulting from poorly anticipated labor surpluses or shortages. Human resource recruiting is a buffer activity that creates an applicant pool that the organization can draw from in the event of a labor shortage that is to be filled with new hires. Organizational recruitment programs affect applications through personnel policies (such as promote-from-within policies or due process provisions) that affect the attributes of the vacancies themselves. They can also impact the nature of people who apply for positions by using different recruitment sources (like recruiting from universities versus advertising in newspapers). Finally, organizations can use recruiters to influence individuals' perceptions of jobs (eliminating misconceptions, clarifying uncertainties) or perceptions of themselves (changing their valences for various work outcomes).

KEY TERMS

Forecasting, 195
Leading indicator, 195
Transitional matrix, 196
Downsizing, 200

Outsourcing, 206
Offshoring, 206
Workforce utilization review, 210
Human resource recruitment, 212

Employment-at-will policies, 213
Due process policies, 213
Direct applicants, 217
Referrals, 217

DISCUSSION QUESTIONS

1. Discuss the effects that an impending labor shortage might have on the following three subfunctions of human resource management: selection and placement, training and career development, and compensation and benefits. Which subfunction might be most heavily impacted? In what ways might these groups develop joint cooperative programs to avert a labor shortage?

2. Discuss the costs and benefits associated with statistical versus judgmental forecasts for labor demand and labor supply. Under what conditions might either of these techniques be infeasible? Under what conditions might both be feasible, but one more desirable than the other?

3. Some companies have detailed affirmative action plans, complete with goals and timetables, for women and minorities, and yet have no formal human resource plan for the organization as a whole. Why might this be the case? If you were a human resource specialist interviewing with this company for an open position, what would this practice imply for the role of the human resource manager in that company?

4. Recruiting people for jobs that entail international assignments is increasingly important for many companies. Where might one go to look for individuals interested in these types of assignments? How might recruiting practices aimed at these people differ from those one might apply to the "average" recruit?

5. Discuss the relative merits of internal versus external recruitment. What types of business strategies might best be supported by recruiting externally, and what types might call for internal recruitment? What factors might lead a firm to decide to switch from internal to external recruitment or vice versa?

SELF-ASSESSMENT EXERCISE

Most employers have to evaluate hundreds of résumés each week. If you want your résumé to have a good chance of being read by prospective employers, you must invest time and energy not only in its content, but also in its look. Review your résumé and answer yes or no to each of the following questions.

1. Does it avoid typos and grammatical errors?
2. Does it avoid using personal pronouns (such as I and me)?
3. Does it clearly identify what you have done and accomplished?
4. Does it highlight your accomplishments rather than your duties?
5. Does it exceed two pages in length?
6. Does it have correct contact information?
7. Does it have an employment objective that is specific and focuses on the employer's needs as well as your own?
8. Does it have at least one-inch margins?
9. Does it use a maximum of two typefaces or fonts?
10. Does it use bullet points to emphasize your skills and accomplishments?
11. Does it avoid use of underlining?
12. Is the presentation consistent? (Example: If you use all caps for the name of your most recent workplace, do you do that for previous workplaces as well?)

The more "yes" answers you gave, the more likely your résumé will attract an employer's attention and get you a job interview!

EXERCISING STRATEGY: BAILOUTS FOR FOREIGN WORKERS?

Due to the near total collapse of the financial industry in the United States in 2008, the United States government provided over $200 billion in bailout money to over 400 banks, 25% of which went to Citigroup and Bank of America, two of the country's largest financial institutions. Given the level of support the U.S. taxpayer was providing these organizations, many were shocked to learn that at the same time these companies were laying off

U.S. workers, they were also taking steps to increase hiring levels of foreign workers. As one outraged U.S. Senator noted, "What has been the response of Wall Street to the loss of 100,000 of their own workers? What these banks have announced is that they are requesting to hire 21,000 foreign workers over the next six years through the H-1B Visa Program to fill these jobs."

The H-1B Visa Program was originally designed to let U.S. companies fill high-skill positions for which no local workers were available. Employers seeking the visas apply to the Department of Labor for each potential hire, and once the applications are approved the employers can petition U.S. Citizenship and Immigration Services for the visa, which lasts for three years and can be extended to six. Most of these visas are generally granted until a cap is reached. Typically this limit is reached in a couple of days after the April 1 application deadline, and many employers in specific industries have lobbied hard to get the cap raised.

For example, Microsoft typically leads the nation in H-1B visas, and HR executives at Microsoft have argued that each H-1B visa issued in the technology sector of the economy creates five new jobs for U.S. workers. As an extreme example, they cite the case of Sergey Brin, the Russian-born co-founder of Google, who first entered the United States on an H-1B visa. In other industries, like nursing and computer programming, there is a chronic shortage of trained personnel, and this means that firms have to scour the world for suitable talent in these areas.

At the same time as many employers are lobbying for raising the limit on H-1B visas, however, many politicians have argued for a reduction in the number of visas in order to protect U.S. jobs. Indeed, the data seems to suggest that this sentiment is being reflected in the number of visas granted. H-1B visas were down 52% in 2010 and the agency that grants the visas doubled the requested evidence needed to support a successful claim. Also, in January of 2010, this same agency established a new policy that effectively prohibits technical consulting firms who act as headhunters for this industry from bringing in any foreigners on H1-B visas. One CEO noted that "The new rules are fundamentally anti-employer on almost any level."

Questions

1. Why are foreign workers a vital source of competitive advantage for U.S. firms in certain industries? What are the limitations of U.S. workers in some of these fields?
2. If it is true that the recent changes in the number of H-1B visas reflect an "antiemployer" attitude, what groups might consider these new polices as "pro-someone else?"
3. How can businesses and government work together to help ensure that there are enough workers, both foreign and domestic, available for high-level openings in U.S. firms in the short term, as well as the long term, and how might short-term and long-term approaches differ?

SOURCES: M. Herbst, "Immigration: One Reform at a Time," *BusinessWeek*, February 2, 2009, p. 50; M. Herbst, "A Narrowing Window for Foreign Workers?" *BusinessWeek*, March 16, 2009, p. 65; N. Leiber, "Why It's Getting Harder to Hire Foreign Workers," *Bloomberg Businessweek*, August 30, 2010, pp. 53–55.

● Managing People

Experienced Workers: Past Practices Put a Premium on Seniority

Despite the fact that most employers were cutting payrolls during the most recent recession, the data revealed that most of the attrition was among younger workers, and that employment levels for workers over 55 years of age actually increased during that time period. Indeed, pay-level data reflected a similar trend. Whereas inflation-adjusted wages for workers in the "25 to 55 age group" dropped on average over 2% in the most recent data, employees in the 55 and older age category experienced wage gains of over 4%. In addition to this, recent data suggest that the labor participation rate for older workers hit a historic high in 2010. Several specific industries seemed to be particularly protective of their older workers, and this can be traced to some of their past practices with respect to managing previous labor surpluses.

For example, in 2009, Boeing cut 10,000 jobs, but almost none of these cuts included their most senior employees.

Part of this can be attributed to Boeing's experience in the 1990s, when similar cuts were obtained by supplying the workforce with voluntary buyout plans. Left to decide on their own, workers with the most experience, and hence best alternative employment opportunities, accepted the buyouts. When the recession ended, however, and the company tried to expand, it was hurt by labor shortages in the jobs that required the most experience. Richard Hartnett, Boeing's Chief of Global Staffing noted in 2009 that "We don't ever want to get ourselves stuck in that situation again," and this time around, when it came to reducing the size of the labor force, few of the cuts were voluntary. Instead, this time Boeing is picking and choosing who stays and who leaves, and more often than not, workers with the higher levels of experience are being kept on.

In the oil industry, past labor surpluses were met with "attrition-related" adjustments. Rather than directly laying workers off, most employers in the industry simply did not hire new workers when older ones retired. The lack of hiring meant that many younger people gave up on that industry as a viable career alternative, and enrollments in undergraduate programs related to the oil industry dropped 85% from 1982 to 2003. With over 40% of their workforce now over the age of 50 and no replacements in sight, employers like Conoco are struggling to keep their most senior employees from retiring with higher pay and more lucrative benefits. As Michael Killalea, Vice President of the International Association of Drilling Contractors notes, "We skipped an entire generation of workers, and we cannot make the transition fast enough without extending the service of our most senior employees."

Finally, another example of this can be seen in the Federal Aviation Authority, the group that oversees airline safety. The majority of air traffic controllers who currently work for this agency were hired in the mid-1980s after then-President Ronald Reagan fired over 10,000 controllers who were illegally striking. Now, 25 years later, most of these controllers are nearing the age of retirement, and the FAA is desperately trying to retain these workers for as long as possible, in order to help ease the transition to a younger, less-experienced workforce. The problem, however, is that strained labor–management relations has created a situation where job dissatisfaction among current controllers is very high, and a mass exodus is taking place. As one departing controller noted, "it is only a matter of time before an accident occurs, and the pervasive feeling among experienced controllers is that I don't want to be there when it happens." This kind of quote strikes fear into the hearts of would-be flyers, and dramatizes the generic need in the economy for all sorts of employers to hold onto their most senior and experienced members.

Questions

1. This article suggests some reasons why, on the supply side, the demand for older workers is high. What are some recent short-term phenomena related to the housing market and the recent financial situation that create a higher supply of older workers relative to the past?

2. What are some long-term phenomena that might also contribute to the increased supply of older workers in the workforce?

3. Our "Competing through Sustainability" box in this chapter described the plight of young workers across the globe, and their struggles to gain meaningful employment. To what extent has the change in labor supply among older workers affected the demand for labor among younger workers, and what can employers, workers, unions, and government do to help balance this equation?

SOURCES: L. Denning, "Older Work Force Has an Ugly Wrinkle," *The Wall Street Journal*, September 2, 2010, pp. 22–23; J. Weber, "This Time, Old Hands Keep Their Jobs," *BusinessWeek*, February 9, 2009, p. 50; M. Herbst, "Big Oil's Talent Hunt," *BusinessWeek*, December 24, 2007, p. 62–63; J. Marquez, "Taking Flight," *Workforce Management*, June 9, 2009, pp. 1–21.

○ TWITTER FOCUS: FOR PERSONAL FINANCIAL ADVISORS, A SMALL STAFFING PLAN WITH A BIG IMPACT

Using Twitter, continue the conversation about HR planning and recruitment by reading the Personal Financial Advisors case at www.mhhe.com/noe8e.

In 1999, Robert Reed started Personal Financial Advisors with one employee. Six years later, Reed realized that if he wanted to grow the business, he needed to get serious about HR planning and recruitment. His strategy was to recruit a financial planner adept at giving presentations to current and potential clients—a task that was not Reed's favorite. Eight months later, Reed made the perfect hire: an experienced financial planner relocating to Louisiana. Hiring someone with the right skill set allowed Reed to focus his efforts on managing investments and providing clients with better-than-average returns while growing the company's overall business.

Engage with your classmates and instructor via Twitter to chat about Reed's recruitment strategy using the case questions posted on the Noe website. Don't have a Twitter account yet? See the instructions for getting started on the Online Learning Center.

○ NOTES

1. P. Coy, "What Falling Prices Tell Us," *BusinessWeek*, February 9, 2009, pp. 24–26.
2. K. Doheny, "Nursing Is in Critical Condition," *Workforce Management*, October 9, 2006, pp. 39–41.
3. M. Dorninng, "The Long Hard Road to Job Creation," *Bloomberg Businessweek*, August 9, 2010, p. 54.
4. M. Whitehouse, "Some Firms Struggle to Hire Despite High Unemployment," *The Wall Street Journal*, August 9, 2010, pp. A1 and A7.
5. J. Millman, "Hot-Dog Maker, Lured for Jobs, Now Can't Fill Them," *The Wall Street Journal*, October 1, 2010, p. C1.
6. R. G. Mathews, "Mining Forms Dig Deeper to Lure Scarce Workers," *The Wall Street Journal*, January 4, 2011, pp. B1–B2.

7. T. R. Homan and Z. Tracer, "The Long-Term Jobless Are Being Left Behind," *Bloomberg Businessweek*, August 9, 2010, pp. 53–54.

8. P. Coy, M. Conlin, and M. Herbst, "The Disposable Worker," *Bloomberg Businessweek*, January 18, 2010, pp. 33–39.

9. N. D. Schwartz, "Will 'Made in the USA' Fade Away?" *Fortune*, November 24, 2003, pp. 98–110.

10. C. Power, "Machines Don't Get Paid Overtime," *Bloomberg Businessweek*, August 2, 2010, p. 13.

11. J. Schneider, "I'll Take a Big Mac, Fries and Hey How's the Weather in Fargo? *Lansing State Journal*, January 15, 2009, p. B1.

12. J. P. Guthrie, "Dumb and Dumber: The Impact of Downsizing on Firm Performance as Moderated by Industry Conditions," *Organization Science* 19 (2008), pp. 108–23.

13. J. McGregor, A. McConnon, and D. Kiley, "Customer Service in a Shrinking Economy," *BusinessWeek*, February 19, 2009, pp. 34–35.

14. D. S. DeRue, J. R. Hollenbeck, M. D. Johnson, D. R. Ilgen, and D. K. Jundt, "How Different Team Downsizing Approaches Influence Team-level Adaptation and Performance," *Academy of Management Journal* 51 (2008), pp. 182–96.

15. C. D. Zatzick and R. D. Iverson, "High-Involvement Management and Workforce Reduction: Competitive Advantage or Disadvantage?" *Academy of Management Journal* 49 (2006), pp. 999–1015.

16. P. P. Shaw, "Network Destruction: The Structural Implications of Downsizing," *Academy of Management Journal* 43 (2000), pp. 101–12.

17. J. Schu, "Internet Helps Keep Goodwill of Downsized Employees," *Workforce*, July 2001, p. 15.

18. C. O. Trevor and A. J. Nyberg, "Keeping Your Headcount When All About You Are Losing Theirs: Downsizing, Voluntary Turnover Rates, and the Moderating Role of HR Practices," *Academy of Management Journal* 51 (2008), pp. 259–76.

19. E. Frauenheim, "Technology Forcing Firms to Shed More Light on Layoffs," *Workforce Management*, January 19, 2009, pp. 7–8.

20. J. Holton, "You've Been Deleted," *Workforce Management*, September 11, 2006, p. 42.

21. E. Thronton, "The Hidden Perils of Layoffs," *BusinessWeek*, March 2, 2009, pp. 52–53.

22. J. E. Hilsenrath, "Adventures in Cost Cutting," *The Wall Street Journal*, May 10, 2004, pp. A1–A3.

23. J. Marquez, "The Would-be Retirees," *Workforce Management*, November 3, 2008, pp. 24–28.

24. P. Coy, "The Lost Generation," *BusinessWeek*, October, 19, 2009, pp. 33–35.

25. J. S. Lublin and S. Thurm, "How Companies Calculate Odds in Buyout Offers," *The Wall Street Journal*, March 27, 2006, pp. B1–B2.

26. S. Gustafson, "38,000 Took Buyouts, Ford Says," *Columbus (Ohio) Dispatch*, November 2006, pp. E1–E2.

27. J. Bennett and J. D. Stoll, "GM Logs 7,500 Buyouts; Chrysler Extends Deadline," *The Wall Street Journal*, March 26, 2009, pp. C1–C2.

28. R. Adams, "New York Times Will Cut Salaries; Washington Post to Offer Buyouts," *The Wall Street Journal*, March 26, 2009, p. C1.

29. E. E. Derez and M. Robinson, "Help Wanted—For Now," *Bloomberg Businessweek*, August 9, 2010, pp. 51–52.

30. S. A. Johnson and B. E. Ashforth, "Externalization of Employment in a Service Environment: The Role of Organizational and Customer Identification," *Journal of Organizational Behavior* 29 (2008), pp. 287–309.

31. P. Coy, M. Conlin, and M. Herbst, "The Disposable Worker," *Bloomberg Businessweek*, January 18, 2010, pp. 33–39.

32. M. L. Kraimer, S. J. Wayne, R. C. Liden, and R. T. Sparrowe, "The Role of Job Security in Understanding the Relationship between Employees' Perceptions of Temporary Workers and Employees' Performance," *Journal of Applied Psychology* 90 (2005), pp. 389–398.

33. J. Feife, R. Schook, B. Schyns, and B. Six, "Does the Form of Employment Make a Difference? Commitment of Traditional, Temporary, and Self-employed Workers," *Journal of Vocational Behavior* 72 (2008), pp. 81–94.

34. C. Hajim, "Bodies in Motion," *Fortune*, February 19, 2007, p. 114.

35. J. Marquez, "Inside Job," *Workforce Management*, February 12, 2006, pp. 19–21.

36. F. Hanson, "Special Report: Mid-market Outsourcing," *Workforce Management*, February 12, 2007, pp. 23–26.

37. P. Engardio, "Let's Offshore the Lawyers," *BusinessWeek*, September 18, 2006, pp. 42–43.

38. M. Kripalani, "Call Center? That's so 2004," *BusinessWeek*, August 7, 2006, pp. 40–41.

39. S. Hamm, "Outsourcing Heads to the Outskirts," *BusinessWeek*, January 22, 2007, p. 56.

40. S. Shellenbarger, "Outsourcing Jobs to the Den," *The Wall Street Journal*, January 2, 2006, p. D1.

41. M. Reitzig and S. Wagner, "The Hidden Costs of Outsourcing: Evidence from Patent Data," *Strategic Management Journal* 11 (2010), pp. 1183–1201.

42. M. Hiltzik, "787 Dreamliner Teaches Boeing a Costly Lesson on Outsourcing," *The Los Angeles Times*, February 15, 2011, p. B1.

43. N. Leiber, "Rural Outsources vs. Bangalore," *Bloomberg Businessweek*, September 27, 2010, pp. 51–52.

44. M. Srivastava and M. Herbst, "The Return of the Outsourced Job," *Bloomberg Businessweek*, January 11, 2010, pp. 16–17.

45. W. Zellner, "Lessons from a Faded Levi-Strauss," *BusinessWeek*, December 15, 2003, p. 44.

46. A. Meisler, "Think Globally, Act Rationally," *Workforce*, January 2004, pp. 40–45.

47. A. Tiwana, "Does Firm Modularity Complement Ignorance? A Field Study of Software Outsourcing Alliances," *Strategic Management Journal* 29 (2008), pp. 1241–52.

48. S. E. Ante, "Shifting Work Offshore? Outsourcer Beware," *BusinessWeek*, January 12, 2004, pp. 36–37.

49. K. Weise, "Send Us Your Educated Masses," *Bloomberg Businessweek*, May 23, 2011, p. 30.

50. J. Light, "Labor Shortage Persists in Some Fields," *The Wall Street Journal*, February 7, 2011, p. C1.

51. S. Hamm and M. Herbst, "America's High-Tech Sweat Shops," *BusinessWeek*, October 12, 2009, pp. 35–39.

52. M. Jordan, "Crackdown on Illegal Workers Grows," *The Wall Street Journal*, January 20, 2011, p. B2.

53. C. Tuna, "Looking for More Tools to Trim Costs," *The Wall Street Journal*, February 23, 2011, p. B4.

54. O. Kharif, "Chopping Hours, Not Heads," *BusinessWeek*, January 5, 2009, p. 85; M. Boyle, "Cutting Costs without Cutting Jobs," *BusinessWeek*, March 9, p. 55.

55. D. Mattioli and S. Murray, "Employers Hit Salaried Staff with Furloughs," *The Wall Street Journal*, February 24, 2009, pp. C1–C3.

56. C. Tuna, "Weighing Furlough vs. Layoff," *The Wall Street Journal*, April 13, 2009, p. B6.

57. G. Shteynberg, L. M. Leslie, A. P. Knight,, and D. M. Mayer, "But Affirmative Action Hurts Us! Race-Related Beliefs Shape Perceptions of White Disadvantage and Policy Unfairness," *Organizational Behavior and Human Decision Processes* 115 (2011), pp. 1–12.

58. R. Cropanzano, J. E. Slaughter, and P. D. Bachiochi, "Organizational Justice and Black Applicants Reactions to Affirmative Action," *Journal of Applied Psychology* 90 (2005), pp. 1168–84.

59. D. A. Harrison, D. A. Kravitz, D. M. Mayer, L. M. Leslie, and D. Lev-Arey, "Understanding Attitudes toward Affirmative Action Programs in Employment: Summary and Meta-analysis of 35 Years of Research," *Journal of Applied Psychology* 91 (2006), pp. 1013–36.

60. I. Hideg and J. L. Michela, "Overcoming Negative Reactions of Nonbeneficiaries of Employment Equity: The Effect of Participation in Policy Formulation," *Journal of Applied Psychology* 96 (2011), pp. 363–76.

61. M. Totty, "New Tools for Frazzled Recruiters," *The Wall Street Journal*, October 23, 2006, p. C11.

62. C. K. Stevens, "Antecedents of Interview Interactions, Interviewers' Ratings, and Applicants' Reactions," *Personnel Psychology* 51 (1998), pp. 55–85.

63. A. E. Barber, J. R. Hollenbeck, S. L. Tower, and J. M. Phillips, "The Effects of Interview Focus on Recruitment Effectiveness: A Field Experiment," *Journal of Applied Psychology* 79 (1994), pp. 886–96.

64. S. J. Marks, "After School," *Human Resources Executive*, June 15, 2001, pp. 49–51.

65. G. Ruiz, "Cardiovascular Device Maker Pinpoints and Tracks Mission Critical Jobs," *Workforce Management*, March 26, 2007, p. 24.

66. M. Magnus, "Recruitment Ads at Work," *Personnel Journal* 64 (1985), pp. 42–63.

67. P. J. Kiker, "Recruitment Battles," *Workforce Management*, October 24, 2005, pp. 20–31.

68. S. Shellenbarger, "Military Recruits: Companies Make New Effort to Hire Spouses of Soldiers," *The Wall Street Journal*, December 15, 2005, p. D1.

69. K. Greene, "AARP Is to Recruit Older Workers for Home Depot," *The Wall Street Journal*, February 6, 2004, p. B5.

70. D. S. Chapman, K. L. Uggerslev, S. A. Carroll, K. A. Piasentin, and D. A. Jones, "Applicant Attraction to Organizations and Job Choice: A Meta-analytic Review of the Correlates of Recruiting Outcomes," *Journal of Applied Psychology* 90 (2005), pp. 928–44.

71. C. Collins and C. K. Stevens, "The Relationship between Early Recruitment-Related Activities and the Application Decisions of New Labor Market Entrants: A Brand Equity Approach to Recruitment," *Journal of Applied Psychology* 87 (2002), pp. 1121–33.

72. F. Lievens and S. Highhouse, "The Relation of Instrumental and Symbolic Attributes to a Company's Attractiveness as an Employer," *Personnel Psychology* 56 (2003), pp. 75–102.

73. J. E. Slaughter, M. J. Zickar, S. Highhouse, and D. C. Mohr, "Personality Trait Inferences about Organizations: Development of a Measure and Assessment of Construct Validity," *Journal of Applied Psychology* 89 (2004), pp. 85–103.

74. D. R. Avery, "Reactions to Diversity in Recruitment Advertising—Are Differences Black and White?" *Journal of Applied Psychology* 88 (2003), pp. 672–79.

75. E. Byron, "Call Me Mike," *The Wall Street Journal*, March 27, 2006, pp. B1, B4.

76. G. Colvin, "How to Manage Your Business in a Recession," *Fortune*, January 19, 2009, pp. 88–93.

77. M. Orey, "Hang the Recession, Let's Bulk Up," *BusinessWeek*, February 2, 2009, pp. 80–81.

78. J. Collins, "How Great Companies Turn Crisis into Opportunity," *Fortune*, February 2, 2009, pp. 49.

79. G. Van Hoye and F. Lievens, "Tapping the Grapevine: A Closer Look at Word-of-Mouth as a Recruitment Source," *Journal of Applied Psychology* 94 (2009), pp. 341–52.

80. J. Mintz, "Large Firms Increasingly Rely on Employee Job Referrals," *The Wall Street Journal*, March 1, 2005, p. B4.

81. J. McGregor, "I Can't Believe They Took the Whole Team," *BusinessWeek*, December 18, 2006, pp. 120–22.

82. B. Dineen and R. A. Noe, "Effects of Customization on Applicant Decisions and Applicant Pool Characteristics in a Web-based Recruiting Context," *Journal of Applied Psychology* 94 (2009), pp. 224–34.

83. "PwC Pays for Priority," *The Wall Street Journal*, October 4, 2010, p. B6.

84. K. Maher, "Blogs Catch on as Recruiting Tool," *The Wall Street Journal*, September 28, 2004, p. B10.

85. A. Singh, "Podcasts Extend Recruiters Reach," *The Wall Street Journal*, April 24, 2006, p. B3.

86. E. White, "Ernst & Young Reaches Out to Recruits on Facebook," *The Wall Street Journal*, January 8, 2007, p. B5.

87. S. Berfield, "Dueling Your Facebook Friends for a New Job," *Bloomberg Businessweek*, March 7, 2011, pp. 35–36.

88. D. Mattioli, "Who's Reading On-Line Resumes? Identity Crooks," *The Wall Street Journal*, October 17, 2006, p B9.

89. M. Bidwell and I. Fernandez-Mateo, "Relationship Duration and Returns to Brokerage in the Staffing Sector," *Organization Science* 21 (2010), pp. 1141–58.

90. A. McConnon, "A Headhunter Searches for a Second Life," *BusinessWeek*, January 26, 2009, pp. 80–81.

91. H. Zhao and R. C. Liden, "Internship: A Recruitment and Selection Perspective," *Journal of Applied Psychology* 96 (2011), pp. 221–229.

92. K. D. Carlson, M. L. Connerly, and R. L. Mecham, "Recruitment Evaluation: The Case for Assessing the Quality of Applicants Attracted," *Personnel Psychology* 55 (2002), pp. 461–94.

93. M. S. Taylor and T. J. Bergman, "Organizational Recruitment Activities and Applicants' Reactions at Different Stages of the Recruitment Process," *Personnel Psychology* 40 (1984), pp. 261–85.

94. L. M. Graves and G. N. Powell, "The Effect of Sex Similarity on Recruiters' Evaluations of Actual Applicants: A Test of the Similarity–Attraction Paradigm," *Personnel Psychology* 48 (1995), pp. 85–98.

95. P. Hom, R. W. Griffeth, L. E. Palich, and J. S. Bracker, "An Exploratory Investigation into Theoretical Mechanisms Underlying Realistic Job Previews," *Personnel Psychology* 51 (1998), pp. 421–51.

96. J. M. Phillips, "The Effects of Realistic Job Previews on Multiple Organizational Outcomes: A Meta-analysis," *Academy of Management Journal* 41 (1998), pp. 673–90.

97. P. G. Irving and J. P. Meyer, "Reexamination of the Met-Expectations Hypothesis: A Longitudinal Analysis," *Journal of Applied Psychology* 79 (1995), pp. 937–49.

98. Y. Ganzach, A. Pazy, Y. Hohayun, "Social Exchange and Organizational Commitment: Decision-Making Training for Job Choice as an Alternative to the Realistic Job Preview," *Personnel Psychology* 55 (2002), pp. 613–37.

99. W. J. Becker, T. Connolly, and J. E. Slaughter, "The Effect of Job Offer Timing on Offer Acceptance, Performance, and Turnover," *Personnel Psychology* 63 (2010), pp. 223–41.

CHAPTER

6

Selection and Placement

LO LEARNING OBJECTIVES

After reading this chapter, you should be able to:

LO 6-1 Establish the basic scientific properties of personnel selection methods, including reliability, validity, and generalizability. *page 232*

LO 6-2 Discuss how the particular characteristics of a job, organization, or applicant affect the utility of any test. *page 240*

LO 6-3 Describe the government's role in personnel selection decisions, particularly in the areas of constitutional law, federal laws, executive orders, and judicial precedent. *page 243*

LO 6-4 List the common methods used in selecting human resources. *page 246*

LO 6-5 Describe the degree to which each of the common methods used in selecting human resources meets the demands of reliability, validity, generalizability, utility, and legality. *page 247*

ENTER THE WORLD OF BUSINESS

Selective Personnel Selection: Staffing Seal Team 6

The midnight raid that killed Osama bin Laden on May 2, 2011, will go down in history as one of the most successful counterterrorist military missions in history. This mission was executed by a group formally known as the United States Special Warfare Development Group. In military circles this group goes by the acronym DEVGRU for short, but the rest of the world knows them more informally as Seal Team 6, one of the most selective organizations in the world. Indeed, the process of being chosen for this elite unit is so rigorous that it takes thousands and thousands of applicants just to staff just a few positions. At the end of this process, however, one has literally selected the best of the best, and as one former member has noted, "it was like being selected for an all-star team."

DEVGRU was first established in 1980 in the wake of the failed hostage rescue mission in Iran. A series of unforeseen problems, human errors, and bad decisions in that mission resulted in the deaths of eight soldiers, and the event was a source of national humiliation almost as bad as the hostage taking incident itself. Vowing this would never happen again, DEVGRU was created, and its founding commanding officer, Richard Marcinko hand-picked the top personnel from a wide variety of Special Operations Personnel within the Navy.

As one might expect, the job requirements associated with these positions were oriented to physical abilities and war-fighting skills. Insiders sometimes suggest that SEAL stands for "Sleep, Eat And Lift," due to the demanding requirements for strength and conditioning. In addition, all members must have skills in "explosive ordnance disposal" (defusing bombs), "close quarters battle" (hand-to-hand fighting), "aerial infiltration" (parachuting), and SERE (survival, evasion, resistance, and escape). However, what one might not expect is that the process goes beyond physical and technical skills and is heavily influenced by recruits' mental ability, personality traits, and above all, integrity.

For example, with respect to cognitive ability, SEAL Team 6 works closely with the CIA and its members have to be able to process and retain huge amounts of information (e.g., building layouts, details about suspects, local customs, and language). In addition, personality characteristics like decisiveness, emotional stability, confidence, and extraversion are critical because these individuals are typically immersed in stressful contexts engaged in collaborative tasks. Finally, due to the secretive nature of their work, each person has to be totally trustworthy. For example, when SEAL Team 6 was involved in the rescue attempt of British aid worker Linda Nosgrove, one member of the team stated after the fact that she died when one her kidnappers triggered his suicide vest. When an internal investigation later revealed that instead, she died when a fragmentation grenade thrown by a member landed where she was hiding, that member was summarily dismissed. In this line of work, the only thing more dangerous than making a mistake is covering one up.

SOURCES: D. Von Drehle, "Death Comes for the Terrorist," *Time*, May 20, 2011, pp. 13–28; M. Benjamin, "SEAL Team 6 Established after Disastrous 1980 Raid," *Time*, May 2, 2011, pp. 16–17; S. Gorman, "U.S. Gains Entry into bin Laden's Pakistan House," *The Wall Street Journal*, May 27, 2011, pp. B1–B2; "Fabled SEAL Team 6 Ends the Hunt for Bin Laden, *The Wall Street Journal*, May 3, 2011, pp. A1, A6.

 **Introduction**

Any organization that intends to compete through people must take the utmost care with how it chooses organizational members. These decisions have a critical impact on the organization's ability to compete, as well as each and every job applicant's life. As our opening vignette shows, some organizations, like SEAL Team 6, go to incredible lengths to ensure that they have chosen the "best of the best" and this supports their ability to accomplish very difficult missions. Although few of the tasks conducted by business organizations are as dramatic as this, the same spirit of aggressively maintaining high hiring standards is critical to success in this domain as well. Jack Welch, the legendary former CEO at General Electric says it best:

> What could possibly be more important than who gets hired? Business is a game, and as with all games, the team that puts the best people on the field and gets them playing together wins. It's that simple.[1]

This is as true at the level of individual firms, as it is with respect to competition between nations. The United States has always been a magnet for talent from other nations, and this country grew economically powerful through the contributions of many different people who emigrated here from other countries. Some have suggested the United States is losing its edge in this regard, however, and that "this is America's most serious long-term threat."[2] That is, social and economic inequality, racial and ethnic bias, growing political intolerance, and a failing educational system are contributing to a state of reverse migration, where highly trained professionals who came to this country are now leaving the United States in larger percentages than those coming in. Innovation and economic growth are fueled by people, and the firms or countries that bring in the best people will be the ones that compete most successfully.

The purpose of this chapter is to familiarize you with ways to minimize errors in employee selection and placement and, in doing so, improve your company's competitive position. The chapter first focuses on five standards that should be met by any selection method. The chapter then evaluates several common selection methods according to those standards.

Selection Method Standards

LO 6-1
Establish the basic scientific properties of personnel selection methods, including reliability, validity, and generalizability.

Personnel selection is the process by which companies decide who will or will not be allowed into organizations. Several generic standards should be met in any selection process. We focus on five: (1) reliability, (2) validity, (3) generalizability, (4) utility, and (5) legality. The first four build off each other in the sense that the preceding standard is often necessary but not sufficient for the one that follows. This is less the case with legal standards. However, a thorough understanding of the first four standards helps us understand the rationale underlying many legal standards.

RELIABILITY

Much of the work in personnel selection involves measuring characteristics of people to determine who will be accepted for job openings. For example, we might be interested in applicants' physical characteristics (like strength or endurance), their cognitive abilities (such as spatial memory or verbal reasoning), or aspects of their personality (like their decisiveness or integrity). Indeed, as we saw in our opening vignette, some organizations like SEAL Team 6 are interested in all of these characteristics and more. Whatever the specific focus, in the end we need to quantify people on these dimensions (assign numbers to them) so we can order them from high to low on the characteristic of interest. Once people are ordered in this way, we can decide whom to hire and whom to reject.

One key standard for any measuring device is its reliability. We define **reliability** as the degree to which a measure is free from random error. If a measure of some supposedly stable characteristic such as intelligence is reliable, then the score a person receives based on that measure will be consistent over time and in different contexts.

Reliability
The consistency of a performance measure; the degree to which a performance measure is free from random error.

Estimating the Reliability of Measurement

Most measurement in personnel selection deals with complex characteristics like intelligence, integrity, and leadership ability. However, to appreciate some of the complexities in measuring people, we will consider something concrete in discussing these concepts: the measurement of height. For example, if we were measuring an applicant's height, we might start by using a 12-inch ruler. Let's say the first person we measure turns out to be 6 feet 1 and $4/16$ inches tall. It would not be surprising to find out that someone else measuring the same person a second time, perhaps an hour later, found this applicant's height to be 6 feet and $12/16$ inches. The same applicant, measured a third time, maybe the next day, might be measured at 6 feet 1 and $8/16$ inches tall.

As this example makes clear, even though the person's height is a stable characteristic, we get slightly different results each time he is assessed. This means that each time the person is assessed, we must be making slight errors. If a measurement device were perfectly reliable, there would be no errors of measurement. If we used a measure of height that was not as reliable as a ruler—for example, guessing someone's height after seeing her walk across the room—we might see an even greater amount of unreliability in the measure. Thus *reliability* refers to the measuring instrument (a ruler versus a visual guess) rather than to the characteristic itself.

We can estimate reliability in several different ways, however; and because most of these rely on computing a correlation coefficient, we will briefly describe and illustrate this statistic. The *correlation coefficient* is a measure of the degree to which two sets of numbers are related. The correlation coefficient expresses the strength of the relationship in numerical form. A perfect positive relationship (as one set of numbers goes up, so does the other) equals $+1.0$; a perfect negative relationship (as one goes up, the other goes down) equals -1.0. When there is no relationship between the sets of numbers, the correlation equals .00. Although the actual calculation of this statistic goes beyond the scope of this book, it will be useful for us to conceptually examine the nature of the correlation coefficient and what this means in personnel selection contexts.

When assessing the reliability of a measure, for example, we might be interested in knowing how scores on the measure at one time relate to scores on the same measure at another time. Obviously, if the characteristic we are measuring is supposedly stable (like intelligence or integrity) and the time lapse is short, this relationship should be strong. If it were weak, then the measure would be inconsistent—hence unreliable. This is called assessing *test–retest reliability*.

Plotting the two sets of numbers on a two-dimensional graph often helps us to appreciate the meaning of various levels of the correlation coefficient. Figure 6.1, for example, examines the relationship between student scholastic aptitude in one's junior and senior years in high school, where aptitude for college is measured in three ways: (1) via the scores on the Scholastic Aptitude Test (SAT), (2) via ratings from a high school counselor on a 1-to-100 scale, and (3) via tossing dice. In this plot, each number on the graphs represents a person whose scholastic aptitude is assessed twice (in the junior and senior years), so in Figure 6.1a, 1_1 represents a person who scored 1580 on the SAT in the junior year and 1500 in the senior year; 20_{20} represents a person who scored 480 in the junior year and 620 in the senior year.

Figure 6.1a shows a very strong relationship between SAT scores across the two years. This relationship is not perfect in that the scores changed slightly from one year to the next, but not a great deal. Indeed, if there were a perfect 1.0 correlation, the plot would show a straight line at a 45-degree angle. Turning to Figure 6.1b, we see that the relationship between the high school counselors' ratings across the two years, while still positive, is not as strong. That is, the counselors' ratings of individual students' aptitudes for college are less consistent over the two years than their test scores. Finally, Figure 6.1c shows a worst-case scenario, where the students' aptitudes are assessed by tossing two six-sided dice. As you would expect, the random nature of the dice means that there is virtually no relationship between scores taken in one year and scores taken the next. Although no one would seriously consider tossing dice to be a measure of aptitude, it is worth noting that research shows that the correlation of overall ratings of job applicants' suitability for jobs based on unstructured interviews is very close to .00. Thus, one cannot assume a measure is reliable without actually checking this directly. Novices in measurement are often surprised at exactly how unreliable many human judgments turn out to be.

There are many steps one can take to increase the reliability of the interview process, such as providing raters with standardized training and common formats for translating observed behaviors into scores on dimensions, but in lieu of these measures, most people tend to be pretty unreliable raters of other people, especially people they are meeting for the first time.[3]

Standards for Reliability

Regardless of what characteristic we are measuring, we want highly reliable measures. Thus, in the previous example, when it comes to measuring students' aptitudes for college, the SAT is more reliable than counselor ratings, which in turn are more reliable than tossing dice. But in an absolute sense, how high is high enough—.50, .70, .90? This is a difficult question to answer specifically because the required reliability depends in part on the nature of the decision being made about the people being measured.

For example, let's assume some college admissions officer was considering several students depicted in Figures 6.1a and 6.1b. Turning first to Figure 6.1b, assume the admissions officer was deciding between Student 1 (1_1) and Student 20 (20_{20}). For this decision, the .50 reliability of the ratings is high enough because the difference between the two students is so large that one would make the same decision for admission regardless of the year in which the rating was taken. That is, Student 1 (with scores of 100 and 80 in the junior and senior year, respectively) is always admitted and Student 20 (with scores of 12 and 42 for junior and senior years, respectively) is always rejected. Thus, although the ratings in this case are not all that reliable in an absolute sense, their reliability is high enough for this decision.

On the other hand, let's assume the same college admissions officer was deciding between Student 1 (1_1) and Student 2 (2_2). Looking at Figure 6.1a, it is clear that even with the highly reliable SAT scores, the difference between these students is so small that one would make a different admission decision depending on what year

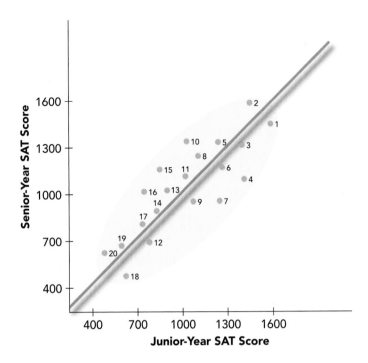

figure 6.1a

Measurements of a
Student's Aptitude

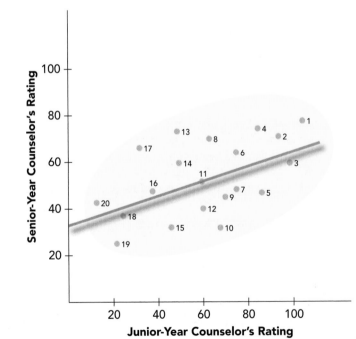

figure 6.1b

one obtained the score. Student 1 would be selected over Student 2 if the junior-year score was used, but Student 2 would be chosen over Student 1 if the senior-year score was used. Thus, even though the reliability of the SAT exam is high in an absolute sense, it is not high enough for this decision. Under these conditions, the admissions officer needs to find some other basis for making the decision regarding these two students (like high school GPA or rank in graduating class).

figure 6.1c

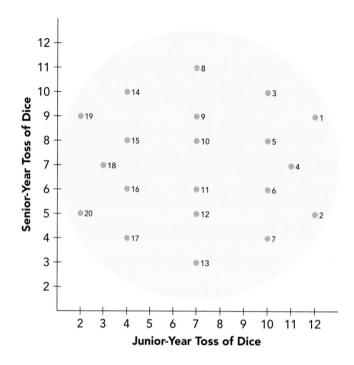

Although these two scenarios clearly show that no specific value of reliability is always acceptable, they also demonstrate why, all else being equal, the more reliable a measure is, the better. For example, turning again to Figures 6.1a and 6.1b, consider Student 9 (9_9) and Student 14 (14_{14}). One would not be able to make a decision between these two students based on scholastic aptitude scores if assessed via counselor ratings, because the unreliability in the ratings is so large that scores across the two years conflict. On the other hand, one would be able to base the decision on scholastic aptitude scores if assessed via the SAT, because the reliability of the SAT scores is so high that scores across the two years point to the same conclusion. Moreover, if there are differences between scores the first time someone takes a test and the second time, research evidence suggests that the second score is usually more predictive of future outcomes.[4]

Validity
The extent to which a performance measure assesses all the relevant—and only the relevant—aspects of job performance.

VALIDITY

We define **validity** as the extent to which performance on the measure is related to performance on the job. A measure must be reliable if it is to have any validity. On the other hand, we can reliably measure many characteristics (like height) that may have no relationship to whether someone can perform a job. For this reason, reliability is a necessary but insufficient condition for validity.

Criterion-Related Validity
A method of establishing the validity of a personnel selection method by showing a substantial correlation between test scores and job-performance scores.

Criterion-Related Validation

One way of establishing the validity of a selection method is to show that there is an empirical association between scores on the selection measure and scores for job performance. If there is a substantial correlation between test scores and job-performance scores, **criterion-related validity** has been established.[5] For example, Figure 6.2 shows

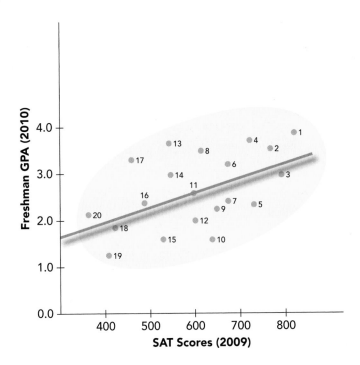

figure 6.2
Relationship
between 2009 SAT
Scores and 2010
Freshman GPA

the relationship between 2009 scores on the Scholastic Aptitude Test (SAT) and 2010 freshman grade point average (GPA). In this example, there is roughly a .50 correlation between the SAT and GPA. This .50 is referred to as a *validity coefficient*. Note that we have used the correlation coefficient to assess both reliability and validity, which may seem somewhat confusing. The key distinction is that the correlation reflects a reliability estimate when we are attempting to assess the same characteristic twice (such as SAT scores in the junior and senior years), but the correlation coefficient reflects a validity coefficient when we are attempting to relate one characteristic (SAT) to performance on some task (GPA).

Criterion-related validity studies come in two varieties. **Predictive validation** seeks to establish an empirical relationship between test scores taken *prior* to being hired and eventual performance on the job. Because of the time and effort required to conduct a predictive validation study, many employers are tempted to use a different design. **Concurrent validation** assesses the validity of a test by administering it to people already on the job and then correlating test scores with existing measures of each person's performance. The logic behind this strategy is that if the best performers currently on the job perform better on the test than those who are currently struggling on the job, the test has validity. (Figure 6.3 compares the two types of validation study.)

Despite the extra effort and time needed for predictive validation, it is superior to concurrent validation for a number of reasons, First, job applicants (because they are seeking work) are typically more motivated to perform well on the tests than are current employees (who already have jobs). Second, current employees have learned many things on the job that job applicants have not yet learned. Therefore, the correlation between test scores and job performance for current employees may not be the same as the correlation between test scores and job performance for less knowledgeable job applicants. Third, current employees tend to be homogeneous—that is, similar to each other on many characteristics. Thus, on many of the characteristics

Predictive Validation
A criterion-related validity study that seeks to establish an empirical relationship between applicants' test scores and their eventual performance on the job.

Concurrent Validation
A criterion-related validity study in which a test is administered to all the people currently in a job and then incumbents' scores are correlated with existing measures of their performance on the job.

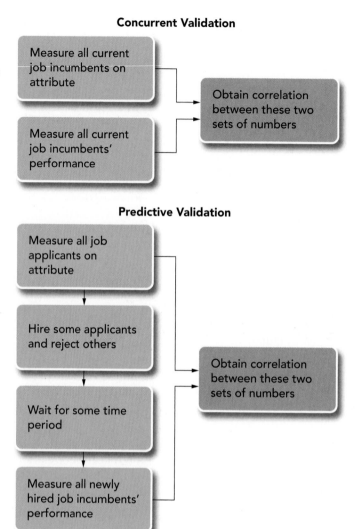

Concurrent Validation

Measure all current job incumbents on attribute

Measure all current job incumbents' performance

Obtain correlation between these two sets of numbers

Predictive Validation

Measure all job applicants on attribute

Hire some applicants and reject others

Wait for some time period

Measure all newly hired job incumbents' performance

Obtain correlation between these two sets of numbers

needed for success on the job, most current employees will show restriction in range. This restricted range makes it hard to detect a relationship between test scores and job-performance scores because few of the current employees will be very low on the characteristic you are trying to validate. For example, if emotional stability is required for a nursing career, it is quite likely that most nurses who have amassed five or six years' experience will score high on this characteristic. Yet to validate a test, you need both high test scorers (who should subsequently perform well on the job) and low test scorers (who should perform poorly on the job). Thus, although concurrent studies can sometimes help one anticipate the results of predictive studies, they do not serve as substitutes.

Obviously, we would like our measures to be high in validity; but as with the reliability standard, we must also ask, how high is high enough? When trying to determine how much validity is enough, one typically has to turn to tests of statistical significance. A test of statistical significance answers the question, "Assuming that there is no true relationship between the predictor and the criterion, what are the odds of seeing a relationship this strong by chance alone?" If these odds are very low, then one might infer that the results from the test were in fact predicting future job performance.

Table 6.1 shows how big a correlation between a selection measure and a measure of job performance needs to be to achieve statistical significance at a level of .05 (that is, there is only a 5 out of 100 chance that one could get a correlation this big by chance alone). Although it is generally true that bigger correlations are better, the size of the sample on which the correlation is based plays a large role as well. Because many of the selection methods we examine in the second half of this chapter generate correlations in the .20s and .30s, we often need samples of 80 to 90 people. A validation study with a small sample (such as 20 people) is almost doomed to failure from the start.

Content Validation

When sample sizes are small, an alternative test validation strategy, content validation, can be used. **Content validation** is performed by demonstrating that the questions or problems posed by the test are a representative sample of the kinds of situations or problems that occur on the job. A test that is content valid exposes the job applicant to situations that are likely to occur on the job, and then tests whether the applicant currently has sufficient knowledge, skill, or ability to handle such situations.

Many of the new simulations that organizations are using are essentially computer-based role-playing games, where applicants play the role of the job incumbent, confronting the exact types of people and problems real-live job incumbents would face. The simulations are just like traditional role-playing games (e.g., "The Sims"), and the applicant's reactions and behaviors are scored to see how well they match with what one would expect from the ideal employee.[6] Because the content of these tests so closely parallels the content of the job, one can safely make inferences from one to the other. Although criterion-related validity is established by empirical means, content validity is achieved primarily through a process of expert judgment.

The ability to use content validation in small sample settings makes it generally more applicable than criterion-related validation. However, content validation has two limitations. First, one assumption behind content validation is that the person who is to be hired must have the knowledge, skills, or abilities at the time she is hired. Second, because subjective judgment plays such a large role in content validation, it is critical to minimize the amount of inference involved on the part of judges. Thus the judges' ratings need to be made with respect to relatively concrete and observable behaviors.

Content Validation
A test-validation strategy performed by demonstrating that the items, questions, or problems posed by a test are a representative sample of the kinds of situations or problems that occur on the job.

SAMPLE SIZE	REQUIRED CORRELATION
5	.75
10	.58
20	.42
40	.30
80	.21
100	.19

table 6.1

Required Level of Correlation to Reach Statistical Significance as a Function of Sample Size

GENERALIZABILITY

Generalizability
The degree to which the validity of a selection method established in one context extends to other contexts.

Generalizability is defined as the degree to which the validity of a selection method established in one context extends to other contexts. Thus, the SAT may be a valid predictor of someone's performance (e.g., as a measure of someone's GPA in an undergraduate program), but, does this same test predict performance in graduate programs? If the test does not predict success in this other situation, then it does not "generalize" to this other context. Thus, rather than rely on the SAT for all types of programs, separate tests like the GMAT, LSAT, MCAT, and GRE may be needed for particular types of graduate schools.

There are two primary "contexts" over which we might like to generalize: different situations (jobs or organizations) and different samples of people. Just as reliability is necessary but not sufficient for validity, validity is necessary but not sufficient for generalizability.

It was once believed, for example, that validity coefficients were situationally specific—that is, the level of correlation between test and performance varied as one went from one organization to another, even though the jobs studied seemed to be identical. Subsequent research has indicated that this is largely false. Rather, tests tend to show similar levels of correlation even across jobs that are only somewhat similar (at least for tests of intelligence and cognitive ability). Correlations with these kinds of tests change as one goes across widely different kinds of jobs, however. Specifically, the more complex the job, the higher the validity of many tests. It was also believed that tests showed differential subgroup validity, which meant that the validity coefficient for any test–job performance pair was different for people of different races or genders. This belief was also refuted by subsequent research, and, in general, one finds very similar levels of correlations across different groups of people.[7]

Because the evidence suggests that test validity often extends across situations and subgroups, *validity generalization* stands as an alternative for validating selection methods for companies that cannot employ criterion-related or content validation. Validity generalization is a three-step process. First, the company provides evidence from previous criterion-related validity studies conducted in other situations that shows that a specific test (such as a test of emotional stability) is a valid predictor for a specific job (like nurse at a large hospital). Second, the company provides evidence from job analysis to document that the job it is trying to fill (nurse at a small hospital) is similar in all major respects to the job validated elsewhere (nurse at a large hospital). Finally, if the company can show that it uses a test that is the same as or similar to that used in the validated setting, then one can "generalize" the validity from the first context (large hospital) to the new context (small hospital).

UTILITY

Utility
The degree to which the information provided by selection methods enhances the effectiveness of selecting personnel in real organizations.

Utility is the degree to which the information provided by selection methods enhances the bottom-line effectiveness of the organization. In general, the more reliable, valid, and generalizable the selection method is, the more utility it will have. On the other hand, many characteristics of particular selection contexts enhance or detract from the usefulness of given selection methods, even when reliability, validity, and generalizability are held constant.

Figures 6.4a and 6.4b, for example, show two different scenarios where the correlation between a measure of extroversion and the amount of sales revenue generated by

LO 6-2
Discuss how the particular characteristics of a job, organization, or applicant affect the utility of any test.

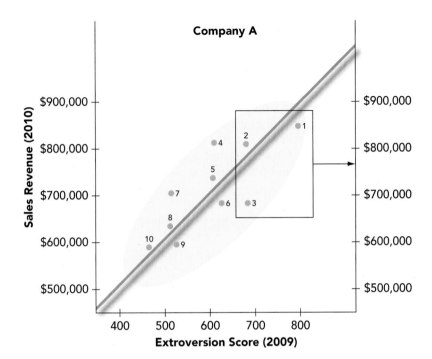

figure 6.4a
Utility of Selecting on Extroversion Scores when Selection Ratio Is High

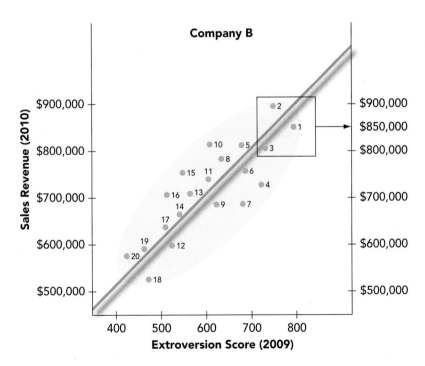

figure 6.4b
Utility of Selecting on Extroversion Scores when Selection Ratio Is Low

a sample of sales representatives is the same for two different companies: Company A and Company B. Although the correlation between the measure of extroversion and sales is the same, Company B derives much more utility or practical benefit from the measure. That is, as indicated by the arrows proceeding out of the boxes (which indicate the people selected), the average sales revenue of the three people selected by Company B (Figure 6.4b) is $850,000 compared to $780,000 from the three people selected by Company A (Figure 6.4a).

The major difference between these two companies is that Company B generated twice as many applicants as Company A. This means that the selection ratio (the percentage of people selected relative to the total number of people tested) is quite low for Company B (3/20) relative to Company A (3/10). Thus, the people selected by Company B have higher amounts of extroversion than those selected by Company A; therefore, Company B takes better advantage of the relationship between extroversion and sales. Thus, the utility of any test generally increases as the selection ratio gets lower, so long as the additional costs of recruiting and testing are not excessive.

As we saw in our opening vignette, the selection ratio for SEAL Team 6 was very, very low, in the sense that thousands of people were tested for just a few positions on the team. Selection ratios tend to get low when the economy is in a recession, and there are more people looking for work than there are jobs, the utility of valid selection techniques is especially high. This is a reason why countercyclical hiring, a notion we mentioned in our last chapter, can be especially effective in terms of establishing long-term competitive advantage. Figure 6.5 shows how the recession of 2008 powerfully affected selection ratios and why this was actually a very good time to be hiring employees.[8]

Many other factors relate to the utility of a test. For example, the value of the product or service produced by the job incumbent plays a role: the more valuable the product or service, the more value there is in selecting the top performers. The cost of the test, of course, also plays a role. More expensive tests will on average have less utility unless they produce more valid predictions. A good recent example of this can be seen in the drug testing industry. Although few would dispute the reliability and validity of a properly conducted drug test, these can be relatively expensive, and employers are increasingly unwilling to pay the cost for these tests given the yield. Most drug tests yield few hard core drug abusers, and one study showed that given the hit rate of one test used in one department of the federal government, it cost the agency $77,000 per detected drug addict. Thus, although roughly 70% of companies were employing drug tests in 1996, that same figure is closer to 60% in 2003, due largely to cost/benefit questions such as this.[9]

figure 6.5

The Effects of an Economic Recession on Selection Ratios

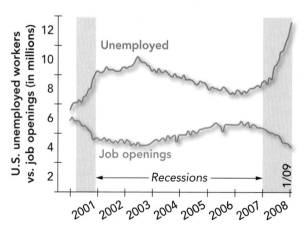

SOURCE: Bureau of Labor Statistics, 2009.

LEGALITY

The final standard that any selection method should adhere to is *legality*. All selection methods should conform to existing laws and existing legal precedents. Employers who are taken to court for illegal discrimination experience high costs associated with litigation, settlements, and awards, and also suffer potential damage to their social reputations as good employers, making recruitment more difficult. For example, a recent class-action charge of racial discrimination accuses the advertising industry of discriminating against African Americans. The suit seeks to secure damages of over $200 million from four of the largest firms in the United States (Interpublic, Omnicon, Publicis, and WPP).[10] A different case against Walmart seeks damages of over $1 billion, and charges that the retailer discriminated against women via a set of subjective and decentralized interview processes that were rife with gender stereotypes that limited their advancement opportunities.[11] Moreover, although the threat of litigation is ever present, this is especially a problem during economic recessions, when it is difficult to find a job. Indeed, the number of discrimination cases filed with the EEOC set a record of over 100,000 in 2010 alone.[12]

LO 6-3
Describe the government's role in personnel selection decisions, particularly in the areas of constitutional law, federal laws, executive orders, and judicial precedent.

Federal Legislation

Three primary federal laws form the basis for a majority of the suits filed by job applicants. First, the Civil Rights Act of 1991 (discussed in Chapter 3), an extension of the Civil Rights Act of 1964, protects individuals from discrimination based on race, color, sex, religion, and national origin with respect to hiring as well as compensation and working conditions. The 1991 act differs from the 1964 act in three important areas.

First, it defines employers' explicit obligation to establish the business necessity of any neutral-appearing selection method that has had adverse impact on groups specified by the law. This is typically done by showing that the test has significant criterion-related or content validity. If the employer cannot show such a difference, which the research suggests will be difficult, then the process may be ruled illegal. It should also be noted that "customer preference" is not a legally defensible means of justifying a process that has adverse impact.

This is not a legal defense, nor is the defense that "our customers prefer to buy from people of this or that race." For example, Walgreens was targeted for a class action suit by the Equal Employment Opportunity Commission for a documented statistical tendency to place African American managers in stores that served largely African American populations. Because managerial salaries at Walgreens are based partially on sales, and sales in these largely urban communities are smaller than more affluent suburban communities and malls, this had the effect of lowering salaries for all African American managers.[13]

Second, the 1991 act allows the individual filing the complaint to have a jury decide whether he or she may recover punitive damages (in addition to lost wages and benefits) for emotional injuries caused by the discrimination. This can generate large financial settlements as well as poor public relations that can hinder the organization's ability to compete.

Finally, the 1991 act explicitly prohibits the granting of preferential treatment to minority groups. Preferential treatment is often attractive because many of the most valid methods for screening people, especially cognitive ability tests and work sample tests, often are high in adverse impact.[14] Thus, there is somewhat of a trade-off in terms of selecting the highest scorers on validated tests on the one hand and creating diversity in the workforce on the other hand.[15] Indeed, as the "Competing through Sustainability" box shows, the complexity of trying to meet both of these desired goals at once is so high that only the U.S. Supreme Court can make the decision in some cases.

One potential way to "have your cake and eat it too" is to simply rank the scores of different races or gender groups within their own groups, and then taking perhaps the top 10% of scorers from each group, instead of the top 10% that would be obtained if one ignored race or gender. Many feel that this practice is justified because it levels the playing field in a context where bias works against African Americans. However, the 1991 act specifically outlaws this practice (sometimes referred to as *race norming*). The reason for this is that adjusting scores in this way has been found to have a number of negative effects, not only on the attitudes of white males who claim it causes reverse discrimination,[16] but on the proposed beneficiaries of such preferential treatment. Research shows that when selection decisions are perceived as being based partially on group membership, it undermines the confidence and hurts the job performance of the women or minority group members the program was designed to help.[17]

Rather than employing race norming, employers can partially achieve both goals of maximizing predicted future performance and diversity in several ways. First, aggressive recruiting of members of protected groups allows an employer to generate a larger pool of protected group members, and, by being highly selective within this larger group, the scores of admitted applicants will more closely match those of all the other groups.[18] Second, as we see later in this chapter, different selection methods have different degrees of adverse impact, and multistage selection batteries that use different methods at different stages can also help.[19] The key is to use methods that have low adverse impact early in the process and only employ the methods that have high adverse impact later. Third, by directly showing the degree to which past unfair practices and unconscious bias has resulted in adverse impact in the past, the nonbeneficiaries of affirmative action programs are much more likely to view them as acceptable as a form of short-term remedy.[20]

Finally, one common approach that does not seem to work is to abandon the kinds of compliance-driven, evidenced-based workforce utilization reviews that we discussed in our last chapter, in favor of softer, "inclusion" initiatives that express the generic value of diversity but fail to document goals and timetables statistically. Some organizations treat diversity more like a marketing campaign than an HR initiative, and it is not uncommon to see companies that won awards for their "inclusion programs" such as Texaco and Bank of America, also later convicted of illegal discrimination. Some observers have noted that there is an almost complete overlap of the lists of the top 50 companies for inclusion and the top 50 companies for advertising expenditures, and the need to complement style with substance cannot be overlooked in this critical area.[21] The simple truth is that best predictors of whether a firm becomes truly diverse and avoids litigation is whether (a) there is a specific person (e.g., a diversity compliance officer) whose sole job is to monitor hiring statistics, (b) this person has the power to change hiring practices, and (c) this person is held strictly accountable in their own performance appraisal for achieving quantifiable results.[22]

Although most litigation that involves the Civil Rights Act seeks to redress bias associated with race and gender, it should also be stressed that the act also protects against bias based on religion. In particular, in the post-9/11 world, evidence is accruing that indicates increased bias against job applicants who are Muslim.[23] Still, perhaps because the United States stresses the values of freedom of religion and freedom of

COMPETING THROUGH SUSTAINABILITY

Supreme Court Outlaws "Do Overs"

Exactly 100 people sat down to take the test that would qualify them to be selected as lieutenants and captains in the New Haven, Connecticut, Fire Department. Out of the 100, 58 test takers were white, 19 were Hispanic, and 23 were African American. When the results of that test came in, it triggered immediate controversy, because while 18 white and 2 Hispanic candidates had scores that would support a promotion, no African Americans qualified for promotion based on their scores. Given the high level of adverse impact of this test on African American applicants, and the fear of being sued for racial discrimination in hiring against this group, the New Haven Fire Commission decided to throw out all the test results. Their commission's plan was to act as if nothing happened and then try to come up with a different way to make promotion decisions.

As you might imagine, this "Do Over" did not sit well with the 20 people whose promotions were denied because of this decision, and this group sued the City of New Haven based upon the unequal treatment clause of the 1964 Civil Rights Act. This controversial case regarding reverse discrimination highlights the difference between the disparate impact clause and the unequal treatment clause of the Civil Rights Act and it seems to pit the two clauses against one another. Indeed, this case, *Ricci versus DeStefano*, was considered so important that it was taken up by the Supreme Court.

On the one hand, it is clear why those who passed the test would be angry. According to the rules that were set up in advance, they won in a fair competition, and yet one person of Italian origin with a passing score was told, "you just had too many vowels in your name." However, it is also clear why African American firefighters, all of whom were denied promotion based on the written test, might also be angry. After all, when one shows up to do battle with a raging fire, one does not bring a Number 2 pencil to get the job done. Thus, when caught between a rock and a hard place, the commission, fearing the paper and pencil test would not be perceived as valid for this task, blinked, and dropped the test like a hot potato.

In a close 5–4 ruling the Supreme Court decided in June of 2009 against the commission, stating that it was unlawful to throw out the test results just out of fear of being sued by those who failed the test. That is, one cannot presume that a test that the commission themselves ordered up, did not assess the required skills for the job without direct evidence. The problem, according to the majority opinion, was that the purpose of Title VII is to promote hiring on the basis of job qualifications rather than on the basis of race and color, but the city made its employment decision because of race. Given the dual goals of trying to integrate the workforce while at the same time being fair to white workers, this will not be the last time we see this kind of controversy. Indeed, as Justice Antonin Scalia noted, "The war between disparate impact and equal protection will be waged sooner or later, and it behooves us to begin thinking about how—and on what terms—to make peace between them."

SOURCES: A. Thernstrom, "The Supreme Court Says No to Quotas," *The Wall Street Journal,* July 1, 2009, p. B1; M. Schoeff, "Ruling Raises Bar on Testing for Employment," *Workforce Management,* July 2009, p. 11; J. A. Burns, "Employment Testing after Ricci: What to Do Now," *Workforce Management,* September 2009, pp. 12–13.

speech, the level of litigation associated with religious-based charges are very small in number compared to what one sees for gender and race. However, as the "Competing through Globalization" box illustrates, in countries like France, where the cultural values lean more heavily toward secularism, the perception of religious discrimination seems more salient.

The Age Discrimination in Employment Act of 1967 is also widely used in personnel selection. Court interpretations of this act also mirror those of the Civil Rights Act, in the sense that if any neutral-appearing practice happens to have adverse impact on those over 40, the burden of proof shifts to the employer, who must show business necessity to avoid a guilty verdict.[24] The act does not protect younger workers (thus there is never a case for "reverse discrimination" here), and like the most recent civil rights act, it allows for jury trials and punitive damages. This act outlaws almost all "mandatory retirement" programs (company policies that dictate that everyone who reaches a set age must retire).

Finally, the Americans with Disabilities Act (ADA) of 1991 protects individuals with physical and mental disabilities (or with a history of the same), and requires that employers make "reasonable accommodation" to disabled individuals whose handicaps may prevent them from performing essential functions of the job as currently designed. "Reasonable accommodation" could include restructuring jobs, modifying work schedules, making facilities accessible, providing readers, or modifying equipment. The ADA does not require an organization to hire someone whose disability prevents him or her from performing either critical or routine aspects of the job nor does it require accommodations that would cause "undue hardship." Technological advancements in the area of accommodations, along with the general shift in jobs from those that are physically demanding to those that are more mentally challenging, is increasing the percentage of jobs that disabled workers can hold.[25] Unfortunately, when there is a downturn in the economy, nondisabled workers start to compete for the very same jobs, which places the disabled at a disadvantage. For example, the percentage of disabled workers in the workforce rose in the period between 2001 and 2006 but sharply fell off in 2007 and 2008 due to the economic recession.[26]

Executive Orders

As noted in Chapter 3, the executive branch of the government also regulates hiring decisions through the use of executive orders. Executive Order 11246 parallels the protections provided by the Civil Rights Act of 1964 but goes beyond the 1964 act in two important ways. First, not only do the executive orders prohibit discrimination, they actually mandate that employers take affirmative action to hire qualified minority applicants.[27] Executive orders also allow the government to suspend all business with a contractor while an investigation is being conducted (rather than waiting for an actual finding), which puts a great deal of pressure on employers to comply with these orders. Executive orders are monitored by the Office of Federal Contract Compliance Programs (OFCCP), which issues guidelines (like the Affirmative Action Program Guidelines published by the Bureau of National Affairs in 1983) to help companies comply.

Types of Selection Methods

LO 6-4
List the common methods used in selecting human resources.

The first half of this chapter laid out the five standards by which we can judge selection measures. In the second half of this chapter, we examine the common selection methods used in various organizations and discuss their advantages and disadvantages in terms of these standards.

Secularism Is Considered Sacred in France

Although many consider France as possessing a very free-spirited and liberal culture, this country takes its religion—or more accurately, its lack of religion—very seriously. In May of 2011, over 50 Muslim women were arrested for doing no more than wearing facial veils in public. This was in accord with a new law put into effect that month that banned veils, extending previous legislation that banned body covering Burquas, and any other "ostentatious religious symbols." In the United States, the combined cultural values of freedom of religion and freedom of speech would make such a law unthinkable, but for the French, the value of secularism, that is, the belief that religion should not enter into any public or state function, is considered sacrosanct.

Indeed, official French policy holds that all citizens of France are considered equal, and thus, the government does not even collect data that would support the kind of affirmative action policies that exist in the United States on the grounds that it is unnecessary. However, labor market data belies this rosy view, at least when it comes to getting good jobs. As one young Muslim student notes, "there are good jobs in France, but they are reserved for certain people, and usually it's white French people." This statement is backed up by labor market data that reveals that the unemployment rate for Muslims in France is three times higher than the rate for the country as a whole. Part of this can be traced to religious-neutral employment practices in France, where job security provisions supported by the government and unions protect the jobs of those already employed, often at the expense of Muslims who are immigrants and relative newcomers to the country.

However, there is also direct evidence from scientific studies that shows that active discrimination in hiring decisions is a major contributor to the problem. For example, as part of a scientific research, Claire Adida and her colleagues sent out fake job applications in response to employment advertisements posted in France where each applicant was identical in their experience and qualifications—with one exception. Half the employers were randomly sent an application from someone with a Muslim sounding name, Khadjia Diouf, and half were sent an application from someone with a Christian name, Aurelie Menard. Despite having the exact same qualifications, "Aurelie" was asked to interview for the position at a rate (28%) that was four times higher than Khadjia (7%), which is direct irrefutable evidence of religious bias.

Ironically, despite this bias, the current trend within the Muslim community is for young people to change their names in a direction that celebrates, rather than hides their religion. That is, first generation Muslim immigrants into France routinely gave their children Christian names in order to help speed the integration process. However, partially in response to the obvious segregation by religion that exists in many French cities, an increasing number of young Muslims are adopting names that reflect their religious group identity as opposed to their French identity.

SOURCES: M. De La Baume, "Enforcing Veil Ban, the French Have Stopped 46 Violators," *The New York Times*, May 11, 2011, p. B1; C. L. Adida, D. D. Laitin, and M. A. Valfort, "Identifying Barriers to Muslim Integration," *Proceeding from the National Academy of Sciences* 107 (2010), pp. 384–90; C. Bremner and M. Tourres, "Melting Pot Cracks as Muslims Reject Christian Names in France," *The Times*, November 15, 2008, p. C2.

INTERVIEWS

A selection interview has been defined as "a dialogue initiated by one or more persons to gather information and evaluate the qualifications of an applicant for employment." The selection interview is the most widespread selection method employed in organizations, and there have been literally hundreds of studies examining their effectiveness.[28]

LO 6-5
Describe the degree to which each of the common methods used in selecting human resources meets the demands of reliability, validity, generalizability, utility, and legality.

Unfortunately, the long history of research on the employment interview suggests that, without proper care, it can be unreliable, low in validity, and biased against a number of different groups. Moreover, interviews are relatively costly because they require at least one person to interview another person, and these persons have to be brought to the same geographic location. Finally, in terms of legality, the subjectivity embodied in the process, as well as the opportunity for unconscious bias effects, often makes applicants upset, particularly if they fail to get a job after being asked apparently irrelevant questions. In the end, subjective selection methods like the interview must be validated by traditional criterion-related or content-validation procedures if they show any degree of adverse impact.

Fortunately, more recent research has pointed to a number of concrete steps that one can employ to increase the utility of the personnel selection interview. First, HR staff should keep the interview structured, standardized, and focused on accomplishing a small number of goals. That is, they should plan to come out of each interview with quantitative ratings on a small number of dimensions that are observable (like interpersonal style or ability to express oneself) and avoid ratings of abilities that may be better measured by tests (like intelligence). In addition to coming out of the interview with quantitative ratings, interviewers should also have a structured note-taking system that will aid recall when it comes to justifying the ratings.[29]

EVIDENCE-BASED HR

In particular, given the interpersonal and subjective nature of the interview situation, one might be concerned that interviewer ratings might be biased by demographic similarity. That is, job applicants might fare better when they are of the same race, gender, and educational background as the interviewer. This "demographic similarity bias," if it indeed exists, would lead to several negative outcomes for a selection process, in terms of validity, legality, and financial utility. However, if an interview is highly structured, and is aimed at generating objective evidence about specific past behavior at work, this effect might be mitigated.

A recent test of the ability of highly structured interviews to reduce demographic similarity bias was conducted by McCarthy, Van Iddekinge, and Campion, who studied the evidence associated with roughly 20,000 interviews for entry-level positions in the U.S. federal government. The results suggested that although female applicants scored slightly higher than men across all interviewers, there were no differences attributable to the gender, race, or background of the interviewers. Thus, the evidence suggests that organizations that adopt carefully administered interviews that conform to the key components of high structure can minimize concerns of applicant discrimination on the basis of gender and race.

SOURCE: J. M. McCarthy, C. H. Van Iddekinge, and M. A. Campion, "Are Highly Structured Interviews Resistant to Demographic Similarity Effects?" *Journal of Applied Psychology* 63 (2010), pp. 325–59.

Situational Interview
An interview procedure where applicants are confronted with specific issues, questions, or problems that are likely to arise on the job.

Second, ask questions dealing with specific situations that are likely to arise on the job, and use these to determine what the person is likely to do in that situation. These types of **situational interview** items have been shown to have quite high predictive validity.[30] Situational judgment items come in two varieties, as shown in Table 6.2. Some items are "experience-based" and require the applicant to reveal an actual experience he or she had in the past when confronting the situation. Other items are "future-oriented" and ask what the person is likely to do when confronting a certain

Experience-based	
Motivating employees:	"Think about an instance when you had to motivate an employee to perform a task that he or she disliked but that you needed to have done. How did you handle that situation?"
Resolving conflict:	"What was the biggest difference of opinion you ever had with a co-worker? How did you resolve that situation?"
Overcoming resistance to change:	"What was the hardest change you ever had to bring about in a past job, and what did you do to get the people around you to change their thoughts or behaviors?"
Future-oriented	
Motivating employees:	"Suppose you were working with an employee who you knew greatly disliked performing a particular task. You needed to get this task completed, however, and this person was the only one available to do it. What would you do to motivate that person?"
Resolving conflict:	"Imagine that you and a co-worker disagree about the best way to handle an absenteeism problem with another member of your team. How would you resolve that situation?"
Overcoming resistance to change:	"Suppose you had an idea for change in work procedures that would enhance quality, but some members of your work group were hesitant to make the change. What would you do in that situation?"

table 6.2

Examples of Experience-Based and Future-Oriented Situational Interview Items

hypothetical situation in the future. Research suggests that these types of items can both show validity but that experience-based items often outperform future-oriented items. Experience-based items also appear to reduce some forms of impression management such as ingratiation better than future-oriented items.[31]

Situational interviews can be particularly effective when assessing sensitive issues dealing with the honesty and integrity of candidates. Clearly, simply asking people directly whether they have integrity will not produce much in the way of useful information. However, questions that pose ethical dilemmas and ask respondents to discuss how they dealt with such situations in the past are often revealing in terms of how different people deal with common dilemmas. For example, by stating "We have all observed someone stretching the rules at work, so give me two examples of situations in which you faced this dilemma and how you dealt with it," the interviewer forces the applicant to reveal how he or she deals with ethical dilemmas as an observer. Since the person is an observer and not the perpetrator in this case, he or she will be less defensive in terms of revealing how he or she deals with ethical issues.[32]

It is also important to use multiple interviewers who are trained to avoid many of the subjective errors that can result when one human being is asked to rate another.

● When more than one person is able to interview a candidate for a position, there is significant advantage in removing any errors or biases that a single individual might make in choosing the correct person for the job. In today's technological world, it is becoming easier for multiple people to give their input in an interview by watching a video tape or listening via conference call if they cannot be there in person.

For example, at Google, there were definite concerns with demographic similarity bias in interviews, because their own analysis of local data was suggesting that managers were hiring people who seemed just like them. To eliminate this problem, Google now compiles elaborate files for each candidate, and then has all interviews conducted by groups rather than individuals. Laszlo Bock, vice president for Google's People Operations, notes that "we do everything to minimize the authority and power of the lone manager in making hiring decisions that are going to affect the entire company."[33] Many companies find that a good way to get "multiple eyes" on an applicant is to conduct digitally taped interviews, and then send the digitalized files (rather than the applicants) around from place to place.

This is seen by some as a cost-effective means of allowing numerous raters to evaluate the candidate under standard conditions. The use of video-based interviews began on college campuses, where technology resources were widely available. However, over time, private start-up companies began selling those same services to the general public.[34] Of course, many employers find that the lack of true interaction that can take place in videos limits their value somewhat and, hence, the use of face-to-face interactive technology like Skype is also on the rise.[35]

Regardless of the medium, limiting the subjectivity of the process is central to much of interviewer training, and research suggests that it is best to ask interviewers to be "witnesses" of facts that can later be integrated via objective formulas, as opposed to being "judges" allowed to idiosyncratically weigh how various facts should be combined to form the final recommendation.[36] In addition to being a witness, the interviewer sometimes has to be the prosecuting attorney, because in some cases the interviewees may be motivated to try to present an overly positive, if not outright false, picture of their qualifications. People seem to be particularly prone to present false information when the competition for jobs is high, and data on résumé fraud indicated a spike in detected fraud during the recent recession of 2007. Part of this spike was attributable to the behavior of applicants, but part of it was also due to the ease with which employers can access basic information on applicants from sources like Google.[37] The data from a 2006 survey of executive recruiters bears this out and reveals that it is common practice for employers to search the web for information on applicants. In fact, 35% of those respondents stated that they eliminated candidates based upon what they learned from web searches—up from 25% the year before.[38] Some of this is attributable directly to content placed on blogs or social networking sites. For example, a former Delta Airlines flight attendant, Ellen Simonetti, was fired because she posted suggestive pictures in her work uniform on her personal website. In the case of Delta, the company had previously been charged with sexism in the content of their marketing and was trying to move away from that image when Simonetti posed in her uniform.[39]

The important point to take away from these lessons is that one needs to manage his or her digital identity the same way one manages his or her résumé. For example, the first step, of course, is to know exactly what pops up on you if your name is searched. If your search turns up something potentially unflattering or embarrassing, posting a correction may be necessary because you can always point to that if some particular content becomes an issue. Finally, you may be able to manage what information pops up for you (and in what order) by hiring a search-engine optimization firm that will create both sites and hits for sites that will drive the incriminating information far, far down the list that is generated for you using various search algorithms.[40]

Interviewers need to be critical and look for inconsistencies or gaps in stories or experiences in those who are providing information. Increasingly, interviewers are seeking training that helps them detect nonverbal signs that someone is trying to be deceptive, such as hand tremors, darting eyes, mumbled speech, and failing to maintain eye contact that may be a cause for concern and increased scrutiny.[41] In fact, one such trained observer in the U.S. Customs Department was credited with thwarting a terrorist mission aimed at disrupting the nation's Millennium Celebrations in Los Angeles. The officer spotted several behavioral manifestations of deceptiveness, then pulled the driver over for a detailed search that uncovered a substantial amount of bombmaking materials.[42]

REFERENCES, BIOGRAPHICAL DATA, AND APPLICATION BLANKS

Just as few employers would think of hiring someone without an interview, nearly all employers also use some method for getting background information on applicants before an interview. This information can be solicited from the people who know the candidate through reference checks.

The evidence on the reliability and validity of reference checks suggests that these are, at best, weak predictors of future success on the job. The main reason for this low validity is that the evaluations supplied in most reference letters are so positive that it is hard to differentiate applicants. This problem with reference letters has two causes. First, the applicant usually gets to choose who writes the letter and can thus choose only those writers who think the highest of her abilities. Second, because letter writers can never be sure who will read the letters, they may justifiably fear that supplying damaging information about someone could come back to haunt them. Thus, it is clearly not in the past employers' interest to reveal too much information beyond job title and years of service. In general, the validity of reference checks increases when the employer goes beyond the list provided by the applicant, and employers who rely heavily on this source tend to seek a large number of references (10 to 12) and contact those people directly by phone for a more interactive and, possibly, open and anonymous exchange of information.[43]

The evidence on the utility of biographical information collected directly from job applicants is much more positive, especially for certain outcomes like turnover.[44] The low cost of obtaining such information significantly enhances its utility, especially when the information is used in conjunction with a well-designed, follow-up interview that complements, rather than duplicates, the biographical information bank.

Again, as with the interview, the biggest concern with the use of biographical data is that applicants who supply the information may be motivated to misrepresent themselves. Résumé fraud is on the rise and one survey indicated that roughly 45% of job applications that were audited contained some amount of inaccurate material. In fact, one company, CareerExcuses.com, even provides a service wherein they will provide false references and fill in gaps in one's résumés for a fee.[45] Background checks can help on this score, but many firms that provide background checks are unreliable themselves. In addition, background checks offer no guarantee, because of the increased sophistication of those in the dishonesty business. Some universities and state prison systems have even been hacked into by companies that try to insert or delete their clients' names from databases.[46]

Although it is not a panacea, to some extent forcing applicants to elaborate on their responses to biodata questions can sometimes be helpful.[47] A good elaboration forces applicants to support their answers with evidence that includes names of other people involved, dates, locations, and objective evidence that would support a thorough cross-checking. Thus, rather than just asking someone if they have ever led a sales team, an elaborated item would force the applicant to name all members of the team, where and when the team was together, and what sales they accomplished, citing specific products, figures, and customers. The evidence suggests that forced elaboration reduces the traditional measures of faking behavior.[48]

Although the use of background checks is increasingly common in the United States, they are rarely used in Europe. There are several reasons for these differences between Europe and the United States. First, in terms of values and culture, in Europe, the applicant's right to privacy trumps the organization's right to know. As noted by Andrew Boling, partner at Baker and McKenzie, a Chicago-based HR outsourcing firm, "outside the United States, individual privacy rights enjoy the same protections that we give to our First Amendment—in Europe what's private, stays private."[49] Thus, a U.S. firm that seeks an employee's consent to do a background check is likely to be denied in Europe, and performing the check without consent would be illegal in many countries.

Second, relative to the United States, one sees far fewer incidences of workplace violence in Europe, and the rates of theft and fraud are also much lower. Similarly, unlike Americans, Europeans tend to carry less debt, and hence background checks for credit problems rarely turn up applicants whose financial situations are so dire that one might be afraid of trusting them around money. At the height of the U.S. financial crisis in 2007, for example, over 40% of people who were screened on credit card balances would have been rejected as viable hires given most standards adopted by companies that do background checks. The percentage of similarly situated bad risks in Europe is simply much lower.[50]

Third, although the greater deference to individual privacy would seem to put the employer at a disadvantage, on the other side of the equation, the legal concept of negligent hiring is also largely unheard of in Europe. This reduces the need for employers to show copious amounts of due diligence in order to protect themselves legally. As in any country, individual employees in Europe may run afoul of the law or commit egregious acts; however, this is an issue between the offender and the law, and one's employing organization is rarely held legally responsible for their actions.

Finally, if one takes away the legal motivation to perform due diligence and avoid negligent hiring suits, the decision to do a background check lies solely on its perceived value in screening out future problems. However, much of the information collected by firms doing background checks is inaccurate, and the objective evidence regarding the effectiveness of these firms in preventing future problems is weak. For example, most fraud is committed by long-term employees who know the firm well, not repeat offenders who move from place to place. Thus, only 7% of convicted fraud perpetrators had any criminal record whatsoever prior to the offense they were convicted for, and hence they would not be caught in any screen. Moreover, in roughly half the cases where a fraud conviction was upheld by a U.S. court, the companies that were harmed *did perform a background check*. Thus, for a whole host of reasons, the use of background checks is likely to stay a uniquely American tradition.[51]

PHYSICAL ABILITY TESTS

Although automation and other advances in technology have eliminated or modified many physically demanding occupational tasks, many jobs still require certain physical abilities or psychomotor abilities. In these cases, tests of physical abilities may be relevant not only to predicting performance but to predicting occupational injuries and disabilities as well.[52] There are seven classes of tests in this area: ones that evaluate (1) muscular tension, (2) muscular power, (3) muscular endurance, (4) cardiovascular endurance, (5) flexibility, (6) balance, and (7) coordination.[53]

The criterion-related validities for these kinds of tests for certain jobs like fire-fighting are quite strong.[54] Unfortunately, these tests, particularly the strength tests, are likely to have an adverse impact on some applicants with disabilities and many female applicants. For example, roughly two-thirds of all males score higher than the highest-scoring female on muscular tension tests.[55]

Because of this there are two key questions to ask in deciding whether to use these kinds of tests. First, is the physical ability essential to performing the job and is it mentioned prominently enough in the job description? Neither the Civil Rights Act nor the ADA requires employers to hire individuals who cannot perform essential job functions, and both accept a written job description as evidence of the essential functions of the job. Second, is there a probability that failure to adequately perform the job would result in some risk to the safety or health of the applicant, co-workers, or clients? The "direct threat" clause of the ADA makes it clear that adverse impact against those with disabilities is warranted under such conditions.

COGNITIVE ABILITY TESTS

Cognitive ability tests differentiate individuals based on their mental rather than physical capacities. Cognitive ability has many different facets, although we will focus only on three dominant ones. **Verbal comprehension** refers to a person's capacity to understand and use written and spoken language. **Quantitative ability** concerns the speed and accuracy with which one can solve arithmetic problems of all kinds. **Reasoning ability,** a broader concept, refers to a person's capacity to invent solutions to many diverse problems.

Some jobs require only one or two of these facets of cognitive ability. Under these conditions, maintaining the separation among the facets is appropriate. For example, the verbal requirements associated with many jobs in the U.S. economy has increased over the years, but this has occurred at a time when we have actually witnessed decreases in scores on standardized tests measuring these skills.[56] For example, a survey of more than 400 large firms suggested that as many as 30% of the applicants for entry-level positions have such poor reading and writing scores that it would be impossible to put them on the job without remedial training.[57] If this is the only cognitive ability that is related to the job, then this would be the only one that should be used to make decisions. However, many jobs that are high in complexity require most, if not all, of the facets, and hence one general test is often as good as many tests of separate facets. Highly reliable commercial tests measuring these kinds of abilities are widely available, and they are generally valid predictors of job performance in many different kinds of contexts, including widely different countries.[58] The validity of these kinds of tests is related to the complexity of the job, however, in that one sees higher criterion-related validation for complex jobs than for simple jobs. The predictive validity for these tests is also higher in jobs that are dynamic and changing over time and thus require

Cognitive Ability Tests
Tests that include three dimensions: verbal comprehension, quantitative ability and reasoning ability.

Verbal Comprehension
Refers to a person's capacity to understand and use written and spoken language.

Quantitative Ability
Concerns the speed and accuracy with which one can solve arithmetic problems of all kinds.

Reasoning Ability
Refers to a person's capacity to invent solutions to many diverse problems.

adaptability on the part of the job incumbent.[59] Thus, jobs in rapidly changing industries like the technology sector often require high levels of cognitive ability to adapt to ever-changing conditions.[60]

One of the major drawbacks to these tests is that they typically have adverse impact on some minority groups. Indeed, the size of the differences is so large that some have advocated abandoning these types of tests for making decisions regarding who will be accepted for certain schools or jobs.[61] The notion of race norming, alluded to earlier, was born of the desire to use these high-utility tests in a manner that avoided adverse impact. Although race norming was made illegal by the recent amendments to the Civil Rights Act, some have advocated the use of banding to both achieve the benefits of testing and minimize its adverse impact. The concept of *banding* suggests that similar groups of people whose scores differ by only a small amount all be treated as having the same score. Then, within any band, preferential treatment is given to minorities. Most observers feel preferential treatment of minorities is acceptable when scores are tied, and banding simply broadens the definition of what constitutes a tied score.

For example, in many classes a score of 90 to 100% may constitute a 4.0 for the course. This means that even though someone scoring 99 outperformed someone with a score of 91, each gets the same grade (a 4.0). Banding uses the same logic for all kinds of tests. Thus, if one was going to use the grade in the class as a selection standard, this would mean that the person with the 91 is equal to the person with the 99 (i.e., they both score a 4.0), and if their scores are tied, preference should be given to the minority. Like race norming, banding is very controversial, especially if the bands are set too wide.[62]

PERSONALITY INVENTORIES

While ability tests attempt to categorize individuals relative to what they can do, personality measures tend to categorize individuals by what they are like. Research suggests that there are five major dimensions of personality, known as "the Big Five": (1) extroversion, (2) adjustment, (3) agreeableness, (4) conscientiousness, and (5) openness to experience. Table 6.3 lists each of these with a corresponding list of adjectives that fit each dimension.

Although it is possible to find reliable, commercially available measures of each of these traits, the evidence for their validity and generalizability is mixed at best.[63] For example, conscientiousness, which captures the concepts of self-regulation and self-motivation, is one of the few factors that displays any validity across a number of different job categories, and many real-world managers rate this as one of the most important characteristics they look for in employees.

table 6.3

The Five Major Dimensions of Personality Inventories

1. Extroversion	Sociable, gregarious, assertive, talkative, expressive
2. Adjustment	Emotionally stable, nondepressed, secure, content
3. Agreeableness	Courteous, trusting, good-natured, tolerant, cooperative, forgiving
4. Conscientiousness	Dependable, organized, persevering, thorough, achievement-oriented
5. Openness to experience	Curious, imaginative, artistically sensitive, broad-minded, playful

Despite their generic lack of validity the use of personality traits in selection contexts has risen over the years, and a 2006 study indicates that 35% of U.S. organizations employ these kinds of tests when selecting personnel.[64] Part of this is attributable to the wider use of team-based structures that put more emphasis on collaboration at work. In contexts where task interdependence between individuals is stressed, personality conflicts become more salient and disruptive relative to situations where individuals are working alone.[65] Team contexts require that people create and maintain roles and relationships, and several traits like agreeableness and conscientiousness seem to promote effective role taking.[66] On the other hand, people who are high in disagreeableness and low in conscientiousness are more prone to engage in counterproductive behavior in group contexts.[67] One important element of staffing in team-based structures, however, relates to how the selection of one team member influences the requirements associated with other team members.[68] In some cases, organizations might try to select people who have very similar values and personality traits in order to create a strong team culture. When there is a strong team culture, everyone shares the same views and traits, promoting harmony and cohesiveness.[69]

In other cases, people putting together a team go out of their way to make sure that the people on the team have different values and personalities. The hope here is that a diversity of opinion that promotes internal debate and creativity.[70] For example, when assembling his leadership team in 2009, President Barack Obama took a "Team of Rivals" approach where, like Abraham Lincoln, he selected people who had previously been critical of him, including his vice president Joe Biden and his secretary of state, Hillary Clinton.[71] Lincoln, Obama had once said, "was confident enough to be willing to have these dissenting voices and confident enough to listen to the American people and to push them outside of their comfort zone."[72] Many considered this move on Obama's part to be a very risky move. On the one hand, by surrounding himself with a team of strong-minded, independent thinkers who would not necessarily act as simple "yes men," he assured himself that he would get a great deal of unbiased and unique thoughts on every conceivable challenge to his administration. On the other hand, could he really count on these individuals to faithfully execute the decisions that he made, especially when one of those decisions was, perhaps, inconsistent with the advice that he was offered?

If one does take this approach to staffing a team, it is critical that one also takes steps to make sure that there are not strong "fault lines" within the group that create strong and opposing subgroups. Diversity can be built into a team, and subgrouping problems avoided with judicious selection. For example, imagine a four-person group comprised of two men and two women, two marketing experts and two engineers, and two people from the United States and two people from France. One way this diversity could configure itself is such that the two males were also both engineers and both from the United States, and the two women were both marketing experts from France. In this configuration, the group has a strong fault line because all three dimensions of diversity converge, and it is easy to predict how this group might break apart into two subgroups. In contrast, the same level of diversity could be configured in a group where one of the men was an engineer, but one of the women was an engineer also. Similarly, one of the marketing experts was a man and one was woman. Finally, one of the men was from France and one was from the United States. In this second configuration, there is no strong fault line, and it is harder to see how the group is likely to fall apart.[73]

The concept of "emotional intelligence" is also important in team contexts and has been used to describe people who are especially effective in fluid and socially intensive contexts. Emotional intelligence is traditionally conceived of having five aspects: (1) self-awareness (knowledge of one's strengths and weaknesses), (2) self-regulation (the ability to keep disruptive emotions in check), (3) self-motivation (how to motivate oneself and persevere in the face of obstacles), (4) empathy (the ability to sense and read emotions in others), and (5) social skills (the ability to manage the emotions of other people). Danial Goleman, one of the primary proponents of this construct, noted that "in the new workplace, with its emphasis on flexibility, teams and a strong customer orientation, this crucial set of emotional competencies is becoming increasingly essential for excellence in every job in every part of the world."[74] Relative to standard measures of ability and personality, there has not been a great deal of scientific research on emotional intelligence, and critics have raised both theoretical and empirical questions about the construct. Theoretically, some have argued that the construct is overly broad and confuses aspects of perception, ability, and temperament that are best conceptualized as separate processes.[75] Empirically, the data seem to suggest that if one holds scores on the variables captured by the five-factor model of personality and scores on tests of cognitive ability constant, there is very little, if any, added predictive power attributable to emotional intelligence.[76] Still, because the general concept of emotional intelligence creates a simple, unified, and holistic package that helps describe why some people do better when working or leading teams, many firms employ it as one part of their staffing process.[77]

In addition to the development of team-based structures, the use of personality measures as screening devices has also increased because of the increased use of multinational structures and the increase in the number of jobs that require that people work in foreign locales. The number of people that are asked to work outside their own country has increased steadily over time, and more often than not, the decision of whom to send where is based primarily on technical skills. However, in one large study of expatriates working in Hong Kong, Japan, and Korea, high levels of emotional stability and openness to experience were two of the strongest predictors of adjustment and performance, and these tended to trump technical expertise when it came to predicting who would succeed and fail. In this study, the cost of an adjustment failure (i.e., someone who has to come home prior to finishing his or her assignment) was estimated at over $150,000 per person, and hence the stakes are high in this context.[78]

Regardless of the nature of the context the validity for almost all of the Big Five factors in terms of predicting job performance also seems to be higher when the scores are not obtained from the applicant but are instead taken from other people.[79] The lower validity associated with self-reports of personality can be traced to three factors. First, people sometimes lack insight into what their own personalities are actually like (or how they are perceived by others), so their scores are inaccurate or unreliable. Second, people's personalities sometimes vary across different contexts. Thus, someone may be very conscientious when it comes to social activities such as planning a family wedding or a fraternity party, but less conscientious when it comes to doing a paid job. Thus, contextualized measures that add the term "at work" to standard personality items often perform better as predictors than standard noncontextualized measures. Third, with some traits like ability, validity coefficients are higher when one uses a curvilinear prediction instead of just a straight linear prediction. That is, with a trait like emotional stability, the best job performers often score in the middle range, and for a lot of jobs, both being too nervous and being too calm can be problematic.[80] This kind of curvilinear finding is rarely found with ability measures, in the sense that people who are "overqualified" on ability typically perform at the highest levels with evidence of a drop-off at extreme levels.[81]

Finally, one factor that also limits the validity of personality items is that, unlike cognitive ability scores, applicants find it easier to fake traits by providing socially desirable responses to questions. Research suggests that when people fill out these inventories when applying for a job, their scores on conscientiousness and emotional stability are much higher relative to when they are just filling out the same questionnaires anonymously for research purposes.[82] In addition, if people fail a personality test and then take the same test again in the future, their scores seem to drastically increase.[83] Several steps can be used to try to reduce faking. For example, if employers simply warn applicants that they are going to cross-check the applicants' self-ratings with other people, this seems to reduce faking.[84] Also, the degree to which people can fake various personality traits is enhanced with questionnaires, and one sees much less faking of traits when interviewers are assessing the characteristics.[85] All of this reinforces the idea that it is better to obtain this information from people other than the job applicant, and that it is better to use this information to reject low scorers but not necessarily hire all higher scores on the basis of self-reports alone.[86]

Finally, as the "Competing through Technology" box illustrates, changes in the technical delivery of personality measures also may hold out some promise for increased validity.

WORK SAMPLES

Work-sample tests attempt to simulate the job in a prehiring context to observe how the applicant performs in the simulated job. The degree of fidelity in work samples can vary greatly. In some cases, applicants respond to a set of standardized hypothetical case studies and role play how they would react to certain situations.[87] Often these standardized role plays employ interactive video technology to create "virtual job auditions."[88] Indeed, simulations involving video-based role-plays seem to be more engaging and display higher levels of predictive validity relative to paper-and-pencil approaches.[89] In other cases, the job applicants are brought to the employers' location and actually perform the job for a short time period as part of a "job tryout."[90] Finally, although not generally considered a test, the practice whereby employers hire someone on a temporary basis and then, after a rather long trial (six months to a year), hire that person permanently is in essence an extended work-sample test.[91] These extended job trials give employers a rich base of experience to base their hiring decisions on, and as one HR manager noted of work samples, "It's foolish of any of us to think our interview skills are so great that we can predict how well someone is going to work in terms of dynamics of a real job with a real team.[92]

In some cases, employers will sponsor competitions where contestants (who at this point are not even considered job applicants) vie for attention by going head-to-head in solving certain job-related problems. These sorts of competitions have been common in some industries like architecture and fashion design, but their use is spreading across many other business contexts. These competitions tend to be cost effective in generating a lot of interest, and some have attracted as many as 1,000 contestants who bring their talents to bear on specific problems faced by the employing organization.[93] Competitions are particularly well-suited for assessing and "discovering" young people who may not have extended track records or portfolios to evaluate.

As part of its own fight in the war for talent, Google sponsors an event called "Google Code Jam," which attracts more than 10,000 contestants a year from all over the world. This one-day competition requires contestants work to solve some very difficult programming problems under relatively high levels of time pressure. For example, finalists have to develop software that would perform unique and difficult searches employing a minimum number of "clicks" or develop a complex interactive war game from scratch in under two hours. The winner of the contest receives $7,000

COMPETING THROUGH TECHNOLOGY

New Technology Reignites Double-Barreled Debate

Imagine you wanted to hire someone for a job that demanded a high level of extraversion, and thus, you needed to construct a test that could differentiate a group of job applicants who were total strangers to you. You decide to ask an applicant if he or she agrees with the question, "I would enjoy chatting with a friend at a noisy bar." If you were to show this question to an expert in test validation 10 years ago, this person would immediately recognize this as a double-barreled item and tell you to break this one item into two items—one about "chatting with a friend" and one about "being in a noisy bar." The reason is that there may be people who may enjoy chatting with a friend, but who would not like to do this in a noisy bar, making the response ambiguous. If you were to ask that same expert about that same question today, however, you might get a different answer.

Nearly 80 years ago, a debate was waged in the scientific literature on test construction between Louis Thurstone and Rensis Likert. Thurstone was an advocate of what was called "Ideal Point Theory," that believed that double-barreled items like the one described above are good, because when paired with other double-barreled items like "I would enjoy chatting with someone I just met at a noisy bar" (indicative of higher extraversion) and "I would enjoy chatting with a friend at a quiet café" (indicative of lower extraversion), the items as a set allow you to "zero in on" exactly where a person stands on extraversion with a great deal of precision. In contrast, Likert was an advocate of a theory called "Dominant Response Theory," that believed that people were either high or low on extraversion, and when their responses to a large number of standard items (on five point agree–disagree scales) were averaged, people who were high would endorse more items than people who were low.

If you have ever taken a test like this lately, you know who won this debate, because Dominant Response Theory totally dominates testing and double-barreled items have become nearly extinct. The ubiquitous five-point agree versus disagree format was embraced by experts because the "Likert-scale" approach was simple and efficient. Even though all agreed that the Ideal Point Theory was much more precise at all levels of the trait, the problem was that it took way too many items to "zero in" on the Ideal Point.

Recently, however, the advent of computer adaptive testing has radically changed the balance in this debate. The real-time computing power that is afforded by taking a test online or on a computer allows the test to "serve up" different items, depending upon how one responded to previous items. This means one can ask fewer questions in the process of zeroing in on the Ideal Point. If the test taker looks extraverted based on Item #1, then Item #2 asks a question that requires even higher levels of extraversion to endorse. In contrast, if the test taker looks introverted based on Item #1, then Item #2 asks a question that requires even lower levels of extraversion to endorse. This type of adaptive test can be routinely programmed and is increasingly used for all kinds of traits and abilities in business and military contexts. Louis Thurstone, who died in 1955 and never lived to see a personal computer, would have been pleased.

SOURCES: F. Drasgow, O. S., Chernyshenko, and S. Stark, "75 Years after Likert: Thurstone Was Right!" *Industrial and Organizational Psychology* 3 (2010), pp 465–76; E. Frauenheim, "Personality Tests Adapt to the Times," *Workforce Management*, February 2010, p. 4; T. M. Kantrowitz and K. A. Tuzinski, "The Ideal Point Model in Action: How the Use of Computer Adaptive Personality Scales Benefits Organizations," *Industrial and Organizational Psychology* 3 (2010), pp. 507–10.

and a guaranteed job at Google's prestigious Research and Development Center, but, in fact, Google usually winds up hiring more than half of the 50 finalists each year (but that is not guaranteed). The finalists in this contest represent the best of the best in terms of the world's top programmers, and as Robert Hughes, director of the Code Jam, notes, "Wherever the best talent is, Google wants them."[94]

With all these advantages of work-sample tests come three drawbacks. First, by their very nature the tests are job-specific, so generalizability is low. Second, partly because a new test has to be developed for each job and partly because of their nonstandardized formats, these tests are relatively expensive to develop. It is much more cost-effective to purchase a commercially available cognitive ability test that can be used for a number of different job categories within the company than to develop a test for each job. For this reason, some have rated the utility of cognitive ability tests higher than work-sample tests, despite the latter's higher criterion-related validity. Finally, at least with respect to work-sample tests developed as contests and competitions, these events tend to attract more male applicants than female applicants. In fact, for evening occupations where roughly 50% of the job incumbents are women, only 15% of the people who show up for competitions for such jobs are female, suggesting this is a practice that could easily lead to adverse impact if not carefully monitored.[95]

In the area of managerial selection, work-sample tests are typically the cornerstone in assessment centers. Generically, the term **assessment center** is used to describe a wide variety of specific selection programs that employ multiple selection methods to rate either applicants or job incumbents on their managerial potential. Someone attending an assessment center would typically experience work-sample tests such as an in-basket test and several tests of more general abilities and personality. Because assessment centers employ multiple selection methods, their criterion-related validity tends to be quite high. Assessment centers seem to tap a number of different characteristics, but "problem-solving ability" stands out as probably the most important skill tapped via this method.[96] The idiosyncratic and unique nature of the different exercises, however, has led some to suggest that the exercises themselves should be scored for winners and losers without making any reference to higher order characteristics like skills, abilities, or traits.[97] Research indicates that one of the best combinations of selection methods includes work-sample tests with a highly structured interview and a measure of general cognitive ability. The validity coefficient expected from such a combined battery often exceeds .60.[98]

Assessment Center
A process in which multiple raters evaluate employees' performance on a number of exercises.

HONESTY TESTS AND DRUG TESTS

Many problems that confront society also exist within organizations, which has led to two new kinds of tests: honesty tests and drug-use tests. Many companies formerly employed polygraph tests, or lie detectors, to evaluate job applicants, but this changed with the passage of the Polygraph Act in 1988. This act banned the use of polygraphs in employment screening for most organizations. However, it did not eliminate the problem of theft by employees. As a result, the paper-and-pencil honesty testing industry was born.

Paper-and-pencil honesty tests come in a number of different forms. Some directly emphasize questions dealing with past theft admissions or associations with people who stole from employers. Other items are less direct and tap more basic traits such as social conformity, conscientiousness, or emotional stability.[99] A large-scale independent review of validity studies suggests they can predict both theft and other disruptive behaviors. Another positive feature of these tests is that one does not see large differences attributable to race or sex, so they are not likely to have adverse impact on these demographic groups.[100]

As is the case with measures of personality, some people are concerned that people confronting an honesty test can fake their way to a passing score. The evidence suggests that people instructed to fake their way to a high score (indicating honesty) can do so. However, it is not clear that this affects the validity of the predictions made using such tests. That is, it seems that despite this built-in bias, scores on the test still predict future theft. Thus, the effect of the faking bias is not large enough to detract from the test's validity.[101]

As with theft, there is a growing perception of the problems caused by drug use among employees. The major controversies surrounding drug tests involve not their reliability and validity but whether they represent an invasion of privacy, an unreasonable search and seizure, or a violation of due process. Urinalysis and blood tests are invasive procedures, and accusing someone of drug use is a serious matter. Employers considering the use of drug tests would be well advised to make sure that their drug-testing programs conform to some general rules. First, these tests should be administered systematically to all applicants for the same job. Second, testing seems more defensible for jobs that involve safety hazards associated with failure to perform.[102] Test results should be reported back to the applicant, who should be allowed an avenue of appeal (and perhaps retesting). Tests should be conducted in an environment that is as unintrusive as possible, and results from those tests should be held in strict confidence. Finally, when testing current employees, the program should be part of a wider organizational program that provides rehabilitation counseling.[103]

A Look Back

COMPOSING SUCCESSFUL TEAMS

In the vignette that opened this chapter we saw how the rigorous selection procedures that went into selecting the members of SEAL Team 6 contributed to this group's success, including how this unit helped end the hunt of Osama bin Laden. Although most business organizations do not necessarily deal with life and death tasks as dramatic as this, the decisions that organizations make regarding who is going to be part of the team and who is going to be turned away, are some of the most important decisions that the firm will make in terms of gaining a competitive advantage. Firms that routinely recruit and select the "best of the best," regardless of the occupation leave their competitors with labor-pool leftovers that will constantly limit their ability to compete. This chapter has summarized hundreds of years of research and demonstrated a large and varied set of tactics that firms can use to make the right hiring decisions when it comes to the selection process.

Questions

1. Based on this chapter, what are the best methods of obtaining information about job applicants?
2. What are the best characteristics to look for in applicants, and how does this depend on the nature of the job?
3. If you could use only two of the methods described in this chapter and could assess only two of the characteristics discussed, which would you choose, and why?

 Please see the Video that corresponds to this chapter at www.mhhe.com/noe8e.

SUMMARY

In this chapter we examined the five critical standards with which all personnel selection methods should conform: reliability, validity, generalizability, utility, and legality. We also looked at nine different selection methods currently used in organizations and evaluated each with respect to these five standards. Table 6.4 summarizes these selection methods and can be used as a guide in deciding which test to use for a specific purpose. Although we discussed each type of test individually, it is important to note in closing that there is no need to use only one type of test for any one job. Indeed, managerial assessment centers use many different forms of tests over a two- or three-day period to learn as much as possible about candidates for important executive positions. As a result, highly accurate predictions are often made, and the validity associated with the judicious use of multiple tests is higher than for tests used in isolation.

KEY TERMS

Reliability, 233
Validity, 236
Criterion-related validity, 236
Predictive validation, 237
Concurrent validation, 237

Content validation, 239
Generalizability, 240
Utility, 240
Situational interview, 248
Cognitive ability tests, 253

Verbal comprehension, 253
Quantitative ability, 253
Reasoning ability, 253
Assessment center, 259

DISCUSSION QUESTIONS

1. We examined nine different types of selection methods in this chapter. Assume that you were just rejected for a job based on one of these methods. Obviously, you might be disappointed and angry regardless of what method was used to make this decision, but can you think of two or three methods that might leave you most distressed? In general, why might the acceptability of the test to applicants be an important standard to add to the five we discussed in this chapter?

2. Videotaping applicants in interviews is becoming an increasingly popular means of getting multiple assessments of that individual from different perspectives. Can you think of some reasons why videotaping interviews might also be useful in evaluating the interviewer? What would you look for in an interviewer if you were evaluating one on videotape?

3. Distinguish between concurrent and predictive validation designs, discussing why the latter is preferred over the former. Examine each of the nine selection methods discussed in this chapter and determine which of these would have their validity most and least affected by the type of validation design employed.

4. Some have speculated that in addition to increasing the validity of decisions, employing rigorous selection methods has symbolic value for organizations. What message is sent to applicants about the organization through hiring practices, and how might this message be reinforced by recruitment programs that occur before selection and training programs that occur after selection?

SELF-ASSESSMENT EXERCISE

Reviews of research about personality have identified five common aspects of personality, referred to as the Big Five personality traits. Find out which are your most prominent traits. Read each of the following statements, marking "Yes" if it describes you and "No" if it does not.

1. In conversations I tend to do most of the talking.
2. Often people look to me to make decisions.
3. I am a very active person.
4. I usually seem to be in a hurry.
5. I am dominant, forceful, and assertive.
6. I have a very active imagination.
7. I have an active fantasy life.
8. How I feel about things is important to me.
9. I find it easy to feel myself what others are feeling.

table 6.4

A Summary of Personnel Selection Methods

METHOD	RELIABILITY	VALIDITY	GENERALIZABILITY	UTILITY	LEGALITY
Interviews	Low when unstructured and when assessing nonobservable traits	Low if unstructured and nonbehavioral	Low	Low, especially because of expense	Low because of subjectivity and potential interviewer bias; also, lack of validity makes job-relatedness low
Reference checks	Low, especially when obtained from letters	Low because of lack of range in evaluations	Low	Low, although not expensive to obtain	Those writing letters may be concerned with charges of libel
Biographical information	High test-retest, especially for verifiable information	High criterion-related validity; low in content validity	Usually job-specific, but have been successfully developed for many job types	High; inexpensive way to collect vast amounts of potentially relevant data	May have adverse impact; thus often develop separate scoring keys based on sex or race
Physical ability tests	High	Moderate criterion-related validity; high content validity for some jobs	Low; pertain only to physically demanding jobs	Moderate for some physical jobs; may prevent expensive injuries and disability	Often have adverse impact on women and people with disabilities; need to establish job-relatedness
Cognitive ability tests	High	Moderate criterion-related validity; content validation inappropriate	High; predictive for most jobs, although best for complex jobs	High; low cost and wide application across diverse jobs in companies	Often have adverse impact on race, especially for African Americans, though decreasing over time
Personality inventories	High	Low to moderate criterion-related validity for most traits; content validation inappropriate	Low; few traits predictive for many jobs, except conscientiousness	Low, although inexpensive for jobs where specific traits are relevant	Low because of cultural and sex differences on most traits, and low job-relatedness in general
Work-sample tests	High	High criterion and content validity	Usually job-specific, but have been successfully developed for many job types	High, despite the relatively high cost to develop	High because of low adverse impact and high job-relatedness
Honesty tests	Insufficient independent evidence	Insufficient independent evidence	Insufficient independent evidence	Insufficient independent evidence	Insufficient history of litigation, but will undergo scrutiny
Drug tests	High	High	High	Expensive, but may yield high payoffs for health-related costs	May be challenged on invasion-of-privacy grounds

10. I think it's interesting to learn and develop new hobbies.
11. My first reaction is to trust people.
12. I believe that most persons are basically well intentioned.
13. I'm not crafty or shy.
14. I'd rather not talk about myself and my accomplishments.
15. I'd rather praise others than be praised myself.
16. I come into situations being fully prepared.
17. I pride myself on my sound judgment.
18. I have a lot of self-discipline.
19. I try to do jobs carefully so they don't have to be done again.

20. I like to keep everything in place so I know where it is.
21. I enjoy performing under pressure.
22. I am seldom sad or depressed.
23. I'm an even-tempered person.
24. I am levelheaded in emergencies.
25. I feel I am capable of coping with most of my problems.

The statements are grouped into categories. Statements 1–5 describe extroversion, 6–10 openness to experience, 11–15 agreeableness, 16–20 conscientiousness, and 21–25 emotional stability. The more times you wrote "Yes" for the statements in a category, the more likely you are to have the associated trait.

EXERCISING STRATEGY: WHO IS SCREENING THE SCREENERS?

In May of 2006, after an extensive legal proceeding following the typical procedures for rules of evidence, an administrative law judge for the Department of Labor concluded that Theron Carter, a 61-year-old unemployed truck driver from Michigan, was a hero. Carter was a whistle-blower, bringing to light safety violations at his place of employment that could have cost the lives of many innocent drivers. Despite being told by his supervisor to ignore a series of violations, Carter persisted in his objections, up to the point that he was eventually fired. The judge concluded that Carter's termination was illegal and ordered the firm to pay him damages and back pay. The only problem, however, is that Carter is still unable to obtain work, because despite eliminating the discharge from his record, the background checking industry still has him listed as "a chronic complainer" based on his former supervisor's report.

One can understand why, in an age when employers are constantly seeing and reading stories in the press regarding workplace violence, theft, and fraud, some would feel the need to closely vet each and every employee. This is especially the case since many employers can be held legally responsible for the illegal acts of people they hire via various negligent hiring lawsuits. Under U.S. law, lawsuits claiming negligent hiring are "uncapped," and hence there is no limit to the liability that employers face if found guilty. For this and other reasons, over the last 10 years, the number of employers who conduct routine background checks has gone from 51% to 96%. In fact, demand for this information is so strong that one is seeing unprecedented growth in the employee background checking industry. Among the major players in this industry, in the period between 2007 and 2008, revenue is up over 20% and profits up over 50%. This has attracted a number of new entrants to the industry, and as one would expect, this type of growth in an essentially unregulated industry has led to a number of problems.

Perhaps the biggest problem within this industry over the last 10 years has been the expanding scope of background investigations. In the early days of the industry, screening companies merely searched for objective information related to past criminal history, and perhaps credit history. Increasingly, however, firms are going well beyond this and assembling "digital dossiers" based upon telephone interviews with friends, co-workers, and former bosses. Untrained call-center employees inquire about work habits, personal character, drug and alcohol consumption practices, and just about anything else that the source wants to talk about. Unlike past criminal convictions, however, that are typically handed out only after passing some due process criterion, almost all of these charges are just gossip and hearsay. Thus, in Theron Carter's case, the background screening firm removed his termination from the record because it was court ordered, but still maintained that he was a chronic complainer, a charge they assert was not specifically addressed by the judge.

Lester Rosen, president of the Employment Screening Resources, notes that "essentially this is the Wild, Wild West—an unregulated industry with easy money and, ironically, not a huge emphasis on hiring quality people to do the screening." Most companies compete on speed and price, and not accuracy, which is more difficult to assess. For this reason, Rosen's firm still sticks strictly to criminal record and credit history checks as their service provided, and leaves the collection of all information regarding skills and personalities to more qualified and trained HR specialists. Since organizations are now increasingly being sued for discrimination claims based upon faulty background checks, this might be a good policy for all organizations. At the very least, as a potential job applicant, you might want to check the accuracy of what these companies are saying about you. Most of these firms will share their information they have about you and correct it for a fee. It is again ironic, that the less accurate you suspect the company is, the more you would probably be willing to pay for that service.

Questions

1. What alternative selection procedures discussed in this chapter could an employer use to screen potential "bad actors" that would not involve outsourced background checks?
2. If one is committed to obtaining outsourced background checks, what evidence might one want to collect that would allow an assessment of the value of the information in terms of the criteria (reliability, validity, and so on) covered in this chapter?
3. In today's digitally networked world, in what ways is it easier for HR managers or line managers to do their own homework on applicants that would obviate the need for outsourced background checks?

SOURCES: F. Hanson, "Burden of Proof," *Workforce Management*, February 2010, pp. 27–33; C. Terhune, "The Trouble with Background Checks," *BusinessWeek*, June 9, 2009, p. 58; F. Hanson and G. Hernandez, "Caution amid the Credit Crunch," *Workforce Management*, February 16, 2009, pp. 35–36; A. Hedger, "Three Ways to Improve Your Employee Screening," *Workforce Management*, March 16, 2009, pp. 26–30.

● MANAGING PEOPLE

Mining for Gold: A Network Approach for Creating Criteria

Traditional approaches to validating employment tests and methods have relied on subjective appraisals from supervisors as the primary criterion. A test was valid if it predicted what future supervisors are likely to say about that person after having worked with him or her for a short time. As you might imagine, the perceptions of these supervisors are often biased, unreliable, and based upon incomplete information. Therefore, one might question what the ability to predict actually implies, and that the need for finding some alternative, more reliable, valid, and less biased criterion has been an ongoing concern in the area of human resources.

Increasingly, the combination of social networking software and the technology to analyze data that can be collected by this software, is ushering in a new age of methods to determine employee value. Data mining, that is, the process of electronically going through massive amounts of data generated by networked computers has proven valuable in many areas of business. In the area of operations, it has been used to streamline supply chains. In marketing, it has been used to more effectively target audiences. Now, in the area of human resource management, it is being used to identify who are the most important and valuable employees within the firm.

For example, at Microsoft, they have software that allows them to code who talks to whom, how often, and about what content. This allows them to see who tends to originate ideas (sparkplugs), who seems to build on them and pass them on (superconnectors), and who seems to hold them up (bottlenecks). Deciding who should get credit for a great idea has always been a contentious and controversial process in organizations that rely on subjective appraisals; however with this new "process tracing technology," once the market identifies an idea as a winner, the organization can really go back and objectively determine its source and trajectory.

In addition to tracing specific ideas, this software also, over the longer haul, can be used to help identify who is at the center, and who is at the periphery of the organization's social network. For example, at IBM, someone who is routinely copied on ideas from a large number of people, from a large number of different departments, and from many different sources (supervisors, peers, subordinates, and clients) is identified as someone who must be playing a leadership major role in the organization. Once identified, these people are fast-tracked for future leadership roles and shielded from downsizing efforts such as those that marked the 2008 recession. Although, as is the case with any objective indicator, one might be able to game this system in different ways, in general, this shows the desire that some companies have to go beyond the single subjective impression of a supervisor when it comes to determining the value of each and every employee.

Questions

1. When it comes to validating tests, what type of predictors that we studied in this chapter may be overestimated and underestimated if one relies just on supervisory evaluations as the criterion?
2. When it comes to validating tests, what type of predictors that we studied in this chapter may be overestimated and underestimated if one relies just on social network data like that described above?
3. How might you reconcile differences in assessed performance if these two sources largely disagreed about the value of any one employee, and how would data on traditional predictors of performance help inform this deliberation?

SOURCES: S. Baker, "How Much Is That Worker Worth?" *BusinessWeek*, March 23, 2009, pp. 46–48; S. Baker, "Putting a Price on Social Networks," *BusinessWeek*, April 8, 2009, pp. 45–47; S. Baker, "Reading the Body Language of Leadership," *BusinessWeek*, March 30, 2009, p. 48.

TWITTER FOCUS: KINAXIS CHOOSES SALES REPS WITH PERSONALITY

Using Twitter, continue the conversation about personnel selection and placement by reading the Kinaxis case at www.mhhe.com/noe8e.

Kinaxis is a global software company specializing in supply-chain management that needed to hire a sales team to serve North American clients. After receiving more than 100 résumés for the openings, the sales director selected 20 candidates for first-round interviews. The interview process helped him cut the list to 10, but he

needed another way to narrow the number of candidates. The company hired a firm to administer personality testing to the remaining candidates, which helped identify the four persons best suited for the sales positions.

Engage with your classmates and instructor via Twitter to chat about Kinaxis's hiring strategy using the case questions posted on the Noe website. Don't have a Twitter account yet? See the instructions for getting started on the Online Learning Center.

NOTES

1. J. Welch and S. Welch, "So Many CEO's Get This Wrong," *BusinessWeek,* July 17, 2006, p. 92.
2. V. Wadhwa, "America's Immigrant Brain Drain," *BusinessWeek,* March 16, 2009, p. 68.
3. K. G. Melchers, N. Lienhardt, M. Von Aartburg, and M. Kleinmann, "Is More Structure Really Better? A Comparison of Frame of Reference Training and Descriptively Anchored Rating Scales to Improve Interviewers' Rating Quality," *Personnel Psychology* 64 (2011), pp. 53–87.
4. F. Lievens, T. Buyse, and P. R. Sackett, "Retest Effects in Operational Selection Settings: Development and Test of a Framework," *Personnel Psychology* 58 (2005), pp. 981–1007.
5. C. H. Van Iddekinge and R. E. Ployhart, "Developments in the Criterion-Related Validation of Selection Procedures: A Critical Review and Recommendations for Practice," *Personnel Psychology* 61 (2008), pp. 871–925.
6. M. V. Rafter, "Assessment Providers Scoring Well," *Workforce Management,* January 19, 2009, pp. 24–25.
7. F. Schmidt, H. Le, I. S. Oh, and J. Shaffer, "General Mental Ability, Job Performance, and Red Herrings: Responses to Osterman, Hauser, and Schmitt," *Academy of Management Perspectives* 21 (2007), pp. 64–76.
8. A. Eccles, "How to Get a Job," *Fortune,* April 13, 2009, pp. 49–56.
9. A. Meisler, "Negative Results," *Workforce,* October 2003, pp. 35–40.
10. B. Helm, "Is Madison Avenue Too White?" *Bloomberg Businessweek,* March 8, 2010, p. 28.
11. O. Kinnander and K. McLaughlin, "Wal-Mart Faces the Big Box of Class Actions," *Bloomberg Businessweek,* March 28, 2011, pp. 31–34.
12. M. Trottman, "Charges of Bias at Work Hit Record," *The Wall Street Journal,* January 12, 2011, p. C1.
13. M. Schoeff, "Walgreen Suit Reflects EEOC's Latest Strategy," *Workforce Management,* March 16, 2007, p. 8.
14. P. Roth, P. Bobko, L. McFarland, and M. Buster, "Work Sample Tests in Personnel Selection: A Meta-analysis of Black-White Differences in Overall Exercise Scores," *Personnel Psychology* 61 (2008), pp. 637–61.
15. R. E. Ployhart and B. C. Holtz, "The Diversity-Validity Dilemma: Strategies for Reducing Racioethnic and Sex Group Differences and Adverse Impact in Selection," *Personnel Psychology* 61 (2008), pp. 153–72.
16. G. Flynn, "The Reverse Discrimination Trap," *Workforce,* June 2003, pp. 106–7.

17. M. E. Heilman, W. S. Battle, C. E. Keller, and R. A. Lee, "Type of Affirmative Action Policy: A Determinant of Reactions to Sex-Based Preferential Selection," *Journal of Applied Psychology* 83 (1998), pp. 190–205.
18. D. A. Newman and J. S. Lyon, "Recruitment Efforts to Reduce Adverse Impact: Targeted Recruiting for Personality, Cognitive Ability and Diversity," *Journal of Applied Psychology* 94 (2009), pp. 298–317.
19. D. M. Finch, B. D. Edwards, and J. C. Wallace, "Multistage Selection Strategies: Simulating the Effects of Adverse Impact and Expected Performance for Various Predictor Combinations," *Journal of Applied Psychology* 94 (2009), pp. 318–40.
20. A. S. Levi and Y. Fried, "Differences between African Americans and Whites in Reactions to Affirmative Action Programs in Training, Promotion, and Layoffs," *Journal of Applied Psychology* 93 (2008), pp. 1118–29.
21. F. Hanson, "Diversity of a Different Color," *Workforce Management,* June 2010, pp. 21–24.
22. L. T. Cullen, "The Diversity Delusion," *Time,* May 2007, p. 45.
23. E. B. King and A. S. Ahmad, "An Experimental Field Study of Interpersonal Discrimination toward Muslim Job Applicants," *Personnel Psychology* 63 (2010), pp. 881–906.
24. A. Gutman, "Smith versus City of Jackson: Adverse Impact in the ADEA (Well Sort Of)," *Industrial Psychologist,* July 2005, pp. 31–32.
25. J. Mullich, "Hiring without Limits," *Workforce,* June 2002, pp. 53–58.
26. M. C. Nazario, "Non-disabled Job Seekers Taking Jobs of Disabled," CNN.com, March 18, 2009.
27. L. T. Cullen, "The Diversity Delusion," *Time,* May 7, 2007, p. 45.
28. R. A. Posthuma, F. R. Morgeson, and M. A. Campion, "Beyond Employment Interview Validity: A Comprehensive Narrative Review of Recent Research and Trends over Time," *Personnel Psychology* 55 (2002), pp. 1–81.
29. C. H. Middendorf and T. H. Macan, "Note-Taking in the Interview: Effects on Recall and Judgments," *Journal of Applied Psychology* 87 (2002), pp. 293–303.
30. M. A. McDaniel, F. P. Morgeson, E. B. Finnegan, M. A. Campion, and E. P. Braverman, "Use of Situational Judgment Tests to Predict Job Performance: A Clarification of the Literature," *Journal of Applied Psychology* 86 (2001), pp. 730–40.
31. A. P. J. Ellis, B. J. West, A. M. Ryan, and R. P. DeShon, "The Use of Impression Management Tactics in Structured

Interviews: A Function of Question Type?" *Journal of Applied Psychology* 87 (2002), pp. 1200–8.

32. W. C. Byham, "Can You Interview for Integrity?" *Across the Board*, March 2004, pp. 34–38.

33. A. Bryant, "Google's Quest to Build a Better Boss," *The New York Times*, March 12, 2011, p. C1.

34. D. Middleton, "Non-Campus Recruiting," *The Wall Street Journal*, February 23, 2010, p. D4.

35. A. Dizik, "Wooing Job Recruiters with Video Resumes," *The Wall Street Journal*, May 2010, p. D4.

36. J. S. Lublin, "What Won't You Do for a Job," *The Wall Street Journal*, June 2, 2009, p. B1.

37. C. Tuna, "How to Spot Resume Fraud," *The Wall Street Journal*, November 13, 2008, p. C1.

38. J. Twist, "Pitfalls of Work Blogs," *BBC News*, May 15, 2006, p. 1.

39. M. Conlin, "You Are What You Post," *BusinessWeek*, March 27, 2006, pp. 52–53.

40. D. Stead, "Just a Click Away," *BusinessWeek*, June 26, 2006, p. 9.

41. S. F. Dingfelder, "To Tell the Truth," *Monitor on Psychology*, March 2004, pp. 22–23.

42. A. Davis, J. Pereira, and W. M. Bulkeley, "Security Concerns Bring Focus on Translating Body Language," *The Wall Street Journal*, August 15, 2002, pp. A1–A3.

43. J. S. Lublin, "Bulletproofing Your References in the Hunt for a New Job," *The Wall Street Journal*, April 7, 2009, p. C1.

44. M. R. Barrick and R. D. Zimmerman, "Reducing Voluntary Turnover through Selection," *Journal of Applied Psychology* 90 (2005), pp. 159–66.

45. J. Bos, "Five Trends in Employee Screening: Is Your Company Prepared?" *Workforce Management*, March 2010, pp. 28–30.

46. S. Pustizzi, "Résumé Fraud Gets Slicker and Easier," CNN.com, March 11, 2004, p. 1.

47. N. Schmitt, F. L. Oswald, B. H. Kim, M. A. Gillespie, L. J. Ramsey, and T. Y. Yoo, "The Impact of Elaboration on Socially Desirable Responding and the Validity of Biodata Measures," *Journal of Applied Psychology* 88 (2003), pp. 979–88.

48. N. Schmitt and C. Kunce, "The Effects of Required Elaboration of Answers to Biodata Questions," *Personnel Psychology* 55 (2002), pp. 569–87.

49. F. Hanson, "Worker Screening Limited Overseas," *Workforce Management*, February 16, 2009, p. 37.

50. F. Hanson and G. Hernandez, "Caution amid the Credit Crunch," *Workforce Management*, February 16, 2009, pp. 35–36;

51. C. Terhune, "The Trouble with Background Checks," *BusinessWeek*, June 9, 2009, p. 58.

52. M. Barnekow-Bergkvist, U. Aasa, K. A. Angquist, and H. Johansson, "Prediction of Development of Fatigue during a Simulated Ambulance Work Task from Physical Performance Tests," *Ergonomics* 47 (2004), pp. 1238–50.

53. J. Hogan, "Structure of Physical Performance in Occupational Tasks," *Journal of Applied Psychology* 76 (1991), pp. 495–507.

54. N. D. Henderson, "Predicting Long-term Firefighter Performance from Measures of Cognitive Ability and Physical Ability Measures," *Personnel Psychology* 63 (2010), pp. 999–1039.

55. J. Hogan, "Physical Abilities," in *Handbook of Industrial & Organizational Psychology*, 2nd ed., ed. M. D. Dunnette and L. M. Hough (Palo Alto, CA: Consulting Psychologists Press, 1991).

56. M. Schoeff, "Skill Levels of U.S. Grads Leave Employers Cold," *Workforce Management*, April 7, 2007, p. 14.

57. J. Smerd, "New Workers Sorely Lacking Literacy Skills," *Workforce Management*, December 10, 2007, pp. 6.

58. J. F. Salagado, N. Anderson, S. Moscoso, C. Bertua, and F. De Fruyt, "International Validity Generalization of GMA and Cognitive Abilities: A European Community Meta-Analysis," *Personnel Psychology* 56 (2003), pp. 573–605.

59. J. A. LePine, J. A. Colquitt, and A. Erez, "Adaptability to Changing Task Contexts: Effects of General Cognitive Ability, Conscientiousness, and Openness to Experience," *Personnel Psychology* 53 (2000), pp. 563–93.

60. P. Burrows, "Einstein Never Tweeted," *Bloomberg Businessweek*, June 7, 2010, pp. 89–91.

61. R. J. Barro, "Why Colleges Shouldn't Dump the SAT," *BusinessWeek*, April 9, 2001, p. 20.

62. M. A. Campion, J. L. Outtz, S. Zedeck, F. S. Schmidt, J. E. Kehoe, K. R. Murphy, and R. M. Guion, "The Controversy over Score Banding in Personnel Selection: Answers to 10 Key Questions," *Personnel Psychology* 54 (2001), pp. 149–85.

63. F. P. Morgeson, M. A. Campion, R. L. Dipboye, J. R. Hollenbeck, K. R. Murphy, and N. Schmitt, "Reconsidering the Use of Personality Tests in Personnel Selection Contexts," *Personnel Psychology* 60 (2007), pp. 683–729.

64. E. Freudenheim, "Personality Testing Controversial, but Poised to Take Off," *Workforce Management*, August 14, 2006, p. 38.

65. V. Knight, "Personality Tests as Hiring Tools," *The Wall Street Journal*, March 15, 2006, p. B1.

66. G. L. Steward, I. S. Fulmer, and M. R. Barrick, "An Exploration of Member Roles as a Multilevel Linking Mechanism for Individual Traits and Team Outcomes," *Personnel Psychology* 58 (2005), pp. 343–65.

67. M. Mount, R. Ilies, and E. Johnson, "Relationship of Personality Traits and Counterproductive Work Behaviors: The Mediation Effects of Job Satisfaction," *Personnel Psychology* 59 (2006), pp. 591–622.

68. S. E. Humphrey, J. R. Hollenbeck, C. J. Meyer, and D. R. Ilgen, "Trait Configurations in Self-managed Teams: A Conceptual Examination of the Use of Seeding for Maximizing and Minimizing Trait Variance in Teams," *Journal of Applied Psychology* 92 (2007), pp. 885–92.

69. A. Hedger, "Employee Screening: Common Challenges, Smart Solutions," *Workforce Management*, March 17, 2008, pp. 39–46.

70. J. Welch and S. Welch, "Team Building: Right and Wrong," *BusinessWeek*, November 24, 2008, p. 130.

71. Y. J. Dreazen and S. Gorman, "Obama National Security Team Set," *The Wall Street Journal*, December 1, 2008, p. A1.

72. J. Williams, "Will Lincoln's 'Team of Rivals' Play Today?" *The Boston Globe*, November 21, 2008, p. A1.

73. A. C. Homan, D. van Knippenberg, G. A. van Kleff, and C. K. W. De Dreu, "Bridging Faultlines by Valuing Diversity: Diversity Beliefs, Information Elaboration, and Performance in Diverse Work Groups," *Journal of Applied Psychology* 92 (2007), pp. 1189–99.

74. D. Goleman, "Sometimes, EQ Is More Important than IQ," CNN.com, January 14, 2005, p. 1.

75. R. D. Roberts, G. Mathews, and M. Zeidner, "Emotional Intelligence: Muddling through Theory and Measurement," *Industrial and Organizational Psychology* 3 (2010), pp. 140–44.

76. D. L. Joseph and D. A. Newman, "Emotional Intelligence: An Integrative Meta-Analysis and Cascading Model," *Journal of Applied Psychology* 95 (2010), pp. 54–78.

77. D. Brady, "Can GE Still Manage?" *Bloomberg Businessweek*, April 25, 2010, pp. 27–32.

78. M. A. Shaffer, D. A. Harrison, H. Gregersen, J. S. Black, L. A. Ferzandi, "You Can Take It With You: Individual

Differences and Expatriate Effectiveness," *Journal of Applied Psychology* 91 (2006), pp. 109–25.

79. J. M. Hunthausen, D. M. Truxillo, T. N. Bauer, and L. B. Hammer, "A Field Study of Frame of Reference Effects on Personality Test Validity," *Journal of Applied Psychology* 88 (2003), pp. 545–51.

80. H. Le, I. S. Oh, S. B. Robbins, R. Ilies, E. Holland, and P. Westrick, "Too Much of a Good Thing? Curvilinear Relationship between Personality Traits and Job Performance," *Journal of Applied Psychology* 96 (2011), pp. 113–33.

81. B. Erdogan, T. N. Bauer, J. M. Peiro, and D. M. Truxillo, "Overqualified Employees: Making the Best of a Potentially Bad Situation for Individuals and Organizations," *Industrial and Organizational Psychology* 4 (2011), pp. 215–32.

82. S. A. Birkland, T. M. Manson, J. L. Kisamore, M. T. Brannick, and M. A. Smith, "Faking on Personality Measures," *International Journal of Selection and Assessment* 14 (December 2006), pp. 317–35.

83. J. P. Hausknecht, "Candidate Persistence and Personality Test Practice Effects: Implications for Staffing System Management," *Personnel Psychology* 63 (2010), pp. 299–324.

84. N. L. Vasilopoulos, J. M. Cucina, and J. M. McElreath, "Do Warnings of Response Verification Moderate the Relationship between Personality and Cognitive Ability?" *Journal of Applied Psychology* 90 (2005), pp. 306–22.

85. C. H. Van Iddekinge, P. H. Raymark, and P. L. Roth, "Assessing Personality with a Structured Employment Interview: Construct-Related Validity and Susceptibility to Response Inflation," *Journal of Applied Psychology* 90 (2005), pp. 536–52.

86. R. Mueller-Hanson, E. D. Heggestad, and G. C. Thornton, "Faking and Selection: Considering the Use of Personality from Select-In and Select-Out Perspectives," *Journal of Applied Psychology* 88 (2003), pp. 348–55.

87. C. Palmeri, "Putting Managers to the Test," *BusinessWeek*, November 20, 2006, p. 82.

88. C. Winkler, "Job Tryouts Go Virtual: Online Job Simulations Provide Sophisticated Candidate Assessments," *HR Magazine*, September 2006, pp. 10–15.

89. M. S. Christian, B. D. Edwards, and J. C. Bradley, "Situational Judgment Tests: Constructs Assessed and a Meta-Analysis of Their Criterion-Related Validities," *Personnel Psychology* 63 (2010), pp. 83–117.

90. E. White, "Walk a Mile in My Shoes," *The Wall Street Journal*, January 16, 2006, p. B3.

91. A. Hedger, "Six Ways to Strengthen Staffing," *Workforce Management*, January 15, 2007.

92. M. Conlin, "Test-Drives in the C-Suite," *BusinessWeek*, December, 19, 2009, p. 54.

93. K. Maher, "Win in a Competition, Land on Square that Offers Job," *The Wall Street Journal*, June 1, 2004, p. B10.

94. J. Puliyenthuruthel, "How Google Searches—For Talent," *BusinessWeek*, April 11, 2005, pp. 32–34.

95. K. E. Klein, "Business Plan Contests: Where Are the Women?" *Bloomberg Businessweek*, February 14, 2011, pp. 48–49.

96. W. Arthur, E. A. Day, T. L. McNelly, and P. S. Edens, "Meta-Analysis of the Criterion-Related Validity of Assessment Center Dimensions," *Personnel Psychology* 56 (2003), pp. 125–54.

97. C. E. Lance, T. A. Lambert, A. G. Gewin, F. Lievens, and J. M. Conway, "Revised Estimates of Dimension and Exercise Variance Components in Assessment Center Postexercise Dimension Ratings," *Journal of Applied Psychology* 89 (2004), pp. 377–85.

98. F. L. Schmidt and J. E. Hunter, "The Validity and Utility of Selection Methods in Personnel Psychology: Practical and Theoretical Implications of 85 Years of Research Findings," *Psychological Bulletin* 124 (1998), pp. 262–74.

99. J. E. Wanek, P. R. Sackett, and D. S. Ones, "Toward an Understanding of Integrity Test Similarities and Differences: An Item-Level Analysis of Seven Tests," *Personnel Psychology* 56 (2003), pp. 873–94.

100. D. S. Ones and C. Viswesvaran, "Gender, Age, and Race Differences on Overt Integrity Tests: Results across Four Large-Scale Job Applicant Data Sets," *Journal of Applied Psychology* 83 (1998), pp. 35–42.

101. M. R. Cunningham, D. T. Wong, and A. P. Barbee, "Self-Presentation Dynamics on Overt Integrity Tests: Experimental Studies of the Reid Report," *Journal of Applied Psychology* 79 (1994), pp. 643–58.

102. M. E. Paronto, D. M. Truxillo, T. N. Bauer, and M. C. Leo, "Drug Testing, Drug Treatment, and Marijuana Use: A Fairness Perspective," *Journal of Applied Psychology* 87 (2002), pp. 1159–66.

103. K. R. Murphy, G. C. Thornton, and D. H. Reynolds, "College Students' Attitudes toward Drug Testing Programs," *Personnel Psychology* 43 (1990), pp. 615–31.

CHAPTER

7

Training

Training Leads to Clean Cars, Satisfied Customers, and Engaged Employees at Mike's Carwash Inc.

Mike's Carwash, based in Indianapolis, Indiana, is a privately owned chain of car washes that has 37 locations in Indiana and Ohio with 650 employees. Opened in 1948, the first Mike's was called "Mike's Minit Man Carwash," named after the type of equipment originally used. Mike's has a reputation for great and speedy service and continues to expand to new locations. Mike's Carwashes are automated and feature equipment systems and technology developed by Mike's employees. Mike's credits some of its success to the family's business smarts but believes that most of its success comes from its employees and its hiring and training practices. Mike's original founders, Joe and Ed Dahm, were known to tell employees that the company was truly in the people business but it just happened to wash cars.

Customer satisfaction is very important to Mike's with the emphasis placed on repeat business by serving customers so they will come back again. The biggest challenge that Mike's faces is providing a consistent enjoyable customer experience. Mike's is constantly trying to improve the customer experience through innovation and new ideas. If a new idea works it is implemented in all locations. Mike's believes that the only way to provide a consistent customer experience is through finding great employees, retaining them, and helping them develop. The company website explains that it is "notoriously picky" when it comes to hiring. For every 50 people Mike's considered hiring, just one is hired. Mike's feels that it is easy to teach the mechanics of how to perform a job, but it is much more difficult to teach someone to care about customers. Also, because about half of promotions to managerial positions come from current employees, Mike's is looking for employees who intend to stay with the company. As a result, the hiring process focuses on identifying employees who have a positive attitude, a desire to work with people, a willingness to go out of their way to please customers, and leadership qualities. To identify new employees with these characteristics, job applicants participate in multiple interviews, pre-employment testing, thorough reference checks, criminal background checks, and drug testing.

Mike's retains and engages its employees through a number of HR practices. Each employee has a development plan and receives performance appraisals twice each year. New employee training involves familiarizing them with best practices and how to help customers in different situations that they will encounter at the car wash. Before employees wait on their first customer they receive two days of orientation and participate in workshops that all focus on customer service, how to treat customers, how to recover from service errors and mistakes, and how to deal with difficult customers. Mike's also provides training to help employees advance in the company. The career path from hourly associate to supervisor to shift manager to assistant manager is well-defined. Movement on the career path is possible through good performance and completing internal certifications that include up to 12 weeks of training and three exams requiring passing grades of at least 80%. Employee engagement and satisfaction is measured by semiannual surveys as well as information gathered from employees who are leaving Mike's. Employees play an important role in the choice and design of training and development activities. A 15- to 20-person team consisting of members who have been nominated by their store manager serve a one-year term as subject matter experts in helping to develop new and modify existing training programs. Team members also are the first trainees in new programs, providing feedback about needed changes and feedback on program effectiveness.

In addition to its regular training programs for new employees and certification programs for advancement, Mike's has developed programs to meet emerging business needs. The economic recession resulted in a decrease in the volume of customers Mike's served as well as revenue. As a result, Mike's recognized the need to increase the spending of its customers by making sure that employees made them aware of value-added services such as underbody washes, tire treatments, and clearcoat. To do this, Mike's developed an online training module and trained managers to encourage employees to complete the training and practice using the selling skills at monthly employee meetings. Mike's recognizes the important role that managers play in helping employees learn. At Mike's managers need to actively support and help deliver training. They are held accountable for training and developing employees in order to advance and succeed. In this program, managers were taught how to identify weaknesses in employees' service recommendation techniques and use weekly coaching sessions to enhance them. Managers were also encouraged to observe and document employees making service recommendations to customers and to provide them with feedback. The results of this program were positive: overall revenue, revenue per customer, customer satisfaction, and mystery shopper scores all increased.

Another business issue that Mike's uses training to resolve is how to maintain a consistent corporate culture across its 37 locations. To address this challenge, Mike's created "In the Loop," a weekly video communication that is shown on a computer terminal in each location. Each 10-minute segment is used to deliver training content, recognize employee and store performance, communicate to employees, and share best practices. Regularly on the video the CEO shares a letter from a satisfied customer and discusses the specific behaviors that the customer experienced that exemplifies Mike's customer service values. Since the development of the video Mike's has seen an increase of more than 100% in the number of positive customer letters, comment cards, and website contacts.

SOURCE: Based on J. Salopek, "Learning-Assisted Service," *T + D*, October 2010, pp. 40–42; website for Mike's Carwash at www.mikescarwash.com; and T. Jones, "Inner Strength," *Modern Car Magazine*, April 2008, pp. 48–53.

Introduction

As the chapter opener shows, training contributes to Mike's Carwash's focus on its employees and customers. Training helps Mike's employees develop skills they need to succeed in their current jobs and develop for future positions. From Mike's perspective, training is strategic because it leads to consistent service that attracts and retains customers, high-quality employees, and positive revenues. Mike's Carwash recognizes that there is stiff competition for consumers' disposable income—success requires smart, motivated employees who can delight customers.

Why is the emphasis on strategic training important? Companies are in business to make money, and every business function is under pressure to show how it contributes to business success or face spending cuts and even outsourcing. To contribute to a company's success, training activities should help the company achieve its business strategy. (Consider how Mike's training contributed to development of employees selling skills).

There is both a direct and an indirect link between training and business strategy and goals. Training can help employees develop skills needed to perform their jobs, which directly affects the business. Giving employees opportunities to learn and develop creates a positive work environment, which supports the business strategy by attracting talented employees as well as motivating and retaining current employees.

Why do Mike's Carwash and many other companies believe that an investment in training can help them gain a competitive advantage? Training can

- Increase employees' knowledge of foreign competitors and cultures, which is critical for success in foreign markets.
- Help ensure that employees have the basic skills to work with new technology, such as robots and computer-assisted manufacturing processes.
- Help employees understand how to work effectively in teams to contribute to product and service quality.
- Ensure that the company's culture emphasizes innovation, creativity, and learning.
- Ensure employment security by providing new ways for employees to contribute to the company when their jobs change, their interests change, or their skills become obsolete.
- Prepare employees to accept and work more effectively with each other, particularly with minorities and women.[1]

In this chapter, we emphasize the conditions through which training practices can help companies gain competitive advantage and how managers can contribute to effective training and other learning intiatives. The chapter begins by discussing a systematic and effective approach to training design. Next we review training methods and training evaluation. The chapter concludes with a discussion of training issues including cross-cultural preparation, managing diversity, and socializing employees.

Training: Its Role in Continuous Learning and Competitive Advantage

As we discussed in Chapter 1, intangible assets including human capital, customer capital, social capital, and intellectual capital help companies gain competitive advantage. Recognizing that formal training, informal learning, and knowledge management are important for the development of intangible assets, many companies now consider training one part of a larger emphasis on continuous learning. Figure 7.1 shows that formal training and development, informal learning, and knowledge management are the key features of a continuous learning philosophy that focuses on performance and supports the business strategy. **Continuous learning** refers to a learning system that requires employees to understand the entire work system and they are expected to acquire new skills, apply them on the job, and share what they have learned with other employees.[2]

Training refers to a planned effort by a company to facilitate learning of job-related competencies, knowledge, skills, and behaviors by employees. The goal of training is for employees to master the knowledge, skills, and behaviors emphasized in training and apply them to their day-to-day activities. Traditionally, companies have relied on formal training through a course, program, or event to teach employees the knowledge, skills, and behaviors they need to successfully perform their jobs. **Formal training** refers to training and development programs, courses, and events that are developed and organized by the company. Typically employees are required to attend or complete these programs, which can include face-to-face training programs (such as instructor-led courses) as well as online programs. U.S. companies make substantial

LO 7-1
Discuss how training, informal learning, and knowledge management can contribute to continuous learning and companies' business strategy.

Continuous Learning
A learning system that requires employees to understand the entire work process and expects them to acquire new skills, apply them on the job, and share what they have learned with other employees.

Training
A planned effort to facilitate the learning of job-related knowledge, skills, and behavior by employees.

Formal Training
Training and development programs and courses that are developed and organized by the company.

figure 7.1
Key Features of
Continuous Learning

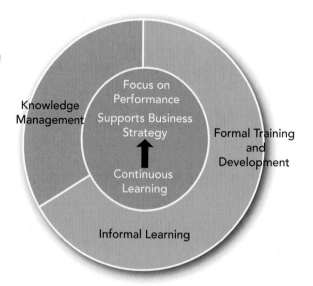

estimates in formal training. One estimate is that in 2009 U.S. organizations spent an estimated $126 billion on formal employee training and development.[3] We will discuss development in Chapter 9, "Employee Development."

Despite companies' significant investments in formal training and development activities, informal learning is also important for facilitating knowledge and skill acquisition.[4] **Informal learning** refers to learning that is learner initiated, involves action and doing, is motivated by an intent to develop, and does not occur in a formal learning setting.[5] Informal learning occurs without an instructor, and its breadth, depth, and timing are controlled by the employee. It occurs on an as-needed basis and may involve an employee learning alone or through face-to-face or technology-aided social interactions. Informal learning can occur through many different ways, including casual unplanned interactions with peers, e-mail, informal mentoring, or company-developed or publicly available social networking websites such as Twitter or Facebook. The application of social media from a marketing strategy to a learning strategy and the availability of Web 2.0 technologies such as social networks, micro-blogs, and wikis allow employees easy access to social learning through collaboration and sharing with one or two or more people.[6] One estimate is that informal learning may account for up to 75% of learning within organizations!

Both formal training and informal learning contribute to the development of intangible assets but especially human capital. Human capital includes knowledge (know what), advanced skills (know how), system understanding and creativity (know why), as well as motivation to deliver high-quality products and services (care why).[7] One reason why informal learning may be especially important is that it may lead to the effective development of *tacit* knowledge, which can be contrasted with *explicit* knowledge.[8] **Explicit knowledge** refers to knowledge that is well documented, easily articulated, and easily transferred from person to person. Examples of explicit knowledge include processes, checklists, flowcharts, formulas, and definitions. Explicit knowledge tends to be the primary focus of formal training. **Tacit knowledge** refers to personal knowledge based on individual experiences that make it difficult to codify. It is best acquired through informal learning. The characteristics of the formal training environment may limit the extent to which tacit knowledge can be acquired, such as the relatively short duration of classroom or online training and limited opportunities

Informal Learning
Learning that is learner initiated, involves action and doing, is motivated by an intent to develop, and does not occur in a formal learning setting.

Explicit Knowledge
Knowledge that is well documented and easily transferred to other persons.

Tacit Knowledge
Knowledge based on personal experience that is difficult to codify.

for practice. Thus, informal learning is central to the development of tacit knowledge. Well-designed formal training programs can help employees acquire explicit knowledge. But to acquire tacit knowledge employees need to interact with peers, colleagues, and experts and have learning experiences that are not usually found in formal training. Informal learning does not replace formal training. Formal training is still needed to prepare employees for their jobs and help them progress to future positions. Informal learning complements training by helping employees gain tacit knowledge that formal training cannot provide.

Knowledge management refers to the process of enhancing company performance by designing and implementing tools, processes, systems, structures, and cultures to improve the creation, sharing, and use of knowledge.[9] Knowledge management contributes to informal learning. For example, Cerner Corporation, a global technology company in Kansas City, Missouri, developed uCern, a knowledge-sharing system for employees and clients to share their knowledge about solutions, projects, and professional interests.[10] Caterpillar Inc. moved toward becoming a continuous learning organization with the help of knowledge management.[11] Thirty years ago Caterpillar Inc., a manufacturer of construction and mining equipment, engines, and gas turbines, had most of its value in plant and equipment. Today, intangible assets account for most of the company's value. Caterpillar's web-based knowledge management system known as Knowledge Network has thousands of communities of practice. They range in size from small teams to hundreds of employees across the world. The communities of practice are useful for employees to gain both explicit and tacit knowledge. They are used to distribute information, post questions, and provide space for reference materials. One community of practice focused on bolted joints and fasteners. This gives specialized engineers who generally work alone in manufacturing facilities the ability to ask other engineers questions or get second opinions on designs and problems. The community of practice has resulted in improved decision making, increased collaboration and teamwork, and better product design and development. For example, members of the Bolted Joints and Fastener Community and the Dealer Service Training Community saved more than $1.5 million from online discussions.

It is important for all aspects of continuous learning, including training, knowledge management, and informal learning, to contribute to and support the business strategy. Continuous learning needs to address performance issues that lead to improved business results. To do so requires that the emphasis on continuous learning aligns with the business strategy, has visible support from senior managers and involves leaders as instructors and teachers, creates a culture or work environment that encourages learning, provides a wide range of learning opportunities including training, informal learning, knowledge management, and employee development, uses traditional methods and innovative technologies to design and deliver learning, and measures the effectiveness and overall business impact of learning.[12]

Campbell's Soup Company is a good example of a company that has embraced a continuous learning philosophy and learning that supports the business strategy.[13] Campbell's is the world's largest soup maker but it is also growing business in healthy beverages (V8 brand) and baked snacks (Pepperidge Farms). Campbell's is currently expanding into Russia and China. In 2000, Campbell's lost about 50% of its market value in one year. A new CEO was hired, Doug Conant, to transform and revitalize the company. The new CEO created the "Campbell's Success Model." The model focuses on winning in the workplace, which will lead to winning in the marketplace, which in turns leads to winning in the community, creating shareholder value, and making a better world. Conant also established operating principles, one of which

Knowledge Management
Process of enhancing company performance by using tools, processes, systems, and cultures to improve the creation, sharing, and use of knowledge.

was the "Campbell Promise." This means that the company needs to first value its employees before they will value the company and its agenda. Campbell's mission is to build the world's most extraordinary food company by nourishing people's lives everywhere, every day.

Conant's learning agenda involved rebuilding training and development by creating a leadership development model. The leadership model includes: inspire trust, create direction, drive organizational alignment, build organizational vitality, execute with excellence, and produce extraordinary results. Developing leaders is seen as strategically important because building an outstanding food company requires outstanding leaders. The CEO Institute was created to develop leadership skills of a cross-section of high-performing experienced and new managers. Campbell's University was created for training and development of all employees. Campbell encourages all employees from individual contributors to senior leaders to learn and grow personally and professionally. Campbell's University includes classrooms and breakout rooms for training and development activities as well as the capability to do virtual training to most of the company's locations around the world. Classes include finance, marketing, and other functional areas as well as the business benefits of diversity and inclusion. Programs and initiatives include mentoring, 360 feedback tools, tuition assistance, and leadership development programs for manufacturing supervisors, general managers, and senior leaders. All employees have a training agenda. This fits the company's mission of building the world's most extraordinary food company by nourishing people's lives every day including its employees. Campbell's believes that the more training and development opportunities provided to employees, the more engaged in work they become. Employee engagement leads to better performance in their roles and better performance for the company in the marketplace.

However, Conant believes that training and development involves more than just courses. It also needs to involve development planning. As a result, employees create a development plan with their managers that includes one or two development issues they want to work on. Conant personally spends time on development plans for Campbell's higher-level managers. He loves to read and learn and believes that for Campbell's to be successful it needs to have a culture that values learning.

⬤ Designing Effective Formal Training Activities

LO 7-2
Explain the role of the manager in identifying training needs and supporting training on the job.

Training Design Process
A systematic approach for developing training programs.

A key characteristic of training activities that contribute to competitiveness is that they are designed according to the instructional design process.[14] **Training design process** refers to a systematic approach for developing training programs. Instructional System Design (ISD) and the ADDIE model (analysis, design, development, implementation, evaluation) are two specific types of training design processes you may know. Table 7.1 presents the six steps of this process, which emphasizes that effective training practices involve more than just choosing the most popular or colorful training method.

Step 1 is to assess needs to determine if training is needed. Step 2 involves ensuring that employees have the motivation and basic skills to master training content. Step 3 addresses whether the training session (or the learning environment) has the factors necessary for learning to occur. Step 4 is to ensure that trainees apply the content of training to their jobs. This requires support from managers and peers for the use of training content on the job as well as getting the employee to understand how to take personal responsibility for skill improvement. Step 5 involves choosing

table 7.1

The Training Process

1. Needs assessment
   - Organizational analysis
   - Person analysis
   - Task analysis
2. Ensuring employees' readiness for training
   - Attitudes and motivation
   - Basic skills
3. Creating a learning environment
   - Identification of learning objectives and training outcomes
   - Meaningful material
   - Practice
   - Feedback
   - Observation of others
   - Administering and coordinating program
4. Ensuring transfer of training
   - Self-management strategies
   - Peer and manager support
5. Selecting training methods
   - Presentational methods
   - Hands-on methods
   - Group methods
6. Evaluating training programs
   - Identification of training outcomes and evaluation design
   - Cost–benefit analysis

a training method. As we shall see in this chapter, a variety of training methods are available ranging from traditional on-the-job training to newer technologies such as the Internet. The key is to choose a training method that will provide the appropriate learning environment to achieve the training objectives. Step 6 is evaluation— that is, determining whether training achieved the desired learning outcomes and/or financial objectives.

The training design process should be systematic yet flexible enough to adapt to business needs. Different steps may be completed simultaneously. Keep in mind that designing training unsystematically will reduce the benefits that can be realized. For example, choosing a training method before determining training needs or ensuring employees' readiness for training increases the risk that the method chosen will not be the most effective one for meeting training needs. Also, training may not even be necessary and may result in a waste of time and money! Employees may have the knowledge, skills, or behavior they need but simply not be motivated to use them. Next we will discuss important aspects of the training design process.

NEEDS ASSESSMENT

The first step in the instructional design process, **needs assessment,** refers to the process used to determine if training is necessary. Figure 7.2 shows the causes and outcomes resulting from needs assessment. As we see, many different "pressure points" suggest that training is necessary. These pressure points include performance problems, new technology, internal or external customer requests for training, job redesign, new legislation, changes in customer preferences, new products, or employees' lack of basic

LO 7-3
Conduct a needs assessment.

Needs Assessment
The process used to determine if training is necessary.

figure 7.2

The Needs Assessment Process

Reasons or "pressure points"

- Legislation
- Lack of basic skills
- Poor performance
- New technology
- Customer requests
- New products
- Higher performance standards
- New jobs
- Business growth or contraction
- Global business expansion

What is the context?

Organization analysis

Task analysis

Person analysis

In what do they need training?

Who needs training?

Outcomes

- What trainees need to learn
- Who receives training
- Type of training
- Frequency of training
- Buy-versus-build training decision
- Training versus other HR options such as selection or job redesign
- How training should be evaluated

Organizational Analysis
A process for determining the business appropriateness of training.

Person Analysis
A process for determining whether employees need training, who needs training, and whether employees are ready for training.

Task Analysis
The process of identifying the tasks, knowledge, skills, and behaviors that need to be emphasized in training.

skills as well as support for the company's business strategy (e.g., growth, global business expansion). Note that these pressure points do not guarantee that training is the correct solution. Consider, for example, a delivery truck driver whose job is to deliver anesthetic gases to medical facilities. The driver mistakenly hooks up the supply line of a mild anesthetic to the supply line of a hospital's oxygen system, contaminating the hospital's oxygen supply. Why did the driver make this mistake, which is clearly a performance problem? The driver may have done this because of a lack of knowledge about the appropriate line hookup for the anesthetic, anger over a requested salary increase that his manager recently denied, or mislabeled valves for connecting the gas supply. Only the lack of knowledge can be addressed by training. The other pressure points require addressing issues related to the consequence of good performance (pay system) or the design of the work environment.

Needs assessment typically involves organizational analysis, person analysis, and task analysis.[15] Organizational analysis considers the context in which training will occur. That is, **organizational analysis** involves determining the business appropriateness of training, given the company's business strategy, its resources available for training, and support by managers and peers for training activities.

Person analysis helps identify who needs training. **Person analysis** involves (1) determining whether performance deficiencies result from a lack of knowledge, skill, or ability (a training issue) or from a motivational or work-design problem; (2) identifying who needs training; and (3) determining employees' readiness for training. **Task analysis** includes identifying the important tasks and knowledge, skill, and behaviors that need to be emphasized in training for employees to complete their tasks.

In practice, organizational analysis, person analysis, and task analysis are usually not conducted in any specific order. However, because organizational analysis is concerned with identifying whether training fits with the company's strategic objectives and whether the company wants to devote time and money to training, it is usually conducted first. Person analysis and task analysis are often conducted at the same time because it is often difficult to determine whether performance deficiencies are a training problem without understanding the tasks and the work environment.

What outcomes result from a needs assessment? As shown in Figure 7.2, needs assessment shows who needs training and what trainees need to learn, including the tasks in which they need to be trained plus knowledge, skill, behavior, or other job requirements. Needs assessment helps determine whether the company will purchase training from a vendor or consultant or develop training using internal resources.

Steelcase spends considerable time and energy on needs assessment.[16] Course designers are responsible for ensuring that all of Steelcase University's training and development capabilities help drive business performance and lead strategic change for the company. The university helps to identify how behaviors need to change to align with new performance standards and future directions. The university tries to understand and provide solutions for critical business needs. Learning consultants serve as team members in key functional groups across the company. The learning consultant becomes aware of business challenges the function is facing and identifies the required business results. This helps identify a learning solution that can overcome behavior gaps. Consultants look for solutions that balance skill and knowledge development, management commitment, and demands of the work environment. If any of the three are missing, performance will not improve. The consultants serve as liaisons between the business unit and a team of project managers, instructional designers, and tech developers to communicate learning needs. The team may provide an already available course that meets the need or create a learning solution specific to the needs of the employees within the function.

ORGANIZATIONAL ANALYSIS

Three factors need to be considered before choosing training as the solution to any pressure point: the company's strategic direction, the training resources available, and support of managers and peers for training activities.

Support of Managers and Peers

Various studies have found that peer and manager support for training is critical. The key factors to success are a positive attitude among peers and managers about participation in training activities; managers' and peers' willingness to tell trainees how they can more effectively use knowledge, skills, or behaviors learned in training on the job; and the availability of opportunities for the trainees to use training content in their jobs.[17] If peers' and managers' attitudes and behaviors are not supportive, employees are not likely to apply training content to their jobs.

Company Strategy

In Chapter 2 we discussed the importance of business strategy for a company to gain a competitive advantage and earlier in this chapter we discussed how Campbell Soup relies on learning to support the company's mission and strategy. As Figure 7.1 highlights, training should help companies achieve the business strategy. Table 7.2 shows possible strategic training and development initiatives and their implications for training practices. **Strategic training and development initiatives** are learning-related actions that a company should take to help achieve its business strategy.[18] The initiatives are based on the business environment, an understanding of the company's goals and resources, and insight into potential training and development options. They provide the company with a road map to guide specific training and development activities. They also show how training

Strategic Training and Development Initiatives
Learning-related actions that a company takes to achieve its business strategy.

table 7.2

Strategic Training and Development Initiatives and Their Implications

STRATEGIC TRAINING AND DEVELOPMENT INITIATIVES	IMPLICATIONS
Diversify the learning portfolio	• Use new technology such as the Internet for training • Facilitate informal learning • Provide more personalized learning opportunities
Expand who is trained	• Train customers, suppliers, and employees • Offer more learning opportunities to nonmanagerial employees
Accelerate the pace of employee learning	• Quickly identify needs and provide a high-quality learning solution • Reduce the time to develop training programs • Facilitate access to learning resources on an as-needed basis
Improve customer service	• Ensure that employees have product and service knowledge • Ensure that employees have skills needed to interact with customers • Ensure that employees understand their roles and decision-making authority
Provide development opportunities and communicate to employees	• Ensure that employees have opportunities to develop • Ensure that employees understand career opportunities and personal growth opportunities • Ensure that training and development addresses employees' needs in current job as well as growth opportunities
Capture and share knowledge	• Capture insight and information from knowledgeable employees • Logically organize and store information • Provide methods to make information available (e.g., resource guides, websites)
Align training and development with the company's strategic direction	• Identify needed knowledge, skills, abilities, or competencies • Ensure that current training and development programs support the company's strategic needs
Ensure that the work environment supports learning and transfer of training	• Remove constraints to learning, such as lack of time, resources, and equipment • Dedicate physical space to encourage teamwork, collaboration, creativity, and knowledge sharing • Ensure that employees understand the importance of learning • Ensure that managers and peers are supportive of training, development, and learning

SOURCE: Based on S. Tannenbaum, "A Strategic View of Organizational Training and Learning," in *Creating, Implementing and Managing Effective Training and Development*, ed. K. Kraiger (San Francisco: Jossey-Bass, 2002), pp. 10–52.

will help the company reach its goals and add value. The plan or goal the company chooses to achieve strategic objectives has a major impact on whether resources (money, trainers' time, program development) should be devoted to addressing a training pressure point.

It is important to identify the prevailing business strategy and goals to ensure that the company allocates enough of its budget to training, that employees receive training on relevant topics, and that employees get the right amount of training.[19] For example, consider how globalization has affected the training practices of KLA-Tencor, a manufacturer of equipment and systems for semiconductor manufacturers.[20] KLA-Tencor has factories in China, Taiwan, Singapore, and India in order to better serve its customers, such as Intel, who also have global locations.

KLA-Tencor needs to train employees in installing and servicing machine tools in its global operations. Employees also need to know how to adjust the machines to maximize productivity so they can educate customers on how to use more effectively. Technology training is provided regionally because trainees needs hands-on experience with the machines. KLA-Tencor finds local instructors who are qualified to teach in the local language. The local instructors are trained in how to deliver the technical training and use the machines. Before teaching courses on their own, the local instructors co-teach a class with another trainer to ensure they are comfortable and proficient in delivering training.

EMC's products helps companies store, protect, and organize employee, customer, and product information.[21] In five years, EMC grew from offering 200 to 300 products to more than 4,000 products based on a business strategy that included acquiring 40 companies whose products complemented EMC's product line. The acquisition strategy meant that a necessary strategic training initiative for EMC was to develop and expand its professional certification program (Proven Professionals). The certification program is critical for the company's technical employees and its customers to understand the value of its products and how to install and support them. The program includes 10 technologies with certification available, and within each certification area, employees and customers can attain associate, specialist, and expert levels.

Yapi Kredi Academy was established to provide learning and development for Yapi ve Kredi Bank's Turkish employees.[22] The bank's executive committee, including the CEO executive vice presidents and an advisory committee, provides the strategic direction and vision for the academy. The advisory committee includes senior managers and individuals from outside the bank who identify trends, challenges, and opportunities in the industry. The bank's need assessment process includes branch visits, surveys, and focus groups, as well as meetings with business units. The academy surveys employees about their satisfaction with the training they receive and their experiences with individual development plans and training offerings. The results are used to determine how to meet learning and development needs. B&W Pantex conducted a review of the technical training program to ensure that it was not wasting its budget and the courses were relevant for current safety and compliance issues in the nuclear weapons industry.[23] A review of the courses included questions about their necessity, relevance of their objectives, and changes in the intended audience. As a result of the review, courses were consolidated and redesigned.

Training Resources

It is necessary to identify whether the company has the budget, time, and expertise for training. For example, if the company is installing computer-based manufacturing equipment in one of its plants, it has three possible strategies to have computer-literate employees. First, the company can use internal consultants to train all affected employees. Second, the company may decide that it is more cost-effective to identify computer-literate employees by using tests and work samples. Employees who fail the test or perform below standards on the work sample can be reassigned to other jobs. Choosing this strategy suggests that the company has decided to devote resources to selection and placement rather than training. Third, if it lacks time or expertise, the company may decide to purchase training from a consultant.

Table 7.3 provides examples of questions to ask vendors and consultants to help evaluate whether they can meet the company's training needs.

table 7.3

Questions to
Ask Vendors and
Consultants

How do your products and services fit our needs?
How much and what type of experience does your company have in designing and delivering training?
What are the qualifications and experiences of your staff?
Can you provide demonstrations or examples of training programs you have developed?
Would you provide references of clients for whom you worked?
What evidence do you have that your programs work?
Will the training program be customized to meet the company's needs?
How long will it take to develop the training program?
How much will your services cost?
What instructional design methods do you use?

SOURCES: Adapted from R. Zemke and J. Armstrong, "Evaluating Multimedia Developers," *Training Magazine,* November 1996, pp. 33–38; B. Chapman, "How to Create the Ideal RFP," *Training,* January 2004, pp. 40–43.

PERSON ANALYSIS

Person analysis helps the manager identify whether training is appropriate and which employees need training. In certain situations, such as the introduction of a new technology or service, all employees may need training. However, when managers, customers, or employees identify a problem (usually as a result of a performance deficiency), it is often unclear whether training is the solution.

A major pressure point for training is poor or substandard performance—that is, a gap between employees' current performance and their expected performance. Poor performance is indicated by customer complaints, low performance ratings, or on-the-job accidents or unsafe behavior. Another potential indicator of the need for training is if the job changes so current performance levels need improvement or employees must complete new tasks.

From a manager's perspective, to determine if training is needed, for any performance problem you need to analyze characteristics of the performer, input, output, consequences, and feedback. How might this be done? You should ask several questions to determine if training is the likely solution to a performance problem.[24]

Assess whether

1. The performance problem is important and has the potential to cost the company a significant amount of money from lost productivity or customers.
2. Employees do not know how to perform effectively. Perhaps they received little or no previous training or the training was ineffective (person characteristics).
3. Employees cannot demonstrate the correct knowledge or behavior. Perhaps they were trained but they infrequently or never used the training content (knowledge, skills, etc.) on the job (input problem).
4. Performance expectations are clear (input) and there are no obstacles to performance such as faulty tools or equipment (output).
5. There are positive consequences for good performance, whereas poor performance is not rewarded. For example, if employees are dissatisfied with their compensation, their peers or a union may encourage them to slow down their pace of work (consequences).

6. Employees receive timely, relevant, accurate, constructive, and specific feedback about their performance (feedback).
7. Other solutions such as job redesign or transferring employees to other jobs are too expensive or unrealistic.

If employees lack the knowledge and skill to perform and the other factors are satisfactory, training is likely the effective solution. If employees have the knowledge and skill to perform, but input, output, consequences, or feedback are inadequate, training may not be the best solution. For example, if poor performance results from faulty equipment, training cannot solve this problem, but repairing the equipment will! If poor performance results from lack of feedback, then employees may not need training, but their managers may need training on how to give performance feedback.

TASK ANALYSIS

A task analysis, defined on page 276, identifies the conditions in which tasks are performed. The conditions include identifying equipment and the environment the employee works in, time constraints (deadlines), safety considerations, or performance standards. Task analysis results in a description of work activities, including tasks performed by the employee and the knowledge, skills, and abilities required to successfully complete the tasks. A *job* is a specific position requiring the completion of specific tasks. A *task* is a statement of an employee's work activity in a specific job. The four steps in a task analysis include identifying the job(s) to be analyzed, developing a list of tasks performed on the job, validating or confirming the tasks, and identifying the knowledge, skills, abilities, and other factors (e.g., equipment, working conditions) needed to successfully perform each task.[25]

Each of the four steps of a task analysis can be seen in this example from a utility company. Trainers were given the job of developing a training system in six months.[26] The purpose of the program was to identify tasks and knowledge, skills, abilities, and other considerations that would serve as the basis for training program objectives and lesson plans.

The first phase of the project involved identifying potential tasks for each job in the utility's electrical maintenance area. Procedures, equipment lists, and information provided by subject matter experts (SMEs) were used to generate the tasks. SMEs included managers, instructors, and senior technicians. The tasks were incorporated into a questionnaire administered to all technicians in the electrical maintenance department. The questionnaire included 550 tasks. Figure 7.3 shows sample items from the questionnaire for the electrical maintenance job. Technicians were asked to rate each task on importance, difficulty, and frequency of performance. The rating scale for frequency included zero. A zero rating indicated that the technician rating the task had never performed the task. Technicians who rated a task zero were asked not to evaluate the task's difficulty and importance.

Customized software was used to analyze the ratings collected via the questionnaire. The primary requirement used to determine whether a task required training was its importance rating. A task rated "very important" was identified as one requiring training regardless of its frequency or difficulty. If a task was rated moderately important but difficult, it also was designated for training. Tasks rated unimportant, not difficult, and done infrequently were not designated for training.

The list of tasks designated for training was reviewed by the SMEs to determine if it accurately described job tasks. The result was a list of 487 tasks. For each of the 487 tasks, two SMEs identified the necessary knowledge, skills, abilities, and other

figure 7.3

Sample Items from Task Analysis Questionnaires for an Electrical Maintenance Job

Job: Electrical Maintenance Worker				
		Task Performance Ratings		
Task #s	**Task Description**	**Frequency of Performance**	**Importance**	**Difficulty**
199-264	Replace a light bulb	0 1 2 3 4 5	0 1 2 3 4 5	0 1 2 3 4 5
199-265	Replace an electrical outlet	0 1 2 3 4 5	0 1 2 3 4 5	0 1 2 3 4 5
199-266	Install a light fixture	0 1 2 3 4 5	0 1 2 3 4 5	0 1 2 3 4 5
199-267	Replace a light switch	0 1 2 3 4 5	0 1 2 3 4 5	0 1 2 3 4 5
199-268	Install a new circuit breaker	0 1 2 3 4 5	0 1 2 3 4 5	0 1 2 3 4 5
		Frequency of Performance 0=never 5=often	**Importance** 1=negligible 5=extremely high	**Difficulty** 1=easiest 5=most difficult

SOURCE: E. F. Holton III and C. Bailey, "Top-to-Bottom Curriculum Redesign," *Training and Development*, March 1995, pp. 40–44. Reprinted with permission of *Training & Development*.

factors required for performance. This included information on working conditions, cues that initiate the task's start and end, performance standards, safety considerations, and necessary tools and equipment. All data were reviewed by plant technicians and members of the training department. More than 14,000 knowledge, skill, ability, and other considerations were clustered into common areas. An identification code was assigned to each group that linked groups to task and knowledge, skill, ability, and other factors. These groups were then combined into clusters that represented qualification areas. That is, the task clusters related to linked tasks that the employees must be certified in to perform the job. The clusters were used to identify training lesson plans and course objectives; trainers also reviewed the clusters to identify prerequisite skills.

ENSURING EMPLOYEES' MOTIVATION FOR LEARNING

LO 7-4
Evaluate employees' motivation for learning.

Motivation to Learn
The desire of the trainee to learn the content of a training program.

The second step in the training design process is to evaluate whether employees are motivated to learn. **Motivation to learn** is the desire of the trainee to learn the content of the training program.[27] That desire includes having the energy to learn, directing that energy toward learning, and being able to exert effort to learn even when faced with difficulties (such as making errors when learning a new skill or having a less than ideal training instructor). Various research studies have shown that motivation is related to knowledge gain, behavior change, or skill acquisition in training programs.[28] Table 7.4 presents factors that influence motivation to learn and the actions that strength them. Motivation to learn influences mastery of all types of training content, including knowledge, behavior, and skills. Managers need to ensure

table 7.4

Factors That Influence Motivation to Learn

FACTOR	DESCRIPTION	ACTIONS TO ENHANCE OR IMPROVE
Self-efficacy	Employee belief that they can successfully learn content of the training program.	Show employees training success of their peers.
		Communicate that purpose of training is to improve not identify area of incompetence. Communicate purpose and activities involved in training. Emphasize that learning is under their personal control.
Benefits or consequences of training	Job-related, personal, career benefits that can result from attending training.	Realistic communication about short- and long-term benefits from training.
Awareness of training needs	Knowledge of skill strengths and weaknesses.	Communicate why they were asked to attend training program. Share performance appraisal information. Encourage trainees to complete self-evaluation of all strengths and weaknesses. Allow employees to participate in choice of training to attend.
Work environment	Proper tools and equipment, materials, supplies, budget time. Managers' and peers' willingness to provide feedback and reinforce use of training content.	Give employees opportunities to practice and apply skills to their work. Encourage employees to provide feedback to each other. Encourage trainees to share training experiences and situations where use of training content was beneficial. Acknowledge use of training content in their work. Provide resources necessary for training content to be used in their work.
Basic skills	Cognitive ability, reading, and writing skills.	Ensure trainees have prerequisite skills needed for understanding and learning training content. Provide remedial training. Use video or other visual training methods. Modify training program to meet trainees' basic skill levels.
Goal orientation	Goals held by employees in a learning situation.	Create a learning goal orientation by deemphasizing competition between trainees, allowing trainees to make errors and to experiment with new knowledge, skills, behavior during training, and setting goals-based learning and experimenting.
Conscientiousness	Tendency to be reliable, hardworking, self-disciplined, and persistent.	Communicate need for learning.

SOURCES: Based on J. Colquitt, J. LePine, and R. Noe, "Toward an Integrative Theory of Training Motivation: A Meta-Analytic Path Analysis of 20 Years of Research," *Journal of Applied Psychology* 85 (2000), pp. 678–707; and R. Noe and J. Colquitt, "Planning for Impact Training: Principles of Training Effectiveness," in K. Kraiger (ed.), *Creating, Implementing, and Managing Effective Training and Development* (San Francisco: Jossey-Bass, 2002), pp. 53–79.

that employees' motivation to learn is as high as possible. They can do this by ensuring employees' self-efficacy; understanding the benefits of training; being aware of training needs, career interests, and goals; understanding work environment characteristics; and ensuring employees' basic skill levels.

The "Competing through Sustainability" box shows efforts to develop the skills of the "hidden workforce" and in return get motivated and committed employees.

CREATING A LEARNING ENVIRONMENT

Learning permanently changes behavior. For employees to acquire knowledge and skills in the training program and apply this information in their jobs, the training program must include specific learning principles. Educational and industrial psychologists and instructional design specialists have identified several conditions under which employees learn best.[29] Table 7.5 shows the events that should take place for learning to occur in the training program and their implications for instruction.

Consider how several companies are creating a positive learning environment using a variety of training methods.[30] Yapi ve Kredi Bank, headquartered in Istanbul, Turkey, developed a program to help managers improve their skills in motivating and coaching their employees. The program included classroom sessions in which trainers reviewed common case studies of common situations in coaching and provided online readings and videos. Senior managers reviewed coaching and development techniques and program participants were given coaching assignments with their peers to complete. B & W Pantex first-line mangers' course focuses on soft skills as well as HR policies, discipline, and supervision using instructor-led training with video presentations and role-plays. The course includes real-life scenarios based on actual situations that have occurred in its facilities. The program also includes on-the-job training in which trained and qualified subject matter experts teach tasks and procedures. Brown-Forman, one of the largest companies in the global wine and spirits industry (its brands include Jack Daniels Tennessee Whiskey, Southern Comfort, Findlandia Vodka, and Herradura Tequillas) created a two-and-a-half-day training program focused on helping the company's marketing professionals build the brand. The company's chief marketing officer visits the class to explain the importance of its content and why the course was developed. In the course, participants work in teams to develop a brand campaign for a sample brand. This includes making presentations and completing exercises. Representatives from Brown-Forman's creative agencies attend the program and part of the program involves interacting with consumers to identify their drinking patterns and preferences. At the end of the program, participant teams present their final project to a panel of senior marketing executives who serve as judges.

ENSURING TRANSFER OF TRAINING

Transfer of Training
The use of knowledge, skills, and behaviors learned in training on the job.

Transfer of training refers to on-the-job use of knowledge, skills, and behaviors learned in training. As Figure 7.4 shows, transfer of training is influenced by the climate for transfer, manager support, peer support, opportunity to use learned capabilities, technology support, and self-management skills. As we discussed earlier, learning is influenced by the learning environment (such as meaningfulness of the material and opportunities for practice and feedback) and employees' readiness for training (for example, their self-efficacy and basic skill level). If no learning occurs in the training program, transfer is unlikely.

Capitalizing on Available but Unrecognized Talent

Many companies rely on welfare-to-work programs and nonprofit community groups to provide employment and training to the unemployed or hard-to-employ. The relationship is beneficial for the employees, the company, and the local community. Employees receive wage-paying jobs, companies get a committed and motivated workforce, and living and working standards are raised in the communities where the companies are located.

Mark Goldsmith, a former Revlon executive, started his own nonprofit organization called Getting Out and Staying Out (GOSO). GOSO is working with more than 200 inmates serving prison sentences in New York. GOSO works with young prisoners who are attending school and have been in prison only a short time period. It provides individual job and education counseling and interview preparation, maintains a job bank of openings from employers willing to hire former inmates, provides educational scholarships, and holds seminars. One seminar taught by a retired construction company executive focused on the skills required to become a successful tradesperson. GOSO has been successful. Fewer than 10% of the 400 released inmates GOSO has worked with have been arrested again, compared with two-thirds of prisoners nationwide who have been rearrested. Seventy-five percent of the former prisoners in GOSO are employed or attending school. Former inmates stop by to share good news about a job, discuss problems they are having at home or work, or return for counseling if they lose or don't get a job, want to change jobs, or decide to go back to school.

The primary mission of Greater Chicago Food Depository, a nonprofit food bank, has been to feed the hungry. The food bank and others around the country affiliated with America's Second Harvest have been offering 30 chef training classes to about 1,000 students. These programs teach low-income students the basics of cooking such as slicing, dicing, sizing, and fricasseeing, as well as advanced skills, with the goal of getting each student a job. Also, the program teaches the students life skills such as punctuality, responsibility, teamwork, and commitment. As one of the executive chef instructors told her 17 students on the first day of class, "When you're out there working and you're fifteen minutes late, I'm already calling someone to do your job." Seventy percent of program graduates find jobs within one month, and more than 65% retain their first job for at least six months. For students who succeed, the program helps them escape from the cycle of poverty.

Project Vacant Streets, a Miami-based program founded by Frank Kelley, a Johnson & Johnson executive, tries to get jobs for persons who are "crisis homeless," that is, everyday people who end up homeless due to losing their jobs because of the recession. One estimate is that 80% of the homeless are crisis homeless with the remaining 20% including individuals who have chronic physical or mental health problems. Many of the crisis homeless are qualified for jobs but have lost their homes and now live in homeless shelters. Project Vacant Streets helps the crisis homeless develop skill sets that can get them back into the workforce. It focuses on emotional, professional, and physical issues needed for success. Kelley works with the program participants to identify their passions, develop their interviewing skills, physical presence, and strategies to leave a lasting impression built around his attitude, communication, external image (ACE) approach. Exercises, simulations, and workshops are delivered to participants to improve their attitudes toward the job search and communicate their positive attitudes to prospective employers. Also, the program involves companies such as Starbucks presenting to the homeless the same types of courses that their employees would receive (e.g., a customer service class). Because of the comprehensive nature of the program Kelley works with a small number of participants at one time. But despite the small numbers he has helped, program participants get jobs in local Miami hotels including the Eden Roc, Hilton, and Doubletree.

SOURCE: Based on M. Weinstein, "Homeless But Hopeful," *Training*, March/April 2010, pp. 22–26; www .unleashyourace.com, website for Frank Kelley; L. Germinsky, "Back to Life, One Man at a Time," from http://blog.tonic .com/project-vacant-streets, August 20, 2009; C. Hymowitz, "Executives Teach Inmates How to Be Employees," *The Wall Street Journal*, March 17, 2008, pp. B1, B3; R. Thurow, "To Tackle Hunger, a Food Bank Tries Training Chefs," *The Wall Street Journal*, November 28, 2006, pp. A1, A13.

table 7.5

Conditions for Learning and Their Importance

CONDITIONS FOR LEARNING	IMPORTANCE AND APPLICATION TO TRAINING
Need to know why they should learn	Employees need to understand the purpose or objectives of the training program to help them understand why they need training and what they are expected to accomplish.
Meaningful training content	Motivation to learn is enhanced when training is related to helping learner (such as related to current job tasks, problems, enhancing skills, or dealing with jobs or company changes). The training context should be similar to the work environment.
Opportunities for practice	Trainees need to demonstrate what is learned (knowledge, skill, behavior) to become more comfortable using it and to commit it to memory. Let trainees choose their practice strategy.
Feedback	Feedback helps learner modify behavior, skill, or use knowledge to meet objectives. Videotape, other trainees, and the trainer are useful feedback sources.
Observe, experience, and interact with training content, other learners, and the instructor	Adults learn best by doing. Gain new perspectives and insights by working with others. Can learn by observing the actions of models or sharing experiences with each other in communities of practice or through social networking. Interact and manipulate content through reading or using tools that allow for building ideas and solving problems, such as worksheets and online interactions.
Good program coordination and administration	Eliminate distractions that could interfere with learning, such as cell-phone calls. Make sure the room is properly organized, comfortable, and appropriate for the training method (e.g., movable seating for team exercises). Trainees should receive announcements of the purpose of training, place, hour, and any pretraining materials such as cases or readings.
Commit training content to memory	Facilitate recall of training content after training. Examples include using concept maps showing relationships among ideas, using multiple types of review (writing, drawing, role-plays), teaching key words, or providing a visual image. Limit instruction to manageable units that don't exceed memory limits; review and practice over multiple days (overlearning).

SOURCES: Based on R. M. Gagne, "Learning Processes and Instruction," *Training Research Journal* 1 (1995/1996), pp. 17–28; M. Knowles, *The Adult Learner*, 4th ed. (Houston: Gulf, 1990); A. Bandura, *Social Foundations of Thought and Action* (Englewood Cliffs, NJ: Prentice Hall, 1986); E. A. Locke and G. D. Latham, *A Theory of Goal Setting and Task Performance* (Englewood Cliffs, NJ: Prentice Hall, 1990); B. Mager, *Preparing Instructional Objectives*, 2nd ed. (Belmont, CA: Lake, 1984); B.J. Smith and B. L. Delahaye, *How to Be an Effective Trainer*, 2nd ed. (New York: John Wiley and Sons, 1987); K. A. Smith-Jentsch, F. G. Jentsch, S. C. Payne, and E. Salas, "Can Pretraining Experience Explain Individual Differences in Learning?" *Journal of Applied Psychology* 81 (1996), pp. 110–16; and H. Nuriddin, "Building the Right Interaction," *T + D*, March 2011, pp. 32–35.

figure 7.4

Work Environment Characteristics Influencing Transfer of Training

Climate for Transfer

One way to think about the work environment's influence on transfer of training is to consider the overall climate for transfer. **Climate for transfer** refers to trainees' perceptions about a wide variety of characteristics of the work environment that facilitate or inhibit use of trained skills or behavior. These characteristics include manager and peer support, opportunity to use skills, and the consequences for using learned capabilities.[31] It is important to recognize that similar factors influence motivation to learn and transfer of training (e.g., peer and manager support, opportunity to use skills). Research has shown that transfer of training climate is significantly related to positive changes in behaviors following training.

Climate for Transfer
Trainees' perceptions of characteristics of the work environment (social support and situational constraints) that can either facilitate or inhibit use of trained skills or behavior.

Manager Support

Manager support refers to the degree to which trainees' managers (1) emphasize the importance of attending training programs and (2) stress the application of training content to the job. Table 7.6 shows what managers should do to support training. For example, at Men's Wearhouse, managers are expected to spend part of their budget

table 7.6

How Managers Can Support Training

Understand the content of the training.
Know how training relates to what you need employees to do.
In performance appraisals, evaluate employees on how they apply training to their jobs.
Support employees' use of training when they return to work.
Ensure that employees have the equipment and technology needed to use training.
Prior to training, discuss with employees how they plan to use training.
Recognize newly trained employees who use training content.
Give employees release time from their work to attend training.
Explain to employees why they have been asked to attend training.
Give employees feedback related to skills or behavior they are trying to develop.
If possible, be a trainer.

SOURCES: Based on R. Bates, "Managers as Transfer Agents," in E. Holton III and T. Baldwin (eds.), *Improving Learning Transfer in Organizations* (San Francisco: Jossey-Bass, 2003), pp. 243–70; and A. Rossett, "That Was a Great Class, but . . ." *Training and Development*, July 1997, p. 21.

on training. As part of Brown-Forman's "BF Way of Selling" program, webinars were created for sales leaders to reinforce the importance of their role in motivating sales employees to use their newly acquired sales skills.[32]

At Ingersoll Rand, to ensure that top managers understand and support the role that training and development can play in the company, a "ladder of engagement" model was created.[33] Top managers are engaged in training and development in many different ways, including providing input into learning program development, serving as trainers or co-trainers, visiting courses as an executive speaker, or serving as advisory council members for Ingersoll Rand's corporate university.

The greater the level of manager support, the more likely that transfer of training will occur.[34] The basic level of support that a manager should provide is acceptance, that is, allowing trainees to attend training. The highest level of support is to participate in training as an instructor (teaching in the program). Managers who serve as instructors are more likely to provide lower-level support functions such as reinforcing use of newly learned capabilities, discussing progress with trainees, and providing opportunities to practice. Managers can also facilitate transfer through use of action plans. An **action plan** is a written document that includes the steps that the trainee and manager will take to ensure that training transfers to the job. The action plan includes (1) a goal identifying what training content will be used and how it will be used (project, problem); (2) strategies for reaching the goal, including resources needed; (3) strategies for getting feedback (such as meetings with the manager); and (4) expected outcome (what will be different?). The action plan includes a schedule of specific dates and times when the manager and trainee agree to meet to discuss the progress being made in using learned capabilities on the job.

At a minimum, special sessions should be scheduled with managers to explain the purpose of the training and set expectations that they will encourage attendance at the training session, provide practice opportunities, reinforce use of training, and follow up with employees to determine the progress in using newly acquired capabilities.

Action Plan
Document summarizing what the trainee and manager will do to ensure that training transfers to the job.

Peer Support

Transfer of training can also be enhanced by creating a support network among the trainees.[35] A **support network** is a group of two or more trainees who agree to meet and discuss their progress in using learned capabilities on the job. This could involve face-to-face meetings or communications via e-mail, Twitter, or other social networking tools. Trainees can share successful experiences in using training content on the job; they can also discuss how they obtained resources needed to use training content or how they coped with a work environment that interfered with use of training content.

Websites or newsletters might be used to show how trainees are dealing with transfer of training issues. Available to all trainees, the newsletter or website might feature interviews with trainees who were successful in using new skills or provide tips for using new skills. Managers may also provide trainees with a mentor—a more experienced employee who previously attended the same training program. The mentor, who may be a peer, can provide advice and support related to transfer of training issues (such as how to find opportunities to use the learned capabilities).

Support Network
Trainees who meet to discuss their progress in using learned capabilities on the job.

Opportunity to Use Learned Capabilities

Opportunity to use learned capabilities (**opportunity to perform**) refers to the extent to which the trainee is provided with or actively seeks experience with newly learned knowledge, skill, and behaviors from the training program.[36] Opportunity to perform

Opportunity to Perform
Trainee is provided with or actively seeks experience using newly learned knowledge, skills, or behavior.

is influenced by both the work environment and trainee motivation. One way trainees can use learned capabilities is through assigned work experiences (problems or tasks) that require their use. The trainees' manager usually plays a key role in determining work assignments. Opportunity to perform is also influenced by the degree to which trainees take personal responsibility to actively seek out assignments that allow them to use newly acquired capabilities. Trainees given many opportunities to use training content on the job are more likely to maintain learned capabilities than trainees given few opportunities.[37]

Technological Support: EPSS and Knowledge Management Systems

Electronic performance support systems (EPSS) are computer applications that can provide, as requested, skills training, information access, and expert advice.[38] EPSSs may be used to enhance transfer of training by giving trainees an electronic information source that they can refer to as needed as they attempt to apply learned capabilities on the job.

At Reuters, the news and financial information company, employees who deal with orders for financial systems information and data needed a way to get their questions answered on an as-needed basis because they did not have the time to attend training sessions.[39] Typical questions included how to register financial traders to access Reuters' information and systems and how to coordinate installation of Reuters' technology on the trading floor. Reuters purchased an EPSS that provides employees with help tabs on their computer screens as they perform tasks. The help tabs provide answers to questions about the steps employees need to complete different processes (such as user registration).

As we discussed earlier in the chapter, many companies are using knowledge management systems to improve the creation, sharing, and use of knowledge. At MWH Global, an engineering and environmental consulting company, a software program was used to analyze the data that employees provided about which colleagues they most frequently interacted with and whom they turned to for expertise.[40] The program plotted a web of interconnecting nodes and lines representing people and relationships. The web provides a corporate map of how work gets done, lists the well-connected technical experts, and helps identify informal connections between people that are missing on a traditional organizational chart.

Knowledge management systems often include communities of practice. **Communities of practice** are groups of employees who work together, learn from each other, and develop a common understanding of how to get work accomplished.

Chicago-based Grant Thornton LLP, part of the Global Six accounting organizations, developed and deployed a knowledge management system known as "K-Source."[41] K-Source was designed to help meet key business goals of growing sales, improving customer service, supporting company values, and increasing efficiency of internal services. K-Source includes an online community of practice for every line of service offered by the company, industry group, and geographic area. Employees are encouraged to contribute to K-Source by a knowledge manager who solicits their participation as well as by including it as part of their performance evaluation goals. Using K-Source employees can create personal profiles, set up personalized news feeds from financial websites, access courses, e-books and webcasts, and participate in online discussions. Datatel, a provider of technology solutions and business services to higher-education institutions in North America, provides a virtual knowledge café for its 500 employees.[42] The café includes discussion forums, frequently asked questions,

Electronic Performance Support Systems (EPSS)
Computer applications that can provide (as requested) skills training, information access, and expert advice.

Communities of Practice
Groups of employees who work together, learn from each other, and develop a common understanding of how to get work accomplished.

and learning plans for different employee positions. Datatel wants its employees to be able to access knowledge and to have conversations in any area that interests them. Datatel also uses a café as part of a productivity improvement initiative. This site includes "ask the experts" discussion boards, job aids, and document sharing.

Self-Management Skills

Training programs should prepare employees to self-manage their use of new skills and behaviors on the job.[43] Specifically, within the training program, trainees should set goals for using skills or behaviors on the job, identify conditions under which they might fail to use them, identify the positive and negative consequences of using them, and monitor their use of them. Also, trainees need to understand that it is natural to encounter difficulty in trying to use skills on the job; relapses into old behavior and skill patterns do not indicate that trainees should give up. Finally, because peers and supervisors on the job may be unable to reward trainees using new behaviors or to provide feedback automatically, trainees need to create their own reward system and ask peers and managers for feedback.

Consider how Vanderbilt University Medical Center (VUMC) emphasizes transfer of training.[44] To improve patient safety and quality, VUMC initiated a team training program. The program teaches participants about patient safety mistakes and how to avoid them, team building, cross-checking and communications, decision making, and performance feedback. Participants are provided classroom training that shows how concepts from aviation flight crew training can be applied to patient safety and quality care by talking about how to create an effective team (crew), how to communicate effectively (briefings), how to recognize potential problems and what to do about them, how to make informed decisions, and how to critique performance (debrief). For example, the module on crew resource management focuses on how crew resource management is applied to health care and how it improves patient safety and quality of care.

Several steps are taken to make sure transfer of training occurs, that is, what is learned in the program is used and supported at work. Before the training starts, VUMC leaders are prepared to help the training succeed. Senior administrators, medical directors, and nursing staff attend a boot camp, which highlights the team training program. A safety climate survey is conducted to determine how each department perceives the VUMC attitudes toward safety practices and patient safety issues. Then, each department is reviewed to find built-in errors that are system problems and to evaluate how the team communicates and deals with conflict. After this, training, observation, coaching, and feedback are provided by medical supervisors. Checklists are provided for certain procedures such as patient handoffs, medication administration, and briefing and debriefing sessions to help participants use the strategies emphasized in training to improve safety and the quality of patient care. Patients also help ensure safety. They are asked to watch a video created by VUMC when they are admitted to the hospital. The video emphasizes the importance of asking questions about medications and medical procedures.

LO 7-5
Discuss the strengths and weaknesses of presentation, hands-on, and group training methods.

SELECTING TRAINING METHODS

A number of different methods can help employees acquire new knowledge, skills, and behaviors. Figure 7.5 provides an overview of the use of training methods across all size companies. The instructor-led classroom still remains the most frequently used

figure 7.5

Overview of Use of
Training Methods

SOURCE: From "2010 Training Industry Report," *Training*, November/December 2010, p. 26.

training method. However, it is important to note that the use of online learning, mobile learning, and social networking for training continues to increase and expectations are that this trend with continue.

Consider these survey results.[45] One estimate is that nearly 40% of executives plan to use tablets such as the iPad into their new training and development initiatives. These devices are expected to be used for learning and performance support but also for coaching and mentoring employees, mobile gaming, and microblogging (e.g., Twitter). Social media tools are reshaping learning by allowing employees to access and control their own learning through relationships and collaborations with others. Social media tools including shared workspaces (space hosted on a webserver where people can share information and documents), social networks (online communities of people such as Facebook and LinkedIn), Wikis (a website with content created and edited by users), blogs (a webpage where entries can be posted and readers can comment), podcasts (downloadable video or audio files that can be accessed on computers or mobile devices), and microblogs are being used for learning. Shared workspaces, social networks, and Wikis are the most commonly used social media.

Regardless of whether the training method is traditional or technology based, for training to be effective it needs to be based on the training design model shown in Table 7.1. Needs assessment, a positive learning environment, and transfer of training are critical for training program effectiveness.

Presentation Methods

Presentation methods refer to methods in which trainees are passive recipients of information. Presentation methods include traditional classroom instruction, distance learning, audiovisual techniques, and mobile technology such as iPods and PDAs. These are ideal for presenting new facts, information, different philosophies, and alternative problem-solving solutions or processes.

Instructor-Led Classroom Instruction. Classroom instruction typically involves having the trainer lecture a group. In many cases the lecture is supplemented with question-and-answer periods, discussion, or case studies. Classroom instruction remains a popular training method despite new technologies such as interactive video

Presentation Methods
Training methods in which trainees are passive recipients of information.

and computer-assisted instruction. Traditional classroom instruction is one of the least expensive, least time-consuming ways to present information on a specific topic to many trainees. The more active participation, job-related examples, and exercises that the instructor can build into traditional classroom instruction, the more likely trainees will learn and use the information presented on the job.

Distance learning is used by geographically dispersed companies to provide information about new products, policies, or procedures as well as skills training and expert lectures to field locations.[46] Distance learning features two-way communications between people. Distance learning currently involves two types of technology.[47] First, it includes teleconferencing. **Teleconferencing** refers to synchronous exchange of audio, video, and/or text between two or more individuals or groups at two or more locations. Trainees attend training programs in training facilities in which they can communicate with trainers (who are at another location) and other trainees using the telephone or personal computer. A second type of distance learning also includes individualized, personal-computer–based training.[48] Employees participate in training anywhere they have access to a personal computer. This type of distance learning may involve multimedia training methods such as web-based training. Course material and assignments can be distributed using the company's intranet, video, or CD-ROM. Trainers and trainees interact using e-mail, bulletin boards, and conferencing systems. Both types of distance learning can also allow trainees to respond to questions posed during the training program using a keypad.

Teleconferencing usually includes a telephone link so that trainees viewing the presentation can call in questions and comments to the trainer. Also, satellite networks allow companies to link up with industry-specific and educational courses for which employees receive college credit and job certification. IBM, Digital Equipment, and Eastman Kodak are among the many firms that subscribe to the National Technological University, which broadcasts courses throughout the United States that technical employees need to obtain advanced degrees in engineering.[49]

An advantage of distance learning is that the company can save on travel costs. It also allows employees in geographically dispersed sites to receive training from experts who would not otherwise be available to visit each location. Intuit finds that a traditional classroom environment is good for introducing software and providing trainees with the opportunity to network. Virtual classroom training is used for courses on special software features, demonstrations, and troubleshooting using application-sharing features. For example, JCPenney, which produces more than 200 different interactive distance learning (IDL) programs each year uses distance learning to reach every associate.[50] Each store has a training room, where up to 12 employees sign on to the program and watch on a large television screen. Each employee has his or her own keypad to interact. Employees are able to watch the satellite broadcast live or later view a tape of the program. Regardless of whether watching the program live or via tape, employees can answer questions such as, "How many square feet does your store have for lingerie?"; at the end of the program, managers and trainers can access a report on how every store answered. Evaluations of the interactive distance learning satellite have been positive. IDL has allowed JCPenney to deliver training to every employee in the company. Eight-six percent of employees report that they use the training to effectively perform their jobs.

Online learning also has disadvantages. FileNeT Corporation was concerned with how its sales force was going to keep up with new software and software updates.[51] FileNeT tried self-paced online learning but discovered that salespeople did not like to read a lot of material about new products on the web. Enrollment in online courses

Teleconferencing
Synchronous exchange of audio, video, or text between individuals or groups at two or more locations.

dwindled, and salespeople flooded the company's training department with requests for one-on-one assistance. To solve the training problem, the company decided to use webcasting. **Webcasting** involves classroom instructions that are provided online through live broadcasts. Webcasting helped spread the sales force training throughout the year rather than cramming it into twice-a-year sales meetings. Webcasting also helped ensure that the salespeople all received the same information. The salespeople liked the webcasts because of the timely information that helped them have conversations with customers. The live sessions were also popular because participants could ask questions. Webcasting has not replaced face-to-face training at FileNeT; classroom training is still about 80% of training, but that percentage has decreased by 10%. Webcasting has also resulted in savings of $500,000 annually (one of the twice-yearly sales meetings was canceled).

Webcasting
Classroom instruction provided online via live broadcasts.

The major disadvantage of distance learning is the potential for lack of interaction between the trainer and the audience. A high degree of interaction between trainees and the trainer is a positive learning feature that is missing from distance learning programs that merely use technology to broadcast a lecture to geographically dispersed employees. All that is done in this case is repurposing a traditional lecture (with its limitations for learning and transfer of training) for a new training technology! That's why establishing a communications link between employees and the trainer is important. Also, on-site instructors or facilitators should be available to answer questions and moderate question-and-answer sessions.

Audiovisual Techniques. *Audiovisual instruction* includes overheads, slides, and video. It has been used for improving communications skills, interviewing skills, and customer-service skills and for illustrating how procedures (such as welding) should be followed. Video is, however, rarely used alone. It is usually used in conjunction with lectures to show trainees real-life experiences and examples. Video is also a major component of behavior modeling and, naturally, interactive video instruction. Morse Bros., located in Tangent, Oregon, is one of only a few ready-mix firms in the Northwest that provide regular training for their drivers. Drivers play a key role in determining the success of the business. Excessive idling at construction sites, avoiding rollovers at construction sites, and product training can reduce costs and raise customer satisfaction. Morse Bros. produces training videos, which are presented by mentor-drivers. The mentor-driver's job is to select the weekly video, schedule viewing sessions, keep attendance records, and guide a wrap-up discussion following each video. The mentor-drivers are trained to call attention to key learning points covered in the video and relate the topics to issues the drivers deal with on the job. Because training sessions are scheduled early in the morning at the beginning of the drivers' shift, time is limited. Videos seldom run more than 10 minutes. For example, one called *Another Pair of Eyes* trains drivers to observe test procedures used by testing agencies at job sites. Samples are tested several times a month. A sample that fails can leave the company liable for demolition and removal of the concrete structure. Morse Bros. provides training on test procedures because samples often fail a test due to contamination (such as dirt) that gets into the test cylinder. At each training session, drivers answer several questions related to the content of the program. At the end of a session, drivers and the mentor-driver discuss anything that might be interfering with the quality of the product or timeliness of delivery. Mentor-drivers then share this information with company managers.[52]

The use of video in training has a number of advantages. First, the trainer can review, slow down, or speed up the lesson, which permits flexibility in customizing the session depending on trainees' expertise. Second, trainees can be exposed

● Mobile technology is useful not only for entertainment, but can also be used for employees who travel and need to be in touch with the office. iPods, IPads, and Personal Digital Assistants also give employees the ability to listen to and participate in training programs at their own leisure.

to equipment, problems, and events that cannot be easily demonstrated, such as equipment malfunctions, angry customers, or emergencies. Third, trainees get consistent instruction; program content is not affected by the interests and goals of a particular trainer. Fourth, videotaping trainees allows them to see and hear their own performance without the interpretation of the trainer. As a result, trainees cannot attribute poor performance to the bias of external evaluators such as the trainer or peers.

Most problems in video result from the creative approach used.[53] These problems include too much content for the trainee to learn, poor dialogue between the actors (which hinders the credibility and clarity of the message), overuse of humor or music, and drama that makes it confusing for the trainee to understand the important learning points emphasized in the video.

Mobile Technologies: iPods, iPads, Cellphones, and Tablet Computers. Mobile technologies such as iPods and tablet computers allow training and learning to occur naturally throughout the workday or at home, allow employees to be connected to communities of learning, and give employees the ability to learn at their own pace by reviewing material or skipping over content they know.[54] The typical users for mobile learning include employees who are part of a workforce that spends most of its time traveling and visiting customers, clients, or various company locations (such as sales, security officers, executives, or inspectors) and has limited time available to spend in traditional training activities or e-learning.

Hilton Worldwide is distributing 1,000 iPads to senior executives. These executives spend almost 8% of their time traveling, making classroom learning difficult.[55] The iPads are loaded with customized apps and videos. SAP, a technology company, gave its employees 1,500 iPads and is expected to distribute an additional 17,000 in 2011. SAP is utilizing the iPad because it can help facilitate personalized learning for salespeople around the world. A new salesperson in China will need a different set of skills and apps than a saleperson who is experienced selling SAP solutions in Canada. Retailers such as Sephora and JCPenney are supplying employees with iPads that they can use as a product reference guide (a performance support tool). Watson Pharmaceuticals has developed an app for its corporate university, allowing pharmaceutical representatives to access videos and product knowledge from their iPhones.

Capital One, a financial services company, provides iPods (portable audio players) for employees enrolled in training courses.[56] More than 2,000 iPods have been distributed as part of the Audio Learning program. The iPods can be used for business or personal reasons such as listening to music. Capital One decided that a new way to deliver training was needed based on employee surveys suggesting that employees did not have the time at work to attend classroom training. As a result, Capital One experimented with an audio channel for learning and found that employees liked learning on iPods and were able to gain access to programs that they would have been unable to attend in a classroom. Employees can access digitized audio, such as MP3 files, which are downloaded to their computers and can be transferred to their iPods. Approximately 30 training programs use the iPod. Employees can access a variety of programs, including leadership development and workshops on conflict management. Books and Harvard Business School cases are provided to employees on the iPod and have been used in executive-level programs to discuss leadership and new-hire programs to understand customer service. Besides using the iPod as a primary training content delivery mechanism, some programs use the iPod to provide books or articles for employees for pre-work before they attend a classroom program, and others use it to enhance transfer of training. For example, scenarios and role-plays discussed in classroom training are recorded and available for iPod upload. Employees can listen to the role-plays, which reinforces the use of the training content on the job and motivates them to think about using what they have learned. Capital One has determined that despite the costs related to purchasing and providing each employee with an iPod, if employees were listening to four to six hours of training content outside the classroom, the company was breaking even. Some of the benefits of the iPod programs include employees' increased enthusiasm for learning (attending courses that use the iPod), employees' willingness to take on new roles and broader job responsibilities, and time savings over traditional learning methods.

Some of the challenges of using mobile technology for learning include ensuring that employees know when and how to take advantage of the technology; encouraging communication, collaboration, and interaction with other employees in communities of practice; and ensuring that employees can connect to a variety of networks no matter their location or mobile device they are using.[57] However, simply digitizing lectures and distributing them to employees will not facilitate learning. Thus, for example, Capital One creates simulated radio shows with phone-in questions and answers given by the announcers to create an audio learning environment that is enjoyable and interesting. The best approach may be to use iPods as part of a blended learning approach involving face-to-face interaction between trainees as well as audio learning.

Hands-on Methods

Hands-on methods are training methods that require the trainee to be actively involved in learning. Hands-on methods include on-the-job training, simulations, business games and case studies, behavior modeling, interactive video, and web-based training. These methods are ideal for developing specific skills, understanding how skills and behaviors can be transferred to the job, experiencing all aspects of completing a task, and dealing with interpersonal issues that arise on the job.

Hands-on Methods
Training methods that actively involve the trainee in learning.

ON-THE-JOB TRAINING (OJT)

On-the-job training (OJT) refers to new or inexperienced employees learning through observing peers or managers performing the job and trying to imitate their behavior. OJT can be useful for training newly hired employees, upgrading experienced employees' skills when new technology is introduced, cross-training employees within a department or work unit, and orienting transferred or promoted employees to their new jobs.

OJT takes various forms, including apprenticeships and self-directed learning programs. (Both are discussed later in this section.) OJT is an attractive training method because, compared to other methods, it needs less investment in time or money for materials, trainer's salary, or instructional design. Managers or peers who are job knowledge experts are used as instructors. As a result, it may be tempting to let them conduct the training as they believe it should be done.

This unstructured approach to OJT has several disadvantages[58] Managers and peers may not use the same process to complete a task. They may pass on bad habits as well as useful skills. Also, they may not understand that demonstration, practice, and feedback are important conditions for effective on-the-job training. Unstructured

On-the-Job Training (OJT)
Peers or managers training new or inexperienced employees who learn the job by observation, understanding, and imitation.

OJT can result in poorly trained employees, employees who use ineffective or dangerous methods to produce a product or provide a service, and products or services that vary in quality.

OJT must be structured to be effective. Table 7.7 shows the principles of structured OJT. Because OJT involves learning by observing others, successful OJT is based on the principles emphasized by social learning theory. These include the use of a credible trainer, a manager or peer who models the behavior or skill, communication of specific key behaviors, practice, feedback, and reinforcement. Reliance Industries, one of India's largest businesses, uses on-the-job training in its Nagothane Manufacturing Division (a refinery that makes polymers and chemicals).[59] Because of rapid company growth and the need for experienced employees, the company needed to help new engineers contribute more quickly. The training staff identified mentors who would help accelerate learning for the new engineers. The mentors and new hires are carefully matched based on an assessment of the mentor's training style and the new employee's learning style. Mentors are paired with up to three new employees each for nine months. The mentors and new employees work together on four learning modules, each module taking two months to complete. Each module includes predetermined lesson plans, and they track their progress using an online portal. The length of time it takes new engineers to contribute at work has decreased from 12 to 6 months.

Apprenticeship
A work-study training method with both on-the-job and classroom training.

Apprenticeship is a work-study training method with both on-the-job training and classroom training.[60] To qualify as a registered apprenticeship program under state or federal guidelines, at least 144 hours of classroom instruction and 2,000 hours, or one year, of on-the-job experience are required.[61] Apprenticeships can be sponsored by individual companies or by groups of companies cooperating with a union. The majority of apprenticeship programs are in the skilled trades, such as plumbing, carpentry, electrical work, and bricklaying.

table 7.7
Principles of On-the-Job Training

PREPARING FOR INSTRUCTION	
1. Break down the job into important steps.	3. Decide how much time you will devote to OJT and when you expect the employees to be competent in skill areas.
2. Prepare the necessary equipment, materials, and supplies.	

ACTUAL INSTRUCTION	
1. Tell the trainees the objective of the task and ask them to watch you demonstrate it.	6. Have the trainees do the entire task and praise them for correct reproduction.
2. Show the trainees how to do it without saying anything.	7. If mistakes are made, have the trainees practice until accurate reproduction is achieved.
3. Explain the key points or behaviors. (Write out the key points for the trainees, if possible.)	8. Praise the trainees for their success in learning the task.
4. Show the trainees how to do it again.	
5. Have the trainees do one or more single parts of the task and praise them for correct reproduction (optional).	

SOURCES: Based on W. J. Rothwell and H. C. Kazanas, "Planned OJT Is Productive OJT," *Training and Development Journal*, October 1990, pp. 53–55; P. J. Decker and B. R. Nathan, *Behavior Modeling Training* (New York: Praeger Scientific, 1985).

The hours and weeks that must be devoted to completing specific skill units are clearly defined. OJT involves assisting a certified tradesperson (a journeyman) at the work site. The on-the-job training portion of the apprenticeship follows the guidelines for effective on-the-job training.[62] Modeling, practice, feedback, and evaluation are involved. First, the employer verifies that the trainee has the required knowledge of the operation or process. Next, the trainer (who is usually a more experienced, licensed employee) demonstrates each step of the process, emphasizing safety issues and key steps. The senior employee provides the apprentice with the opportunity to perform the process until all are satisfied that the apprentice can perform it properly and safely.

A major advantage of apprenticeship programs is that learners can earn pay while they learn. This is important because programs can last several years. Learners' wages usually increase automatically as their skills improve. Also, apprenticeships are usually effective learning experiences because they involve learning why and how a task is performed in classroom instruction provided by local trade schools, high schools, or community colleges. Apprenticeships also usually result in full-time employment for trainees when the program is completed. From the company's perspective, apprenticeship programs meet specific business needs and help to attract talented employees.

At its manufacturing facility in Toledo, Ohio, Libbey Glass has apprenticeship programs in mold making, machine repair, millwrighting, and maintenance repair.[63] Each apprentice requires the support of a journeyman for each work assignment. The program also requires apprentices to be evaluated every 1,000 hours to meet Department of Labor standards. The reviews are conducted by a committee including representatives of management and department journeymen. The committee also develops tests and other evaluation materials. The committee members cannot perform their normal duties during the time they are reviewing apprentices so their workload has to be spread among other employees or rescheduled for some other time. The benefits of the program include the development of employees who are more receptive to change in the work environment, the ability to perform work at Libbey instead of having to outsource jobs to contract labor, and an edge for Libbey in attracting talented employees who like the idea that after completing an apprenticeship they are eligible for promotions to other positions in the company, including management positions. Also, the apprenticeship program helps Libbey tailor training and work experiences to meet specific needs in maintenance repair, which is necessary to create and repair production mold equipment used in making glass products.

Apprentice-type programs are also used to prepare new managers. The president and chief executive officer of Goldcorp Inc., a company in the mining industry, offers the chance for MBAs to apply for a nine-month apprenticeship.[64] The apprentice shadows Goldcorp's CEO, observing board meetings, negotiations, and the process of acquiring mines, and travels to learn important aspects of the mining industry. Goldcorp hopes the apprenticeships will attract more graduates to the mining industry, which many would not consider because of the mining industry's image as an unsafe, dirty business.

One disadvantage of many apprenticeship programs is limited access for minorities and women.[65] Another disadvantage is that there is no guarantee that jobs will be available when the program is completed. Finally, apprenticeship programs prepare trainees who are well trained in one craft or occupation. Due to the changing nature of jobs (thanks to new technology and use of cross-functional teams), many employers may be reluctant to employ workers from apprenticeship programs. Employers may believe that because apprentices are narrowly trained in one occupation or with one company, program graduates may have only company-specific skills and may be unable to acquire new skills or adapt their skills to changes in the workplace.

Simulation
A training method that represents a real-life situation, allowing trainees to see the outcomes of their decisions in an artificial environment.

Simulations. A **simulation** is a training method that represents a real-life situation, with trainees' decisions resulting in outcomes that mirror what would happen if the trainee were on the job. Simulations, which allow trainees to see the impact of their decisions in an artificial, risk-free environment, are used to teach production and process skills as well as management and interpersonal skills.

At United Parcel Service (UPS), technology has made the drivers' job more complex.[66] They have to handle the truck safely, be proficient on the DIAD (handheld computer), and understand how to stay safe during a package delivery. As a result, UPS developed the Integrad training center in Maryland. Integrad includes a package car simulator designed to teach new hires how to load and unload packages from shelves, the floor, and the rear door—meeting company time standards for such activities while minimizing stress and strain that cause injuries. The average driver has to step off and on the truck at least 120 times on his or her route, which can strain ankles if done incorrectly. Trainees deliver packages with trainer and trainees serving as customers in a simulated town with stores, streets, and even a loading dock.

Rogers Wireless Communications, a cell phone company, uses a simulation to train sales skills and product knowledge.[67] An online role-playing simulator that is used includes a variety of animated customers including a busy mother and a punk rocker, each providing a different customer service challenge. The simulation training has helped improve ratings of "mystery shoppers" at Rogers retail stores. Pitney Bowes, a mail-equipment and service company, uses an interactive spreadsheet program to simulate the company's product lines, key processes, and business culture. Executive teams are given a set of monthly revenue and product goals. They have to make a series of decisions including how many sales representatives to hire and how much time to invest in finding new clients. The decisions are plugged into the spreadsheet and both short- and long-term financial results are provided. The simulation has helped executives develop innovative ideas for transforming the sales organization with positive bottom-line dollar results.

Avatars
Computer depictions of humans that can be used as imaginary coaches, co-workers, and customers in simulations.

Avatars refer to computer depictions of humans that are being used as imaginary coaches, co-workers, and customers in simulations.[68] In second life (see www.second-life.com), a virtual world built by its residents, avatars are used. Typically, trainees see the avatar who appears throughout the training course. For example, a sales training course at CDW Corporation, a technology products and service company, guides trainees through mock interviews with customers. The avatar introduces the customer situation, and the trainee hears the customer speaking in a simulated phone conversation. The trainee has to determine with help from the avatar what is happening in the sales process by reading the customer's voice. Loews Corporation's hotel chain uses "Virtual Leader," a program that helps participants learn how to be effective in meetings (e.g., how to build alliances, how to get a meeting agenda approved). As trainees attend the simulated meetings what they say (or don't say) results in scores that relate to their influence in the meeting.

Virtual Reality
Computer-based technology that provides trainees with a three-dimensional learning experience. Trainees operate in a simulated environment that responds to their behaviors and reactions.

A recent development in simulations is the use of virtual reality technology. **Virtual reality** is a computer-based technology that provides trainees with a three-dimensional learning experience. Using specialized equipment or viewing the virtual model on the computer screen, trainees move through the simulated environment and interact with its components.[69] Technology is used to stimulate multiple senses of the trainee.[70] Devices relay information from the environment to the senses. For example, audio interfaces, gloves that provide a sense of touch, treadmills, or motion platforms are used to create a realistic, artificial environment. Devices also communicate information about the trainee's movements to a computer. These devices allow the trainee to experience the perception of actually being in a particular environment. For example, Motorola's advanced manufacturing courses for employees learning to run the Pager Robotic Assembly facility use virtual reality. Employees are fitted with a head-mount display that allows them to view the virtual world, which includes the actual lab space, robots, tools, and the assembly operation. The trainees hear and see the actual sounds and sights as if they were using the real equipment. Also, the equipment responds to the employees' actions (such as turning on a switch or dial).

Second Life is one example of a computer-based, simulated online virtual world, including a three-dimensional representation of the real world and a place to host learning programs or experiences. In Second Life, trainees use an avatar to interact with each other in classrooms, webinars, simulations, or role-play exercises. Second Life allows for employees to learn alone or with their peers or teams. Second Life can be used to create virtual classrooms, but its strength is the ability to create virtual reality simulations that actively involve the learner—such as putting the trainees' avatar in a realistic role-play where they have to deal with an upset customer. Paidera, a technology company that provides English-as-a-second-language training, uses a virtual world to teach English.[71] Trainees create an avatar and enter the virtual world to practice language skills in real situations. For example, trainees talk to cab drivers or order food at a restaurant, all of which require use of English.

Employees at Silicon Image learn about making silicon chips by exploring a virtual world in Second Life that represents a corporate campus and by interacting with avatars.[72] Employees can visit the company's departments while watching videos and slide shows explaining what work is done within each unit. British Petroleum used Second Life to train new gas station employees in the safety features of gasoline storage tanks and piping systems.[73] BP builds three-dimensional replicas of the tank and pipe systems at a gas station. Trainees are able to see the underground storage tanks and piping systems and observe how safety devices control gasoline flow, which they could never do in real life.

As you can see from the example, simulations can be effective for several reasons.[74] First, trainees can use them on their desktop, eliminating the need to travel to a central training location. Second, simulations are meaningful, get trainees involved in learning, and are emotionally engaging (they can be fun!). This helps increase employees' willingness to practice, retain, and improve their skills. Third, simulators provide a consistent message of what needs to be learned; trainees can work at their own pace; and, compared to face-to-face instruction, simulators can incorporate more situations or problems that a trainee might encounter. Fourth, simulations can safely put employees in situations that would be dangerous in the real world. Fifth, simulations have been found to result in positive outcomes such as training being completed in a shorter time compared to traditional training courses, and providing a positive return on investment. The use of simulations has been limited by their development costs. As the development costs of simulations continue to decrease they will likely become a more popular training method. The costs of simulations varies. A customized simulation can cost between $200,000 and $300,000, while a simulation purchased from a supplier without any customization costs $100 to $200 per trainee.[75] Leased space in a virtual world can range from $5,000 to $100,000 annually depending on the size and type of space leased (e.g., private, customized island).[76]

Business Games and Case Studies. Situations that trainees study and discuss (case studies) and business games in which trainees must gather information, analyze it, and make decisions are used primarily for management skill development. One organization that has effectively used case studies is the Central Intelligence Agency (CIA).[77] The cases are historically accurate and use actual data. For example, "The Libyan Attack" is used in management courses to teach leadership qualities. "The Stamp Case" is used to teach new employees about the agency's ethics structure. The CIA uses approximately 100 cases. One-third are focused on management; the rest focus on operations training, counterintelligence, and analysis. The cases are used in the training curriculum where the objectives include teaching students to analyze and resolve complex, ambiguous situations. The CIA found that for the cases used in training programs to be credible and meaningful to trainees, the material had to be as authentic as possible and stimulate students to make decisions similar to those they must make in their work environment. As a result, to ensure case accuracy, the CIA uses retired officers to research and write cases. The CIA has even developed a case writing workshop to prepare instructors to use the case method.

Games stimulate learning because participants are actively involved and they mimic the competitive nature of business. The types of decisions that participants make in games include all aspects of management practice, including labor relations (such as agreement in contract negotiations), marketing (the price to charge for a new product), and finance (financing the purchase of new technology). For example, at NetApp Inc., 25 managers participated in a game in which they played the role of top executives of an imaginary company modeled after their employer.[78] The managers worked in five-person teams to produce the strongest sales and operating profit, faced with challenges such as balancing long-term investments against short-term results. Managers received information including market analyses based on actual NetApp data and a menu of strategic initiatives such as improving college recruiting. The teams had to choose strategies and allocate employees and money. They had to respond to issues such as large customers seeking to add last-minute product features, considering whether to add the features and their related costs or refuse and risk angering an important client. The teams saw the consequences of their decisions. For example, one team declined to add the product features, which resulted in a decline in customer satisfaction and market share. At the end of the simulation, the sales and total profits of each team, as well as the effect of their strategies, were discussed.

Documentation on learning from games is anecdotal.[79] Games may give team members a quick start at developing a framework for information and help develop cohesive groups. For some groups (such as senior executives), games may be more meaningful training activities (because the game is realistic) than presentation techniques such as classroom instruction.

Cases may be especially appropriate for developing higher-order intellectual skills such as analysis, synthesis, and evaluation. These skills are often required by managers, physicians, and other professional employees. Cases also help trainees develop the willingness to take risks given uncertain outcomes, based on their analysis of the situation. To use cases effectively, the learning environment must let trainees prepare and discuss their case analyses. Also, face-to-face or electronic communication among trainees must be arranged. Because trainee involvement is critical for the effectiveness of the case method, learners must be willing and able to analyze the case and then communicate and defend their positions.

There are a number of available sources for preexisting cases (e.g., Harvard Business School). It is especially important to review preexisting cases to determine how meaningful they will be to the trainee.

Behavior Modeling. Research suggests that behavior modeling is one of the most effective techniques for teaching interpersonal skills.[80] Each training session, which typically lasts four hours, focuses on one interpersonal skill, such as coaching or communicating ideas. Each session presents the rationale behind key behaviors, a DVD of a model performing key behaviors, practice opportunities using role-playing, evaluation of a model's performance in the videotape, and a planning session devoted to understanding how the key behaviors can be used on the job. In the practice sessions, trainees get feedback regarding how closely their behavior matches the key behaviors demonstrated by the model. The role-playing and modeled performance are based on actual incidents in the employment setting in which the trainee needs to demonstrate success.

Interactive Video. Interactive video combines the advantages of video and computer-based instruction. Instruction is provided one-on-one to trainees via a personal computer. Trainees use the keyboard or touch the monitor to interact with the program. Interactive video is used to teach technical procedures and interpersonal skills. The training program may be stored on a DVD or the company intranet. For example, the Shoney's and Captain D's restaurant chains have more than 350 restaurants in more than 20 states.[81] More than 8,000 employees each year must be trained on the basics of the operational parts of the business, including how to make french fries, hush puppies, and coleslaw. Also, each year 600 new managers must be trained in business issues and back-office operations of the restaurants. The biggest challenge that Shoney's faced was how to consistently train geographically dispersed employees. Shoney's solution was to implement OneTouch, a live integrated video and two-way voice and data application that combines synchronous video, voice, and data and live web pages so that team members can interact with trainers. OneTouch can be delivered to desktop PCs as well as to warehouses and repair bays. Desktop systems can be positioned in any appropriate locations in the restaurant. Individuals or groups of employees can gather around the PC for training. The training modules include such topics as orientation, kitchen, and dining room. Each module is interactive. Topics are introduced and are followed up by quizzes to ensure that learning occurs. For example, the coleslaw program shows trainees what the coleslaw ingredients are and where they can be found in the restaurant. The coleslaw program includes a video that trainees can watch and practice with. After they practice, they have to complete a quiz, and their manager has to verify that they completed the topic before they move on to the next program. The training is consistent and is easy to update so as to ensure it is current. The program also allows kitchen and counter staff to learn each other's skills, which gives Shoney's flexibility in its staffing (e.g., counter employees who know how to cook). The main disadvantage of interactive video is the high cost of developing the courseware. This may be a particular problem for courses in which frequent updates are necessary.[82]

E-Learning. **E-learning** or online learning refers to instruction and delivery of training by computers through the Internet or company intranets.[83] E-learning includes web-based training, distance learning, virtual classrooms, and use of CD-ROMs. E-learning can include task support, simulation training, distance learning, and learning portals. There are three important characteristics of e-learning. First, e-learning involves electronic networks that enable information and instruction to be delivered, shared, and updated instantly. Second, e-learning is delivered to the trainee

LO 7-6
Explain the potential advantages of e-learning for training.

E-Learning
Instruction and delivery of training by computers through the Internet or company intranet.

via computers with Internet technology. Third, it focuses on learning solutions that go beyond traditional training to include information and tools that improve performance.

Figure 7.6 depicts the features of e-learning, which include collaboration and sharing, links to resources, learner control, delivery, and administration. As Figure 7.6 shows, e-learning not only provides training content but lets learners control what they learn, the speed at which they progress through the program, how much they practice, and even when they learn. E-learning also allows learners to collaborate or interact with other trainees and experts, and it provides links to other learning resources such as reference materials, company websites, and other training programs. Text, video, graphics, and sound can present course content. E-learning may also include various aspects of training administration such as course enrollment, testing and evaluating trainees, and monitoring learning progress. Various delivery methods can be incorporated into e-learning including distance learning, DVD, and the Internet.

These features of e-learning give it advantages over other training methods. E-learning initiatives are designed to contribute to strategic business objectives.[84]

figure 7.6

Characteristics of E-Learning

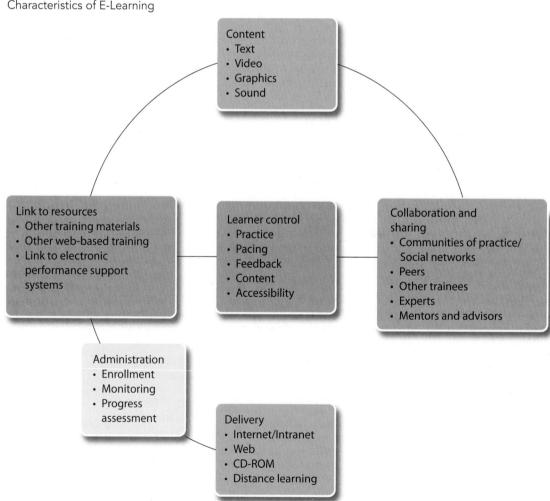

E-learning supports company initiatives such as attracting customers, devising new ways to operate such as e-business, or quickly developing products or new services. E-learning may involve a larger audience than traditional training programs, which focused on employees; it may involve partners, suppliers, vendors, and potential customers.

For example, Ritz Camera Centers uses an e-learning program to help keep employees up-to-date on product information and enhance their selling skills.[85] E-learning was selected because the company needed a systematic way to reach all associates quickly, with easily managed and updated materials. Ritz Camera employees access short training courses online on a wide variety of technologies and brands. Each module provides insight into product features, competitive differences, and benefits. Training modules are created monthly and can stay live for up to a year based on product cycles. The modules feature training assessments in the form of a quiz that must be passed. In addition, Ritz can track employees' participation through a web portal.

Learning is enhanced through e-learning because trainees are more engaged through the use of video, graphics, sound, and text, which appeal to multiple senses of the learner. Also, e-learning requires that learners actively participate in practice, questions, and interaction with other learners and experts.

Besides enhancing the training experience, e-learning can reduce training costs and time. E-learning brings training to geographically dispersed employees at their locations, reducing travel costs.

Sanofi-Aventis U.S. was behind its competition in product knowledge within the diabetes sales force.[86] The company needed a training solution that the sales force could complete in the field or while traveling. As a result, the company developed a self-paced e-learning solution—a virtual campus called Diabetes University. Learners can be guided through the campus by a "professor" and participate in different types of learning activities including games, videos, and narrated text.

Effective e-learning is grounded on a thorough needs assessment and complete learning objectives. **Repurposing** refers to directly translating an instructor-led, face-to-face training program online. Online learning that merely repurposes an ineffective training program will remain ineffective. Unfortunately, in their haste to develop online learning, many companies are repurposing bad training! The best e-learning combines the advantages of the Internet with the principles of a good learning environment. Effective online learning takes advantage of the web's dynamic nature and ability to use many positive learning features, including linking to other training sites and content through the use of hyperlinks, and allowing the trainee to collaborate with other learners. Online learning also gives learner control over the pace of learning, exercises, and use of links to other material and peer and expert networks. Online learning allows activities typically led by the instructor (presentation, visuals, slides), trainees (discussion, questions), and group interaction (discussion of application of training content) to be incorporated into training without trainees or the instructor having to be physically present in a training room. Effective online learning gives trainees meaningful content, relevant examples, and the ability to apply content to work problems and issues. Also, trainees can practice and receive feedback through problems, exercises, assignments, and tests.

Repurposing
Directly translating instructor-led training online.

Blended Learning. Because of the limitations of online learning related to technology (e.g., insufficient bandwidth, lack of high-speed web connections), because of trainee preference for face-to-face contact with instructors and other learners, and because of employees' inability to find unscheduled time during their workday to devote to learning from their desktops, many companies are moving to a hybrid, or blended,

Blended Learning
Delivering content and instruction with a combination of technology-based and face-to-face methods.

learning approach. **Blended learning** refers to combining technology methods, such as e-learning or mobile learning, with face-to-face instruction, for delivery of learning content and instruction. Blended learning approaches capitalize on the strengths of face-to-face and technological instruction. For example, time savings and reduced costs can be gained by having employees first complete online learning, focusing on acquiring knowledge, and then meet face-to-face at a training session to discuss how the knowledge can be applied to the workplace using cases, games, simulations, or classroom discussion. The "Competing though Technology" box shows how companies are using technology for blended learning and to encourage informal learning.

Learning Management System (LMS)
Technology platform that automates the administration, development, and delivery of a company's training program.

Learning Management System. A **learning management system (LMS)** refers to a technology platform that can be used to automate the administration, development, and delivery of all of a company's training programs. An LMS can provide employees, managers, and trainers with the ability to manage, deliver, and track learning activities.[87] LMSs are becoming more popular for several reasons. An LMS can help companies reduce travel and other costs related to training, reduce time for program completion, increase employees' accessibility to training across the business, and provide administrative capabilities to track program completion and course enrollments. An LMS allows companies to track all of the learning activity in the business. VCA Animal Hospitals has a geographically dispersed workforce with 13,000 workers in over 500 animal hospitals across 40 states.[88] It used to rely on training based on PowerPoint presentations with audio narration but recognized that it had to improve the quality of its courses. VCA Animal Hospitals purchased a new LMS which now allows for more engaging training methods including video clips of veterinarians discussing medical practices, simulations, online collaboration between learners and learners and the instructors, and safety inspection checklists. The LMS is used for online courses, registering veterinarians for classroom-based courses, and tracking who has completed training and how well they scored on posttraining tests. Vanguard, the financial services firm, uses an LMS that allows its employees, known as crew members, to get learning recommendations from Vanguard's University based on their career interests, development goals, and relevant content for their current jobs.[89] It also makes it easier for crew members to find and access videos, audio clips, interactive Flash demonstrations, and articles and enroll in classes. The LMS categorizes informal learning sources such as podcasts, articles, and videoclips with formal learning solutions including online and classroom-based courses. Informal and formal learning solutions as well as outside courses offered by vendors can also be found using a keyword search. Gales Residential develops, builds, and manages multifamily communities and mixed-use developments in urban markets such as Houston, Texas, and Washington, D.C.[90] Gales Residential associates, primarily Millenials and Generation X, wanted a system that was exciting and easily customizable. Associates can use the LMS to take assessments and courses that are linked to their development plans. The LMS also gives associates access to e-learning courses and a WebEx Training Center through which instructors can lead live virtual classes. The LMS has helped the company reduce travel and hotel costs by 21%.

Group- or Team-Building Methods
Training techniques that help trainees share ideas and experiences, build group identity, understand the dynamics of interpersonal relationships, and get to know their own strengths and weaknesses and those of their co-workers.

Group- or Team-Building Methods

Group- or team-building methods are training methods designed to improve team or group effectiveness. Training is directed at improving the trainees' skills as well as team effectiveness. In group-building methods, trainees share ideas and experiences, build group identity, understand the dynamics of interpersonal relationships,

Blended Learning and Informal Learning Made Easier

Many companies are capitalizing on new technology to help employees learn informally and share knowledge both informally on an as-needed basis and formally during scheduled training courses. This involves the use of blended learning approaches which combine face-to-face instruction and technology-based learning methods including online learning, social networking tools, and knowledge management systems. Online training can be used to provide consistent delivery of training content involving transfer of information (knowledge and skills) to geographically dispersed employees who can work at their own pace, practice, and collaborate with the trainer and trainee online. Then, trainees can be brought to a central location for face-to-face training (classroom, action learning, games, and role-plays), which can emphasize the application of knowledge and skills using cases and problems that require the application of training content. Face-to-face instruction is also more useful for facilitating interaction between trainees, collaboration, networking, and discussion.

Dunkin' Donuts training uses a blended learning approach involving online, classroom, and on-site work with follow-up and reinforcement. Franchisees attend an introductory course that focuses on the business as well as their roles and responsibilities (and those of the franchisor). This helps the franchisees learn from and build relationships with important individuals and teams at the corporation. Franchisees then complete 60 hours of online training on their own time in how donuts are made, equipment maintenance, food safety, and shift management. A five-and-half-week instructor-led course and certification program runs at the same time as the online training. Both the online and instructor-led course are designed to simulate restaurant experiences with the goal of facilitating on-the-job practice that occurs in the restaurant. Practice sessions are supported with skills checklists to monitor progress and review training materials. Before opening the restaurant, franchisees train their new staffs, working side-by-side with regional market trainers or operations managers from Dunkin' Donuts. The goal is to have all employees working efficiently and effectively when the new restaurant opens. Extensive training also occurs after the restaurant opens. Market and network trainers and operations managers visit the store to evaluate them and provide ongoing training, support, and coaching. Based on the store evaluations, new training programs are developed to improve problem areas. The success of the training programs is measured in several different ways. Each of the training programs measures learning through the franchisee's ability to perform skills in restaurant operations. Dunkin' Donuts also asks franchisees for feedback on the training programs.

Advantage Sales & Marketing (ASM), a sales and marketing agency based in Irvine, California, added social networking to its sales training program (Accelerated Career Excellence in Sales—ACES) which teaches individuals to become business development managers. The five-month learning program involves participants meeting face-to-face for a two-day training session and then returning to their home sales markets. The remaining time in the program is spent working in the field with mentors and completing online training modules. During the program, employees have access to the ACES workplace community online for interaction with senior sales leaders, peers, mentors, and other salespersons in the program. Adding the social networking platform to the training program has encouraged employees to share knowledge. For example, one learner in the program contacted all of the ACES mentors to identify best practices on a specific topic. He compiled this information into a document which he shared with the entire learner community. Verizon uses social networking tools to train employees to support new products and devices. Device

Blog, Device Forum, and Learning Communities help ensure that employees are ready to support customers when new products and devices are introduced to the market, engage Verizon's multigenerational workforce, and facilitate peer-to-peer learning. Device Blog makes available information and updates on wireless devices (such as DROID), FAQs (frequently asked questions), how-to-videos, and troubleshooting tips. Device Forums enable retail employees to learn from peers and product manufacturers. Employees can ask each other questions, share issues, post tips, make suggestions, and access product experts. Learning communities are accessed through the Device Blog. They include video blogs, message boards, links to online training modules, and product

demonstrations. In addition to these tools, employees have access to My Network for collaborating with their peers, knowledge and document sharing, and creating working groups. Some instructors also use it for posting supplemental content for learners' use.

Special People In Northeast, Inc. (SPIN) a nonprofit organization that provides services to individuals with disabilities, makes webcasts as well as videos, "how-to manuals," and process flowcharts electronically available to employees to ensure that knowledge of key employees is documented and current practices and procedures are available and shared. Intel encourages informal learning two ways: through knowledge sharing and providing employees with "performer support." Both knowledge

sharing and performer support are part of Planet Blue, a social media platform for Intel employees. Employees also have access to Intelpedia, an internal wiki, that employees can edit. Intelpedia has millions of pages and thousands of employees have contributed to it. Intelpedia helped create a culture for using technology-based information-sharing solutions at Intel.

SOURCES: Based on W. Webb, "Training = Franchise Success," *Training*, October 2008, pp. 54–55; M. Weinstein, "A Better Blend," *Training*, September 2008, pp. 30–39; M. Weinstein, "Netting Know-How," *Training*, September/October 2010, pp. 26–29; J. Roy, "Transforming Informal Learning into a Competitive Advantage," *T + D*, October 2010, pp. 23–25; P. Galagan, "Unformal, the New Normal?" *T + D*, September 2010, pp. 29–31; and M. Weinstein, "Verizon Connects to Success," *Training*, January/February 2011, pp. 40–42.

and get to know their own strengths and weaknesses and those of their co-workers. Group techniques focus on helping teams increase their skills for effective teamwork. A number of training techniques are available to improve work group or team performance, to establish a new team, or to improve interactions among different teams. They include trust falls (in which each trainee stands on a table and falls backward into the arms of fellow group members), paintball games, NASCAR pit crews, cooking, obstacle courses, and even drumming! All involve examination of feelings, perceptions, and beliefs about the functioning of the team; discussion; and development of plans to apply what was learned in training to the team's performance in the work setting. Group-building methods fall into three categories: adventure learning, team training, and action learning.

Group-building methods often involve experiential learning. *Experiential learning* training programs involve gaining conceptual knowledge and theory; taking part in a behavioral simulation; analyzing the activity; and connecting the theory and activity with on-the-job or real-life situations.[91]

For experiential training programs to be successful, several guidelines should be followed. The program needs to tie in to a specific business problem. The trainees need to be moved outside their personal comfort zones but within limits so as not to reduce trainee motivation or ability to understand the purpose of the program. Multiple learning modes should be used, including audio, visual, and kinesthetic. When preparing activities for an experiential training program, trainers should ask trainees for input on the program goals. Clear expectations about the purpose, expected outcomes, and trainees' role in the program are important. Finally, training programs that include experiential learning should be linked to changes in employee attitudes, behaviors, and other business results.

California-based Quantum Corporation developed a project to overhaul the company's online infrastructure across global operations.[92] The project included a diverse group of team members from the information technology, engineering, marketing, and graphic design departments. The team consisted of very talented employees who were not used to working with each other. Many of the team members were geographically dispersed, which increased the difficulties in working together. Quantum hired an actors' group to lead the team through a series of improvisational activities designed to get the team members to share personal stories. Using music, props, lighting, and costumes, the actors interpreted the stories told by team members. The actors portrayed team members who, for example, expressed isolation and frustration. Other times, team members would play the parts. The sessions allowed each team member to ask questions of the actors or each other. The team came away from the activity with more empathy and understanding for each other. Development of the personal relationships created positive interpersonal bonds that helped the team meet deadlines and complete projects.

Adventure Learning. **Adventure learning** develops teamwork and leadership skills using structured outdoor activities.[93] Adventure learning appears to be best suited for developing skills related to group effectiveness, such as self-awareness, problem solving, conflict management, and risk taking. Adventure learning may involve strenuous, challenging physical activities such as dogsledding or mountain climbing. It can also use structured individual and group outdoor activities such as climbing walls, going through rope courses, making trust falls, climbing ladders, and traveling from one tower to another using a device attached to a wire that connects the two towers.

For example, a Chili's restaurant manager in adventure learning was required to scale a three-story-high wall.[94] About two-thirds away from the top of the wall the manager became very tired. She successfully reached the top of the wall using the advice and encouragement shouted from team members on the ground below. When asked to consider what she learned from the experience, she reported that the exercise made her realize that reaching personal success depends on other people. At her restaurant, everyone has to work together to make the customers happy.

Adventure learning can also include demanding activities that require coordination and place less of a physical strain on team members. For example, Cookin' Up Change is one of many team-building courses offered around the United States by chefs, caterers, hotels, and cooking schools.[95] These courses have been used by companies such as Honda and Microsoft. The underlying idea is that cooking classes help strengthen communications and networking skills by requiring team members to work together to create a full-course meal (a culinary feast!). Each team has to decide who does what kitchen tasks (e.g., cooking, cutting, cleaning) and prepares the main course, salads, or dessert. Often team members are required to switch assignments in midpreparation to see how the team reacts to change.

For adventure learning programs to succeed, the exercises should be related to the types of skills that participants are expected to develop. Also, after the exercises, a skilled facilitator should lead a discussion about what happened in the exercise, what was learned, how the exercise relates to the job situation, and how to set goals and apply what was learned on the job.[96]

Adventure Learning
Learning focused on the development of teamwork and leadership skills by using structured outdoor activities.

Does adventure learning work? Participants often report that they gained a greater understanding of themselves and the ways they interact with their co-workers. One key to the success of an adventure learning program may be the insistence that whole work groups participate together so that group dynamics that inhibit effectiveness can emerge and be discussed.

The physically demanding nature of adventure learning and the requirement that trainees often have to touch each other in the exercises may increase the company's risk for negligence claims due to personal injury, intentional infliction of emotional distress, and invasion of privacy. Also, the Americans with Disabilities Act (discussed in Chapter 3) raises questions about requiring employees with disabilities to participate in physically demanding training experiences.[97]

Team Training. Team training coordinates the performance of individuals who work together to achieve a common goal. Such training is an important issue when information must be shared and individuals affect the overall performance of the group. For example, in the military as well as the private sector (think of nuclear power plants or commercial airlines), much work is performed by crews, groups, or teams. Success depends on coordination of individual activities to make decisions, team performance, and readiness to deal with potentially dangerous situations (like an overheating nuclear reactor).

Cross-Training
Team members understand and practice each other's skills.

Coordination Training
Trains the team in how to share information and decisions.

Team Leader Training
Training the team manager or facilitator.

Team training strategies include cross-training and coordination training.[98] In **cross-training** team members understand and practice each other's skills so that members are prepared to step in and take another member's place. **Coordination training** trains the team in how to share information and decisions to maximize team performance. Coordination training is especially important for commercial aviation and surgical teams, who monitor different aspects of equipment and the environment but must share information to make the most effective decisions regarding patient care or aircraft safety and performance. **Team leader training** refers to training the team manager or facilitator. This may involve training the manager how to resolve conflict within the team or help the team coordinate activities or other team skills.

United Airlines (UAL) is having its supervisors "lead" ramp employees in attending Pit Instruction & Training (Pit Crew U), which focuses on the preparation, practice, and teamwork of NASCAR pit crews. United is using the training to develop standardized methods to safely and efficiently unload, load, and send off its airplanes.[99] Pit Instruction & Training, located outside of Charlotte, North Carolina, has a quarter-mile race track and a pit road with places for six cars. The school offers programs to train new racing pit crews, but most of its business comes from companies interested in having their teams work as safely, efficiently, and effectively as NASCAR pit crews. The training is part of a multimillion-dollar investment that includes updating equipment and providing luggage scanners. The purpose of the training is to reinforce the need for ramp teams to be orderly and communicate, and to help standardize tasks of ramp team members, along with increasing morale. Training has been optional for ramp employees and they have survived layoffs and been asked to make wage concessions to help the company get out of bankruptcy. United already has started scheduling shorter ground times at some airports, anticipating the positive results of the program. Shorter ground times translate into more daily flights without having to buy more airplanes. United hopes to cut the average airplane ground time by eight minutes to make the airline more competitive.

The keys for safety, speed, and efficiency for NASCAR pit crews is that each member knows what tasks to do (change tires, use air gun, add gasoline, clean up spills) and, when the crew has finished servicing the race car, moves new equipment into position anticipating the next pit stop. The training involves the ramp workers actually working as pit crews. They learn how to handle jacks, change tires, and fill fuel tanks on race cars. They are videotaped and timed just like real pit crews. They receive feedback from professional pit crew members who work on NASCAR teams and trainers. Also, the training requires them to deal with circumstances they might encounter on the job. For one pit stop, lug nuts had been sprinkled intentionally in the area where the car stops to see if the United employees would notice them and clean them up. On their jobs ramp employees are responsible for removing debris from the tarmac so it doesn't get sucked into jet engines or harm equipment. For another pit stop, teams had to work with fewer members, as sometimes occurs when ramp crews are understaffed due to absences.

Action Learning. In **action learning** teams or work groups get an actual business problem, work on solving it and commit to an action plan, and are accountable for carrying out the plan.[100] Typically, action learning involves between 6 and 30 employees; it may also include customers and vendors. There are several variations on the composition of the group. In one variation the group includes a single customer for the problem being dealt with. Sometimes the groups include cross-functional team members (members from different company departments) who all have a stake in the problem. Or the group may involve employees from multiple functions who all focus on their own functional problems, each contributing to helping solve the problems identified. For example, ATC, a public transportation services management company in Illinois, used action learning to help boost profitability by reducing operating costs.[101] Employees were divided into Action Workout Teams to identify ways of reducing costs and to brainstorm effective solutions. The process assumed that employees closest to where the work gets done have the best ideas about how to solve problems. Teams of five to seven employees met once a week for a couple of hours for 45 to 60 days. For example, a team working on parts inventory might have had a parts clerk, a couple of people from maintenance, a supervisor, and an operations employee. These teams studied problems and issues such as overtime, preventive maintenance, absenteeism, parts inventory, and inefficient safety inspection procedures. The teams brainstormed ideas, prioritized them according to their highest potential, developed action plans, installed them, tested them, and measured the outcomes. The solutions that the teams generated resulted in more than $1.8 million in savings for the company.

Six Sigma and black belt training programs involve principles of action learning. **Six Sigma training** provides employees with measurement and statistical tools to help reduce defects and to cut costs.[102] Six Sigma is a quality standard with a goal of only 3.4 defects per million processes. There are several levels of Six Sigma training, resulting in employees becoming certified as green belts, champions, or black belts.[103] To become black belts, trainees must participate in workshops and written assignments coached by expert instructors. The training involves four 4-day sessions over about 16 weeks. Between training sessions, candidates apply what they learn to assigned projects and then use them in the next training session. Trainees are also required to complete not only oral and written exams but also two or more projects that have a significant impact on the company's bottom line. After completing black belt training, employees are able to develop, coach, and lead Six Sigma teams; mentor and advise management on determining Six Sigma projects; and provide Six Sigma tools and statistical methods to team members. After black belts lead several project teams, they can take additional training and be certified as master black belts. Master black

Action Learning
Teams work on an actual business problem, commit to an action plan, and are accountable for carrying out the plan.

Six Sigma Training
An action training program that provides employees with defect-reducing tools to cut costs and certifies employees as green belts, champions, or black belts.

belts can teach other black belts and help senior managers integrate Six Sigma into the company's business goals.

McKesson Corporation trained 15 to 20 black belts and reassigned them to their original business units as their team's Six Sigma representatives.[104] When the two-year commitment ends, the black belts return to the business at higher positions, helping to spread the approach throughout the organization and ensuring that key leaders are committed to the Six Sigma philosophy. In most divisions of the company, Six Sigma training is mandated for senior vice presidents, who attend training that introduces Six Sigma and details how to identify a potential Six Sigma project. Across the company, every manager and director is expected to attend basic training. The Six Sigma effort has shown benefits every year since the program started.

Advice for Choosing a Training Method

LO 7-7
Design a training session to maximize learning.

As a manager, you will likely be asked to choose a training method. Given the large number of training methods available to you, this task may seem difficult. One way to choose a training method is to compare methods. The first step in choosing a method is to identify the type of learning outcome that you want training to influence. These outcomes include verbal information, intellectual skills, cognitive strategies, attitudes, and motor skills. Training methods may influence one or several learning outcomes. Once you have identified a learning method, the next step is to consider the extent to which the method facilitates learning and transfer of training, the costs related to development and use of the method, and its effectiveness.

For learning to occur, trainees must understand the objectives of the training program, training content should be meaningful, and trainees should have the opportunity to practice and receive feedback. Also, a powerful way to learn is through observing and interacting with others. Transfer of training refers to the extent to which training will be used on the job. In general, the closer the training content and environment prepare trainees for use of learning outcomes on the job, the greater the likelihood that transfer will occur. Two types of costs are important: development costs and administrative costs. Development costs relate to design of the training program, including costs to buy or create the program. Administrative costs are incurred each time the training method is used. These include costs related to consultants, instructors, materials, and trainers.

Several trends are worth noting. First, there is considerable overlap between learning outcomes across the training methods. Group-building methods are unique because they focus on individual as well as team learning (e.g., improving group processes). If you are interested in improving the effectiveness of groups or teams, you should choose one of the group-building methods (e.g., action learning, team training, adventure learning). Second, comparing the presentation methods to the hands-on methods illustrates that most hands-on methods provide a better learning environment and transfer of training than do the presentation methods. The presentation methods are also less effective than the hands-on methods. E-learning or blended learning can be an effective training method for geographically dispersed trainees if it includes meaningful content, links to other resources, collaboration and sharing, and learner control. E-learning and other technology-driven training methods have higher development costs, but travel and housing cost savings will likely offset development costs over time. As the previous "Competing through Technology" box shows, many companies recognize the strengths and weaknesses of both technology-based training methods (such as iPods or e-learning) and face-to-face instruction. As a result, they are using both in a blended learning approach. The training budget for developing training methods can influence the method chosen. If you have a limited budget for developing new training methods, use structured on-the-job training—a relatively inexpensive yet effective hands-on method. If you have a larger budget, you might want to consider hands-on methods that facilitate transfer of training, such as simulators.

EVALUATING TRAINING PROGRAMS

Examining the outcomes of a program helps in evaluating its effectiveness. These outcomes should be related to the program objectives, which help trainees understand the purpose of the program. **Training outcomes** can be categorized as cognitive outcomes, skill-based outcomes, affective outcomes, results, and return on investment.[105] Table 7.8 shows the types of outcomes used in evaluating training programs and what is measured and how it is measured.

Which training outcomes measure is best? The answer depends on the training objectives. For example, if the instructional objectives identified business-related outcomes such as increased customer service or product quality, then results outcomes should be included in the evaluation. Both reaction and cognitive outcomes are usually collected before the trainees leave the training site. As a result, these measures do not help determine the extent to which trainees actually use the training content in their jobs (transfer of training). Skill-based, affective, and results outcomes measured following training can be used to determine transfer of training—that is, the extent to

LO 7-8
Choose an appropriate evaluation design based on training objectives and analysis of constraints.

Training Outcomes
A way to evaluate the effectiveness of a training program based on cognitive, skill-based, affective, and results outcomes.

table 7.8

Outcomes Used in Evaluating Training Programs

OUTCOME	WHAT IS MEASURED	HOW MEASURED	EXAMPLE
Cognitive outcomes	• Acquisition of knowledge	• Pencil-and-paper tests • Work sample	• Safety rules • Electrical principles • Steps in appraisal interview
Skill-based outcomes	• Behavior • Skills	• Observation • Work sample • Ratings	• Jigsaw use • Listening skills • Coaching skills • Airplane landings
Affective outcomes	• Motivation • Reaction to program • Attitudes	• Interviews • Focus groups • Attitude surveys	• Satisfaction with training • Beliefs regarding other cultures
Results	• Company payoff	• Observation • Data from information system or performance records	• Absenteeism • Accidents • Patents
Return on investment	• Economic value of training	• Identification and comparison of costs and benefits of the program	• Dollars

which training has changed behavior, skills, or attitudes or directly influenced objective measures related to company effectiveness (such as sales).

The Union Sanitary District located in Union City, California, uses a balanced scorecard to link employee learning and development to customer, financial, and internal process objectives (balanced scorecard was discussed in Chapter 1). The measures include number of training modules developed, number of employees trained, number of employees assessed as competent, number of accidents, injuries, and lost time, the ratio of safety events delivered versus planned, and employee satisfaction surveys.[106]

Reasons for Evaluating Training

Many companies are beginning to invest millions of dollars in training programs to gain a competitive advantage. Firms with high-leverage training practices not only invest large sums of money in developing and administering training programs but also evaluate training programs. Why should training programs be evaluated?

1. To identify the program's strengths and weaknesses. This includes determining whether the program is meeting the learning objectives, the quality of the learning environment, and whether transfer of training to the job is occurring.
2. To assess whether the content, organization, and administration of the program (including the schedule, accommodations, trainers, and materials) contribute to learning and the use of training content on the job.
3. To identify which trainees benefited most or least from the program.
4. To gather marketing data by asking participants whether they would recommend the program to others, why they attended the program, and their level of satisfaction with the program.
5. To determine the financial benefits and costs of the program.
6. To compare the costs and benefits of training to nontraining investments (such as work redesign or better employee selection).
7. To compare the costs and benefits of different training programs to choose the best program.

Kelly Services is a good example of a company that has investigated the benefits of training based on evaluation data.[107] Kelly Services, a company in the temporary staffing industry, revised its training programs to try and reduce the time it takes new employees to become productive and to reduce their turnover. Kelly Services created a new employee orientation program and developed 13 new sales courses. Kelly uses multiple approaches to evaluate its training programs. It uses anecdotal and quantitative data to demonstrate a causal relationship between learning and outcomes such as course completion rates, course enrollments, cost per trainee, and trainee reactions. For the news sales courses, sales were 84% higher for employees who had completed at least one of the courses compared to employees who did not participate in the program. Evaluation of the new employee orientation program showed that turnover decreased 13% and productivity was 27% higher for employees who participated in the program compared to those who did not.

Evaluation Designs

As shown in Table 7.9, a number of different evaluation designs can be applied to training programs. Table 7.9 compares each evaluation design on the basis of who is involved (trainees and/or a comparison group that does not receive training),

table 7.9

Comparison of Evaluation Designs

DESIGN	GROUPS	MEASURES		COST	TIME	STRENGTH
		PRETRAINING	POSTTRAINING			
Posttest only	Trainees	No	Yes	Low	Low	Low
Pretest/posttest	Trainees	Yes	Yes	Low	Low	Medium
Posttest only with comparison group	Trainees and comparison	No	Yes	Medium	Medium	Medium
Pretest/posttest with comparison group	Trainees and comparison	Yes	Yes	Medium	Medium	High
Time series	Trainees	Yes	Yes, several	Medium	Medium	Medium

when outcome measures are collected (pretraining, posttraining), the costs, the time needed to conduct the evaluation, and the strength of the design for ruling out alternative explanations for the results (e.g., are improvements due to factors other than the training?). In general, designs that use pretraining and posttraining measures of outcomes and include a comparison group reduce the risk that factors other than training itself are responsible for the evaluation results. This builds confidence to use the results to make decisions. The trade-off is that evaluations using these designs are more costly and time-consuming to conduct than evaluations not using pretraining or posttraining measures or comparison groups.

There is no one appropriate evaluation design. Several factors need to be considered in choosing one:[108]

- Size of the training program.
- Purpose of training.
- Implications if a training program does not work.
- Company norms regarding evaluation.
- Costs of designing and conducting an evaluation.
- Need for speed in obtaining program effectiveness information.

For example, if a manager is interested in determining how much employees' communications skills have changed as a result of a behavior-modeling training program, a pretest/posttest comparison group design is necessary. Trainees should be randomly assigned to training and no-training conditions. These evaluation design features give the manager a high degree of confidence that any communication skill change is the result of participating in the training program.[109] This type of evaluation design is also necessary if the manager wants to compare the effectiveness of two training programs.

Consider the evaluation design that Mayo Clinic used to compare two methods for training new managers.[110] The Mayo Clinic, located in Rochester, Minnesota, is one of the world's leading centers of medical education and research. Recently, Mayo has undergone considerable growth, adding a new hospital and clinic in the Phoenix area. As a result, employees who were not fully prepared were moved into management positions. This resulted in increased employee dissatisfaction and employee turnover rates. After a needs assessment indicated that employees were leaving because of dissatisfaction with management, Mayo decided to initiate a new training program designed to help the new managers improve their skills. There was some debate whether the training would be best administered one-on-one with a coach or in a classroom. Because of the higher cost of using coaching instead of classroom training, Mayo decided to conduct an evaluation using a posttest comparison group design. Before training all managers, Mayo held three training sessions. No more than 75 managers were included in each session. Within each session managers were divided into three groups: a group that received four days of classroom training, a group that received one-on-one training from a coach, and a group that received no training (a comparison group). Mayo collected reaction (did the trainees like the program?), learning, transfer, and results outcomes. The evaluation found no statistically significant differences in the effects of the coaching compared to classroom training. As a result, Mayo decided to rely on classroom courses for new managers and consider coaching only for managers with critical and immediate job issues.

Determining Return on Investment

Cost–Benefit Analysis
The process of determining the economic benefits of a training program using accounting methods.

Cost–benefit analysis is the process of determining the economic benefits of a training program using accounting methods, which involves determining training costs and benefits. Training cost information is important for several reasons:

1. To understand total expenditures for training, including direct and indirect costs.
2. To compare the costs of alternative training programs.
3. To evaluate the proportion of money spent on training development, administration, and evaluation, as well as to compare moneys spent on training for different groups of employees (such as exempt versus nonexempt).
4. To control costs.[111]

Determining Costs. As we discussed earlier, training costs include direct and indirect costs.[112] One method for comparing costs of alternative training programs is the resource requirements model.[113] This model compares equipment, facilities, personnel, and materials costs across different stages of the training process (training design, implementation, needs assessment, development, and evaluation). The resource requirements model can help determine overall differences in costs between training programs. Also, costs incurred at different stages of the training process can be compared across programs.

Determining Benefits. To identify the potential benefits of training, the company must review the original reasons for the training. For example, training may have been conducted to reduce production costs or overtime costs or to increase repeat business. A number of methods may help identify the benefits of training:

1. Technical, academic, and practitioner literature summarizes the benefits that have been shown to relate to a specific training program.
2. Pilot training programs assess the benefits for a small group of trainees before a company commits more resources.
3. Observing successful job performers can help a company determine what they do differently than unsuccessful job performers.[114]
4. Trainees and their managers can provide estimates of training benefits.

Making the Analysis. To calculate return on investment, follow these steps:

1. Identify outcomes (e.g., quality, accidents).
2. Place a value on the outcomes.

3. Determine the change in performance after eliminating other potential influences on training results.
4. Obtain an annual amount of benefits (operational results) from training by comparing results after training to results before training (in dollars).
5. Determine the training costs (direct costs + indirect costs + development costs + overhead costs + compensation for trainees).
6. Calculate the total savings by subtracting the training costs from benefits (operational results).
7. Calculate the ROI by dividing benefits (operational results) by costs. The ROI gives an estimate of the dollar return expected from each dollar invested in training.

Recall our discussion earlier in the chapter on the evaluation of the new manager training program at Mayo Clinic.[115] To determine Mayo's return on investment, the human resource department calculated that one-third of the 84 employees retained (29 employees) would have left Mayo as a result of dissatisfaction. The department believed their retention was due to the impact of the training. The department calculated that the cost of a single employee turnover was 75% of average total compensation, or $42,000 per employee at Mayo. Multiplying $42,000 by 29 employees retained equals a savings of $609,000. However, the cost of the training program needs to be considered. If the annual cost of the training program ($125,000) was subtracted from the savings, the new savings were $484,000. These numbers were based on estimates but even if the net savings figure were cut in half, the ROI is still over 100%. Being able to quantify the benefits delivered by the program has given the human resource department greater credibility at Mayo.

EVIDENCED-BASED HR

Grant Thornton, the public accounting and consulting firm, introduced a new tax service methodology and tools to approximately 1,400 tax professionals in more than 50 offices. The training solution, known as Tax Symphony, involved blended learning which included a three-day national and local office classroom program, web-based performance support, and webcasts. The new methodology was introduced during a tax conference. After the conference the content was taught at local offices using avatars presenting prerecorded audio clips combined with group application activities. Evaluation results showed that 86% of the program participants completing the posttest passed it with an average passing score of 85%. Average posttest scores improved by 11 percentage points over national classroom posttest scores. Using avatars instead of real instructors in local offices saved $72,000 in costs.

SOURCE: Based on "Grant Thornton," *T + D*, October 2010, p. 75.

Special Training Issues

To meet the competitive challenges of sustainability, globalization, and technology discussed in Chapter 1, companies must successfully deal with several special training issues. The special training issues include preparing employees to work in different cultures abroad, managing workforce diversity, and socializing and orienting new employees.

LO 7-9
Design a cross-cultural preparation program.

CROSS-CULTURAL PREPARATION

Expatriate
Employee sent by his or her company to manage operations in a different country.

As we mentioned in Chapter 1, companies today are challenged to expand globally. Because of the increase in global operations, employees often work outside their country of origin or work with employees from other countries. An **expatriate** works in a country other than his or her country of origin. The most frequently selected locations for expatriate assignments include the United States, China, United Kingdom, Singapore, Germany, and Japan.[116] Many U.S. companies are using international rotational assignments as a training tool. Microsoft has 14 divisions using international rotational programs. Companies are also increasing the movement of employees from one global location to another. These involve management or technical positions moving from one country, like India, to China or Vietnam. This type of relocation is less expensive than moving a U.S.-based manager (who would have to be paid wages comparable to what they would earn in the United States) to China. Unfortunately, only about 25% of companies make cultural training mandatory for international assignments.[117] This may be because of mistaken beliefs that employees who have already been on international assignments or traveled internationally will be able to adapt to a new culture.

Because of a growing pool of talented labor around the world, greater use of host-country nationals is occurring.[118] *Host-country nationals* are employees with citizenship in the country where a company is located. A key reason is that a host-country national can more easily understand the values and customs of the workforce than an expatriate can. Also, training and transporting U.S. employees and their families to a foreign assignment and housing them there tend to be more expensive than hiring a host-country national. We discuss international human resource management in detail in Chapter 15. Here the focus is on understanding how to prepare employees for expatriate assignments.

Cross-Cultural Preparation
The process of educating employees (and their families) who are given an assignment in a foreign country.

Cross-cultural preparation educates employees (expatriates) and their families who are to be sent to a foreign country. To successfully conduct business in the global marketplace, employees must understand the business practices and the cultural norms of different countries.

Steps in Cross-Cultural Preparation

To prepare employees for cross-cultural assignments, companies need to provide cross-cultural training. Most U.S. companies send employees overseas without any preparation. As a result, the number of employees who return home before completing their assignments is higher for U.S. companies than for European and Japanese companies.[119] One estimate is that U.S. companies lose more than $2 billion a year as a result of failed overseas assignments.

To succeed overseas, expatriates (employees on foreign assignments) need to be

1. Competent in their areas of expertise.
2. Able to communicate verbally and nonverbally in the host country.
3. Flexible, tolerant of ambiguity, and sensitive to cultural differences.
4. Motivated to succeed, able to enjoy the challenge of working in other countries, and willing to learn about the host country's culture, language, and customs.
5. Supported by their families.[120]

One reason for U.S. expatriates' high failure rate is that companies place more emphasis on developing employees' technical skills than on preparing them to work in other cultures. Research suggests that the comfort of an expatriate's spouse and family is the most important determinant of whether the employee will complete the assignment.[121] Studies have also found that personality characteristics are related to expatriates' desire to terminate the assignment and performance in the assignment.[122] Expatriates who were extroverted (outgoing), agreeable (cooperative and tolerant), and conscientious (dependable, achievement oriented) were more likely to want to stay on the assignment and perform well. This suggests that cross-cultural training may be effective only when expatriates' personalities predispose them to be successful in assignments in other cultures.

The key to a successful foreign assignment is a combination of training and career management for the employee and family. The "Competing through Globalization" box shows how training and social networks can be used for language and cultural training. Foreign assignments involve three phases: predeparture, on-site, and repatriation (preparing to return home). Training is necessary in all three phases.

Predeparture Phase

Before departure, employees need to receive language training and an orientation to the new country's culture and customs. It is critical that the family be included in orientation programs.[123] Expatriates and their families need information about housing, schools, recreation, shopping, and health care facilities in the areas where they will live. Expatriates also must discuss with their managers how the foreign assignment fits into their career plans and what types of positions they can expect upon return.

Cross-cultural training methods include presentational techniques, such as lectures that expatriates and their families attend on the customs and culture of the host country, immersion experiences, or actual experiences in the home country in culturally diverse communities.[124] Experiential exercises, such as miniculture experiences, allow expatriates to spend time with a family in the United States from the ethnic group of the host country. For example, an Indian trainer took 20 managers from Advanced Micro Devices on a two-week immersion trip during which the group traveled to New Delhi, Bangalore, and Mumbai, meeting with business persons and government officials.[125] The program required six months of planning, including providing the executives with information on foods to eat, potential security issues, and how to interact in business meetings. For example, Indians prefer a relatively indirect way into business discussions, so the managers were advised to discuss current events and other subjects before talking business.

Research suggests that the degree of difference between the United States and the host country (cultural novelty), the amount of interaction with host country citizens and host nationals (interaction), and the familiarity with new job tasks and work environment (job novelty) all influence the "rigor" of the cross-cultural training method used.[126] Hands-on and group-building methods are most effective (and most needed) in assignments with a high level of cultural and job novelty that require a good deal of interpersonal interaction with host nationals.

On-Site Phase

On-site training involves continued orientation to the host country and its customs and cultures through formal programs or through a mentoring relationship. Expatriates and their families may be paired with an employee from the host country who helps them understand the new, unfamiliar work environment and community.[127] Companies are also using the web to help employees on expatriate assignments get

Learning through Training and Networking Helps Global Business

Globalization introduces many issues that companies need to successfully deal with to be successful. Some of these issues include the need to speak the local language and understand the culture, to keep employees connected with each other, and to introduce common learning experiences while holding down travel costs related to bringing employees together face-to-face in one location.

English is the common language at many multinational companies. But failing to speak the native language can cause employees to risk being misinterpreted or fail to understand informal conversations. Speaking and understanding the local language can help employees avoid misunderstandings and gain greater respect from business partners, subordinates, and customers.

At Intel, employees with a business need can take classes in Mandarin, Japanese, and Spanish at various offices throughout the United States, free of charge. The courses are not designed for expatriates destined for assignments abroad, but instead target employees who, through technology, are in direct contact with foreign clients or who work on cross-cultural teams within the company. With 78,000 employees in 294 offices in 48 countries, Intel has teams that are regularly made up of employees from different cultures working in different locations. The optional

12-week courses, taught at three levels by contracting companies, are designed to help minimize the culture gaps within these teams. The classes meet for two hours a week and cost the company approximately $300 per person. Employees are allowed to repeat courses.

The language classes are part of a larger in-house cultural-training curriculum for Intel employees. The company also offers optional one-day classes with titles such as "Working with Russia" and "Doing Business with the Japanese," which are designed to give employees basic information that they need to build relationships and do business cross-culturally. Class size is about 15 students, and subjects include culture, history and an overview of various countries and their business practices.

VF Asia Limited is a Hong Kong–based unit of VF Corporation. VF Corporation is the world's largest apparel company owner of many brands including Nautica, Wrangler, Jansport, and North Face. VF Asia's SELF program (Self Enhancement Learning Fundamentals) is an online customer training program that includes instruction on topics that help employees understand and communicate with individuals from the diverse cultures throughout Asia with whom they do business. Course topics include business etiquette, holding successful meetings,

and negotiations. VF Asia's training team maintains a partnership with the VF Corporation organization development team. Both teams work together to develop and implement global initiatives to ensure they are customized to local needs and requirements.

To save on travel costs Sodexo, Inc., a food and facilities management company located in Gaithersburg, Maryland, decided to hold its annual diversity inclusion conference in a virtual setting rather than having 450 employees travel to Sodexo Group Headquarters in Paris, France. Conference participants logged into a website, heard prerecorded opening comments from the top manager at Sodexco France, and moved from "room to room" as they would at a live conference using an avatar to listen to live presentations and panel discussions, visit exhibits, and participate in chat room discussion and networking events. In an interactive theater, participants could also watch actors role-playing diversity scenarios that occur in the workplace. Holding the conference virtually saved the company approximately $1.8 million in travel-related costs and an estimated 900 work days.

IBM uses social networking tools to connect its employees around the world. IBM's site, known as w3, contributes to the global integration of the company. The w3 On Demand answers to questions.[128] Expatriates can use a website to get answers to questions such as, How do I conduct a meeting here? or What religious philosophy might have influenced today's negotiation behavior? Knowledge management software allows employees to contribute, organize, and access knowledge specific to their expatriate assignment.

A major reason that employees refuse expatriate assignments is that they can't afford to lose their spouse's income or are concerned that their spouse's career could be derailed by being out of the workforce for a few years.[129] Some "trailing" spouses decide to use the time to pursue educational activities that could contribute to their long-term career goals. But it is difficult to find these opportunities in an unfamiliar place. Pfizer, the pharmaceutical firm, is taking action to help trailing spouses. It provides a $10,000 allowance that the spouse can use in many different ways. A person at the expatriate location is assigned to help the spouse with professional development and locating educational or other resources. In countries where spouses are allowed to work, Pfizer tries to find them jobs within the company. Pfizer also provides cross-cultural counseling and language assistance. The company tries to connect the family with the expatriate community. Several multinational companies including Hewlett-Packard, Axalto, and Group Danon have partnered to develop an online employment resource that tries to get expatriate spouses jobs posted by other member companies.[130] However, work permit restrictions requiring potential employers to demonstrate that the spouse has skills that are not locally available remains a major restriction to spouse employment.

Repatriation Phase

Repatriation prepares expatriates for return to the parent company and country from the foreign assignment. Expatriates and their families are likely to experience high levels of stress and anxiety when they return because of the changes that have occurred since their departure. Employees should be encouraged to self-manage the repatriation process.[131] Before they go on the assignment they need to consider what skills they want to develop and the types of jobs that might be available in the company for an employee with those skills. Because the company changes and colleagues, peers, and managers may leave while the expatriate is on assignment, they need to maintain contact with key company and industry contacts. Otherwise, on return the employees' reentry shock will be heightened when they have to deal with new colleagues, a new job, and a company culture that may have changed. This includes providing expatriates with company newsletters and community newspapers and ensuring that they receive personal and work-related mail from the United States while they are on foreign assignment. It is also not uncommon for employees and their families to have

Repatriation
The preparation of expatriates for return to the parent company and country from a foreign assignment.

to readjust to a lower standard of living in the United States than they had in the foreign country, where they may have enjoyed maid service, a limousine, private schools, and clubs. Salary and other compensation arrangements should be worked out well before employees return from overseas assignments.

Aside from reentry shock, many expatriates decide to leave the company because the assignments they are given upon returning to the United States have less responsibility, challenge, and status than their foreign assignments.[132] As noted earlier, career planning discussions need to be held before the employees leave the United States to ensure that they understand the positions they will be eligible for upon repatriation.

Royal Dutch Shell, a joint Dutch and United Kingdom oil and gas company, has one of the world's largest expatriate workforces. To avoid expatriates who feel undervalued and leave the company, Royal Dutch gets involved with expatriates and their career. Resource planners track workers abroad, helping to identify their next assignment. Most expatriates know their next assignment three to six months before the move, and all begin the next assignment with a clear job description. Expatriates who have the potential to reach top-level management positions are placed in the home office every third assignment to increase their visibility to company executives. Expatriates are also assigned technical mentors who evaluate their skills and help them improve their skills through training at Royal Dutch's training center.

Because of family issues, poor economic times, and security issues, many companies are using virtual expatriates, relying more on short-time assignments, frequent business travel, and international commutes in which an employee lives in one country and works in another.[133] *Virtual expatriates* have an assignment to manage an operation abroad without being located permanently in that country. The employees periodically travel to the overseas location, return, and later use video conferencing and communications technology to manage the operation.[134] Virtual expatriates eliminate exposing the family to the culture shock of an overseas move. This setup also allows the employee to manage globally while keeping in close touch with the home office. Virtual expatriates are less expensive than traditional expatriates, who can cost companies over three times as much as a host national employee. One major disadvantage of virtual expatriates is that visiting a foreign operation on a sporadic basis may lengthen the time needed to build a local management team, so it will take longer to solve problems because of the lack of a strong personal relationship with local employees. One of the potential difficulties of short-term international assignments is that employees may be perceived as foreigners rather than colleagues because they haven't had the time to build relationships and develop trust among co-workers in their short-term location. Another is that traveling can take a physical and emotional toll on employees as they try to juggle business responsibilities with maintaining contact with family and friends. Procter & Gamble helps employees on short-term assignments by providing a trip fund that is based on the length of time an employee is on an extended business trip. For example, a U.S.-based employee working in western Europe for six months would get a fund containing the cost of five business-class round-trips. The employee can use money from the fund to take trips home or to cover family visits to the employee's location.

MANAGING WORKFORCE DIVERSITY AND INCLUSION

LO 7-10
Develop a program for effectively managing diversity.

Diversity can be considered any dimension that differentiates a person from another.[135] For example at Verizon diversity means embracing differences and variety including age, ethnicity, education, sexual orientation, work style, race, gender, and more.

Inclusion refers to creating an environment in which employees share a sense of belonging, mutual respect, and commitment from others so they can perform their best work.[136]

The goals of diversity training are (1) to eliminate values, stereotypes, and managerial practices that inhibit employees' personal development and therefore (2) to allow employees to contribute to organizational goals regardless of their race, sexual orientation, gender, family status, religious orientation, or cultural background.[137] Equal Opportunity Employment laws help ensure that women and minorities are adequately represented in a company's labor force. That is, companies have focused on ensuring equal access to jobs. As was discussed in Chapter 1, the impact of culture on the workplace, and specifically on training and development, has received heightened attention. Cultural factors that companies need to consider include the terrorist attacks of 9/11 and threats from Al-Quaida; employees' fear of discussing cultural differences; more work being conducted in teams whose members have many different characteristics; the realization that people from diverse cultures represent an important customer market; and, especially for professional and technical jobs, the availability of highly trained employees that has many companies seeking workers from overseas. These new immigrants need diversity training to help them understand such facets of American culture as obsession with time, individualistic attitudes, and capitalistic ideas.[138]

Managing diversity and inclusion involves creating an environment that allows all employees to contribute to organizational goals and experience personal growth. This environment includes access to jobs as well as fair and positive treatment of all employees. The company must develop employees who are comfortable working with people from a wide variety of ethnic, racial, and religious backgrounds. Managing diversity may require changing the company culture. It includes the company's standards and norms about how employees are treated, competitiveness, results orientation, innovation, and risk taking. The value placed on diversity is grounded in the company culture.

More generally, a survey of diversity training efforts found that[139]

Managing Diversity and Inclusion
The process of creating an environment that allows all employees to contribute to organizational goals and experience personal growth.

- The most common area addressed through diversity efforts is the pervasiveness of stereotypes, assumptions, and biases.
- Fewer than one-third of companies do any kind of long-term evaluation or follow-up. The most common indicators of success were reduced grievances and lawsuits, increased diversity in promotions and hiring, increased self-awareness of biases, and increased consultation of HRM specialists on diversity-related issues.
- Most programs lasted only one day or less.
- Three-fourths of the survey respondents indicated that they believed the typical employee leaves diversity training with positive attitudes toward diversity. However, more than 50% reported that the programs have no effect over the long term.
- Twenty-nine percent of survey respondents reported that no tools were provided to reinforce diversity training, and 22% reported that no development or advancement issues were addressed.

Diversity may enhance performance when organizations have an environment that promotes learning from diversity. There is no evidence to support the direct relationship between diversity and business.[140] Rather, a company will see the success of its diversity efforts only if it makes a long-term commitment to managing diversity. Successful diversity requires that it be viewed as an opportunity for employees to (1) learn from each other how to better accomplish their work, (2) be provided with a supportive and cooperative organizational culture, and (3) be taught leadership and process skills that can facilitate effective team functioning. Diversity is a reality in labor and customer markets and is a social expectation and value. Managers should focus on building an organizational environment, on human resource practices, and on managerial and team skills that all capitalize on diversity. As you will see in the discussion that follows, managing diversity requires difficult cultural change, not just slogans on the wall!

Table 7.10 shows the characteristics associated with the long-term success of diversity programs. It is critical that a diversity program be tied to business objectives. For example, cultural differences affect the type of skin cream consumers believe they need or the fragrance they may be attracted to. Understanding cultural differences is part of understanding the consumer (which is critical to the success of companies such as Avon). Top management support can be demonstrated by creating a structure to support the initiative.

Consider Sodexo's diversity effort.[141] Sodexo is the leading food and facilities management company in the United States, Canada, and Mexico, daily serving 10 million customers. With employees in 80 countries representing 128 nationalities connecting with customers on a daily basis, a policy of inclusion is not an option or a choice—it is a business necessity. Sodexo is focused on gender representation, generational opportunities in the workplace, people with disabilities, and ethnic minority representation. As a result, diversity and inclusion are core elements of the business strategy. Sodexo believes that diversity and inclusion is a fundamental business objective focused on employees (e.g., work culture, recruitment, talent development, work life effectiveness), customers, clients, and shareholders (e.g., supplier diversity, cross-market

table 7.10

Characteristics Associated with Diversity Programs' Long-Term Success

- Top management provides resources, personally intervenes, and publicly advocates diversity.
- The program is structured.
- Capitalizing on a diverse workforce is defined as a business objective.
- Capitalizing on a diverse workforce is seen as necessary to generate revenue and profits.
- The program is evaluated using metrics such as sales, retention, and promotion rates.
- Manager involvement is mandatory.
- The program is seen as a culture change, not a one-shot program.
- Managers and demographic groups are not blamed for problems.
- Behaviors and skills needed to successfully interact with others are taught.
- Managers are rewarded on progress toward meeting diversity goals.
- Management collects employee feedback and responds to it.
- Create a safe and open culture that all employees want to belong to, in which employees can discover and appreciate differences and where the benefits of diversity are recognized by all employees.

SOURCES: M. Jayne and R. Dipboye, "Leveraging Diversity to Improve Business Performance: Research Findings and Recommendations for Organizations," *Human Resource Management* 43 (2004); pp. 409–24; S. Rynes and B. Rosen, "What Makes Diversity Programs Work?" *HR Magazine*, October 1994, pp. 67–73; S. Rynes and B. Rosen, "A Field Survey of Factors Affecting the Adoption and Perceived Success of Diversity Training," *Personnel Psychology* 48 (1995), pp. 247–70; J. Gordon, "Different from What? Diversity as a Performance Issue," *Training*, May 1995, pp. 25–33; Corporate Leadership Council, *The Evolution of Corporate Diversity* (Washington, DC: Corporate Executive Board, 2002); R. Anand and M. Winters, "A Retrospective View of Corporate Diversity Training from 1964 to the Present," *Academy of Management Learning & Education* 7 (2008), pp. 356–72; C. Chavez and J. Weisinger, "Beyond Diversity Training: A Social Infusion for Cultural Inclusion," *Human Resource Management* 47 (2008), pp. 331–50.

diversity council, diversity consulting), and communities (e.g., Sodexo Foundation, Community Partners). For example, some of the objectives include understanding and living the business case for diversity and inclusion; increasing awareness of how diversity relates to business challenges; creating and fostering a diverse work environment by developing management practices that drive hiring, promotion, and retention of talent; engaging in relationship management and customer service to attract and retain diverse clients and customers; and partnering with women and minority businesses to deliver food and facility management services. Diversity and inclusion are core competencies at Sodexo. Diversity and inclusion are part of employees' training and managers' annual performance review; new employee orientation emphasizes Sodexo's values and expectations regarding diversity and inclusion.

Sodexo separates Equal Employment Opportunity (EEO) and legal compliance training from diversity training. At Sodexo, diversity training is part of the managing diversity strategy. **Diversity training** refers to learning efforts that are designed to change employee attitudes about diversity and/or develop skills needed to work with a diverse workforce. Every three years, employees are required to take EEO and affirmative action refresher courses. Top management is also involved in and committed to managing diversity. The senior executives program includes ongoing classroom training that is reinforced with community involvement, sponsoring employee groups, and mentoring diverse employees. Executives are engaged in learning the business case for diversity and are personally held accountable for the company's diversity agenda. Every manager takes an eight-hour introductory class (Spirit of Diversity). Sodexo's diversity training involves learning labs focused on skill building and diversity awareness. Examples of these learning labs include Generations in the Workplace, Disability Awareness Training, Cross-Cultural Communications, and Improving Team Effectiveness through Inclusion. The company's learning and development team develops customized learning solutions for different functions and work teams. For example, a course related to selling to a diverse client base was developed and offered to the sales force, and a cross-cultural communications program was provided for recruiters.

In addition to diversity training activities, Sodexo has six employee network groups—such as the African American Leadership Forum, People Respecting Individuality, Diversity, and Equality, Honoring Our Nation's Finest with Opportunity and Respect (HONOR), and the Intergenerational Network Group. These network groups provide forums for employees' professional development and sharing input and ideas to support the companys' diversity efforts. Sodexo's "Champions of Diversity" program rewards and recognizes employees who advance diversity and inclusion.

To emphasize the importance of diversity for the company, at Sodexo each manager has a diversity scorecard that evaluates their success in recruitment, retention, promotion, and development of all employees. The scorecard includes both quantitative goals as well as evaluation of behaviors such as participating in training, mentoring, and doing community outreach. A proportion of their pay bonuses is determined by success in these areas.

Sodexo has found that its diversity training and efforts to manage diversity are having a positive impact on business results. Its mentoring program has led to increased productivity, engagement, and retention of women and people of color. There was an estimated return on investment of $19 for every dollar spent on the program. Sodexo also has been awarded several new business contracts and retained clients because of its involvement in managing diversity. Sodexo has also been recognized for its diversity and inclusion efforts, which helps attract talented employees by signaling that the company cares about the well-being of all of its employees. Sodexo was ranked

Diversity Training
Learning efforts that are designed to change employee attitudes about diversity and develop skills needed to work with a diverse workforce.

number 2 on the 2011 DiversityInc Top 50 Companies for Diversity list. This marks the sixth consecutive year that the company has been recognized by DiversityInc for the success of its diversity efforts. Sodexo is also recognized as a top company for executive women and ranked among the top 10 companies for Latinos, blacks, global diversity, and people with disabilities. Most effective programs to manage diversity, such as Sodexo's diversity program, include the key components shown in Table 7.11.

As should be apparent from this discussion, successful diversity programs involve more than just an effective training program. They require an ongoing process of culture change that includes top management support as well as diversity policies and practices in the areas of recruitment and hiring, training and development, and administrative structures, such as conducting diversity surveys and evaluating managers' progress on diversity goals.[142] They also focus on enhancing diversity and inclusion with suppliers, vendors, and in the communities where the company conducts business.

Socialization and Orientation

Organizational socialization is the process by which new employees are transformed into effective members of the company. As Table 7.12 shows, effective socialization involves being prepared to perform the job effectively, learning about the organization, and establishing work relationships. Socialization involves three phases: anticipatory socialization, encounter, and settling in.[143] Figure 7.7 shows the three phases and the actions that should be taken to help employees at each phase.

Anticipatory socialization occurs before the individual joins the company. Through **anticipatory socialization,** expectations about the company, job, working conditions, and interpersonal relationships are developed through interactions with representatives of the company (recruiters, prospective peers, and managers) during recruitment and selection. The expectations are also based on prior work experiences in similar jobs. The **encounter phase** occurs when the employee begins a new job. No matter how realistic the information provided during interviews and site visits, individuals beginning new jobs will experience shock and surprise.[144] In the **settling-in phase,** employees begin to feel comfortable with their job demands and social relationships. They begin to resolve work conflicts (like too much work or conflicting job demands) and conflicts between work and nonwork activities. Employees are interested in the company's evaluation of their performance and in learning about potential career opportunities within the company.

Employees need to complete all three socialization phases to fully contribute to the company. For example, employees who do not feel that they have established good working relationships with co-workers will likely spend time and energy worrying about those relationships rather than being concerned with product development or customer service. Employees who experience successful socialization are more motivated, more committed to the company, and more satisfied with their jobs.[145]

SOCIALIZATION, ORIENTATION, AND ONBOARDING PROGRAMS

Socialization and orientation programs play an important role in socializing employees. Orientation involves familiarizing new employees with company rules, policies, and procedures. Typically, a program includes information about the company, department in which the employees will be working, and the community they will live in.

Organizational Socialization
The process used to transform new employees into effective company members.

Anticipatory Socialization
Process that helps individuals develop expectations about the company, job, working conditions, and interpersonal relationships.

Encounter Phase
Phase of socialization that occurs when an employee begins a new job.

Settling-in Phase
Phase of socialization that occurs when employees are comfortable with job demands and social relationships.

table 7.11

Key Components of Effective Managing Diversity Programs

Top Management Support
- Make the business case for diversity.
- Include diversity as part of the business strategy and corporate goals.
- Participate in diversity programs, and encourage all managers to attend.
- Ensure that the composition of the executive management team mirrors the diversity of the workforce.

Recruitment and Hiring
- Ask search firms to identify wider arrays of candidates.
- Enhance the interviewing, selection, and hiring skills of managers.
- Expand college recruitment at historically minority colleges.

Identifying and Developing Talent
- Form a partnership with internship programs that target minority students for management careers.
- Establish a mentoring process.
- Refine the company's global succession planning system to improve identification of talent.
- Improve the selection and development of managers and leaders to help ensure that they are capable of maximizing team performance.
- Ensure that all employees, especially women and minorities, have access to management development and leadership programs.

Employee Support
- Form resource groups or employee network groups, including employees with common interests, and use them to help the company develop business goals and understand the issues they are concerned with (e.g., Asian Pacific employees, women, gays, lesbians, transgenders, Native Americans, veterans, Hispanics).
- Celebrate cultural traditions, festivities, and holidays.
- Make work/life balance initiatives (such as flextime, telecommuting, eldercare) available to all employees.

Ensuring Fair Treatment
- Conduct extensive diversity training.
- Implement an alternative dispute resolution process.
- Include women and minorities on all human resources committees throughout the company.

Holding Managers Accountable
- Link managers' compensation to their success in meeting diversity goals and creating openness and inclusion in the workplace.
- Use employee attitude or engagement surveys to track employees' attitudes such as inclusion, fairness, opportunities for development, work/life balance, and perceptions of the company culture.
- Implement 360-degree feedback for all managers and supervisors.

Improving Relationships with External Stakeholders
- Increase marketing to diverse communities.
- Provide customer service in different languages.
- Broaden the company's base of suppliers and vendors to include businesses owned by minorities and women.
- Provide scholarships and educational and neighborhood grants to diverse communities and their members.

SOURCES: Based on R. Anand and M. Winters, "A Retrospective View of Corporate Diversity Training from 1964 to the Present," *Academy of Management Learning & Education* 7 (2008), pp. 356–72; C. Chavez and J. Weisinger, "Beyond Diversity Training: A Social Infusion for Cultural Inclusion," *Human Resource Management* 47 (2008), pp. 331–50; V. Smith, "Texaco Outlines Comprehensive Initiatives," *Human Resource Executive*, February 1997, p. 13; Verizon's diversity program available at the company website, www.verizon.com.

table 7.12

What Employees Should Learn and Develop through the Socialization Process

History	The company's traditions, customs, and myths; background of members
Company goals	Rules, values, or principles directing the company
Language	Slang and jargon unique to the company; professional technical language
Politics	How to gain information regarding the formal and informal work relationships and power structures in the company
People	Successful and satisfying work relationships with other employees
Performance proficiency	What needs to be learned; effectiveness in using and acquiring the knowledge, skills, and abilities needed for the job

SOURCE: Based on G. T. Chao, A. M. O'Leary-Kelly, S. Wolf, H. Klein, and P. D. Gardner, "Organizational Socialization: Its Content and Consequences," *Journal of Applied Psychology* 79 (1994), pp. 730–43.

Although the content of orientation programs is important, the process of orientation cannot be ignored. Too often, orientation programs consist of completing payroll forms and reviewing personnel policies with managers or human resource representatives. Although these are important activities, the new employee has little opportunity to ask questions, interact with peers and managers, or become familiar with the company's culture, products, and service.

Effective orientation programs actively involve the new employee. Table 7.13 shows the characteristics of effective orientation. An important characteristic of effective orientation is that peers, managers, and senior co-workers are actively involved in helping new employees adjust to the work group.[146]

Several companies offer programs that include the characteristics shown in Table 7.13.[147] For example, through its "52 weeks" program, Qualcomm uses e-mail to distribute 52 short stories, written to share the company's history, factors that make it successful, and future business directions. Each new employee receives one story per week throughout his or her first year. Each story relates company history and demonstrates how the corporate culture was formed. The stories cover the first employee meeting in the company parking lot and the development of the chip division. The stories help employees understand that innovation, doing whatever it takes, and camaraderie are Qualcomm values.

Clarkston Consulting, a management and technology consulting company with approximately 300 employees, has an orientation program that includes learning about the company after accepting a job offer as well as during the first days on the job.[148] An onboarding team consisting of trainers, recruiters, human resource representatives, and current employees maintain contact with each new employee using a Wiki. The Wiki provides information about the company culture, and a discussion blog is also accessible. Once they join the company, employees have eight weeks of instructor-led and e-learning training, a book assignment with a discussion, and individual and team assignments simulating actual projects with clients. Biweekly conference calls are arranged for new employees so they can share their knowledge and experiences.

Similarly, new hires at Sierra Nevada Corporation, a company in the defense and aerospace industry, are contacted by the company's talent acquisition and

figure 7.7

Phases of Socialization and Necessary Company Actions

Anticipatory Socialization
- Provide a realistic job preview as well as accurate information about the positive and negative aspects of the job, including working conditions, company, and location.

Encounter
- Provide training, challenging work, and orientation, thus reducing shock and surprise. Manager can help new employees understand their roles, provide information about the company, and empathize with stress of new job.

Settling In
- Provide performance evaluation and information on career opportunities.

SOURCES: Based on D. T. Hall, *Careers In and Out of Organizations* (Thousand Oaks, CA: Sage Publications, 2002); J. D. Kammeyer-Mueller and C. R. Wanberg, "Unwrapping the Organizational Entry Process: Disentangling Multiple Antecedents and Their Pathway to Adjustment," *Journal of Applied Psychology* 88 (2003), pp. 779–94; G. M. McEnvoy and W. F. Cascio, "Strategies for Reducing Employee Turnover: A Meta-analysis," *Journal of Applied Psychology* 70 (1985), pp. 342–53; M. R. Louis, "Surprise and Sensemaking: What Newcomers Experience in Entering Unfamiliar Organizational Settings," *Administrative Science Quarterly* 25 (1980), pp. 226–51; R. F. Morrison and T. M. Brantner, "What Enhances or Inhibits Learning a New Job? A Basic Career Issue," *Journal of Applied Psychology* 77 (1992), pp. 926–40; D. A. Major, S. W. J. Kozlowski, G. T. Chao, and P. D. Gardner, "A Longitudinal Investigation of Newcomer Expectations, Early Socialization Outcomes, and the Moderating Effect of Role Development Factors," *Journal of Applied Psychology* 80 (1995), pp. 418–31.

table 7.13

Characteristics of Effective Orientation Programs

Employees are encouraged to ask questions.
Program includes information on both technical and social aspects of the job.
Orientation is the responsibility of the new employee's manager.
Debasing or embarrassing new employees is avoided.
Formal and informal interactions with managers and peers occur.
Programs involve relocation assistance (such as house hunting or information sessions on the community for employees and their spouses).
Employees learn about the company's products, services, and customers.

training teams before orientation.[149] The program includes a review of the company's history, culture, vision, and values. New hires' first day on the job includes a meet-and-greet lunch date with their manager. Employees consider onboarding for 90 days which includes e-learning, mentoring, on-the-job training, and a performance review.

Many companies are using technology to make orientation more interactive and reduce travel costs. For example, Arrow Electronics—an electronics component and computer products company with 11,000 employees in more than 200 locations in 53 countries—used to have a five-day orientation that introduced the industry and Arrow's culture, values, and history to new employees.[150] However, the program was not cost-effective because it was limited to the company's North American employees, which meant all new employees had to travel to one location to attend the program. Arrow now delivers the same content through an interactive computer game. New employees can view modules on industry basics, corporate history, and culture. Each module is followed by a quiz-show-based game to assess what employees learned, and they receive immediate feedback. The program is self-paced, can be accessed around the world, and can be completed in several different languages. The program has saved Arrow money. Total costs for game development were approximately 10% of what was spent on the classroom orientation. IBM uses Second Life for new hires to learn about corporate culture and business processes by having their avatars attend meetings, watch presentations, and interact with other avatars in a virtual IBM community.

Onboarding gives new managers an introduction to the work they will be supervising and an understanding of the culture and operations of the entire company. For example, at Pella Corporation, an Iowa-based manufacturer of windows and doors, new managers are sent on a tour of production plants, meeting and observing employees and department heads. These tours ensure that the managers will get a better sense of the market and how the company's products are designed, built, and distributed.[151]

A LOOK BACK

As the chapter opener highlighted, Mike's Carwash uses training to support the company's business strategy. Mike's provides extensive training focused on selling and providing services.

Questions

1. Suppose a manager asked you to determine whether training was supporting a company's business strategy. How would you conduct this type of analysis? What kind of information would you look for?
2. How does Mike's support training? What else should a company do to support training activities to maximize their effectiveness?

 Please see the Video that corresponds to this chapter at www.mhhe.com/noe8e.

SUMMARY

Technological innovations, new product markets, and a diverse workforce have increased the need for companies to reexamine how their training practices contribute to learning. In this chapter we discussed a systematic approach to training, including needs assessment, design of the learning environment, consideration of employee readiness for training, and transfer-of-training issues. We reviewed numerous training methods and stressed that the key to successful training was to choose a method that would best accomplish the objectives of training. We also emphasized how training can contribute to effectiveness through establishing a link with the company's strategic direction and demonstrating through cost–benefit analysis how training contributes to profitability. Managing diversity and cross-cultural preparation are two training issues that are relevant given company needs to capitalize on a diverse workforce and global markets.

● KEY TERMS

Continuous learning, 271	Opportunity to perform, 288	Adventure learning, 307
Training, 271	Electronic performance support	Cross-training, 308
Formal training, 271	systems (EPSS), 289	Coordination training, 308
Informal learning 272	Communities of practice, 289	Team leader training, 308
Explicit Knowledge, 272	Presentation methods, 291	Action learning, 309
Tacit Knowledge, 272	Teleconferencing, 292	Six Sigma training, 309
Knowledge management, 273	Webcasting, 293	Training outcomes, 311
Training design process, 274	Hands-on methods, 295	Cost–benefit analysis, 314
Needs assessment, 275	On-the-job training (OJT), 295	Expatriate, 316
Organizational analysis, 276	Apprenticeship, 296	Cross-cultural preparation, 316
Person analysis, 276	Simulation, 298	Repatriation, 319
Task analysis, 276	Avatar, 298	Managing diversity and inclusion, 321
Strategic training and development	Virtual reality, 298	Diversity training, 323
initiatives, 277	E-learning, 301	Organizational socialization, 324
Motivation to learn, 282	Repurposing, 303	Anticipatory socialization, 324
Transfer of training, 284	Blended learning, 304	Encounter phase, 324
Climate for transfer, 287	Learning management system	Settling-in phase, 324
Action plan, 288	(LMS), 304	
Support network, 288	Group- or team-building methods, 304	

● DISCUSSION QUESTIONS

1. Noetron, a retail electronics store, recently invested a large amount of money to train sales staff to improve customer service. The skills emphasized in the program include how to greet customers, determine their needs, and demonstrate product convenience. The company wants to know whether the program is effective. What outcomes should it collect? What type of evaluation design should it use?

2. "Melinda," bellowed Toran, "I've got a problem and you've got to solve it. I can't get people in this plant to work together as a team. As if I don't have enough trouble with the competition and delinquent accounts, now I have to put up with running a zoo. It's your responsibility to see that the staff gets along with each other. I want a human relations training proposal on my desk by Monday." How would you determine the need for human relations training? How would you determine whether you actually had a training problem? What else could be responsible?

3. Assume you are general manager of a small seafood company. Most training is unstructured and occurs on the job. Currently, senior fish cleaners are responsible for teaching new employees how to perform the job. Your company has been profitable, but recently wholesale fish dealers that buy your product have been complaining about the poor quality of your fresh fish. For example, some fillets have not had all the scales removed and abdomen parts remain attached to the fillets. You have decided to change the on-the-job training received by the fish cleaners. How will you modify the training to improve the quality of the product delivered to the wholesalers?

4. A training needs analysis indicates that managers' productivity is inhibited because they are reluctant to delegate tasks to their subordinates. Suppose you had to decide between using adventure learning and interactive video for your training program. What are the strengths and weaknesses of each technique? Which would you choose? Why? What factors would influence your decision?

5. To improve product quality, a company is introducing a computer-assisted manufacturing process into one of its assembly plants. The new technology is likely to substantially modify jobs. Employees will also be required to learn statistical process control techniques. The new technology and push for

quality will require employees to attend numerous training sessions. More than 50% of the employees who will be affected by the new technology completed their formal education more than 10 years ago. Only about 5% of the company's employees have used the tuition reimbursement benefit. How should management maximize employees' readiness for training?

6. A training course was offered for maintenance employees in which trainees were supposed to learn how to repair and operate a new, complex electronics system. On the job, maintenance employees were typically told about a symptom experienced by the machine operator and were asked to locate the trouble. During training, the trainer would pose various problems for the maintenance employees to solve. He would point out a component on an electrical diagram and ask, "What would happen if this component was faulty?" Trainees would then trace the circuitry on a blueprint to uncover the symptoms that would appear as a result of the problem. You are receiving complaints about poor troubleshooting from maintenance supervisors of employees who have completed the program. The trainees are highly motivated and have the necessary prerequisites. What is the problem with the training course? What recommendations do you have for fixing this course?

7. What factors contribute to the effectiveness of web training programs?

8. Choose a job you are familiar with. Design a new employee orientation program for that job. Explain how your program contributes to effective socialization.

9. Why might employees prefer blended learning to training using only iPods?

10. What learning condition do you think is most necessary for learning to occur? Which is least critical? Why?

11. What can companies do to encourage informal learning?

● SELF-ASSESSMENT EXERCISE

● EXERCISING STRATEGY: GROWTH THROUGH ACQUISITION HELPS FARMERS COMPETITIVE POSITION

In 2009 Farmers Insurance Group of companies acquired AIG's Personal Auto Group which included 21st Century Insurance Company. This expanded Farmers position in the auto insurance marketplace. The acquisition was part of the company's strategy of broad distribution and product operations. The acquisition presented several challenges including adding 6,000 new employees located in different locations who need to be trained to join Farmers. The University of Farmers provided training including a six-week program that focused on the fundamentals of products, sales, and service. The university also created a personal coaching strategy to strengthen newly acquired employees' performance and make them feel comfortable as part of the Farmer's organization.

Questions

1. What role should socialization play when a company completes the acquisition of another company? Explain the importance of socialization for the acquiring company and for the acquired company's employees.

2. What would you measure to determine the business impact of Farmers' training of the acquired company's employees (AIG Personal Auto Group)?

SOURCE: Based on J. Salopek, "Thriving through Change, Cultivating Growth," *T + D*, October 2010, pp. 53–54.

Learning Isn't Perishable at Wegmans Food Markets

At Wegmans Food Markets, learning is how the company differentiates itself from other supermarkets. Learning is not part of the competitive strategy: it *is* the competitive strategy.

Wegmans Food Markets is known as much for carrying 700 different types of cheeses as it is for being one of the best companies to work for. In 2010 Wegmans was named to *Fortune* magazine's list of the "100 Best Companies to Work For," ranked number 3. This marks the 14th consecutive year Wegmans has appeared on the annual list since it was first published in 1998. The company also is financially successful. In 2010 its annual sales were $5.6 billion. Wegmans makes a considerable investment in training. On average, the supermarket industry spends about eight hours of training per new employee. Wegmans' employees average about 50 hours of training per year. The company has branched out of its traditional locations in New York, Pennsylvania, and New Jersey to open stores in Virginia and Maryland and is planning a store opening in Massachusetts.

Wegmans likely offers more customer convenience services and stores within a store than any other supermarket chain. These include a café, pâtisserie French pastry shop, nature's marketplace (natural foods), pharmacy, bakery, and deli and cheese shop. Because the level of service is as important as is product knowledge, Wegmans offers classroom training as well as hands-on training. Because Wegmans is a food business, learning with the five senses is very important. Employees are put through rigorous courses in areas such as operations, product knowledge, and cooking. But employees first receive training about the products they are selling, what makes them good, and how to prepare them. Wegmans believes that with knowledge, employees can provide real value to customers. Part of the company's strategy is to help customers understand the products so they will buy a new product. Wegmans mails *Menu* magazine to about 1 million addresses four times a year. It also developed an iPhone app and a blog, Fresh Stores. It has recipes, cooking techniques, and product advice. Customers come to the stores looking for products needed for the recipes and tips on how to prepare them. As a result, cooking coaches and sales staff go through a session each week on how to make a meal of the week. This training increases their product knowledge and makes them comfortable selling products.

Wegmans wants to teach people the company values. The values include caring, empowering employees to make decisions that improve their work and the company, respecting employees, pursuit of excellence, and making a difference in the communities it serves. Wegmans tries to find people who will care about the customers and care about their Wegmans teammates. High food safety standards are also important and are emphasized in technical training.

Wegmans also has special programs for teenagers who work in the stores. For example, the company has an apprenticeship program with about 250 people in it each year. The apprentices take on a team project on some aspect of the department they are working in. After studying for five months, the teams give presentations. The company also offers work-study programs. The three-year work-study program offers more than 1,500 hours of paid, school-supervised work experience, supported by related instruction at school. Students may receive high school credits for this experience. With the support of a mentor, students complete structured rotations through a variety of departments—bakery, produce, seafood, and other departments—based on career interests. The students learn and enhance their customer service, teamwork, product knowledge, food safety, and technical skills. Students in their last rotation during their senior year in high school focus on gaining new experiences in merchandising, product preparation, selling skills, and department sales concepts and finish off the program by completing a senior research project. Students who successfully finish the program receive either a full-time employment opportunity or, if attending college, a Scholarship Award and an opportunity to compete for the Store Operations Summer Internship program immediately after high school graduation. The Wegmans Scholarship Program encourages all employees to pursue educational goals. Wegmans has awarded more than $77 million in scholarships to more than 24,000 employees since the beginning of the Scholarship Program. About 4,000 employees have active scholarships each year while they attend colleges and universities. Why does Wegmans invest time and money in training students? Wegmans has a lot of young adults working in the stores and they are responsible for making a difference to customers by providing excellent service. Also, Wegmans believes that the success of all of its learning programs helps contribute to the company reputation as the employer of first choice, builds community goodwill, and helps retain employees who are committed to continuous improvement.

How does Wegmans Food Markets measure the return on its investment in training? CEO Danny Wegman says, "People are continuing to learn and have more confidence. We don't have a formula for measuring that, but we ask ourselves 'Are we being successful as a company? Are we getting good feedback from our people on the various courses we are offering? Do they feel they [the courses] are relevant to their success as individuals and part of the company?' "

Questions

1. Would you consider learning to contribute to the business strategy at Wegmans Food Markets? Explain.
2. Is there a difference between a company supporting learning and a company supporting training? Explain.
3. What outcomes or types of data would you collect if you were asked to evaluate the effectiveness of Wegmans

scholarship program? Identify the data or outcome you would collect and why you would collect it.
4. How could technology-based training methods such as online training or social networking be useful for learning at Wegmans?

SOURCES: Based on www.wegmans.com website for Wegmans Food Markets; D. Owens, "Treating Employees Like Customers," *HR Magazine*, October 2009, pp. 28–29; T. Bingham and P. Galagan, "A Higher Level of Learning," *TD*, September 2005, pp. 32–36; and M. Enis, "Challenge for Talent," *Supermarket News*, May 4, 2009, online from Business and Company Resource Center.

● TWITTER FOCUS: HOW NICK'S PIZZA DELIVERS TRAINING RESULTS

Using Twitter, continue the conversation about training by reading the Nick's Pizza & Pub case at www.mhhe.com/noe8e.

Instead of hiring expert managers and creating a lot of rules for its employees, Nick's is choosy about who gets hired for every position and provides them with enough training to operate skillfully and exercise sound judgment in a competitive business environment. Training begins with a two-day orientation where employees learn the company's purpose, values, and culture and participate in role-playing activities to practice the lessons learned. Next

it's on to skills training—where every employee learns how to make a pizza. The next training level involves certification for a specific job within the company. Employees are also encouraged to take additional training courses to learn more jobs and earn pay increases.

Engage with your classmates and instructor via Twitter to chat about Nick's training program using the case questions posted on the Noe website. Don't have a Twitter account yet? See the instructions for getting started on the Online Learning Center.

● NOTES

1. R. Hughes and K. Beatty, "Five Steps to Leading Strategically," *Training and Development*, July 2001, pp. 32–38; I. I. Goldstein and P. Gilliam, "Training Systems Issues in the Year 2000," *American Psychologist* 45 (1990), pp. 134–43; E. Salas and J. A. Cannon-Bowers, "The Science of Training: A Decade of Progress," *Annual Review of Psychology* 52 (2002), pp. 471–99.
2. U. Sessa and M. London, *Continuous Learning in Organizations* (Mahwah, NJ: Lawrence Erlbaum, 2006).
3. L. Patel, *2010 State of the Industry Report* (Alexandria, VA: American Society for Training & Development, 2010).
4. J. Roy, "Transforming Informal Learning into a Competitive Advantage," *T + D*, October 2010, pp. 23–25; P. Galagan, "Unformal, the New Normal," *T + D*, September 2010, pp. 29–31.
5. S. I. Tannenbaum, R. Beard, L. A. McNall, and E. Salas, "Informal Learning and Development in Organizations," in S. W. J. Kozlowski and E. Salas (eds.), *Learning, Training, and Development in Organizations* (New York: Routledge, 2010), pp. 303–32; D. J. Bear, H. B. Tompson, C. L. Morrison, M. Vickers, A. Paradise, M. Czarnowsky, M. Soyars, and K. King, *Tapping the Potential of Informal Learning. An ASTD research study* (Alexandria, VA: American Society for Training and Development, 2008).
6. T. Bingham and M. Conner, *The New Social Learning* (Alexandria, VA: ASTD Press, 2010).
7. J. Quinn, P. Andersen, and S. Finkelstein, "Leveraging Intellect," *Academy of Management Executive* 10 (1996), pp. 7–39.
8. I. Nonaka and H. Takeuchi, *The Knowledge-Creating Company: How Japanese Companies Create the Dynamics of Innovation* (New York: Oxford University Press, 1995).
9. S. E. Jackson, M. A. Hitt, and A. S. Denisi, eds., *Managing Knowledge for Sustained Competitive Advantage: Designing Strategies for Effective Human Resource Management* (San Francisco: Jossey-Bass, 2003); A. Rossett, "Knowledge Management Meets Analysis," *Training and Development*, May 1999, pp. 63–68; R. Davenport, "Why Does Knowledge Management Still Matter?" *T + D* 59 (2005), pp. 19–23.
10. "Training Top 125," *Training*, January/February 2011, p. 57.
11. V. Powers, "Virtual Communities at Caterpillar Foster Knowledge Sharing," *TD*, June 2004, pp. 40–45.
12. L. Patel, *2010 State of the Industry Report* (Alexandria, VA: American Society for Training and Development, 2010); M. Weinstein, "Long-Range Learning Plans," *Training*, November/December 2010, pp. 38–41.
13. T. Bingham and P. Galagan, "M,m M,m Good," *T + D*, March 2011, pp. 36–43; N. Reardon, "Making Leadership Personal," *T + D*, March 2011, pp. 44–48; www.campbellsoupcompany.com, website for Campbell's Soup Company.
14. R. Noe, *Employee Training and Development*, 5th ed. (New York: Irwin/McGraw-Hill, 2010).
15. Ibid.
16. Based on Steelcase company website, www.steelcase.com; G. Wolfe, "Steelcase: Demonstrating the Connection between Learning and Strategic Business Results," *TD*, April 2005, pp. 28–34; T. Bingham and P. Galagan, "At c-Level: James P. Hackett, President and CEO, Steelcase," *TD*, April 2005, pp. 22–26.

17. J. B. Tracey, S. I. Tannenbaum, and M. J. Kavanaugh, "Applying Trained Skills on the Job: The Importance of the Work Environment," *Journal of Applied Psychology* 80 (1995), pp. 239–52; E. Holton, R. Bates, and W. Ruona, "Development of a Generalized Learning Transfer System Inventory," *Human Resource Development Quarterly* 11(2001), pp. 333–60; E. Helton III and T. Baldwin, eds., *Improving Learning Transfer in Organizations* (San Francisco: Jossey-Bass, 2003); J. S. Russell, J. R. Terborg, and M. L. Powers, "Organizational Performance and Organizational Level Training and Support," *Personnel Psychology* 38 (1985), pp. 849–63.

18. S. Tannenbaum, "A Strategic View of Organizational Training and Learning," in *Creating, Implementing, and Managing Effective Training and Development,* ed. K. Kraiger (San Francisco: Jossey-Bass, 2002), pp. 10–52.

19. Ibid.

20. H. Dolezalek, "It's a Small World," *Training,* January 2008, pp. 22–26.

21. H. Dolezalek, "EMC's Competitive Advantage," *Training,* February 2009, pp. 42–46.

22. J. Salopek, "From Learning Department to Learning Partner," *T + D,* October 2010, pp. 48–50.

23. J. Salopek, "Keeping Knowledge Safe and Sound," *T + D,* October 2010, pp. 64–66.

24. C. Reinhart, "How to Leap Over Barrier to Performance," *Training and Development,* January 2000, pp. 20–29; G. Rummter and K. Morrill, "The Results Chain," *T + D,* February 2005, pp. 27–35; O. Rummter, "In Search of the Holy Performance Grail," *Training and Development,* April 1996, pp. 26–31.

25. C. E. Schneier, J. P. Guthrie, and J. D. Olian, "A Practical Approach to Conducting and Using Training Needs Assessment," *Public Personnel Management,* Summer 1988, pp. 191–205; I. Goldstein, "Training in Organizations," in *Handbook of Industrial/Organizational Psychology,* 2nd ed., ed. M. D. Dunnette and L. M. Hough (Palo Alto, CA: Consulting Psychologists Press, 1991), vol. 2, pp. 507–619.

26. E. F. Holton III and C. Bailey, "Top-to-Bottom Curriculum Redesign," *Training and Development,* March 1995, pp. 40–44.

27. R. A. Noe, "Trainees' Attributes and Attitudes: Neglected Influences on Training Effectiveness," *Academy of Management Review* 11 (1986), pp. 736–49.

28. T. T. Baldwin, R. T. Magjuka, and B. T. Loher, "The Perils of Participation: Effects of Choice on Trainee Motivation and Learning," *Personnel Psychology* 44 (1991), pp. 51–66; S. I. Tannenbaum, J. E. Mathieu, E. Salas, and J. A. Cannon-Bowers, "Meeting Trainees' Expectations: The Influence of Training Fulfillment on the Development of Commitment, Self-Efficacy, and Motivation," *Journal of Applied Psychology* 76 (1991), pp. 759–69.

29. C. E. Schneier, "Training and Development Programs: What Learning Theory and Research Have to Offer," *Personnel Journal,* April 1974, pp. 288–93; M. Knowles, "Adult Learning," in *Training and Development Handbook,* 3rd ed., ed. R. L. Craig (New York: McGraw-Hill, 1987), pp. 168–79; R. Zemke and S. Zemke, "30 Things We Know for Sure about Adult Learning," *Training,* June 1981, pp. 45–52; B. J. Smith and B. L. Delahaye, *How to Be an Effective Trainer,* 2nd ed. (New York: John Wiley and Sons, 1987).

30. "Spirited Learning," *T + D,* October 2009, pp. 56–58; J. Salopek, "From Learning Department to Learning Partner," *T + D,* October 2010, pp. 48–50; J. Salopek, "Keeping Knowledge Safe and Sound," *T + D,* October 2010, pp. 64–66.

31. E. Holton III and T. Baldwin, eds, *Improving Learning Transfer in Organizations* (San Francisco: Jossey-Bass, 2003); J. B. Tracey, S. I. Tannenbaum, and M. J. Kavanaugh, "Applying Trained Skills on the Job: The Importance of the Work Environment," *Journal of Applied Psychology* 80 (1995), pp. 239–52; P. E. Tesluk, J. L. Farr, J. E. Mathieu, and R. J. Vance, "Generalization of Employee Involvement Training to the Job Setting: Individual and Situational Effects," *Personnel Psychology* 48 (1995), pp. 607–32; J. K. Ford, M. A. Quinones, D. J. Sego, and J. S. Sorra, "Factors Affecting the Opportunity to Perform Trained Tasks on the Job," *Personnel Psychology* 45 (1992), pp. 511–27.

32. "Spirited Learning," *T + D,* October 2009, pp. 56–58.

33. R. Smith, "Aligning Learning with Business Strategy," *T + D* November 2008, pp. 40–43.

34. J. M. Cusimano, "Managers as Facilitators," *Training and Development* 50 (1996), pp. 31–33.

35. C. M. Petrini, ed., "Bringing It Back to Work," *Training and Development Journal,* December 1990, pp. 15–21.

36. Ford, Quinones, Sego, and Sorra, "Factors Affecting the Opportunity to Perform Trained Tasks on the Job."

37. M. A. Quinones, J. K. Ford, D. J. Sego, and E. M. Smith, "The Effects of Individual and Transfer Environment Characteristics on the Opportunity to Perform Trained Tasks," *Training Research Journal* 1 (1995/96), pp. 29–48.

38. G. Stevens and E. Stevens, "The Truth about EPSS," *Training and Development* 50 (1996), pp. 59–61.

39. M. Weinstein, "Wake-up Call," *Training,* June 2007, pp. 48–50.

40. J. MacGregor, "The Office Chart That Really Counts," *BusinessWeek,* February 27, 2006, pp. 48–49.

41. "Grant Thornton LLP (USA)," *T + D,* October 2010, p. 74.

42. J. Salopek, "Re-discovering Knowledge," *T + D,* October 2010, pp. 36–38.

43. R. D. Marx, "Relapse Prevention for Managerial Training: A Model for Maintenance of Behavior Change," *Academy of Management Review* 7 (1982), pp. 433–41; G. P. Latham and C. A. Frayne, "Self-Management Training for Increasing Job Attendance: A Follow-up and Replication," *Journal of Applied Psychology* 74 (1989), pp. 411–16.

44. P. Keller, "Soaring to New Safety Heights," *TD,* January 2006, pp. 51–54. Also see "About Us" on the Vanderbilt University Medical Center website at www.mc.vanderbilt.edu.

45. B. Mirza, "Social Media Tools Redefine Learning," *HR Magazine,* December 2010, p. 74; L. Patel, "The Rise of Social Media," *T + D,* July 2010, pp. 60–61; J. Meister, E. Kaganer, and R. Von Feldt, "2011: The Year of the Media Tablet as a Learning Tool," *T + D,* April 2011, pp. 28–31.

46. "Putting the Distance into Distance Learning," *Training,* October 1995, pp. 111–18.

47. D. Picard, "The Future Is Distance Training," *Training,* November 1996, pp. s3–s10.

48. A. F. Maydas, "On-line Networks Build the Savings into Employee Education," *HR Magazine,* October 1997, pp. 31–35.

49. J. M. Rosow and R. Zager, *Training: The Competitive Edge* (San Francisco: Jossey-Bass, 1988).

50. M. Weinstein, "Satellite Success," *Training,* January 2007, pp. 36–38.

51. S. Alexander, "Reducing the Learning Burden," *Training,* September 2002, pp. 32–34.

52. T. Skylar, "When Training Collides with a 35-Ton Truck," *Training,* March 1996, pp. 32–38.

53. R. B. Cohn, "How to Choose a Video Producer," *Training,* July 1996, pp. 58–61.

54. E. Wagner and P. Wilson, "Disconnected," *TD*, December 2005, pp. 40–43; J. Bronstein and A. Newman, "IM Learning," *TD*, February 2006, pp. 47–50.

55. J. Meister, E. Kaganer, and R. Von Feldt, "2011: The Year of the Media Tablet as a Learning Tool," *T + D*, April 2011, pp. 28–31.

56. M. Weinstein, "Ready or Not, Here Comes Podcasting," *Training*, January 2006, pp. 22–23; D. Sussman, "Now Here This," *TD*, September 2005, pp. 53–54; J. Pont, "Employee Training on iPod Playlist," *Workforce Management*, August 2005, p. 18; S. Boehle, "iPod Corporation," *Training*, September 6, 2007, pp. 17–19.

57. E. Wagner and P. Wilson, "Disconnected," *TD*, December 2005, pp. 40–43.

58. B. Filipczak, "Who Owns Your OJT?" *Training*, December 1996, pp. 44–49.

59. "Reliance Industries Limited, Nagothane Manufacturing Division," *T + D*, October 2008, p. 78.

60. R. W. Glover, *Apprenticeship Lessons from Abroad* (Columbus, OH: National Center for Research in Vocational Education, 1986).

61. Commerce Clearing House, Inc., *Orientation–Training* (Chicago, IL: Personnel Practices Communications, Commerce Clearing House, 1981), pp. 501–905.

62. A. H. Howard III, "Apprenticeships," in *The ASTD Training and Development Handbook*, pp. 803–13.

63. M. Rowh, "The Rise of the Apprentice," *Human Resource Executive*, January 2006, pp. 38–43.

64. A. Ciaccio, "You're Hired: Goldcorp Stint Touts Opportunities in Mining," *The Wall Street Journal*, September 25, 2005, p. B6.

65. *Eldredge v. Carpenters JATC* (1981), 27 Fair Employment Practices (Bureau of National Affairs), p. 479.

66. M. Weinstein, "Virtually Integrated," *Training*, April 2007, p. 10; A. Hira, "The Making of a UPS Driver," *Fortune*, November 12, 2007, pp. 118–29; P. Ketter, "What Can Training Do for Brown," *T + D*, May 2008, pp. 30–36.

67. C. Cornell, "Better than the Real Thing?" *Human Resource Executive*, August 2005, pp. 34–37.

68. J. Borzo, "Almost Human," *The Wall Street Journal*, May 24, 2004, pp. R1, R10; J. Hoff, "My Virtual Life," *BusinessWeek*, May 1, 2006, pp. 72–78.

69. N. Adams, "Lessons from the Virtual World," *Training*, June 1995, pp. 45–48.

70. Ibid.

71. H. Dolezalek, "Virtual Vision," *Training*, October 2007, pp. 40–46.

72. R. Flandez, "Small Business Link: Chip Maker Trains in the Virtual World," *The Wall Street Journal* (April 3, 2008), B6.

73. P. Galagan, "Second That," *T+D*, February 2008, pp. 34–37.

74. Cornell, "Better than the Real Thing?"; E. Frauenheim, "Can Video Games Win Points as Teaching Tools?" *Workforce Management*, April 10, 2006, pp. 12–14; S. Boehle, "Simulations: The Next Generation of e-Learning," *Training*, January 2005, pp. 22–31; Borzo, "Almost Human"; T. Sitzmann, "A Meta-Analytic Examination of the Instructional Effectiveness of Computer-Based Simulation Games," *Personnel Psychology* 64 (2011), pp. 489–528.

75. L. Freifeld, "Solid Sims," *Training*, October 2007, p. 48.

76. "What Things Cost: What Does It Cost to Use a Virtual World Learning Environment?" *T + D*, November 2008, p. 88.

77. T. W. Shreeve, "On the Case at the CIA," *Training and Development*, March 1997, pp. 53–54.

78. P. Dvorak, "Theory & Practice: Simulation Shows What It Is Like to Be the Boss; Middle Managers at NetApp Receive Useful Taste of Reality," *The Wall Street Journal*, March 31, 2008, p. B7.

79. M. Hequet, "Games That Teach," *Training*, July 1995, pp. 53–58.

80. G. P. Latham and L. M. Saari, "Application of Social Learning Theory to Training Supervisors through Behavior Modeling," *Journal of Applied Psychology* 64 (1979), pp. 239–46.

81. E. Hollis, "Shoney's: Workforce Development on the Side," *Chief Learning Officer*, March 2003, pp. 32–34.

82. W. Hannum, *The Application of Emerging Training Technology* (Alexandria, VA: American Society for Training and Development, 1990).

83. M. Rosenberg, *E-Learning: Strategies for Delivering Knowledge in the Digital Age* (New York: McGraw-Hill, 2001).

84. P. Galagan, "The E-Learning Revolution," *Training and Development*, December 2000, pp. 24–30; D. Khirallah, "A New Way to Learn," *Information Week Online* (May 22, 2000).

85. S. Murphy, "Ritz Camera Focuses on Web-Based Teaching Tools," in "Techtalk Tuesday" at www.chainstoreage.com, December 23, 2008.

86. "Sanofi-Aventis U.S.," *T + D*, October 2009, p. 83.

87. "Learning Management Systems: An Executive Summary," *Training*, March 2002, p. 4.

88. "LMS Goes to the Dogs," *Training*, September/October 2010, p. 8.

89. L. Freifeld, "LMS Lessons," *Training*, September/October 2010, pp. 20–24.

90. "A New Lease on Learning," *Training*, October 2009, pp. 44–46.

91. D. Brown and D. Harvey, *An Experiential Approach to Organizational Development* (Englewood Cliffs, NJ: Prentice Hall, 2000); J. Schettler, "Learning by Doing," *Training*, April 2002, pp. 38–43; G. Kranz, "From Fire Drills to Funny Skills," *Workforce Management*, May 2011, pp. 28–32.

92. Schettler, "Learning by Doing."

93. R. J. Wagner, T. T. Baldwin, and C. C. Rowland, "Outdoor Training: Revolution or Fad?" *Training and Development Journal*, March 1991, pp. 51–57; C. J. Cantoni, "Learning the Ropes of Teamwork," *The Wall Street Journal*, October 2, 1995, p. A14.

94. C. Steinfeld, "Challenge Courses Can Build Strong Teams," *Training and Development*, April 1997, pp. 12–13.

95. D. Mishev, "Cooking for the Company," *Cooking Light*, August 2004, pp. 142–47.

96. P. F. Buller, J. R. Cragun, and G. M. McEvoy, "Getting the Most Out of Outdoor Training," *Training and Development Journal*, March 1991, pp. 58–61.

97. C. Clements, R. J. Wagner, C. C. Roland, "The Ins and Outs of Experiential Training," *Training and Development*, February 1995, pp. 52–56.

98. J. Cannon-Bowers and C. Bowers, "Team Development and Functioning," in S. Zedeck (ed.), *APA Handbook of Industrial and Organizational Psychology* (Washington, DC: American Psychological Association, 2011), vol. 1, pp. 597–650. L. Delise, C. Gorman, A. Brooks, J. Rentsch, and D. Steele-Johnson, "The Effects of Team Training on Team Outcomes: A Meta-Analysis," *Performance Improvement Quarterly* 22 (2010), pp. 53–80.

99. S. Carey, "Racing to Improve," *The Wall Street Journal*, March 24, 2006, pp. B1, B6.

100. P. Froiland, "Action Learning," *Training*, January 1994, pp. 27–34.

101. "A Team Effort," *Training*, September 2002, p. 18.

102. H. Lancaster, "This Kind of Black Belt Can Help You Score Some Points at Work," *The Wall Street Journal*, September 14,

1999, p. B1; S. Gale, "Building Frameworks for Six Sigma Success," *Workforce*, May 2003, pp. 64–66.

103. J. DeFeo, "An ROI Story," *Training and Development*, July 2000, pp. 25–27.

104. S. Gale, "Six Sigma Is a Way of Life," *Workforce*, May 2003, pp. 67–68.

105. K. Kraiger, J. K. Ford, and E. Salas, "Application of Cognitive, Skill-Based, and Affective Theories of Learning Outcomes to New Methods of Training Evaluation," *Journal of Applied Psychology* 78 (1993), pp. 311–28; J. J. Phillips, "ROI: The Search for Best Practices," *Training and Development*, February 1996, pp. 42–47; D. L. Kirkpatrick, "Evaluation of Training," in *Training and Development Handbook*, 2nd ed., ed. R. L. Craig (New York: McGraw-Hill, 1976), pp. 18-1 to 18–27.

106. "Training Top 125," *Training*, January/February 2011, p. 93.

107. P. Harris, "Learning, at Your Service," *T + D*, October 2010, pp. 57–58.

108. A. P. Carnevale and E. R. Schulz, "Return on Investment: Accounting for Training," *Training and Development Journal*, July 1990, pp. S1–S32; P. R. Sackett and E. J. Mullen, "Beyond Formal Experimental Design: Toward an Expanded View of the Training Evaluation Process," *Personnel Psychology* 46 (1993), pp. 613–27; S. I. Tannenbaum and S. B. Woods, "Determining a Strategy for Evaluating Training: Operating within Organizational Constraints," *Human Resource Planning* 15 (1992), pp. 63–81; R. D. Arvey, S. E. Maxwell, and E. Salas, "The Relative Power of Training Evaluation Designs under Different Cost Configurations," *Journal of Applied Psychology* 77 (1992), pp. 155–60.

109. D. A. Grove and C. O. Ostroff, "Program Evaluation," in *Developing Human Resources*, ed. K. N. Wexley (Washington, DC: BNA Books, 1991), pp. 185–219.

110. D. Sussman, "Strong Medicine Required," *TD*, November 2005, pp. 34–38.

111. Carnevale and Schulz, "Return on Investment."

112. Ibid.; G. Kearsley, *Costs, Benefits, and Productivity in Training Systems* (Boston: Addison-Wesley, 1982).

113. Ibid.

114. D. G. Robinson and J. Robinson, "Training for Impact," *Training and Development Journal*, August 1989, pp. 30–42.

115. Sussman, "Strong Medicine Required."

116. I. Speizer, "Rolling through the Downturn," *Workforce Management*, August 11, 2008, pp. 31–37.

117. Ibid.

118. B. Ettorre, "Let's Hear It for Local Talent," *Management Review*, October 1994, p. 9; S. Franklin, "A New World Order for Business Strategy," *Chicago Tribune*, May 15, 1994, sec. 19, pp. 7–8.

119. R. L. Tung, "Selection and Training of Personnel for Overseas Assignments," *Columbia Journal of World Business* 16 (1981), pp. 18–78.

120. W. A. Arthur Jr. and W. Bennett Jr., "The International Assignee: The Relative Importance of Factors Perceived to Contribute to Success," *Personnel Psychology* 48 (1995), pp. 99–114; G. M. Spreitzer, M. W. McCall Jr., and Joan D. Mahoney, "Early Identification of International Executive Potential," *Journal of Applied Psychology* 82 (1997), pp. 6–29.

121. J. S. Black and J. K. Stephens, "The Influence of the Spouse on American Expatriate Adjustment and Intent to Stay in Pacific Rim Overseas Assignments," *Journal of Management* 15 (1989), pp. 529–44; M. Shaffer and D. A. Harrison, "Forgotten Partners of International Assignments: Development and Test of a Model of Spouse Adjustment," *Journal of Applied Psychology* 86 (2001), pp. 238–54.

122. M. Shaffer, D. A. Harrison, H. Gregersen, J. S. Black, and L. A. Ferzandi, "You Can Take It with You: Individual Differences and Expatriate Effectiveness," *Journal of Applied Psychology* 91 (2006), pp. 109–25; P. Caligiuri, "The Big Five Personality Characteristics as Predictors of Expatriate's Desire to Terminate the Assignment and Supervisor-Rated Performance," *Personnel Psychology* 53 (2000), pp. 67–88.

123. E. Dunbar and A. Katcher, "Preparing Managers for Foreign Assignments," *Training and Development Journal*, September 1990, pp. 45–47.

124. J. S. Black and M. Mendenhall, "A Practical but Theory-Based Framework for Selecting Cross-Cultural Training Methods," in *Readings and Cases in International Human Resource Management*, ed. M. Mendenhall and G. Oddou (Boston: PWS-Kent, 1991), pp. 177–204.

125. P. Tam, "Culture Course," *The Wall Street Journal*, May 25, 2004, pp. B1, B12.

126. S. Ronen, "Training the International Assignee," in *Training and Development in Organizations*, ed. I. L. Goldstein (San Francisco: Jossey-Bass, 1989), pp. 417–53.

127. P. R. Harris and R. T. Moran, *Managing Cultural Differences* (Houston: Gulf, 1991).

128. J. Carter, "Globe Trotters," *Training*, August 2005, pp. 22–28.

129. C. Solomon, "Unhappy Trails," *Workforce*, August 2000, pp. 36–41.

130. J. Ramirez, "Lost in the Shuffle," *Human Resource Executive*, January 2006, pp. 54–57.

131. H. Lancaster, "Before Going Overseas, Smart Managers Plan Their Homecoming," *The Wall Street Journal*, September 28, 1999, p. B1; A. Halcrow, "Expats: The Squandered Resource," *Workforce*, April 1999, pp. 42–48.

132. Harris and Moran, *Managing Cultural Differences*.

133. J. Cook, "Rethinking Relocation," *Human Resources Executive*, June 2, 2003, pp. 23–26.

134. J. Flynn, "E-Mail, Cellphones, and Frequent-Flier Miles Let 'Virtual' Expats Work Abroad but Live at Home," *The Wall Street Journal*, October 25, 1999, p. A26; J. Flynn, "Multinationals Help Career Couples Deal with Strains Affecting Expatriates," *The Wall Street Journal*, August 8, 2000, p. A19; C. Solomon, "The World Stops Shrinking," *Workforce*, January 2000, pp. 48–51.

135. H. Dolezalek, "The Path to Inclusion," *Training*, May 2008, pp. 52–54.

136. E. McKeown, "Quantifiable Inclusion Strategies," *T + D*, October 2010, p. 16.

137. S. E. Jackson and Associates, *Diversity in the Workplace: Human Resource Initiatives* (New York: Guilford Press, 1992).

138. M. Lee, "Post-9/11 Training," *TD*, September 2002, pp. 33–35.

139. S. Rynes and B. Rosen, "A Field Study of Factors Affecting the Adoption and Perceived Success of Diversity Training," *Personnel Psychology* 48 (1995), pp. 247–70; Aparna, "Why Diversity Training Doesn't Work . . . Right Now," *T + D*, November 2008, pp. 52–57.

140. T. Kochan, K. Bezrukova, R. Ely, S. Jackson, A. Joshi, K. Jehn, J. Leonard, D. Levine, and D. Thomas, "The Effects of Diversity on Business Performance: Report of the Diversity Research Network," *Human Resource Management* 42 (2003), pp. 8–21; F. Hansen, "Diversity's Business Case Just Doesn't Add Up," *Workforce*, June 2003, pp. 29–32; M. J. Wesson and C. I. Gogus, "Shaking Hands with the Computer: An Examination of Two Methods of Newcomer Socialization," *Journal of Applied Psychology* 90 (2005), pp. 1018–26; H. J. Klein and N. A., Weaver, "The Effectiveness of an Organizational-Level Orientation

Training Program in the Socialization of New Hires," *Personnel Psychology* 53 (2000), pp. 47–66.

141. R. Anand and M. Winters, "A Retrospective View of Corporate Diversity Training from 1964 to the Present," *Academy of Management Learning & Education*, 7 (2008), pp. 356–72; Dolezalek, "The Path to Inclusion." Also, see www.sodexousa.com. "Sodexo 2010 Diversity and Inclusion Annual Report," available at www.sodexousa.com website for Sodexo USA, accessed June 20, 2011.

142. C. T. Schreiber, K. F. Price, and A. Morrison, "Workforce Diversity and the Glass Ceiling: Practices, Barriers, Possibilities," *Human Resource Planning* 16 (1994), pp. 51–69.

143. D. C. Feldman, "A Contingency Theory of Socialization," *Administrative Science Quarterly* 21 (1976), pp. 433–52; D. C. Feldman, "A Socialization Process That Helps New Recruits Succeed," *Personnel* 57 (1980), pp. 11–23; J. P. Wanous, A. E. Reichers, and S. D. Malik, "Organizational Socialization and Group Development: Toward an Integrative Perspective," *Academy of Management Review* 9 (1984), pp. 670–83; C. L. Adkins, "Previous Work Experience and Organizational Socialization: A Longitudinal Examination," *Academy of Management Journal* 38 (1995), pp. 839–62; E. W. Morrison, "Longitudinal Study of the Effects of Information Seeking on Newcomer Socialization," *Journal of Applied Psychology* 78 (1993), pp. 173–83.

144. M. R. Louis, "Surprise and Sense Making: What Newcomers Experience in Entering Unfamiliar Organizational Settings," *Administrative Science Quarterly* 25 (1980), pp. 226–51.

145. For example see J. D. Kammeyer-Mueller and C. R. Wanberg, "Unwrapping the Organizational Entry Process: Disentangling Multiple Antecedents and Their Pathway to Adjustment," *Journal of Applied Psychology* 88 (2003), pp. 779–94; M. R. Buckley, D. B. Fedor, J. G. Veres, D. S. Wiese, and S. M. Carraher, "Investigating Newcomer Expectations and Job-Related Outcomes," *Journal of Applied Psychology* 83 (1998), pp. 452–61; G. W. Maier and J. C. Brunstein, "The Role of Personal Work Goals in Newcomers' Job Satisfaction and Organizational Commitment: A Longitudinal Analysis," *Journal of Applied Psychology* 86 (2001), pp. 1034–42.

146. D. C. Feldman, *Managing Careers in Organizations* (Glenview, IL: Scott Foresman, 1988); D. Reed-Mendenhall and C. W. Millard, "Orientation: A Training and Development Tool," *Personnel Administrator* 25, no. 8 (1980), pp. 42–44; M. R. Louis, B. Z. Posner, and G. H. Powell, "The Availability and Helpfulness of Socialization Practices," *Personnel Psychology* 36 (1983), pp. 857–66; C. Ostroff and S. W. J. Kozlowski Jr., "Organizational Socialization as a Learning Process: The Role of Information Acquisition," *Personnel Psychology* 45 (1992), pp. 849–74; D. R. France and R. L. Jarvis, "Quick Starts for New Employees," *Training and Development*, October 1996, pp. 47–50.

147. J. Schettler, "Welcome to ACME Inc.," *Training*, August 2002, pp. 36–43; J. Salopek, "A Story to Tell," *TD*, October 2005, pp. 54–56; D. Sussman, "A Monstrous Welcome," *TD*, April 2005, pp. 401–41; D. Sussman, "Getting Up to Speed," *TD*, December 2005, pp. 49–51.

148. "Clarkston Consulting," *T + D*, October 2008, p. 73.

149. "Training Top 125," *Training*, January/February 2011, p. 91.

150. J. Arnold, "Gaming Technology Used to Orient New Hires," *SHRM 2009 HR Trendbook* (Alexandria, VA: Society for Human Resource Management), pp. 36–38.

151. K. Rhodes, "Breaking in the Top Dogs," *Training*, February 2000, pp. 67–71.

PART 3

Assessment and Development of HRM

Chapter 8
Performance Management

Chapter 9
Employee Development

Chapter 10
Employee Separation and Retention

CHAPTER

8 Performance Management

Performance Management Helps Turn Around a Health Care Organization

In 2000 financial distress was plaguing Scripps Health, a private nonprofit community health system located in San Diego, California. The company was losing money, the chief executive officer resigned, turnover among nurses was high, and employee morale was poor. Under the leadership of a new CEO, a new strategic plan was developed that included streamlining business operations, increasing the efficiencies of operations, and improving employee satisfaction and performance. Implementation of the strategic plan was successful.

A new performance management system that focused on leadership development, metrics, recognition of employees and business unit performance, and using compensation to motivate employees was a key contributor to the successful turnaround of Scripps Health. Scripps Health performance management system plays an important role in helping Scripps Health motivate and engage employees, which leads to delighting customers through providing excellent patient care and service.

Patient admissions and donations are high and employee turnover dropped below industry standards. Today, Scripps Health system includes five acute-care hospitals, more than 20 primary and specialty care outpatient clinics, home health care services, and more than 2,500 affiliated physicians and 13,000 employees. Scripps also provides health education and wellness events and programs such as exercise classes, heart health seminars, parenting classes, and fund raising events across San Diego County. Since 2008 Scripps has been named one of the 100 Best Companies to Work For by *Fortune* magazine.

Performance managements is part of Scripps' annual planning, business strategy, financial and operations processes through collaboration between HR, finance, strategic planning, and operations departments. This helps ensure that the performance management process helps Scripps meet its strategic business goals and employees engage in behaviors that support the achievement of these goals. The performance appraisal evaluates employees on annual objectives and behaviors related to the Scripps core values (respect, quality, and efficiency). The performance management process is aligned for all employees in the organization including board and senior executive management and staff employees. Also, Scripps Health performance management process encourages managers and employees to work together in evaluating performance, setting measurable goals, indentifying areas for performance improvement, and recognizing excellent performance.

HR introduced an automated, online performance evaluation that simplified the performance management process. Managers can more easily track employee performance strengths and weaknesses and ensure performance appraisals are valid by linking them to the job description. The online system makes it easier for managers to set personal, employee, and department goals that are linked to functional and organizational goals (a process known as "cascading" goal setting). Also, the online performance management system helps managers review and track their own, their employees', and the department's progress in reaching performance goals.

One of the most important uses for performance management systems is to help motivate and reward employees for effective performance. Scripps Health uses its performance management system to help determine pay increases and reward bonuses. Employees can receive annual pay increases up to 5% based on their performance appraisals. Scripps also has a gainsharing program called "Success Shares" which helps motivate and reward teamwork. Gainsharing programs such as Success Shares are designed to reward outstanding patient care and employee contributions toward financial performance based on the overall performance of their department or business unit. Employees only receive rewards if department or business unit goals and objectives are met or exceeded. Rewards are calculated using formulas which include a combination of patient satisfaction scores and financial objectives. For example, in 2007 Scripps paid out $7.8 million to more than 9,300 employees. On average these employees received $900 with a maximum payout of five days' pay.

For successful performance management, employees need to receive effective and timely performance feedback from their managers.

Employees need to receive feedback on a day-to-day basis as well as during the formal annual performance review. In addition, managers need to understand how to set goals that link employee performance to department and business goals. To facilitate effective performance management, Scripps managers receive extensive performance management education and training. Also, managers' performance evaluation includes leadership competencies including character, relationships, serve, change, and results which help hold them accountable for evaluating and developing employees.

SOURCES: Based on S. J. Wells, "Prescription for a Turnaround," *HR Magazine*, June 2009, pp. 88–94; website for Scripps Health at www.scripps.org.

Introduction

Companies that seek competitive advantage through employees must be able to manage the behavior and results of all employees. Traditionally, the formal performance appraisal system was viewed as the primary means for managing employee performance. Performance appraisal was an administrative duty performed by managers and was primarily the responsibility of the human resource function. Managers now view performance appraisal as an annual ritual—they quickly complete the form and use it to catalog all the negative information they have collected on an employee over the previous year. Because they may dislike confrontation and feel that they don't know how to give effective evaluations, some managers spend as little time as possible giving employees feedback. Not surprisingly, most managers and employees dislike performance appraisals. "Time-consuming," "frustrating," "dread," "burden," and "pain" are some of the words that come to employees' minds when giving or receiving performance reviews.[1] Some of the reasons include the lack of consistency of use of performance appraisals across the company; inability to differentiate among different performance levels; and the inability of the appraisal system to provide useful data for development, to help employees build their skills and competencies, or to build a high-performance culture.[2]

Some have argued that all performance appraisal systems are flawed to the point that they are manipulative, abusive, autocratic, and counterproductive. It is important to realize that the criticisms voiced about annual performance appraisals shown in Table 8.1 are not the result of evaluating employee performance. Rather, they result from how the performance management system is developed and used. As the chapter opener illustrated, if done correctly, performance appraisal can provide several valuable benefits to both employees and the company. An important part of appraising performance is to establish employee goals, which should be tied to the company's strategic goals. The performance appraisal process tells top performers that they are valued by the company. It requires managers to at least annually communicate to

table 8.1

Examples of
Problems with
Traditional Annual
Performance
Reviews

"Feedback needs to happen more than once or twice a year. We thought that the traditional annual review was a crutch for managers to do just that and no more."
—Rebecca Henry, director of human resources at Zappos

The annual performance review is ". . . physical and mental turmoil. I don't think that people realize when you're about to go into one of these review sessions, the heart rate goes up, the palms get sweaty, it's a physical reaction."—Jacob Palmer, a recruiter for Zappos

"No one could convince me that there was any value to it. You've got to be able to explain the process to a 10-year-old. You want to talk to me once a year about what I did for the whole year? What if I told my kids that I was going to give them a once-a-year discussion on their behavior? Sometimes we do stupid things."
—Dan Walker, former chief talent officer at Apple Inc.

". . . mainstream management is embedded in, and relies on, a culture of domination . . . the performance review is the biggest hammer management has."
—Samuel A. Culbert, author of *Get Rid of the Performance Review*

"Even surprise good reviews are bad because if employees don't know they're doing well, you are not reinforcing that behavior, or you run the risk of losing a real good employee."—Cindy Gerathy, HR manager at Belimo Aircontrols Inc.

SOURCE: From A. Fox, "Curing What Ails Performance Reviews," *HR Magazine*, January 2009, pp. 52–56; S. Culbert, *Get Rid of the Performance Review* (New York: Business Plus, 2010); and R. Pyrillis, "The Reviews Are In," *Workforce Management*, May 2011, pp. 20–25.

employees their performance strengths and deficiencies. A good appraisal process ensures that all employees doing similar jobs are evaluated according to the same standards. The use of technology, such as the web, can reduce the administrative burden of performance appraisal and improve the accuracy of performance reviews. Also, a properly conducted appraisal can help the company identify the strongest and weakest employees. It can help legally justify many HRM decisions such as promotions, salary increases, discipline, and layoffs.

We believe that performance appraisal is only one part of the broader process of performance management. We define **performance management** as the process through which managers ensure that employees' activities and outputs are congruent with the organization's goals. Performance management is central to gaining competitive advantage.

Our performance management system has three parts: defining performance, measuring performance, and feeding back performance information. First, a performance management system specifies which aspects of performance are relevant to the organization, primarily through job analysis (discussed in Chapter 4). Second, it measures those aspects of performance through **performance appraisal**, which is only one method for managing employee performance. Third, it provides feedback to employees through **performance feedback** sessions so they can adjust their performance to the organization's goals. Performance feedback is also fulfilled through tying rewards to performance via the compensation system (such as through merit increases or bonuses), a topic to be covered in Chapters 11 and 12.

In this chapter, we examine a variety of approaches to performance management. First we provide a brief summary of current performance management practices. Next, we present a model of performance that helps us examine the system's purposes. Then

Performance Management
The means through which managers ensure that employees' activities and outputs are congruent with the organization's goals.

Performance Appraisal
The process through which an organization gets information on how well an employee is doing his or her job.

Performance Feedback
The process of providing employees information regarding their performance effectiveness.

we discuss specific approaches to performance management and the strengths and weaknesses of each. We also look at various sources of performance information. The errors resulting from subjective assessments of performance are presented, as well as the means for reducing those errors. Then we discuss some effective components to performance feedback. Finally, we address components of a legally defensible performance management system.

The Practice of Performance Management

Several recent surveys of human resource professionals suggest that most companies' performance management practices require annual paper-driven reviews that include both behaviors and business goals.[3] While many companies use performance management to manage employee performance and make pay decisions, less than 25% of the companies use performance management to help manage talent through identifying training needs and developing leadership talent. Sixty-six percent of companies used the same performance management system across all levels of the organization. Unfortunately, more than 60% of employees say reviews don't help their future performance. Eight in ten companies conduct performance appraisals and of those 72% report being only somewhat satisfied, not very satisfied, or extremely dissatisfied with the appraisal process. Forty-five percent of employees feel that their manager consistently communicates to them about their performance throughout the year and in between formally scheduled performance reviews. Only 28% of companies have automated their performance management system.

The Process of Performance Management

LO 8-1
Identify the major determinants of effective performance management.

As you may have already figured out from the chapter introduction and your own experiences, many employees and managers dislike the annual performance review. Although performance management does include the once or twice a year appraisal or evaluation meeting, effective performance management is a process, not an event. Figure 8.1 shows the performance management process. As shown in the process model, providing feedback and the formal performance evaluation are important but they are not the only important parts of an effective performance management process that contributes to the company's competitive advantage.[4] Also, visible CEO and senior management support for the system are necessary. This ensures that the system is consistently used across the company, appraisals are completed on time, and giving and receiving performance feedback is an accepted part of the company culture. The first two steps of the performance management process involve identifying what the company is trying to accomplish (goals or objectives), a set of key performance dimensions that represent critical factors or drivers that influence the goals or objectives, and then develop performance measures for the key performance dimensions.[5] The first step in the performance management process starts with understanding and identifying important performance outcomes or results. Typically, these outcomes or results benefit customers, the employees' peers or team, and the organization itself. The company's and department or team's strategy, mission, and values play an important part in determining these outcomes. Chapter 2 pointed out that

figure 8.1

Model of the Effective Performance Management Process

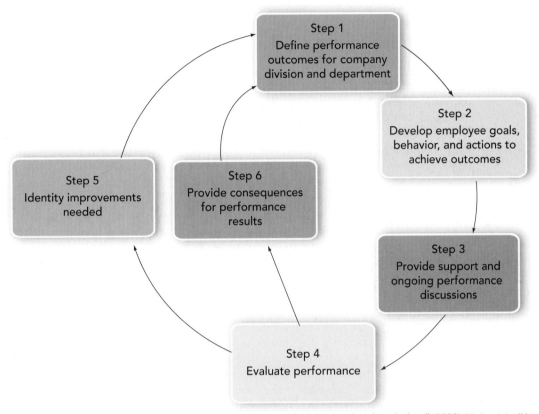

SOURCE: Based on E. Pulakos, *Performance Management* (Oxford, England: Wiley-Blackwell, 2009); H. Aguinis, "An Expanded View of Performance Management," in J. W. Smith and M. London (eds.), *Performance Management* (San Francisco: Jossey-Bass, 2009), pp. 1–43; and J. Russell and L. Russell, "Talk Me through It: The Next Level of Performance Management," *T + D*, April 2010, pp. 42–48.

most companies pursue some type of strategy to reach revenue, profit, and market share goals. Divisions, departments, teams, and employees must align their goals and behaviors, and choose to engage in activities that help achieve the organization's strategy and goals. The second step of the process involves understanding the process (or how) to achieve the goals established in the first step. This includes identifying measurable goals, behaviors, and activities that will help the employee achieve the performance results. The goals, behaviors, and activities should be measurable so that the manager and employee can determine if they have been achieved. The goals, activities, and behaviors should be part of the employee's job description. Step three in the process, organizational support, involves providing employees with training, necessary resources and tools, and frequent feedback communication between the employee and manager focusing on accomplishments as well as issues and challenges influencing performance. For effective performance management managers and employees have to value feedback and regularly exchange it. Managers need to make time to provide feedback as well as train in how to give and receive it. Step four involves performance evaluation, that is, when the manager and employee discuss and compare the targeted performance goal and supporting behaviors with the actual results. This typically involves the annual or biannual formal performance review. As we will see later in the chapter there are many ways to help make this formal review more of a performance conversation designed to identify and discuss opportunities to improve and less of a one-way evaluation by the manager. One way to make the formal evaluation more effective is for managers to engage in frequent performance conversations with employees rather than wait for the annual review (step 3). The final steps of the performance management cycle involve the employee and manager identifying what the employee (with help from the manager) can do to capitalize on performance strengths and address weaknesses (step 5) and providing consequences for achieving (or failing to achieve) performance outcomes (step 6). This includes identifying training needs, adjusting the type or frequency of feedback the managers provides to the employee, clarifying, adjusting, or modifying performance outcomes, and discussions of behaviors or activities that need improvement or relate to new priorities based on changes or new areas of emphasis in organizational or department goals. Achieving performance results may relate to compensation (salary increases, cash bonuses), recognition, promotion, development opportunities, and continued employment. This depends on the purposes the company decides on for the performance management system (see our discussion in the section "Purposes of Performance Management"). Finally, it is important to realize that what employees accomplish (or fail to accomplish) and their consequences help shape changes in the organizational business strategy and performance goals and the ongoing performance management process. Evaluating the effectiveness of the performance management system is necessary to determine needed changes. This could include gathering comments about the managers' and employees' concerns about the system, analyzing rating data to determine if they are being affected by rating errors, reviewing objectives for their quality, and studying the relationship between employees meeting objectives and department and organizational results.

 # Purposes of Performance Management

LO 8-2
Discuss the three general purposes of performance management.

The purposes of performance management systems are of three kinds: strategic, administrative, and developmental.

STRATEGIC PURPOSE

First and foremost, a performance management system should link employee activities with the organization's goals. One of the primary ways strategies are implemented is through defining the results, behaviors, and, to some extent, employee characteristics that are necessary for carrying out those strategies, and then developing measurement and feedback systems that will maximize the extent to which employees exhibit the characteristics, engage in the behaviors, and produce the results.

Performance management is critical for companies to execute their talent management strategy, that is, to identify employees' strengths and weaknesses, link employees to appropriate training and development activity, and reward good performance with pay and other incentives. The "Competing through Globalization" box shows how performance management can help develop global business.

A Mix of Metrics Are Needed to Support Local and Company Performance

WD-40 Company's products are found under the sink, in the garage, and in toolboxes of consumers around the world. WD-40 Company produces lubricants, heavy-duty hand cleaners, toilet bowl cleaners, bathroom cleaners, and carpet stain and room odor eliminators. It's most well-known product is the versatile lubricant WD-40 that can be used to help loosen rusty nuts and bolts and even as a stain and gum remover! Do you know what WD-40 stands for? WD-40 means Water Displacement, 40th attempt. That's the name from the lab book used by the chemist who developed WD-40 in 1953. The chemist was attempting to create a solution to prevent corrosion (which involves displacing water). The chemist's persistence paid off when he perfected the formula on his 40th try.

WD-40 is a global consumer products company, headquartered in San Diego, California, with operations in the United States, Asia, Canada, Europe, and Latin America. The majority of WD-40's revenue comes from outside the United States. Until 2008, 80% of bonus payouts for employees in countries in North America, Europe, and Asia were determined by overall financial performance and 20% by financial performance within the employee's country. The results of an employee survey in 2008 showed that employees wanted more of their bonus to be linked to performance measures under their control, that is, country-specific performance. In response, HR at WD-40 created the Double Vision Program, which places a greater focus on country-specific performance while still rewarding global business results. Net invoiced sales and operating cash flow based on earnings before interest, taxes, depreciation, and amoritization are the two performance metrics used in the program. Eighty percent of the bonus is now based on local performance, according to the achievement of sales and profit targets established by the CEO and board for the entire company. Of the 80%, 50% is determined by meeting sales targets and 30% by meeting profit goals, and 20% is determined by global, corporate earnings results. The HR team collaborates with the finance department to distribute quarterly earnings and sales reports to every employee. This helps employees understand how they are performing on the numbers and gives them time to try and positively influence the numbers before the year-end bonuses are determined. Also, employees have a clear vision of how their activities influence both the company's country-specific performance and overall corporate performance.

SOURCE: Based on E. Krell, "All for Incentives, Incentives for All," *HR Magazine,* January 2011, pp. 35–38 and www.wd40.com website for WD-40 Company.

ADMINISTRATIVE PURPOSE

Organizations use performance management information (performance appraisals, in particular) in many administrative decisions: salary administration (pay raises), promotions, retention–termination, layoffs, and recognition of individual performance.[6] Despite the importance of these decisions, however, many managers, who are the source of the information, see the performance appraisal process only as a necessary evil they must go through to fulfill their job requirements. They feel uncomfortable evaluating others and feeding those evaluations back to the employees. Thus, they tend to rate everyone high or at least rate them the same, making the performance appraisal information relatively useless. For example, one manager stated, "There is really no getting around the fact that whenever I evaluate one

of my people, I stop and think about the impact—the ramifications of my decisions on my relationship with the guy and his future here. . . . Call it being politically minded, or using managerial discretion, or fine-tuning the guy's ratings, but in the end, I've got to live with him, and I'm not going to rate a guy without thinking about the fallout."[7]

DEVELOPMENTAL PURPOSE

A third purpose of performance management is to develop employees who are effective at their jobs. When employees are not performing as well as they should, performance management seeks to improve their performance. The feedback given during a performance evaluation process often pinpoints the employee's weaknesses. Ideally, however, the performance management system identifies not only any deficient aspects of the employee's performance but also the causes of these deficiencies—for example, a skill deficiency, a motivational problem, or some obstacle holding the employee back.

● Performance management is critical for executing a talent management system and involves one-on-one contact with managers to ensure that proper training and development are taking place.

Managers are often uncomfortable confronting employees with their performance weaknesses. Such confrontations, although necessary to the effectiveness of the work group, often strain everyday working relationships. Giving high ratings to all employees enables a manager to minimize such conflicts, but then the developmental purpose of the performance management system is not fully achieved.[8]

An important step in performance management is to develop the measures by which performance will be evaluated. We next discuss the issues involved in developing and using different measures of performance.

⦿ Performance Measures Criteria

LO 8-3
Identify the five criteria for effective performance management systems.

In Chapter 4 we discussed how, through job analysis, one can analyze a job to determine exactly what constitutes effective performance. Once the company has determined, through job analysis and design, what kind of performance it expects from its employees, it needs to develop ways to measure that performance. This section presents the criteria underlying job performance measures. Later sections discuss approaches to performance measurement, sources of information, and errors.

Although people differ about criteria to use to evaluate performance management systems, we believe that five stand out: strategic congruence, validity, reliability, acceptability, and specificity.

STRATEGIC CONGRUENCE

Strategic Congruence
The extent to which the performance management system elicits job performance that is consistent with the organization's strategy, goals, and culture.

Strategic congruence is the extent to which a performance management system elicits job performance that is congruent with the organization's strategy, goals, and culture. If a company emphasizes customer service, then its performance management system should assess how well its employees are serving the company's customers. Strategic congruence emphasizes the need for the performance management system to guide employees in contributing to the organization's success. This requires systems flexible enough to adapt to changes in the company's strategic posture.

Many companies such as Hewlett-Packard, Federal Express, and Coca-Cola have introduced measures of critical success factors (CSFs) into their performance management systems.[9] CSFs are factors in a company's business strategy that give it a competitive edge. Companies measure employee behavior that relates to attainment of CSFs, which increases the importance of these behaviors for employees. Employees can be held accountable and rewarded for behaviors that directly relate to the company attaining the CSFs.

Sprint, the Overland, Kansas-based company that provides wireless services, has three pillars for its strategy.[10] The strategic pillars include improving the customer experience, strengthening the brand, and generating cash and increase profits. To support the strategy, the performance management system involves managers assessing employees on a pass–fail basis using three to five criteria, each of which is linked to a strategic objective. Sprint provides performance management tools that allow tracking of metrics such as what percent of employees receive coaching as part of their ongoing appraisal. Also, in Sprint's call centers and retail stores where most employees work, employees can go online and see their individual performance objectives and their progress toward achieving them. Sprint's managers set performance objectives based on changing internal company as well as market conditions. To motivate employees to achieve objectives (and the bonuses determined by reaching the objectives), achievement of objectives is based on two 6-month periods. This gives the company the flexibility to adjust performance objectives at least two times during the year, which is important when financial forecasts change or new products are introduced, such as being the first company to introduce a national 4G wireless network.

One challenge that companies face is how to measure customer loyalty, employee satisfaction, and other nonfinancial performance areas that affect profitability. To effectively use nonfinancial performance measures managers need to:[11]

- Develop a model of how nonfinancial performance measures link to the company's strategic goals. Identify the performance areas that are critical to success.
- Using already existing databases, identify data that exists on key performance measures (e.g., customer satisfaction, employee satisfaction surveys). If data are not available, identify a performance area that affects the company's strategy and performance. Develop measures for those performance areas.
- Use statistical and qualitative methods for testing the relationship between the performance measures and financial outcomes. Regression and correlation analysis as well as focus groups and interviews can be used. For example, studies show that employees' involvement, satisfaction, and enthusiasm for work are significantly related to business performance including customer satisfaction, productivity, and profitability.[12]
- Revisit the model to ensure that the nonfinancial performance measures are appropriate and determine whether new measures should be added. This is important to understand the drivers of financial performance and to ensure that the model is appropriate as the business strategy and economic conditions change.
- Act on conclusions that the model demonstrates. For example, Sears found that employee attitudes about the supervision they received and the work environment had a significant impact on customer satisfaction and shareholder results. As a result, Sears invested in managerial training to help managers do a better job of holding employees accountable for their jobs while giving them autonomy to perform their roles.[13]
- Audit whether the actions taken and the investments made produced the desired result.

Most companies' appraisal systems remain constant over a long time and through a variety of strategic emphases. However, when a company's strategy changes, its employees' behavior needs to change too.[14] The fact that appraisal systems often do not change may account for why many managers see performance appraisal systems as having little impact on a firm's effectiveness.

VALIDITY

Validity is the extent to which a performance measure assesses all the relevant—and only the relevant—aspects of performance. This is often referred to as "content validity." For a performance measure to be valid, it must not be deficient or contaminated. As you can see in Figure 8.2, one of the circles represents "true" job performance—all the aspects of performance relevant to success in the job. On the other hand, companies must use some measure of performance, such as a supervisory rating of performance on a set of dimensions or measures of the objective results on the job. Validity is concerned with maximizing the overlap between actual job performance and the measure of job performance (the green portion in the figure).

A performance measure is deficient if it does not measure all aspects of performance (the cranberry portion in the figure). An example is a system at a large university that assesses faculty members based more on research than teaching, thereby relatively ignoring a relevant aspect of performance.

A contaminated measure evaluates irrelevant aspects of performance or aspects that are not job related (the gold portion in the figure). The performance measure should seek to minimize contamination, but its complete elimination is seldom possible. An example of a contaminated measure is the use of actual sales figures for evaluating salespersons across very different regional territories. Often sales are highly dependent upon the territory (number of potential customers, number of competitors, economic conditions) rather than the actual performance of the salesperson. A salesperson who works harder and better than others might not have the highest sales totals because the territory simply does not have as much sales potential as others. Thus, these figures alone would be a measure that is strongly affected by things beyond the control of the individual employee.

RELIABILITY

Reliability refers to the consistency of a performance measure. One important type of reliability is *interrater reliability:* the consistency among the individuals who evaluate the employee's performance. A performance measure has interrater reliability if two

figure 8.2

Contamination and Deficiency of a Job Performance Measure

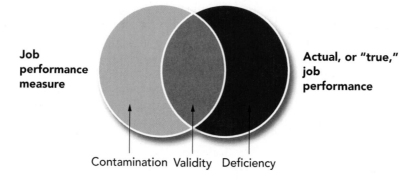

Job performance measure

Actual, or "true," job performance

Contamination Validity Deficiency

individuals give the same (or close to the same) evaluations of a person's job performance. Evidence seems to indicate that most subjective supervisory measures of job performance exhibit low reliability.[15] With some measures, the extent to which all the items rated are internally consistent is important (*internal consistency reliability*).

In addition, the measure should be reliable over time (*test–retest reliability*). A measure that results in drastically different ratings depending on when the measures are taken lacks test–retest reliability. For example, if salespeople are evaluated based on their actual sales volume during a given month, it would be important to consider their consistency of monthly sales across time. What if an evaluator in a department store examined sales only during May? Employees in the lawn and garden department would have high sales volumes, but those in the men's clothing department would have somewhat low sales volumes. Clothing sales in May are traditionally lower than other months. One needs to measure performance consistently across time.

ACCEPTABILITY

Acceptability refers to whether the people who use a performance measure accept it. Many elaborate performance measures are extremely valid and reliable, but they consume so much of managers' time that they refuse to use it. Alternatively, those being evaluated by a measure may not accept it.

Acceptability is affected by the extent to which employees believe the performance management system is fair. As Table 8.2 shows, there are three categories of perceived fairness: procedural, interpersonal, and outcome fairness. The table also shows specifically how the performance management system's development, use, and outcomes

Acceptability
The extent to which a performance measure is deemed to be satisfactory or adequate by those who use it.

table 8.2

Categories of Perceived Fairness and Implications for Performance Management Systems

FAIRNESS CATEGORY	IMPORTANCE FOR PERFORMANCE MANAGEMENT SYSTEM	IMPLICATIONS
Procedural fairness	Development	• Give managers and employees opportunity to participate in development of system. • Ensure consistent standards when evaluating different employees. • Minimize rating errors and biases.
Interpersonal fairness	Use	• Give timely and complete feedback. • Allow employees to challenge the evaluation. • Provide feedback in an atmosphere of respect and courtesy.
Outcome fairness	Outcomes	• Communicate expectations regarding performance evaluations and standards. • Communicate expectations regarding rewards.

SOURCE: Adapted from S. W. Gilliland and J. C. Langdon, "Creating Performance Management Systems That Promote Perceptions of Fairness," in *Performance Appraisal: State of the Art in Practice*, ed. J. W. Smither. Copyright © 1998 by Jossey-Bass, Inc. This material is used by permission of John Wiley & Sons, Inc.

affect perceptions of fairness. In developing and using a performance management system, managers should take the steps shown in the column labeled "Implications" in Table 8.2 to ensure that the system is perceived as fair. Research suggests that performance management systems that are perceived as unfair are likely to be legally challenged, be used incorrectly, and decrease employee motivation to improve.[16]

Specificity
The extent to which a performance measure gives detailed guidance to employees about what is expected of them and how they can meet these expectations.

SPECIFICITY

Specificity is the extent to which a performance measure tells employees what is expected of them and how they can meet these expectations. Specificity is relevant to both the strategic and developmental purposes of performance management. If a measure does not specify what an employee must do to help the company achieve its strategic goals, it does not achieve its strategic purpose. Additionally, if the measure fails to point out employees' performance problems, it is almost impossible for the employees to correct their performance.

Approaches to Measuring Performance

LO 8-4
Discuss the four approaches to performance management, the specific techniques used in each approach, and the way these approaches compare with the criteria for effective performance management systems.

An important part of effective performance management is establishing how we evaluate performance. In this section we explore different ways to evaluate performance: the comparative approach, the attribute approach, the results approach, and the quality approach. We also evaluate these approaches against the criteria of strategic congruence, validity, reliability, acceptability, and specificity. As you will see, all of these approaches have strengths and weaknesses. As a result, many companies' performance evaluations use a combination of approaches. To effectively contribute to organizational business strategy and goals, effective performance evaluation systems should measure both what gets accomplished (objectives) and how it gets accomplished (behaviors). Figure 8.3 shows an example of a performance management system that evaluates behavior and results. The results (project development) are linked to the goals of the business. The performance standards include behaviors that the employee must demonstrate to reach the results. The system provides feedback to the employee and holds both the employee and manager accountable for changing behavior.

THE COMPARATIVE APPROACH

The comparative approach to performance measurement requires the rater to compare an individual's performance with that of others. This approach usually uses some overall assessment of an individual's performance or worth and seeks to develop some ranking of the individuals within a work group. At least three techniques fall under the comparative approach: ranking, forced distribution, and paired comparison.

Ranking

Simple ranking requires managers to rank employees within their departments from highest performer to poorest performer (or best to worst). *Alternation ranking,* on the other hand, consists of a manager looking at a list of employees, deciding who is the best employee, and crossing that person's name off the list. From the remaining names, the manager decides who the worst employee is and crosses that name off the list—and so forth.

figure 8.3

Example of a Performance Management System That Includes Behavior and Results

Accountabilities and Key Results	Performance Standards	Interim Feedback	Actual Results	Performance Rating	Areas for Development	Action
Key result areas that the employee will accomplish during the review period. Should align with company values, business goals, and job description.	How the key result area will be measured (quality, cost, quantity). Focus on work methods and accomplishments.	Employee and manager discuss performance on an ongoing basis.	Review actual performance for each key result.	Evaluate performance on each key result. 1 = Outstanding 2 = Highly effective 3 = Acceptable 4 = Unsatisfactory	Specific knowledge, skills, and behaviors to be developed that will help employee achieve key results.	What employee and manager will do to address development needs.
Project Development Manage the development of project scope, cost estimate studies, and schedules for approval.	Develop preliminary project material for approval within four weeks after receiving project scope. Eighty percent of new projects receive approval. Initial cost estimates are within 5% of final estimates.	Preliminary project materials are developed on time.	By end of year, approvals were at 75%, 5% less than standard.	3	Increase knowledge of project management software.	Read articles, research, and meet with software vendors.

Ranking has received specific attention in the courts. As discussed in Chapter 3, in the *Albermarle v. Moody* case the validation of the selection system was conducted using employee rankings as the measure of performance. The court actually stated, "There is no way of knowing precisely what criteria of job performance that supervisors were considering, whether each supervisor was considering the same criteria—or whether, indeed, any of the supervisors actually applied a focused and stable body of criteria of any kind."[17]

Forced Distribution

The *forced distribution* method also uses a ranking format, but employees are ranked in groups. This technique requires the manager to put certain percentages of employees into predetermined categories. Most commonly, employees are grouped into three, four, or five categories usually of unequal size indicating the best workers, the worst workers, and one or more categories in between. For example, at General Electric managers were to place employees into top (20%), middle (70%), and bottom (10%) categories. The bottom 10% usually receive no bonuses and can be terminated. The forced distribution method forces managers to categorize employees based on distribution rules, not on their performance. American International Group (AIG), the government-controlled insurance company, is using a forced distribution system in which AIG employees are ranked on a scale of 1 to 4.[18] Using this system only 10% of employees receive the top ranking of "1," 20% of employees receive a ranking of "2," 50% of employees receive a ranking of "3," and 20% receive the lowest ranking of "4." Employees with higher rankings receive much more year-end incentive pay such as bonuses than those with lower rankings (employees ranked in the top 10% will get much greater bonuses compared to their peers). Unlike the GE system, employees who receive the lowest ranking are not forced to leave. The CEO advocated the implementation of the forced distribution system to ensure that the company is paying the best people for their performance and to better differentiate poor from high performers. The company had previously used ranking systems but found that over half of employees were evaluated as high performers. Also, the CEO wants to send a message of accountability to the American taxpayers who helped bail out the company.

Advocates of these systems say that they are the best way to identify high-potential employees who should be given training, promotions, and financial rewards and to identify the poorest performers who should be helped or asked to leave. Top-level managers at many companies have observed that despite corporate performance and return to shareholders being flat or decreasing, compensation costs have continued to spiral upward and performance ratings continue to be high. They question how there can be such a disconnect between corporate performance and employees' evaluations and compensation. Forced distribution systems provide a mechanism to help align company performance and employee performance and compensation. Employees in the bottom 10% cause performance standards to be lowered, influence good employees to leave, and keep good employees from joining the company.

A forced distribution system helps managers tailor development activities to employees based on their performance. For example, as shown in Table 8.3, poor performers are given specific feedback about what they need to improve in their job and a timetable is set for their improvement. If they do not improve their performance, they are dismissed. Top performers are encouraged to participate in development activities such as job experiences, mentoring, and completion of leadership programs which will help prepare them for top management positions. The use of a forced distribution

RANKING OR DISTRIBUTION CATEGORY	PERFORMANCE AND DEVELOPMENT PLAN
A Above average exceptional A1 performer	• Accelerate development through challenging job assignments • Provide mentor from leadership team • Recognize and reward contributions • Praise employees for strengths • Consider leadership potential • Nominate for leadership development programs
B Average meets expectations steady performer	• Offer feedback on how B can become a high performer • Encourage development of strengths and improvement of weaknesses • Recognize and reward employee contributions • Consider enlarging job
C Below expectations poor performance	• Give feedback and agree upon what specific skills, behavior, and/or results need to be improved with timetable for accomplishment • Move to job that better matches skills • Ask to leave the company

table 8.3

Performance and Development Based on Forced Distribution and Ranking

SOURCES: Based on B. Axelrod, H. Handfield-Jones, and E. Michaels, "A New Game Plan for C Players," *HBR*, January 2002, pp. 80–88; A. Walker, "Is Performance Management as Simple as ABC?" *T + D*, February 2007, pp. 54–57; T. De Long and V. Vijayaraghavan, "Let's Hear It for B Players," *HBR*, June 2003, pp. 96–102.

system is seen as a way for companies to increase performance, motivate employees, and open the door for new talent to join the company to replace poor performers.[19] Advocates say these systems force managers to make hard decisions about employee performance based on job-related criteria, rather than to be lenient in evaluating employees. Critics, on the other hand, say the systems in practice are arbitrary, may be illegal, and cause poor morale.[20] For example, one workgroup might have 20% poor performers while another might have only high performers, but the process mandates that 10% of employees be eliminated from both groups. Also, in many forced distribution systems an unintended consequence is the bottom category tends to consist of minorities, women, and people over 40 years of age, causing discrimination lawsuits (we discuss legal issues affecting performance management later in the chapter). Finally, it is difficult to rank employees into distinctive categories when criteria are subjective or when it is difficult to differentiate employees on the criteria (such as teamwork or communications skills).

Research simulating different features of a forced system and other factors that influence company performance (e.g., voluntary turnover rate, validity of selection methods) suggests that forced distribution rating systems can improve the potential performance of a company's workforce.[21] Companies that have clear goals and management criteria, train evaluators, use the rankings along with other HR metrics, and reward good performance may find them useful. The majority of improvement appears to occur during the first several years the system is used, mainly because of the large number of poorly performing employees who are identified and fired. Keep in mind that despite the potential advantages of forced choice systems for improving a company's workforce performance, the potential negative side effects on morale, teamwork, recruiting, and shareholder perceptions should be considered before adopting such a system. Forced ranking is ethical as long as the system is clearly communicated, the system is part of a positive dimension of the organization culture (innovation, continuous improvement), and the employees have the chance to appeal decisions.

Paired Comparison

The *paired comparison* method requires managers to compare every employee with every other employee in the work group, giving an employee a score of 1 every time he or she is considered the higher performer. Once all the pairs have been compared, the manager computes the number of times each employee received the favorable decision (i.e., counts up the points), and this becomes the employee's performance score.

The paired comparison method tends to be time-consuming for managers and will become more so as organizations become flatter with an increased span of control. For example, a manager with 10 employees must make 45 ($10 \times 9/2$) comparisons. However, if the group increases to 15 employees, 105 comparisons must be made.

Evaluating the Comparative Approach

The comparative approach to performance measurement is an effective tool in differentiating employee performance; it virtually eliminates problems of leniency, central tendency, and strictness. This is especially valuable if the results of the measures are to be used in making administrative decisions such as pay raises and promotions. In addition, such systems are relatively easy to develop and in most cases easy to use; thus, they are often accepted by users.

One problem with these techniques, however, is their common failure to be linked to the strategic goals of the organization. Although raters can evaluate the extent to which individuals' performances support the strategy, this link is seldom made explicit. In addition, because of the subjective nature of the ratings, their actual validity and reliability depend on the raters themselves. Some firms use multiple evaluators to reduce the biases of any individual, but most do not. At best, we could conclude that their reliability and validity are modest.

These techniques lack specificity for feedback purposes. Based only on their relative rankings, individuals are completely unaware of what they must do differently to improve their ranking. This puts a heavy burden on the manager to provide specific feedback beyond that of the rating instrument itself. Finally, many employees and managers are less likely to accept evaluations based on comparative approaches. Evaluations depend on how employees' performance relates to other employees in a group, team, or department (normative standard) rather than on absolute standards of excellent, good, fair, and poor performance.

THE ATTRIBUTE APPROACH

The attribute approach to performance management focuses on the extent to which individuals have certain attributes (characteristics or traits) believed desirable for the company's success. The techniques that use this approach define a set of traits—such as initiative, leadership, and competitiveness—and evaluate individuals on them.

table 8.4

Example of a Graphic Rating Scale

> The following areas of performance are significant to most positions. Indicate your assessment of performance on each dimension by circling the appropriate rating.

PERFORMANCE DIMENSION	RATING				
	DISTINGUISHED	EXCELLENT	COMMENDABLE	ADEQUATE	POOR
Knowledge	5	4	3	2	1
Communication	5	4	3	2	1
Judgment	5	4	3	2	1
Managerial skill	5	4	3	2	1
Quality performance	5	4	3	2	1
Teamwork	5	4	3	2	1
Interpersonal skills	5	4	3	2	1
Initiative	5	4	3	2	1
Creativity	5	4	3	2	1
Problem solving	5	4	3	2	1

Graphic Rating Scales

The most common form that the attribute approach to performance management takes is the *graphic rating scale*. Table 8.4 shows a graphic rating scale used in a manufacturing company. As you can see, a list of traits is evaluated by a five-point (or some other number of points) rating scale. The manager considers one employee at a time, circling the number that signifies how much of that trait the individual has. Graphic rating scales can provide a number of different points (a discrete scale) or a continuum along which the rater simply places a check mark (a continuous scale).

The legal defensibility of graphic rating scales was questioned in the *Brito v. Zia* (1973) case. In this case, Spanish-speaking employees had been terminated as a result of their performance appraisals. These appraisals consisted of supervisors' rating subordinates on a number of undefined dimensions such as volume of work, quantity of work, job knowledge, dependability, and cooperation. The court criticized the subjective appraisals and stated that the company should have presented empirical data demonstrating that the appraisal was significantly related to actual work behavior.

Mixed-Standard Scales

Mixed-standard scales were developed to get around some of the problems with graphic rating scales. To create a mixed-standard scale, we define the relevant performance dimensions and then develop statements representing good, average, and poor performance along each dimension. These statements are then mixed with the statements from other dimensions on the actual rating instrument. An example of a mixed-standard scale is presented in Table 8.5.

As we see in the table, the rater is asked to complete the rating instrument by indicating whether the employee's performance is above (+), at (0), or below (−) the statement. A special scoring key is then used to score the employee's performance

table 8.5

An Example of a
Mixed-Standard
Scale

Three traits being assessed:
 Initiative (INTV)
 Intelligence (INTG)
 Relations with others (RWO)

Levels of performance in statements:
 High (H)
 Medium (M)
 Low (L)

Instructions: Please indicate next to each statement whether the employee's performance is above (+), equal to (0), or below (−) the statement.

INTV	H	1. This employee is a real self-starter. The employee always takes the initiative and his/her superior never has to prod this individual.	+
INTG	M	2. While perhaps this employee is not a genius, s/he is a lot more intelligent than many people I know.	+
RWO	L	3. This employee has a tendency to get into unnecessary conflicts with other people.	0
INTV	M	4. While generally this employee shows initiative, occasionally his/her superior must prod him/her to complete work.	+
INTG	L	5. Although this employee is slower than some in understanding things, and may take a bit longer in learning new things, s/he is of average intelligence.	+
RWO	H	6. This employee is on good terms with everyone. S/he can get along with people even when s/he does not agree with them.	−
INTV	L	7. This employee has a bit of a tendency to sit around and wait for directions.	+
INTG	H	8. This employee is extremely intelligent, and s/he learns very rapidly.	−
RWO	M	9. This employee gets along with most people. Only very occasionally does s/he have conflicts with others on the job, and these are likely to be minor.	−

Scoring Key:

	STATEMENTS			SCORE
	HIGH	MEDIUM	LOW	
	+	+	+	7
	0	+	+	6
	−	+	+	5
	−	0	+	4
	−	−	+	3
	−	−	0	2
	−	−	−	1

Example score from preceding ratings:

	STATEMENTS			SCORE
	HIGH	MEDIUM	LOW	
Initiative	+	+	+	7
Intelligence	0	+	+	6
Relations with others	−	−	0	2

for each dimension. Thus, for example, an employee performing above all three statements receives a 7. If the employee is below the good statement, at the average statement, and above the poor statement, a score of 4 is assessed. An employee below all three statements is given a rating of 1. This scoring is applied to all the dimensions to determine an overall performance score.

Note that mixed-standard scales were originally developed as trait-oriented scales. However, this same technique has been applied to instruments using behavioral rather than trait-oriented statements as a means of reducing rating errors in performance appraisal.[22]

Evaluating the Attribute Approach

Attribute-based performance methods are the most popular methods in organizations. They are quite easy to develop and are generalizable across a variety of jobs, strategies, and organizations. In addition, if much attention is devoted to identifying those attributes relevant to job performance and carefully defining them on the rating instrument, they can be as reliable and valid as more elaborate measurement techniques.

However, these techniques fall short on several of the criteria for effective performance management. There is usually little congruence between the techniques and the company's strategy. These methods are used because of the ease in developing them and because the same method (list of traits, comparisons) is generalizable across any organization and any strategy. In addition, these methods usually have very vague performance standards that are open to different interpretations by different raters. Because of this, different raters often provide extremely different ratings and rankings. The result is that both the validity and reliability of these methods are usually low.

Virtually none of these techniques provides any specific guidance on how an employee can support the company's goals or correct performance deficiencies. In addition, when raters give feedback, these techniques tend to elicit defensiveness from employees. For example, how would you feel if you were told that on a five-point scale, you were rated a "2" in maturity? Certainly you might feel somewhat defensive and unwilling to accept that judgment, as well as any additional feedback. Also, being told you were rated a "2" in maturity doesn't tell you how to improve your rating.

THE BEHAVIORAL APPROACH

The behavioral approach to performance management attempts to define the behaviors an employee must exhibit to be effective in the job. The various techniques define those behaviors and then require managers to assess the extent to which employees exhibit them. We discuss five techniques that rely on the behavioral approach.

Behaviorally Anchored Rating Scales

A *behaviorally anchored rating scale* (BARS) is designed to specifically define performance dimensions by developing behavioral anchors associated with different levels of performance.[23] An example of a BARS is presented in Figure 8.4. As you can see, the performance dimension has a number of examples of behaviors that indicate specific levels of performance along the dimension.

To develop a BARS, we first gather a large number of critical incidents that represent effective and ineffective performance on the job. These incidents are classified into performance dimensions, and the ones that experts agree clearly represent a particular

figure 8.4

Task-BARS Rating
Dimension: Patrol
Officer

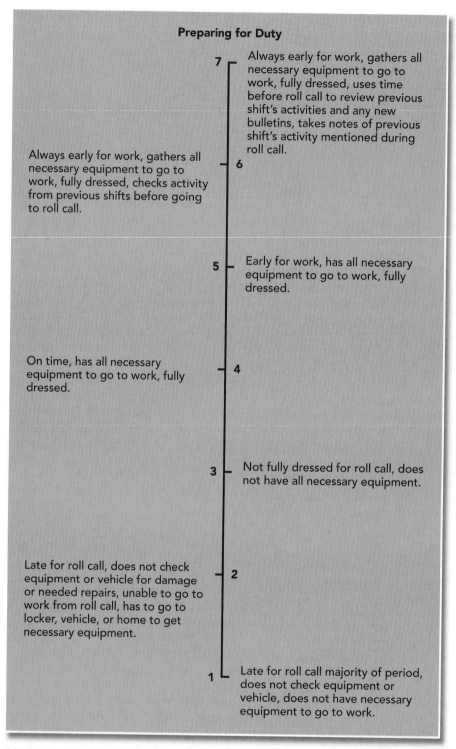

Preparing for Duty

7 — Always early for work, gathers all necessary equipment to go to work, fully dressed, uses time before roll call to review previous shift's activities and any new bulletins, takes notes of previous shift's activity mentioned during roll call.

6 —

Always early for work, gathers all necessary equipment to go to work, fully dressed, checks activity from previous shifts before going to roll call.

5 — Early for work, has all necessary equipment to go to work, fully dressed.

On time, has all necessary equipment to go to work, fully dressed.

4 —

3 — Not fully dressed for roll call, does not have all necessary equipment.

Late for roll call, does not check equipment or vehicle for damage or needed repairs, unable to go to work from roll call, has to go to locker, vehicle, or home to get necessary equipment.

2 —

1 — Late for roll call majority of period, does not check equipment or vehicle, does not have necessary equipment to go to work.

SOURCE: Adapted from R. Harvey, "Job Analysis," in *Handbook of Industrial & Organizational Psychology*, 2nd ed., ed. M. Dunnette and L. Hough (Palo Alto, CA: Consulting Psychologists Press, 1991), p. 138.

level of performance are used as behavioral examples (or anchors) to guide the rater. The manager's task is to consider an employee's performance along each dimension and determine where on the dimension the employee's performance fits using the behavioral anchors as guides. This rating becomes the employee's score for that dimension.

Behavioral anchors have advantages and disadvantages. They can increase inter-rater reliability by providing a precise and complete definition of the performance dimension. A disadvantage is that they can bias information recall—that is, behavior that closely approximates the anchor is more easily recalled than other behavior.[24] Research has also demonstrated that managers and their subordinates do not make much of a distinction between BARS and trait scales.[25]

Behavioral Observation Scales

A *behavioral observation scale* (BOS) is a variation of a BARS. Like a BARS, a BOS is developed from critical incidents.[26] However, a BOS differs from a BARS in two basic ways. First, rather than discarding a large number of the behaviors that exemplify effective or ineffective performance, a BOS uses many of them to more specifically define all the behaviors that are necessary for effective performance (or that would be considered ineffective performance). Instead of using, say, 4 behaviors to define 4 levels of performance on a particular dimension, a BOS may use 15 behaviors. An example of a BOS is presented in Table 8.6.

A second difference is that rather than assessing which behavior best reflects an individual's performance, a BOS requires managers to rate the frequency with which the employee has exhibited each behavior during the rating period. These ratings are then averaged to compute an overall performance rating.

table 8.6

An Example of a Behavioral Observation Scale (BOS) for Evaluating Job Performance

Overcoming Resistance to Change						
(1) Describes the details of the change to subordinates.						
Almost Never	1	2	3	4	5	Almost Always
(2) Explains why the change is necessary.						
Almost Never	1	2	3	4	5	Almost Always
(3) Discusses how the change will affect the employee.						
Almost Never	1	2	3	4	5	Almost Always
(4) Listens to the employee's concerns.						
Almost Never	1	2	3	4	5	Almost Always
(5) Asks the employee for help in making the change work.						
Almost Never	1	2	3	4	5	Almost Always
(6) If necessary, specifies the date for a follow-up meeting to respond to the employee's concerns.						
Almost Never	1	2	3	4	5	Almost Always
Total = _____						

Below Adequate	Adequate	Full	Excellent	Superior
6–10	11–15	16–20	21–25	26–30

Scores are set by management.

SOURCE: From Gary Latham and Ken Wexley, *Increasing Productivity Through Performance Appraisal* (Prentice Hall Series in Human Resources), 2E, © 1994. Reproduced by permission of Pearson Education, Inc., Upper Saddle River, New Jersey.

The major drawback of a BOS is that it may require more information than most managers can process or remember. A BOS can have 80 or more behaviors, and the manager must remember how frequently an employee exhibited each of these behaviors over a 6- or 12-month rating period. This is taxing enough for one employee, but managers often must rate 10 or more employees.

A direct comparison of BOS, BARS, and graphic rating scales found that both managers and employees prefer BOS for differentiating good from poor performers, maintaining objectivity, providing feedback, suggesting training needs, and being easy to use among managers and subordinates.[27]

Competencies
Sets of skills, knowledge, abilities, and personal characteristics that enable employees to successfully perform their jobs.

Competency Models

Competencies are sets of skills, knowledge, abilities, and personal characteristics that enable employees to successfully perform their jobs.[28] A **competency model** identifies and provides descriptions of competencies that are common for an entire occupation, organization, job family, or a specific job. Competency models can be used for performance management. However, one of the strengths of competency models is that they are useful for a variety of HR practices including recruiting, selection, training, and development. Competency models can be used to help identify the best employees to fill open positions, and as the foundation for development plans that allow the employee and manager to target specific strengths and development areas.

Competency models
Identify and provide descriptions of competencies that are common for an occupations, organization, job family, or specific job.

Table 8.7 shows the competency model that Luxottica Retail, known for premium, luxury, and sports eyewear sold through LensCrafters, Sunglass Hut, and Pearle Vision, developed for its associates in field and store positions.[29] The competency model

table 8.7

Luxottica Retail's Competency Model

Leadership and Managerial
Leadership
Coach and develop others
Motivate others
Foster teamwork
Think strategically
Functional
Global perspective
Financial acumen
Business key performance indicators
Foundational
Critical thinking
Foster open communications
Build relationships and interpersonal skills
Develop and manage oneself
Adaptability and flexibility
Customer focus
Act with integrity
Diversity and multiculturalism
Drive and commitment

SOURCE: From C. Spicer, "Building a Competency Model," *HR Magazine*, April 2009, pp. 34–36. Copyright 2009. Reproduced with permission of Society for Human Resource Management via Copyright Clearance Center.

includes leadership and managerial, functional, and foundational competencies. The goal was to define and identify competencies that managers could use for hiring, performance management, and training. Also, competencies would help associates identify and develop the skills they need to apply for different jobs. To effectively use competency models for performance evaluation they must be up-to-date, drive business performance, be job-related (valid), be relevant (or customized) for all of the company's business units, and provide sufficient detail to make an accurate assessment of employees' performance. At Luxottica Retail developing competencies started with meeting with business leaders to understand their current and future business strategies. Business drivers were identified and questionnaires, focus groups, and meetings with managers and associates were used to identify important competencies and examples of behaviors related to each. Competencies across business units and brands are reviewed every four or five years or whenever a major change in jobs or business strategy occurs to ensure they are relevant. Also, the weighting given to each set of competencies in the performance evaluation is reviewed to ensure that they are appropriate (e.g., what weights should be given to the functional skills). Depending on their relevance for a specific job, various combinations of these competencies are used for evaluating associates' performances. Associates are rated on a 1–5 scale for each competency with 5 meaning far exceeds expectations. HR, training and development, and operations teams worked together to define the levels of each competency, that is, what does it mean and what does the competency look like when an employee is rated "meets expectations" versus "below expectations"? This was necessary to ensure that managers are using a similar frame of reference when they evaluate associates using the competencies.

Evaluation of the Behavioral Approach

The behavioral approach can be very effective. It can link the company's strategy to the specific behavior necessary for implementing that strategy. It provides specific guidance and feedback for employees about the performance expected of them. Most of the techniques rely on in-depth job analysis, so the behaviors that are identified and measured are valid. Because those who will use the system develop the measures, the acceptability is also often high. Finally, with a substantial investment in training raters, the techniques are reasonably reliable.

The major weaknesses have to do with the organizational context of the system. Although the behavioral approach can be closely tied to a company's strategy, the behaviors and measures must be constantly monitored and revised to ensure that they are still linked to the strategic focus. This approach also assumes that there is "one best way" to do the job and that the behaviors that constitute this best way can be identified. One study found that managers seek to control behaviors when they perceive a clear relationship between behaviors and results. When this link is not clear, they tend to rely on managing results.[30] The behavioral approach might be best suited to less complex jobs (where the best way to achieve results is somewhat clear) and least suited to complex jobs (where there are multiple ways, or behaviors, to achieve success).

THE RESULTS APPROACH

The results approach focuses on managing the objective, measurable results of a job or work group. This approach assumes that subjectivity can be eliminated from the measurement process and that results are the closest indicator of one's contribution to organizational effectiveness.[31] We examine two performance management systems that use results: the balanced scorecard and the productivity measurement and evaluation system.

The Use of Objectives

The use of objectives is popular in both private and public organizations.[32] In a results-based system, the top management team first defines the company's strategic goals for the coming year. These goals are passed on to the next layer of management, and these managers define the goals they must achieve for the company to reach its goals. This goal-setting process cascades down the organization so that all managers set goals that help the company achieve its goals.[33] These goals are used as the standards by which an individual's performance is evaluated.[34]

Results-based systems have three common components.[35] They require setting effective goals. The most effective goals are SMART goals. That is, the goals are specific (clearly stated, define the result to be achieved), measurable (compared to a standard), attainable (difficult but achievable), relevant (link to organizational success factors or goals), and timely (measured in deadline, due dates, cycles, or schedules). Different types of measurements can be used for goals or objectives including timeliness (e.g., responds to requests within 12 hours), quality (report provided clear information with no revisions necessary), quantity (increased sales 25%), or financial metrics (e.g., reduced purchasing costs 10%). (An example of objectives used in a financial service firm is presented in Table 8.8.) The goals are not usually set unilaterally by management but with the managers' and subordinates' participation. And the manager gives objective feedback throughout the rating period to monitor progress toward the goals.

Research on objectives has revealed two important findings regarding their effectiveness.[36] Of 70 studies examined, 68 showed productivity gains, while only 2 showed productivity losses, suggesting that objectives usually increase productivity. Also, productivity gains tend to be highest when there is substantial commitment to the objectives program from top management: an average increase of 56% when commitment was high, 33% when commitment was moderate, and 6% when commitment was low.

Clearly, use of an objectives system can have a very positive effect on an organization's performance. Considering the process through which goals are set (involvement of staff in setting objectives), it is also likely that use of an objectives system effectively links individual employee performance with the firm's strategic goals.

table 8.8

An Example of an Objectives Measure of Job Performance

KEY RESULT AREA	OBJECTIVE	% COMPLETE	ACTUAL PERFORMANCE
Loan portfolio management	Increase portfolio value by 10% over the next 12 months	90	Increased portfolio value by 9% over the past 12 months
Sales	Generate fee income of $30,000 over the next 12 months	150	Generated fee income of $45,000 over the past 12 months

Evaluation of objectives, based on results or business-based metrics, removes the subjectivity from the evaluation process—employees either meet the objectives or they do not. For example, Long Island Jewish Medical Center implemented a computer-based performance management system that breaks the nurses' job description into measurable goals in order to keep infection rates for the unit low and patient-satisfaction scores high.[37]

Balanced Scorecard

Some companies use the balanced scorecard to measure performance (we discussed the use of the balanced scorecard in Chapter 1). The balanced scorecard includes four perspectives of performance including financial, customer, internal or operations, and learning and growth (see Table 1.9 in Chapter 1). The financial perspective focuses on creating sustainable growth in shareholder value, the customer perspective defines value for customers (e.g., service, quality), the internal or operations perspective focuses on processes that influence customer satisfaction, and the learning and growth perspective focuses on the company's capacity to innovate and continuously improve. Each of these perspectives are used to translate the business strategy into organizational, managerial, and employee objectives. Employee performance is linked with the business strategy through communicating and educating employees on the elements of the balanced scorecard, translating strategic objectives into measures for departments and employees, and linking rewards to performance measures.[38] Employees need to know the corporate objectives, how they translate into objectives for each business unit, and develop their own and team objectives that are consistent with the business unit and company objectives. Effective balanced scorecards allow employees to understand the business strategy by looking only at the scorecard and the strategy map (the cause-and-effect relationships among the measures). For example, for the customer perspective of the balanced scorecard an airline might have on-time performance as a critical success factor.[39] Gate agents, ground, maintenance, and scheduling represent groups of employees who impact on-time performance. Gate agents have four roles that can influence boarding speed including check-in timeliness, effectively dealing with connections, flight documentation, and the boarding process. Gate agents' performance in these four roles should be evaluated because they impact key performance indicators related to on-time performance including cost savings, customer satisfaction, customer losses, and operational costs.

Productivity Measurement and Evaluation System (ProMES)

The main goal of ProMES is to motivate employees to improve team or company-level productivity.[40] It is a means of measuring and feeding back productivity information to employees.

Team members try to map the relationship between specific outcomes and productivity and the relationships between effect and performance, performance and outcomes, and outcomes relationship to satisfaction of employee needs. ProMES consists of four steps. First, people in an organization identify the products, or the set of activities or objectives, the organization expects to accomplish. The organization's productivity depends on how well it produces these products. At a repair shop, for example, a product might be something like "quality of repair." Second, the staff defines indicators of the products. Indicators are measures of how well the products are being generated by the organization. Quality of repair could be indicated by (1) return rate (percentage of items returned that did not function immediately after repair) and (2) percentage of quality-control inspections passed. Third, the staff establishes the contingencies between the amount of the indicators and the level of evaluation associated with that amount. Fourth, a feedback system is developed that provides employees and work groups with information about their specific level of performance on each of the indicators. An overall productivity score can be computed by summing the effectiveness scores across the various indicators.

Research thus far strongly suggests this technique is effective in increasing productivity. (Figure 8.5 illustrates the productivity gains in the repair shop described previously.) The research also suggests the system is an effective feedback mechanism. However, users found it time-consuming to develop the initial system.

Evaluation of the Results Approach

The results approach minimizes subjectivity, relying on objective, quantifiable indicators of performance. Thus, it is usually highly acceptable to both managers and employees. Another advantage is that it links an individual's results with the organization's strategies and goals.

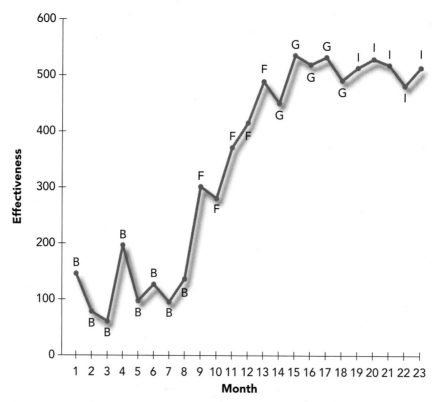

figure 8.5

Increases in Productivity for a Repair Shop Using ProMES Measures

SOURCE: P. Pritchard, S. Jones, P. Roth, K. Stuebing, and S. Ekeberg, "The Evaluation of an Integrated Approach to Measuring Organizational Productivity," *Personnel Psychology,* 42, (1989), pp. 69–115. Used by permission.

However, there are a number of challenges in using objective performance measures. Objective measurements can be both contaminated and deficient—contaminated because they are affected by things that are not under the employee's control and deficient because not all the important aspects of job performance are amenable to objective measurement. For example, consider how an economic recession can influence sales goals or, for a teacher, parental support for studying can influence student's achievement test scores. Another disadvantage is that individuals may focus only on aspects of their performance that are measured, neglecting those that are not. For example, if the large majority of employees' goals relate to productivity, it is unlikely they will be concerned with customer service. One study found that objective performance goals led to higher performance but that they also led to helping co-workers less.[41] It is important to identify if goals should be set at the individual, team, or department level. Setting employees' objectives may not be appropriate if work is team-based. Individual objectives may undermine behaviors related to team success such as sharing information and collaboration. A final disadvantage is that, although results measures provide objective feedback, the feedback may not help employees learn how they need to change their behavior to increase their performance. If baseball players are in a hitting slump, simply telling them that their batting average is .190 may not motivate them to raise it. Feedback focusing on the exact behavior that needs to be changed (like taking one's eye off the ball or dropping one's shoulder) would be more helpful.[42]

John Deere takes specific actions to avoid these problems.[43] At the start of each fiscal year, managers and employees meet to discuss objectives for the year. A mid-year review is then conducted to check on the employees' progress in meeting the goals. The year-end review meeting focuses on evaluating goal accomplishment. Goal achievement at the end of the year is linked to pay increases and other rewards. All company objectives are supported by division objectives that are available for employees to view online. Employees also have available a learning and activities courseware catalog they can use to help develop skills needed to achieve their performance objectives.

THE QUALITY APPROACH

Thus far we have examined the traditional approaches to measuring and evaluating employee performance. Fundamental characteristics of the quality approach include a customer orientation, a prevention approach to errors, and continous improvement. Improving customer satisfaction is the primary goal of the quality approach. Customers can be internal or external to the organization. A performance management system designed with a strong quality orientation can be expected to

- Emphasize an assessment of both person and system factors in the measurement system.
- Emphasize that managers and employees work together to solve performance problems.
- Involve both internal and external customers in setting standards and measuring performance.
- Use multiple sources to evaluate person and system factors.[44]

Based on this chapter's earlier discussion of the characteristics of an effective performance management system, it should be apparent to you that these characteristics are not just unique to the quality approach but are characteristics of an effective appraisal system!

Advocates of the quality approach believe that most U.S. companies' performance management systems are incompatible with the quality philosophy for a number of reasons:

1. Most existing systems measure performance in terms of quantity, not quality.
2. Employees are held accountable for good or bad results to which they contribute but do not completely control.
3. Companies do not share the financial rewards of successes with employees according to how much they have contributed to them.
4. Rewards are not connected to business results.[45]

Sales, profit margins, and behavioral ratings are often collected by managers to evaluate employees' performance. These are person-based outcomes. An assumption of using these types of outcomes is that the employee completely controls them. However, according to the quality approach, these types of outcomes should not be used to evaluate employees' performance because they do not have complete control over them (i.e., they are contaminated). For example, for salespersons, performance evaluations (and salary increases) are often based on attainment of a sales quota. Salespersons' abilities and motivation are assumed to be directly responsible for their performance. However, quality approach advocates argue that better determinants of whether a salesperson reaches the quota are "systems factors" (such as competitors' product price changes) and economic conditions (which are not under the salesperson's control).[46] Holding employees accountable for outcomes affected by systems factors is believed to result in dysfunctional behavior, such as falsifying sales reports, budgets, expense accounts, and other performance measures, as well as lowering employees' motivation for continuous improvement.

Quality advocates suggest that the major focus of performance evaluations should be to provide employees with feedback about areas in which they can improve. Two types of feedback are necessary: (1) subjective feedback from managers, peers, and customers about the personal qualities of the employee and (2) objective feedback based on the work process itself using statistical quality control methods.

At Just Born, the company that makes Peeps and Mike and Ike candy, the performance management process is designed with a strong quality orientation.[47] The performance management system is designed to facilitate employee improvement (a forward-looking approach) rather than focus entirely on what the employee has accomplished during the past year. Also, managers and employees are encouraged to work together to solve performance problems.

The performance management system is part of the company's broader people development system (PDS) which is designed to ensure that learning and development align with business strategy and drive business results while ensuring employees have the skills to succeed in their current and future jobs. The PDS includes the performance management process, learning and career development processes, and succession planning process. Information from each of these systems is shared to ensure that employees are developing the skills through training and on-the-job experiences needed for their current jobs as well as preparing for their future career interests. Just Born's performance management system starts with a planning meeting between the employee and their manager. At this meeting the employee's role and strategic goals of the department are discussed. The manager and employee agree on up to four personal objectives that will help the department meet its objectives and the employee achieve the specific deliverables described in the job description. Two competencies that the employee needs to deliver or improve on are identified. The manager and employee work together to develop a learning plan to help the employee gain the competencies. During the year, the employee and manager meet to discuss the progress in meeting the deliverables and improving the competencies. Pay decisions made at the end of each fiscal year are based on the achievement of performance objectives and learning goals.

Just Born also uses the Wow . . . Now improvement process, a customized Kaizen process to improve business processes and results. The Wow . . . Now improvement process includes teaching employees how to identify improvement opportunities, collect data, make improvements, measure results, and, based on the results, refine practices. Kaizen, the Japanese word for improvement, is one of the underlying principles of lean manufacturing and total quality management (we discussed lean manufacturing in Chapter 1). **Kaizen** refers to practices participated in by employees from all levels of the company that focus on continuous improvement of business processes.[48] As the Wow . . . Now improvement process illustrates, Kaizen involves considering a continuous cycle of activities including planning, doing, checking, and acting (PDCA). Statistical process control techniques are used by employees to identify causes of problems and potential solutions. They include process-flow analysis, cause-and-effect diagrams, control charts, histograms, and scattergrams.

Kaizen
Employee practices that emphasize continuous improvement of business processes.

Statistical process control techniques are very important in the quality approach. These techniques provide employees with an objective tool to identify causes of problems and potential solutions. These techniques include process-flow analysis, cause-and-effect diagrams, Pareto charts, control charts, histograms, and scattergrams. *Process-flow analysis* identifies each action and decision necessary to complete work, such as waiting on a customer or assembling a television set. Process-flow analysis is useful for identifying redundancy in processes that increase manufacturing or service time. In *cause-and-effect diagrams*, events or causes that result in undesirable outcomes are identified. Employees try to identify all possible causes of a problem. The feasibility of the causes is not evaluated, and as a result, cause-and-effect diagrams produce a large list of possible causes. A *Pareto chart* highlights the most important cause of a problem. In a Pareto chart, causes are listed in decreasing order of importance, where *importance* is usually defined as the frequency with which that cause resulted in a problem. The assumption of Pareto analysis is that the majority of problems are the result of a small number of causes. Figure 8.6 shows a Pareto chart listing the reasons managers give for not selecting current employees for a job vacancy. *Control charts* involve collecting data at multiple points in time. By collecting data at different times, employees can identify what factors contribute to an outcome and when they tend to occur. Figure 8.7 shows the percentage of employees hired internally for a company for each quarter between 1993 and 1995. Internal hiring increased dramatically during the third quarter of 1994. The use of control charts helps employees understand the number of internal candidates who can be expected to be hired each year. Also, the control chart shows that the amount of internal hiring conducted during the third quarter of 1994 was much larger than normal. *Histograms* display distributions of large sets of data. Data are grouped

figure 8.6

Pareto Chart

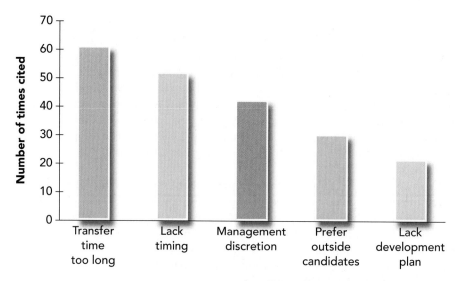

Reasons given for not selecting employees

SOURCE: From Clara Carter, *HR Magazine*. Copyright 1992. Reproduced with permission of Society for Human Resource Management via Copyright Clearance Center.

figure 8.7

Control Chart

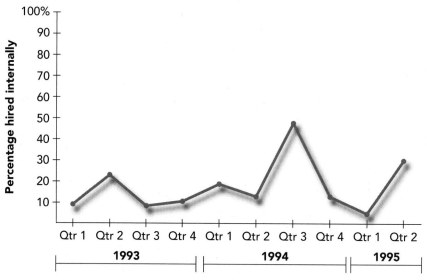

SOURCE: From Clara Carter, *HR Magazine*. Copyright 1992. Reproduced with permission of Society for Human Resource Management via Copyright Clearance Center.

into a smaller number of categories or classes. Histograms are useful for understanding the amount of variance between an outcome and the expected value or average outcome.

Scattergrams show the relationship between two variables, events, or different pieces of data. Scattergrams help employees determine whether the relationship between two variables or events is positive, negative, or zero.

Evaluation of the Quality Approach

The quality approach relies primarily on a combination of the attribute and results approaches to performance measurement. However, traditional performance appraisal systems focus more on individual employee performance, while the quality approach adopts a systems-oriented focus.[49] Many companies may be unwilling to completely abandon their traditional performance management system because it serves as the basis for personnel selection validation, identification of training needs, or compensation decisions. Also, the quality approach advocates evaluation of personal traits (such as cooperation), which are difficult to relate to job performance unless the company has been structured into work teams.

In summary, organizations can take five approaches to measuring performance: comparative, attribute, behavioral, results, and quality. Table 8.9 summarizes the various approaches to measuring performance based on the criteria we set forth earlier and illustrates that each approach has strengths and weaknesses. As a result, effective performance evaluations involve a combination of approaches including assessment of objectives and behaviors. The "Competing through Sustainability" box shows how companies with strong values are incorporating them into their performance management system.

LO 8-5
Choose the most effective approach to performance measurement for a given situation.

table 8.9

Evaluation of Approaches to Performance Measurement

APPROACH	STRATEGIC CONGRUENCE	VALIDITY	RELIABILITY	ACCEPTABILITY	SPECIFICITY
Comparative	Poor, unless manager takes time to make link	Can be high if ratings are done carefully	Depends on rater, but usually no measure of agreement used	Moderate; easy to develop and use but resistant to normative standard	Very low
Attribute	Usually low; requires manager to make link	Usually low; can be fine if developed carefully	Usually low; can be improved by specific definitions of attributes	High; easy to develop and use	Very low
Behavioral	Can be quite high	Usually high; minimizes contamination and deficiency	Usually high	Moderate; difficult to develop, but accepted well for use	Very high
Results	Very high	Usually high; can be both contaminated and deficient	High; main problem can be test–retest— depends on timing of measure	High; usually developed with input from those to be evaluated	High regarding results, but low regarding behaviors necessary to achieve them
Quality	Very high	High, but can be both contaminated and deficient	High	High; usually developed with input from those to be evaluated	High regarding results, but low regarding behaviors necessary to achieve them

Core Values Make the Place: How Employees Perform Is as Important as What Was Accomplished

Most companies have a unique set of core values that they believe contribute to business success through distinguishing them from competitors and helping create a brand image in the eyes of customers, clients, employees, and the general public. For example, VivaKi Nerve Center in Chicago, the research, development, and production unit of the advertising and communications firm Publicis Groupe's VivaKi, has a set of core values called The Way We Work. These values include "work hard playfully," "develop disruptive innovate solutions," "count on infectious talent and radical thinking," and "believe change ignites new energy and conversations." Studies have shown that companies' fixation on hitting financial targets often works against producing sustainable growth. One study found that the highest financial returns were achieved at companies whose CEOs had challenging financial goals and communicated a vision of the company beyond making profits such as creating an innovative product, providing greater customer service, or improving the quality of life. Despite the importance of values it is challenging to define them in behavioral terms so they can be measured and included as part of a performance management system. Also, the results of a Society for Human Resource Management survey on performance management highlight the complexity of values for performance management. Survey results showed that over 85% of HR professionals agree it is more difficult to manage employee behaviors underlying values than it is to manage job performance.

A number of companies are taking on the challenge of redesigning their performance management systems to ensure that they are evaluating not only *what* employees get accomplished but *how* they get it accomplished. Online retailer Zappos.com dumped its traditional performance review for an approach in which employees would no longer be rated on how they accomplished tasks but instead on how well their behavior reflects Zappos' 10 core values such as "delivering Wow service," "demonstrating humility," or "doing more with less." Zappos is famous for its unique corporate culture. The changes to the performance management system are designed to ensure that employees embodied the cultural values which the company believes are key for its success. With the new values-based performance management system managers record how many times they notice employees exhibiting behaviors supporting the core values. Managers are asked to provide specific examples of how an employee displays the behaviors. The performance evaluation form includes 22 questions on different behaviors. The evaluations are not used for discipline or promotion decisions. Instead, employees are encouraged to try to improve low scores. To help employees understand the values and their implication for work behavior, Zappos offers free classes focused on understanding each of its cultural values and their relationship to employees' behavior. Eastern Idaho Regional Medical Center (EIRMC) in Idaho Falls evaluates employees on seven values and their underlying behavior. The values and example behavior in parentheses include accountability (works to achieve individual, department, and hospital goals), I am EIRMC and I CARE (demonstrates the use of the center's caring model with every patient and visitor), integrity (manages conflict appropriately), respect (respects co-workers by being on time), quality (identifies a potential problem and also potential solutions), loyalty (builds teamwork by being a good team member and not backbiting), and enjoyment (greets and welcomes each person with a smiling face and a kind word). EIRMC uses a five-point scale to rate employees on the values. The scale values range from 1 meaning the employee exceeds expectations to 5 meaning their performance is unacceptable.

Because values impact morale, patient satisfaction, turnover, and finances, confronting employees about behaviors that breach company values is crucial. Assessing and changing behaviors that are incongruent with company values means that at the end of the day the company stands for something and reinforces the culture and the way the company conducts its business. All employees, including top leaders, need to be held accountable for living the values. For example, at EIRMC a nurse was disciplined for yelling and swearing at another nurse during a procedure with a patient. The nurse believed he was showing his passion for patient care and demonstrating his willingness to protect them. HR had to help the nurse understand that he had violated EIRMC's respect and integrity values, despite his good intentions. After several meetings the nurse understood and accepted the violation and has since repaired the relationships he damaged.

SOURCE: Based on K. Tyler, "Evaluating Values," *HR Magazine*, April 2011, pp. 57–62; R. Pyrillis, "The Reviews Are In," *Workforce Management*, May 2011, pp. 20–25; and C. Hymowitz, "When Meeting the Targets Becomes the Strategy, CEO Is on the Wrong Path," *The Wall Street Journal*, March 8, 2005, p. B1.

Choosing a Source for Performance Information

Whatever approach to performance management is used, it is necessary to decide whom to use as the source of the performance measures. Each source has specific strengths and weaknesses. We discuss five primary sources: managers, peers, subordinates, self, and customers. To increase the effect of performance management systems include many companies both managers and self-assessment of performance. This helps facilitate a conversation about performance during the appraisal meeting and on a more frequent basis.

LO 8-6
Discuss the advantages and disadvantages of the different sources of performance information.

MANAGERS

Managers are the most frequently used source of performance information. It is usually safe to assume that supervisors have extensive knowledge of the job requirements and that they have had adequate opportunity to observe their employees—in other words, that they have the ability to rate their employees. In addition, because supervisors have something to gain from the employees' high performance and something to lose from low performance, they are motivated to make accurate ratings.[50] Finally, feedback from supervisors is strongly related to performance and to employee perceptions of the accuracy of the appraisal if managers attempt to observe employee behavior or discuss performance issues in the feedback session.[51]

LO 8-7
Choose the most effective source(s) for performance information for any situation.

Burlington Northern Santa Fe Corporation of Fort Worth, Texas, improved its performance management process by holding leaders accountable in setting annual goals, creating individual development plans, providing feedback and coaching to employees, and self-evaluation.[52] An online performance management system supports the process. The company's executive team creates the overall company objectives, which cascade down to each department and individual employees who can now see how they contribute to the company's success. The online system allows managers and employees to see how they and the department are progressing on the objectives. Required to be engaged in the performance management process, managers are more focused on the necessary communications, coaching, and giving feedback, and they are more inclined to seek out training to be sure that they have the necessary communications, feedback, and coaching skills. Managers' effectiveness is monitored by periodic employee surveys that ask questions about whether the manager discusses performance, whether the dialogue with the manager is two-way, and whether the employee receives ongoing feedback.

Problems with using supervisors as the source of performance information can occur in particular situations. In some jobs, for example, the supervisor does not have an adequate opportunity to observe the employee performing his job duties. For example, in outside sales jobs, the supervisor does not have the opportunity to see the salesperson at work most of the time. This usually requires that the manager occasionally spend a day accompanying the salesperson on sales calls. However, on those occasions the employee will be on best behavior, so there is no assurance that performance that day accurately reflects performance when the manager is not around.

Also, some supervisors may be so biased against a particular employee that to use the supervisor as the sole source of information would result in less-than-accurate measures for that individual. Favoritism is a fact of organizational life, but it is one that must be minimized as much as possible in performance management.[53] Thus, the performance evaluation system should seek to minimize the opportunities for favoritism to affect ratings. One way to do this is not to rely on only a supervisor's evaluation of an employee's performance.

PEERS

Another source of performance information is the employee's co-workers. Peers are an excellent source of information in a job such as law enforcement, where the supervisor does not always observe the employee. Peers have expert knowledge of job requirements, and they often have the most opportunity to observe the employee in day-to-day activities. Peers also bring a different perspective to the evaluation process, which can be valuable in gaining an overall picture of the individual's performance. In fact, peers have been found to provide extremely valid assessments of performance in several different settings.[54]

One disadvantage of using peer ratings is the potential for friendship to bias ratings.[55] Little empirical evidence suggests that this is often a problem, however. Another disadvantage is that when the evaluations are made for administrative decisions, peers often find the situation of being both rater and ratee uncomfortable. When these ratings are used only for developmental purposes, however, peers react favorably.[56]

SUBORDINATES

Upward Feedback
Managerial performance appraisal that involves subordinates' evaluations of the manager's behavior or skills.

Subordinates are an especially valuable source of performance information when managers are evaluated. Subordinates often have the best opportunity to evaluate how well a manager treats employees. **Upward feedback** refers to appraisals that involve collecting subordinates' evaluations of manager's behavior or skills. Dell Inc., the Texas-based computer company, recently took steps to focus not only on financial goals but also on making the company a great place to work to attract and keep talented employees.[57] To help develop what Dell calls a "winning culture," Dell added a people management component to its results-oriented performance management system. Managers are now rated by their employees on semiannual "Tell Dell" surveys. Managers who receive less than 50% favorable scores on five questions receive less favorable compensation, bonus, and promotion opportunities and are required to take additional training. Table 8.10 shows the five questions. Managers are expected to work continuously to improve their scores. Their goal is to receive at

- Even if I were offered a comparable position with similar pay and benefits at another company, I would stay at Dell.
- I receive ongoing feedback that helps me to improve my performance.
- My manager/supervisor supports my efforts to balance my work and personal life.
- My manager/supervisor is effective at managing people.
- I can be successful at Dell and still retain my individuality.

table 8.10

Example of Upward Feedback Survey Questions from "Tell Dell" Surveys

SOURCE: Based on A. Pomeroy, "Agent of Change," *HR Magazine*, May 2005, pp. 52–56.

least 75% favorable ratings from employees on the five questions. One study found that managers viewed receiving upward feedback more positively when receiving feedback from subordinates who were identified, but subordinates preferred to provide anonymous feedback. When subordinates were identified, they inflated their ratings of the manager.[58]

One problem with subordinate evaluations is that they give subordinates power over their managers, thus putting the manager in a difficult situation.[59] This can lead to managers' emphasizing employee satisfaction over productivity. However, this happens only when administrative decisions are made from these evaluations. As with peer evaluations, it is a good idea to use subordinate evaluations only for developmental purposes. To assure subordinates that they need not fear retribution from their managers, it is necessary to use anonymous evaluations and at least three subordinates for each manager.

SELF

Although self-ratings are not often used as the sole source of performance information, they can still be valuable.[60] Obviously, individuals have extensive opportunities to observe their own behavior, and they usually have access to information regarding their results on the job. The YMCA of Greater Rochester, New York, added employee self-evaluation as part of its performance review process to address concerns that employees had little input into the appraisal process. It didn't help facilitate conversation between employees and managers, and both parties dreaded formal appraisal meetings.[61] In the revamped process, self-evaluation allows employees to give examples of good performance and to request training to improve their weaknesses. Before they are finalized, performance ratings are based on a discussion between the manager and employee. Self-evaluations have lessened the fear and anxiety associated with the old appraisal process. Employees feel they have a voice and the opportunity to influence the appraisal process. Managers are relieved because the burden for evaluation is no longer completely their responsibility. Now, employees provide them with feedback and insight into their performance which help determine performance ratings.

One problem with self-ratings, however, is a tendency toward inflated assessments. Research has found that self-ratings for personal traits as well as overall performance ratings tend to be lenient compared to ratings from other sources.[62] This stems from two sources. If the ratings are going to be used for administrative decisions (like pay raises), it is in the employees' interests to inflate their ratings. And there is ample evidence in the social psychology literature that individuals attribute their poor performance to external causes, such as a co-worker who they think has not provided them with timely information. Although self-ratings are less inflated when supervisors provide frequent performance feedback, it is not advisable to use them for administrative purposes.[63] The best use of self-ratings is as a prelude to the performance feedback session to get employees thinking about their performance and to focus discussion on areas of disagreement.

CUSTOMERS

As discussed in Chapter 1, service industries are expected to account for a major portion of job growth.[64] As a result, many companies are involving customers in their evaluation systems. One writer has defined *services* this way: "Services is something which can be bought and sold but which you cannot drop on your foot."[65] Because of the unique nature of services—the product is often produced and consumed on the spot—supervisors, peers, and subordinates often do not have the opportunity to observe employee behavior. Instead, the customer is often the only person present to observe the employee's performance and thus is the best source of performance information.

Many companies in service industries have moved toward customer evaluations of employee performance. Marriott Corporation provides a customer satisfaction card in every room and mails surveys to a random sample of customers after their stay in a Marriott hotel. Whirlpool's Consumer Services Division conducts on-site (using the service technicians' handheld computers), mail, and telephone surveys of customers after factory service technicians have serviced their appliances. These surveys allow the company to evaluate an individual technician's customer-service behaviors while in the customer's home.

Using customer evaluations of employee performance is appropriate in two situations.[66] The first is when an employee's job requires direct service to the customer or linking the customer to other services within the company. Second, customer evaluations are appropriate when the company is interested in gathering information to determine what products and services the customer wants. That is, customer evaluations serve a strategic goal by integrating marketing strategies with human resource activities and policies. Customer evaluations collected for this purpose are useful for both evaluating the employee and helping to determine whether changes in other HRM activities (such as training or the compensation system) are needed to improve customer service.

The weakness of customer surveys is their expense, particularly if printing, postage, telephone, and labor are involved. On-site surveys completed using handheld computers help eliminate these expenses.

In conclusion, the best source of performance information often depends on the particular job. One should choose the source or sources that provide the best opportunity to observe employee behavior and results. Often, eliciting performance information from a variety of sources results in a performance management process that is accurate and effective. In fact, one recent popular trend in organizations is called **360-degree appraisals**.[67] This technique consists of having multiple raters (boss, peers, subordinates, customers) provide input into a manager's evaluation. The major advantage of the technique is that it provides a means for minimizing bias in an otherwise subjective evaluation technique. It has been used primarily for strategic and developmental purposes and is discussed in greater detail in Chapter 9.[68]

360-Degree Appraisal
A performance appraisal process for managers that includes evaluations from a wide range of persons who interact with the manager. The process includes self-evaluations as well as evaluations from the manager's boss, subordinates, peers, and customers.

EVIDENCE-BASED HR

Fallon Clinic is a group medical practice that has more than 1,700 employees. Three hundred and fifty of these employees are doctors and advanced practitioners and the remaining employees are nurses, therapists, lab technicians, and administrative and clerical support. Overall, clinic locations have approximately 1.5 million patient visits each year. Fallon Clinic recognizes that there are specific staff and clinical behaviors that are critical for patient satisfaction. The best way to evaluate a patient's experience at the clinic is to experience it through the patient's eyes. Fallon Clinic created the "Patient Shadowing Program" which involves staff members "shadowing" consenting patients on their appointments to observe the patient experience. The observation criteria used by the staff members includes behaviors, included on rating templates, that are the basis for positive patient interactions. Volunteers, selected because they have strong interpersonal, communications, and feedback skills, are trained on how to use the templates. The raters, known as "shadow coaches," observe the patient's entire visit from registration to checkout. The coaches prepare written reports and hold feedback sessions that include the observed employees as well as their managers. Since the program began over 113 physicians have been observed. This has resulted in a 6% average increase in their patient satisfaction scores and a 298% return-on-investment over the costs related to using an external consultant.

SOURCE: Based on "Linking Training to Care," *T + D*, October 2009, pp. 64–66.

Use of Technology in Performance Management

Technology is influencing performance management systems in three ways. As we have seen in the chapter many companies are moving to web-based online paperless performance management systems. These systems help companies ensure that performance goals across all levels of the organization are aligned, provide managers and employees with greater access to performance information and tools for understanding and using the data, and improve the efficiency of the performance management process. Consider the use of online performance management at Sereno, a biotechnology company, and Amcor Sunclipse, a nationwide distribution company headquartered in California.[69] Sereno uses an online performance management system that allows all managers to see the performance of any employee that they are responsible for as well as the total distribution of ratings. Senior managers can see how every manager rated their people and analyze the relationship between department productivity and the total average performance of employees in the department. If there is a lack of relationship it suggests that employees are being overrated. At Amcor Sunclipse, annual appraisals were consistently late, there was no consistency in appraisals, they had little connection to company objectives, and weren't useful in assigning employees to training programs or filling open positions. The new online process allows e-mail notification to employees and their manager to complete performance evaluations and makes it easier to weight the relative value of different performance goals. For example, all employees are measured on safety behaviors but safety is a more critical part of some jobs (such as manufacturing jobs) than others. The online system can be set up to automatically weight performance areas (safety, reduce waste, etc.) based on how important they are to the job. For example, for a manufacturing supervisor improving safety might count for 40% of their overall performance rating compared to 5% for an office worker.

Second, social networking tools such as Facebook, Twitter, and MySpace are increasingly being used to deliver timely feedback. As emphasized in the effective performance management model (see Figure 8.1) performance feedback is a critical part of the performance management process that should not be limited to quarterly, midyear, or annual formal performance evaluations. The "Competing through Technology" box shows how social networking tools are being used for performance feedback.

Third, companies are relying on electronic tracking and monitoring systems and software to ensure that employees are working when and how they should be and to block access to visiting certain websites (such as those containing pornographic images). These systems include hand and fingerprint recognition systems, global positioning systems (GPS), and systems that can track employees using cell phones and handheld computers.

For example, at the New York law firm Akin & Smith LLC, paralegals, receptionists, and clerks clock in by placing their finger on a sensor kept at a secretary's desk. The managing partners believe the system improves productivity and keeps everyone honest, holding them to their lunch times.[70]

Economic Advantages Corporation, a mortgage service company with offices in Vermont and New York, installed an attendance tracking system. The new system implies that the company's salaried workers, client services representatives, get paid by the hour. Automated Waste Disposal, based in Danbury, Connecticut, was concerned with the amount of overtime hours of garbage collectors and sales staff. The operations manager installed a global positioning system (GPS) in garbage trucks and sales vehicles. The tracking technology has reduced the need for overtime hours to complete work, eliminating employees getting "lost" during the day and visiting friends or local restaurants during work hours.[71]

Meijer, a retail supercenter offering groceries and 40 other departments (including furniture, automotive, fashion, and health and beauty), is one of several retailers using software designed to improve the efficiency of cashiers.[72] The store's computer times how long it takes to complete each customer transaction, taking into account the kinds of merchandise being purchased as well as whether customers are paying with cash, credit, gift cards, or store credit. Each week the cashiers receive scores. If the cashier falls below the baseline score too many times, they may be carefully monitored by their manager, moved to a lower-paying job, or even lose their job!

The rationale behind the system is to maximize efficiency to improve customer service. Meijer suggests that the system has helped managers identify slow cashiers and work with them to improve their efficiency. It also allows the company to establish standards for identifying which newly hired cashiers in the 90-day probationary period should be transferred or fired. However, interviews with cashiers suggest that it has increased their stress and decreased other customer service behaviors not related to efficiency, such as making eye contact with customers, or rushing older or physically challenged customers who might need help unloading and paying for their merchandise. Some customers like the quicker checkout times, but others feel that the cashiers are not as friendly with them because they are rushed at checkout.

Despite the potential increased productivity and efficiency benefits that can result from these systems, they still present privacy concerns. Critics argue that these system threaten to reduce the workplace to an electronic sweatshop in which employees are

Social Networking Tools Help Make Performance Management a Daily Event

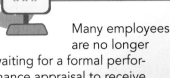

Many employees are no longer waiting for a formal performance appraisal to receive feedback or help them understand how to improve. Employees are increasingly relying on social networking for performance feedback whether or not the organization is using Facebook, Twitter, or MySpace as part of the performance management process. This is especially true for Generation Y employees who have grown up electronically connected to each other through social networking tools that enable personal and professional connections. Although baby boomers may be more likely to believe that feedback involves judgment compared to younger generations who see feedback as an opportunity to learn, high performers of all ages across generations are likely to seek and value feedback.

Recognizing the potential use of social networking for performance management and capitalizing on the employees' needs for feedback from peers as well as their managers, forward-thinking companies are developing websites or purchasing software to help make performance management more of an ongoing dynamic process. Use of social networking as a performance management tool is likely to be more prevalent in companies that have a culture emphasizing open communications rather than those that believe they need managers to tightly control and monitor performance. For example, Accenture has developed a Facebook-type program called Performance Multiplier that allows employees to update their performance and post weekly performance goals. Rypple's performance management platform resembles a Facebook page. Employees and managers can send each other colorful "badges" to recognize good performance. The badges include slogans such as "you rock" or "kicking butt." Rypple also allows employees to receive feedback and coaching from peers. Employees can post short questions about their performance such as "What did you think about my speech?" or "How can I handle angry customers better?" The questions are e-mailed to managers, peers, and anyone else from whom the employee wants to receive feedback. The responses are gathered together so they are anonymous and sent back to the employee, providing a quick and timely performance review. Some companies are also posting performance review forms on Wikis to improve the accuracy and validity of evaluations by allowing all parties who have observed an employee's performance, including managers, peers, and customers, to provide input into the process and valuable feedback to employees.

SOURCES: A. Brown, "Crossing the Generational Divide," *Financial Post*, April 14, 2011, from www.financialpost.com; P. Galagan, "Dude How'd I Do?" *T + D*, July 2009, pp. 26–28; and J. McGregor, "Performance Review Takes a Page from Facebook," *BusinessWeek*, March 12, 2009, p. 58.

treated as robots that are monitored to maximize productivity for every second they are at work. Also, electronic monitoring systems such as GPS threaten employees' rights and dignity to work without being monitored.

Some argue that electronic tracking systems are needlessly surveilling and tracking employees when there is no reason to believe that anything is wrong. Good managers know what their employees are doing, and electronic systems should not be a substitute for good management. Critics also argue that such systems result in less productivity and motivation, demoralize employees, and create unnecessary stress. A mentality is created that employees have to always be at their desks to be productive. Advocates, on the other hand, counter that these systems ensure that time is not abused, they improve scheduling, and they help managers identify lazy workers. To avoid the potential negative effects of electronic monitoring, managers must communicate why employees are being monitored. Monitoring can also be used as a way for more experienced employees to coach less experienced employees.

REDUCING RATER ERRORS, POLITICS, AND INCREASING RELIABILITY AND VALIDITY OF RATINGS

LO 8-8
Distinguish types of rating errors, and explain how to minimize each in a performance evaluation.

Research consistently reveals that humans have tremendous limitations in processing information. Because we are so limited, we often use "heuristics," or simplifying mechanisms, to make judgments, whether about investments or about people.[73] These heuristics, which appear often in subjective measures of performance, can lead to rater errors. Performance evaluations may also be purposefully distorted to achieve personal or company goals (appraisal politics). Table 8.11 shows the different types of rating errors. Similar to me error is based on stereotypes the rater has about how individuals with certain characteristics are expected to perform.[74] Leniency, strictness, and central tendency are known as distributional errors because the rater tends to use only one part of the rating scale.

Appraisal Politics
A situation in which evaluators purposefully distort ratings to achieve personal or company goals.

Appraisal politics refer to evaluators purposefully distorting a rating to achieve personal or company goals. Research suggests that several factors promote appraisal politics. These factors are inherent in the appraisal system and the company culture. Appraisal politics are most likely to occur when raters are accountable to the employee being rated, there are competing rating goals, and a direct link exists between performance appraisal and highly desirable rewards. Also, appraisal politics are likely to occur if top executives tolerate distortion or are complacent toward it, and if distortion strategies are part of "company folklore" and are passed down from

table 8.11

Typical Rater Errors

RATER ERROR	DESCRIPTION
Similar to me	Individuals who are similar to us in race, gender, background, interest, beliefs, etc., receive higher ratings than those who are not.
Contrast	Ratings influenced by comparison between individuals instead of an objective standard (e.g., employee receives lower than deserved rating because he/she is compared to outstanding peers).
Leniency	Rater gives high ratings to all employees regardless of their performance.
Strictness	Rater gives low ratings to all employees regardless of their performance.
Central tendency	Rater gives middle or average ratings to all employees despite their performance.
Halo	Rater gives employee high ratings on all aspects of performance because of their overall positive impression of the employee.
Horns	Rater gives employee low ratings on all aspects of performance because of an overall negative impression of the employee.

senior employees to new employees. For example, employees at King Pharmaceutical resisted development of a centralized performance system.[75] King Pharmaceutical is built from smaller acquired companies, each with a unique culture. Each department within the company had developed its own way of figuring out how to evaluate performance and link it to pay.

There are two training approaches to reducing rating errors.[76] *Rater error training* attempts to make managers aware of rating errors and helps them develop strategies for minimizing those errors.[77] These programs consist of having the participants view videotaped vignettes designed to elicit rating errors such as "contrast." They then make their ratings and discuss how the error influenced the rating. Finally, they get tips to avoid committing those errors. This approach has been shown to be effective for reducing errors, but there is evidence that reducing rating errors can also reduce accuracy.[78]

Rater accuracy training, also called *frame-of-reference training*, attempts to emphasize the multidimensional nature of performance and to get raters to understand and use the same idea of high, medium, and low performance when making evaluations. This involves providing examples of performance for each dimension and then discussing the actual or "correct" level of performance that the example represents.[79] Accuracy training seems to increase accuracy, provided that in addition the raters are held accountable for ratings, job-related rating scales are used, and raters keep records of the behavior they observe.[80]

An important way to help ensure that performance is evaluated consistently across managers and to reduce the influence of rating errors and politics on appraisals is to hold calibration meetings.[81] **Calibration meetings** provide a way to discuss employees' performance with the goal of ensuring that similar standards are applied to their evaluations. These meeting include managers responsible for conducting performance appraisals and their managers and are facilitated by an internal HR representative or an external consultant. In the meetings, each employee's performance rating and the manager's reasons for the ratings are discussed. Managers have the opportunity to discuss the definition of each performance rating and ask questions. The calibration meetings help managers identify if their ratings are too positive or negative or tend to be based on employees' most recent performance. Managers are more likely to provide accurate evaluations that are well-documented when they know they may have to justify them in a calibration meeting. Calibration meetings can also help eliminate politics by discussing how performance ratings relate to business results. Also, in addition to rater training and calibration meetings, to minimize appraisal politics, managers should keep in mind the characteristics of a fair appraisal system, shown earlier in Table 8.2. Thus, managers should also:

Calibration Meetings
Meetings attended by managers in which employee performance ratings are discussed and evidence supporting the ratings is provided. The purpose of the meetings is to reduce the influence of rating errors and politics on performance appraisals.

- Build top management support for the appraisal system and actively discourage distortion.
- Give raters some latitude to customize performance objectives and criteria for their ratees.
- Recognize employee accomplishments that are not self-promoted.
- Provide employees with access to information regarding which behaviors are desired and acceptable at work.
- Encourage employees to actively seek and use feedback to improve performance.
- Make sure constraints such as budget do not drive the process.
- Make sure appraisal processes are consistent across the company.
- Foster a climate of openness to encourage employees to be honest about weaknesses.[82]

Performance Feedback

LO 8-9
Conduct an effective
performance feedback
session.

Once the expected performance has been defined and employees' performances have been measured, it is necessary to feed that performance information back to the employees so they can correct any deficiencies. The performance feedback process is complex and provokes anxiety for both the manager and the employee.

Few of us feel comfortable sitting in judgment of others. The thought of confronting others with what we perceive to be their deficiencies causes most of us to shake in our shoes. If giving negative feedback is painful, receiving it can be excruciating—thus the importance of the performance feedback process.

THE MANAGER'S ROLE IN AN EFFECTIVE PERFORMANCE FEEDBACK PROCESS

If employees are not made aware of how their performance is not meeting expectations, their performance will almost certainly not improve. In fact, it may get worse. Effective managers provide specific performance feedback to employees in a way that elicits positive behavioral responses. Because of the importance of performance feedback for an effective performance management system many companies are training managers on how to provide feedback. For example, Lubrizol Corporation, a chemical manufacturer based in Wickliffe, Ohio, requires that managers enroll in a two-day training course designed to help them provide meaningful feedback.[83] The company's goal is to become recognized as the best developer of people. The training course focuses on how managers give feedback, who they need help from, and how they can hold themselves accountable. To provide effective performance feedback managers should consider the following recommendations.[84]

Feedback Should Be Given Frequently, Not Once a Year. There are two reasons for this. First, managers have a responsibility to correct performance deficiencies immediately on becoming aware of them. If performance is subpar in January, waiting until December to appraise the performance could mean an 11-month productivity loss. Second, a major determinant of the effectiveness of a feedback session is the degree to which the subordinate is not surprised by the evaluation. An easy rule to follow is that employees should receive such frequent performance feedback that they already know almost exactly what their formal evaluation will be.

Surveys results from several companies suggest that many employees, especially those in Generation Y (employees born after 1980), want more frequent and candid performance feedback from managers beyond what is provided once or twice a year during their formal performance review.[85] As a result, Ernst & Young LLC created an online "Feedback Zone" that prompts employees twice a year to request feedback but also allows them to request or submit feedback at any time.

Create the Right Context for the Discussion. Managers should choose a neutral location for the feedback session. The manager's office may not be the best place for a constructive feedback session because the employee may associate the office with unpleasant conversations. Managers should describe the meeting as an opportunity to discuss the role of the employee, the role of the manager, and the relationship between them. Managers should also acknowledge that they would like the meeting to be an open dialogue.

Ask the Employee to Rate His or Her Performance before the Session. Having employees complete a self-assessment before the feedback session can be very productive.

It requires employees to think about their performance over the past rating period, and it encourages them to think about their weaknesses. Although self-ratings used for administrative decisions are often inflated, there is evidence that they may actually be lower than supervisors' ratings when done for developmental purposes. Another reason a self-assessment can be productive is that it can make the session go more smoothly by focusing discussion on areas where disagreement exists, resulting in a more efficient session. Finally, employees who have thought about past performance are more able to participate fully in the feedback session.

Encourage the Employee to Participate in the Session. Managers can take one of three approaches in performance feedback sessions. In the "tell-and-sell" approach, managers tell the employees how they have rated them and then justify these ratings. In the "tell-and-listen" approach, managers tell employees how they have rated them and then let the employees explain their side of the story. In the "problem-solving" approach, managers and employees work together to solve performance problems in an atmosphere of respect and encouragement. In spite of the research demonstrating the superiority of the problem-solving approach, most managers still rely on the tell-and-sell approach.

When employees participate in the feedback session, they are consistently satisfied with the process. (Recall our discussion of fairness earlier in this chapter.) Participation includes allowing employees to voice their opinions of the evaluation, as well as discuss performance goals. One study found that, other than satisfaction with one's supervisor, participation was the single most important predictor of satisfaction with the feedback session.[86]

Recognize Effective Performance through Praise. One usually thinks of performance feedback sessions as focusing on the employee's performance problems. This should never be the case. The purpose of the session is to give accurate performance feedback, which entails recognizing effective performance as well as poor performance. Praising effective performance provides reinforcement for that behavior. It also adds credibility to the feedback by making it clear that the manager is not just identifying performance problems.

Focus on Solving Problems. A common mistake that managers make in providing performance feedback is to try to use the session as a chance to punish poorly performing employees by telling them how utterly lousy their performance is. This only reduces the employees' self-esteem and increases defensiveness, neither of which will improve performance.

To improve poor performance, a manager must attempt to solve the problems causing it. This entails working with the employee to determine the actual cause and then agreeing on how to solve it. For example, a salesperson's failure to meet a sales goal may be the result of lack of a proper sales pitch, lack of product knowledge, or stolen sales by another salesperson. Each of these causes requires a different solution. Without a problem-solving approach, however, the correct solution might never be identified.

Focus Feedback on Behavior or Results, Not on the Person. One of the most important things to do when giving negative feedback is to avoid questioning the employee's worth as a person. This is best accomplished by focusing the discussion on the employee's behaviors or results, not on the employee. Saying "You're screwing up! You're just not motivated!" will bring about more defensiveness and ill feelings than stating "You did not meet the deadline that you agreed to because you spent too much time on another project."

Minimize Criticism. Obviously, if an individual's performance is below standard, some criticism must take place. However, an effective manager should resist the temptation to reel off a litany of offenses. Having been confronted with the performance problem, an employee often agrees that a change is in order. However, if the manager continues to come up with more and more examples of low performance, the employee may get defensive.

Agree to Specific Goals and Set a Date to Review Progress. The importance of goal setting cannot be overemphasized. It is one of the most effective motivators of performance.[87] Research has demonstrated that it results in increased satisfaction, motivation to improve, and performance improvement.[88] Besides setting goals, the manager must also set a specific follow-up date to review the employee's performance toward the goal. This provides an added incentive for the employee to take the goal seriously and work toward achieving it.

What Managers Can Do to Diagnose Performance Problems and Manage Employees' Performance

LO 8-10
Identify the cause of a performance problem.

As we emphasized in the previous discussion, employees need performance feedback to improve their current job performance. As we discuss in Chapter 9, "Employee Development," performance feedback is also needed for employees to develop their knowledge and skills for the future. In addition to understanding how to effectively give employees performance feedback, managers need to be able to diagnose the causes of performance problems and take actions to improve and maintain employee performance. For example, giving performance feedback to marginal employees may not be sufficient for improving their performance.

DIAGNOSING THE CAUSES OF POOR PERFORMANCE

Many different reasons can cause an employee's poor performance. For example, poor performance can be due to lack of employee ability, misunderstanding of performance expectations, lack of feedback, or the need for training an employee who does not have the knowledge and skills needed to meet the performance standards. When diagnosing the causes of poor performance it is important to consider whether the poor performance is detrimental to the business. That is, is poor performance critical to completing the job and does it affect business results? If it is detrimental, then the next step is to conduct a performance analysis to determine the cause of poor performance. The different factors that should be considered in analyzing poor performance are shown in Figure 8.8. For example, if an employee understands the expected level of performance, has been given sufficient feedback, understands the consequences, but lacks the knowledge and skills needed to meet the performance standard, this suggests that the manager may want to consider training the employee to improve performance, moving the employee to a different job that better fits that person's skills, or discharging the employee and making sure that selection methods to find a new employee measure the level of knowledge and skills needed to perform the job.

After conducting the performance analysis, managers should meet with the employee to discuss the results, agree to the next steps that the manager and employee

Input

Does the employee recognize what he or she is supposed to do?

Are the job flow and procedures logical?

Do employees have the resources (tools, equipment, technology, time) needed for successful performance?

Are other job demands interfering with good performance in this area?

figure 8.8

Factors to Consider in Analyzing Poor Performance

Employee Characteristics

Does the employee have the necessary skills and knowledge needed?

Does the employee know why the desired performance level is important?

Is the employee mentally, physically, and emotionally able to perform at the expected level?

Feedback

Has the employee been given information about his or her performance?

Is performance feedback relevant, timely, accurate, specific, and understandable?

Performance Standard/Goals

Do performance standards exist?

Does the employee know the desired level of expected performance?

Does the employee believe she or he can reach the performance standard?

Consequences

Are consequences (rewards, incentives) aligned with good performance?

Are the consequences of performance valuable to the employee?

Are performance consequences given in a timely manner?

Do work group or team norms encourage employees not to meet performance standards?

SOURCES: Based on G. Rummler, "In Search of the Holy Performance Grail," *Training and Development,* April 1996, pp. 26–31; C. Reinhart, "How to Leap over Barriers to Performance," *Training and Development,* January 2000, pp. 20–24; F. Wilmouth, C. Prigmore, and M. Bray, "HPT Models: An Overview of the Major Models in the Field," *Performance Improvement* 41 (2002), pp. 14–21.

will take to improve performance (e.g., training, providing resources, giving more feedback), discuss the consequences of failing to improve performance, and set a time line for improvement. This type of discussion is most beneficial if it occurs more frequently than the quarterly or yearly performance review, so performance issues can be quickly dealt with before they have adverse consequences for the company (and the employee). Below we discuss the actions that should be considered for different types of employees.

ACTIONS FOR MANAGING EMPLOYEES' PERFORMANCE

Table 8.12 shows actions for the manager to take with four different types of employees. As the table highlights, managers need to take into account employees' ability, motivation, or both in considering ways to improve performance. To determine an employee's level of ability, a manager should consider if he or she has the knowledge, skills, and abilities needed to perform effectively. Lack of ability may be an issue if an employee is new or the job has recently changed. To determine employees' level of motivation, managers need to consider if employees are doing a job they want to do and if they feel they are being appropriately paid or rewarded. A sudden negative change in an employee's performance may indicate personal problems.

Employees with high ability and motivation include likely good and outstanding performers (*solid performers*). Table 8.12 emphasizes that managers should not ignore employees with high ability and high motivation. Managers should provide development opportunities to keep them satisfied and effective. Some individuals who are outstanding or good performers may be candidates for leadership positions within the company. As a result they will need challenging development experiences and exposure to different aspects of the business. These employees would be considered "A players" (see Table 8.3). We discuss development experiences in Chapter 9. Other employees may not desire positions with managerial responsibility. These

table 8.12

Ways to Manage Employees' Performance

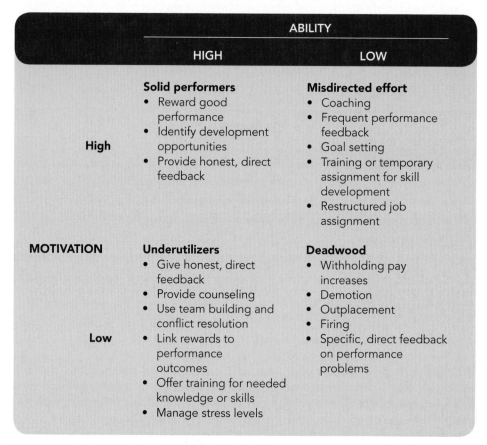

SOURCE: Based on M. London, *Job Feedback* (Mahwah, NJ: Lawrence Erlbaum Associates, 1997), pp. 96–97. Used by permission.

employees need development opportunities to help keep them engaged in their work and to avoid obsolescence. These employees would be considered B players in Table 8.3. Finally, there are different reasons why employees are considered poor performers (C players shown in Table 8.3). Poor performance resulting from lack of ability but not motivation (*misdirected effort*) may be improved by skill development activities such as training or temporary assignments. Managers with employees who have the ability but lack motivation (*underutilizers*) need to consider actions that focus on interpersonal problems or incentives. These actions include making sure that incentives or rewards that the employee values are linked to performance and making counseling available to help employees deal with personal problems or career or job dissatisfaction. Chronic poor performance by employees with low ability and motivation (*deadwood*) indicates that outplacement or firing may be the best solution.

Developing and Implementing a System That Follows Legal Guidelines

We now discuss the legal issues and constraints affecting performance management. Because performance measures play a central role in such administrative decisions as promotions, pay raises, and discipline, employees who sue an organization over these decisions ultimately attack the measurement systems on which the decisions were made. Two types of cases have dominated: discrimination and unjust dismissal.

In discrimination suits, the plaintiff often alleges that the performance measurement system unjustly discriminated against the plaintiff because of age, race, or gender. Many performance measures are subjective, and we have seen that individual biases can affect them, especially when those doing the measuring harbor racial or gender stereotypes. For example, in 2002, Ford Motors settled two class action lawsuits for $10.5 million.[89] Ford said it needed a forced ranking system because its culture discouraged candor in performance evaluations. Ford Motors Performance Management System involved grading 1,800 middle managers as A, B, or C. Managers who received a C for one year received no bonus; two years at the C level meant possible demotion and termination. Ten percent of the managers were to be graded as C. But some employees claimed the system had a negative impact on older, white workers because they received a larger proportion of C grades. Eventually, Ford eliminated the forced ranking system.

In *Brito v. Zia*, the Supreme Court essentially equated performance measures with selection tests.[90] It ruled that the *Uniform Guidelines on Employee Selection Procedures* apply to evaluating the adequacy of a performance appraisal instrument. This ruling presents a challenge to those involved in developing performance measures, because a substantial body of research on race discrimination in performance rating has demonstrated that both white and black raters give higher ratings to members of their own racial group, even after rater training.[91] There is also evidence that the discriminatory biases in performance rating are worse when one group makes up a small percentage of the workgroup. When the vast majority of the group is male, females receive lower ratings; when the minority is male, males receive lower ratings.[92]

In the second type of suit, an unjust dismissal suit, the plaintiff claims that the dismissal was for reasons other than those the employer claims. For example, an employee who works for a defense contractor might blow the whistle on the company for defrauding the government. If the company fires the employee, claiming poor performance, the employee may argue that the firing was, in fact, because of blowing the whistle on the employer—in other words, that the dismissal was unjust. The court case will likely focus on the performance measurement system used as the basis for claiming the employee's performance was poor. Unjust dismissal also can result from terminating for poor performance an employee who has a history of favorable reviews and raises. This may occur especially when a new evaluation system is introduced that results in more experienced older employees receiving unsatisfactory reviews. Rewarding poor performers or giving poor performers positive evaluations because of an unwillingness to confront a performance issue undermines the credibility of any performance management system. This makes it difficult to defend termination decisions based on a performance appraisal system.

Because of the potential costs of discrimination and unjust dismissal suits, an organization needs to determine exactly what the courts consider a legally defensible performance management system. Based on reviews of such court decisions, we offer the following characteristics of a system that will withstand legal scrutiny.[93]

1. The system should be developed by conducting a valid job analysis that ascertains the important aspects of job performance. The requirements for job success should be clearly communicated to employees.
2. The system should be based on either behaviors or results; evaluations of ambiguous traits should be avoided. Also, performance discussions should focus on work behavior and results other than questioning potential underlying reasons for behavior and results such as a physical or mental disability.
3. Raters should be trained in how to use the system rather than simply given the materials and left to interpret how to conduct the appraisal.
4. There should be some form of review by upper-level managers of all the performance ratings, and there should be a system for employees to appeal what they consider to be an unfair evaluation.
5. The organization should provide some form of performance counseling or corrective guidance to help poor performers improve their performance before being dismissed. Both short- and long-term performance goals should be included.
6. Multiple raters should be used, particularly if an employee's performance is unlikely to be seen by only one rating source such as manager or customer. At a minimum, employees should be asked to comment on their appraisals. There should be a dialogue between the manager and the employee.
7. Performance evaluations need to be documented.

A LOOK BACK

The chapter opener on Scripps Health discussed how its performance management system helped it recover from financial problems.

Questions

1. How does Scripps Health ensure that employees' performance helps reach the organization's strategic objectives?
2. Scripps evaluates employees based on objective measures such as business goals as well as behaviors related to the organization's values. Is it a good idea to include both objective measures and behaviors in a performance appraisal system? Explain your answer.

Please see the Video that corresponds to this chapter at
www.mhhe.com/noe8e.

SUMMARY

Measuring and managing performance is a challenging enterprise and one of the keys to gaining competitive advantage. Performance management systems serve strategic, administrative, and developmental purposes—their importance cannot be overestimated. A performance measurement system should be evaluated against the criteria of strategic congruence, validity, reliability, acceptability, and specificity. Measured against these criteria, the comparative, attribute, behavioral, results, and quality approaches have different strengths and weaknesses. Thus, deciding which approach and which source of performance information are best depends on the job in

question. Effective managers need to be aware of the issues involved in determining the best method or combination of methods for their particular situations. In addition, once performance has been measured, a major component of a manager's job is to feed that performance information back to employees in a way that results in improved performance rather than defensiveness and decreased motivation. Managers should take action based on the causes for poor performance: ability, motivation, or both. Managers must be sure that their performance management system can meet legal scrutiny, especially if it is used to discipline or fire poor performers.

KEY TERMS

Performance management, 341
Performance appraisal, 341
Performance feedback, 341
Strategic congruence, 346
Validity, 348

Reliability, 348
Acceptability, 349
Specificity, 350
Competencies, 360
Competency model, 360

Kaizen, 367
Upward feedback, 372
360-degree appraisal, 374
Appraisal politics, 378
Calibration meetings, 379

DISCUSSION QUESTIONS

1. What are examples of administrative decisions that might be made in managing the performance of professors? Developmental decisions?
2. What would you consider the strategy of your university (e.g., research, undergraduate teaching, graduate teaching, a combination)? How might the performance management system for faculty members fulfill its strategic purpose of eliciting the types of behaviors and results required by this strategy?
3. What do you think is the most important step shown in the model of the effective performance management process? Justify your answer.
4. What sources of performance information would you use to evaluate faculty members' performance?
5. What are the advantages and disadvantages of a performance management system that evaluates values?
6. Think of the last time you had a conflict with another person, either at work or at school. Using

the guidelines for performance feedback, how would you provide effective performance feedback to that person?
7. Explain what fairness has to do with performance management.
8. Why might a manager intentionally distort appraisal results? What would you recommend to minimize this problem?
9. Can computer monitoring of performance ever be acceptable to employees? Explain.
10. A delivery driver contaminated a hospital's oxygen supply by refilling the hospital's main oxygen supply line with trichloroethane, a mild anesthetic. Following detection of the contamination, all patients were switched to oxygen tanks and no patients were injured. How would you diagnose the cause of this performance problem? Explain.
11. How can the use of technology benefit the performance management process?

SELF-ASSESSMENT EXERCISE

How do you like getting feedback? To test your attitudes toward feedback, take the following quiz. Read each statement, and write A next to each statement you agree with. If you disagree with the statement, write D.

_____ 1. I like being told how well I am doing on a project.

_____ 2. Even though I may think I have done a good job, I feel a lot more confident when someone else tells me so.

_____ 3. Even when I think I could have done something better, I feel good when other people think well of me for what I have done.

_____ 4. It is important for me to know what people think of my work.

_____ 5. I think my instructor would think worse of me if I asked him or her for feedback.

_____ 6. I would be nervous about asking my instructor how she or he evaluates my behavior in class.

_____ 7. It is not a good idea to ask my fellow students for feedback; they might think I am incompetent.

_____ 8. It is embarrassing to ask other students for their impression of how I am doing in class.

_____ 9. It would bother me to ask the instructor for feedback.

_____ 10. It is not a good idea to ask the instructor for feedback because he or she might think I am incompetent.

_____ 11. It is embarrassing to ask the instructor for feedback.

_____ 12. It is better to try to figure out how I am doing on my own, rather than to ask other students for feedback.

For statements 1–4, add the total number of As: _____

For statements 5–12, add the total number of As: _____

For statements 1–4, the greater the number of As, the greater your preference for and trust in feedback from others. For statements 5–12, the greater the number of As, the greater the risk you believe there is in asking for feedback.

How might this information be useful in understanding how you react to feedback in school or on the job?

SOURCES: Based on D. B. Fedor, R. B. Rensvold, and S. M. Adams, "An Investigation of Factors Expected to Affect Feedback Seeking: A Longitudinal Field Study," *Personnel Psychology* 45 (1992), pp. 779–805; S. J. Asford, "Feedback Seeking in Individual Adaptation: A Resource Perspective," *Academy of Management Journal* 29 (1986), pp. 465–87.

EXERCISING STRATEGY: CASCADING GOALS

Baxter Healthcare Corporation has an automated goal-alignment system that about half of its 55,000 employees participate in. At Baxter the process starts with the company's top strategic goals known as the four Bs (Best Team, Best Partner, Best Investments, Best Citizen). The executive team creates goals under each category. The top 150 executives then develop their goals which are distributed to employees. The goals are collected in a performance management system. A website provides guidance on how to write goals, and achievement results are shared with the company's performance review and compensation systems. A manager of e-procurement of suppliers at Baxter who reports to the VP of purchasing says, "The biggest value is the digitization and consistent fashion of performance information. Historically we'd put this information into filing cabinets and pull it out once or twice a year. What this process is, really, is a tool that provides me with an opportunity to better understand Baxter's expectations of me and my team."

Questions

1. How does this type of goal-setting process contribute to effective performance management?

2. Baxter uses a website to provide guidance on how to write goals. What are the characteristics of effective goals and objectives that should be emphasized on the website?

3. What are the potential disadvantages of relying entirely on goals or objectives for performance management? What recommendations would you give, if any, to Baxter to increase the effectiveness of this system?

SOURCE: K. Tyler, "Performance Art," *HR Magazine*, August 2005, pp. 58–63; M. Hayes, "Goals Oriented," *Information Week*, March 10, 2003, from *Information Week* website at www.informationweek.com; D. Silverstone, "Paperless Performance Reviews," *HR Professional*, February 2005, www.hrpao.org/HRPAO/KnowledgeCentre/HRProfessional/newscluster/ Paperless+Performance+Reviews.htm, retrieved: February 19, 2005; and M. Totty, "The Dreaded Performance Review," *The Wall Street Journal*, November 27, 2006, p. R7.

● MANAGING PEOPLE

Lions . . . Tigers . . . and Bears . . . and Performance Management

The Zoological Society of San Diego, which operates the San Diego Zoo, the San Diego Zoo's Wild Animal Park, and the Conservation and Research for Endangered Species scientific center, employs 2,600 people and has revenues of more than $160 million per year. For many years, performance appraisals were not a high priority. Measurement metrics used to rate employees were inconsistent, and managers not completing appraisals faced no consequences. Different versions of the one-page appraisal form were used. Managers evaluated employees on how well they thought they were doing rather than specific goals. Managers received annual cost-of-living raises not linked to their performance.

As part of the Zoological Society's emphasis on accountability outlined in the strategic plan, a new performance management system for its 225 managerial employees was recently developed. The goals for the system were to establish employee goals related to the organization's goals, include both a midyear and end-of-year performance review, and require year-end-review ratings be used to determine performance-based pay increases. Employee teams were used to help design the system. One team evaluated vendors from which a new appraisal system could be purchased. The other team investigated skills characterizing an effective leader. Use of the teams led to performance appraisals based on two categories: goals and leadership competencies. Goals and leadership competencies each make up 50% of the overall employee appraisal. At the beginning of each year, managers choose five goals, with three linked to the organization's objectives, such as visitor satisfaction or revenue, and the other two targeted to the manager's specific work area. Employees are rated on six leadership competencies, each including five subfactors. For example, "professionalism" includes ratings on teamwork, communications, interpersonal relations, Zoological Society mission, and customer focus.

The Zoological Society chose a web-based system that helps guide managers through the appraisal process. The system allows employees to record accomplishments in an online journal they can share with their manager. This helps ensure the accuracy of performance reviews. It is especially useful for employees of the Zoological Society who are involved with many different conservation and other projects that their manager may not know about. The system also includes tools such as a "comment helper," which provides phrases to use in giving feedback, and a "language sensitivity checker," which flags offensive words and suggests alternatives. Despite the use of the web-based system, HR requires that the appraisal must be given in person, with the manager printing and reviewing it or discussing the results with the employee as they review it on the computer screen. The manager must certify that a personal meeting occurred.

HR believes that the web-based appraisal process has helped the zoo attract talented employees. Employees are attracted to companies that have clearly defined performance goals and objectives, offer timely feedback, and determine salary based on performance. Long-time employees like the system because it helps encourage discussions with managers, goal setting, and raises based on performance. Michele Stancer, who has been working at the zoo for 28 years, says, "If you perform well, you will get more. I think people should be held accountable. I've been here a long time. You see people who are 'working in retirement,' and that's not good for anyone."

Questions

1. The chapter discusses five criteria for effective performance appraisals: strategic congruence, validity, reliability, acceptability, and specificity. Evaluate the Zoological Society's appraisal system on each criterion, that is, decide whether the appraisal system meets the criterion, falls short of the criterion, or exceeds the criterion. Provide evidence of each.

2. What are the strengths and weaknesses of web-based appraisal systems such as the one used by the Zoological Society? What changes would you recommend for the Zoological Society's system to improve its weaknesses?

SOURCES: Based on T. Henneman, "Employee Performance Management: What's Gnu at the Zoo?" *Workforce Management Online* (September 2006); J. McGregor, "Performance Review Takes a Page from Facebook," *BusinessWeek*, March 12, 2009, p. 58.

◯ TWITTER FOCUS: APPRAISALS MATTER AT MEADOW HILLS VETERINARY CENTER

Using Twitter, continue the conversation about performance management by reading the Meadow Hills Veterinary Center case at www.mhhe.com/noe8e.

Performance management is an important activity at Meadow Hills Veterinary Center in Washington State. Each employee meets with the company's practice manager and owners twice a year to discuss performance. The company tries to keep appraisal meetings positive by not waiting until meeting with employees to address performance problems. When employees don't perform up to expectations, managers evaluate whether changes are needed in training or hiring. This effective approach to performance management has reduced the employee turnover rate from 25% to 10%.

Engage with your classmates and instructor via Twitter to chat about Meadow Hills' performance appraisal process using the case questions posted on the Noe website. Don't have a Twitter account yet? See the instructions for getting started on the Online Learning Center.

NOTES

1. A. Bradley, "Taking the Formality out of Performance Reviews," *T + D*, June 2010, p. 18; R. Pyrillis, "The Reviews Are In," *Workforce Management*, May 2011, pp. 20–25.
2. M. Laff, "Performance Management Gives a Shaky Performance," *T + D*, September 2007, p. 18; A. Fox, "Curing What Ails Performance Reviews," *HR Magazine*, January 2009, pp. 52–56.
3. A. Freedman, "Balancing Values, Results in Reviews," *Human Resource Executive*, August 2006, pp. 62–63; G. Ruiz, "Performance Management Underperforms," *Workforce Management*, December 2006, pp. 47–49; A. Fox, "Curing What Ails Performance Reviews," *HR Magazine*, January 2009; A. Bradley, "Taking the Formality out of Performance Reviews," *T + D*, June 2010, p. 18; E. Pulakos, *Performance Management* (Oxford, England: Wiley-Blackwell, 2009).
4. E. Pulakos, *Performance Management* (Oxford, England: Wiley-Blackwell, 2009); H. Aguinis, "An Expanded View of Performance Management," in J. W. Smith and M. London (eds.), *Performance Management* (San Francisco: Jossey-Bass, 2009), pp. 1–43; J. Russell and L. Russell, "Talk Me Through It: The Next Level of Performance Management," *T + D*, April 2010, pp. 42–48; J. Dahling and A. O'Malley, "Supportive Feedback Environments Can Mend Broken Performance Management Systems," *Industrial and Organizational Psychology* 4 (2011), pp. 201–3; E. Pulakos and R. O'Leary, "Why Is Performance Management Broken?" *Industrial and Organizational Psychology* 4 (2011), pp. 146–64.
5. J. Harbour, "The Three 'Ds' of Successful Performance Measurement: Design, Data, and Display," *Performance Improvement* 50 (February 2011), pp. 5–12.
6. J. Cleveland, K. Murphy, and R. Williams, "Multiple Uses of Performance Appraisal: Prevalence and Correlates," *Journal of Applied Psychology* 74 (1989), pp. 130–35.
7. C. Longenecker, "Behind the Mask: The Politics of Employee Appraisal," *Academy of Management Executive* 1 (1987), p. 183.
8. M. Beer, "Note on Performance Appraisal," in *Readings in Human Resource Management*, ed. M. Beer and B. Spector (New York: Free Press, 1985).
9. C. G. Banks and K. E. May, "Performance Management: The Real Glue in Organizations," in *Evolving Practices in Human Resource Management*, ed. A. Kraut and A. Korman (San Francisco: Jossey-Bass, 1999), pp. 118–45.
10. E. Krell, "All for Incentives, Incentives for All," *HR Magazine*, January 2011, pp. 35–38.
11. C. D. Ittner and D. F. Larcker, "Coming Up Short on Nonfinancial Performance Measurement," *Harvard Business Review*, December 2003, pp. 88–95.
12. J. K. Harter, F. Schmidt, and T. L. Hayes, "Business-Unit Level Relationships between Employee Satisfaction, Employee Engagement, and Business Outcomes: A Meta-Analysis," *Journal of Applied Psychology* 87 (2002), pp. 268–79.
13. A. J. Rucci, S. P. Kim, and R. T. Quinn, "The Employee-Customer-Profit Chain at Sears," *Harvard Business Review*, January–February 1998, pp. 82–97.
14. R. Schuler and S. Jackson, "Linking Competitive Strategies with Human Resource Practices," *Academy of Management Executive* 1 (1987), pp. 207–19.
15. L. King, J. Hunter, and F. Schmidt, "Halo in a Multidimensional Forced-Choice Performance Evaluation Scale," *Journal of Applied Psychology* 65 (1980), pp. 507–16.
16. B. R. Nathan, A. M. Mohrman, and J. Millman, "Interpersonal Relations as a Context for the Effects of Appraisal Interviews on Performance and Satisfaction: A Longitudinal Study," *Academy of Management Journal* 34 (1991), pp. 352–69; M. S. Taylor, K. B. Tracy, M. K. Renard, J. K. Harrison, and S. J. Carroll, "Due Process in Performance Appraisal: A Quasi-experiment in Procedural Justice," *Administrative Science Quarterly* 40 (1995), pp. 495–523; J. M. Werner and M. C. Bolino, "Explaining U.S. Courts of Appeals Decisions Involving Performance Appraisal: Accuracy, Fairness, and Validation," *Personnel Psychology* 50 (1997), pp. 1–24.
17. *Albermarle Paper Company v. Moody*, 10 FEP 1181 (1975).
18. S. Ng and J. Lublin, "AIG Pay Plan: Rank and Rile," *The Wall Street Journal*, February 11, 2010, p. R8.
19. S. Bates, "Forced Ranking," *HR Magazine*, June 2003, pp. 63–68; A. Meisler, "Deadman's Curve," *Workforce Management*, July 2003, pp. 44–49; M. Lowery, "Forcing the Issue," *Human Resource Executive* (October 16, 2003), pp. 26–29.
20. Ibid.
21. S. Scullen, P. Bergey, and L. Aiman-Smith, "Forced Choice Distribution Systems and the Improvement of Workforce Potential: A Baseline Simulation," *Personnel Psychology* 58 (2005), pp. 1–32.
22. F. Blanz and E. Ghiselli, "The Mixed Standard Scale: A New Rating System," *Personnel Psychology* 25 (1973), pp. 185–99; K. Murphy and J. Constans, "Behavioral Anchors as a Source of Bias in Rating," *Journal of Applied Psychology* 72 (1987), pp. 573–77.
23. P. Smith and L. Kendall, "Retranslation of Expectations: An Approach to the Construction of Unambiguous Anchors for Rating Scales," *Journal of Applied Psychology* 47 (1963), pp. 149–55.
24. Murphy and Constans, "Behavioral Anchors"; M. Piotrowski, J. Barnes-Farrel, and F. Esrig, "Behaviorally Anchored Bias: A Replication and Extension of Murphy and Constans," *Journal of Applied Psychology* 74 (1989), pp. 823–26.
25. U. Wiersma and G. Latham, "The Practicality of Behavioral Observation Scales, Behavioral Expectation Scales, and Trait Scales," *Personnel Psychology* 39 (1986), pp. 619–28.
26. G. Latham and K. Wexley, *Increasing Productivity through Performance Appraisal* (Boston: Addison-Wesley, 1981).

27. Wiersma and Latham, "The Practicality of Behavioral Observation Scales, Behavioral Expectation Scales, and Trait Scales."

28. M. Campion, A. Fink, B. Ruggeberg, L. Carr, G. Phillips, and R. Odman, "Doing Competencies Well: Best Practices in Competency Modeling," *Personnel Psychology* 64 (2011), pp. 225–62; J. Shippmann, R. Ash, M. Battista, L. Carr, L. Eyde, B. Hesketh, J. Kehow, K. Pearlman, and J. Sanchez, "The Practice of Competency Modeling," *Personnel Psychology* 53 (2000), pp. 703–40; A. Lucia and R. Lepsinger, *The Art and Science of Competency Models* (San Francisco: Jossey-Bass, 1999).

29. C. Spicer, "Building a Competency Model," *HR Magazine*, April 2009, pp. 34–36.

30. S. Snell, "Control Theory in Strategic Human Resource Management: The Mediating Effect of Administrative Information," *Academy of Management Journal* 35 (1992), pp. 292–327.

31. T. Patten Jr., *A Manager's Guide to Performance Appraisal* (New York: Free Press, 1982).

32. M. O'Donnell and R. O'Donnell, "MBO—Is It Passe?" *Hospital and Health Services Administration* 28, no. 5 (1983), pp. 46–58; T. Poister and G. Streib, "Management Tools in Government: Trends over the Past Decade," *Public Administration Review* 49 (1989), pp. 240–48.

33. E. Locke and G. Latham, *A Theory of Goal Setting and Task Performance* (Englewood Cliffs, NJ: Prentice Hall, 1990).

34. S. Carroll and H. Tosi, *Management by Objectives* (New York: Macmillan, 1973).

35. G. Odiorne, *MBO II: A System of Managerial Leadership for the 80's* (Belmont, CA: Pitman, 1986); E. Pulakos, *Performance Management* (Oxford, England: Wiley-Blackwell, 2009).

36. R. Rodgers and J. Hunter, "Impact of Management by Objectives on Organizational Productivity," *Journal of Applied Psychology* 76 (1991), pp. 322–26.

37. J. Light, "Performance Reviews by Numbers," *The Wall Street Journal*, June 29, 2010, p. D4.

38. R. S. Kaplan and D. P. Norton, "Using the Balanced Scorecard as a Strategic Management System," *Harvard Business Review*, July–August 2007, pp. 150–161.

39. W. Schiemann, "Aligning Performance Management with Organizational Strategy, Values, and Goals," in J. W. Smither and M. London (eds.), *Performance Management* (San Francisco: Jossey-Bass, 2009), pp. 45–87.

40. R. Pritchard, S. Jones, P. Roth, K. Stuebing, and S. Ekeberg, "The Evaluation of an Integrated Approach to Measuring Organizational Productivity," *Personnel Psychology* 42 (1989), pp. 69–115; R. Pritchard, M. Harrell, D. DiazGranados, and M. Guzman, "The Productivity Measurement and Enhancement System: A Meta-Analysis," *Journal of Applied Psychology* 93 (2008), pp. 340–67.

41. P. Wright, J. George, S. Farnsworth, and G. McMahan, "Productivity and Extra-Role Behavior: The Effects of Goals and Incentives on Spontaneous Helping," *Journal of Applied Psychology* 78, no. 3 (1993), pp. 374–81.

42. Latham and Wexley, *Increasing Productivity through Performance Appraisal*.

43. J. Liedman, "The Ongoing Conversation," *Human Resource Executive*, November 2006, pp. 71–74; R. Davenport, "John Deere Champions Workforce Development," *TD*, April 2006, pp. 41–43.

44. R. L. Cardy, "Performance Appraisal in a Quality Context: A New Look at an Old Problem," in *Performance Appraisal: State of the Art in Practice*, ed. J. W. Smither (San Francisco: Jossey-Bass, 1998), pp. 132–62.

45. E. C. Huge, *Total Quality: An Executive's Guide for the 1990s* (Homewood, IL: Richard D. Irwin, 1990): see Chapter 5, "Measuring and Rewarding Performance," pp. 70–88; W. E. Deming, *Out of Crisis* (Cambridge, MA: MIT Center for Advanced Engineering Study, 1986).

46. M. Caroselli, *Total Quality Transformations* (Amherst, MA: Human Resource Development Press, 1991); Huge, *Total Quality*.

47. M. Sallie-Dosunmu, "Born to Grow," *T + D*, May 2006, pp. 33–37.

48. A. Brunet and S. New, "Kaizen in Japan: An Empirical Study," *International Journal of Production and Operations Management* 23 (2003), pp. 1426–46.

49. D. E. Bowen and E. E. Lawler III, "Total Quality-Oriented Human Resource Management," *Organizational Dynamics* 21 (1992), pp. 29–41.

50. R. Heneman, K. Wexley, and M. Moore, "Performance Rating Accuracy: A Critical Review," *Journal of Business Research* 15 (1987), pp. 431–48.

51. T. Becker and R. Klimoski, "A Field Study of the Relationship between the Organizational Feedback Environment and Performance," *Personnel Psychology* 42 (1989), pp. 343–58; H. M. Findley, W. F. Giles, and K. W. Mossholder, "Performance Appraisal and Systems Facets: Relationships with Contextual Performance," *Journal of Applied Psychology* 85 (2000), pp. 634–40.

52. K. Ellis, "Developing for Dollars," *Training*, May 2003, pp. 34–39.

53. L. Axline, "Performance Biased Evaluations," *Supervisory Management*, November 1991, p. 3.

54. K. Wexley and R. Klimoski, "Performance Appraisal: An Update," in *Research in Personnel and Human Resource Management* (vol. 2), ed. K. Rowland and G. Ferris (Greenwich, CT: JAI Press, 1984).

55. F. Landy and J. Farr, *The Measurement of Work Performance: Methods, Theory, and Applications* (New York: Academic Press, 1983).

56. G. McEvoy and P. Buller, "User Acceptance of Peer Appraisals in an Industrial Setting," *Personnel Psychology* 40 (1987), pp. 785–97.

57. A. Pomeroy, "Agent of Change," *HR Magazine*, May 2005, pp. 52–56.

58. D. Antonioni, "The Effects of Feedback Accountability on Upward Appraisal Ratings," *Personnel Psychology* 47 (1994), pp. 349–56.

59. K. Murphy and J. Cleveland, *Performance Appraisal: An Organizational Perspective* (Boston: Allyn & Bacon, 1991).

60. J. Bernardin and L. Klatt, "Managerial Appraisal Systems: Has Practice Caught Up with the State of the Art?" *Public Personnel Administrator*, November 1985, pp. 79–86.

61. A. Fox, "Curing What Ails Performance Reviews," *HR Magazine*, January 2009.

62. H. Heidemeier and K. Moser, "Self-Other Agreement in Job Performance Rating: A Meta-Analytic Test of a Process Model," *Journal of Applied Psychology* 94 (2008), pp. 353–70.

63. R. Steel and N. Ovalle, "Self-Appraisal Based on Supervisor Feedback," *Personnel Psychology* 37 (1984), pp. 667–85; L. E. Atwater, "The Advantages and Pitfalls of Self-Assessment in Organizations," in J. Smither (ed.) *Performance Appraisal: State of the Art in Practice* (San Francisco: Jossey-Bass, 1998) pp. 331–65.

64. M. W. Horrigan, "Employment Projections to 2012: Concepts and Context," *Monthly Labor Review* 127 (2004), pp. 3–11.

65. E. Gummerson, "Lip Services—A Neglected Area of Service Marketing," *Journal of Services Marketing* 1 (1987), pp. 1–29.

66. J. Bernardin, B. Hagan, J. Kane, and P. Villanova, "Effective Performance Management: A Focus on Precision, Customers, and Situational Constraints," in *Performance Appraisal: State of the Art in Practice*, ed. J. W. Smither (San Francisco: Jossey-Bass, 1998), pp. 3–48.

67. R. Hoffman, "Ten Reasons You Should Be Using 360-Degree Feedback," *HR Magazine*, April 1995, pp. 82–84.

68. S. Sherman, "How Tomorrow's Best Leaders Are Learning Their Stuff," *Fortune*, November 27, 1995, pp. 90–104; W. W. Tornow, M. London, and Associates, *Maximizing the Value of 360-Degree Feedback* (San Francisco: Jossey-Bass, 1998); D. A. Waldman, L. E. Atwater, and D. Antonioni, "Has 360-Degree Feedback Gone Amok?" *Academy of Management Executive* 12 (1988), pp. 86–94.

69. K. Tyler, "Performance Art," *HR Magazine*, August 2005, pp. 58–63; M. Hayes, "Goals Oriented," *Information Week*, March 10, 2003, from *Information Week* website at www.informationweek.com; D. Silverstone, "Paperless Performance Reviews," *HR Professional*, February 2005, www.hrpao.org/HRPAO/KnowledgeCentre/HRProfessional/newscluster/Paperless+Performance+Reviews.htm, retrieved February 19, 2005; M. Totty, "The Dreaded Performance Review," *The Wall Street Journal*, November 27, 2006, p. R7.

70. K. Maher, "Big Employer Is Watching," *The Wall Street Journal*, November 4, 2003, pp. B1 and B6.

71. D. Onley, "Technology Gives Big Brother Capability," *HR Magazine*, July 2005, pp. 99–102.

72. V. O'Connell, "Stores Count Seconds to Cut Labor Costs," *The Wall Street Journal*, November 17, 2008, pp. A1, A15.

73. A. Tversky and D. Kahneman, "Availability: A Heuristic for Judging Frequency and Probability," *Cognitive Psychology* 5 (1973), pp. 207–32.

74. K. Wexley and W. Nemeroff, "Effects of Racial Prejudice, Race of Applicant, and Biographical Similarity on Interviewer Evaluations of Job Applicants," *Journal of Social and Behavioral Sciences* 20 (1974), pp. 66–78.

75. G. Ruiz, "Lessons from the Front Lines," *Workforce Management*, December 2006, pp. 50–52.

76. D. Smith, "Training Programs for Performance Appraisal: A Review," *Academy of Management Review* 11 (1986), pp. 22–40.

77. G. Latham, K. Wexley, and E. Pursell, "Training Managers to Minimize Rating Errors in the Observation of Behavior," *Journal of Applied Psychology* 60 (1975), pp. 550–55.

78. J. Bernardin and E. Pence, "Effects of Rater Training: Creating New Response Sets and Decreasing Accuracy," *Journal of Applied Psychology* 65 (1980), pp. 60–66.

79. E. Pulakos, "A Comparison of Rater Training Programs: Error Training and Accuracy Training," *Journal of Applied Psychology* 69 (1984), pp. 581–88; E. Dierdorff, E. Surface, and K. Brown, "Frame-of-Reference Training Effectiveness: Effects of Goal Orientation and Self-Efficacy on Affective, Cognitive, Skill-Based and Transfer Outcomes," *Journal of Applied Psychology* 95 (2010), pp. 1181–1191.

80. H. J. Bernardin, M. R. Buckley, C. L. Tyler, and D. S. Wiese, "A Reconsideration of Strategies in Rater Training," in G. R. Ferris (ed.), *Research in Personnel and Human Resource Management* (Greenwich, CT: JAI Press, 2000), vol. 18, pp. 221–74.

81. J. Sammer, "Calibrating Consistency," *HR Magazine*, January 2008, pp. 73–75.

82. S. W. J. Kozlowski, G. T. Chao, and R. F. Morrison, "Games Raters Play: Politics, Strategies, and Impression Management in Performance Appraisal," in *Performance Appraisal: State of the Art in Practice*, pp. 163–205; C. Rosen, P. Levy, and R. Hall, "Placing Perceptions of Politics in the Context of the Feedback Environment, Employee Attitudes, and Job Performance," *Journal of Applied Psychology* 91 (2006), pp. 211–20.

83. R. Pyrillis, "The Reviews Are In," *Workforce Management*, May 2011, pp. 20–25.

84. K. Wexley, V. Singh, and G. Yukl, "Subordinate Participation in Three Types of Appraisal Interviews," *Journal of Applied Psychology* 58 (1973), pp. 54–57; K. Wexley, "Appraisal Interview," in *Performance Assessment*, ed. R. A. Berk (Baltimore: Johns Hopkins University Press, 1986), pp. 167–85; D. Cederblom, "The Performance Appraisal Interview: A Review, Implications, and Suggestions," *Academy of Management Review* 7 (1982), pp. 219–27; B. D. Cawley, L. M. Keeping, and P. E. Levy, "Participation in the Performance Appraisal Process and Employee Reactions: A Meta-analytic Review of Field Investigations," *Journal of Applied Psychology* 83, no. 3 (1998), pp. 615–63; H. Aguinis, *Performance Management* (Upper Saddle River, NJ: Pearson Prentice Hall, 2007); C. Lee, "Feedback, Not Appraisal," *HR Magazine*, November 2006, pp. 111–14.

85. B. Hite, "Employers Rethink How They Give Feedback," *Wall Street Journal*, October 13, 2008, p. B5.

86. W. Giles and K. Mossholder, "Employee Reactions to Contextual and Session Components of Performance Appraisal," *Journal of Applied Psychology* 75 (1990), pp. 371–77.

87. E. Locke and G. Latham, *A Theory of Goal Setting and Task Performance* (Englewood Cliffs, NJ: Prentice Hall, 1990).

88. H. Klein, S. Snell, and K. Wexley, "A Systems Model of the Performance Appraisal Interview Process," *Industrial Relations* 26 (1987), pp. 267–80.

89. S. Bates, "Forced Ranking," *HR Magazine*, June 2003, pp. 63–68; A. Meisler, "Deadman's Curve," *Workforce Management*, July 2003, pp. 44–49; M. Lowery, "Forcing the Issue," *Human Resource Executive* (October 16, 2003), pp. 26–29.

90. *Brito v. Zia Co.*, 478 F.2d 1200 (10th Cir 1973).

91. K. Kraiger and J. Ford, "A Meta-Analysis of Ratee Race Effects in Performance Rating," *Journal of Applied Psychology* 70 (1985), pp. 56–65; S. Needleman, "Monitoring the Monitors: Small Firms Increasingly Are Keeping Tabs on Their Workers, Keystroke by Keystroke," *The Wall Street Journal*, August 16, 2010, p. R8.

92. P. Sackett, C. DuBois, and A. Noe, "Tokenism in Performance Evaluation: The Effects of Work Groups Representation on Male–Female and White–Black Differences in Performance Ratings," *Journal of Applied Psychology* 76 (1991), pp. 263–67.

93. G. Barrett and M. Kernan, "Performance Appraisal and Terminations: A Review of Court Decisions since *Brito v. Zia* with Implications for Personnel Practices," *Personnel Psychology* 40 (1987), pp. 489–503; H. Field and W. Holley, "The Relationship of Performance Appraisal System Characteristics to Verdicts in Selected Employment Discrimination Cases," *Academy of Management Journal* 25 (1982), pp. 392–406; J. M. Werner and M. C. Bolino, "Explaining U.S. Courts of Appeals Decisions Involving Performance Appraisal: Accuracy, Fairness, and Validation," *Personnel Psychology* 50 (1997), pp. 1–24; J. Segal, "Performance Management Blunders," *HR Magazine*, November 2010, pp. 75–77.

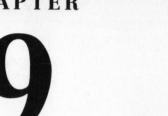

CHAPTER

9

Employee Development

LO LEARNING OBJECTIVES

After reading this chapter, you should be able to:

LO 9-1   Explain how employee development contributes to strategies related to employee retention, developing intellectual capital, and business growth. *page 397*

LO 9-2   Discuss the steps in the development planning process. *page 399*

LO 9-3   Explain the employees' and company's responsibilities in planning development. *page 400*

LO 9-4   Discuss current trends in using formal education for development. *page 405*

LO 9-5   Relate how assessment of personality type, work behaviors, and job performance can be used for employee development. *page 409*

LO 9-6   Explain how job experiences can be used for skill development. *page 415*

LO 9-7   Develop successful mentoring programs. *page 422*

LO 9-8   Describe how to train managers to coach employees. *page 425*

LO 9-9   Discuss what companies are doing for management development issues, including succession planning, melting the glass ceiling, and helping dysfunctional managers. *page 427*

ENTER THE WORLD OF BUSINESS

Management Development Helps Fatten Chicken, Beef, and Pork Business

Tyson Foods, Inc., headquartered in Springdale, Arkansas, is one of the world's largest processors and marketers of chicken, beef, and pork. The company produces a wide variety of protein-based and prepared food products and is the recognized market leader in the retail and food-service markets it serves. Tyson provides products and services to customers throughout the United States and more than 90 countries. The company has approximately 117,000 employees (known as Team Members) in more than 400 facilities and offices in the United States and around the world.

Tyson Foods recognizes that its success depends on the development of its managers. Specifically, Tyson needs to identify employees with high leadership potential and quickly develop them into leaders and managers capable of leading process improvements and cost efficiencies to drive and sustain business profits. To accomplish this Tyson, with the help of consulting firm SVI, created a two-year development program known as Leaders into Champions (LINC). The objectives of LINC were to create a group of managers who were ready to take executive management positions, ensure they had the correct skills and attitudes to drive innovation and create competitive advantage in the business, expand their involvement and influence within the industry and within Tyson Foods, and provide development opportunities.

To identify participants in the LINC program, leaders from every business unit are asked to nominate high potential leaders who received performance evaluations in the top 5%. A selection process then occurs that includes a review of operational results, peer and manager recommendations, and an evaluation of future growth potential. Nominees are also asked to present to an executive panel their most personal challenges that helped shape them. Asking nominees to share these challenges communicates to them that the LINC program will require courage, honesty, and sharing with others. Following the presentations 20 managers are chosen for the LINC program.

The LINC program begins by having participants read the book *The Organization Champion* and complete an assessment that measures participants' skills in being an organization champion. The assessment is used by LINC participants to identify their strengths and areas for improvement and is used to create individual development plans. Next, participants complete a two-day event that helps them consider their life perspectives. Through the event participants focus on what they are good at doing, what makes them come alive, and how they uniquely contribute to the company. LINC participants have opportunities to directly interact with Tyson's executives in monthly meetings either in person at company headquarters or using video conferencing. A business unit executive hosts each meeting and shares information on the business, their own personal challenges that helped shape them, and present a leadership-competency–based topic. The meetings are useful for development for both participants and executives. LINC participants gain exposure and networking opportunities with executives and executives have the opportunity to "size up" high-potential leaders who may someday work in their business unit. The monthly meetings also involve peer coaching that takes place among LINC participants. LINC participants share ideas and provide feedback to each other.

The second year of the program includes an experiential event designed to measure the development progress of the participants. It requires participants to rely on what they have learned. After the experiential event, participants are given an assignment based on their interests, that forces them to experience new challenges and exposes them to different parts of the business (stretch assignments). The stretch assignments involve important roles that require LINC participants to face actual business challenges and opportunities. Participants need to develop new skills to successfully complete the stretch assignments. These assignments might include participation in an action learning team, research project, or executive internship. Stretch assignments have resulted in new products and competitive advantages for Tyson Foods.

Overall, the LINC program has been successful. LINC is considered the best development program within Tyson Foods and most of the LINC participants are promoted into executive positions.

SOURCE: Based on M. Thompson, "What Makes Tyson's High-Potential Leadership Program Critical to Company Success?" *T + D*, April 2011, pp. 98–100; www.tysonfoods.com, website for Tyson Foods.

Introduction

As the Tyson Food example illustrates, employee development is a key contributor to a company's competitive advantage by helping high-potential managers understand their strengths, weaknesses, and interests and by showing them how new jobs and expanded job responsibilities are available to them to meet their personal growth needs. This helps retain valuable managers who might otherwise leave to join clients or competitors. It is also important to emphasize that development is important for all employees, not just managers. Employee development is a necessary component of a company's efforts to compete in the new economy, to meet the challenges of global competition and social change, and to incorporate technological advances and changes in work design. Employee development is key to ensuring that employees have the competencies necessary to serve customers and create new products and customer solutions. Regardless of the business strategy, development is important for retaining talented employees. Also because companies (and their employees) must constantly learn and change to meet customer needs and compete in new markets, the emphasis placed on both training and development has increased. As we noted in Chapter 1, employee commitment and retention are directly related to how employees are treated by their managers.

This chapter begins by discussing the relationship between development, training, and careers. Choosing an approach is one part of development planning. Second, before employees choose development activities, the employee and the company must have an idea of the employee's development needs and the purpose of development. Identifying the needs and purpose of development is part of its planning. The second section of the chapter describes the steps of the development planning process. Employee and company responsibilities at each step of the process are emphasized. Third, we look at development approaches, including formal education, assessment, job experiences, and interpersonal relationships. The chapter emphasizes the types of skills, knowledge, and behaviors that are strengthened by each development method. The chapter concludes with a discussion of special issues in employee development, including succession planning and using development to help women and minorities move into upper-level management positions (referred to as "melting the glass ceiling").

The Relationship among Development, Training, and Careers

DEVELOPMENT AND TRAINING

Development refers to formal education, job experiences, relationships, and assessment of personality and abilities that help employees prepare for the future. The Tyson Foods example illustrates that although development can occur through participation in planned programs, it often results from performing different types of work. Because it is future-oriented, it involves learning that is not necessarily related to the employee's current job.[1] Table 9.1 shows the differences between training and development. Traditionally, training focuses on helping employees' performance in their current jobs. Development prepares them for other positions in the company and increases their ability to move into jobs that may not yet exist.[2] Development also helps employees prepare for changes in their current jobs that may result from new technology, work designs, new customers, or new product markets. Development is especially critical for talent management, particularly for senior managers and employees with leadership potential (recall our discussion of attracting and retaining talent in Chapter 1). Companies report that the most important talent management challenges they face include developing existing talent and attracting and retaining existing leadership talent.[3] Chapter 7 emphasized the strategic role of training. As training continues to become more strategic (that is, related to business goals), the distinction between training and development will blur. Both training and development will be required and will focus on current and future personal and company needs.

DEVELOPMENT AND CAREERS

Traditionally, careers have been described in various ways.[4] Careers have been described as a sequence of positions held within an occupation. For example, a university faculty member can hold assistant, associate, and full professor positions. A career has also been described in the context of mobility within an organization. For example, an engineer may begin her career as a staff engineer. As her expertise, experience, and performance increase, she may move through advisory engineering, senior engineering, and senior technical positions. Finally, a career has been described as a characteristic of the employee. Each employee's career consists of different jobs, positions, and experiences.

Today's careers are known as protean careers.[5] A **protean career** is based on self-direction with the goal of psychological success in one's work. Employees take major responsibility for managing their careers. For example, an engineer may decide to take a sabbatical from her position to work in management at the United Way Agency for a year. The purpose of this assignment could be to develop her managerial skills as well as help her personally evaluate if she likes managerial work more than engineering.

LO 9-1
Explain how employee development contributes to strategies related to employee retention, developing intellectual capital, and business growth.

Development
The acquisition of knowledge, skills, and behaviors that improve an employee's ability to meet changes in job requirements and in client and customer demands.

Protean Career
A career that is based on self-direction with the goal of psychological success in one's work.

	TRAINING	DEVELOPMENT
Focus	Current	Future
Use of work experiences	Low	High
Goal	Preparation for current job	Preparation for changes
Participation	Required	Voluntary

table 9.1

Comparison between Training and Development

Psychological Success
The feeling of pride and accomplishment that comes from achieving life goals.

The protean career has several implications for employee development. The goal of the new career is **psychological success:** the feeling of pride and accomplishment that comes from achieving life goals that are not limited to achievements at work (such as raising a family and having good physical health). Psychological success is more under the employee's control than the traditional career goals, which were not only influenced by employee effort but were controlled by the availability of positions in the company. Psychological success is self-determined rather than solely determined through signals the employee receives from the company (like salary increase and promotion). Psychological success appears to be especially important to the new generation of persons entering the workforce. For example, consider Jacqueline Strayer. Since graduating from college in 1976, she has held a series of positions with different companies including General Electric, GTE, United Technologies, and William Mercer.[6] At the same time, she earned a master's degree in professional studies in film and television and is currently working on a doctorate in management. Her motivation is finding interesting, challenging positions rather than trying to be promoted to a top management position. She is also passionate about running, so she wants to work with an employer that has a fitness center.

Employees need to develop new skills rather than rely on a static knowledge base. This has resulted from companies' need to be more responsive to customers' service and product demands. As we emphasized in Chapter 7, "Training," learning is continuous, often informal, and involves creating and sharing knowledge.

The emphasis on continuous learning has altered the direction and frequency of movement within careers (career pattern).[7] Traditional career patterns consisted of a series of steps arranged in a linear hierarchy, with higher steps related to increased authority, responsibility, and compensation. Expert career patterns involve a lifelong commitment to a field or specialization (such as law, medicine, or management). These types of career patterns will not disappear. Rather, career patterns involving movement across specializations or disciplines (a spiral career pattern) will become more prevalent. These new career patterns mean that developing employees (as well as employees taking control of their own careers) will require providing them with the opportunity to (a) determine their interests, skill strengths, and weaknesses and (b) based on this information, seek appropriate development experiences that will likely involve job experiences and relationships as well as formal courses.

The most appropriate view of today's careers are that they are "boundaryless and often change."[8] It may include movement across several employers or even different occupations. Statistics indicate that the average employment tenure for all American workers is only five years.[9] One study found that 60% of employees of all ages rate time and flexibility as very important reasons for staying with a company.[10] But Gen Xers (those in their mid-20s to late 40s) were more likely to leave a job than baby boomers (those in their mid-40s to late 50s). Some 51% of employees under age 40 reported they were looking for a new job within the next year, compared to only 25% of those 40 or older. For example, Craig Matison, 33 years old, took a job with Cincinnati Bell Information System, a unit of Cincinnati Bell Corporation that manages billing for phone and cable companies.[11] Although he had been on the job only six months, he was already looking to make his next career move. Not wanting to stay on the technical career path, he regularly explored company databases for job postings, looking for sales and marketing opportunities within the company.

"Boundaryless" means that careers may involve identifying more with a job or profession than with the present employer. A career can also be considered boundaryless in the sense that career plans or goals are influenced by personal or family demands and values. One way that employees cope with changes in their personal lives as well as in employment relationships is to rearrange and shift their roles and responsibilities. Employees can change their careers throughout their life based on awareness of strengths and weaknesses, perceived need to balance work and life, and the need to find stimulating and exciting work.[12] Career success may not be tied to promotions but to achieving goals that are personally meaningful to the employee rather than those set by parents, peers, or the company. As we discuss later in the chapter, careers are best managed through partnerships between employees and their company that create a positive relationship through which employees are committed to the organization but can take personal control for managing their own careers to benefit themselves and the company.

As this discussion shows, to retain and motivate employees companies need to provide a system to identify and meet employees' development needs. This is especially important to retain good performers and employees who have potential for managerial positions. This system is often known as a **development planning** or **career management system.** We discuss these systems in the following section.

> **Development planning system**
> A system to retain and motivate employees by identifying and meeting their development needs (also called *career management systems*).

Development Planning Systems

Companies' development planning systems vary in the level of sophistication and the emphasis they place on different components of the process. Steps and responsibilities in the development planning system are shown in Figure 9.1.

> **LO 9-2**
> Discuss the steps in the development planning process.

Self-Assessment

Self-assessment refers to the use of information by employees to determine their career interests, values, aptitudes, and behavioral tendencies. It often involves psychological tests such as the Myers-Briggs Type Indicator (described later in the chapter), the Strong-Campbell Interest Inventory, and the Self-Directed Search.

figure 9.1

Steps and Responsibilities in the Career Management Process

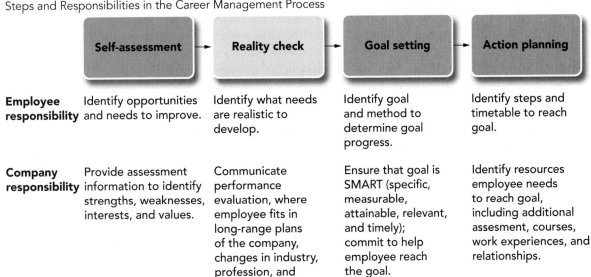

	Self-assessment	Reality check	Goal setting	Action planning
Employee responsibility	Identify opportunities and needs to improve.	Identify what needs are realistic to develop.	Identify goal and method to determine goal progress.	Identify steps and timetable to reach goal.
Company responsibility	Provide assessment information to identify strengths, weaknesses, interests, and values.	Communicate performance evaluation, where employee fits in long-range plans of the company, changes in industry, profession, and workplace.	Ensure that goal is SMART (specific, measurable, attainable, relevant, and timely); commit to help employee reach the goal.	Identify resources employee needs to reach goal, including additional assesment, courses, work experiences, and relationships.

The Strong-Campbell helps employees identify their occupational and job interests; the Self-Directed Search identifies employees' preferences for working in different types of environments (like sales, counseling, landscaping, and so on). Tests may also help employees identify the relative values they place on work and leisure activities.

Through the assessment, a development need can be identified. This need can result from gaps between current skills and/or interests and the type of work or position the employee wants. For example, Verizon Wireless provides an online tool that allows employees to assess their current skills and abilities in order to benchmark themselves against job openings throughout the company. The assessment allows employees to identify capabilities they are lacking and provides them with specific information about what they can do to develop skills through training, job experience, or enrolling in an academic program.[13]

Reality Check

Reality check refers to the information employees receive about how the company evaluates their skills and knowledge and where they fit into the company's plans (potential promotion opportunities, lateral moves). Usually this information is provided by the employee's manager as part of performance appraisal. Some companies also use the 360-degree feedback assessment which involves employees completing a self-evaluation of their behaviors or competencies as well as managers, peers, direct reports, and even customers provide smaller evaluations. (360-degree feedback is discussed later in the chapter.) It is not uncommon in well-developed systems for the manager to hold separate performance appraisals and development discussions.

For example, as part of Caterpillar's performance management process, career development is discussed between the employee and his or her manager.[14] To facilitate this discussion, employees complete a data sheet that serves as an internal résumé. The data sheet includes information about the employee's skills, education, academic degrees, languages spoken, and previous positions. Managers are expected to indicate an employee's readiness for a new job, whether the job will be a promotion or lateral move, and what education or training the employee needs to be ready for the move. Managers discuss with employees where they want to go next and what they have to do to prepare themselves for the next position. Managers also identify where they think the employee has the best opportunities in different functional areas and provide an overall rating of potential and promotability.

Goal Setting

Goal setting refers to the process of employees developing short- and long-term development objectives. These goals usually relate to desired positions (such as becoming sales manager within three years), level of skill application (use one's budgeting skills to improve the unit's cash flow problems), work setting (move to corporate marketing within two years), or skill acquisition (learn how to use the company's human resource information system). These goals are usually discussed with the manager and written into a development plan. A development plan for a product manager is shown in Figure 9.2. Development plans usually include descriptions of strengths and weaknesses, career goals, and development activities for reaching the career goal. An effective development plan focuses on development needs that are most relevant to the organization's strategic objectives.

figure 9.2

Development Plan

Name:	**Title:** Project Manager	**Immediate Manager:**

Competencies

Please identify your three greatest strengths and areas for improvement.

Strengths
- Strategic thinking and execution (confidence, command skills, action orientation)
- Results orientation (competence, motivating others, perseverance)
- Spirit for winning (building team spirit, customer focus, respect colleagues)

Areas for Improvement
- Patience (tolerance of people or processes and sensitivity to pacing)
- Written communications (ability to write clearly and succinctly)
- Overly ambitious (too much focus on successful completion of projects rather than developing relationships with individuals involved in the projects)

Development Goals

Please describe your overall career goals.
- **Long-term:** Accept positions of increased responsibility to a level of general manager (or beyond). The areas of specific interest include but are not limited to product and brand management, technology and development, strategic planning, and marketing.
- **Short-term:** Continue to improve my skills in marketing and brand management while utilizing my skills in product management, strategic planning, and global relations.

Next Assignments

Identify potential next assignments (including timing) that would help you develop toward your goals.
- Manager or director level in planning, development, product, or brand management. Timing estimated to be Spring 2012.

Training and Development Needs

List both training and development activities that will either help you develop in your current assignment or provide overall development.
- Master's degree classes will allow me to practice and improve my written communications skills. The dynamics of my current position, teamwork, and reliance on other individuals allow me to practice patience and to focus on individual team members' needs along with the success of the projects.

Employee _____ **Date** _____
Immediate Manager _____ **Date** _____
Mentor _____ **Date** _____

Consider Just Born's Career Development Process (CDP) used by high-performing employees to identify their career path within the company and ready themselves for their next position.[15] The development plan involves identifying both short- and long-term career goals. Employees commit to two goals to help them progress in their career. Just Born provides a competency dictionary on the company's intranet that can be used for identifying development needs. The CDP gives both employees and their managers the opportunity to discuss future career plans and becomes a reality check by raising expectations and increasing performance standards. Employees initiate the career development program by first defining future job interests, identifying work experiences that help prepare for the future job, and establishing the long-term career goal. The CDP is discussed with the employee's manager. The manager can support the CDP or suggest changes. If employees' future job interests are outside their current department, the interests are communicated to the manager of that department.

Action Planning

During this phase, employees determine how they will achieve their short- and long-term career goals. Action plans may involve any one or combination of development approaches discussed later the chapter (such as enrolling in courses and seminars, getting additional assessment, obtaining new job experiences, or finding a mentor or coach).[16] The development approach used depends on the needs and developmental goal.

Examples of Career Management and Development Systems

Effective career development systems include several important features (see Table 9.2). Several companies' development systems include one or more of these features. Sprint's individual development plan is based on five core competencies: act with integrity, focus on the customer, deliver results, build relationships, and develop leadership.[17] These competencies are used by each business unit to establish its strategy as well as by each manager and employee in creating development plans. The competencies are the foundations for development conversations between managers and employees. Among the resources available to support the development plan is a development activities guide, which includes audiotapes, books, and specific courses designed to improve each of the competencies, as well as a website where employees can learn about the process. At Automatic Data Processing (ADP) managers are trained to promote development and they are held accountable in part of their

table 9.2

Design Factors of Effective Development Systems

1. System is positioned as a response to a business need or supports the business strategy.
2. Employees and managers participate in development of the system.
3. Employees are encouraged to take an active role in career management and development.
4. Evaluation is ongoing and used to improve the system.
5. Business units can customize the system for their own purposes (with some constraints).
6. Employees have access to development and career information sources (including advisors and positions available).
7. Senior management and the company culture support the development system.
8. The development system is linked to other human resource practices such as performance management, training, and recruiting systems.
9. A large, diverse talent pool is created.
10. Development plans and talent evaluation information are available and accessible to all managers.

SOURCE: Based on B. Baumann, J. Duncan, S. E. Former, and Z. Leibowitz, "Amoco Primes the Talent Pump," *Personnel Journal*, February 1996, pp. 79–84; D. Hall, *Careers In and Out of Organizations* (Thousand Oaks, CA: Sage, 2002).

performance evaluation for the number of employees they have coached and prepared for promotion.[18] Managers receive training on how to hold effective development discussions. Employees can attend information sessions where they can learn about career options within ADP from other employees holding many different positions. ADP also provides a web-based tool for its sales associates, which they can use to access sales and sales leadership career descriptions and opportunities across the company's markets, products, and international locations. General Mills's development plan follows the process shown in Figure 9.2. Each employee completes a development plan that asks employees to consider four areas:

- *Professional goals and motivation:* What professional goals do I have? What excites me to grow professionally?
- *Talents or strengths:* What are my talents and strengths?
- *Development opportunities:* What development needs are important to improve?
- *Development objectives and action steps:* What will be my objective for this plan? What steps can I take to meet the objectives?

Every year managers and employees are expected to have a development discussion and create an individual development plan. Speakers, online tools, and workshops to help employees complete the development plan and prepare for a development discussion with their manager increase the visibility and emphasize the importance of the development planning process. Evaluation data showed that more than 80% of employees report having an effective and motivating development plan. Also, annual survey results show that General Mills ranks 20% to 30% higher on continued improvement and impact of learning and growth compared to companies it is benchmarked against.

The "Competing through Technology" box shows how companies are using online systems for development and career management.

Approaches to Employee Development

Four approaches are used to develop employees: formal education, assessment, job experiences, and interpersonal relationships.[19] Many companies use a combination of these approaches. Figure 9.3 shows the frequency of use of different employee development practices. Larger companies are more likely to use leadership training and development planning more frequently than smaller companies. Children's Healthcare of Atlanta, a medical system specializing in pediatric care, has a Center for Leadership that includes assessment, workshops, action learning, and personal coaches.[20] High-performing employees with potential to become managers complete a full day of assessment that includes participating in a business simulation requiring them to pretend they are managing a division of a major company. They also complete a personality inventory. Employees are given feedback about their behavior in the simulation and the results of the personality inventory. Employees attend five workshops each year that focus on helping employees work with the feedback they received during the assessment. The workshops cover topics such as leading change, developing a business strategy, and creating a personal vision. Action learning requires participants to work in teams on a topic that is of strategic importance to the medical system. Coaches work with the employees to identify long-term improvement goals. The "Competing through Globalization" box shows how the InterContinental Hotel Group is using virtual technology to facilitate global management development.

E-Learning and the Internet Help Employees Manage Careers and Employers Build Management Talent

Many companies are realizing the value of using technology for career management and building management talent. Walgreens, the neighborhood drugstore and retailer's online career development site, Blueprints, allows employees to manage their own career. Career management products available on Blueprints include e-learning modules, competencies and performance standards for different jobs, and descriptions of roles, career paths, and job rotations related to specific career goals. In the hospitality industry, White Lodging Services provides each leader with a career steward who provides them with mentoring and coaching needed for their success. Each leader has a "2 Sheet" which is an online dashboard that provides a snapshot of the leader's performance over time based on the company's balanced scorecard, presents their short- and long-term goals and actions to reach the goals, and identifies the training they have completed and what types of training they will need to achieve their goals. MasterCard Worldwide's Career Management Center supports mobility, career coaching, and career transitions. The online system provides mentoring resources, job postings, development suggestions, and access to an online personal coach. At Baylor Health Care System new managers are required to take six e-learning courses and three classroom courses as well as to develop a leadership improvement plan based on an assessment they take in one of those courses. The results of the assessment are mapped to development activities such as project and committee work and mentoring. Experienced managers can assess their skills through a web-based talent management system and can plan development activities using an individual planning resource guide.

IBM's Blue Opportunities reinforces to employees that growing their careers is important to obtain challenging and interesting work and that they need to take responsibility, working with their managers, for identifying training and development activities that interest them. Blue Opportunities highlights the company's training and development opportunities such as short- and long-term job rotation, on-site job shadowing, and cross-functional projects on an employee-only Internet site that is accessible to employees in the United States and other global locations. The goals of Blue Opportunities are developing employees' skills and knowledge and offering them potential job or career changes. Blue Opportunities provides a way for employees to develop skills across business units and explore career options that they would not have previously considered.

The Role of the Manager @ IBM is an expert system that provides a customized learning portfolio for each manager based on their background, training, and management style. The expert system guides managers through prework that has to be completed prior to attending learning labs. Learning is reinforced through use of a knowledge management system that allows managers to post suggestions and store ideas. Managers who have completed the Role of the Manager @ IBM program have created action plans that have generated revenues of $184 million.

SOURCES: T. Shawel, "Homegrown Career Development," *HR Magazine*, April 2011, pp. 36–38; "Training Top 125," *Training*, January/February 2011, pp. 54–93; T. Barron, "IBM's New Fangled, Old-Fashioned Pep," *T + D*, April 2004, pp. 64–65; D. Robb, "Succeeding with Succession," *HR Magazine*, January 2006, pp. 89–92; N. Lewis and P. Orton, "The Five Attributes of Innovative E-Learning," *Training and Development*, June 2000, pp. 47–51; N. Davis, "One-on-One Training Crosses Continents," *HR Magazine*, November 2007, pp. 54–56.

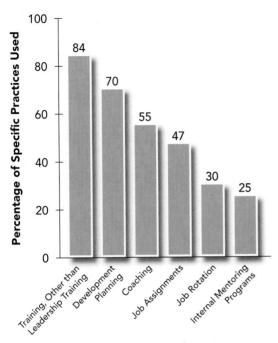

figure 9.3

Frequency of
Use of Employee
Development
Practices

SOURCE: Based on E. Esen and J. Collison, *Employee Development* (Alexandria, VA: SHRM Research, 2005).

Keep in mind that although much development activity is targeted at managers, all levels of employees may be involved in development. For example, most employees typically receive performance appraisal feedback (a development activity related to assessment) at least once per year. As we discussed in Chapter 8, as part of the appraisal process they are asked to complete individual development plans outlining (1) how they plan to change their weaknesses and (2) their future plans (including positions or locations desired and education or experience needed). Next we explore each type of development approach.

FORMAL EDUCATION

Formal education programs include off-site and on-site programs designed specifically for the company's employees, short courses offered by consultants or universities, executive MBA programs, and university programs in which participants actually live at the university while taking classes. These programs may involve lectures by business experts, business games and simulations, adventure learning, and meetings with customers.

Many companies such as Bank of Montreal and General Electric rely primarily on in-house development programs offered by training and development centers or corporate universities, rather than sending employees to programs offered by universities.[21] Companies rely on in-house programs because they can be tied directly to business needs, can be easily evaluated using company metrics, and can get senior-level management involved. The Bank of Montreal (BMO) has invested more than $400 million in training and development, including building the Institute for Learning, with high-tech classrooms, rooms to accommodate out-of-town employees, a presentation hall, restaurants, and a gym.[22] Each year 8,000 employees receive training at the Institute for Learning. A wide range of courses and programs are offered that are linked to the bank's business strategies.

LO 9-4
Discuss current trends in using formal education for development.

Formal Education Programs
Employee development programs, including short courses offered by consultants or universities, executive MBA programs, and university programs.

Management Development Is Served 24/7 in InterContinental Hotel Group's Leaders' Lounge

InterContinental Hotel Group (IHG), an Atlanta-based company, operates by a simple strategy: "Great hotels guests love." IHG operates brands such as InterContinental, Crowne Plaza, Hotel Indigo, Holiday Inn, Holiday Inn Express, Staybridge Suites, and Candlewood Suites. These brands include 4,400 hotels with 652,000 rooms, in over one hundred countries around the world. The company believes that how its employees feel about its brands and how they deliver the guest experience is what distinguishes it from the competition. "Winning Ways," IHG's core values, help guide and motivate employees to improve their personal and professional lives, take ownership, work together, and engage in responsible behavior. IHG makes four promises to employees: Room to Have a Great Start, Room to Be Involved, Room to Grow, and Room for You. The "Room to Grow" promise means that employees are given support for development opportunities and to pursue a rewarding career. "Room to Grow" ensures that employees know what success means for their jobs, they receive regular, high-quality feedback, they have opportunities to develop in their current and future roles, and they are aware of career opportunities within IHG around the world.

In step with its Room to Grow promise IHG wanted to create a way to connect and develop its global corporate and hotel-level managers who had indicated in surveys that they did not feel connected to each other and senior management. To develop managers' leadership skills IHG created a virtual leadership development community, the Leaders' Lounge, for employees in general manager positions in its hotels as well as for employees holding corporate director or higher-level positions. The Leaders' Lounge features short and concise information on leadership provided in articles, tips, videos, downloadable tools, and best practices within IHG. Employees who access the site can use social networks to post tips and react to the leadership content. There are several dedicated areas within the Leaders' Lounge including the "Leadership Gym," which features assessment tools designed to help employees identify their leadership strengths and weaknesses, and "Problem Solver" which asks employees for input on leadership issues. Also, included is a section for users to access e-learning opportunities on business topics including finance, customer service, and coaching skills ("The Academy").

Use of "The Academy" also allowed IHG to move several modules of its Senior Leadership Program online, generating cost savings resulting from reducing travel costs related to global managers having to travel to the training site.

There is compelling evidence that the Leaders' Lounge has been effective for developing managers. The Lounge costs 5% of the costs for a typical three-day on-site leadership workshop. More than 70% of Lounge members use it in any one month, averaging six times per year. More than 3,000 leadership tools have been downloaded and shared with leadership teams around the world. Lounge members across the globe have taken content from the Lounge and used it to build local learning workshops and training sessions. Surveys for hotel general managers who make up 75% of the Leaders' Lounge membership show that their engagement scores increased approximately 3% in 2010.

SOURCE: Based on www.ihgplc.com website for InterContinental Hotels Group; P. Harris, "Where People Power Makes the Difference," *T + D*, October 2010, pp. 32–34; "Best Practices and Outstanding Initiatives: InterContinental Hotels Group Leaders' Lounge," *Training*, January/February 2011, pp. 96–97.

They include management leadership training, risk management training, project management programs, and a four-year MBA program in financial services offered through a partnership with the Dalhousie School of Management and the Institute for Canadian Bankers. BMO believes the programs provide immediate benefit to the company because they often require participants to provide solutions to issues the company is facing. Evaluation and feedback are used to determine the success of specific programs. BMO uses many different types of evaluation including skill tests and performance evaluations conducted by managers after the participant returns to the job to determine transfer of training. BMO also looks at the relationship between the bank's education spending and its performance. Employee surveys are used to determine the quality and relevance of programs.

General Electric (GE) has one of the oldest and most widely known management development centers in the world. GE invests approximately $1 billion each year for training and education programs for its employees.[23] Over the past 17 years, the 189 most senior executives in the company spent at least 12 months in training and professional development. GE develops managers at the John F. Welch Leadership Center at Crotonville, New York.[24] The facility has residence buildings where participants stay while attending programs as well as classrooms for courses, programs, and seminars. Each year GE employees chosen by their managers based on their performance and potential attend management development programs. The programs include professional skills development and specialized courses in areas such as risk analysis and loan structuring. All of the programs emphasize theory and practical application. Course time is spent discussing business issues facing GE. The programs are taught by in-house instructors, university faculty members, and even CEO Jeff Immelt. Examples of management development programs available at GE are shown in Table 9.3. As you can see, GE uses a combination of coursework and job experiences to develop entry-level

table 9.3

Examples of Leadership Development Programs at General Electric

PROGRAM	SUMMARY	QUALIFICATIONS TO ATTEND
Commercial Leadership Program: Commercial and Industrial	Formal courses, including Selling@GE, Marketing@GE, and negotiation skills. Challenging assignments in key sales and marketing roles within a business.	Bachelor's degree in engineering or industrial distribution; minimum 3.0 GPA; prior internship or co-op experience, willingness to relocate; demonstrated interest in sales career and results oriented.
Experienced Commercial Leadership Program (ECLP): Sales and Marketing	Four 6-month business rotations within a GE business; two rotations are marketing focused and two are sales focused. Every 3 months, review self-assessment and manager evaluations to identify accomplishments, development needs, and career interests. Strengthen commercial business and leadership skills by completing classroom and online training and in-residence symposiums at the John F. Welch Learning Center.	MBA; 4–6 years marketing or sales experience; demonstrated achievement and leadership in sales or marketing leadership, communications, and analytical skills; willingness to relocate; expertise aligned with a GE business; unrestricted U.S. work authorization.

SOURCE: Based on "Undergraduate Leadership Programs" and "Masters and MBA Leadership Programs" at www.gecareers.com (April 6, 2009).

and top levels of management. Other programs such as the Business Manager Course and the Executive Development Course involve action learning. As discussed in Chapter 7, action learning involves assigning a real problem that GE is facing to program participants who must present their recommendations to Jeff Immelt. Besides programs and courses for management development GE also holds seminars to better understand customer expectations and leadership conferences designed specifically for African Americans, women, or Hispanic managers to discuss leading and learning.

A number of institutions in the United States and abroad provide executive education including Harvard, Stanford, Columbia, INSEAD, and IMD. There are several important trends in executive education. Leadership, entrepreneurship, and e-business are the most important topics in executive education programs. Programs directed at developing executives' understanding of global business issues and management of change are other important parts of executive development.[25] Many companies who compete in the global economy with a worldwide workforce are using a blended learning approach for management development (we discussed blended learning in Chapter 7). For example, Xerox Corporation's Emerging Leaders Program (ELP) is a five-month program that includes a two-hour program kickoff using web-based conferencing, e-modules that employees complete at their own pace, face-to-face meetings, online assessment, coaching, and mentoring.[26] Employees from North America and Europe have participated in ELP. Each session in the European ELP includes high-potential managers from 14 countries who work in different functions and speak different languages. The most challenging part of ELP involves working as a cross-functional, cross-cultural, geographically dispersed team to identify, plan, and begin a business project based on the strategic initiatives. Each team presents their results to vice presidents and executives at the conclusion of the program.

There is another trend in executive education: business schools or other educational institutions have begun offering companies in-house, custom programs to help managers gain real-world skills and study problems in real-world environments—without requiring the managers to disrupt their work by requiring them to travel to campus. These programs supplement formal courses from consultants or university faculty with other types of development activities. For example, Duke Corporate Education conducts custom programs for ArcelorMittal, which was formed by the merger of two steel companies.[27] One of the challenges the company faces is how to get its managers to understand the global challenges facing the steel industry. As a result, the program involves middle managers visiting steel plants in both mature and emerging markets to gain an understanding of the technology and management processes of a more established steel plant compared with a growing steel plant. The managers are asked to develop proposals for improving the growing plant, such as how to identify environmental problems and expanding health and safety features. The Haas School of Business at the University of California, Berkeley, worked with StatoilHydro, the Norwegian oil and gas company that focuses on preparing employees to work in different cultures. The program includes challenges such as working with contractors who may not have the employees or equipment to complete a project on time or learning to deal with local government officials.

Managers who attend the Center for Creative Leadership development program take psychological tests; receive feedback from managers, peers, and direct reports; participate in group-building activities (like adventure learning, discussed in Chapter 7); receive counseling; and set improvement goals and write development plans.[28]

Enrollment in executive education programs or MBA programs may be limited to managers or employees identified to have management potential. As a result, many companies also provide tuition reimbursement as a benefit for all employees to encourage them to develop. **Tuition reimbursement** refers to the practice of reimbursing

Tuition Reimbursement
The practice of reimbursing employees' costs for college and university courses and degree programs.

employees' costs for college and university courses and degree programs. Companies spend about $10 billion on tuition reimbursement for courses offered by nonprofit colleges and universities as well as for-profit universities like Capella University.[29] These courses include face-to-face classroom instruction, online learning, and blended learning. For example, United Technology's Employee Scholar Program allows employees to receive 100% tuition reimbursement of all educational costs including tuition, registration fees, and books. Courses do not have to be related to the employee's job. Employees receive three hours each week to study or attend class. Employees who earn a degree receive $10,000 of company stock. The company has paid more than $60 million for the program. About 15% of employees use the program.

EVIDENCE-BASED HR

The recession had a significant impact on the leadership skills at Blue Cross Blue Shield North of North Carolina. Managers were unprepared to achieve company goals or lead emerging business opportunities. As a result, the company initiated a management development program that was offered to all 600 formal leaders and emerging leaders. The program consisted of a customized curriculum focusing on all levels of management. Courses addressed competencies in supply chain management, goal setting, and process and metric management. The program included instructor-led training, e-learning, action learning teams, and learning labs. Action learning involved cross-functional project teams of five employees working on business issues identified by senior managers. The program resulted in the company reducing costs by more than $1 million reengineering work processes, and reducing turnover. The program also resulted in an 18% increase in internal promotions, a 29% increase in self-assessed performance, and quality scores that exceeded an 80% benchmark.

SOURCE: Based on "Blue Cross Blue Shield North of North Carolina," *T + D*, October 2010, p. 72.

ASSESSMENT

Assessment involves collecting information and providing feedback to employees about their behavior, communication style, or skills.[30] The employees, their peers, managers, and customers may provide information. Assessments are used for several reasons. First, assessment is most frequently used to identify employees with managerial potential and to measure current managers' strengths and weaknesses. Assessment is also used to identify managers with the potential to move into higher-level executive positions, and it can be used with work teams to identify the strengths and weaknesses of individual team members and the decision processes or communication styles that inhibit the team's productivity. Assessments can help employees understand their tendencies, needs, the type of work environment they prefer, and the type of work they might prefer to do.[31] This information, along with the performance evaluations they receive from the company, can help employees decide what type of development goals might be most appropriate for them (e.g., leadership position, increase scope of their current position).

Companies vary in the methods and the sources of information they use in developmental assessment. Many companies use employee performance evaluations. Companies with sophisticated development systems use psychological tests to measure employees' skills, interests, personality types, and communication styles. Self, peer, and managers' ratings of employees' interpersonal styles and behaviors may also be collected. Popular assessment tools include personality tests, assessment center performance appraisal, and 360-degree feedback.

LO 9-5
Relate how assessment of personality type, work behaviors, and job performance can be used for employee development.

Assessment
Collecting information and providing feedback to employees about their behavior, communication style, or skills.

Personality Tests and Inventories

Tests are used to determine if employees have the personality characteristics necessary to be successful in specific managerial jobs or jobs involving international assignments. Personality tests typically measure five major dimensions: extroversion, adjustment, agreeableness, conscientiousness, and inquisitiveness (see Table 6.3 in Chapter 6). For example, Carmeuse North America uses personality tests in its leadership development program. The personality tests for employees who have been identified as having high potential for top management positions will be used to guide employees into development activities including coaching and formal courses.[32] Starwood Vacation Ownership, a subsidiary of Starwood Hotels and Resorts, uses several assessment tools to determine if the top managers value the commercial success of the business as well as tolerance for ambiguity, the ability to create and communicate a business strategy, the ability to build business partnerships, and the ability to develop staff. The assessment identifies managers who are ready for international assignments, may not fit their current position, or need coaching to better understand the company culture.[33] CareSource, a Medicaid-managed care provider in Dayton, Ohio, has a defined process for identifying and developing employees who have the potential to be strong leaders and effective managers.[34] Assessment of fit with the organizational values and culture which emphasize serving the underserved, begins with the recruiting process. The company uses multiple assessment tools to evaluate managers' competencies (recall our discussion of competencies in Chapter 8, "Performance Management"). These assessments include the Myers-Briggs Type Indicator (discussed below), the Gallup's Strength Finder to identify managers' strengths and develop plans for using their strengths with their employee team, and the Leadership Practices Inventory, which provides managers with an idea of their leadership skills as evaluated by peers, their boss, and their own self-assessment, and is used to build a personal leadership development plan. Also twice a year, using the performance management system, they are evaluated on competencies and behavior that CareSource believes are characteristics of an effective leader and manager: a service orientation, organizational awareness, teamwork, communications, and organizational leadership. Based on the assessment results, managers with high leadership potential are encouraged to participate in a variety of development activities.

Myers-Briggs Type Inventory (MBTI)®
A personality assessment tool used for team building and leadership development that identifies employees' preferences for energy, information gathering, decision making, and lifestyle.

The Myers-Briggs Type Inventory (MBTI)® refers to an assessment that is based on Carl Jung's personality type theory. This theory emphasizes that we have a fundamental personality type that shapes and influences how we understand the world, process information, and socialize. The assessment determines which one of 16 personality types fits best. The 16 unique personality types are based on preferences for introversion (I) or extraversion (E), sensing (S) or intuition (N), thinking (T) or feeling (F), and judging (J) or perceiving (P). The assessment tool identifies individuals' preferences for energy (introversion versus extroversion), information gathering (sensing versus intuition), decision making (thinking versus feeling), and lifestyle (judging versus perceiving).[35] Each personality type has implications for work habits and interpersonal relationships. For example, individuals who are introverted, sensing, thinking, and judging (known as ISTJs) tend to be serious, quiet, practical, orderly, and logical. These persons can organize tasks, be decisive, and follow through on plans and goals. ISTJs have several weaknesses because they do not tend to use the opposite preferences: extroversion, intuition, feeling, and perceiving. These weaknesses include problems dealing with unexpected opportunities, appearing too task-oriented or impersonal to colleagues, and making overly quick decisions. Visit the website www.cpp.com for more information on the personality types.

Hallmark Cards has helped people express their feelings and celebrate important events and occasions for over one hundred years.[36] Hallmark executives want to change the company's culture from that of a manufacturing company focused on developing products to a consumer-based company focusing on engaging its key customers. It recognizes the importance of developing leaders that can view situations from different perspectives, provide support to each other and work together, inspire employees, and efficiently implement new ideas. To help make this cultural shift Hallmark Cards is using the MBTI to help managers increase their self-insight into how their actions and communications are perceived by other employees and managers as well as how they tend to interact in teams, and their work and leadership styles.

Hallmark Cards has realized several positive results from using the MBTI. The speed of managers' decision making and clarity of communications to employees have improved. There has been a noticeable improvement in employees feeling comfortable expressing their thoughts and managers communicating in ways that appeal to all employee types.

Assessment Center

At an **assessment center** multiple raters or evaluators (assessors) evaluate employees' performance on a number of exercises.[37] An assessment center is usually an off-site location such as a conference center. From 6 to 12 employees usually participate at one time. Assessment centers are primarily used to identify if employees have the personality characteristics, administrative skills, and interpersonal skills needed for managerial jobs. They are also increasingly being used to determine if employees have the necessary skills to work in teams.

The types of exercises used in assessment centers include leaderless group discussions, interviews, in-baskets, and role-plays.[38] In a **leaderless group discussion,** a team of five to seven employees is assigned a problem and must work together to solve it within a certain time period. The problem may involve buying and selling supplies, nominating a subordinate for an award, or assembling a product. In the **interview,** employees answer questions about their work and personal experiences, skill strengths and weaknesses, and career plans. An **in-basket** is a simulation of the administrative tasks of the manager's job. The exercise includes a variety of documents that may appear in the in-basket on a manager's desk. The participants read the materials and decide how to respond to them. Responses might include delegating tasks, scheduling meetings, writing replies, or completely ignoring the memo! **Role-plays** refer to the participant taking the part or role of a manager or other employee. For example, an assessment center participant may be asked to take the role of a manager who has to give a negative performance review to a subordinate. The participant is told about the subordinate's performance and is asked to prepare for and actually hold a 45-minute meeting with the subordinate to discuss the performance problems. The role of the subordinate is played by a manager or other member of the assessment center design team or company. The assessment center might also include interest and aptitude tests to evaluate an employee's vocabulary, general mental ability, and reasoning skills. Personality tests may be used to determine if employees can get along with others, their tolerance for ambiguity, and other traits related to success as a manager.

Assessment center exercises are designed to measure employees' administrative and interpersonal skills. Skills typically measured include leadership, oral and written communication, judgment, organizational ability, and stress tolerance. Table 9.4 shows an example of the skills measured by the assessment center. As we see, each

Assessment Center
A process in which multiple raters evaluate employees' performance on a number of exercises.

Leaderless Group Discussion
Process in which a team of five to seven employees solves an assigned problem together within a certain time period.

Interview
Employees are questioned about their work and personal experiences, skills, and career plans.

In-Basket
A simulation of the administrative tasks of a manager's job.

Role-Plays
A participant taking the part or role of a manager or other employee.

table 9.4

Examples of Skills Measured by Assessment Center Exercises

			EXERCISES		
	IN-BASKET	SCHEDULING EXERCISE	LEADERLESS GROUP DISCUSSION	PERSONALITY TEST	ROLE-PLAY
SKILLS					
Leadership (Dominance, coaching, influence, resourcefulness)	X		X	X	X
Problem solving (Judgment)	X	X	X		X
Interpersonal (Sensitivity, conflict resolution, cooperation, oral communication)			X	X	X
Administrative (Organizing, planning, written communications)	X	X	X		
Personal (Stress tolerance, confidence)			X	X	X

X indicates skill measured by exercise.

exercise gives participating employees the opportunity to demonstrate several different skills. For example, the exercise requiring scheduling to meet production demands evaluates employees' administrative and problem-solving ability. The leaderless group discussion measures interpersonal skills such as sensitivity toward others, stress tolerance, and oral communication skills.

Managers are usually used as assessors. The managers are trained to look for employee behaviors that are related to the skills that will be assessed. Typically, each assessor observes and records one or two employees' behaviors in each exercise. The assessors review their notes and rate each employee's level of skills (for example, 5 = high level of leadership skills, 1 = low level of leadership skills). After all employees have completed the exercises, the assessors discuss their observations of each employee. They compare their ratings and try to agree on each employee's rating for each of the skills.

As we mentioned in Chapter 6, research suggests that assessment center ratings are related to performance, salary level, and career advancement.[39] Assessment centers may also be useful for development because employees who participate in the process receive feedback regarding their attitudes, skill strengths, and weaknesses.[40] For example, Steelcase, the office furniture manufacturer based in Grand Rapids, Michigan, uses assessment centers for first-level managers.[41] The assessment center exercises include in-basket, interview simulation, and a timed scheduling exercise requiring participants to fill positions created by absences. Managers are also required to confront an employee on a performance issue, getting the employee to commit to improve. Because the exercises relate closely to what managers are required to do at work, feedback given to managers based on their performance in the assessment center can target specific skills or competencies that they need to be successful managers.

Performance Appraisals and 360-Degree Feedback Systems

As we mentioned in Chapter 8, **performance appraisal** is the process of measuring employees' performance. Performance appraisal information can be useful for employee development under certain conditions.[42] The appraisal system must tell employees specifically about their performance problems and how they can improve their performance. This includes providing a clear understanding of the differences between current performance and expected performance, identifying causes of the performance discrepancy, and developing action plans to improve performance. Managers must be trained in frequent performance feedback. Managers also need to monitor employees' progress in carrying out action plans.

Recall our discussion in Chapter 8 of how Just Born uses performance appraisals for evaluation and development.[43] The appraisal starts with a planning meeting between employee and manager. The strategic initiatives of the department are discussed along with the employee's role. The employee and manager agree on four personal objectives that will help the department reach its goals as well as key performance outcomes related to the employee's job description. Competencies the employee needs to reach the personal objectives are identified. The manager and employee jointly develop a plan for improving or learning the competencies. During the year, the manager and employee monitor the progress toward reaching the performance and personal objectives and achievement of the learning plan. Pay decisions made at the end of each year are based on the achievement of both performance and learning objectives.

A recent trend in performance appraisals for management development is the use of upward feedback and 360-degree feedback. **Upward feedback** refers to appraisal that involves collecting subordinates' evaluations of managers' behaviors or skills. The 360-degree feedback process is a special case of upward feedback. In **360-degree feedback systems,** employees' behaviors or skills are evaluated not only by subordinates but by peers, customers, their bosses, and themselves. The raters complete a questionnaire asking them to rate the person on a number of different dimensions. Table 9.5 provides an example of the types of skills related to management success that are rated in a 360-degree feedback questionnaire. Typically, raters are asked to assess the manager's strength in a particular item or whether development is needed. Raters may also be asked to identify how frequently they observe a competency or skill (e.g., always, sometimes, seldom, never).

The results of a 360-degree feedback system show how the manager was rated on each item. The results also show how self-evaluations differ from evaluations from the other raters. Typically managers review their results, seek clarification from the raters, and set specific development goals based on the strengths and weaknesses identified.[44] Table 9.6 shows the type of activities involved in using 360-degree feedback for development.[45]

The benefits of 360-degree feedback include collecting multiple perspectives of managers' performance, allowing employees to compare their own personal evaluations with the views of others, and formalizing communications about behaviors and skills ratings between employees and their internal and external customers. Several studies have shown that performance improves and behavior changes as a result of participating in upward feedback and 360-degree feedback systems.[46] The most change occurs in individuals who receive lower ratings from others than they gave themselves (overraters).

Potential limitations of 360-degree feedback include the time demands placed on the raters to complete the evaluations, managers seeking to identify and punish raters who provided negative information, the need to have a facilitator help interpret results, and companies' failure to provide ways that managers can act on the feedback they receive (development planning, meeting with raters, taking courses).

Performance Appraisal
The process through which an organization gets information on how well an employee is doing his or her job.

Upward Feedback
A performance appraisal process for managers that includes subordinates' evaluations.

360-Degree Feedback Systems
A performance appraisal system for managers that includes evaluations from a wide range of persons who interact with the manager. The process includes self-evaluations as well as evaluations from the manager's boss, subordinates, peers, and customers.

table 9.5

Skills Related to Managerial Success

Resourcefulness	Can think strategically, engage in flexible problem solving, and work effectively with higher management.
Doing whatever it takes	Has perseverance and focus in the face of obstacles.
Being a quick study	Quickly masters new technical and business knowledge.
Building and mending relationships	Knows how to build and maintain working relationships with co-workers and external parties.
Leading subordinates	Delegates to subordinates effectively, broadens their opportunities, and acts with fairness toward them.
Compassion and sensitivity	Shows genuine interest in others and sensitivity to subordinates' needs.
Straightforwardness and composure	Is honorable and steadfast.
Setting a developmental climate	Provides a challenging climate to encourage subordinates' development.
Confronting problem subordinates	Acts decisively and fairly when dealing with problem subordinates.
Team orientation	Accomplishes tasks through managing others.
Balance between personal life and work	Balances work priorities with personal life so that neither is neglected.
Decisiveness	Prefers quick and approximate actions to slow and precise ones in many management situations.
Self-awareness	Has an accurate picture of strengths and weaknesses and is willing to improve.
Hiring talented staff	Hires talented people for the team.
Putting people at ease	Displays warmth and a good sense of humor.
Acting with flexibility	Can behave in ways that are often seen as opposites.

SOURCE: Adapted with permission from C. D. McCauley, M. M. Lombardo, and C. J. Usher, "Diagnosing Management Development Needs: An Instrument Based on How Managers Develop," *Journal of Management* 15 (1989), pp. 389–403.

table 9.6

Activities in Using 360-Degree Feedback for Development

1. **Understand strengths and weaknesses.**
   Review ratings for strengths and weaknesses.
   Identify skills or behaviors where self and others' (manager, peer, customer) ratings agree and disagree.
2. **Identify a development goal.**
   Choose a skill or behavior to develop.
   Set a clear, specific goal with a specified outcome.
3. **Identify a process for recognizing goal accomplishment.**
4. **Identify strategies for reaching the development goal.**
   Establish strategies such as reading, job experiences, courses, and relationships.
   Establish strategies for receiving feedback on progress.
   Establish strategies for reinforcing the new skill or behavior.

In effective 360-degree feedback systems, reliable or consistent ratings are provided, raters' confidentiality is maintained, the behaviors or skills assessed are job-related (valid), the system is easy to use, and managers receive and act on the feedback.[47]

Technology allows 360-degree questionnaires to be delivered to the raters via their personal computers. This increases the number of completed questionnaires returned, makes it easier to process the information, and speeds feedback reports to managers.

Regardless of the assessment method used, the information must be shared with the employee for development to occur. Along with assessment information, the employee needs suggestions for correcting skill weaknesses and using skills already learned. These suggestions might be to participate in training courses or develop skills through new job experiences. Based on the assessment information and available development opportunities, employees should develop action plans to guide their self-improvement efforts.

At AlliedBarton Security Systems, its 360-degree feedback report maps onto the company's core values and what it calls its Leadership Non-Negotiables.[48] The process is linked to an online talent tool kit which gives managers leadership tips based on their 360-degree feedback. Capital One has developed an effective 360-degree feedback system.[49] Capitol One, a consumer credit company, has included a number of features in its 360-degree feedback system to minimize the chance that the ratings will be used as ways to get back at an employee or turned into popularity contests. The 360-degree assessments are based on the company's competency model, so raters are asked for specific feedback on a competency area. Rather than a lengthy form that places a large burden on raters to assess many different competencies, Capital One's assessment asks the raters to concentrate on three or four strengths or development opportunities. It also seeks comments rather than limiting raters to merely circling numbers corresponding to how much of each competency the employee has demonstrated. These comments often provide specific information about what aspect of a competency needs to be developed or identifies work situations in which a competency needs to be improved. This comment system helps tailor development activities to fit competency development. To increase the chances that the assessment will result in change, the feedback from the 360-degree assessment is linked to development plans, and the company offers coaching and training to help employees strengthen their competencies. Employees are encouraged to share feedback with their co-workers. This creates a work environment based on honest and open feedback that helps employees personally grow.

● The Rainforest Alliance Certified seal of approval ensures that goods and services were produced in compliance with strict guidelines protecting the environment, wildlife, workers, and local communities.

JOB EXPERIENCES

Most employee development occurs through **job experiences**:[50] relationships, problems, demands, tasks, or other features that employees face in their jobs. A major assumption of using job experiences for employee development is that development is most likely to occur when there is a mismatch between the employee's skills and past experiences and the skills required for the job. To succeed in their jobs, employees must stretch their skills—that is, they are forced to learn new skills, apply their skills and knowledge in a new way, and master new experiences.[51] New job assignments help take advantage of employees' existing skills, experiences, and contacts, while helping them develop new ones.[52] General Electric uses experienced managers to

LO 9-6
Explain how job experiences can be used for skill development.

Job Experiences
The relationships, problems, demands, tasks, and other features that employees face in their jobs.

integrate newly acquired companies. The Rainforest Alliance, an international non-profit organization with 265 employees that helps product makers employ sustainable land practices, is challenged by quick growth (it has doubled in size since 2003) and the need it created to identify and develop managerial staff.[53] The Rainforest Alliance gives many junior employees the chance to lead research and other initiatives and, if they are successful, promotes them to manage the initiatives. For example, one employee who is now the coordinator of a new climate initiative, started with the company as an administrative assistant, but she was asked to take on more responsibilities, including researching climate change. Junior employees also can take part in internship programs in foreign offices to learn more about the organization and work on the "front lines" in implementing sustainable land practices.

Most of what we know about development through job experiences comes from a series of studies conducted by the Center for Creative Leadership.[54] Executives were asked to identify key career events that made a difference in their managerial styles and the lessons they learned from these experiences. The key events included those involving the job assignment (such as fixing a failing operation), those involving interpersonal relationships (getting along with supervisors), and the specific type of transition required (situations in which the executive did not have the necessary background). The job demands and what employees can learn from them are shown in Table 9.7.

One concern in the use of demanding job experiences for employee development is whether they are viewed as positive or negative stressors. Job experiences that are seen as positive stressors challenge employees to stimulate learning. Job challenges viewed as negative stressors create high levels of harmful stress for employees exposed to them. Recent research findings suggest that all of the job demands, with the exception of obstacles, are related to learning.[55] Managers reported that obstacles and job demands related to creating change were more likely to lead to negative stress than the other job demands. This suggests that companies should carefully weigh the potential negative consequences before placing employees in development assignments involving obstacles or creating change.

Although the research on development through job experiences has focused on executives and managers, line employees can also learn from job experiences. As we noted earlier, for a work team to be successful, its members now need the kinds of skills that only managers were once thought to need (such as dealing directly with customers, analyzing data to determine product quality, and resolving conflict among team members). Besides the development that occurs when a team is formed, employees can further develop their skills by switching work roles within the team.

Figure 9.4 shows the various ways that job experiences can be used for employee development. These include enlarging the current job, job rotation, transfers, promotions, downward moves, and temporary assignments. For companies with global operations (multinationals), it is not uncommon for employee development to involve international assignments that require frequent travel or relocation.

Enlarging the Current Job

Job Enlargement
Adding challenges or new responsibilities to an employee's current job.

Job enlargement refers to adding challenges or new responsibilities to employees' current jobs. This could include special project assignments, switching roles within a work team, or researching new ways to serve clients and customers. For example, an engineering employee may join a task force developing new career paths for technical employees. Through this project work, the engineer may lead certain aspects of career

table 9.7

Job Demands and the Lessons Employees Learn from Them

Making transitions	*Unfamiliar responsibilities:* The manager must handle responsibilities that are new, very different, or much broader than previous ones. *Proving yourself:* The manager has added pressure to show others she can handle the job.
Creating change	*Developing new directions:* The manager is responsible for starting something new in the organization, making strategic changes in the business, carrying out a reorganization, or responding to rapid changes in the business environment. *Inherited problems:* The manager has to fix problems created by a former incumbent or take over problem employees. *Reduction decisions:* Decisions about shutting down operations or staff reductions have to be made. *Problems with employees:* Employees lack adequate experience, are incompetent, or are resistant.
Having high level of responsibility	*High stakes:* Clear deadlines, pressure from senior managers, high visibility, and responsibility for key decisions make success or failure in this job clearly evident. *Managing business diversity:* The scope of the job is large with responsibilities for multiple functions, groups, products, customers, or markets. *Job overload:* The sheer size of the job requires a large investment of time and energy. *Handling external pressure:* External factors that affect the business (e.g., negotiating with unions or government agencies; working in a foreign culture; coping with serious community problems) must be dealt with.
Being involved in nonauthority relationships	*Influencing without authority:* Getting the job done requires influencing peers, higher management, external parties, or other key people over whom the manager has no direct authority.
Facing obstacles	*Adverse business conditions:* The business unit or product line faces financial problems or difficult economic conditions. *Lack of top management support:* Senior management is reluctant to provide direction, support, or resources for current work or new projects. *Lack of personal support:* The manager is excluded from key networks and gets little support and encouragement from others. *Difficult boss:* The manager's opinions or management style differs from those of the boss, or the boss has major shortcomings.

SOURCE: C. D. McCauley, L. J. Eastman, and J. Ohlott, "Linking Management Selection and Development through Stretch Assignments," *Human Resource Management* 84 (1995), pp. 93–115. Copyright © 1995 Wiley Periodicals, Inc., a Wiley Company.

path development (such as reviewing the company's career development process). As a result, the engineer not only learns about the company's career development system, but uses leadership and organizational skills to help the task force reach its goals. Some companies are enlarging jobs by giving two managers the same responsibilities and job title and allowing them to divide the work (two-in-a-box).[56] This helps managers learn from a more experienced employee; helps companies fill jobs that require multiple skills; and, for positions requiring extensive travel, ensures that one employee is always on site to deal with work-related issues. For example, at Cisco Systems, the head of the Cisco routing group, who was trained as an engineer but now works in business development, shared a job with an engineer. Each employee was exposed to the other's skills, which has helped both perform their jobs better.

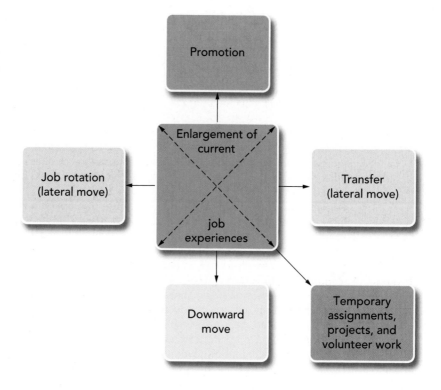

figure 9.4

How Job Experiences Are Used for Employee Development

Job Rotation

Job Rotation

The process of systematically moving a single individual from one job to another over the course of time. The job assignments may be in various functional areas of the company or movement may be between jobs in a single functional area or department.

Job rotation gives employees a series of job assignments in various functional areas of the company or movement among jobs in a single functional area or department. Cianbro Corporation, a construction company, uses a rotational program for new hires that exposes them to estimating, engineering, and field experience.[57] The Financial Department provides a program that includes rotations through field assignments, business unit assignments, and a corporate rotation. At the senior level, top talent are rotated to provide them with the exposure and experiences they need to succeed in senior management positions in the company. India-based Tata Consultancy Services job rotation program sends native employees to operations in China, Hungary, and South America.[58] The program helps the company have skilled employees who are prepared to work in any of the company's offices in 42 countries. Employees also gain an understanding of the culture of the country they work in. It also helps improve customer service because the company can draw on the strength of its entire workforce, rather than just relying on employees who are located close to the customer. The assignments typically last 18 to 24 months, involving learning from both the customers and the local employees based at the location. After the assignment is completed, the employee usually works on the same kinds of projects they worked on in the overseas assignment, which helps transfer the knowledge gained to their home operations.

Job rotation helps employees gain an overall appreciation of the company's goals, increases their understanding of different company functions, develops a network of contacts, and improves problem-solving and decision-making skills.[59] For example, Sanofi-Aventis Pharmaceuticals encourages high performing sales professionals to take on a temporary project or assignment with the Commercial Training Department to determine if they are interested in a training specialist role.[60] The length of the project assignments vary from a few days to several weeks depending on the needs of the employee and training unit. Sales professionals who accept a full-time training positions rotate to another role in the corporate office in two to three years (such as Marketing), go back to the field in a different sales unit, or accept a promotion to the district sales manager position. Job rotation has also been shown to be related to skill acquisition, salary growth, and promotion rates. But there are several potential problems with job rotation for both the employee and the work unit. The rotation may create a short-term perspective on problems and solutions in rotating employees and their peers. Employees' satisfaction and motivation may be adversely affected because they find it difficult to develop functional specialties and they don't spend enough time in one position to receive a challenging assignment. Productivity losses and workload increases may be experienced by both the department gaining a rotating employee and the department losing the employee due to training demands and loss of a resource.

Transfers, Promotions, and Downward Moves

Upward, lateral, and downward mobility is available for development purposes in most companies.[61] In a **transfer,** an employee is assigned a job in a different area of the company. Transfers do not necessarily increase job responsibilities or compensation. They are likely lateral moves (a move to a job with similar responsibilities). **Promotions** are advancements into positions with greater challenges, more responsibility, and more authority than in the previous job. Promotions usually include pay increases.

Transfers may involve relocation within the United States or to another country. This can be stressful not only because the employee's work role changes, but if the employee is in a two-career family, the spouse must find new employment. Also, the family has to join a new community. Transfers disrupt employees' daily lives, interpersonal relationships, and work habits.[62] People have to find new housing, shopping, health care, and leisure facilities, and they may be many miles from the emotional support of friends and family. They also have to learn a new set of work norms and procedures; they must develop interpersonal relationships with their new managers and peers; and they are expected to be as productive in their new jobs as they were in their old jobs even though they may know little about the products, services, processes, or employees for whom they are responsible.

Because transfers can provoke anxiety, many companies have difficulty getting employees to accept them. Research has identified the employee characteristics associated with a willingness to accept transfers:[63] high career ambitions, a belief that one's future with the company is promising, and a belief that accepting a transfer is necessary for success in the company. Employees who are not married and not active in the community are generally most willing to accept transfers. Among married employees, the spouse's willingness to move is the most important influence on whether an employee will accept a transfer.

A **downward move** occurs when an employee is given less responsibility and authority.[64] This may involve a move to another position at the same level (lateral demotion), a temporary cross-functional move, or a demotion because of poor performance. Temporary cross-functional moves to lower-level positions, which give employees experience working in different functional areas, are most frequently used for employee development. For example, engineers who want to move into management often take lower-level positions (like shift supervisor) to develop their management skills.

Transfer
The movement of an employee to a different job assignment in a different area of the company.

Promotions
Advancement into positions with greater challenge, more responsibility, and more authority than the employee's previous job.

Downward Move
A job change involving a reduction in an employee's level of responsibility and authority.

Because of the psychological and tangible rewards of promotions (such as increased feelings of self-worth, salary, and status in the company), employees are more willing to accept promotions than lateral or downward moves. Promotions are more readily available when a company is profitable and growing. When a company is restructuring or experiencing stable or declining profits'—especially if numerous employees are interested in promotions and the company tends to rely on the external labor market to staff higher-level positions—promotion opportunities may be limited.[65]

Unfortunately, many employees have difficulty associating transfers and downward moves with development. They see them as punishments rather than as opportunities to develop skills that will help them achieve long-term success with the company. Many employees decide to leave a company rather than accept a transfer. Companies need to successfully manage transfers not only because of the costs of replacing employees but because of the costs directly associated with them. For example, GTE spends approximately $60 million a year on home purchases and other relocation costs such as temporary housing and relocation allowances.[66] One challenge companies face is learning how to use transfers and downward moves as development opportunities—convincing employees that accepting these opportunities will result in long-term benefits for them.

To ensure that employees accept transfers, promotions, and downward moves as development opportunities, companies can provide

- Information about the content, challenges, and potential benefits of the new job and location.
- Involvement in the transfer decision by sending the employees to preview the new location and giving them information about the community.
- Clear performance objectives and early feedback about their job performance.
- A host at the new location to help them adjust to the new community and workplace.
- Information about how the job opportunity will affect their income, taxes, mortgage payments, and other expenses.
- Reimbursement and assistance in selling and purchasing or renting a place to live.
- An orientation program for the new location and job.
- Information on how the new job experiences will support the employee's career plans.
- Assistance for dependent family members, including identifying schools and child care and elder care options.
- Help for the spouse in identifying and marketing skills and finding employment.[67]

Externship
When a company allows an employee to take a full-time operational role at another company.

Externship refers to a company allowing employees to take a full-time operational role at another company. Mercer Management, a consulting firm, uses externship to develop employees interested in gaining experience in a specific industry.[68] Mercer Management promises to employ the externs after their assignments end. For example, one employee who had been a Mercer consultant became a vice president of Internet services for Binney & Smith, the maker of Crayola crayons. He had served as a consultant on an Internet project for Binney & Smith. But he wanted to actually implement his recommendations rather than just give them to the client and move on to another project—so he started working at Binney & Smith. He remains on Mercer Management's payroll, though his salary comes from Binney & Smith. Mercer believes that employees who participate in the externship program will remain committed to the company because they have had the opportunity to learn and grow professionally and have not had to disrupt their personal and professional lives with a job search. Although externships give employees other employment options and some employees will leave, Mercer believes that it not only is a good development strategy but also helps in recruitment. The externship program signals to potential employees that Mercer is creative and flexible with its employees.

Temporary Assignments, Projects, Volunteer Work, and Sabbaticals

Employee exchange is one type of temporary assignment. Procter & Gamble (P&G) and Google have started to swap employees.[69] Employees from the two companies participate in each other's training programs and attend meetings where business plans are discussed. Both companies hope to benefit from the employee swap. Procter & Gamble is trying to increase its understanding of how to market laundry detergent, toilet paper, and skin cream products to a new generation of consumers who spend more time online than watching television. Google wants to gain more ad revenue by persuading companies to shift from showcasing their brands on television to video-sharing sites such as YouTube. The idea of the employee swap occurred when P&G recognized that a switch to a smaller Tide laundry soap bottle with a more concentrated formula did not include an online campaign, where buyers could find answers as to why the bottle decreased in size. Employees of both companies have benefited from the swap. Google employees have learned that Tide's bright orange packaging is a critical part of the brand and have adopted P&G's marketing language. P&G employees have recognized that online ad campaigns can increase brand awareness—even for products such as diapers that are not purchased online. P&G has invited mommy-bloggers to visit their baby division to better understand how their diapers can meet their needs.

Temporary assignments can include a **sabbatical** (a leave of absence from the company to renew or develop skills). Employees on sabbatical often receive full pay and benefits. Sabbaticals let employees get away from the day-to-day stresses of their jobs and acquire new skills and perspectives. Sabbaticals also allow employees more time for personal pursuits such as writing a book or spending more time with young children. Sabbaticals are common in a variety of industries ranging from consulting firms to the fast-food industry.[70] Fallon Worldwide, an advertising agency, offers a program called Dreamcatchers to staff members who want to work on a project or travel.[71] Dreamcatchers was developed to help the agency avoid having employees burn out and lose their creative edge. Employees have taken time off to write novels, kayak, and motorcycle through the Alps. Fallon Worldwide matches employee contributions of up to $1,000 annually for two years and offers up to two extra weeks of paid vacation. The agency partners believe that the program has helped in the retention of key employees and the recruiting of new ones. The partners also believe that the program helps recharge employees' creativity, which is key for employees to do their best work for customers.

Volunteer assignments can also be used for development. Volunteer assignments may give employees opportunities to manage change, teach, have a high level of responsibility, and be exposed to other job demands shown earlier in Table 9.7. For General Mills, volunteer assignments and involvement with community projects is one of the ways the company lives its corporate values.[72] Employees work in a wide variety of charities, with duties ranging from serving meals to the homeless, painting child care center rooms, or serving as corporate board members. Besides providing valuable services to community organizations, General Mills believes volunteer assignments help employees improve team relationships and develop leadership and strategic thinking skills.

Sabbatical
A leave of absence from the company to renew or develop skills.

INTERPERSONAL RELATIONSHIPS

LO 9-7
Develop successful
mentoring programs.

Employees can also develop skills and increase their knowledge about the company and its customers by interacting with a more experienced organization member. Mentoring and coaching are two types of interpersonal relationships that are used to develop employees.

Mentoring

Mentor
An experienced, productive senior employee who helps develop a less experienced employee.

A **mentor** is an experienced, productive senior employee who helps develop a less experienced employee (the protégé). Because of the lack of potential mentors and recognizing that employees can benefit from relationships with peers and colleagues some companies have initiated and supported group and peer mentoring. In **group mentoring programs,** a successful senior employee is paired with a group of four to six less experienced protégés. One potential advantage of peer mentoring is that protégés are encouraged to learn from each other as well as from a more experienced senior employee. Also, group mentoring acknowledges the reality that it is difficult for one mentor to provide an employee with all the guidance and support they need. Group mentoring provides a development network for employees: a small group an employee can use for mentoring support and also have an interest in their learning and development. The leader helps protégés understand the organization, guides them in analyzing their experiences, and helps them clarify career directions. Each member of the group may complete specific assignments, or the group may work together on a problem or issue.[73]

Group Mentoring Program
A program pairing a successful senior employee with a group of four to six less experienced protégés.

Most mentoring relationships develop informally as a result of interests or values shared by the mentor and protégé. Research suggests that employees with certain personality characteristics (like emotional stability, the ability to adapt their behavior based on the situation, and high needs for power and achievement) are most likely to seek a mentor and be an attractive protégé for a mentor.[74] Mentoring relationships can also develop as part of a formal mentoring program, that is, a planned company effort to bring together successful senior employees with less experienced employees. Table 9.8 shows examples of how companies are using formal mentoring programs. Mentoring programs have many important purposes including socializing new employees, developing managers, and providing opportunities for women and minorities to share experiences and gain the exposure and skills needed to move into management positions.

Developing Successful Mentoring Programs. One major advantage of formalized mentoring programs is that they ensure access to mentors for all employees, regardless of gender or race. An additional advantage is that participants in the mentoring relationship know what is expected of them.[75] One limitation of formal mentoring programs is that mentors may not be able to provide counseling and coaching in a relationship that has been artificially created.[76] To overcome this limitation, it is important that mentors and protégés spend time discussing work styles, their personalities, and their backgrounds, which helps build the trust needed for both parties to be comfortable with their relationship.[77] Toshiba America Medical Systems doesn't have a formal mentoring program. However, Toshiba encourages informal mentoring from the first day employees are hired. Both managers and HR business partners take the time to help new employees meet their colleagues and show them around the workplace.[78]

Table 9.9 presents the characteristics of a successful formal mentoring program. Mentors should be chosen based on interpersonal and technical skills. They also need to be trained.[79] For mentors, protégés, and the company to get the most out of mentoring, tools and support are needed.[80] For example, at the University of New Mexico

table 9.8

Examples of Mentoring Programs

SCC Soft Computer—Every new hire is assigned a mentor. The mentor creates a personalized learning passport including the new employee's photo and identifies the competency areas the new hire needs to develop. After identifying the competency the mentor is responsible for, the mentor follows up with the employee. When the employee's personal learning passport is complete they are eligible for advancement.

Microsoft—The mentoring program includes career development mentoring and peer mentoring. Career development mentoring focuses on career and professional development through structured, year-long cross-group mentoring. Peer mentoring is less structured and focuses on transfer of work-related knowledge among members of the same work team.

The Sacramento Municipal Utility District (SMUD)—Includes a one-year mentoring program in its Building Leadership Talent program. The program matches protégés with mentors who are outside their business unit. SMUD provides an orientation and half-day session for the mentors that includes skill building, role-playing, a process model for effective mentoring, templates for documenting goals and progress toward meeting the goals, skill practice, and web-based training.

Sodexo—Peer-to-peer mentoring is a program managed directly by Sodexo's Network Groups. Networks are organized around a common dimension of diversity and are created by employees who want to raise awareness in Sodexo of their identity groups. They include network groups based on national orientation, race, sexual preference, military service, and intergenerations. The Spirit of Mentoring Bridge Programs are informal divisional pairings in which newly hired and front-line managers come together to expand professional development opportunities and increase the depth and diversity of Sodexo's management.

Agilent Technologies—The Next Generation Leadership Program accelerates development for top talent by matching senior executives with high potential.

McDonald's—Offers a virtual online mentoring program that employees can use to build their skill sets and develop relationships.

SOURCES: Based on www.sodexousa.com, website for Sodexo, Inc.; "Best Practices and Outstanding Initiatives," *Training*, January/February 2011, pp. 94–98; "Training Top 125," *Training*, January/February 2011, pp. 54–93: R. Emelo, "Conversations with Mentoring Leaders," *T + D*, June 2011, pp. 32–37.

Hospitals (UNMH) a "Mentorship Program Partnering Guide" provides information on the mentor and protégé roles, monthly meeting structure, and ideas for development activities and how to build relationships. Yum! Brands provides goal sheets, discussion guides, websites, books, and self-guided e-learning modules.

A key to successful mentoring programs is that the mentor and protégé are well-matched and can interact with each other face-to-face or virtually using video-conferencing. American Fidelity Assurance Company (AFA) created a specialized mentoring program for developing leaders.[81] Current leaders serve as mentors but also can serve as protégés. In the program participants are paired based on assessment results and protégé goals and objectives. Paying attention to mentor–protégé pairings has paid off: 88% of protégés indicated that their mentors played a key role in reaching their goals and 88% plan to continue the mentoring relationship. At UNMH quarterly "Speed Networking" sessions are an important part of the mentoring program. These sessions provide the opportunity for up to 15 mentors to meet and interact with 15 protégés. These sessions provide the protégé with exposure to the guidance and tips of multiple leaders and the opportunity to network. Microsoft provides an online portal that provides assistance in matching mentors and protégés and a social networking function that helps employees connect with each other.

table 9.9

Characteristics of Successful Formal Mentoring Programs

1. Mentor and protégé participation is voluntary. Relationship can be ended at any time without fear of punishment.
2. The mentor–protégé matching process does not limit the ability of informal relationships to develop. For example, a mentor pool can be established to allow protégés to choose from a variety of qualified mentors.
3. Mentors are chosen on the basis of their past record in developing employees, willingness to serve as a mentor, and evidence of positive coaching, communication, and listening skills.
4. Mentor–protégé matching is based on how the mentor's skills can help meet the protégé's needs.
5. The purpose of the program is clearly understood. Projects and activities that the mentor and protégé are expected to complete are specified.
6. The length of the program is specified. Mentor and protégé are encouraged to pursue the relationship beyond the formal period.
7. A minimum level of contact between the mentor and protégé is specified. Mentors and protégés need to determine when they will meet, how often, and how they will communicate outside the meetings.
8. Protégés are encouraged to contact one another to discuss problems and share successes.
9. The mentor program is evaluated. Interviews with mentors and protégés give immediate feedback regarding specific areas of dissatisfaction. Surveys gather more detailed information regarding benefits received from participating in the program.
10. Employee development is rewarded, which signals to managers that mentoring and other development activities are worth their time and effort.

Web-based matching systems are also available to help match mentors and protégés. Software is also available to track mentors' and protégés' work, help build development plans, and schedule mentor and protégé meetings.[82] For example, at SAIC, a company specializing in technology solutions, a web-based tool is used to provide online forms, make calendar appointments, set goals for mentoring relationships, and outline an action plan to ensure that protégé needs are discussed.

Career Support
Coaching, protection, sponsorship, and providing challenging assignments, exposure, and visibility.

Benefits of Mentoring Relationships. Both mentors and protégés can benefit from a mentoring relationship. Research suggests that mentors provide career and psychosocial support to their protégés. **Career support** includes coaching, protection, sponsorship, and providing challenging assignments, exposure, and visibility. **Psychosocial support** includes serving as a friend and a role model, providing positive regard and acceptance, and creating an outlet for the protégé to talk about anxieties and fears. Additional benefits for the protégé include higher rates of promotion, higher salaries, and greater organizational influence.[83]

Psychosocial Support
Serving as a friend and role model, providing positive regard and acceptance, and creating an outlet for a protégé to talk about anxieties and fears.

Mentoring relationships provide opportunities for mentors to develop their interpersonal skills and increase their feelings of self-esteem and worth to the organization. For individuals in technical fields such as engineering or health services, the protégé may help them gain knowledge about important new scientific developments in their field (and therefore prevent them from becoming technically obsolete). Tamara Trummer summarizes some of the benefits she gained from mentoring relationships: "I found mentors in two of my earlier companies, both male and female managers who 'taught me the ropes' in an informal sense by giving me inside information about the company, certain executives—and even such practical things as how to conduct business travel and handle an expense account."[84] One mentor arranged for her to travel from the remote manufacturing plant where she worked to the corporate office and set up meetings to meet key employees she would have to work with. Her mentors have also included co-workers, peers, and even subordinates who have taught her computer software skills. As a result of her positive experiences as a protégé Trummer now mentors others employees.

Mentoring can also occur between mentors and protégés from different organizations and can allow small business owners access to experienced mentors they might not otherwise meet.[85] Websites such as MicroMentor are available to help small business owners find online mentors. For example, Sturdy McKee wanted to expand his physical therapy practice but needed help understanding financial statements so he could plan the growth of his business and seek outside funding. Using MicroMentor, he completed a personal profile, listed his goals, and then searched potential mentor profiles. Sturdy and his mentor had weekly phone conversations discussing the basics of balance sheets and financial vocabulary. As a result of his positive experience, Sturdy has mentored other entrepreneurs seeking help on how to start a physical therapy practice.

The "Competing through Sustainability" box shows how mentoring programs can lead to value for different company stakeholders.

Coaching

A **coach** is a peer or manager who works with an employee to motivate him, help him develop skills, and provide reinforcement and feedback. There are three roles that a coach can play.[86] The main reasons coaches are used include developing high-potential managers, acting as a sounding board for managers, or specifically trying to change behaviors that are making managers ineffective.[87] Part of coaching may be one-on-one with an employee (such as giving feedback). Another role is to help employees learn for themselves. This involves helping them find experts who can assist them with their concerns and teaching them how to obtain feedback from others. Third, coaching may involve providing resources such as mentors, courses, or job experiences that the employee may not be able to gain access to without the coach's help. Becton Dickinson uses peer coaching as part of its leadership development programs.[88] The topics discussed include job challenges as a development method, ambiguity as a change agent, and how to influence others. Evaluation of the peer coaching has found that coaches gain confidence in their abilities and participants learn about the topics discussed. Wachovia Corporation, a financial services company, has an executive coaching program that uses both internal and external coaches.[89] Participants in the executive leadership development program receive 360-degree assessments that they take to their internal coaches, who are from a different division in the company. Together the manager and coach review the assessment results and agree on an action plan. The coaches are trained how to coach and understand the positive and negative aspects of 360-degree feedback. Research suggests that coaching improves managers' use of 360-degree feedback by helping them set specific improvement goals and solicit ideas for improvement, which results in improved performance.[90]

PG&E, an energy company hired a coach to work with a skilled manager whose brash personality was hurting her relationships with her associates and her career.[91] The coach videotaped her as she role-played an actual clash that she had had with another manager over a new information system. During the confrontation (and the role-play) she was aloof, abrasive, cold, and condescending. The coach helped her

LO 9-8
Describe how to train managers to coach employees.

Coach
A peer or manager who works with an employee to motivate her, help her develop skills, and provide reinforcement and feedback.

COMPETING THROUGH SUSTAINABILITY

Mentoring Programs Have Potential to Pay Individual, Corporate, and Societal Dividends

A company's sustainability is determined by the extent to which it satisfies the needs of shareholders, customers, employees, community, and society. The Women's Alliance at Xerox, General Electric, and The Economical Insurance Group are using mentoring programs to help encourage women and minorities to move into management positions and develop management talent that can help sustain a business strategy.

The Women's Alliance (TWA) at Xerox is using electronic self-service mentor matching software to help women overcome one of the problems they face in establishing a mentoring relationship: finding a suitable mentor. Mentors and mentees both complete online profiles, which include information on their background and interests, areas of expertise, development needs (mentees), and what they hope to gain by participating in

the mentoring program. After completing the profile, a TWA mentee can use the search capability to locate a match from the pool of mentors. An e-mail is sent to the selected mentor, who reviews the mentee's profile and accepts or declines the invitation.

Top females at General Electric are assigned leadership roles within GE's Women's Network (GEWN) local and regional groups so they can get leadership experience. The women also have the opportunity to meet and talk with members of GE's senior management team by attending speaker seminars, workshops, and networking dinners. The network opportunities help the women form an ongoing relationship with a senior leader, which can develop into a mentoring relationship.

The Economical Insurance Group (TEIG), one of the largest property and casualty insurance groups in Canada, is focused

on women's leadership development. TEIG's women's leadership development program includes an instructor-led workshop focusing on the fundamentals of achievement, leadership, and legacy specific to women in the company. Following the workshop female leaders were invited to participate in the TEIG Women's Leadership Network, held quarterly. The network meetings use the company's virtual classroom to discuss business ideas and challenges unique to women and to share leadership experiences.

SOURCES: Based on A. Poe, "Establishing Positive Mentoring Relationships," *HR Magazine*, February 2002, pp. 62–69; H. Dolezalek, "Got High Potentials?" *Training* 44 (2007), pp. 18–22; B. Carvin, "The Great Mentor Match," *T + D*, January 2009, pp. 46–50; and L. Freifeld, "TEIG Locks In on Leadership," *Training*, January/February 2011, pp. 34–39.

see the limitations of her approach. She apologized to colleagues and listened to their ideas. Coaching helped this manager learn how to maintain her composure and focus on what is being said rather than on the person.

The best coaches should be empathetic, supportive, practical, and self-confident but not appear as someone who knows all the answers or wants to tell others what to do.[92] Employees who are going to be coached need to be open-minded and interested, not defensive, closed-minded, or concerned with their reputation. Both the coach and the employee to be coached take risks in the relationship. Coaches use their expertise and experiences to help an employee. Employees are vulnerable by honestly communicating about their weaknesses.

To develop coaching skills, training programs need to focus on four issues related to managers' reluctance to provide coaching.[93] First, managers may be reluctant to discuss performance issues even with a competent employee because they want to avoid confrontation. This is especially an issue when the manager is less of an expert than the employee. Second, managers may be better able to identify performance problems than to help employees solve them. Third, managers may also feel that the employee interprets coaching as criticism. Fourth, as companies downsize and operate with fewer employees, managers may feel that there is not enough time for coaching.

Special Issues in Employee Development
MELTING THE GLASS CEILING

A major development issue facing companies today is how to get women and minorities into upper-level management positions—how to break the **glass ceiling.** Surveys show that in Fortune 500 companies women represent less than 3% of CEOs and approximately 14% of executive officers.[94] Two-thirds of companies lack specific programs targeted at the needs of women leaders. Twenty-three percent of companies offer some activities or programs targeted to the needs of women. These activities include flexible scheduling, diversity recruiting, and coaching and mentoring. One of the dilemmas is that companies may be reluctant to treat women any differently than men from a leadership development perspective despite acknowledging that women lack executive sponsors or mentors, have insufficient experience, and need better work/life balance. The glass ceiling is a barrier to advancement to the higher levels of the organization. This barrier may be due to stereotypes or company systems that adversely affect the development of women or minorities.[95] The glass ceiling is likely caused by lack of access to training programs, appropriate developmental job experiences, and developmental relationships (such as mentoring).[96] Women and minorities often have trouble finding mentors because of their lack of access to the "old boy network," managers' preference to interact with other managers of similar status rather than with line employees, and intentional exclusion by managers who have negative stereotypes about women's and minorities' abilities, motivation, and job preferences.[97] Research has found no gender differences in access to job experiences involving transitions or creating change.[98] However, male managers receive significantly more assignments involving high levels of responsibility (high stakes, managing business diversity, handling external pressure) than female managers of similar ability and managerial level. Also, female managers report experiencing more challenge due to lack of personal support (a type of job demand considered to be an obstacle that has been found to relate to harmful stress) than male managers. Career encouragement from peers and senior managers does help women advance to the higher management levels.[99] Managers making developmental assignments need to carefully consider whether gender biases or stereotypes are influencing the types of assignments given to women versus men.

Also, the "Competing through Sustainability" box highlights how Xerox, General Electric, and TEIG are using networking and mentoring to melt the glass ceiling. Consider Safeway's efforts.[100] Safeway has 1,775 grocery stores in the United States and Canada. To meet the challenges of specialty grocers and big-box, low-price competitors such as Walmart and Target, and recognizing that 70% of its customers were women, Safeway took steps to help develop women for advancement into management. A women's initiative, Championing Change for Women: An Integrated Strategy, includes programs that focus on leadership development, mentoring, and work/life balance. Safeway typically promotes from within and has focused on the retail level as a source for potential managers through the company's Retail Leadership Development (RLD) program. Ninety percent of Safeway's 1,800 store

Glass Ceiling
A barrier to advancement to higher-level jobs in the company that adversely affects women and minorities. The barrier may be due to lack of access to training programs, development experiences, or relationships (e.g., mentoring).

managers moved up through the company's management ranks through the program, and all but 1 of the company's 10 division presidents began their careers working in one of the stores.

To help women and minorities achieve top-level management positions, the RLD was used to increase the number of women and minorities who complete the program. Those who complete the program are assigned to a store or an assistant manager position that can lead to corporate-level leadership positions. To help support women's efforts to gain leadership positions, Safeway ensures that women who work part-time and use flexible schedules have similar opportunities for coaching, advancement, and development as employees who are on traditional work schedules. The company also realized that frequent relocations did not work for some employees, especially women. As a result, rejecting a relocation to a different location is no longer considered a career-busting decision.

Safeway also provides a women's leadership network for women interested in advancing into management. The network sponsors events such as presentations at different company locations that highlight the success of Safeway women and provide learning opportunities. Executives who attend these presentations meet with women who have been identified as candidates for management positions and are targeted for development opportunities in stores. These discussions focus on the women's career interests, and the executives suggest job opportunities and encourage them to apply for positions that can help them advance to the next management level. Safeway's mentoring program emphasizes that a manager's first protégé should be a woman because of the lack of female mentors. Safeway's work/life balance program, which includes flextime, allows all women, regardless of their family status, to have a healthy balance between work and life. Safeway realizes that its managers are responsible for helping women reach management positions. As a result, all managers attend a Managing Diversity Workshop. Managers are evaluated on their success in meeting diversity goals. Managers who reach their targets can increase their pay bonus by 10%.

Safeway's women's initiative has been successful. Since 2000, the number of female store managers has increased by 42%. The number of women who have qualified for and completed the RLD program increased 31% over the past five years. A research report prepared by Lehman Brothers showed that the program increased the company's sales and earnings. Enhancing its reputation as an employer of choice for women and minorities, Safeway received the Catalyst Award, which is presented annually to outstanding companies that promote the career advancement of women and minorities. Table 9.10 provides recommendations for melting the glass ceiling and helping retain talented women.

table 9.10

Recommendations for Melting the Glass Ceiling

Make sure senior management supports and is involved in the program.
Make a business case for change.
Make the change public.
Gather data on problems causing the glass ceiling using task forces, focus groups, and questionnaires.
Create awareness of how gender attitudes affect the work environment.
Force accountability through reviews of promotion rates and assignment decisions.
Promote development for all employees.

SOURCE: Based on D. McCracken, "Winning the Talent War for Women," *Harvard Business Review,* November–December 2000, pp. 159–67.

SUCCESSION PLANNING

Many companies are losing sizable numbers of upper-level managers due to retirement and company restructurings that reduced the number of potential upper-level managers. They are finding that their middle managers are not ready to move into upper management positions due to skill weaknesses or lack of needed experience. This creates the need for succession planning. Succession planning refers to the process of identifying and tracking high-potential employees. **Succession planning** helps organizations in several different ways.[101] It requires senior management to systematically review leadership talent in the company. It ensures that top-level managerial talent is available. It provides a set of development experiences that managers must complete to be considered for top management positions; this avoids premature promotion of managers who are not ready for upper management ranks. Succession planning systems also help attract and retain managerial employees by providing them with development opportunities that they can complete if upper management is a career goal for them. **High-potential employees** are those the company believes are capable of being successful in higher-level managerial positions such as general manager of a strategic business unit, functional director (such as director of marketing), or chief executive officer (CEO).[102] High-potential employees typically complete an individual development program that involves education, executive mentoring and coaching, and rotation through job assignments. Job assignments are based on the successful career paths of the managers whom the high-potential employees are being prepared to replace. High-potential employees may also receive special assignments, such as making presentations and serving on committees and task forces.

Table 9.11 shows the process used to develop a succession plan. The first step is to identify what positions are included in the succession plan, such as all management positions or only certain levels of management. The second step is to identify which employees are part of the succession planning system. For example, in some companies only high-potential employees are included in the succession plan. Third, the company needs to identify how positions will be evaluated. For example, will the emphasis be on competencies needed for each position or on the experiences an individual needs

Succession Planning
The identification and tracking of high-potential employees capable of filling higher-level managerial positions.

High-Potential Employees
Employees the company believes are capable of being successful in high-level management positions.

1. Identify what positions are included in the plan.
2. Identify the employees who are included in the plan.
3. Develop standards to evaluate positions (e.g., competencies, desired experiences, desired knowledge, developmental value).
4. Determine how employee potential will be measured (e.g., current performance and potential performance).
5. Develop the succession planning review.
6. Link the succession planning system with other human resource systems, including training and development, compensation, performance management, and staffing systems.
7. Determine what feedback is provided to employees.
8. Measure the effectiveness of the succession plan.

table 9.11

The Process of Developing a Succession Plan

SOURCES: Based on W. Rothwell, "The Future of Succession Planning," *T + D*, September 2010, pp. 51–54; B. Dowell, "Succession Planning," in *Implementing Organizational Interventions*, ed. J. Hedge and E. Pulaskos (San Francisco: Jossey-Bass, 2002), pp. 78–109; R. Barnett and S. Davis, "Creating Greater Success in Succession Planning," *Advances in Developing Human Resources* 10 (2008), pp. 721–39.

to have before moving into the position? Fourth, the company should identify how employee potential will be measured. That is, will employees' performance in their current jobs as well as ratings of potential be used? Will employees' position interests and career goals be considered? Fifth, the succession planning review process needs to be developed. Typically, succession planning reviews first involve employees' managers and human resources. A talent review could also include an overall assessment of leadership talent in the company, an identification of high-potential employees, and a discussion of plans to keep key managers from leaving the company. Sixth, succession planning is dependent on other human resource systems, including compensation, training and development, and staffing. Incentives and bonuses may be linked to completion of development opportunities. Activities such as training courses, job experiences, mentors, and 360-degree feedback can be used to meet development needs. Companies need to make decisions such as will they fill an open management position internally with a less-experienced employee who will improve in the role over time, or will they hire a manager from outside the company who can immediately deliver results. Seventh, employees need to be provided with feedback on future moves, expected career paths, and development goals and experiences. Finally, the succession planning process needs to be evaluated. This includes identifying and measuring appropriate results outcomes (such as reduced time to fill manager positions, increased use of internal promotions) as well as collecting measures of satisfaction with the process (reaction outcomes) from employees and managers. Also, modifications that will be made to the succession planning process need to be identified, discussed, and implemented.

To prepare for the expected shortage of health care managers, Gunderson Lutheran Health System in La Crosse, Wisconsin, developed a succession planning process to identify and develop high-potential candidates in one of four leadership levels: physician executives, physician administrative leadership, administrative executives, and administrative leaders at the director level.[103] Selection of candidates was based on demonstrating a high level of competency in nine areas including operations, finance, strategic thinking, building partnerships and teams, staff development, change management, performance management, and leadership development. Candidates also needed to demonstrate an interest and willingness for promotion, to participate in a leadership assessment process to determine skill gaps and development needs, to receive development feedback and coaching to get a realistic view of current performance and develop skills and competencies for future positions, to accept assignments that provided development opportunities, and to invest the time and effort required to learn new skills and review their progress with their vice president or manager and a review group headed by the vice president of Operations and Human Resources. Behavioral interviews, 360-degree assessment, the Myers-Briggs Type Indicator, and assessments of values and leadership skills are used to identify individuals' strengths and development needs or gaps. Based on the assessment, individual development plans are discussed and agreed upon with the review group. Development plans are based on both the candidate's and organizational needs. The development plans include activities such as coaching, continuing education, mentoring, project assignments, committee appointments, job enlargement, job rotation, or cross-functional assignments. For example, projects have included work in developing an electronic medical record and assignments. New job experiences include moving an administrative director from the rehabilitation area into the human resources operation role for three years before moving into a larger role overseeing all hospital operations. These activities allow candidates to learn while the leadership team can evaluate how they perform when given increased responsibility and stretch assignments.

Gunderson measures the impact of development activities and the success of the succession planning process through performance and feedback from peers and colleagues. The review group studies annual progress. Sixty high-potential employees in all levels of leadership have been identified and their career paths discussed. Four high-potential directors have been promoted into chief roles and six high-potential managers into director roles. Nine high-potential managers and directors now have expanded roles.

One of the important issues in succession planning is deciding whether to tell employees if they are on or off the list of potential candidates for higher-level manager positions.[104] There are several advantages and disadvantages that companies need to consider. One advantage to making a succession planning list public or telling employees who are on the list is that they are more likely to stay with the company because they understand they likely will have new career opportunities. Another is that high-potential employees who are not interested in other positions can communicate their intentions. This helps the company avoid investing costly development resources in them and allows the company to have a more accurate idea of its high-potential managerial talent. The disadvantages of identifying high-potential employees are those not on the list may become discouraged and leave the company or changes in business strategy or the employees' performance could take them off the list. Also, employees might not believe they have had a fair chance to compete for leadership positions if they already know that a list of potential candidates has been established. One way to avoid these problems is to let employees know they are on the list but not discuss a specific position they will likely reach. Another is to frequently review the list of candidates and clearly communicate plans and expectations. Managers at Midmark Corporation, a medical equipment manufacturer based in Versailles, Ohio, identify successors every six months as part of the company's performance review process and produce a potential list of candidates. Some employees are also labeled as high potential and others are identified as having high potential for leadership positions. Employees with high potential for leadership positions are considered for challenging development assignments involving overseas relocation. Using interviews the company determines if employees on the succession list are interested and qualified for leadership positions.

A Look Back

The chapter opener described Tyson Foods' development program (LINC) for managers identified as having high potential.

Questions

1. Tyson uses "stretch assignments" as part of the development program. How can stretch assignments help managers develop? What type of job experiences might be considered "stretch assignments"?
2. What should be included in the managers' development plan?
3. Would the development activities for LINC participants vary from the development activities used for successful managers who do not have high potential and/or interest in top leadership positions at Tyson Foods? Why? Explain the similarities and differences.

Please see the Video that corresponds to this chapter at www.mhhe.com/noe8e.

SUMMARY

This chapter emphasized the various development methods that companies use: formal education, assessment, job experiences, and interpersonal relationships. Most companies use one or more of these approaches to develop employees. Formal education involves enrolling employees in courses or seminars offered by the company or educational institutions. Assessment involves measuring the employee's performance, behavior, skills, or personality characteristics. Job experiences include job enlargement, rotating to a new job, promotions, or transfers. A more experienced, senior employee (a mentor) can help employees better understand the company and gain exposure and visibility to key persons in the organization. Part of a manager's job responsibility may be to coach employees. Regardless of the development approaches used, employees should have a development plan to identify (1) the type of development needed, (2) development goals, (3) the best approach for development, and (4) whether development goals have been reached. For development plans to be effective, both the employee and the company have responsibilities that need to be completed.

KEY TERMS

Development, 397
Protean career, 397
Psychological success, 398
Development planning system, 399
Formal education programs, 405
Tuition reimbursement, 408
Assessment, 409
Myers-Briggs Type Inventory (MBTI)®, 410
Assessment center, 411
Leaderless group discussion, 411

Interview, 411
In-basket, 411
Role-plays, 411
Performance appraisal, 413
Upward feedback, 413
360-degree feedback systems, 413
Job experiences, 415
Job enlargement, 416
Job rotation, 418
Transfer, 419
Promotions, 419

Downward move, 419
Externship, 420
Sabbatical, 421
Mentor, 422
Group mentoring programs, 422
Career support, 424
Psychosocial support, 424
Coach, 425
Glass ceiling, 427
Succession planning, 429
High-potential employees, 429

DISCUSSION QUESTIONS

1. How could assessment be used to create a productive work team?
2. List and explain the characteristics of effective 360-degree feedback systems.
3. Why do companies develop formal mentoring programs? What are the potential benefits for the mentor? For the protégé?
4. Your boss is interested in hiring a consultant to help identify potential managers among current employees of a fast-food restaurant. The manager's job is to help wait on customers and prepare food during busy times, oversee all aspects of restaurant operations (including scheduling, maintenance, on-the-job training, and food purchase), and help motivate employees to provide high-quality service. The manager is also responsible for resolving disputes that might occur between employees. The position involves working under stress and coordinating several activities at one time. She asks you to outline the type of assessment program you believe would do the best job of identifying employees who will be successful managers. What will you tell her?
5. Many employees are unwilling to relocate because they like their current community, and spouses and children prefer not to move. Yet employees need to develop new skills, strengthen skill weaknesses, and be exposed to new aspects of the business to prepare for management positions. How could an employee's current job be changed to develop management skills?
6. What is coaching? Is there one type of coaching? Explain.
7. Why are many managers reluctant to coach their employees?
8. Why should companies be interested in helping employees plan their development? What benefits can companies gain? What are the risks?
9. What are the manager's roles in a development system? Which role do you think is most difficult for the typical manager? Which is the easiest role? List the reasons why managers might resist involvement in career management.

10. Should a company identify and formally acknowledge its high-potential managers or should it be kept secret? Should managers know they are considered high-potential managers? Explain your positions.
11. Nationwide Financial, a 5,000-employee life insurance company based in Columbus, Ohio, found that its management development program contained four types of managers. One type, unknown leaders, have the right skills but their talents are unknown to top managers in the company. Another group, arrogant leaders, believe they have all the skills they need. What types of development program would you recommend for these managers?

SELF-ASSESSMENT EXERCISE

The Department of Labor's Occupational Information Network (O*NET) is designed to meet the goal of promoting the education, training, counseling, and employment needs of the American workforce. Go to http://online.onetcenter.org/. Click on Skills Search. Complete the skills search and then click Go. What occupations match your skills? How might Skills Search be useful for career management?

EXERCISING STRATEGY: TRUSTMARK'S LEADERSHIP DEVELOPMENT PROGRAM

Trustmark provides more than 2 million people with flexible medical, life, and disability benefits and fitness and wellness services. The company, headquartered in Lake Forest, Illinois, has more than 6,200 full- and part-time employees working in 25 locations across the United States. Trustmark experienced steady growth until mid-1990 when it experienced financial pressures forcing it to reevaluate its operations. Trustmark concentrated on core competencies, sold off businesses, and focused on generating capital. Once the company was financially sound, Trustmark executives moved to create a culture that would be open to innovation and opportunity. The challenge was to create a culture where all employees felt they could challenge the status quo and seek new opportunities. The key to creating the culture was effective leadership and developing leaders who supported it.

Trustmark used workshops and 360-degree feedback to help the "Trustmark Renaissance," a radical change in the organizational culture and mind-set, succeed. The leadership program includes sessions, attended by senior leaders, directors, and managers, during which participants learn about leadership practices such as how to inspire a shared vision, challenge the process, enable others to act, and encourage with the heart. During these sessions participants also receive feedback from their 360-degree assessments. Participants also get one-on-one coaching where they can discuss their leadership challenges and their feedback. Participants are asked to identify development areas to focus on during the next step in the process, a two-day workshop. At the workshop, participants learn more about the leadership practices and how to improve the areas identified in their feedback. Participants leave the workshop with an improvement plan for improving their leadership effectiveness. Participants are paired with partners who are expected to provide postworkshop support, exchange action plans, and commit to follow-up to ensure success in using what they learned.

Questions
1. What development activities are used in this program? Why are they important?
2. What data or outcomes should be collected to monitor the effectiveness of the leadership development program? Explain the business reason for your choice of outcomes or data.

SOURCE: Based on T. Welch, "Setting the Stage for a Renaissance at Trustmark," *T + D*, December 2010, pp. 70–72.

MANAGING PEOPLE

It's Not Leadership Development as Usual at Qualcomm

Qualcomm, the San Diego, California–based world leader in next-generation mobile technologies, has received kudos for its products, work culture, and employee practices. For example, in 2010 Qualcomm was recognized by *Fast Company* as one of the most innovative American companies. For 13 years, including 2011, Qualcomm has been considered one of best places to work by *Fortune*. Qualcomm was also recognized as one of India's top 25 great places to work for the fourth straight year. CareerBliss.com rated Qualcomm the fourth happiest place to work in 2011 based on employee evaluations. Qualcomm exceeded the industry average in growth opportunities, compensation, benefits, work/life balance, career advancement, and job security. Qualcomm is also a global corporate citizen committed to improving the communities in which the company operates and where its employees live. That includes partnering with local agencies and organizations in countries around the world to apply the power of a 3G wireless network to help close the digital divide that exists in many parts of the world. This is particularly important in developing regions that lack traditional telecom infrastructure and where people may be struggling to make ends meet. Projects now under way or now being planned include improving access to health care for Andean villagers near Peru's Machu Picchu and working with teenage students in North Carolina to improve their math skills.

One of the reasons for the company's success is its unusual approach to leadership development. Unlike other companies, Qualcomm does not try to identify a few high-potential employees and give them specialized development activities to help prepare them for executive positions. Instead the company's philosophy is to use development to help as many employees as possible develop leadership skills. Qualcomm's vice president for learning and development explains the company philosophy: "We don't tag people. . . . Leaders develop at different paces and blossom at different stages of their careers—and different stages in the company's development. We believe that if we treat everyone as eligible for leadership training, the best leaders are going to emerge when they're ready and when you need them . . . flexibility and being able to adapt to the market is really crucial. It doesn't make sense to spend a lot of resources grooming someone for a specific position when we don't know if we're going to be in that business in the future. We want to be in the position that if a business opportunity suddenly emerges in India and we need a person to run it, we can look at the entire talent pool and decide who is best suited for the job."

Qualcomm's leadership development program includes an introductory program in basic managerial skills which helps train project managers with technical expertise in how to manage. Experienced managers participate in the Leadership Skills program which focuses on studying specific business issues Qualcomm is facing and identifying solutions to these issues. Executives and directors participate in the Executive Leadership Essential's program. A blended learning approach is used for leadership development. This involves studying Qualcomm case histories or taking online training courses, after which employees return to their jobs and try to apply what they have learned. Later, employees meet again to share their successes and discuss challenges they face in using what they learned. Employees are encouraged to meet between formal development sessions to help each other understand the material and how it can be applied to their workplace.

Qualcomm relies on only a few metrics to evaluate the effectiveness of the leadership development program. The metrics used include the company's financial performance, employee satisfaction, and retention and promotion numbers. "It's not all that complicated," according to the vice president for learning and development. "If you've got good leaders, for example, you tend to be able to retain workers, but if you've got poor leaders, you usually don't."

Questions

1. What other types of development activities should Qualcomm consider for its leadership development program? Explain the rationale for your recommendations.
2. How would giving a manager a project such as helping a health clinic in the small isolated mountain valley Peruvian village of Coya, which serves as many as 500 patients a week, improve its ability to access advice and offer the best care to its patients be an effective developmental experience? Explain. What managerial skills or competencies could be improved through such an assignment?

SOURCE: Based on www.qualcomm.com website for Qualcomm; P. J Kiger, "The Leadership Formula," *Workforce Magazine*, May 2010, pp. 25–30; A. Fox, "Achieving Integration," *HR Magazine*, April 2010, pp. 43–51.

⬤ TWITTER FOCUS: EMPLOYEE SABBATICAL BENEFITS OTHERS AT LITTLE TOKYO SERVICE CENTER

Using Twitter, continue the conversation about employee development by reading the Little Tokyo Service Center case at www.mhhe.com/noe8e.

With more than 100 employees, the Little Tokyo Service Center (LTSC) in Los Angeles, California, provides a range of social services for Asians and Pacific Islanders. The center's executive director, Bill Watanabe, was encouraged to take a sabbatical—not because he was "burned out" but because his absence would help other

LTSC employees learn to operate more independently. After a three-month break, Watanabe felt personally restored and found his absence also provided developmental opportunities for others who worked at the center.

Engage with your classmates and instructor via Twitter to chat about Watanabe's sabbatical using the case questions posted on the Noe website. Don't have a Twitter account yet? See the instructions for getting started on the Online Learning Center.

● NOTES

1. D. Day, *Developing Leadership Talent* (Alexandria, VA: SHRM Foundation, 2007); M. London, *Managing the Training Enterprise* (San Francisco: Jossey-Bass, 1989); C. McCauley and S. Heslett, "Individual Development in the Workplace," in *Handbook of Industrial, Work, and Organizational Psychology*, Vol. 1, ed. N. Anderson, D. Ones, H. Sinangil, and C. Visweveran (London: Sage Publications, 2001), pp. 313–35.

2. R. W. Pace, P. C. Smith, and G. E. Mills, *Human Resource Development* (Englewood Cliffs, NJ: Prentice Hall, 1991); W. Fitzgerald, "Training versus Development," *Training and Development Journal*, May 1992, pp. 81–84; R. A. Noe, S. L. Wilk, E. J. Mullen, and J. E. Wanek, "Employee Development: Issues in Construct Definition and Investigation of Antecedents," in *Improving Training Effectiveness in Work Organizations*, ed. J. K. Ford (Mahwah, NJ: Lawrence Erlbaum, 1997), pp. 153–89.

3. Towers Perrin HR Services, *Talent Management: The State of the Art* (Chicago, IL: Towers Perrin, 2005). Available at www.towersperrin.com.

4. J. H. Greenhaus and G. A. Callanan, *Career Management*, 2nd ed. (Fort Worth, TX: Dryden Press, 1994); D. C. Feldman, *Managing Careers in Organizations* (Glenview, IL: Scott Foresman, 1988); D. Hall, *Careers In and Out of Organizations* (Thousand Oaks, CA: Sage, 2002).

5. D. T. Hall, "Protean Careers of the 21st Century," *Academy of Management Executive* 11 (1996), pp. 8–16; Hall, *Careers In and Out of Organizations*.

6. K. Kathryn, "Three Generations, Three Perspectives," *The Wall Street Journal*, March 29, 2004, p. R8.

7. K. R. Brousseau, M. J. Driver, K. Eneroth, and R. Larsson, "Career Pandemonium: Realigning Organizations and Individuals," *Academy of Management Executive* 11 (1996), pp. 52–66.

8. M. B. Arthur, "The Boundaryless Career: A New Perspective of Organizational Inquiry," *Journal of Organization Behavior* 15 (1994), pp. 295–309; P. H. Mirvis and D. T. Hall, "Psychological Success and the Boundaryless Career," *Journal of Organization Behavior* 15 (1994), pp. 365–80; M. Lazarova and S. Taylor, "Boundaryless Careers, Social Capital, and Knowledge Management: Implications for Organizational Performance," *Journal of Organizational Behavior* 30 (2009), pp. 119–39; D. Feldman and T. Ng, "Careers: Mobility, Embeddedness, and Success," *Journal of Management* 33 (2007), pp. 350–77.

9. B. P. Grossman and R. S. Blitzer, "Choreographing Careers," *Training and Development*, January 1992, pp. 67–69.

10. Harris Interactive, Emerging workforce study (Ft. Lauderdale, FL: Spherion, 2005); Available at www.spherion.com/pressroom/; L. Chao, "What GenXers Need to Be Happy at Work," *The Wall Street Journal*, November 29, 2005, p. B6; E. Kaplan-Leiserson, "The Changing Workforce," *TD*, February 2005, pp. 10–11.

11. J. S. Lubin and J. B. White, "Throwing Off Angst, Workers Are Feeling in Control of Their Careers," *The Wall Street Journal*, September 11, 1997, pp. A1, A6.

12. L. Mainiero and S. Sullivan, "Kaleidoscope Careers: An Alternative Explanation for the 'Opt-Out' Revolution," *Academy of Management Executive* 19 (2005), pp. 106–23; S. Sullivan and L. Mainiero, "Benchmarking Ideas for Fostering Family-Friendly Workplaces," *Organizational Dynamics* 36 (2007), pp. 45–62.

13. B. Yovovich, "Golden Opportunities," *Human Resource Executive*, August 2008, pp. 30–34.

14. S. Needleman, "New Career, Same Employer," *The Wall Street Journal*, April 21, 2008, p. B9.

15. M. Sallie-Dosunmu, "Born to Grow," *TD*, May 2006, pp. 34–37.

16. D. T. Jaffe and C. D. Scott, "Career Development for Empowerment in a Changing Work World," in *New Directions in Career Planning and the Workplace*, ed. J. M. Kummerow (Palo Alto, CA: Consulting Psychologists Press, 1991), pp. 33–60; L. Summers, "A Logical Approach to Development Planning," *Training and Development* 48 (1994), pp. 22–31; D. B. Peterson and M. D. Hicks, *Development First* (Minneapolis, MN: Personnel Decisions, 1995).

17. K. Ellis, "Individual Development Plans: The Building Blocks of Development," *Training*, December 2004, pp. 20–25; "Training Top 10 Hall of Fame," *Training*, February 2010, pp. 60, 62.

18. "Training Top 125 2010," *Training*, February 2010, pp. 64–101.

19. R. Noe, *Employee Training and Development*, 5th ed. (New York: McGraw-Hill, Irwin, 2010).

20. M. Weinstein, "Teaching the Top," *Training*, February 2005, pp. 30–33.

21. C. Waxer, "Course Review," *Human Resource Executive*, December 2005, pp. 46–48.

22. C. Waxer, "Bank of Montreal Opens Its Checkbook in the Name of Employee Development," *Workforce Management*, October 24, 2005, pp. 46–48.

23. www.ge.com/company/culture/leaderhip_learning.html, January 15, 2009.

24. R. Knight, "GE's Corporate Boot Camp cum Talent Spotting Venue," *Financial Times Business Education*, March 20, 2006, p. 2; J. Durett, "GE Hones Its Leaders at Crotonville," *Training*, May 2006, pp. 25–27.

25. J. Bolt, *Executive Development* (New York: Harper Business, 1989); M. A. Hitt, B. B. Tyler, C. Hardee, and D. Park, "Understanding Strategic Intent in the Global Marketplace," *Academy of Management Executive* 9 (1995), pp. 12–19.

26. Center for Creative Leadership, "Xerox Corporation" (2007), from website, www.ccl.org.

27. "Client Stories," www.dukece.com, website of Duke Corporate Education.

28. L. Bongiorno, "How'm I Doing," *BusinessWeek*, October 23, 1995, pp. 72, 74.

29. Waxer, "Course Review."

30. Day, *Developing Leadership Talent*.

31. M. Weinstein, "Personalities & Performance," *Training*, July/August 2008, pp. 36–40.

32. E. Krell, "Personality Counts," *HR Magazine*, November 2005, pp. 47–52.

33. C. Cornell, "The Value of Values," *Human Resource Executive*, November 2004, pp. 68–72.

34. M. Weinstein, "The X Factor," *Training*, May/June 2011, pp. 65–67.

35. S. K. Hirsch, *MBTI Team Member's Guide* (Palo Alto, CA: Consulting Psychologists Press, 1992); A. L. Hammer, *Introduction to Type and Careers* (Palo Alto, CA: Consulting Psychologists Press, 1993); J. Llorens, "Taking Inventory of Myers-Briggs," *T + D*, April 2010, pp. 18–19.

36. J. Overbo, "Using Myers-Briggs Personality Type to Create a Culture Adapted to the New Century," *T + D*, February 2010, pp. 70–72.

37. G. C. Thornton III and W. C. Byham, *Assessment Centers and Managerial Performance* (New York: Academic Press, 1982); L. F. Schoenfeldt and J. A. Steger, "Identification and Development of Management Talent," in *Research in Personnel and Human Resource Management*, ed. K. N. Rowland and G. Ferris (Greenwich, CT: JAI Press, 1989), vol. 7, pp. 151–81.

38. Thornton and Byham, *Assessment Centers and Managerial Performance*.

39. B. B. Gaugler, D. B. Rosenthal, G. C. Thornton III, and C. Bentson, "Metaanalysis of Assessment Center Validity," *Journal of Applied Psychology* 72 (1987), pp. 493–511; D. W. Bray, R. J. Campbell, and D. L. Grant, *Formative Years in Business: A Long-Term AT&T Study of Managerial Lives* (New York: Wiley, 1974).

40. R. G. Jones and M. D. Whitmore, "Evaluating Developmental Assessment Centers as Interventions," *Personnel Psychology* 48 (1995), pp. 377–88.

41. J. Schettler, "Building Bench Strength," *Training*, June 2002, pp. 55–58.

42. S. B. Silverman, "Individual Development through Performance Appraisal," in *Developing Human Resources*, pp. 5–120 to 5–151.

43. M. Sallie-Dosunmu, "Born to Grow," *TD*, May 2006, pp. 34–37.

44. J. S. Lublin, "Turning the Tables: Underlings Evaluate Bosses," *The Wall Street Journal*, October 4, 1994, pp. B1, B14; D. O'Reilly, "360-Degree Feedback Can Change Your Life," *Fortune*, October 17, 1994, pp. 93–100; J. F. Milliman, R. A. Zawacki, C. Norman, L. Powell, and J. Kirksey, "Companies Evaluate Employees from All Perspectives," *Personnel Journal*, November 1994, pp. 99–103.

45. Center for Creative Leadership, *Skillscope for Managers: Development Planning Guide* (Greensboro, NC: Center for Creative Leadership, 1992); G. Yukl and R. Lepsinger, "360-Degree Feedback," *Training*, December 1995, pp. 45–50.

46. L. Atwater, P. Roush, and A. Fischthal, "The Influence of Upward Feedback on Self- and Follower Ratings of Leadership," *Personnel Psychology* 48 (1995), pp. 35–59; J. F. Hazucha, S. A. Hezlett, and R. J. Schneider, "The Impact of 360-Degree Feedback on Management Skill Development," *Human Resource Management* 32 (1993), pp. 325–51; J. W. Smither, M. London, N. Vasilopoulos, R. R. Reilly, R. E. Millsap, and N. Salvemini, "An Examination of the Effects of an Upward Feedback Program over Time," *Personnel Psychology* 48 (1995), pp. 1–34; J. Smither and A. Walker, "Are the Characteristics of Narrative Comments Related to Improvements in Multi-rater Feedback Ratings over Time?" *Journal of Applied Psychology* 89 (2004), pp. 575–81; J. Smither, M. London, and R. Reilly, "Does Performance Improve Following Multisource Feedback? A Theoretical Model, Meta-analysis, and Review of Empirical Findings," *Personnel Psychology* 58 (2005), pp. 33–66.

47. D. Bracken, "Straight Talk about Multirater Feedback," *Training and Development*, September 1994, pp. 44–51; K. Nowack, J. Hartley, and W. Bradley, "How to Evaluate Your 360-Feedback Efforts," *Training and Development*, April 1999, pp. 48–52; M. Levine, "Taking the Burn out of the 360-Degree Hot Seat," *T + D*, August 2010, pp. 40–45.

48. "Training Top 125," *Training*, January/February 2011, pp. 54–93.

49. A. Freedman, "The Evolution of 360s," *Human Resource Executive*, December 2002, pp. 47–51.

50. M. W. McCall Jr., M. M. Lombardo, and A. M. Morrison, *Lessons of Experience* (Lexington, MA: Lexington Books,

1988); L. Dragoni, P. Tesluk, J. Russell, and I. Oh, "Understanding Managerial Development: Integrating Developmental Assignments, Learning Orientation, and Access to Developmental Opportunities in Predicting Managerial Competencies," *Academy of Management Journal* 52 (2009), pp. 731–43.

51. R. S. Snell, "Congenial Ways of Learning: So Near yet So Far," *Journal of Management Development* 9 (1990), pp. 17–23.

52. R. Morrison, T. Erickson, and K. Dychtwald, "Managing Middlescence," *Harvard Business Review*, March 2006, pp. 78–86.

53. *The Wall Street Journal*, October 13, 2008, p. R6.

54. McCall, Lombardo, and Morrison, *Lessons of Experience*; M. W. McCall, "Developing Executives through Work Experiences," *Human Resource Planning* 11 (1988), pp. 1–11; M. N. Ruderman, P. J. Ohlott, and C. D. McCauley, "Assessing Opportunities for Leadership Development," in *Measures of Leadership*, pp. 547–62; C. D. McCauley, L. J. Estman, and P. J. Ohlott, "Linking Management Selection and Development through Stretch Assignments," *Human Resource Management* 34 (1995), pp. 93–115.

55. C. D. McCauley, M. N. Ruderman, P. J. Ohlott, and J. E. Morrow, "Assessing the Developmental Components of Managerial Jobs," *Journal of Applied Psychology* 79 (1994), pp. 544–60; J. LePine, M. LePine, and C. Jackson, "Challenge and Hindrance Stress: Relationships with Exhaustion, Motivation to Learn, and Learning Performance," *Journal of Applied Psychology* 89 (2004) pp. 883–91.

56. S. Thurm, "Power-Sharing Prepares Managers," *The Wall Street Journal*, December 5, 2005, p. B4.

57. "Training Top 125," *Training*, January/February 2011, pp. 54–93.

58. M. Weinstein, "Foreign but Familiar," *Training*, January 2009, pp. 20–23.

59. M. London, *Developing Managers* (San Francisco: Jossey-Bass, 1985); M. A. Campion, L. Cheraskin, and M. J. Stevens, "Career-Related Antecedents and Outcomes of Job Rotation," *Academy of Management Journal* 37 (1994), pp. 1518–42; M. London, *Managing the Training Enterprise* (San Francisco: Jossey-Bass, 1989).

60. "Training Top 125," *Training*, January/February 2011, pp. 54–93.

61. D. C. Feldman, *Managing Careers in Organizations* (Glenview, IL: Scott Foresman, 1988); D. Hall, *Careers In and Out of Organizations* (Thousand Oaks, CA: Sage, 2002).

62. J. M. Brett, L. K. Stroh, and A. H. Reilly, "Job Transfer," in *International Review of Industrial and Organizational Psychology: 1992*, ed. C. L. Cooper and I. T. Robinson (Chichester, England: John Wiley and Sons, 1992); D. C. Feldman and J. M. Brett, "Coping with New Jobs: A Comparative Study of New Hires and Job Changers," *Academy of Management Journal* 26 (1983), pp. 258–72.

63. R. A. Noe, B. D. Steffy, and A. E. Barber, "An Investigation of the Factors Influencing Employees' Willingness to Accept Mobility Opportunities," *Personnel Psychology* 41 (1988), pp. 559–80; S. Gould and L. E. Penley, "A Study of the Correlates of Willingness to Relocate," *Academy of Management Journal* 28 (1984), pp. 472–78; J. Landau and T. H. Hammer, "Clerical Employees' Perceptions of Intraorganizational Career Opportunities," *Academy of Management Journal* 29 (1986), pp. 385–405; R. P. Duncan and C. C. Perruci, "Dual Occupation Families and Migration," *American Sociological Review* 41 (1976), pp. 252–61; J. M. Brett and A. H. Reilly, "On the Road Again: Predicting the Job Transfer Decision," *Journal of Applied Psychology* 73 (1988), pp. 614–620.

64. D. T. Hall and L. A. Isabella, "Downward Moves and Career Development," *Organizational Dynamics* 14 (1985), pp. 5–23.

65. H. D. Dewirst, "Career Patterns: Mobility, Specialization, and Related Career Issues," in *Contemporary Career Development Issues*, ed. R. F. Morrison and J. Adams (Hillsdale, NJ: Lawrence Erlbaum, 1991), pp. 73–108.

66. N. C. Tompkins, "GTE Managers on the Move," *Personnel Journal*, August 1992, pp. 86–91.

67. J. M. Brett, "Job Transfer and Well-Being," *Journal of Applied Psychology* 67 (1992), pp. 450–63; F. J. Minor, L. A. Slade, and R. A. Myers, "Career Transitions in Changing Times," in *Contemporary Career Development Issues*, pp. 109–20; C. C. Pinder and K. G. Schroeder, "Time to Proficiency Following Job Transfers," *Academy of Management Journal* 30 (1987), pp. 336–53; G. Flynn, "Heck No—We Won't Go!" *Personnel Journal*, March 1996, pp. 37–43.

68. R. E. Silverman, "Mercer Tries to Keep Employees Through Its 'Externship' Program," *The Wall Street Journal*, November 7, 2000, p. B18.

69. E. Byron, "A New Odd Couple: Google, P&G Swap Workers to Spur Innovation," The *Wall Street Journal*, November 19, 2008, pp. A1, A18.

70. C. J. Bachler, "Workers Take Leave of Job Stress," *Personnel Journal*, January 1995, pp. 38–48.

71. F. Jossi, "Taking Time Off from Advertising," *Workforce*, April 2002, p. 15.

72. M. Weinstein, "Charity Begins @ Work," *Training*, May 2008, pp. 56–58; K. Ellis, "Pass It On," *Training*, June 2005, pp. 14–19.

73. B. Kaye and B. Jackson, "Mentoring: A Group Guide," *Training and Development*, April 1995, pp. 23–27.

74. D. B. Turban and T. W. Dougherty, "Role of Protégé Personality in Receipt of Mentoring and Career Success," *Academy of Management Journal* 37 (1994), pp. 688–702; E. A. Fagenson, "Mentoring: Who Needs It? A Comparison of Protégés' and Nonprotégés' Needs for Power, Achievement, Affiliation, and Autonomy," *Journal of Vocational Behavior* 41 (1992), pp. 48–60.

75. A. H. Geiger, "Measures for Mentors," *Training and Development Journal*, February 1992, pp. 65–67.

76. K. E. Kram, *Mentoring at Work: Developmental Relationships in Organizational Life* (Glenview, IL: Scott Foresman, 1985); K. Kram, "Phases of the Mentoring Relationship," *Academy of Management Journal* 26 (1983), pp. 608–25; G. T. Chao, P. M. Walz, and P. D. Gardner, "Formal and Informal Mentorships: A Comparison of Mentoring Functions and Contrasts with Nonmentored Counterparts," *Personnel Psychology* 45 (1992), pp. 619–36; C. Wanberg, E. Welsh, and S. Hezlett, "Mentoring Research: A Review and Dynamic Process Model," in *Research in Personnel and Human Resources Management*, ed. J. Martocchio and G. Ferris (New York: Elsevier Science, 2003), pp. 39–124.

77. E. White, "Making Mentorships Work," *The Wall Street Journal*, October 23, 2007, p. B11; E. Holmes, "Career Mentors Today Seem Short on Advice but Give a Mean Tour," *The Wall Street Journal*, August 28, 2007, p. B1; J. Sandberg, "With Bad Mentors It's Better to Break Up than to Make Up," *The Wall Street Journal*, March 18, 2008, p. B1.

78. M. Weinstein, "Please Don't Go," *Training*, May/June 2011, pp. 28–34.

79. L. Eby, M. Butts, A. Lockwood, and A. Simon, "Protégés' Negative Mentoring Experiences: Construct Development and Nomological Validation," *Personnel Psychology* 57 (2004),

pp. 411–47; M. Boyle, "Most Mentoring Programs Stink—but Yours Doesn't Have To," *Training*, August 2005, pp. 12–15.

80. R. Emelo, "Conversations with Mentoring Leaders," *T + D*, June 2011, pp. 32–37.

81. M. Weinstein, "Please Don't Go," *Training*, May/June 2011, pp. 28–34; "Training Top 125," *Training*, January/February 2011, pp. 54–93.

82. M. Weinstein, "Tech Connects," *Training*, September 2008, pp. 58–59.

83. G. F. Dreher and R. A. Ash, "A Comparative Study of Mentoring among Men and Women in Managerial, Professional, and Technical Positions," *Journal of Applied Psychology* 75 (1990), pp. 539–46; T. D. Allen, L. T. Eby, M. L. Poteet, E. Lentz, and L. Lima, "Career Benefits Associated with Mentoring for Protégés: A Meta-Analysis," *Journal of Applied Psychology* 89 (2004), pp. 127–36; R. A. Noe, D. B. Greenberger, and S. Wang, "Mentoring: What We Know and Where We Might Go," in *Research in Personnel and Human Resources Management*, ed. G. Ferris and J. Martucchio (New York: Elsevier Science, 2002), pp. 129–74; R. A. Noe, "An Investigation of the Determinants of Successful Assigned Mentoring Relationships," *Personnel Psychology* 41 (1988), pp. 457–79; B. J. Tepper, "Upward Maintenance Tactics in Supervisory Mentoring and Nonmentoring Relationships," *Academy of Management Journal* 38 (1995), pp. 1191–205; B. R. Ragins and T. A. Scandura, "Gender Differences in Expected Outcomes of Mentoring Relationships," *Academy of Management Journal* 37 (1994), pp. 957–71.

84. S. Wells, "Tending Talent," *HR Magazine*, May 2009, pp. 53–60.

85. K. Spors, "Websites Offer Access to Mentors," *The Wall Street Journal*, June 3, 2008, p. B7.

86. D. B. Peterson and M. D. Hicks, *Leader as Coach* (Minneapolis, MN: Personnel Decisions, 1996).

87. D. Coutu and C. Kauffman, "What Coaches Can Do for You," *Harvard Business Review*, January 2009, pp. 91–97.

88. J. Toto, "Untapped World of Peer Coaching," *TD*, April 2006, pp. 69–71; R. Barner, "The 5 Hidden Roles of the Managerial Coach," *T + D*, June 2011, pp. 38–45.

89. H. Johnson, "The Ins and Outs of Executive Coaching," *Training*, May 2004, pp. 36–41.

90. J. Smither, M. London, R. Flautt, Y. Vargas, and L. Kucine, "Can Working with an Executive Coach Improve Multisource Ratings over Time? A Quasi-Experimental Field Study," *Personnel Psychology* 56 (2003), pp. 23–44.

91. J. Lublin, "Did I Just Say That?! How You Can Recover from Foot-in-Mouth," *The Wall Street Journal*, June 18, 2002, p. B1.

92. Toto, "Untapped World of Peer Coaching."

93. R. Zemke, "The Corporate Coach," *Training*, December 1996, pp. 24–28.

94. "Most Employers Lacking a Strategy for Developing Women Leaders," press release from October 25, 2010, at www.mercer.com, website of Mercer, a global provider of consulting, outsourcing, and investment services; R. Pyrillis, "Programs That Help Women Take the Lead," *Workforce Management*, January 2011, pp. 3–4.

95. U.S. Department of Labor, *A Report on the Glass Ceiling Initiative* (Washington, DC: U.S. Department of Labor, 1991).

96. P. J. Ohlott, M. N. Ruderman, and C. D. McCauley, "Gender Differences in Managers' Developmental Job Experiences," *Academy of Management Journal* 37 (1994), pp. 46–67; D. Mattioli, "Programs to Promote Female Managers Win Citations," *The Wall Street Journal*, January 30, 2007, p. B7.

97. U.S. Department of Labor, *A Report on the Glass Ceiling Initiative*; R. A. Noe, "Women and Mentoring: A Review and Research Agenda," *Academy of Management Review* 13 (1988), pp. 65–78; B. R. Ragins and J. L. Cotton, "Easier Said Than Done: Gender Differences in Perceived Barriers to Gaining a Mentor," *Academy of Management Journal* 34 (1991), pp. 939–51.

98. L. A. Mainiero, "Getting Anointed for Advancement: The Case of Executive Women," *Academy of Management Executive* 8 (1994), pp. 53–67; J. S. Lublin, "Women at Top Still Are Distant from CEO Jobs," *The Wall Street Journal*, February 28, 1995, pp. B1, B5; P. Tharenov, S. Latimer, and D. Conroy, "How Do You Make It to the Top? An Examination of Influences on Women's and Men's Managerial Advancement," *Academy of Management Journal* 37 (1994), pp. 899–931.

99. P. Tharenou, "Going Up? Do Traits and Informal Social Processes Predict Advancement in Management?" *Academy of Management Journal* 44 (2001), pp. 1005–17.

100. A. Pomeroy, "Cultivating Female Leaders," *HR Magazine*, February 2007, pp. 44–50.

101. W. J. Rothwell, *Effective Succession Planning*, 4th ed. (New York: AMACOM, 2010).

102. C. B. Derr, C. Jones, and E. L. Toomey, "Managing High-Potential Employees: Current Practices in Thirty-Three U.S. Corporations," *Human Resource Management* 27 (1988), pp. 273–90.

103. N. Noelke, "Leveraging the Present to Build the Future," *HR Magazine*, March 2009, pp. 34–36.

104. M. Steen, "Where to Draw the Line on Revealing Who's Next in Line," *Workforce Management*, June 2011, pp. 16–18.

CHAPTER

10

Employee Separation and Retention

ENTER THE WORLD OF BUSINESS

Heading for the Exit: Flight Attendant Becomes Hero

It had happened a hundred times before. This time it happened in JFK Airport in New York on a plane that just landed from Pittsburgh. A passenger left her seat too soon, and opened up the storage compartment above her seat. The flight attendant, Steven Slater, then did what he always did. He calmly asked her to return to her seat until the airplane came to a complete stop. The passenger ignored him, and then Slater did what he always did. He calmly went to help her get seated again. The passenger verbally attacked Slater and wound up hitting him over the head with the oversized bag that she was wrestling out of the overhead bin. After this, Slater did something that no one else *ever did*. He returned to the intercom and let loose with an obscenity-laced invective directed at the woman. He then made a dramatic departure by pulling the trigger on the emergency inflatable exit chute, sliding off into retirement—but only after grabbing two beers from the beverage cart for the trip.

Perhaps the only thing more remarkable than Slater's outrageous escape was the public's reaction to it. Despite the unsafe and, in fact, illegal nature of Slater's act, he immediately became an American folk hero. Within two days of the event, over 180,000 people had joined Facebook pages devoted to him where they all shared fantasies about how they too would like to make dramatic exits from their own jobs. One of his fans, a former flight attendant from Queens, spoke for many when she stated, "Enough is enough—good for him."

The reaction of Slater and his fan base speaks volumes to both the difficult nature of the specific job of flight attendant, as well as the larger collective mood of the American workforce. With respect to the flight attendant's job, this is an arduous task characterized by low pay, long hours, and demanding customers, some of whom are crying babies, drunks, or phobic to heights, crowds, or enclosed conditions. Within this charged context, they must enact strict safety and security procedures that have to be followed without exception or face disciplinary charges. In addition to the stressful nature of the work, Slater himself was struggling with work–family conflict, as he juggled his highly unpredictable work schedule with the demands of simultaneously trying to care for his dying mother.

Turning to the larger workforce, Steven Slater's frustration mirrored the mood of many American workers who were fed up with their current jobs and looking for the first opportunity to quit. Large-scale surveys of the American workforce documented that "feeling of loyalty to one's employer" hit an all-time low in *2009*, and in 2010, the number of employees who voluntarily left their jobs surpassed the number of people involuntarily laid off for the first time since 2008. This spells future trouble for many employers, and as one HR executive noted, "We're trying to catch people even before they start looking for a new job, which will become even more important as the economy improves and more opportunities at competitors opens up." For many employers, however, this all may be too little, too late, and they may be unable to recapture the loyalty of all of these "Steven Slater wannabes."

SOURCES: D. Leonard, "Mad as Hell," *Bloomberg Businessweek*, August 16, 2010, pp. 5–6; A. Newman and R. Rivera, "Fed up Flight Attendant Makes Sliding Exit," *The New York Times*, August 9, 2010, pp. B1–B2; and J. Poniewozik, "Steven Slater, Road Warrior: JetBlue Mints a Folk Hero," *Time*, August 10, 2010, p. 34.

⊙ Introduction

Every executive recognizes the need for satisfied, loyal customers. If the firm is publicly held, it is also safe to assume that every executive appreciates the need to have satisfied, loyal investors. Customers and investors provide the financial resources that allow the organization to survive. However, not every executive understands the need to generate satisfaction and loyalty among employees, and as we see in this opening vignette highlighting Steven Slater and JetBlue, one disgruntled employee can do a great deal of damage to the company's reputation. Yet, retention rates among employees are related to retention rates among customers.[1] In fact, research has established a direct link between employee retention rates and sales growth and companies that are cited as one of the "100 Best Companies to Work For" routinely outperform their competition on many other financial indicators of performance. For example Figure 10.1 shows the average annual returns for the "100 Best Companies to Work For" over various time periods ending in 2005. The figure reveals that sustained (10 years) competitive advantage in capital markets is directly attributable to successfully managing the workforce.[2] This is especially the case in service industries, where disgruntled workers often create large numbers of dissatisfied customers.[3]

Lack of experience and cohesiveness within work units destroys efficiency, and the costs associated with constantly replacing workers erodes a firm's competitive position.[4] For example, after bankruptcy proceedings in 2007 forced United Airlines to cut the pay of flight attendants to 1985 levels, the high level of dissatisfaction within the ranks of these workers on the front line immediately spilled over into customer ratings of service. Thus, just at a time when United was finally putting its financial problems behind it, new problems related to customer service threatened to throw them back into bankruptcy court again. As Greg Davidowitch, president of the Associated United Flight Attendants noted, "You can't run a service business when you are at war with your employees."[5] Indeed, study after study has shown a direct causal connection between poor worker attitudes on the one hand, and poor customer service on the other.[6] This is an especially timely fact because a recent 2010 survey suggests that only 45% of current employees report being satisfied with their jobs, one of the lowest percentages in recorded history.[7]

figure 10.1

Stock Performance: Average Annual Return Best Companies to Work For vs. S&P 500

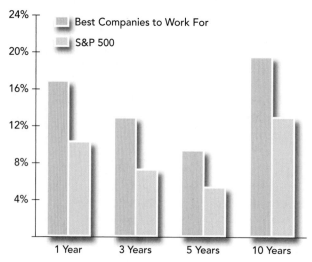

SOURCE: M. Boyle, "Happy People, Happy Returns," *BusinessWeek*, January 22, 2007, p. 100.

In addition to holding onto key personnel, another hallmark of successful firms is their ability and willingness to dismiss employees who are engaging in counter-productive behavior. Indeed, it is somewhat ironic that one of the keys to retaining productive employees is ensuring that these people are not being made miserable by supervisors or co-workers who are engaging in unproductive, disruptive, or dangerous behavior. Unfortunately, surveys indicate that many managers—indeed as many as 70%—struggle to give frank and honest feedback to poorly performing subordinates, and then wind up experiencing and tolerating poor performance for very long periods.[8] It is precisely for this reason that many organizations have resorted to forced distribution rating systems like those we discussed earlier in Chapter 8, which require some percentage of employees to be given "unsatisfactory" ratings. However, in the absence of honest, accurate, and diagnostic feedback, even these systems do little to spur improvement. For example, at Microsoft, employees felt that some managers who were poor at giving negative feedback just used the distribution system as a crutch. As one Microsoft worker noted, managers would just say, "I really wanted to give to you a 4, but I had the curve so I had to give you a 3."[9] Feedback like that does not give the employee any sense of justice—and does nothing to promote focused improvement.

Thus, to compete effectively, organizations must take steps to ensure that good performers are motivated to stay with the organization, whereas chronically low performers are allowed, encouraged, or, if necessary, forced to leave. Retaining top performers is not always easy, however. Competing organizations are constantly looking to steal top performers, and "poaching talent" is becoming an increasingly common way for organizations to build themselves up, while at the same time, tearing their competitors down.[10] It is also not nearly as easy to fire employees as many people think. The increased willingness of people to sue their employer, combined with an unprecedented level of violence in the workplace, has made discharging employees who lack talent legally complicated and personally dangerous.[11]

The purpose of this chapter (the last in Part 3 of this book) is to focus on employee separation and retention. The material presented in Part 3's previous two chapters ("Performance Management" and "Employee Development") can be used to help establish who are the current effective performers as well as who is likely to respond well to future developmental opportunities. This chapter completes Part 3 by discussing what can be done to retain high-performing employees who warrant further development as well as managing the separation process for low-performing employees who have not responded well to developmental opportunities.

Since much of what needs to be done to retain employees involves compensation and benefits, this chapter also serves as a bridge to Part 4, which addresses these issues in more detail. The chapter is divided into two sections. The first examines **involuntary turnover,** that is, turnover initiated by the organization (often among people who would prefer to stay). The second deals with **voluntary turnover,** that is, turnover initiated by employees (often whom the company would prefer to keep). Although both types of turnover reflect employee separation, they are clearly different phenomena that need to be examined separately.

Involuntary Turnover
Turnover initiated by the organization (often among people who would prefer to stay).

Voluntary Turnover
Turnover initiated by employees (often whom the company would prefer to keep).

Managing Involuntary Turnover

Despite a company's best efforts in the area of personnel selection, training, and design of compensation systems, some employees will occasionally fail to meet performance requirements or will violate company policies while on the job. When this happens, organizations need to invoke a discipline program that could ultimately lead to the

LO 10-1
Distinguish between involuntary and voluntary turnover, and discuss how each of these forms of turnover can be leveraged for competitive advantage.

individual's discharge. For a number of reasons, discharging employees can be a very difficult task that needs to be handled with the utmost care and attention to detail.

First, legal aspects to this decision can have important repercussions for the organization. Historically, in the absence of a specified contract, either the employer or the employee could sever the employment relationship at any time. The severing of this relationship could be for "good cause," "no cause," or even "bad cause." Over time, this policy has been referred to as the **employment-at-will doctrine.** This employment-at-will doctrine has eroded significantly over time, however. Today employees who are fired sometimes sue their employers for wrongful discharge. Some judges have been willing to consider employees who meet certain criteria regarding longevity, promotions, raises, and favorable past performance reviews as having an implied contract to dismissal only for good cause—even in the face of direct language in the company handbook that states an employment-at-will relationship.[12]

Employment-at-Will Doctrine
The doctrine that, in the absence of a specific contract, either an employer or employee could sever the employment relationship at any time.

A wrongful discharge suit typically attempts to establish that the discharge either (1) violated an implied contract or covenant (that is, the employer acted unfairly) or (2) violated public policy (that is, the employee was terminated because he or she refused to do something illegal, unethical, or unsafe). Wrongful discharge suits can also be filed as a civil rights infringement if the person discharged is a member of a protected group. The number of such "protected groups" is large, however, and includes racial minorities, women, older workers (over 40 years of age), homosexuals, disabled workers (including the obese), whistle-blowers, people who have filed workers compensation claims, and if one counts reverse discrimination claims—Caucasians. Indeed, as noted by Lisa Cassilly, a defense attorney for the firm Alston and Bird, "It's difficult to find someone who doesn't have some capacity to claim protected status."[13] This means that in almost any instance when someone is fired for poor performance, the alternative possibility that this person was a victim of discrimination can be raised.

Not surprisingly, this has led to an increase in litigation, such that while there were roughly 8,000 wrongful termination lawsuits filed in 1991, by 2006 the number of lawsuits filed annually was close to 15,000. Moreover, because the Civil Rights Act of 1991 allowed for jury trials and "punitive" damages, in some well-known cases, the size of the awards are attention-getting. For example, in a recent case at General Electric, an employee was awarded more than $11 million in a wrongful discharge suit.[14] The vividness of these highly publicized cases often distorts the perceptions of how infrequently plaintiffs actually win such cases, however. For example, Figure 10.2 shows the base rate probabilities for various outcomes in such cases. As you can see, a plaintiff rarely achieves a victory in this kind of case should it survive appeal (odds are roughly one-tenth of 1 percent). However, the high legal cost associated with winning the case is often enough to make some employers reluctant to fire workers. When this happens, the employer's short-term emphasis on staying out of court has come into conflict with the long-term need to develop a competitive workforce.

For example, one reaction to this dilemma is enduring long stretches of poor performance in order to create the extensive "paper trail" that would support a negative action. While HR professionals often point the finger of blame at supervisors who have not done a diligent job documenting past performance problems, supervisors often turn around and accuse HR of being "nervous Nellies" who never seem satisfied with the amount of evidence provided by supervisors. Moreover, keeping poor performers in their roles does not directly affect HR professionals every day, like it does supervisors, who have to watch helplessly as the morale of the rest of the workforce erodes. Indeed, there is nothing more corrosive to team-based structures than wide variability in effort and performance between different members. As one member of

Out of 10,000 Employment Suits	Stage of Lawsuit	Cumulative Cost for a Company to Defend a Single Lawsuit
FILING		
7,000	Settle (most settlements are for nuisance value)	$10,000
SUMMARY JUDGMENT		
2,400	Get resolved by summary judgment and other pretrial rulings	$100,000
START OF TRIAL		
600	Go to trial	$175,000
END OF TRIAL		
186	Trials are won by plaintiffs	$250,000*
APPEAL		
13**	Plaintiff victories survive appeal	$300,000

figure 10.2

Probable Outcomes of Wrongful Discharge Suits

*Assumes a five-day trial.

**Out of 22 trial losses typically appealed by companies.

SOURCES: M. Orey, "Fear of Firing," *BusinessWeek*, April 23, 2007, p. 60; Cornell Law School; *Hofstra Labor & Employment Law Journal*; BW reporting.

a research team in a pharmaceutical firm noted with respect to the idea of "carrying" a poor performer for fear of litigation, "As a female and also of a minority race, I am appalled and saddened by this scenario as I must bear the weight of this constant underperformer."[15]

Another questionable reaction is to initiate punitive actions short of termination, in an effort to get the employee to quit on his or her own. This reaction is often a result of frustrated supervisors, who, unable to fire someone because of HR, resort to punishing the employee in other ways. This might include giving the person a low-level work assignment, a downsized office, or some other form of undesirable treatment. The problem with this approach, however, is that it might be construed as "retaliation," and the employer could be sued for this, even if the original discrimination suit is dismissed. In 2005 and 2006, 30% of EEOC filings were this type of "retaliation lawsuits," which was three times the percentage just 10 years ago.[16] In fact, some attorneys advise any clients who are expecting a poor performance appraisal or some other adverse job event to file a discrimination suit as part of a preemptive attack that sets up the groundwork for a subsequent "retaliation" lawsuit.

Finally, a third unsustainable reaction is to pay off the employee with thousands of dollars in excess severance pay in return for waiving their right to sue for wrongful dismissal. That is, even if the employer feels the case is unwarranted, in order to avoid litigation itself, the employer may offer the terminated employee $20,000 or more to waive their right to sue. The problem with this strategy is that it sets the expectation that all poor performers are entitled to compensation on their way out the door, and this eventually increases the amount of potential future litigation by rewarding frivolous charges. A more effective and sustainable strategy for employers would be to develop a reputation that you will defend the firm's right to terminate low performers, rather than invite bullying by an overly aggressive attorney or employee. As defense attorney Mark Dichter notes, "I can design HR policies that can virtually eliminate your risk of facing employment claims, but you'll have a pretty lousy workforce. At the end of the day, you have to run your business."[17]

The costs associated with letting poor performers stay on within the organization cannot be discounted. Organizations that introduce forced distribution rating systems where low performers are systematically identified and, where necessary, eliminated from payrolls often experience quick improvement gains in the range of 40%. Over time, research shows that the gains achieved by such programs get smaller and smaller, but the initial jump illustrates how many organizations drift into a situation where tolerating low performance has become an unsustainable business practice.[18] This fact is even being realized in many European countries where worker protections embody a critical cultural value. Recent legislation passed in both France and Germany have simplified the procedures that firms have to go through to eliminate poor performers and lowered the bar for the evidence that has to be provided in such cases.[19]

In addition to the financial risks associated with having to legally defend a dismissal, there are issues related to personal safety. Although the fact that some former employees use the court system to get back at their former employers may be distressing, even more problematic are employees who respond to a termination decision with violence directed at the employer. Violence in the workplace has become a major organizational problem and workplace homicide is the fastest-growing form of murder in the United States.[20] For example, in 2010, a truck driver for a beer distributor in Hartford, Connecticut, was dismissed, and then came back and fatally shot seven co-workers and his supervisors. This is not an isolated incident and requests for crisis counseling center services for laid-off workers actually doubled in the period between 2008 and 2010.[21] In the wake of these trends, many HR executives were shocked by the recent passage of "Bring Your Gun to Work" laws like those passed in the state of Indiana and North Dakota in 2011. The "Bring Your Gun to Work" laws are generally backed by the American Rifle Association (ARA) and are seen as part of protecting the Second Amendment in the face of company polices that prohibit guns at the workplace. For example, Weyerhaeuser bans guns on company policy in an effort to promote a safe work environment, but when the company fired workers who brought guns to work based on this policy, they were sued by the ARA.[22]

Given the critical financial and personal risks associated with employee dismissal, it is easy to see why the development of a standardized, systematic approach to discipline and discharge is critical to all organizations. These decisions should not be left solely to the discretion of individual managers or supervisors. In the next section we explore aspects of an effective discipline and discharge policy.

PRINCIPLES OF JUSTICE

As we noted earlier in Chapter 8, **outcome fairness** refers to the judgment that people make with respect to the *outcomes received* relative to the outcomes received by other people with whom they identify (referent others). Clearly, a situation where one person is losing his or her job while others are not is conducive to perceptions

---

Outcome Fairness
The judgment that people make with respect to the outcomes received relative to the outcomes received by other people with whom they identify.

LO 10-2
List the major elements that contribute to perceptions of justice and how to apply these in organizational contexts involving discipline and dismissal.

of outcome unfairness on the part of the discharged employee. The degree to which this potentially unfair act translates into the type of anger and resentment that might spawn retaliation in the form of violence or litigation, however, depends on perceptions of procedural and interactional justice.

Whereas outcome justice focuses on the ends, procedural and interactional justice focus on means. If methods and procedures used to arrive at and implement decisions that impact the employee negatively are seen as fair, the reaction is likely to be much more positive than if this is not the case. **Procedural justice** focuses specifically on the *methods used to determine the outcomes received*. Table 10.1 details six key principles that determine whether people perceive procedures as being fair. Even given all the negative ramifications of being dismissed from one's job, the person being dismissed may accept the decision with minimum anger if the procedures used to arrive at the decision are consistent, unbiased, accurate, correctable, representative, and ethical. When the procedures for the decisions are perceived in this fashion, the individual does not feel unfairly singled out, and this helps maintain his or her faith in the system as a whole, even if he or she is unhappy with the specific decision that was triggered by the system.[23]

Lack of bias and informational accuracy are the most critical features of the six, and the potential for subjective judgments to be biased by gender or racial differences means that employers often have to go beyond simple supervisor evaluations in most cases.[24] In an effort to ensure that they have an airtight case many employers have turned to private investigators to collect objective evidence where necessary. For example, when a Florida hospital suspected a worker who claimed she was out with the flu for three days was actually totally healthy, they hired a private investigator to look into the case. In fact, the woman had gone to Universal Studio theme parks those days and the investigation uncovered photos of her from three different roller coaster rides (which routinely photograph riders and then try to sell the pictures to them), as well as a video where she volunteered as part of an animal act—all time-stamped and dated. Needless to say, this led to a termination that the worker was not interested in challenging.[25]

Whereas procedural justice deals with how a decision was made, **interactional justice** refers to the *interpersonal nature of how the outcomes were implemented*. For example, in many documented cases, after giving employees the news of their termination, employers immediately have security guards whisk them out of the building

Procedural Justice
A concept of justice focusing on the methods used to determine the outcomes received.

Interactional Justice
A concept of justice referring to the interpersonal nature of how the outcomes were implemented.

table 10.1

Six Determinants of Procedural Justice

(1) **Consistency.** The procedures are applied consistently across time and other persons.
(2) **Bias suppression.** The procedures are applied by a person who has no vested interest in the outcome and no prior prejudices regarding the individual.
(3) **Information accuracy.** The procedure is based on information that is perceived to be true.
(4) **Correctability.** The procedure has built-in safeguards that allow one to appeal mistakes or bad decisions.
(5) **Representativeness.** The procedure is informed by the concerns of all groups or stakeholders (co-workers, customers, owners) affected by the decision, including the individual being dismissed.
(6) **Ethicality.** The procedure is consistent with prevailing moral standards as they pertain to issues like invasion of privacy or deception.

table 10.2

Four Determinants of Interactional Justice

(1) **Explanation.** Emphasize aspects of procedural fairness that justify the decision.
(2) **Social sensitivity.** Treat the person with dignity and respect.
(3) **Consideration.** Listen to the person's concerns.
(4) **Empathy.** Identify with the person's feelings.

with their various personal items haphazardly thrown together in cardboard boxes. This strips the person of their dignity, as well as their job, and employees who witness this happen to a co-worker show a drastically lower level of organizational commitment from that day forward.[26] Table 10.2 lists the four key determinants of interactional justice. When the decision is explained well and implemented in a fashion that is socially sensitive, considerate, and empathetic, this helps defuse some of the resentment that might come about from a decision to discharge an employee. As one human research director noted, the key is to ensure that the affected individual "walks out with their dignity and self-respect intact."[27] Going through these steps is especially important if the individual who is being managed is already high in hostility, and hence a threat to respond in violent fashion.[28]

PROGRESSIVE DISCIPLINE AND ALTERNATIVE DISPUTE RESOLUTION

Except in the most extreme cases, employees should generally not be terminated for a first offense. Rather, termination should come about at the end of a systematic discipline program. Effective discipline programs have two central components: documentation (which includes specific publication of work rules and job descriptions that should be in place prior to administering discipline) and progressive punitive measures. Thus, as shown in Table 10.3, punitive measures should be taken in steps of increasing magnitude, and only after having been clearly documented. This may start with an unofficial warning for the first offense, followed by a written reprimand for additional offenses. At some point, later offenses may lead to a temporary suspension. Before a company suspends an employee, it may even want to issue a "last chance notification," indicating that the next offense will result in termination. Such procedures may seem exasperatingly slow, and they may fail to meet one's emotional need for quick and satisfying retribution. In the end, however, when problem employees are discharged, the chance that they can prove they were discharged for poor cause has been minimized.

Alternative Dispute Resolution (ADR)
A method of resolving disputes that does not rely on the legal system. Often proceeds through the four stages of open door policy, peer review, mediation, and arbitration.

At various points in the discipline process, the individual or the organization might want to bring in outside parties to help resolve discrepancies or conflicts. As a last resort, the individual might invoke the legal system to resolve these types of conflicts, but in order to avoid this, more and more companies are turning to **alternative dispute resolution (ADR)** techniques that show promise in resolving disputes in a timely, constructive, cost-effective manner. Alternative dispute resolution can take on many different forms, but in general, ADR proceeds through the four stages

OFFENSE FREQUENCY	ORGANIZATIONAL RESPONSE	DOCUMENTATION
First offense	Unofficial verbal warning	Witness present
Second offense	Official written warning	Document filed
Third offense	Second official warning, with threat of temporary suspension	Document filed
Fourth offense	Temporary suspension and "last chance notification"	Document filed
Fifth offense	Termination (with right to go to arbitration)	Document filed

table 10.3

An Example of a Progressive Discipline Program

shown in Table 10.4. Each stage reflects a somewhat broader involvement of different people, and the hope is that the conflict will be resolved at earlier steps. However, the last step may include binding arbitration, where an agreed upon neutral party resolves the conflict unilaterally if necessary. The key word in this context is "neutral," and if there is one common complaint about ADR systems it is that, more often than not, arbitrators wishing to do more business lean in favor of the organizations that are paying their salaries, and not the workers. As Damon Silvers, the general counsel for the AFL-CIO noted, "There is a mountain of evidence that these kinds of things are captive of the industry," and this makes some workers reluctant to abide by their rulings.[29] This reluctance sometimes leads to lawsuits being filed anyway; hence, on the flip side, some employers find that ADR, rather than streamlining the process, just adds another layer to the problem.[30]

Whereas ADR is effective in dealing with problems related to performance and interpersonal differences in the workplace, many of the problems that lead an organization to want to terminate an individual's employment relate to drug or alcohol abuse. In these cases, the organization's discipline and dismissal program should also incorporate an employee assistance program. Due to the increased prevalence of EAPs in organizations, we describe them in detail here.

Stage 1: Open-door policy
The two people in conflict (e.g., supervisor and subordinate) attempt to arrive at a settlement together. If none can be reached, they proceed to

Stage 2: Peer review
A panel composed of representatives from the organization that are at the same level of those people in the dispute hears the case and attempts to help the parties arrive at a settlement. If none can be reached, they proceed to

Stage 3: Mediation
A neutral third party from outside the organization hears the case and, via a nonbinding process, tries to help the disputants arrive at a settlement. If none can be reached, the parties proceed to

Stage 4: Arbitration
A professional arbitrator from outside the organization hears the case and resolves it unilaterally by rendering a specific decision or award. Most arbitrators are experienced employment attorneys or retired judges.

table 10.4

Stages in Alternative Dispute Resolution

EMPLOYEE ASSISTANCE AND WELLNESS PROGRAMS

Employee Assistance Programs (EAPs)
Employer programs that attempt to ameliorate problems encountered by workers who are drug dependent, alcoholic, or psychologically troubled.

An **employee assistance program (EAP)** is a referral service that supervisors or employees can use to seek professional treatment for various problems. EAPs vary widely, but most share some basic elements. First, the programs are usually identified in official documents published by the employer (such as employee handbooks). Supervisors (and union representatives, where relevant) are trained to use the referral service for employees whom they suspect of having health-related problems. Employees are also trained to use the system to make self-referrals when necessary. Finally, costs and benefits of the programs (as measured in positive employee outcomes such as return-to-work rates) are evaluated, typically annually.

The key to the effectiveness of an EAP is striking the right balance between collecting information that can be used to promote employee health on the one hand and the employee's right to privacy on the other. In particular, in an age of digitalization, organizations can do a great deal to help employees provide more detailed and accurate information to their health care providers. For example, most people who go to their physician fill out a form on their past history over and over again; in many cases, because they do not feel well or feel rushed, they wind up preparing inaccurate and unreliable histories. This can lead to treatment errors and complications that are bad for the patient and drive up the health care costs that companies have to pay. To help solve this problem, Walmart provides employees with a digital tool that allows them to enter their health data once, very slowly and carefully, and then keeps this in digitalized form so that it can be accessed by health care providers whenever it is needed. This reduces errors and costs, but it also places a great deal of personal information that needs to be protected in the hands of the employer.[31]

Whereas EAPs deal with employees who have developed problems at work because of health-related issues, employee wellness programs take a proactive and preemptive focus on trying to prevent health-related problems in the first place. Some of these programs take a very positive approach and are not very controversial. For example, accounting firm Grant Thornton spent roughly $200,000 in 2008 to help more than 200 of their employees train for and run in marathons. Most of these employees reported that they would not have taken this step toward a more active lifestyle without this kind of support.[32]

Some organizations even reach beyond the employee and offer incentives to the worker's spouse and family. After all, if the organization is actually insuring everyone in the family, there are savings to be made by placing the focus on the whole family. For example, Aetna offers a $1,200 reward for employees who can get their spouse and children to sign up for its corporate wellness program. These kinds of financial incentives typically pay for themselves because research suggests that for large employers, every $1 spent on wellness results in a savings of $3.27 when it comes to costs.[33]

Not all employees will necessarily respond to positive incentives like this, however, and hence some companies take a more punitive approach to wellness. Scott's Miracle Gro Company is at the forefront of firms that are taking extreme steps to curtail rising health care costs. Scott's has a "no-tobacco policy" that bars all employees from smoking or chewing tobacco (which was common in the company). In addition to this, employees being considered for employment are asked the following questions: Do you drink alcohol, and how much? Do you suffer from high cholesterol or high blood pressure? Are you depressed or burned-out? How stressful are your relationships with your spouse or children? What were the causes of death for your parents? All of this seems highly intrusive and an invasion of privacy on the part of the employer; however, the company only took this step when it became clear that its workforce was in such bad physical shape that the costs it was incurring for health care expenses was destroying its ability to compete effectively. Indeed, Miracle Gro's health care expenditures had essentially doubled from roughly $10 million in 1999 to $20 million in 2003—and were projected to go up another 20% the next year.[34]

Although perhaps on the edge of how far it is willing to go to reduce these costs, Miracle Gro is certainly not alone in terms of its concerns about such costs. For example, cell phone service provider Sprint realized in 2004 that its annual increase for health care expenditures was going up $50 million a year, and that it would take a 12% increase in sales revenue each year to simply cover that cost—an increase that was twice the industry average. Delta Airlines performed a similar analysis and discovered that it was paying more than $5,000 annually per employee for health care, and that this was going up close to 10% a year. More pointedly, Delta's analysis revealed that much of this cost was attributable to a small percentage of its workers. For example, as Lynn Zonakis, director of health strategy and resources, noted, "We saw that $1/10$ of 1% of our participants were responsible for 10% of our health care costs, and that 1% was responsible for 33% of our cost."[35]

Most employers that run the numbers come to similar conclusions that a small percentage of workers drive a big percentage of costs, and it is not difficult to predict which workers are in this group. Indeed, the very factors that Miracle Gro screens for reflect this list of valid predictors. Thus, although this may seem invasive from the employees' perspective because a lot of the troublesome behavior occurs outside of work, much of this becomes job-related when the costs are born by the employer. Indeed, a recent survey of 135 executives at *Fortune* 500 firms indicated that more than 60% of them believed that employees who exhibit unhealthy behaviors such as smoking or failing to manage obesity should be required to pay a greater share of health insurance premiums.[36] Indeed, employees who smoke are often further subgrouped and ostracized by policies that make them smoke outside company facilities. As one smoker who works for a publisher noted, "It's a little bit humiliating when you realize that you look like a herd of dumb animals corralled outside the building."[37]

In the meantime, individual employers have to make their own decisions regarding how to balance privacy concerns with cost concerns and how much pressure to place on employees whose lifestyles put them at risk. They also have to decide how intrusive they are going to be into employees' lives, knowing that some will lie and falsify records in order to avoid more costly premiums or losing their jobs. For example, at the Whirlpool plant in Benton Harbor, Michigan, 40 workers who were caught on videotape smoking in the parking lot had to be fired because they claimed they were nonsmokers on their benefits enrollment form.[38]

Although financial costs are often the driving force behind these programs, one should not lose sight of the fact that the quality of life enjoyed by employees both on and off the job is also affected. For example, while some employees were suing Miracle Gro over its program, another employee, Joe Pellegrini, was celebrating the fact that the very same program saved his life. Although physically fit, Pellegrini's health assessment indicated a high level of cholesterol, and the company forced him to see a physician. That trip to the doctor revealed a 95% blockage in a heart valve that would have probably killed him within five days. Obviously, Pellegrini has a different perception of Miracle Gro's policies than most employees, noting that when it came to his own life, "It was that close."[39]

OUTPLACEMENT COUNSELING

Outplacement Counseling
Counseling to help displaced employees manage the transition from one job to another.

The permanent nature of an employee termination not only leaves the person angry, it also leads to confusion as to how to react and in a quandary regarding what happens next. If the person feels there is nothing to lose and nowhere else to turn, the potential for violence or litigation is higher than most organizations are willing to tolerate. Therefore, many organizations provide **outplacement counseling,** which tries to help dismissed employees manage the transition from one job to another. There is a great deal of variability in the services offered via outplacement programs, typically including career counseling, job search support, résumé critiques, job interviewing training, and provision of networking opportunities. The number of companies offering outplacement support has increased dramatically in recent years. This was most clearly evident in the recession of 2008, when the percentage of employers offering this service was 55% compared with just 39% during the 2001 recession. Although it may seem counterintuitive to help someone find a new job after just concluding they did not perform well in their last job, most outplacement services frame this as just a bad fit between the person and the job, and work to find jobs where the fit is better.[40]

Outplacement counseling is aimed at helping people realize that losing a job is not the end of the world and that other opportunities exist. Indeed, for many people, losing a job can be a critical learning experience that plants the seed for future success. For example, when John Morgridge was fired from his job as branch manager at Honeywell, it made him realize that his own assertiveness and need for independence were never going to cut it in a large, bureaucratic institution like Honeywell. Morgridge took his skills and went on to build computer network maker Cisco Systems, which is now worth more than $1 billion.[41] This is a success story for Morgridge, but the fact that a major corporation like Honeywell let his talent go certainly reflects a lost opportunity for the company. Retaining people who can make such contributions is a key to gaining and maintaining competitive advantage. The second half of this chapter is devoted to issues related to retention.

Managing Voluntary Turnover

In the first section of this chapter, our focus was on how to help employees who were not contributing to the organization's goal in a manner that protected the firm's ability to compete, and on how to support former employees' transition into alternative employment. In this second section, we focus on the other side of the separation equation—preventing employees who are highly valued by the organization from leaving (and perhaps even joining the competition). At the organizational level, turnover results in lowered work unit performance, which, in turn, harms the firm's financial performance.[42] This causal chain is especially strong when the organization is losing its top performers. Research suggests that some of the organization's top performers are up to 300% more productive than average employees, and retaining these workers is especially difficult.[43] Moreover, in organizations that rely on long-term customer contacts, the loss of workers who are central to customer networks can be especially disruptive.[44]

In general, at least when it comes to complex jobs, there seems to be a curvilinear relationship between past performance and future turnover, in the sense that the worst and best performers tend to leave more frequently than those at the average. Low performers often see the "writing on the wall" and quit before they are fired, especially if there is evidence that their relatively poor performance is actually getting worse over time.[45] In contrast, the best performers often have many other employment opportunities and are subjected to repeated poaching attempts that eventually take their toll unless the organization can keep coming up with pay raises.[46] In fact, the fear that one's best employees might leave has fueled a debate about whether it pays to provide a great deal of expensive employee development, a debate that was at least partially resolved by the evidence provided in our "Evidence-Based HR" box.

EVIDENCE-BASED HR

A high degree of investment in employees via training and development programs is sometimes seen as a double-edged sword. On the one hand, the organization clearly benefits from the increased skill level of employees as long as the employee is working for that particular company. However, enhanced levels of skills might also make that same employee more marketable, and thus, there is always the chance that the employee might take those enhanced skill sets to a different, perhaps even competing employer. This makes investing in human resources a little bit different than investing in technology, and may explain why some firms are more comfortable investing in the latter relative to the former. On the other hand, the very act of investing in employees may send a critical signal to people that the organization cares for them, and this message might actually wind up increasing loyalty and reducing turnover.

Thus, the evidence related to the question of whether or not employee training and development increases or decreases turnover is critically important and was provided by a recent study conducted by Maria Kraimer and her colleagues. Employing a sample of 290 employees of a *Fortune* 500 firm, this research team found that if there were ample opportunities for promotion within the organization, then enhanced employee development actually resulted in lower turnover probabilities (.02). However, in contrast, when there were few opportunities for promotion within the organization, enhanced employee development actually did lead to higher turnover. In fact, the probability of turnover for people who had access to developmental experiences but who perceived few opportunities for promotion were 15 times higher (.33) relative to those who saw promotion opportunities. Thus, the key is to align their HR practices so that they support one another, and hence employee development needs to also be paired with internal promotion practices in order to truly reap the benefits of such programs.

SOURCE: M. L. Kraimer, S. E. Seibert, S. J. Wayne, R. C. Liden, and J. Bravo, "Antecedents and Outcomes of Organizational Support for Development: The Critical Role of Career Opportunities," *Journal of Applied Psychology* 96 (2011), pp. 485–500.

In 2007, Yahoo witnessed a mass exodus of engineers and vice presidents who left to either join small startups or even worse—Google, one of Yahoo's top competitors. The stream of attrition started with lower level workers, but as one former vice president notes, "Now it's the people who have institutional knowledge who are leaving." Google was the top destination spot for most of this talent because the firm was widely recognized as being a great place to work. Google is renowned for its outrageous employee benefits, which include 11 free gourmet cafeterias, five fully staffed on-site doctors' offices, on-site car washes and oil changes, free on-site washers and dryers, unlimited sick days, all-expense-paid ski trips, free shuttles with WiFi for commuters, lap pool, climbing wall, and volleyball courts.

Google's employees respond to all of this by working incredibly long hours and by putting all headhunter calls into their autoreject bin. Most employees are committed to the organization's general well-being not for annual raises but because they are heavily vested in stock options that will make them all millionaires if the company can maintain its current trajectory. Teamwork is demanded and salaries, while not high for the industry, tend to be uniform in order to promote collaboration and teamwork while discouraging "lone wolves." Individuals are given autonomy to run their own experimental projects (up to 20% of their time can be devoted to these), but collective decisions on most large-scale group projects are arrived at via open and spirited public debates that tend to unfold very quickly. In contrast, many workers who are leaving Yahoo complain that most large Yahoo projects have to be signed off by multiple division heads, which both slows the process and minimizes the sense of employee ownership. As noted by one former Yahoo employee, who now works for Google, "Hard core geeks are here because there's no place they'd rather be," which is pretty convincing evidence with respect to who is winning and losing the war for talent in this industry.[47]

In this section of the chapter, we examine the job withdrawal process that characterizes voluntary employee turnover, and we illustrate the central role that job satisfaction plays in this process. Replacing workers is an expensive undertaking, and recent estimates for 2008 place this cost at roughly $50,000 for professional or managerial workers and $25,000 for clerical or manufacturing employees.[48] Replacement costs reflect just a tip of the iceberg, however, when it comes to the costs of job dissatisfaction and turnover. There is also a demonstrable relationship between employee satisfaction and customer satisfaction at the individual level,[49] and turnover rates and customer satisfaction at the organizational level.[50] Indeed, the whole employee satisfaction–firm performance relationship can become part of a virtuous cycle, where firms with more highly satisfied employees perform better and increase their profits, which in turn they use to shore up employee pay and benefits—further adding to their competitive advantage.[51] We will discuss what aspects of job satisfaction seem most critical to retention and how to measure these facets and we show how survey–feedback interventions, designed around these measures, can be used to strategically manage the voluntary turnover process.

PROCESS OF JOB WITHDRAWAL

Job withdrawal is a set of behaviors that dissatisfied individuals enact to avoid the work situation. The right side of Figure 10.3 shows a model grouping the overall set of behaviors into three categories: behavior change, physical job withdrawal, and psychological job withdrawal.

We present the various forms of withdrawal in a progression, as if individuals try the next category only if the preceding is either unsuccessful or impossible to implement. This theory of **progression of withdrawal** has a long history and many adherents.[52] For example, someone who is dissatisfied with the job or organization might not be able to just jump to another job right away but will instead either disengage temporarily (through absenteeism or tardiness) or psychologically (through lower job involvement and organizational commitment) until the right opportunity comes along.[53] During an economic recession like the one experienced in 2008, for example, many employers bent on cutting costs engaged in practices that created dissatisfied employees. The poor job market did not really allow these employees to leave, but many were just biding their time. As one HR executive noted, "People have long

Progression of Withdrawal
Theory that dissatisfied individuals enact a set of behaviors in succession to avoid their work situation.

figure 10.3

An Overall Model of the Job Dissatisfaction–Job Withdrawal Process

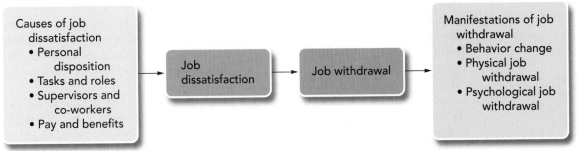

memories. What they don't have right now are a whole lot of career options. And they will judge their employer by how equitably they feel they were treated during the down market."[54] Others have suggested that there is no tight progression in that any one of the categories can compensate for another, and people choose the category that is most likely to redress the specific source of dissatisfaction.[55] Still other theories maintain that turnover is set up by a general level of persistent dissatisfaction that then is triggered abruptly by some single disruptive event at work that either pushes the employee away (such as a dispute with a supervisor or co-worker) or pulls the employee away (an alternative employment opportunity).[56] This model focuses on "the straw that breaks the camel's back" but shares with all the other theories an emphasis on job dissatisfaction as the necessary but insufficient cause of turnover. Regardless of what specific theory one endorses, there is a general consensus that withdrawal behaviors are clearly related to one another, and they are all at least partially caused by job dissatisfaction.[57]

Behavior Change

One might expect that an employee's first response to dissatisfaction would be to try to change the conditions that generate the dissatisfaction. This can lead to supervisor–subordinate confrontation, perhaps even conflict, as dissatisfied workers try to bring about changes in policy or upper-level personnel. Although at first this type of conflict can feel threatening to the manager, on closer inspection, this is really an opportunity for the manager to learn about and perhaps solve an important problem. For example, Don McAdams, a manager at Johnsonville Foods, recalls an incident where one particular employee had been very critical of the company's incentive system. McAdams listened to the person's concerns and then asked him to head a committee charged with developing a better incentive system. At first the employee was taken aback, but he eventually accepted the challenge and became so enthusiastic about the project that he was the one who presented the new system to the general membership. Because this person was known to be highly critical of the old system, he had a high level of credibility with the other workers, who felt, "If this guy likes it, it must be pretty good." In the end, this critic-turned-champion was immensely successful in solving a specific organizational problem.[58]

Less constructively, employees can initiate change through **whistle-blowing** (making grievances public by going to the media).[59] Whistle-blowers are often dissatisfied individuals who cannot bring about internal change and, out of a sense of commitment or frustration, take their concerns to external constituencies. For example,

Whistle-blowing Making grievances public by going to the media or government.

Russell Tice was an employee of the U.S. National Security Agency (NSA) whose job was to electronically eavesdrop (i.e., spy) on our nation's enemies. He was devoted to his job and noted that "the mentality at NSA was we need to get these guys and we're going to do whatever it takes to get them." However, when his job was changed in the wake of 9/11 to focus on calls being made by U.S. citizens, he was concerned that without the proper warrants, this type of surveillance of his fellow Americans was illegal. No one at NSA would take Tice's concerns seriously, and so he took his concerns to the *New York Times,* which eventually published an article that accused the Bush administration of conducting widespread illegal wiretapping. The White House first denied the allegations, but when the evidence became too overwhelming to dispute, the administration admitted that the program was inappropriate and hence ended its existence. Tice eventually had his security clearance revoked, but he noted that it was worth it. "We need to clean up the intelligence community. We've had abuses and they need to be addressed."[60]

Although this type of whistle-blowing activity has always taken place, the advent of websites like Wikileaks has provided a more obvious and convenient outlet for this activity. Wikileaks is most famous for collecting and publishing information provided by government and military sources, but it has also threatened private companies such as Bank of America.[61]

Physical Job Withdrawal

If the job conditions cannot be changed, a dissatisfied worker may be able to solve the problem by leaving the job. This could take the form of an internal transfer if the dissatisfaction is job-specific (the result of an unfair supervisor or unpleasant working conditions). On the other hand, if the source of the dissatisfaction relates to organizationwide policies (lack of job security or below-market pay levels), organizational turnover is likely.

Many employees who would like to quit their jobs have to stay on if they have no other employment opportunities. This was certainly true during the most recent recession and, in 2011, when the recession was easing, many CEOs started making the rounds to hold town hall meeting with employees to get ideas about boosting morale. For example, Robert Moritz, head of PricewaterhouseCooper, noted that "As the economy turns around, there is more of a risk in losing people so we've increased our efforts to talk to workers."[62]

Another way of physically removing oneself from the dissatisfying work short of quitting altogether is to be absent. One recent survey indicated that, on average, companies spend 15% of their payroll costs to make up for absent or tardy workers.[63] Part of the reason that absenteeism is costly is that, like a virus, it often spreads from one worker to another, even if no one is really sick with any communicable health disorder. The evidence suggests that there are strong social norms associated with absenteeism, and that it "snowballs" in groups so that once it gets rolling it becomes more and more acceptable.[64] The large impact of social influences on absenteeism can be traced to the fact that there is not a great deal of standardized practice when it comes to how and when people report in sick, and this creates a great deal of interpretive latitude for individual workers, especially when they do not get paid for reporting in sick. Indeed, 40% of workers in the private sector do not get paid for sick days, and the U.S. Congress is considering legislation, the Healthy Families Act, that would guarantee seven paid sick days for anyone working at a company with 15 or more employees.[65] To get around the nonstandardized way various units treat the issue, some companies like Walmart have centralized the process by which an employee requests a day off, taking it out of the hands of local managers. Walmart employees seeking a day off need to call a 1-800 number and provide a standardized set of documentation supporting the reason underlying the request.[66]

Psychological Withdrawal

When dissatisfied employees are unable to change their situation or remove themselves physically from their jobs, they may psychologically disengage themselves from their jobs. Although they are physically on the job, their minds may be somewhere else.

This psychological disengagement can take several forms. First, if the primary dissatisfaction has to do with the job itself, the employee may display a very low level of job involvement. **Job involvement** is the degree to which people identify themselves with their jobs. People who are uninvolved with their jobs consider their work an unimportant aspect of their lives. A second form of psychological disengagement, which can occur when the dissatisfaction is with the employer as a whole, is a low level of organizational commitment. **Organizational commitment** is the degree to which an employee identifies with the organization and is willing to put forth effort on its behalf. Individuals who feel they have been unjustly treated by their employer often respond by reducing their level of commitment and are often looking for the first good chance to quit their jobs.

They may also respond to perceived unjust treatment by trying to get back at the employer via theft, fraud, or sabotage. Indeed, although theft by employees is a constant concern among all employers, history reveals that during economic recessions, cases of fraud and malfeasance often rise as fast as the stock market falls. Part of the problem, of course, is that when people are struggling to make ends meet they are also subject to greater levels of temptation. This might be especially the case if they believe that they are about to be laid off, and hence are angry and perceive an act of theft as a just, retaliatory behavior aimed at the organization. The other part of the problem, however, is that during hard times, organizations become more vigilant of bottom line concerns and, in the hunt to reduce costs, often trip over irregularities that might not have been noticed during more flush periods. As security consultant Brian Mich notes, "it is often hard to tell which is the chicken or the egg in these cases, but the evidence that recessions cause a spike in documented employee theft is irrefutable."[67]

For example, in the case of the most recent recession, one 2009 survey revealed that roughly 20% of managers polled were able to document an increase in theft of both financial and physical assets from 2006 to 2008. A separate study by PricewaterhouseCooper found that companies lost an average of $2.4 million to fraud in 2007, up from $1.7 million in 2005. Ironically, the evidence from fraud cases suggests that it is often the most educated and trusted employees that do the most damage. For example, the average organizational tenure of employees convicted of fraud is roughly eight years, and most have graduate degrees. This is a group of smart employees who have earned trust and worked their way into the best position to know exactly how to get away with various fraud schemes.[68]

Instead of hoping to just trip over theft and fraud cases as part of an overall cost-cutting hunt, however, organizations are increasingly using electronic means of sleuthing to catch people in the act. For example, at Wendy's and Chili's restaurant franchises, managers have begun to install fingerprint scanners on cash registers to more definitively link each transaction to specific employees. This has cut down on theft and also

Job Involvement
The degree to which people identify themselves with their jobs.

Organizational Commitment
The degree to which an employee identifies with the organization and is willing to put forth effort on its behalf.

reduced conflict within the chains that was formerly caused by employees who were constantly arguing about who rang up what transactions. At IBM, tracking technology installed into computers has allowed the organization to track down stolen laptops (or machines that employees falsely report being stolen) on the Internet.[69]

JOB SATISFACTION AND JOB WITHDRAWAL

LO 10-3
Specify the relationship between job satisfaction and various forms of job withdrawal, and identify the major sources of job satisfaction in work contexts.

Job Satisfaction
A pleasurable feeling that results from the perception that one's job fulfills or allows for the fulfillment of one's important job values.

Frame of Reference
A standard point that serves as a comparison for other points and thus provides meaning.

As we see in Figure 10.3, the key driving force behind all the different forms of job withdrawal is **job satisfaction,** which we will define as a pleasurable feeling that results from the perception that one's job fulfills or allows for the fulfillment of one's important job values.[70] This definition reflects three important aspects of job satisfaction. First, job satisfaction is a function of *values,* defined as "what a person consciously or unconsciously desires to obtain." Second, this definition emphasizes that different employees have different views of which values are important, and this is critical in determining the nature and degree of their job satisfaction. One person may value high pay above all else; another may value the opportunity to travel; another may value staying within a specific geographic region. The third important aspect of job satisfaction is perception. An individual's perceptions may not be a completely accurate reflection of reality, and different people may view the same situation differently.

In particular, people's perceptions are often strongly influenced by their frame of reference. A **frame of reference** is a standard point that serves as a comparison for other points and thus provides meaning. For example, an upper-level executive who offers a 6% salary increase to a lower-level manager might expect this to make the manager happy because inflation (the executive's frame of reference) is only 3%. The manager, on the other hand, might find the raise quite unsatisfactory because it is less than the 9% raise received by a colleague who does similar work (the manager's frame of reference). Often the most salient frame of reference for job satisfaction is the person's current level of satisfaction and changes in the direction of job satisfaction predict turnover over and above the absolute level of turnover itself. That is, two people could report a level of "moderate" satisfaction with their jobs, but if one person was formerly high, and the other person was formerly low, the person with the negative trend has a much higher probability of leaving relative to the person with the positive trend.[71]

SOURCES OF JOB DISSATISFACTION

Many aspects of people and organizations can cause dissatisfaction among employees. Managers and HR professionals need to be aware of these because they are the levers which can raise job satisfaction and reduce employee withdrawal. This is an issue that is particularly salient in the current economy where pressures to raise productivity have pushed many workers to the limit.

Unsafe Working Conditions

Earlier in this chapter we discussed the employer's role in helping employees stay healthy via employee assistance programs for specific problems like drug addiction and alcohol dependency, as well as general wellness initiatives to promote health and reduce health care–related expenditures. Obviously, if employers care this much about the risk employees are exposed to off the job, there needs to be an even more important emphasis on risk exposure that occurs on the job.

Of course, each employee has a right to safe working conditions, and previously in this book (see Chapter 3) we reviewed the Occupational Safety and Health Act of 1970 (OSHA), which spells out those rights in a very detailed fashion. We also discussed in that chapter how to develop safety awareness programs that identify and communicate job hazards, as well as how to reinforce safe work practices that would allow one to pass an OSHA inspection. Although our emphasis in that chapter on safety was primarily directed at legal compliance, we need to revisit the topic in this chapter, because OSHA is not the only audience that is likely to evaluate the safety of jobs. The perception and reaction of the organization's own employees to working conditions has implications for satisfaction, retention, and competitive advantage that go well beyond merely meeting the legal requirements. That is, if applicants or job incumbents conclude that their health or lives are at risk because of the job, attracting and retaining workers will be impossible. For example, one of the managers of the Massey Energy Company sent an e-mail to workers that stated that "if any of you have been asked by your group presidents, your supervisors, engineers, safety inspectors, or anyone else to do anything other than run coal (i.e., build overcasts, do construction jobs, whatever) you need to ignore them and run coal." This message, which did not exactly put "safety first," was highlighted in a subsequent investigation into the deadliest coal mine accident in 40 years, which killed 29 workers at Massey's Upper Big Branch mine in West Virginia.[72]

Although broad statistics suggest that on-the-job injury rates have plummeted over time, many attribute this to fears among employees that if they report an injury, they might be fired, especially if there is any chance that the worker may have performed what could be construed by anyone as an unsafe act. This kind of "blame-the-worker" attitude results in what many consider to be a severe "underreporting" problem when it comes to workplace injuries. For example, Jeff Repper, a retired employee at AK Steel, spoke for many when he noted, "At a steel mill, you don't turn the small or medium injuries in or else you'll get time off without pay."[73] Clearly, these kinds of practices send the wrong message regarding the value of human resources, and as the "Competing through Sustainability" box highlights, the organizational and societal costs that are associated with not emphasizing safety typically vastly outweigh the costs of compliance.

Not all jobs pose safety risks, but the nature of the work in a whole host of jobs makes managing safety-related perceptions critical. This includes jobs such as fishing boat operators, timber cutters, airline pilot/flight attendants, structural metal workers, garbage collectors, and taxi drivers/chauffeurs, which all have been identified as jobs where people are most likely to be involved in fatal accidents. In fact, in these job categories alone, close to 1,000 people die annually. Other jobs that rate low in terms of fatal accidents rate higher in nonfatal accidents, and this includes many jobs in eating establishments, hospitals, nursing homes, convenience stores, and the long-haul trucking industry. Still other jobs pose risks in terms of contracting occupational diseases due to exposure to chemicals. Finally, some jobs create health risks simply because of the long hours and high stress that are associated with them.[74] This was highlighted recently by several cases in the aviation industry where air traffic controllers who were working at night were found to be sleeping on the job because of extended hours. For example, in one case, a lone controller was working on less than two hours' sleep in the previous 24 hours, and this was a contributing factor in the crash of ComAir Flight 191 in Lexington, Kentucky.[75] In general, working at night runs counter to the basic physiology of the human body and disrupts one's natural circadian rhythm, which in turn causes a whole host of physical problems. Thus, working at night has to be considered a safety issue in any job that states this as a task requirement in the job description.[76]

Safety Lapses Sink Deep Water Horizon

When it came to accidents and safety violations, British Petroleum (BP) had a history. In 2005, a blast at its refinery in Texas City, Texas, killed 15 people and seriously injured another 180. When it came to Gulf of Mexico Operations, British Petroleum had warnings. In fact, there were 10 reported major incidents in the Gulf in 2007 alone. Vice president of Gulf of Mexico Production, Richard Morrison, noted at the end of that year that "we are experiencing an unprecedented frequency of serious incidents in our operations. We are extremely fortunate that one or more of our co-workers has not been seriously injured or killed."

The good fortune ended abruptly on April 20, 2010, when the Deep Water Horizon rig, a floating oil well larger than two football fields, exploded due to an undetected natural gas leak. The explosion killed 11 people and injured another 17, and sent the giant rig to an underwater burial under a mile of seawater. In addition to this human cost, the accident was an environmental disaster. It took months to cap the well over which the Deep Water Horizon was perched, and in the meantime, over 200 million gallons of oil spewed into the Gulf, threatening the delicate ecosystem of flora, fauna, and beaches in that region. The cost of the accident to the financial standing of BP was also monumental. BP put aside $41 billion to pay for the spill, but by the summer of 2011 that fund was already tapped out.

Investigations into the disaster revealed a large number of human errors and problems in the area of human resource management on the part of BP, its partners, and government regulators that contributed to the disaster. First, on the BP side, cost-cutting efforts at the company led to massive layoffs of workers, which in turn resulted in a shortage of people with the skills to conduct self-inspections. Those individuals were then provided financial incentives and bonuses that, when push came to shove, placed efficiency goals ahead of safety goals. This was exacerbated by coordination failures between BP and its partners who actually owned the rig and drilling equipment. Indeed, in the first week of the disaster, BP CEO Tony Hayward was quick to point the finger at Transocean, noting that "It is not our rig, not our equipment, not our systems."

Of course, both BP and Transocean are regulated by the U.S. government via the Minerals Management Service (MMS), but many believe that the workers of this unit were hardly up to the task of monitoring and controlling those they supervised. An internal report conducted by the Department of the Interior found that several MMS employees had "frequently consumed alcohol at industry functions, had used cocaine, and marijuana, and had sexual relationships with oil and gas representatives." Indeed, this crack staff was scheduled to award BP with a prize for safety, a mere two weeks after the incident. As an official government report noted in January of 2011, "This disaster would not have happened if the companies involved had been guided by an unrelenting commitment to safety first. And it would not have happened if the responsible government regulators had the capacity and will to demand world class safety standards."

SOURCES: G. Chazen, B. Faucon, and B. Gasselman, "Safety and Cost Drives Clashed as CEO Hayward Remade BP," *The Wall Street Journal*, June 29, 2010, pp. B1–B6; J. Mervin, "Counting the Cost of the BP Disaster One Year On," BBC News, April 19, 2011; P. Coy and S. Reed, "Lessons of the Spill," *Bloomberg Businessweek*, May 10, 2010, pp. 48–55; and S. Smith, "Commission Spreads Blame for the Gulf Oil Disaster," CNN.com, January 5, 2011.

Although one would think that workers and managers would do this naturally, the fact is the longer one is exposed to a particular risk environment the more comfortable one gets in that environment and the less vigilant one becomes. Upper level management needs to continually emphasize and stress compliance with worker safety regulations and carefully monitor statistics related to workplace accidents. Many employers link financial bonuses to attaining specific safety-related goals, and this helps keep employees focused on doing the job the right way every day.[77] These programs more than pay for themselves over time. Research suggests that it is not unusual for a mid-size company that reduces accidents by 10% to see a $50,000 reduction in premiums. Assuming that the firm has a profit margin of 5%, this is essentially the equivalent of bringing in another $1 million in sales. Based on these numbers, Jim Hatherley, a vice president at Liberty Mutual Group, notes that "the companies that have better profit-and-loss statements are the ones that take everything more seriously, including safety. When they look at safety as a business issue, they win."[78]

Personal Dispositions

Because dissatisfaction is an emotion that ultimately resides within the person, it is not surprising that many who have studied these outcomes have focused on individual differences. For example, in Chapter 6, we described the Five Factor Model of Personality, and several of these traits have been linked to higher turnover intentions and actual turnover. In general, turnover is more likely to be an issue for employees who are low in emotional stability, low in conscientiousness, and low in agreeableness.[79]

Negative affectivity is a term used to describe a dispositional dimension that reflects pervasive individual differences in satisfaction with any and all aspects of life. Individuals who are high in negative affectivity report higher levels of aversive mood states, including anger, contempt, disgust, guilt, fear, and nervousness across all contexts (work and nonwork). People who are high in negative affectivity tend to focus extensively on the negative aspects of themselves and others. They also tend to persist in their negative attitudes even in the face of organizational interventions, such as increased pay levels, that generally increase the levels of satisfaction of other people.[80] Research has even shown that negative affectivity in early adolescence is predictive of overall job dissatisfaction in adulthood. There were also significant relationships between work attitudes measured over 5-year[81] and 10-year[82] periods, even for workers who changed employers and/or occupations. All of this implies that some individuals tend to bring low satisfaction with them to work. Thus these people may be relatively dissatisfied regardless of what steps the organization or the manager takes.

The evidence on the linkage between these kinds of traits and job satisfaction suggests the importance of personnel selection as a way of raising overall levels of employee satisfaction. If job satisfaction remains relatively stable across time and jobs because of characteristics like negative affectivity, this suggests that transient changes in job satisfaction will be difficult to sustain in these individuals, who will typically revert to their "dispositional" or adaptation level over time. Thus, some employers actually try to screen for this when selecting job candidates. For example, at Zappos, the online retailer of shoes and apparel, CEO Tony Hsei notes that "We do our best to hire positive people and put them where their positive thinking is reinforced."[83] Interviews should assess the degree to which any job applicant has a history of chronic dissatisfaction with employment. The logic is, if an applicant states that

Negative Affectivity
A dispositional dimension that reflects pervasive individual differences in satisfaction with any and all aspects of life.

COMPETING THROUGH TECHNOLOGY

Downloading a Positive Mood

Psychologists and sociologists have long studied the determinants of happiness and it is fair to say that when it comes to being happy, this is now more of a science than it is an art. In fact, the field of "Positive Psychology" reversed psychology's traditional focus on negative states such as depression, anger, and grief, and shifted the attention to states such as joy, enthusiasm, and optimism. At first, much of this research suggested that positive emotionality was a stable dispositional characteristic that was not particularly "malleable" or "trainable." For example, poor people who won the lottery or healthy people who became disabled often returned to the similar levels of happiness they experienced prior to these major life-changing events.

However, more recent research has shown that there are measurable effects for some happiness-inducing interventions, and that these effects are so reliable that applications for iPhones and iPads have been developed to help people download a happy mood. For example, the act of expressing gratitude directly to another person has an immediate positive effect on one's mood, and

at regular intervals, a "Live Happy" application will remind you to do this on a regular basis. Similarly, complimenting a person on some trait or characteristic that you truly admire can have a similar effect, and is prompted by your Live Happy application. Savoring positive experiences is also an act with reliable effects on moods, and this same application will, on a regular basis, send you some of your favorite photos of friends or family or special places in order to jump start a positive feeling. Recalling and replaying days in your life that brought you a great deal of joy is also a source of positive mood, and once programmed, the Live Happy application will serve those up for you, again, on a regular basis.

At a very general level, these external prompts help "train" people who are usually unhappy, to do the sort of things that happy people do naturally on a regular basis. As you might expect, power of any one mood enhancing intervention often wears off over time, and thus, the warm feeling one gets out of writing a thank you letter becomes smaller and smaller the more the act is repeated. Thus, the key to these

interventions is to expose the person to a wide variety of different mood manipulations. To date this kind of intervention has not found its way directly into the workplace with a specific target aimed at job satisfaction, but that day might not be far off.

"Happiness coaching" in the workplace is now common, and most of these programs are based on the same principles that have been derived from the science of positive psychology. Firms such as UBS, American Express, KPMG, and Goodwin Proctor have employed these programs to help boost employee morale and generally found positive results. With current levels of job satisfaction at the lowest level ever recorded in the 22 year history of the annual Conference Board survey, employers would certainly seem happy to express their gratitude for any technology that can be used to help reverse those numbers.

SOURCES: C. Wallis, "The Science of Happiness Turns 10," *Time*, July 8, 2009, pp. 20–21; E. Leis-Newman, "Unhappy? There's an App for That," *Monitor on Psychology*, June 2011, pp. 29–31; and S. Shellenbarger, "Thinking Happy Thoughts at Work," *The Wall Street Journal*, January 27, 2010, p. D2.

he was dissatisfied with his past six jobs, what makes Hsei think that person won't be dissatisfied with this one? Despite the strong evidence for the stability of negative affectivity, as the "Competing through Technology" box illustrates, researchers are exploring technologically mediated interventions that might be able to help people that have negative affectivity think and act like someone who has positive affectivity.

Tasks and Roles

As a predictor of job dissatisfaction, nothing surpasses the nature of the task itself. Many aspects of a task have been linked to dissatisfaction. Several elaborate theories relating task characteristics to worker reactions have been formulated and extensively tested. We discussed several of these in Chapter 4. In this section we focus on three primary aspects of tasks that affect job satisfaction: the complexity of the task, the amount of flexibility in where and when the work is done, and, finally, the value the employee puts on the task.[84]

With a few exceptions, there is a strong positive relationship between task complexity and job satisfaction. That is, the boredom generated by simple, repetitive jobs that do not mentally challenge the worker leads to frustration and dissatisfaction.[85] One of the major interventions aimed at reducing job dissatisfaction by increasing job complexity is job enrichment. As the term suggests, this intervention is directed at jobs that are "impoverished" or boring because of their repetitive nature or low scope. Many job enrichment programs are based on the job characteristics theory discussed earlier in Chapter 4.

For example, many job enrichment programs provide increased opportunities for workers to have input into important organizational decisions that involve their work, and this has been routinely found to reduce role conflict and ambiguity. For example, at Crouse Hospital in upstate New York, turnover was reduced from 49% to 18% after initiating a program that promoted formal, small-group discussion about how to improve patient care at every level of the organization. In addition to the reduction in turnover, cost savings and increased customer service led to an $11 million net gain in 2007 that compared very favorably to the $15 million net loss the hospital recorded prior to the program.[86]

In some cases, job enrichment programs may have to be complemented with training programs to ensure people have the skills to expand their jobs. For example, at University of Chicago Hospital, many technical employees struggled with interpersonal tasks associated with customers, resulting in conflict with clients and stress at work. Training programs in customer service, critical thinking, and situational judgment were provided, and the technicians were each encouraged to develop their own "Ideal Patient Encounter" associated for their specific job. Complaints from patients dropped precipitously, and the reduction in conflict led to less stress for the technicians, as well as a 33% reduction in turnover in those job categories. With this type of training, participants decide on their most important work values. They then learn how to pinpoint goals, identify roadblocks to successful goal accomplishment, and seek the collaboration of co-workers in achieving these goals. In general, skills training gives job incumbents the ability to better predict, understand, and control events occurring on the job, which in turn increases their ability to make their own decisions.[87]

Another task-based intervention is **job rotation.** This is a process of systematically moving a single individual from one job to another over the course of time. Although employees may not feel capable of putting up with the dissatisfying aspects of a particular job indefinitely, they often feel they can do so temporarily. Job rotation can do more than simply spread out the dissatisfying aspects of a particular job. It can increase work complexity for employees and provide valuable cross-training in jobs so that employees eventually understand many different jobs. This makes for a more flexible workforce and increases workers' appreciation of the other tasks that have to be accomplished for the organization to complete its mission.

Because of the degree to which nonwork roles often spill over and affect work roles, and vice versa, a third critical aspect of work that affects satisfaction and retention is the degree to which scheduling is flexible. To help employees manage their multiple roles, companies have turned to a number of family-friendly policies to both recruit new talent and hold

Job Rotation
The process of systematically moving a single individual from one job to another over the course of time. The job assignments may be in various functional areas of the company or movement may be between jobs in a single functional area or department.

onto the talent they already have. These policies may include provisions for child care, elder care, flexible work schedules, job sharing, telecommuting, and extended maternal and paternal leaves.[88] Although these programs create some headaches for managers in terms of scheduling work and reporting requirements, they have a number of demonstrable benefits. First, the provision of these sorts of benefits is a recruitment aid that helps employers attract potential job applicants.[89] Second, once hired, flexible work arrangements result in reduced absenteeism. Third, over the long term, these programs result in higher levels of employee commitment to the organization.[90] They have also been linked to increased organizational citizenship behaviors on the part of individual employees.[91] Standardized training programs to help supervisors initiate and sustain friendly-family policies have been developed and validated in several different contexts.[92] Indeed, as the "Competing through Globalization" box illustrates, the value of such programs for retaining valued employees, especially women, have resulted in the spread of these practices to other countries such as India.

By far, the most important aspect of work in terms of generating satisfaction is the degree to which it is meaningfully related to core values of the worker. The term **prosocial motivation** is often used explicitly to capture the degree to which people are motivated to help other people. When people believe that their work has an important impact on other people, they are much more willing to work longer hours.[93] This prosocial motivation could be directed at co-workers and has been found to relate to helping behavior.[94] This form of motivation can also be triggered by recognizing that one's work has a positive impact on those who benefit from one's service, such as customers or clients.[95] In contrast, when one's social needs are thwarted, they often react negatively and in self-defeating ways that drive people further away from them.[96]

For example, Genentech is a small San Francisco–based biotech pharmaceutical company that competes directly with the largest and most well-funded pharmaceutical giants in the industry including Merck, Lilly, and Johnson & Johnson. From the outset, Genentech knew that the ultimate success of its venture depended on attracting and retaining the best minds within the field of bioscience, despite having less capital relative to the competition.

Genentech focused its mission on developing and testing "big ideas," particularly as this relates to life and death issues (e.g., drugs to fight cancer) in the field of health care. It then searched out scientists who had passionate feelings about work in this area, and surrounded them with a supportive corporate culture that was more like working in a small, close-knit research university than a large pharmaceutical company. Researchers were given the autonomy to pursue their own ideas in a context where every success was celebrated (often in a sophomoric fashion), and every failure was treated as a learning experience rather than a career-ending catastrophe. The strategy was a "swing for the fences" approach emphasizing hitting a few home runs, rather than trying to incrementally tinker with existing products. As CEO Art Levinson notes, "At the end of the day, we want to make drugs that really matter—that's the transcendent issue," and this is captured in the corporate motto: "In Business for Life."

This strategy was clearly a risky bet, since in this industry, up to $800 million may be spent to invent a new drug, only to have 90% of these drugs fail to reach the market, but so far this bet has paid off. According to Wall Street estimates, Genentech's year-end revenues for 2006 stood at $6.6 billion, three times what the company earned in 2002, and the stock price doubled from $47 to $95 a share between 2005 and 2006. The company has attracted many of the top graduating doctoral students, as well as many scientists who have left their larger, more conservative and hierarchical competitors. As one industry analyst noted, "From the day the company was founded, Genentech's culture has been its competitive advantage."[97]

Prosocial Motivation
The degree to which people are energized to do their jobs because it helps other people.

Family-Friendly Practices Come to Bangalore

There was once a time when the number of hard-working, skilled, and English-proficient workers in India was so high that the country could run its economy with half of its labor force. However, times are changing, and many large Indian employers are struggling in terms of finding new employees and holding onto experienced employees as the economy comes off the most recent recession. Call centers and other basic service companies are experiencing attrition rates of over 50%, and even the most admired employers in the country such as Tata Consulting Services, Wipro, and HCL Industries reported turnover rates in excess of 20%. In fact, a recent report from the Indian Chambers of Commerce and industry states, "high attrition rates might prove to be fatal for the survival and growth of India's business processing outsourcing sector."

Thus, the days of trying to run the country's economy with an almost totally male workforce may be over. In terms of culture, India is a relatively male-dominated society, and as one HR executive has noted, "The measures of daughterly guilt are much higher in India women than in the West." Thus, while it is true that many young women work in India, very few ever develop their expertise through long-term experience because most never return to the workforce after having children. In addition, responsibilities for taking care of aging parents in India also fell disproportionately on women, often limiting their ability to return to work even after their children had grown.

These cultural effects can be readily seen in the labor force statistics. At roughly 35%, the labor force participation rate for women in India is much lower than other developed countries, including those at similar stages of development such as Brazil, Russia, or China. This figure is especially low given the fact that women make up 42% of college graduates in India.

In response to these developments, many Indian employers are working harder than ever to help retain female employees, and the kinds of family-friendly policies that have been popular in the United States are now taking root in Indian firms. In addition to the traditional kinds of support one would see in the West, such as day care and elder care, Indian family-friendly policies take on their own unique flavor and often target their attention to parents and in-laws. For example, German pharmaceutical giant Boehringer Ingelheim, realizing that parents disapprove of their daughters traveling alone will pay for an employee to take their mother with them on business trips. Google provides point-to-point taxi service to any woman who is caring for a parent or in-law. Ernst & Young throws office parties for parents and in-laws so that they can come into the office and see what their daughters are doing, who they are working with. These practices help to attract, develop, and retain well-educated women, and at least at Ernst & Young, this is part of the firm's overall competitive labor market strategy. Ernst & Young's goal is to have an equal number of male and female workers, and this has made it the employer of choice for talented Indian women.

SOURCES: B. Einhorn, "Scarce Talent, Rising Wages, Balky Clients," *Bloomberg Businessweek*, May 30, 2011, pp. 13–14; B. Einhorn, "Bangalore's Paying to Keep the Talent," *Bloomberg Businessweek*, May 24, 2010, pp. 14–15; M. Srivastava, "In India, 101 Employees Pose Big Problems," *Bloomberg Businessweek*, January 17, 2011, pp. 13–14; and "Keeping Women on the Job in India," *Bloomberg Businessweek*, March 7, 2011, pp. 11–12.

Supervisors and Co-workers

The two primary sets of people in an organization who affect job satisfaction are co-workers and supervisors. A person may be satisfied with her supervisor and co-workers for one of two reasons. First, she may have many of the same values, attitudes, and philosophies that the co-workers and supervisors have. Research shows the diversity in values and beliefs can create a "misfit" between the person and the work group that increases the likelihood of turnover.[98] In other cases, even if there is an initial misfit between a new employee and his or her leader and co-workers, some highly adaptable newcomers can adjust their attitudes and beliefs in order to create a fit, and those that cannot adjust leave.[99] Over time, this creates an environment where groups can become increasingly homogeneous, and this "attraction–selection–attrition" cycle can be a powerful determinant of the organization's culture.[100] Indeed, even if one cannot generate a unifying culture throughout an entire organization, it is worth noting that increases in job satisfaction can be derived simply from congruence among supervisors and subordinates at one level.[101]

Second, people may be satisfied with their supervisor and co-workers because they provide support that helps them achieve their own goals. Social support means the degree to which the person is surrounded by other people who are sympathetic and caring. Considerable research indicates that social support is a strong predictor of job satisfaction and lower employee turnover.[102] In contrast, abusive supervision is a major cause of turnover, and some organizations find that they can reduce turnover in some units by 25% to 33% in a single year simply by removing a specific supervisor who lacks interpersonal skills.[103]

Because of the powerful role played by supervisors and other more experienced workers in terms of supporting the organization's culture, some organizations are going to great lengths to develop the mentoring skills of their managers and other highly experienced workers.[104] In fact, recent statistics show that the number of *Fortune* 500 companies that provided formal mentoring programs jumped from 10% in 2002 to over 50% in 2007. Much of this is attributed to the fact that many organizations are facing a wave of retirements as baby boomers prepare to leave the workforce, and organizations are scrambling to develop systems that would promote critical knowledge transfer from older to younger workers. As William Arnone, a human capital consultant at Ernst & Young, notes, "Companies know there is a looming 'wisdom withdrawal' but they're putting off addressing it."[105]

Because a supportive environment reduces dissatisfaction, many organizations foster team building both on and off the job (such as via softball or bowling leagues). The idea is that group cohesiveness and support for individual group members will be increased through exposure and joint efforts. Although management certainly cannot ensure that each stressed employee develops friends, it can make it easier for employees to interact—a necessary condition for developing friendship and rapport. In fact, results of surveys indicate that endorsing the item "Most of my closest friendships are with people at work" is one of the most powerful tools for predicting turnover.[106]

Pay and Benefits

We should not discount the influence of the job incumbent, the job itself, and the surrounding people in terms of influencing job satisfaction, but for most people, work is their primary source of income and financial security. Pay is also seen as an indicator of status within the organization as well as in society at large. Thus, for many individuals, the standing of their pay relative to those within their organization, or the standing of their pay relative to others doing similar work for other employers, becomes even more important than the level of pay itself.[107] Thus, for some people, pay is a reflection of self-worth, so pay satisfaction takes on critical significance when it comes to retention.[108] Indeed, the role of pay and benefits is so large that we devote the entire next part of this book to these topics. Within this chapter we focus

CHAPTER 10 Employee Separation and Retention **467**

primarily on satisfaction with two aspects of pay (pay levels and benefits) and how these are assessed within the organization. Methods for addressing these issues are discussed in Part 4 of this book.

One of the main dimensions of satisfaction with pay deals with pay levels relative to market wages. Indeed, when it comes to retention, employees being recruited away from one organization by another are often lured with promises of higher pay levels. In fact, exit surveys of high-performing employees who have left their organization indicate "better pay" as the reason in over 70% of the cases compared to only 33% who indicate "better opportunity." Ironically, when the managers of those same workers are polled, 68% cite "better opportunity" versus 45% who indicate it was "better pay," suggesting quite a difference of opinion.[109] Satisfaction with benefits is another important dimension of overall pay satisfaction. Because many individuals have a difficult time ascertaining the true dollar value of their benefits package, however, this dimension may not always be as salient to people as pay itself. To derive competitive advantage from benefits' expenditures, it is critical not only to make them highly salient to employees, however, but also link them to the organization's strategic direction.

MEASURING AND MONITORING JOB SATISFACTION

Most attempts to measure job satisfaction rely on workers' self-reports. There is a vast amount of data on the reliability and validity of many existing scales as well as a wealth of data from companies that have used these scales, allowing for comparisons across firms. Established scales are excellent places to begin if employers wish to assess the satisfaction levels of their employees. An employer would be foolish to "reinvent the wheel" by generating its own versions of measures of these broad constructs. Of course, in some cases, organizations want to measure their employees' satisfaction with aspects of their work that are specific to that organization (such as satisfaction with one particular health plan versus another). In these situations the organization may need to create its own scales, but this will be the exception rather than the rule.

One standardized, widely used measure of job satisfaction is the Job Descriptive Index (JDI). The JDI emphasizes various facets of satisfaction: pay, the work itself, supervision, co-workers, and promotions. Table 10.5 presents several items from the JDI scale. Other scales exist for those who want to get even more specific about different facets of satisfaction. For example, although the JDI we just examined assesses satisfaction with pay, it does not break pay up into different dimensions.[110] The Pay Satisfaction Questionnaire (PSQ) focuses on these more specific dimensions (pay levels, benefits, pay structure, and pay raises); thus this measure gives a more detailed view of exactly what aspects of pay are most or least satisfying.[111]

Clearly there is no end to the number of satisfaction facets that we might want to measure, but the key in operational contexts, where the main concern is retention, is making sure that scores on whatever measures taken truly relate to voluntary turnover among valued people. For example, satisfaction with co-workers might be low, but if this aspect of satisfaction is not too central to employees, it may not translate into voluntary turnover. Similarly, in an organization that bases raises on performance, low performers might report being dissatisfied with raises, but this may not reflect any operational problem. Indeed, the whole strategic purpose of many pay-for-performance plans is to create this type of dissatisfaction among low performers to motivate them to higher levels of performance.

table 10.5

Sample Items from a Standardized Job Satisfaction Scale (the JDI)

Instructions: Think of your present work. What is it like most of the time? In the blank beside each word given below, write

__Y__ for "Yes" if it describes your work

__N__ for "No" if it does NOT describe your work

__?__ if you cannot decide

Work Itself	**Pay**	**Promotion Opportunities**
__?__ Routine	__?__ Less than I deserve	__?__ Dead-end job
__?__ Satisfying	__?__ Highly paid	__?__ Unfair policies
__?__ Good	__?__ Insecure	__?__ Based on ability

Supervision	**Co-workers**
__?__ Impolite	__?__ Intelligent
__?__ Praises good work	__?__ Responsible
__?__ Doesn't supervise enough	__?__ Boring

SOURCE: W. K. Balzar, D. C. Smith, D. E. Kravitz, S. E. Lovell, K. B. Paul, B. A. Reilly, and C. E. Reilly, *User's Manual for the Job Descriptive Index (JDI)* (Bowling Green, OH: Bowling Green State University, 1990).

SURVEY-FEEDBACK INTERVENTIONS

LO 10-4
Design a survey feedback intervention program, and use this to promote retention of key organizational personnel.

Regardless of what measures are used or how many facets of satisfaction are assessed, a systematic, ongoing program of *employee survey research* should be a prominent part of any human resource strategy for a number of reasons. First, it allows the company to monitor trends over time and thus prevent problems in the area of voluntary turnover before they happen. For example, Figure 10.4 shows the average profile for different facets of satisfaction for a hypothetical company in 2007, 2009, and 2011. As the figure makes clear, the level of satisfaction with promotion opportunities in this company has eroded over time, whereas the satisfaction with co-workers has improved. If there was a strong relationship between satisfaction with promotion opportunities and voluntary turnover among high performers, this would constitute a threat that the organization might need to address via some of the techniques discussed in our previous chapter, "Employee Development." For example, Sun Healthcare Group found exactly this kind of trend in its survey of nurses, aides, and other caregivers. The company responded to this feedback by creating the Career Pathways Initiative that allowed the employees to develop new skills and grow professionally. The program provided time off and financial support—some of which was obtained from seeking a federal grant—to workers who wanted to go back to school and obtain higher degrees. Many former nurses aides became fully certified nursing assistants, many nursing assistants became licensed practical nurses (LPNs) and registered nurses (RNs), and many LPNs and RNs became nurse practitioners and physician assistants. The organization not only wound up having a higher skilled staff, in addition, turnover was reduced by 20% after the initiation of the program.[112]

A second reason for engaging in an ongoing program of employee satisfaction surveys is that it provides a means of empirically assessing the impact of changes in policy (such as introduction of a new performance appraisal system) or personnel (e.g., introduction of a new CEO) on worker attitudes. Figure 10.5 shows the average profile for different satisfaction facets for a hypothetical organization one year before and one year after a merger. An examination of the profile makes it clear that

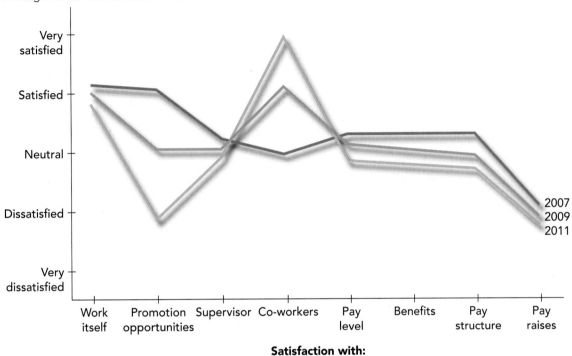

figure 10.4

Average Profile for Different Facets of Satisfaction over Time

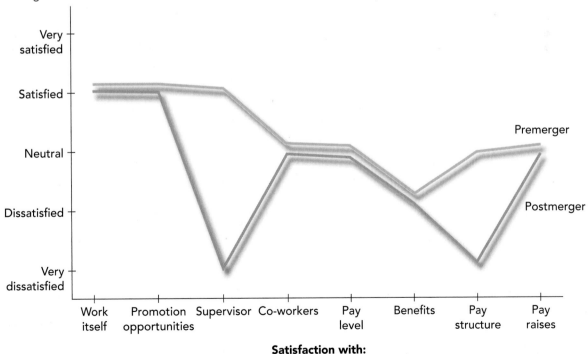

figure 10.5

Average Profile for Different Facets of Satisfaction before and after a Major Event since the merger, satisfaction with supervision and pay structure have gone down dramatically, and this has not been offset by any increase in satisfaction along other dimensions. Again, this might point to the need for training programs for supervisors (like those discussed in Chapter 7) or changes in the pay system (like those discussed in Chapter 11). This was the exact pattern of results that was found by HCL Technologies, an India-based technology services provider. More specifically, the company learned from its survey that its variable pay-for-performance program was creating too many wild swings in the workers' paychecks, and many were leaving to take jobs with more stable month-to-month paychecks. The company responded by reducing the variable component in pay from 30% to just 10%. The result was an increase in customer satisfaction, a 140% growth in revenue, and a 50% reduction in turnover.[113]

Third, when these surveys incorporate standardized scales like the JDI, they often allow the company to compare itself with others in the same industry along these dimensions. For example, Figure 10.6 shows the average profile for different satisfaction facets for a hypothetical organization and compares this to the industry average. Again, if we detect major differences between one organization and the industry as a whole (on overall pay levels, for example), this might allow the company to react and change its policies before there is a mass exodus of people moving to the competition.

According to Figure 10.6, the satisfaction with pay levels is low relative to the industry, but this is offset by higher-than-industry-average satisfaction with benefits and the work itself. As we showed in Chapter 6 ("Selection and Placement"), the organization might want to use this information to systematically screen people. That is, the fit between the person and the organization would be best if the company

figure 10.6

Average Profile for Different Facets of Satisfaction versus the Industry Average

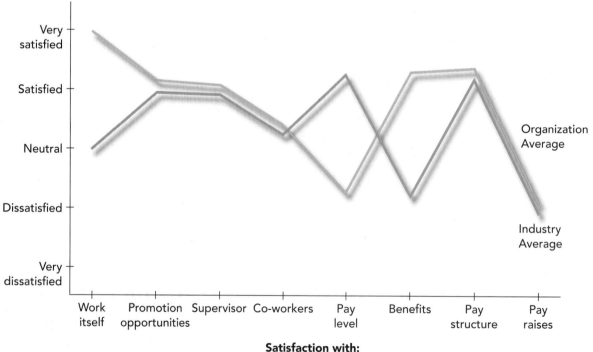

selected applicants who reported being most interested in the nature of the work itself and benefits, and rejected those applicants whose sole concern was with pay levels.

Within the organization, a systematic survey program also allows the company to check for differences between units and hence benchmark "best practices" that might be generalized across units. For example, Figure 10.7 shows the average profile for five different regional divisions of a hypothetical company. The figure shows that satisfaction with pay raises is much higher in one of the regions relative to the others. If the overall amount of money allocated to raises was equal through the entire company, this implies that the manner in which raises are allocated or communicated in the Midwest region might be something that the other regions should look into.

Although findings such as these are leading more companies to do such surveys, conducting an organizational opinion survey is not something that should be taken lightly. Especially in the beginning, surveys such as this often raise expectations. If people fail to see any timely actions taken on matters identified as problems in the survey, satisfaction is likely to be even lower than it would be in the absence of a survey.

Finally, although the focus in this section has been on surveys of current employees, any strategic retention policy also has to consider surveying people who are about to become ex-employees. Exit interviews with departing workers can be a valuable tool for uncovering systematic concerns that are driving retention problems. If properly conducted, an exit interview can reveal the reasons why people are leaving, and perhaps even set the stage for their later return. Indeed, in the new economy, it is now so common for people who once left their firm to return that they are given a special name—"boomerangs." A good exit interview sets the stage for this

figure 10.7

Average Profile for Different Facets of Satisfaction for Different Regional Divisions

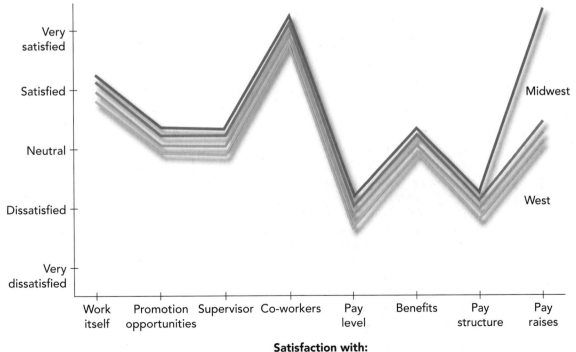

phenomenon because if a recruiter is armed with information about what caused a specific person to leave (such as an abusive supervisor or a lack of family-friendly policies), when the situation changes, the person may be willing to come back.[114] Indeed, in the war for talent, the best way to manage retention is to engage in a battle for every valued employee, even in situations when it looks like the battle may have been lost.

A LOOK BACK

WORKER HEADS FOR EXIT

In the story that opened this chapter, we saw how one specific dissatisfied worker, Steven Slater, quit his flight attendant job at JetBlue with an unusual amount of flair and drama. Clearly, in service jobs like this, there is little hope that dissatisfaction within the ranks of workers will not spill over into dissatisfaction within the ranks of customers. Thus, managing the emotional experience of human resources has to be at the center of any company's competitive strategy.

Questions

1. What are some of the major causes of job dissatisfaction and turnover that are experienced by flight attendants, in general, and Steven Slater on that one memorable day?
2. What are some specific interventions that companies like JetBlue can use to decrease stress and job dissatisfaction, and how might the more general culture of companies like JetBlue need to change in order to promote employee engagement and loyalty?
3. What role can employee attitude surveys play in maintaining a loyal and engaged workforce? What are some of the challenges associated with getting accurate and reliable information from employee surveys, and how can a survey process "backfire" in terms of harming, rather than helping a firm's efforts?

 Please see the Video that corresponds to this chapter at www.mhhe.com/noe8e.

SUMMARY

This chapter examined issues related to employee separation and retention. Involuntary turnover reflects a separation initiated by the organization, often when the individual would prefer to stay a member of the organization. Voluntary turnover reflects a separation initiated by the individual, often when the organization would prefer that the person stay a member. Organizations can gain competitive advantage by strategically managing the separation process so that involuntary turnover is implemented in a fashion that does not invite retaliation, and voluntary turnover among high performers is kept to a minimum. Retaliatory reactions to organizational discipline and dismissal decisions can be minimized by implementing these decisions in a manner that promotes feelings of procedural and interactive justice. Voluntary turnover can be minimized by measuring and monitoring employee levels of satisfaction with critical facets of job and organization, and then addressing any problems identified by such surveys.

KEY TERMS

Involuntary turnover, 443
Voluntary turnover, 443
Employment-at-will doctrine, 444
Outcome fairness, 446
Procedural justice, 447
Interactional justice, 447
Alternative dispute resolution
 (ADR), 448

Employee assistance programs
 (EAPs), 450
Outplacement counseling, 452
Progression of withdrawal, 454
Whistle-blowing, 455
Job involvement, 457
Organizational commitment, 457
Job satisfaction, 458

Frame of reference, 458
Negative affectivity, 461
Job rotation, 463
Prosocial motivation, 464

DISCUSSION QUESTIONS

1. The discipline and discharge procedures described in this chapter are systematic but rather slow. In your opinion, should some offenses lead to immediate dismissal? If so, how would you justify this to a court if you were sued for wrongful discharge?
2. Organizational turnover is generally considered a negative outcome, and many organizations spend a great deal of time and money trying to reduce it. What situations would indicate that an increase in turnover might be just what an organization needs? Given the difficulty of terminating employees, what organizational policies might promote the retention of high-performing workers but voluntary turnover among low performers?
3. Three popular interventions for enhancing worker satisfaction are job enrichment, job rotation, and role

analysis. What are the critical differences between these interventions, and under what conditions might one be preferable to the others?
4. If off-the-job stress and dissatisfaction begin to create on-the-job problems, what are the rights and responsibilities of the human resource manager in helping the employee to overcome these problems? Are intrusions into such areas an invasion of privacy, a benevolent and altruistic employer practice, or simply a prudent financial step taken to protect the firm's investment?
5. Discuss the advantages of using published, standardized measures in employee attitude surveys. Do employers ever need to develop their own measures for such surveys? Where would one turn to learn how to do this?

SELF-ASSESSMENT EXERCISE

The characteristics of your job influence your overall satisfaction with the job. One way to be satisfied at work is to find a job with the characteristics that you find desirable. The following assessment is a look at what kind of job is likely to satisfy you.

The following phrases describe different job characteristics. Read each phrase, then circle a number to indicate how much of the job characteristic you would like. Use the following scale: 1 = very little; 2 = little; 3 = a moderate amount; 4 = much; 5 = very much.

1. The opportunity to perform a number of different activities each day   1 2 3 4 5
2. Contributing something significant to the company   1 2 3 4 5
3. The freedom to determine how to do my job   1 2 3 4 5
4. The ability to see projects or jobs through to completion, rather than performing only one piece of the job   1 2 3 4 5

5. Seeing the results of my work, so I can get an idea of how well I am doing the job   1 2 3 4 5
6. A feeling that the quality of my work is important to others in the company   1 2 3 4 5
7. The need to use a variety of complex skills   1 2 3 4 5
8. Responsibility to act and make decisions independently of managers or supervisors   1 2 3 4 5
9. Time and resources to do an entire piece of work from beginning to end   1 2 3 4 5
10. Getting feedback about my performance from the work itself   1 2 3 4 5

Add the scores for the pairs of items that measure each job characteristic. A higher score for a characteristic means that characteristic is more important to you.

Skill Variety: The degree to which a job requires you to use a variety of skills.

Item 1: ____ + Item 7: ____ = ____

Task Identity: The degree to which a job requires completion of a whole and identifiable piece of work.

Item 4: ____ + Item 9: ____ = ____

Task Significance: The degree to which a job has an impact on the lives or work of others.

Item 2: ____ + Item 6: ____ = ____

Autonomy: The degree to which a job provides freedom, empowerment, and discretion in scheduling the work and determining processes and procedures for completing the work.

Item 3: ____ + Item 8: ____ = ____

Feedback: The degree to which carrying out job-related tasks and activities provides you with direct and clear information about your effectiveness.

Item 5 ____ + Item 10: ____ = ____

SOURCE: Adapted from R. Daft and R. Noe, *Organizational Behavior* (New York: Harcourt, 2001).

● EXERCISING STRATEGY: HOME DEPOT: A FIXER UPPER

The business model at Home Depot is built around homes, and the hope that people will be buying homes, selling homes, and improving homes. Thus, when confronted with the worst housing market in three decades, it is not that surprising that the company and its employees were experiencing stress. In terms of financial stress, in May of 2008, Home Depot reported a 66% drop in first-quarter profits, along with a 7% drop in sales. Expansion plans were scrapped and 15 of its flagship stores were closed, affecting 1,300 employees. This created stress among the surviving workers, and triggered higher rates of turnover among the most-skilled and knowledgeable workers who had the best alternative employment opportunities.

When Nardelli and his hand-picked vice president for human resources, Dennis Donovan, resigned in 2007, this created an opportunity for transformation, and new CEO, Frank Blake, and new vice president for human resources, Tim Crow, decided that restoring employee morale was the single most important change that had to be made at the retail chain. In Crow's words, "If people aren't happy, they aren't going to be happy to customers. That's why morale is so important in our business and that's my focus." Crow's strategy for achieving this goal for enhanced morale had three basic components.

First, Crow wanted to reestablish a sense of employee ownership of the work. Many Home Depot employees had already become disaffected because of a perception that CEO Robert Nardelli had so centralized all decision making in the organization that people felt they had little say in how to do their own work. This stood in stark contrast to the philosophy of the Home Depot's founders, Arthur Blank and Bernie Marcus, who empowered store managers and encouraged them to be entrepreneurial in orientation. In order to promote this new spirit, Crow eliminated the practice of having one HR professional in every store. Although a strategic HR team was made available to store managers on an "as needed basis" the expectation was that store managers would be given more control over hiring and promotion decisions. The more transactional aspects of HR were then in-sourced to a 220 person HR call center.

Second, Crow was bent on increasing the skill level of the workers so that they are more confident about being able to do an effective job. During the Nardelli regime, Home Depot began hiring more part-time workers, with limited skill sets, and this resulted in customer service ratings that lagged far behind competitors like Lowe's. Training was often based on an e-learning model where workers logged into a training site and slogged through material alone. Crow overturned this and replaced it with a model where workers interact face-to-face with one another on the store floor and share stories of specific successes and failures they have had with respect to customer service. Many of the best sales personnel that had left the store were rerecruited and the ratio of part-time workers to full-time workers went from 20% to close to 80%.

Finally, Crow wanted to align the rewards and recognition programs at Home Depot to boost morale. In fact, even though sales and profits were down, the amount of money that Home Depot rewarded managers who reached their sales goals actually doubled in the last two years. The company also introduced a systematic system that raises pay for each certified skill that an associate learns. Each department (e.g., plumbing) has a certification test, and the more tests the associate passes, the more he or she is paid. This level of skill is also recognized via a badge system that makes it clear to everyone on the floor who knows what. Although it is too early to tell how all of these changes will turn out, one immediate impact has been made with respect to employee turnover, which went down by 15% from 2007 to 2008.

Questions

1. The belief at Home Depot was that if their workers aren't happy, their customers are probably not going to be happy either. What are some of the major causes of job dissatisfaction and turnover that were targeted by Home Depot, and why are those so central to address in service-oriented industries?

2. What were some of the sources of job satisfaction that were not addressed by Home Depot, and what might have been done along these other lines to change the culture?

3. Despite their documented value in comprehensively addressing sources of job dissatisfaction, employee attitude surveys did not seem to play a large role in the remake of

Home Depot. Other than surveys, what are alternative methods for taking an organization's pulse, and how can these methods be used to complement surveys?

SOURCES: J. Marquez, "Rallying the Home Team," *Workforce Management*, July 14, 2008, pp. 24–28; R. J. Grossman, "Remodeling HR at Home Depot," *HRMagazine*, November 1, 2008, pp. 3–13; and G. Ruiz, "Home Depot's New HR Leader Faces Tall Order," *Workforce Management*, February 12, 2007, pp. 24–28.

● MANAGING PEOPLE

The Cost of Burnout

The wars that are being waged in Iraq and Afghanistan are now the longest ever endured by an all-volunteer army in U.S. history. As with any war, casualties are to be expected; however, one surprising source of military deaths has been a series of suicides within the ranks of military recruiters. In 2008, the suicide rate for military recruiters was three times the rate for the next highest job category, making it one of the most dangerous positions in the army. In the Houston Recruiting Battalion alone, four separate suicides were reported in a 12-month period, and army Staff Sergeant Amanda Henderson lost both her supervisor and her husband to suicides in a five-week period. Those two most recent deaths finally caught the public's attention, and an investigation ordered by Texas Senator John Cornyn uncovered a number of issues related to working conditions within the recruiter's ranks that appeared to be direct causes of the suicides.

One of the most obvious problems with the army recruiting jobs was that the goals required of recruiters were almost impossible to meet. Official policy, stated in a letter from Major General Thomas Bostick in 2006, was labeled "Must Do Two," and recruiters were told that "all of your training is geared toward prospecting and/or processing at least two enlistments monthly." This was converted at the Houston brigade into a set of work rules that seemed to require a 13-hour workday, bridged by conference calls that took place at 7 AM and 10 PM each day. Even working a 13-hour day was rarely enough to meet the required standards, however, and many recruiters were encouraged (or apparently in some cases, ordered directly) to break other rules just to make quota. For example, some recruiters were told to coach unqualified applicants on how to lie on their application forms or help applicants pass drug tests that otherwise would have disqualified them for service. As one recruiter noted, "there is one set of values for the Army, and when you go to the Recruiting Command, you're basically forced to do things outside of what would normally be considered moral or ethical."

Failure to make one's quota then resulted in very harsh punishment that included attending mandatory

"low production training sessions" that were all-day affairs held on Saturdays. Recruiters at these sessions were told to write long essays detailing their specific failures over the course of the previous week, as well as the lessons they learned from these experiences that might help them during the next week. One of the suicide victims in Texas had just come out of one of these sessions where he was publically berated and humiliated by his commander. That particular recruiter was actually a decorated battlefield soldier who could take just about anything the enemy threw at him, but reached the limit of what he could take from those who were supposedly on the same side.

Although it might be easy for readers to just chalk all of this up to unique features associated with working in a military context, this would be a mistake. The exact same pattern of practices was found when an investigation was conducted at a Paris design center, operated by French automaker Renault. In an attempt to meet the goal of boosting sales by 800,000 cars in 2007, the CEO of Renault demanded that the design center double the number of models under development from 13 to 26. This led to 16-hour workdays, which were attributed as causal factors associated with the suicides of three engineers at the Paris facility. The suicide notes left by the engineers mirrored the conditions uncovered by Senator Cornyn's investigation in Texas, documenting the stress that the engineers experienced due to "unreasonable workloads, high pressure management tactics, exhaustion, and humiliating criticism in front of colleagues during performance reviews." Working conditions such as these may promote a short-term jump in performance, but are unsustainable. They create a recipe for disaster and constitute an indictment of the organization's leaders and human resource professionals.

Questions

1. What are some of the unique aspects of military occupations and culture that would heighten one's sensitivity to concerns regarding stress and suicides in that context?

2. What other occupations or industries might be susceptible to the same kinds of concerns for stress and suicide as those experienced by military personnel?
3. What aspects of the work and supervision experienced by the army recruiters in this case that have absolutely nothing to do with this specific military context might generically raise concerns regarding stress and suicide?

SOURCES: M. Thompson, "Why Are Army Recruiters Killing Themselves?" *Time*, April 2, 2009, pp. 32–36; M. Roberts, "Army General to Investigate Recruiter Suicides," *USA Today*, November 7, 2008, pp. A1–A2; and J. Goudreau, "Dispatches from the War on Stress," *BusinessWeek*, August 6, 2007, pp. 74–76.

⬤ TWITTER FOCUS: LEARNING TO SHOW APPRECIATION AT DATOTEL

Using Twitter, continue the conversation about employee retention by reading the Datotel case at www.mhhe.com/noe8e.

Datotel is a St. Louis company that provides IT services and storage for its client companies. Founder David Brown believes in making sure employees know how much the company appreciates them, even as everyone scrambles to keep up with the demands of this expanding small business. When a manager notes that an employee has done something extraordinary, Brown asks one of the other managers—in addition to the employee's direct supervisor—to thank the employee in person. The company also conducts business based on its core values: passion, integrity, fun, teamwork, "superior business value," and "improving the community in which we work."

Engage with your classmates and instructor via Twitter to chat about Datotel's strategy for employee retention using the case questions posted on the Noe website. Don't have a Twitter account yet? See the instructions for getting started on the Online Learning Center.

⬤ NOTES

1. J. D. Shaw, M. K. Duffy, J. L. Johnson, and D. E. Lockhart, "Turnover, Social Capital Losses, and Performance," *Academy of Management Journal* 48 (2005), pp. 594–606.
2. M. Boyle, "Happy People, Happy Returns," *Fortune*, January 22, 2007, p. 100.
3. S. S. Masterson, "A Trickle-Down Model of Organizational Justice: Relating Employees' and Customers' Perceptions of and Reactions to Fairness," *Journal of Applied Psychology* 86 (2001), pp. 594–604.
4. G. R. Bushe, "When People Come and Go," *The Wall Street Journal*, August 23, 2010, p. B6.
5. D. Foust, "Why United Is Ready to Unite," *BusinessWeek*, December 3, 2007, pp. 22–23.
6. M. Riketta, "The Causal Relation between Job Attitudes and Performance: A Meta-analysis of Panel Studies," *Journal of Applied Psychology* 93 (2008), pp. 472–81.
7. S. E. Needleman, "Business Owners Try to Motivate Employees," *The Wall Street Journal*, January 14, 2010, p. B5.
8. K. Sulkowicz, "Straight Talk at Review Time," *BusinessWeek*, September 10, 2007, p. 16.
9. M. Conlin and J. Greene, "How to Make a Microserf Smile," *BusinessWeek*, September 10, 2007, pp. 57–59.
10. F. Hanson, "'Poaching' Can Be Pricey, but Benefits May Outweigh Costs," *Workforce Management*, January 30, 2006, pp. 37–39.
11. S. A. Feeney, "The High Cost of Employee Violence," *Workforce*, August 2003, pp. 23–24.
12. M. Heller, "A Return to At-Will Employment," *Workforce*, May 2001, pp. 42–46.
13. M. Orey, "Fear of Firing," *BusinessWeek*, April 23, 2007, pp. 52–62.
14. M. Conlin, "Litigation Inoculation," *BusinessWeek*, May 28, 2007, p. 35.
15. G. Casellas, "Fired Up over Firing," *BusinessWeek*, May 14, 2007, p. 76.
16. C. Holahan, "Virtually Addicted," *BusinessWeek*, December 14, 2006, p. 41.
17. Orey, "Fear of Firing."
18. S. E. Scullen, P. K. Bergey, and L. Aimon-Smith, "Forced Distribution Rating Systems and the Improvement of Workforce Potential: A Baseline Simulation," *Personnel Psychology* 58 (2005), pp. 1–32.
19. J. Rossant and J. Ewing, "Every Little Reform Counts," *BusinessWeek*, March 7, 2005, pp. 54–55.
20. J. McGregor, "Sweet Revenge," *BusinessWeek*, January 22, 2007, pp. 65–70.
21. L. Waldman, "Work Shooting Kills Nine," *The Wall Street Journal*, August 4, 2010, p. A3.
22. S. Armour, "A 'Bring Your Gun to Work' Movement Builds," *Bloomberg Businessweek*, April 4, 2011, p. 38.
23. C. M. Holmvall and D. R. Bobocel, "What Fair Procedures Say about Me: Self-Construals and Reactions to Procedural Fairness," *Organizational Behavior and Human Decision Processes* 105 (2008), pp. 147–68.
24. E. J. Castilla and S. Bernard, "The Paradox of Meritocracy in Organizations," *Administrative Science Quarterly* 55 (2010), pp. 543–76.
25. E. Spitznagel, "The Sick Day Bounty Hunters," *Bloomberg Businessweek*, December 6, 2010, pp. 93–95.
26. H. Y. Li, J. B. Bingham, and E. E. Umphress, "Fairness from the Top: Perceived Procedural Justice and Collaborative Problem Solving in New Product Development," *Organization Science* 18 (2007), pp. 200–16.
27. P. Dvorak, "Firing Workers Who Are a Bad Fit," *The Wall Street Journal*, May 1, 2006, p. B5.

28. T. A. Judge, B. A. Scott, and R. Ilies, "Hostility, Job Attitudes and Workplace Deviance: A Test of a Multilevel Model," *Journal of Applied Psychology* 91 (2006), pp. 126–38.

29. M. Orey, "The Vanishing Trial," *BusinessWeek*, April 30, 2007, pp. 38–39.

30. M. Orey, "Arbitration Aggravation," *BusinessWeek*, April 30, 2007, pp. 38–39.

31. R. Jana, "A Shot in the Arm for E-Health," *BusinessWeek*, December 8, 2008, pp. 58–59.

32. K. Doheny, "Going the Extra Mile," *Workforce Management*, January 19, 2009, pp. 27–28.

33. "Your Boss to Your Kids: Slim Down," *Bloomberg Businessweek*, February 1, 2010, p. 67.

34. M. Colin, "Get Healthy—Or Else," *BusinessWeek*, February 26, 2007, pp. 58–69.

35. J. Marquez, "Being Healthy May Be Its Own Reward, but a Little Cash Can Also Help Keep Workers Fit," *Workforce Management*, September 2005, pp. 66–69.

36. D. Stevens, "Target: Fat Smokers," *Workforce Management*, December 10, 2007, p. 26.

37. J. Stein, "The Secret Cult of Smokers," *Bloomberg Businessweek*, May 10, 2010, pp. 73–75.

38. J. Marquez, "Wellness: Bad Side Effects," *Workforce Management*, May 5, 2008, pp. 1–3.

39. V. Leo, "Wellness—Or Orwellness?" *BusinessWeek*, March 19, 2007, p. 82.

40. S. E. Needleman, "More Employers Help the Laid Off Find Jobs," *The Wall Street Journal*, April 1, 2009, pp. C1.

41. J. Jones, "How to Bounce Back if You're Bounced Out," *BusinessWeek*, January 27, 1998, pp. 22–23.

42. J. D. Shaw, N. Gupta, and J. E. Delery, "Alternative Conceptualizations of the Relationship between Voluntary Turnover and Organizational Performance," *Academy of Management Journal* 48 (2005), pp. 50–68.

43. J. Sullivan, "Not All Turnover Is Equal," *Workforce Management*, May 21, 2007, p. 42.

44. J. Lublin, "Keeping Clients by Keeping Workers," *The Wall Street Journal*, November 20, 2006, p. B1.

45. W. J. Becker and R. Cropanzano, "Dynamic Aspects of Voluntary Turnover: An Integrated Approach to Curvilinearity in the Performance–Turnover Relationship," *Journal of Applied Psychology* 96 (2011), pp. 233–46.

46. A. Nyberg, "Retaining Your High Performers: Moderators of the Performance–Job Satisfaction–Voluntary Turnover Relationship," *Journal of Applied Psychology* 95 (2010), pp. 440–53.

47. A. Lashinsky, "Search and Enjoy," *Fortune*, January 22, 2007, pp. 70–82.

48. J. Banks, "Turnover Costs," *Workforce Management*, June 23, 2008, p. 22.

49. S. C. Payne and S. S. Weber, "Effects of Service Provider Attitudes and Employment Status on Citizenship Behaviors and Customer's Attitudes and Loyalty Behavior," *Journal of Applied Psychology* 91 (2006), pp. 365–78.

50. G. A. Gelade and M. Ivery, "The Impact of Human Resource Management and Work Climate on Organizational Performance," *Personnel Psychology* 56 (2003), pp. 383–404.

51. B. Schneider, P. J. Hanges, D. B. Smith, and A. N. Salvaggio, "Which Come First, Employee Attitudes or Organizational Financial and Market Performance?" *Journal of Applied Psychology* 88 (2003), pp. 838–51.

52. J. G. Rosse, "Relations among Lateness, Absence and Turnover: Is There a Progression of Withdrawal?" *Human Relations* 41 (1988), pp. 517–31.

53. E. R. Burris, J. R. Detert, and D. S. Chiaburu, "Quitting before Leaving: The Mediating Effects of Psychological Attachment and Detachment on Voice," *Journal of Applied Psychology* 93 (2008), pp. 912–22.

54. B. Conaty, "Cutbacks: Don't Neglect the Survivors," *Bloomberg Businessweek*, January 11, 2010, p. 68.

55. C. Hulin, "Adaptation, Persistence and Commitment in Organizations," in *Handbook of Industrial & Organizational Psychology* 2nd ed., ed. M. D. Dunnette and L. M. Hough (Palo Alto, CA: Consulting Psychologists Press, 1991), pp. 443–50.

56. C. Sablynski, T. Mitchell, T. Lee, J. Burton, and B. Holtom, "Turnover: An Integration of Lee and Mitchell's Unfolding Model and Job Embeddedness Construct and Hulin's Withdrawal Construct," in *The Psychology of Work*, ed. J. Brett and F. Drasgow (Mahwah, NJ: Lawrence Erlbaum Associates, 2002).

57. D. A. Harrison, D. A. Newman, and P. L. Roth, "How Important Are Job Attitudes? Meta-Analytic Comparisons of Integrative Behavioral Outcomes and Time Sequences," *Academy of Management Journal* 49 (2006), pp. 305–25.

58. J. Cook, "Positively Negative," *Human Resource Executive* (June 15, 2001), pp. 101–4.

59. M. P. Miceli and J. P. Near, "Characteristics of Organizational Climate and Perceived Wrongdoing Associated with Whistle-Blowing Decisions," *Personnel Psychology* 38 (1985), pp. 525–44.

60. V. Walter and A. Patel, "NSA Whistleblower Alleges Illegal Spying," *ABCNews.com*, January 10, 2006, p. 1.

61. H. Son and A. Lee, "B of A was Unprepared for Wikileaks, Chief Moynihan Says," *Bloomberg Businessweek*, March 23, 2011, p. 23.

62. D. Mattioli, "CEOs Welcome Recovery to Look after Staff," *The Wall Street Journal*, April 5, 2010, p. B5.

63. S. F. Gale, "Sickened by Costs of Absenteeism, Companies Look for Solutions," *Workforce*, September 2003, pp. 72–75.

64. P. Bamberger and M. Biron, "Group Norms and Excessive Absenteeism: The Role of Peer Referent Others," *Organizational Behavior and Human Decision Processes* 103 (2007), pp. 179–96.

65. J. Warren, "Cough if You Need Sick Leave," *Bloomberg Businessweek*, June 7, 2010, p. 33.

66. M. Conlin, "Shirking Working: The War on Hooky," *BusinessWeek*, November 12, 2007, pp. 70–71.

67. S. E. Needleman, "Businesses Say Theft by Their Workers Is Up," *The Wall Street Journal*, December 11, 2008, pp. C1–C2.

68. S. Covel, "Small Businesses Face More Fraud in Downturn," *The Wall Street Journal*, February 19, 2009, p. C2.

69. M. Conlin, "To Catch a Corporate Thief," *Business Week*, February 16, 2009, p. 52.

70. E. A. Locke, "The Nature and Causes of Job Dissatisfaction," in *The Handbook of Industrial & Organizational Psychology*, ed. M. D. Dunnette (Chicago: Rand McNally, 1976), pp. 901–69.

71. G. Chen, R. E. Ployhart, H. C. Thomas, N. Anderson, and P. D. Bliese, "The Power of Momentum: A New Model of Dynamic Relationships between Job Satisfaction Change and Turnover Intentions," *Academy of Management Journal* 54 (2011), pp. 159–81.

72. K. Maher, S. Power, and S. Hughes, "Massey Defends Its Safety Practices," *The Wall Street Journal*, April 22, 2010, p. B3.

73. B. Elgin, "Caution: Stats May Be Slippery," *Bloomberg Businessweek*, March 11, 2010, pp. 57–59.

74. F. Jones, D. B. O'Connor, M. Conner, B. McMillan, and E. Ferguson, "Impact of Daily Mood, Work Hours and Iso-strain Variables on Self-Reported Health Behaviors," *Journal of Applied Psychology* 92 (2007), pp. 1731–40.

75. J. Jacoby, "Air Traffic Control Staffing under Scrutiny," CNN. com, March 25, 2011.

76. M. Price, "The Risks of Night Work," *Monitor on Psychology*, January 2011, pp. 39–41.

77. L. Woellert, "Does Welding Make You Sick?" *BusinessWeek*, July 10, 2006, p. 32.

78. J. Bailey, "Improving Safety for Workers Also Improves Company Health," *The Wall Street Journal*, May 1, 2006, p. B3.

79. R. D. Zimmerman, "Understanding the Impact of Personality Traits on Individuals' Turnover Decisions: A Meta-analysis," *Personnel Psychology* 61 (2008), pp. 309–48.

80. T. Begley and C. Lee, "The Role of Negative Affectivity in Pay-at-Risk Reactions: A Longitudinal Study," *Journal of Applied Psychology*, 2005, pp. 382–88.

81. B. M. Staw, N. E. Bell, and J. A. Clausen, "The Dispositional Approach to Job Attitudes: A Lifetime Longitudinal Test," *Administrative Science Quarterly* 31 (1986), pp. 56–78; B. M. Staw and J. Ross, "Stability in the Midst of Change: A Dispositional Approach to Job Attitudes," *Journal of Applied Psychology* 70 (1985), pp. 469–80.

82. R. P. Steel and J. R. Rentsch, "The Dispositional Model of Job Attitudes Revisited: Findings of a 10-Year Study," *Journal of Applied Psychology* 82 (1997), pp. 873–79.

83. J. M. O'Brian, "Zappos Knows How to Kick It," *Fortune*, January 2, 2009, pp. 55–60.

84. E. F. Stone and H. G. Gueutal, "An Empirical Derivation of the Dimensions along Which Characteristics of Jobs Are Perceived," *Academy of Management Journal* 28 (1985), pp. 376–96.

85. L. W. Porter and R. M. Steers, "Organizational, Work and Personal Factors in Employee Absenteeism and Turnover," *Psychological Bulletin* 80 (1973), pp. 151–76.

86. P. J. Kiger, "Crouse Hospital," *Workforce Management*, October 20, 2008, p. 17.

87. D. Isen, "Reduce Employee Turnover, Build Customer Loyalty," *Workforce Management*, May 19, 2008, p. 34.

88. E. C. Dierdorff and J. K. Ellington, "It's the Nature of the Work: Examining Behavior-based Sources of Work-Family Conflict," *Journal of Applied Psychology* 93 (2008), pp. 883–92.

89. B. L. Rau and M. M. Hyland, "Role Conflict and Flexible Work Arrangements: The Effects on Applicant Attraction," *Personnel Psychology* 55 (2002), pp. 111–36.

90. G. Flynn, "The Legalities of Flextime," *Workforce*, October 2001, pp. 62–66.

91. S. L. Lambert, "Added Benefits: The Link between Work–Life Benefits and Organizational Citizenship Behaviors," *Academy of Management Journal* 43 (2000), pp. 801–15.

92. L. B. Hammer, E. E. Kossek, W. K. Anger, T. Bodner, and K. L. Zimmerman, "Clarifying Work–Family Intervention Processes: The Role of Work–Family Supportive Supervisor Behaviors," *Journal of Applied Psychology* 96 (2011), pp. 134–50.

93. A. M. Grant, "Relational Job Design and the Motivation to Make a Prosocial Difference," *Academy of Management Review* 32 (2007), pp. 393–417.

94. A. M. Grant, "Does Intrinsic Motivation Fuel the Prosocial Fire? Motivational Synergy in Predicting Persistence, Performance, and Productivity," *Journal of Applied Psychology* 93 (2007), pp. 48–58.

95. A. M. Grant, "The Significance of Task Significance," *Journal of Applied Psychology* 93 (2007), pp. 108–24.

96. A. M. Grant, E. M. Campbell, G. Chen, K. Cottone, D. Lapedia, and K. Lee, "Impact and Art of Motivation Maintenance: The Effects of Contact with Beneficiaries on Persistance Behavior," *Organizational Behavior and Human Decision Processes* 103 (2007), pp. 53–67.

97. B. Morris, "The Best Place to Work Now," *Fortune*, January 20, 2006, pp. 79–86.

98. J. M. Sacco and N. Schmitt, "A Dynamic Multi-level Model of Demographic Diversity and Misfit Effects," *Journal of Applied Psychology* 90 (2005), pp. 203–31.

99. M. Wang, Y. J. Zhan, E. McCune, and D. Truxillo, "Understanding Newcomers' Adaptability and Work-Related Outcomes: Testing the Mediating Roles of Perceived P-E Fit Variables," *Personnel Psychology* 64 (2011), pp. 163–89.

100. R. E. Ployhart, J. A. Weekley, and K. Baughman, "The Structure and Function of Human Capital Emergence: A Multilevel Examination of the Attraction–Selection–Attrition Model," *Academy of Management Journal* 49 (2006), pp. 661–77.

101. B. M. Meglino, E. C. Ravlin, and C. L. Adkins, "A Work Values Approach to Corporate Culture: A Field Test of the Value Congruence Process and Its Relationship to Individual Outcomes," *Journal of Applied Psychology* 74 (1989), pp. 424–33.

102. R. Eisenberger, F. Stinghamber, C. Vandenberghe, I. L. Sucharski, and L. Rhoades, "Perceived Supervisor Support: Contributions to Perceived Organizational Support and Employee Retention," *Journal of Applied Psychology* 87 (2002), pp. 565–73.

103. P. Lattman, "Does Thank You Help Keep Associates?" *The Wall Street Journal*, January 24, 2007.

104. S. C. Payne and A. H. Huffman, "A Longitudinal Examination of the Influence of Mentoring on Organizational Commitment and Turnover," *Academy of Management Journal* 48 (2005), pp. 158–168.

105. S. Berfield, "Mentoring Can Be Messy," *BusinessWeek*, January 29, 2007, pp. 80–81.

106. G. C. Ganster, M. R. Fusiler, and B. T. Mayes, "Role of Social Support in the Experience of Stress at Work," *Journal of Applied Psychology* 71 (1986), pp. 102–11.

107. C. O. Trevor and D. L. Wazeter, "Contingent View of Reactions to Objective Pay Conditions: Interdependence among Pay Structure Characteristics and Pay Relative to Internal and External Referents," *Journal of Applied Psychology* 91 (2006), pp. 1260–75.

108. S. C. Currall, A. J. Towler, T. A. Judge, and L. Kohn, "Pay Satisfaction and Organizational Outcomes," *Personnel Psychology* 58 (2005), pp. 613–40.

109. E. White, "Opportunity Knocks, and It Pays a Lot Better," *The Wall Street Journal*, November 13, 2006, p. B3.

110. H. G. Heneman and D. S. Schwab, "Pay Satisfaction: Its Multidimensional Nature and Measurement," *International Journal of Applied Psychology* 20 (1985), pp. 129–41.

111. T. Judge and T. Welbourne, "A Confirmatory Investigation of the Dimensionality of the Pay Satisfaction Questionnaire," *Journal of Applied Psychology* 79 (1994), pp. 461–66.

112. J. Smerd, "Healthcare Staffing Firm Tackles its Perennial Turnover Problem," *Workforce Management*, March 2007, p. 32.

113. E. Frauenheim, "Tech Services Provider Sees Reduced Turnover and Explosive Revenue Growth After Making Employee Satisfaction Its Top Priority," *Workforce Management*, October 20, 2008, p. 25.

114. J. Lynn, "Many Happy Returns," CNNMoney.com (March 2, 2001), pp. 1–2.

PART 4

Compensation of Human Resources

CHAPTER

11

Pay Structure Decisions

ENTER THE WORLD OF BUSINESS

Wage Growth in China Means Companies Have Decisions to Make

Coach, a U.S. company that makes purses and accessories, now has 85% of its manufacturing operations in China. However, it plans to reduce that to 40 to 50%. Why? Labor costs in China have increased significantly in recent years, including a 20% increase this past year alone, and companies are anticipating continued significant wage increases going forward. Thus, China, especially in the coastal areas, is losing its labor cost advantage in attracting and keeping manufacturing. Note that wages (and total labor costs) are still much, much lower in China than in countries such as the United States, Japan, and western European countries (e.g., Germany). However, the production Coach plans to move from China will likely go to countries such as India, Vietnam, and the Philippines, where it expects to have lower labor costs than it has in China for the forseeable future. Likewise, Yue Yuen Industrial, the world's largest maker of shoes, has begun to move manufacturing from China to Bangladesh and Cambodia. Foxconn, which is owned by Taiwan-based Hon Hai Precision Industry Company Ltd, makes iPhones and other products for Apple in China and has faced scrutiny of how its workers in China

are treated. In response, Foxconn raised wages for workers at its Shenzhen factory in China from 900 yuan per month to 1,200 yuan per month and then, four months later from 1,200 yuan per month to 2,000 yuan (about 300 U.S. dollars) per month. So, wages more than doubled in four months. Foxconn plans to grow its workforce in China from 920,000 to 1.3 million, but not in the higher-wage, coastal area where its Shenzhen plant is located. Rather, it will look to the less expensive inland areas of China for lower wages and, it hopes, smaller growth in wages. Workers at other plants in China (e.g., at Honda Motor Company) have gone on strike to achieve higher wages. The Chinese government seems to be supportive of higher wages as a way to head off labor unrest. In summary, although one reason companies locate production in China is to capitalize on its low labor costs, companies are finding that labor costs can change quickly. That can have major implications for product prices and competiveness and so must be monitored closely and incorporated into decision making about where to locate production.

SOURCES: John Gapper and Barney Jopson, "Coach to Cut Output in China," *Financial Times*, May 13, 2011; Ben Blanchard, Foxconn to Raise Wages Again at China Plant, www.reuters.com, accessed October 19, 2010; Joe Manget and Pierre Mercier, "As Wages Rise, Time to Leave China?" *Bloomberg Businessweek*, December 1, 2010; and Shai Oster, "China's Rising Wages Propel U.S. Prices," *The Wall Street Journal*, May 9, 2011.

Introduction

LO 11-1
List the main decision areas and concepts in employee compensation management.

From the employer's point of view, pay is a powerful tool for furthering the organization's strategic goals. First, pay has a large impact on employee attitudes and behaviors. It influences the kind of employees who are attracted to (and remain with) the organization, and it can be a powerful tool for aligning current employees' interests with those of the broader organization. Second, employee compensation is typically a significant organizational cost and thus requires close scrutiny. As Table 11.1 shows, total compensation (cash and benefits) averages 22% of revenues and varies both within and across industries. In the chapter opener, the goal of Coach and other companies in this case is simple, but important: keep labor costs in check to achieve maximum profit. Companies often look for ways to reduce labor costs without jeopardizing their relationships with their workforces. They also want to have an efficient workforce in place and ready to go when the demand for their products picks up again. For example, when Toyota paused automobile assembly at U.S. plants due to slow sales, it did not lay off workers. It did offer a voluntary buyout plan under which workers signing up received 10 weeks of salary plus 2 weeks salary for every year worked. Workers who remained worked 36 hour rather than 40-hour weeks and reallocated their time to receive increased training and look for new ways to reduce costs.

From the employees' point of view, policies having to do with wages, salaries, and other earnings affect their overall income and thus their standard of living. Both the level of pay and its seeming fairness compared with others' pay are important. Pay is also often considered a sign of status and success. Employees attach great importance to pay decisions when they evaluate their relationship with the organization. Therefore, pay decisions must be carefully managed and communicated.

Total compensation, as noted, consists of cash compensation (salary, merit increases, bonuses, stock options, and other incentives) and benefits (e.g., health insurance, paid vacation, unemployment compensation). In the current chapter, we focus on salary levels. In Chapter 12, we address merit increase and incentive issues. In Chapter 13, we examine benefits decisions. Total rewards, total returns, and inducements are concepts that include not only total compensation, but also any other (nonmonetary) rewards (interesting or fulfilling work, good co-workers, development opportunities, recognition) that are associated with the employment relationship. These nonmonetary rewards are discussed in Chapters 4, 5, and 10. An organization must choose to what degree its total rewards strategy depends on monetary rewards (compensation) and what mix of compensation components will be used.

table 11.1

Total Compensation as a Percentage of Revenues

INDUSTRY	PERCENTILE		
	25TH	50TH	75TH
Hospitals/health care	43%	46%	49%
Manufacturing	22	27	34
Insurance/health care	6	8	11
All industries	13	22	32

SOURCES: Data from Saratoga Institute, *Human Capital Benchmarking Report 2000,* and Saratoga/PricewaterhouseCoopers, *Key Trends in Human Capital: A Global Perspective, 2006.*

Salary level decisions can be broken into two areas: pay structure and individual pay. In this chapter we focus on **pay structure**, which in turn entails a consideration of pay level and job structure. **Pay level** is defined here as the average pay (including wages, salaries, and bonuses) of jobs in an organization. (Benefits could also be included, but these are discussed separately in Chapter 13.) **Job structure** refers to the relative pay of jobs in an organization. Consider the same two jobs in two different organizations. In Organization 1, jobs A and B are paid an annual average compensation of $40,000 and $60,000, respectively. In Organization 2, the pay rates are $45,000 and $55,000, respectively. Organizations 1 and 2 have the same pay level ($50,000), but the job structures (relative rates of pay) differ.

Both pay level and job structure are characteristics of organizations and reflect decisions about jobs rather than about individual employees. This chapter's focus is on why and how organizations attach pay policies to jobs. In the next chapter we look within jobs to discuss the different approaches that can determine the pay of individual employees as well as the advantages and disadvantages of these different approaches.

Why is the focus on jobs in developing a pay structure? As the number of employees in an organization increases, so too does the number of human resource management decisions. In determining compensation, for example, each employee must be assigned a rate of pay that is acceptable in terms of external, internal, and individual equity (defined later) and in terms of the employer's cost. Although each employee is unique and thus requires some degree of individualized treatment, standardizing the treatment of similar employees (those with similar jobs) can help greatly to make compensation administration and decision making more manageable and more equitable. Thus pay policies are often attached to particular jobs rather than tailored entirely to individual employees.

Pay Structure
The relative pay of different jobs (job structure) and how much they are paid (pay level).

Pay Level
The average pay, including wages, salaries, and bonuses, of jobs in an organization.

Job Structure
The relative pay of jobs in an organization.

Equity Theory and Fairness

In discussing the consequences of pay decisions, it is useful to keep in mind that employees often evaluate their pay relative to that of other employees. Equity theory suggests that people evaluate the fairness of their situations by comparing them with those of other people.[1] According to the theory, a person (p) compares her own ratio of perceived outcomes O (pay, benefits, working conditions) to perceived inputs I (effort, ability, experience) to the ratio of a comparison other (o).

$$O_p/I_p <, >, \text{or} = O_o/I_o?$$

If p's ratio (O_p/I_p) is smaller than the comparison other's ratio (O_o/I_o), underreward inequity results. If p's ratio is larger, overreward inequity results, although evidence suggests that this type of inequity is less likely to occur and less likely to be sustained because p may rationalize the situation by reevaluating her outcomes less favorably or inputs (self-worth) more favorably.[2]

The consequences of p's comparisons depend on whether equity is perceived. If equity is perceived, no change is expected in p's attitudes or behavior. In contrast, perceived inequity may cause p to restore equity. Some ways of restoring equity are counterproductive, including (1) reducing one's own inputs (not working as hard), (2) increasing one's outcomes (such as by theft), or (3) leaving the situation that generates perceived inequity (leaving the organization or refusing to work or cooperate with employees who are perceived as overrewarded).

Equity theory's main implication for managing employee compensation is that to an important extent, employees evaluate their pay by comparing it with what others get paid, and their work attitudes and behaviors are influenced by such comparisons. For example, consider the contract that shortstop Alex Rodriguez (now a New York Yankee) signed in 2000 with the Texas Rangers baseball team. One provision stated that during the 2001 to 2004 seasons, his base compensation must be at least $2 million higher than any other shortstop in major league baseball. A second provision permitted Rodriguez to void seasons after 2008 unless his 2009 and 2010 base compensation was at least $1 million higher than any position player in major league baseball. Otherwise, Rodriguez would be free to leave his current team. These provisions that pegged Rodriguez's pay to other players' pay provide a compelling example of the importance of being paid well in *relative* terms. (We later learned that "A-Rod" apparently felt compelled to break some rules in hopes of helping his on-field performance live up to his pay.)

Another implication is that employee perceptions are what determine their evaluation. The fact that management believes its employees are paid well compared with those of other companies does not necessarily translate into employees' beliefs. Employees may have different information or make different comparisons than management. For example, Toyota recently set a goal to move from using wages in the U.S. auto industry as the standard of comparison to using the (lower) prevailing wages in the state where each plant is located. To do so, however, Toyota recognizes its "challenge will be how to educate team members and managers . . . so they can understand and accept [this] change."

Two types of employee social comparisons of pay are especially relevant in making pay level and job structure decisions. (See Table 11.2.) First, *external equity* pay comparisons focus on what employees in other organizations are paid for doing the same general job. Such comparisons are likely to influence the decisions of applicants to accept job offers as well as the attitudes and decisions of employees about whether to stay with an organization or take a job elsewhere. (See Chapters 5 and 10.) The organization's choice of pay level influences its employees' external pay comparisons and their consequences. A market pay survey is the primary administrative tool organizations use in choosing a pay level.

table 11.2

Pay Structure Concepts and Consequences

PAY STRUCTURE DECISION AREA	ADMINISTRATIVE TOOL	FOCUS OF EMPLOYEE PAY COMPARISONS	CONSEQUENCES OF EQUITY PERCEPTIONS
Pay level	Market pay surveys	External equity	External employee movement (attraction and retention of quality employees); labor costs; employee attitudes
Job structure	Job evaluation	Internal equity	Internal employee movement (promotion, transfer, job rotation); cooperation among employees; employee attitudes

Second, *internal equity* pay comparisons focus on what employees within the same organization, but in different jobs, are paid. Employees make comparisons with lower-level jobs, jobs at the same level (but perhaps in different skill areas or product divisions), and jobs at higher levels. These comparisons may influence general attitudes of employees; their willingness to transfer to other jobs within the organization; their willingness to accept promotions; their inclination to cooperate across jobs, functional areas, or product groups; and their commitment to the organization. The organization's choice of job structure influences its employees' internal comparisons and their consequences. Job evaluation is the administrative tool organizations use to design job structures.

In addition, employees make internal equity pay comparisons with others performing the same job. Such comparisons are most relevant to the following chapter, which focuses on using pay to recognize individual contributions and differences.

We now turn to ways to choose and develop pay levels and pay structures, the consequences of such choices, and the ways two administrative tools—market pay surveys and job evaluation—help in making pay decisions.

Developing Pay Levels

MARKET PRESSURES

Any organization faces two important competitive market challenges in deciding what to pay its employees: product market competition and labor market competition.

LO 11-2
Describe the major administrative tools used to manage employee compensation.

Product Market Competition

First, organizations must compete effectively in the product market. In other words, they must be able to sell their goods and services at a quantity and price that will bring a sufficient return on their investment. Organizations compete on multiple dimensions (quality, service, and so on), and price is one of the most important dimensions. An important influence on price is the cost of production.

An organization that has higher labor costs than its product market competitors will have to charge higher average prices for products of similar quality. Thus, for example, if labor costs are 30% of revenues at Company A and Company B, but Company A has labor costs that are 20% higher than those of Company B, we would expect Company A to have product prices that are higher by $(0.30 \times 0.20) = 6\%$. At some point, the higher price charged by Company A will contribute to a loss of its business to competing companies with lower prices (like Company B). Until recently, in the automobile industry, hourly labor cost (including not only wages, but also retiree and active worker benefits such as health care) in assembly plants averaged $75 for the U.S. Big Three (Chrysler, General Motors, Ford), compared to $52 for Toyota and Honda plants in the United States. On average, it takes roughly 30 hours to assemble a car. So, the labor cost per car for the Big Three was $30 \times \$75 = \$2,250$, compared to $30 \times \$52 = \$1,560$ for Toyota and Honda. That labor cost disadvantage would have to be offset by superior vehicle quality, performance, and so forth for the Big Three to make a profit. The bankruptcies at Chrysler and General Motors indicate that was not possible. More recently, the U.S. Big Three have reduced their labor costs to $58 per hour by hiring some workers at lower wages and by reducing benefits costs. That is a major improvement, but continues to be a higher hourly labor cost than at Honda and Toyota, as well as at the new Volkswagen plant in Chattanooga,

Tennessee, estimated to be $27 per hour initially.[3] (See the "Competing through Globalization" box.) That $27 per hour cost to build Volkswagen Passats in Tennessee is much lower than Volkswagen's hourly labor cost to build cars in Germany, which is estimated to be about $100.[4] (A major part of the labor cost difference is the strength of the euro relative to the dollar.) Due to this labor cost saving (and due to lower costs for parts, transportation, and so forth), Volkswagen will reduce the price of a Passat from $28,000 (when it was built in Germany) to $20,000.

Therefore, *product market competition* places an *upper bound* on labor costs and compensation. This upper bound is more constrictive when labor costs are a larger share of total costs and when demand for the product is affected by changes in price (i.e., when demand is *elastic*). Unless higher labor costs are offset by higher worker productivity or desirable product features that allow a higher product price, it will be difficult to sustain these relatively high costs in a competitive product market. As we have noted, Volkswagen will be able to lower the price of its Passat by producing it in the United States where its labor costs will be lower than in Germany and lower than those of U.S. competitors.

What components make up labor costs? A major component is the average cost per employee. This is made up of both direct payments (such as wages, salaries, and bonuses) and indirect payments (such as health insurance, Social Security, and unemployment compensation). A second component of labor cost is the staffing level (number of employees). Not surprisingly, financially troubled organizations often seek to cut costs by focusing on one or both components. Staff reductions, hiring freezes, wage and salary freezes, and sharing benefits costs with employees are several ways of enhancing the organization's competitive position in the product market.

Labor Market Competition

A second important competitive market challenge is *labor market competition*. Essentially, labor market competition is the amount an organization must pay to compete against other companies that hire similar employees. These labor market competitors typically include not only companies that have similar products but also those in different product markets that hire similar types of employees. If an organization is not competitive in the labor market, it will fail to attract and retain employees of sufficient numbers and quality. For example, even if a computer manufacturer offers newly graduated electrical engineers the same pay as other computer manufacturers, if automobile manufacturers and other labor market competitors offer salaries $5,000 higher, the computer company may not be able to hire enough qualified electrical engineers. Labor market competition places a *lower bound* on pay levels. The "Competing through Sustainability" box shows how Google recently reacted to growing labor market competition.

EMPLOYEES AS A RESOURCE

Because organizations have to compete in the labor market, they should consider their employees not just as a cost but as a resource in which the organization has invested and from which it expects valuable returns. Although controlling costs directly affects an organization's ability to compete in the product market, the organization's competitive position can be compromised if costs are kept low at the expense of employee productivity and quality. Having higher labor costs than your competitors is not necessarily a concern if you also have the best and most effective workforce, one that produces products more efficiently and with better quality.

VW Chops Labor Costs in U.S.

Volkswagen AG on Tuesday will celebrate the opening of a new Tennessee auto plant in Chattanooga that gives the German auto maker much lower U.S. labor costs than not only its Detroit rivals but its Japanese competitors on American soil. The new VW plant will pay starting workers about $27 an hour in wages and benefits, roughly half the $52 an hour cost of labor at the Detroit Three auto makers and some non-union U.S. plants owned by Toyota Motor Corp. and Honda Motor Co. It comes as Korea's Hyundai Motor Co. and Kia Motors Corp., whose Alabama and Georgia plant labor costs are similar to VW's, are gaining share against Detroit and Tokyo rivals.

During the auto bailout, unions at GM and Chrysler agreed to sharply lower the pay for new hires, but there haven't been that many workers coming in at the lower levels. As a result, their labor costs remain far higher than those of new plants in the South.

"Any current wage or benefit gap between the Detroit Three and transplants could grow as transplants add capacity in the lower-wage U.S. South," said Brian Johnson, the lead auto analyst for Barclays Capital.

VW plans to build its Passat, a sedan that will be priced at $20,000, about the same as the Honda Accord and Chevrolet Malibu, making it competitive with the other volume sedans in the segment. The current model starts at nearly $28,000, but the price is coming down.

Over the next three years, VW is expected to boost the average worker's wage from $14.50 to $19.50, pushing up the total cost for a worker to roughly $38 an hour, according to the Center for Automotive Research in Ann Arbor, Michigan.

Ford Motor Co., GM, and Chrysler have battled for years to lower the gap between themselves and Japanese auto makers that assemble vehicles in the U.S. Years ago, Detroit had labor costs of around $70 an hour, but in the last few years the three companies have won concessions from the United Auto Workers union. Ford's labor cost is now about $58 an hour, according to the company.

One key UAW concession allows GM, Ford, and Chrysler to hire new workers at a wage of $14 an hour, about half the pay of veteran workers. New workers also get less costly benefits, such as 401k retirement accounts instead of a life-long pension program. The number of workers who get this "second-tier" pay package is limited, however.

The Detroit Three and the UAW are scheduled to begin negotiating a new labor contract this year and GM, Ford, and Chrysler are expected to seek to increase the percentage of workers making the lower, entry-level wage up from the 20% cap today.

The string of non-union auto plants that have gone up in the South is a reflection of the U.S.'s increased competitiveness in auto manufacturing. Both BMW AG and Daimler AG produce vehicles in the U.S. and export them to markets around the world.

VW, the world's most profitable auto maker last year, is hoping its new plant makes the company more competitive in the U.S. market. It hasn't made money in the U.S. for the past decade because unfavorable exchange rates between the dollar and the euro have increased the cost of German-built cars sold in the U.S.

SOURCE: Excerpted from "VW Chops Labor Costs in U.S., by Mike Ramsey, *Wall Street Journal*, May 23, 2011. Reproduced with permission of Dow Jones & Company, Inc. via Copyright Clearance Center.

COMPETING THROUGH SUSTAINABILITY
Google Battles to Keep Talent

Google Inc. is fighting off Facebook Inc. and other fast-growing Internet firms that are poaching its staff, a reversal for a company that has long been one of Silicon Valley's hottest job destinations.

Facebook and other start-ups have a recruiting tool that Google can no longer claim: They are private companies that haven't yet gone public, and can lure workers with pre-IPO stock. Recruiters say Facebook and others also pay competitively, with average annual salaries for engineers typically starting at $120,000.

Facebook today has about 1,700 employees, up from 1,000 a year ago. Twitter now has 300 employees, up from 99 a year ago. LinkedIn said it started the year with 450 employees and expects to end the year with 900.

Much of the most recent hiring battles have centered on Facebook and Google. According to data from LinkedIn, 137 Facebook employees previously worked at Google. Among Google's recent departures to Facebook: Lars Rasmussen, co-founder of Google Maps. Google Chrome architect Matthew Papakipos, Android senior product manager Erick Tseng,

and top Google ad executive David Fischer also decamped to Facebook earlier this year.

To help attract new recruits and preempt defections, Google Tuesday said it was giving a 10% raise to its more than 23,000 employees. Google Chief Executive Eric Schmidt wrote in an all-hands e-mail, "We want to continue to attract the best people to Google." Google declined to comment Wednesday.

To be sure, Google is also on a hiring spree and increased its workforce by 19%, or 3,600 people, over the past year. To acquire some high-profile talent, Google has ramped up acquisitions of start-ups such as social app maker Slide Inc. And while Facebook is a huge draw now, it too has become too large for some employees, who have left to start other projects.

Hiring wars aren't uncommon in Silicon Valley, with mature tech companies long battling with up-and-coming start-ups for workers. A few years ago, Google was snaring workers from Yahoo Inc., Microsoft, and others. Now, as Google's growth has slowed, it is finding the tables have turned.

Amir Efrati and Eric Savitz explain how the 10% raise

given by Google signals an escalating war between Google and Facebook, Inc., for top talent.

"Google isn't the hot place to work" and has "become the safe place to work," said Robert Greene, who recruits engineers for start-ups such as Facebook.

Facebook's social-networking technology and smaller size is also appealing, say some job seekers. Software engineer Murali Vajapeyam, 29, who left Oracle Corp. this year, said he interviewed at Google and Facebook.

"Facebook is more interesting," said Mr. Vajapeyam, who didn't land an offer with Facebook and ultimately elected to join a San Francisco software start-up in September.

Google and Facebook's recruiting battles come as the two companies increasingly appear to be moving onto each other's turf. Among other things, Mr. Schmidt has spoken about adding social-networking elements to Google's services.

SOURCE: Excerpted from "Google Battles to Keep Talent," by Amir Efrati and Pui-Wing Tam, *Wall Street Journal*, November 10, 2010. Reproduced with permission of Dow Jones & Company, Inc. via Copyright Clearance Center.

Pay policies and programs are one of the most important human resource tools for encouraging desired employee behaviors and discouraging undesired behaviors. Therefore, they must be evaluated not just in terms of costs but in terms of the returns they generate—how they attract, retain, and motivate a high-quality workforce. For example, if the average revenue per employee in Company A is 20% higher than in Company B, it may not be important that the average pay in Company A is 10% higher than in Company B.

DECIDING WHAT TO PAY

Although organizations face important external labor and product market pressures in setting their pay levels, a range of discretion remains.[5] How large the range is depends on the particular competitive environment the organization faces. Where the range is broad, an important strategic decision is whether to pay above, at, or below the market average. The advantage of paying above the market average is the ability to attract and retain the top talent available and help generate positive job attitudes (e.g., satisfaction), all of which can translate into a highly effective and productive workforce. The disadvantage, however, is the added cost.[6]

Under what circumstances do the benefits of higher pay outweigh the higher costs? According to **efficiency wage theory**, one circumstance is when organizations have technologies or structures that depend on highly skilled employees. For example, organizations that emphasize decentralized decision making may need higher-caliber employees. Another circumstance where higher pay may be warranted is when an organization has difficulties observing and monitoring its employees' performance. It may therefore wish to provide an above-market pay rate to ensure the incentive to put forth maximum effort. The theory is that employees who are paid more than they would be paid elsewhere will be reluctant to shirk because they wish to retain their good jobs.[7]

Efficiency Wage Theory
A theory stating that wages influence worker productivity.

MARKET PAY SURVEYS

To compete for talent, organizations use **benchmarking**, a procedure in which an organization compares its own practices against those of the competition. In compensation management, benchmarking against product market and labor market competitors is typically accomplished through the use of one or more pay surveys, which provide information on going rates of pay among competing organizations.

The use of pay surveys requires answers to several important questions:[8]

Benchmarking
Comparing an organization's practices against those of the competition.

1. Which employers should be included in the survey? Ideally, they would be the key labor market and product market competitors.
2. Which jobs are included in the survey? Because only a sample of jobs is ordinarily used, care must be taken that the jobs are representative in terms of level, functional area, and product market. Also, the job content must be sufficiently similar.
3. If multiple surveys are used, how are all the rates of pay weighted and combined? Organizations often have to weight and combine pay rates because different surveys are often tailored toward particular employee groups (labor markets) or product markets. The organization must decide how much relative weight to give to its labor market and product market competitors in setting pay.

Several factors affect decisions on how to combine surveys.[9] Product market comparisons that focus on labor costs are likely to deserve greater weight when (1) labor costs represent a large share of total costs, (2) product demand is elastic (it changes in response to product price changes), (3) the supply of labor is inelastic, and (4) employee skills are specific to the product market (and will remain so). In contrast, labor market comparisons may be more important when (1) attracting and retaining qualified employees is difficult and (2) the costs (administrative, disruption, and so on) of recruiting replacements are high.

As this discussion suggests, knowing what other organizations are paying is only one part of the story. It is also necessary to know what those organizations are getting in return for their investment in employees. To find that out, some organizations examine ratios such as revenues/employees and revenues/labor cost. The first ratio includes the staffing component of employee cost but not the average cost per employee. The second ratio, however, includes both. Note that comparing these ratios across organizations requires caution. For example, different industries rely on different labor and capital resources. So comparing the ratio of revenues to labor costs of a petroleum company (capital intensive, high ratio) to a hospital (labor intensive, low ratio) would be like comparing apples and oranges. But within industries, such comparisons can be useful. Besides revenues, other return-on-investment data might include product quality, customer satisfaction, and potential workforce quality (such as average education and skill levels).

Rate Ranges

Rate Ranges
Different employees in the same job may have different pay rates.

As the preceding discussion suggests, obtaining a single "going rate" of market pay is a complex task that involves a number of subjective decisions; it is both an art and a science. Once a market rate has been chosen, how is it incorporated into the pay structure? Typically—especially for white-collar jobs—it is used for setting the midpoint of pay ranges for either jobs or pay grades (discussed next). Market survey data are also often collected on minimum and maximum rates of pay as well. The use of **rate ranges** permits a company to recognize differences in employee performance, seniority, training, and so forth in setting individual pay (discussed in the next chapter). For some blue-collar jobs, however, particularly those covered by collective bargaining contracts, there may be a single rate of pay for all employees within the job.

Key Jobs and Nonkey Jobs

Key Jobs
Benchmark jobs, used in pay surveys, that have relatively stable content and are common to many organizations.

Nonkey Jobs
Jobs that are unique to organizations and that cannot be directly valued or compared through the use of market surveys.

In using pay surveys, it is necessary to make a distinction between two general types of jobs: key jobs (or benchmark jobs) and nonkey jobs. **Key jobs** have relatively stable content and—perhaps most important—are common to many organizations. Therefore, it is possible to obtain market pay survey data on them. Note, however, that to avoid too much of an administrative burden, organizations may not gather market pay data on all such jobs. In contrast to key jobs, **nonkey jobs** are, to an important extent, unique to organizations; thus, by definition, they cannot be directly valued or compared through the use of market surveys. Therefore, they are treated differently in the pay-setting process.

DEVELOPING A JOB STRUCTURE

Job Evaluation
An administrative procedure used to measure internal job worth.

Although external comparisons of the sort we have been discussing are important, employees also evaluate their pay using internal comparisons. So, for example, a vice president of marketing may expect to be paid roughly the same amount as a vice president of information systems because they are at the same organizational level, with similar levels of responsibility and similar impacts on the organization's performance. A job structure can be defined as the relative worth of various jobs in the organization, based on these types of internal comparisons. We now discuss how such decisions are made.

Job Evaluation

Compensable Factors
The characteristics of jobs that an organization values and chooses to pay for.

One typical way of measuring internal job worth is to use an administrative procedure called **job evaluation**. A job evaluation system is composed of compensable factors and a weighting scheme based on the importance of each **compensable factor** to the organization. Simply stated, compensable factors are the characteristics of jobs that an organization values and chooses to pay for. These characteristics may include job complexity, working conditions, required education, required experience, and responsibility. Most job evaluation systems use several compensable factors. Job analysis (discussed in Chapter 4) provides basic descriptive information on job attributes, and the job evaluation process assigns values to these compensable factors.

Scores can be generated in a variety of ways, but they typically include input from a number of people. A job evaluation committee commonly generates ratings. Although there are numerous ways to evaluate jobs, the most widely used is the point-factor system, which yields job evaluation points for each compensable factor.[10]

The Point-Factor System

After generating scores for each compensable factor on each job, job evaluators often apply a weighting scheme to account for the differing importance of the compensable factors to the organization. Weights can be generated in two ways. First, *a priori* weights can be assigned, which means factors are weighted using expert judgments about the importance of each compensable factor. Second, weights can be derived empirically based on how important each factor seems in determining pay in the labor market. (Statistical methods such as multiple regression can be used for this purpose.) For the sake of simplicity, we assume in the following example that equal a priori weights are chosen, which means that the scores on the compensable factors can be simply summed.

Table 11.3 shows an example of a three-factor job evaluation system applied to three jobs. Note that the jobs differ in the levels of experience, education, and complexity required. Summing the scores on the three compensable factors provides an internally oriented assessment of relative job worth in the organization. In a sense, the computer programmer job is worth 41% (155/110 − 1) more than the computer operator job, and the systems analyst job is worth 91% (210/110 − 1) more than the computer operator job. Whatever pay level is chosen (based on benchmarking and competitive strategy), we would expect the pay differentials to be somewhat similar to these percentages. The internal job evaluation and external survey-based measures of worth can, however, diverge.

DEVELOPING A PAY STRUCTURE

In the example provided in Table 11.4, there are 15 jobs, 10 of which are key jobs. For these key jobs, both pay survey and job evaluation data are available. For the five nonkey jobs, by definition, no survey data are available, only job evaluation information. Note that, for simplicity's sake, we work with data from only two pay surveys and we use a weighted average that gives twice as much weight to survey 1. Also, our

JOB TITLE	COMPENSABLE FACTORS			
	EXPERIENCE	EDUCATION	COMPLEXITY	TOTAL
Computer operator	40	30	40	110
Computer programmer	40	50	65	155
Systems analyst	65	60	85	210

table 11.3

Example of a Three-Factor Job Evaluation System

table 11.4

Job Evaluation and Pay Survey Data

JOB	KEY JOB?	JOB TITLE	JOB EVALUATION	SURVEY 1 (S1)	SURVEY 2 (S2)	SURVEY COMPOSITE (2/3*S1 + 1/3*S2)
A	y	Computer operator	110	$2,012	$1,731	$1,919
B	y	Engineering tech I	115	2,206	1,908	2,106
C	y	Computer programmer	155	2,916	2,589	2,807
D	n	Engineering tech II	165	—	—	—
E	n	Compensation analyst	170	—	—	—
F	y	Accountant	190	3,613	3,099	3,442
G	y	Systems analyst	210	4,275	3,854	4,134
H	n	Computer programmer—senior	225	—	—	—
I	y	Director of personnel	245	4,982	4,506	4,823
J	y	Accountant—senior	255	5,205	4,270	4,893
K	y	Systems analyst—senior	270	5,868	5,652	5,796
L	y	Industrial engineer	275	5,496	4,794	5,262
M	n	Chief accountant	315	—	—	—
N	y	Senior engineer	320	7,026	6,572	6,875
O	n	Senior scientist	330	—	—	—

SOURCE: Adapted from S. Rynes, B. Gerhart, G.T. Milkovich, and J. Boudreau, *Current Compensation Professional Institute* (Scottsdale, AZ: American Compensation Association, 1988). Reprinted with permission.

example works with a single structure. Many organizations have multiple structures that correspond to different job families (like clerical, technical, and professional) or product divisions.

How are the data in Table 11.4 combined to develop a pay structure? First, it is important to note that both internal and external comparisons must be considered in making compensation decisions. However, because the pay structures suggested by internal and external comparisons do not necessarily converge, employers must carefully balance them. Studies suggest that employers may differ significantly in the degree to which they place priority on internal- or external-comparison data in developing pay structures.[11]

At least three pay-setting approaches, which differ according to their relative emphasis on external or internal comparisons, can be identified.[12]

Market Survey Data

Pay Policy Line
A mathematical expression that describes the relationship between a job's pay and its job evaluation points.

The approach with the greatest emphasis on external comparisons (market survey data) is achieved by directly basing pay on market surveys that cover as many key jobs as possible. For example, the rate of pay for job A in Table 11.5 would be $1,919; for job B, $2,106; and for job C, $2,807. For nonkey jobs (jobs D, E, H, M, and O), however, pay survey information is not available, and we must proceed differently. Basically, we develop a market **pay policy line** based on the key jobs (for which there are both job evaluation and market pay survey data available). As Figure 11.1 shows, the data can be plotted with a line of best fit estimated. This line can be generated using a statistical procedure (regression analysis). Doing so yields the

table 11.5

Pay Midpoints under Different Approaches

JOB	KEY JOB?	JOB TITLE	JOB EVALUATION	(1) SURVEY + POLICY	(2) PAY MIDPOINTS POLICY	(3) GRADES
A	y	Computer operator	110	$1,919	$1,835	$2,175
B	y	Engineering tech I	115	2,106	1,948	2,175
C	y	Computer programmer	155	2,807	2,856	3,310
D	n	Engineering tech II	165	3,083	3,083	3,310
E	n	Compensation analyst	170	3,196	3,196	3,310
F	y	Accountant	190	3,442	3,650	3,310
G	y	Systems analyst	210	4,134	4,104	4,444
H	n	Computer programmer—senior	225	4,444	4,444	4,444
I	y	Director of personnel	245	4,823	4,898	4,444
J	y	Accountant—senior	255	4,893	5,125	5,579
K	y	Systems analyst—senior	270	5,796	5,465	5,579
L	y	Industrial engineer	275	5,262	5,579	5,579
M	n	Chief accountant	315	6,486	6,486	6,713
N	y	Senior engineer	320	6,875	6,600	6,713
O	n	Senior scientist	330	6,826	6,826	6,713

SOURCE: Adapted from S. Rynes, B. Gerhart, G. T. Milkovich, and J. Boudreau, *Current Compensation Professional Institute* (Scottsdale, AZ: American Compensation Association, 1988). Reprinted with permission.

equation −$661 + $22.69 × job evaluation points. In other words, the predicted monthly salary (based on fitting a line to the key job data) is obtained by plugging the number of job evaluation points into this equation. Thus, for example, job D, a non-key job, would have a predicted monthly salary of −$661 + $22.69 × 165 = $3,083.

As Figure 11.1 also indicates, it is not necessary to fit a straight line to the job evaluation and pay survey data. In some cases, a pay structure that provides increasing

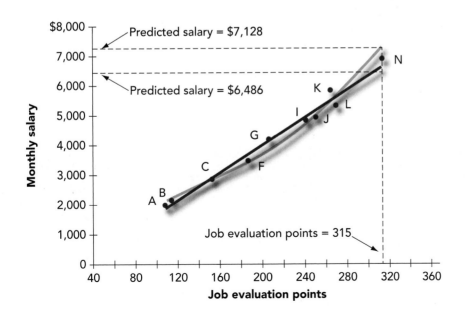

figure 11.1

Pay Policy Lines, Linear and Natural Logarithmic Functions

monetary rewards to higher-level jobs may be more consistent with the organization's goals or with the external market. For example, nonlinearity may be more appropriate if higher-level jobs are especially valuable to organizations and the talent to perform such jobs is rare. The curvilinear function in Figure 11.1 is described by the equation

$$\text{Natural logarithm of pay} = \$6.98 + (0.006 \times \text{job evaluation points})$$

Pay Policy Line

A second pay-setting approach that combines information from external and internal comparisons is to use the pay policy line to derive pay rates for both key and nonkey jobs. This approach differs from the first approach in that actual market rates are no longer used for key jobs. This introduces a greater degree of internal consistency into the structure because the pay of all the jobs is directly linked to the number of job evaluation points.

Pay Grades

Pay Grades
Jobs of similar worth or content grouped together for pay administration purposes.

A third approach is to group jobs into a smaller number of pay classes or **pay grades**. Table 11.6 (see also Table 11.5, last column), for example, demonstrates one possibility: a five-grade structure. Each job within a grade would have the same rate range (i.e., would be assigned the same midpoint, minimum, and maximum). The advantage of this approach is that the administrative burden of setting separate rates of pay for hundreds (even thousands) of different jobs is reduced. It also permits greater flexibility in moving employees from job to job without raising concerns about, for example, going from a job having 230 job evaluation points to a job with 215 job evaluation points. What might look like a demotion in a completely job-based system is often a nonissue in a grade-based system. Note that the **range spread** (the distance between the minimum and maximum) is larger at higher levels, in recognition of the fact that performance differences are likely to have more impact on the organization at higher job levels. (See Figure 11.2.)

Range Spread
The distance between the minimum and maximum amounts in a pay grade.

The disadvantage of using grades is that some jobs will be underpaid and others overpaid. For example, job C and job F both fall within the same grade. The midpoint for job C under a grade system is $3,310 per month, or about $400 or so more than under the two alternative pay-setting approaches. Obviously, this will contribute to higher labor costs and potential difficulties in competing in the product market.

table 11.6

Sample Pay Grade Structure

PAY GRADE	JOB EVALUATION POINTS RANGE		MONTHLY PAY RATE RANGE		
	MINIMUM	MAXIMUM	MINIMUM	MIDPOINT	MAXIMUM
1	100	150	$1,740	$2,175	$2,610
2	150	200	2,648	3,310	3,971
3	200	250	3,555	4,444	5,333
4	250	300	4,463	5,579	6,694
5	300	350	5,370	6,713	8,056

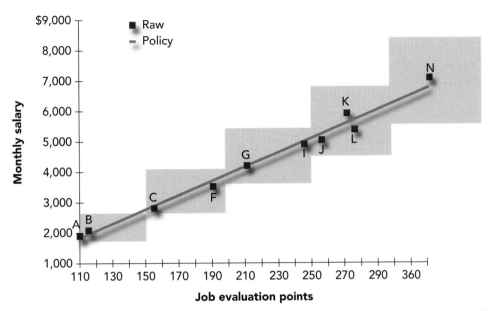

figure 11.2

Sample Pay Grade Structure

Unless there is an expected return to this increased cost, the approach is questionable. Job F, on the other hand, is paid between $130 and $340 less per month under the grades system than it would be otherwise. Therefore, the company may find it more difficult to compete in the labor market.

CONFLICTS BETWEEN MARKET PAY SURVEYS AND JOB EVALUATION

An examination of Table 11.5 suggests that the relative worth of jobs is quite similar overall, whether based on job evaluation or pay survey data. However, some inconsistencies typically arise, and these are usually indicated by jobs whose average survey pay is significantly below or above the pay policy line. The closest case in Table 11.5 is job L, for which the average pay falls significantly below the policy line. One possible explanation is that a relatively plentiful supply of people in the labor market are capable of performing this job, so the pay needed to attract and retain them is lower than would be expected given the job evaluation points. Another kind of inconsistency occurs when market surveys show that a job is paid higher than the policy line (like job K). Again, this may reflect relative supply and demand, in this case driving pay higher.

How are conflicts between external and internal equity resolved, and what are the consequences? The example of the vice presidents of marketing and information technology may help illustrate the type of choice faced. The marketing VP job may receive the same number of job evaluation points, but market survey data may indicate that it typically pays less than the information technology VP job, perhaps because of tighter supply for the latter. Does the organization pay based on the market survey (external comparison) or on the job evaluation points (internal comparison)?

Emphasizing the internal comparison would suggest paying the two VPs the same. In doing so, however, either the VP of marketing would be "overpaid" or the VP of information technology would be "underpaid." The former drives up labor costs (product market problems); the latter may make it difficult to attract and retain a quality VP of information technology (labor market problems).

LO 11-3
Explain the importance of competitive labor market and product market forces in compensation decisions.

Another consideration has to do with the strategy of the organization. In some organizations (like Pepsi and Nike) the marketing function is critical to success. Thus, even though the market for marketing VPs is lower than that for information technology VPs, an organization may choose to be a pay leader for the marketing position (pay at the 90th percentile, for example) but only meet the market for the information technology position (perhaps pay at the 50th percentile). In other words, designing a pay structure requires careful consideration of which positions are most central to dealing with critical environmental challenges and opportunities in reaching the organization's goals.[13]

What about emphasizing external comparisons? Two potential problems arise. First, the marketing VP may be dissatisfied because she expects a job of similar rank and responsibility to that of the information technology VP to be paid similarly. Second, it becomes difficult to rotate people through different VP positions (for training and development) because going to the marketing VP position might appear as a demotion to the VP of information technology.

There is no one right solution to such dilemmas. Each organization must decide which objectives are most essential and choose the appropriate strategy. However, there seems to be a growing sentiment that external comparisons deserve greater weight because organizations are finding it increasingly difficult to ignore market competitive pressures.

MONITORING COMPENSATION COSTS

Pay structure influences compensation costs in a number of ways. Most obviously, the pay level at which the structure is pegged influences these costs. However, this is only part of the story. The pay structure represents the organization's intended policy, but actual practice may not coincide with it. Take, for example, the pay grade structure presented earlier. The midpoint for grade 1 is $2,175, and the midpoint for grade 2 is $3,310. Now, consider the data on a group of individual employees in Table 11.7. One frequently used index of the correspondence between actual and intended pay is the **compa-ratio**, computed as follows:

Compa-Ratio
An index of the correspondence between actual and intended pay.

Grade compa-ratio = Actual average pay for grade/Pay midpoint for grade

table 11.7

Compa-Ratios for Two Grades

EMPLOYEE	JOB	PAY	MIDPOINT	EMPLOYEE COMPA-RATIOS
	Grade 1			
1	Engineering tech I	$2,306	$2,175	1.06
2	Computer programmer	2,066	2,175	.95
3	Engineering tech I	2,523	2,175	1.16
4	Engineering tech I	2,414	2,175	1.11
				1.07
	Grade 2			
5	Computer programmer	3,906	3,310	1.18
6	Accountant	3,773	3,310	1.14
7	Accountant	3,674	3,310	1.11
				1.15

The compa-ratio directly assesses the degree to which actual pay is consistent with the pay policy. A compa-ratio less than 1.00 suggests that actual pay is lagging behind the policy, whereas a compa-ratio greater than 1.00 indicates that pay (and costs) exceeds that of the policy. Although there may be good reasons for compa-ratios to differ from 1.00, managers should also consider whether the pay structure is allowing costs to get out of control.

GLOBALIZATION, GEOGRAPHIC REGION, AND PAY STRUCTURES

As Figure 11.3 shows, market pay structures can differ substantially across countries both in terms of their level and in terms of the relative worth of jobs. Compared with the labor markets in Germany and the United States, markets in Slovakia and Korea provide much lower levels of pay overall and much lower payoffs to skill, education, and advancement. These differences create a dilemma for global companies. For example, should a German engineer posted to Korea be paid according to the standard in Germany or Korea? If the Germany standard is used, a sense of inequity is likely to exist among peers in Korea. If the Korea market standard is used, it may be all but impossible to find a German engineer willing to accept an assignment in Korea. Typically, expatriate pay and benefits (like housing allowance and tax equalization) continue to be linked more closely to the home country. However, this link appears to be slowly weakening and now depends more on the nature and length of the assignment.[14]

Within the United States, Runzheimer International reports that most companies have either a formal or an informal policy that provides for pay differentials based on geographic location.[15] These differentials are intended to prevent inequitable treatment of employees who work in more expensive parts of the country. For example, according to Salary.com the cost of living index for New York City is 91% higher than in Madison, Wisconsin. Therefore, an employee receiving annual pay of $50,000 in Madison in 2011 would require annual pay of $95,554 in New York City to retain the same purchasing power. The most common company approach is to move an employee higher in the pay structure to compensate for higher living costs. However,

Geographic location is an important factor for Human Resources to consider when establishing a pay structure. Living in New York City is more expensive than other places, and employers need to factor in living costs when deciding upon salaries in order to hire a strong workforce.

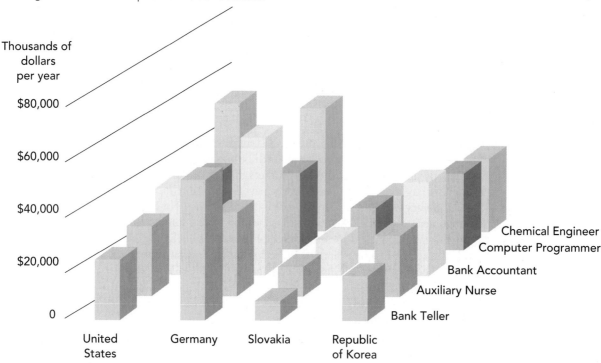

figure 11.3

Earnings in Selected Occupations in Four Countries

SOURCE: International Labor Organization website, at http://laborsta.ilo.org, accessed February 16, 2009. Earnings converted to U.S. dollars using 2008 year-end exchange rates.

the drawback of this approach is that it may be difficult to adjust the salary downward if costs in that location fall or the employee moves to a lower-cost area. Thus, some percentage of the companies choose to pay an ongoing supplement that changes or disappears in the event of such changes.

EVIDENCE-BASED HR

Walmart's legendary obsession with cost containment shows up in countless ways, including aggressive control of employee benefits and wages. Managing labor costs isn't a crazy idea, of course. But stingy pay and benefits don't necessarily translate into lower costs in the long run.

Consider Costco and Walmart's Sam's Club, which compete fiercely on low-price merchandise. Among warehouse retailers, Costco—with 338 stores and 67,600 full-time employees in the United States—is number one, accounting for about 50% of the market. Sam's Club—with 551 stores and 110,200 employees in the United States—is number two, with about 40% of the market.

Although the businesses are direct competitors and quite similar overall, a remarkable disparity shows up in their wage and benefits structures. The average wage at Costco is $17 an hour. Walmart does not break out the pay of its Sam's Club workers, but a full-time worker at Walmart makes $10.11 an hour on average, and a variety of sources suggest that Sam's Club's pay scale is similar to Walmart's. A 2005 *New York*

Times article by Steven Greenhouse reported that at $17 an hour, Costco's average pay is 42% higher than Sam's Club's ($9.86 an hour). Interviews that a colleague and I conducted with a dozen Sam's Club employees in San Francisco and Denver put the average hourly wage at about $10. And a 2004 *BusinessWeek* article by Stanley Holmes and Wendy Zellner estimated Sam's Club's average hourly wage at $11.52.

On the benefits side, 82% of Costco employees have health insurance coverage, compared with less than half at Walmart. And Costco workers pay just 8% of their health premiums, whereas Walmart workers pay 33% of theirs. Ninety-one percent of Costco's employees are covered by retirement plans, with the company contributing an annual average of $1,330 per employee, while 64% of employees at Sam's Club are covered, with the company contributing an annual average of $747 per employee.

Costco's practices are clearly more expensive, and Wall Street has been known to complain that Costco cares more about its employees (and customers) than it does about its shareholders. But they have an offsetting cost-containment effect: turnover is unusually low, at 17% overall and just 6% after one year's employment. In contrast, turnover at Walmart is 44% a year—close to the industry average. In skilled and semiskilled jobs, the fully loaded cost of replacing a worker who leaves (excluding lost productivity) is typically 1.5 to 2.5 times the worker's annual salary. To be conservative, let's assume that the total cost of replacing an hourly employee at Costco or Sam's Club is only 60% of his or her annual salary. If a Costco employee quits, the cost of replacing him or her is therefore $21,216. If a Sam's Club employee leaves, the cost is $12,617. At first glance, it may seem that the low-wage approach at Sam's Club would result in lower turnover costs. But if its turnover rate is the same as Walmart's, Sam's Club loses more than twice as many people as Costco does: 44% versus 17%. By *this calculation*, the total annual cost to Costco of employee churn is $244 million, whereas the total annual cost to Sam's Club is $612 million. That's $5,274 per Sam's Club employee, versus $3,628 per Costco employee.

In return for its generous wages and benefits, Costco gets one of the most loyal and productive workforces in all of retailing—and, probably not coincidentally, the lowest shrinkage (employee theft) figures in the industry. While Sam's Club and Costco generated $37 billion and $43 billion, respectively, in U.S. sales last year, Costco did it with 38% fewer employees—admittedly, in part by selling to higher-income shoppers and offering more high-end goods. As a result, Costco generated $21,805 in U.S. operating profit per hourly employee, compared with $11,615 at Sam's Club. Costco's stable, productive workforce more than offsets its higher costs.

These figures challenge the common assumption that labor rates equal labor costs. Costco's approach shows that when it comes to wages and benefits, a cost-leadership strategy need not be a race to the bottom.

SOURCES: W. F. Cascio, "The High Cost of Low Wages," *Harvard Business Review* 84 (December 2006), p. 23; and J. Chu and K. Rockwood, "CEO Interview: Costco's Jim Sinegal, *Fast Company*, October 13, 2008.

The Importance of Process: Participation and Communication

Compensation management has been criticized for following the simplistic belief that "if the right technology can be developed, the right answers will be found."[16] In reality, however, any given pay decision is rarely obvious to the diverse groups that make up organizations, regardless of the decision's technical merit or basis in theory.

LO 11-4
Discuss the significance of process issues such as communication in compensation management.

Of course, it is important when changing pay practices to decide which program or combination of programs makes most sense, but how such decisions are made and how they are communicated also matter.[17]

PARTICIPATION

Employee participation in compensation decision making can take many forms. For example, employees may serve on task forces charged with recommending and designing a pay program. They may also be asked to help communicate and explain its rationale. This is particularly true in the case of job evaluation as well as many of the programs discussed in the next chapter. To date, for what are perhaps obvious reasons, employee participation in pay level decisions remains fairly rare.

It is important to distinguish between participation by those affected by policies and those who must actually implement the policies. Managers are in the latter group (and often in the former group at the same time). As in other areas of human resource management, line managers are typically responsible for making policies work. Their intimate involvement in any change to existing pay practices is, of course, necessary.

COMMUNICATION

A dramatic example of the importance of communication was found in a study of how an organization communicated pay cuts to its employees and the effects on theft rates and perceived equity.[18] Two organization units received 15% across-the-board pay cuts. A third unit received no pay cut and served as a control group. The reasons for the pay cuts were communicated in different ways to the two pay-cut groups. In the "adequate explanation" pay-cut group, management provided a significant amount of information to explain its reasons for the pay cut and also expressed significant remorse. In contrast, the "inadequate explanation" group received much less information and no indication of remorse. The control group received no pay cut (and thus no explanation).

The control group and the two pay-cut groups began with the same theft rates and equity perceptions. After the pay cut, the theft rate was 54% higher in the "adequate explanation" group than in the control group. But in the "inadequate explanation" condition, the theft rate was 141% higher than in the control group. In this case communication had a large, independent effect on employees' attitudes and behaviors.

Communication is likely to have other important effects. We know, for example, as emphasized by equity theory that not only actual pay but the comparison standard influences employee attitudes.[19] Under two-tier wage plans, employees doing the same jobs are paid two different rates, depending on when they were hired. Moreover, the lower-paid employees do not necessarily move into the higher-paying tier. Common sense might suggest that the lower-paid employees would be less satisfied, but this is not necessarily true. In fact, a study by Peter Cappelli and Peter Sherer found that the lower-paid employees were more satisfied on average.[20] Apparently, those in the lower tier used different (lower) comparison standards than those in the higher tier. The lower-tier employees compared their jobs with unemployment or lower-paying jobs they had managed to avoid. As a result, they were more satisfied, despite being paid less money for the same work. This finding does not mean that two-tier wage plans are likely to be embraced by an organization's workforce. It does, however, support equity theory through its focus on the way employees compare their pay with other jobs and the need for managers to take this into consideration. Employees increasingly have access to salary survey information, which is likely to result in more comparisons and thus a greater need for effective communication.

Managers play the most crucial communication role because of their day-to-day interactions with their employees. Therefore, they must be prepared to explain why the pay structure is designed as it is and to judge whether employee concerns about the structure need to be addressed with changes to the structure. One common issue is deciding when a job needs to be reclassified because of substantial changes in its content. If an employee takes on more responsibility, she will often ask the manager for assistance in making the case for increased pay for the job.

Current Challenges

PROBLEMS WITH JOB-BASED PAY STRUCTURES

The approach taken in this chapter, that of defining pay structures in terms of jobs and their associated responsibilities, remains the most widely used in practice. However, job-based pay structures have a number of potential limitations.[21] First, they may encourage bureaucracy. The job description sets out specific tasks and activities for which the incumbent is responsible and, by implication, those for which the incumbent is not responsible. Although this facilitates performance evaluation and control by the manager, it can also encourage a lack of flexibility and a lack of initiative on the part of employees: "Why should I do that? It's not in my job description." Second, the structure's hierarchical nature reinforces a top-down decision making and information flow as well as status differentials, which do not lend themselves to taking advantage of the skills and knowledge of those closest to production. Third, the bureaucracy required to generate and update job descriptions and job evaluations can become a barrier to change because wholesale changes to job descriptions can involve a tremendous amount of time and cost. Fourth, the job-based pay structure may not reward desired behaviors, particularly in a rapidly changing environment where the knowledge, skills, and abilities needed yesterday may not be very helpful today and tomorrow. Fifth, the emphasis on job levels and status differentials encourages promotion-seeking behavior but may discourage lateral employee movement because employees are reluctant to accept jobs that are not promotions or that appear to be steps down.

LO 11-5
Describe new developments in the design of pay structures.

RESPONSES TO PROBLEMS WITH JOB-BASED PAY STRUCTURES

Delayering and Banding

In response to the problems caused by job-based pay structures, some organizations are **delayering**, or reducing the number of job levels to achieve more flexibility in job assignments and in assigning merit increases. Pratt and Whitney, for example, changed from 11 pay grades and 3,000 job descriptions for entry-level through middle-management positions to 6 pay grades and several hundred job descriptions.[22] These broader groupings of jobs are also known as *broad bands*. Table 11.8 shows how banding might work for a small sample of jobs.

IBM greatly reduced the bureaucratic nature of the system, going from 5,000 job titles and 24 salary grades to a simpler 1,200 jobs and 10 bands. Within their broad bands, managers were given more discretion to reward high performers and to choose

Delayering
Reducing the number of job levels within an organization.

table 11.8

Example of Pay Bands

TRADITIONAL STRUCTURE		BANDED STRUCTURE	
GRADE	TITLE	BAND	TITLE
14	Senior accountant	6	Senior accountant
12	Accountant III		
10	Accountant II	5	Accountant
8	Accountant I		

SOURCE: P. LeBlanc, *Perspectives in Total Compensation, 2*, no. 3, (March 1992), pp. 1–6. Used with permission of the National Practice Director, Sibson & Company, Inc.

pay levels that were competitive in the market for talent. Sometimes, technology can drive major changes in pay structure and labor cost as the "Competing through Technology" box shows.

One possible disadvantage of delayering and banding is a reduced opportunity for promotion. Therefore, organizations need to consider what they will offer employees instead. In addition, to the extent that there are separate ranges within bands, the new structure may not represent as dramatic a change as it might appear. These distinctions can easily become just as entrenched as they were under the old system. Broad bands, with their greater spread between pay minimums and maximums, can also lead to weaker budgetary control and rising labor costs. Alternatively, the greater spread can permit managers to better recognize high performers with high pay. It can also permit the organization to reward employees for learning.

Paying the Person: Pay for Skill, Knowledge, and Competency

A second, related response to job-based pay structure problems has been to move away from linking pay to jobs and toward building structures based on individual characteristics such as skill or knowledge.[23] Competency-based pay is similar but usually refers to a plan that covers exempt employees (such as managers). The basic idea is that if you want employees to learn more skills and become more flexible in the jobs they perform, you should pay them to do it. (See Chapter 7 for a discussion of the implications of skill-based pay systems on training.) According to Gerald Ledford, however, it is "a fundamental departure" because employees are now "paid for the skills they are capable of using, not for the job they are performing at a particular point in time."[24]

Skill-Based Pay
Pay based on the skills employees acquire and are capable of using.

Skill-based pay systems seem to fit well with the increased breadth and depth of skill that changing technology continues to bring.[25] For example, in a production environment, workers might be expected not only to operate machines but also to take responsibility for maintenance and troubleshooting, quality control, even modifying computer programs.[26] Toyota concluded years ago that "none of the specialists [e.g., quality inspectors, many managers, and foremen] beyond the assembly worker was actually adding any value to the car. What's more . . . assembly workers could probably do most of the functions of specialists much better because of their direct acquaintance with conditions on the line."[27]

In other words, an important potential advantage of skill-based pay is its contribution to increased worker flexibility, which in turn facilitates the decentralization of decision making to those who are most knowledgeable. It also provides the opportunity for leaner staffing levels because employee turnover or absenteeism can now be covered by current employees who are multiskilled.[28] In addition, multiskilled employees are

Armies of Expensive Lawyers Replaced by Cheaper Software

When five television studios became entangled in a Justice Department antitrust lawsuit against CBS, the cost was immense. As part of the obscure task of "discovery"—providing documents relevant to a lawsuit—the studios examined six million documents at a cost of more than $2.2 million, much of it to pay for a platoon of lawyers and paralegals who worked for months at high hourly rates.

But that was in 1978. Now, thanks to advances in artificial intelligence, "e-discovery" software can analyze documents in a fraction of the time for a fraction of the cost. In January, for example, Blackstone Discovery of Palo Alto, California, helped analyze 1.5 million documents for less than $100,000.

Some programs go beyond just finding documents with relevant terms at computer speeds. They can extract relevant concepts—like documents relevant to social protest in the Middle East—even in the absence of specific terms, and deduce patterns of behavior that would have eluded lawyers examining millions of documents.

"From a legal staffing viewpoint, it means that a lot of people who used to be allocated to conduct document review are no longer able to be billed out," said Bill Herr, who as a lawyer at a major chemical company used to muster auditoriums of lawyers to read documents for weeks on end.

"People get bored, people get headaches. Computers don't."

Computers are getting better at mimicking human reasoning—as viewers of "Jeopardy!" found out when they saw Watson beat its human opponents—and they are claiming work once done by people in high-paying professions. The number of computer chip designers, for example, has largely stagnated because powerful software programs replace the work once done by legions of logic designers and draftsmen.

Software is also making its way into tasks that were the exclusive province of human decision makers, like loan and mortgage officers and tax accountants.

These new forms of automation have renewed the debate over the economic consequences of technological progress.

David H. Autor, an economics professor at the Massachusetts Institute of Technology, says the United States economy is being "hollowed out." New jobs, he says, are coming at the bottom of the economic pyramid, jobs in the middle are being lost to automation and outsourcing, and now job growth at the top is slowing because of automation.

"There is no reason to think that technology creates unemployment," Professor Autor said. "Over the long run we find things for people to do. The harder question is, does changing technology always lead to better jobs? The answer is no."

Automation of higher-level jobs is accelerating because of progress in computer science and linguistics. Only recently have researchers been able to test and refine algorithms on vast data samples, including a huge trove of e-mail from the Enron Corporation. Nowhere are these advances clearer than in the legal world.

Last year, Clearwell software was used by the law firm DLA Piper to search through a half-million documents under a court-imposed deadline of one week. Clearwell's software analyzed and sorted 570,000 documents (each document can be many pages) in two days. The law firm used just one more day to identify 3,070 documents that were relevant to the court-ordered discovery motion.

Clearwell's software uses language analysis and a visual way of representing general concepts found in documents to make it possible for a single lawyer to do work that might have once required hundreds.

"The catch here is information overload," said Aaref A. Hilaly, Clearwell's chief executive. "How do you zoom in to just the specific set of documents or facts that are relevant to the specific question? It's not about search; it's about sifting, and that's what e-discovery software enables."

Some specialists acknowledge that the technology has limits. "The documents that the process kicks out still have to be read by someone," said Herbert L. Roitblat of OrcaTec, a consulting firm in Altanta.

Quantifying the employment impact of these new technologies is difficult. Mike Lynch, the founder of Autonomy, is convinced that "legal is a sector that will likely employ fewer, not more, people in the U.S. in the future." He estimated that the shift from manual document discovery to e-discovery would lead to a manpower reduction in which one lawyer would suffice for work that once required 500 and that the newest generation of software, which can detect duplicates and find clusters of important documents on a particular topic, could cut the head count by another 50%.

The computers seem to be good at their new jobs. Mr. Herr, the former chemical company lawyer, used e-discovery software to reanalyze work his company's lawyers did in the 1980s and 1990s. His human colleagues had been only 60% accurate, he found. "Think about how much money had been spent to be slightly better than a coin toss," he said.

important in cases where different products require different manufacturing processes or where supply shortages or other problems call for adaptive or flexible responses—characteristics typical, for example, of many newer so-called advanced manufacturing environments (like flexible manufacturing and just-in-time systems).[29] More generally, it has been suggested that skill-based plans also contribute to a climate of learning and adaptability and give employees a broader view of how the organization functions. Both changes should contribute to better use of employees' know-how and ideas. Consistent with the advantages just noted, a field study found that a change to a skill-based plan led to better quality and lower labor costs in a manufacturing plant.[30]

Of course, skill-based and competency-based approaches also have potential disadvantages.[31] First, although the plan will likely enhance skill acquisition, the organization may find it a challenge to use the new skills effectively. Without careful planning, it may find itself with large new labor costs but little payoff. In other words, if skills change, work design must change as quickly to take full advantage. Second, if pay growth is based entirely on skills, problems may arise if employees "top out" by acquiring all the skills too quickly, leaving no room for further pay growth. (Of course, this problem can also afflict job-based systems.) Third, and somewhat ironically, skill-based plans may generate a large bureaucracy—usually a criticism of job-based systems. Training programs need to be developed. Skills must be described, measured, and assigned monetary values. Certification tests must be developed to determine whether an employee has acquired a certain skill. Finally, as if the challenges in obtaining market rates under a job-based system were not enough, there is almost no body of knowledge regarding how to price combinations of skills (versus jobs) in the marketplace. Obtaining comparison data from other organizations will be difficult until skill-based plans become more widely used.

CAN THE U.S. LABOR FORCE COMPETE?

LO 11-6
Explain where the United States stands from an international perspective on pay issues.

We often hear that U.S. labor costs are simply too high to allow U.S. companies to compete effectively with companies in other countries. The average hourly labor costs (cash and benefits) for manufacturing production workers in the United States and in other advanced industrialized and newly industrialized countries are given in Table 11.9 in U.S. dollars.

	1985	1990	1995	2000	2005	2009
Industrialized						
United States	$13.01	$14.91	$17.19	$19.76	$29.74	33.53
Canada	10.95	15.95	16.10	16.04	26.81	29.60
Czech Republic				2.83	7.28	11.21
Germany[a]	9.57	21.53	30.26	23.38	38.18	46.52
Japan	6.43	12.64	23.82	22.27	25.56	30.36
Newly industrialized						
Mexico	1.60	1.80	1.51	2.08	5.36	5.38
Brazil				4.38	5.05	8.32
Taiwan	1.49	3.90	5.85	7.30	7.93	7.76
South Korea	1.25	3.82	7.29	8.19	15.13	14.20
China					0.62[b]	1.36[c]

table 11.9

Average Hourly Labor Cost (Cash and Benefits) for Production Workers in Manufacturing by Country and Year

SOURCE: Bureau of Labor Statistics, U.S. Department of Labor,. www.bls.gov/fls/#compensation, extracted June 2, 2011.

[a] West Germany for 1985 and 1990 data.

[b] 2006.

[c] 2008.

Based solely on a cost approach, it would perhaps make sense to try to shift many types of production from a country like Germany to other countries, particularly the newly industrialized countries. Would this be a good idea? Not necessarily. There are several factors to consider.

Instability of Country Differences in Labor Costs

First, note that relative labor costs are very unstable over time. For example, in 1985, U.S. labor costs were (13.01/9.57) or 36% greater than those of (West) Germany. But by 1990, the situation was reversed, with (West) German labor costs exceeding those of the United States by (21.53/14.77), or 46%, and remaining higher. Did German employers suddenly become more generous while U.S. employers clamped down on pay growth? Not exactly. Because all our figures are expressed in U.S. dollars, currency exchange rates influence such comparisons, and these exchange rates often fluctuate significantly from year to year. For example, in 1985, when German labor costs were 74% of those in the United States, the U.S. dollar was worth 2.94 German marks. But in 1990 the U.S. dollar was worth 1.62 German marks. If the exchange rate in 1990 were still 1 to 2.94, the average German hourly wage in U.S. dollars would have been $11.80, or about 80% of the U.S. average. In any event, relative to countries like Germany, U.S. labor costs are now a bargain; this explains, in part, decisions by BMW, Mercedes-Benz, and Volkswagen to locate production facilities in South Carolina, Alabama, and Tennessee, respectively, where labor costs are lower than Germany's by a substantial amount. The euro, Germany's current currency, rose from €1 = US$.89 at the end of 2001 to €1 = US$1.44 by mid-2011, reinforcing the rising labor cost in Germany relative to the United States (when expressed in U.S. dollars).

Skill Levels

Second, the quality and productivity of national labor forces can vary dramatically. This is an especially important consideration in comparisons between labor costs in industrialized countries like the United States and developing countries like Mexico. For example, the high school graduation rate in the United States is 77% versus 44% in Mexico.[32] Thus, lower labor costs may reflect the lower average skill level of the workforce; certain types of skilled labor may be less available in low–labor-cost countries. On the other hand, any given company needs only enough skilled employees for its own operations. Some companies have found that low labor costs do not necessarily preclude high quality.

Productivity

Third, and most directly relevant, are data on comparative productivity and unit labor costs, essentially meaning labor cost per hour divided by productivity per hour worked. One indicator of productivity is gross domestic product (or total output of the economy) per person. On this measure, the United States fares well. These figures (in U.S. dollars) for 2009 are represented in Figure 11.4. The combination of lower labor costs and higher productivity translates into lower unit labor costs in the United States than in Japan and western Europe.[33]

Nonlabor Considerations

Fourth, any consideration of where to locate production cannot be based on labor considerations alone. For example, although the average hourly labor cost in Country A may be $15 versus $10 in Country B, if labor costs are 30% of total operating costs

figure 11.4

Gross Domestic Product per Person, 2009

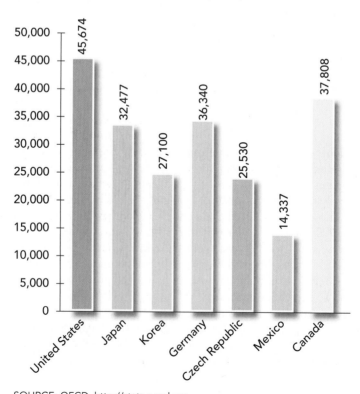

SOURCE: OECD, http://stats.oecd.org.

and nonlabor operating costs are roughly the same, then the total operating costs might be $65 (50 + 15) in Country A and $60 (50 + 10) in Country B. Although labor costs in Country B are 33% less, total operating costs are only 7.7% less. This may not be enough to compensate for differences in skills and productivity, customer wait time, transportation costs, taxes, and so on. Further, the direct labor component of many products, particularly high-tech products (such as electronic components), may often be 5% or less. Thus the effect on product price-competitiveness may be insignificant.[34]

In fact, an increasing number of organizations have decided that it is more important to focus on nonlabor factors in deciding where to locate production. Being close to where customers are matters a great deal. Product development speed may be greater when manufacturing is physically close to the design group. Quick response to customers (like making a custom replacement product) is difficult when production facilities are on the other side of the world. Inventory levels can be dramatically reduced through the use of manufacturing methods like just-in-time production, but suppliers need to be in close physical proximity.

On the other hand, some firms are aggressively offshoring jobs (including professional or knowledge worker jobs) primarily to reduce labor costs. For example, financial services firms like Goldman Sachs and Citigroup now have significant numbers of employees in India doing statistical and research work at much lower pay levels.[35] As another example, IBM began to move thousands of programmer jobs overseas to countries like China where the hourly cost would be $12.50 an hour versus $56 an hour in the United States, potentially saving more than $100 million per year.[36]

EXECUTIVE PAY

LO 11-7
Explain the reasons for the controversy over executive pay.

The issue of executive pay has been given widespread attention in the press. In a sense, the topic has received more coverage than it deserves because there are very few top executives and their compensation accounts for only a small share of an organization's total labor costs. On the other hand, top executives have a disproportionate ability to influence organization performance, so decisions about their compensation are critical. They can also be symbolic. During the recent financial crisis, the U.S. government, as part of the Troubled Asset Relief Program (TARP), decided it was appropriate to further regulate executive pay in firms receiving government "bailout" money. Top executives also help set the tone or culture of the organization. If, for example, the top executive's pay seems unrelated to the organization's performance, staying high even when business is poor, employees may not understand why some of their own pay should be at risk and depend on how the organization is performing.

How much do executives make? Table 11.10 provides some data. Long-term compensation, typically in the form of stock plans, is the major component of CEO pay, which means that CEO pay varies with the performance of the stock market (see the "change in S&P 500" column). Table 11.11 shows that some CEOs are paid well above the averages shown in Table 11.10.

As Table 11.12 shows, U.S. top executives are also the highest paid in the world. (These figures are lower than those from *BusinessWeek* and *Forbes* because the latter reports pertain to larger companies.) The fact that the differential between top-executive pay and that of an average manufacturing worker is so much higher in the United States than in some other countries has been described as creating a "trust gap"—that

table 11.10

CEO Compensation

| | CEO PAY | | | | | | | |
YEAR	SALARY PLUS BONUS	STOCK GAINS	OTHER	TOTAL PAY	CHANGE IN CEO PAY	CHANGE IN S&P 500	WORKER PAY*	CEO PAY/ WORKER PAY**
2011	$3 million	$3 million	$3 million	$ 9.0 million	6%	—	$33,800	266
2010	3 million	2 million	3 million	8.5 million	−25	14%	33,129	257
2009	3 million	6 million	3 million	11.4 million	−11	27	32,093	355
2008	3 million	6 million	3 million	12.8 million	−18	−38	31,617	405
2007	4 million	8 million	4 million	15.6 million	34	5	30,682	508
2006	4 million	6 million	2 million	11.6 million	3	16	29,529	393
2005	3 million	6 million	2 million	11.3 million	51	5	28,305	399
2004	3 million	3 million	2 million	7.5 million	6	11	27,513	273
2003	3 million	3 million	1 million	7.1 million	−37	29	26,939	264
2002	3 million	7 million	1 million	11.3 million	−9	−22	26,351	429
2001	3 million	8 million	2 million	12.4 million	−5	−12	25,677	483
2000	3 million	6 million	4 million	13.1 million	56	−9	25,013	524
1995	2 million	1 million	1 million	3.0 million	25	38	20,804	144
1990	2 million	1 million	0 million	2.4 million	4	−3	18,187	132

SOURCES: CEO pay data from *Forbes* magazine website; Worker pay data from U.S. Bureau of Labor Statistics, Employment and Earnings, table B-2.

Through the year 1999, *Forbes* data pertain to the 800 largest U.S. companies. Beginning with year 2000, data pertain to the 500 largest U.S. companies.

* Establishment survey data on earnings of production and nonsupervisory workers on private nonfarm payrolls.

** Ratio of CEO pay to hourly employee pay.

is, in employees' minds, a "frame of mind that mistrusts senior management's intentions, doubts its competence, and resents its self-congratulatory pay." The issue becomes more salient when many of the same companies with high executive pay simultaneously engage in layoffs or other forms of employment reduction. Employees might ask, "If the company needs to cut costs, why not cut executive pay rather than our jobs?"[37] The issue is one of perceived fairness. One study, in fact, reported that business units with higher pay differentials between executives and rank-and-file employees had lower customer satisfaction, which was speculated to result from employees' perceptions of inequity coming through in customer relations.[38] Perhaps more important than how much top executives are paid is how they are paid (i.e., whether performance-based). This is an issue we return to in the next chapter.

table 11.11

Highest-Paid CEOs

	TOTAL COMPENSATION
Stephen J. Hemsley, United Health Group	$102 million
Edward A. Mueller, Qwest Communications	66 million
Robert A. Iger, Walt Disney	53 million

SOURCE: *Forbes* magazine website, accessed June 2, 2011.

COUNTRY	CEO TOTAL REMUNERATION	CEO/MANUFACTURING EMPLOYEE TOTAL REMUNERATION MULTIPLE
United States	$2,160,000	39
Canada	1,100,000	24
Mexico	1,000,000	60
Brazil	849,000	60
Argentina	431,000	45
France	1,200,000	23
Germany	1,180,000	20
China	211,000	36
India	291,000	51
Japan	543,000	11
Korea	584,000	23

table 11.12

Total Remuneration of CEOs in Selected Countries (U.S. dollars)

Notes: Data based on a company with $500 million in sales; total remuneration includes salary, bonus, company contributions, perquisites, and long-term incentives. Table 11.12 values are based on much smaller companies than those in Table 11.10, thus explaining the table differences.

SOURCE: Towers Perrin, "2005–2006 Worldwide Total Remuneration," Stamford, CT, 2006.

Government Regulation of Employee Compensation

EQUAL EMPLOYMENT OPPORTUNITY

Equal employment opportunity (EEO) regulation (such as Title VII of the Civil Rights Act) prohibits sex- and race-based differences in employment outcomes such as pay, unless justified by business necessity (like pay differences stemming from differences in job performance). In addition to regulatory pressures, organizations must deal with changing labor market and demographic realities. At least two trends are directly relevant in discussing EEO. First, women have gone from 33% of all employees in 1960 to 47% in 2011. Second, between 1960 and 2011, Whites have gone from 90% to 82% of all employees. White men account for 44% of all U.S. employment and that percentage will probably continue to decline, making attention to EEO issues in compensation even more important.

Is there equality of treatment in pay determination? Typically, the popular press focuses on raw earnings ratios. For example, in 2010, among full-time workers, the ratio of female-to-male median earnings was 0.81, the ratio of Black-to-White earnings was 0.80, and Hispanic–Latino-to-White earnings was 0.70.[39] These percentages have generally risen over the last two to three decades, but significant race and sex differences in pay clearly remain.[40] In contrast, Asian Americans earn 12% more than Whites. Among executives, women appear to have lower pay than men partly due to less use of performance-based (e.g., stock and bonus-related) pay.[41]

The usefulness of raw percentages is limited, however, because some portion of earnings differences arises from differences in legitimate factors: education, labor market experience, and occupation. Adjusting for such factors reduces earnings differences based on race and sex, but significant differences remain. With few exceptions, such adjustments rarely account for more than half of the earnings differential.[42]

LO 11-8
Describe the regulatory framework for employee compensation.

What aspects of pay determination are responsible for such differences? In the case of women, it is suggested that their work is undervalued. Another explanation rests on the "crowding" hypothesis, which argues that women were historically restricted to entering a small number of occupations. As a result, the supply of workers far exceeded demand, resulting in lower pay for such occupations. If so, market surveys would only perpetuate the situation.

Comparable Worth
A public policy that advocates remedies for any undervaluation of women's jobs (also called *pay equity*).

Comparable worth (or pay equity) is a public policy that advocates remedies for any undervaluation of women's jobs. The idea is to obtain equal pay, not just for jobs of equal content (already mandated by the Equal Pay Act of 1963) but for jobs of equal value or worth, on the basis of Title VII of the Civil Rights Act. Typically, job evaluation is used to measure worth. Table 11.13, which is based on Washington State data from one of the first comparable worth cases, suggests that measures of worth based on internal comparisons (job evaluation) and external comparisons (market surveys) can be compared. In this case many disagreements between the two measures appear. Internal comparisons suggest that women's jobs are underpaid, whereas external comparisons are less supportive of this argument. For example, although the licensed practical nurse job receives 173 job evaluation points and the truck driver position receives 97 points, the market rate (and thus the state of Washington employer rate) for the truck driver position is $1,493 per month versus only $1,030 per month for the nurse. The truck driver is paid nearly 127% more than the pay policy line would predict, whereas the nurse is paid only 75% of the pay policy line prediction.

One potential problem with using job evaluation to establish worth independent of the market is that job evaluation procedures were never designed for this purpose.[43]

table 11.13

Job Evaluation Points, Monthly Prevailing Market Pay Rates, and Proportion of Incumbents in Job Who Are Female

BENCHMARK TITLE	MONTHLY EVALUATION POINTS	PREVAILING RATES[a]	PREVAILING RATE AS PERCENTAGE OF PREDICTED[b]	PERCENTAGE OF FEMALE INCUMBENTS
Warehouse worker	97	$1,286	109.1%	15.4%
Truck driver	97	1,493	126.6	13.6
Retail sales clerk	121	921	74.3	100.0
Highway engineering tech	133	1,401	110.4	11.1
Word processing equipment operator	138	1,082	83.2	98.3
Licensed practical nurse	173	1,030	75.3	89.5
Maintenance carpenter	197	1,707	118.9	2.3
Secretary	197	1,122	78.1	98.5
Civil engineer	287	1,885	116.0	0.0
Highway engineer 3	345	1,980	110.4	3.0
Registered nurse	348	1,368	76.3	92.2
Senior computer systems analyst	384	2,080	113.1	17.8
Personnel representative	410	1,956	101.2	45.6

SOURCE: Reprinted with permission of *Public Personnel Management*, published by the International Personnel Management Association.

[a]Prevailing market rate as of July 1, 1980. Midpoint of job range set equal to this amount.

[b]Predicted salary is based on regression of prevailing market rate on job evaluation points $2.43 × Job evaluation points + 936.19, r = 0.77.

Rather, as demonstrated earlier, their major use is in helping to capture the market pay policy and then applying that to nonkey jobs for which market data are not available. In other words, job evaluation has typically been used to help apply the market pay policy, quite the opposite of replacing the market in pay setting.

As with any regulation, there are also concerns that EEO regulation obstructs market forces, which, according to economic theory, provide the most efficient means of pricing and allocating people to jobs. In theory, moving away from a reliance on market forces would result in some jobs being paid too much and others too little, leading to an oversupply of workers for the former and an undersupply for the latter. In addition, some empirical evidence suggests that a comparable worth policy would not have much impact on the relative earnings of women in the private sector.[44] One limitation of such a policy is that it targets single employers, ignoring that men and women tend to work for different employers.[45] To the extent that segregation by employer contributes to pay differences between men and women, comparable worth would not be effective. In other words, to the extent that sex-based pay differences are the result of men and women working in different organizations with different pay levels, such policies will have little impact.

Perhaps most important, despite potential problems with market rates, the courts have consistently ruled that using the going market rates of pay is an acceptable defense in comparable worth litigation suits.[46] The rationale is that organizations face competitive labor and product markets. Paying less or more than the market rate will put the organization at a competitive disadvantage. Thus there is no comparable worth legal mandate in the U.S. private sector.

On the other hand, by the early 1990s, almost one-half of the states had begun or completed comparable worth adjustments to public-sector employees' pay. In addition, in 1988 the Canadian province of Ontario mandated comparable worth in both the private and public sectors. Further, although comparable worth is not mandated in the U.S. private sector, the Department of Labor (Office of Federal Contracts Compliance), which enforces Executive Order 11246, put into place new enforcement standards and guidelines in 2006 that prohibit race or sex-based "systemic compensation discrimination," which it defines as a situation "where there are statistically significant compensation disparities (as established by a regression analysis) between similarly situated employees, after taking into account the legitimate factors which influence compensation, such as: education, prior work experience, performance, productivity, and time in the job."[47] Further, passage of the 2009 Lilly Ledbetter Fair Pay Act means that employers may face claims in situations where a discriminatory decision (e.g., too small of a pay raise) was made many years earlier, but the effect (lower pay) continues into the more current period.

Some work has focused on pinpointing where women's pay falls behind that of men. One finding is that the pay gap is wider where bonus and incentive payments (not just base salary) are examined. Other evidence indicates that women lose ground at the time they are hired and actually do better once they are employed for some time.[48] One interpretation is that when actual job performance (rather than the limited general qualification information available on applicants) is used in decisions, women may be less likely to encounter unequal treatment. If so, more attention needs to be devoted to ensuring fair treatment of applicants and new employees.[49] On the other hand, a "glass ceiling" is believed to exist in some organizations that allows women (and minorities) to come within sight of the top echelons of management, but not advance to them.

It is likely, however, that organizations will differ in terms of where women's earnings disadvantages arise. For example, advancement opportunities for women and other protected groups may be hindered by unequal access to the "old boy" or informal network. This, in turn, may be reflected in lower rates of pay. Mentoring programs have been suggested as one means of improving access. Indeed, one study found that mentoring was successful, having a significant positive effect on the pay of both men and women, with women receiving a greater payoff in percentage terms than men.[50]

MINIMUM WAGE, OVERTIME, AND PREVAILING WAGE LAWS

Fair Labor Standards Act (FLSA)
The 1938 law that established the minimum wage and overtime pay.

The 1938 **Fair Labor Standards Act (FLSA)** establishes a **minimum wage** for jobs, which new stands at $7.25 per hour. State laws may specify higher minimum wages. The FLSA also permits a subminimum training wage that is approximately 85% of the minimum wage, which employers are permitted to pay most employees under the age of 20 for a period of up to 90 days.

Minimum Wage
The lowest amount that employers are legally allowed to pay; the 1990 amendment of the Fair Labor Standards Act permits a subminimum wage to workers under the age of 20 for a period of up to 90 days.

The FLSA also requires that employees be paid at a rate of one and a half times their hourly rate for each hour of overtime worked beyond 40 hours in a week. The hourly rate includes not only the base wage but also other components such as bonuses and piece-rate payments. The FLSA requires overtime pay for any hours beyond 40 in a week that an employer "suffers or permits" the employee to perform, regardless of whether the work is done at the workplace or whether the employer explicitly asked or expected the employee to do it. If the employer knows the employee is working overtime but neither moves to stop it nor pays time and a half, a violation of the FLSA may have occurred. A department store was the target of a lawsuit that claimed employees were "encouraged" to, among other things, write thank-you notes to customers outside of scheduled work hours but were not compensated for this work. Although the company denied encouraging this off-the-clock work, it reached an out-of-court settlement to pay between $15 million and $30 million in back pay (plus legal fees of $7.5 million) to approximately 85,000 sales representatives it employed over a three-year period.[51]

Exempt
Employees who are not covered by the Fair Labor Standards Act. Exempt employees are not eligible for overtime pay.

Executive, professional, administrative, outside sales, and certain "computer employees" occupations are **exempt** from FLSA coverage. *Nonexempt* occupations are covered and include most hourly jobs. One estimate is that just over 20% of employees fall into the exempt category.[52] Exempt status depends on job responsibilities and salary. All exemptions (except for outside sales) require that an employee be paid no less than $455 per week. The job responsibility criteria vary. For example, the executive exemption is based on whether two or more people are supervised, whether there is authority to hire and fire (or whether particular weight is given to the employee's recommendations), and whether the employee's primary duty is managing the enterprise, recognized department, or subdivision of the enterprise. The Wage and Hour Division, Employment Standards Administration (www.dol.gov/esa), U.S. Department of Labor, and its local offices can provide further information on these definitions. (The exemptions do *not* apply to police, firefighters, paramedics, and first responders.)

Two pieces of legislation—the 1931 Davis-Bacon Act and the 1936 Walsh-Healy Public Contracts Act—require federal contractors to pay employees no less than the prevailing wages in the area. Davis-Bacon covers construction contractors receiving federal money of more than $2,000. Typically, prevailing wages have been based on relevant union contracts, partly because only 30% of the local labor force is required to be used in establishing the prevailing rate. Walsh-Healy covers all government contractors receiving $10,000 or more in federal funds.

Finally, employers must take care in deciding whether a person working on their premises is classified as an employee or independent contractor. We address this issue in Chapter 13.

A LOOK BACK

We began this chapter by looking at how foreign companies in China are responding to increases in labor costs and how U.S. companies and their workers have had to make dramatic changes to reduce labor costs in hopes of helping the companies survive, as well as save jobs. We also saw other strategies to control labor costs in these difficult times. For example, some companies are offshoring work to countries (e.g., China and India, but also the United States), in part, to make labor costs more competitive. We have seen in this chapter that pay structure decisions influence the success of strategy execution by influencing not only labor costs, but also employee perceptions of equity, and the way that different structures provide flexibility and incentives for employees to learn and be productive.

Questions

1. What types of changes have the companies discussed in this chapter made to their pay structures to support execution of their business strategies?
2. Would other companies seeking to better align their pay structures with their business strategies benefit from imitating the changes made at these companies?

 Please see the Video that corresponds to this chapter at www.mhhe.com/noe8e.

SUMMARY

In this chapter we have discussed the nature of the pay structure and its component parts, the pay level, and the job structure. Equity theory suggests that social comparisons are an important influence on how employees evaluate their pay. Employees make external comparisons between their pay and the pay they believe is received by employees in other organizations. Such comparisons may have consequences for employee attitudes and retention. Employees also make internal comparisons between what they receive and what they perceive others within the organization are paid. These types of comparisons may have consequences for internal movement, cooperation, and attitudes (like organization commitment). Such comparisons play an important role in the controversy over executive pay, as illustrated by the focus of critics on the ratio of executive pay to that of lower-paid workers.

Pay benchmarking surveys and job evaluation are two administrative tools widely used in managing the pay level and job structure components of the pay structure, which influence employee social comparisons. Pay surveys also permit organizations to benchmark their labor costs against other organizations. Globalization is increasing the need for organizations to be competitive in both their labor costs and productivity.

The nature of pay structures is undergoing a fundamental change in many organizations. One change is the move to fewer pay levels to reduce labor costs and bureaucracy. Second, some employers are shifting from paying employees for narrow jobs to giving them broader responsibilities and paying them to learn the necessary skills.

Finally, a theme that runs through this chapter and the next is the importance of process in managing employee compensation. How a new program is designed, decided on, implemented, and communicated is perhaps just as important as its core characteristics.

KEY TERMS

Pay structure, 483
Pay level, 483
Job structure, 483
Efficiency wage theory, 489
Benchmarking, 489
Rate ranges, 490
Key jobs, 490

Nonkey jobs, 490
Job evaluation, 490
Compensable factors, 490
Pay policy line, 492
Pay grades, 494
Range spread, 494
Compa-ratio, 496

Delayering, 501
Skill-based pay, 502
Comparable worth, 510
Fair Labor Standards
    Act (FLSA), 512
Minimum wage, 512
Exempt, 512

DISCUSSION QUESTIONS

1. You have been asked to evaluate whether your organization's current pay structure makes sense in view of what competing organizations are paying. How would you determine what organizations to compare your organization with? Why might your organization's pay structure differ from those in competing organizations? What are the potential consequences of having a pay structure that is out of line relative to those of your competitors?

2. Top management has decided that the organization is too bureaucratic and has too many layers of jobs to compete effectively. You have been asked to suggest innovative alternatives to the traditional "job-based" approach to employee compensation and to list the advantages and disadvantages of these new approaches.

3. If major changes of the type mentioned in Question 2 are to be made, what types of so-called process issues need to be considered? Of what relevance is equity theory in helping to understand how employees might react to changes in the pay structure?

4. Are executive pay levels unreasonable? Why or why not?

5. Your company plans to build a new manufacturing plant but is undecided where to locate it. What factors would you consider in choosing in which country (or state) to build the plant?

6. You have been asked to evaluate whether a company's pay structure is fair to women and minorities. How would you go about answering this question?

SELF-ASSESSMENT EXERCISE

Consider your current job or a job you had in the past. For each of the following pay characteristics, indicate your level of satisfaction by using the following scale: 1 = very dissatisfied; 2 = somewhat dissatisfied; 3 = neither satisfied nor dissatisfied; 4 = somewhat satisfied; 5 = very satisfied.

_____ 1. My take-home pay
_____ 2. My current pay
_____ 3. My overall level of pay
_____ 4. Size of my current salary
_____ 5. My benefit package
_____ 6. Amount the company pays toward my benefits
_____ 7. The value of my benefits
_____ 8. The number of benefits I receive
_____ 9. My most recent raise
_____10. Influence my manager has over my pay
_____11. The raises I have typically received in the past
_____12. The company's pay structure
_____13. Information the company gives about pay issues of concern to me
_____14. Pay of other jobs in the company

_____ 15. Consistency of the company's pay policies
_____ 16. How my raises are determined
_____ 17. Differences in pay among jobs in the company
_____ 18. The way the company administers pay

These 18 items measure four dimensions of pay satisfaction. Find your total score for each set of item numbers to measure your satisfaction with each dimension.
Pay Level
Total of items 1, 2, 3, 4, 9, 11: _____
Benefits
Total of items 5, 6, 7, 8: _____
Pay Structure and Administration
Total of items 12, 13, 14, 15, 17, 18: _____
Pay Raises
Total of items 10, 11, 16: _____

Considering the principles discussed in this chapter, how could your company improve (or how could it have improved) your satisfaction on each dimension?

SOURCE: Based on H. G. Heneman III and D. P. Schwab, "Pay Satisfaction: Its Multidimensional Nature and Measurement," *International Journal of Psychology* 20 (1985), pp. 129–41.

EXERCISING STRATEGY: CHANGING COMPENSATION TO SUPPORT CHANGES IN CORPORATE STRATEGY

By realigning its strategy and compensation and benefits programs, Corning Inc., once a traditional economy company, hopes to compete successfully in the new economy. First, the company divested itself of several business units, including Corning Consumer Products. These divestitures reduced its annual revenues from $5 billion to $3 billion. Next Corning pursued a "high-octane" growth strategy in optical communications (optical fiber, cable systems, photo technologies, optical networking devices), environmental technologies, display technologies, and specialty materials. To support this shift in corporate strategy, Corning sought to support growth by creating an environment that bolstered innovation, risk taking, teaming, and speed. One major change was in its compensation system. The salary structure was streamlined from 11 grades to 5 broad bands for exempt employees and from 7 grades to 3 broad bands for nonexempt employees. In a new economy company, products have a short life cycle and change in markets is a way of life. This means that the nature of work also changes rapidly, so the detailed job descriptions and traditional promotion paths of the past may not fit this fluid environment. By changing its salary structure, Corning hopes to increase its ability to move quickly in responding to and anticipating customer needs in rapidly changing markets by encouraging flexibility, teamwork, and learning among its employees. Decentralizing more pay decisions to managers contributes to this flexibility, and giving employees an increasing stake in the success of the company by making more employees eligible for stock options contributes to the increased focus on teamwork. Finally, employee compensation is increasingly tied to individual employee learning and performance as the broad bands allow managers more flexibility to recognize outstanding achievements.

Questions

1. What are the pros and cons of Corning's new pay structure?
2. How did shifting product market conditions affect Corning's restructuring and its success?

SOURCE: B. Parus, "How an Old Economy Company Became a New Economy Enterprise," *Workspan* 44:6 (June 2001), pp. 34–41.

MANAGING PEOPLE

Workers at Harley and Sub-Zero Accept Pay Freezes and Cuts to Keep Their Jobs from Moving

At Harley-Davidson, the company that makes the iconic motorcycle, union workers in Wisconsin agreed to an unusually long contract of seven years. During that seven-year period, the company has the right to freeze wages. There will also be higher health care expenses for workers. The company will also be allowed to use more casual workers who receive lower wages and probably will not receive health or retirement benefits. Why did workers accept this contract? Harley said that it needed to cut millions of dollars in costs to be profitable in an industry where sales have weakened and the timing of a recovery is unknown. Harley lost $55 million in the past year. One way to cut costs would be to move production to other states with lower labor costs or to move production to lower-cost countries. Harley put on the table the possibility that it would completely close its Wisconsin factories without the worker concessions and resulting labor cost savings. By voting to accept the concessions, workers received a verbal commitment that the factories would stay open, but no written guarantee. Some jobs will still be moved out of Wisconsin despite the concessions. But, some workers saw little alternative. As one put it, "I am too young to retire and too old to start over."

A similar situation took place at Sub-Zero/Wolf, an appliance manufacturer. The company threatened to move jobs from Wisconsin to a lower-cost plant in Kentucky if workers did not agree to concessions. The unionized workers ended up agreeing to a 20% pay cut, followed by a freeze of wages and benefits for the following four years. As a result, the company will still move some jobs to other locations, but most jobs will now remain in Wisconsin.

Questions

1. Why do companies ask workers for wage and benefit cuts or freezes? Is it the right thing to do?
2. Why do workers agree to these concessions? What negotiating leverage do they have in dealing with the company? What changes have occurred over time that have reduced the negotiating leverage that workers have?
3. What are the future prospects for workers in manufacturing? Does it differ from state to state or country to country? Explain.

SOURCES: Michael Sears, "Harley Workers OK Deal," *Milwaukee Journal Sentinel*, September 13, 2010; Karen Rivedal, "Jobs Stay at Sub-Zero/Wolf," *Wisconsin State Journal*, September 11, 2010.

● TWITTER FOCUS: CHANGING THE PAY LEVEL AT EIGHT CROSSINGS

Using Twitter, continue the conversation about pay structure by reading the Eight Crossings case at www.mhhe .com/noe8e.

Eight Crossings provides transcription services for physicians, attorneys, and health care facilities. Employees work at the company's office or in their homes. Sending files electronically provided a competitive advantage that helped grow the business at a tremendous pace. The downside to using electronic files was that it exposed Eight Crossings to increased competition from low-wage locations such as India. To keep

competitive with offshore vendors, Eight Crossings told its employees they would not be paid for "boilerplate text" that appeared in most documents, which was generated automatically by transcription software. This cut brought pay levels down to the market rate and kept the company competitive.

Engage with your classmates and instructor via Twitter to chat about pay structure decisions at Eight Crossings using the case questions posted on the Noe website. Don't have a Twitter account yet? See the instructions for getting started on the Online Learning Center.

● NOTES

1. J. S. Adams, "Inequity in Social Exchange," in *Advances in Experimental Social Psychology*, ed. L. Berkowitz (New York: Academic Press, 1965); P. S. Goodman, "An Examination of Referents Used in the Evaluation of Pay," *Organizational Behavior and Human Performance* 12 (1974), pp. 170–95; C. O. Trevor and D. L. Wazeter, "A Contingent View of Reactions to Objective Pay Conditions: Interdependence among Pay Structure Characteristics and Pay Relative to Internal and External Referents," *Journal of Applied Psychology* 91 (2006), pp. 1260–1275; M. M. Harris, F. Anseel, and F. Lievens, "Keeping Up with the Joneses: A Field Study of the Relationships among Upward, Lateral, and Downward Comparisons and Pay Level Satisfaction," *Journal of Applied Psychology* 93, no. 3 (May 2008), pp. 665–73; and Gordon D. A. Brown, Jonathan Gardner, Andrew J. Oswald, Jing Qian, "Does Wage Rank Affect Employees' Well-being?" *Industrial Relations* 47, no. 3 (July 2008), p. 355.

2. J. B. Miner, *Theories of Organizational Behavior* (Hinsdale, IL: Dryden Press, 1980); and B. Gerhart and S. L. Rynes, *Compensation: Theory, Evidence, and Strategic Implications* (Thousand Oaks, CA: Sage, 2003).

3. Mike Ramsey, "VW Chops Labor Costs in U.S.," *The Wall Street Journal*, May 23, 2011, extracted June 2, 2011. http://online.wsj .com/article/SB100014240527487040839045763355011323964 40.html

4. Bill Poovey, "Volkswagen's New Passat Makes Hometown Debut" January 13, 2011, http://finance.yahoo.com/news/Volks wagens-new-Passat-makes-apf-3319550755.html?x=0, extracted June 2, 2011.

5. B. Gerhart and G. T. Milkovich, "Organizational Differences in Managerial Compensation and Financial Performance," *Academy of Management Journal* 33 (1990), pp. 663–91; E. L. Groshen, "Why Do Wages Vary among Employers?" *Economic Review* 24 (1988), pp. 19–38; Gerhart and Rynes, *Compensation*.

6. M. L. Williams, M. A. McDaniel, N. T. Nguyen, "A Meta-Analysis of the Antecedents and Consequences of Pay Level Satisfaction," *Journal of Applied Psychology* 91 (2006), pp. 392–413; M. C. Sturman, C. O. Trevor, J. W. Boudreau, and B. Gerhart, "Is It Worth It to Win the Talent War? Evaluating the Utility of Performance-Based Pay," *Personnel Psychology* 56 (2003), pp. 997–1035; B. Klaas and J. A. McClendon, "To Lead, Lag or Match: Estimating the Financial Impact of Pay Level Policies," *Personnel Psychology* 49 (1996), pp. 121–41; S. C. Currall,

A. J. Towler, T. A. Judge, and L. Kohn, "Pay Satisfaction and Organizational Outcomes," *Personnel Psychology* 58 (2005), pp. 613–40; M. P. Brown, M. C. Sturman, and M. J. Simmering, "Compensation Policy and Organizational Performance: The Efficiency, Operational, and Financial Implications of Pay Levels and Pay Structures," *Academy of Management Journal* 46 (2003), pp. 752–62; Eric A. Verhoogen, Stephen V. Burks, and Jeffrey P. Carpenter, "Fairness and Freight-Handlers: Local Labor Market Conditions and Wage-Fairness Perceptions in a Trucking Firm," *Industrial &Labor Relations Review* 60, no. 4 (July 2007), p. 477; T. A. Judge, R. F. Piccolo, N. P. Podsakoff, J. C. Shaw, and B. L. Rich, "The Relationship between Pay and Job Satisfaction: A Meta-Analysis of the Literature," *Journal of Vocational Behavior* 77 (2010), pp. 157–67; M. Subramony, N. Krause, J. Norton, and G. N. Burns, "The Relationship between Human Resource Investments and Organizational Performance: A Firm-Level Examination of Equilibrium Theory," *Journal of Applied Psychology* 93 (2008), pp. 778–88.

7. G. A. Akerlof, "Gift Exchange and Efficiency-Wage Theory: Four Views," *American Economic Review* 74 (1984), pp. 79–83; and J. L. Yellen, "Efficiency Wage Models of Unemployment," *American Economic Review* 74 (1984), pp. 200–5.

8. S. L. Rynes and G. T. Milkovich, "Wage Surveys: Dispelling Some Myths about the Market Wage," *Personnel Psychology* 39 (1986), pp. 71–90.

9. B. Gerhart and G. T. Milkovich, "Employee Compensation: Research and Practice," in *Handbook of Industrial and Organizational Psychology*, 2nd ed., ed. M. D. Dunnette and L. M. Hough (Palo Alto, CA: Consulting Psychologists Press, 1992).

10. G. T. Milkovich, J. M. Newman, and B. Gerhart, *Compensation*, 10th ed. (New York: McGraw-Hill/Irwin, 2010).

11. B. Gerhart, G. T. Milkovich, and B. Murray, "Pay, Performance, and Participation," in *Research Frontiers in Industrial Relations and Human Resources*, ed. D. Lewin, O. S. Mitchell, and P. D. Sherer (Madison, WI: IRRA, 1992).

12. C. H. Fay, "External Pay Relationships," in *Compensation and Benefits*, ed. L. R. Gomez-Mejia (Washington, DC: Bureau of National Affairs, 1989).

13. J. P. Pfeffer and A. Davis-Blake, "Understanding Organizational Wage Structures: A Resource Dependence Approach," *Academy of Management Journal* 30 (1987), pp. 437–55; and M. A. Carpenter and J. B. Wade, "Micro-Level Opportunity Structures as

Determinants of Non-CEO Executive Pay," *Academy of Management Journal* 45 (2002), pp. 1085–1103.

14. C. M. Solomon, "Global Compensation: Learn the ABCs," *Personnel Journal*, July 1995, p. 70; and R. A. Swaak, "Expatriate Management: The Search for Best Practices," *Compensation and Benefits Review*, March–April 1995, p. 21.

15. *1997–1998 Survey of Geographic Pay Differential Policies and Practices* (Rochester, WI: Runzeimer International). Actually, data from the American Chamber of Commerce Research Association (ACCRA) estimate the cost of living in New York City (in 2001) to be 239.2, compared to 100 for the average metropolitan area.

16. E. E. Lawler III, *Pay and Organizational Development* (Reading, MA: Addison-Wesley, 1981).

17. R. Folger and M. A. Konovsky, "Effects of Procedural and Distributive Justice on Reactions to Pay Raise Decisions," *Academy of Management Journal* 32 (1989), pp. 115–30; H. G. Heneman III and T. A. Judge, "Compensation Attitudes," in S. L. Rynes and B. Gerhart, eds., *Compensation in Organizations* (San Francisco: Jossey-Bass, 2002), pp. 61–103; J. Greenberg, "Determinants of Perceived Fairness of Performance Evaluations," *Journal of Applied Psychology* 71 (1986), pp. 340–42; and H. G. Heneman III, "Pay Satisfaction," *Research in Personnel and Human Resource Management* 3 (1985), pp. 115–39.

18. J. Greenberg, "Employee Theft as a Reaction to Underpayment of Inequity: The Hidden Cost of Pay Cuts," *Journal of Applied Psychology* 75 (1990), pp. 561–68.

19. Adams, "Inequity in Social Exchange"; C. J. Berger, C. A. Olson, and J. W. Boudreau, "The Effect of Unionism on Job Satisfaction: The Role of Work-Related Values and Perceived Rewards," *Organizational Behavior and Human Performance* 32 (1983), pp. 284–324; P. Cappelli and P. D. Sherer, "Assessing Worker Attitudes under a Two-Tier Wage Plan," *Industrial and Labor Relations Review* 43 (1990), pp. 225–44; and R. W. Rice, S. M. Phillips, and D. B. McFarlin, "Multiple Discrepancies and Pay Satisfaction," *Journal of Applied Psychology* 75 (1990), pp. 386–93.

20. Cappelli and Sherer, "Assessing Worker Attitudes."

21. R. M. Kanter, *When Giants Learn to Dance* (New York: Simon & Schuster, 1989); E. E. Lawler III, *Strategic Pay* (San Francisco: Jossey-Bass, 1990); "Farewell, Fast Track," *Business-Week*, December 10, 1990, pp. 192–200; and R. L. Heneman, G. E. Ledford, Jr., and M. T. Gresham, "The Changing Nature of Work and Its Effects on Compensation Design and Delivery," in S. L. Rynes and B. Gerhart, eds., *Compensation in Organizations*.

22. P. R. Eyers, "Realignment Ties Pay to Performance," *Personnel Journal*, January 1993, p. 74.

23. Lawler, *Strategic Pay*; G. Ledford, "3 Cases on Skill-Based Pay: An Overview," *Compensation and Benefits Review*, March–April 1991, pp. 11–23; G. E. Ledford, "Paying for the Skills, Knowledge, Competencies of Knowledge Workers," *Compensation and Benefits Review*, July–August 1995, p. 55; Heneman et al., "The Changing Nature of Work"; G. Ledford, "Factors Affecting the Long-term Success of Skill-based Pay," *WorldatWork Journal*, First Quarter (2008), pp. 6–18; J. Canavan, "Overcoming the Challenge of Aligning Skill-based Pay Levels to the External Market," *WorldatWork Journal*, First Quarter (2008), pp. 18–24; and E. C. Dierdorff and E. A. Surface, "If You Pay for Skills, Will They Learn? Skill Change and Maintenance Under a Skill-Based Pay System," *Journal of Management* 34 (2008), pp. 721–43.

24. Ledford, "3 Cases."

25. Heneman et al., "The Changing Nature of Work."

26. T. D. Wall, J. M. Corbett, R. Martin, C. W. Clegg, and P. R. Jackson, "Advanced Manufacturing Technology, Work Design, and Performance: A Change Study," *Journal of Applied Psychology* 75 (1990), pp. 691–97.

27. James P. Womack, Daniel T. Jones, Daniel Roos, and Donna S. Carpenter, *The Machine That Changed the World: Based on the Massachusetts Institute of Technology 5-Million Dollar 5-Year Study on the Future of the Automobile* (New York: Rawson Assoc., 1990), p. 56.

28. Lawler, *Strategic Pay*.

29. Ibid.; Gerhart and Milkovich, "Employee Compensation."

30. B. C. Murray and B. Gerhart, "An Empirical Analysis of a Skill-Based Pay Program and Plant Performance Outcomes," *Academy of Management Journal* 41, no. 1 (1998), pp. 68–78.

31. Ibid.; N. Gupta, D. Jenkins, and W. Curington, "Paying for Knowledge: Myths and Realities," *National Productivity Review*, Spring 1986, pp. 107–23; J. D. Shaw, N. Gupta, A. Mitra, and G. E. Ledford, "Success and Survival of Skill-Based Pay Plans," *Journal of Management* 31 (2005), pp. 28–49.

32. *Education at a Glance—OECD Indicators* 2010, www.OECD.org.

33. C. Sparks and M. Greiner, "U.S. and Foreign Productivity and Labor Costs," *Monthly Labor Review*, February 1997, pp. 26–35.

34. E. Faltermayer, "U.S. Companies Come Back Home," *Fortune*, December 30, 1991, pp. 106ff; M. Hayes, "Precious Connection: Companies Thinking about Using Offshore Outsourcing Need to Consider More than Just Cost Savings," *Information Week Online*, www.informationweek.com (October 20, 2003).

35. Heather Timmons, "Cost-Cutting in New York, but a Boom in India," *New York Times*, August 12, 2008, p. C1. Reprinted with permission of PARS International.

36. William Bulkeley, "IBM Documents Give Rare Look at Sensitive Plans on 'Offshoring,'" *The Wall Street Journal*, January 19, 2004; David Wessel, "Big U.S. Firms Shift Hiring Abroad," *The Wall Street Journal*, April 19, 2011.

37. A. Farnham, "The Trust Gap," *Fortune*, December 4, 1989, pp. 56ff; and Scott McCartney, "AMR Unions Express Fury," *The Wall Street Journal*, April 17, 2003.

38. D. M. Cowherd and D. I. Levine, "Product Quality and Pay Equity between Lower-Level Employees and Top Management: An Investigation of Distributive Justice Theory," *Administrative Science Quarterly* 37 (1992), pp. 302–20.

39. Bureau of Labor Statistics, *Current Population Surveys* (website).

40. Ibid.

41. C. Kulich, G. Trojanowski, M. K. Ryan, S. A. Haslam, and L. D. R. Renneboog, "Who Gets the Carrot and Who Gets the Stick? Evidence of Gender Disparities in Executive Remuneration," *Strategic Management Journal* 32 (2011), pp. 301–21; and F. Munôz-Bullón, "Gender-Level Differences among High-Level Executives," *Industrial Relations* 49 (2010), pp. 346–70.

42. B. Gerhart, "Gender Differences in Current and Starting Salaries: The Role of Performance, College Major, and Job Title," *Industrial and Labor Relations, Review* 43 (1990), pp. 418–33; G. G. Cain, "The Economic Analysis of Labor-Market Discrimination: A Survey," in *Handbook of Labor Economics*, ed. O. Ashenfelter and R. Layard (New York: North-Holland, 1986), pp. 694–785; F. D. Blau and L. M. Kahn, "The Gender Pay Gap: Have Women Gone as Far as They Can?" *Academy of Management Perspectives*, February 2007, pp. 7–23.

43. D. P. Schwab, "Job Evaluation and Pay-Setting: Concepts and Practices," in *Comparable Worth: Issues and Alternatives*, ed. E. R. Livemash (Washington, DC: Equal Employment Advisory Council, 1980).

44. B. Gerhart and N. El Cheikh, "Earnings and Percentage Female: A Longitudinal Study," *Industrial Relations* 30 (1991), pp. 62–78; R. S. Smith, "Comparable Worth: Limited Coverage and the

Exacerbation of Inequality," *Industrial and Labor Relations Review* 61 (1988), pp. 227–39.

45. W. T. Bielby and J. N. Baron, "Men and Women at Work: Sex Segregation and Statistical Discrimination," *American Journal of Sociology* 91 (1986), pp. 759–99.

46. Rynes and Milkovich, "Wage Surveys"; and G. T. Milkovich, J. M. Newman, and B. Gerhart, *Compensation*, 10th ed. (New York: McGraw-Hill/Irwin, 2010).

47. U.S. Department of Labor website, at www.dol.gov/esa/regs/ compliance/ofccp/faqs/comstrds.htm.

48. Gerhart, "Gender Differences in Current and Starting Salaries"; B. Gerhart and G. T. Milkovich, "Salaries, Salary Growth, and Promotions of Men and Women in a Large, Private Firm," in *Pay Equity: Empirical Inquiries*, ed. R. Michael, H. Hartmann, and B. O'Farrell (Washington, DC: National Academy Press, 1989); K. W. Chauvin and R. A. Ash, "Gender Earnings Differentials in Total Pay, Base Pay, and Contingent Pay," *Industrial and Labor Relations Review* 47 (1994), pp. 634–49; M. M. Elvira and M. E. Graham, "Not Just a Formality: Pay System Formalization and Sex-Related Earnings Effects," *Organization Science* 13 (2002), pp. 601–17.

49. Gerhart, "Gender Differences in Current and Starting Salaries"; B. Gerhart and S. Rynes, "Determinants and Consequences of Salary Negotiations by Graduating Male and Female MBAs," *Journal of Applied Psychology* 76 (1991), pp. 256–62.

50. G. F. Dreher and R. A. Ash, "A Comparative Study of Mentoring among Men and Women in Managerial, Professional, and Technical Positions," *Journal of Applied Psychology* 75 (1990), pp. 539–46.

51. G. A. Patterson, "Nordstrom Inc. Sets Back-Pay Accord on Suit Alleging 'Off-the-Clock' Work," *The Wall Street Journal*, January 12, 1993, p. A2; for additional information on overtime legal issues, see A. Weintraub and J. Kerstetter, "Revenge of the Overworked Nerds," *BusinessWeek Online*, www.businessweek.com (December 8, 2003).

52. R. I. Henderson, *Compensation Management in a Knowledge-Based World* (Upper Saddle River, NJ: Prentice Hall, 2003).

CHAPTER

12

Recognizing Employee Contributions with Pay

Enter the World of Business

Companies Gradually Re-Start Merit Increase and Bonus Programs

During tough economic times, companies took many actions to control labor costs, including freezing merit pay increases and bonuses. Now, companies are re-starting those programs or investing more in them as they anticipate an eventual uptick in competition for employees, especially top employees.

Employers continue to move toward a growing emphasis on using bonuses because they do not become part of an employee's base salary. A merit increase does become part of base salary and, as described by Aon Hewitt's Ken Abosch, "it's a fixed cost for life."

Surveys, however, indicate that companies are increasingly re-starting their merit pay programs as well. Increases in the coming year are expected to be in the neighborhood of 2.5 to 3%. In addition, according to Mercer, only about 2% of companies plan pay freezes this year, which is down from 31% a few years ago.

Companies still need to keep an eye on costs, so they are looking for ways to leverage their pay increases as effectively as possible. One strategy is to strengthen the connection between employee pay and performance. Mercer projects that top performers will receive pay increases of 4.5%, whereas low-rated workers can expect an increase of around 0.5%. Their data also indicate that fewer employees receive high performance ratings, meaning that fewer actually receive the larger pay increases. They believe that more companies are using forced ranking/distribution systems, which limit the number of high performance ratings that managers can give out to their units. One longtime consultant observed that it is now harder to get a high rating than it was in the past.

In some cases, employers are already seeing increased competition for employees and do not want to wait until it is too late to adjust their pay programs to head off losses of key employees and difficulties in recruiting new top talent. For example, both chemical-maker BASF's North American unit and accounting firm PricewaterhouseCoopers LLP ended their pay freezes earlier than anticipated.

SOURCES: Ruth Mantell, "Companies tie more of workers' pay to performance," MarketWatch, www.marketwatch.com, May 17, 2011, accessed May 30, 2011; Todd Henneman, "Special Report on Compensation: Cracks in the Ice," *Workforce Management*, November 2010, www.workforce.com, accessed April 4, 2011; and Dana Mattioli, "Raises Creep Back onto Salary Scene," *The Wall Street Journal*, May 3, 2010.

Introduction

The opening story illustrates how firms increasingly seek to use compensation to motivate performance, while at the same time controlling fixed compensation costs. The chapter opening also demonstrates how firms react and manage compensation differently as product market and labor conditions change.

The preceding chapter discussed setting pay for jobs. In this chapter we focus on using pay to recognize and reward employees' contributions to the organization's success. Employees' pay does not depend solely on the jobs they hold. Instead, differences in performance (individual, group, or organization), seniority, skills, and so forth are used as a basis for differentiating pay among employees.[1] In some cases, large amounts of compensation can be at stake.

Several key questions arise in evaluating different pay programs for recognizing contributions. First, what are the costs of the program? Second, what is the expected return (in terms of influences on attitudes and behaviors) from such investments? Third, does the program fit with the organization's human resource strategy and its overall business strategy? Fourth, what might go wrong with the plan in terms of unintended consequences? For example, will the plan encourage managers and employees to pay more attention to some objectives (e.g., short-term sales) than to some others (e.g., customer service, long-term customer satisfaction, and long-term sales)?

Organizations have a relatively large degree of discretion in deciding how to pay, especially compared with the pay level decisions discussed in the previous chapter. The same organizational pay level (or "compensation pie") can be distributed (shared) among employees in many ways. Whether each employee's share is based on individual performance, profits, seniority, or other factors, the size of the pie (and thus the cost to the organization) can remain the same.

Regardless of cost differences, different pay programs can have very different consequences for productivity and return on investment. Indeed, a study of 150 organizations found not only that the largest differences between organizations had to do with how (rather than how much) they paid, but that these differences also resulted in different levels of profitability.[2]

 How Does Pay Influence Individual Employees?

Pay plans are typically used to energize, direct, or control employee behavior. Equity theory, described in the previous chapter, is relevant here as well. Most employees compare their own pay with that of others, especially those in the same job. Perceptions of inequity may cause employees to take actions to restore equity. Unfortunately, some of these actions (like quitting, reduced effort, or lack of cooperation) may not help the organization.

Three additional theories also help explain compensation's effects: reinforcement, expectancy, and agency theories.

REINFORCEMENT THEORY

E. L. Thorndike's Law of Effect states that a response followed by a reward is more likely to recur in the future. The implication for compensation management is that high employee performance followed by a monetary reward will make future high performance more likely. By the same token, high performance not followed by a reward will make it less likely in the future. The theory emphasizes the importance of a person's actual experience of a reward.

EXPECTANCY THEORY

Although **expectancy theory** also focuses on the link between rewards and behaviors, it emphasizes expected (rather than experienced) rewards. In other words, it focuses on the effects of incentives. Behaviors (job performance) can be described as a function of ability and motivation. In turn, motivation is hypothesized to be a function of expectancy, instrumentality, and valence perceptions. Compensation systems differ according to their impact on these motivational components. Generally speaking, the main influence of compensation is on instrumentality: the perceived link between behaviors and pay. Valence of pay outcomes should remain the same under different pay systems. Expectancy perceptions (the perceived link between effort and performance) often have more to do with job design and training than pay systems. A possible exception would be skill-based pay, which directly influences employee training and thus expectancy perceptions.

Although expectancy theory implies that linking an increased amount of rewards to performance will increase motivation and performance, some authors have used cognitive evaluation theory to question this assumption, arguing that monetary rewards may increase extrinsic motivation but decrease intrinsic motivation. Extrinsic motivation depends on rewards (such as pay and benefits) controlled by an external source, whereas intrinsic motivation depends on rewards that flow naturally from work itself (like performing interesting work).[3] In other words, paying a child to read books may diminish the child's natural interest in reading, and the child may in the future be less likely to read books unless there are monetary incentives. Although monetary incentives may reduce intrinsic motivation in some settings (such as education), the evidence suggests that such effects are small and probably not very relevant to most work settings, where monetary payment is the norm.[4] Therefore, while it is important to keep in mind that money is not the only effective way to motivate behavior and that monetary rewards will not always be the answer to motivation problems, it does not appear that monetary rewards run much risk of compromising intrinsic motivation in most work settings.

Expectancy Theory
The theory that says motivation is a function of valence, instrumentality, and expectancy.

AGENCY THEORY

This theory focuses on the divergent interests and goals of the organization's stakeholders and the ways that employee compensation can be used to align these interests and goals. We cover agency theory in some depth because it provides especially relevant implications for compensation design.

An important characteristic of the modern corporation is the separation of ownership from management (or control). Unlike the early stages of capitalism, where owner and manager were often the same, today, with some exceptions (mostly smaller companies), most stockholders are far removed from the day-to-day operation of companies. Although this separation has important advantages (like mobility of financial capital and diversification of investment risk), it also creates agency costs—the interests of the **principals** (owners) and their **agents** (managers) may no longer converge. What is best for the agent, or manager, may not be best for the owner.

Agency costs can arise from two factors. First, principals and agents may have different goals (goal incongruence). Second, principals may have less than perfect information on the degree to which the agent is pursuing and achieving the principal's goals (information asymmetry).

Principal
In agency theory, a person (e.g., an owner) who seeks to direct another person's behavior.

Agent
In agency theory, a person (e.g., a manager) who is expected to act on behalf of a principal (e.g., an owner).

KEPCO, South Korea's largest energy firm, recently announced that it will implement a merit-based pay system.

Consider three examples of agency costs that can occur in managerial compensation.[5] First, although shareholders seek to maximize their wealth, management may spend money on things such as perquisites (corporate jets, for example)or "empire building" (making acquisitions that do not add value to the company but may enhance the manager's prestige or pay). Second, managers and shareholders may differ in their attitudes toward risk. Shareholders can diversify their investments (and thus their risks) more easily than managers (whose only major source of income may be their jobs), so managers are typically more averse to risk. They may be less likely to pursue projects or acquisitions with high potential payoff. It also suggests a preference on the part of managers for relatively little risk in their pay (high emphasis on base salary, low emphasis on uncertain bonuses or incentives). Indeed, research shows that managerial compensation in manager-controlled firms is more often designed in this manner.[6] Third, decision-making horizons may differ. For example, if managers change companies more than owners change ownership, managers may be more likely to maximize short-run performance (and pay), perhaps at the expense of long-term success.

Agency theory is also of value in the analysis and design of nonmanagers' compensation. In this case, interests may diverge between managers (now in the role of principals) and their employees (who take on the role of agents).

In designing either managerial or nonmanagerial compensation, the key question is, How can such agency costs be minimized? Agency theory says that the principal must choose a contracting scheme that helps align the interests of the agent with the principal's own interests (that is, it reduces agency costs). These contracts can be classified as either behavior-oriented (such as merit pay) or outcome-oriented (stock options, profit sharing, commissions, and so on).[7]

At first blush, outcome-oriented contracts seem to be the obvious solution. If profits are high, compensation goes up. If profits drop, compensation goes down. The interests of "the company" and employees are aligned. An important drawback, however, is that such contracts also increase the agent's risk. And because agents are averse to risk, they may require higher pay (a compensating wage differential) to make up for it.[8] Thus, there is a trade-off between risk and incentives that must be considered. Outcome-oriented contracts are typically a major component of executive compensation.[9]

Behavior-based contracts, on the other hand, do not transfer risk to the agent and thus do not require a compensating wage differential. However, the principal must be able to overcome the information asymmetry issue. To do so the principal must either invest in monitoring (e.g., add more supervisors) and information or else revert, at least in part, to structuring the contract so that pay is linked at least partly to outcomes.[10]

Which type of contract should an organization use? It depends partly on the following factors:[11]

- *Risk aversion.* Risk aversion among agents makes outcome-oriented contracts less likely.
- *Outcome uncertainty.* Profit is an example of an outcome. Agents are less willing to have their pay linked to profits to the extent that there is a risk of low profits. They would therefore prefer a behavior-oriented contract.
- *Job programmability.* As jobs become less programmable (less routine), outcome-oriented contracts become more likely because monitoring becomes more difficult.[12]
- *Measurable job outcomes.* When outcomes are more measurable, outcome-oriented contracts are more likely.
- *Ability to pay.* Outcome-oriented contracts contribute to higher compensation costs because of the risk premium.
- *Tradition.* A tradition or custom of using (or not using) outcome-oriented contracts will make such contracts more (or less) likely.

In summary, the reinforcement, expectancy, and agency theories all focus on the fact that behavior–reward contingencies can shape behaviors. However, agency theory is of particular value in compensation management because of its emphasis on the risk–reward trade-off, an issue that needs close attention when companies consider variable pay plans, which can carry significant risk.

How Does Pay Influence Labor Force Composition?

Traditionally, using pay to recognize employee contributions has been thought of as a way to influence the behaviors and attitudes of current employees, whereas pay level and benefits have been seen as a way to influence so-called membership behaviors: decisions about whether to join or remain with the organization. However, there is increasing recognition that individual pay programs may also affect the nature and composition of an organization's workforce.[13] For example, it is possible that an organization that links pay to performance may attract more high performers than an organization that does not link the two. There may be a similar effect with respect to job retention.[14]

Continuing the analysis, different pay systems appear to attract people with different personality traits and values.[15] Organizations that link pay to individual performance may be more likely to attract individualistic employees, whereas organizations relying more heavily on team rewards are more likely to attract team-oriented employees. The implication is that the design of compensation programs needs to be carefully coordinated with the organization and human resource strategy. Increasingly, both in the United States and abroad, employers are seeking to establish stronger links between pay and performance.

Programs

In compensating employees, an organization does not have to choose one program over another. Instead, a combination of programs is often the best solution. For example, one program may foster teamwork and cooperation but not enough individual initiative. Another may do the opposite. Used in conjunction, a balance may

LO 12-2
Describe the fundamental pay programs for recognizing employees' contributions to the organization's success.

be attained. Such balancing of objectives, combined with careful alignment with the organization and human resource strategy, may help increase the probability that a pay-for-performance program has its intended effects and reduce the probability of unintended consequences and problems.[16] In some cases, an organization may, at least temporarily, design an incentive plan to focus everyone's attention on one critical objective. As the "Competing through Technology" box shows, this is what BP did to focus on safety in using technology.

Table 12.1 provides an overview of the programs for recognizing employee contributions. Each program shares a focus on paying for performance. The programs differ according to three design features: (1) payment method, (2) frequency of payout, and (3) ways of measuring performance. In a perhaps more speculative vein, the table also suggests the potential consequences of such programs for (1) performance motivation of employees, (2) attraction of employees, (3) organization culture, and (4) costs. Finally, there are two contingencies that may influence whether each pay program fits the situation: (1) management style and (2) type of work. We now discuss the different programs and some of their potential consequences in more depth.

MERIT PAY

In merit pay programs, annual pay increases are usually linked to performance appraisal ratings. (See Chapter 8.) Some type of merit pay program exists in almost all organizations (although evidence on merit pay effectiveness is surprisingly scarce).[17] As the chapter opening demonstrated, some employers have moved toward a form of merit pay that relies on bonuses rather than increases to base pay. One reason for the widespread use of merit pay is its ability to define and reward a broad range of performance dimensions. (See Table 12.2 for an example.) Indeed, given the pervasiveness of merit pay programs, we devote a good deal of attention to them here.

Basic Features

Merit Increase Grid
A grid that combines an employee's performance rating with the employee's position in a pay range to determine the size and frequency of his or her pay increases.

Many merit pay programs work off of a **merit increase grid.** As Table 12.3 indicates, the size and frequency of pay increases are determined by two factors. The first factor is the individual's performance rating (better performers receive higher pay). The second factor is position in range (that is, an individual's compa-ratio). So, for example, an employee with a performance rating that exceeds expectations and a compa-ratio of 120 would receive a pay increase of roughly 3%. By comparison, an employee with a performance rating of exceeds expectations and a compa-ratio of 85 would receive an increase of around 7%. (Note that the general magnitude of increases in such a table is influenced by inflation rates.) One reason for factoring in the compa-ratio is to control compensation costs and maintain the integrity of the pay structure. If a person with a compa-ratio of 120 received a merit increase of 7%, she would soon exceed the pay range maximum. Not factoring in the compa-ratio would also result in uncontrolled growth of compensation costs for employees who continue to perform the same job year after year. Instead, some organizations think in terms of assessing where the employee's pay is now and where it should be, given a particular performance level. Consider Table 12.4. An employee who consistently performs at the highest level is

BP Links Pay to Safety in Fourth Quarter

BP PLC, which faced accusations that it precipitated the Gulf of Mexico oil spill by placing profits before safety, said in an internal memo to its staff that safety would be the sole criterion for rewarding employee performance in its operating business for the fourth quarter.

BP's new chief executive, Bob Dudley, announced the step in an e-mail to employees that was viewed by *The Wall Street Journal.* While the move shows Mr. Dudley acting on a promise to change the culture at BP, it's likely to be greeted skeptically because of BP's past safety lapses and the fierce attacks the company sustained after the Gulf disaster.

Yet even as it has defended its safety efforts in recent years, the company has begun to signal that it recognizes that improvement is necessary.

The need to show it is taking safety seriously is even more acute given the fact that past claims about safety improvements weren't borne out by the facts on the ground.

Beginning last year, Mr. Dudley's predecessor, Tony Hayward, boasted that he had fixed a safety culture that appeared broken following a fatal refinery fire at Texas City, Texas, in 2005, only to be proved wrong by the Deepwater Horizon disaster.

That means even more skepticism is likely to greet Mr. Dudley's efforts to do what Mr. Hayward had claimed was already accomplished. Shortly before taking the reins as CEO of the beleaguered energy giant October 1, Mr. Dudley unveiled a big restructuring aimed at toughening oversight of safety in all BP's operating units. He also said he would be reviewing the way the company rewards performance, with a bigger stress on safety.

In advance of that review, Mr. Dudley said in the memo that the sole criterion for judging performance in the 2010 fourth quarter would be "each business's progress in reducing operational risks and achieving excellent safety and compliance standards." The memo stressed that all existing performance contracts for the first three quarters of 2010 would be honored.

Mr. Dudley said the objective was "to ensure that a low-probability, high-impact incident such as the Deepwater Horizon tragedy never happens again." The key to achieving that goal, he said, is "the rigorous identification and management of every risk we face."

"We're determined to leave no stone unturned in the pursuit of our focus on safety," added spokesman Andrew Gowers.

Mark Reilly, a partner with the Chicago-based compensation consulting firm Compensation Consulting Consortium LLC, said safety-linked incentives are typical in dangerous industries like mining and construction, but safety isn't normally the sole criterion for rewards. "I think part of it's to help with its image, but the reality is that this incident almost bankrupt the company, and they can't afford another one," he said.

Mr. Reilly has helped companies incorporate safety incentives into their compensation models. "People react to incentive measures and it does affect their behavior," he said.

SOURCE: From Guy Chazan and Dana Mattioli, "BP Links Pay to Safety in Fourth Quarter," *The Wall Street Journal,* October 19, 2010. Reproduced with permission of Dow Jones & Company, Inc. via Copyright Clearance Center.

targeted to be paid at 111 to 120% of the market (that is, a compa-ratio of 111 to 120). To the extent that the employee is far from that pay level, larger and more frequent pay increases are necessary to move the employee to the correct position. On the other hand, if the employee is already at that pay level, smaller pay increases will be needed. The main objective in the latter case would be to provide pay increases that are sufficient to maintain the employee at the targeted compa-ratio.

table 12.1

Programs for Recognizing Employee Contributions

	MERIT PAY	INCENTIVE PAY	PROFIT SHARING	OWNERSHIP	GAIN SHARING	SKILL-BASED
Design features						
Payment method	Changes in base pay	Bonus	Bonus	Equity changes	Bonus	Change in base pay
Frequency of payout	Annually	Weekly	Semiannually or annually	When stock sold	Monthly or quarterly	When skill or competency acquired
Performance measures	Supervisor's appraisal of individual performance	Individual output, productivity, sales	Company profit	Company stock returns	Production or controllable costs of stand-alone work unit	Skill or competency acquisition of individuals
Consequences						
Performance motivation	Relationship between pay and performance varies	Clear performance–reward connection	Stronger in smaller firms	Stronger in smaller firms	Stronger in smaller units	Encourages learning
Attraction	Over time pays better performers more	Pays higher performers more	Helps with all employees if plan pays out	Can help lock in employees	Helps with all employees if plan pays out	Attracts learning-oriented employees
Culture	Individual competition	Individual competition	Knowledge of business and cooperation	Sense of ownership and cooperation	Supports cooperation, problem solving	Learning and flexible organization
Costs	Requires well-developed performance appraisal system	Setting and maintaining acceptable standards	Relates costs to ability to pay	Relates costs to ability to pay	Setting and maintaining acceptable standards	Training and certification
Contingencies						
Management style	Some participation desirable	Control	Fits participation	Fits participation	Fits participation	Fits participation
Type of work	Individual unless group appraisals done	Stable, individual, easily measurable	All types	All types	All types	Significant skill depth or breadth

SOURCE: Adapted and modified from E. E. Lawler III, "Pay for Performance: A Strategic Analysis," in *Compensation and Benefits*, ed. L. R. Gomez-Mejia (Washington, DC: Bureau of National Affairs, 1989).

table 12.2

Performance
Dimensions for
Lower to Midlevel
Managers, Arrow
Electronics

1. Exercises good business judgment
2. Inspires enthusiasm, energy, understanding, loyalty for company goals
3. Attracts, grows, and retains outstanding talent
4. Shows initiative
5. Has position-specific knowledge
6. Delivers results
7. Builds internal good will

SOURCE: R. Riphahn (2011), Evidence on Incentive Effects of Subjective Performance Evaluations,"
Industrial and Labor Relations Review, 64.

In controlling compensation costs, another factor that requires close attention is the distribution of performance ratings. (See Chapter 8.) In many organizations, 60% to 70% of employees fall into the top two (out of four to five) performance rating categories.[18] This means tremendous growth in compensation costs because most employees will eventually be above the midpoint of the pay range, resulting in compa-ratios well over 100. To avoid this, some organizations provide guidelines regarding the percentage of employees who should fall into each performance category, usually limiting the percentage that can be placed in the top two categories. These guidelines are enforced differently, ranging from true guidelines to strict forced-distribution requirements.[19]

In general, merit pay programs have the following characteristics. First, they identify individual differences in performance, which are assumed to reflect differences in ability or motivation. By implication, system constraints on performance are not seen as significant. Second, the majority of information on individual performance is collected from the immediate supervisor. Peer and subordinate ratings are rare, and where they exist, they tend to receive less weight than supervisory ratings.[20] Third, there is a policy of linking pay increases to performance appraisal results.[21] Fourth, the feedback under such systems tends to occur infrequently, often once per year at the formal performance review session. Fifth, the flow of feedback tends to be largely unidirectional, from supervisor to subordinate.

Criticisms of Traditional Merit Pay Programs

Criticisms of this process have been raised. For example, W. Edwards Deming, a leader of the total quality management movement, argued that it is unfair to rate individual performance because "apparent differences between people arise almost entirely from

table 12.3

Merit Increase Grid

RECOMMENDED SALARY INCREASES BY PERFORMANCE RATING AND COMPA-RATIO		
COMPA-RATIO[a]		
80% TO 90%	**91% TO 110%**	**111% TO 120%**
Performance rating		
Exceeds expectations 7%	5%	3%
Meets expectations 4%	3%	2%
Below expectations 2%	0%	0%

[a]Employee salary/midpoint of their salary range.

table 12.4

Performance Ratings and Compa-Ratio Targets

PERFORMANCE RATING	COMPA-RATIO TARGET
Exceeds expectations	111–120
Meets expectations	91–110
Below expectations	Below 91

the system that they work in, not from the people themselves."[22] Examples of system factors include co-workers, the job, materials, equipment, customers, management, supervision, and environmental conditions. These are believed to be largely outside the worker's control, instead falling under management's responsibility. Deming argued that the performance rating is essentially "the result of a lottery."[23]

Deming also argued that the individual focus of merit pay discourages teamwork: "Everyone propels himself forward, or tries to, for his own good, on his own life preserver. The organization is the loser."[24] As an example, if people in the purchasing department are evaluated based on the number of contracts negotiated, they may have little interest in materials quality, even though manufacturing is having quality problems.

Deming's solution was to eliminate the link between individual performance and pay. This approach reflects a desire to move away from recognizing individual contributions. What are the consequences of such a move? It is possible that fewer employees with individual-achievement orientations would be attracted to and remain with the organization. One study of job retention found that the relationship between pay growth and individual performance over time was weaker at higher performance levels. As a consequence, the organization lost a disproportionate share of its top performers.[25] In other words, too little emphasis on individual performance may leave the organization with average and poor performers.[26]

Thus, although Deming's concerns about too much emphasis on individual performance are well taken, one must be careful not to replace one set of problems with another. Instead, there needs to be an appropriate balance between individual and group objectives. At the very least, ranking and forced-distribution performance-rating systems need to be considered with caution, lest they contribute to behavior that is too individualistic and competitive.

Another criticism of merit pay programs is the way they measure performance. If the performance measure is not perceived as being fair and accurate, the entire merit pay program can break down. One potential impediment to accuracy is the almost exclusive reliance on the supervisor for providing performance ratings, even though peers, subordinates, and customers (internal and external) often have information on a person's performance that is as good as or better than that of the supervisor. A 360-degree performance feedback approach (discussed in Chapter 9) gathers feedback from each of these sources. To date, however, organizations have mainly used such data for development purposes and have been reluctant to use these multisource data for making pay decisions.[27]

In general, process issues, including communication, expectation setting, and credibility/fairness, are important in administering merit pay and pay-for-performance in general.[28] In any situation where rewards are distributed, employees appear to assess fairness along two dimensions: distributive (based on how much they receive) and procedural (what process was used to decide how much).[29] Some of the most important aspects of procedural fairness, or justice, appear in Table 12.5. These items suggest that employees desire clear and consistent performance standards, as well as opportunities to provide input, discuss their performance, and appeal any decision they believe to be incorrect.

Indicate the extent to which your supervisor did each of the following:
1. Was honest and ethical in dealing with you.
2. Gave you an opportunity to express your side.
3. Used consistent standards in evaluating your performance.
4. Considered your views regarding your performance.
5. Gave you feedback that helped you learn how well you were doing.
6. Was completely candid and frank with you.
7. Showed a real interest in trying to be fair.
8. Became thoroughly familiar with your performance.
9. Took into account factors beyond your control.
10. Got input from you before a recommendation.
11. Made clear what was expected of you.

Indicate how much of an opportunity existed, after the last raise decision, for you to do each of the following things:
12. Make an appeal about the size of a raise.
13. Express your feelings to your supervisor about the salary decision.
14. Discuss, with your supervisor, how your performance was evaluated.
15. Develop, with your supervisor, an action plan for future performance.

table 12.5

Aspects of Procedural Justice in Pay Raise Decisions

SOURCE: From R. Folger and M. A. Konorsky, "Effects of Procedural and Distributive Justice on Reactions to Pay Raise Decisions," *Academy of Management Journal*, Volume 32 1989, p. 115. Reproduced with permission of Academy of Management via Copyright Clearance Center.

Perhaps the most basic criticism is that merit pay does not really exist. High performers, it is argued, are not paid significantly more than mediocre or even poor performers in most cases.[30] For example, with a merit increase budget of 4% to 5%, suppose high performers receive 6% raises, versus 3.5% to 4% raises for average performers. On a salary of $40,000 per year, the difference in take-home pay would not be more than about $300 per year, or about $6 per week. Critics of merit pay point out that this difference is probably not significant enough to influence employee behaviors or attitudes. Indeed, as Figure 12.1 indicates, many employees do not believe there is any payoff to higher levels of performance.

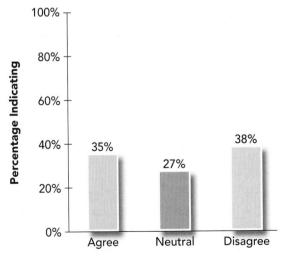

figure 12.1

Percentage of Employees Who Agree That Better Performance Leads to Better Increases

SOURCE: Hay Group, *Managing Performance: Survey of Employees in 335 Companies*, Philadelphia: Hay Group, 2002. Reprinted with permission.

Of course, small differences in pay can accumulate into large differences over time. The present value of the salary advantage would be $29,489 (based on a discount rate of 5%). For example, over a 30-year career, an initial annual salary difference of $740 with equal merit increases thereafter of 7% would accumulate into a career salary advantage of $75,738.[31] Whether employees think in these terms is open to question. But even if they do not, nothing prevents an organization from explaining to employees that what may appear to be small differences in pay can add up to large differences over time. It should also be kept in mind that merit ratings are often closely linked to promotions, which in turn are closely linked to salary. Thus, even in merit pay settings where performance differences are not recognized in the short run, high performers are likely to have significantly higher career earnings because of a faster rate of promotion.

Finally, the accumulation effect just described can also be seen as a drawback if it contributes to an entitlement mentality. Here the concern is that a big merit increase given early in an employee's career remains part of base salary "forever." It does not have to be re-earned each year, and the cost to the organization grows over time, perhaps more than either the employee's performance or the organization's profitability would always warrant. Merit bonuses (payouts that do not become part of base salary), in lieu of traditional merit increases, are thus used by some organizations instead.

EVIDENCE-BASED HR

In a bid to reduce high turnover rates among restaurant employees, Applebee's, the United States's biggest casual-dining chain by number of restaurants, reviews and ranks its hourly employees, and then rewards managers for retaining their better workers. When it first started this program, Applebee's turnover rate was 146%, well above even the industrywide casual-dining turnover rate of around 100%.

At Applebee's, Overland Park, Kansas, managers must now divide hourly workers into "A" players, the top 20%; B, the middle 60%; and C, the bottom 20%. The managers then are eligible for merit raises and bonuses based on how well they retain employees in the top 80%. The practice is unusual in the restaurant industry, where managers tend to worry more about staffing the next shift than career development and performance evaluation. "Among the hourly retail or service employees, there is certainly a tendency to say, 'Let's bring warm bodies in here,' and then to just try to hold down turnover in general," says Rick Beal, a senior compensation consultant at Watson Wyatt Worldwide, a human resources consulting firm in Washington, DC. Beal says rewarding managers for retaining the better workers is a great idea in theory, but will prove effective only if employers develop straightforward, and simple, ways to judge hourly workers. "Otherwise you're going to burn more time than it's worth," he says.

Applebee's says the system is time-consuming, but worth the effort. Before introducing the system, Applebee's measured overall turnover but didn't use the numbers to evaluate managers. Then, executives realized, "there is a different value if you lose a top-20 person than if you lose a bottom-20 person," says John Prutsman, who is in charge of human resources for the restaurants. In order to reward managers for keeping the best people, the company had to develop a system for reviewing hourly workers, including the grading criteria. Today, Applebee's evaluates all hourly employees twice a year on nine counts, including reliability, attitude, guest service, and teamwork. First, employees complete a self-evaluation. Then, managers grade employees.

Managers, in turn, get rewarded on how well they retain the top 80%, or their As and Bs. To win employees' loyalty, managers can give out small raises; award them

"Applebucks," points toward prizes such as bicycles, radios, or DVD players; or distribute special pins for highly ranked employees. Workers generally aren't told their grades. Many managers also employ their own motivational tricks, such as displaying posters of employee photos or not scheduling employees to work on their birthdays and anniversaries. Applebee's credits the system with helping to reduce annual turnover among hourly employees at company-owned restaurants almost by half in four years, to 84% from 146%. Applebee's owns 485 restaurants; a further 1,301 are franchises, where Applebee's doesn't control the retention practices but shares its techniques with the franchisees.

Linda Saleeby, general manager at an Applebee's in Chester, Virginia, for several years, says the evaluation process takes her management team about six weeks from start to finish. But she says the benefits extend beyond reduced turnover. She says employees like knowing what is expected of them and generally where they stand. "They know what it is we're focusing on," she says. "I don't think any kind of time we spend on people is a waste of time or hassle, because it's such a huge portion of our business," she says.

Saleeby has benefited from the system, too, by earning raises and bonuses based partly on her high retention scores. This is important in an industry where manager turnover is also high (27%) and where evidence shows that retention of managers goes hand-in-hand with higher store sales. Some of her techniques include giving out ice-cream bars to employees who work on Saturdays, meeting with parents of newly hired teen workers, and holding "round-table meetings" with employees to give them a say in things like scheduling. She likes the focus on the top 80%. "There's a certain number of people, despite all the tools you use to hire them, that just don't work out," she says.

SOURCES: E. White, "Theory & Practice: How To Reduce Turnover; Restaurant Chain Retains Workers Using Rankings and Rewards," *The Wall Street Journal*, November 21, 2005, p. B5; D. Berta, "People Report: Worker Turnover Rate Continues to Climb," *Nation's Restaurant News*, November 20, 2006; and D. Berta, "People Report: Reduced Turnover Helps Restaurants Fight Recession," *Nation's Restaurant News*, November 24, 2008.

INDIVIDUAL INCENTIVES

Like merit pay, individual incentives reward individual performance, but with two important differences. First, payments are not rolled into base pay. They must be continuously earned and re-earned. Second, performance is usually measured as physical output (such as number of water faucets produced) rather than by subjective ratings. Individual incentives have the potential to significantly increase performance. Locke and his colleagues found that monetary incentives increased production output by a median of 30%—more than any other motivational device studied.[32]

Nevertheless, individual incentives are relatively rare for a variety of reasons.[33] Most jobs (like those of managers and professionals) have no physical output measure. Instead, they involve what might be described as "knowledge work." Also, many potential administrative problems (such as setting and maintaining acceptable standards) often prove intractable. Third, individual incentives may do such a good job of motivating employees that they do whatever they get paid for and nothing else. (See the Dilbert cartoon in Figure 12.2.) Fourth, as the name implies, individual incentives typically do not fit well with a team approach. Fifth, they may be inconsistent with the goals of acquiring multiple skills and proactive problem solving. Learning new skills often requires employees to slow or stop production. If the

figure 12.2
How Incentives Sometimes Work "Too Well"

employees are paid based on production volume, they may not want to slow down or stop. Sixth, some incentive plans reward output volume at the expense of quality or customer service.

Therefore, although individual incentives carry potential advantages, they are not likely to contribute to a flexible, proactive, problem-solving workforce. In addition, such programs may not be particularly helpful in the pursuit of total quality management objectives.

PROFIT SHARING AND OWNERSHIP

Profit Sharing

Profit Sharing

A compensation plan in which payments are based on a measure of organization performance (profits) and do not become part of the employees' base salary.

At the other end of the individual–group continuum are profit sharing and stock ownership plans. Under **profit sharing,** payments are based on a measure of organization performance (profits), and the payments do not become part of the base salary. Profit sharing has two potential advantages. First, it may encourage employees to think more like owners, taking a broad view of what needs to be done to make the organization more effective. Thus, the sort of narrow self-interest encouraged by individual incentive plans (and perhaps also by merit pay) is presumably less of an issue. Instead, increased cooperation and citizenship are expected. Second, because payments do not become part of base pay, labor costs are automatically reduced during difficult economic times, and wealth is shared during good times. Consequently, organizations may not need to rely on layoffs as much to reduce costs during tough times.[34]

Does profit sharing contribute to better organization performance? The evidence is not clear. Although there is consistent support for a correlation between profit sharing payments and profits, questions have been raised about the direction of causality.[35] For example, Ford, Chrysler, and GM all have profit sharing plans in their contracts with the United Auto Workers (UAW). (See Table 12.6 for provisions of the GM–UAW plan.) The average profit sharing payment at Ford one year was $4,000 per worker versus an average of $550 per worker at GM and $8,000 at Chrysler. Given that the profit sharing plans are similar, it seems unlikely they caused Ford and Chrysler to be more profitable. Rather, it would appear that profits were higher at Ford for other reasons, resulting in higher profit sharing payments.

table 12.6

Profit Sharing in the
General Motors–
UAW Contract

2.14   **"Profits"** . . . means income earned by U.S. operations before income taxes and "extraordinary" items. . . . Profits are before any profit sharing charges are deducted. Profits also are before incentive program charges for U.S. operations.

2.18   **"Total Profit Share"** . . . means an obligation of the corporation for any plan year in an amount equal to the sum of:
   (a) 6% of the portion of profits . . . which exceeds 0.0% of sales and revenues . . . but does not exceed 1.8% . . . ;
   (b) 8% of the portion of profits . . . which exceeds 1.8% of sales and revenues . . . but does not exceed 2.3% . . . ;
   (c) 10% of the portion of profits . . . which exceeds 2.3% of sales and revenues . . . but does not exceed 4.6% . . . ;
   (d) 14% of the portion of profits . . . which exceeds 4.6% of sales and revenues . . . but does not exceed 6.9% . . . ;
   (e) 17% of the portion of profits . . . which exceeds 6.9% of sales and revenues.

4.02   **Allocation of Profit Sharing Amount to Participants**
The portion of the total profit share for the plan year allocated to this plan . . . will be allocated to each participant entitled to a distribution . . . in the proportion that (a) the participant's compensation hours for the plan year bears to (b) the total compensated hours for all participants in the plan entitled to a distribution for the plan year.

SOURCE: From John Fossum, *Labor Relations: Development, Structure Processes* 10E, 2009. Copyright © 2009 The McGraw-Hill Companies, Inc. Reprinted with permission.

This example also helps illustrate the fundamental drawback of profit sharing. Why should automobile workers at GM receive profit sharing payments that are only 1/15 the size received by those doing the same type of work at Chrysler? Is it because Chrysler UAW members performed 15 times better than their counterparts at GM that year? Probably not. Rather, workers are likely to view top management decisions regarding products, engineering, pricing, and marketing as more important. As a result, with the exception of top (and perhaps some middle) managers, most employees are unlikely to see a strong connection between what they do and what they earn under profit sharing. This means that performance motivation is likely to change very little under profit sharing. Consistent with expectancy theory, motivation depends on a strong link between behaviors and valued consequences such as pay (instrumentality perceptions).

Another factor that reduces the motivational impact of profit sharing plans is that most plans are of the deferred type. Roughly 16% of full-time employees in medium-size and large private establishments participate in profit sharing plans, but only 1% of employees overall (about 6% of those in profit sharing plans) are in cash plans where profits are paid to employees during the current time period.[36]

Not only may profit sharing fail to increase performance motivation, but employees may also react very negatively when they learn that such plans do not pay out during business downturns.[37] First, they may not feel they are to blame because they have been performing their jobs well. Other factors are beyond their control, so why should they be penalized? Second, what seems like a small amount of at-risk pay for a manager earning $80,000 per year can be very painful to someone earning $15,000 or $20,000.

Consider the case of the Du Pont Fibers Division, which had a plan that linked a portion of employees' pay to division profits.[38] After the plan's implementation, employees' base salary was about 4% lower than similar employees in other divisions unless 100% of the profit goal (a 4% increase over the previous year's profits) was reached. Thus, there was what might be called downside risk. However, there was also considerable upside opportunity: if 100% of the profit goal was exceeded, employees would earn more than similar employees in other divisions. For example, if the division reached 150% of the profit goal (6% growth in profits), employees would receive 12% more than comparable employees in other divisions.

Initially, the plan worked fine. The profit goal was exceeded, and employees earned slightly more than employees in other divisions. In the following year, however, profits were down 26%, and the profit goal was not met. Employees received no profit sharing bonus; instead, they earned 4% less than comparable employees in other divisions. Profit sharing was no longer seen as a very good idea. Du Pont management responded to employee concerns by eliminating the plan and returning to a system of fixed base salaries with no variable (or risk) component. This outcome is perhaps not surprising from an agency theory perspective, which suggests that employees must somehow be compensated to assume increased risk.

One solution some organizations choose is to design plans that have upside but not downside risk. In such cases, when a profit sharing plan is introduced, base pay is not reduced. Thus, when profits are high, employees share in the gain, but when profits are low, they are not penalized. Such plans largely eliminate what is purported to be a major advantage of profit sharing: reducing labor costs during business downturns. During business upturns, labor costs will increase. Given that the performance benefits of such plans are not assured, an organization runs the risk under such plans of increasing its labor costs with little return on its investment.

In summary, although profit sharing may be useful as one component of a compensation system (to enhance identification with broad organizational goals), it may need to be complemented with other pay programs that more closely link pay to outcomes that individuals or teams can control (or "own"), particularly in larger companies. In addition, profit sharing runs the risk of contributing to employee dissatisfaction or higher labor costs, depending on how it is designed.

Ownership

Recent data show that 20 million Americans own stock in their company.[39] Employee ownership is similar to profit sharing in some key respects, such as encouraging employees to focus on the success of the organization as a whole. In fact, with ownership, this focus may be even stronger. Like profit sharing, ownership may be less motivational the larger the organization. And because employees may not realize any financial gain until they actually sell their stock (typically upon leaving the organization), the link between pay and performance may be even less obvious than under profit sharing. Thus, from a reinforcement theory standpoint (with its emphasis on actually experiencing rewards), the effect on performance motivation may be limited.

Stock Options
An employee ownership plan that gives employees the opportunity to buy the company's stock at a previously fixed price.

One way of achieving employee ownership is through **stock options,** which give employees the opportunity to buy stock at a fixed price. Say the employees receive options to purchase stock at $10 per share in 2012, and the stock price reaches $30 per share in 2017. They have the option of purchasing stock ("exercising" their stock options) at $10 per share in 2017, thus making a tidy return on investment if the shares are then sold. If the stock price goes down to $8 per share in the year 2017, however, there will be no financial gain. Therefore, employees are encouraged to act in ways that will benefit the organization.

For many years, stock options had typically been reserved for executives in larger, established companies. More recently, there was a trend toward pushing eligibility farther down in the organization.[40] In fact, many companies, including PepsiCo, Merck, McDonald's, Wal-Mart, and Procter & Gamble, began granting stock options to employees at all levels. Among start-up companies like these in the technology sector, these broad-based stock option programs have long been popular and companies like Microsoft and Cisco Systems attribute much of their growth and success to these option plans. Some studies suggest that organization performance is higher when a large percentage of top and midlevel managers are eligible for long-term incentives such as stock options, which is consistent with agency theory's focus on the problem of encouraging managers to think like owners.[41] However, it is not clear whether these findings would hold up for lower-level employees, particularly in larger companies, who may see much less opportunity to influence overall organization performance.

The Golden Age of stock options has faded some. Investors have long questioned the historically favorable tax treatment of employee stock options. In 2004, the Financial Accounting Standards Board (FASB) issued SFAS 123R, a landmark change, requiring companies to expense options on their financial statements, which reduces reported net income, dramatically in some cases. Microsoft decided to eliminate stock options in favor of actual stock grants. This is partly in response to the new accounting standards and partly in recognition of the fact that Microsoft's stock price is not likely to grow as rapidly as it once did, making options less effective in recruiting, retaining, and motivating its employees. It appears that many companies are cutting back on stock options overall, and especially for nonexecutive employees.

Those companies that continue to use broad-based stock options have encountered difficulties in keeping employees motivated during years when there has been a steep decline in stock prices. For example, in 2009 Google's stock price dropped to $306, down from $741 in 2007, putting many employee stock options "underwater" (i.e., the stock price was under the option/exercise price), meaning that employees were not able to make any gain from exercising their options. Google's answer to this situation was an option exchange where employees turned in their underwater options in return for options having an exercise price equal to the current (lower) stock price. The hope was that employee motivation and retention would be reinvigorated.[42]

Employee stock ownership plans (ESOPs), under which employers give employees stock in the company, are the most common form of employee ownership, with the number of employees in such plans increasing from 4 million in 1980 to over 11 million in 2007 in the United States.[43] In Japan, 91% of companies listed on Japanese stock markets have an ESOP, and these companies appear to have higher average productivity than non-ESOP companies.[44] ESOPs raise a number of unique issues. On the negative side, they can carry significant risk for employees. An ESOP must, by law, invest at least 51% of assets in its company's stock, resulting in less diversification of investment risk (in some cases, no diversification). Consequently, when employees buy out companies in poor financial condition to save their jobs, or when the ESOP is used to fund pensions, employees risk serious financial difficulties if the company does poorly.[45] This is not just a concern for employees, because, as agency theory suggests, employees may require higher pay to offset increased risks of this sort.

Employee Stock Ownership Plan (ESOP)
An employee ownership plan that gives employers certain tax and financial advantages when stock is granted to employees.

ESOPs can be attractive to organizations because they have tax and financing advantages and can serve as a takeover defense (under the assumption that employee owners will be "friendly" to management). ESOPs give employees the right to vote their securities (if registered on a national exchange).[46] As such, some degree of participation in a select number of decisions is mandatory, but overall participation in decision making appears to vary significantly across organizations with ESOPs. Some studies suggest that the positive effects of ownership are larger in cases where employees have greater participation,[47] perhaps because the "employee–owner comes to psychologically experience his/her ownership in the organization."[48]

GAINSHARING, GROUP INCENTIVES, AND TEAM AWARDS

Gainsharing

Gainsharing
A form of compensation based on group or plant performance (rather than organizationwide profits) that does not become part of the employee's base salary.

Gainsharing programs offer a means of sharing productivity gains with employees. Although sometimes confused with profit sharing plans, gainsharing differs in two key respects. First, instead of using an organization-level performance measure (profits), the programs measure group or plant performance, which is likely to be seen as more controllable by employees. Second, payouts are distributed more frequently and not deferred. In a sense, gainsharing programs represent an effort to combine the best features of organization-oriented plans like profit sharing and individual-oriented plans like merit pay and individual incentives. Like profit sharing, gainsharing encourages pursuit of broader goals than individual-oriented plans do. But, unlike profit sharing, gainsharing can motivate employees much as individual plans do because of the more controllable nature of the performance measure and the frequency of payouts. Indeed, studies indicate that gainsharing improves performance.[49]

One type of gainsharing, the Scanlon plan (developed in the 1930s by Joseph N. Scanlon, president of a local union at Empire Steel and Tin Plant in Mansfield, Ohio), provides a monetary bonus to employees (and the organization) if the ratio of labor costs to the sales value of production is kept below a certain standard. Table 12.7 shows a modified (i.e., costs in addition to labor are included) Scanlon plan. Because actual costs ($850,000) were less than allowable costs ($907,500) in the first and second periods, there is a gain of $57,500. The organization receives 45% of the savings, and the employees receive the other 55%, although part of the employees' share is set aside in the event that actual costs exceed the standard in upcoming months (as Table 12.7 shows did occur).

Gainsharing plans like the Scanlon plan and pay-for-performance plans in general often encompass more than just a monetary component. As Table 12.8 indicates, there is often a strong emphasis on taking advantage of employee know-how to improve the production process through teams and suggestion systems. A number of recommendations have been made about the organization conditions that should be in place for gainsharing to succeed. Commonly mentioned factors include (1) management commitment, (2) a need to change or a strong commitment to continuous improvement, (3) management's acceptance and encouragement of employee input, (4) high levels of cooperation and interaction, (5) employment security, (6) information sharing on productivity and costs, (7) goal setting, (8) commitment of all involved parties to the process of change and improvement, and (9) agreement on a performance standard and calculation that is understandable, seen as fair, and closely related to managerial objectives.[50]

table 12.7

Example of Gainsharing (Modified Scanlon Plan) Report

ITEMS	AVERAGE OF 1ST AND 2ND PERIODS	AVERAGE OF 2ND AND 3RD PERIODS
1. Sales in dollars	$1,000,000	$1,000,000
2. Inventory change and work in process	100,000	100,000
3. Sales value of production	1,100,000	1,100,000
4. Allowable costs (82.5% × 3 above)	907,500	907,500
5. Actual costs	850,000	917,500
6. Gain (4 – 5 above)	57,500	−10,000
7. Employee share (55% of 6 above)	31,625	−5,500
8. Monthly reserve (20% of 7 above)	6,325	−5,500
*If no bonus, 100% of 7 above		
9. Bonus to be distributed (7 – 8)	25,300	0
10. Company share (45% of 6 above)	25,875	−4,500
11. Participating payroll	132,000	132,000
12. Bonus percentage (9/11)	19.2%	0.0%
13. Monthly reserve (8 above)	6,325	−5,500
14. Reserve at the end of last period	0	6,325
15. Year-end reserve to date	6,325	825

SOURCE: From *Gainsharing and Goalsharing,* by K. Mericle and D. O. Kim. Copyright © 2004 Praeger. Reproduced with permission of ABC-CLI0, LLC.

Group Incentives and Team Awards

Whereas gainsharing plans are often plantwide, group incentives and team awards typically pertain to a smaller work group.[51] Group incentives (like individual incentives) tend to measure performance in terms of physical output, whereas team award plans may use a broader range of performance measures (like cost savings, successful

table 12.8

Employee Involvement Plans for Nonmanagement Employees

TYPE OF EMPLOYEE INVOLVEMENT PROGRAM	PERCENTAGE USING PROGRAM	MEDIAN PERCENTAGE OF EMPLOYEES PARTICIPATING	MEDIAN NUMBER OF HOURS SPENT PER PARTICIPATING EMPLOYEE PER YEAR
Individual suggestion plans	42%	20%	5
Ad hoc problem solving groups	44	20	22
Team group suggestion plans	28	25	10
Employee–management teams	19	15	40
Quality circles	26	16	50
Percentage of all plans using any type of employee involvement program	66		

SOURCE: From Jerry L. McAdams, "Design, Implementation, and Results: Employee Involvement and Performance Reward Plans," *Compensation and Benefits Review,* March–April 1995, pp. 45–55. Reproduced with permission of Sage Publications, Inc. via Copyright Clearance Center.

completion of product design, or meeting deadlines). As with individual incentive plans, these plans have a number of potential drawbacks. Competition between individuals may be reduced, but it may be replaced by competition between groups or teams. Also, consistent with our earlier discussion of pay effects on workforce composition, any plan that does not adequately recognize differences in individual performance risks demotivating top performers or losing them. Finally, as with any incentive plan, a standard-setting process must be developed that is seen as fair by employees, and these standards must not exclude important dimensions such as quality.

BALANCED SCORECARD

As the preceding discussion indicates, every pay program has advantages and disadvantages. Therefore, rather than choosing one program, some companies find it useful to design a mix of pay programs, one that has just the right chemistry for the situation at hand. Relying exclusively on merit pay or individual incentives may result in high levels of work motivation but unacceptable levels of individualistic and competitive behavior and too little concern for broader plant or organization goals. Relying too heavily on profit sharing and gainsharing plans may increase cooperation and concern for the welfare of the entire plant or organization, but it may reduce individual work motivation to unacceptable levels. However, a particular mix of merit pay, gainsharing, and profit sharing could contribute to acceptable performance on all these performance dimensions.

One approach that seeks to balance multiple objectives is the balanced scorecard (see Chapter 1), which Kaplan and Norton describe as a way for companies to "track financial results while simultaneously monitoring progress in building the capabilities and acquiring the intangible assets they would need for future growth."[52]

Table 12.9 shows how a mix of measures might be used by a manufacturing firm to motivate improvements in a balanced set of key business drivers.

Managerial and Executive Pay

Because of their significant ability to influence organization performance, top managers and executives are a strategically important group whose compensation warrants special attention, including its competitiveness in the labor market.[53] In the previous chapter we discussed how much this group is paid. Here we focus on the issue of how their pay is determined.

Business magazines such as *Forbes* and *Bloomberg Businessweek* often publish lists of top executives who did the most for their pay and those who did the least. The latter group has been the impetus for much of the attention to executive pay. The problem seems to be that in some companies, top executive pay is high every year, regardless of profitability or stock market performance. One study, for example, found that CEO pay changes by $3.25 for every $1,000 change in shareholder wealth. Although this relationship was interpreted to mean that "the compensation of top executives is virtually independent of corporate performance," later work demonstrates, to the contrary, that executive pay, in most companies, is significantly aligned with shareholder return."[54]

How can executive pay be linked to organization performance? From an agency theory perspective, the goal of owners (shareholders) is to encourage the agents (managers and executives) to act in the best interests of the owners. This may mean

table 12.9

Illustration of Balanced Scorecard Incentive Concept

PERFORMANCE MEASURE	INCENTIVE SCHEDULE				
	TARGET INCENTIVE	PERFORMANCE	% TARGET	ACTUAL PERFORMANCE	INCENTIVE EARNED
Financial • Return on capital employed	$100	20% + 16–20% 12–16% Below 12%	150% 100% 50% 0%	18%	$100
Customer • Product returns	$ 40	1 in: 1,000 + 900–999 800–899 Below 800	150% 100% 50% 0%	1 in 876	$ 20
Internal • Cycle time reduction (%)	$ 30	9% + 6–9% 3–6% 0–3%	150% 100% 50% 0%	11%	$ 45
Learning and growth • Voluntary employee turnover	$ 30	Below 5% 5–8% 8–12%	150% 100% 50%	7%	$ 30
Total	$200				$195

SOURCE: F. C. McKenzie and M. P. Shilling, "Avoiding Performance Traps: Ensuring Effective Incentive Design and Implementation," *Compensation and Benefits Review,* July–August 1998, pp. 57–65. Reproduced with permission of Sage Publications, Inc. via Copyright Clearance Center.

less emphasis on noncontingent pay, such as base salary, and more emphasis on outcome-oriented "contracts" that make some portion of executive pay contingent on the organization's profitability or stock performance.[55] Among midlevel and top managers, it is common to use both short-term bonus and long-term incentive plans to encourage the pursuit of both short- and long-term organization performance objectives. Indeed, the bulk of executive compensation comes from restricted stock, stock options, and other forms of long-term compensation. Putting pay "at risk" in this manner can be a strong incentive. However, agency theory suggests that while too little pay at risk may weaken the incentive effect, too much pay at risk can also be a problem if executives take too big of risks with firm assets.[56] The banking and mortgage industry problems of late provide an example. The "Competing through Sustainability" box describes how financial services company Goldman Sachs is addressing such issues.

To what extent do organizations use such pay-for-performance plans, and what are their consequences? Research suggests that organizations vary substantially in the extent to which they use both long-term and short-term incentive programs. Further, greater use of such plans among top and midlevel managers is associated with higher subsequent levels of profitability. As Table 12.10 indicates, greater reliance on short-term bonuses and long-term incentives (relative to base pay) resulted in substantial improvements in return on assets.[57] For top executives, aligning compensation with past shareholder return is associated with his or her future shareholder returns.[58]

COMPETING THROUGH SUSTAINABILITY

Goldman Sachs May Pay Bonuses Tied to Profit, Revenue

Goldman Sachs Group Inc., weighing 2010 pay packages for a year that could rank as Wall Street's second best, said it may grant bonuses that depend on future earnings, in addition to stock performance.

The awards would go to "key employees" and be tied to a variety of financial measures including revenue, net income and return on equity, a gauge of profitability, the New York–based company said yesterday in a regulatory filing. Awards may consist of cash, securities, or other equity-linked components, and carry provisions allowing their cancellation or return.

The plan "is a tool the compensation committee may use to further align incentive compensation with long-term performance," said Stephen Cohen, a company spokesman. Cohen declined to provide figures on potential payouts, saying that awards haven't been set.

Regulators have pushed banks to design pay packages for top employees that would discourage excessive risk-taking, after a financial crisis wiped out firms including Lehman Brothers Holdings Inc. and led to government bailouts. Most firms have interpreted the guidance to emphasize deferred stock awards over cash bonuses.

Goldman Sachs's new program aims to ensure "that the firm's incentive–compensation structure is balanced and consistent with the safety and soundness of the firm," according to the filing. It won't fuel "imprudent risk-taking," it said.

"Improper Risk"

The payouts may be halted or reclaimed if the firm determines, for example, that an employee engaged in "materially improper risk analysis or failed sufficiently to raise concerns about risks," according to the filing.

Earlier, we saw how the balanced scorecard approach could be applied to paying manufacturing employees. It is also useful in designing executive pay. Table 12.11 shows how the choice of performance measures can be guided by a desire to balance shareholder, customer, and employee objectives. Sears sees financial results as a lagging indicator that tells the company how it has done in the past, whereas customer and employee metrics like those in Table 12.11 are leading indicators that tell the company how its financial results will be in the future. Importantly, Sears

table 12.10

The Relationship between Managerial Pay and Organization Return on Assets

		PREDICTED RETURN ON ASSETS	
BONUS/BASE RATIO	LONG-TERM INCENTIVE ELIGIBILITY	%	$[a]
10%	28%	5.2%	$250 million
20	28	5.6	269 million
10	48	5.9	283 million
20	48	7.1	341 million

[a]Based on the assets of the average *Fortune* 500 company in 1990.
SOURCE: B. Gerhart and G. T. Milkovich, "Organizational Differences in Managerial Compensation and Financial Performance," *Academy of Management Journal* 33 (1990), pp. 663–91.

STAKEHOLDER	MEASURES
Shareholder value	Economic value added
	Earnings per share
	Cash flow
	Total cost productivity
Customer value	Quality
	Market share
	Customer satisfaction
Employee value	High-performance culture index
	High-performance culture deployment
	Training and development diversity

table 12.11

Whirlpool's Three-Stakeholder Scorecard

SOURCE: From E. Gubman, *The Talent Solution*, 1998. Copyright © 1998 The McGraw-Hill Companies, Inc. Reprinted with permission.

conducted empirical research to validate these presumed linkages.[59] Thus, Sears ties its executive compensation to achievement of objectives to "(1) drive profitable growth, (2) become customer-centric, (3) foster the development of a diverse, high-performance culture, and (4) focus on productivity and returns."[60]

Finally, there is pressure from regulators and shareholders to better link pay and performance. The Securities and Exchange Commission (SEC) requires companies to report compensation levels for the five highest paid executives and the company's performance relative to that of competitors over a five-year period. In 2006, the SEC put additional rules into effect that require better disclosure of the value of executive perquisites and retirement benefits. In 2010, the Dodd-Frank Wall Street Reform and Consumer Protection Act was signed into law in the United States. It regulates executive compensation in financial institutions, requiring, for example, that shareholders have a "say on pay," meaning that they have the right to a (nonbinding) vote on executive pay plans.

Large retirement fund investors such as TIAA-CREF and CalPERS have proposed guidelines to better ensure that boards of directors act in shareholders' best interests when making executive pay decisions, rather than being beholden to management. Some of the governance practices believed to be related to director independence (Dodd-Frank has similar provisions) from management are shown in Table 12.12. In addition, when a firm's future is at risk, the board may well need to demonstrate its independence from management by taking dramatic action, which may include removing the chief executive.

Process and Context Issues

In Chapter 11 we discussed the importance of process issues such as communication and employee participation. Earlier in the present chapter we discussed the importance of fairness, both distributive and procedural. Significant differences in how such issues are handled can be found both across and within organizations, suggesting that organizations have considerable discretion in this aspect of compensation management.[61] As such, it represents another strategic opportunity to distinguish one's organization from the competition.

LO 12-6
Explain the importance of process issues such as communication in compensation management.

table 12.12

Guidelines for Board of Directors Independence and Leadership

1. **Majority of independent directors:** At a minimum, a majority of the board consists of directors who are independent. Boards should strive to obtain board composition made up of a substantial majority of independent directors.
2. **Independent executive session:** Independent directors meet periodically (at least once a year) alone in an executive session, without the CEO. The independent board chair or lead (or presiding) independent director should preside over this meeting.
3. **Independent director definition:** Each company should disclose in its annual proxy statement the definition of "independence" relied upon by its board.
4. **Independent board chairperson:** The board should be chaired by an independent director. The CEO and chair roles should only be combined in very limited circumstances; in these situations, the board should provide a written statement in the proxy materials discussing why the combined role is in the best interest of shareowners, and it should name a lead independent director to fulfill duties that are consistent with those provided in other company material.
5. **Examine separate chair/CEO positions:** When selecting a new chief executive officer, boards should reexamine the traditional combination of the "chief executive" and "chair" positions.
6. **Board role of retiring CEO:** Generally, a company's retiring CEO should not continue to serve as a director on the board and at the very least be prohibited from sitting on any of the board committees.
7. **Board access to management:** The board should have a process in place by which all directors can have access to senior management.
8. **Independent board committees:** Committees who perform the audit, director nomination, and executive compensation functions should consist entirely of independent directors.
9. **Board oversight:** The full board is responsible for the oversight function on behalf of shareowners. Should the board decide to have other committees (e.g., executive committee) in addition to those required by law, the duties and membership of such committees should be fully disclosed.
10. **Board resources:** The board, through its committees, should have access to adequate resources to provide independent counsel advice, or other tools that allow the board to effectively perform its duties on behalf of shareowners.

SOURCE: "Global Principles of Accountable Corporate Governance," The California Public Employees' Retirement System, August 18, 2008.

EMPLOYEE PARTICIPATION IN DECISION MAKING

Consider employee participation in decision making and its potential consequences. Involvement in the design and implementation of pay policies has been linked to higher pay satisfaction and job satisfaction, presumably because employees have a better understanding of and greater commitment to the policy when they are involved.[62]

What about the effects on productivity? Agency theory provides some insight. The delegation of decision making by a principal to an agent creates agency costs because employees may not act in the best interests of top management. In addition, the more agents there are, the higher the monitoring costs.[63] Together, these suggest that delegation of decision making can be very costly.

On the other hand, agency theory suggests that monitoring would be less costly and more effective if performed by employees because they have knowledge about the workplace and behavior of fellow employees that managers do not have. As such, the right compensation system might encourage self-monitoring and peer monitoring.[64]

Researchers have suggested that two general factors are critical to encouraging such monitoring: monetary incentives (outcome-oriented contracts in agency theory) and an environment that fosters trust and cooperation. This environment, in turn, is a function of employment security, group cohesiveness, and individual rights for employees—in other words, respect for and commitment to employees.[65]

COMMUNICATION

Another important process issue is communication. Earlier, we spoke of its importance in the administration of merit pay, both from the perspective of procedural fairness and as a means of obtaining the maximum impact from a merit pay program.[66] More generally, a change in any part of the compensation system is likely to give rise to employee concerns. Rumors and assumptions based on poor or incomplete information are always an issue in administering compensation, partly because of its importance to employee economic security and well-being. Therefore, in making any changes, it is crucial to determine how best to communicate reasons for the changes to employees. Some organizations now rely heavily on video messages from the chief executive officer to communicate the rationale for major changes. Brochures that include scenarios for typical employees are also used, as are focus group sessions where small groups of employees are interviewed to obtain feedback about concerns that can be addressed in later communication programs.

PAY AND PROCESS: INTERTWINED EFFECTS

The preceding discussion treats process issues such as participation as factors that may facilitate the success of pay programs. At least one commentator, however, has described an even more important role for process factors in determining employee performance:

> Worker participation apparently helps make alternative compensation plans . . . work better—and also has beneficial effects of its own. . . . It appears that changing the way workers are treated may boost productivity more than changing the way they are paid.[67]

This suggestion raises a broader question: How important are pay decisions, per se, relative to other human resource practices? Although it may not be terribly useful to attempt to disentangle closely intertwined programs, it is important to reinforce the notion that human resource programs, even those as powerful as compensation systems, do not work alone.

Consider gainsharing programs. As described earlier, pay is often only one component of such programs. (See Table 12.8.) How important are the nonpay components?[68] There is ample evidence that gainsharing programs that rely almost exclusively on the monetary component can have substantial effects on productivity.[69] On the other hand, a study of an automotive parts plant found that adding a participation component (monthly meetings with management to discuss the gainsharing plan and ways to increase productivity) to a gainsharing pay incentive plan raised productivity. In a related study, employees were asked about the factors that motivated them to engage in active participation (such as suggestion systems). Employees reported that the desire to earn a monetary bonus was much less important than a number of nonpay factors, particularly the desire for influence and control in how their work was done.[70] A third study reported that productivity and profitability were both enhanced by the addition of employee participation in decisions, beyond the improvement derived from monetary incentives such as gainsharing.[71]

Organization Strategy and Compensation Strategy: A Question of Fit

Although much of our focus has been on the general, or average, effects of different pay programs, it is also useful to think in terms of matching pay strategies to organization strategies. To take an example from medicine, using the same medical treatment regardless of the symptoms and diagnosis would be foolish. In choosing a pay strategy, one must consider how effectively it will further the organization's overall business strategy. Consider again the findings reported in Table 12.10. The average effect of moving from a pay strategy with below-average variability in pay to one with above-average variability is an increase in return on assets of almost two percentage points (from 5.2% to 7.1%). But in some organizations, the increase could be smaller. In fact, greater variability in pay could contribute to a lower return on assets in some organizations. In other organizations, greater variability in pay could contribute to increases in return on assets of greater than two percentage points. Obviously, being able to tell where variable pay works and where it does not could have substantial consequences.

As the "Competing through Globalization" box shows, sometimes groups of companies decide pay-for-performance is needed to compete more effectively and to better execute strategy, even if the new pay plan goes against tradition.

In Chapter 2 we discussed directional business strategies, two of which were growth (internal or external) and concentration ("sticking to the knitting"). How should compensation strategies differ according to whether an organization follows a growth strategy or a concentration strategy? Table 12.13 provides some suggested matches. Basically, a growth strategy's emphasis on innovation, risk taking, and new markets is linked to a pay strategy that shares risk with employees but also gives them the opportunity for high future earnings by having them share in whatever success the organization has.[72] This means relatively low levels of fixed compensation in the short run but the use of bonuses and stock options, for example, that can pay off handsomely in the long run. Stock options have been described as the pay program "that built Silicon Valley," having been used by companies such as Apple, Microsoft, and others.[73] When such companies become successful, everyone from top managers to secretaries can become millionaires if they own stock. Growth organizations are also thought to benefit from a less bureaucratic orientation, in the sense of having more decentralization and flexibility in pay decisions and in recognizing individual skills,

table 12.13

Matching Pay Strategy and Organization Strategy

| | ORGANIZATION STRATEGY | |
PAY STRATEGY DIMENSIONS	CONCENTRATION	GROWTH
Risk sharing (variable pay)	Low	High
Time orientation	Short-term	Long-term
Pay level (short run)	Above market	Below market
Pay level (long-run potential)	Below market	Above market
Benefits level	Above market	Below market
Centralization of pay decisions	Centralized	Decentralized
Pay unit of analysis	Job	Skills

SOURCE: Adapted from L. R. Gomez-Mejia and D. B. Balkin, *Compensation, Organizational Strategy, and Firm Performance* (Cincinnati: South-Western, 1992), Appendix 4b.

Companies in Asia Make Greater Use of Pay-for-Performance Plans

For both executives and employees in general, some Asian companies are moving away from traditional methods of pay to a greater emphasis on performance. For executives, there is less emphasis on base pay. Instead, executives are being given the opportunity to increase their variable pay plans in the form of short-term and long-term incentives, which means that their pay will depend on how they and their companies perform.

Moving beyond executives, Asian companies are also putting greater emphasis on performance in deciding what to pay other employees. As an example, KEPCO, the largest energy firm in South Korea, recently announced that it will implement a merit-based pay system to replace its current system in which salaries depend on years of service with the company. KEPCO sees this change to replace seniority with performance as the main determinant of employee pay as a key part of its plan to make the company more efficient and profitable and to build a more innovative corporate culture.

SOURCES: "Asian Companies Shifting to 'Pay for Performance' Schemes," *Business World,* March 19, 2010; and Kim Hyuncheol, "KEPCO to Adopt Results-Based Annual Salary System," *Korea Times,* March 15, 2010.

rather than being constrained by job or grade classification systems. On the other hand, concentration-oriented organizations are thought to require a very different set of pay practices by virtue of their lower rate of growth, more stable workforce, and greater need for consistency and standardization in pay decisions. As noted earlier, Microsoft has eliminated stock options in favor of stock grants to its employees, in part because it is not the growth company it once was.

A LOOK BACK

In this chapter, we discussed the potential advantages and disadvantages of different types of incentive or pay-for-performance plans. We also saw that these pay plans can have both intended and unintended consequences. Designing a pay-for-performance strategy typically seeks to balance the pros and cons of different plans and reduce the chance of unintended consequences. To an important degree, pay strategy will depend on the particular goals and strategy of the organization and its units. For example, Microsoft determined that its pay strategy needed to be revised (less emphasis on stock options, more on stock grants) to support a change in its business strategy and to recognize the slower-paced growth of its stock price. At the beginning of this chapter, we saw that many organizations are working to link pay to performance and reduce fixed labor costs.

Questions

1. Does money motivate? Use the theories and examples discussed in this chapter to address this question.
2. Think of a job that you have held. Design an incentive plan. What would be the potential advantages and disadvantages of your plan? If your money was invested in the company, would you adopt the plan?

Please see the Video that corresponds to this chapter at www.mhhe.com/noe8e.

SUMMARY

Our focus in this chapter has been on the design and administration of programs that recognize employee contributions to the organization's success. These programs vary as to whether they link pay to individual, group, or organization performance. Often, it is not so much a choice of one program or the other as it is a choice between different combinations of programs that seek to balance individual, group, and organization objectives.

Wages, bonuses, and other types of pay have an important influence on an employee's standard of living. This carries at least two important implications. First, pay can be a powerful motivator. An effective pay strategy can substantially promote an organization's success; conversely, a poorly conceived pay strategy can have

detrimental effects. Second, the importance of pay means that employees care a great deal about the fairness of the pay process. A recurring theme is that pay programs must be explained and administered in such a way that employees understand their underlying rationale and believe it is fair.

The fact that organizations differ in their business and human resource strategies suggests that the most effective compensation strategy may differ from one organization to another. Although benchmarking programs against the competition is informative, what succeeds in some organizations may not be a good idea for others. The balanced scorecard suggests the need for organizations to decide what their key objectives are and use pay to support them.

KEY TERMS

Expectancy theory, 523
Principal, 523
Agent, 523

Merit increase grid, 526
Profit sharing, 534
Stock options, 536

Employee stock ownership plan
 (ESOP), 537
Gainsharing, 538

DISCUSSION QUESTIONS

1. To compete more effectively, your organization is considering a profit sharing plan to increase employee effort and to encourage employees to think like owners. What are the potential advantages and disadvantages of such a plan? Would the profit sharing plan have the same impact on all types of employees? Is the size of your organization an important consideration? Why? What alternative pay programs should be considered?

2. Gainsharing plans have often been used in manufacturing settings but can also be applied in service organizations. How could performance standards be developed for gainsharing plans in hospitals, banks, insurance companies, and so forth?

3. Your organization has two business units. One unit is a long-established manufacturer of a product that

competes on price and has not been subject to many technological innovations. The other business unit is just being started. It has no products yet, but it is working on developing a new technology for testing the effects of drugs on people via simulation instead of through lengthy clinical trials. Would you recommend that the two business units have the same pay programs for recognizing individual contributions? Why?

4. Beginning with the opening vignette and continuing throughout the chapter, we have seen many examples of companies (e.g., Goldman Sachs and Applebee's) making changes to how they pay for performance. Do you believe the changes at these companies make sense? What are the potential payoffs and pitfalls of their new pay strategies?

SELF-ASSESSMENT EXERCISE

Pay is only one type of incentive that can motivate you to perform well and contribute to your satisfaction at work. This survey will help you understand what motivates you at work. Consider each aspect of work and rate its importance to you, using the following scale: 5 = very important, 4 = somewhat important, 3 = neutral, 2 = somewhat unimportant, 1 = very unimportant.

Salary or wages	1	2	3	4	5
Cash bonuses	1	2	3	4	5
Boss's management style	1	2	3	4	5
Location of workplace	1	2	3	4	5
Commute	1	2	3	4	5
Job security	1	2	3	4	5
Opportunity for advancement	1	2	3	4	5

Work environment	1	2	3	4	5
Level of independence in job	1	2	3	4	5
Level of teamwork required for job	1	2	3	4	5
Other (enter your own):					
_____	1	2	3	4	5
_____	1	2	3	4	5
_____	1	2	3	4	5

Which aspects of work received a score of 5? A score of 4? These are the ones you believe motivate you to perform well and make you happy in your job. Which aspects of work received a score of 1 or 2? These are least likely to motivate you. Is pay the only way to motivate you?

SOURCE: Based on the "Job Assessor" found at www.salarymonster.com, accessed August 2002.

EXERCISING STRATEGY: PAYING FOR GOOD EMPLOYEE RELATIONS

Organizations understand that reaching financial objectives, or satisfying shareholders, depends to a considerable degree on how well they manage relationships with other important stakeholders such as customers and employees. One suggestion has been to link compensation, in part, to customer satisfaction and employee satisfaction. Is this a good idea in the case of employee satisfaction? There is some disagreement on this issue. Eastman Kodak has, since 1995, used employee opinion survey results as one factor in deciding executive bonuses. Likewise, United Airlines, which is employee-owned, is moving to a system where executive bonuses will depend to some degree on employee-satisfaction surveys. Although the idea of rewarding managers for good employee relations has some intuitive appeal, there may be unintended consequences. Indeed, Gordon Bethune, CEO of Continental Airlines, described such an idea as "absolutely stupid." Bethune argues, "Being an effective leader and having a company where people enjoy coming to work is not a popularity contest. When you run popularity contests, you tend to do things that may get you more points. That may not be good for shareholders and may not be good for the company." This is not to say that Bethune and Continental do not see employee relations as an important part of their competitive advantage. Continental was named the 2001

airline of the year by *Air Transport World* and number 18 on *Fortune's* 2001 list of best companies to work for in America. And many companies use employee opinion survey results to adjust their employee relations policies as needed. Rather, the issue is whether an incentive plan that explicitly rewards employee satisfaction will produce only intended positive consequences or might also produce unintended, less desirable consequences. Eastman Kodak and United are two examples of companies that have decided some direct incentive makes sense, even if it is small relative to other factors (like financial performance) that determine executive pay. Other companies, even those that use strong employee relations as an important source of competitive advantage, have been too concerned about unintended consequences to use explicit incentives.

Questions
1. Should companies worry about employee attitudes? Why or why not?
2. If positive employee attitudes are an objective, should organizations directly link pay incentives to attitudes?

SOURCE: "Bottom-up Pay: Companies Regularly Survey How Employees Feel about Their Bosses, But They Rarely Use Ratings to Set Compensation," *The Wall Street Journal*, April 6, 2000, pp. R5+.

MANAGING PEOPLE

PEOPLE scrutinize just about everything Walmart does. As Michael T. Duke, the company's chief executive, put it recently, "What we do and how we perform is watched closely not only by our customers and shareholders, but also by the whole world."

All of which makes a recent decision about *executive pay* at this giant retailer downright puzzling. In a proxy statement filed a few weeks ago, Walmart's compensation committee said it had replaced a crucial metric for assessing executives' performance: same-store sales, referring to stores that have been open for at least a year. Instead of that measure, Walmart is using total sales companywide, or at its major units, Wal-Mart Stores and Sam's Club.

Why? The change was "intended to align our performance share goals more closely with our evolving business strategy, which emphasizes productive growth, leverage and returns," Walmart said.

The timing was certainly curious. The switch came amid a sustained decline in Walmart's same-store sales, which have been falling for nearly two years. The company's total sales, however, rose 3.4% in the latest fiscal year.

Shifting the goal posts meant more money for Mr. Duke in the latest fiscal year than he would have received under the old arrangement. His compensation totaled $18.7 million, more than $16 million of which was performance-based.

Certainly, past statements about why the board chose to include this measure suggest that it's important. Walmart said in its 2008 proxy that its board had used "comparable-store sales as a performance metric because it believes it is a key driver of shareholder returns, and because investors look to comparable-store sales as an important measure of performance in the retail industry." The committee later added that "the combination of these performance metrics was likely to incentivize our executives to achieve performance that is in the best interests of our company and our shareholders."

But now, Walmart has jettisoned same-store sales from the mix. Explaining the decision, the proxy said the compensation committee concluded that "the combination of these performance metrics was likely to incentivize our executives to achieve performance that is in line with the best interests of our company and our shareholders."

Talk about trying to have it both ways.

KEEP in mind that when Walmart included same-store sales in its pay calculations, that measure had a sizable effect on Mr. Duke's compensation, accounting for 30% of the weighted factors determining his performance pay in fiscal 2010.

The switch at Walmart last year followed a shift in 2009 that allowed the company to set performance targets annually. In previous years, the board had set performance targets for three-year periods. The goals had to be met over that time before company executives could receive certain incentive pay awards.

The company's proxy said that shifting to annual targets allowed the board "to set more effective performance goals based on more current information and over a more realistic time frame."

But Mr. Flickinger said Walmart's pay packages seemed especially unfortunate in light of the company's decision late last year to end its longtime profit-sharing programs

for lower-level workers. This arrangement was created by Sam Walton, the company's founder, and was a source of considerable pride to him.

"Profit-sharing has pretty much been the carrot that's kept Walmart headed forward," Mr. Walton wrote in his 1992 autobiography, "Sam Walton: Made in America."

Last year, before Walmart eliminated that profit-sharing program, it said it paid roughly $1.1 billion in profit-sharing and 401(k) matches to employees. In the future, it will offer only the 401(k) match.

"Taking away profit-sharing was the ultimate Ebenezer Scrooge story of the last holiday season," Mr. Flickinger said. "Ebenezer makes all the money, and all the poor Cratchits working in the Walmart stores become poorer and poorer."

At least one Walmart shareholder has expressed concern that the company's directors are awarding bonuses to executives despite lagging performance.

"As the union that represents retail workers we are troubled that these bonus payouts come when front-line Walmart associates are getting wages and benefits cut, and seeing their hours reduced," says John Marshall, senior analyst in the capital stewardship program of the United Food and Commercial Workers. "Walmart's serious under-staffing is part of the reason same-store sales continue to decline, which ultimately hurts the stock price."

WALMART's annual shareholder meeting is scheduled for June 3. It will be interesting to see whether other shareholders speak out about the changes in the performance pay structure. Shareholder meetings have been fairly quiet this year, but Walmart's shares have not kept up with either the overall stock market or retail store indexes for the last three years.

A flagging share price has a funny way of focusing otherwise complacent stockholders.

Questions

1. Which performance measures do you believe should be used to evaluate the CEO of Walmart?
2. Why do you think the board changed the performance measure used to evaluate the CEO of Walmart? Make a case that supports the board's decision and then make a case that is critical of the board's decision. After thinking through both sides, do you think the board made the correct choice?
3. The article compares the compensation of the CEO with that of rank-and-file employees. Do you feel this comparison is relevant? Why or why not? Do you believe that employees compare their pay to that of the CEO? Explain why or why not.

⦿ TWITTER FOCUS: EMPLOYEES OWN BOB'S RED MILL

Using Twitter, continue the conversation about recognizing employee contributions with pay by reading the Bob's Red Mill case at www.mhhe.com/noe8e.

Bob Moore, founder and president of Bob's Red Mill Natural Foods, called together employees on his 81st birthday to tell them he was giving them the company. Moore had set up an employee stock ownership plan, placing company stock in a trust fund, and established a profit-sharing plan. All employees with three years of service were immediately fully vested in the plans. As they retire,

employees will receive cash for their stock shares. Instead of selling the business to one of many potential suitors, Moore gave the company to the employees because of their commitment to the company and to its mission of providing foods that make consumers healthier.

Engage with your classmates and instructor via Twitter to chat about Bob Moore's decision using the case questions posted on the Noe website. Don't have a Twitter account yet? See the instructions for getting started on the Online Learning Center.

⦿ NOTES

1. We draw freely in this chapter on several literature reviews: B. Gerhart and G. T. Milkovich, "Employee Compensation: Research and Practice," in *Handbook of Industrial and Organizational Psychology*, vol. 3, 2nd ed., ed. M. D. Dunnette and L. M. Hough (Palo Alto, CA: Consulting Psychologists Press, 1992); B. Gerhart and S. L. Rynes, *Compensation: Theory, Evidence, and Strategic Implications* (Thousand Oaks, CA: Sage, 2003); B. Gerhart, "Compensation Strategy and Organization Performance," in S. L. Rynes and B. Gerhart, eds., *Compensation in Organizations: Current Research and Practice* (San Francisco: Jossey-Bass, 2000), pp. 151–94; B. Gerhart, S. L. Rynes, and I. S. Fulmer, "Compensation," *Academy of Management Annals* 3 (2009).

2. B. Gerhart and G. T. Milkovich, "Organizational Differences in Managerial Compensation and Financial Performance," *Academy of Management Journal* 33 (1990), pp. 663–91.

3. E. Deci and R. Ryan, *Intrinsic Motivation and Self-Determination in Human Behavior* (New York: Plenum, 1985); A. Kohn, "Why Incentive Plans Cannot Work," *Harvard Business Review*, September–October 1993.

4. R. Eisenberger and J. Cameron, "Detrimental Effects of Reward: Reality or Myth?" *American Psychologist* 51, no. 11 (1996), pp. 1153–66; S. L. Rynes, B. Gerhart, and L. Parks, "Personnel Psychology: Performance Evaluation and Compensation," *Annual Review of Psychology* (2005); M. Fang and B. Gerhart, "Does Pay for Performance Diminish Intrinsic Interest? A Workplace Test Using Cognitive Evaluation Theory and the Attraction-Selection-Attrition Model," *International Journal of Human Resource Management* (forthcoming); M. Gagné and E. L. Deci, "Self-Determination Theory and Work Motivation," *Journal of Organizational Behavior* 26, pp. 331–362.

5. D. R. Dalton, M. A. Hitt, S. T. Certo, and C. M. Dalton, "The Fundamental Agency Problem and Its Mitigation: Independence, Equity, and the Market for Corporate Control," *Academy of Management Annals* 1 (2007), pp. 1–64; R. A. Lambert and D. F. Larcker, "Executive Compensation, Corporate Decision Making, and Shareholder Wealth," in *Executive Compensation*, ed. F. Foulkes (Boston: Harvard Business School Press, 1989), pp. 287–309.

6. L. R. Gomez-Mejia, H. Tosi, and T. Hinkin, "Managerial Control, Performance, and Executive Compensation," *Academy of Management Journal* 30 (1987), pp. 51–70; H. L. Tosi Jr. and

L. R. Gomez-Mejia, "The Decoupling of CEO Pay and Performance: An Agency Theory Perspective," *Administrative Science Quarterly* 34 (1989), pp. 169–89.

7. K. M. Eisenhardt, "Agency Theory: An Assessment and Review," *Academy of Management Review* 14 (1989), pp. 57–74.

8. R. E. Hoskisson, M. A. Hitt, and C. W. L. Hill, "Managerial Incentives and Investment in R&D in Large Multiproduct Firms," *Organizational Science* 4 (1993), pp. 325–41; M. Bloom and G. T. Milkovich, "Relationships among Risk, Incentive Pay, and Organizational Performance," *Academy of Management Journal* 41 (1998), pp. 283–97.

9. A. J. Nyberg, I. S. Fulmer, B. Gerhart, and M. A. Carpenter, "Agency Theory Revisited: CEO Return and Shareholder Interest Alignment," *Academy of Management Journal* 53 (2010), pp. 1029–49.

10. Eisenhardt, "Agency Theory."

11. Ibid.; E. J. Conlon and J. M. Parks, "Effects of Monitoring and Tradition on Compensation Arrangements: An Experiment with Principal–Agent Dyads," *Academy of Management Journal* 33 (1990), pp. 603–22; K. M. Eisenhardt, "Agency- and Institutional-Theory Explanations: The Case of Retail Sales Compensation," *Academy of Management Journal* 31 (1988), pp. 488–511; Gerhart and Milkovich, "Employee Compensation."

12. G. T. Milkovich, J. Hannon, and B. Gerhart, "The Effects of Research and Development Intensity on Managerial Compensation in Large Organizations," *Journal of High Technology Management Research* 2 (1991), pp. 133–50.

13. G. T. Milkovich and A. K. Wigdor, *Pay for Performance* (Washington, DC: National Academy Press, 1991); Gerhart and Milkovich, "Employee Compensation"; Gerhart and Rynes, *Compensation: Theory, Evidence, and Strategic Implications*; A. Nyberg, "Retaining Your High Performers: Moderators of the Performance-Job Satisfaction-Voluntary Turnover Relationship," *Journal of Applied Psychology* 95, no. 3 (2010), pp. 440–53; C. O. Trevor, G. Reilly, and B. Gerhart, "Reconsidering Pay Dispersion's Effect on the Performance of Interdependent Work: Reconciling Sorting and Pay Inequality," *Academy of Management Journal* (forthcoming).

14. C. Trevor, B. Gerhart, and J. W. Boudreau, "Voluntary Turnover and Job Performance: Curvilinearity and the Moderating Influences of Salary Growth and Promotions," *Journal of Applied Psychology* 82 (1997), pp. 44–61; C. B. Cadsby, F. Song, and

F. Tapon, "Sorting and Incentive Effects of Pay-for-Performance: An Experimental Investigation," *Academy of Management Journal* 50 (2007), pp. 387–405; A. Salamin and P. W. Hom, "In Search of the Elusive U-Shaped Performance-Turnover Relationship: Are High Performing Swiss Bankers More Liable to Quit?" *Journal of Applied Psychology* 90 (2005), pp. 1204–16; J. D. Shaw, and N. Gupta, "Pay System Characteristics and Quit Patterns of Good, Average, and Poor Performers," *Personnel Psychology* 60 (2007), pp. 903–28.

15. R. D. Bretz, R. A. Ash, and G. F. Dreher, "Do People Make the Place? An Examination of the Attraction–Selection–Attrition Hypothesis," *Personnel Psychology* 42 (1989), pp. 561–81; T. A. Judge and R. D. Bretz, "Effect of Values on Job Choice Decisions," *Journal of Applied Psychology* 77 (1992), pp. 261–71; D. M. Cable and T. A. Judge, "Pay Performances and Job Search Decisions: A Person–Organization Fit Perspective," *Personnel Psychology* 47 (1994), pp. 317–48.

16. E. E. Lawler III, *Strategic Pay* (San Francisco: Jossey-Bass, 1990); Gerhart and Milkovich, "Employee Compensation"; Gerhart and Rynes, *Compensation: Theory, Evidence, and Strategic Implications*; B. Gerhart, C. Trevor, and M. Graham, "New Directions in Employee Compensation Research" in G. R. Ferris (ed.), *Research in Personnel and Human Resources Management* (London: JAI Press, 1996), pp. 143–203; M. Beer and M. D. Cannon, "Promise and Peril in Implementing Pay-for-Performance," *Human Resource Management* 43 (2004), pp. 3–20.

17. R. D. Bretz, G. T. Milkovich, and W. Read, "The Current State of Performance Appraisal Research and Practice," *Journal of Management* 18 (1992), pp. 321–52; R. L. Heneman, "Merit Pay Research," *Research in Personnel and Human Resource Management* 8 (1990), pp. 203–63; Milkovich and Wigdor, *Pay for Performance*; Rynes, Gerhart, and Parks, "Personnel Psychology: Performance Evaluation and Compensation."

18. Bretz et al., "Current State of Performance Appraisal."

19. B. D. Blume, T. T. Baldwin, and R. S. Rubin, "Reactions to Different Types of Forced Distribution Performance Evaluation Systems," *Journal of Business and Psychology* 24, no. 1 (2009), pp. 77–91.

20. Bretz et al., "Current State of Performance Appraisal."

21. Ibid.

22. W. E. Deming, *Out of the Crisis* (Cambridge, MA: Center for Advanced Engineering Study, Massachusetts Institute of Technology, 1986), p. 110.

23. Ibid.

24. Ibid.

25. Trevor et al., "Voluntary Turnover."

26. Gerhart and Rynes, *Compensation: Theory, Evidence, and Strategic Implications*.

27. Rynes, Gerhart, and Parks, "Personnel Psychology: Performance Evaluation and Compensation."

28. J. Schaubroeck, J. D. Shaw, M. K. Duffy, "An Under-Met and Over-Met Expectations Model of Employee Reactions to Merit Raises," *Journal of Applied Psychology* 93 (2008) pp. 424–34; S. Kepes, J. Delery, and N. Gupta, "Contingencies in the Effects of Pay Range on Organizational Effectiveness," *Personnel Psychology* 62 (2009), pp. 497–531; M. S. Chien, J. S. Lawler, and J. F. Uen, "Performance-Based Pay, Procedural Justice and Job Performance for RD Professionals: Evidence from the Taiwanese High-Tech Sector" (2010), *International Journal of Human Resource Management* 21, no. 12 (2010), pp. 2234–48; P. Bamberger and E. Belogolovsky, "The Impact of Pay Secrecy on Individual Task Performance," *Personnel Psychology* 63, no. 4 (2010), pp. 965–96.

29. R. Folger and M. A. Konovsky, "Effects of Procedural and Distributive Justice on Reactions to Pay Raise Decisions," *Academy of Management Journal* 32 (1989), pp. 115–30; J. Greenberg, "Determinants of Perceived Fairness of Performance Evaluations," *Journal of Applied Psychology* 71 (1986), pp. 340–42.

30. Rynes, Gerhart, and Parks, "Personnel Psychology: Performance Evaluation and Compensation."

31. B. Gerhart and S. Rynes, "Determinants and Consequences of Salary Negotiations by Graduating Male and Female MBAs," *Journal of Applied Psychology* (1991), pp. 256–62; Gerhart and Rynes, *Compensation: Theory, Evidence, and Strategic Implications*.

32. E. A. Locke, D. B. Feren, V. M. McCaleb, K. N. Shaw, and A. T. Denny, "The Relative Effectiveness of Four Methods of Motivating Employee Performance," in *Changes in Working Life*, ed. K. D. Duncan, M. M. Gruenberg, and D. Wallis (New York: Wiley, 1980), pp. 363–88; for a summary of additional evidence, see also Gerhart and Rynes, *Compensation: Theory, Evidence, and Strategic Implications*.

33. Gerhart and Milkovich, "Employee Compensation."

34. This idea has been referred to as the "share economy." See M. L. Weitzman, "The Simple Macroeconomics of Profit Sharing," *American Economic Review* 75 (1985), pp. 937–53. For supportive empirical evidence, see the following studies: J. Chelius and R. S. Smith, "Profit Sharing and Employment Stability," *Industrial and Labor Relations Review* 43 (1990), pp. 256S–73S; B. Gerhart and L. O. Trevor, "Employment Stability under Different Managerial Compensation Systems," working paper 1995 (Cornell University: Center for Advanced Human Resource Studies); D. L. Kruse, "Profit Sharing and Employment Variability: Microeconomic Evidence on the Weitzman Theory," *Industrial and Labor Relations Review* 44 (1991), pp. 437–53.

35. Gerhart and Milkovich, "Employee Compensation"; M. L. Weitzman and D. L. Kruse, "Profit Sharing and Productivity," in *Paying for Productivity*, ed. A. S. Blinder (Washington, DC: Brookings Institution, 1990); D. L. Kruse, *Profit Sharing: Does It Make a Difference?* (Kalamazoo, MI: Upjohn Institute, 1993); M. Magnan and S. St-Onge, "The Impact of Profit Sharing on the Performance of Financial Services Firms," *Journal of Management Studies* 42 (2005), pp. 761–91.

36. "GM/UAW: The Battle Goes On," *Ward's Auto World* (May 1995), p. 40; E. M. Coates III, "Profit Sharing Today: Plans and Provisions," *Monthly Labor Review* (April 1991), pp. 19–25.

37. Gerhart and Rynes, *Compensation: Theory, Evidence, and Strategic Implications*.

38. American Management Association, *CompFlash*, April 1991, p. 3.

39. "New Data Show Widespread Employee Ownership in U.S.," National Center for Employee Ownership, www.nceo.org/library/widespread.html.

40. "Executive Compensation: Taking Stock," *Personnel* 67 (December 1990), pp. 7–8; "Another Day, Another Dollar Needs Another Look," *Personnel* 68 (January 1991), pp. 9–13; J. Blasi, D. Kruse, and A. Bernstein, *In the Company of Owners* (New York: Basic Books, 2003).

41. Gerhart and Milkovich, "Organizational Differences in Managerial Compensation."

42. Scott Thurm, Joann S. Lublin, and Jessica E. Vascellaro, "Google's 'One-to-One' Exchange Could Prompt Others to Follow," *The Wall Street Journal*, January 23, 2009. Copyright © 2009 by Dow Jones & Co., Inc. Reproduced with permission of Dow Jones & Co., Inc. via Copyright Clearance Center.

43. Corey Rosen, *EBRI Databook on Employee Benefits* (Washington, DC: Employee Benefit Research Institute, 1995) www.nceo.org (National Center for Employee Ownership website), updated February 14, 2008.

44. D. Jones and T. Kato, "The Productivity Effects of Employee Stock Ownership Plans and Bonuses: Evidence from Japanese Panel Data," *American Economic Review* 185, no. 3 (June 1995), pp. 391–414.

45. "Employees Left Holding the Bag," *Fortune* (May 20, 1991), pp. 83–93; M. A. Conte and J. Svejnar, "The Performance Effects of Employee Ownership Plans," in Blinder, *Paying for Productivity*, pp. 245–94.

46. Conte and Svejnar, "Performance Effects of Employee Ownership Plans."

47. Ibid.; T. H. Hammer, "New Developments in Profit Sharing, Gainsharing, and Employee Ownership," in *Productivity in Organizations*, ed. J. P. Campbell, R. J. Campbell and Associates (San Francisco: Jossey-Bass, 1988); K. J. Klein, "Employee Stock Ownership and Employee Attitudes: A Test of Three Models," *Journal of Applied Psychology* 72 (1987), pp. 319–32.

48. J. L. Pierce, S. Rubenfeld, and S. Morgan, "Employee Ownership: A Conceptual Model of Process and Effects," *Academy of Management Review* 16 (1991), pp. 121–44.

49. R. T. Kaufman, "The Effects of Improshare on Productivity," *Industrial and Labor Relations Review* 45 (1992), pp. 311–22; M. H. Schuster, "The Scanlon Plan: A Longitudinal Analysis," *Journal of Applied Behavioral Science* 20 (1984), pp. 23–28; M. M. Petty, B. Singleton, and D. W. Connell, "An Experimental Evaluation of an Organizational Incentive Plan in the Electric Utility Industry," *Journal of Applied Psychology* 77 (1992), pp. 427–36; W. N. Cooke, "Employee Participation Programs, Group-Based Incentives, and Company Performance: A Union–Nonunion Comparison," *Industrial and Labor Relations Review* 47 (1994), pp. 594–609; J. B. Arthur and L. Aiman-Smith, "Gainsharing and Organizational Learning: An Analysis of Employee Suggestions over Time," *Academy of Management Journal* 44 (2001), pp. 737–54; J. B. Arthur and G. S. Jelf, "The Effects of Gainsharing on Grievance Rates and Absenteeism over Time," *Journal of Labor Research* 20 (1999), pp. 133–45.

50. T. L. Ross and R. A. Ross, "Gainsharing: Sharing Improved Performance," in *The Compensation Handbook*, 3rd ed., ed. M. L. Rock and L. A. Berger (New York: McGraw-Hill, 1991).

51. T. M. Welbourne and L. R. Gomez-Mejia, "Optimizing Team Incentives in the Workplace," in *The Compensation Handbook*, 3rd ed. (New York: McGraw-Hill, 2000), pp. 275–290; E. Siemsen, S. Balasubramanian, and A. V. Roth, "Incentives That Induce Task-Related Effort, Helping, and Knowledge Sharing in Workgroups," *Management Science* 10 (2007), pp. 1533–50.

52. R. S. Kaplan and D. P. Norton, "Using the Balanced Scorecard as a Strategic Management System," *Harvard Business Review*, January–February 1996, pp. 75–85.

53. I. S. Fulmer, "The Elephant in the Room: Labor Market Influences on CEO Compensation," *Personnel Psychology* 62, no. 4 (2009), pp. 659–95.

54. M. C. Jensen and K. J. Murphy, "Performance Pay and Top-Management Incentives," *Journal of Political Economy* 98 (1990), pp. 225–64; A stronger relationship between CEO pay and performance was found by R. K. Aggarwal and A. A. Samwick, "The Other Side of the Trade-off: The Impact of Risk on Executive Compensation," *Journal of Political Economy* 107 (1999), pp. 65–105; A. J. Nyberg, I. S. Fulmer, B. Gerhart, and M. A. Carpenter, "Agency Theory Revisited: CEO Returns and Shareholder Interest Alignment, *Academy of Management Journal* 53

(2010), pp. 1029–49. Also, these observed relationships actually translate into significant changes in CEO pay in response to modest changes in financial performance of a company, as made clear by Gerhart and Rynes, *Compensation: Theory, Evidence, and Strategic Implications*; B. Gerhart, S. L. Rynes, and I. S. Fulmer, "Pay and Performance: Individuals, Groups, and Executives," *Academy of Management Annals* 3 (2009), pp. 251–315.

55. M. C. Jensen and K. J. Murphy, "CEO Incentives—It's Not How Much You Pay, but How," *Harvard Business Review* 68 (May–June 1990), pp. 138–53. The definitive resource on executive pay is B. R. Ellig, *The Complete Guide to Executive Compensation*, 2nd ed. (New York: McGraw-Hill); B. Gerhart, S. L. Rynes, and I. S. Fulmer, "Pay and Performance: Individuals, Groups, and Executives," *Academy of Management Annals* 3 (2009), pp. 251–315.

56. C. E. Devers, A. A. Cannella, G. P. Reilly, and M. E. Yoder, "Executive Compensation: A Multidisciplinary Review of Recent Developments," *Journal of Management* 33 (2007), pp. 1016–72; W. G. Sanders and D. C. Hambrick, "Swinging for the Fences: The Effects of CEO Stock Options on Company Risk Taking and Performance," *Academy of Management Journal* 50 (2007), pp. 1055–78; Genhart, Rynes, and Fulmer, "Pay and Performance."

57. Gerhart and Milkovich, "Organizational Differences in Managerial Compensation."

58. M. Hanlon, S. Rajgopal, and T. Shevlin, "Are Executive Stock Options Associated with Future Earnings?" *Journal of Accounting and Economics* 36 (2003), pp. 3–43; A. J. Nyberg, I. S. Fulmer, B. Gerhart, and M. Carpenter "Agency Theory Revisited: CEO Return and Shareholder Interest Alignment," *Academy of Management Journal* 53, no. 5 (2010), pp. 1029–49.

59. See Anthony J. Rucci, Steven P. Kirn, and Richard T. Quinn, "The Employee-Customer-Profit Chain at Sears," *Harvard Business Review*, January-February 1998, pp. 82–97; Christopher D. Ittner and David F. Larcker, "Coming Up Short on Nonfinancial Performance Measurement," *Harvard Business Review*, November 2003, pp. 88–95.

60. Sears, Roebuck proxy statement to shareholders, March 22, 2004. Available at www.sec.gov.

61. J. Cutcher-Gershenfeld, "The Impact on Economic Performance of a Transformation in Workplace Relations," *Industrial and Labor Relations Review* 44 (1991), pp. 241–60; Irene Goll, "Environment, Corporate Ideology, and Involvement Programs," *Industrial Relations* 30 (1991), pp. 138–49.

62. L. R. Gomez-Mejia and D. B. Balkin, *Compensation, Organizational Strategy, and Firm Performance* (Cincinnati: South-Western, 1992); G. D. Jenkins and E. E. Lawler III, "Impact of Employee Participation in Pay Plan Development," *Organizational Behavior and Human Performance* 28 (1981), pp. 111–28.

63. D. I. Levine and L. D. Tyson, "Participation, Productivity, and the Firm's Environment," in Blinder, *Paying for Productivity*.

64. T. Welbourne, D. Balkin, and L. Gomez-Mejia, "Gainsharing and Mutual Monitoring: A Combined Agency–Organizational Justice Interpretation," *Academy of Management Journal* 38 (1995), pp. 881–99.

65. Ibid.

66. A. Colella, R. L. Paetzold, A. Zardkoohi, and M. J. Wesson, "Exposing Pay Secrecy," *Academy of Management Review* 32 (2007), pp. 55–71; J. Schaubroeck et al., "An Under-Met and Over-Met Expectations Model of Employee Reactions to Merit Raises," *Journal of Applied Psychology* 93, no. 2 (March 2008), pp. 424–34.

67. Blinder, *Paying for Productivity*.

68. Hammer, "New Developments in Profit Sharing"; Milkovich and Wigdor, *Pay for Performance*; D. J. B. Mitchell, D. Lewin, and E. E. Lawler III, "Alternative Pay Systems, Firm Performance and Productivity," in Blinder, *Paying for Productivity*.

69. Kaufman, "The Effects of Improshare on Productivity"; M. H. Schuster, "The Scanlon Plan: A Longitudinal Analysis," *Journal of Applied Behavioral Science* 20 (1984), pp. 23–28; J. A. Wagner III, P. Rubin, and T. J. Callahan, "Incentive Payment and Nonmanagerial Productivity: An Interrupted Time Series Analysis of Magnitude and Trend," *Organizational Behavior and Human Decision Processes* 42 (1988), pp. 47–74.

70. C. R. Gowen III and S. A. Jennings, "The Effects of Changes in Participation and Group Size on Gainsharing Success: A Case Study," *Journal of Organizational Behavior Management* 11 (1991), pp. 147–69.

71. L. Hatcher, T. L. Ross, and D. Collins, "Attributions for Participation and Nonparticipation in Gainsharing-Plan Involvement Systems," *Group and Organization Studies* 16 (1991), pp. 25–43; Mitchell et al., "Alternative Pay Systems."

72. B. R. Ellig, "Compensation Elements: Market Phase Determines the Mix," *Compensation and Benefits Review* 13 (3) (1981), pp. 30–38; L. R. Gomez-Mejia and D. B. Balkin, *Compensation, Organizational Strategy, and Firm Performance* (Cincinnati, Ohio: South-Western Publishing, 1992); M. K. Kroumova and J. C. Sesis, "Intellectual Capital, Monitoring, and Risk: What Predicts the Adoption of Employee Stock Options?" *Industrial Relations* 45 (2006), pp. 734–52; Y. Yanadori and J. H. Marler, "Compensation Strategy: Does Business Strategy Influence Compensation in High-Technology Firms?" *Strategic Management Journal* 27 (2006), pp. 559–70; B. Gerhart, "Compensation Strategy and Organizational Performance" in S. L. Rynes and B. Gerhart (eds.), *Compensation in Organizations* (San Francisco: Jossey-Bass, 2000).

73. A. J. Baker, "Stock Options—a Perk That Built Silicon Valley," *The Wall Street Journal*, June 23, 1993, p. A20.

CHAPTER

13

Employee Benefits

LO **LEARNING OBJECTIVES**

After reading this chapter, you should be able to:

LO 13-1 Discuss the growth in benefits costs and the underlying reasons for that growth. *page 559*

LO 13-2 Explain the major provisions of employee benefits programs. *page 561*

LO 13-3 Discuss how employee benefits in the United States compare with those in other countries. *page 571*

LO 13-4 Describe the effects of benefits management on cost and workforce quality. *page 573*

LO 13-5 Explain the importance of effectively communicating the nature and value of benefits to employees. *page 584*

LO 13-6 Describe the regulatory constraints that affect the way employee benefits are designed and administered. *page 588*

ENTER THE WORLD OF BUSINESS

Employers Push Costs for Health on Workers

As health care costs continue their relentless climb, companies are increasingly passing on higher premium costs to workers.

The shift is occurring, policy analysts and others say, as employers feel more pressure from the weak economy and the threat of even more expensive coverage under the new health care law.

In contrast to past practices of absorbing higher prices, some companies chose this year to keep their costs the same by passing the entire increase in premiums for family coverage onto their workers, according to a new survey released on Thursday by the Kaiser Family Foundation, a nonprofit research group.

Workers' share of the cost of a family policy jumped an average of 14%, an increase of about $500 a year. The cost of a policy rose just 3%, to an average of $13,770.

Workers are now paying nearly $4,000 for family coverage, according to the survey, and their costs have increased much faster than those of employers.

Since 2005, while wages have increased just 18%, workers' contributions to premiums have jumped 47%, almost twice as fast as the rise in the policy's overall cost.

Workers also increasingly face higher deductibles, forcing them to pay a larger share of their overall medical bills. "The long-term trend is pretty clear," said Drew E. Altman, the chief executive of the Kaiser Foundation, which conducted the survey this year with the Health Research and Educational Trust, a research organization affiliated with the American Hospital Association. "Insurance is getting stingier and less comprehensive."

Companies may be at a point where they are no longer willing or able to protect their workers' health benefits, said Helen Darling, the president of the National Business Group on Health, an organization representing employers that provide coverage.

She says that companies expect that their costs will only go up more under the new health care law because it requires them to provide more benefits, like coverage for preventive care.

"There's a sense we can't keep up," Ms. Darling said. "We can't afford to continue to subsidize what's happening." Her group's own survey, conducted last month, found that almost two-thirds of employers said they planned to increase the percentage their workers would have to contribute toward premiums next year.

More employers may be changing their view of providing health benefits, moving toward contributing only a fixed amount rather than maintaining certain levels of coverage, she said. "It's a portent of the future," Ms. Darling said.

Some examples around the country offer examples of the choices being made by employers and their workers.

Faced with a potential increase in the premiums paid that would bring the cost of family coverage to about $1,000 a month, the executives at a trucking business in Salt Lake City chose to switch to a plan that had a $6,000 annual deductible.

The company, Utility Trailer Sales of Utah, and a related company were able to reduce their monthly premiums by nearly $200, to $647 a family, according to the chief financial officer, Clair Heslop.

Mr. Heslop acknowledged that people with chronic conditions or the need for expensive medicines had felt the impact of the change. "It's hit them hard," he said. "They're paying the bill because they're consuming the goods."

The Kaiser survey found a significant increase in the number of employees who had a deductible of at least $1,000, to 27% this year, from 22% in 2009. Almost half of workers who are covered by a small employer with fewer than 200 workers have an annual deductible of that amount.

Once employers have a better handle on the new federal health care legislation, they may well pursue different strategies, including moving toward a system in which they are responsible for only a fixed amount of the cost of coverage, said Tracy Watts, a partner with Mercer Health and Benefits, which advises companies about the health benefits they offer. "There's going to be a lot of studying about what are the longer-term strategies, what makes sense," she said.

 # Introduction

If we think of benefits as a part of total employee compensation, many of the concepts discussed in the two previous chapters on employee compensation apply here as well. This means, for example, that both cost and behavioral objectives are important. The cost of benefits adds an average of 43% to every dollar of payroll, thus accounting for about 30% of the total employee compensation package. Controlling labor costs is not possible without controlling benefits costs. On the behavioral side, benefits seem to influence whether potential employees come to work for a company, whether they stay, when they retire—perhaps even how they perform (although the empirical evidence, especially on the latter point, is surprisingly limited).[1] Different employees look for different types of benefits. Employers need to regularly reexamine their benefits to see whether they fit the needs of today rather than yesterday. The chapter-opening story also makes clear that employers are increasingly focused on cost control, passing health care cost increases onto employees through higher premiums and deductibles.

Although it makes sense to think of benefits as part of total compensation, benefits have unique aspects. First, there is the question of legal compliance. Although direct compensation is subject to government regulation, the scope and impact of regulation on benefits is far greater. Some benefits, such as Social Security, are mandated by law. Others, although not mandated, are subject to significant regulation or must meet certain criteria to achieve the most favorable tax treatment; these include pensions and savings plans. The heavy involvement of government in benefits decisions reflects the central role benefits play in maintaining economic security.

A second unique aspect of benefits is that organizations so typically offer them that they have come to be institutionalized. Providing medical and retirement benefits of some sort remains almost obligatory for many (e.g., large) employers. A large employer that did not offer such benefits to its full-time employees would be highly unusual, and the employer might well have trouble attracting and retaining a quality workforce.

A third unique aspect of benefits, compared with other forms of compensation, is their complexity. It is relatively easy to understand the value of a dollar as part of a salary, but not as part of a benefits package. The advantages and disadvantages of different types of medical coverage, pension provisions, disability insurance, and investment options for retirement funds are often difficult to grasp, and their value (beyond a general sense that they are good to have) is rarely as clear as the value of one's salary. Most fundamentally, employees may not even be aware of the benefits available to them; and if they are aware, they may not understand how to use them. When employers spend large sums of money on benefits but employees do not understand the benefits or attach much value to them, the return on employers' benefits investment will be fairly dismal.[2] Thus, one reason for giving more responsibility to employees for retirement planning and other benefits is to increase their understanding of the value of such benefits. As the chapter opening indicates, however, there is a risk to this approach.

Reasons for Benefits Growth

In thinking about benefits as part of total compensation, a basic question arises: why do employers choose to channel a significant portion of the compensation dollar away from cash (wages and salaries) into benefits? Economic theory tells us that people prefer a dollar in cash over a dollar's worth of any specific commodity because the cash can be used to purchase the commodity or something else.[3] Thus, cash is less restrictive. Several factors, however, have contributed to less emphasis on cash and more on benefits in compensation. To understand these factors, it is useful to examine the growth in benefits over time and the underlying reasons for that growth.

LO 13-1
Discuss the growth in benefits costs and the underlying reasons for that growth.

Figure 13.1 gives an indication of the overall growth in benefits. Note that in 1929, on the eve of the Great Depression, benefits added an average of only 3% to every dollar of payroll. By 1955 this figure had grown to 17%, and it has continued to grow, now accounting for about 43 cents on top of every payroll dollar.

figure 13.1

Growth of Employee Benefits, Percentage of Wages and Salaries and of Total Compensation, 1929–2011

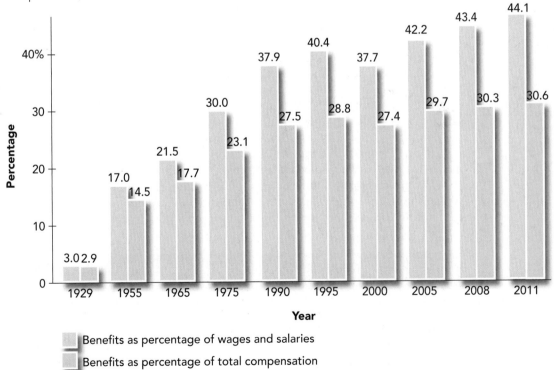

SOURCES: Data through 1990, U.S. Chamber of Commerce Research Center, *Employee Benefits 1990, Employee Benefits 1997, Employee Benefits 2000* (Washington, DC: U.S. Chamber of Commerce, 1991, 1997, and 2000). Data from 1995 onward, "Employer Cost for Employee Compensation," www.bls.gov.

Many factors contributed to this tremendous growth.[4] First, during the 1930s several laws were passed as part of Franklin Roosevelt's New Deal, a legislative program aimed at buffering people from the devastating effects of the Great Depression. The Social Security Act and other legislation established legally required benefits (such as the Social Security retirement system) and modified the tax structure in such a way as to effectively make other benefits—such as workers' compensation (for work-related injuries) and unemployment insurance—mandatory. Second, wage and price controls instituted during World War II, combined with labor market shortages, forced employers to think of new ways to attract and retain employees. Because benefits were not covered by wage controls, employers channeled more resources in this direction. Once institutionalized, such benefits tended to remain even after wage and price controls were lifted.

Third, the tax treatment of benefits programs is often more favorable for employees than the tax treatment of wages and salaries, meaning that a dollar spent on benefits has the potential to generate more value for the employees than the same dollar spent

Marginal Tax Rate
The percentage of an additional dollar of earnings that goes to taxes.

on wages and salaries. The **marginal tax rate** is the percentage of additional earnings that goes to taxes. Consider the hypothetical employee in Table 13.1 and the effect on take-home pay of a $1,000 increase in salary. The total effective marginal tax rate is higher for higher-paid employees and also varies according to state and city. (New York State and New York City are among the highest.) A $1,000 annual raise for the employee earning $50,000 per year would increase net pay $594.50 ($1,000 × [1 − 0.4055]). In contrast, an extra $1,000 put into benefits would lead to an increase of $1,000 in "take-home benefits."

Employers, too, realize tax advantages from certain types of benefits. Although both cash compensation and most benefits are deductible as operating expenses, employers (like employees) pay Social Security tax on salaries below a certain amount ($106,800 in 2011) and Medicare tax on the entire salary, as well as other taxes like workers' compensation and unemployment compensation. However, no such taxes are paid on most employee benefits. The bottom line is that the employer may be able to provide more value to employees by spending the extra $1,000 on benefits instead of salary.

The tax advantage of benefits also takes another form. Deferring compensation until retirement allows the employee to receive cash, but at a time (retirement) when the employee's tax rate is sometimes lower because of a lower income level. More important, perhaps, is that investment returns on the deferred money typically accumulate tax free, resulting in much faster growth of the investment.

A fourth factor that has influenced benefits growth is the cost advantage that groups typically realize over individuals. Organizations that represent large groups of employees can purchase insurance (or self-insure) at a lower rate because of economies of scale,

table 13.1

Example of Marginal Tax Rates for an Employee Salary of $50,000

	NOMINAL TAX RATE	EFFECTIVE TAX RATE
Federal	25.0%	25.0%
State (New York)	6.8	5.1
City (New York)	3.7	2.8
Social Security	6.2	6.2
Medicare	1.45	1.45
Total tax rate		40.55

Note: State and city taxes are deductible on the federal tax return, reducing their effective tax rate.

20 days of free backup care for 3- to 6-month-olds	Goldman Sachs
Paid week off for new grandparents	MBNA
Pregnant employees can take a paid month off before their due date	Eli Lilly
Use of the company plane for family emergencies	BE&K
Dinner with the president and CEO after 10 years	Cerner
A free stay at any company-run hotel	Four Seasons
Pet insurance	Timberland
$4 on-site haircuts	Worthington Industries
$10,000 total benefit for infertility treatments and adoption aid	CMP Media
10 paid hours a month for volunteer work	Fannie Mae
35 extra vacation days on 10th year and every fifth year after	Moog
1,200-acre camping and recreational area for employee use	Steelcase
Life Cycle account of $10,000 to help employees cross major thresholds such as buying first house or paying tuition	Xerox

table 13.2

Differentiating via Benefits

SOURCE: Brian Ballou and Norman H. Goodwin, "Quality of Work Life," *Strategic Finance*, October 2007, pp. 40–48.

which spread fixed costs over more employees to reduce the cost per person. Insurance risks can be more easily pooled in large groups, and large groups can also achieve greater bargaining power in dealing with insurance carriers or medical providers.

A fifth factor influencing the growth of benefits was the growth of organized labor from the 1930s through the 1950s. This growth was partly a result of another piece of New Deal legislation, the National Labor Relations Act, which greatly enhanced trade unions' ability to organize workers and negotiate contracts with employers. Benefits were often a key negotiation objective. (Indeed, they still are. Benefits issues continue to be a common reason for work stoppages.) Unions were able to successfully pursue their members' interests in benefits, particularly when tax advantages provided an incentive for employers to shift money from cash to benefits. For unions, a new benefit such as medical coverage was a tangible success that could have more impact on prospective union members than a wage increase of equivalent value, which might have amounted to only a cent or two per hour. Also, many nonunion employers responded to the threat of unionization by implementing the same benefits for their own employees, thus contributing to benefits growth.

Finally, employers may also provide unique benefits as a means of differentiating themselves in the eyes of current or prospective employees. In this way, employers communicate key aspects of their culture that set them apart from the rest of the pack. Table 13.2 shows some examples.

Benefits Programs

Most benefits fall into one of the following categories: social insurance, private group insurance, retirement, pay for time not worked, and family-friendly policies.[5] Table 13.3, based on Bureau of Labor Statistics (BLS) data, provides an overview of

LO 13-2

Explain the major provisions of employee benefits programs.

table 13.3

Percentage of Full-Time Workers in U.S. Private Sector with Access to Selected Benefits Programs, by Establishment Size, 2010

	ESTABLISHMENTS HAVING 100 WORKERS OR MORE	ESTABLISHMENTS HAVING LESS THAN 100 WORKERS
Medical care	86%	60%
Dental care	50[a]	24[a]
Short-term disability insurance	52[a]	25[a]
Long-term disability insurance	42[a]	18[a]
All retirement	84	52
Defined benefit pension	35[b]	9[b]
Defined contribution plan	71[b]	42[b]
Life insurance	78	44
Paid leave		
Sickness	78	54
Vacation	78	70
Personal	53	27

[a] 2006.
[b] 2008.
SOURCE: www.bls.gov.

the prevalence of specific benefits programs. As Table 13.3 shows, the percentage of employees covered by these benefits programs increases with establishment size. Among the largest employers, these percentages would be higher still. Likewise, as shown in Table 13.4, benefits (and total compensation) costs also increase with establishment size.

SOCIAL INSURANCE (LEGALLY REQUIRED)

Social Security

Among the most important provisions of the Social Security Act of 1935 was the establishment of old-age insurance and unemployment insurance. The act was later amended to add survivor's insurance (1939), disability insurance (1956), hospital insurance (Medicare Part A, 1965), and supplementary medical insurance (Medicare Part B, 1965) for the elderly. Together these provisions constitute the federal Old Age, Survivors, Disability, and Health Insurance (OASDHI) program. More than 90% of U.S. employees are covered by the program, the main exceptions being

table 13.4

Total Hourly Compensation and Benefits Costs, U.S. Private Sector, by Establishment Size, 2011

		ESTABLISHMENT SIZE	
	ALL	1–99 EMPLOYEES	500 OR MORE EMPLOYEES
Total compensation	$30.07	$23.21	$40.53
Wages and salaries	20.91	17.17	26.83
Benefits	9.15	6.04	13.70

SOURCE: www.bls.gov.

railroad and federal, state, and local government employees, who often have their own plans. Note, however, that an individual employee must meet certain eligibility requirements to receive benefits. To be fully insured typically requires 40 quarters of covered employment and minimum earnings of $1,120 per quarter in 2011. However, the eligibility rules for survivors' and disability benefits are somewhat different.

Social Security retirement (old-age insurance) benefits for fully insured workers begin at age 65 years and 6 months (full benefits) or age 62 (at a permanent reduction in benefits) for those born in 1940. The full retirement age now rises with birth year, reaching age 67 for those born in 1960 or later. Although the amount of the benefit depends on one's earnings history, benefits go up very little after a certain level (the maximum monthly benefit at full retirement age in 2011 was $2,366); thus high earners help subsidize benefit payments to low earners. Cost-of-living increases are provided each year that the consumer price index increases.

An important attribute of the Social Security retirement benefit is that it is free from state tax in about half of the states and entirely free from federal tax. However, the federal tax code has an earnings test for those who are still earning wages (and not yet at full retirement age). In 2011, beneficiaries between age 62 and the full retirement age were allowed to make $14,160; in the year an individual reaches full retirement age, the earnings test is $37,680. If these amounts are exceeded, the Social Security benefit is reduced $1 for every $2 in excess earnings for those under the full retirement age and $1 for every $3 in the year a worker reaches the full retirement age. These provisions are important because of their effects on the work decisions of those between 62 and full retirement age. The earnings test increases a person's incentive to retire (otherwise full Social Security benefits are not received), and if she continues to work, the incentive to work part-time rather than full-time increases.

A major change made in January 2000 is that there is no earnings test once full retirement age is reached. Therefore, these workers no longer incur any earnings penalty (and thus have no tax-related work disincentive).

How are retirement and other benefits financed? Both employers and employees are assessed a payroll tax of 7.65% (a total of 15.3%) on the first $110,100 of the employee's earnings. Of the 7.65%, 6.2% funds OASDHI and 1.45% funds Medicare (Part A). In addition, the 1.45% Medicare tax is assessed on all earnings. For 2011 only, the employee 6.2% OASDHI tax is reduced to 4.2%.

What are the behavioral consequences of Social Security benefits? Because they are legally mandated, employers do not have discretion in designing this aspect of their benefits programs. However, Social Security does affect employees' retirement decisions. The eligibility age for benefits and any tax penalty for earnings influence retirement decisions. The elimination of the tax penalty on earnings for those at full retirement age should mean a larger pool of older workers in the labor force for employers to tap into.

Unemployment Insurance

Established by the 1935 Social Security Act, this program has four major objectives: (1) to offset lost income during involuntary unemployment, (2) to help unemployed workers find new jobs, (3) to provide an incentive for employers to stabilize employment, and (4) to preserve investments in worker skills by providing income during short-term layoffs (which allows workers to return to their employer rather than start over with another employer).

The unemployment insurance program is financed largely through federal and state taxes on employers. Although, strictly speaking, the decision to establish the program is left to each state, the Social Security Act created a tax incentive structure that quickly led every state to establish a program. The federal tax rate is currently 0.8% on the first $7,000 of wages. The state tax rate varies, the minimum being 5.4% on the first $7,000 of wages. Many states have a higher rate or impose the tax on a greater share of earnings. As a percent of total wages, the average tax rate paid by employers ranges from 0.1% in Virginia to 1.5% in Arkansas.[6]

A very important feature of the unemployment insurance program is that no state imposes the same tax on every employer. Instead, the size of the tax depends on the employer's experience rating. Employers that have a history of laying off a large share of their workforces pay higher taxes than those who do not. In some states, an employer that has had very few layoffs may pay no state tax. In contrast, an employer with a poor experience rating could pay a tax as high as 5% to 10%, depending on the state.[7]

Unemployed workers are eligible for benefits if they (1) have a prior attachment to the workforce (often 52 weeks or four quarters of work at a minimum level of pay); (2) are available for work; (3) are actively seeking work (including registering at the local unemployment office); and (4) were not discharged for cause (such as willful misconduct), did not quit voluntarily, and are not out of work because of a labor dispute.

Benefits also vary by state, but they are typically about 50% of a person's earnings and last for 26 weeks. Extended benefits for up to 13 weeks are also available in states with a sustained unemployment rate above 6.5%. Emergency extended benefits are also sometimes funded by Congress. All states have minimum and maximum weekly benefit levels. In contrast to Social Security retirement benefits, unemployment benefits are taxed as ordinary income.

Because unemployment insurance is, in effect, legally required, management's discretion is limited here, too. Management's main task is to keep its experience rating low by avoiding unnecessary workforce reductions (e.g., by relying, on the sorts of actions described in Chapter 5).

Workers' Compensation

Workers' compensation laws cover job-related injuries and death.[8] Prior to enactment of these laws, workers suffering work-related injuries or diseases could receive compensation only by suing for damages. Moreover, the common-law defenses available to employers meant that such lawsuits were not usually successful. In contrast, these laws operate under a principle of no-fault liability, meaning that an employee does not need to establish gross negligence by the employer. In return, employers receive immunity from lawsuits. (One exception is the employer who intentionally contributes to a dangerous workplace.) Employees are not covered when injuries are self-inflicted or stem from intoxication or "willful disregard of safety rules."[9] Approximately 90% of all U.S. workers are covered by state workers' compensation laws, although again there are differences among states, with coverage ranging from 70% to more than 95%.

Workers' compensation benefits fall into four major categories: (1) disability income, (2) medical care, (3) death benefits, and (4) rehabilitative services.

Disability income is typically two-thirds of predisability earnings, although each state has its own minimum and maximum. In contrast to unemployment insurance benefits, disability benefits are tax free. The system is financed differently by different states, some having a single state fund, most allowing employers to purchase coverage from private insurance companies. Self-funding by employers is also permitted in most states. The cost to the employer is based on three factors. The first factor is the nature of the occupations and the risk attached to each. Premiums for low-risk occupations may be less than 1% of payroll; the cost for some of the most hazardous occupations may be as high as 100% of payroll. The second factor is the state where work is located. For example, the loss of a leg may be worth $264,040 in Pennsylvania versus $67,860 in Colorado.[10] The third factor is the employer's experience rating.

The experience rating system again provides an incentive for employers to make their workplaces safer. Dramatic injuries (like losing a finger or hand) are less prevalent than minor ones, such as sprains and strains. Back strain is the most expensive benign health condition in developed countries. Each year in the United States, 3 to 4% of the population is temporarily disabled and 1% is permanently and totally disabled.[11] Many actions can be taken to reduce workplace injuries, such as work redesign and training, and to speed the return to health, and thus to work (e.g., exercise).[12] Some changes can be fairly simple (such as permitting workers to sit instead of having them bend over). It is also important to hold managers accountable (in their performance evaluations) for making workplaces safer and getting employees back to work promptly following an injury. With the passage of the Americans with Disabilities Act, employers came under even greater pressure to deal effectively and fairly with workplace injuries. See the discussion in Chapter 3 on safety awareness programs for some of the ways employers and employees are striving to make the workplace safer.

PRIVATE GROUP INSURANCE

As we noted earlier, group insurance rates are typically lower than individual rates because of economies of scale, the ability to pool risks, and the greater bargaining power of a group. This cost advantage, together with tax considerations and a concern for employee security, helps explain the prevalence of employer-sponsored insurance plans. We discuss two major types: medical insurance and disability insurance. Note that these programs are not legally required; rather, they are offered at the discretion of employers.

Medical Insurance

Not surprisingly, public opinion surveys indicate that medical benefits are by far the most important benefit to the average person.[13] As Table 13.3 indicates, most full-time employees in medium-size and large companies get such benefits. Three basic types of medical expenses are typically covered: hospital expenses, surgical expenses, and physicians' visits. Other benefits that employers may offer include dental care, vision care, birthing centers, and prescription drug programs. Perhaps the most important issue in benefits management is the challenge of providing quality medical benefits while controlling costs, a subject we return to in a later section.

The **Consolidated Omnibus Budget Reconciliation Act (COBRA)** of 1985 requires employers to permit employees to extend their health insurance coverage at group rates for up to 36 months following a "qualifying event" such as termination (except for gross misconduct), a reduction in hours that leads to the loss of health insurance, death, and other events. The beneficiary (whether the employee, spouse, or dependent) must have access to the same services as employees who have not lost their health insurance. Note that the beneficiaries do not get free coverage. Rather, they receive the advantage of purchasing coverage at the employer rather than the individual rate.

Consolidated Omnibus Budget Reconciliation Act (COBRA)
The 1985 act that requires employers to permit employees to extend their health insurance coverage at group rates for up to 36 months following a qualifying event, such as a layoff.

Disability Insurance

Two basic types of disability coverage exist.[14] As Table 13.3 indicates, 25% to 52% of employees are covered by short-term disability plans and 18% to 42% are covered by long-term disability plans. Short-term plans typically provide benefits for six months or less, at which point long-term plans take over, potentially covering the person for life. The salary replacement rate is typically between 50% and 70%, although short-term plans are sometimes higher. There are often caps on the amount that can be paid each month. Federal income taxation of disability benefits depends on the funding method. Where employee contributions completely fund the plan, there is no federal tax. Benefits based on employer contributions are taxed. Finally, disability benefits, especially long-term ones, need to be coordinated with other programs, such as Social Security disability benefits.

RETIREMENT

Earlier we discussed the old-age insurance part of Social Security, a legally required source of retirement income. Although this remains the largest single component of the elderly's overall retirement income (39%), the combination of private pensions (18%) and earnings from assets (savings and other investments like stock) account for an even larger share (16%). The remainder of the elderly's income comes from earnings (24%) and other sources (3%).[15]

Employers have no legal obligation to offer private retirement plans, but many do. As we note later, if a private retirement plan is provided, it must meet certain standards set forth by the Employee Retirement Income Security Act.

Pension Benefit Guaranty Corporation (PBGC)
The agency that guarantees to pay employees a basic retirement benefit in the event that financial difficulties force a company to terminate or reduce employee pension benefits.

Employee Retirement Income Security Act (ERISA)
The 1974 act that increased the fiduciary responsibilities of pension plan trustees, established vesting rights and portability provisions, and established the Pension Benefit Guaranty Corporation (PBGC).

Defined Benefit

A *defined benefit plan* guarantees ("defines") a specified retirement benefit level to employees based typically on a combination of years of service and age as well as on the employee's earnings level (usually the five highest earnings years). For instance, an organization might guarantee a monthly pension payment of $1,500 to an employee retiring at age 65 with 30 years of service and an average salary over the final 5 years of $40,000. As Table 13.3 indicates, full-time employees in 35% of larger companies and 9% in smaller companies are covered by such plans. (As recently as the mid-1990s 50% of larger companies and 15% of smaller companies had such plans.) The replacement ratio (pension payment/final salary) ranges from about 21% for a worker aged 55 with 30 years of service who earned $35,000 in her last year to about 36% for a 65-year-old worker with 40 years of service who earned the same amount. With Social Security added in, the ratio for the 65-year-old worker increases to about 77%.[16]

Defined benefit plans insulate employees from investment risk, which is borne by the company. In the event of severe financial difficulties that force the company to terminate or reduce employee pension benefits, the **Pension Benefit Guaranty Corporation (PBGC)** provides some protection of benefits. Established by the **Employee Retirement Income Security Act (ERISA)** of 1974, the PBGC guarantees a basic benefit, not necessarily complete pension benefit replacement, for employees who were eligible for pensions at the time of termination. It insures the retirement benefits of 45 million workers in more than 27,000 plans and currently is responsible for the current and future pensions of more than 1.4 million people.[17] The maximum annual benefit is limited to the lesser of an employee's annual gross income during a PBGC-defined period or $54,000 for plans terminated in 2011. Thus, higher-paid employees, who would have received higher pensions under the company plan, can experience major cuts in pensions if the PBGC must take over the plan. Payouts are not adjusted for cost-of-living changes. The PBGC is funded by an annual contribution of $35 per (single-employer) plan participant, plus an additional variable rate premium for underfunded plans.[18] Note that the PBGC does not guarantee health care benefits.

Defined Contribution

Unlike defined benefit plans, *defined contribution plans* do not promise a specific benefit level for employees upon retirement. Rather, an individual account is set up for each employee with a guaranteed size of contribution. The advantage of such plans for employers is that they shift investment risk to employees and present fewer administrative challenges because there is no need to calculate payments based on age and service and no need to make payments to the PBGC. As Table 13.3 indicates, defined contribution plans are especially preferred in smaller companies, perhaps because of small employers' desire to avoid long-term obligations or perhaps because small companies tend to be younger, often being founded since the trend toward defined contribution plans. Some companies have both defined benefit and defined contribution plans.

There is a wide variety of defined contribution plans, a few of which are briefly described here. One of the simplest is a money purchase plan, under which an employer specifies a level of annual contribution (such as 10% of salary). At retirement age, the employee is entitled to the contributions plus the investment returns. The term "money purchase" stems from the fact that employees often use the money to purchase an annuity rather than taking it as a lump sum. Profit sharing plans and employee stock ownership plans are also often used as retirement vehicles. Both permit contributions (cash and stock, respectively) to vary from year to year, thus allowing employers to avoid fixed obligations that may be burdensome in difficult financial times. Section 401(k) plans (named after the tax code section) permit employees to defer compensation on a pretax basis. Annual contributions in 2011 are limited to $16,500.[19] For those age 50 or over, an additional $5,500 per year in catch-up contributions is also permitted. Additionally, many employers match some portion of employee contributions. A final incentive is tax based. For example, based on our earlier Table 13.1, $10,000 contributed to a 401(k) plan would only be worth $(1 - 0.4055) \times \$10,000 = \$5,945$ if taken in salary.

Defined contribution plans continue to grow in importance, while, as we saw earlier, defined benefit plans have become less common. An important implication is that defined contribution plans put the responsibility for wise investing squarely on the shoulders of the employee. These investment decisions will become more critical because 401(k) plans continue to grow rapidly, covering 165 million people in 2007, up from 16 million in 1978.[20] Several factors affect the amount of income that will be available to an employee upon retirement. First, the earlier the age at which investments are made, the longer returns can accumulate. As Figure 13.2 shows, an annual investment of $3,000 made between ages 21 and 29 will be worth much more at age 65 than a similar investment made between ages 31 and 39. Second, different investments have different historical rates of return. Between 1946 and 1990, the average annual return was 11.4% for stocks, 5.1% for bonds, and 5.3% for cash (bank savings accounts).[21] As Figure 13.2 shows, if historical rates of return were to continue, an investment in a mix of 60% stock, 30% bonds, and 10% cash between the ages of 21 and 29 would be worth almost four times as much at age 65 as would the

figure 13.2

The Relationship of
Retirement Savings
to Age When
Savings Begins and
Type of Investment
Portfolio

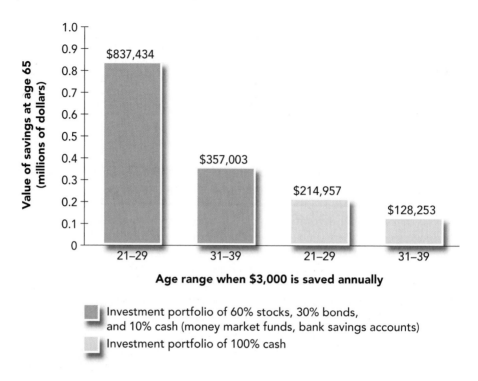

Investment portfolio of 60% stocks, 30% bonds,
and 10% cash (money market funds, bank savings accounts)

Investment portfolio of 100% cash

same amount invested in a bank savings account. A third consideration is the need to counteract investment risk by diversification because stock and bond prices can be volatile in the short run. Although stocks have the greatest historical rate of return, that is no guarantee of future performance, particularly over shorter time periods. (This fact becomes painfully obvious during dramatic drops in stock market values.) Thus some investment advisers recommend a mix of stock, bonds, and cash, as shown in Figure 13.2, to reduce investment risk. Younger investors may wish to have more stock, while those closer to retirement age typically have less stock in their portfolios.

It's also important—indeed, extraordinarily important—not to invest too heavily in any single stock. Some Enron employees had 100% of their 401(k) assets in Enron stock. When the price dropped from $90 to less than $1 in 2001, their retirement money was gone. Risk is further compounded by risk of job loss when one's employer struggles financially. Employees at Bear Stearns, a storied Wall Street firm, also learned the hard way what can happen when you put all your eggs in one basket—company stock. When the stock price fell from its peak of $160 to $2 when Bear was purchased by JP Morgan Chase, the value of employee-owned shares fell from $6.3 billion to $79 million, a loss of 99%. So, repeat after me: *Always* diversify and don't put all your retirement eggs in one basket.[22]

The Pension Protection Act of 2006 requires defined contribution plans holding publicly traded securities to provide employees with (1) the opportunity to divest employer securities and (2) at least three investment options other than employer securities.

Cash Balance Plan
Retirement plan in which the employer sets up an individual account for each employee and contributes a percentage of the employee's salary; the account earns interest at a predefined rate.

Cash Balance Plans

One way to combine the advantages of defined benefit plans and defined contribution plans is to use a **cash balance plan**. This type of retirement plan consists of individual accounts, as in a 401(k) plan. But in contrast to a 401(k), all the contributions come from the employer. Usually, the employer contributes a percentage of the employee's salary, say, 4% or 5%. The money in the cash balance plan earns interest according to a predetermined rate, such as the rate paid on U.S. Treasury bills. Employers guarantee this rate as in a defined benefit plan. This arrangement helps employers plan their contributions and helps employees predict their retirement benefits. If employees change jobs, they generally can roll over the balance into an individual retirement account.

Many organizations have switched from traditional defined benefit plans to cash balance plans. The change, like any major change, requires employers to consider the effects on employees as well as on the organization's bottom line. Defined benefit plans are most generous to older employees with many years of service, and cash balance plans are most generous to young employees who will have many years ahead in which to earn interest. For an organization with many experienced employees, switching from a defined benefit plan can produce great savings in pension benefits. In that case, the older workers are the greatest losers, unless the organization adjusts the program to retain their benefits.

In recent years, however, few if any companies converted their defined benefit plans to cash balance plans because of legal uncertainties. In a closely watched case, IBM was sued for age discrimination after converting its plan in 1999. A district court ruled in 2003 that IBM had discriminated, but this was overturned in 2006 by the Seventh Circuit Court of Appeals. Also, the Pension Protection Act of 2006 seeks to clarify the legal requirements of such plans. As of 2008, all five appelate courts that had reviewed age discrimination–based cases against companies using cash balance plans had rejected the claims. Thus, renewed movement to cash balance plans may occur. IBM, however, announced in 2006 that it would freeze its pension and cash balance plan benefits and instead place greater emphasis on its 401(k) plan.

Funding, Communication, and Vesting Requirements

ERISA does not require organizations to have pension plans, but those that are set up must meet certain requirements. In addition to the termination provisions discussed earlier, plans must meet certain guidelines on management and funding. For example, employers are required to make yearly contributions that are sufficient to cover future obligations. (As noted previously, underfunded plans require higher premiums.) ERISA also specifies a number of reporting and disclosure requirements involving the IRS, the Department of Labor, and employees.[23] Employees, for example, must receive within 90 days after entering a plan a **summary plan description (SPD)** that describes the plan's funding, eligibility requirements, risks, and so forth. Upon request, an employer must also make available to an employee an individual benefit statement, which describes the employee's vested and unvested benefits. Obviously, employers may wish to provide such information on a regular basis anyway as a means of increasing the understanding and value employees attach to their benefits.

ERISA guarantees employees that when they become participants in a pension plan and work a specified minimum number of years, they earn a right to a pension upon retirement. These are referred to as *vesting rights*.[24] Vested employees have the right to their pension at retirement age, regardless of whether they remain with the employer until that time. Employee contributions to their own plans are always completely vested. The vesting of employer-funded pension benefits must take place under one

Summary Plan Description (SPD)
A reporting requirement of the Employee Retirement Income Security Act (ERISA) that obligates employers to describe the plan's funding, eligibility requirements, risks, and so forth within 90 days after an employee has entered the plan.

of two schedules. Employers may choose to vest employees after five years; until that time, employers can provide zero vesting if they choose. Alternatively, employers may vest employees over a three- to seven-year period, with at least 20% vesting in the third year and each year thereafter. These two schedules represent minimum requirements; employers are free to vest employees more quickly. These are the two choices relevant to the majority of employers. However, so-called top-heavy plans, where pension benefits for "key" employees (like highly paid top managers) exceed a certain share of total pension benefits, require faster vesting for nonkey employees. On the other hand, multiemployer pension plans need not provide vesting until after 10 years of employment.

These requirements were put in place to prevent companies from terminating employees before they reach retirement age or before they reach their length-of-service requirements in order to avoid paying pension benefits. It should also be noted that transferring employees or laying them off as a means of avoiding pension obligations is not legal either, even if such actions are motivated partly by business necessity.[25] On the other hand, employers are free to choose whichever of the two vesting schedules is most advantageous. For example, an employer that experiences high quit rates during the fourth and fifth years of employment may choose five-year vesting to minimize pension costs.

The traditional defined benefit pension plan discourages employee turnover or delays it until the employer can recoup the training investment in employees.[26] Even if an employee's pension benefit is vested, it is usually smaller if the employee changes employers, mainly because the size of the benefit depends on earnings in the final years with an employer. Consider an employee who earns $30,000 after 20 years and $60,000 after 40 years.[27] The employer pays an annual retirement benefit equal to 1.5% of final earnings times the number of years of service. If the employee stays with the employer for 40 years, the annual benefit level upon retirement would be $36,000 (0.015 × $60,000 × 40). If, instead, the employee changes employers after 20 years (and has the same earnings progression), the retirement benefit from the first employer would be $9,000 (0.015 × $30,000 × 20). The annual benefit from the second employer would be $18,000 (0.015 × $60,000 × 20). Therefore, staying with one employer for 40 years would yield an annual retirement benefit of $36,000, versus a combined annual retirement benefit of $27,000 ($9,000 + $18,000) if the employee changes employers once. It has also been suggested that pensions are designed to encourage long-service employees, whose earnings growth may eventually exceed their productivity growth, to retire. This is consistent with the fact that retirement benefits reach their maximum at retirement age.[28]

The fact that in recent years many employers have sought to reduce their work-forces through early retirement programs is also consistent with the notion that pensions are used to retain certain employees while encouraging others to leave. One early retirement program approach is to adjust years-of-service credit upward for employees willing to retire, resulting in a higher retirement benefit for them (and less monetary incentive to work). These workforce reductions may also be one indication of a broader trend toward employees becoming less likely to spend their entire careers with a single employer.[29] On one hand, if more mobility across employers becomes necessary or desirable, the current pension system's incentives against (or penalties for) mobility may require modification. On the other hand, perhaps increased employee mobility will reinforce the continued trend toward defined contribution plans [like 401(k)s], which have greater portability (ease of transfer of funds) across employers.[30]

PAY FOR TIME NOT WORKED

At first blush, paid vacation, holidays, sick leave, and so forth may not seem to make economic sense. The employer pays the employee for time not spent working, receiving no tangible production value in return. Therefore, some employers may see little direct advantage. Perhaps for this reason, a minimum number of vacation days (20) is mandated by law in the European Community. As many as 30 days of vacation is not uncommon for relatively new employees in Europe. By contrast, there is no legal minimum in the United States, but 10 days is typical for large companies. U.S. workers must typically be with an employer for 20 to 25 years before they receive as much paid vacation as their western European counterparts.[31]

Sick leave programs often provide full salary replacement for a limited period of time, usually not exceeding 26 weeks. The amount of sick leave is often based on length of service, accumulating with service (one day per month, for example). Sick leave policies need to be carefully structured to avoid providing employees with the wrong incentives. For example, if sick leave days disappear at the end of the year (rather than accumulate), a "use it or lose it" mentality may develop among employees, contributing to greater absenteeism. Organizations have developed a number of measures to counter this.[32] Some allow sick days to accumulate, then pay employees for the number of sick days when they retire or resign. Employers may also attempt to communicate to their employees that accumulated sick leave is better saved to use as a bridge to long-term disability, because the replacement rate (the ratio of sick leave or disability payments to normal salary) for the former is typically higher. Sick leave payments may equal 100% of usual salary, whereas the replacement ratio for long-term disability might be 50%, so the more sick leave accumulated, the longer an employee can avoid dropping to 50% of usual pay when unable to work.

Although vacation and other paid leave programs help attract and retain employees, there is a cost to providing time off with pay, especially in a global economy. The fact that vacation and other paid leave practices differ across countries contributes to the differences in labor costs described in Chapter 11. Consider that, on average, in manufacturing, German workers work 344 fewer hours per year than their U.S. counterparts, who work 1,847 hours per year. (See Figure 13.3.) In other words, German workers are at work approximately 9 fewer weeks per year than their U.S. counterparts. It is perhaps not surprising then that German manufacturers have looked outside Germany for alternative production sites. (However, you might consider what you might do with the equivalent of an extra 9 weeks away from work. Hmm . . .)

FAMILY-FRIENDLY POLICIES

To ease employees' conflicts between work and nonwork, organizations may use *family-friendly policies* such as family leave policies and child care. Although the programs discussed here would seem to be targeted to a particular group of employees, these programs often have "spillover effects" on other employees, who see them as symbolizing a general corporate concern for human resources, thus promoting loyalty even among employee groups that do not use the programs and possibly resulting in improved organizational performance.[33] Evidence suggests that firms using family-friendly policies have better quality management practices overall that are positively associated with organization performance.[34]

Since 1993 the **Family and Medical Leave Act** requires organizations with 50 or more employees within a 75-mile radius to provide as much as 12 weeks of unpaid

LO 13-3
Discuss how employee benefits in the United States compare with those in other countries.

Family and Medical Leave Act
The 1993 act that requires employers with 50 or more employees to provide up to 12 weeks of unpaid leave after childbirth or adoption; to care for a seriously ill child, spouse, or parent; or for an employee's own serious illness.

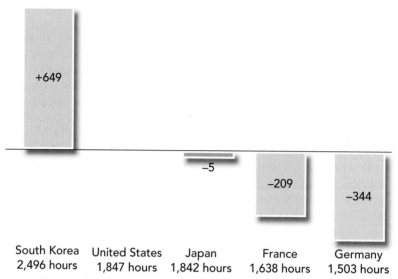

Normal Annual
Hours Worked
Relative to United
States

SOURCE: U.S. Department of Labor, *A Charting of International Labor Comparisons, 2010.* Original data from Organization for Economic Cooperation and Development.

leave after childbirth or adoption; to care for a seriously ill child, spouse, or parent; or for an employee's own serious illness. Employees are guaranteed the same or a comparable job on their return to work. Employees with less than one year of service or who work under 25 hours per week or who are among the 10% highest paid are not covered.

Many employers had already taken steps to deal with this issue, partly to help attract and retain key employees. Less than 10% of American families fit the image of a husband working outside the home and a wife who stays home to take care of the children.[35]

The United States still offers significantly less unpaid leave than most western European countries and Japan. Moreover, paid family leave remains rare in the United States (fewer than 5% are eligible for paid leave, despite some state laws), in even sharper contrast to western Europe and Japan, where it is typically mandated by law.[36] Until the passage of the Americans with Disabilities Act, the only applicable law was the Pregnancy Discrimination Act of 1978, which requires employers that offer disability plans to treat pregnancy as they would any other disability.

Experience with the Family and Medical Leave Act suggests that a majority of those opting for this benefit fail to take the full allotment of time. This is especially the case among female executives. Many of these executives find they do not enjoy maternity leave as much as they expected they would and miss the challenges associated with their careers. Others fear that their careers would be damaged in the long run by missing out on opportunities that might arise while they are out on leave.[37]

Child Care

U.S. companies increasingly provide some form of child care support to their employees. This support comes in several forms that vary in their degree of organizational involvement.[38] The lowest level of involvement, offered by 36% of companies, is when an organization supplies and helps employees collect information about the cost and quality of available child care. At the next level, organizations provide vouchers or discounts for employees to use at existing child care facilities (5% of companies). At the highest level, firms provide child care at or near their worksites (9% of companies). Toyota's Child Development Program provides 24-hours-a-day care for children of workers at its Georgetown, Kentucky, plant. This facility is designed to meet the needs of employees working evening and night shifts who want their children to be on the same schedule. In this facility, the children are kept awake all night. At the end of the night shift, the parents pick up their children and the whole family goes home to bed.[39]

● Toyota employees check in on their kids at the Georgetown location onsite child care.

An organization's decision to staff its own child care facility should not be taken lightly. It is typically a costly venture with important liability concerns. Moreover, the results, in terms of reducing absenteeism and enhancing productivity, are often mixed.[40] One reason for this is that many organizations are "jumping on the day care bandwagon" without giving much thought to the best form of assistance for their specific employees.

As an alternative example, Memphis-based First Tennessee Bank, which was losing 1,500 days of productivity a year because of child care problems, considered creating its own on-site day care center. Before acting, however, the company surveyed its employees. This survey indicated that the only real problem with day care occurred when the parents' regular day care provisions fell through because of sickness on the part of the child or provider. Based on these findings, the bank opted to establish a sick-child care center, which was less costly and smaller in scope than a full-time center and yet still solved the employees' major problem. As a result, absenteeism dropped so dramatically that the program paid for itself in the first nine months of operation.[41]

Managing Benefits: Employer Objectives and Strategies

LO 13-4
Describe the effects of benefits management on cost and workforce quality.

Although the regulatory environment places some important constraints on benefits decisions, employers retain significant discretion and need to evaluate the payoff of such decisions.[42] As discussed earlier, however, this evaluation needs to recognize that employees have come to expect certain things from employers. Employers who do not meet these expectations run the risk of violating what has been called an "implicit contract" between the employer and its workers. If employees believe their employers feel little commitment to their welfare, they can hardly be expected to commit themselves to the company's success.

Clearly, there is much room for progress in the evaluation of benefits decisions.[43] Despite some of the obvious reasons for benefits—group discounts, regulation, and minimizing compensation-related taxes—organizations do not do as well as they could in spelling out what they want their benefits package to achieve and evaluating how well they are succeeding. Research suggests that most organizations do not have written benefits objectives.[44] Obviously, without clear objectives to measure progress, evaluation is difficult (and less likely to occur). Table 13.5 provides an example of one organization's written benefits objectives.

table 13.5

One Company's
Written Benefits
Objectives

- To establish and maintain an employee benefit program that is based primarily on the employees' needs for leisure time and on protection against the risks of old age, loss of health, and loss of life.
- To establish and maintain an employee benefit program that complements the efforts of employees on their own behalf.
- To evaluate the employee benefit plan annually for its effect on employee morale and productivity, giving consideration to turnover, unfilled positions, attendance, employees' complaints, and employees' opinions.
- To compare the employee benefit plan annually with that of other leading companies in the same field and to maintain a benefit plan with an overall level of benefits based on cost per employee that falls within the second quintile of these companies.
- To maintain a level of benefits for nonunion employees that represents the same level of expenditures per employee as for union employees.
- To determine annually the costs of new, changed, and existing programs as percentages of salaries and wages and to maintain these percentages as much as possible.
- To self-fund benefits to the extent that a long-run cost savings can be expected for the firm and catastrophic losses can be avoided.
- To coordinate all benefits with social insurance programs to which the company makes payments.
- To provide benefits on a noncontributory basis except for dependent coverage, for which employees should pay a portion of the cost.
- To maintain continual communications with all employees concerning benefit programs.

SOURCE: *Employee Benefits,* 3rd ed., Burton T. Beam Jr. and John J. McFadden. © 1992 by Dearborn Financial Publishing, Inc. Published by Dearborn Financial Publishing, Inc., Chicago. All rights reserved.

SURVEYS AND BENCHMARKING

As with cash compensation, an important element of benefits management is knowing what the competition is doing. Survey information on benefits packages is available from private consultants, the U.S. Chamber of Commerce, and the Bureau of Labor Statistics (BLS).[45] BLS data of the sort in Table 13.3 and the more detailed information on programs and provisions available from consultants are useful in designing competitive benefits packages. To compete effectively in the product market, cost information is also necessary. A good source is again the BLS, which provides information on benefits costs for specific categories as well as breakdowns by industry, occupation, union status, and organization size. Figure 13.4 shows some of these data for 2011.

COST CONTROL

In thinking about cost control strategies, it is useful to consider several factors. First, the larger the cost of a benefit category, the greater the opportunity for savings. Second, the growth trajectory of the benefit category is also important: even if costs are currently acceptable, the rate of growth may result in serious costs in the future. Third, cost containment efforts can only work to the extent that the employer has significant discretion in choosing how much to spend in a benefit category. Much of the cost of

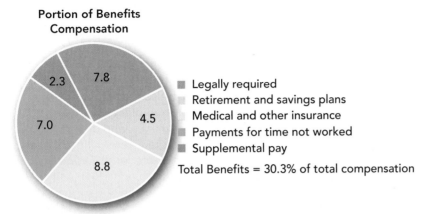

Portion of Benefits Compensation

■ Legally required
■ Retirement and savings plans
■ Medical and other insurance
■ Payments for time not worked
■ Supplemental pay

Total Benefits = 30.3% of total compensation

figure 13.4

Employee Benefits
Cost by Category

SOURCE: "Employer Cost for Employee Compensation," March 2011, www.bls.gov.

legally required benefits (like Social Security) is relatively fixed, which constrains cost reduction efforts. Even with legally required benefits, however, employers can take actions to limit costs because of "experience ratings," which impose higher taxes on employers with high rates of unemployment or workers' compensation claims.

One benefit—medical and other insurance—stands out as a target for cost control for two reasons. Its costs are substantial; they have, except for the 1994 to 1999 period, grown at a significant pace, and this growth is expected to continue. Second, employers have many options for attacking costs and improving quality.

Health Care: Controlling Costs and Improving Quality

As Table 13.6 indicates, the United States spends more on health care than any other country in the world. U.S. health care expenditures have gone from 5.3% of the gross national product ($27 billion) in 1960 to 16% (over $2 trillion) today. Yet the percentage of full-time workers receiving job-related health benefits has declined, with more than 51 million Americans uninsured as of 2009.[46] The United States also trails Japan and western Europe on measures of life expectancy and infant mortality.

	LIFE EXPECTANCY AT BIRTH, FEMALE	INFANT MORTALITY RATE (PER 1,000)	HEALTH EXPENDITURES AS A PERCENTAGE OF GDP
Japan	86	3	8%
Korea	83	4	6
Canada	83	5	10
United Kingdom	82	5	9
France	85	4	11
Germany	83	4	11
Mexico	78	15	6
United States	81	7	16

table 13.6

Health Care Costs
and Outcomes in
Various Countries

SOURCES: Organization for Economic Cooperation and Development, *OECD Health*. Data 2010, www.OECD.org and World Bank, *World Development Report 2011*, www.worldbank.org.

Some Companies Shift Health Costs to Better-Paid

With health care costs climbing even higher during this enrollment season, more employers are adopting a tiered system to pass on the bulk of those costs to their employees by assigning bigger contributions to workers in top salary brackets and offering some relief to workers who make less money.

For years, employees have seen what they pay toward health care go up as companies ask them to contribute more to premiums and deductibles. But now, as people enroll in health plans for the coming year, the sticker shock is more jolting than ever because so many companies are passing on to their workers most, if not all, of the higher costs.

A worker's share of a family policy is approaching $4,000 a year on average, and is most certainly going to keep rising through the next few years. For lower-salaried workers, those costs have only compounded their struggle in a brutal economy.

More and more companies in the last year or so have begun signaling their recognition of the added burden shouldered by workers in low- and middle-income jobs by varying the premiums they pay based on salary.

Vanderbilt University, for instance, has adopted a wage-based benefit program for 2011 under which premiums will remain the same for employees who make $50,000 or less, while everyone else will pay up to $75 more a month. "We're trying to help those lower-paid employees cope with hard economic times," said Jerry Fife, a vice chancellor.

Corporations had absorbed some higher costs in recent years, along with their workers, but have recently passed all, on average, onto employees. In 2010 alone, a worker's share of the cost of a family policy jumped an average of 14% from the previous year, according to a recent survey by the Kaiser Family Foundation. In real money, that is an additional $500 a year deducted from a paycheck.

Across the country, the percentage of workers with coverage in large companies whose premiums vary with their wages climbed to 17% in 2010, up from 14% two years ago. About 20% of employees who are covered by large companies in the Northeast, which has suffered from a combination of high unemployment and steep medical costs, have the premiums they pay tied to their wages, according to Kaiser.

"If health care reform hadn't happened, there would be more companies going in this direction," said Ms. Darling, alluding to the period between the law's passage this year and 2014, when it is expected to take full effect.

Some corporations have gone further than others in trying to spare their lowest-paid workers, even as they increased the cost of premiums for everyone else. This year, for example, employees at Bank of America who make $100,000 or more a year will pay at least 14% more for coverage for 2011.

But workers who make less will actually see their contributions decrease, although their deductibles and co-payments will stay the same. Employees earning less than $50,000 could see as much as a 50% drop in the amount deducted from their paychecks, as compared to 2010. The bank says it is making up the difference.

The concept of tiered plans is not new, with employers that typically offer generous benefits, like universities, being quicker to try it. General Electric, for example, has long divided its workforce into separate tiers to determine how much an employee has to contribute toward insurance coverage.

Some companies may be reluctant to ask certain of their employees to pay more, especially if workers belong to unions that have negotiated a certain level of benefits for all their members.

Other companies could be wary of a system that could be viewed as unfair since salary may not be the best indication of household income. Some low-paid employees whose spouse is a high earner may not need the help, while a single person with a higher salary could. The other concern is not being able to move away from a wage-based benefit structure once it is in place.

For most workers, however, the trend has been very clear: the increase in health care costs has easily outstripped any rise in their incomes. Since 2005, while wages have increased 18%, workers' contributions to premiums have jumped 47%, almost twice as fast as the rise in the policy's overall cost, according to Kaiser.

Companies have also become increasingly creative in the ways they shift costs. Instead of simply raising premiums or increasing the size of the deductible workers must pay

before their coverage kicks in, employers are increasingly asking their workers to pay more of the cost of coverage for their dependents, or to pay more of their share of a hospital stay or an emergency room visit. "Employers do a bit here and do a bit there," said Gary Claxton, a policy expert at Kaiser.

The result is that employees may be paying more, but they may not know how much. Mark Rukavina, the director of the Access Project, an advocacy group, said, "You need multiple spreadsheets to figure this out."

More companies are adopting plan designs that require employees to pay more of their own medical bills under specific circumstances so workers are

increasingly feeling the pinch. Companies "are taking the usual cost–trend reduction measures, but more of them are doing it," said Beth Umland, director of health and benefits research at Mercer, the consulting firm.

This has clouded exactly how much more workers are paying. "Employers have shifted costs for the past 10 years," says Joshua Miley, a principal at HighRoads, a health benefits management consultant. "The confusion allows them to push it further."

Unlike workers in most western European countries, who have nationalized health systems, the majority of Americans receiving health insurance get it through their (or a family member's) employers.[47] Consequently, health insurance, like pensions, discourages employee turnover because not all employers provide health insurance benefits.[48] Not surprisingly, the fact that many Americans receive coverage through their employers has meant that many efforts at controlling costs and increasing quality and coverage have been undertaken by employers. These efforts, broadly referred to as managed care, fall into six major categories: (1) plan design, (2) use of alternative providers, (3) use of alternative funding methods, (4) claims review, (5) education and prevention, and (6) external cost control systems.[49] Examples appear in Table 13.7.

One trend in plan design has been to shift costs to employees through the use of deductibles, coinsurance, exclusions and limitations, and maximum benefits.[50] These costs can be structured such that employees act on incentives to shift to less expensive plans.[51] The "Competing through Sustainability" box indicates that some employers shift more costs to higher-paid employees. Another trend has been to focus on reducing, rather than shifting, costs through such activities as preadmission testing and second surgical opinions. The use of alternative providers like **health maintenance organizations (HMOs)** and **preferred provider organizations (PPOs)** has also increased. HMOs differ from more traditional providers by focusing on preventive care and outpatient treatment, requiring employees to use only HMO services, and providing benefits on a prepaid basis. Many HMOs pay physicians and other health care workers a flat salary instead of using the traditional fee-for-service system, under which a physician's pay may depend on the number of patients seen. Paying on a salary basis is intended to reduce incentives for physicians to schedule more patient visits or medical procedures than might be necessary. (Of course, there is the risk

Health Maintenance Organization (HMO)
A health care plan that provides benefits on a prepaid basis for employees who are required to use only HMO medical service providers.

Preferred Provider Organization (PPO)
A group of health care providers who contract with employers, insurance companies, and so forth to provide health care at a reduced fee.

table 13.7

Ways Employers Use Managed Care to Control Health Care Costs

Plan design
Cost shifting to employees
   Deductibles
   Coinsurance
   Exclusions and limitations
   Maximum benefits
Cost reduction
   Preadmission testing
   Second surgical opinions
   Coordination of benefits
   Alternatives to hospital stays (such as home health care)
Alternative providers
Health maintenance organizations (HMOs)
Preferred provider organizations (PPOs)
Alternative funding methods
Self-funding
Claims review
Health education and preventive care
Wellness programs
Employee assistance programs (EAPs)
Encouragement of external control systems
National Council on Health Planning and Development
Employer coalitions

SOURCE: Adapted from B. T. Beam Jr. and J. J. McFadden, *Employee Benefits,* 3rd ed. (Chicago: Dearborn Financial Publishing, 1992).

that incentives will be reduced too much, resulting in inadequate access to medical procedures and specialists.) PPOs are essentially groups of health care providers that contract with employers, insurance companies, and so forth to provide health care at a reduced fee. They differ from HMOs in that they do not provide benefits on a prepaid basis and employees often are not required to use the preferred providers. Instead, employers may provide incentives for employees to choose, for example, a physician who participates in the plan. In general, PPOs seem to be less expensive than traditional delivery systems but more expensive than HMOs.[52] Another trend in employers' attempts to control costs has been to vary required employee contributions based on the employee's health and risk factors rather than charging each employee the same premium. Indeed, some companies go further, refusing to employ people with risk factors such as smokers. See Exercising strategy at the end of the chapter for more on this issue. Some employers now offer a "Medical tourism" benefit, which means sending patients to other countries where medical procedures can sometimes be done much more cheaply. For example, Hannaford Brothers, a Maine-based grocery chain, will pay for an employee (and significant other) to travel to Singapore for a knee or hip replacement. Doing so saves the company roughly $30,000 to $40,000 and saves the employee about $3,000 in out-of-pocket costs (i.e., the deductible). And, the employee and travel companion get to experience another country.[53]

Employee Wellness Programs. Employee wellness programs (EWPs) focus on changing behaviors both on and off work time that could eventually lead to future health problems. The "Computing through Globalization" box gives an example of how Toyota changed its employee behaviors. EWPs are preventive in nature; they

Is Working for Toyota Really Good for Your Health?

TOKYO—Working for Toyota Motor Corp. might actually make you healthier. Both smoking rates and obesity levels have come down among Toyota employees over the past four years.

Last year, 36% of its Japanese workforce lit up the occasional cigarette, compared with about 42% in 2006. At the same time, the percentage of workers with a body mass index over 24.2—a common measure of obesity—had dropped to 24.7% from 28.5%.

These are just two outtakes from the automaker's recently released 2010 Sustainability Report, which outlines Toyota's latest efforts to be environmentally friendly and socially responsible.

Toyota attributes the health improvements to company campaigns to curb consumption of tobacco and junk food. Toyota pledged to step up the promotion of exercise in the workplace this year.

Indeed, anyone visiting the company's global manufacturing and engineering campus in Toyota City around lunchtime might be forgiven for assuming a marathon race was on. The sidewalks are often crammed with workers doing their daily jog.

SOURCE: From Hans Greimel, "Is Working for Toyota Really Good for Your Health?" *Automotive News*, October 14, 2010. Reprinted with permission, Automotive News. Copyright Crain Communications, May 2011.

attempt to manage health care costs (and workers' compensation costs) by decreasing employees' needs for services. Typically, these programs aim at specific health risks such as high blood pressure, high cholesterol levels, smoking, and obesity. They also try to promote positive health influences such as physical exercise and good nutrition.[54] See the Evidence-Based HR discussion of return on investment for EWPs.

EWPs are either passive or active. Passive programs use little or no outreach to individuals, nor do they provide ongoing support to motivate them to use the resources. Active wellness centers assume that behavior change requires not only awareness and opportunity but support and reinforcement.

One example of a passive wellness program is a health education program. Health education programs have two central goals: raising awareness levels of health-related issues and informing people on health-related topics. In these kinds of programs, a health educator usually conducts classes or lunchtime lectures (or coordinates outside speakers). The program may also have various promotions (like an annual mile run or a "smoke-out") and include a newsletter that reports on current health issues.

Another kind of passive employee wellness program is a fitness facility. In this kind of program, the company sets up a center for physical fitness equipped with aerobic and muscle-building exercise machines and staffed with certified athletic trainers. The facility is publicized within the organization, and employees are free to use it on their own time. Aetna, for example, has created five state-of-the-art health clubs that serve more than 7,500 workers.[55] Northwestern Mutual Life's fitness facilities are open 24 hours a day to its 3,300 employees.[56] Health education classes related to smoking cessation and weight loss may be offered in addition to the facilities. Although fitness facility programs are usually more expensive than health education programs, both are classified as passive because they rely on individual employees to identify their problems and take corrective action.

In contrast, active wellness centers assume that behavior change also requires encouragement and assistance. One kind of active wellness center is the outreach and follow-up model. This type of wellness center contains all the features of a passive

EVIDENCE-BASED HR
What's the Hard Return on Employee Wellness Programs?

The ROI data will surprise you, and the softer evidence may inspire you.

Since 1995, the percentage of Johnson & Johnson employees who smoke has dropped by more than two-thirds.

The number who have high blood pressure or who are physically inactive also has declined—by more than half. That's great, obviously, but should it matter to managers? Well, it turns out that a comprehensive, strategically designed investment in employees' social, mental, and physical health pays off. J&J's leaders estimate that wellness programs have cumulatively saved the company $250 million on health care costs over the past decade; from 2002 to 2008, the return was $2.71 for every dollar spent.

Wellness programs have often been viewed as a nice extra, not a strategic imperative. Newer evidence tells a different story. With tax incentives and grants available under recent federal health care legislation, U.S. companies can use wellness programs to chip away at their enormous health care costs, which are only rising with an aging workforce.

Government incentives or not, healthy employees cost you less. Doctors Richard Milani and Carl Lavie demonstrated that point by studying, at a single employer, a random sample of 185 workers and their spouses. The participants were not heart patients, but they received cardiac rehabilitation and exercise training from an expert team. Of those classified as high risk when the study started (according to body fat, blood pressure, anxiety, and other measures), 57% were converted to low-risk status by the end of the six-month program. Furthermore, medical claim costs had declined by $1,421 per participant, compared with those from the previous year. A control group showed no such improvements. The bottom line: Every dollar invested in the intervention yielded $6 in health care savings.

We've found similar results in our own experience. In 2001 MD Anderson Cancer Center created a workers' compensation and injury care unit within its employee health and well-being department, staffed by a physician and a nurse case manager. Within six years, lost work days declined by 80% and modified-duty days by 64%. Cost savings, calculated by multiplying the reduction in lost work days by average pay rates, totaled $1.5 million; workers' comp insurance premiums declined by 50%.

What's more, healthy employees stay with your company. A study by Towers Watson and the National Business Group on Health shows that organizations with highly effective wellness programs report significantly lower voluntary attrition than do those whose programs have low effectiveness (9% vs. 15%). At the software firm SAS Institute, voluntary turnover is just 4%, thanks in part to such a program; at the Biltmore tourism enterprise, the rate was 9% in 2009, down from 19% in 2005. According to Vicki Banks, Biltmore's director of benefits and compensation, "Employees who participate in our wellness programs do not leave." Nelnet, an education finance firm, asks departing employees in exit interviews what they will miss most. The number one answer: the wellness program.

SOURCE: From Leonard Berry, Ann Mirabito, and William Baun, "What's the Hard Return on Employee Wellness Programs?" *Harvard Business Review*, Dec. 2010, Vol. 88, Issue 12, pp. 104–12.

model, but it also has counselors who handle one-on-one outreach and provide tailored, individualized programs for employees. Typically, tailored programs obtain baseline measures on various indicators (weight, blood pressure, lung capacity, and so on) and measure individuals' progress relative to these indicators over time. The programs set goals and provide small, symbolic rewards to individuals who meet their goals.

This encouragement needs to be particularly targeted to employees in high-risk categories (like those who smoke, are overweight, or have high blood pressure) for two reasons. First, a small percentage of employees create a disproportionate amount of health care costs; therefore, targeted interventions are more efficient. Second, research shows that those in high-risk categories are the most likely to perceive barriers (like family problems or work overload)[57] to participating in company-sponsored fitness programs. Thus untargeted interventions are likely to miss the people that most need to be included.

Research on these different types of wellness centers leads to several conclusions.[58] First, the costs of health education programs are significantly less than those associated with either fitness facility programs or the follow-up model. Second, as indicated in Figure 13.5, all three models are effective in reducing the risk factors associated with cardiovascular disease (obesity, high blood pressure, smoking, and lack of exercise). However, the follow-up model is significantly better than the other two in reducing the risk factors.

Whether the added cost of follow-up programs compared with health education programs is warranted is a judgment that only employers, employees, and unions can make. However, employers like Sony and Quaker Oats believe that incentives are worth the extra cost, and their employees can receive up to several hundred dollars

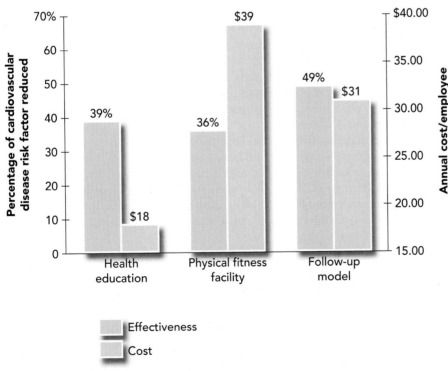

figure 13.5

The Cost and Effectiveness of Three Different Types of Employee Wellness Designs

SOURCE: J. C. Erfurt, A. Foote, and M. A. Heirich, "The Cost Effectiveness of Worksite Wellness Programs for Hypertension Control, Weight Loss, Smoking Cessation and Exercise," *Personnel Psychology* 45 (1992), pp. 5–27. Used with permission.

for reducing their risk factors. There appears to be no such ambiguity associated with the fitness facility model, however. This type of wellness center costs as much or more than the follow-up model but is only as effective as the health education model. Providing a fitness facility that does not include systematic outreach and routine long-term follow-up to assist people with risk factors is not cost-effective in reducing health risks. "Attendants may sit in the fitness center like the 'Maytag repairman' waiting for people to come."[59]

Health Care Costs and Quality: Ongoing Challenges. In 2010, the average annual premium for family coverage was $13,770, with employers paying $9,773 (71%) and employees paying $3,997 (29%) on average.[60] (These numbers pertain only to employers that provide health care benefits.) Premiums for employer-sponsored health care (family coverage) grew by 14.4% in 2010, and since 2000, premium costs have increased 147%. Thus, control of health care costs is an ongoing challenge.

Two important phenomena are often encountered in cost control efforts. First, piecemeal programs may not work well because steps to control one aspect (such as medical cost shifting) may lead employees to "migrate" to other programs that provide medical treatment at no cost to them (like workers' compensation). Second, there is often a so-called Pareto group, which refers to a small percentage (perhaps 20%) of employees being responsible for generating the majority (often 60% to 80%) of health care costs. Obviously, cost control efforts will be more successful to the extent that the costs generated by the Pareto group can be identified and managed effectively.[61]

Although cost control will continue to require a good deal of attention, there is a growing emphasis on monitoring health care quality, which has been described as "the next battlefield." A major focus is on identifying best medical practices by measuring and monitoring the relative success of alternative treatment strategies using large-scale databases and research.[62] In addition, employers increasingly cooperate with one another to develop "report cards" on health care provider organizations to facilitate better choices by their employers and to receive improved health care. General Motors, Ford, and Chrysler, for example, have developed this type of system and made it web-accessible.[63]

In addition, several companies, including Intel, Walmart, and British Petroleum, have announced a plan to provide digital health records to their employees. By doing so, they hope that costs will be reduced and better care delivered by providing consumers, hospitals, doctors, and pharmacies accurate and accessible data.[64]

Finally, the recently passed Patient Protection and Affordable Care Act (PPACA) will have a major impact on employer cost control efforts. For example, employers must now allow children to stay on parents' plans through age 26. Beginning in 2014, employers must offer health care coverage to full-time employees or else pay a penalty. Beginning in 2018, employers having health plan premium costs above a certain level will have to pay an excise tax.[65]

Staffing Responses to Control Benefits Cost Growth

Employers may change staffing practices to control benefits costs. First, because benefits costs are fixed (in that they do not usually go up with hours worked), the benefits cost per hour can be reduced by having employees work more hours. However, there are drawbacks to having employees work more hours. The Fair Labor Standards Act (FLSA), introduced in Chapter 11, requires that nonexempt employees be paid time-and-a-half for hours in excess of 40 per week. Yet the decline in U.S. work hours tapered off in the late 1940s; work hours have actually gone up since then. It is estimated that Americans were working the equivalent of one month longer in 1987 than they were in 1969, and these higher levels have continued.[66] Increased benefits were identified as one of the major reasons for this.

A second possible effect of FLSA regulations (although this is more speculative) is that organizations will try to have their employees classified as exempt whenever possible (although such attempts may run afoul of FLSA law). The growth in the number of salaried workers (many of whom are exempt) may also reflect an effort by organizations to limit the benefits cost per hour without having to pay overtime. A third potential effect is the growth in part-time employment and the use of temporary workers, which may be a response to rising benefits costs. Part-time workers are less likely to receive benefits than full-time workers although labor market shortages in recent years have reduced this difference.[67] Benefits for temporary workers are also usually quite limited.

Third, employers may be more likely to classify workers as independent contractors rather than employees, which eliminates the employer's obligation to provide legally required employee benefits. However, the Internal Revenue Service (IRS) scrutinizes such decisions carefully, as Microsoft and other companies have discovered. Microsoft was compelled to reclassify a group of workers as employees (rather than as independent contractors) and to grant them retroactive benefits. The IRS looks at several factors, including the permanency of the relationship between employer and worker, how much control the employer exercises in directing the worker, and whether the worker offers services to only that employer. Permanency, control, and dealing with a single employer are viewed by the IRS as suggestive of an employment relationship.

NATURE OF THE WORKFORCE

Although general considerations such as cost control and "protection against the risks of old age, loss of health, and loss of life" (see Table 13.5) are important, employers must also consider the specific demographic composition and preferences of their current workforces in designing their benefits packages.

At a broad level, basic demographic factors such as age and sex can have important consequences for the types of benefits employees want. For example, an older workforce is more likely to be concerned about (and use) medical coverage, life insurance, and pensions. A workforce with a high percentage of women of childbearing age may care more about disability leave. Young, unmarried men and women often have less interest in benefits generally, preferring higher wages and salaries.

Although some general conclusions about employee preferences can be drawn based on demographics, more finely tuned assessments of employee benefit preferences need to be done. One approach is to use marketing research methods to assess employees' preferences the same way consumers' demands for products and services are assessed.[68] Methods include personal interviews, focus groups, and questionnaires. Relevant questions might include

- What benefits are most important to you?
- If you could choose one new benefit, what would it be?
- If you were given x dollars for benefits, how would you spend it?

As with surveys generally, care must be taken not to raise employee expectations regarding future changes. If the employer is not prepared to act on the employees' input, surveying may do more harm than good.

The preceding discussion may imply that the current makeup of the workforce is a given, but this is not the case. As discussed earlier, the benefits package may influence the composition of the workforce. For example, a benefits package that has strong medical benefits and pensions may be particularly attractive to older people or those with families. An attractive pension plan may be a way to attract workers who wish to make a long-term commitment to an organization. Where turnover costs are high, this type of strategy may have some appeal. On the other hand, a company that has very lucrative health care benefits may attract and retain people with high health care costs. Sick leave provisions may also affect the composition of the workforce. Organizations need to think about the signals their benefits packages send and the implications of these signals for workforce composition. In this vein, Table 13.8 shows the benefits used by Google, a company that has twice topped *Fortune*'s list of "100 Best Companies to Work For," to attract and retain its desired workforce.

COMMUNICATING WITH EMPLOYEES

LO 13-5
Explain the importance of effectively communicating the nature and value of benefits to employees.

Effective communication of benefits information to employees is critical if employers are to realize sufficient returns on their benefits investments. Research makes it clear that current employees and job applicants often have a very poor idea of what benefits provisions are already in place and the cost or market value of those benefits. One study asked employees to estimate both the amount contributed by the employer to their medical insurance and what it would cost the employees to provide their own health insurance. Table 13.9 shows that employees significantly underestimated both the cost and market value of their medical benefits. In the case of family coverage, employees estimated that the employer contributed $24, only 38% of the employer's actual contribution. This employer was receiving a very poor return on its benefits investment: $0.38 for every $1.00 spent.[69] As we saw earlier, the average employer today providing health care benefits spends $9,325 per year for family coverage. One wonders whether today's employees are any more aware of this fact.

table 13.8

Employee Benefits at Google

- Up to $8,000/year in tuition reimbursement
- On-site perks include medical and dental facilities; oil change and bike repair; valet parking; free washers and dryers; and free breakfast, lunch, and dinner on a daily basis at 11 gourmet restaurants
- Unlimited sick leave
- 27 days of paid time off after one year of employment
- Global Education Leave program enables employees to take a leave of absence to pursue further education for up to 5 years and $150,000 in reimbursement.
- Free shuttles equipped with WiFi from locations around the Bay Area to headquarter offices.
- Fuel-efficiency vehicle incentive program ($5,000 incentive to purchase a hybrid car)
- A climbing wall
- Classes on a variety of subjects from estate planning and home purchasing to foreign-language lessons in French, Spanish, Japanese, and Mandarin.

SOURCES: The Great Place to Work® Institute, 2008, www.greatplacetowork.com; 100 best companies to work for 2011, http://money.cnn.com, accessed May 31, 2011.

COVERAGE	EMPLOYER CONTRIBUTION			MARKET VALUE[a]		
	ACTUAL	EMPLOYEE PERCEPTION	RATIO	ACTUAL	EMPLOYEE PERCEPTION	RATIO
Individual	$34	$23	68%	$ 61	$37	61%
Family	64	24	38	138	43	31

table 13.9

Employee Perceptions versus Actual Cost and Market Value of Employer Contributions to Employee Medical Insurance

Note: Dollar values in table represent means across three different insurance carriers for individual coverage and three different carriers for family coverage.

[a]Defined as the amount a nonemployee would have to pay to obtain the same level of coverage.

SOURCE: Adapted from M. Wilson, G. B. Northcraft, and M. A. Neale, "The Perceived Value of Fringe Benefits," *Personnel Psychology* 38 (1985), pp. 309–20. Used with permission.

The situation with job applicants is no better. One study of MBAs found that 46% believed that benefits added 15% or less on top of direct payroll. Not surprisingly, perhaps, benefits were dead last on the applicants' priority lists in making job choices.[70] A study of undergraduate business majors found similar results, with benefits ranked 15th (out of 18) in importance in evaluating jobs. These results must be interpreted with caution, however. Some research suggests that job attributes can be ranked low in importance, not because they are unimportant per se, but because all employers are perceived to be about the same on that attribute. If some employers offered noticeably poorer benefits, the importance of benefits could become much greater.

Organizations can help remedy the problem of applicants' and employees' lack of knowledge about benefits. One study found that employees' awareness of benefits information was significantly increased through several media, including memoranda, question-and-answer meetings, and detailed brochures. The increased awareness, in turn, contributed to significant increases in benefits satisfaction. Another study suggests, however, that increased employee knowledge of benefits can have a positive or negative effect, depending on the nature of the benefits package. For example, there was a negative, or inverse, correlation between cost to the employee and benefits satisfaction overall, but the correlation was more strongly negative among employees with greater knowledge of their benefits.[71] The implication is that employees will be least satisfied with their benefits if their cost is high and they are well informed.

One thing an employer should consider with respect to written benefits communication is that more than 27 million employees in the United States may be functionally illiterate. Of course, there are many alternative ways to communicate benefits information. (See Table 13.10.) Nevertheless, most organizations spend little to communicate information about benefits, and much of this is spent on general written communications. Considering that Bureau of Labor Statistics data cited earlier indicate that private-sector organizations spend an average of roughly $18,000 per worker per year on benefits, together with the complex nature of many benefits and the poor understanding of most employees, the typical communication effort may be inadequate.[72]

On a more positive note, organizations are increasingly using web-based tools to personalize and tailor communications to individual employees. (See the "Competing through Technology" box.) In addition, effective use of traditional approaches (e.g., booklets) can have a large effect on employee awareness.[73] Web-based tools have also enabled many organizations to eliminate benefits-related jobs now that employees can get answers to many benefits questions on their own.

table 13.10

Benefits Communication Media Examples for Different Audiences and Purposes

MEDIA	AUDIENCE	PURPOSE
Enrollment package	All employees (English and Spanish)	Announce changes or new hire enrollment only by deadline
Meetings	Local employees	Provide information on benefits and changes
Teleconference messaging	Remote employees	Provide information on benefits and changes
Intranet	All employees (personalized)	Provide information on benefits, training, and employment policies
E-mail alerts	Supervisors	Provide employees with information
Summary plan descriptions	All employees	Make available compliance information
Paycheck attachments	All employees	Provide information on benefits
Webcasts	Regional managers	Share context for changes and their roles and responsibilities

SOURCE: From A. Parsons and K. Groh, "The New Road Effective Communications," *Compensation Benefits Review*, Vol. 38, 2006, p. 57. Reproduced with permission of Sage Publications, Inc. via Copyright Clearance Center.

Rather than a single standard benefits package for all employees, flexible benefit plans (flex-plans or cafeteria-style plans) permit employees to choose the types and amounts of benefits they want for themselves. The plans vary according to such things as whether minimum levels of certain benefits (such as health care coverage) are prescribed and whether employees can receive money for having chosen a "light" benefits package (or have to pay extra for more benefits). One example is vacation, where some plans permit employees to give up vacation days for more salary or, alternatively, purchase extra vacation days through a salary reduction.

What are the potential advantages of such plans?[74] In the best case, almost all of the objectives discussed previously can be positively influenced. First, employees can gain a greater awareness and appreciation of what the employer provides them, particularly with plans that give employees a lump sum to allocate to benefits. Second, by permitting employee choice, there should be a better match between the benefits package and the employees' preferences. This, in turn, should improve employee attitudes and retention.[75] Third, employers may achieve overall cost reductions in their benefits programs. Cafeteria plans can be thought of as similar to defined contribution plans, whereas traditional plans are more like defined benefit plans. The employer can control the size of the contribution under the former, but not under the latter, because the cost and utilization of benefits is beyond the employer's control. Costs can also be controlled by designing the choices so that employees have an incentive to choose more efficient options. For example, in the case of a medical flex-plan, employees who do not wish to take advantage of the (presumably more cost-effective) HMO have to pay significant deductibles and other costs under the alternative plans.

One drawback of cafeteria-style plans is their administrative cost, especially in the initial design and start-up stages. However, software packages and standardized flex-plans developed by consultants offer some help in this regard. Another possible drawback to these plans is adverse selection. Employees are most likely to choose benefits that they expect to need the most. Someone in need of dental work would choose

Employers Ending the Paper Chase by Communicating Benefits Online

Last fall, an employee of Affiliated Computer Services Inc. attended a benefits fair at 2 a.m.

Though he was the sole attendee, he had access to crucial benefits information, viewed presentations by his human resources representatives and could have chatted about benefits with co-workers—had any been up that late. He was attending ACS's first virtual benefits fair, which ran 24/7 for three weeks and facilitated the enrollment of 40,000 of its employees.

"Our employees accessed benefits information, got answers to their questions and completed their enrollments online," says Rohail Khan, managing director for total benefits outsourcing for the Norwalk, Connecticut-based information technology and business process outsourcing company. "ACS could monitor where employees searched within the virtual site for information and how long they stayed."

Traditional benefits fairs are costly and only attracted about 11% of the ACS employee population in the past, Khan says. "Our testing showed a virtual fair costs less, provides a better vehicle for employees to engage with the information, allows spouses and family members to participate and ultimately leads to more informed enrollment decisions," he says. "We know that the future of enrollment is to engage employees and affect behavioral outcomes, and this application provided an enrollment experience that was easy to access and relevant."

"In a virtual environment, you can have company spokespeople walking around the space or manning information booths to add personality and credibility," says Joerg Rathenberg, vice president of products at Intercall, a conferencing service provider. Rathenberg says that ACS attendees were able to move in and out of the fair to the enrollment site or a call center. "The idea is to have all resources in one place, available at any time."

The concept of engagement vs. education began evolving a decade ago with communications around consumer-driven health care plans as employees sought more information to choose their medical plan option, says Elizabeth Bierbower, chief operating officer for Humana Specialty Benefits in Green Bay, Wisconsin.

Humana recently developed a series of health care videos titled Stay Smart, Stay Healthy featuring a hand that writes and pastes information on topics such as COBRA, Medicare, and health savings accounts on a white board. Interactive tools allow users to tailor benefit information to their individual needs and even ask questions.

"People are visual and tech-savvy today," Bierbower says. "Most employees use the Internet, and our mission is to educate and engage consumers about their health care and voluntary benefits by helping them relate those products to their own needs."

According to MetLife's ninth annual Study of Employee Benefits Trends released in March, 55% of employees polled do not believe their benefits materials are clear and comprehensive, while 25% are satisfied with their benefits communications. Employee suggestions for improvement include making benefits information available online, tailoring information to life events, and issuing more frequent communications.

John Moses, a principal in Aon Hewitt, says Aon Hewitt is taking a marketing approach to benefits communications. "Our focus is on the short-term want, not the long-term need, and the employee is the hero of the story," he says. "Logic doesn't always sell. Telling employees to reduce their body mass index to 25 is not motivating. Telling them they will look and feel better if they lose weight is more likely to result in the desired action."

Moses says their idea is to create the optimal mix of communications to drive employee behaviors, whether it's exercising, saving money or eating a healthier diet.

"You do that by making it easy for employees to do the right thing, with simple, easy-to-understand information that focuses on the benefit to them."

SOURCE: From, "Employers Ending the Paper Chase by Communicating Benefits Online," by Lisa Beyer. May 2011, *Workforce Management*. Reprinted with permission, Workforce Management Magazine. Copyright Crain Communications, May 2011.

as much dental coverage as possible. As a result, employer costs can increase significantly as each employee chooses benefits based on their personal value. Another result of adverse selection is the difficulty in estimating benefits costs under such a plan, especially in small companies. Adverse selection can be controlled, however, by limiting coverage amounts, pricing benefits that are subject to adverse selection higher, or using a limited set of packaged options, which prevents employees from choosing too many benefits options that would be susceptible to adverse selection.

Flexible Spending Accounts

A flexible spending account permits pretax contributions to an employee account that can be drawn on to pay for uncovered health care expenses (like deductibles or copayments). A separate account of up to $5,000 per year is permitted for pretax contributions to cover dependent care expenses. The federal tax code requires that funds in the health care and dependent care accounts be earmarked in advance and spent during the plan year. Remaining funds revert to the employer. Therefore, the accounts work best to the extent that employees have predictable expenses. The major advantage of such plans is the increase in take-home pay that results from pretax payment of health and dependent care expenses. Consider again the hypothetical employee with annual earnings of $50,000 and an effective total marginal tax rate of 41% from Table 13.1. The take-home pay from an additional $10,000 in salary with and without a flexible dependent care account is as follows:

	NO FLEXIBLE SPENDING CARE ACCOUNT	FLEXIBLE SPENDING CARE ACCOUNT
Salary portion	$10,000	$10,000
Pretax dependent care contribution	0	−5,000
Taxable salary	10,000	5,000
Tax (41%)	−4,100	−2,050
Aftertax cost of dependent care	−5,000	0
Take-home pay	$ 900	$ 2,950

Therefore, the use of a flexible spending account saves the employee $2,050 ($2,950 − $900) per year.

General Regulatory Issues

LO 13-6
Describe the regulatory constraints that affect the way employee benefits are designed and administered.

Although we have already discussed a number of regulatory issues, some additional ones require attention.

NONDISCRIMINATION RULES AND QUALIFIED PLANS

As a general rule, all benefits packages must meet certain rules to be classified as qualified plans. What are the advantages of a qualified plan? Basically, it receives more favorable tax treatment than a nonqualified plan. In the case of a qualified retirement plan, for example, these tax advantages include (1) an immediate tax deduction for employers for their contributions to retirement funds, (2) no tax liability for the employee at the time of the employer deduction, and (3) tax-free investment returns (from stocks, bonds, money markets, or the like) on the retirement funds.[76]

What rules must be satisfied for a plan to obtain qualified status? Each benefit area has different rules. It would be impossible to describe the various rules here, but some general observations are possible. Taking pensions as an example again, vesting requirements must be met. More generally, qualified plans must meet so-called nondiscrimination rules. Basically, this means that a benefit cannot discriminate in favor of "highly compensated employees." One rationale behind such rules is that the tax benefits of qualified benefits plans (and the corresponding loss of tax revenues for the U.S. government) should not go disproportionately to the wealthy.[77] Rather, the favorable tax treatment is designed to encourage employers to provide important benefits to a broad spectrum of employees. The nondiscrimination rules discourage owners or top managers from adopting plans that benefit them exclusively.

SEX, AGE, AND DISABILITY

Beyond the Pregnancy Discrimination Act's requirements that were discussed earlier in the chapter, a second area of concern for employers in ensuring legal treatment of men and women in the benefits area has to do with pension benefits. Women tend to live longer than men, meaning that pension benefits for women are more costly, all else being equal. However, in its 1978 *Manhart* ruling, the Supreme Court declared it illegal for employers to require women to contribute more to a defined benefit plan than men: Title VII protects individuals, and not all women outlive all men.[78]

Two major age-related issues have received attention under the Age Discrimination in Employment Act (ADEA) and later amendments such as the Older Workers Benefit Protection Act (OWBPA). First, employers must take care not to discriminate against workers over age 40 in the provision of pay or benefits. As one example, employers cannot generally cease accrual (stop the growth) of retirement benefits at some age (like 65) as a way of pressuring older employees to retire.[79] Second, early retirement incentive programs need to meet the following standards to avoid legal liability: (1) the employee is not coerced to accept the incentive and retire, (2) accurate information is provided regarding options, and (3) the employee is given adequate time (is not pressured) to make a decision.

Employers also have to comply with the Americans with Disabilities Act (ADA), which went into effect in 1992. The ADA specifies that employees with disabilities must have "equal access to whatever health insurance coverage the employer provides other employees." However, the act also notes that the terms and conditions of health insurance can be based on risk factors as long as this is not a subterfuge for denying the benefit to those with disabilities. Employers with risk-based programs in place would be in a stronger position, however, than employers who make changes after hiring employees with disabilities.[80]

MONITORING FUTURE BENEFITS OBLIGATIONS

Financial Accounting Statement (FAS) 106, issued by the Financial Accounting Standards Board, became effective in 1993. This rule requires that any benefits (excluding pensions) provided after retirement (the major one being health care) can no longer be funded on a pay-as-you-go basis. Rather, they must be paid on an accrual

Financial Accounting Statement (FAS) 106
The rule issued by the Financial Accounting Standards Board in 1993 requiring companies to fund benefits provided after retirement on an accrual rather than a pay-as-you-go basis and to enter these future cost obligations on their financial statements.

basis, and companies must enter these future cost obligations on their financial statements. The effect on financial statements can be substantial.

Increasing retiree health care costs (and the change in accounting standards) have also led some companies to require white-collar employees and retirees to pay insurance premiums for the first time in history and to increase copayments and deductibles. Survey data indicate that some companies are ending retiree health care benefits altogether. GM, for example, recently eliminated retiree health care benefits for white-collar workers. Union contracts prevented GM from eliminating the blue-collar plan.

However, as part of its bankruptcy proceeding it reached a settlement with the United Auto Workers union (UAW) to create a voluntary employee benefit association (VEBA) trust. GM agreed to contribute roughly $35 billion to fund the VEBA. Ford ($13.2 billion) and Chrysler ($7.1 billion) also reached agreements to set up VEBAs. By one estimate, the VEBAs moved $100 billion in retiree health care obligations off the financial statements of the three U.S. automakers, playing a major role in reducing labor cost per vehicle produced. Also, the VEBAs, like defined contribution plans, make the cost for the companies certain. After paying to set up the VEBAs, they have no future obligations to cover retiree health care. It is up to the UAW to administer the VEBA.[81]

Other companies have reduced benefits or increased retiree contributions. Obviously, such changes hit the elderly hard, especially those with relatively fixed incomes. Not surprisingly, legal challenges have arisen. The need to balance the interests of shareholders, current employees, and retirees in this area will be one of the most difficult challenges facing managers in the future.

A Look Back

We have seen that many organizations have become less paternalistic in their employee benefits strategies. Employees now have more responsibility, and sometimes more risk, regarding their benefits choices. One change has been in the area of retirement income plans, where employers have moved toward greater reliance on defined contribution plans. Such plans require employees to understand investing; otherwise, their retirement years may not be so happy. The risk to employees is especially great when defined contribution plans invest a substantial portion of their assets in company stock. One reason companies do this is because they wish to move away from an entitlement mentality and instead link benefits to company performance. However, if the company has financial problems, employees risk losing not only their jobs, but also their retirement money. As we saw in the beginning of the chapter, another change has been in the area of health care benefits. Employees are being asked to increase the proportion of costs that they pay and also to use data on health care quality to make better choices about health care.

Questions

1. Why do employers offer benefits? Is it because the law requires it, because it makes good business sense, or because it is the right thing to do? How much responsibility should employers have for the health and well-being of their

employees? Take the perspective of both a shareholder and an employee in answering this question.
2. If you were advising a new company on how to design its health care plan, what would you recommend?

 Please see the Video that corresponds to this chapter at www.mhhe.com/noe8e.

● SUMMARY

Effective management of employee benefits is an important means by which organizations successfully compete. Benefits costs are substantial and continue to grow rapidly in some areas, most notably health care. Control of such costs is necessary to compete in the product market. At the same time, employers must offer a benefits package that permits them to compete in the labor market. Beyond investing more money in benefits, this attraction and retention of quality employees can be helped by better communication of the value of the benefits package and by allowing employees to tailor benefits to their own needs through flexible benefits plans.

Employers continue to be a major source of economic security for employees, often providing health insurance, retirement benefits, and so forth. Changes to benefits can have a tremendous impact on employees and retirees. Therefore, employers carry a significant social responsibility in making benefits decisions. At the same time, employees need to be aware that they will increasingly become responsible for their own economic security. Health care benefit design is changing to encourage employees to be more informed consumers, and retirement benefits will depend more and more on the financial investment decisions employees make on their own behalf.

● KEY TERMS

Marginal tax rate, 560
Consolidated Omnibus Budget
   Reconciliation Act
   (COBRA), 565
Pension Benefit Guaranty
   Corporation (PBGC), 566

Employee Retirement Income
   Security Act (ERISA), 566
Cash balance plan, 568
Summary plan description
   (SPD), 569
Family and Medical Leave Act, 571

Health maintenance organization
   (HMO), 577
Preferred provider organization
   (PPO), 577
Financial Accounting Statement
   (FAS) 106, 589

● DISCUSSION QUESTIONS

1. The chapter-opening story described how employers are shifting more employee health care costs to employees. What are the likely consequences of this change? Where does the social responsibility of employers end, and where does the need to operate more efficiently begin?
2. Your company, like many others, is experiencing double-digit percentage increases in health care costs. What suggestions can you offer that may reduce the rate of cost increases?
3. Why is communication so important in the employee benefits area? What sorts of programs can a company use to communicate more effectively? What are the

potential positive consequences of more effective benefits communication?
4. What are the potential advantages of flexible benefits and flexible spending accounts? Are there any potential drawbacks?
5. Although benefits account for a large share of employee compensation, many feel there is little evidence on whether an employer receives an adequate return on the benefits investment. One suggestion has been to link benefits to individual, group, or organization performance. Explain why you would or would not recommend this strategy to an organization.

SELF-ASSESSMENT EXERCISE

One way companies determine which types of benefits to provide is to use a survey asking employees which types of benefits are important to them. Read the following list of employee benefits. For each benefit, mark an X in the column that indicates whether it is important to you or not.

Benefit	Important to Have	Not Important to Have	% Employers Offering
Dependent-care flexible spending account			70%
Flextime			64
Ability to bring child to work in case of emergency			30
Elder-care referral services			21
Adoption assistance			21
On-site child care center			6
Gym subsidy			28
Vaccinations on site (e.g., flu shots)			61
On-site fitness center			26
Casual dress days (every day)			53
Organization-sponsored sports teams			39
Food services/subsidized cafeteria			29
Travel-planning services			27
Dry-cleaning services			15
Massage therapy services at work			12
Self-defense training			6
Concierge services			4

Compare your importance ratings for each benefit to the corresponding number in the right-hand column that indicates the percentage of employers that offer the benefit. Are you likely to find jobs that provide the benefits you want? Explain.

SOURCE: Based on Figure 2, "Percent of Employers Offering Work/Life Benefits (by Year)," in *Workplace Visions* 4 (2002), p. 3, published by the Society for Human Resource Management.

EXERCISING STRATEGY: COMPANIES LEARN THAT IT PAYS TO KEEP EMPLOYEES FIT

Physical fitness—or at least wellness—does matter, as more and more companies and their insurers are learning. A healthy workforce means better productivity and fewer workdays lost, not to mention reduced medical costs by keeping injuries and illnesses to a minimum. A study published by the Presidents' Council on Physical Fitness and Sports found that fitness programs provided by companies saved from $1.15 to $5.52 for every dollar spent.

At 3Com, the network communications company, employees spend their lunch hours at the WellCom Center, a 13,500-square-foot fitness facility right on site. There they can cycle, walk a treadmill, lift weights, take a fitness class, or relax in the sauna. Or they can play a game of basketball or beach volleyball outside. Afterward, they can cool off at the juice bar with a fruit smoothie. The center is open 24 hours a day, seven days a week, to meet the needs of employees who work at all hours. More than 40% of the 4,200 workers at 3Com are WellCom members, and 70% take advantage of the center's seminars on wellness, smoking cessation, or weight loss. "A healthy workforce is good for employees and good for 3Com," says Peter Sandman, a manager of strategic planning at the company. "It helps recruiting and it helps retention, especially in a competitive environment like Silicon Valley [California]."

Applied Materials Inc. of Santa Clara, California, conducted its own study that showed that for fitness center participants, medical payments were reduced by 20%, hospital admissions were 70% lower, costs for accident-related disability claims were 30% less, and workers' compensation claims were 79% less than those of employees who didn't use the company's fitness center. Even a five-minute stretch break has been shown to reduce strains and sprains by as much as 65%. "Just moving and getting away from their PC makes them feel better," says Judy Webster, director of corporate wellness for the company.

Boeing's health care package also includes access to its fitness centers as part of its overall recreation program. "When you're happy and healthy, you're able to perform at your best," explains the aircraft manufacturer's website. The recreation program includes indoor and outdoor facilities as well as discount packages for sports and cultural events. These companies have embraced the wisdom of the old adage, "an ounce of prevention is worth a pound of cure," and it has literally paid off.

Questions

1. Why don't more companies emphasize employee wellness? Does it work better for some companies than for others?
2. The companies here have on-site facilities. Is that the right model for all companies?

SOURCES: Boeing website, www.boeing.com, accessed October 30, 2001; D. Beck, "Your Company Needs Its Own Best Practices," *Career Journal* from *The Wall Street Journal* (July 30–August 5, 2001), www.careerjournal.com; M. Chase, "Healthy Assets," *The Wall Street Journal* (May 1, 2000), http://interactive.wsj.

● **MANAGING PEOPLE**

Smokers Now Face Another Risk from Their Habit: It Could Cost Them a Shot at a Job

More hospitals and medical businesses in many states are adopting strict policies that make smoking a reason to turn away job applicants, saying they want to increase worker productivity, reduce health care costs, and encourage healthier living.

The policies reflect a frustration that softer efforts—like banning smoking on company grounds, offering cessation programs, and increasing health care premiums for smokers—have not been powerful-enough incentives to quit.

The new rules essentially treat cigarettes like an illegal narcotic. Applications now explicitly warn of "tobacco-free hiring," job seekers must submit to urine tests for nicotine, and new employees caught smoking face termination.

This shift—from smoke-free to smoker-free workplaces—has prompted sharp debate over whether the policies establish a troubling precedent of employers intruding into private lives to ban a habit that is legal.

"If enough of these companies adopt these policies and it really becomes difficult for smokers to find jobs, there are going to be consequences," said Dr. Michael Siegel, a professor at the Boston University School of Public Health, who has written about the trend. "Unemployment is also bad for health."

There is no reliable data on how many businesses have adopted such policies. But people tracking the issue say there are enough examples to suggest the policies are becoming more mainstream, and in some states courts have upheld the legality of refusing to employ smokers.

For example, hospitals in Florida, Georgia, Massachusetts, Missouri, Ohio, Pennsylvania, Tennessee, and Texas, among others, stopped hiring smokers in the last year and more are openly considering the option.

"We've had a number of inquiries over the last 6 to 12 months about how to do this," said Paul Terpeluk, a director at the Cleveland Clinic, which stopped hiring smokers in 2007 and has championed the policy. "The trend line is getting pretty steep, and I'd guess that in the next few years you'd see a lot of major hospitals go this way."

A number of these organizations have justified the new policies as advancing their institutional missions of promoting personal well-being and finding ways to reduce the growth in health care costs.

About one in five Americans still smoke, and smoking remains the leading cause of preventable deaths. And employees who smoke cost, on average, $3,391 more a year each for health care and lost productivity, according to federal estimates.

"We felt it was unfair for employees who maintained healthy lifestyles to have to subsidize those who do not," said Steven C. Bjelich, chief executive of St. Francis Medical Center in Cape Girardeau, Missouri, which stopped hiring smokers last month. "Essentially that's what happens."

Two decades ago—after large companies like Alaska Airlines, Union Pacific, and Turner Broadcasting adopted such policies—29 states and the District of Columbia passed laws, with the strong backing of the tobacco lobby and the American Civil Liberties Union, that prohibit discrimination against smokers or those who use "lawful products." Some of those states, like Missouri, make an exception for health care organizations.

A spokesman for Philip Morris said the company was no longer actively working on the issue, though it remained strongly opposed to the policies.

One concern voiced by groups like the National Workrights Institute is that such policies are a slippery slope—that if they prove successful in driving down health care costs, employers might be emboldened to crack down on other behavior by their workers, like drinking alcohol, eating fast food, and participating in risky hobbies like motorcycle riding. The head of the Cleveland Clinic was both praised and criticized when he mused in an interview two years ago that, were it not illegal, he would expand the hospital policy to refuse employment to obese people.

"There is nothing unique about smoking," said Lewis Maltby, president of the Workrights Institute, who has lobbied vigorously against the practice. "The number of things that we all do privately that have negative impact on our health is endless. If it's not smoking, it's beer. If it's not beer, it's cheeseburgers. And what about your sex life?"

While most of the companies applied their rules only to new employees, a few eventually mandated that existing employees must quit smoking or lose their jobs. There is also disagreement over whether to fire employees who are caught smoking after they are hired. The Truman Medical Centers, here in Kansas City, for example, will investigate accusations of tobacco use by employees. In one recent case a new employee returned from a lunch break smelling of smoke and, when confronted by his supervisor, admitted that he had been smoking, said Marcos DeLeon, head of human resources for the hospital. The employee was fired.

Taking a drag of her cigarette outside the University of Kansas School of Nursing, just beyond the sign warning that smoking is prohibited on campus, Mandy Carroll explained that she was well aware of the potential consequences of her pack-a-day habit: both her parents died of smoking-related illnesses. But Ms. Carroll, a 26-year-old nursing student, said she opposed any effort by hospitals to "discriminate" against her and other smokers.

"Obviously we know the effects of smoking, we see it every day in the hospital," Ms. Carroll said. "It's a stupid choice, but it's a personal choice."

Others do not mind the strict policy. John J. Stinson, 68, said he had been smoking for more than three decades when he decided to apply for a job at the Cleveland Clinic, helping incoming patients, nearly three years ago.

It turned out to be the motivation he needed: he passed the urine test and has not had a cigarette since. "It's a good idea," Mr. Stinson said.

Questions

1. Should companies be allowed to require their employees not to smoke? Why or why not?
2. Do you feel that companies should be able to restrict other employee activities?
3. Do you believe it is discrimination to not hire people who smoke? Define discrimination. Explain your view on whether employers are engaging in discrimination in this case.

SOURCE: From *New York Times*, "Smokers Now Face Another Risk from Their Habit: It Could Cost Them a Shot at a Job," by Steve Hebert, February 10, 2011. © 2011 The New York Times. All rights reserved. Used by permission and protected by Copyright Laws of the United States.

● TWITTER FOCUS: BABIES WELCOMED AT T3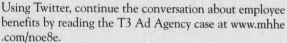

Using Twitter, continue the conversation about employee benefits by reading the T3 Ad Agency case at www.mhhe.com/noe8e.

T3 is an independent advertising agency started by Gay Warren Gaddis, a woman who encouraged employees to bring their babies to work. She counted on the employees to work flexibly in the presence of their children. Once babies reach nine months or start to crawl, parents are expected to make arrangements for day care. Bringing babies to work is not the only employee benefit at T3. The company also offers medical, dental, and vision insurance; various life insurance policies; disability insurance; a 401(k) plan; paid time for vacations, holidays, and sick leave; and discounts on gym memberships and cell phone plans.

Engage with your classmates and instructor via Twitter to chat about T3's employee benefits using the case questions posted on the Noe website. Don't have a Twitter account yet? See the instructions for getting started on the Online Learning Center.

● NOTES

1. James H. Dulebohn, Janice C. Molloy, Shaun M. Pichler, and Brian Murray, "Employee Benefits: Literature Review and Emerging Issues," *Human Resource Management Review* 19 (2009), pp. 86–103; Joseph J. Martocchio, *Employee Benefits*, 2nd ed. (New York: McGraw-Hill, 2006).
2. H. W. Hennessey, "Using Employee Benefits to Gain a Competitive Advantage," *Benefits Quarterly* 5, no. 1 (1989), pp. 51–57; B. Gerhart and G.T. Milkovich, "Employee Compensation: Research and Practice," in *Handbook of Industrial and Organizational Psychology*, vol. 3, 2nd ed., ed. M. D. Dunnette and L. M. Hough (Palo Alto, CA: Consulting Psychologists Press, 1992); J. Swist, "Benefits Communications: Measuring Impact and Value," *Employee Benefit Plan Review*, September 2002, pp. 24–26.
3. R. Ehrenberg and R. S. Smith, *Modern Labor Economics: Theory and Public Policy*, 7th ed. (Upper Saddle River, NJ: Addison Wesley Longman, 2000).
4. B. T. Beam Jr. and J. J. McFadden, *Employee Benefits*, 6th ed. (Chicago: Dearborn Financial Publishing, 2000).
5. The organization and description in this section draws heavily on Beam and McFadden, *Employee Benefits*.
6. See www.doleta.gov for further information.

7. J. A. Penczak, "Unemployment Benefit Plans," in *Employee Benefits Handbook*, 3rd ed., ed. J. D. Mamorsky (Boston: Warren, Gorham & Lamont, 1992).

8. J. V. Nackley, *Primer on Workers' Compensation* (Washington, DC: Bureau of National Affairs, 1989).

9. Beam and McFadden, *Employee Benefits*, p. 81.

10. www.dol.gov/esa.

11. A. H. Wheeler, "Pathophysiology of Chronic Back Pain," www.emedicine.com (2002).

12. J. R. Hollenbeck, D. R. Ilgen, and S. M. Crampton, "Lower Back Disability in Occupational Settings: A Review of the Literature from a Human Resource Management View," *Personnel Psychology* 45 (1992), pp. 247–78; J. J. Martocchio, D. A. Harrison, and H. Berkson, "Connections between Lower Back Pain, Interventions, and Absence from Work: A Time-Based Meta-Analysis," *Personnel Psychology* (2000), p. 595.

13. Employee Benefit Research Institute, "Value of Employee Benefits Constant in a Changing World," www.ebri.org (March 28, 2002).

14. Beam and McFadden, *Employee Benefits*.

15. Social Security Administration, "Fast Facts and Figures about Social Security." Data for 2001, published 2003, www.ssa.gov.

16. K. A. Bender, "Pension Integration and Retirement Benefits," *Monthly Labor Review*, February 2001, pp. 49–58, http://stats.bls.gov/opub/mlr.

17. www.pbgc.gov.

18. Ibid.

19. www.irs.gov. Those age 50 and over have higher contribution limits.

20. R. A. Ippolito, "Toward Explaining the Growth of Defined Contribution Plans," *Industrial Relations* 34 (1995), pp. 1–20; Profit Sharing/401(k) Council of America, http://www.psca.org/portals/0/docs/PDFs/2007%20Defined%Contribution%20Growth.pdf.

21. J. Fierman, "How Secure Is Your Nest Egg?" *Fortune*, August 12, 1991, pp. 50–54.

22. A. R. Sorking, "JP Morgan Pays $2 a Share for Bear Stearns," *The New York Times*, March 17, 2008; P. Lattman and J. Strasburg," We Are All in a Daze, Says One Employee, Life Savings Wiped Out, "*The Wall Street Journal*, March 18, 2008; D. Maxey, J. L. Pessin, and I. Salisbury, "The Job/Stock Double Whammy: Bear Saga Shows Perils of Loading Up on Employer Equity," *The Wall Street Journal*, March 18, 2008.

23. Beam and McFadden, *Employee Benefits*.

24. B. J. Coleman, *Primer on Employee Retirement Income Security Act*, 3rd ed. (Washington, DC: Bureau of National Affairs, 1989).

25. *Continental Can Company v. Gavalik*, summary in *Daily Labor Report* (December 8, 1987): "Supreme Court Lets Stand Third Circuit Ruling That Pension Avoidance Scheme Is ERISA Violation," No. 234, p. A-14.

26. A. L. Gustman, O. S. Mitchell, and T. L. Steinmeier, "The Role of Pensions in the Labor Market: A Survey of the Literature," *Industrial and Labor Relations* 47 (1994), pp. 417–38.

27. D. A. DeCenzo and S. J. Holoviak, *Employee Benefits* (Englewood Cliffs, NJ: Prentice Hall, 1990).

28. E. P. Lazear, "Why Is There Early Retirement?" *Journal of Political Economy* 87 (1979), pp. 1261–84; Gustman et al., "The Role of Pensions."

29. P. Cappelli, *The New Deal at Work: Managing the Market-Driven Workforce* (Boston: Harvard Business School Press, 1999).

30. S. Dorsey, "Pension Portability and Labor Market Efficiency," *Industrial and Labor Relations* 48, no. 5 (1995), pp. 276–92.

31. Commission of the European Communities, European Community Directive 93/104/EC, issued November 23, 1993, and amended June 22, 2000, by Directive 2000/34/EC, http://europa/eu.int/comm/index_en.htm.

32. DeCenzo and Holoviak, *Employee Benefits*.

33. S. L. Grover and K. J. Crooker, "Who Appreciates Family Responsive Human Resource Policies: The Impact of Family-Friendly Policies on the Organizational Attachment of Parents and Nonparents," *Personnel Psychology* 48 (1995), pp. 271–88; T. J. Rothausen, J. A. Gonzalez, N. E. Clarke, and L. L. O'Dell, "Family-Friendly Backlash: Fact or Fiction? The Case of Organizations' On-Site Child Care Centers," *Personnel Psychology* 51 (1998), p. 685; M. A. Arthur, "Share Price Reactions to Work–Family Initiatives: An Institutional Perspective," *Academy of Management Journal* 46 (2003), p. 497; J. E. Perry-Smith and T. Blum, "Work–Family Human Resource Bundles and Perceived Organizational Performance," *Academy of Management Journal* 43 (2000), pp. 1107–17.

34. N. Bloom, T. Kretschmer, and J. Van Reenen (2011), "Are Family-Friendly Workplace Practices a Valuable Firm Resource?" *Strategic Management Journal* 32 (2011), pp. 343–67.

35. "The Employer's Role in Helping Working Families." For examples of child care arrangements in some well-known companies (e.g., AT&T, Apple, Exxon, IBM, Merck), see "A Look at Child-Care Benefits," *USA Today*, March 14, 1989, p. 4B; U.S. Census Bureau, "America's Families and Living Arrangements," June 2001, www.census.gov.

36. J. Waldfogel, "International Policies toward Parental Leave and Child Care," *Future of Children* 11, no. 1 (2001), pp. 99–111.

37. P. Hardin, "Women Execs Should Feel at Ease about Taking Full Maternity Leave," *Personnel Journal*, September 1995, p. 19.

38. "The Families and Work Institute's 1998 Business Work–Life Study," www.familiesandwork.org. Results based on a nationally representative survey of employers having 100 or more employees.

39. J. Fierman, "It's 2 A.M.: Let's Go to Work," *Fortune*, August 21, 1995, pp. 82–88.

40. E. E. Kossek, "Diversity in Child Care Assistance Needs: Employee Problems, Preferences, and Work-Related Outcomes," *Personnel Psychology* 43 (1990), pp. 769–91.

41. "A Bank Profits from Its Work/Life Program," *Workforce*, February 1997, p. 49.

42. R. Broderick and B. Gerhart, "Nonwage Compensation," in *The Human Resource Management Handbook*, ed. D. Lewin, D. J. B. Mitchell, and M. A. Zadi (San Francisco: JAI Press, 1996).

43. Dulabohn et al., "Employee Benefits."

44. Hennessey, "Using Employee Benefits to Gain a Competitive Advantage."

45. U.S. Bureau of Labor Statistics, "Employer Cost for Employee Compensation," www.bls.gov; U.S. Chamber of Commerce Research Center, Employee Benefits Study, annual (Washington, D.C.: U.S. Chamber of Commerce).

46. www.census.gov.

47. Employee Benefit Research Institute, *EBRI's Fundamentals of Employee Benefit Programs*, ebri.org, 6th ed., 2009.

48. A. C. Monheit and P. F. Cooper, "Health Insurance and Job Mobility: The Effects of Public Policy on Job-Lock," *Industrial and Labor Relations Review* 48 (1994), pp. 86–102.

49. Beam and McFadden, *Employee Benefits*.

50. R. Lieber, "New Way to Curb Medical Costs: Make Employees Feel the Sting," *The Wall Street Journal*, June 23, 2004, p. A1.

51. M. Barringer and O. S. Mitchell, "Workers' Preferences among Company-Provided Health Insurance Plans," *Industrial and Labor Relations Review* 48 (1994), pp. 141–52.

52. Beam and McFadden, *Employee Benefits*.

53. Jared Shelly, "Transformation Vacation," *Human Resource Executive*, November 1, 2008.

54. Wellness Councils of America, "101 Ways to Wellness," www.welcoa.org, 2001; Wellness Councils of America, "A Guide to Developing Your Worksite Wellness Program," www.welcoa.org, 1997; Simona Covell, "Companies Win as Workers Lose Pounds," *The Wall Street Journal*, July 10, 2008, p. B6. Copyright © 2008 by Dow Jones & Co., Inc. Reproduced with permission of Dow Jones & Co., Inc. via Copyright Clearance Center.

55. S. Tully, "America's Healthiest Companies," *Fortune*, June 12, 1995, pp. 98–106.

56. G. Flynn, "Companies Make Wellness Work," *Personnel Journal*, February 1995, pp. 63–66.

57. D. A. Harrison and L. Z. Liska, "Promoting Regular Exercise in Organizational Fitness Programs: Health-Related Differences in Motivational Building Blocks," *Personnel Psychology* 47 (1994), pp. 47–71.

58. J. C. Erfurt, A. Foote, and M. A. Heirich, "The Cost-Effectiveness of Worksite Wellness Programs for Hypertension Control, Weight Loss, Smoking Cessation and Exercise," *Personnel Psychology* 45 (1992), pp. 5–27.

59. Ibid.

60. The Henry J. Kaiser Family Foundation and Health Research and Educational Trust, *Survey of Employer Health Benefits 2010*, www.kff.org.

61. H. Gardner, unpublished manuscript (Cheyenne, WY: Options & Choices, 1995).

62. H. B. Noble, "Quality Is Focus for Health Plans," *The New York Times*, July 3, 1995, p. A1; J. D. Klinke, "Medicine's Industrial Revolution," *The Wall Street Journal*, August 21, 1995, p. A8.

63. J. B. White, "Business Plan," *The Wall Street Journal*, October 19, 1998, p. R18.

64. G. McWilliams, "Big Employers Plan Electronic Health Records," *The Wall Street Journal*, November 29, 2006, p. B1.

65. Towers Watson, Health Care Reform, www.towerswatson.com, May 2010; D. Mattioli, "Firms Feel Pain from Health Law," *The Wall Street Journal*, December 13, 2010.

66. J. Schor, *The Overworked American: The Unexpected Decline of Leisure* (New York: Basic Books, 1991); U.S. Bureau of Labor Statistics, "Workers Are on the Job More Hours over the Course of a Year," *Issues in Labor Statistics*, February 1997.

67. Hewitt Associates. http://www.hewitt.com.

68. Beam and McFadden, *Employee Benefits*.

69. M. Wilson, G. B. Northcraft, and M. A. Neale, "The Perceived Value of Fringe Benefits," *Personnel Psychology* 38 (1985), pp. 309–20. Similar results were found in other studies reviewed by H. W. Hennessey, P. L. Perrewe, and W. A. Hochwarter, "Impact of Benefit Awareness on Employee and Organizational Outcomes: A Longitudinal Field Experiment," *Benefits Quarterly* 8, no. 2 (1992), pp. 90–96; MetLife, Employee Benefits Benchmarking Report, www.metlife.com. Accessed June 24, 2007.

70. R. Huseman, J. Hatfield, and R. Robinson, "The MBA and Fringe Benefits," *Personnel Administrator* 23, no. 7 (1978), pp. 57–60. See summary in H. W. Hennessey Jr., "Using Employee Benefits to Gain a Competitive Advantage," *Benefits Quarterly* 5, no. 1 (1989), pp. 51–57.

71. Hennessey et al., "Impact of Benefit Awareness"; the same study found no impact of the increased awareness and benefits satisfaction on overall job satisfaction. G. F. Dreher, R. A. Ash, and R. D. Bretz, "Benefit Coverage and Employee Cost: Critical Factors in Explaining Compensation Satisfaction," *Personnel Psychology* 41 (1988), pp. 237–54.

72. M. C. Giallourakis and G. S. Taylor, "An Evaluation of Benefit Communication Strategy," *Employee Benefits Journal* 15, no. 4 (1991), pp. 14–18; Employee Benefits Research Institute, "How Readable Are Summary Plan Descriptions for Health Care Plans," *EBRI Notes*, October 2006, ebri.org.

73. J. Abraham, R. Feldman, and C. Carlin, "Understanding Employee Awareness of Health Care Quality Information: How Can Employers Benefit?" *Health Services Research* 39 (2004), pp. 1799–1816; J. H. Marler, S. L. Fisher, and W. Ke, "Employee Self-Service Technology Acceptance: A Comparison of Pre-Implementation and Post-Implementation Relationships," *Personal Psychology* 62 (2009), pp. 327–58.

74. Beam and McFadden, *Employee Benefits*; M. W. Barringer and G. T. Milkovich, "A Theoretical Explanation of the Adoption and Design of Flexible Benefit Plans: A Case of Human Resource Innovation," *Academy of Management Review* 23 (1998), pp. 305–24.

75. For supportive evidence, see A. E. Barber, R. B. Dunham, and R. A. Formisano, "The Impact of Flexible Benefits on Employee Satisfaction: A Field Study," *Personnel Psychology* 45 (1992), pp. 55–75; E. E. Lawler, *Pay and Organizational Development* (Reading, MA: Addison-Wesley, 1981).

76. Beam and McFadden, *Employee Benefits*.

77. Ibid.

78. *Los Angeles Dept. of Water & Power v. Manhart*, 435 US SCt 702 (1978), 16 EPD, 8250.

79. S. K. Hoffman, "Discrimination Litigation Relating to Employee Benefits," *Labor Law Journal*, June 1992, pp. 362–81.

80. Ibid., p. 375.

81. S. J. Sacher and J. Day, "The New VEBAs," BNA *Pension and Benefits* blog, June 1, 2010. http://pblog.bna.com, extracted June 3, 2011; P. C. Borzi, "Retiree Health VEBAs: A New Twist on an Old Paradigm. Implications for Retirees, Unions, and Employers," The Henry J. Kaiser Family Foundation, March 2009.

PART 5

Special Topics in Human Resource Management

Chapter 14
Collective Bargaining and Labor Relations

Chapter 15
Managing Human Resources Globally

Chapter 16
Strategically Managing the HRM Function

CHAPTER

14

Collective Bargaining and Labor Relations

LO **LEARNING OBJECTIVES**

After reading this chapter, you should be able to:

ENTER THE WORLD OF BUSINESS

UAW Open to More Jobs at a Second-Tier Pay Level

ORION TOWNSHIP, Mich.—The United Automobile Workers union might allow carmakers to put more new workers on a lower wage scale to create more jobs and reopen idled plants. A UAW official, Joe Ashton, said that creating jobs is a priority entering this fall's negotiations with the three Detroit carmakers and that it will "look at anything, when it comes to negotiations, that will retain jobs."

He said the union would ask GM to reopen plants in Spring Hill, Tenn., and Janesville, Wis., which GM placed on standby status as part of its bankruptcy reorganization in case more production capacity was needed in the future, and to keep operating a plant in Shreveport, La., that is scheduled to shut in mid-2012.

GM's vice president for labor relations, Cathy Clegg, said the company would reopen the two standby plants if needed but that it had enough capacity to meet current demand.

Mr. Ashton and Ms. Clegg said GM already was planning to call back all of the approximately 2,000 workers on layoff status by year's end and would undoubtedly need to hire some additional workers, but they declined to say how many or where.

GM's Orion assembly plant is preparing to build a pair of subcompact cars, the Chevrolet Sonic and Buick Verano, later this year. GM considered closing the plant, located north of Detroit, but reversed course after the UAW agreed to a deal that allows 40% of its 1,550 hourly workers to be paid about half as much as the others.

GM said the arrangement was necessary so it could profitably build such small, inexpensive cars in the United States, something none of its competitors do. The deal expands on a 2007 provision in the UAW's contracts with GM, the Ford Motor Company, and the Chrysler Group that allows newly hired workers to earn about $14 an hour instead of the standard rate of about $28. No current workers have been moved down to the lower tier.

The two-tier wage system was controversial within the union when it was created, but comments by Mr. Ashton and by the UAW's president, Bob King, last week, signaled that the union was increasingly embracing it as a means of creating jobs.

He noted that, because workers on the second tier can be moved to the first when positions open up, the system can encourage automakers to bring some work in-house that had been done by suppliers or in other countries. The Chevrolet Aveo, which the Michigan-built Sonic will replace, is imported from South Korea.

"The UAW leaders clearly do not like the two-tier wage," observed Harley Shaiken, of the University of California, Berkeley. "But they view the creation of domestic jobs as urgent. I think the trade-off they're looking at is that it is far easier to raise that wage in future negotiations than to reopen plants that have been permanently shuttered."

Introduction

As the chapter opening indicates, unions can help achieve important worker goals, including high wages. However, with global competition, high wages, without high worker productivity, threatens a company's survival. In the case of the U.S. automobile industry, companies, together with their unionized workers, have had to take aggressive steps to reduce costs for the company and worker jobs to survive. This common goal is what binds management and labor together in a search for improved competitiveness.

 The Labor Relations Framework

LO 14-1
Describe what is meant by collective bargaining and labor relations.

John Dunlop, former secretary of labor and a leading industrial relations scholar, suggested in the book *Industrial Relations Systems* (1958) that a successful industrial relations system consists of four elements: (1) an environmental context (technology, market pressures, and the legal framework, especially as it affects bargaining power); (2) participants, including employees and their unions, management, and the government; (3) a "web of rules" (rules of the game) that describe the process by which labor and management interact and resolve disagreements (such as the steps followed in settling contract grievances); and (4) ideology.[1] For the industrial relations system to operate properly, the three participants must, to some degree, have a common ideology (like acceptance of the capitalist system) and must accept the roles of the other participants. Acceptance does not translate into convergence of interests, however. To the contrary, some degree of worker–management conflict is inevitable because, although the interests of the two parties overlap, they also diverge in key respects (such as how to divide the economic profits).[2]

Therefore, according to Dunlop and other U.S. scholars of like mind, an effective industrial relations system does not eliminate conflict. Rather, it provides institutions (and a "web of rules") that resolve conflict in a way that minimizes its costs to management, employees, and society. The collective bargaining system is one such institution, as are related mechanisms such as mediation, arbitration, and participation in decision making. These ideas formed the basis for the development in the 1940s of schools and departments of industrial and labor relations to train labor relations professionals who, working in both union and management positions, would have the skills to minimize costly forms of conflict such as strikes (which were reaching record levels at the time) and maximize integrative (win–win) solutions to such disagreements.

A more recent industrial relations model, developed by Harry Katz and Thomas Kochan, is particularly helpful in laying out the types of decisions management and unions make in their interactions and the consequences of such decisions for attainment of goals in areas such as wages and benefits, job security, and the rights and responsibilities of unions and managements.[3] According to Katz and Kochan, these choices occur at three levels.

First, at the strategic level, management makes basic choices such as whether to work with its union(s) or to devote its efforts to developing nonunion operations. Environmental factors (or competitive challenges) offer both constraints and opportunities in implementing strategies. For example, if public opinion toward labor unions becomes negative during a particular time period, some employers may see that as an opportunity to rid themselves of unions, whereas other employers may seek a better working relationship with their unions. Similarly, increased competition may dictate the need to increase productivity or reduce labor costs, but whether this is accomplished by shifting work to nonunion facilities or by working with unions to become more competitive is a strategic choice that management faces.

Although management has often been the initiator of change in recent years, unions face a similar choice between fighting changes to the status quo and being open to new labor–management relationships (like less adversarial forms of participation in decision making, such as labor–management teams).

Katz and Kochan suggest that labor and management choices at the strategic level in turn affect the labor–management interaction at a second level, the functional level, where contract negotiations and union organizing occur, and at the final workplace level, the arena in which the contract is administered. Although the relationships between labor and management at each of the three levels are somewhat interdependent, the relationship at the three levels may also differ. For example, while management may have a strategy of building an effective relationship with its unions at the strategic level, there may be significant day-to-day conflicts over work rules, grievances, and so forth at any given facility or bargaining unit (workplace level).

The labor relations framework depicted in Figure 14.1 incorporates many of the ideas discussed so far, including the important role of the environment (the competitive challenges); union, management, and societal goals; and a separation

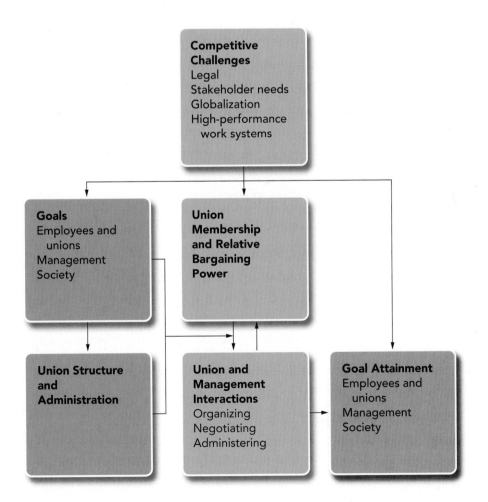

figure 14.1

A Labor Relations Framework

of union–management interactions into categories (union organizing, contract negotiation, contract administration) that can have important influences on one another but may also be analyzed somewhat independently. The model also highlights the important role that relative bargaining power plays in influencing goals, union–management interactions, and the degree to which each party achieves its goals. Relative bargaining power, in turn, is significantly influenced by the competitive environment (legal, social, quality, high-performance work systems, and globalization competitive challenges) and the size and depth of union membership.[4]

We now describe the components of this model in greater depth. The remainder of the chapter is organized into the following sections: the goals and strategies of society, management, and unions; union structure (including union administration and membership); the legal framework, perhaps the key aspect of the competitive environment for labor relations; union and management interactions (organizing, contract negotiation, contract administration); and goal attainment. Environmental factors (other than legal) and bargaining power are discussed in the context of these sections. In addition, two special topics, international comparisons and public sector labor relations, are discussed.

Goals and Strategies

SOCIETY

LO 14-2
Identify the labor relations goals of management, labor unions, and society.

In one sense, labor unions, with their emphasis on group action, do not fit well with the individualistic orientation of U.S. capitalism. However, industrial relations scholars such as Beatrice and Sidney Webb and John R. Commons argued in the late 1800s and early 1900s that individual workers' bargaining power was far smaller than that of employers, who were likely to have more financial resources and the ability to easily replace workers.[5] Effective institutions for worker representation (like labor unions) were therefore seen as a way to make bargaining power more equal.

Labor unions' major benefit to society is the institutionalization of industrial conflict, which is therefore resolved in the least costly way. Thus, although disagreements between management and labor continue, it is better to resolve disputes through discussion (collective bargaining) than by battling in the streets. As an influential group of industrial relations scholars put it in describing the future of advanced industrial relations around the world, "Class warfare will be forgotten. The battles will be in the corridors instead of the streets, and memos will flow instead of blood."[6] In this sense, collective bargaining not only has the potential to reduce economic losses caused by strikes but may also contribute to societal stability. For this reason, industrial relations scholars have often viewed labor unions as an essential component of a democratic society.[7] These were some of the beliefs that contributed to the enactment of the National Labor Relations Act (NLRA) in 1935, which sought to provide an environment conducive to collective bargaining and has since regulated labor and management activities and interactions.

Even Senator Orrin Hatch, described by *BusinessWeek* as "labor's archrival on Capitol Hill," has spoken of the need for unions:

> There are always going to be people who take advantage of workers. Unions even that out, to their credit. We need them to level the field between labor and management. If you didn't have unions, it would be very difficult for even enlightened employers not to take advantage of workers on wages and working conditions, because of [competition from] rivals. I'm among the first to say I believe in unions.[8]

Although an industrial relations system based on collective bargaining has drawbacks, so too do the alternatives. Unilateral control by management sacrifices workers' rights. Extensive involvement of government and the courts can result in conflict resolution that is expensive, slow, and imposed by someone (a judge) with much less firsthand knowledge of the circumstances than either labor or management.

MANAGEMENT

One of management's most basic decisions is whether to encourage or discourage the unionization of its employees. It may discourage unions because it fears higher wage and benefit costs, the disruptions caused by strikes, and an adversarial relationship with its employees or, more generally, greater constraints placed on its decision-making flexibility and discretion. Historically, management has used two basic strategies to avoid unionization.[9] It may seek to provide employment terms and conditions that employees will perceive as sufficiently attractive and equitable so that they see little gain from union representation. Or it may aggressively oppose union representation, even where there is significant employee interest. Use of the latter strategy has increased significantly during the last 20 to 30 years.

If management voluntarily recognizes a union or if employees are already represented by a union, the focus is shifted from dealing with employees as individuals to employees as a group. Still, certain basic management objectives remain: controlling labor costs and increasing productivity (by keeping wages and benefits in check) and maintaining management prerogatives in important areas such as staffing levels and work rules. Of course, management always has the option of trying to decertify a union (that is, encouraging employees to vote out the union in a decertification election) if it believes that the majority of employees no longer wish to be represented by the union.

LABOR UNIONS

Labor unions seek, through collective action, to give workers a formal and independent voice in setting the terms and conditions of their work. Table 14.1 shows typical provisions negotiated by unions in collective bargaining contracts. Labor unions attempt to represent their members' interests in these decisions.

A major goal of labor unions is bargaining effectiveness, because with it comes the power and influence to make the employees' voices heard and to effect changes in the workplace.[10] The right to strike is one important component of bargaining power. In turn, the success of a strike (actual or threatened) depends on the relative magnitude of the costs imposed on management versus those imposed on the union. A critical factor is the size of union membership. More members translate into a greater ability to halt or disrupt production and also into greater financial resources for continuing a strike in the face of lost wages.

Union Structure, Administration, and Membership

A necessary step in discussing labor–management interactions is a basic knowledge of how labor and management are organized and how they function. Management has been described throughout this book. We now focus on labor unions.

table 14.1

Typical Provisions in Collective Bargaining Contracts

Establishment and administration of the agreement
Bargaining unit and plant supplements
Contract duration and reopening and renegotiation provisions
Union security and the checkoff
Special bargaining committees
Grievance procedures
Arbitration and mediation
Strikes and lockouts
Contract enforcement

Functions, rights, and responsibilities
Management rights clauses
Plant removal
Subcontracting
Union activities on company time and premises
Union–management cooperation
Regulation of technological change
Advance notice and consultation

Wage determination and administration
General provisions
Rate structure and wage differentials
Allowances
Incentive systems and production bonus plans
Production standards and time studies
Job classification and job evaluation
Individual wage adjustments
General wage adjustments during the contract period

Job or income security
Hiring and transfer arrangements
Employment and income guarantees
Reporting and call-in pay
Supplemental unemployment benefit plans
Regulation of overtime, shift work, etc.
Reduction of hours to forestall layoffs
Layoff procedures; seniority; recall
Worksharing in lieu of layoff
Attrition arrangements
Promotion practices
Training and retraining
Relocation allowances
Severance pay and layoff benefit plans
Special funds and study committees

Plant operations
Work and shop rules
Rest periods and other in-plant time allowances
Safety and health
Plant committees
Hours of work and premium pay practices
Shift operations
Hazardous work
Discipline and discharge

Paid and unpaid leave
Vacations and holidays
Sick leave
Funeral and personal leave
Military leave and jury duty

Employee benefit plans
Health and insurance plans
Pension plans
Profit-sharing, stock purchase, and thrift plans
Bonus plans

Special groups
Apprentices and learners
Workers with disabilities and older workers
Women
Veterans
Union representatives
Nondiscrimination clauses

SOURCE: From Harry Katz, Thomas Kochan, and Alexander Colvin, *An Introduction to Collective Bargaining and Industrial Relations* 4E, 2008. Copyright © 2008. The McGraw-Hill Companies.

NATIONAL AND INTERNATIONAL UNIONS

Most union members belong to a national or international union. In turn, most national unions are composed of multiple local units, and most are affiliated with the American Federation of Labor and Congress of Industrial Organizations (AFL-CIO).

The largest national unions are listed in Table 14.2. (The National Education Association, with 3.2 million members, is not affiliated with the AFL-CIO.) An

table 14.2

Largest Labor Unions in the United States

ORGANIZATION	NUMBER OF MEMBERS
1. National Education Association	3,200,000
2. Service Employees International Union	1,800,000
3. International Brotherhood of Teamsters	1,400,000
4. American Federation of State, County, and Municipal Employees	1,378,000
5. United Food and Commercial Workers International Union	1,300,000
6. American Federation of Teachers	1,111,000
7. International Brotherhood of Electrical Workers	617,000
8. Communications Workers of America	582,000
9. United Steel, Paper and Forestry, Rubber, Manufacturing, Energy, Allied Industrial, and Service Workers International Union	504,000
10. United Automobile, Aerospace, and Agricultural Implement Workers of America International Union	455,000
11. International Association of Machinists and Aerospace Workers	313,000
12. International Union of Operating Engineers	280,000
13. International Association of Fire Fighters	243,000
14. American Federation of Government Employees	227,000
15. United Association of Journeymen and Apprentices of the Plumbing and Pipe Fitting Industry of the United States and Canada	220,000
16. American Postal Workers Union, AFL-CIO	210,000
17. National Association of Letter Carriers	209,000

SOURCE: D. Gifford, Directory of U.S. Labor Organizations, 2010 edition. Copyright © 2010 by the Bureau of National Affairs, Washington, DC 20037. For copies of BNA Books publications call toll free 1-800-960-1220.

important characteristic of a union is whether it is a craft or industrial union. The electrical workers' and carpenters' unions are craft unions, meaning that the members all have a particular skill or occupation. Craft unions often are responsible for training their members (through apprenticeships) and for supplying craft workers to employers. Requests for carpenters, for example, would come to the union hiring hall, which would decide which carpenters to send out. Thus craft workers may work for many employers over time, their constant link being to the union. A craft union's bargaining power depends greatly on the control it can exercise over the supply of its workers.

In contrast, industrial unions are made up of members who are linked by their work in a particular industry (such as steelworkers and autoworkers). Typically they represent many different occupations. Membership in the union is a result of working for a particular employer in the industry. Changing employers is less common than it is among craft workers, and employees who change employers remain members of the same union only if they happen to move to other employers covered by that union. Whereas a craft union may restrict the number of, say, carpenters to maintain higher wages, industrial unions try to organize as many employees in as wide a range of skills as possible.

LOCAL UNIONS

Even when a national union plays the most critical role in negotiating terms of a collective bargaining contract, negotiation occurs at the local level as well as over work rules and other issues that are locally determined. In addition, administration of the contract is largely carried out at the local union level. Consequently, the bulk of day-to-day interaction between labor and management takes place at the local union level.

The local of an industrial-based union may correspond to a single large facility or to a number of small facilities. In a craft-oriented union, the local may cover a city or a region. The local union typically elects officers (like president, vice president, treasurer). Responsibility for contract negotiation may rest with the officers, or a bargaining committee may be formed for this purpose. Typically the national union provides assistance, ranging from background data about other settlements and technical advice to sending a representative to lead the negotiations.

Individual members' participation in local union meetings includes the election of union officials and strike votes. However, most union contact is with the shop steward, who is responsible for ensuring that the terms of the collective bargaining contract are enforced. The shop steward represents employees in contract grievances. Another union position, the business representative, performs some of the same functions, especially where the union deals with multiple employers, as is often the case with craft unions.

AMERICAN FEDERATION OF LABOR AND CONGRESS OF INDUSTRIAL ORGANIZATIONS (AFL-CIO)

The AFL-CIO is not a labor union but rather an association that seeks to advance the shared interests of its member unions at the national level, much as the Chamber of Commerce and the National Association of Manufacturers do for their member employers. As Figure 14.2 indicates, there are 54 affiliated national and international unions and thousands of locals. An important responsibility of the AFL-CIO is to represent labor's interests in public policy issues such as civil rights, economic policy, safety, and occupational health. It also provides information and analysis that member unions can use in their activities: organizing new members, negotiating new contracts, and administering contracts.

UNION SECURITY

The survival and security of a union depends on its ability to ensure a regular flow of new members and member dues to support the services it provides. Therefore, unions typically place high priority on negotiating two contract provisions with an employer that are critical to a union's security or viability: checkoff provisions and union membership or contribution. First, under a **checkoff provision,** the employer, on behalf of the union, automatically deducts union dues from employees' paychecks.

A second union security provision focuses on the flow of new members (and their dues). The strongest union security arrangement is a **closed shop,** under which a person must be a union member (and thus pay dues) before being hired. A closed shop is, however, illegal under the NLRA. A **union shop** requires a person to join the union within a certain amount of time (30 days) after beginning employment. An **agency shop** is similar to a union shop but does not require union membership, only that dues be paid.

Checkoff Provision
A union contract provision that requires an employer to deduct union dues from employees' paychecks.

Closed Shop
A union security provision requiring a person to be a union member before being hired. Illegal under NLRA.

Union Shop
A union security provision that requires a person to join the union within a certain amount of time after being hired.

Agency Shop
A union security provision that requires an employee to pay union membership dues but not to join the union.

figure 14.2

AFL-CIO Organization Chart

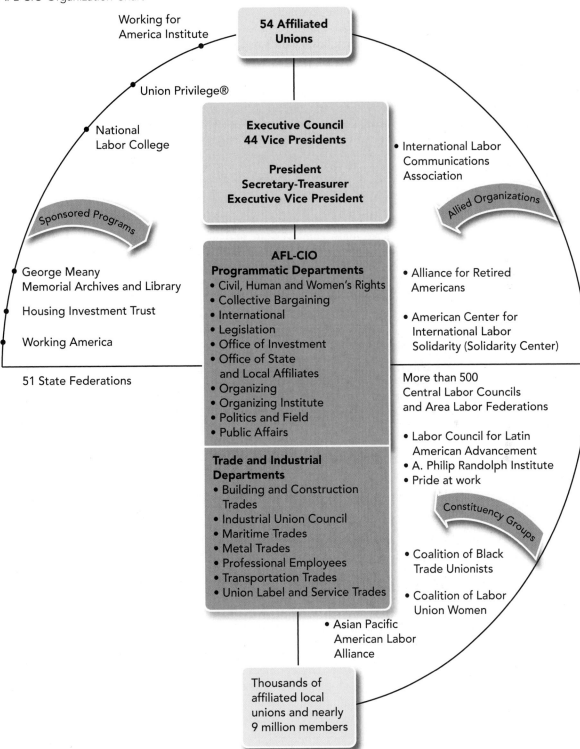

SOURCE: AFL-CIO, www.aflcio.org, accessed March 18, 2007.

Maintenance of Membership
Union rules requiring members to remain members for a certain period of time (such as the length of the union contract).

Maintenance of membership rules do not require union membership but do require that employees who choose to join must remain members for a certain period of time (such as the length of the contract).

Under the 1947 Taft–Hartley Act (an amendment to the NLRA), states may pass so-called **right-to-work laws,** which make union shops, maintenance of membership, and agency shops illegal. The idea behind such laws is that compulsory union membership (or making employees pay union dues) infringes on the employee's right to freedom of association. From the union perspective, a big concern is "free riders," employees who benefit from union activities without belonging to a union. By law, all members of a bargaining unit, whether union members or not, must be represented by the union. If the union is required to offer service to all bargaining unit members, even those who are not union members, it may lose its financial viability.

Right-to-Work Laws
State laws that make union shops, maintenance of membership, and agency shops illegal.

UNION MEMBERSHIP AND BARGAINING POWER

At the strategic level, management and unions meet head-on over the issue of union organizing. Increasingly, employers are actively resisting unionization in an attempt to control costs and maintain their flexibility. Unions, on the other hand, must organize new members and hold on to their current members to have the kind of bargaining power and financial resources needed to achieve their goals in future organizing and to negotiate and administer contracts with management. For this reason we now discuss trends in union membership and possible explanations for those trends.

Since the 1950s, when union membership rose to 35% of employment, membership has consistently declined as a percentage of employment. It now stands at 11.9% of all employment and 6.9% of private-sector employment.[11] As Figure 14.3 indicates, this decline shows no indication of reversing.[12]

What factors explain the decline in union membership? Several have been identified.[13]

Structural Changes in the Economy

At the risk of oversimplifying, we might say that unions have traditionally been strongest in urban workplaces (especially those outside the South) that employ middle-aged men in blue-collar jobs. However, much recent job growth has occurred among women and youth in the service sector of the economy. Although unionizing such groups is possible, unions have so far not had much success organizing these groups in the private sector. Despite the importance of structural changes in the economy, studies show that they account for no more than one-quarter of the overall union membership decline.[14]

Increased Employer Resistance

Almost one-half of large employers in a survey reported that their most important labor goal was to be union-free. This contrasts sharply with 50 years ago, when Jack Barbash wrote that "many tough bargainers [among employers] prefer the union to a situation where there is no union. Most of the employers in rubber, basic steel and the automobile industry fall in this category." The idea then was that an effective union could help assess and communicate the interests of employees to management, thus helping management make better decisions. But product-market pressures, such as foreign competition and deregulation (e.g., trucking, airlines, telecommunications), have contributed

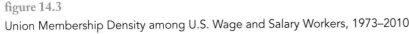

figure 14.3

Union Membership Density among U.S. Wage and Salary Workers, 1973–2010

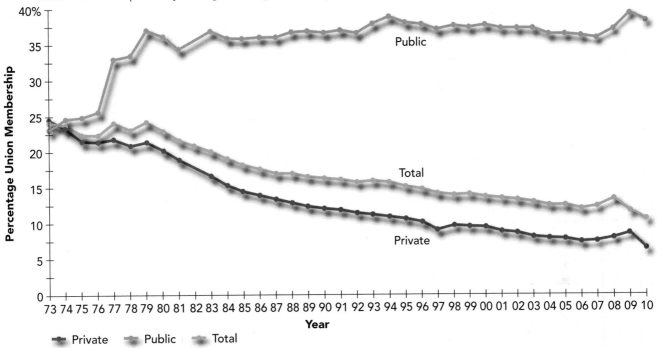

SOURCE: From B. T. Hirsch and D. A. MacPherson, *Union Membership and Earnings Data Book 2001* (Washington, DC: The Bureau of National Affairs, Inc., 2001). Reprinted with permission. Data for 2001 to 2010 obtained from U.S. Bureau of Labor Statistics, www.bls.gov.

to increasing employer resistance to unions.[15] These changes in the competitive environment have contributed to a change in management's perspective and goals.[16]

In the absence of significant competition from foreign producers, unions were often able to organize entire industries. For example, the UAW organized all four major producers in the automobile industry (GM, Ford, Chrysler, and American Motors). The UAW usually sought and achieved the same union–management contract at each company. As a consequence, a negotiated wage increase in the industry could be passed on to the consumer in the form of higher prices. No company was undercut by its competitors because the labor cost of all major producers in the industry was determined by the same union–management contract, and the U.S. public had little option but to buy U.S.-made cars. However, the onset of foreign competition in the automobile market changed the competitive situation as well as the UAW's ability to organize the industry.[17] U.S. automakers were slow to recognize and respond to the competitive threat from foreign producers, resulting in a loss of market share and employment.

Competitive threats have contributed to increased employer resistance to union organizing and, in some cases, to an increased emphasis on ridding themselves of existing unions. Unionized workers receive, on average, 10% to 15% higher wages than their nonunion counterparts and this advantage is still larger if benefits are also included. Many employers have decided that they can no longer compete with these higher labor costs, and union membership has suffered as a result.[18] One measure of increased employer resistance is the dramatic increase in the late 1960s in the number of unfair employer labor practices (violations of sections of the NLRA such as section 8(a)(3), which prohibits firing employees for union organizing, as we discuss later) even though the number of elections held did not change much. (See Figure 14.4.) The use of remedies such as back pay for workers also grew, but the costs to employers of such penalties does not appear to have been sufficient to prevent the growth in employer unfair labor practices. Not surprisingly, the union victory rate in representation elections decreased from almost 59% in 1960 to below 50% by 1975. Although the union victory rate in recent years has been over 50%, the number of elections has declined by more than 50% since the 1960s and 1970s. Moreover, decertification elections have gone from about 4% of elections in 1960 to 15% to 20% of elections in recent years.[19] Given the significant decline in both elections and union membership percentage, the increases in the number of unfair labor practice charges and back pay awards is all the more notable.

Finally, even if a union wins the right to represent employees, its ability to successfully negotiate a contract with the employer is not guaranteed. Indeed, refusal to bargain by the employer is the unfair labor practice most frequently filed (over half of all charges) against employers. As a result, only one in seven union representation election petitions with the National Labor Relations Board (NLRB) results in both a

figure 14.4

Employer Resistance to Union Organizing, 1950–2009

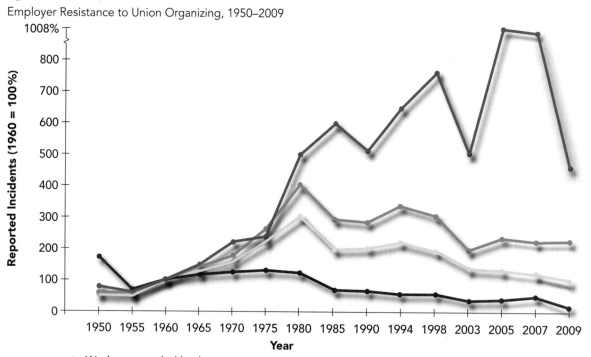

NOTE: 8(a)(3) charges refer to the section of the NLRA that makes it an unfair employer labor practice to discriminate against (e.g., fire) employees who engage in union activities such as union organizing.

SOURCE: Adapted and updated from R. B. Freeman and J. L. Medoff, *What Do Unions Do?* (New York: Basic Books, 1984). Data for 1985, 1989, 1990, 1994, 1998, 2003, 2005, 2007, and 2009 from National Labor Relations Board annual reports.

union victory *and* successful negotiation of a first contract. Further, where an unfair labor practice charge was filed against an employer during the organizing campaign, the chance of union success was substantially lower.[20]

At a personal level, some managers may face serious consequences if a union successfully organizes a new set of workers or mounts a serious organizing drive. One study indicated that 8% of the plant managers in companies with organizing drives were fired, and 10% of those in companies where the union was successful were fired (compared with 2% in a control group).[21] Furthermore, only 3% of the plant managers facing an organizing drive were promoted, and none of those ending up with a union contract were promoted (compared with 21% of the managers in the control group). Therefore, managers are often under intense pressure to oppose unionization attempts.

Substitution with HRM

A major study of the human resource management strategies and practices among large, nonunion employers found that union avoidance was often an important employee relations objective.[22] Top management's values in such companies drive specific policies such as promotion from within, an influential personnel–human resource department, and above-average pay and benefits. These policies, in turn, contribute to a number of desirable outcomes such as flexibility, positive employee attitudes, and responsive and committed employees, which ultimately lead to higher productivity and better employee relations. In other words, employers attempt to remain nonunion by offering most of the things a union can offer, and then some, while still maintaining a productivity advantage over their competitors. Of course, one aspect of union representation that employers cannot duplicate is the independent employee voice that a union provides.

Substitution by Government Regulation

Since the 1960s, regulation of many employment areas has increased, including equal employment opportunity, pensions, and worker displacement. Combined with existing regulations, this increase may result in fewer areas in which unions can provide worker rights or protection beyond those specified by law. Yet western European countries generally have more regulations and higher levels of union membership than the United States.[23]

Worker Views

Industrial relations scholars have long argued that the absence in the United States of a history of feudalism and of strong class distinctions found in western Europe have contributed to a more pragmatic, business-oriented (versus class-conscious) unionism. Although this may help explain the somewhat lower level of union membership in the United States, its relevance in explaining the downward trend is not clear. Further, when U.S. workers are asked about their interest in joining a union, interest is substantial.[24]

Union Actions

In some ways, unions have hurt their own cause. First, corruption in unions such as the Teamsters may have had a detrimental effect. Second, questions have been raised about how well unions have adapted to recent changes in the economic structure.

Employee groups and economic sectors with the fastest growth rates tend to have the lowest rates of unionization.[25] Women are less likely to be in unions than men (11.3% versus 13.3%), and nonmanufacturing industries such as finance, insurance, and real estate have a lower union representation (1.8%) than does manufacturing (10.9%). The South is also less heavily organized than the rest of the country, with, for example, South Carolina having a unionization rate of 4.5%, compared with 25.2% in New York State.[26] For example, none of the foreign-owned automobile assembly plants (e.g., BMW, Mercedes-Benz, Toyota), most of which are located in the South, are unionized (although they would be in their home countries). One reason for the smaller union presence in southern states is the existence of right-to-work laws (see our earlier discussion) in such states.

Legal Framework

LO 14-3
Explain the legal environment's impact on labor relations.

Although competitive challenges have a major impact on labor relations, the legal framework of collective bargaining is an especially critical determinant of union membership and relative bargaining power and, therefore, of the degree to which employers, employees, and society are successful in achieving their goals. The legal framework also constrains union structure and administration and the manner in which unions and employers interact. Perhaps the most dramatic example of labor laws' influence is the 1935 passage of the Wagner Act (also known as the National Labor Relations Act or NLRA), which actively supported collective bargaining rather than impeding it. As a result, union membership nearly tripled, from 3 million in 1933 (7.7% of all employment) to 8.8 million (19.2% of employment) by 1939.[27] With increased membership came greater union bargaining power and, consequently, more success in achieving union goals.

Before the 1930s, the legal system was generally hostile to unions. The courts generally viewed unions as coercive organizations that hindered free trade. Unions' focus on collective voice and collective action (strikes, boycotts) did not fit well with the U.S. emphasis on capitalism, individualism, freedom of contract, and property rights.[28]

The Great Depression of the 1930s, however, shifted public attitudes toward business and the free-enterprise system. Unemployment rates as high as 25% and a 30% drop in the gross national product between 1929 and 1933 focused attention on employee rights and on the shortcomings of the system as it existed then. The nation was in a crisis, and President Franklin Roosevelt responded with dramatic action, the New Deal. On the labor front, the 1935 NLRA ushered in a new era of public policy for labor unions, enshrining collective bargaining as the preferred mechanism for settling labor–management disputes.

The introduction to the NLRA states:

It is in the national interest of the United States to maintain full production in its economy. Industrial strife among employees, employers, and labor organizations interferes with full production and is contrary to our national interest. Experience has shown that labor disputes can be lessened if the parties involved recognize the legitimate rights of each in their relations with one another. To establish these rights under the law, Congress enacted the National Labor Relations Act. Its purpose is to define and protect the rights of employees and employers, to encourage collective bargaining, and to eliminate certain practices on the part of labor and management that are harmful to the general welfare.[29]

The rights of employees are set out in Section 7 of the act, including the "right to self-organization, to form, join, or assist labor organizations, to bargain collectively through representatives of their own choosing, and to engage in other concerted activities for the purpose of collective bargaining. The act also gives employees the right to refrain from any or all of such activities except [in cases] requiring membership in a labor organization as a condition of employment."[30] Examples of protected activities include

- Union organizing.
- Joining a union, whether it is recognized by the employer or not.
- Going out on strike to secure better working conditions.
- Refraining from activity on behalf of the union.[31]

Although the NLRA has broad coverage in the private sector, Table 14.3 shows that there are some notable exclusions.

UNFAIR LABOR PRACTICES—EMPLOYERS

The NLRA prohibits certain activities by both employers and labor unions. Unfair labor practices by employers are listed in Section 8(a) of the NLRA. Section 8(a)(1) prohibits employers from interfering with, restraining, or coercing employees in exercising their rights to join or assist a labor organization or to refrain from such activities. Section 8(a)(2) prohibits employer domination of or interference with the formation or activities of a labor union. Section 8(a)(3) prohibits discrimination in any aspect of employment that attempts to encourage or discourage union-related activity. Section 8(a)(4) prohibits discrimination against employees for providing testimony relevant to enforcement of the NLRA. Section 8(a)(5) prohibits employers from refusing to bargain collectively with a labor organization that has standing under the act. Examples of employer unfair labor practices are listed in Table 14.4.

UNFAIR LABOR PRACTICES—LABOR UNIONS

Originally the NLRA did not list any union unfair labor practices. These were added through the 1947 **Taft-Hartley Act.** The 1959 *Landrum-Griffin Act* further regulated unions' actions and their internal affairs (like financial disclosure and conduct of elections). Section 8(b)(1)(a) of the NLRA states that a labor

Taft-Hartley Act, 1947
The 1947 act that outlawed unfair union labor practices.

table 14.3
Are You Excluded from the NLRA's Coverage?

The NLRA specifically excludes from its coverage individuals who are
- Employed as a supervisor.
- Employed by a parent or spouse.
- Employed as an independent contractor.
- Employed in the domestic service of any person or family in a home.
- Employed as agricultural laborers.
- Employed by an employer subject to the Railway Labor Act.
- Employed by a federal, state, or local government.
- Employed by any other person who is not an employer as defined in the NLRA.

SOURCE: www.nlrb.gov/publications/engulp.html.

table 14.4

Examples of Employer Unfair Labor Practices

- Threatening employees with loss of their jobs or benefits if they join or vote for a union.
- Threatening to close down a plant if organized by a union.
- Questioning employees about their union membership or activities in a manner that restrains or coerces them.
- Spying or pretending to spy on union meetings.
- Granting wage increases that are timed to discourage employees from forming or joining a union.
- Taking an active part in organizing a union or committee to represent employees.
- Providing preferential treatment or aid to one of several unions trying to organize employees.
- Discharging employees for urging other employees to join a union or refusing to hire applicants because they are union members.
- Refusing to reinstate workers when job openings occur because the workers participated in a lawful strike.
- Ending operation at one plant and opening the same operation at another plant with new employees because employees at the first plant joined a union.
- Demoting or firing employees for filing an unfair labor practice or for testifying at an NLRB hearing.
- Refusing to meet with employees' representatives because the employees are on strike.
- Refusing to supply the employees' representative with cost and other data concerning a group insurance plan covering employees.
- Announcing a wage increase without consulting the employees' representative.
- Failing to bargain about the effects of a decision to close one of employer's plants.

SOURCE: National Labor Relations Board, *Basic Guide to the National Labor Relations Act* (Washington, DC: U.S. Government Printing Office, 1997). Available at www.nlrb.gov.

organization is not to "restrain or coerce employees in the exercise of the rights guaranteed in section 7" (described earlier). Table 14.5 provides examples of union unfair labor practices.

ENFORCEMENT

Enforcement of the NLRA rests with the National Labor Relations Board, which is composed of a five-member board, the general counsel, and 33 regional offices. The basis for the NLRA is the commerce clause of the U.S. Constitution. Therefore, the NLRB's jurisdiction is limited to employers whose operations affect commerce generally and interstate commerce in particular. In practice, only purely local firms are likely to fall outside the NLRB's jurisdiction. Specific jurisdictional standards (nearly 20) that vary by industry are applied. Two examples of businesses that are covered (and the standards) are retail businesses that had more than $500,000 in annual business and newspapers that had more than $200,000 in annual business.

The NLRB's two major functions are to conduct and certify representation elections and prevent unfair labor practices. In both realms, it does not initiate action. Rather, it responds to requests for action. The NLRB's role in representation elections is discussed in the next section. Here we discuss unfair labor practices.

Unfair labor practice cases begin with the filing of a charge, which is investigated by a regional office. A charge must be filed within six months of the alleged unfair practice, and copies must be served on all parties. (Registered mail is recommended.) If the NLRB finds the charge to have merit and issues a complaint, there are two possible actions. It may defer to a grievance procedure agreed on by the employer and

table 14.5

Examples of Union Unfair Labor Practices

- Mass picketing in such numbers that nonstriking employees are physically barred from entering the plant.
- Acts of force or violence on the picket line or in connection with a strike.
- Threats to employees of bodily injury or that they will lose their jobs unless they support the union's activities.
- Fining or expelling members for crossing a picket line that is unlawful.
- Fining or expelling members for filing unfair labor practice charges or testifying before the NLRB.
- Insisting during contract negotiations that the employer agree to accept working conditions that will be determined by a group to which it does not belong.
- Fining or expelling union members for the way they apply the bargaining contract while carrying out their supervisory responsibilities.
- Causing an employer to discharge employees because they spoke out against a contract proposed by the union.
- Making a contract that requires an employer to hire only members of the union or employees "satisfactory" to the union.
- Insisting on the inclusion of illegal provisions in a contract.
- Terminating an existing contract and striking for a new one without notifying the employer, the Federal Mediation and Conciliation Service, and the state mediation service (where one exists).
- Attempting to compel a beer distributor to recognize a union (the union prevents the distributor from obtaining beer at a brewery by inducing the brewery's employees to refuse to fill the distributor's orders).
- Picketing an employer to force it to stop doing business with another employer who has refused to recognize the union (a "secondary boycott").

SOURCE: National Labor Relations Board, *A Guide to Basic Law and Procedures under the National Labor Relations Act* (Washington, DC: U.S. Government Printing Office, 1997). Available at www.nlrb.gov.

union. Otherwise, a hearing is held before an administrative law judge. The judge makes a recommendation, which can be appealed by either party. The NLRB has the authority to issue cease-and-desist orders to halt unfair labor practices. It can also order reinstatement of employees, with or without back pay. In 2009, for example, $77.6 million in back pay was awarded and 1,559 workers were offered reinstatement (of whom 78% accepted). Note, however, that the NLRA is not a criminal statute, and punitive damages are not available. If an employer or union refuses to comply with an NLRB order, the board has the authority to petition the U.S. Court of Appeals. The court can choose to enforce the order, remand it to the NLRB for modification, change it, or set it aside altogether.

Union and Management Interactions: Organizing

To this point we have discussed macro trends in union membership. Here we shift our focus to the more micro questions of why individual employees join unions and how the organizing process works at the workplace level.

LO 14-4

Describe the major labor–management interactions: organizing, contract negotiations, and contract administration.

WHY DO EMPLOYEES JOIN UNIONS?

Virtually every model of the decision to join a union focuses on two questions.[32] First, is there a gap between the pay, benefits, and other conditions of employment that employees actually receive versus what they believe they should receive? Second, if such a gap exists and is sufficiently large to motivate employees to try to remedy the situation, is union membership seen as the most effective or instrumental means of change? The outcome of an election campaign hinges on how the majority of employees answer these two questions.

THE PROCESS AND LEGAL FRAMEWORK OF ORGANIZING

The NLRB is responsible for ensuring that the organizing process follows certain steps. At the most general level, the NLRB holds a union representation election if at least 30% of employees in the bargaining unit sign authorization cards (see Figure 14.5). If more than 50% of the employees sign authorization cards, the union may request that the employer voluntarily recognize it. If 50% or fewer of the employees sign, or if the employer refuses to recognize the union voluntarily, the NLRB conducts a secret-ballot election. The union is certified by the NLRB as the exclusive representative of employees if more than 50% of employees vote for the union. If more than one union appears on the ballot and neither gains a simple majority, a runoff election is held. Once a union has been certified as the exclusive representative of a group of employees, no additional elections are permitted for one year. After the negotiation of a contract, an election cannot be held for the contract's duration or for three years, whichever comes first. The parties to the contract may agree not to hold an election for longer than three years, but an outside party cannot be barred for more than three years.

As mentioned previously, union members' right to be represented by leaders of their own choosing was expanded under the Taft-Hartley Act to include the right to vote an existing union out—that is, to decertify it. The process follows the same steps as a representation election. A decertification election is not permitted when a contract is in effect. Research indicates that when decertification elections are held, unions typically do not fare well, losing the majority of the time.[33]

figure 14.5
Authorization Card

YES, I WANT THE IAM

I, the undersigned employee of

(Company)_____

authorize the International Association of Machinists and Aerospace Workers (IAM) to act as my collective bargaining agent for wages, hours and working conditions. I agree that this card may be used either to support a demand for recognition or an NLRB election, at the discretion of the union.

Name (print)_____ Date _____

Home Address_____ Phone_____

City_____ State _____ Zip_____

Job Title————————— Dept.————— Shift ————

Sign Here X
_____

Note: This authorization to be SIGNED and DATED in employee's own handwriting.
YOUR RIGHT TO SIGN THIS CARD IS PROTECTED BY FEDERAL LAW.

RECEIVED BY (Initial) _____

SOURCE: From John Fossum, *Labor Relations: Development, Structure and Processes*, 8E, 2002. Copyright © 2002 The McGraw-Hill Companies Inc. Reprinted with permission.

The NLRB also is responsible for determining the appropriate bargaining unit and the employees who are eligible to participate in organizing activities. A unit may cover employees in one facility or multiple facilities within a single employer, or the unit may cover multiple employers. In general, employees on the payroll just prior to the ordering of an election are eligible to vote, although this rule is modified in some cases where, for example, employment in the industry is irregular. Most employees who are on strike and who have been replaced by other employees are eligible to vote in an election (such as a decertification election) that occurs within 12 months of the onset of the strike.

As shown in Table 14.3, the following types of employees cannot be included in bargaining units: agricultural laborers, independent contractors, supervisors, and managers. Beyond this, the NLRB attempts to group together employees who have a community of interest in their wages, hours, and working conditions. In many cases this grouping will be sharply contested, with management and the union jockeying to include or exclude certain employee subgroups in the hope of influencing the outcome of the election.

Organizing Campaigns: Management and Union Strategies and Tactics

Tables 14.6 and 14.7 list common issues that arise during most campaigns.[34] Unions attempt to persuade employees that their wages, benefits, treatment by employers, and opportunity to influence workplace decisions are not sufficient and that the union will be effective in obtaining improvements. Management emphasizes that it

UNION ISSUES	PERCENTAGE OF CAMPAIGNS
Union will prevent unfairness and will set up a grievance procedure and seniority system.	82%
Union will improve unsatisfactory wages.	79
Union strength will give employees voice in wages, working conditions.	79
Union, not outsider, bargains for what employees want.	73
Union has obtained gains elsewhere.	70
Union will improve unsatisfactory sick leave and insurance.	64
Dues and initiation fees are reasonable.	64
Union will improve unsatisfactory vacations and holidays.	61
Union will improve unsatisfactory pensions.	61
Employer promises and good treatment may not be continued without union.	61
Employees choose union leaders.	55
Employer will seek to persuade or frighten employees to vote against union.	55
No strike without vote.	55
Union will improve unsatisfactory working conditions.	52
Employees have legal right to engage in union activity.	52

table 14.6

Prevalence of Certain Union Issues in Campaigns

SOURCE: From John Fossum, *Labor Relations: Development, Structure and Processes*, 5E, 1992. Copyright © 1992 The McGraw-Hill Companies Inc. Reprinted with permission.

table 14.7

Prevalence
of Certain
Management Issues
in Campaigns

MANAGEMENT ISSUES	PERCENTAGE OF CAMPAIGNS
Improvements not dependent on unionization.	85%
Wages good, equal to, or better than under union contract.	82
Financial costs of union dues outweigh gains.	79
Union is outsider.	79
Get facts before deciding; employer will provide facts and accept employee decision.	76
If union wins, strike may follow.	70
Loss of benefits may follow union win.	67
Strikers will lose wages; lose more than gain.	67
Unions not concerned with employee welfare.	67
Strike may lead to loss of jobs.	64
Employer has treated employees fairly and/or well.	60
Employees should be certain to vote.	54

SOURCE: From John Fossum, *Labor Relations: Development, Structure and Processes*, 5E, 1992. Copyright © 1992 The McGraw-Hill Companies Inc. Reprinted with permission.

has provided a good package of wages, benefits, and so on. It also argues that, whereas a union is unlikely to provide improvements in such areas, it will likely lead to certain costs for employees, such as union dues and the income loss resulting from strikes.

As Table 14.8 indicates, employers use a variety of methods to oppose unions in organizing campaigns, some of which may go beyond what the law permits, especially in the eyes of union organizers. This perception is supported by our earlier discussion, which noted a significant increase in employer unfair labor practices since the late 1960s. (See Figure 14.4.)

Why would employers increasingly break the law? Fossum suggests that the consequences (like back pay and reinstatement of workers) of doing so are "slight."[35] His review of various studies suggests that discrimination against employees involved in union organizing decreases union organizing success significantly and that the cost of back pay to union activists reinstated in their jobs is far smaller than the costs that would be incurred if the union managed to organize and gain better wages, benefits, and so forth.

Still, the NLRB attempts to maintain a noncoercive atmosphere under which employees feel they can exercise free choice. It will set aside an election if it believes that either the union or the employer has created "an atmosphere of confusion or fear of reprisals."[36] Examples of conduct that may lead to an election result being set aside include

- Threats of loss of jobs or benefits by an employer or union to influence votes or organizing activities.
- A grant of benefits or a promise of benefits as a means of influencing votes or organizing activities.
- An employer or union making campaign speeches to assembled groups of employees on company time less than 24 hours before an election.
- The actual use or threat of physical force or violence to influence votes or organizing activities.[37]

table 14.8

Percentage of Firms Using Various Methods to Oppose Union Organizing Campaigns

Survey of employers	
Consultants used	41%
Unfair labor practice charges filed against employer	24
Survey of union organizers	
Consultants and/or lawyers used	70
Unfair labor practices by employer	
Charges filed	36
Discharges or discriminatory layoffs	42[a]
Company leaflets	80
Company letters	91
Captive audience speech	91[b]
Supervisor meetings with small groups of employees	92
Supervisor intensity in opposing union	
Low	14
Moderate	34
High	51

[a]This percentage is larger than the figure for charges filed because it includes cases in which no unfair labor practice charge was actually filed against the employer.

[b]Refers to management's requiring employees to attend a session on company time at which the disadvantages of union membership are emphasized.

SOURCE: R. B. Freeman and M. M. Kleiner, "Employer Behavior in the Face of Union Organizing Drives," *Industrial and Labor Relations Review* 43, no. 4 (April 1990), pp. 351–65. © Cornell University.

Supervisors have the most direct contact with employees. Thus, as Table 14.9 indicates, it is critical that they be proactive in establishing good relationships with employees if the company wishes to avoid union organizing attempts. It is also important for supervisors to know what not to do should a drive take place.

In response to organizing difficulties, the union movement has tried alternative approaches. **Associate union membership** is not linked to an employee's workplace and does not provide representation in collective bargaining. Instead the union provides other services, such as discounts on health and life insurance or credit cards.[38] In return, the union receives membership dues and a broader base of support for its activities. Associate membership may be attractive to employees who wish to join a union but cannot because their workplace is not organized by a union.

Corporate campaigns seek to bring public, financial, or political pressure on employers during the organizing (and negotiating) process.[39] For example, the Building and Construction Trades Department of the AFL-CIO successfully lobbied Congress to eliminate $100 million in tax breaks for a Toyota truck plant in Kentucky until Toyota agreed to use union construction workers and pay union wages.[40] The Amalgamated Clothing and Textile Workers Union (ACTWU) corporate campaign against J. P. Stevens during the late 1970s was one of the first and best known. The ACTWU organized a boycott of J. P. Stevens products and threatened to withdraw its pension funds from financial institutions where J. P. Stevens officers acted as directors. J. P. Stevens subsequently agreed to a contract with the ACTWU.[41]

Associate Union Membership
A form of union membership by which the union receives dues in exchange for services (e.g., health insurance, credit cards) but does not provide representation in collective bargaining.

Corporate Campaigns
Union activities designed to exert public, financial, or political pressure on employers during the union-organizing process.

table 14.9

What Supervisors
Should and Should
Not Do to Stay
Union-Free

WHAT TO DO:

Report any direct or indirect signs of union activity to a core management group.
Deal with employees by carefully stating the company's response to pro-union
arguments. These responses should be coordinated by the company to maintain
consistency and to avoid threats or promises.
Take away union issues by following effective management practice all the time:
    Deliver recognition and appreciation.
    Solve employee problems.
    Protect employees from harassment or humiliation.
    Provide business-related information.
    Be consistent in treatment of different employees.
    Accommodate special circumstances where appropriate.
    Ensure due process in performance management.
    Treat all employees with dignity and respect.

WHAT TO AVOID:

Threatening employees with harsher terms and conditions of employment or
employment loss if they engage in union activity.
Interrogating employees about pro-union or anti-union sentiments that they or
others may have or reviewing union authorization cards or pro-union petitions.
Promising employees that they will receive favorable terms or conditions of
employment if they forgo union activity.
Spying on employees known to be, or suspected of being, engaged in pro-union
activities.

SOURCE: From J. A. Segal, *HR Magazine.* Copyright © 1998. Reproduced with permission of Society
for Human Resource Management via the Copyright Clearance Center.

Unions also hope to use their financial assets to influence companies. Recent
estimates suggest that unions directly control roughly $250 billion in pension funds
and share control with employers over another $1.04 trillion.[42] In addition, public
sector pension funds control another $2.0 trillion. The AFL-CIO and the United
Steelworkers have also set up a separate fund, the Heartland Labor Capital Network,
which invests in worker-friendly companies.[43]

In some success stories unions have eschewed elections in favor of strikes and
negative publicity to pressure corporations to accept a union. The Hotel Employees
and Restaurant Employees (HERE) organized 9,000 workers in 2001, with 80% of
these memberships resulting from pressure on employers rather than a vote. The
Union of Needletrade, Industrial, and Textile Employees (UNITE), which organized 15,000 workers in 2001, has also succeeded with this approach. After losing an election by just two votes among employees of Up-to-Date Laundry, which
cleans linens for Baltimore hotels and hospitals, UNITE decided to try other tactics, including a corporate campaign. It called a strike to demand that Up-to-Date
recognize the union. It also persuaded several major customers of the laundry to
threaten to stop using the laundry's services, shared claims of racial and sexual
harassment with state agencies and the National Association for the Advancement of Colored People (NAACP), and convinced the Baltimore city council to

require testimony from Up-to-Date. Eventually, the company gave in, recognized the union, and negotiated a contract that raised the workers' $6-an-hour wages and gave them better benefits.

Another winning union organizing strategy is to negotiate employer neutrality and card-check provisions into a contract. Under a *neutrality provision*, the employer pledges not to oppose organizing attempts elsewhere in the company. A *card-check provision* is an agreement that if a certain percentage—by law, at least a majority—of employees sign an authorization card, the employer will recognize their union representation. An impartial outside agency, such as the American Arbitration Association, counts the cards. The Communication Workers of America negotiated these provisions in its dispute with Verizon. Evidence suggests that this strategy can be very effective for unions.

Union and Management Interactions: Contract Negotiation

The majority of contract negotiations take place between unions and employers that have been through the process before. In most cases, management has come to accept the union as an organization that it must work with. But when the union has just been certified and is negotiating its first contract, the situation can be very different. In fact, unions are unable to negotiate a first contract in 27% to 37% of the cases.[44] As noted previously, more than half of all unfair labor practice charges filed against employers pertain to the refusal to negotiate.

Labor–management contracts differ in their bargaining structures—that is, the range of employees and employers that are covered. As Table 14.10 indicates, the contracts differ, first, according to whether narrow (craft) or broad (industrial) employee

table 14.10

Types and Examples of Bargaining Structures

EMPLOYER INTERESTS COVERED	EMPLOYEE INTERESTS COVERED		
	MULTIEMPLOYER (CENTRALIZED)	SINGLE-EMPLOYER— MULTIPLANT	SINGLE-EMPLOYER— SINGLE PLANT (DECENTRALIZED)
Craft (Narrow)	Construction trades Interstate trucking Longshoring Hospital association	Airline Teacher Police Firefighters Railroad	Craft union in small manufacturing plant Hospital
Industrial or Multiskill (Broad)	Coal mining (underground) Basic steel (pre-1986) Hotel association	Automobiles Steel (post-1986) Farm equipment State government Textile	Industrial union in small manufacturing plant

SOURCE: From Harry Katz, et al, *An Introduction to Collective Bargaining and Industrial Relations* 4E, 2008. Copyright © 2008. The McGraw-Hill Companies Inc. Reprinted with permission.

interests are covered. Second, they differ according to whether they cover multiple employers or multiple plants within a single employer. (A single employer may have multiple plants, some union and some nonunion.) Different structures have different implications for bargaining power and the number of interests that must be incorporated in reaching an agreement.

THE NEGOTIATION PROCESS

Richard Walton and Robert McKersie suggested that labor–management negotiations could be broken into four subprocesses: distributive bargaining, integrative bargaining, attitudinal structuring, and intraorganizational bargaining.[45] **Distributive bargaining** focuses on dividing a fixed economic "pie" between the two sides. A wage increase, for example, means that the union gets a larger share of the pie, management a smaller share. It is a win–lose situation. **Integrative bargaining** has a win–win focus; it seeks solutions beneficial to both sides. So if management needs to reduce labor costs, it could reach an agreement with the union to avoid layoffs in return for the union agreeing to changes in work rules that might enhance productivity.

Attitudinal structuring refers to the relationship and trust between labor and management negotiators. Where the relationship is poor, it may be difficult for the two sides to engage in integrative bargaining because each side hesitates to trust the other side to carry out its part of the deal. For example, the union may be reluctant to agree to productivity-enhancing work-rule changes to enhance job security if, in the past, it has made similar concessions but believes that management did not stick to its assurance of greater job security. Thus the long-term relationship between the two parties can have a very important impact on negotiations and their outcomes.

Intraorganizational bargaining reminds us that labor–management negotiations involve more than just two parties. Within management, and to an even greater extent within the union, different factions can have conflicting objectives. High-seniority workers, who are least likely to be laid off, may be more willing to accept a contract that has layoffs (especially if it also offers a significant pay increase for those whose jobs are not at risk). Less senior workers would likely feel very differently. Thus negotiators and union leaders must simultaneously satisfy both the management side and their own internal constituencies. If they do not, they risk the union membership's rejecting the contract, or they risk being voted out of office in the next election. Management, too, is unlikely to be of one mind about how to approach negotiations. Some will focus more on long-term employee relations, others will focus on cost control, and still others will focus on what effect the contract will have on stockholders.

MANAGEMENT'S PREPARATION FOR NEGOTIATIONS

Clearly, the outcome of contract negotiations can have important consequences for labor costs and labor productivity and, therefore, for the company's ability to compete in the product market. Adapting Fossum's discussion, we can divide management preparation into the following seven areas, most of which have counterparts on the union side.[46]

Distributive Bargaining
The part of the labor–management negotiation process that focuses on dividing a fixed economic "pie."

Integrative Bargaining
The part of the labor–management negotiation process that seeks solutions beneficial to both sides.

Attitudinal Structuring
The aspect of the labor–management negotiation process that refers to the relationship and level of trust between the negotiators.

Intraorganizational Bargaining
The part of the labor–management negotiation process that focuses on the conflicting objectives of factions within labor and management.

1. *Establishing interdepartmental contract objectives:* The employer's industrial relations department needs to meet with the accounting, finance, production, marketing, and other departments and set contract goals that will permit each department to meet its responsibilities. As an example, finance may suggest a cost figure above which a contract settlement would seriously damage the company's financial health. The bargaining team needs to be constructed to take these various interests into account.

2. *Reviewing the old contract:* This step focuses on identifying provisions of the contract that might cause difficulties by hindering the company's productivity or flexibility or by leading to significant disagreements between management and the union.

3. *Preparing and analyzing data:* Information on labor costs and the productivity of competitors, as well as data the union may emphasize, needs to be prepared and analyzed. The union data might include cost-of-living changes and agreements reached by other unions that could serve as a target. Data on employee demographics and seniority are relevant for establishing the costs of such benefits as pensions, health insurance, and paid vacations. Finally, management needs to know how much it would be hurt by a strike. How long will its inventory allow it to keep meeting customer orders? To what extent are other companies positioned to step in and offer replacement products? How difficult would it be to find replacement workers if the company decided to continue operations during a strike?

4. *Anticipating union demands:* Recalling grievances over the previous contract, having ongoing discussions with union leaders, and becoming aware of settlements at other companies are ways of anticipating likely union demands and developing potential counterproposals.

5. *Establishing the cost of possible contract provisions:* Wages have not only a direct influence on labor costs but often an indirect effect on benefit costs (such as Social Security and paid vacation). Recall that benefits add 35 to 40 cents to every dollar's worth of wages. Also, wage or benefit increases that seem manageable in the first year of a contract can accumulate to less manageable levels over time.

6. *Preparing for a strike:* If management intends to operate during a strike, it may need to line up replacement workers, increase its security, and figure out how to deal with incidents on the picket line and elsewhere. If management does not intend to operate during a strike (or if the company will not be operating at normal levels), it needs to alert suppliers and customers and consider possible ways to avoid the loss of their business. This could even entail purchasing a competitor's product in order to have something to sell to customers.

7. *Determining strategy and logistics:* Decisions must be made about the amount of authority the negotiating team will have. What concessions can it make on its own, and which ones require it to check with top management? On which issues can it compromise, and on which can it not? Decisions regarding meeting places and times must also be made.

NEGOTIATION STAGES AND TACTICS

Negotiations go through various stages.[47] In the early stages, many more people are often present than in later stages. On the union side, this may give all the various internal interest groups a chance to participate and voice their goals.

This, in turn, helps send a message to management about what the union feels it must do to satisfy its members, and it may also help the union achieve greater solidarity. Union negotiators often present an extensive list of proposals at this stage, partly to satisfy their constituents and partly to provide themselves with issues on which they can show flexibility later in the process. Management may or may not present proposals of its own; sometimes it prefers to react to the union's proposals.

During the middle stages, each side must make a series of decisions, even though the outcome is uncertain. How important is each issue to the other side? How likely is it that disagreement on particular issues will result in a strike? When and to what extent should one side signal its willingness to compromise on its position?

In the final stage, pressure for an agreement increases as the deadline for a strike approaches. Public negotiations may be only part of the process. Negotiators from each side may have one-on-one meetings or small-group meetings where public relations pressures are reduced. In addition, a neutral third party may become involved, someone who can act as a go-between or facilitator. In some cases, the only way for the parties to convince each other of their resolve (or to convince their own constituents of the other party's resolve) is to allow an impasse to occur.

Various books suggest how to avoid impasses by using mutual gains or integrative bargaining tactics. For example, *Getting to Yes* (New York: Penguin Books, 1991), by Roger Fisher and William Ury, describes four basic principles:

1. Separate the people from the problem.
2. Focus on interests, not positions.
3. Generate a variety of possibilities before deciding what to do.
4. Insist that the results be based on some objective standard.

BARGAINING POWER, IMPASSES, AND IMPASSE RESOLUTION

Employers' and unions' conflicting goals are resolved through the negotiation process just described. An important determinant of the outcome of this process is the relative bargaining power of each party, which can be defined as the "ability of one party to achieve its goals when faced with opposition from some other party to the bargaining process."[48] In collective bargaining, an important element of power is the relative ability of each party to withstand a strike. The "Competing through Technology" box describes recent strikes in China and how workers used technology to communicate during these strikes. Although strikes are rare, the threat of a strike often looms large in labor–management negotiations. The relative ability to take a strike, whether one occurs or not, is an important determinant of bargaining power and, therefore, of bargaining outcomes.

MANAGEMENT'S WILLINGNESS TO TAKE A STRIKE

Management's willingness to take a strike comes down to two questions:

1. *Can the company remain profitable over the long run if it agrees to the union's demands?* The answer is more likely to be yes to the extent that higher labor costs can be passed on to consumers without losing business. This, in turn, is most likely when

In China, Labor Movement Enabled by Technology

The 1,700 workers who went on strike at the Honda Lock auto parts factory here in Zhongshan, China, are mostly poor migrants with middle-school educations. But they are surprisingly tech-savvy.

Hours into a strike that began last week, they started posting detailed accounts of the walkout online, spreading word not only among themselves but also to restive and striking workers elsewhere in China.

They fired off cellphone text messages urging colleagues to resist pressure from factory bosses. They logged onto a state-controlled website—workercn.cn—that is emerging as a digital hub of the Chinese labor movement. And armed with desktop computers, they uploaded video of Honda Lock's security guards roughing up employees.

"We videotaped the strike with our cellphones and decided to post the video online to let other people know how unfairly we were treated," said a 20-year-old Honda employee who asked not to be named because of the threat of retaliation.

The disgruntled workers in this southern Chinese city took their cues from earlier groups of web-literate strikers at other Honda factories, who in mid-May set up Internet forums and made online bulletin board postings about their own battle with the Japanese automaker over wages and working conditions.

But they have also tapped into a broader communications web enabling the working class throughout China to share grievances and strategies. Some strike leaders now say they spend much of their time perusing the web for material on China's labor laws.

Wielding cellphones and keyboards, members of China's emerging labor movement so far seem to be outwitting official censors in an effort to build broad support for what they say is a war against greedy corporations and their local government allies.

And it might not be possible if the Chinese government had not made a concerted effort in the last decade to shrink the country's digital divide by lowering the cost of mobile phone and Internet service in this country—a modernization campaign that has given China the world's biggest Internet population (400 million) and allowed even the poorest of the poor to log onto the Internet and air their labor grievances.

"This is something people haven't paid attention to—migrant workers can organize using these technologies," said Guobin Yang, a professor at Barnard College and author of "The Power of the Internet in China: Citizen Activism Online."

"Usually we think of this kind of thing being used by middle-class youths and intellectuals," Professor Yang said.

The web and digital devices, analysts say, have become vehicles of social change in much the way the typewriter and mimeograph machine were the preferred media during the pro-democracy protests in Beijing in 1989—before the government put down that movement in the June 1989 Tiananmen Square crackdown that left hundreds dead.

A looming question now, in fact, is whether and when the government might seek to quash the current worker uprisings if they become too big a threat to the established social order. Already, the government has started cracking down on strike-related websites and deleted many of the blog posts about the strikes.

But the activists say they are getting around some of those restraints by shifting to different platforms (including a Skype-like network called YY Voice) and using code words to discuss protest gatherings.

For years, labor activists have been exposing the harsh working conditions in Chinese factories by smuggling cell-phone images and video out of coastal factories and posting documents showing labor law violations on the web. New and notable is that these formerly covert activities have become open and pervasive.

A month earlier, at Honda's transmission factory in Foshan, strike leaders organized and communicated with more than 600 workers by, among other means, setting up Internet chat rooms.

"I created one myself the night before the strike, and that had 40 people," said Xiao Lang, one of the two Honda strike leaders in Foshan. Mr. Xiao was fired by Honda soon after leading the walkout. "We discussed all kinds of things on it," he said of the QQ chat room, "such as when to meet, when to walk out and how much pay we want."

Workers at other Honda factories say they followed the Foshan developments online and began considering their own actions.

The Chinese government allowed the state-run media to publish and broadcast news about the first Foshan strike. But when the strike news went viral, the government issued a notice virtually banning coverage. The workers' own communications effort, however, never let up.

The Honda Lock workers here await the results of a government-led negotiation for higher wages and better working conditions. Even though last weekend they were offered wage increases of only 11%, many of the workers say they are still confident they will get a raise of as much as 50%—to as much as $234 a month—just as the Honda workers in Foshan did.

"This couldn't have happened if we didn't hear about how they were doing things in Foshan," said the worker who has used computers since age 7. "We followed their lead. So why shouldn't we get the same pay raise as they did?"

the price increase is small because labor costs are a small fraction of total costs or there is little price competition in the industry. Low price competition can result from regulated prices, from competition based on quality (rather than price), or from the union's organizing all or most of the employers in the industry, which eliminates labor costs as a price factor.

Unions share part of management's concern with long-term competitiveness because a decline in competitiveness can translate into a decline in employment levels. On the other hand, the majority of union members may prefer to have higher wages, despite employment declines, particularly if a minority of the members (those with low seniority) suffer more employment loss and the majority keep their employment with higher wages.

2. *Can the company continue to operate in the short run despite a strike?* Although "hanging tough" on its bargaining goals may pay off for management in the long run, the short-run concern is the loss of revenues and profits from production being disrupted. The cost to strikers is a loss of wages and possibly a permanent loss of jobs.

Under what conditions is management most able to take a strike? The following factors are important:[49]

1. *Product demand:* Management is less able to afford a strike when the demand for its product is strong because that is when more revenue and profits are lost.
2. *Product perishability:* A strike by certain kinds of employees (farm workers at harvest time, truckers transporting perishable food, airline employees at peak travel periods) will result in permanent losses of revenue, thus increasing the cost of the strike to management.
3. *Technology:* An organization that is capital intensive (versus labor intensive) is less dependent on its employees and more likely to be able to use supervisors or others as replacements. Telephone companies are typically able to operate

through strikes, even though installing new equipment or services and repair work may take significantly longer than usual.

4. *Availability of replacement workers:* When jobs are scarce, replacement workers are more available and perhaps more willing to cross picket lines. Using replacement workers to operate during a strike raises the stakes considerably for strikers who may be permanently replaced. Most strikers are not entitled to reinstatement until there are job openings for which they qualify. If replacements were hired, such openings may not occur for some time (if at all).

5. *Multiple production sites and staggered contracts:* Multiple sites and staggered contracts permit employers to shift production from the struck facility to facilities that, even if unionized, have contracts that expire at different times (so they are not able to strike at the same time).

6. *Integrated facilities:* When one facility produces something that other facilities need for their products, the employer is less able to take a strike because the disruption to production goes beyond that single facility. The just-in-time production system, which provides very little stockpiling of parts, further weakens management's ability to take a strike.

7. *Lack of substitutes for the product:* A strike is more costly to the employer if customers have a readily available alternative source from which to purchase the goods or services the company provides.

Management has several factors to consider before taking a strike. Most negotiations do not result in a strike since it is often not in the best interests of either party.

Bargaining outcomes also depend on the nature of the bargaining process and relationship, which includes the types of tactics used and the history of labor relations. The vast majority of labor–management negotiations do not result in a strike because a strike is typically not in the best interests of either party. Furthermore, both the union and management usually realize that if they wish to interact effectively in the future, the experience of a strike can be difficult to overcome. When strikes do occur, the conduct of each party during the strike can also have a lasting effect on labor–management relations. Violence by either side or threats of job loss by hiring replacements can make future relations difficult.

IMPASSE RESOLUTION PROCEDURES: ALTERNATIVES TO STRIKES

Given the substantial costs of strikes to both parties, procedures that resolve conflicts without strikes have arisen in both the private and public sectors. Because many public sector employees do not have the right to strike, alternatives are particularly important in that arena.

Three often-used impasse resolution procedures are mediation, fact finding, and arbitration. All of them rely on the intervention of a neutral third party, most typically provided by the Federal Mediation and Conciliation Service (FMCS), which must be notified 60 days prior to contract expiration and 30 days prior to a planned change in contract terms (including a strike). **Mediation** is the least formal but most widely used of the procedures (in both the public and private sectors). One survey

Mediation
A procedure for resolving collective bargaining impasses by which a mediator with no formal authority acts as a facilitator and go-between in the negotiations.

found it was used by nearly 40% of all large private sector bargaining units.[50] A mediator has no formal authority but, rather, acts as a facilitator and go-between in negotiations.

Fact Finder
A person who reports on the reasons for the labor–management dispute and the views and arguments of both sides and offers a nonbinding recommendation for settling the dispute.

A **fact finder,** most commonly used in the public sector, typically reports on the reasons for the dispute, the views and arguments of both sides, and (in some cases) a recommended settlement, which the parties are free to decline. That these recommendations are made public may give rise to public pressure for a settlement. Even if a fact finder's settlement is not accepted, the hope is that he or she will identify or frame issues in such a way as to facilitate an agreement. Sometimes, for the simple reason that fact finding takes time, the parties reach a settlement during the interim.

Arbitration
A procedure for resolving collective bargaining impasses by which an arbitrator chooses a solution to the dispute.

The most formal type of outside intervention is **arbitration,** under which a solution is actually chosen by an arbitrator (or arbitration board). In some instances the arbitrator can fashion a solution (conventional arbitration). In other cases the arbitrator must choose either the management's or union's final offer (final offer arbitration) on either the contract as a whole or on an issue-by-issue basis. Traditionally, arbitrating the enforcement or interpretation of contract terms (rights arbitration) has been widely accepted, whereas arbitrating the actual writing or setting of contract terms (interest arbitration, our focus here) has been reserved for special circumstances. These include some public sector negotiations, where strikes may be especially costly (such as those by police or firefighters) and a very few private-sector situations, where strikes have been especially debilitating to both sides (the steel industry in the 1970s).[51] One reason for avoiding greater use of interest arbitration is a strong belief that the parties closest to the situation (unions and management, not an arbitrator) are in the best position to effectively resolve their conflicts.

Union and Management Interactions: Contract Administration

GRIEVANCE PROCEDURE

Although the negotiation process (and the occasional resulting strike) receive the most publicity, the negotiation process typically occurs only about every three years, whereas contract administration goes on day after day, year after year. The two processes—negotiation and administration—are linked, of course. Vague or incomplete contract language developed in the negotiation process can make administration of the contract difficult. Such difficulties can, in turn, create conflict that can spill over into the next negotiation process.[52] Furthermore, events during the negotiation process—strikes, the use of replacement workers, or violence by either side—can lead to management and labor difficulties in working successfully under a contract.

A key influence on successful contract administration is the grievance procedure for resolving labor–management disputes over the interpretation and execution of the contract. During World War II, the War Labor Board helped institutionalize the use of arbitration as an alternative to strikes to settle disputes that arose during the term of the contract. The soon-to-follow Taft-Hartley Act further reinforced this preference. Today the great majority of grievance procedures have binding arbitration as a final step, and only a minority of strikes occur during the term of a contract. (Most occur during the negotiation stage.) Strikes during the term of a contract can be especially disruptive because they are more unpredictable than strikes during the negotiation phase, which occur only at regular intervals.

Beyond its ability to reduce strikes, a grievance procedure can be judged using three criteria.[53] First, how well are day-to-day contract questions resolved? Time delays and heavy use of the procedure may indicate problems. Second, how well does the grievance procedure adapt to changing circumstances? For example, if the company's business turns downward and the company needs to cut costs, how clear are the provisions relating to subcontracting of work, layoffs, and so forth? Third, in multiunit contracts, how well does the grievance procedure permit local contract issues (like work rules) to be included and resolved?[54]

From the employees' perspective, the grievance procedure is the key to fair treatment in the workplace, and its effectiveness rests both on the degree to which employees feel they can use it without fear of recrimination and whether they believe their case will be carried forward strongly enough by their union representative. The **duty of fair representation** is mandated by the NLRA and requires that all bargaining unit members, whether union members or not, have equal access to and representation by the union in the grievance procedure. Too many grievances may indicate a problem, but so may too few. A very low grievance rate may suggest a fear of filing a grievance, a belief that the system is not effective, or a belief that representation is not adequate.

As Table 14.11 suggests, most grievance procedures have several steps prior to arbitration. Moreover, the majority of grievances are settled during the earlier steps of

Duty of Fair Representation
The National Labor Relations Act requirement that all bargaining unit members have equal access to and representation by the union.

table 14.11

Steps in a Typical Grievance Procedure

Employee-initiated grievance
Step 1
a. Employee discusses grievance or problem orally with supervisor.
b. Union steward and employee may discuss problem orally with supervisor.
c. Union steward and employee decide (1) whether problem has been resolved or (2) if not resolved, whether a contract violation has occurred.
Step 2
a. Grievance is put in writing and submitted to production superintendent or other designated line manager.
b. Steward and management representative meet and discuss grievance. Management's response is put in writing. A member of the industrial relations staff may be consulted at this stage.
Step 3
a. Grievance is appealed to top line management and industrial relations staff representatives. Additional local or international union officers may become involved in discussions. Decision is put in writing.
Step 4
a. Union decides on whether to appeal unresolved grievance to arbitration according to procedures specified in its constitution and/or bylaws.
b. Grievance is appealed to arbitration for binding decision.
Discharge grievance
a. Procedure may begin at step 2 or step 3.
b. Time limits between steps may be shorter to expedite the process.
Union or group grievance
a. Union representative initiates grievance at step 1 or step 2 on behalf of affected class of workers or union representatives.

SOURCE: From Harry Katz et al, *An Introduction to Collective Bargaining and Industrial Relations*, 4E, 2008. Copyright © 2008 The McGraw-Hill Companies Inc. Reprinted with permission.

the process, which is desirable both to reduce time delays and to avoid the costs of arbitration. If the grievance does reach arbitration, the arbitrator makes the final ruling in the matter. A series of Supreme Court decisions in 1960, commonly known as the Steelworkers' Trilogy, established that the courts should essentially refrain from reviewing the merits of arbitrators' decisions and, instead, limit judicial review to the question of whether the issue was subject to arbitration under the contract.[55] Furthermore, unless the contract explicitly states that an issue is not subject to arbitration, it will be assumed that arbitration is an appropriate means of deciding the issue. Giving further strength to the role of arbitration is the NLRB's general policy of deferring to arbitration.

What types of issues most commonly reach arbitration? Data from the FMCS on a total of 2,473 grievances show that discharge and disciplinary issues topped the list with 913 cases.[56] Other frequent issues include the use of seniority in promotion, layoffs, transfers, work assignments, and scheduling (309 cases); wages (178); and benefits (127).

What criteria do arbitrators use to reach a decision? In the most common case— discharge or discipline—the following due process questions are important:[57]

1. *Did the employee know what the rule or expectation was and what the consequences of not adhering to it were?*
2. *Was the rule applied in a consistent and predictable way?* In other words, are all employees treated the same?
3. *Are facts collected in a fair and systematic manner?* An important element of this principle is detailed record keeping. Both employee actions (such as tardiness) and management's response (verbal or written warnings) should be carefully documented.
4. *Does the employee have the right to question the facts and present a defense?* An example in a union setting is a hearing with a shop steward present.
5. *Does the employee have the right to appeal a decision?* An example is recourse to an impartial third party, such as an arbitrator.
6. *Is there progressive discipline?* Except perhaps for severe cases, an arbitrator will typically look for evidence that an employee was alerted as early as possible that behavior was inappropriate and the employee was given a chance to change prior to some form of severe discipline, such as discharge.
7. *Are there unique mitigating circumstances?* Although discipline must be consistent, individuals differ in terms of their prior service, performance, and discipline record. All of these factors may need to be considered.

NEW LABOR–MANAGEMENT STRATEGIES

LO 14-5
Describe new, less adversarial approaches to labor–management relations.

Jack Barbash described the nature of the traditional relationship between labor and management (during both the negotiation and administration phases) as follows:

> Bargaining is a love–hate, cooperation–conflict relationship. The parties have a common interest in maximizing the total revenue which finances their respective returns. But they take on adversarial postures in debating how the revenue shall be divided as between wages and profits. It is the adversarial posture which has historically set the tone of the relationship.[58]

Although there have always been exceptions to the adversarial approach, there are signs of a more general transformation to less adversarial workplace relations (at least where the union's role is accepted by management).[59] This transformation has two basic objectives: (1) to increase the involvement of individuals and work groups in overcoming adversarial relations and increasing employee commitment, motivation, and problem solving and (2) to reorganize work so that work rules are minimized and flexibility in managing people is maximized. These objectives are especially important for companies that need to be able to shift production quickly in response to changes in markets and customer demands. The specific programs aimed at achieving these objectives include employee involvement in decision making, self-managing employee teams, labor–management problem-solving teams, broadly defined jobs, and sharing of financial gains and business information with employees. Examples include the labor–management relationships at Ford, Harley-Davidson, and Chrysler's Global Engine Manufacturing Alliance (GEMA) plant in Dundee, Michigan.[60]

GEMA is not only an example of a new approach to labor relations. It also has the blessing of the United Auto Workers (UAW). Why? According to the president of the UAW local, "It's a question of survival." Hourly workers at the GEMA plant are highly educated and skilled and rotate through different jobs to provide skill flexibility to support production flexibility, engage workers, and reduce repetitive motion injuries. Unlike a traditional plant where there can be scores of hourly job classifications/titles, GEMA has only two: team member of team leader. There are no supervisors. Team leaders, rather than only observing, work alongside teams of six team members. The guiding principles are captured by what are called the "four As": "anyone can do anything anytime, anywhere." That is much different from the more typical idea of "if it's not in my job description, I don't have to do it, I won't do it, and if I did do it, I would probably get in trouble." The UAW was concerned at first with the "four As" approach because without narrow job descriptions, management has more discretion, workers less discretion, in what workers do each day. As the UAW put it, it could allow management to "pull out anybody, anytime." However, the need for flexibility in production is so central to the success of the plant in a global competitive environment and to Chrysler being willing to make future investments (the key to jobs) in the plant that the UAW leadership agreed. The team approach, job rotation, and flexibility expectations translate into higher expectations skill and education requirements. Hourly workers at the plant must have a two-year technical degree, hold a skilled journeyman's card, or have had several years of experience in advanced manufacturing.[61]

Union resistance to such programs has often been substantial, precisely because the programs seek to change workplace relations and the role that unions play. (As another example, the "Competing through Sustainability" box describes how U.S. automobile companies hope to negotiate to use merit pay for UAW members, something the UAW has long fundamentally opposed.) Without the union's support, these programs are less likely to survive and less likely to be effective if they do survive.[62] Union leaders have often feared that such programs will weaken unions' role as an independent representative of employee interests. Indeed, according to the NLRA, to "dominate or interfere with the formation or administration of any labor organization or contribute financial or other support to it" is an unfair labor practice. An example of a prohibited practice is "taking an active part in organizing a union or committee to represent employees."[63]

One case that has received much attention is that of Electromation, a small electrical parts manufacturer. In 1992 the NLRB ruled that the company had violated Section 8(a)(2) of the NLRA by setting up worker–management committees (typically about six workers and one or two managers) to solve problems having to do with absenteeism and pay scales.[64] The original complaint was filed by the Teamsters union, which was trying to organize the (nonunion) company and felt that the committees were, in

COMPETING THROUGH SUSTAINABILITY

Merit Pay Pressure on UAW Is Rising

DETROIT—A push for a merit-pay system for hourly workers is emerging as a key issue in contract talks that will get under way this year between the three Detroit car makers and the United Auto Workers union.

"We need to somehow link the performance of the business to the workers. I am quite willing to start working with the UAW to try and get this done," Chrysler Chief Executive Officer Sergio Marchionne said Wednesday. "I think it is important for all of us, not just the UAW."

Executives at General Motors Co. sparked the issue this week at the Detroit auto show when they said union wages for factory workers should be tied to employee performance and the company's financial well-being in a system similar to one used for its salaried workers.

GM wants more flexibility to entice workers to strive toward improved productivity and quality while freeing the company from having to raise wages when times are tough, company executives say. Others inside Ford Motor Co. and Chrysler Group LLC said altering the pay structure could be essential to keeping the newly revived companies competitive.

UAW President Bob King said in an interview Wednesday that he wants to make sure his members "are getting their fair share of the upside and have a fair system to do it in the long term." He declined specifically to say whether the union would be open to a restructuring of the pay system. "I really believe in the sacredness in keeping that confidential. You can make a lot more progress if people aren't in a public forum," he said.

The UAW is caught in a tough place now that a union-controlled trust owns significant stakes in GM and Chrysler after their government-backed reorganizations last year. The welfare of tens of thousands of union retirees is now directly tied to the fortunes of the auto makers.

As part of the bankruptcies, the UAW also agreed to not strike at GM or Chrysler until September 2015.

At the same time, some union members expect a new contract to restore some of the concessions the union made over the last four years to keep the Detroit Three afloat. One concession allows the car makers to pay newly hired workers about $14 an hour—half of what existing workers get.

The union's fortunes, most directly through the healthcare trust for retirees, are also tied to making sure that the companies operate more efficiently to improve their bottom line.

The trust sold 89 million GM shares in November as part of the company's initial public offering, leaving it with a 10.7% stake if warrants are included. It owns 63.5% of Chrysler, though it hopes to sell part of that when Chrysler has its own IPO, possibly later this year.

The UAW doesn't have a no-strike agreement with Ford. Any strike could stunt Ford's turn-around and force the company to rethink plans to hire 7,000 workers over the next two years in the United States, most of them hourly, unionized workers.

A Ford spokeswoman said that "we are looking at various proposals linking employee compensation to company performance, which could include quality as a metric."

SOURCE: From Matthew Dolan, "Merit-Pay Pressure on UAW Is Rising," *The Wall Street Journal*, April 19, 2011, B1. Reproduced with permission of Dow Jones & Company, Inc. via Copyright Clearance Center.

effect, illegally competing with them to be workers' representatives. Similarly, Polaroid dissolved an employee committee that had been in existence for over 40 years in response to the U.S. Department of Labor's claim that it violated the NLRA. The primary functions of the employee committee had been to represent employees in grievances and to advise senior management on issues such as pay and company rules and regulations. In a third case, the NLRB ruled in 1993 that seven worker–management safety committees at DuPont were illegal under the NLRB because they were dominated by management. The committee members were chosen by management and their decisions were subject to the approval of the management members of the committees. Finally, the committees made decisions about issues that were mandatory subjects of bargaining with the employees' elected representative—the chemical workers' union.[65] The impact of such cases will be felt both in nonunion companies, as union organizers move to fill the worker representation vacuum, and in unionized companies, as managers find they must deal more directly and effectively with their unions.

In 1994 the Commission on the Future of Worker–Management Relations (also referred to as the Dunlop Commission, after its chair, former Secretary of Labor John Dunlop) recommended that Congress clarify Section 8(a)(2) and give employers more freedom to use employee involvement programs without risking legal challenges. In 1996 the U.S. Congress passed the Teamwork for Employees and Managers Act, which supporters said would remove legal roadblocks to greater employee involvement. Critics claimed the act went too far and would bring back employer-dominated labor organizations, which existed prior to the passage of the NLRA in 1935. The Clinton administration vetoed the bill, meaning that employers will continue to face some uncertainty about legal issues. Table 14.12 provides some guidance on when the use of teams might be illegal.

Employers must take care that employee involvement meets the legal test, but the NLRB has clearly supported the legality of involvement in important cases. For example, in a 2001 ruling, the NLRB found that the use of seven employee participation committees at a Crown Cork & Seal aluminum can manufacturing plant did not violate federal labor law. The committees in question make and implement decisions regarding a wide range of issues, including production, quality, training, safety, and certain types of worker discipline. The NLRB determined that these committees were not employer-dominated labor organizations, which would have violated federal labor law. Instead of "dealing with" management in a bilateral manner where proposals are made that are either rejected or accepted by management, the teams and committees exercise authority, delegated by management, to operate the plant within certain parameters. Indeed, the NLRB noted that rather than "dealing with management," the evidence indicated that within delegated areas of authority, the teams and committees "are management." This authority was found to be similar to that delegated to a first-line supervisor. Thus the charge that the teams and committees did not have final decision-making authority (and so were not acting in a management capacity) did not weigh heavily with the NLRB, which noted, "Few, if any, supervisors in a conventional

table 14.12

When Teams May Be Illegal

Primary factors to look for that could mean a team violates national labor law:	
Representation	Does the team address issues affecting nonteam employees? (Does it represent other workers?)
Subject matter	Do these issues involve matters such as wages, grievances, hours of work, and working conditions?
Management involvement	Does the team deal with any supervisors, managers, or executives on any issue?
Employer domination	Did the company create the team or decide what it would do and how it would function?

SOURCE: From *BusinessWeek*, January 25, 1993. Reprinted with permission.

table 14.13

Patterns in Labor–Management Relations Using Traditional and Transformational Approaches

DIMENSION	PATTERN	
	TRADITIONAL	TRANSFORMATIONAL
Conflict resolution		
Frequency of conflicts	High	Low
Speed of conflict resolution	Slow	Fast
Informal resolution of grievances	Low	High
Third- and fourth-step grievances	High	Low
Shop-floor cooperation		
Formal problem-solving groups (such as quality, reducing scrap, employment security)	Low	High
Informal problem-solving activity	Low	High
Worker autonomy and feedback		
Formal autonomous work groups	Low	High
Informal worker autonomous activity	Low	High
Worker-initiated changes in work design	Low	High
Feedback on cost, quality, and schedule	Low	High

SOURCE: Adapted from J. Cutcher-Gershenfeld, "The Impact on Economic Performance of a Transformation in Workplace Relations," *Industrial and Labor Relations Review* 44 (1991), pp. 241–60. Reprinted with permission.

plant have authority that is final and absolute." Instead, it was noted that managers typically make recommendations that move up through "the chain of command."[66]

Although there are legal concerns to address, some evidence suggests that these new approaches to labor relations—incorporating greater employee participation in decisions, using employee teams, multiskilling, rotating jobs, and sharing financial gains—can contribute significantly to an organization's effectiveness,[67] as well as to workers' wages and job satisfaction.[68] Indeed, these practices are now often referred to as "high performance work practices" or systems. One study, for example, compared the features of traditional and transformational approaches to labor relations at Xerox.[69] As Table 14.13 indicates, the transformational approach was characterized by better conflict resolution, more shop-floor cooperation, and greater worker autonomy and feedback in decision making. Furthermore, compared with the traditional approach, transformational labor relations were found to be associated with lower costs, better product quality, and higher productivity. The Commission on the Future of Worker–Management Relations concluded that the evidence is "overwhelming that employee participation and labor–management partnerships are good for workers, firms, and the national economy." National survey data also indicate that most employees want more influence in workplace decisions and believe that such influence leads to more effective organizations.[70]

Labor Relations Outcomes

The effectiveness of labor relations can be evaluated from management, labor, and societal perspectives. Management seeks to control costs and enhance productivity and quality. Labor unions seek to raise wages and benefits and exercise control over how employees spend their time at work (such as through work rules). Each of the

YEAR	STOPPAGES	NUMBER OF WORKERS (THOUSANDS)	PERCENTAGE OF TOTAL WORKING TIME
1950	424	1,698	0.26%
1955	363	2,055	0.16
1960	222	896	0.09
1965	268	999	0.10
1970	381	2,468	0.29
1975	235	965	0.09
1980	187	795	0.09
1985	54	324	0.03
1990	44	185	0.02
1995	31	192	0.02
2000	39	394	0.06
2002	19	46	0.005
2004	17	171	0.01
2006	20	70	0.01
2008	15	72	0.03
2010	11	45	<0.005

table 14.14

Work Stoppages Involving 1,000 or More Workers

SOURCE: http://stats.bls.gov.

three parties typically seeks to avoid forms of conflict (like strikes) that impose significant costs on everyone. In this section we examine several outcomes.

STRIKES

Table 14.14 presents data on strikes in the United States that involved 1,000 or more employees. Because strikes are more likely in large units, the lack of data on smaller units is probably not a major concern, although such data would, of course, raise the figure on the estimated time lost to strikes. For example, for the 1960s, this estimate is 0.12% using data on strikes involving 1,000 or more employees versus 0.17% for all strikes. Although strikes impose significant costs on union members, employers, and society, it is clear from Table 14.14 that strikes are the exception rather than the rule. Very little working time is lost to strikes in the United States (with annual work hours of 1,800, less than 6 minutes per union member in 2010), and their frequency in recent years is generally low by historical standards. Does this mean that the industrial relations system is working well? Not necessarily. Some would view the low number of strikes as another sign of labor's weakness.

WAGES AND BENEFITS

In 2010, private-sector unionized workers received, on average, wages 9% (down from a 21% difference in 2008) higher than their nonunion counterparts.[71] Total compensation was 29% (down from a 40% difference in 2008) 75% higher for union-covered employees because of an even larger effect of unions on benefits.[72] However, these are raw differences. To assess the net effect of unions on wages more accurately, adjustments must be made.[73] We now briefly highlight a few of these.

The union wage effect is likely to be overestimated to the extent that unions can more easily organize workers who are already highly paid or who are more productive. The gap is likely to be underestimated to the extent that nonunion employers raise wages and benefits in response to the perceived "union threat" in the hope that their employees will then have less interest in union representation. When these and other factors are taken into account, the net union advantage in wages, though still substantial, is reduced by as much as one-half. The union benefits advantage is also reduced, but it remains larger than the union wage effect, and the union effect on total compensation is therefore larger than the wage effect alone.[74]

Beyond differences in pay and benefits, unions typically influence the way pay and promotions are determined. Whereas management often seeks to deal with employees as individuals, emphasizing performance differences in pay and promotion decisions, unions seek to build group solidarity and avoid the possibly arbitrary treatment of employees. To do so, unions focus on equal pay for equal work. Any differences among employees in pay or promotions, they say, should be based on seniority (an objective measure) rather than on performance (a subjective measure susceptible to favoritism). It is very common in union settings for there to be a single rate of pay for all employees in a particular job classification.

Although wages and benefits are higher for union members, job satisfaction is lower, on average.[75] Reasons include less positive perceptions of supervision, promotion opportunities, and the interest and discretion in their work.

PRODUCTIVITY

There has been much debate regarding the effects of unions on productivity.[76] Unions are believed to decrease productivity in at least three ways: (1) the union pay advantage causes employers to use less labor and more capital per worker than they would otherwise, which reduces efficiency across society; (2) union contract provisions may limit permissible workloads, restrict the tasks that particular workers are allowed to perform, and require employers to use more employees for certain jobs than they otherwise would; and (3) strikes, slowdowns, and working-to-rule (slowing down production by following every workplace rule to an extreme) result in lost production.[77]

On the other hand, unions can have positive effects on productivity.[78] Employees, whether members of a union or not, communicate to management regarding how good a job it is doing by either the "exit" or "voice" mechanisms. "Exit" refers to simply leaving the company to work for a better employer. "Voice" refers to communicating one's concerns to management without necessarily leaving the employer. Unions are believed to increase the operation and effectiveness of the voice mechanism.[79] This, in turn, is likely to reduce employee turnover and its associated costs. More broadly, voice can be seen as including the union's contribution to the success of labor–management cooperation programs that make use of employee suggestions and increased involvement in decisions. A second way that unions can increase productivity is (perhaps ironically) through their emphasis on the use of seniority in pay, promotion, and layoff decisions. Although management typically prefers to rely more heavily on performance in such decisions, using seniority has a potentially important advantage—namely, it reduces competition among workers. As a result, workers may be less reluctant to share their knowledge with less senior workers because they do not have to worry about less senior workers taking their jobs. Finally, the introduction of a union may have a "shock effect" on management, pressuring it into tightening standards and accountability and paying greater heed to employee input in the design and management of production.[80]

Although there is evidence that unions have both positive and negative effects on productivity, most studies have found that union workers are more productive than nonunion workers. Nevertheless, it is generally recognized that most of the findings on this issue are open to a number of alternative explanations, making any clear conclusions difficult. For example, if unions raise productivity, why has union representation of employees declined over time, even within industries?[81] A related concern is that unionized establishments are more likely to survive where there is some inherent productivity advantage unrelated to unionism that actually offsets a negative impact of unionism. If so, these establishments would be overrepresented, whereas establishments that did not survive the negative impact of unions would be underrepresented. Consequently, any negative impact of unions on productivity would be underestimated.

PROFITS AND STOCK PERFORMANCE

Even if unions do raise productivity, a company's profits and stock performance may still suffer if unions raise costs (such as wages) or decrease investment by a greater amount. Evidence shows that unions have a large negative effect on profits and that union coverage tends to decline more quickly in firms experiencing lower shareholder returns, suggesting that some firms become more competitive partly by reducing union strength.[82] Similarly, one study finds that each dollar of unexpected increase in collectively bargained labor costs results in a dollar reduction in shareholder wealth. Other research suggests that investment in research and development is lower in unionized firms.[83] Strikes, although infrequent, lower shareholder returns in both the struck companies and firms (like suppliers) linked to those companies.[84] These research findings describe the average effects of unions. The consequences of more innovative union–management relationships for profits and stock performance are less clear.

The International Context

Except for China, Russia, and Ukraine, the United States has more union members than any other country. Yet, as Table 14.15 indicates, aside from France and Korea, the United States has the lowest unionization rate (union density) of any country

LO 14-6

Explain how changes in competitive challenges (e.g., product market competition and globalization) are influencing labor–management interactions.

| COUNTRY | MEMBERSHIP | | COVERAGE |
	NUMBER (THOUSANDS)	PERCENTAGE OF EMPLOYMENT (DENSITY)	PERCENTAGE OF EMPLOYMENT
United States	15,776	12	14
Canada	4,037	27	32
Japan	10,531	18	24
Korea	1,606	10	—
Australia	1,867	19	50
Netherlands	1,575	19	82
France	1,830	8	95
United Kingdom	6,524	27	35

table 14.15

Union Membership and Union Coverage, Selected Countries

SOURCES: J. Visser, "Union Membership Statistics in 24 Countries," *Monthly Labor Review,* January 2006, pp. 38–49; OECD, *StatExtracts, Trade Union Density,* http://stats.oecd.org, extracted June 2, 2011.

in the table. Even more striking are differences in union coverage, the percentage of employees whose terms and conditions of employment are governed by a union contract. (See Table 14.15.) In parts of western and northern Europe, it is not uncommon to have coverage rates of 80% to 90%, meaning that the influence of labor unions far outstrips what would be implied by their membership levels.[85] Why are the unionization rate and coverage comparatively low? One explanation is that the United States does not have as strong a history of deep class-based divisions in society as other countries do. For example, labor and social democratic political parties are commonplace in western Europe, and they are major players in the political process. Furthermore, the labor movement in western and northern Europe is broader than that in the United States. It extends not just to the workplace but—through its own or closely related political parties—directly into the national political process.

What is the trend in union membership rates and coverage? In the United States, we saw earlier that the trend is clearly downward, at least in the private sector. Although there have also been declines in membership rates in many other countries, coverage rates have stayed high in many of these countries. In the United States, deregulation and competition from foreign-owned companies have forced companies to become more efficient. Combined with the fact that the union wage premium in the United States is substantially larger than in other advanced industrialized countries, it is not surprising that management opposition would be higher in the United States than elsewhere.[86] This, in turn, may help explain why the decline in union influence has been especially steep in the United States.

It seems likely that—with the growing globalization of markets—labor costs and productivity will continue to be key challenges. The European Union (EU) added 10 new member countries in 2004, and 2 more in 2007, bringing its total to 27 countries and 495 million people, or about 60% larger than the United States. The newer EU countries (e.g., Bulgaria, the Czech Republic, Poland, Romania, Slovakia) have much lower wages than the existing EU countries. Closer to home, we have the North American Free Trade Agreement among the United States, Canada, and Mexico. These common market agreements mean that goods, services, and production will continue to move more freely across international borders. Where substantial differences in wages, benefits, and other costs of doing business (such as regulation) exist, there will be a tendency to move to areas that are less costly, unless skills are unavailable or productivity is significantly lower there. Unless labor unions can increase their productivity sufficiently or organize new production facilities, union influence is likely to decline.

In addition to membership and coverage, the United States differs from western Europe in the degree of formal worker participation in decision making. Works' councils (joint labor–management decision-making institutions at the enterprise level) and worker representation on supervisory boards of directors (codetermination) are mandated by law in countries such as Germany. The Scandinavian countries, Austria, and Luxembourg have similar legislation. German works' councils make decisions about changes in work or the work environment, discipline, pay systems, safety, and other human resource issues. The degree of codetermination on supervisory boards depends on the size and industry of the company. For example, in German organizations having more than 2,000 employees, half of the board members must be worker representatives. (However, the chairman of the board, a management representative, can cast a tie-breaking vote.) In contrast, worker representation on boards of directors in the United States is still rare.[87]

The works' councils exist in part because collective bargaining agreements in countries such as Germany tend to be oriented toward industrywide or regional issues,

Collective negotiation is not a new concept in China; it can be traced back to the 2000 Trial Act of Collective Negotiation on Salary. However, collective negotiation has become a bigger issue following strikes in Shenzhen and nearby cities in the Guangdong province. These strikes were triggered when workers in some foreign-owned factories asked for increased wages but were not responded to in a "timely and serious" fashion.

The Collective Negotiation Act, issued by the legislature of the Shenzhen Special Economic Zone (SEZ), is now under public hearing. The draft act aims to ensure stable labor relations by requiring good-faith negotiation between employers and workers' organizations (trade unions) to reach agreement on wages and working conditions. According to the draft, workers in the Shenzhen SEZ can request collective bargaining if 50% of the workers' wages are below 50% of the average earnings of the Shenzhen SEZ, and employers will be required to commence collective negotiations with labor unions.

Apart from the Shenzhen SEZ, local legislatures in some 20 other cities/provinces have enacted, or are in the process of enacting, collective bargaining acts to require collective negotiations in some circumstances.

One significant aspect of the new labor law lies in the independent role it envisions for labor unions. Currently in China, union leaders typically also act as senior management and participate actively in the company's operating decisions—a conflict of interests that inhibits them from effectively representing workers and protecting their interests.

The development of collective negotiation will most heavily impact labor-intensive industries, such as shoe and clothing manufacturers where most factory workers are paid between CY1,100 and CY1,500 per month, far below 50% of the average earnings in the Shenzhen SEZ (currently CY3,900). Anticipating an increase in labor costs, some employers in these industries are considering moving their plants from Shenzhen and other coastal cities to northern or western cities in China where labor costs are still low.

Employers should pay close attention to any collective labor contracts in their industries or in the districts where they are located. According to the draft act in the Shenzhen SEZ, if any employer or labor union fails to reach an agreement on their specific disputes, the terms of any current collective contracts in their industries or districts can be enforced on their company if approved by local authorities.

SOURCE: From Towers Watson, "China: Collective Negotiation—An Emerging Trend," *Global News Briefs*, September 30, 2010. Reprinted with permission.

with less emphasis on local issues. However, competitive forces have led employers to increasingly opt out of centralized bargaining, even in the countries best known for centralized bargaining, like Sweden and Germany.[88]

The "Competing through Globalization" box shows that the regulatory framework for labor unions in China is changing and that consequences for employers can be important.

The Public Sector

Unlike the private sector, union membership in the public sector grew in the 1960s and 1970s and remained fairly stable through the 1980s. As we saw earlier in Figure 14.3, in 2010 some 36.2% of government employees were union members. Like the NLRA in the private sector, changes in the legal framework contributed

LO 14-7

Explain how labor relations in the public sector differ from labor relations in the private sector.

significantly to union growth in the public sector. One early step was the enactment in Wisconsin of collective bargaining legislation in 1959 for its state employees.[89] Executive Order 10988 provided collective bargaining rights for federal employees in 1962. By the end of the 1960s, most states had passed similar laws. The Civil Service Reform Act of 1978, Title VII, later established the Federal Labor Relations Authority (modeled after the NLRB). Many states have similar administrative agencies to administer their own laws.

An interesting aspect of public sector union growth is that much of it has occurred in the service industry and among white-collar employees—groups that have traditionally been viewed as difficult to organize. The American Federation of State, County, and Municipal Employees (AFSCME), with more than 1.6 million members, has several hundred thousand members in health care and in white-collar occupations.[90]

In contrast to the private sector, strikes are illegal at the federal level of the public sector and in most states. At the local level, all states prohibit strikes by police (Hawaii being a partial exception) and firefighters (Idaho being the exception). Teachers and state employees are somewhat more likely to have the right to strike, depending on the state. In 2006, of the 20 work stoppages involving 1,000 or more workers, 8 were in state and local government. In 2010, 6 of the 11 major work stoppages were in the public sector.

A Look Back

The membership rate, and thus influence, of labor unions in the United States and in many other countries has been on the decline in the private sector. In the meantime, however, as we saw in the opening to this chapter, there continue to be companies where labor unions represent a large share of employees and thus play a major role in the operation and success of those companies. In such companies, whatever the national trend, effective labor relations are crucial for both companies and workers.

Questions

1. Many people picture labor union members as being men in blue-collar jobs in manufacturing plants. Is that accurate? Are there certain types of jobs where an employer can be fairly certain that employees will not join a union? Give examples.
2. Why do people join labor unions? Would you be interested in joining a labor union if given the opportunity? Why or why not? As a manager, would you prefer to work with a union or would you prefer that employees be unrepresented by a union? Explain.
3. What led to a change in labor relations at the Global Engine Manufacturing Alliance? What was the nature of the change and do you think it is an important and sustainable change?

 Please see the Video that corresponds to this chapter at www.mhhe.com/noe8e.

SUMMARY

Labor unions seek to represent the interests of their members in the workplace. Although this may further the cause of industrial democracy, management often finds that unions increase labor costs while setting limits on the company's flexibility and discretion in decision making. As a result, the company may witness a diminished ability to compete effectively in a global economy. Not surprisingly, management in nonunion companies often feels compelled to actively resist the unionization of its employees. This, together with a host of economic, legal, and other factors, has contributed to union losses in membership and bargaining power in the private sector. There are some indications, however, that managements and unions are seeking new, more effective ways of working together to enhance competitiveness while giving employees a voice in how workplace decisions are made.

KEY TERMS

Checkoff provision, 606
Closed shop, 606
Union shop, 606
Agency shop, 606
Maintenance of membership, 608
Right-to-work laws, 608

Taft-Hartley Act, 1947, 613
Associate union membership, 619
Corporate campaigns, 619
Distributive bargaining, 622
Integrative bargaining, 622
Attitudinal structuring, 622

Intraorganizational bargaining, 622
Mediation, 627
Fact finder, 628
Arbitration, 628
Duty of fair representation, 629

DISCUSSION QUESTIONS

1. Why do employees join unions?
2. What has been the trend in union membership in the United States, and what are the underlying reasons for the trend?
3. What are the consequences for management and owners of having a union represent employees?
4. What are the general provisions of the National Labor Relations Act, and how does it affect labor–management interactions?
5. What are the features of traditional and nontraditional labor relations? What are the potential advantages of the "new" nontraditional approaches to labor relations?
6. How does the U.S. industrial and labor relations system compare with systems in other countries, such as those in western Europe?

SELF-ASSESSMENT EXERCISE

Would you join a union? Each of the following phrases expresses an opinion about the effects of a union on employees' jobs. For each phrase, circle a number on the scale to indicate whether you agree that a union would affect your job as described by the phrase.

Having a union would result in . . .	Strongly Disagree				Strongly Agree
1. Increased wages	1	2	3	4	5
2. Improved benefits	1	2	3	4	5
3. Protection from being fired	1	2	3	4	5
4. More promotions	1	2	3	4	5
5. Better work hours	1	2	3	4	5
6. Improved productivity	1	2	3	4	5
7. Better working conditions	1	2	3	4	5
8. Fewer accidents at work	1	2	3	4	5
9. More interesting work	1	2	3	4	5
10. Easier handling of employee problems	1	2	3	4	5
11. Increased work disruptions	5	4	3	2	1
12. More disagreements between employees and management	5	4	3	2	1
13. Work stoppages	5	4	3	2	1

Add up your total score. The highest score possible is 65, the lowest 13. The higher your score, the more you see value in unions, and the more likely you would be to join a union.

SOURCE: Based on S. A. Youngblood, A. S. DeNisi, J. L. Molleston, and W. H. Mobley, "The Impact of Work Environment, Instrumentality Beliefs, Perceived Union Image, and Subjective Norms on Union Voting Intentions," *Academy of Management Journal* 27 (1984), pp. 576–90.

EXERCISING STRATEGY: HOW NISSAN LAPS DETROIT

Jonathan Gates slaps a wide slab of tan-colored, hard foam rubber on his workbench. He fastens a numbered tag in one corner and some black foam insulation at the edges. As soon as he puts a number on the piece of foam, which will become the top of a dashboard for a Nissan Quest minivan, the vehicle has an identity. All of the parts for a big chunk of the minivan's interior, decked out with the customer's choice of colors, fabrics, and options, will come together in the next 42 minutes.

Gates and his co-workers fill a crucial role at Nissan Motor Co.'s new Canton, Mississippi, assembly plant: Almost everything a driver touches inside a new Quest, Titan pickup, or Armada sport-utility vehicle is put together in a single module, starting at Gates's workbench. "This is the most important job," he says. And yet, amazingly, Gates doesn't even work for Nissan. He works for Lextron/Visteon Automotive Systems, a parts supplier that also builds the center console between the front seats and a subassembly of the car's front end. The finished modules pass over a wall to be bolted into a car or truck body rolling down the assembly line. Lextron/Visteon does the work faster than Nissan could and pays $3 an hour less than the carmaker pays assembly workers. Nissan is using a similar strategy for its vehicle frames, seats, electrical systems, and completed doors.

It's a level of efficiency that Detroit auto makers are only beginning to attempt. Along with other features in Nissan's eight-month-old, $1.4 billion factory, the wholesale integration of outside suppliers is another reason why General Motors, Ford, and Chrysler are still playing catch-up with Japanese car manufacturers. The Big Three have made great strides in productivity in recent years: General Motors Corp.'s best plants now actually beat Toyota's factories. But overall, every time Detroit gets close, the competition seems to get a little better.

Nissan's secret? Sure, its plants use cheaper, nonunion labor. Besides lower wages, its Smyrna, Tennessee, workers get about $3 an hour less in benefits than Big Three assemblers represented by the United Auto Workers. But there's more to it. Outsourcing offers huge savings, whereas the Big Three must negotiate the outsourcing of subassembly work with the union. And Nissan's plants are far more flexible in adjusting to market twists and turns. Nissan's Canton plant can send a minivan, pickup truck, and sport-utility vehicle down the same assembly line, one after the other, without interruption. At first glance, a Nissan factory does not look much different than one you would see in Detroit or St. Louis. But talk to the workers, and it soon becomes clear how relentlessly the company squeezes mere seconds out of the assembly process.

The United Auto Workers is slowly allowing more outsourcing. But the UAW wants to outsource work only to union-friendly suppliers. And even then it has to be negotiated. Nissan, meanwhile, has free rein to outsource jobs. Two of Smyrna's vehicles—the Maxima and Altima sedans—were engineered to be built using modules built by suppliers. Every vehicle built in Canton was designed that way. All together, buying modules saves 15% to 30% on the total cost of that section of the car, according to the Center for Automotive Research (CAR) in Ann Arbor, Michigan. And the Big Three? GM is the most "modular" of the domestic manufacturers, but only a few of its plants have been designed to build cars using many big modules.

Detroit is slowly making headway. Prudential says half of GM's 35 North American assembly lines can make multiple vehicles. GM's two-year-old Cadillac plant in Lansing, Michigan, will make three luxury vehicles: the CTS and STS sedans and SRX SUV. It has also been designed to get some large, preassembled modules from suppliers. GM is using the Cadillac plant as a model for upgrading other plants. "We're getting much more flexible," says Gary L. Cowger, president of GM North America.

But it's much easier to design a new factory to be flexible from the ground up than to refurbish those built 30 or more years ago. And with so much excess capacity, the Big Three have no room to build new plants. Even if they could match the Japanese in productivity, they would have to account for the costs of laid-off workers, whose contracts entitle them to 75% of their pay.

By contrast, Nissan runs a tight ship and works its employees harder. During the UAW's failed attempt to organize Smyrna in 2001, workers told the union that line speeds were too fast and people were getting injured, says Bob King, the UAW's vice president of organizing. The union says that in 2001, Nissan reported 31 injuries per 1,000 workers—twice the average at Big Three plants—according to logs reported to the Occupational Safety and Health Administration.

Nissan does not dispute the OSHA figures, but it denies its assembly lines are any less safe than Detroit's. Although the company won't release current numbers, executives do say that they have taken steps to reduce injuries. For instance, the company has workers do four different jobs during a typical eight-hour shift, to try to cut down on repetitive-motion injuries. Nissan claims that injury rates have fallen 60% in the past two years.

Questions

1. Can unionized plants compete with Nissan's nonunion plants?
2. Why isn't there a union at Nissan? Would a union be a good thing or a bad thing for Nissan workers? Nissan shareholders?

● MANAGING PEOPLE

Boeing's Labour Problems: Moving Factories to Flee Unions

Boeing decided a few years ago to build its 787 Dreamliner not in Washington State, but in South Carolina, a "right-to-work" state, which means it is illegal for companies and unions in that state to sign a contract in which anyone who works at the company has to join the union. That makes it extremely difficult to organise effective unions, and Boeing hoped it wouldn't have as many strikes at a plant in South Carolina as it had experienced at its plants in Seattle in recent years. The unions sued over the move, and the National Labor Relations Board has now awarded them a preliminary order blocking the factory from operating pending an investigation into whether the company's shift of production to a union-hostile state in order to avoid union activity constituted "anti-union animus."

To lay the groundwork here, it's important to understand what "right-to-work" means. Such laws specifically ban employers and unions from signing contracts stipulating that anyone who works at the company has to join the union. That's a basic step that unions always try to negotiate for, since without it they find it very hard to establish themselves as the negotiating partner with management.

Anyway, here's a sentence I found most amusing in a *Wall Street Journal* editorial: "Boeing management did what it judged to be best for its shareholders and customers and looked elsewhere." Boeing's motivation for shifting production to an anti-union state was not to benefit customers. If Boeing felt it could raise prices for the airplanes it builds without losing market share, it would do so in a second, regardless of whether that was "best for its customers." Companies try to lower operating costs in order to raise profits or cut prices and win market share, not out of a selfless desire to benefit customers.

But the more important flaw here is that the reason why Boeing might have judged its decision to move production to South Carolina "best for its shareholders" was that it didn't think it violated labour law to flee your union. If it did violate labour law, then Boeing made a bad decision and delivered negative value to its shareholders. To put things another way, if America had labour laws that were uniform from state to state like any other normal economic power, rather than a race-to-the-bottom system where states are pressured to weaken labour laws in order to entice employers, then there would have been no reason for Boeing to move production. There is simply no moral content to Boeing's decision to move production to South Carolina. Boeing doesn't get brownie points for

engaging in regulatory arbitrage and stiffing its unions just because it judged that move to be best for shareholders. Congratulating Boeing for trying to deliver shareholder value is like congratulating it for building and selling airplanes. That's simply what the company does. Boeing's decision was a judgment about how to play, given its evaluation of the rules of the game. The question of whether companies should be allowed to flee their unions is a question about what the rules of the game ought to be, in order to deliver value to the economy and to society.

Does anyone think that the United States would be a dramatically less prosperous country if it had uniform labour and business law throughout its territory? Have right-to-work laws in 22 states made such an immense contribution to American prosperity that without them America would not be the world's largest and wealthiest economy? Really? Seriously? Would American technological ingenuity have been crippled if the whole country had to follow the labour laws that obtain in Silicon Valley?

I don't think so. I think if there were no right-to-work states, American GDP wouldn't be significantly different than it is today. And if America did have uniform labour laws, then Boeing's decision as to whether to produce in Puget Sound or South Carolina would have nothing whatsoever to do with unions. If labour laws in South Carolina and Washington were equivalent, the only thing the workers in Puget Sound would have to worry about is whether their demands would lead the company to lose market share or to move production overseas. The first might be a real worry; the latter is a marginal issue for Boeing workers because the company is a defence industry–supported national champion firm.

Now maybe unionised Boeing workers should be more worried about hurting the company's market share as it competes with EADS and with regional-jet builders like Embraer and Bombardier. It certainly sounds like the company has a strike problem. But EADS's labour force is hardly non-unionised. If Boeing is having more trouble with its unions than its competitors are, it's possible that the fault lies with the company, rather than with the unions. What's happening here is that anti-labour laws in certain states allow companies to shift investment to those states in order to get around their unions. The issue is whether employers can use a threat to move production to a union-hostile state as a negotiating tactic in collective bargaining.

Questions

1. In a capitalist society and in a competitive global market, a company should be able to choose where it locates its production. Do you agree? Why or why not?
2. Does Boeing have a legitimate concern regarding the effect of strikes at its Washington operations on its ability to compete? What effect do strikes have on company profits?
3. Should Boeing simply do a better job of managing labor relations with its union? If you say yes,

how should it go about doing a better job? If you say no, explain why you do not think that will be effective.
4. Should all U.S. states have the same labor laws? Is it accurate to say that in most other countries, laws are the same throughout the country?

SOURCE: From *The Economist*, "Boeing's Labour Problems: Moving Factories to Flee Unions," April 25, 2011. © The Economist Newspaper Limited, London 2011. Reprinted with permission.

TWITTER FOCUS: REPUBLIC GETS SERIOUS

Using Twitter, continue the conversation about collective bargaining and labor relations by reading the Serious Materials case at www.mhhe.com/noe8e.

Serious Materials is a maker of eco-friendly building products that stepped in to buy Republic Windows and Doors. Republic's owners, with little warning, closed the plant without giving workers severance pay and secretly began to transfer machinery to a nonunion plant in another state. The employee's union filed complaints against Republic with the National Labor Relations Board. At the same time, the owner of Serious Materials

bought the Republic facility and saw it as a chance to expand the business into the Midwest. When he decided to make an offer, the owner talked first to the employee's union rather than to Republic's creditors. This unusual move helped seal the business deal, and all 300 employees were rehired by Serious.

Engage with your classmates and instructor via Twitter to chat about Serious Materials's actions using the case questions posted on the Noe website. Don't have a Twitter account yet? See the instructions for getting started on the Online Learning Center.

NOTES

1. J. T. Dunlop, *Industrial Relations Systems* (New York: Holt, 1958).
2. C. Kerr, "Industrial Conflict and Its Mediation," *American Journal of Sociology* 60 (1954), pp. 230–45.
3. T. A. Kochan, *Collective Bargaining and Industrial Relations* (Homewood, IL: Richard D. Irwin, 1980), p. 25; H. C. Katz and T. A. Kochan, *An Introduction to Collective Bargaining and Industrial Relations*, 3rd ed. (New York: McGraw-Hill, 2004).
4. Katz and Kochan, *An Introduction to Collective Bargaining*.
5. S. Webb and B. Webb, *Industrial Democracy* (London: Longmans, Green, 1897); J. R. Commons, *Institutional Economics* (New York: Macmillan, 1934).
6. C. Kerr, J. T. Dunlop, F. Harbison, and C. Myers, "Industrialism and World Society," *Harvard Business Review*, February 1961, pp. 113–26.
7. T. A. Kochan and K. R. Wever, "American Unions and the Future of Worker Representation," in *The State of the Unions*, ed. G. Strauss et al. (Madison, WI: Industrial Relations Research Association, 1991).
8. "Why America Needs Unions, but Not the Kind It Has Now," *BusinessWeek*, May 23, 1994, p. 70.
9. Katz and Kochan, *An Introduction to Collective Bargaining*.
10. J. Barbash, *The Elements of Industrial Relations* (Madison, WI: University of Wisconsin Press, 1984).
11. U.S. Bureau of Labor Statistics, www.bls.gov.
12. J. T. Bennett and B. E. Kaufman, *The Future of Private Sector Unionism in the United States* (Armonk, NY: M. E. Sharpe, 2002).
13. Katz and Kochan, *An Introduction to Collective Bargaining*. Katz and Kochan in turn build on work by J. Fiorito and C. L. Maranto, "The Contemporary Decline of Union Strength," *Contemporary Policy Issues* 3 (1987), pp. 12–27.
14. G. N. Chaison and J. Rose, "The Macrodeterminants of Union Growth and Decline," in *The State of the Unions*, George Strauss et al. (eds.) (Madison, WI: Industrial Relations Research Association, 1991).
15. D. L. Belman and K. A. Monaco, "The Effects of Deregulation, Deunionization, Technology, and Human Capital on the Work and Work Lives of Truck Drivers," *Industrial and Labor Relations Review* 54 (2001), pp. 502–24.
16. T. A. Kochan, R. B. McKersie, and J. Chalykoff, "The Effects of Corporate Strategy and Workplace Innovations in Union Representation," *Industrial and Labor Relations Review* 39 (1986), pp. 487–501; Chaison and Rose, "The Macrodeterminants of Union Growth"; J. Barbash, *Practice of Unionism* (New York: Harper, 1956), p. 210; W. N. Cooke and D. G. Meyer, "Structural and Market Predictors of Corporate Labor Relations Strategies," *Industrial and Labor Relations Review* 43 (1990), pp. 280–93; T. A. Kochan and P. Cappelli, "The Transformation of the Industrial Relations and Personnel Function," in *Internal Labor Markets*, ed. P. Osterman (Cambridge, MA: MIT Press, 1984); J. Logan, "The Union Avoidance Industry in the United States," *British Journal of Industrial Relations* 44 (2006), pp. 651–75.

17. Kochan and Cappelli, "The Transformation of the Industrial Relations and Personnel Function."

18. S. B. Jarrell and T. D. Stanley, "A Meta-Analysis of the Union–Nonunion Wage Gap," *Industrial and Labor Relations Review* 44 (1990), pp. 54–67; P. D. Lineneman, M. L. Wachter, and W. H. Carter, "Evaluating the Evidence on Union Employment and Wages," *Industrial and Labor Relations Review* 44 (1990), pp. 34–53; L. Mischel and M. Walters, "How Unions Help All Workers," Economic Policy Institute Briefing Paper (2003).

19. National Labor Relations Board annual reports.

20. John-Paul Ferguson, "The Eyes of the Needles: A Sequential Model of Union Organizing Drives, 1999–2004," *Industrial & Labor Relations Review* 62, no. 1 (October 2008), p. 3.

21. R. B. Freeman and M. M. Kleiner, "Employer Behavior in the Face of Union Organizing Drives," *Industrial and Labor Relations Review* 43 (1990), pp. 351–65.

22. F. K. Foulkes, "Large Nonunionized Employers," in *U.S. Industrial Relations 1950–1980: A Critical Assessment*, eds. J. Steiber et al. (Madison, WI: Industrial Relations Research Association, 1981).

23. Katz and Kochan, *An Introduction to Collective Bargaining.*

24. R. B. Freeman and J. Rogers, *What Workers Want* (Ithaca, NY: Cornell University Press, 1999).

25. E. E. Herman, J. L. Schwarz, and A. Kuhn, *Collective Bargaining and Labor Relations* (Englewood Cliffs, NJ: Prentice Hall, 1992), p. 32.

26. www.bls.gov; AFL-CIO website.

27. Herman et al., *Collective Bargaining*, p. 33.

28. Kochan, *Collective Bargaining and Industrial Relations*, p. 61.

29. National Labor Relations Board, *A Guide to Basic Law and Procedures under the National Labor Relations Act* (Washington, DC: U.S. Government Printing Office, 1991).

30. Ibid.

31. Ibid.

32. H. N. Wheeler and J. A. McClendon, "The Individual Decision to Unionize," in *The State of the Unions.*

33. National Labor Relations Board annual reports, www.nlrb.gov.

34. J. G. Getman, S. B. Goldberg, and J. B. Herman, *Union Representation Elections: Law and Reality* (New York: Russell Sage Foundation, 1976).

35. J. A. Fossum, *Labor Relations*, 8th ed. (New York: McGraw-Hill, 2002), p. 149.

36. National Labor Relations Board, *A Guide to Basic Law*, p. 17.

37. Ibid.

38. Herman et al., *Collective Bargaining*; P. Jarley and J. Fiorito, "Associate Membership: Unionism or Consumerism?" *Industrial and Labor Relations Review* 43 (1990), pp. 209–24.

39. Katz and Kochan, *An Introduction to Collective Bargaining*; R. L. Rose, "Unions Hit Corporate Campaign Trail," *The Wall Street Journal*, March 8, 1993, p. B1.

40. P. Jarley and C. L. Maranto, "Union Corporate Campaigns: An Assessment," *Industrial and Labor Relations Review* 44 (1990), pp. 505–24.

41. Katz and Kochan, *An Introduction to Collective Bargaining.*

42. A. Fung, T. Hebb, and J. Rogers (eds.), *Working Capital: The Power of Labor's Pensions* (Ithaca, NY: Cornell University Press, 2001).

43. A. Bernstein, "Working Capital: Labor's New Weapon?" *BusinessWeek*, September 27, 1997; A. Michaud, "Investments with the Union Label," *BusinessWeek*, August 22, 2001.

44. Chaison and Rose, "The Macrodeterminants of Union Growth."

45. R. E. Walton and R. B. McKersie, *A Behavioral Theory of Negotiations* (New York: McGraw-Hill, 1965).

46. Fossum, *Labor Relations.* See also C. S. Loughran, *Negotiating a Labor Contract: A Management Handbook*, 2nd ed. (Washington, DC: Bureau of National Affairs, 1990).

47. C. M. Steven, *Strategy and Collective Bargaining Negotiations* (New York: McGraw-Hill, 1963); Katz and Kochan, *An Introduction to Collective Bargaining.*

48. Kochan, *Collective Bargaining and Industrial Relations.*

49. Fossum, *Labor Relations.*

50. Kochan, *Collective Bargaining and Industrial Relations*, p. 272.

51. Herman et al., *Collective Bargaining.*

52. Katz and Kochan, *An Introduction to Collective Bargaining.*

53. Kochan, *Collective Bargaining and Industrial Relations*, p. 386.

54. Alternative criteria would be efficiency, equity, and worker voice. John W. Budd and Alexander J. S. Colvin, "Improved Metrics for Workplace Dispute Resolution Procedures: Efficiency, Equity, and Voice," *Industrial Relations* 47, no. 3 (July 2008), p. 460.

55. *United Steelworkers v. American Manufacturing Co.*, 363 U.S. 564 (1960); *United Steelworkers v. Warrior Gulf and Navigation Co.*, 363 U.S. 574 (1960); *United Steelworkers v. Enterprise Wheel and Car Corp.*, 363 U.S. 593 (1960).

56. Original data from U.S. Federal Mediation and Conciliation Service, *Fiftieth Annual Report, Fiscal Year 2006* (Washington, DC: U.S. Government Printing Office, 2006); www.fmcs.gov.

57. J. R. Redecker, *Employee Discipline: Policies and Practices* (Washington, DC: Bureau of National Affairs, 1989).

58. Barbash, *The Elements of Industrial Relations*, p. 6.

59. T. A. Kochan, H. C. Katz, and R. B. McKersie, *The Transformation of American Industrial Relations* (New York: Basic Books, 1986), chap. 6.

60. J. B. Arthur, "The Link between Business Strategy and Industrial Relations Systems in American Steel Minimills," *Industrial and Labor Relations Review* 45 (1992), pp. 488–506; M. Schuster, "Union Management Cooperation," in *Employee and Labor Relations*, ed. J. A. Fossum (Washington, DC: Bureau of National Affairs, 1990); E. Cohen-Rosenthal and C. Burton, *Mutual Gains: A Guide to Union–Management Cooperation*, 2nd ed. (Ithaca, NY: ILR Press, 1993); T. A. Kochan and P. Osterman, *The Mutual Gains Enterprise* (Boston: Harvard Business School Press, 1994); E. Applebaum and R. Batt, *The New American Workplace* (Ithaca, NY: ILR Press, 1994). J. Marquez, "Streamlined Model: Engine of Change," *Workforce Management*, July 17, 2006, pp. 1, 20–30; B. Visnic, "Harbour—Topping Chrysler JV Engine Plant Attracting Foreign Attention," *Edmunds Auto Observer*, July 20, 2008, www.autoobserver.com.

61. J. McCracken, "Desperate to Cut Costs, Ford Gets Union's Help," *The Wall Street Journal*, March 2, 2007, p. A1; M. Oneal, "Model Partnership: Automakers, Labor Could Learn from Harley-Davidson's Kansas City Operation," *Columbus Dispatch*, May 27, 2006 (original article in *Chicago Tribune*).

62. A. E. Eaton, "Factors Contributing to the Survival of Employee Participation Programs in Unionized Settings," *Industrial and Labor Relations Review* 47, no. 3 (1994), pp. 371–89.

63. National Labor Relations Board, *A Guide to Basic Law.*

64. A. Bernstein, "Putting a Damper on That Old Team Spirit," *BusinessWeek*, May 4, 1992, p. 60.

65. Bureau of National Affairs, "Polaroid Dissolves Employee Committee in Response to Labor Department Ruling," *Daily Labor Report*, June 23, 1992, p. A3; K. G. Salwen, "DuPont Is Told

It Must Disband Nonunion Panels," *The Wall Street Journal*, June 7, 1993, p. A2.

66. "NLRB 4-0 Approves Crown Cork & Seal's Use of Seven Employee Participation Committees," *HR News*, September 3, 2001.

67. Kochan and Osterman, *Mutual Gains*; J. P. MacDuffie, "Human Resource Bundles and Manufacturing Performance: Organizational Logic and Flexible Production Systems in the World Auto Industry," *Industrial and Labor Relations Review* 48, no. 2 (1995), pp. 197–221; W. N. Cooke, "Employee Participation Programs, Group-Based Incentives, and Company Performance: A Union–Nonunion Comparison," *Industrial and Labor Relations Review* 47, no. 4 (1994), pp. 594–609; C. Doucouliagos, "Worker Participation and Productivity in Labor-Managed and Participatory Capitalist Firms: A Meta-Analysis," *Industrial and Labor Relations Review* 49, no. 1 (1995), pp. 58–77; L. W. Hunter, J. P. MacDuffie, and L. Doucet, "What Makes Teams Take? Employee Reactions to Work Reforms," *Industrial and Labor Relations Review* 55 (2002), pp. 448–72; S. J. Deery and R. D. Iverson, "Labor-Management Cooperation: Antecedents and Impact on Organizational Performance," *Industrial and Labor Relations Review* 58 (2005), pp. 588–609; James Combs, Yongmei Liu, Angela Hall, and David Ketchen, "How Much Do High-Performance Work Practices Matter? A Meta-Analysis of Their Effects on Organizational Performance," *Personnel Psychology* 59, no. 3 (2006), pp. 501–28; T. Rabl, M. Jayasinghe, B. Gerhart, and T. M. Köhlmann, "How Much Does Country Matter? A Meta-Analysis of the HPWP Systems-Business Performance Relationship," *Academy of Management Annual Meeting Proceedings*, August 2011.

68. Robert D. Mohr and Cindy Zoghi, "High-Involvement Work Design and Job Satisfaction," *Industrial & Labor Relations Review* 61, no. 3 (April 2008), pp. 275–296; Paul Osterman, "The Wage Effects of High Performance Work Organization in Manufacturing," *Industrial and Labor Relations Review* 59 (2006), pp. 187–204.

69. J. Cutcher-Gershenfeld, "The Impact of Economic Performance of a Transformation in Workplace Relations," *Industrial and Labor Relations Review* 44 (1991), pp. 241–60.

70. R. B. Freeman and J. Rogers, *Proceedings of the Industrial Relations Research Association*, 1995. A survey of workers represented by the United Autoworkers at six Chrysler manufacturing plants found generally positive worker reactions to the implementation of work teams, streamlined job classifications, and skill-based pay. See L. W. Hunter, J. P. MacDuffie, and L. Doucet, "What Makes Teams Take? Employee Reactions to Work Reforms," *Industrial and Labor Relations Review* 55 (2002), p. 448. A study of the airline industry, moreover, concludes that relational factors, such as conflict and workplace culture, also play an important role in firm performance. See J. H. Gittell, A. vonNordenflycht, and T. A. Kochan, "Mutual Gains or Zero Sum? Labor Relations and Firm Performance in the Airline Industry," *Industrial and Labor Relations Review* 57 (2004), p. 163.

71. http://stats.bls.gov, Employer Costs for Employee Compensation (ECEC).

72. Ibid.

73. Mckinley L. Blackburn, "Are Union Wage Differentials in the United States Falling?" *Industrial Relations* 47, no. 3 (July 2008), p. 390.

74. Jarrell and Stanley, "A Meta-Analysis"; R. B. Freeman and J. Medoff, *What Do Unions Do?* (New York: Basic Books, 1984); L. Mishel and M. Walters, "How Unions Help All Workers," *Economic Policy Institute Briefing Paper*, August 2003, www.epinet.org.

75. T. H. Hammer and A. Augar, "The Impact of Unions on Job Satisfaction, Organizational Commitment, and Turnover," *Journal of Labor Research* 26 (2005), pp. 241–66; B. Artz "The Impact of Union Experience on Job Satisfaction," *Industrial Relations: A Journal of Economy and Society* 49 (2010), pp. 387–405.

76. J. T. Addison and B. T. Hirsch, "Union Effects on Productivity, Profits, and Growth: Has the Long Run Arrived?" *Journal of Labor Economics* 7 (1989), pp. 72–105.

77. R. B. Freeman and J. L. Medoff, "The Two Faces of Unionism," *Public Interest* 57 (Fall 1979), pp. 69–93.

78. Ibid.; L. Mishel and P. Voos, *Unions and Economic Competitiveness* (Armonk, NY: M. E. Sharpe, 1991); M. Ash and J. A. Seago, "The Effect of Registered Nurses' Unions on Heart-Attack Mortality," *Industrial and Labor Relations Review* 57 (2004), p. 422; C. Doucouliagos and P. Laroche, "What Do Unions Do to Productivity? A Meta-Analysis," *Industrial Relations* 42 (2003), pp. 650–91.

79. Freeman and Medoff, "Two Faces."

80. S. Slichter, J. Healy, and E. R. Livernash, *The Impact of Collective Bargaining on Management* (Washington, DC: Brookings Institution, 1960); Freeman and Medoff, "Two Faces."

81. Freeman and Medoff, *What Do Unions Do?*; Herman et al., R. B. Freeman J. L. Medoff 1984. What Do Unions Do? New York: Basic Books. *Collective Bargaining*; Addison and Hirsch, "Union Effects on Productivity"; Katz and Kochan, *An Introduction to Collective Bargaining*; Lineneman et al., "Evaluating the Evidence."

82. B. E. Becker and C. A. Olson, "Unions and Firm Profits," *Industrial Relations* 31, no. 3 (1992), pp. 395–415; B. T. Hirsch and B. A. Morgan, "Shareholder Risks and Returns in Union and Nonunion Firms," *Industrial and Labor Relations Review* 47, no. 2 (1994), pp. 302–18. Hristos Doucouliagos and Partice Laroche, "Unions and Profits: A Meta-Regression Analysis," *Industrial Relations* 48, no. 1 (January 2008), p. 146.

83. Addison and Hirsch, "Union Effects on Productivity." See also B. T. Hirsch, *Labor Unions and the Economic Performance of Firms* (Kalamazoo, MI: W. E. Upjohn Institute, 1991); J. M. Abowd, "The Effect of Wage Bargains on the Stock Market Value of the Firm," *American Economic Review* 79 (1989), pp. 774–800; Hirsch, *Labor Unions*.

84. B. E. Becker, and C. A. Olson, "The Impact of Strikes on Shareholder Equity," *Industrial and Labor Relations Review* 39, no. 3 (1986), pp. 425–38; O. Persons, "The Effects of Automobile Strikes on the Stock Value of Steel Suppliers," *Industrial and Labor Relations Review* 49, no. 1 (1995), pp. 78–87.

85. C. Brewster, "Levels of Analysis in Strategic HRM: Questions Raised by Comparative Research," Conference on Research and Theory in HRM, Cornell University, October 1997.

86. C. Chang and C. Sorrentino, "Union Membership in 12 Countries," *Monthly Labor Review* 114, no. 12 (1991), pp. 46–53; D. G. Blanchflower and R. B. Freeman, "Going Different Ways: Unionism in the U.S. and Other Advanced O.E.C.D. Countries" (Symposium on the Future Role of Unions, Industry, and Government in Industrial Relations. University of Minnesota),

cited in Chaison and Rose, "The Macrodeterminants of Union Growth," p. 23.

87. J. P. Begin and E. F. Beal, *The Practice of Collective Bargaining* (Homewood, IL: Richard D. Irwin, 1989); T. H. Hammer, S. C. Currall, and R. N. Stern, "Worker Representation on Boards of Directors: A Study of Competing Roles," *Industrial and Labor Relations Review* 44 (1991), pp. 661–80; Katz and Kochan, *An Introduction to Collective Bargaining*; H. Gunter and G. Leminsky, "The Federal Republic of Germany," in *Labor in the Twentieth Century*, ed. J. T. Dunlop and W. Galenson (New York: Academic Press, 1978), pp. 149–96.

88. "Adapt or Die," *The Economist*, July 1, 1995, p. 54; G. Steinmetz, "German Firms Sour on Stem That Keeps Peace with Workers: Centralized Bargaining, a Key to Postwar Gains, Inflates Costs, Companies Fear," *The Wall Street Journal*, October 17, 1995, p. A1; H. C. Katz, W. Lee, and J. Lee, *The New Structure of Labor Relations: Tripartism and Decentralization* (Ithaca, NY: ILR Press/Cornell University, 2004).

89. J. F. Burton and T. Thomason, "The Extent of Collective Bargaining in the Public Sector," in *Public Sector Bargaining*, ed. B. Aaron, J. M. Najita, and J. L. Stern (Washington, DC: Bureau of National Affairs, 1988).

90. www.afscme.org.

CHAPTER

15

Managing Human Resources Globally

LO **LEARNING OBJECTIVES**

After reading this chapter, you should be able to:

LO 15-1 Identify the recent changes that have caused companies to expand into international markets. *page 651*

LO 15-2 Discuss the four factors that most strongly influence HRM in international markets. *page 653*

LO 15-3 List the different categories of international employees. *page 662*

LO 15-4 Identify the four levels of global participation and the HRM issues faced within each level. *page 662*

LO 15-5 Discuss the ways companies attempt to select, train, compensate, and reintegrate expatriate managers. *page 667*

Globalizing GE

General Electric is one of the most well known and most admired companies in the world. During CEO Jack Welch's reign, GE became the company whose practices other companies tried to imitate. GE popularized the processes of re-engineering, e-business, and Six Sigma, among others. However, one of the other areas where GE led was in the area of globalization. GE was one of the first U.S. companies to establish a strong presence in China and India, and this was often driven by the search for lower labor costs. In fact, Welch was once quoted as saying that he wished he could just place his manufacturing plants on huge barges and float the barges to whatever country had the current lowest labor costs.

However, today globalization is less about labor costs (although they are still important, as you will see), and more about access to talent and access to markets. While GE has been reducing its global workforce in response to the economic crisis, it is becoming a company with more of a global than a U.S. footprint. In fact, between 2005 and 2010 GE reduced its U.S. workforce by 28,000, but its non–U.S. workforce by only 1,000.

Current CEO Jeffrey Immelt stated, "We've globalized around markets, not cheap labor. The era of globalization around cheap labor is over. Today we go to Brazil, we go to China, we go to India, because that's where the customers are." In 2000, 30% of GE's business was overseas, whereas today, that number is 60%. In addition, today 54% of GE employees are overseas, compared to 46% in 2000.

As more and more companies follow GE's lead, what do you think are the human resource issues that they have to consider?

SOURCE: From D. Wessel, "Big U.S. Firms Shift Hiring Abroad," *The Wall Street Journal*, April 19, 2011, B.1. Reproduced with permission of Dow Jones & Company, Inc., via Copyright Clearance Center.

Introduction

The environment in which business competes is rapidly becoming globalized. More and more companies are entering international markets by exporting their products overseas, building plants in other countries, and entering into alliances with foreign companies. Back in the middle of the 1980s, 61 of the top 100 organizations had their headquarters in the United States. By 2004, that number had dropped to 35, and, as you can see in Table 15.1, of the world's largest 25 organizations in 2010, only 10 are headquartered in the United States, with 9 in Europe and 6 in Asia in 2010. Of *Fortune* magazine's Global 500 (the 500 largest companies), 133 are headquartered in the United States, 68 in Japan, 61 in China, 35 in France, 34 in Germany, 30 in the United Kingdom, 12 in the Netherlands, and 14 in South Korea. In addition, for the first time in history, an automaker from outside the United States (Toyota) became the largest in worldwide sales, surpassing General Motors in the first quarter of 2007. However, production disruptions at Toyota following the earthquake and tsunami in Japan in 2010 allowed GM to barely regain the lead.

Forbes magazine lists its top 2000 global companies, and identifies a subset that exhibits exceptional growth rates which they dub "Global High Performers." In

table 15.1

Fortune Global 500—25 Largest Organizations Ranked by Revenues

RANK	COMPANY	REVENUES ($ MILLIONS)	PROFITS ($ MILLIONS)
1	Wal-Mart Stores, Inc.	421,849	16,389
2	Royal Dutch Shell	378,152	20,127
3	ExxonMobil	354,674	30,460
4	BP	308,928	−3,719
5	Sinopec Group	273,422	7,629
6	China National Petroleum	240,192	14,367
7	State Grid	226,294	4,556
8	Toyota Motor	221,760	4,766
9	Japan Post Holdings	203,958	4,891
10	Chevron	196,337	19,024
11	Total	186,055	14,001
12	ConocoPhillips	184,966	11,358
13	Volkswagen	168,041	9,053
14	AXA	162,236	3,641
15	Fannie Mae	153,825	−14,014
16	General Electric	151,628	11,644
17	ING Group	147,052	3,678
18	Glencore International	144,978	1,291
19	Berkshire Hathaway	136,185	12,967
20	General Motors	135,592	6,172
21	Bank of America Corp.	134,194	−2,238
22	Samsung Electronics	133,781	13,669
23	ENI	131,756	8,368
24	Daimler	129,481	5,957
25	Ford Motor	128,954	6,561

SOURCE: From "The World's Biggest Companies," *Fortune*. © 2011 Time Inc. Used under license.

2011, 69 of the 130 high-performer companies (those standing out from their peers in growth, return to investors, and future prospects) were headquartered outside of the United States.[1]

In addition, cross-border mergers (e.g., Merck/Schering-Plough, New York Stock Exchange/Deutche Bourse, etc.) are increasing. In fact, in 2011, 30% of all mergers were of companies headquartered in different countries, and the total value of cross-border mergers was up by 56%.[2]

Indeed, most organizations now function in the global economy. Thus U.S. businesses are entering international markets at the same time foreign companies are entering the U.S. market.

What is behind the trend toward expansion into global markets? Companies are attempting to gain a competitive advantage, which can be provided by international expansion in a number of ways. First, these countries are new markets with large numbers of potential customers. For companies that are producing below their capacity, they provide a means of increasing sales and profits. Second, many companies are building production facilities in other countries as a means of capitalizing on those countries' lower labor costs for relatively unskilled jobs. For example, many of the *maquiladora* plants (foreign-owned plants located in Mexico that employ Mexican laborers) provide low-skilled labor at considerably lower cost than in the United States. In 2009, the average manufacturing hourly wage in Mexico was $5.38, versus more than $24.00 in the United States.[3] Third, the rapid increase in telecommunications and information technology enables work to be done more rapidly, efficiently, and effectively around the globe. With the best college graduates available for $2.00 an hour in India versus $12–$18 an hour in the United States, companies can hire the best talent (resulting in better work) at a lower cost. And because their day is our night, work done in the United States can be handed off to those in India for a 24/7 work process.[4]

Deciding whether to enter foreign markets and whether to develop plants or other facilities in other countries, however, is no simple matter, and many human resource issues surface.

This chapter discusses the human resource issues that must be addressed to gain competitive advantage in a world of global competition. This is not a chapter on international human resource management (the specific HRM policies and programs companies use to manage human resources across international boundaries).[5] The chapter focuses instead on the key factors that must be addressed to strategically manage human resources in an international context. We discuss some of the important events that have increased the global nature of business over the past few years. We then identify some of the factors that are most important to HRM in global environments. Finally, we examine particular issues related to managing expatriate managers. These issues present unique opportunities for firms to gain competitive advantage.

Current Global Changes

Several recent social and political changes have accelerated the movement toward international competition. The effects of these changes have been profound and far-reaching. Many are still evolving. In this section we discuss the major developments that have accentuated the need for organizations to gain a competitive advantage through effectively managing human resources in a global economy.

LO 15-1
Identify the recent changes that have caused companies to expand into international markets.

EUROPEAN ECONOMIC COMMUNITY

European countries have managed their economies individually for years. Because of the countries' close geographic proximity, their economies have become intertwined. This created a number of problems for international businesses; for example, the regulations of one country, such as France, might be completely different from those of another country, such as Germany. In response, most of the European countries agreed to participate in the European Economic Community (EEC), which began in 1992. The EEC is a confederation of most of the European nations that agree to engage in free trade with one another, with commerce regulated by an overseeing body called the European Commission (EC). Under the EEC, legal regulation in the participating countries has become more, although not completely, uniform. Assuming the EEC's trend toward free trade among members continues, Europe has become one of the largest free markets in the world. In addition, as of 1999, all of the members of the European Economic Community share a common currency, the euro. This ties the members' economic fates even more closely with one another. In addition to the previous 15 EU states, as of May 1, 2004, 12 EU accession states—Bulgaria, Cyprus, the Czech Republic, Estonia, Hungary, Latvia, Lithuania, Malta, Poland, Romania, Slovakia, and Slovenia—were added to the EU, expanding the economic zone covered by the European Union.

NORTH AMERICAN FREE TRADE AGREEMENT

The North American Free Trade Agreement (NAFTA) is an agreement among Canada, the United States, and Mexico that has created a free market even larger than the European Economic Community. The United States and Canada already had a free trade agreement since 1989, but NAFTA brought Mexico into the consortium. The agreement was prompted by Mexico's increasing willingness to open its markets and facilities in an effort to promote economic growth.[6] As previously discussed, the *maquiladora* plants exemplify this trend. In addition, some efforts have been made to expand the membership of NAFTA to other Latin American countries, such as Chile.

NAFTA has increased U.S. investment in Mexico because of Mexico's substantially lower labor costs for low-skilled employees. This has had two effects on employment in the United States. First, many low-skilled jobs went south, decreasing employment opportunities for U.S. citizens who lack higher-level skills. Second, it has increased employment opportunities for Americans with higher-level skills beyond those already being observed.[7]

THE GROWTH OF ASIA

An additional global market that is of economic consequence to many firms lies in Asia. Whereas Japan has been a dominant economic force for over 20 years, recently countries such as Singapore, Hong Kong, and Malaysia have become significant economic forces. In addition, China, with its population of more than 1 billion and trend toward opening its markets to foreign investors, presents a tremendous potential market for goods. In fact, a consortium of Singaporean companies and governmental agencies has jointly developed with China a huge industrial township in eastern China's Suzhou City that will consist of ready-made factories for sale to foreign companies.[8] While Asia has been affected by the recent recession, the main impact has only been to slow its rate of growth.

GENERAL AGREEMENT ON TARIFFS AND TRADE

The General Agreement on Tariffs and Trade (GATT) is an international framework of rules and principles for reducing trade barriers across countries around the world. It currently consists of more than 100 member-nations. The most recent round of GATT negotiations resulted in an agreement to cut tariffs (taxes on imports) by 40%, reduce government subsidies to businesses, expand protection of intellectual property such as copyrights and patents, and establish rules for investing and trading in services. It also established the World Trade Organization (WTO) to resolve disputes among GATT members.

These changes—the European Economic Community, NAFTA, the growth of Asia, and GATT—all exemplify events that are pushing companies to compete in a global economy. These developments are opening new markets and new sources of technology and labor in a way that has never been seen in history. However, this era of increasing international competition accentuates the need to manage human resources effectively to gain competitive advantage in a global marketplace. This requires understanding some of the factors that can determine the effectiveness of various HRM practices and approaches.

Factors Affecting HRM in Global Markets

Companies that enter global markets must recognize that these markets are not simply mirror images of their home country. Countries differ along a number of dimensions that influence the attractiveness of direct foreign investment in each country. These differences determine the economic viability of building an operation in a foreign location, and they have a particularly strong impact on HRM in that operation. Researchers in international management have identified a number of factors that can affect HRM in global markets, and we focus on four factors, as depicted in Figure 15.1: culture, education–human capital, the political–legal system, and the economic system.[9]

LO 15-2
Discuss the four factors that most strongly influence HRM in international markets.

figure 15.1

Factors Affecting Human Resource Management in International Markets

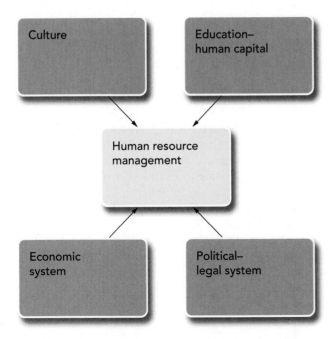

CULTURE

By far the most important factor influencing international HRM is the culture of the country in which a facility is located. Culture is defined as "the set of important assumptions (often unstated) that members of a community share."[10] These assumptions consist of beliefs about the world and how it works and the ideals that are worth striving for.[11]

Culture is important to HRM for two reasons. First, it often determines the other three factors affecting HRM in global markets. Culture can greatly affect a country's laws, in that laws are often the codification of right and wrong as defined by the culture. Culture also affects human capital, because if education is greatly valued by the culture, then members of the community try to increase their human capital. Finally, as we discuss later, cultures and economic systems are closely intertwined.[12]

However, the most important reason that culture is important to HRM is that it often determines the effectiveness of various HRM practices. Practices found to be effective in the United States may not be effective in a culture that has different beliefs and values.[13] For example, U.S. companies rely heavily on individual performance appraisal, and rewards are tied to individual performance. In Japan, however, individuals are expected to subordinate their wishes and desires to those of the larger group. Thus, individual-based evaluation and incentives are not nearly as effective there and, in fact, are seldom observed among Japanese organizations.[14]

In this section we examine a model that attempts to characterize different cultures. This model illustrates why culture can have a profound influence on HRM.

Hofstede's Cultural Dimensions

**Individualism–
Collectivism**
One of Hofstede's cultural dimensions; describes the strength of the relation between an individual and other individuals in a society.

In a classic study of culture, Geert Hofstede identified four dimensions on which various cultures could be classified.[15] In a later study he added a fifth dimension that aids in characterizing cultures.[16] The relative scores for 10 major countries are provided in Table 15.2. **Individualism–collectivism** describes the strength of the relation between an individual and other individuals in the society—that is, the degree to which people act as individuals rather than as members of a group. In individualist cultures, such as the United States, Great Britain, and the Netherlands, people are expected to look after their own interests and the interests of their immediate families. The individual is expected to stand on her own two feet rather than be protected by the group. In collectivist cultures, such as Colombia, Pakistan, and Taiwan, people are expected to look after the interest of the larger community, which is expected to protect people when they are in trouble.

Power Distance
One of Hofstede's cultural dimensions; describes how a culture deals with hierarchical power relationships.

The second dimension, **power distance,** concerns how a culture deals with hierarchical power relationships—particularly the unequal distribution of power. It describes the degree of inequality among people that is considered to be normal. Cultures with small power distance, such as those of Denmark and Israel, seek to eliminate inequalities in power and wealth as much as possible, whereas countries with large power distances, such as India and the Philippines, seek to maintain those differences.

Differences in power distance often result in miscommunication and conflicts between people from different cultures. For example, in Mexico and Japan individuals are always addressed by their titles (Señor Smith or Smith-san, respectively). Individuals from the United States, however, often believe in minimizing power distances by using first names. Although this is perfectly normal, and possibly even advisable in the United States, it can be offensive and a sign of disrespect in other cultures.

	PD[a]	ID	MA	UA	LT
United States	40 L[b]	91 H	62 H	46 L	29 L
Germany	35 L	67 H	66 H	65 M	31 M
Japan	54 M	45 M	95 H	92 H	80 H
France	68 H	71 H	43 M	86 H	30[c] L
Netherlands	38 L	80 H	14 L	53 M	44 M
Hong Kong	68 H	25 L	57 H	29 L	96 H
Indonesia	78 H	14 L	46 M	48 L	25[c] L
West Africa	77 H	20 L	46 M	54 M	16 L
Russia	95[c] H	50[c] M	40[c] L	90[c] H	10[c] L
China	80[c] H	20[c] L	50[c] M	60[c] M	118 H

table 15.2
Cultural Dimension Scores for 10 Countries

[a]PD = power distance; ID = individualism; MA = masculinity; UA = uncertainty avoidance; LT = long-term orientation.

[b]H = top third; M = medium third; L = bottom third (among 53 countries and regions for the first four dimensions; among 23 countries for the fifth).

[c]Estimated.

SOURCE: From "Cultural Constraints in Management Theories," by Geert Hofstede, *Academy of Management Executive*, February 1993, Vol. 7, No. 1, p. 91. Reproduced with permission of Academy of Management, via Copyright Clearance Center.

The third dimension, **uncertainty avoidance,** describes how cultures seek to deal with the fact that the future is not perfectly predictable. It is defined as the degree to which people in a culture prefer structured over unstructured situations. Some cultures, such as those of Singapore and Jamaica, have weak uncertainty avoidance. They socialize individuals to accept this uncertainty and take each day as it comes. People from these cultures tend to be rather easygoing and flexible regarding different views. Other cultures, such as those of Greece and Portugal, socialize their people to seek security through technology, law, and religion. Thus these cultures provide clear rules as to how one should behave.

The **masculinity–femininity dimension** describes the division of roles between the sexes within a society. In "masculine" cultures, such as those of Germany and Japan, what are considered traditionally masculine values—showing off, achieving something visible, and making money—permeate the society. These societies stress assertiveness, performance, success, and competition. "Feminine" cultures, such as those of Sweden and Norway, promote values that have been traditionally regarded as feminine, such as putting relationships before money, helping others, and preserving the environment. These cultures stress service, care for the weak, and solidarity.

Finally, the fifth dimension comes from the philosophy of the Far East and is referred to as the **long-term–short-term orientation.** Cultures high on the long-term orientation focus on the future and hold values in the present that will not necessarily provide an immediate benefit, such as thrift (saving) and persistence. Hofstede found that many Far Eastern countries such as Japan and China have a long-term orientation. Short-term orientations, on the other hand, are found in the United States, Russia, and West Africa. These cultures are oriented toward the past and present and promote respect for tradition and for fulfilling social obligations.

The current Japanese criticism of management practices in the United States illustrates the differences in long-term–short-term orientation. Japanese managers, traditionally exhibiting a long-term orientation, engage in 5- to 10-year planning. This

Uncertainty Avoidance
One of Hofstede's cultural dimensions; describes how cultures seek to deal with an unpredictable future.

Masculinity–Femininity Dimension
One of Hofstede's cultural dimensions; describes the division of roles between the sexes within a society.

Long-Term–Short-Term Orientation
One of Hofstede's cultural dimensions; describes how a culture balances immediate benefits with future rewards.

leads them to criticize U.S. managers, who are traditionally much more short-term in orientation because their planning often consists of quarterly to yearly time horizons.

These five dimensions help us understand the potential problems of managing employees from different cultures. Later in this chapter we will explore how these cultural dimensions affect the acceptability and utility of various HRM practices. However, it is important to note that these differences can have a profound influence on whether a company chooses to enter a given country. One interesting finding of Hofstede's research was the impact of culture on a country's economic health. He found that countries with individualist cultures were more wealthy. Collectivist cultures with high power distance were all poor.[17] Cultures seem to affect a country's economy through their promotion of individual work ethics and incentives for individuals to increase their human capital.

Implications of Culture for HRM

Cultures have an important impact on approaches to managing people. As we discuss later, the culture can strongly affect the education–human capital of a country, the political–legal system, and the economic system. As Hofstede found, culture also has a profound impact on a country's economic health by promoting certain values that either aid or inhibit economic growth.

More important to this discussion, however, is that cultural characteristics influence the ways managers behave in relation to subordinates, as well as the perceptions of the appropriateness of various HRM practices. First, cultures differ strongly on such things as how subordinates expect leaders to lead, how decisions are handled within the hierarchy, and (most important) what motivates individuals. For example, in Germany, managers achieve their status by demonstrating technical skills, so employees look to them to assign their tasks and resolve technical problems. In the Netherlands, on the other hand, managers focus on seeking consensus among all parties and must engage in an open-ended exchange of views and balancing of interests.[18] Clearly, these methods have different implications for selecting and training managers in the different countries.

Second, cultures may influence the appropriateness of HRM practices. For example, as previously discussed, the extent to which a culture promotes an individualistic versus a collectivist orientation will impact the effectiveness of individually oriented human resource management systems. In the United States, companies often focus selection systems on assessing an individual's technical skill and, to a lesser extent, social skills. In collectivist cultures, on the other hand, companies focus more on assessing how well an individual will perform as a member of the work group.

Culture often influences how employees value certain aspects of their work environment. In an interesting study comparing call center workers in India (a collectivist culture) and the United States (an individualistic culture), researchers found that in the United States person–job fit was the stronger predictor of turnover relative to India, where person–organization fit, links to the organization, and links to the community were the stronger predictors of turnover.[19]

Similarly, cultures can influence compensation systems. Individualistic cultures such as those found in the United States often exhibit great differences between the highest- and lowest-paid individuals in an organization, with the highest-paid individual often receiving 200 times the salary of the lowest. Collectivist cultures, on the other hand, tend to have much flatter salary structures, with the top-paid individual receiving only about 20 times the overall pay of the lowest-paid one.

Cultural differences can affect the communication and coordination processes in organizations. Collectivist cultures, as well as those with less of an authoritarian orientation, value group decision making and participative management practices more highly than do individualistic cultures. When a person raised in an individualistic culture must work closely with those from a collectivist culture, communication problems and conflicts often appear. Much of the emphasis on "cultural diversity" programs in organizations focuses on understanding the cultures of others in order to better communicate with them.

EVIDENCE-BASED HR

While national culture is important, recent research also suggests that its importance may be overstated. Researchers reexamining Hofstede's original work found that while differences existed across nations, significant cultural differences also existed within nations. They further found that the differences in cultures across organizations within countries was larger than the differences across countries. Their results imply that while one cannot ignore national culture, one must not think that certain HR practices may not be effective simply based on a regard for national culture. People of varying cultural backgrounds within a nation will be drawn to organizations whose cultures better match their individual, as opposed to national, value systems.

SOURCE: B. Gerhart and M. Fang, "National Culture and Human Resource Management: Assumptions and Evidence," *International Journal of Human Resource Management* 16, no. 6 (June 2005), pp. 971–86.

EDUCATION–HUMAN CAPITAL

A company's potential to find and maintain a qualified workforce is an important consideration in any decision to expand into a foreign market. Thus a country's human capital resources can be an important HRM issue. *Human capital* refers to the productive capabilities of individuals—that is, the knowledge, skills, and experience that have economic value.[20]

A country's human capital is determined by a number of variables. A major variable is the educational opportunities available to the labor force. In the Netherlands, for instance, government funding of school systems allows students to go all the way through graduate school without paying.[21] Similarly, the free education provided to citizens in the former Soviet bloc resulted in high levels of human capital, in spite of the poor infrastructure and economy that resulted from the socialist economic systems. In contrast, some Third World countries, such as Nicaragua and Haiti, have relatively low levels of human capital because of a lack of investment in education.

A country's human capital may profoundly affect a foreign company's desire to locate there or enter that country's market. Countries with low human capital attract facilities that require low skills and low wage levels. This explains why U.S. companies desire to move their currently unionized low-skill–high-wage manufacturing and assembly jobs to Mexico, where they can obtain low-skilled workers for substantially lower wages. Similarly, Japan ships its messy, low-skill work to neighboring countries while maintaining its high-skill work at home.[22] Countries like Mexico, with relatively low levels of human capital, might not be as attractive for operations that consist of more high-skill jobs.

Countries with high human capital are attractive sites for direct foreign investment that creates high-skill jobs. In Ireland, for example, more than 25% of 18-year-olds

COMPETING THROUGH GLOBALIZATION

Immigrants Crowd Out Local Workers

During the current economic crisis, a great debate has arisen over immigration, both legal and illegal, in the United States. Those opposing immigration point out that immigrants who are willing to work for lower wages are taking jobs from American workers and driving down wages. However, this debate is not unique to the United States.

The oil-rich countries of the Middle East face similar problems. The Gulf Cooperation Council (GCC), which includes Kuwait, Saudi Arabia, Bahrain, Oman, Qatar, and the United Arab Emirates, employs over 15 million "guest workers." Whereas Arab manpower (i.e, from places like Jordan, Yemen, Syria, and Egypt) used to be the bulk of this workforce, today over 11 million of these guest workers come from countries east of the Persian Gulf, mostly from India, China, and Pakistan.

As demonstrations across the Middle East have largely been characterized as "pro-democracy" ones, they have largely been fueled by resentment over the lack of opportunity. By some reports the number of unemployed people in the Arabic-speaking world exceeds 20 million, and could rise as high as 100 million by 2020.

Yet as unemployment rises across the region, jobs increasingly go to Asian guest workers. These workers are more skilled, especially in terms of their English language which is important in the information and service sectors. In addition, the Asian workers are less likely to bring their families. They are also easier to lay off and send home. Finally, they tend to work for lower wages because they bring Asian wage expectations to an area where locals were used to soaring wages during the petroleum boom years. Muhammad Malallah, a management consultant in Amman explains, "The Arab employee is seen as someone who is demanding and as someone who poses a political risk. The Indian employee does not. The Pakistani does not."

SOURCE: From J. Millman and J. Parkinson, "Transfer of Jobs to Asian Workers Feeds Discontent," *The Wall Street Journal,* March 4, 2011. Reproduced with permission of Dow Jones & Company, Inc., via Copyright Clearance Center.

attend college, a rate much higher than other European countries. In addition, Ireland's economy supports only 1.1 million jobs for a population of 3.5 million. The combination of high education levels, a strong work ethic, and high unemployment makes the country attractive for foreign firms because of the resulting high productivity and low turnover. The Met Life insurance company set up a facility for Irish workers to analyze medical insurance claims. It has found the high levels of human capital and the high work ethic provide such a competitive advantage that the company is currently looking for other work performed in the United States to be shipped to Ireland. Similarly, as already discussed, the skills of newly graduated technology workers in India are as high or higher than those found among their counterparts in the United States. In addition, because jobs are not as plentiful in India, the worker attitudes are better in many of these locations.[23] The "Competing through Globalization" box describes the clash between guest workers and local workers in the oil-rich countries of the Middle East.

POLITICAL–LEGAL SYSTEM

The regulations imposed by a country's legal system can strongly affect HRM. The political–legal system often dictates the requirements for certain HRM practices, such as training, compensation, hiring, firing, and layoffs. In large part, the legal system is an outgrowth of the culture in which it exists. Thus the laws of a particular country often reflect societal norms about what constitutes legitimate behavior.[24]

For example, the United States has led the world in eliminating discrimination in the workplace. Because of the importance this has in our culture, we also have legal safeguards such as equal employment opportunity laws (discussed in Chapter 3) that strongly affect the hiring and firing practices of firms. As a society, we also have strong beliefs regarding the equity of pay systems; thus the Fair Labor Standards Act (discussed in Chapter 11), among other laws and regulations, sets the minimum wage for a variety of jobs. We have regulations that dictate much of the process for negotiation between unions and management. These regulations profoundly affect the ways human resources are managed in the United States.

Similarly, the legal regulations regarding HRM in other countries reflect their societal norms. For example, in Germany employees have a legal right to "codetermination" at the company, plant, and individual levels. At the company level, a firm's employees have direct influence on the important decisions that affect them, such as large investments or new strategies. This is brought about through having employee representatives on the supervisory council (*Aufsichtsrat*). At the plant level, codetermination exists through works councils. These councils have no rights in the economic management of the company, but they can influence HRM policies on such issues as working hours, payment methods, hirings, and transfers. Finally, at the individual level, employees have contractual rights, such as the right to read their personnel files and the right to be informed about how their pay is calculated.[25]

The EEC provides another example of the effects of the political–legal system on HRM. The EEC's Community Charter of December 9, 1989, provides for the fundamental social rights of workers. These rights include freedom of movement, freedom to choose one's occupation and be fairly compensated, guarantee of social protection via Social Security benefits, freedom of association and collective bargaining, equal treatment for men and women, and a safe and healthful work environment, among others. The "Competing through Technology" box describes how new social media is posing a threat to China's political ruling class.

ECONOMIC SYSTEM

A country's economic system influences HRM in a number of ways. As previously discussed, a country's culture is integrally tied to its economic system, and these systems provide many of the incentives for developing human capital. In socialist economic systems there are ample opportunities for developing human capital because the education system is free. However, under these systems, there is little economic incentive to develop human capital because there are no monetary rewards for increasing human capital. In addition, in former Soviet bloc countries, an individual's investment in human capital did not always result in a promotion. Rather, it was investment in the Communist Party that led to career advancements.

In capitalist systems the opposite situation exists. There is less opportunity to develop human capital without higher costs. (You have probably observed tuition increases at U.S. universities.) However, those who do invest in their individual human capital, particularly through education, are more able to reap monetary rewards, thus providing more incentive for such investment. In the United States, individuals' salaries usually reflect differences in human capital (high-skill workers receive higher compensation than low-skill workers). In fact, research estimates that an individual's wages increase by between 10% and 16% for each additional year of schooling.[26]

China Seeks to Solve Structural Problems before Technology Boosts Unrest

We all watched as technology such as Twitter and Facebook provided the platform for organizing a series of antigovernment protests in countries such as Tunisia and Egypt. With the increasing tension in the Middle East as pro-democracy and disaffected citizens seek to overthrow their governments, China seeks to avoid such conflicts by focusing on boosting the incomes of its less wealthy citizens.

At the National People's Congress the government unveiled its five-year plan (through 2015) committing to raising income levels at the rate of economic growth and calling for companies to match increases in worker wages to productivity gains. For the past five years income levels have not kept up with economic growth. Wen Jiabao, China's premier, acknowledges that problems such as inflation could

threaten social stability and economic growth. Premier Wen stated that China seeks to eradicate poverty by 2020 and to greatly increase its poverty line beyond the current 1,196 yuan ($182) per person a year.

While efforts to boost incomes provide a long-term strategy for maintaining social stability, in the short term, in response to increasing appeals for antigovernment protests China has launched a massive security crackdown. These appeals have gone out on Twitter and other websites that the Chinese government blocks. However, those who use proxies or virtual private networks are able to get around China's Internet controls. The government has detained dozens of political activists and deployed thousands of uniformed and plainclothes police in locations where online activists

have called for silent "strolling" protests. It has also stepped up Internet controls and required foreign journalists to gain permission to report from anywhere in the Beijing city center. Finally, the government projects a 14% increase in security spending on items like police, courts, and jails, even faster than the growth in China's defense spending.

The question or challenge facing China's government is whether or not it can hold off the rising antigovernment sentiments spread instantaneously via technology long enough to fix the structural problems underlying those sentiments.

SOURCE: From B. Davis and J. Page, "China's Focus Turns to Its Poor," *The Wall Street Journal*, March 7, 2011. Reproduced with permission of Dow Jones & Company, Inc., via Copyright Clearance Center.

In addition to the effects of an economic system on HRM, the health of the system can have an important impact. For example, we referred earlier to lower labor costs in India. In developed countries with a high level of wealth, labor costs tend to be quite high relative to those in developing countries. While labor costs are related to the human capital of a country, they are not perfectly related, as shown by Figure 15.2. This chart provides a good example of the different hourly labor costs for manufacturing jobs in various countries.

An economic system also affects HRM directly through its taxes on compensation packages. Thus, the differential labor costs shown in Figure 15.2 do not always reflect the actual take-home pay of employees. Socialist systems are characterized by tax systems that redistribute wealth by taking a higher percentage of a person's income as she moves up the economic ladder. Capitalist systems attempt to reward individuals for their efforts by allowing them to keep more of their earnings. Companies that do business in other countries have to present compensation packages to expatriate managers that are competitive in take-home, rather than gross, pay. HRM responses to these issues affecting expatriate managers will be discussed in more detail later in this chapter.

figure 15.2

2010 Average Gross Hourly Compensation for Production Workers in Several Countries

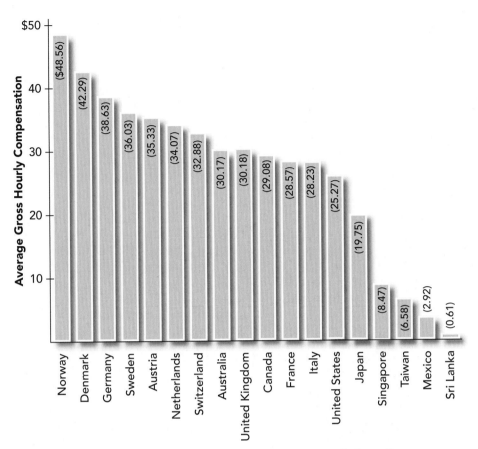

SOURCE: U.S. Bureau of Labor Statistics, www.bls.gov/news.release/pdf/ichcc.pdf.

These differences in economies can have a profound impact on pay systems, particularly among global companies seeking to develop an international compensation and reward system that maintains cost controls while enabling local operations to compete in the war for talent. One recent study examining how compensation managers design these systems indicates that they look at a number of factors including the global firm strategy, the local regulatory/political context, institutions and stakeholders, local markets, and national culture. While they try to learn from the best practices that exist globally, they balance these approaches with the constraints imposed by the local environment.[27] However, not just the hourly labor costs, but also the total cost of employees, affect decisions about where to locate workers. The "Competing through Sustainability" box describes how Coca-Cola is attempting to help build South Africa's economy in a sustainable way.

In conclusion, every country varies in terms of its culture, human capital, legal system, and economic system. These variations directly influence the types of HRM systems that must be developed to accommodate the particular situation. The extent to which these differences affect a company depends on how involved the company is in global markets. In the next sections we discuss important concepts of global business and various levels of global participation, particularly noting how these factors come into play.

Managing Employees in a Global Context

TYPES OF INTERNATIONAL EMPLOYEES

LO 15-3
List the different categories of international employees.

Parent Country
The country in which a company's corporate headquarters is located.

Host Country
The country in which the parent country organization seeks to locate or has already located a facility.

Third Country
A country other than a host or parent country.

Expatriate
An employee sent by his or her company in one country to manage operations in a different country.

Parent-Country Nationals (PCNs)
Employees who were born and live in a parent country.

Host-Country Nationals (HCNs)
Employees who were born and raised in the host, not the parent, country.

Third-Country Nationals (TCNs)
Employees born in a country other than the parent or host country.

LO 15-4
Identify the four levels of global participation and the HRM issues faced within each level.

Before discussing the levels of global participation, we need to distinguish between parent countries, host countries, and third countries. A **parent country** is the country in which the company's corporate headquarters is located. For example, the United States is the parent country of General Motors. A **host country** is the country in which the parent country organization seeks to locate (or has already located) a facility. Thus Great Britain is a host country for General Motors because GM has operations there. A **third country** is a country other than the host country or parent country, and a company may or may not have a facility there.

There are also different categories of employees. **Expatriate** is the term generally used for employees sent by a company in one country to manage operations in a different country. With the increasing globalization of business, it is now important to distinguish among different types of expatriates. **Parent-country nationals (PCNs)** are employees who were born and live in the parent country. **Host-country nationals (HCNs)** are those employees who were born and raised in the host, as opposed to the parent, country. Finally, **third-country nationals (TCNs)** are employees born in a country other than the parent country and host country but who work in the host country. Thus, a manager born and raised in Brazil employed by an organization located in the United States and assigned to manage an operation in Thailand would be considered a TCN.

Research shows that countries differ in their use of various types of international employees. One study revealed that Japanese multinational firms have more ethnocentric HRM policies and practices (they tend to use Japanese expatriate managers more than local host-country nationals) than either European or U.S. firms. This study also found that the use of ethnocentric HRM practices is associated with more HRM problems.[28]

LEVELS OF GLOBAL PARTICIPATION

We often hear companies referred to as "multinational" or "international." However, it is important to understand the different levels of participation in international markets. This is especially important because as a company becomes more involved in international trade, different types of HRM problems arise. In this section we examine Nancy Adler's categorization of the various levels of international participation from which a company may choose.[29] Figure 15.3 depicts these levels of involvement.

Domestic

Most companies begin by operating within a domestic marketplace. For example, an entrepreneur may have an idea for a product that meets a need in the U.S. marketplace. This individual then obtains capital to build a facility that produces the product or service in a quantity that meets the needs of a small market niche. This requires recruiting, hiring, training, and compensating a number of individuals who will be involved in the production process, and these individuals are usually drawn from the local labor market. The focus of the selection and training programs is often on the employees' technical competence to perform job-related duties and to some extent on interpersonal skills. In addition, because the company is usually involved in only one labor market, determining the market rate of pay for various jobs is relatively easy.

COMPETING THROUGH SUSTAINABILITY

Coca-Cola's Sustainability in South Africa

Coca-Cola South Africa today announced the opening of its new Valpré plant and the introduction of PlantBottle™ packaging to Africa. The new state-of-the-art facility will fill Valpré Spring Water in Heidelberg, southeast of Johannesburg. Selected for its close proximity to markets and distribution sites in the Guateng Region and a similar source water profile as Valpré's, the new plant will help Coca-Cola South Africa meet the needs of the increasing demand for bottled water in the country.

South Africa's Minister of Water and Environmental Affairs Ms. Bomo Molewa said, "The opening of the new Valpré plant in Heidelberg, and the launch of PlantBottle™, supports government's mandate to create infrastructure, develop skills, increase the number of women in the workforce and ensure sustainable development with a focus on minimizing the impact on the environment. It is a notable example of the kind of development that we encourage all South African industries to adopt."

The new Valpré plant is undergoing Leadership in Energy and Environmental Design (LEED) certification—an internationally recognized program that is the accepted benchmark for design, construction, and operation of high-performance green buildings. The design of the facility maximizes recycled materials and makes optimal use of water and solar energy. It has a "zero to landfill" target.

The Company today also launches Coca-Cola's innovative PlantBottle™ packaging. This packaging has revolutionized the beverage industry as the first-ever recyclable PET plastic beverage bottle made from up to 30% plant that is 100% recyclable. This is the 10th market to launch the bottle in the world and the first in Africa.

South African National Bottled Water Association (SANBWA) executive director, Charlotte Metcalf, said both the plant and new bottle significantly advance the bottling industry's "green" strategy. "With the new Heidelberg plant, Valpré will reduce its carbon footprint, lower its water usage ratio, adopt energy efficient lighting and production technologies, and boost its solid waste recovery—all while providing its market with a sustainable product packaged in a bottle that takes a giant step towards using renewable resource."

In addition to the environmental aspects of the plant and the new PlantBottle™, the Heidelberg plant is run by a team of talented, black women operators. This reinforces Coca-Cola's commitment to positively impact the communities in which it operates. In 2010, Muhtar Kent, chairman and CEO of Coca-Cola, announced the Company's 5 BY 20 pledge which aims to empower 5 million women by 2020 through the Coca-Cola system. This is one of several programs in South Africa to meet this challenge.

SOURCE: The Coca-Cola Company, "Coca-Cola South Africa Opens Green Valpré Plant and Launches Innovative PlantBottle™ Packaging," *Coca-Cola: The Coca-Cola Company,* July 7, 2011; web, July 28, 2011, http://www.thecoca-colacompany.com/dynamic/press_center/2011/07/green-valpre-plant-and-plantbottle-packaging.html.

As the product grows in popularity, the owner might choose to build additional facilities in different parts of the country to reduce the costs of transporting the product over large distances. In deciding where to locate these facilities, the owner must consider the attractiveness of the local labor markets. Various parts of the country may have different cultures that make those areas more or less attractive according to the work ethics of the potential employees. Similarly, the human capital in the different areas may vary greatly because of differences in educational systems. Finally, local pay rates may differ. It is for these reasons that the U.S. economy in the past 10 years has experienced a movement of jobs from northern states, which are characterized by

figure 15.3

Levels of Global Participation

strong unions and high labor costs, to the Sunbelt states, which have lower labor costs and are less unionized.

Incidentally, even domestic companies face problems with cultural diversity. In the United States, for example, the representation of women and minorities is increasing within the workforce. These groups come to the workplace with worldviews that differ from those of the traditional white male. Thus, we are seeing more and more emphasis on developing systems for managing cultural diversity within single-country organizations, even though the diversity might be on a somewhat smaller scale than the diversity of cultures across national boundaries.[30]

In a recent meta-analysis of the effects of cultural diversity on the functioning of multicultural work groups, Stahl et al. (2010) found that cultural diversity leads to process losses through increased task conflict and decreased social integration. On the other hand, it leads to process gains through increasing creativity and satisfaction.[31]

It is important to note that companies functioning at the domestic level face an environment with very similar cultural, human capital, political–legal, and economic situations, although some variation might be observed across states and geographic areas.

International

As more competitors enter the domestic market, companies face the possibility of losing market share; thus they often seek other markets for their products. This usually requires entering international markets, initially by exporting products but ultimately by building production facilities in other countries. The decision to participate in international competition raises a host of human resource issues. All the problems regarding locating facilities are magnified. One must consider whether a particular location provides an environment where human resources can be successfully acquired and managed.

Now the company faces an entirely different situation with regard to culture, human capital, the political–legal system, and the economic system. For example, the availability of human capital is of utmost importance, and there is a substantially greater variability in human capital between the United States and other countries than there is among the various states in the United States.

A country's legal system may also present HRM problems. For example, France has a relatively high minimum wage, which drives labor costs up. In addition, regulations make it extremely difficult to fire or lay off an employee. In Germany companies are legally required to offer employees influence in the management of the firm. Companies that develop facilities in other countries have to adapt their HRM practices to conform to the host country's laws. This requires the company to gain expertise in the country's HRM legal requirements and knowledge about how to deal with the country's legal system, and it often requires the company to hire one or more HCNs. In fact, some countries legally require companies to hire a certain percentage of HCNs for any foreign-owned subsidiary.

Finally, cultures have to be considered. To the extent that the country's culture is vastly different from that of the parent organization, conflicts, communication problems, and morale problems may occur. Expatriate managers must be trained to identify these cultural differences, and they must be flexible enough to adapt their styles to those of their host country. This requires an extensive selection effort to identify individuals who are capable of adapting to new environments and an extensive training program to ensure that the culture shock is not devastating.

Multinational

Whereas international companies build one or a few facilities in another country, they become multinational when they build facilities in a number of different countries, attempting to capitalize on lower production and distribution costs in different locations. The lower production costs are gained by shifting production from higher-cost locations to lower-cost locations. For example, some of the major U.S. automakers have plants all over the world. They continue to shift their production from the United States, where labor unions have gained high wages for their members, to *maquiladora* facilities in Mexico, where the wages are substantially lower. Similarly, these companies minimize distribution and labor costs by locating facilities in central and eastern European countries such as Poland, Hungary, and the Slovak Republic for manufacturing and assembling automobiles to sell in the European market.

The HRM problems multinational companies face are similar to those international companies face, only magnified. Instead of having to consider only one or two countries' cultural, human capital, legal, and economic systems, the multinational company must address these differences for a large number of countries. This accentuates the need to select managers capable of functioning in a variety of settings, give them necessary training, and provide flexible compensation systems that take into account the different market pay rates, tax systems, and costs of living.

Multinational companies now employ many "inpatriates"—managers from different countries who become part of the corporate headquarters staff. This creates a need to integrate managers from different cultures into the culture of the parent company. In addition, multinational companies now take more expatriates from countries other than the parent country and place them in facilities of other countries. For example, a manager from Scotland, working for a U.S. company, might be assigned to run an operation in South Africa. This practice accentuates the need for cross-cultural training to provide managerial skills for interaction with individuals from different cultures.

Global

Many researchers now propose a fourth level of integration: global organizations. Global organizations compete on state-of-the-art, top-quality products and services and do so with the lowest costs possible. Whereas multinational companies attempt to develop identical products distributed worldwide, global companies increasingly emphasize flexibility and mass customization of products to meet the needs of particular clients. Multinational companies are usually driven to locate facilities in a country as a means of reaching that country's market or lowering production costs, and the company must deal with the differences across the countries. Global firms, on the other hand, choose to locate a facility based on the ability to effectively, efficiently, and flexibly produce a product or service and attempt to create synergy through the cultural differences.

This creates the need for HRM systems that encourage flexible production (thus presenting a host of HRM issues). These companies proactively consider the cultures, human capital, political–legal systems, and economic systems to determine where production facilities can be located to provide a competitive advantage. Global companies have multiple headquarters spread across the globe, resulting in less hierarchically structured organizations that emphasize decentralized decision making. This results in the need for human resource systems that recruit, develop, retain, and use managers and executives who are competent transnationally.

A transnational HRM system is characterized by three attributes.[32] **Transnational scope** refers to the fact that HRM decisions must be made from a global rather than a national or regional perspective. This creates the need to make decisions that balance the need for uniformity (to ensure fair treatment of all employees) with the need for flexibility (to meet the needs of employees in different countries). **Transnational representation** reflects the multinational composition of a company's managers. Global participation does not necessarily ensure that each country is providing managers to the company's ranks. This is a prerequisite if the company is to achieve the next attribute. **Transnational process** refers to the extent to which the company's planning and decision-making processes include representatives and ideas from a variety of cultures. This attribute allows for diverse viewpoints and knowledge associated with different cultures, increasing the quality of decision making.

These three characteristics are necessary for global companies to achieve cultural synergy. Rather than simply integrating foreigners into the domestic organization, a successful transnational company needs managers who will treat managers from other cultures as equals. This synergy can be accomplished only by combining selection, training, appraisal, and compensation systems in such a way that managers have a transnational rather than a parochial orientation. However, a survey of 50 companies in the United States and Canada found that global companies' HRM systems are far less transnational in scope, representation, and process than the companies' strategic planning systems and organizational structures.[33]

In conclusion, entry into international markets creates a host of HRM issues that must be addressed if a company is to gain competitive advantage. Once the choice has been made to compete in a global arena, companies must seek to manage employees who are sent to foreign countries (expatriates and third-country nationals). This causes the need to shift from focusing only on the culture, human capital, political–legal, and economic influences of the host country to examining ways to manage the expatriate managers who must be located there. Selection systems must be developed that allow the company to identify managers capable of functioning in a new culture. These managers must be trained to identify the important aspects of the new culture in which they will live as well as the relevant legal–political and economic systems.

Transnational Scope
A company's ability to make HRM decisions from an international perspective.

Transnational Representation
Reflects the multinational composition of a company's managers.

Transnational Process
The extent to which a company's planning and decision-making processes include representatives and ideas from a variety of cultures.

Finally, these managers must be compensated to offset the costs of uprooting themselves and their families to move to a new situation vastly different from their previous lives. In the next section we address issues regarding management of expatriates.

MANAGING EXPATRIATES IN GLOBAL MARKETS

We have outlined the major macro-level factors that influence HRM in global markets. These factors can affect a company's decision whether to build facilities in a given country. In addition, if a company does develop such facilities, these factors strongly affect the HRM practices used. However, one important issue that has been recognized over the past few years is the set of problems inherent in selecting, training, compensating, and reintegrating expatriate managers.

According to a recent study by the National Foreign Trade Council (NFTC), there were 250,000 Americans on assignments overseas and that number was expected to increase. In addition, the NFTC estimates that the average one-time cost for relocating an expatriate is $60,000.[34] The importance to the company's profitability of making the right expatriate assignments should not be underestimated. Expatriate managers' average compensation package is approximately $250,000,[35] and the cost of an unsuccessful expatriate assignment (that is, a manager returning early) is approximately $100,000.[36] The failure rate for expatriate assignments among U.S. firms had been estimated at between 15% and 40%. However, more recent research suggests that the current figure is much lower. Some recent studies of European multinationals put the rate at 5% for most firms. While the failure rate is generally recognized as higher among U.S. multinationals, it is doubtful that the number reaches the 15% to 40% range.[37]

In the final section of the chapter, we discuss the major issues relevant to the management of expatriate managers. These issues cover the selection, training, compensation, and reacculturation of expatriates.

LO 15-5
Discuss the ways companies attempt to select, train, compensate, and reintegrate expatriate managers.

Selection of Expatriate Managers

One of the major problems in managing expatriate managers is determining which individuals in the organization are most capable of handling an assignment in a different culture. Expatriate managers must have technical competence in the area of operations; otherwise they will be unable to earn the respect of subordinates. However, technical competence has been almost the sole variable used in deciding who to send on overseas assignments, despite the fact that multiple skills are necessary for successful performance in these assignments.[38]

A successful expatriate manager must be sensitive to the country's cultural norms, flexible enough to adapt to those norms, and strong enough to make it through the inevitable culture shock. In addition, the manager's family must be similarly capable of adapting to the new culture. These adaptive skills have been categorized into three dimensions:[39] (1) the self dimension (the skills that enable a manager to maintain a positive self-image and psychological well-being), (2) the relationship dimension (the skills required to foster relationships with the host-country nationals), and (3) the perception dimension (those skills that enable a manager to accurately perceive and evaluate the host environment). One study of international assignees found that they considered the following five factors to be important in descending order of importance: family situation, flexibility and adaptability, job knowledge and motivation, relational skills, and extracultural openness.[40] Table 15.3 presents a series of considerations and questions to ask potential expatriate managers to assess their ability to adapt to a new cultural environment.

table 15.3

Interview Worksheet for International Candidates

Motivation
- Investigate reasons and degree of interest in wanting to be considered.
- Determine desire to work abroad, verified by previous concerns such as personal travel, language training, reading, and association with foreign employees or students.
- Determine whether the candidate has a realistic understanding of what working and living abroad requires.
- Determine the basic attitudes of the spouse toward an overseas assignment.

Health
- Determine whether any medical problems of the candidate or his or her family might be critical to the success of the assignment.
- Determine whether he or she is in good physical and mental health, without any foreseeable change.

Language ability
- Determine potential for learning a new language.
- Determine any previous language(s) studied or oral ability (judge against language needed on the overseas assignment).
- Determine the ability of the spouse to meet the language requirements.

Family considerations
- How many moves has the family made in the past among different cities or parts of the United States?
- What problems were encountered?
- How recent was the last move?
- What is the spouse's goal in this move?
- What are the number of children and the ages of each?
- Has divorce or its potential, or death of a family member, weakened family solidarity?
- Will all the children move? Why or why not?
- What are the location, health, and living arrangements of grandparents and the number of trips normally made to their home each year?
- Are there any special adjustment problems that you would expect?
- How is each member of the family reacting to this possible move?
- Do special educational problems exist within the family?

Resourcefulness and initiative
- Is the candidate independent; can he make and stand by his decisions and judgments?
- Does she have the intellectual capacity to deal with several dimensions simultaneously?
- Is he able to reach objectives and produce results with whatever personnel and facilities are available, regardless of the limitations and barriers that might arise?
- Can the candidate operate without a clear definition of responsibility and authority on a foreign assignment?
- Will the candidate be able to explain the aims and company philosophy to the local managers and workers?
- Does she possess sufficient self-discipline and self-confidence to overcome difficulties or handle complex problems?
- Can the candidate work without supervision?
- Can the candidate operate effectively in a foreign environment without normal communications and supporting services?

Adaptability
- Is the candidate sensitive to others, open to the opinions of others, cooperative, and able to compromise?
- What are his reactions to new situations and efforts to understand and appreciate differences?
- Is she culturally sensitive, aware, and able to relate across the culture?
- Does the candidate understand his own culturally derived values?
- How does the candidate react to criticism?
- What is her understanding of the U.S. government system?
- Will he be able to make and develop contacts with peers in the foreign country?
- Does she have patience when dealing with problems?
- Is he resilient; can he bounce back after setbacks?

(continued)

table 15.3

Interview Worksheet for International Candidates (*concluded*)

Career planning
- Does the candidate consider the assignment anything other than a temporary overseas trip?
- Is the move consistent with her progression and that planned by the company?
- Is his career planning realistic?
- What is the candidate's basic attitude toward the company?
- Is there any history or indication of interpersonal problems with this employee?

Financial
- Are there any current financial and/or legal considerations that might affect the assignment, such as house purchase, children and college expenses, car purchases?
- Are financial considerations negative factors? Will undue pressures be brought to bear on the employee or her family as a result of the assignment?

SOURCE: Reprinted with permission from *Multinational People Management*, pp. 55–57, by D. M. Noer. Copyright © 1989 by the Bureau of National Affairs, Inc., Washington, DC 20037.

One construct that has been emerging in the expatriate literature is cultural intelligence (CQ). This characteristic refers to an individual's ability to adapt across cultures through sensing the different cues regarding appropriate behavior across cultural settings or in multicultural settings. In fact, one set of researchers found that CQ was related to cultural adjustment and task performance among a sample of international executives.[41]

Little evidence suggests that U.S. companies have invested much effort in attempting to make correct expatriate selections. One researcher found that only 5% of the firms surveyed administered any tests to determine the degree to which expatriate candidates possessed cross-cultural skills.[42] More recent research reveals that only 35% of firms choose expatriates from multiple candidates and that those firms emphasize only technical job-related experience and skills in making these decisions.[43] These findings glaringly demonstrate that U.S. organizations need to improve their success rate in overseas assignments. As discussed in Chapter 6, the technology for assessing individuals' knowledge, skills, and abilities has advanced. The potential for selection testing to decrease the failure rate and productivity problems of U.S. expatriate managers seems promising. For instance, recent research has examined the "Big Five" personality dimensions as predictors of expatriate success (remember these from Chapter 6). For instance, one study distinguished between expatriate success as measured by not terminating the assignment and success as measured by supervisory evaluations of the expatriate. The researcher found that agreeableness, emotional stability, and extraversion were negatively related to the desire to terminate the assignment (i.e., they wanted to stay on the assignment longer), and conscientiousness was positively related to supervisory evaluations of the expatriate.[44]

A final issue with regard to expatriate selection is the use of women in expatriate assignments. For a long time U.S. firms believed that women would not be successful managers in countries where women have not traditionally been promoted to management positions (such as in Japan and other Asian countries). However, recent evidence indicates that this is not true. Robin Abrams, an expatriate manager for Apple Computer's Hong Kong office, states that nobody cares whether "you are wearing trousers or a skirt if you have demonstrated core competencies." In fact, some women believe that the novelty of their presence among a group of men increases their credibility with locals. In fact, some research suggests that male and female expatriates can perform equally well in international assignments, regardless of the country's cultural predispositions toward women in management. However, female expatriates self-rate their adjustment lower in countries that have few women in the workforce.[45] Also research has shown that female expatriates were perceived as being effective regardless of the cultural toughness of the host country.[46] And the fact is that female expatriates feel more strongly than their supervisors that prejudice does not limit women's ability to be successful.[47]

Training and Development of Expatriates

Once an expatriate manager has been selected, it is necessary to prepare that manager for the upcoming assignment. Because these individuals already have job-related skills, some firms have focused development efforts on cross-cultural training. A review of the cross-cultural training literature found support for the belief that cross-cultural training has an impact on effectiveness.[48] However, in spite of this, cross-cultural training is hardly universal. According to one 1995 survey, nearly 40% of the respondents offered no cross-cultural preparation to expatriates.[49]

What exactly is emphasized in cross-cultural training programs? The details regarding these programs were discussed in Chapter 7. However, for now, it is important to know that most attempt to create an appreciation of the host country's culture so that expatriates can behave appropriately.[50] This entails emphasizing a few aspects of cultural sensitivity. First, expatriates must be clear about their own cultural background, particularly as it is perceived by the host nationals. With an accurate cultural self-awareness, managers can modify their behavior to accentuate the effective characteristics while minimizing those that are dysfunctional.[51]

Second, expatriates must understand the particular aspects of culture in the new work environment. Although culture is an elusive, almost invisible phenomenon, astute expatriate managers must perceive the culture and adapt their behavior to it. This entails identifying the types of behaviors and interpersonal styles that are considered acceptable in both business meetings and social gatherings. For example, Germans value promptness for meetings to a much greater extent than do Latin Americans. Table 15.4 displays some ways body language conveys different messages in different countries.

Finally, expatriates must learn to communicate accurately in the new culture. Some firms attempt to use expatriates who speak the language of the host country, and a few provide language training. However, most companies simply assume that the host-country nationals all speak the parent-country's language. Although this assumption might be true, seldom do these nationals speak the parent-country language fluently. Thus, expatriate managers must be trained to communicate with others when language barriers exist. Table 15.5 offers some tips for communicating across language barriers.

Effective cross-cultural training helps ease an expatriate's transition to the new work environment. It can also help avoid costly mistakes, such as the expatriate who attempted to bring two bottles of brandy into the Muslim country of Qatar. The brandy was discovered by customs; not only was the expatriate deported, the company was also "disinvited" from the country.[52]

table 15.4

International Body Language

COUNTRY	NONVERBAL MESSAGES
Argentina	If the waiter approaches pointing to the side of his head and making a spinning gesture with their finger, don't think they've lost it—they're trying to say you have a phone call.
Bangladesh	Bursting to go to the toilet? Hold it. It is considered very rude to excuse yourself from the table to use the bathroom.
Bolivia	Don't make "the sign of the fig" (thumb protruding between index and middle finger), historically a sign that you couldn't care less—it is very insulting.
Bulgaria	Bulgarians nod the head up and down to mean no, not yes. To say yes, a Bulgarian nods the head back and forth.
China	In Eastern culture, silence really can be golden. So don't panic if long periods of silence form part of your meeting with Chinese clients. It simply means they are considering your proposal carefully.
Egypt	As across the Arab world the left hand is unclean, use your right to accept business cards and to greet someone. Use only your right hand for eating.
Fiji	To show respect to your Fijian hosts when addressing them, stand with your arms folded behind your back.
France	The French don't like strong handshakes, preferring a short, light grip or air kissing. If your French colleague is seen to be playing an imaginary flute, however, it means he thinks you are not being truthful.
Germany	When Germans meet across a large conference table and it is awkward to reach over and shake hands, they will instead rap their knuckles lightly on the table by way of a greeting.
Greece	Beware of making the okay sign to Greek colleagues as it signifies bodily orifices. A safer bet is the thumbs-up sign. The thumbs-down, however, is the kind of gesture reserved for when a Greek motorist cuts you off on the highway.
Hong Kong	When trying to attract someone's attention, don't use your index finger with palm extended upward. This is how the Cantonese call their dogs.
India	Beware of whistling in public—it is the height of rudeness here.
Japan	Japan is a real minefield for Western businesspeople, but one that always gets to them is the way the Japanese heartily slurp their noodles at lunch. Far from being rude, it actually shows appreciation of the food in Japanese culture.
Jordan	No matter how hungry you are, it is customary to refuse seconds from your host twice before finally accepting a third time.
Lebanon	Itchy eyebrow? Don't scratch it. Licking your little finger and brushing it across your eyebrow is provocative.
Malaysia	If you find a Malaysian standing with hands on hips before you, you've clearly said something wrong. It means he's livid.
Mexico	Mexicans are very tactile and often perform a bizarre handshake whereby, after pressing together the palms, they will slide their hands upward to grasp each other's thumbs.
Netherlands	The Dutch may seem open-minded, but if Dutch people tap the underside of their elbow, it means they think you're unreliable.
Pakistan	The overt display of a closed fist is an incitement to war.
Philippines	The "Roger Moore" is a common greeting here—a quick flash of the eyebrows supersedes the need for handshakes.
Russia	The Russians are highly tactile meet and greeters, with bear hugs and kisses directly on the lips commonplace. Don't take this habit to nearby Uzbekistan, however. They'd probably shoot you.
Saudi Arabia	If a Saudi man takes another's hand on the street, it's a sign of mutual respect.
Samoa	When your new Samoan host offers you a cup of the traditional drink, kava, make sure to deliberately spill a few drops on the ground before taking your first sip.
Turkey	Be careful not to lean back on your chair and point the sole of your foot at anyone in a meeting in Istanbul. Pointing with the underside of the foot is highly insulting.

SOURCES: http://www.businesstravelerusa.com/articles.php?articleID=490 Business Traveler Center; R. Axtell, *Gestures: The Dos and Taboos of Body Language Around the World*, (New York: John Wiley and Sons, 1991); P. Harris and R. Moran, *Managing Cultural Differences*, 3rd ed. (Houston, TX: Gulf Publishing Company, 1991); R. Linowes, "The Japanese Manager's Traumatic Entry into the United States: Understanding the American-Japanese Cultural Divide," *Academy of Management Executive* 7, no. 4 (1993), p. 26; D. Doke, "Perfect Strangers," *HR Magazine*, December 2004, pp. 62–68.

table 15.5

Communicating across Language Barriers

Verbal behavior
- *Clear, slow speech*. Enunciate each word. Do not use colloquial expressions.
- *Repetition*. Repeat each important idea using different words to explain the same concept.
- *Simple sentences*. Avoid compound, long sentences.
- *Active verbs*. Avoid passive verbs.

Nonverbal behavior
- *Visual restatements*. Use as many visual restatements as possible, such as pictures, graphs, tables, and slides.
- *Gestures*. Use more facial and hand gestures to emphasize the meaning of words.
- *Demonstration*. Act out as many themes as possible.
- *Pauses*. Pause more frequently.
- *Summaries*. Hand out written summaries of your verbal presentation.

Attribution
- *Silence*. When there is a silence, wait. Do not jump in to fill the silence. The other person is probably just thinking more slowly in the nonnative language or translating.
- *Intelligence*. Do not equate poor grammar and mispronunciation with lack of intelligence; it is usually a sign of second-language use.
- *Differences*. If unsure, assume difference, not similarity.

Comprehension
- *Understanding*. Do not just assume that they understand; assume that they do not understand.
- *Checking comprehension*. Have colleagues repeat their understanding of the material back to you. Do not simply ask whether they understand or not. Let them explain what they understand to you.

Design
- *Breaks*. Take more frequent breaks. Second-language comprehension is exhausting.
- *Small modules*. Divide the material into smaller modules.
- *Longer time frame*. Allocate more time for each module than usual in a monolingual program.

Motivation
- *Encouragement*. Verbally and nonverbally encourage and reinforce speaking by nonnative language participants.
- *Drawing out*. Explicitly draw out marginal and passive participants.
- *Reinforcement*. Do not embarrass novice speakers.

SOURCE: From Nancy Adler, *International Dimensions of Organizational Behavior*, 2nd ed., pp. 84–85. Copyright © 1991. South-Western, a part of Cengage Learning, Inc. Reproduced by permission. www.cengage.com/permissions.

Compensation of Expatriates

One of the more troublesome aspects of managing expatriates is determining the compensation package. As previously discussed, these packages average $250,000, but it is necessary to examine the exact breakdown of these packages. Most use a balance sheet approach to determine the total package level. This approach entails developing a total compensation package that equalizes the purchasing power of the expatriate manager with that of employees in similar positions in the home country and provides incentives to offset the inconveniences incurred in the location. Purchasing power includes all of the expenses associated with the expatriate assignment. Expenses include goods and services (food, personal care, clothing, recreation, and transportation), housing (for a principal residence), income taxes (paid to federal and local governments), reserve (savings, payments for benefits, pension contributions), and shipment and storage (costs associated with moving and/or storing personal belongings). A typical balance sheet is shown in Figure 15.4.

As you can see from this figure, the employee starts with a set of costs for taxes, housing, goods and services, and reserve. However, in the host country, these costs are significantly higher. Thus the company must make up the difference between costs in the home and those in the host country, and then provide a premium and/or incentive for the employee to go through the trouble of living in a different environment.

Total pay packages have four components. First, there is the base salary. Determining the base salary is not a simple matter, however. Fluctuating exchange rates between countries may make an offered salary a raise some of the time, a pay cut at other times. In addition, the base salary may be based on comparable pay in the parent country, or it may be based on the prevailing market rates for the job in the host

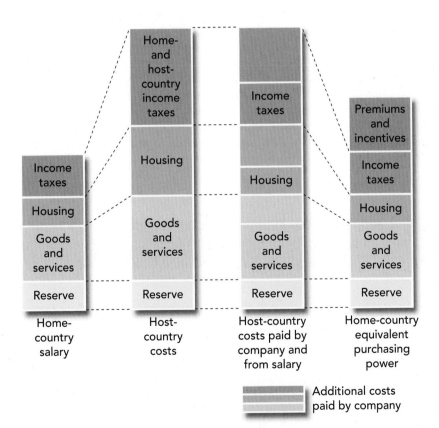

figure 15.4

The Balance Sheet for Determining Expatriate Compensation

SOURCE: From C. Reynolds, "Compensation of Overseas Personnel," in Joseph Famularo, *Handbook of Human Resource Administration*, 2nd ed., 1986. Copyright © 1986 The McGraw-Hill Companies, Inc. Reprinted with permission.

country. Expatriates are often offered a salary premium beyond that of their present salary as an inducement to accept the expatriate assignment.

Tax equalization allowances are a second component. They are necessary because of countries' different taxation systems in high-tax countries. For example, a senior executive earning $100,000 in Belgium (with a maximum marginal tax rate of 70.8%) could cost a company almost $1 million in taxes over five to seven years.[53] Under most tax equalization plans, the company withholds the amount of tax to be paid in the home country, then pays all of the taxes accrued in the host country.

A third component, benefits, presents additional compensation problems. Most of the problems have to do with the transportability of the benefits. For example, if an expatriate contributing to a pension plan in the United States is moved to a different country, does the individual have a new pension in the host country, or should the individual be allowed to contribute to the existing pension in her home country? What about health care systems located in the United States? How does the company ensure that expatriate employees have equal health care coverage? For example, in one company, the different health care plans available resulted in situations where it might cost significantly less to have the employee fly to the United States to have a procedure performed rather than to have it done in the host country. However, the health plans did not allow this alternative.

Finally, allowances are often offered to make the expatriate assignment less unattractive. Cost-of-living allowances are payments that offset the differences in expenditures on day-to-day necessities between the host country and the parent country. For instance, Table 15.6 shows the differences in cost of living among some of the larger international cities. Housing allowances ensure that the expatriate can maintain the same home-country living standard. Education allowances reimburse expatriates for the expense of placing their children in private English-speaking schools. Relocation allowances cover all the expenses of making the actual move to a new country, including transportation to and from the new location, temporary living expenses, and shipping and/or storage of

table 15.6

Global Cost of Living Survey: Ranking of Selected Cities among the Top 50 International Cities, 2010

TOP TEN MOST EXPENSIVE CITIES		
RANK	CITY	INDEX
1	Tokyo	161
2	Oslo	156
3	Osaka Kobe	153
4	Paris	150
5	Zurich	148
6	Sydney	143
7	Melbourne	141
8	Frankfurt	140
9	Geneva	138
10	Singapore	137

SOURCE: Economist Intelligence Unit (2011), "Worldwide Cost of Living 2011." www.eiu.com.

John H. Doe
Name

1 October 2004
Effective date

Singapore
Location of assignment

Manager, SLS./Serv. AP/ME
Title

Houston, Texas
Home base

1234
Emp. no.

202
LCA code

202
Tax code

Reason for Change: International Assignment

	Old	New
Monthly base salary		$5,000.00
Living cost allowance		$1,291.00
Foreign service premium		$ 750.00
Area allowance		-0-
Gross monthly salary		$7,041.00
Housing deduction		$ 500.00
Hypothetical tax		$ 570.00
Other		
Net monthly salary		$5,971.00

Prepared by   **Date**

Vice President, Human Resources   **Date**

personal possessions. Figure 15.5 illustrates a typical summary sheet for an expatriate manager's compensation package.

The cost of a U.S. expatriate working in another country is approximately three to four times that of a comparable U.S. employee.[54] In addition, "about 38% of multinational companies surveyed by KPMG LLP for its 2006 Global Assignment Policies and Practices say overseas assignment programs are 'more generous than they need to be.' "[55] These two facts combined have put pressure on global organizations to rethink their tax equalization strategy and expatriate packages.

Reacculturation of Expatriates

A final issue of importance to managing expatriates is dealing with the reacculturation process when the managers reenter their home country. Reentry is no simple feat. Culture shock takes place in reverse. The individual has changed, the company has changed, and the culture has changed while the expatriate was overseas. According to one source, 60% to 70% of expatriates did not know what their position would be upon their return, and 46% ended up with jobs that gave them reduced autonomy and authority.[56] Twenty percent of workers want to leave the company when they return from an overseas assignment, and this presents potentially serious morale and productivity problems.[57] In fact, the most recent estimates are that 25% of expatriate managers leave the company within one year of returning from their expatriate assignments.[58] If these repatriates leave, the company has virtually no way to recoup its substantial investment in human capital.[59]

Companies are increasingly making efforts to help expatriates through reacculturation. Two characteristics help in this transition process: communication and validation.[60] *Communication* refers to the extent to which the expatriate receives information and recognizes changes while abroad. The closer the contact with the home organization while abroad, the more proactive, effective, and satisfied the expatriate will be upon reentry. *Validation* refers to the amount of recognition received by the expatriate upon return home. Expatriates who receive recognition from their peers and their bosses for their foreign work and their future potential contribution to the company have fewer troubles with reentry compared with those who are treated as if they were "out of the loop." Given the tremendous investment that firms make in expatriate employees, usually aimed at providing global experience that will help the company, firms certainly do not want to lose expatriates after their assignments have concluded.

Finally, one research study noted the role of an expatriate manager's expectations about the expatriate assignment in determining repatriation adjustment and job performance. This study found that managers whose job expectations (constraints and demands in terms of volume and performance standards) and nonwork expectations (living and housing conditions) were met exhibited a greater degree of repatriation adjustment and higher levels of job performance.[61] Monsanto has an extensive repatriation program that begins long before the expatriate returns. The program entails providing extensive information regarding the potential culture shock of repatriation and information on how family members, friends, and the office environment might have changed. Then, a few months after returning, expatriate managers hold "debriefing" sessions with several colleagues to help work through difficulties. Monsanto believes that this program provides them with a source of competitive advantage in international assignments.[62]

In sum, a variety of HR practices can support effective expatriation. In general, the selection system must rigorously assess potential expatriates' skills and personalities and even focus on the candidate's spouse. Training should be conducted prior to and during the expatriate assignment, and the assignment itself should be viewed as a career development experience. Effective reward systems must go beyond salary and benefits, and while keeping the employee "whole" and even offering a monetary premium, should also provide access to career development and learning opportunities. Finally, serious efforts should be made to manage the repatriation process.[63] A summary of the key points is provided in Table 15.7.

table 15.7

Human Resource
Practices That
Support Effective
Expatriation

Staffing and Selection
- Communicate the value of international assignments for the company's global mission.
- Ensure that those with the highest potential move internationally.
- Provide short-term assignments to increase the pool of employees with international experience.
- Recruit employees who have lived or who were educated abroad.

Training and Career Development
- Make international assignment planning a part of the career development process.
- Encourage early international experience.
- Create learning opportunities during the assignment.
- Use international assignments as a leadership development tool.

Performance Appraisal and Compensation
- Differentiate performance management based on expatriate roles.
- Align incentives with expatriation objectives.
- Tailor benefits to the expatriate's needs.
- Focus on equality of opportunities, not cash.
- Emphasize rewarding careers rather than short-term outcomes.

Expatriation and Repatriation Activities
- Involve the family in the orientation program at the beginning and the end of the assignment.
- Establish mentor relationships between expatriates and executives from the home location.
- Provide support for dual careers.
- Secure opportunities for the returning manager to use knowledge and skills learned while on the international assignment.

SOURCE: From Paul Evans and Vladimir Pucik, *The Global Challenge: Frameworks for International Human Resource Management*, 2002. Copyright © 2002 The McGraw-Hill Companies. Reprinted with permission.

A Look Back

GE's increasing global footprint results in a host of HR issues. The expanding international customer base requires that GE's leadership ranks increasingly reflect a demographic that mirrors it. This also requires that those in leadership roles have significant levels of experience outside their home countries in order to gain a greater appreciation for other cultures, regulatory systems, and political/legal systems.

In addition, GE's HR systems must be consistent enough across the globe to ensure a common platform for evaluating and managing talent (for example, its classic "Session C" process), but at the same time have a level of flexibility that enables it to adapt to managing local workforces with practices and processes that are both legal and culturally acceptable.

GE's global footprint exemplifies the challenges in managing across a variety of countries, and their practices continue to be a model from which other firms will learn.

Questions

1. What do you think about companies like GE that may be downsizing their U.S. workforce while expanding their overseas workforces?
2. What do you think are the three most important human resource challenges a multinational company such as GE faces?

Please see the Video that corresponds to this chapter at www.mhhe.com/noe8e.

SUMMARY

Today's organizations are more involved in international commerce than ever before, and the trend will continue. Recent historic events such as the development of the EEC, NAFTA, the economic growth of Asia, and GATT have accelerated the movement toward a global market. Companies competing in the global marketplace require top-quality people to compete successfully. This requires that managers be aware of the many factors that significantly affect HRM in a global environment, such as culture, human capital, and the political–legal and economic systems, and that they understand how these factors come into play in the various levels of global participation. Finally, it requires that they be adept at developing HRM systems that maximize the effectiveness of all human resources, particularly with regard to expatriate managers. Managers cannot overestimate the importance of effectively managing human resources to gain competitive advantage in today's global marketplace.

KEY TERMS

Individualism–collectivism, 654
Power distance, 654
Uncertainty avoidance, 655
Masculinity–femininity
   dimension, 655
Long-term–short-term
   orientation, 655

Parent country, 662
Host country, 662
Third country, 662
Expatriate, 662
Parent-country nationals
   (PCNs), 662
Host-country nationals (HCNs), 662

Third-country nationals
   (TCNs), 662
Transnational scope, 666
Transnational representation, 666
Transnational process, 666

DISCUSSION QUESTIONS

1. What current trends and/or events (besides those mentioned at the outset of the chapter) are responsible for the increased internationalization of the marketplace?
2. According to Hofstede (in Table 15.2), the United States is low on power distance, high on individuality, high on masculinity, low on uncertainty avoidance, and low on long-term orientation. Russia, on the other hand, is high on power distance, moderate on individuality, low on masculinity, high on uncertainty avoidance, and low on long-term orientation. Many U.S. managers are transplanting their own HRM practices into Russia while companies seek to develop operations there. How acceptable and effective do you think the following practices will be and why? (a) Extensive assessments of individual abilities for selection? (b) Individually based appraisal systems? (c) Suggestion systems? (d) Self-managing work teams?
3. The chapter notes that political–legal and economic systems can reflect a country's culture. The former Eastern bloc countries seem to be changing their political–legal and economic systems. Is this change brought on by their cultures, or will culture have an impact on the ability to change these systems? Why?

4. Think of the different levels of global participation. What companies that you are familiar with exhibit the different levels of participation?
5. Think of a time when you had to function in another culture (on a vacation or job). What were the major obstacles you faced, and how did you deal with them?

Was this a stressful experience? Why? How can companies help expatriate employees deal with stress?
6. What types of skills do you need to be able to manage in today's global marketplace? Where do you expect to get those skills? What classes and/or experiences will you need?

● SELF-ASSESSMENT EXERCISE

The following list includes a number of qualities that have been identified as being associated with success in an expatriate assignment. Rate the degree to which you possess each quality, using the following scale:

1 = very low
2 = low
3 = moderate
4 = high
5 = very high

_____ Resourcefulness/resilience
_____ Adaptability/flexibility
_____ Emotional stability
_____ Ability to deal with ambiguity/uncertainty/differences
_____ Desire to work with people who are different
_____ Cultural empathy/sensitivity

_____ Tolerance of others' views, especially when they differ from your own
_____ Sensitivity to feelings and attitudes of others
_____ Good health and wellness

Add up your total score for the items. The higher your score, the greater your likelihood of success. Qualities that you rated low would be considered weaknesses for an expatriate assignment. Keep in mind that you will also need to be technically competent for the assignment, and your spouse and family (if applicable) must be adaptable and willing to live abroad.

SOURCE: Based on "Rating Scale on Successful Expatriate Qualities," from P. R. Harris and R. T. Moran, *Managing Cultural Differences*, 3rd ed. (Houston: Gulf, 1991), p. 569.

● EXERCISING STRATEGY: TERRORISM AND GLOBAL HUMAN RESOURCE MANAGEMENT

Globalization has continued to increase as companies expand their operations in a number of countries, employing an increasingly global workforce. Although this process has resulted in a number of positive outcomes, it has also occasionally presented new types of problems for firms to face.

On September 11, 2001, terrorists with Middle Eastern roots (alleged to be part of Osama bin Laden's al Qaeda network) hijacked four U.S. planes, crashing two of them into the World Trade Center's twin towers and one into the Pentagon (a fourth was crashed in Pennsylvania in a scuffle with passengers). President George W. Bush and U.K. Prime Minister Tony Blair, after their demands that the Taliban government in Afghanistan turn over bin Laden and his leaders were ignored, began military action against that country on October 7, 2001. Both the terrorist acts and the subsequent war on terrorism have created a host of issues for multinational companies.

First, companies doing business overseas, particularly in Muslim-dominated countries such as the Arab states and Indonesia, must manage their expatriate workforce (particularly U.S. and British citizens) in what has the potential to become hostile territory. These employees fear for their security, and some have asked to return to their home countries.

Second, companies with global workforces must manage across what have become increasingly nationalistic boundaries. Those of us in the United States may view the terrorist attacks as an act of war and our response as being entirely justified. However, those in the Arab world, while not justifying the terrorist attacks, may similarly feel that the military response toward Afghanistan (and later Iraq) is hostile aggression. One executive at a global oil company noted the difficulty in managing a workforce that is approximately 25% Arab. He stated that many of the Arab executives have said, "While we know that you are concerned about the events of September 11, you should know that we are equally concerned about the events of October 7 and since."

Questions

1. How can a global company manage the inevitable conflicts that will arise among individuals from different religious, racial, ethnic, and national groups who must work together within firms? How can these conflicts be overcome to create a productive work environment?
2. What will firms have to do differently in managing expatriates, particularly U.S. or British citizens who are asked to take assignments in predominantly Muslim countries?

MANAGING PEOPLE

The Toyota Way to No. I

Toyota's top U.S. executive on how it managed to become the world's No. 1 carmaker and why the company can hang on to the top spot It happened. Toyota passed General Motors in worldwide sales globally in the first quarter. We knew it was coming. It's likely that the trend will continue and hold up for the entire year, and for years to come.

As the baton gets passed this year, there's a mix of opinions and perspectives in the auto industry about whether Toyota is succeeding fairly. Does its lack of health-care and pension responsibilities, which hobble GM, Ford, and DaimlerChrysler's Chrysler division, allow Toyota an advantage on an unlevel playing field? Does Japan's insular economy, which has made it so difficult for U.S. auto makers to achieve sales in Japan, offer an unfair advantage? Do charges that the Japanese government weakens the yen against the dollar to keep prices down and profit up abroad hold water?

Toyota isn't accepting the No. 1 position comfortably. It makes some of its executives nervous to be the chased, rather than the chaser. Yuki Funo is the chairman and CEO of Toyota Motor Sales USA—the top Japanese executive for Toyota in North America. He recently sat down with *BusinessWeek* Senior Correspondent David Kiley to discuss some of the issues confronting Toyota as it achieves top-dog status. Edited excerpts form their conversation follow:
Have you been talking among yourselves about protecting your culture, which could be vulnerable to change as you become the world's largest automaker?
As far as Toyota culture goes . . . we regard ourselves as Japanese, but more important than the Japanese nature of our company is the "Toyota Way," which is embodied in our concepts and systems.

Toyota Way is more than just a Japanese Way. It's about constant improvement. If it was a Japanese Way only, then we wouldn't have Japanese companies that perform poorly or go into bankruptcy. Toyota doesn't monopolize this idea. And it has to translate beyond Japanese culture to be successful. We employ close to 400,000 worldwide, excluding dealers. If we include dealers, it might be about 1 million.

Of that, a significant number are Japanese. But there are people from every culture working for Toyota that share the concept and this way of doing business. From that viewpoint, growing larger doesn't suggest that we're stepping out of anything that's part of our culture.
Someone I know says Toyota really believes and nurtures the idea that the company should be able to build a car with no problems or flaws. When this person does business with Ford and GM, it's different, they tell me.

Those companies strive to be better, but you don't get the idea they think a perfect car is possible.
With the Toyota Way . . . one of the key elements is *kaizen*: continuous improvement. There's no end to it. It's a never-ending journey. Respect for people is another important element. Employees. Customers. Suppliers. When it comes to consumers, they demand changes from time to time. We have to always keep watching what the consumer wants. If we base our business on what the customer wants, there's no end to the improvement we can achieve.
I remember a story related to me by a supplier company: They entered into a contract to supply axles for pickup trucks. It was the first contract his company had with Toyota. He said he was awarded the contract with no discussion of price. It was all based on whether his company's processes and quality were acceptable to Toyota. He was flabbergasted. Is that a common way Toyota does business?
Toyota's thinking based on the Toyota Way is teamwork with suppliers. This teamwork is going to be a long-lasting relationship. Price is only one element. Trust is a more important element. The relationship is a sharing concept, and should always be win–win. Price is important, too. But trust is perhaps more so. This is an idea that American business schools have come to preach. IBM, General Electric, and other companies talk about how important the mission of the company is. Toyota is only doing intelligently what the business schools are teaching.

In the church when you get married, the priest or minister doesn't ask each partner how much each will get from the other in terms of money. You're asked about how well you get along. What is your commitment to one another? Now, in real-life situations, some companies practice this, and some don't. Some practice this in the United States. Some don't. It's the same in Japan. So there are fantastic achievements in both countries, and there are bankruptcies in both countries. So, it isn't a Japanese issue or an American issue. It's a company-culture issue.
Growth comes from both new products and boosting volume of existing products. Will your sales growth come more from new products or from existing products in new geographic markets?
I think 15% global market share isn't low, but it's not that high either. There are a lot of opportunities for our product lineup as it is. But now that we have gone into full-size pickups with the new product, we fill in a significant segment.

I think we need to pursue more niches in the future. We had a car at the Detroit Auto Show that could be a replacement for the former Supra sports car. But what's more important is to keep improving the products we have. Like Camry—what consumers want out of Camry is always changing. That's my understanding of how to keep a product strong for the future. We will look after Camry customers by looking after Camry as a product. Same goes with RAV4 and others.

From time to time, a GM or Ford exec will complain about an uneven playing field: a health-care advantage for Toyota, or monetary policy that favors Japanese products. Do you and your colleagues read that and pay attention?

We always read the stuff in the newspapers. We know health care is a very difficult situation for the Big Three. It's a fact of life that they incur more costs. That's the political and economic history of the United States. A decision was made some years back on what they would give to workers. To some degree, the problem is of their own creation.

Not all the workers in every industry receive as high a medical benefit as in the auto industry. Who decided that? It's their management. They complain sometimes about the currency valuation. It's very difficult. For example, the biggest economy in the world is the United States. Bigger than Japan. It's the Big Three who have an advantage in operating in the biggest economy in the world. For myself, I invested in my English education. If you're born here, there's no need to invest in that. So, that's not a level playing field. It's very difficult to define what a level playing field is.

You would think that GM and Ford execs, given the fact they all grew up here, should have a better idea of how to design and package a family sedan and mini-van, yet these are two product segments where you and Honda have done especially well against the Big Three.

Increasingly, we're doing the development of our vehicles in the States. The Camry chief engineer is a Japanese man. Why the heck does he develop the most favorite car in the United States? That Camry car doesn't sell in Japan. It's a failure. Why? He applies himself to understanding what the customer wants. He visits here and learns things.

If we talk about the level playing field, what is it? He had to overcome such a big handicap being Japanese to create a car that's the top seller in America. It's very difficult to talk about what the level playing field is.

U.S. companies are saying that while they're improving manufacturing processes, costs, etc. they will never out-Toyota Toyota. They have decided the best way to outdo you as they close the gap on those things is by out-designing you. Do you feel a greater pressure to compete on expressive design than you once did?

Toyota, if you look at the history, our design hasn't been very expressive. If we aren't careful, design could fall into the dull category. Our designers have been seeing design as a critical challenge. If you look at the last 5 to 10 years, designers have done a great job of advancing here.

Look at the FJ Cruiser. People look at that and say, "Who designed that? Toyota? I can't believe it." Every organization has strengths and weaknesses. Twenty years ago, Toyota had no confidence in how we would operate manufacturing in the United States. That's why we regard the NUMMI joint-venture plant [where Toyota builds the Matrix and Corolla alongside the Pontiac Vibe] with GM as very beneficial. GM helped us a great deal.

The corporate advertising you have been running seems to be quite effective. Some of your Detroit rivals resent the fact that you're acting and talking like an American company.

We have a lot of dialogue about what should be the corporate message. That advertising is what we wanted to accomplish. We knew that many people didn't know what we have been doing in the United States for 50 years. In San Antonio, Texas, for example, we gave a lot of money to the local family-literacy program. We have been giving money to this organization nationally for 20 years. But we had never advertised it. People need to have a clearer and more correct image of Toyota.

Is your decision to advertise more aggressively a response to those kinds of remarks by people like Ford President of the Americas Mark Fields or GM Vice Chairman Bob Lutz?

More important than the political consideration, Toyota is known as a product. No one knows what Toyota is. Toyota is a faceless organization. It doesn't have a human element in the eyes of the consumer. Toyota is just a car.

Toyota is bigger than that though. It's people. We have some 40,000 people working for us in the United States. We need to have more of a face. That we are people. That's the most critical thing we have been trying to achieve.

Perhaps you would like to star in some ads yourself? DaimlerChrysler Chairman Dieter Zetsche did that last year as "Dr. Z." Do you want to be known as "Dr. T"?

No. We want to show everybody in the company. The heroes. Not one single person.

Questions

1. As you look at how Toyota has surpassed GM and the other U.S. automakers, in what ways do you think its workforce has provided a competitive advantage?
2. What do you think are the major HR issues that Toyota will face in the future?

SOURCE: From D. Kiley, "The Toyota Way to No.1," *BusinessWeek*, April 26, 2007. Used with permission of Bloomberg L. P. Copyright © 2007. All rights reserved.

⬤ Twitter Focus: Is Translating a Global Business? 🐦

Using Twitter, continue the conversation about managing HR globally by reading the Translations case at www.mhhe.com/noe8e.

As barriers to global business continue to fall, more people are encountering language differences among the companies they work with, sell to, or buy from on a daily basis. One field that continues to grow globally is the business of providing translations. The case discusses three different companies that have capitalized on translating information into various languages and how this global approach has become important in the business environment.

Engage with your classmates and instructor via Twitter to chat about translating languages as a global business using the case questions posted on the Noe website. Don't have a Twitter account yet? See the instructions for getting started on the Online Learning Center.

⬤ Notes

1. "The World's Biggest Companies," *Forbes*, April 26, 2011, http://www.wistv.com/Global/story.asp?S=14514970&clienttype=printable.
2. "For Mergers, It's a Small World after All," CNN Money.com, February 15, 2011, http://money.cnn.com/2011/02/15/markets/thebuzz/index.htm.
3. U.S. Department of Labor, "International Comparisons of Hourly Compensation Costs for Production Workers in Manufacturing, 1975–2007," Bureau of Labor Statistics news release, www.bls.gov.
4. D. Kirkpatrick, "The Net Makes It All Easier—Including Exporting U.S. Jobs," *Fortune*, http://www.fortune.com/fortune/print/0,15935,450755,00.html (May 2003).
5. R. Schuler, "An Integrative Framework of Strategic International Human Resource Management," *Journal of Management* (1993), pp. 419–60.
6. L. Rubio, "The Rationale for NAFTA: Mexico's New 'Outward Looking' Strategy," *Business Economics* (1991), pp. 12–16.
7. H. Cooper, "Economic Impact of NAFTA: It's a Wash, Experts Say," *The Wall Street Journal*, interactive edition (June 17, 1997).
8. J. Mark, "Suzhou Factories Are Nearly Ready," *Asian Wall Street Journal*, August 14, 1995, p. 8.
9. R. Peiper, *Human Resource Management: An International Comparison* (Berlin: Walter de Gruyter, 1990).
10. V. Sathe, *Culture and Related Corporate Realities* (Homewood, IL: Richard D. Irwin, 1985).
11. M. Rokeach, *Beliefs, Attitudes, and Values* (San Francisco: Jossey-Bass, 1968).
12. L. Harrison, *Who Prospers? How Cultural Values Shape Economic and Political Success* (New York: Free Press, 1992).
13. N. Adler, *International Dimensions of Organizational Behavior*, 2nd ed. (Boston: PWS-Kent, 1991).
14. R. Yates, "Japanese Managers Say They're Adopting Some U.S. Ways," *Chicago Tribune*, February 29, 1992, p. B1.
15. G. Hofstede, "Dimensions of National Cultures in Fifty Countries and Three Regions," in *Expectations in Cross-Cultural Psychology*, eds. J. Deregowski, S. Dziurawiec, and R. C. Annis (Lisse, Netherlands: Swets and Zeitlinger, 1983).
16. G. Hofstede, "Cultural Constraints in Management Theories," *Academy of Management Executive* 7 (1993), pp. 81–90.
17. G. Hofstede, "The Cultural Relativity of Organizational Theories," *Journal of International Business Studies* 14 (1983), pp. 75–90.
18. G. Hofstede, "Cultural Constraints in Management Theories."
19. A. Ramesh, and M. Gelfland, "Will They Stay or Will They Go? The Role of Job Embeddedness in Predicting Turnover in Individualistic and Collectivistic Cultures," *Journal of Applied Psychology* 95, no. 5 (2010), pp. 807–23.
20. S. Snell and J. Dean, "Integrated Manufacturing and Human Resource Management: A Human Capital Perspective," *Academy of Management Journal* 35 (1992), pp. 467–504.
21. N. Adler and S. Bartholomew, "Managing Globally Competent People," *The Executive* 6 (1992), pp. 52–65.
22. B. O'Reilly, "Your New Global Workforce," *Fortune*, December 14, 1992, pp. 52–66.
23. A. Hoffman, "Are Technology Jobs Headed Offshore?" Monster.com, http://technology.monster.com/articles/offshore.
24. J. Ledvinka and V. Scardello, *Federal Employment Regulation in Human Resource Management* (Boston: PWS-Kent, 1991).
25. P. Conrad and R. Peiper, "Human Resource Management in the Federal Republic of Germany," in *Human Resource Management: An International Comparison*, ed. R. Peiper (Berlin: Walter de Gruyer, 1990).
26. R. Solow, "Growth with Equity through Investment in Human Capital," The George Seltzer Distinguished Lecture, University of Minnesota.
27. M. Bloom, G. Milkovich, and A. Mitra, "Toward a Model of International Compensation and Rewards: Learning from How Managers Respond to Variations in Local Host Contexts," working paper 00-14 (Center for Advance Human Resource Studies, Cornell University: 2000).
28. R. Kopp, "International Human Resource Policies and Practices in Japanese, European, and United States Multinationals," *Human Resource Management* 33 (1994), pp. 581–99.
29. Adler, *International Dimensions of Organizational Behavior*.
30. S. Jackson and Associates, *Diversity in the Workplace: Human Resource Initiatives* (New York: Guilford Press, 1991).
31. G. Stahl, M. Maznevski, A. Voight, and K. Jonsen, "Unraveling the Effects of Cultural Diversity in Teams: A Meta-Analysis of Research on Multicultural Work Groups," *Journal of International Business Studies* 41 (2010), pp. 690–709.
32. Adler and Bartholomew, "Managing Globally Competent People."
33. Ibid.
34. S. Dolianski, "Are Expats Getting Lost in the Translation?" *Workforce*, February 1997.
35. L. Copeland and L. Griggs, *Going International* (New York: Random House, 1985).

36. K. F. Misa and J. M. Fabriacatore, "Return on Investments of Overseas Personnel," *Financial Executive* 47 (April 1979), pp. 42–46.

37. N. Forster, "The Persistent Myth of High Expatriate Failure Rates: A Reappraisal," *International Journal of Human Resource Management* 8, no. 4 (1997), pp. 414–34.

38. M. Mendenhall, E. Dunbar, and G. R. Oddou, "Expatriate Selection, Training, and Career-Pathing: A Review and Critique," *Human Resource Management* 26 (1987), pp. 331–45.

39. M. Mendenhall and G. Oddou, "The Dimensions of Expatriate Acculturation," *Academy of Management Review* 10 (1985), pp. 39–47.

40. W. Arthur and W. Bennett, "The International Assignee: The Relative Importance of Factors Perceived to Contribute to Success," *Personnel Psychology* 48 (1995), pp. 99–114.

41. K. Ng, and C. Earley, "Culture and Intelligence: Old Constructs, New Frontiers," *Group and Organization Management* 31 (2006), pp. 4–19; S. Ang, L. Van Dyne, C. Koh, K. Y. Ng, K. J. Templer, C. Tay, and N. A. Chandrasekar, "Cultural Intelligence: Its Measurement and Effects on Cultural Judgment and Decision Making, Cultural Adaptation, and Task Performance," *Management and Organization Review* 3 (2007), pp. 335–71.

42. R. Tung, "Selecting and Training of Personnel for Overseas Assignments," *Columbia Journal of World Business* 16, no. 2 (1981), pp. 68–78.

43. Moran, Stahl, and Boyer, Inc., *International Human Resource Management* (Boulder, CO: Moran, Stahl, & Boyer, 1987).

44. P. Caligiuri, "The Big Five Personality Characteristics as Predictors of Expatriates' Desire to Terminate the Assignment and Supervisor Rated Performance," *Personnel Psychology* 53 (2000), pp. 67–88.

45. P. Caligiuri and R. Tung, "Comparing the Success of Male and Female Expatriates from a U.S.-based Multinational Company," *International Journal of Human Resource Management* 10, no. 5 (1999), pp. 763–82.

46. L. Stroh, A. Varma, and S. Valy-Durbin, "Why Are Women Left at Home? Are They Unwilling to Go on International Assignments?" *Journal of World Business* 35, no. 3 (2000), pp. 241–55.

47. A. Harzing, *Managing the Multinationals: An International Study of Control Mechanisms* (Cheltenham: Edward Elgar, 1999).

48. J. S. Black and M. Mendenhall, "Cross-Cultural Training Effectiveness: A Review and Theoretical Framework for Future Research," *Academy of Management Review* 15 (1990), pp. 113–36.

49. B. Fitzgerald-Turner, "Myths of Expatriate Life," *HR Magazine* 42, no. 6 (June 1997), pp. 65–74.

50. P. Dowling and R. Schuler, *International Dimensions of Human Resource Management* (Boston: PWS-Kent, 1990).

51. Adler, *International Dimensions of Organizational Behavior.*

52. Dowling and Schuler, *International Dimensions of Human Resource Management.*

53. R. Schuler and P. Dowling, *Survey of ASPA/I Members* (New York: Stern School of Business, New York University, 1988).

54. C. Joinson, "No Returns: Localizing Expats Saves Companies Big Money and Can Be a Smooth Transition with a Little Due Diligence by HR," *HR Magazine* 11, no. 47 (2002), p. 70.

55. J. J. Smith, "Firms Say Expats Getting Too Costly, but Few Willing to Act" (2006), *SHRM Online*, retrieved March 9, 2007, www.shrm.org/global/library_published/subject/nonIC/CMS_018300.asp.

56. C. Solomon, "Repatriation: Up, Down, or Out?" *Personnel Journal* (1995), pp. 28–37.

57. "Workers Sent Overseas Have Adjustment Problems, a New Study Shows," *The Wall Street Journal,* June 19, 1984, p. 1.

58. J. S. Black, "Repatriation: A Comparison of Japanese and American Practices and Results," *Proceedings of the Eastern Academy of Management Bi-annual International Conference* (Hong Kong, 1989), pp. 45–49.

59. J. S. Black, "Coming Home: The Relationship of Expatriate Expectations with Repatriation Adjustment and Job Performance," *Human Relations* 45 (1992), pp. 177–92.

60. Adler, *International Dimensions of Organizational Behavior.*

61. Black, "Coming Home."

62. C. Solomon, "Repatriation: Up, Down, or Out?"

63. P. Evans, V. Pucik, and J. Barsoux, *The Global Challenge: International Human Resource Management* (New York: McGraw-Hill, 2002), p. 137.

CHAPTER

16 Strategically Managing the HRM Function

ENTER THE WORLD OF BUSINESS

Googling HR

How would you like to lead the HR function at Google? Google, in addition to being one of the most successful technology companies in the world and having a brand that exemplifies "cool" has been recognized over 100 times in the last five years as an exceptional employer, including being named the #1 Best Company to Work for in the United States (and many other countries), the #1 Top Diversity Employer overall, as well as #1 in the categories of Physical Disability, Asian/Native Hawaiian/Pacific Islander, American Indian/Alaskan Native, Latino/Hispanic, Middle Eastern, Black/African American, Asian/Indian, and GLBT.

Laszlo Bock leads Google's People Operations function, which has responsibility for all areas related to the attraction, development, and retention of "Googlers." He joined Google after having held a number of executive leadership positions at GE Capital as well as a stint as a management consultant at McKinsey and Company. When he joined Google, HR's (and it was called "HR" then . . . now renamed "People Operations") focus was almost entirely on recruiting, with little thought to the effectiveness or even the cost of the programs: Their goal was just to find as many great people as possible.

Because he came to Google unencumbered by the traditional administrative HR mindset, he sought to create an innovative and impactful People function. He wanted to develop a function that could understand its clients' businesses and anticipate their needs better than a traditional HR function. He wanted a function working on things that matter to the company, and to be able to show that it was having an impact. To do this, he had to set out a vision and strategy for the function, with a clear emphasis on the roles that the function would play in the organization. He also had to develop the technologies and processes that would enable the leaders and managers at Google to effectively manage the "Googlers." Finally, he had to hire, train, motivate, and retain the right kinds of HR people with the right kinds of skills to execute that HR strategy. If you were Laszlo Bock, what would you have done to lead the People Operations function at Google?

SOURCE: Personal Communication, June 2010.

Introduction

Throughout this book we have emphasized how human resource management practices can help companies gain a competitive advantage. We identified specific practices related to managing the internal and external environment; designing work and measuring work outcomes; and acquiring, developing, and compensating human resources. We have also discussed the best of current research and practice to show how they may contribute to a company's competitive advantage.

As we said in Chapter 1, the role of the HRM function has been evolving over time. As we see in this chapter's opening story, it has now reached a crossroads. Although it began as a purely administrative function, most HR executives now see the function's major role as being much more strategic. However, this evolution has resulted in a misalignment between the skills and capabilities of members of the function and the new requirements placed on it. Virtually every HRM function in top companies is going through a transformation process to create a function that can play this new strategic role while successfully fulfilling its other roles. This transformation process is also going on globally. Managing this process is the subject of this chapter. First we discuss the various activities of the HRM function. Then we examine how to develop a market- or customer-oriented HRM function. We then describe the current structure of most HRM functions. Finally, we explore measurement approaches for assessing the effectiveness of the function.

Activities of HRM

LO 16-1
Describe the roles that HRM plays in firms today and the categories of HRM activities.

To understand the transformation going on in HRM, one must understand HRM activities in terms of their strategic value. One way of classifying these activities is depicted in Figure 16.1. Transactional activities (the day-to-day transactions such as benefits administration, record keeping, and employee services) are low in their strategic value. Traditional activities such as performance management, training, recruiting, selection, compensation, and employee relations are the nuts and bolts of HRM. These activities have moderate strategic value because they often form the practices and systems to ensure strategy execution. Transformational activities create long-term capability and adaptability for the firm. These activities include knowledge management, management development, cultural change, and strategic redirection and renewal. Obviously, these activities comprise the greatest strategic value for the firm.

As we see in the figure, most HRM functions spend the vast majority of their time on transactional activities, with substantially less on traditional and very little on transformational activities. However, virtually all HRM functions, in order to add value to the firm, must increase their efforts in the traditional and transformational activities. To do this, however, requires that HR executives (1) develop a strategy for the HRM function, (2) assess the current effectiveness of the HRM function, and (3) redesign, reengineer, or outsource HRM processes to improve efficiency and effectiveness. These issues will be discussed in the following sections.

Strategic Management of the HRM Function

In light of the various roles and activities of the HRM function, we can easily see that it is highly unlikely that any function can (or should) effectively deliver on all roles and all activities. Although this is a laudable goal, resource constraints in

figure 16.1

Categories of HRM Activities and Percentages of Time Spent on Them

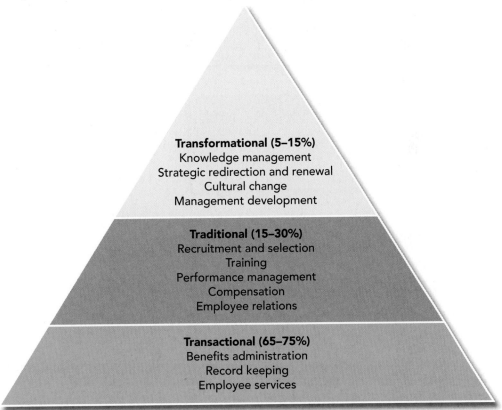

Transformational (5–15%)
Knowledge management
Strategic redirection and renewal
Cultural change
Management development

Traditional (15–30%)
Recruitment and selection
Training
Performance management
Compensation
Employee relations

Transactional (65–75%)
Benefits administration
Record keeping
Employee services

SOURCE: P. Wright, G. McMahan, S. Snell, and B. Gerhart, *Strategic Human Resource Management: Building Human Capital and Organizational Capability.* Technical report. Cornell University, 1998.

terms of time, money, and head count require that the HR executive make strategic choices about where and how to allocate these resources for maximum value to the firm.

Chapter 2 explained the strategic management process that takes place at the organization level and discussed the role of HRM in this process. HRM has been seen as a strategic partner that has input into the formulation of the company's strategy and develops and aligns HRM programs to help implement the strategy. However, for the HRM function to become truly strategic in its orientation, it must view itself as a separate business entity and engage in strategic management in an effort to effectively serve the various internal customers.

In this respect, one recent trend within the field of HRM, consistent with the total quality management philosophy, is for the HR executive to take a customer-oriented approach to implementing the function. In other words, the strategic planning process that takes place at the level of the business can also be performed with the HRM function. HR executives in more progressive U.S. companies have begun to view the HRM function as a strategic business unit and have tried to define that business in terms of their customer base, their customers' needs, and the

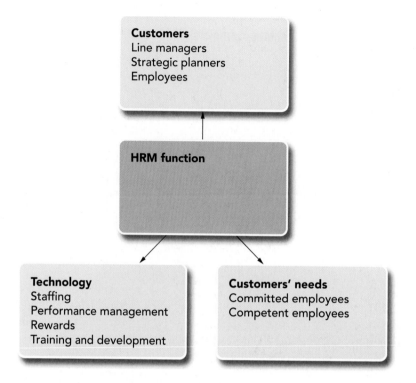

technologies required to satisfy customers' needs (Figure 16.2). For example, Weyerhaeuser Corporation's human resources department identified 11 characteristics that would describe a quality human resource organization; these are presented in Table 16.1.

A customer orientation is one of the most important changes in the HRM function's attempts to become strategic. It entails first identifying customers. The most obvious example of HRM customers are the line managers who require HRM services.

table 16.1

Characteristics
of HRM Quality
at Weyerhaeuser
Corporation

- Human resources products and services are linked to customer requirements.
- Customer requirements are translated into internal service applications.
- Processes for producing products and services are documented with cost/value relationships understood.
- Reliable methods and standardized processes are in place.
- Waste and inefficiency are eliminated.
- Problem solving and decision making are based on facts and data.
- Critical success variables are tracked, displayed, and maintained.
- Human resources employees are trained and educated in total quality tools and principles.
- Human resource systems have been aligned to total quality implementation strategies.
- Human resource managers provide leadership and support to organizations on large-scale organizational change.
- Human resource professionals function as "strategic partners" in managing the business and implementing total quality principles.

In addition, the strategic planning team is a customer in the sense that it requires the identification, analysis, and recommendations regarding people-oriented business problems. Employees are also HRM customers because the rewards they receive from the employment relationship are determined and/or administered by the HRM department.

In addition, the products of the HRM department must be identified. Line managers want to have high-quality employees committed to the organization. The strategic planning team requires information and recommendations for the planning process as well as programs that support the strategic plan once it has been identified. Employees want compensation and benefit programs that are consistent, adequate, and equitable, and they want fair promotion decisions. At Southwest Airlines, the "People" department administers customer surveys to all clients as they leave the department to measure how well their needs have been satisfied.

Finally, the technologies through which HRM meets customer needs vary depending on the need being satisfied. Selection systems ensure that applicants selected for employment have the necessary knowledge, skills, and abilities to provide value to the organization. Training and development systems meet the needs of both line managers and employees by giving employees development opportunities to ensure they are constantly increasing their human capital and, thus, providing increased value to the company. Performance management systems make clear to employees what is expected of them and assure line managers and strategic planners that employee behavior will be in line with the company's goals. Finally, reward systems similarly benefit all customers (line managers, strategic planners, and employees). These systems assure line managers that employees will use their skills for organizational benefit, and they provide strategic planners with ways to ensure that all employees are acting in ways that will support the strategic plan. Obviously, reward systems provide employees with an equitable return for their investment of skills and effort.

Building an HR Strategy
THE BASIC PROCESS

How do HR functions build their HR strategies? Recent research has examined how HR functions go about the process of building their HR strategies that should support the business strategies. Conducting case studies on 20 different companies, Wright and colleagues describe the generic approach as somewhat consistent with the process for developing a business strategy.[1]

LO 16-2
Discuss how the HRM function can define its mission and market.

As depicted in Figure 16.3, the function first scans the environment to determine the trends or events that might have an impact on the organization (e.g., future talent shortage, increasing immigrant population, aging of the workforce).

figure 16.3

Basic Process for HR Strategy

figure 16.4

IBM Priorities and
the On-Demand Era

IBM Strategic Priorities on Demand	
1. Delivering business value 2. Offering world class open infrastructure 3. Developing innovative leadership technology 4. Exploiting new profitable growth opportunities 5. Creating brand leadership and a superior customer experience 6. **Attracting, motivating, and retaining the best talent in our industry**	"An enterprise whose business processes—integrated end-to-end across the company and with key partners, suppliers, and customers—can respond with speed to any customer demand, market opportunity or external threat." —Sam Palmisano, *IBM Chairman and CEO*

It then examines the strategic business issues or needs (e.g., is the company growing, expanding internationally, needing to develop new technologies?). For instance, Figure 16.4 displays IBM's major business strategy priorities. As can be seen in this example, a clear strategic priority is the attraction, motivation, and retention of talent.

From these issues, the HR strategy team needs to identify the specific people issues that will be critical to address in order for the business to succeed (a potential leadership vacuum, lack of technological expertise, lack of diversity, etc.). All of this information is used in designing the HR strategy, which provides a detailed plan regarding the major priorities and the programs, policies, and processes that must be developed or executed. Finally, this HR strategy is communicated to the relevant parties, both internal and external to the function. Again, IBM's HR strategy, depicted in Figure 16.5, shows how IBM seeks to differentiate itself in the labor market as well as the major priority areas that the HR strategy seeks to address.

figure 16.5

IBM HR Strategy

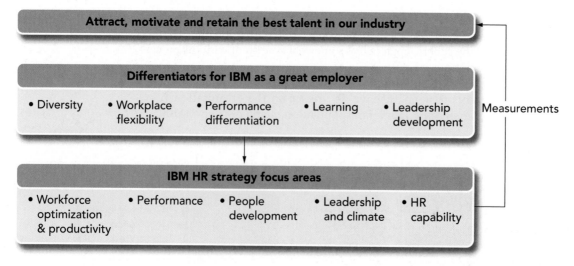

Thus, the HR strategy is a framework that guides individuals in HR by helping them understand where and how they will impact the company. At Google this four-pronged People Operations strategy consists of:

1. "Find them, Grow them, Keep them." The idea is to find great people to work for Google, grow and develop their skills, and do everything possible to keep them at Google.
2. "Put our users first." This goal echoes what Google does as a company, also illustrates how those in HR should think about the users of people operations, which are all the other Google employees.
3. "Put on your own oxygen mask before assisting others." The thinking behind this goal is in many organizations HR is doing all this work in the company for others and they forget to grow and develop their own people. Eventually this cripples the function's ability to serve the rest of the organization because the very best, most talented people get recruited out of HR to go be heads of HR at other companies.
4. "This space intentionally left blank." In Google's environment things change very, very quickly and that creates a lot of uncertainty. Uncertainty causes people to put less discretionary effort into their work, to be less satisfied, less collaborative, more competitive with fellow employees as well as making them more likely to leave the company. Hence, this goal is an attempt to explicitly recognize the dynamic nature of Google's internal and external environment.[2]

INVOLVING LINE EXECUTIVES

This generic process provides for the potential to involve line executives in a number of ways. Because the HR strategy seeks to address business issues, involving those in charge of running the business can increase the quality of information from which the HR strategy is created. This involvement can occur in a few ways. First, line executives could simply provide input, by either surveying or interviewing them regarding the business challenges and strategy. Second, they could be members of the team that actually develops the HR strategy. Third, once the strategy is developed, they could receive communications with the HR strategy information. Finally, they could have to formally approve the strategy, in essence "signing off" that the HR strategy fully supports the business strategy. The most progressive organizations use all four forms of involvement, asking a large group of executives for input, having one or two executives on the team, communicating the HR strategy broadly to executives, and having the senior executive team formally approve it.

CHARACTERIZING HR STRATEGIES

As you can see in Figure 16.6, the variety of ways that HR strategies can be generated results in various levels of linkage with the business. In general, four categories of this relationship can be identified.

First, at the most elementary level, "HR-focused" HR functions' articulation of people outcomes stems more from an analysis of what their functions currently do than from an understanding of how those people outcomes relate to the larger business. Second, "people-linked" functions have clearly identified, articulated, and aligned their HR activities around people issues and outcomes, but not business

figure 16.6

Approaches to
Developing an HR
Strategy

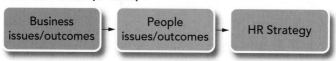

An Outside-In Perspective

Business-Driven (5 cases)

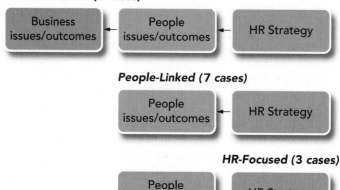

issues and outcomes. Third, "business-linked" HR functions begin with an assessment of what HR is doing, then identify the major people outcomes they should focus on, and, in a few cases, how those might translate into positive business outcomes. Finally, "business-driven" functions have fully developed HR strategies which begin by identifying the major business needs and issues, consider how people fit in and what people outcomes are necessary, and then build HR systems focused on meeting those needs.

The HR strategy must help address the issues that the business faces which will determine its success. As finding, attracting, and retaining talent has become a critical issue, virtually every HR function is addressing this as part of the HR strategy (as can be seen in IBM's HR strategy).

Measuring HRM Effectiveness

LO 16-3

Explain the approaches to
evaluating the effectiveness
of HRM practices.

The strategic decision-making process for the HRM function requires that decision makers have a good sense of the effectiveness of the current HRM function. This information provides the foundation for decisions regarding which processes, systems, and skills of HR employees need improvement. Often HRM functions that have been heavily involved in transactional activities for a long time tend to lack systems, processes, and skills for delivering state-of-the-art traditional activities and are thoroughly unable to contribute in the transformational arena. Thus diagnosis of the effectiveness of the HRM function provides critical information for its strategic management.

In addition, having good measures of the function's effectiveness provides the following benefits:[3]

- *Marketing the function:* Evaluation is a sign to other managers that the HRM function really cares about the organization as a whole and is trying to support operations, production, marketing, and other functions of the company. Information regarding cost savings and benefits is useful to prove to internal customers that HRM practices contribute to the bottom line. Such information is also useful for gaining additional business for the HRM function.
- *Providing accountability:* Evaluation helps determine whether the HRM function is meeting its objectives and effectively using its budget.

APPROACHES FOR EVALUATING EFFECTIVENESS

Two approaches are commonly used to evaluate the effectiveness of HRM practices: the audit approach and the analytic approach.

Audit Approach

The **audit approach** focuses on reviewing the various outcomes of the HRM functional areas. Both key indicators and customer satisfaction measures are typically collected. Table 16.2 lists examples of key indicators and customer satisfaction measures for staffing, equal employment opportunity, compensation, benefits, training, performance management, safety, labor relations, and succession planning. The development of electronic employee databases and information systems has made it much easier to collect, store, and analyze the functional key indicators (more on this later in the chapter) than in the past, when information was kept in file folders.

We previously discussed how HRM functions can become much more customer-oriented as part of the strategic management process. If, in fact, the function desires to be more customer-focused, then one important source of effectiveness data can be the customers. Just as firms often survey their customers to determine how effectively the customers feel they are being served, the HRM function can survey its internal customers.

One important internal customer is the employees of the firm. Employees often have both direct contact with the HRM function (through activities such as benefits administration and payroll) and indirect contact with the function through their involvement in activities such as receiving performance appraisals, pay raises, and training programs. Many organizations such as AT&T, Motorola, and General Electric use their regular employee attitude survey as a way to assess the employees as users/customers of the HRM programs and practices.[4] However, the problem with assessing effectiveness only from the employees' perspective is that often they are responding not from the standpoint of the good of the firm, but, rather, from their own individual perspective. For example, employees notoriously and consistently express dissatisfaction with pay level (who doesn't want more money?), but to simply ratchet up pay across the board would put the firm at a serious labor cost disadvantage.

Thus, many firms have gone to surveys of top line executives as a better means of assessing the effectiveness of the HRM function. The top-level line executives can see how the systems and practices are impacting both employees and the overall effectiveness of the firm from a strategic standpoint. This can also be useful for

Audit Approach
Type of assessment of HRM effectiveness that involves review of customer satisfaction or key indicators (like turnover rate or average days to fill a position) related to an HRM functional area (such as recruiting or training).

table 16.2

Examples of Key Indicators and Customer Satisfaction Measures for HRM Functions

KEY INDICATORS	CUSTOMER SATISFACTION MEASURES
Staffing Average days taken to fill open requisitions Ratio of acceptances to offers made Ratio of minority/women applicants to representation in local labor market Per capita requirement costs Average years of experience/education of hires per job family	Anticipation of personnel needs Timeliness of referring qualified workers to line supervisors Treatment of applicants Skill in handling terminations Adaptability to changing labor market conditions
Equal employment opportunity Ratio of EEO grievances to employee population Minority representation by EEO categories Minority turnover rate	Resolution of EEO grievances Day-to-day assistance provided by personnel department in implementing affirmative action plan Aggressive recruitment to identify qualified women and minority applicants
Compensation Per capita (average) merit increases Ratio of recommendations for reclassification to number of employees Percentage of overtime hours to straight time Ratio of average salary offers to average salary in community	Fairness of existing job evaluation system in assigning grades and salaries Competitiveness in local labor market Relationship between pay and performance Employee satisfaction with pay
Benefits Average unemployment compensation payment (UCP) Average workers' compensation payment (WCP) Benefit cost per payroll dollar Percentage of sick leave to total pay	Promptness in handling claims Fairness and consistency in the application of benefit policies Communication of benefits to employees Assistance provided to line managers in reducing potential for unnecessary claims
Training Percentage of employees participating in training programs per job family Percentage of employees receiving tuition refunds Training dollars per employee	Extent to which training programs meet the needs of employees and the company Communication to employees about available training opportunities Quality of introduction/orientation programs
Employee appraisal and development Distribution of performance appraisal ratings Appropriate psychometric properties of appraisal forms	Assistance in identifying management potential Organizational development activities provided by HRM department
Succession planning Ratio of promotions to number of employees Ratio of open requisitions filled internally to those filled externally	Extent to which promotions are made from within Assistance/counseling provided to employees in career planning
Safety Frequency/severity ratio of accidents Safety-related expenses per $1,000 of payroll Plant security losses per square foot (e.g., fires, burglaries)	Assistance to line managers in organizing safety programs Assistance to line managers in identifying potential safety hazards Assistance to line managers in providing a good working environment (lighting, cleanliness, heating, etc.)

(continued)

table 16.2

Examples of Key Indicators and Customer Satisfaction Measures for HRM Functions *(concluded)*

KEY INDICATORS	CUSTOMER SATISFACTION MEASURES
Labor relations Ratio of grievances by pay plan to number of employees Frequency and duration of work stoppages Percentage of grievances settled	Assistance provided to line managers in handling grievances Efforts to promote a spirit of cooperation in plant Efforts to monitor the employee relations climate in plant
Overall effectiveness Ratio of personnel staff to employee population Turnover rate Absenteeism rate Ratio of per capita revenues to per capita cost Net income per employee	Accuracy and clarity of information provided to managers and employees Competence and expertise of staff Working relationship between organizations and HRM department

SOURCE: Reprinted with permission. Excerpts from Chapter 15, "Evaluating Human Resource Effectiveness," pp. 187–222, by Anne S. Tsui and Luis R. Gomez-Mejia, from *Human Resource Management: Evolving Roles and Responsibilities*, edited by Lee Dyer. Copyright © 1988 by The Bureau of National Affairs, Inc., Washington, DC, 20037. To order BNA publications call toll free 1-800-960-1220.

determining how well HR employees' perceptions of their function's effectiveness align with the views of their line colleagues. For example, a study of 14 firms revealed that HR executives and line executives agreed on the relative effectiveness of HR's delivery of services such as staffing and training systems (that is, which were most and least effectively delivered) but not on the absolute level of effectiveness. As Figure 16.7 shows, HR executives' ratings of their effectiveness in different roles also diverged significantly from line executives'. In addition, line executives viewed HRM as being significantly less effective with regard to HRM's actual contributions to the firm's overall effectiveness, as we see in Figure 16.8.[5]

The Analytic Approach

The **analytic approach** focuses on either (1) determining whether the introduction of a program or practice (like a training program or a new compensation system) has the intended effect, (2) estimating the financial costs and benefits resulting from an HRM practice, or (3) using analytical data to increase organizational effectiveness. For example, in Chapter 7 we discussed how companies can determine a training program's impact on learning, behavior, and results. Evaluating a training program is one strategy for determining whether the program works. Typically, in an overall evaluation of effectiveness, we are interested in determining the degree of change associated with the program.

The second strategy involves determining the dollar value of the training program, taking into account all the costs associated with the program. Using this strategy, we are not concerned with how much change occurred but rather with the dollar value (costs versus benefits) of the program. Table 16.3 lists the various types of cost–benefit analyses that are done. The human resource accounting approach attempts to place a dollar value on human resources as if they were physical resources (like plant

Analytic Approach
Type of assessment of HRM effectiveness that involves determining the impact of, or the financial cost and benefits of, a program or practice.

figure 16.7
Comparing HR and Line Executives' Evaluations of the Effectiveness of HRM Roles

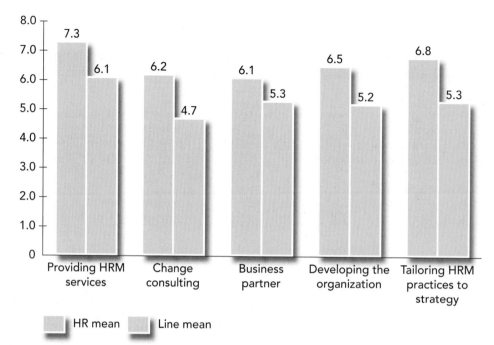

SOURCE: P. Wright, G. McMahan, S. Snell, and B. Gerhart, "Comparing Line and HR Executives' Perceptions of HR Effectiveness: Services, Roles, and Contributions," CAHRS (Center for Advanced Human Resource Studies) working paper 98-29, School of ILR, Cornell University, Ithaca, NY.

figure 16.8

Comparing HR and Line Executives' Evaluations of the Effectiveness of HRM Contributions

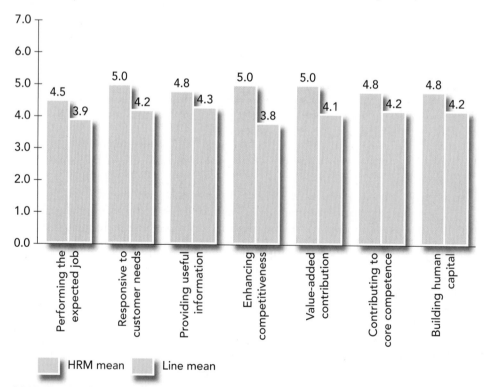

SOURCE: P. Wright, G. McMahan, S. Snell, and B. Gerhart, "Comparing Line and HR Executives' Perceptions of HR Effectiveness: Services, Roles, and Contributions," CAHRS (Center for Advanced Human Resource Studies) working paper 98-29, School of ILR, Cornell University, Ithaca, NY.

Human resource accounting
- Capitalization of salary
- Net present value of expected wage payments
- Returns on human assets and human investments

Utility analysis
- Turnover costs
- Absenteeism and sick leave costs
- Gains from selection programs
- Impact of positive employee attitudes
- Financial gains of training programs

SOURCE: Based on A. S. Tsui and L. R. Gomez-Mejia, "Evaluating HR Effectiveness," in *Human Resource Management: Evolving Roles and Responsibilities,* ed. L. Dyer (Washington, DC: Bureau of National Affairs, 1988), pp. 1–196.

and equipment) or financial resources (like cash). Utility analysis attempts to estimate the financial impact of employee behaviors (such as absenteeism, turnover, job performance, and substance abuse).

For example, wellness programs are a popular HRM program for reducing health care costs through reducing employees' risk of heart disease and cancer. One study evaluated four different types of wellness programs. Part of the evaluation involved determining the costs and benefits associated with the four programs over a three-year period.[6] A different type of wellness program was implemented at each site. Site A instituted a program involving raising employees' awareness of health risks (distributing news articles, blood pressure testing, health education classes). Site B set up a physical fitness facility for employees. Site C raised awareness of health risks and followed up with employees who had identified health risks. Site D provided health education and follow-up counseling and promoted physical competition and health-related events. Table 16.4 shows the effectiveness and cost-effectiveness of the Site C and Site D wellness models.

The analytic approach is more demanding than the audit approach because it requires the detailed use of statistics and finance. A good example of the level of sophistication that can be required for cost–benefit analysis is shown in Table 16.5. This table shows the types of information needed to determine the dollar value of a new selection test for entry-level computer programmers.

	SITE C	SITE D
Annual direct program costs, per employee per year	$30.96	$38.57
Percentage of cardiovascular disease risks[a] for which risk was moderately reduced or relapse prevented	48%	51%
Percentage of preceding entry per annual $1 spent per employee	1.55%	1.32%
Amount spent per 1% of risks reduced or relapse prevented	$.65	$.76

[a]High blood pressure, overweight, smoking, and lack of exercise.

SOURCE: J. C. Erfurt, A. Foote, and M. A. Heirich, "The Cost-Effectiveness of Worksite Wellness Programs," *Personnel Psychology* 45 (1992), p. 22.

table 16.5

Example of Analysis Needed to Determine the Dollar Value of a Selection Test

Cost–benefit information

Current employment	4,404
Number separating	618
Number selected	618
Average tenure	9.69 years

Test information

Number of applicants	1,236
Testing cost per applicant	$10
Total test cost	$12,360
Average test score	0.80 SD
Test validity	0.76
SD_y (per year)[a]	$10,413

Computation

Quantity = Average tenure × Applicants selected
= 9.69 years × 618 applicants
= 5,988 person-years

Quality = Average test score × Test validity × SD_y
= 0.80 × 0.76 × $10,413
= $6,331 per year

Utility = (Quantity × Quality) − Costs
= (5,988 person-year × $6,331 per year) − $12,360
= $37.9 million

[a]SD_y = Dollar value of one standard difference in job performance. Approximately 40% of average salary.

SOURCES: From J. W. Boudreau, "Utility Analysis," in *Human Resource Management: Evolving Roles and Responsibilities,* ed. L. Dyer (Washington, DC: Bureau of National Affairs, 1988), p. 150; F. L. Schmidt, J. E. Hunter, R. C. McKenzie, and T. W. Muldrow, "Impact of Valid Selection Procedures on Work-Force Productivity," *Journal of Applied Psychology* 64 (1979), pp. 609–26.

Finally, HR analytics can be used by the function to increase the effectiveness of the firm. For instance, Google's analytical approach to HR has revealed which backgrounds and capabilities are correlated with high performance as well as the leading cause of attrition—an employee's feeling that he or she is underused at the company. It also discovered that the ideal number of recruiting interviews is 5, down from a previous average of 10.

In addition, Project Oxygen was aimed at developing great managers (named because good management, like oxygen, keeps the company alive). The analytics team poured through performance management scores, employee surveys, and other data to group managers based on two dimensions: their task performance and their people performance. They then conducted a double-blind study focusing on those who were top (or bottom) on both dimensions, in order to identify eight behaviors that characterized good managers.[7]

Improving HRM Effectiveness

LO 16-4
Describe the new structures for the HRM function.

Once a strategic direction has been established and HRM's effectiveness evaluated, leaders of the HRM function can explore how to improve its effectiveness in contributing to the firm's competitiveness. Returning briefly to Figure 16.1, which depicted the different activities of the HRM function, often the improvement focuses on two

figure 16.9
Improving HRM Effectiveness

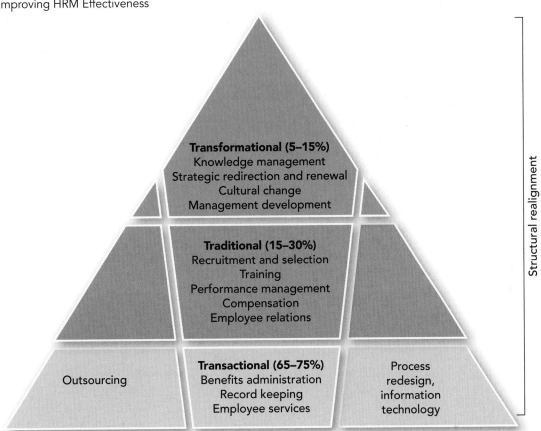

aspects of the pyramid. First, within each activity, HRM needs to improve both the efficiency and effectiveness in performing each of the activities. Second, often there is a push to eliminate as much of the transactional work as possible (and some of the traditional work) to free up time and resources to focus more on the higher-value-added transformational work. Redesign of the structure (reporting relationships) and processes (through outsourcing and information technology) enables the function to achieve these goals simultaneously. Figure 16.9 depicts this process.

RESTRUCTURING TO IMPROVE HRM EFFECTIVENESS

Traditional HRM functions were structured around the basic HRM subfunctions such as staffing, training, compensation, appraisal, and labor relations. Each of these areas had a director who reported to the VP of HRM, who often reported to a VP of finance and administration. However, for the HRM function to truly contribute strategically to firm effectiveness, the senior HR person must be part of the top management team (reporting directly to the chief executive officer), and there must be a different structural arrangement within the function itself.

A recent generic structure for the HRM function is depicted in Figure 16.10. As we see, the HRM function effectively is divided into three divisions: the centers for expertise, the field generalists, and the service center.[8] The centers for expertise usually

figure 16.10

Old and New
Structures for the
HRM Organization

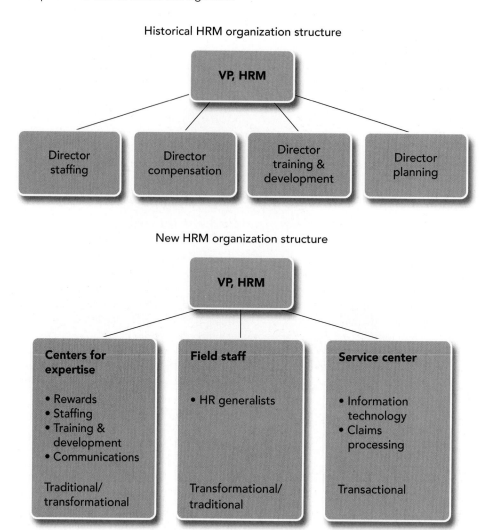

SOURCE: P. Wright, G. McMahan, S. Snell, and B. Gerhart, *Strategic Human Resource Management: Building Human Capital and Organizational Capability.* Technical report. Cornell University, 1998.

consist of the functional specialists in the traditional areas of HRM such as recruitment, selection, training, and compensation. These individuals ideally act as consultants in the development of state-of-the-art systems and processes for use in the organization. The field generalists consist of the HRM generalists who are assigned to a business unit within the firm. These individuals usually have dual reporting relationships to both the head of the line business and the head of HRM (although the line business tends to take priority). They ideally take responsibility for helping the line executives in their business strategically address people issues, and they ensure that the HRM systems enable the business to execute its strategy. Finally, the service center consists of individuals who ensure that the transactional activities are delivered throughout the organization. These service centers often leverage information technology to efficiently deliver employee services. For example, organizations such as Chevron have created call-in service centers where employees can dial a central number where service center employees are available to answer their questions and process their requests and transactions.

Such structural arrangements improve service delivery through specialization. Center for expertise employees can develop current functional skills without being distracted by transactional activities, and generalists can focus on learning the business environment without having to maintain expertise in functional specializations. Finally, service center employees can focus on efficient delivery of basic services across business units.

OUTSOURCING TO IMPROVE HRM EFFECTIVENESS

Restructuring the internal HRM function and redesigning the processes represent internal approaches to improving HRM effectiveness. However, increasingly HR executives are seeking to improve the effectiveness of the systems, processes, and services the function delivers through outsourcing. **Outsourcing** entails contracting with an outside vendor to provide a product or service to the firm, as opposed to producing the product using employees within the firm.

Why would a firm outsource an HRM activity or service? Usually this is done for one of two reasons: either the outsourcing partner can provide the service more cheaply than it would cost to do it internally, or the partner can provide it more effectively than it can be performed internally. Early on, firms resorted to outsourcing for efficiency reasons. Why would using an outsourced provider be more efficient than having internal employees provide a service? Usually it is because outsourced providers are specialists who are able to develop extensive expertise that can be leveraged across a number of companies.

For example, consider a relatively small firm that seeks to develop a pension system for employees. To provide this service to employees, the HRM function would need to learn all of the basics of pension law. Then it would need to hire a person with specific expertise in administering a pension system in terms of making sure that employee contributions are withheld and that the correct payouts are made to retired employees. Then the company would have to hire someone with expertise in investing pension funds. If the firm is small, requirements of the pension fund might not fill the time (80 hours per week) of these two new hires. Assume that it takes only 20 total hours a week for these people to do their jobs. The firm would be wasting 60 hours of employee time each week. However, a firm that specializes in providing pension administration services to multiple firms could provide the 20 hours of required time to that firm and three other firms for the same cost as had the firm performed this activity internally. Thus the specialist firm could charge the focal firm 50% of what it would cost the small firm to do the pensions internally. Of that 50%, 25% (20 hours) would go to paying direct salaries and the other 25% would be profit. Here the focal firm would save 50% of its expenses while the provider would make money.

Now consider the aspect of effectiveness. Because the outsourced provider works for a number of firms and specializes in pensions, its employees develop state-of-the-art knowledge of running pension plans. They can learn unique innovations from one company and transfer that learning to a new company. In addition, employees can be more easily and efficiently trained because all of them will be trained in the same processes and procedures. Finally, with experience in providing constant pension services, the firm is able to develop a capability to perform these services that could never be developed by two individuals working 25% of the time on these services.

What kind of services are being outsourced? Firms primarily outsource transactional activities and services of HRM such as pension and benefits administration as well as payroll. However, a number of traditional and some transformational activities have been outsourced as well.

LO 16-5
Describe how outsourcing HRM activities can improve service delivery efficiency and effectiveness.

Outsourcing
An organization's use of an outside organization for a broad set of services.

IMPROVING HRM EFFECTIVENESS THROUGH PROCESS REDESIGN

Reengineering
Review and redesign of work processes to make them more efficient and improve the quality of the end product or service.

In addition to structural arrangements, process redesign enables the HRM function to more efficiently and effectively deliver HRM services. Process redesign often uses information technology, but information technology applications are not a requirement. Thus we will discuss the general issue of process reengineering and then explore information technology applications that have aided HRM in process redesign.

Reengineering is a complete review of critical work processes and redesign to make them more efficient and able to deliver higher quality. Reengineering is especially critical to ensuring that the benefits of new technology can be realized. Applying new technology to an inefficient process will not improve efficiency or effectiveness. Instead, it will increase product or service costs related to the introduction of the new technology.

Reengineering can be used to review the HRM department functions and processes, or it can be used to review specific HRM practices such as work design or the performance management system. The reengineering process involves the four steps shown in Figure 16.11: identify the process to be reengineered, understand the process, redesign the process, and implement the new process.[9]

Identifying the Process

Managers who control the process or are responsible for functions within the process (sometimes called "process owners") should be identified and asked to be part of the reengineering team. Team members should include employees involved in the process (to provide expertise) and those outside the process, as well as internal or external customers who see the outcome of the process.

Understanding the Process

Several things need to be considered when evaluating a process:

- Can jobs be combined?
- Can employees be given more autonomy? Can decision making and control be built into the process through streamlining it?

figure 16.11

The Reengineering Process

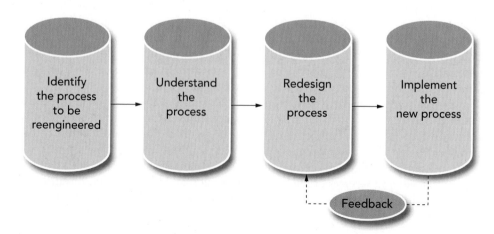

- Are all the steps in the process necessary?
- Are data redundancy, unnecessary checks, and controls built into the process?
- How many special cases and exceptions have to be dealt with?
- Are the steps in the process arranged in their natural order?
- What is the desired outcome? Are all of the tasks necessary? What is the value of the process?

Various techniques are used to understand processes. Data-flow diagrams are useful to show the flow of data among departments. Figure 16.12 shows a data-flow diagram for payroll data and the steps in producing a paycheck. Information about the employee and department are sent to the general account. The payroll check is issued based on a payment voucher that is generated from the general accounting ledger. Data-entity relationship diagrams show the types of data used within a business function and the relationship among the different types of data. In scenario analysis, simulations of real-world issues are presented to data end users. The end users are asked to indicate how an information system could help address their particular situations and what data should be maintained to deal with those situations. Surveys and focus groups collect information about the data collected, used, and stored in a functional area, as well as information about time and information-processing requirements. Users may be asked to evaluate the importance, frequency, and criticality of automating specific tasks within a functional area. For example, how critical is it to have an

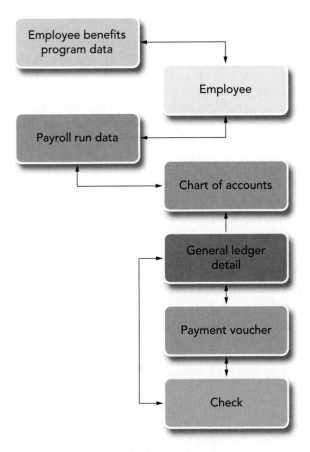

figure 16.12

A Data-Flow Diagram for Payroll Data

applicant tracking system that maintains data on applicants' previous work experience? Cost–benefit analyses compare the costs of completing tasks with and without an automated system or software application. For example, the analysis should include the costs in terms of people, time, materials, and dollars; the anticipated costs of software and hardware; and labor, time, and material expenses.[10]

Redesigning the Process

During the redesign phase, the team develops models, tests them, chooses a prototype, and determines how to integrate the prototype into the organization.

LO 16-7
Discuss the types of new technologies that can improve the efficiency and effectiveness of HRM.

Implementing the Process

The company tries out the process by testing it in a limited, controlled setting before expanding companywide. For example, J. M. Huber Corporation, a New Jersey–based conglomerate that has several operating divisions scattered throughout the United States, used reengineering to avoid installing new software onto inefficient processes.[11] HR staff began by documenting and studying the existing work flow and creating a strategy for improving efficiency. Top management, midlevel managers, and human resources staff worked together to identify the processes that they most wanted to improve. They determined that the most critical issue was to develop a client–server system that could access data more easily than the mainframe computer they were currently using. Also, the client–server system could eliminate many of the requisitions needed to get access to data, which slowed down work. The HRM department's efforts have streamlined record-keeping functions, eliminated redundant steps, and automated manual processes. The fully automated client–server system allows employees to sign up and change benefits information using an interactive voice-response system that is connected to the company's database. In addition, managers have easier access to employees' salary history, job descriptions, and other data. If an employee is eligible for a salary increase and the manager requests a change and it is approved, the system will process it (without entry by a clerical worker), and the changes will be seen on the employee's paycheck. Results of the reengineering effort are impressive. The redesigned processes have reduced the number of problems that HRM has to give to other departments by 42%, cut work steps by 26%, and eliminated 20% of the original work. Although the company is spending more than $1 million to make the technology work, it estimates that the investment should pay for itself in five years.

New Technologies
Current applications of knowledge, procedures, and equipment that have not been previously used. Usually involves replacing human labor with equipment, information processing, or some combination of the two.

Transaction Processing
Computations and calculations used to review and document HRM decisions and practices.

IMPROVING HRM EFFECTIVENESS THROUGH USING NEW TECHNOLOGIES—HRM INFORMATION SYSTEMS

Several new and emerging technologies can help improve the effectiveness of the HRM function. **New technologies** are current applications of knowledge, procedures, and equipment that have not been used previously. New technology usually involves automation—that is, replacing human labor with equipment, information processing, or some combination of the two. The "Competing through Technology" box describes how IBM used technology to onboard and connect new employees.

In HRM, technology has already been used for three broad functions: transaction processing, reporting, and tracking; decision support systems; and expert systems.[12] **Transaction processing** refers to computations and calculations used to

Building Career Success@IBM

When you have over 400,000 employees, with half of them having spent less than five years in the company, and 40% working from either a client location or home, how do you connect employees in a way that gives them access to knowledge and people that they will need to be productive and grow in their career? IBM has developed the "Success@IBM" platform as an extensive technology-based tool to onboard and connect new employees over a two-year time frame.

The platform consists of four basic parts. "Discover IBM" provides customized learning plans which offer insights into IBM's values, history, people, and business. "Share and Connect" allows new employees to connect with each other and with experienced IBMers to build a support network for career and technical guidance. "Grow My Career" provides a road map for how to pursue a variety of learning and career paths. Finally, "Find Support" helps to connect new hires with mentors, coaches and websites and answer the frequently asked questions that newcomers have.

Michael Cannon, IBM's manager of "new employee experience," says they developed the two-year onboarding program in a way that keeps employees simultaneously focused on their immediate jobs and their futures. "People come to IBM starry-eyed and excited and that's great. But where the rubber meets the road—learning and doing the work—can't be provided in a typical orientation program. We needed something much more substantive and that meant a longer time period."

So far the platform seems to be a raging success. Randy MacDonald, IBM's senior vice president of Human Resources says that the program for new hires "provides employees with the building blocks to succeed in their new roles and to grow their careers at IBM."

SOURCE: T. Starner, "Big Blue Welcomes You," *HR Executive*, September 16, 2010, pp. 30–33.

review and document HRM decisions and practices. This includes documenting relocation, training expenses, and course enrollments and filling out government reporting requirements (such as EEO-1 reports, which require companies to report information to the government regarding employees' race and gender by job category). **Decision support systems** are designed to help managers solve problems. They usually include a "what if" feature that allows users to see how outcomes change when assumptions or data change. These systems are useful, for example, for helping companies determine the number of new hires needed based on different turnover rates or the availability of employees with a certain skill in the labor market. **Expert systems** are computer systems incorporating the decision rules of people deemed to have expertise in a certain area. The system recommends actions that the user can take based on the information provided by the user. The recommended actions are those that a human expert would take in a similar situation (such as a manager interviewing a job candidate). We discuss expert systems in more detail later in this chapter.

The newest technologies being applied to HRM include interactive voice technology, client–server architecture, relational databases, imaging, and development of specialized software. These technologies improve effectiveness through increasing access to information, improving communications, improving the speed with which HRM transactions and information can be gathered, and reducing the costs and facilitating the administration of HRM functions such as

Decision Support Systems
Problem-solving systems which usually include a "what-if" feature that allows users to see how outcomes change when assumptions or data change.

Expert Systems
Computer systems incorporating the decision rules of people recognized as experts in a certain area.

● Technology has helped employers find leaner, more flexible ways of working. Human resource professionals are increasingly using new technology to streamline HR functions.

Network
A combination of desktop computers, computer terminals, and mainframes or minicomputers that share access to databases and a method to transmit information throughout the system.

Client–Server Architecture
Computer design that provides a method to consolidate data and applications into a single host system (the client).

recruiting, training, and performance management. Technology enables

- Employees to gain complete control over their training and benefits enrollments (more self-service).
- The creation of a paperless employment office.
- Streamlining the HRM department's work.
- Knowledge-based decision support technology, which allows employees and managers to access knowledge as needed.
- Employees and managers to select the type of media they want to use to send and receive information.
- Work to be completed at any time and place.
- Closer monitoring of employees' work.[13]

There is evidence that new technology is related to improvements in productivity. Improvements in productivity have been credited largely to downsizing, restructuring, and reengineering. But technology is also responsible because new technology has allowed companies to find leaner, more flexible ways of operating.[14] A study of companies in a variety of industries found that investments in computers provided a better return than investments in other kinds of capital.[15] Technology requires companies to have appropriately skilled and motivated people and streamlined work processes. In some cases technology is replacing human capital.[16] For example, Statewide, the regional telephone unit of Pacific Telesis Group, used to dispatch about 20,000 trucks a day to fix customers' lines. New technology has enabled the company to find broken lines using computer signals. As a result, fewer truck dispatches (and fewer drivers) are necessary.

Interactive Voice Technology

Interactive voice technology uses a conventional personal computer to create an automated phone-response system. This technology is especially useful for benefits administration. For example, at Hannaford Brothers, a supermarket chain spread through the northeastern United States, the HRM department installed an interactive voice-response system that allows employees to get information on their retirement accounts, stock purchases, and benefits plans by using the touchtone buttons on their phone.[17] Employees can also directly enroll in programs and speak to an HRM representative if they have questions. As a result of the technology, the company was able to reduce the size of the HRM staff and more quickly serve employees' benefits needs.

Networks and Client–Server Architecture

Traditionally, different computer systems (with separate databases) are used for payroll, recruiting, and other human resource management functions. A **network** is a combination of desktop computers, computer terminals, and mainframes or minicomputers that share access to databases and a means to transmit information throughout the system. A common form of network involves client–server architecture. **Client–server architecture** provides the means of consolidating data and applications into a single system (the client).[18] The data can be accessed by multiple users. Also, software applications can be stored on the server and "borrowed" by other users. Client–server architecture allows easier access to data, faster response time, and maximum use of the computing power of the personal computer.

For example, a pharmaceutical company with 50,000 employees worldwide uses client–server technology to create an employee information system that integrates data from six databases.[19] The available data include financial, operational, and human resource information. A manager at a European location can compare her plant's human resource costs with those for the entire company or a plant in Ohio, and at the same time senior management can use the same data to compare the productivity of the Ohio plant with a plant in Maine.

Relational Databases

Databases contain several data files (topics), which are made up of employee information (records) containing data fields. A data field is an element or type of information such as employee name, Social Security number, or job classification.

In a **relational database** information is stored in separate files, which look like tables. These files can be linked by common elements (fields) such as name, identification number, or location. This contrasts with the traditional file structure, in which all data associated with an employee was kept in one file. In the relational database shown in Figure 16.13, employees' personal information is located in one file and salary information in another, but both topics of information can be accessed via the employees' Social Security numbers.

Users of relational databases can file and retrieve information according to any field or multiple fields across different tables or databases. They provide an easy way to organize data. Also, the number of data fields that can be kept for any employee using a relational database is limitless. The ability to join or merge data from several

Relational Database
A database structure that stores information in separate files that can be linked by common elements.

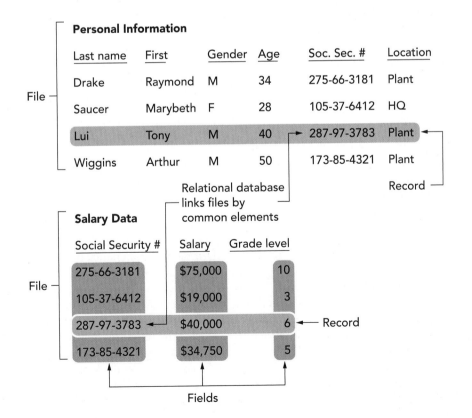

figure 16.13

Example of a Relational Database

different tables or to view only a subset of data is especially useful in human resource management. Databases that have been developed to track employee benefit costs, training courses, and compensation, for example, contain separate pieces of employee information that can be accessed and merged as desired by the user. Relational technology also allows databases to be established in several different locations. Users in one plant or division location can access data from any other company location. Consider an oil company. Human resources data—such as the names, salaries, and skills of employees working on an oil rig in the Gulf of Mexico—can be stored at company headquarters. Databases at the oil rig site itself might contain employee name, safety equipment issued, and appropriate skill certification. Headquarters and oil rig managers can access information on each database as needed.

Imaging

Imaging
A process for scanning documents, storing them electronically, and retrieving them.

Imaging refers to scanning documents, storing them electronically, and retrieving them.[20] Imaging is particularly useful because paper files take a large volume of space and are difficult to access. Imaging has been used in applicant tracking and in benefits management. Applicants' résumés can be scanned and stored in a database so they will be available for access at a later date. Some software applications (such as Resumix) allow the user to scan the résumé based on key items such as job history, education, or experience. At Warner-Lambert, the compensation and benefits department provides HR-related services for over 15,000 retirees.[21] Eight employees retire or die each month; approximately 100 employees terminate each month. This "exit" activity created a tremendous volume of paper for each employee, as well as requests for data from analysts in the department. Locating and refiling the data was very time-consuming and inefficient. Using imaging, the compensation and benefits department was able to better serve its customers by reducing the time needed to locate a file or handle a phone inquiry from a retiree, providing the ability for sharing files among analysts simultaneously, eliminating the need to refile, and reducing the physical space needed to store the files.

Expert Systems

As we discussed earlier, expert systems are technologies that mimic a human expert. Expert systems have three elements:

- A knowledge base that contains facts, figures, and rules about a specific subject.
- A decision-making capability that draws conclusions from those facts and figures to solve problems and answer questions.
- A user interface that gathers and gives information to the person using the system.

The use of expert systems in HRM is relatively new. Some companies use expert systems to help employees decide how to allocate their money for benefits, help managers schedule the labor requirements for projects, and assist managers in conducting selection interviews. Pic 'n Pay (a chain of shoe stores) uses an expert system for the initial job interview. Candidates call a toll-free phone number. The candidates then respond to 100 questions, and the computer records the responses and scores them. At headquarters, a team of trained interviewers evaluates the responses and designs a list of follow-up questions, which are administered by the hiring manager. The expert system reduced employee turnover by 50% and reduced losses due to theft by 39%. Also, hiring of minorities has risen 8%, implying that decision biases may be less significant using the expert system.[22]

A large international food processor uses an expert system called Performer, designed to provide training and support to its plant operators. One of the problems the company was facing was determining why potato chips were being scorched in the fryer operation. An operator solved the problem using Performer. He selected the "troubleshooting" menu, then "product texture/flavor," then "off oil flavor." The program listed probable causes, beginning with high oxidation during frying. The operator chose that cause, and the system recommended adjusting the cooking line's oil flush, providing detailed steps for that procedure. Following those steps resolved the problem.[23]

Expert systems can deliver both high quality and lower costs. By using the decision processes of experts, the system enables many people to arrive at decisions that reflect the expert's knowledge. An expert system helps avoid the errors that can result from fatigue and decision biases. The efficiencies of an expert system can be realized if it can be operated by fewer employees or less skilled (and likely less costly) employees than the company would otherwise require.

Groupware

Groupware (electronic meeting software) is a software application that enables multiple users to track, share, and organize information and to work on the same document simultaneously.[24] Companies have been using groupware to improve business processes such as sales and account management, to improve meeting effectiveness, and to identify and share knowledge in the organization. (See our earlier discussion of creating a learning organization in Chapter 7.) The database contains updated news on competitors and customers, information from public news sources, salespeople's reports, an in-house directory of experts, and attendees' notes from conventions and conferences. Many companies are also creating their own "intranet," a private company network that competes with groupware programs such as Lotus Notes. Intranets are cheaper and simpler to use than groupware programs but pose potential security problems because of the difficulty of keeping people out of the network.[25]

Groupware
Software that enables multiple users to track, share, and organize information and to work on the same database or document simultaneously.

Software Applications for HRM
IMPROVING HRM EFFECTIVENESS THROUGH NEW TECHNOLOGIES—E-HRM

Since the mid-1990s, as HRM functions sought to play a more strategic role in their organizations, the first task was to eliminate transactional tasks in order to free up time to focus on traditional and transformational activities. Part of building a strategic HR function requires moving much of the transactional work away from being done by people so that the people can have time available to work on strategic activities. Consequently, the use of technology can both make HR more strategic and by doing so increase the value that HR adds to the business.[26] As indicated in Figure 16.9, outsourcing of many of these activities provided one mechanism for reducing this burden. However, more relevant today is the focus on the use of information technology to handle these tasks. Early on this was achieved by the development and implementation of information systems that were run by the HRM function but more recently have evolved into systems that allow employees to serve themselves. Thus, for example, employees can access the system and make their benefit enrollment,

figure 16.14

Change in Delivery

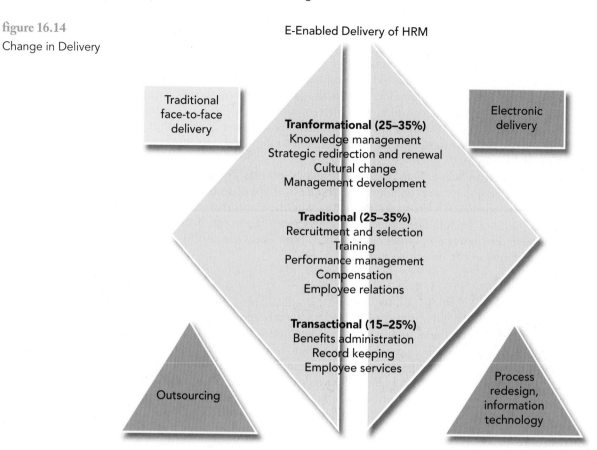

E-Enabled Delivery of HRM

Tranformational (25–35%)
Knowledge management
Strategic redirection and renewal
Cultural change
Management development

Traditional (25–35%)
Recruitment and selection
Training
Performance management
Compensation
Employee relations

Transactional (15–25%)
Benefits administration
Record keeping
Employee services

Traditional face-to-face delivery

Electronic delivery

Outsourcing

Process redesign, information technology

changes, or claims online. Clearly, technology has freed HRM functions from transactional activities to focus on more strategic actions.

However, the speed requirements of e-business force HRM functions to explore how to leverage technology for the delivery of traditional and transformational HRM activities. This does not imply that over time all of HRM will be executed over the web, but that a number of HRM activities currently delivered via paper or face-to-face communications can be moved to the web with no loss (and even gains) in effectiveness and efficiency. This is illustrated by Figure 16.14. We explore some examples next.

In a world dominated by social media, companies like Google are now using it for internal purposes. Google developed "Magnet," an employee information system that benefits both employees and the company by building community and capability. Not surprisingly, given Google's search capability, this system allows employees to search for people and positions that they might be interested in.

Figure 16.15 displays the personal web page for Sunil Chandra, the leader behind Magnet. As you can see, this page lets people know what kinds of skills and experiences he developed over the years (e.g., crazy/creative ideas, globalization, etc.). It also shows his previous work experience and education. On the right side of the page you can find links to other Googlers who have similar experience (e.g., worked at McKinsey and Company) or education (went to University of Wollongong). If you were to click on the McKinsey or Wollongong link you would immediately see a list of all the Googlers with similar experience or education. This enables Googlers to

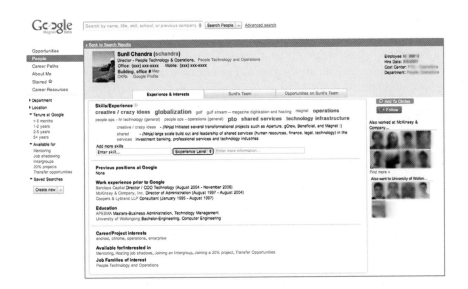

figure 16.15

Personal Web Page
for Sunil Chandra

quickly connect with those they may have worked with, gone to school with, or just want to get to know.

Also, to build community, the bottom links show that Sunil would be interested in projects such as "android" or "chrome," and job families in people technology. It also shows he is available for mentoring, hosting job shadows (e.g., following him around for a day to see what he does), and so on. Again, this allows Googlers who might be interested in finding a mentor to do a quick search and find that Sunil is one of the people who would be available to act as a mentor.

Notice across the top that in addition to his personal/professional information, there are also buttons for "Sunil's Team" (if you wanted to know who works for him) and for "Opportunities on Sunil's Team" (if you might be interested in working for him). In particular, the opportunities button would provide descriptions of jobs or part-time projects that Sunil is seeking people for as well as the kinds of skills those people would need. So again, if you were interested in using your "technology infra-structure" skills and Sunil had a role available requiring that skill, if you were to search that skill, it would list Sunil's role as one of the many across Google that require it.

So, Google's Magnet employee information system uses Google's search capability to build both community and capability. It builds community by providing a technology framework to enable people to connect with those having similar experiences and/or interests. It builds capability by helping connect employee skill sets with the skill needs that exist across Google.

Recruitment and Selection

Traditional recruitment and selection processes have required considerable face-to-face communications with recruitment firms and potential employees, labor-intensive assessment devices, and significant monitoring of managerial decisions to ensure that hiring patterns and decisions do not run afoul of regulatory requirements. However, technology has transformed these processes.

For example, online recruiting accounts for one of every eight hires according to k-force.com's poll of 300 U.S. companies. IBM employees now fill out forms on the web to identify contract help they need, and that information is immediately sent to

14 temp agencies. Within an hour agencies respond with résumés for review, allowing IBM to cut hiring time from 10 days to 3 and save $3 million per year.

Finally, technology has enabled firms to monitor hiring processes to minimize the potential for discriminatory hiring decisions. For example, Home Depot was accused of forcing female applicants into cashier jobs while reserving the customer service jobs for males. While not admitting guilt, as part of their consent decree Home Depot uses technology to identify people who have skills for jobs they are not applying for based on key words in their résumés. In addition, the technology forces managers to interview diverse candidate sets before making decisions.

Compensation and Rewards

Compensation systems in organizations probably reflect the most pervasive form of bureaucracy within HRM. In spite of the critical role they play in attracting, motivating, and retaining employees, most systems consist of rigid, time-consuming, and ineffective processes. Managers fill out what they believe to be useless forms, ignore guidelines, and display a general disdain for the entire process.

Leveraging technology may allow firms to better achieve their compensation goals with considerably less effort. For example, one problem many merit or bonus pay plans face is that managers refuse to differentiate among performers, giving everyone similar pay increases. This allows them to spend less time thinking about how to manage (rate and review) performance as well as minimizes the potential conflict they might face. Thus, employees do not see linkages between performance and pay, resulting in lower motivation among all employees and higher turnover among top performers (and possibly lower turnover among bottom performers). To minimize this, Cypress Semiconductors requires managers to distinguish between equity and merit and forces distributions with regard to both concepts.[27] For example, equity means that the top-ranked performer in any group of peers should make 50% more than the lowest-ranked performer, and people with comparable performance should receive comparable salaries. With regard to merit, there must be at least a 7% spread between the lowest and highest pay raises (if the lowest raise is 3%, then the highest must be at least 10%). If ratings and raises are input into a system, the firm can monitor and control the rating process to ensure that adequate differentiations are made consistent with the policy.

Training and Development

Exploring different vehicles for delivering training (PC, video, and the like) certainly is not a new concept. In addition, a number of firms have begun delivering training via the web. Their experience suggests that some types of training can be done effectively via the Internet or an intranet, whereas others might not. For example, companies such as IBM and Dell both boast that they have developed Internet-based training for some parts of their workforce.

Interestingly, the challenge of speedy delivery of HRM services brings the concept of Internet-based training to the forefront. In today's competitive environment, firms compete to attract and retain both customers and talented employees. How well a firm develops and treats existing employees largely determines how well it achieves these outcomes. Yet the challenges of speed, project focus, and changing technology create environments that discourage managers from managing their people, resulting in a situation where employees may not feel respected or valued.

This presents a challenge to firms to provide both the incentive and the skills for managers to treat employees as assets rather than commodities. Consider how

Internet-based training might facilitate this. Assume that you work for Widget.com, a fast-growing, fast-paced e-business. You arrive at work Monday morning, and your e-mail contains a high-priority message with either an attachment or a link to a URL. It is your Monday morning challenge from the CEO, and you know that the system will track whether you link and complete this challenge. When you link to it, you see a digital video of your CEO telling you how people are Widget.com's competitive advantage, and that when they don't feel valued, they leave. Thus his challenge to you is to make your employees feel valued today. To do so, you will in the next 10 minutes learn how to express appreciation to an employee. You receive six learning points; you observe a digitized video model performing the learning points; you review the learning points again and take a quiz. You then see the CEO giving you the final challenge: that in the next 15 minutes you are to take one of your employees aside and express your appreciation using the skill you just developed.

Notice the advantages of this process. First, it was not time-consuming like most three-day or one-week training programs. The entire process (training and demonstration with a real employee) took less than 30 minutes; you have developed a skill; and an employee now probably feels better about the organization. It communicated a real organizational value or necessary competency. It didn't require any travel expenses to a training facility. It did not overwhelm you with so much information that you would be lucky to remember 10% of what you were exposed to. Finally, it was a push, rather than pull, approach to training. The firm did not wait for you to realize you had a deficiency and then go search and sign up for training. It pushed the training to you.

Thus technology allows firms to deliver training and development for at least some skills or knowledge faster, more efficiently, and probably more effectively. It can quickly merge training, communication, and immediate response to strategic contingencies.

Creating and nurturing a committed workforce presents a tremendous challenge to firms today. According to a recent survey conducted by Monster.com, 61% of Americans consider themselves overworked and 86% are not satisfied with their jobs.[28] Such findings suggest that firms need to find ways to monitor commitment levels, identify potential obstacles to commitment, and respond quickly to eliminate those obstacles. In large part, attitude surveys have constituted the platform from which these activities were managed in the past.

Consider the traditional attitude survey. Surveys are administered to employees over a period of four to six weeks. The data are entered and analyzed, requiring another six to eight weeks. A group interprets the results to identify the major problem areas, and task forces are formed to develop recommendations; this process easily takes another four to six months. Finally, decisions must be made about implementing the task force recommendations. In the end, at best employees might see responses to their concerns 12 to 18 months after the survey—and then the survey administrators cannot understand why employees think that completing the survey is a waste of time.

Now consider how technology can shorten that cycle. E-pulse represents one attempt to create a platform for almost real-time attitude surveys. Developed by Theresa Welbourne at the University of Michigan, E-pulse is a scalable survey device administered online. Normally three questions are asked regarding how employees feel about work, but more questions can be added to get feedback on any specific issue. The survey goes out online, and when employees complete it, the data are immediately entered and analyzed. In essence, the part of the process that took four months in the past has been reduced to a day.

Next the firm can decide how it wants to use the information. For example, it could be broken down by business, site, or work unit, with the relevant information going to the leader of the chosen unit of analysis. In essence, a supervisor could receive almost immediate feedback about the attitudes of his or her work group, or a general manager about his or her business unit. The supervisor or manager can respond immediately, even if only to communicate that she or he realizes a problem exists and will take action soon.

One must recognize that although the technology provides for faster HRM, only a more systemic approach will ensure better and smarter HRM. For example, disseminating the information to the supervisors and managers may be faster, but unless those individuals possess good problem-solving and communication skills, they may either ignore the information or, worse yet, exacerbate the problem with inappropriate responses. As we noted with regard to training, this systemic approach requires knocking down traditional functional walls to deliver organizational solutions rather than functional programs. Thus the challenge is to get beyond viewing the technology as a panacea or even as a functional tool, but rather as a catalyst for transforming the HRM organization. The "Competing through Sustainability" box describes how companies can manage downsizing processes while maintaining a sustainable employment relationship.

The Future for HR Professionals

The future for careers in the human resource profession seems brighter than ever. An increasing number of successful companies such as Microsoft have made the top HR job a member of the senior management team, reporting directly to the chief executive officer. CEOs recognize the importance of their workforce in driving competitive success. Firms need to seek the balance between attracting, motivating, and retaining the very best talent and keeping labor and administrative costs as low as possible. Finding such a balance requires HR leaders who have a deep knowledge of the business combined with a deep knowledge of HR issues, tools, processes, and technologies.

For a reader who is just getting a first glimpse of the HRM function, to portray what a vastly different role HRM must play today compared to 20 or even 10 years ago is impossible. As noted earlier, HRM has traditionally played a largely administrative role—simply processing paperwork plus developing and administering hiring, training, appraisal, compensation, and benefits systems—and all of this has been unrelated to the strategic direction of the firm. In the early 1980s HRM took on more of a one-way linkage role, helping to implement strategy. Now strategic decision makers are realizing the importance of people issues and so are calling for HRM to become the "source of people expertise" in the firm.[29] This requires that HR managers possess and use knowledge of how people can and do play a role in competitive advantage as well as the policies, programs, and practices that can leverage the firm's people as a source of competitive advantage. This leads to an entirely new set of competencies for today's strategic HR executive.[30]

In the future, HR professionals will need four basic competencies to become partners in the strategic management process (see Figure 2.7).[31] First, they will need "business competence"—knowing the company's business and understanding its economic financial capabilities. This calls for making logical decisions that support the company's strategic plan based on the most accurate information possible. Because in almost all companies the effectiveness of decisions must be

COMPETING THROUGH SUSTAINABILITY

Managing after the Layoffs

As the U.S. economy has tumbled, more and more companies have engaged in layoffs as a necessary component of reducing costs. However, the economic downturn will transform to economic growth at some point, thus requiring firms to think about how to manage their employees under challenging circumstances in ways that will enable them to manage well under munificent conditions.

As one would expect, employees feel tremendous uncertainty as they observe their companies' downsizings. Sirota Survey Intelligence's surveys show that the percentage of employees who felt valued fell to 44% in 2002 from 67% prior to the layoffs resulting from 9/11. The research reveals that employees miss co-workers and friends, experience higher levels of stress, and see less teamwork. However, central to employee morale is trust in management. Sirota suggests the following strategies for building sustainable relationships with the workforce:

1. Communicate—quickly, openly, honestly. It is important to answer the most pressing questions right away, such as whether or not the company will be downsizing further.
2. Allow for their emotional response. Survivors naturally feel emotions such as anger, concern, insecurity, depression, and guilt, and managers need to reassure employees that these feelings are natural.
3. Address work frustrations due to the cutbacks. Cutbacks usually result in increased workloads for survivors, and this can damage teamwork at a time when teamwork is even more important. Managers need to engage employees in rethinking how work can be done differently.

4. Demonstrate continuing long-term interest in the careers of the survivors. People want to know that they have a future and that the company still wants to invest in them. In the absence of training budgets, "stretch" assignments can challenge people to gain new skills that will make them even more promotable when the company begins to grow again.
5. Assess whether it's working—don't guess. Use facts and data to gauge how employees are reacting and performing. Employee surveys, focus groups, and one-on-one discussion can provide important data while also communicating that employees' views are still valued.

SOURCE: Douglas Klein, "Five Strategies for Managing after Layoffs," January 1, 2009. http://www.hreonline.com/HRE/story.jsp?storyId=156838048&query=sustainability.

---

evaluated in terms of dollar values, the HR executive must be able to calculate the costs and benefits of each alternative in terms of its dollar impact.[32] In addition, it requires that the nonmonetary impact be considered. The HR executive must be fully capable of identifying the social and ethical issues attached to HRM practices.

Second, HR professionals will need "professional–technical knowledge" of state-of-the-art HRM practices in areas such as staffing, development, rewards, organizational design, and communication. New selection techniques, performance appraisal methods, training programs, and incentive plans are constantly being developed. Some of these programs can provide value whereas others may be no more than the products of today's HRM equivalent of snake oil. HR executives must be able to critically evaluate the new techniques offered as state-of-the-art HRM programs and use only those that will benefit the company.

Third, they must be skilled in the "management of change processes," such as diagnosing problems, implementing organizational changes, and evaluating results. Every time a company changes its strategy in even a minor way, the entire company has to change. These changes result in conflict, resistance, and confusion among the people who must implement the new plans or programs. The HR executive must have the skills to oversee the change in a way that ensures its success. In fact, one survey of *Fortune* 500 companies found that 87% of the companies had their organization development/change function as part of the HR department.[33]

Finally, these professionals must also have "integration competence," meaning the ability to integrate the three other competencies to increase the company's value. This requires that, although specialist knowledge is necessary, a generalist perspective must be taken in making decisions. This entails seeing how all the functions within the HRM area fit together to be effective and recognizing that changes in any one part of the HRM package are likely to require changes in other parts of the package.

Google has sought to achieve this integration with what they call the "three-thirds" staffing model. This consist of the following groups of people with complimentary skill sets:

1. One-third traditional HR people—subject matter experts in benefits, compensation, employee relations, learning, and recruiting. Their expertise, pattern recognition, and emotional intelligence serve as the foundation for developing the services and programs.
2. One-third consultants—high-end strategy experts with a background in management consulting who thrive on solving big, amorphous problems and bring a deliberate, business approach to people issues.
3. One-third analytics professionals—masters and doctoral-level folks who measure, analyze, and provide insight into all that the people operations function does, and to prove what really works. They have a healthy appetite for the impossible and drive experimentation to ensure that Google is as innovative on the people side as it is on the product side.

This staffing model has enabled Google to build the required skill base and integrate the various people to build a world-class HR organization.[34]

The Role of the Chief Human Resource Officer

LO 16-8
List the competencies the HRM executive needs to become a strategic partner in the company.

Having discussed the increasing importance of HR and the new strategic role of HR professionals, in closing we examine the role of the leader of the HR function. These chief human resource officers (CHROs) bear the responsibility for leading the HR function as well as ensuring that HR systems and processes deliver value to the company. Only recently have researchers attempted to examine what these HR leaders do and how they affect the business.

Strategic Advisor
A role of the CHRO that focuses on the formulation and implementation of the firm's strategy.

A recent survey identified seven roles that CHROs have to play to one degree or another, and then asked *Fortune* 150 CHROs to identify how they spend their time across those roles. As can be seen in Figure 16.16, CHROs reported spending the second most time (21%) as a **strategic advisor** to the executive team. This role entails sharing the people expertise as part of the decision-making process, as well as shaping how the human capital of the firm fits into its strategy. This also was the role

What percent of your time would you say you spend in each of the following roles?

- Firm representative 5%
- Other 0%
- Workforce sensor 8%
- Functional leader 22%
- Strategic advisor 21%
- Executive coach 17%
- Talent architect 17%
- Board liaison 10%

figure 16.16

Percentage of Time CHROs Spend in Each Role

that was most frequently cited as having the greatest impact on the firm. One CHRO described the importance of the strategic advisor role as:

> HR is critical, but it's a tool in the firm's portfolio. First to truly impact the success of the firm, the CHRO needs to have a broad credibility that only comes from understanding every facet of the business at a level deep enough to be able to add business value in discussions with every leader. That means understanding the firm's economics, customer behavior, products, technology, etc. at a level deep enough to steer and shape decisions in these areas. From that flows the trust and credibility to counter the "conventional wisdom" on how best to manage people and shape the firm's talent agenda. Without this broader credibility, the CHRO can talk about talent, but risks not having sufficient context to make the right decisions. Second, from the CEO's perspective, the most useful thing is the integration of the people strategy with every other part of the firm's operations. The only way to truly integrate these areas is to be actively involved in the broader discussions as well.[35]

The role of **talent architect** also sees a significant portion of time spent (17%) and was also frequently cited as the role in which the CHRO has the greatest impact on the business. Playing the role of talent architect requires that CHROs help the executive team see the importance of talent, identify present and future talent gaps, and come to own the talent agenda. One CHRO described the importance of this role this way:

> Keeping the senior team focused on the strategic talent needs of the business allows proper identification of talent gaps and future needs, thus allowing time to develop best talent and design appropriate experiential assignments.[36]

CHROs report spending as much time in the role of **counselor/confidante/coach** as they do in the talent architect role (17%), and a number of CHROs listed this role as one of the roles with the greatest impact. This role seemingly is a broad one, and it can entail anything from behavioral or performance counseling to being the personal sounding board for the CEO. Perhaps as pressure mounts on CEOs from investors and analysts, the CHRO is the most trusted advisor that can be counted on to give

Talent Architect
A role of the CHRO that focuses on building and identifying the human capital critical to the present and future of the firm.

Counselor/ Confidante/Coach
A role of the CHRO that focuses on counseling or coaching team members or resolving interpersonal or political conflicts among team members.

Leader of the HR Function
A role of the CHRO that focuses on working with HR team members regarding the development, design, and delivery of HR services.

Liaison to the Board
A role of the CHRO that focuses on preparation for board meetings, phone calls with board members, and attendance at board meetings.

Workforce Sensor
A role of the CHRO that focuses on identifying workforce morale issues or concerns.

Representative of the Firm
A role of the CHRO that focuses on activities with external stakeholders, such as lobbying, speaking to outside groups, etc.

personal advice or simply to listen to the CEO's problems. One poignant comment regarding this role was:

> If I do my job right, I am the copper wire that connects all the outlets of the firm together effectively. This includes OD work (which some might put in the strategic advisor category), performance counseling and relationship building, business consulting and the strategic elements of talent acquisition and planning.[37]

The **leader of the HR function** is the role in which CHROs spent the most time, but it is not seen as one that has the greatest impact. This role deals with ensuring that the HR function is aligning its activities and priorities toward the needs of the business, and it usually entails meeting with direct reports to provide guidance and check on progress. However, CHROs increasingly rely on their direct reports to design and deliver HR services while they shift their attention to advising and counseling the top executive team.

The "Competing through Globalization" box illustrates the different challenges CHROs face in building their functions in U.S. versus European organizations.

Liaison to the board entails all of the activities in which CHROs engage with the board of directors, including discussions of executive compensation, CEO performance, CEO succession, and performance of other members of the executive leadership team. This role is increasing in importance, although it has a long way to go before equaling the strategic advisor, talent architect, and counselor/confidante/coach roles.

The role of **workforce sensors** entails taking the pulse of the employee population to identify any morale or motivation issues. This is a role in which CHROs do not spend much time, and few viewed it as having the greatest impact on the business.

Finally, CHROs to some extent become the face of the organization to outside constituents such as labor unions, nongovernmental organizations, and the press. They spend the least amount of time in the **representative of the firm** role (see Table 16.6).

The new strategic role for HRM presents both opportunities and challenges. HRM has the chance to profoundly impact the way organizations compete through people. On the other hand, with this opportunity comes serious responsibility and accountability.[38] HRM functions of the future must consist of individuals who view themselves as businesspeople who happen to work in an HRM function, rather than HRM people who happen to work in a business. The "Competing through Globalization" box describes how European CHROs differ in their HR function priorities relative to those in the U.S.

table 16.6
Roles of the CHRO

Strategic advisor to the executive team—activities focused specifically on the formulation and implementation of the firm's strategy.

Counselor/confidante/coach to the executive team—activities focused on counseling or coaching team members or resolving interpersonal or political conflicts among team members.

Liaison to the board of directors—preparation for board meetings, phone calls with board members, attendance at board meetings.

Talent architect—activities focused on building and identifying the human capital critical to the present and future of the firm.

Leader of the HR function—working with HR team members regarding the development, design, and delivery of HR services.

Workforce sensor—activities focused on identifying workforce morale issues or concerns.

Representative of the firm—activities with external stakeholders, such as lobbying, speaking to outside groups, etc.

HR in Europe versus the United States

As the saying goes, "context matters," and this is certainly true in the field of HR. As discussed in previous chapters, countries and regions have different institutional and legal requirements regarding the management of people, thus making a one-size-fits-all approach to HR at best ineffective, and at worst, illegal. However, when viewing the basic challenges and requirements of HR, one finds some consistent similarities and a few significant differences.

In a recent survey of chief HR officers in the United States and Europe, the CHROs were asked a number of questions including, "What is your CEO's agenda for HR?" "What are the major obstacles to achieving the CEO's agenda?" and about how much time they spent in the various CHRO roles. In terms of consistencies, both European and U.S. CHROs expressed that "talent" topped the CEO's agenda with over 90% of both groups listing it. In addition, both groups suggested that the major obstacle to achieving the CEO's agenda was the competencies of those in the HR function. Finally, both groups tend to spend similar time in the roles of strategic advisor, talent architect, and counselor/confidante/coach.

On the other hand, a consistent difference between Europe and the United States is the quality of the HR function. For instance, while 58% of U.S. CHROs listed the competence of their HR people as an obstacle to achieving the agenda, a staggering 97% of European CHROs listed this. In addition, European CHROs expressed spending more time as the leader of the HR function relative to those from the United States (30% vs. 25%). And far more U.S. CHROs noted "building a great HR team" as having made them more effective in their role relative to those in Europe (15% vs. 3%).

Thus, it appears that for all the struggles U.S. multinationals have faced in transforming their HR functions, the struggle is even greater in Europe.

SOURCE: P. Wright, M. Stewart, and O. Moore, "The CHRO Challenge 2011: Building Organizational, Functional, and Personal Talent," 2011, http://www.ilr.cornell.edu/cahrs/upload/2011-CHRO-Survey-Report.pdf.

A LOOK BACK

HR AT GOOGLE CONTINUES

As you have seen throughout this chapter, Laszlo Bock and Google have been innovating constantly in how they approach the role that the People Operations function can play and how it plays that role in the organization. However, this also illustrates that transforming an HR function is always a journey and not a destination. HR functions must constantly be sensing the changing needs of the business, developing strategies to help the business meet its goals, and delivering new systems and processes in an efficient and effective manner.

Questions

1. What do you think it would be like to work for Google? In what ways might Google's HR function have an impact on you as an employee there in terms of making your work experience better?
2. In what ways would you expect Google's HR approach to be different from a manufacturing organization like General Motors? How does an HR strategy tend to reflect the nature of the business?

Please see the Video that corresponds to this chapter at www.mhhe.com/noe8e.

SUMMARY

The roles required of the HRM function have changed as people have become recognized as a true source of competitive advantage. This has required a transformation of the HRM function from focusing solely on transactional activities to an increasing involvement in strategic activities. In fact, according to a recent study, 64% of HR executives said that their HRM function is in a process of transformation.[39] The strategic management of the HRM function will determine whether HRM will transform itself to a true strategic partner or simply be blown up.

In this chapter we have explored the various changing roles of the HRM function. HRM today must play roles as an administrative expert, employee advocate, change agent, and strategic partner. The function must also deliver transactional, traditional, and transformational services and activities to the firm, and it must be both efficient and effective. HR executives must strategically manage the HRM function just as the firm must be strategically managed. This requires that HRM develop measures of the function's performance through customer surveys and analytical methods. These measures can form the basis for planning ways to improve performance. HRM performance can increase through new structures for the function, through using reengineering and information technology, and through outsourcing.

KEY TERMS

Audit approach, 693
Analytic approach, 695
Outsourcing, 701
Reengineering, 702
New technologies, 704
Transaction processing, 704
Decision support systems, 705

Expert systems, 705
Network, 706
Client–server architecture, 706
Relational database, 707
Imaging, 708
Groupware, 709
Strategic advisor, 716

Talent architect, 717
Counselor/confidante/
   coach, 717
Leader of the HR function, 718
Liaison to the board, 718
Workforce sensor, 718
Representative of the firm, 718

DISCUSSION QUESTIONS

1. Why have the roles and activities of the HRM function changed over the past 20 to 30 years? What has been driving this change? How effectively do you think HRM has responded?

2. How can the processes for strategic management discussed in Chapter 2 be transplanted to manage the HRM function?

3. Why do you think that few companies take the time to determine the effectiveness of HRM practices? Should a company be concerned about evaluating HRM practices? Why? What might people working in the HRM function gain by evaluating the function?

4. How might imaging technology be useful for recruitment? For training? For benefits administration? For performance management?

5. Employees in your company currently choose and enroll in benefits programs after reading communications brochures, completing enrollment forms, and sending them to their HR rep. A temporary staff has to be hired to process the large amount of paperwork that is generated. Enrollment forms need to be checked, sorted, batched, sent to data entry, keypunched, returned, and filed. The process is slow and prone to errors. How could you use process reengineering to make benefits enrollment more efficient and effective?

6. Some argue that outsourcing an activity is bad because the activity is no longer a means of distinguishing the firm from competitors. (All competitors can buy the same service from the same provider, so it cannot be a source of competitive advantage.) Is this true? If so, why would a firm outsource any activity?

● SELF-ASSESSMENT EXERCISE

How ethical are you? Read each of the following descriptions. For each, circle whether you believe the behavior described is ethical or unethical.

1. A company president found that a competitor had made an important scientific discovery that would sharply reduce the profits of his own company. The president hired a key employee of the competitor in an attempt to learn the details of the discovery.

    Ethical
    Unethical

2. To increase profits, a general manager used a production process that exceeded legal limits for environmental pollution.

    Ethical
    Unethical

3. Because of pressure from her brokerage firm, a stockbroker recommended a type of bond that she did not consider to be a good investment.

    Ethical
    Unethical

4. A small business received one-fourth of its revenues in the form of cash. On the company's income tax forms, the owner reported only one-half of the cash receipts.

    Ethical
    Unethical

5. A corporate executive promoted a loyal friend and competent manager to the position of divisional vice president in preference to a better qualified manager with whom she had no close ties.

    Ethical
    Unethical

6. An employer received applications for a supervisor's position from two equally qualified applicants. The employer hired the male applicant because he thought some employees might resent being supervised by a female.

    Ethical
    Unethical

7. An engineer discovered what he perceived to be a product design flaw that constituted a safety hazard. His company declined to correct the flaw. The engineer decided to keep quiet, rather than taking his complaint outside the company.

    Ethical
    Unethical

8. A comptroller selected a legal method of financial reporting that concealed some embarrassing financial facts. Otherwise, those facts would have been public knowledge.

    Ethical
    Unethical

9. A company paid a $350,000 "consulting" fee to an official of a foreign country. In return, the official promised to help the company obtain a contract that should produce a $10 million profit for the company.

    Ethical
    Unethical

10. A member of a corporation's board of directors learned that his company intended to announce a stock split and increase its dividend. On the basis of this favorable information, the director bought additional shares of the company's stock. Following the announcement of the information, he sold the stock at a gain.

    Ethical
    Unethical

Now score your results. How many actions did you judge to be unethical?

All of these actions are unethical. The more of the actions you judged to be unethical, the better your understanding of ethical business behavior.

SOURCE: Based on S. Morris et al., "A Test of Environmental, Situational, and Personal Influences on the Ethical Intentions of CEOs," *Business and Society* 34 (1995), pp. 119–47.

● EXERCISING STRATEGY: TRANSFORMING THE BUSINESS AND HR AT XEROX

In 1958, Xerox launched the Xerox 914, the first automatic, plain-paper office copier. This product went on to become the top-selling industrial product of all time. Xerox's successful xerography technology gave it a sustainable competitive advantage that endured for years. However, all good things must come to an end, and in Xerox's case, that end was the late 1990s. By 2000, Xerox experienced its biggest slide in history, and the consensus among analysts within the industry was that Xerox was working with "an unsustainable business model," meaning unless things changed drastically, Xerox would soon cease to exist. In 2000 Xerox had $17.1 billion in debt, with only $154 million in cash on hand. By 2001, Xerox's stock, which had peaked at $63, fell to about $4—a loss of 90% of its market capitalization. And as if that was not enough, it also faced an accounting investigation by the Securities and Exchange Commission for how it accounted for its customer leases on copiers.

Enter new VP of HR Pat Nazemetz in 1999 and new CEO Anne Mulcahy in 2000 to try to right a sinking ship. Mulcahy put the company on a starvation diet. This entailed selling major operations in China and Hong Kong, reducing global headcount to 61,100 from 91,500 through selloffs, early retirements, and layoffs, and implementing drastic cost controls. While Mulcahy's strategy has brought Xerox back to life (2003 saw Xerox triple its net income to $360 million) as an organization, the HR function had to drive the change in the business while simultaneously transforming the function.

While many HR functions look to outsource, Xerox transformed its HR function largely internally. According to Nazemetz, outsourcing providers say "'Let us in, let us take over your HR function and we can take 10% to 30% out of your cost base.' We began trimming down, finding synergies and opportunities to get more efficient. We found the savings ourselves."

The largest single savings came from consolidating and expanding the HR Service Center. The Center began with purely transactional work (e.g., address changes), then added web-based processes to handle routine work. The Center now conducts research and analysis to HR operations and handles employee-relations issues. This has enabled HR to reduce headcount without reducing levels of service.

Also, as with any organization that has shed 30% of its workforce, employee morale was and continues to be an issue. Even before the fall, HR had been taking the pulse of employees through their "hearts and minds" surveys. This intranet-based survey taps into a number of employee attitudes and seeks to identify the problem areas for HR and line executives to focus on. Employees have noted concerns with items like "Company supports risk-taking," "Company considers impact on employees," "Senior-management behavior is consistent with words," and "Trust level is high."

"People often ask me how Xerox has found success," says Mulcahy. "My answer is that you have to have a strategy and a plan, but [more importantly], what you really need is excellence of execution, and that starts and ends with a talented, motivated group of people aligned around a common set of goals. Our HR people came through with a series of alignment workshops and retention incentives just when we needed them [to] make Xerox the stronger, better company it is today."

Questions

1. After having gone through the massive downsizing, morale obviously has presented challenges. While Xerox employees seem to understand the need for change (minds), they may not emotionally embrace it (hearts). How can Xerox gain both "hearts" and "minds"?
2. Xerox's HR function focuses on three initiatives: (a) employee value proposition (what can employees expect from the company, and what can the company expect from employees?), (b) performance culture (how can the company develop a culture that encourages continuous improvement and high performance from all employees?), and (c) "three exceptional candidates" (how can HR deliver a pipeline of three-deep bench talent for every position within the organization?). From everything you have learned, how might Xerox address each of these issues?

● MANAGING PEOPLE

Saving Starbucks' Soul

Chairman Howard Schultz is on a mission to take his company back to its roots. Oh, yeah—he also wants to triple sales in five years. *"A heady aroma of coffee reached out and drew me in. I stepped inside and saw what looked like a temple for the worship of coffee . . . it was my Mecca. I had arrived."—Howard Schultz on his first visit to Starbucks in 1981.*

On April 3, Starbucks launches a pair of confections called Dulce de Leche Latte and Dulce de Leche Frappuccino. A 16-oz. Grande latte has a robust 440 calories (about the same as two packages of M&M's) and costs about $4.50 in New York City—or about three times as much as McDonald's most expensive premium coffee. Starbucks Corp. describes its latest concoctions, which took 18 months to perfect, this way: "Topped with whipped cream and a dusting of toffee sprinkles, Starbucks' version of this traditional delicacy is a luxurious tasty treat."

If you find yourself at Starbucks in the next few weeks, letting a Dulce de Leche Latte slide over your taste buds, you might wonder how this drink came to be. It's a tale worth hearing. On the surface it's a story about how the Starbucks marketing machine conjures and sells café romance to millions of people around the world. On a deeper level it's a story about how a company, along with its messianic leader, is struggling to hold on to its soul.

Ask Schultz for the key to Starbucks and he'll tell you it's all about storytelling. Starbucks is centered on two oft-repeated tales: Schultz's trip to Seattle in 1981, where he first enjoyed gourmet coffee, and a 1983 trip to Milan, where he discovered espresso bar culture. Not only are these journeys useful touchstones for recruits, they also provide the original marketing story for a company that prides itself on giving customers an authentic experience.

"The one common thread to the success of these stories and the company itself," says Schultz, "is that they have to be true—and they have to be authentic."

True Believers

Stories alone aren't enough, though, to fuel Starbucks' other obsession: to grow really, really big. By 2012, Schultz aims to nearly triple annual sales, to $23.3 billion. The company also plans to have 40,000 stores worldwide, up from 13,500 today, not long after that, to hit its profit targets. Starbucks has become expert at something that's decidedly unromantic—streamlining operations. Over the past 10 years the company has redesigned the space behind the counter to boost barista efficiency. Automatic espresso machines speed the time it takes to serve up a shot. Coffee is vacuum-sealed, making it easier to ship over long distances. To boost sales, the company sells everything from breath mints to CDs to notebooks. Add it up and you have an experience that's nothing like the worn wooden counters of the first store in Pike Place Market or an Italian espresso bar.

Somewhere along the way that disconnect began to gnaw at Schultz. Most recently it manifested itself in a note he wrote to his senior team. The Valentine's Day memo, which leaked to the web, cut to the heart of what he sees as the company's dilemma. "We have had to make a series of decisions," Schultz wrote, "that, in retrospect, have led to the watering down of the Starbucks experience, and what some might call the commoditization of our brand."

Now, Schultz is asking his lieutenants to redouble their efforts to return to their roots. "We're constantly—I don't want to say battling—but we don't want to be that big company that's corporate and slick," says Michelle Gass, senior vice-president and chief merchant for global products. "We don't. We still think about ourselves as a small entrepreneurial company." That's a tricky business when you have 150,000 employees in 39 countries. But keeping that coffee joie de vivre alive inside Starbucks is crucial to Schultz's entire philosophy. Who better to sell something than a true believer?

In 2004, Starbucks introduced something called the Coffee Master program for its employees. It's a kind of extra-credit course that teaches the staff how to discern the subtleties of regional flavor. Graduates (there are now 25,000) earn a special black apron and an insignia on their business cards. The highlight is the "cupping ceremony," a tasting ritual traditionally used by coffee traders. After the grounds have steeped in boiling water, tasters "crest" the mixture, penetrating the crust on top with a spoon and inhaling the aroma. As employees slurp the brew, a Starbucks Coffee Educator encourages them to taste a Kenyan coffee's "citrusy" notes or the "mushroomy" flavor of a Sumatran blend.

If the ritual reminds you of a wine tasting, that's intentional. Schultz has long wanted to emulate the wine business. Winemakers, after all, command a premium by focusing on provenance: the region of origin, the vineyard, and, of course, the grape that gives the wine its particular notes—a story, in other words. Bringing wine's cachet to coffee would help take the brand upmarket and allow Starbucks to sell premium beans.

The product and marketing people call the strategy "Geography is a Flavor." And in 2005 they began selling this new story with whole-bean coffee. The company reorganized the menu behind the counter, grouping coffees by geography instead of by "smooth" or "bold." It replaced the colorful Starbucks coffee bags with clean white packages emblazoned with colored bands representing the region of origin. Later, for those connoisseurs willing to pay $28 a pound, Starbucks introduced single-origin beans called "Black Apron Exclusives."

The next step was to reach the masses who buy drinks in the stores. The team decided to launch a series of in-store promotions, each with a new set of drinks, that would communicate regional idiosyncrasies to customers. The first promotion, the team decided, would highlight Central and South America, where Starbucks buys more than 70% of its beans.

The sort of authenticity Schultz loves to talk about is hard to pull off when you're the size of Starbucks. Telling a story to a mass audience sometimes requires smoothing over inconvenient cultural nuances. Plus, the marketing folks have to work quickly to stay abreast of beverage trends, not to mention ahead of such rivals as Dunkin' Donuts and McDonald's. Diving deep is not an option.

A year ago, 10 Starbucks marketers and designers got on a plane and went looking for inspiration in Costa Rica. "It's being able to say: This is how and why this [drink] is made," says Angie McKenzie, who runs new product design. "Not because someone told us or we read it somewhere." The Starbucks team spent five days in Costa Rica, traveling on a minivan owned by TAM Tours. Later, a smaller group toured Mexico City and Oaxaca as well.

Made in China

The mission was to find products that would evoke an authentic vibe in the United States. That's harder than it sounds. Philip Clark, a merchandising executive, wanted to sell traditional Costa Rican mugs. But the ones typically used to drink coffee were drab and brown; they wouldn't pop on store shelves. Plus, they broke easily. Then he found Cecilia de Figueres, who handpaints ceramic mugs in a mountainside studio an hour from the capital, San Jose. The artist favors bright floral patterns; they would pop nicely. Starbucks paid de Figueres a flat fee for her designs. Each mug will have a tag bearing her name and likeness; on the bottom it will say "Made in China."

Starbucks will weave artisans and other Costa Ricans into the in-store promotional campaign. Painter Eloy Zuñiga Guevara will appear on a poster with a decidedly homespun Latin aesthetic. (And if customers want some authenticity to take home with them, they can buy one of five paintings of Costa Rican farmers that Guevara produced for Starbucks. They will sell for $25 apiece.) A second poster will feature Costa Rican coffee farmers from whom Starbucks buys beans. A third will show a grand-motherly figure cooking up dulce de leche on a gas stove. (She's a paid model from Seattle.) Each poster will feature the tagline "I am Starbucks."

Having devised a story, Starbucks needed a drink that would say "Latin America." Beverage brainstorming takes place in the Liquid Lab, an airy space painted in Star-bucks' familiar blue, green, and orange hues. The room features huge bulletin boards plastered with the latest bev-erage trends. In this case it didn't take an anthropologist to figure out which drink Starbucks should use to promote its Latin American theme.

Dulce de leche is a caramel-and-milk dessert enjoyed throughout much of the region. What's more, Häagen-Dazs introduced dulce de leche ice cream in 1998, and Starbucks followed suit with its own ice cream in 1999. So Americans are familiar with the flavor, says McKenzie, but "it still has a nice exotic edge to it." Besides, she adds, caramel and milk go great with coffee.

Even so, concocting a drink is never simple at Starbucks. The research-and-development department routinely tack-les 70 beverage projects a year, with 8 of them leading to new drinks. A drink must not only appeal to a broad swath of coffee drinkers but also be easy for a barista to make quickly so as to maximize sales per store (hello, Wall Street). "The store . . . is a little manufacturing plant," says Gass, and yet it must seem as though the drink is being handcrafted spe-cially for the customer (hello, Howard Schultz).

Creating the Dulce de Leche Latte and Frappuccino fell to Debbie Ismon, a 26-year-old beverage developer who holds a degree in food science and has worked at Starbucks for 2 1/2 years. In late June 2006, the design team brought her a small sample they'd whipped up that they felt embodied the right tastes, plus a written description of the characteristics they hoped to see. For the next four months, Ismon fiddled with various ratios of caramel, cooked milk, and sweetness "notes." After the design group decided which version tasted most "in-concept," Ismon mixed up three different flavors for the big taste test. One hundred or so random Starbucks employees filed in, sampled the drinks, and rated them on computer screens. The process was repeated two more times for each drink. Finally, 18 months after starting the process, Starbucks had its two latest premium beverages.

If previous drinks, such as Caramel Macchiato, are any guide, Starbucks' Dulce de Leche drinks will sell briskly. That should please Wall Street and perhaps even help perk up the stock, which is down 20% from its May 2006 high on worries that operating margins are falling and that Starbucks could miss its ambitious growth targets.

And as you wait in line for your Dulce de Leche Latte, you might ask yourself: Are you paying $4.50 for a caffeine jolt and caramel topping? Or have you simply been dazzled by Howard Schultz's storytelling magic?

Questions

1. What are some of the HRM issues inherent in Howard Schultz's concerns?
2. How would an effective strategic HRM function con-tribute to keeping Starbucks on track?

SOURCE: From B. Helm, "Saving Starbucks' Soul," *BusinessWeek*, April 9, 2007, pp. 56–61. Used with permission of Bloomberg L. P. Copyright © 2007. All rights reserved.

TWITTER FOCUS: EMPLOYEES MAKE A DIFFERENCE AT AMY'S ICE CREAMS

Using Twitter, continue the conversation about strategi-cally managing the HRM function by reading the Amy's Ice Creams case at www.mhhe.com/noe8e.

Fun is the name of the game for employees as well as customers at Amy's Ice Creams in the Austin, Texas, area. Founder Amy Miller's goal is to manage her employ-ees in a different way—one that combines informal fun with care for others. The employee selection process involves handing candidates a white paper bag with the

instruction to "make something creative." Service to the community is also an important employee activity at Amy's—employees choose the charities the company will support.

Engage with your classmates and instructor via Twit-ter to chat about Amy's unique approach to HRM using the case questions posted on the Noe website. Don't have a Twitter account yet? See the instructions for getting started on the Online Learning Center.

NOTES

1. P. Wright, S. Snell, and P. Jacobsen, "Current Approaches to HR Strategies: Inside-Out vs. Outside-In," *Human Resource Planning* (in press).
2. Personal communication, June 2010.
3. A. S. Tsui and L. R. Gomez-Mejia, "Evaluating HR Effectiveness," in *Human Resource Management: Evolving Roles and Responsibilities*, ed. L. Dyer (Washington, DC: Bureau of National Affairs, 1988), pp. 1-187–1-227.
4. D. Ulrich, "Measuring Human Resources: An Overview of Practice and a Prescription for Results," *Human Resource Management* 36, no. 3 (1997), pp. 303–20.
5. P. Wright, G. McMahan, S. Snell, and B. Gerhart, "Comparing Line and HR Executives' Perceptions of HR Effectiveness: Services, Roles, and Contributions," CAHRS (Center for Advanced Human Resource Studies) working paper 98-29, School of ILR, Cornell University, Ithaca, NY.
6. J. C. Erfurt, A. Foote, and M. A. Heirich, "The Cost-Effectiveness of Worksite Wellness Programs," *Personnel Psychology* 15 (1992), p. 22.
7. T. H. Davenport, J. Haris, and J. Shapiro, "Competing on Talent Analytics," *Harvard Business Review*, October 2010, pp. 52–59.
8. P. Wright, G. McMahan, S. Snell, and B. Gerhart, *Strategic HRM: Building Human Capital and Organizational Capability*, Technical report. Cornell University, Ithaca, NY, 1998.
9. T. B. Kinni, "A Reengineering Primer," *Quality Digest*, January 1994, pp. 26–30; "Reengineering Is Helping Health of Hospitals and Its Patients," *Total Quality Newsletter*, February 1994, p. 5; R. Recardo, "Process Reengineering in a Finance Division," *Journal for Quality and Participation*, June 1994, pp. 70–73.
10. L. Quillen, "Human Resource Computerization: A Dollar and Cents Approach," *Personnel Journal*, July 1989, pp. 74–77.
11. S. Greengard, "New Technology Is HR's Route to Reengineering," *Personnel Journal*, July 1994, pp. 32c–32o.
12. R. Broderick and J. W. Boudreau, "Human Resource Management, Information Technology, and the Competitive Edge," *Academy of Management Executive* 6 (1992), pp. 7–17.
13. S. E. O'Connell, "New Technologies Bring New Tools, New Rules," *HR Magazine*, December 1995, pp. 43–48; S. F. O'Connell, "The Virtual Workplace Moves at Warp Speed," *HR Magazine*, March 1996, pp. 51–57.
14. E. Brynjolfsson and L. Hitt, "The Productivity Paradox of Information Technology," *Communications of the ACM*, December 1993, pp. 66–77.
15. "Seven Critical Success Factors for Using Information Technology," *Total Quality Newsletter*, February 1994, p. 6.
16. J. E. Rigdon, "Technological Gains Are Cutting Costs in Jobs and Services," *The Wall Street Journal*, February 24, 1995, pp. A1, A5, A6.
17. S. Greengard, "How Technology Is Advancing HR," *Personnel Journal*, September 1993, pp. 80–90.
18. T. L. Hunter, "How Client/Server Is Reshaping the HRIS," *Personnel Journal*, July 1992, pp. 38–46; B. Busbin, "The Hidden Costs of Client/Server," *The Review*, August–September 1995, pp. 21–24.
19. D. Drechsel, "Principles for Client/Server Success," *The Review*, August–September 1995, pp. 26–29.
20. A. L. Lederer, "Emerging Technology and the Buy–Wait Dilemma: Sorting Fact from Fantasy," *The Review*, June–July 1993, pp. 16–19.
21. D. L. Fowler, "Imaging in HR: A Case Study," *The Review*, October–November 1994, pp. 29–33.
22. "Dial a Job Interview," *Chain Store Age Executive*, July 1994, pp. 35–36.
23. P. A. Galagan, "Think Performance: A Conversation with Gloria Gery," *Training and Development*, March 1994, pp. 47–51.
24. J. Clark and R. Koonce, "Meetings Go High-Tech," *Training and Development*, November 1995, pp. 32–38; A. M. Townsend, M. E. Whitman, and A. R. Hendrickson, "Computer Support Adds Power to Group Processes," *HR Magazine*, September 1995, pp. 87–91.
25. B. Ziegler, "Internet Software Poses Big Threat to Notes, IBM's Stake in Lotus," *The Wall Street Journal*, November 7, 1995, pp. A1, A8.
26. S. Shrivastava and J. Shaw, "Liberating HR through Technology," *Human Resource Management* 42, no. 3 (2003), pp. 201–17.
27. C. O'Reilly and P. Caldwell, *Cypress Semiconductor (A): Vision, Values, and Killer Software* (Stanford University Case Study, HR-8A, 1998).
28. "61 Percent of Americans Consider Themselves Overworked and 86 Percent Are Not Satisfied with Their Job, According to Monster's 2004 Work/Life Balance Survey," *Business Wire*, August 3, 2004.
29. G. McMahan and R. Woodman, "The Current Practice of Organization Development within the Firm: A Survey of Large Industrial Corporations," *Group and Organization Studies* 17 (1992), pp. 117–34.
30. B. Becker, M. Huselid, and D. Ulrich, *The HR Scorecard: Linking People, Strategy, and Performance* (Cambridge, MA: HBS Press, 2001).
31. D. Ulrich and A. Yeung, "A Shared Mindset," *Personnel Administrator*, March 1989, pp. 38–45.
32. G. Jones and P. Wright, "An Economic Approach to Conceptualizing the Utility of Human Resource Management Practices," *Research in Personnel/Human Resources* 10 (1992), pp. 271–99.
33. R. Schuler and J. Walker, "Human Resources Strategy: Focusing on Issues and Actions," *Organizational Dynamics*, Summer 1990, pp. 5–19.
34. Company documents.
35. P. Wright, "Strategies and Challenges of the Chief Human Resource Officer: Results of the First Annual Cornell/CAHRS Survey of CHROs," Technical report, 2009.
36. Ibid.
37. Ibid.
38. J. Paauwe, *Human Resource Management and Performance: Unique Approaches for Achieving Long-Term Viability* (Oxford: Oxford University Press, 2004).
39. S. Csoka and B. Hackett, *Transforming the HR Function for Global Business Success* (New York: Conference Board, 1998), Report 1209-19RR.

GLOSSARY

Acceptability The extent to which a performance measure is deemed to be satisfactory or adequate by those who use it.

Action learning Teams work on an actual business problem, commit to an action plan, and are accountable for carrying out the plan.

Action plan Document summarizing what the trainee and manager will do to ensure that training transfers to the job.

Action steps The part of a written affirmative plan that specifies what an employer plans to do to reduce underutilization of protected groups.

Adventure learning Learning focused on the development of teamwork and leadership skills by using structured outdoor activities.

Agency shop A union security provision that requires an employee to pay union membership dues but not to join the union.

Agent In agency theory, a person (e.g., a manager) who is expected to act on behalf of a principal (e.g., an owner).

Alternative dispute resolution (ADR) A method of resolving disputes that does not rely on the legal system. Often proceeds through the four stages of open door policy, peer review, mediation, and arbitration.

Alternative work arrangements Independent contractors, on-call workers, temporary workers, and contract company workers who are not employed full-time by the company.

Americans with Disabilities Act (ADA) A 1990 act prohibiting individuals with disabilities from being discriminated against in the workplace.

Analytic approach Type of assessment of HRM effectiveness that involves determining the impact of, or the financial costs and benefits of, a program or practice.

Anticipatory socialization Process that helps individuals develop expectations about the company, job, working conditions, and interpersonal relationships.

Appraisal politics A situation in which evaluators purposefully distort a rating to achieve personal or company goals.

Apprenticeship A work-study training method with both on-the-job and classroom training.

Arbitration A procedure for resolving collective bargaining impasses by which an arbitrator chooses a solution to the dispute.

Assessment Collecting information and providing feedback to employees about their behavior, communication style, or skills.

Associate union membership A form of union membership by which the union receives dues in exchange for services (e.g., health insurance, credit cards) but does not provide representation in collective bargaining.

Attitudinal structuring The aspect of the labor–management negotiation process that refers to the relationship and level of trust between the negotiators.

Audiovisual instruction Includes overheads, slides, and video.

Audit approach Type of assessment of HRM effectiveness that involves review of customer satisfaction or key indicators (e.g., turnover rate, average days to fill a position) related to an HRM functional area (e.g., recruiting, training).

Avatars Computer depictions of humans that can be used as imaginary coaches, co-workers, and customers in simulations.

Balanced scorecard A means of performance measurement that gives managers a chance to look at their company from the perspectives of internal and external customers, employees, and shareholders.

Benchmarking Comparing an organization's practices against those of the competition.

Benchmarks© An instrument designed to measure the factors that are important to managerial success.

Blended learning Delivering content and instruction with a combination of technology-based and face-to-face methods.

Bona fide occupational qualification (BFOQ) A job qualification based on race, sex, religion, and so on that an employer asserts is a necessary qualification for the job.

Calibration meetings A way to discuss employees' performance with the goal of ensuring that similar standards are applied to their evaluations.

Career support Coaching, protection, sponsorship, and providing challenging assignments, exposure, and visibility.

Cash balance plan Retirement plan in which the employer sets up an individual account for each employee and contributes a percentage of the employee's salary; the account earns interest at a predetermined rate.

Centralization Degree to which decision-making authority resides at the top of the organizational chart.

Checkoff provision A union contract provision that requires an employer to deduct union dues from employees' paychecks.

Client–server architecture Computer design that provides a method to consolidate data and applications into a single host system (the client).

Climate for transfer Trainees' perceptions of characteristics of the work environment (social support and situational constraints) that can either facilitate or inhibit use of trained skills or behavior.

Closed shop A union security provision requiring a person to be a union member before being hired. Illegal under NLRA.

Coach A peer or manager who works with an employee to motivate her, help her develop skills, and provide reinforcement and feedback.

Cognitive ability tests Tests that include three dimensions: verbal comprehension, quantitative ability, and reasoning ability.

Communities of practice Groups of employees who work together, learn from each other, and develop a common understanding of how to get work accomplished.

Comparable worth A public policy that advocates remedies for any undervaluation of women's jobs (also called *pay equity*).

Compa-ratio An index of the correspondence between actual and intended pay.

Compensable factors The characteristics of jobs that an organization values and chooses to pay for.

Competencies Sets of skills, knowledge, and abilities and personal characteristics that enable employees to perform their jobs.

Competency model Identifies and provides a description of competencies that are common for an entire occupation, organization, job family, or specific job.

Competitiveness A company's ability to maintain and gain market share in its industry.

Concentration strategy A strategy focusing on increasing market share, reducing costs, or creating and maintaining a market niche for products and services.

Concurrent validation A criterion-related validity study in which a test is administered to all the people currently in a job and then incumbents' scores are correlated with existing measures of their performance on the job.

Consolidated Omnibus Budget Reconciliation Act (COBRA) The 1985 act that requires employers to permit employees to extend their health insurance coverage at group rates for up to 36 months following a qualifying event, such as a layoff.

Content validation A test validation strategy performed by demonstrating that the items, questions, or problems posed by a test are a representative sample of the kinds of situations or problems that occur on the job.

Continuous learning A learning system that requires employees to understand the entire work process and expects them to acquire new skills, apply them on the job, and share what they have learned with other employees.

Coordination training Training a team in how to share information and decision-making responsibilities to maximize team performance.

Corporate campaigns Union activities designed to exert public, financial, or political pressure on employers during the union-organizing process.

Cost–benefit analysis The process of determining the economic benefits of a training program using accounting methods.

Counselor/confidante/coach to the executive team A role of the CHRO that focuses on counseling or coaching team members or resolving interpersonal or political conflicts among team members.

Criterion-related validity A method of establishing the validity of a personnel selection method by showing a substantial correlation between test scores and job performance scores.

Cross-cultural preparation The process of educating employees (and their families) who are given an assignment in a foreign country.

Cross-training Training in which team members understand and practice each other's skills so that members are prepared to step in and take another member's place should he or she temporarily or permanently leave the team.

Decision support systems Problem-solving systems that usually include a "what-if" feature that allows users to see how outcomes change when assumptions or data change.

Delayering Reducing the number of job levels within an organization.

Departmentalization Degree to which work units are grouped based on functional similarity or similarity of workflow.

Development The acquisition of knowledge, skills, and behaviors that improve an employee's ability to meet changes in job requirements and in client and customer demands.

Development planning system A system to retain and motivate employees by identifying and meeting their development needs (also called *career management systems*).

Direct applicants People who apply for a job vacancy without prompting from the organization.

Disparate impact A theory of discrimination based on facially neutral employment practices that disproportionately exclude a protected group from employment opportunities.

Disparate treatment A theory of discrimination based on different treatment given to individuals because of their race, color, religion, sex, national origin, age, or disability status.

Distributive bargaining The part of the labor–management negotiation process that focuses on dividing a fixed economic "pie."

Diversity training Refers to learning efforts that are designed to change employees' attitudes about diversity and/or develop skills needed to work with a diverse workforce.

Downsizing The planned elimination of large numbers of personnel, designed to enhance organizational effectiveness.

Downward move A job change involving a reduction in an employee's level of responsibility and authority.

Due process policies Policies by which a company formally lays out the steps an employee can take to appeal a termination decision.

Duty of fair representation The National Labor Relations Act requirement that all bargaining unit members have equal access to and representation by the union.

Efficiency wage theory A theory stating that wage influences worker productivity.

E-learning Instruction and delivery of training by computers through the Internet or company intranet.

Electronic business (e-business) Any business that a company conducts electronically.

Electronic human resource management (e-HRM) The processing and transmission of digitized information used in HRM.

Electronic performance support systems (EPSS) Computer applications that can provide (as requested) skills training, information access, and expert advice.

Employee assistance programs (EAPs) Employer programs that attempt to ameliorate problems encountered by workers who are drug dependent, alcoholic, or psychologically troubled.

Employee engagement The degree to which employees are fully involved in their work and the strength of their job and company commitment.

Employee Retirement Income Security Act (ERISA) The 1974 act that increased the fiduciary responsibilities of pension plan trustees, established vesting rights and portability provisions, and established the Pension Benefit Guaranty Corporation (PBGC).

Employee stock ownership plan (ESOP) An employee ownership plan that provides employers certain tax and financial advantages when stock is granted to employees.

Employment-at-will doctrine The doctrine that, in the absence of a specific contract, either an employer or employee could sever the employment relationship at any time.

Employment-at-will policies Policies which state that either an employer or employee can terminate the employment relationship at any time, regardless of cause.

Empowering Giving employees the responsibility and authority to make decisions.

Encounter phase Phase of socialization that occurs when an employee begins a new job.

Equal employment opportunity (EEO) The government's attempt to ensure that all individuals have an equal opportunity for employment, regardless of race, color, religion, sex, age, disability, or national origin.

Equal Employment Opportunity Commission (EEOC) The government commission established to ensure that all individuals have an equal opportunity for employment, regardless of race, color, religion, sex, age, disability, or national origin.

Ergonomics The interface between individuals' physiological characteristics and the physical work environment.

Evidence-based HR Demonstrating that human resource practices have a positive influence on the company's bottom line or key stakeholders (employees, customers, community, shareholders).

Exempt Employees who are not covered by the Fair Labor Standards Act. Exempt employees are not eligible for overtime pay.

Expatriate Employee sent by his or her company to manage operations in a different country.

Expectancy theory The theory that says motivation is a function of valence, instrumentality, and expectancy.

Expert systems Computer systems incorporating the decision rules of people recognized as experts in a certain area.

Explicit knowledge Knowledge that is well-documented and easily transferred to other persons.

External analysis Examining the organization's operating environment to identify strategic opportunities and threats.

External growth strategy An emphasis on acquiring vendors and suppliers or buying businesses that allow a company to expand into new markets.

External labor market Persons outside the firm who are actively seeking employment.

Externship When a company allows an employee to take a full-time operational role at another company.

Fact finder A person who reports on the reasons for a labor–management dispute, the views and arguments of both sides, and a nonbinding recommendation for settling the dispute.

Fair Labor Standards Act (FLSA) The 1938 law that established the minimum wage and overtime pay.

Family and Medical Leave Act The 1993 act that requires employers with 50 or more employees to provide up to 12 weeks of unpaid leave after childbirth or adoption; to care for a seriously ill child, spouse, or parent; or for an employee's own serious illness.

Financial Accounting Statement (FAS) 106 The rule issued by the Financial Accounting Standards Board in 1993 requiring companies to fund benefits provided after retirement on an accrual rather than a pay-as-you-go basis and to enter these future cost obligations on their financial statements.

Forecasting The attempts to determine the supply of and demand for various types of human resources to predict areas within the organization where there will be future labor shortages or surpluses.

Formal education programs Employee development programs, including short courses offered by consultants or universities, executive MBA programs, and university programs.

Formal training Training and development programs and courses that are developed and organized by the company.

Four-fifths rule A rule that states that an employment test has disparate impact if the hiring rate for a minority group is less than four-fifths, or 80 %, of the hiring rate for the majority group.

Frame of reference A standard point that serves as a comparison for other points and thus provides meaning.

Gainsharing A form of group compensation based on group or plant performance (rather than organization-wide profits) that does not become part of the employee's base salary.

General duty clause The provision of the Occupational Safety and Health Act that states an employer has an overall obligation to furnish employees with a place of employment free from recognized hazards.

Generalizability The degree to which the validity of a selection method established in one context extends to other contexts.

Glass ceiling A barrier to advancement to higher-level jobs in the company that adversely affects women and minorities. The barrier may be due to lack of access to training programs, development experiences, or relationships (e.g., mentoring).

Goals What an organization hopes to achieve in the medium- to long-term future.

Goals and timetables The part of a written affirmative action plan that specifies the percentage of women and minorities that an employer seeks to have in each job group and the date by which that percentage is to be attained.

Group mentoring program A program pairing a successful senior employee with a group of four to six less experienced protégés.

Group- or team-building methods Training methods that help trainees share ideas and experiences, build group identity, understand the dynamics of interpersonal relationships, and get to know their own strengths and weaknesses and those of their co-workers.

Groupware Software application that enables multiple users to track, share, and organize information and to work on the same database or document simultaneously.

Hands-on methods Training methods that require the trainee to be actively involved in learning.

Health maintenance organization (HMO) A health care plan that provides benefits on a prepaid basis for employees who are required to use only HMO medical service providers.

High-performance work systems Work systems that maximize the fit between employees and technology.

High-potential employees Employees the company believes are capable of being successful in high-level management positions.

Host country The country in which the parent-country organization seeks to locate or has already located a facility.

Host-country nationals (HCNs) Employees born and raised in a host, not parent, country.

HR or workforce analytics The practice of using data from HR databases and other data sources to make evidence-based human resource decisions.

HR dashboard HR metrics (such as productivity and absenteeism) that are accessible by employees and managers through the company intranet or human resource information system.

Human resource information system (HRIS) A system used to acquire, store, manipulate, analyze, retrieve, and distribute information related to human resources.

Human resource management (HRM) The policies, practices, and systems that influence employees' behavior, attitudes, and performances.

Human resource recruitment The practice or activity carried on by the organization with the primary purpose of identifying and attracting potential employees.

Imaging A process for scanning documents, storing them electronically, and retrieving them.

In-basket A simulation of the administrative tasks of a manager's job.

Inclusion Creating an environment in which employees share a sense of belonging, mutual respect, and commitment with others so they can perform their best work.

Individualism–collectivism One of Hofstede's cultural dimensions; describes the strength of the relation between an individual and other individuals in a society.

Informal learning Learning that is learner initiated, involves action and doing, is motivated by an intent to develop, and does not occur in a formal learning setting.

Intangible assets A type of company asset including human capital, customer capital, social capital, and intellectual capital.

Integrative bargaining The part of the labor–management negotiation process that seeks solutions beneficial to both sides.

Intellectual capital Creativity, productivity, and service provided by employees.

Interactional justice A concept of justice referring to the interpersonal nature of how the outcomes were implemented.

Internal analysis The process of examining an organization's strengths and weaknesses.

Internal growth strategy A focus on new market and product development, innovation, and joint ventures.

Internal labor force Labor force of current employees.

Interview Employees are questioned about their work and personal experiences, skills, and career plans.

Intraorganizational bargaining The part of the labor–management negotiation process that focuses on the conflicting objectives of factions within labor and management.

Involuntary turnover Turnover initiated by the organization (often among people who would prefer to stay).

ISO 9000:2000 A series of quality assurance standards developed by the International Organization for Standardization in Switzerland and adopted worldwide.

Job analysis The process of getting detailed information about jobs.

Job description A list of the tasks, duties, and responsibilities that a job entails.

Job design The process of defining the way work will be performed and the tasks that will be required in a given job.

Job enlargement Adding challenges or new responsibilities to an employee's current job.

Job enrichment Ways to add complexity and meaningfulness to a person's work.

Job evaluation An administrative procedure used to measure internal job worth.

Job experience The relationships, problems, demands, tasks, and other features that employees face in their jobs.

Job hazard analysis technique A breakdown of each job into basic elements, each of which is rated for its potential for harm or injury.

Job involvement The degree to which people identify themselves with their jobs.

Job redesign The process of changing the tasks or the way work is performed in an existing job.

Job rotation The process of systematically moving a single individual from one job to another over the course of time. The job assignments may be in various functional areas of the company or movement may be between jobs in a single functional area or department.

Job satisfaction A pleasurable feeling that results from the perception that one's job fulfills or allows for the fulfillment of one's important job values.

Job specification A list of the knowledge, skills, abilities, and other characteristics (KSAOs) that an individual must have to perform a job.

Job structure The relative pay of jobs in an organization.

Kaizen Practices participated by employees from all levels of the company that focus on continuous improvement of business processes.

Key jobs Benchmark jobs, used in pay surveys, that have relatively stable content and are common to many organizations.

Knowledge management Process of enhancing company performance by designing and using tools, systems, and cultures to improve creation, sharing, and use of knowledge.

Knowledge workers Employees who own the intellectual means of producing a product or service.

Leader of the HR function A role of the CHRO that focuses on working with HR team members regarding the development, design, and delivery of HR services.

Leaderless group discussion Process in which a team of five to seven employees solves an assigned problem within a certain time period.

Leading indicator An objective measure that accurately predicts future labor demand.

Lean thinking A way to do more with less effort, equipment, space, and time, but providing customers with what they need and want.

Learning management system (LMS) Technology platform that automates the administration, development, and delivery of a company's training program.

Learning organization An organization whose employees are continuously attempting to learn new things and apply what they have learned to improve product or service quality.

Liaison to the board of directors A role of the CHRO that focuses on preparation for board meetings, phone calls with board members, and attendance at board meetings.

Long-term–short-term orientation One of Hofstede's cultural dimensions; describes how a culture balances immediate benefits with future rewards.

Maintenance of membership Union rules requiring members to remain members for a certain period of time (e.g., the length of the union contract).

Malcolm Baldrige National Quality Award An award established in 1987 to promote quality awareness, to recognize quality achievements of U.S. companies, and to publicize successful quality strategies.

Managing diversity The process of creating an environment that allows all employees to contribute to organizational goals and experience personal growth.

Marginal tax rate The percentage of an additional dollar of earnings that goes to taxes.

Masculinity–femininity dimension One of Hofstede's cultural dimensions; describes the division of roles between the sexes within a society.

Mediation A procedure for resolving collective bargaining impasses by which a mediator with no formal authority acts as a facilitator and go-between in the negotiations.

Mentor An experienced, productive senior employee who helps develop a less experienced employee.

Merit increase grid A grid that combines an employee's performance rating with his or her position in a pay range to determine the size and frequency of his or her pay increases.

Minimum wage The lowest amount that employers are legally allowed to pay; the 1990 amendment of the Fair Labor Standards Act permits a subminimum wage to workers under the age of 20 for a period of up to 90 days.

Motivation to learn The desire of the trainee to learn the content of a training program.

Myers-Briggs Type Inventory (MBTI)® A psychological test used for team building and leadership development that identifies employees' preferences for energy, information gathering, decision making, and lifestyle.

Needs assessment The process used to determine if training is necessary.

Negative affectivity A dispositional dimension that reflects pervasive individual differences in satisfaction with any and all aspects of life.

Network A combination of desktop computers, computer terminals, and mainframes or minicomputers that share access to databases and a method to transmit information throughout the system.

New technologies Current applications of knowledge, procedures, and equipment that have not been previously used. Usually involves replacing human labor with equipment, information processing, or some combination of the two.

Nonkey jobs Jobs that are unique to organizations and that cannot be directly valued or compared through the use of market surveys.

Objective The purpose and expected outcome of training activities.

Occupational Safety and Health Act (OSHA) The 1970 law that authorizes the federal government to establish and enforce occupational safety and health standards for all places of employment engaging in interstate commerce.

Offshoring A special case of outsourcing where the jobs that move actually leave one country and go to another.

Onshoring Exporting jobs to rural parts of the United States.

On-the-job training (OJT) Peers or managers training new or inexperienced employees who learn the job by observation, understanding, and imitation.

Opportunity to perform   The trainee is provided with or actively seeks experience using newly learned knowledge, skills, or behavior.

Organizational analysis   A process for determining the business appropriateness of training.

Organizational commitment   The degree to which an employee identifies with the organization and is willing to put forth effort on its behalf.

Organizational socialization   The process by which new employees are transformed into effective members of a company.

Outcome fairness   The judgment that people make with respect to the outcomes received relative to the outcomes received by other people with whom they identify.

Outplacement counseling   Counseling to help displaced employees manage the transition from one job to another.

Output   A job's performance standards.

Outsourcing   An organization's use of an outside organization for a broad set of services.

Parent country   The country in which a company's corporate headquarters is located.

Parent-country nationals (PCNs)   Employees who were born and live in a parent country.

Pay grades   Jobs of similar worth or content grouped together for pay administration purposes.

Pay level   The average pay, including wages, salaries, and bonuses, of jobs in an organization.

Pay policy line   A mathematical expression that describes the relationship between a job's pay and its job evaluation points.

Pay structure   The relative pay of different jobs (job structure) and how much they are paid (pay level).

Pension Benefit Guaranty Corporation (PBGC)   The agency that guarantees to pay employees a basic retirement benefit in the event that financial difficulties force a company to terminate or reduce employee pension benefits.

Performance appraisal   The process through which an organization gets information on how well an employee is doing his or her job.

Performance feedback   The process of providing employees information regarding their performance effectiveness.

Performance management   The means through which managers ensure that employees' activities and outputs are congruent with the organization's goals.

Person analysis   A process for determining whether employees need training, who needs training, and whether employees are ready for training.

Power distance   One of Hofstede's cultural dimensions; concerns how a culture deals with hierarchical power relationships—particularly the unequal distribution of power.

Predictive validation   A criterion-related validity study that seeks to establish an empirical relationship between applicants' test scores and their eventual performance on the job.

Preferred provider organization (PPO)   A group of health care providers who contract with employers, insurance companies, and so forth to provide health care at a reduced fee.

Presentation methods   Training methods in which trainees are passive recipients of information.

Principal   In agency theory, a person (e.g., the owner) who seeks to direct another person's behavior.

Procedural justice   A concept of justice focusing on the methods used to determine the outcomes received.

Profit sharing   A compensation plan in which payments are based on a measure of organization performance (profits) and do not become part of the employees' base salary.

Progression of withdrawal   Theory that dissatisfied individuals enact a set of behaviors to avoid the work situation.

Promotions   Advances into positions with greater challenge, more responsibility, and more authority than the employee's previous job.

Prosocial motivation   The degree to which people are motivated to help other people.

Protean career   A career that is frequently changing due to both changes in the person's interests, abilities, and values and changes in the work environment.

Psychological success   The feeling of pride and accomplishment that comes from achieving life goals.

Psychosocial support   Serving as a friend and role model, providing positive regard and acceptance, and creating an outlet for a protégé to talk about anxieties and fears.

Quantitative ability   Concerns the speed and accuracy with which one can solve arithmetic problems of all kinds.

Range spread   The distance between the minimum and maximum amounts in a pay grade.

Rate ranges   Different employees in the same job may have different pay rates.

Realistic job preview   Provides accurate information about the attractive and unattractive aspects of a job, working conditions, company, and location to ensure that potential employees develop appropriate expectations.

Reasonable accommodation   Making facilities readily accessible to and usable by individuals with disabilities.

Reasoning ability   Refers to a person's capacity to invent solutions to many diverse problems.

Recruitment   The process of seeking applicants for potential employment.

Reengineering   Review and redesign of work processes to make them more efficient and improve the quality of the end product or service.

Referrals   People who are prompted to apply for a job by someone within the organization.

Relational database   A database structure that stores information in separate files that can be linked by common elements.

Reliability   The consistency of a performance measure; the degree to which a performance measure is free from random error.

Repatriation   The preparation of expatriates for return to the parent company and country from a foreign assignment.

Representative of the firm   A role of the CHRO that focuses on activities with external stakeholders, such as lobbying, speaking to outside groups, etc.

Repurposing   Directly translating instructor-led training online.

Right-to-work laws   State laws that make union shops, maintenance of membership, and agency shops illegal.

Role behaviors   Behaviors that are required of an individual in his or her role as a job holder in a social work environment.

Role-play   A participant taking the part or role of a manager or other employee.

Sabbatical   A leave of absence from the company to renew or develop skills.

Safety awareness programs   Employer programs that attempt to instill symbolic and substantive changes in the organization's emphasis on safety.

Sarbanes-Oxley Act of 2002   A congressional act passed in response to illegal and unethical behavior by managers and executives. The act sets stricter rules for business, especially accounting practices including requiring more open and consistent disclosure of financial data, CEOs' assurance that data are completely accurate, and provisions that affect the employee–employer relationship (e.g., development of a code of conduct for senior financial officers).

Selection   The process by which an organization attempts to identify applicants with the necessary knowledge, skills, abilities, and other characteristics that will help it achieve its goals.

Self-service   Giving employees online access to human resources information.

Settling-in phase   Phase of socialization that occurs when employees are comfortable with job demands and social relationships.

Shared service model   A way to organize the HR function that includes centers of expertise or excellence, service centers, and business partners.

Simulation   A training method that represents a real-life situation, allowing trainees to see the outcomes of their decisions in an artificial environment.

Situational interview   An interview procedure where applicants are confronted with specific issues, questions, or problems that are likely to arise on the job.

Six Sigma process   System of measuring, analyzing, improving, and controlling processes once they meet quality standards.

Six Sigma training   An action training program that provides employees with defect-reducing tools to cut costs and certifies employees as green belts, champions, or black belts.

Skill-based pay   Pay based on the skills employees acquire and are capable of using.

Specificity   The extent to which a performance measure gives detailed guidance to employees about what is expected of them and how they can meet these expectations.

Stakeholders   The various interest groups who have relationships with and, consequently, whose interests are tied to the organization (e.g., employees, suppliers, customers, shareholders, community).

Standard deviation rule   A rule used to analyze employment tests to determine disparate impact; it uses the difference between the expected representation for minority groups and the actual representation to determine whether the difference between the two is greater than would occur by chance.

Stock options   An employee ownership plan that gives employees the opportunity to buy the company's stock at a previously fixed price.

Strategic advisor to the executive team   A role of the CHRO that focuses on the formulation and implementation of the firm's strategy.

Strategic choice   The organization's strategy; the ways an organization will attempt to fulfill its mission and achieve its long-term goals.

Strategic congruence   The extent to which the performance management system elicits job performance that is consistent with the organization's strategy, goals, and culture.

Strategic human resource management (SHRM)   A pattern of planned human resource deployments and activities intended to enable an organization to achieve its goals.

Strategic training and development initiatives Learning-related actions that a company takes to achieve its business strategy.

Strategy formulation The process of deciding on a strategic direction by defining a company's mission and goals, its external opportunities and threats, and its internal strengths and weaknesses.

Strategy implementation The process of devising structures and allocating resources to enact the strategy a company has chosen.

Succession planning The identification and tracking of high-potential employees capable of filling higher-level managerial positions.

Summary plan description (SPD) A reporting requirement of the Employee Retirement Income Security Act (ERISA) that obligates employers to describe the plan's funding, eligibility requirements, risks, and so forth within 90 days after an employee has entered the plan.

Support network Trainees who meet to discuss their progress in using learned capabilities on the job.

Sustainability The ability of a company to make a profit without sacrificing the resources of its employees, the community, or the environment. Based on an approach to organizational decision making that considers the long-term impact of strategies on stakeholders (e.g., employees, shareholders, suppliers, community).

Tacit knowledge Knowledge based on personal experience that is difficult to codify.

Taft-Hartley Act The 1947 act that outlawed unfair union labor practices.

Talent architect A role of the CHRO that focuses on building and identifying the human capital critical to the present and future of the firm.

Talent management Attracting, retaining, developing, and motivating highly skilled employees and managers.

Task analysis The process of identifying the tasks, knowledge, skills, and behaviors that need to be emphasized in training.

Team leader training Training of the team manager or facilitator.

Technic of operations review (TOR) Method of determining safety problems via an analysis of past accidents.

Teleconferencing Synchronous exchange of audio, video, or text between individuals or groups at two or more locations.

Third country A country other than a host or parent country.

Third-country nationals (TCNs) Employees born in a country other than a parent or host country.

360-degree appraisal (feedback systems) A performance appraisal process for managers that includes evaluations from a wide range of persons who interact with the manager. The process includes self-evaluations as well as evaluations from the manager's boss, subordinates, peers, and customers.

Total quality management (TQM) A cooperative form of doing business that relies on the talents and capabilities of both labor and management to continually improve quality and productivity.

Training A planned effort to facilitate the learning of job-related knowledge, skills, and behavior by employees.

Training design process A systematic approach for developing training programs.

Training outcomes A way to evaluate the effectiveness of a training program based on cognitive, skill-based, affective, and results outcomes.

Transaction processing Computations and calculations used to review and document HRM decisions and practices.

Transfer The movement of an employee to a different job assignment in a different area of the company.

Transfer of training The use of knowledge, skills, and behaviors learned in training on the job.

Transitional matrix Matrix showing the proportion or number of employees in different job categories at different times.

Transnational process The extent to which a company's planning and decision-making processes include representatives and ideas from a variety of cultures.

Transnational representation Reflects the multinational composition of a company's managers.

Transnational scope A company's ability to make HRM decisions from an international perspective.

Tuition reimbursement The practice of reimbursing employees' costs for college and university courses and degree programs.

Uncertainty avoidance One of Hofstede's cultural dimensions; describes how cultures seek to deal with an unpredictable future.

Union shop A union security provision that requires a person to join the union within a certain amount of time after being hired.

Upward feedback A performance appraisal process for managers that includes subordinates' evaluations.

Utility   The degree to which the information provided by selection methods enhances the effectiveness of selecting personnel in real organizations.

Utilization analysis   A comparison of the race, sex, and ethnic composition of an employer's workforce with that of the available labor supply.

Validity   The extent to which a performance measure assesses all the relevant—and only the relevant—aspects of job performance.

Verbal comprehension   Refers to a person's capacity to understand and use written and spoken language.

Virtual reality   Computer-based technology that provides trainees with a three-dimensional learning experience. Trainees operate in a simulated environment that responds to their behaviors and reactions.

Virtual teams   Teams that are separated by time, geographic distance, culture and/or organizational boundaries and rely exclusively on technology for interaction between team members.

Voluntary turnover   Turnover initiated by employees (often whom the company would prefer to keep).

Webcasting   Classroom instruction provided online via live broadcasts.

Whistle-blowing   Making grievances public by going to the media or government.

Workforce sensor   A role of the CHRO that focuses on identifying workforce morale issues or concerns.

Workforce utilization review   A comparison of the proportion of workers in protected subgroups with the proportion that each subgroup represents in the relevant labor market.

Photo Credits

Name and Company Index

SUBJECT INDEX